D0842226

TENNYSON

THE AUTHOR AND CHARACTERS OF THE "IDYLS OF THE KING."—By Gustave Doré

WORKS

ALFRED TENNYSON.—From the photograph by Mrs. Cameron

1

THE

COMPLETE POETICAL WORKS

OF

ALFRED, LORD TENNYSON

POET LAUREATE

554

TENNYSON'S BIRTH-PLACE, LINCOLNSHIRE

WITH AN INTRODUCTORY SKETCH BY ANNE THACKERAY RITCHIE

Illustrated

27

NEW YORK

HARPER & BROTHERS, PUBLISHERS

FRANKLIN SQUARE

1884

LORD TENNYSON AT HOME

ALFRED TENNYSON.

BY

ANNE THACKERAY RITCHIE.

[Reprinted from *Harper's Magazine* for December, 1883.]

I.

THERE is a place called Somersby in Lincolnshire, where an old white rectory stands on the slope of a hill, and the winding lanes are shadowed by tall ashes and elm-trees, and where two brooks meet at the bottom of the glebe field. It is a place far away from us in silence' and in distance, lying upon the "ridgèd wolds." They bound the horizon of the rectory garden, whence they are to be seen flowing to meet the sky. I have never known Somersby, but I have often heard it described, and the pastoral country all about, and the quiet, scattered homes. One can picture the rectory to one's self with something of a monastic sweetness and quiet; an ancient Norman cross is standing in the churchyard, and perhaps there is still a sound in the air of the bleating of flocks. It all comes before one as one reads the sketch of Tennyson's native place in the *Homes and Haunts of the British Poets:* the village not far from the fens, "in a pretty pastoral district of softly sloping hills and large ash-trees, . . . the little glen in the neighborhood, called by the old monkish name of Holywell." Mr. Tennyson sometimes speaks of this glen, which he remembers white with snowdrops in the season; and who will not recall the exquisite invocation:

"Come from the woods that belt the gray hill-side,
The seven elms, the poplars four
That stand beside my father's door,
And chiefly from the brook that loves
To purl o'er matted cress and ribbèd sand,
Or dimple in the dark of rushy coves. . . .
    O! hither lead thy feet!
Pour round mine ears the livelong bleat
Of the thick-fleecèd sheep from wattled folds,
    Upon the ridgèd wolds."

The wind that goes blowing where it listeth, once, in the early beginning of this century, came sweeping through the garden of this old Lincolnshire rectory, and, as the wind blew, a sturdy child of five years old with shining locks stood opening his arms upon the blast and letting himself be blown along, and as he travelled on he made his first line of poetry and said, "I hear a voice that's speaking in the wind," and he tossed his arms, and the gust whirled on, sweeping into the great abyss of winds. One might, perhaps, still trace in the noble familiar face of our Poet Laureate the features of this child, one of many deep-eyed sons and daughters born in the quiet rectory among the elm-trees.

Alfred Tennyson was born on the 6th of August, 1809. He has heard many and many a voice calling to him since the time when he listened to the wind as he played alone in his father's garden, or joined the other children at their games and jousts. They were a noble little clan of poets and of knights, coming of a knightly race, with castles to defend, with mimic tournaments to fight. Somersby was so far away from the world, so behindhand in its echoes (which must have come there softened through all manner of green and tranquil things, and, as it were, hushed into pastoral silence), that though the early part of the century was stirring with the clang of legions, few of its rumors seem to have reached the children. They never heard, at the time, of the battle of Waterloo. They grew up together, playing their own games, living their own life; and where is such life to be found as that of a happy, eager family of boys and girls, before Doubt, the steps of Time, the shocks of Chance, the blows of Death, have come to shake their creed?

These handsome children had beyond most children that wondrous toy at their command which some people call imagination. The boys played great games like Arthur's knights; they were champions and warriors defending a stone heap, or again they would set up opposing camps with a king in the midst of each. The king was a willow wand stuck into the ground, with an outer circle of immortals to defend him of firmer, stiffer sticks. Then each party would come with stones, hurling at each other's king, and trying to overthrow him. Perhaps as the day wore on they became romancers, leaving the jousts deserted. When dinner-time came, and they all sat round

LADY TENNYSON.—After the painting at Aldworth by G. F. Watts, R. A.

the table, each in turn put a chapter of his history underneath the potato-bowl—long, endless histories, chapter after chapter diffuse, absorbing, unending, as are the stories of real life of which each sunrise opens on a new part; some of these romances were in letters, like *Clarissa Harlowe*. Alfred used to tell a story which lasted for months, and which was called "The Old Horse."

Alfred's first verses, so I once heard him say, were written upon a slate which his brother Charles put into his hand one Sunday at Louth, when all the elders of the party were going into church, and the child was left alone. Charles gave him a subject —the flowers in the garden—and when he came back from church little Alfred brought the slate to his brother, all covered with written lines of blank verse. They were made on the models of Thomson's *Seasons*, the only poetry he had ever read. One can picture it all to one's self, the flowers in the garden, the verses, the little poet with waiting eyes, and the young brother scanning the lines. "Yes, you can write," said Charles, and he gave Alfred back the slate.

I have also heard another story of his grandfather, later on, asking him to write an elegy on his grandmother, who had recently died, and, when it was written, putting ten shillings into his hands and saying, "There, that is the first money you have ever earned by your poetry, and, take my word for it, it will be the last."

The Tennysons are a striking example of the theory of family inheritance. Alfred was one of twelve children, of whom the eldest, Frederick, who was educated at Eton, is known as the author of a very imaginative volume of poems. Charles was the second son, and Alfred, whose name is more widely known, was the third. He and Charles were sent for a few years to the Grammar School at Louth, where the Laureate still remembers walking, adorned with blue ribbons in a procession for the proclamation of the coronation of George the Fourth. The old wives said at the time that the boys made the prettiest part of the show.

Charles Tennyson — Charles Turner he was afterward called, for he took the name with a property which he inherited—was little Alfred's special friend and brother. In his own most sweet degree, Charles Ten-

Mr. Spedding quotes the picture of a summer's daybreak:

"But one sole star, none other anywhere:
A wild-rose odor from the fields was borne;
The lark's mysterious joy filled earth and air,
And from the wind's top met the hunter's horn;
The aspen trembled wildly; and the morn
Breathed up in rosy clouds divinely fair."

Charles Tennyson was in looks not unlike his younger brother. He was stately, too,

TENNYSON'S CHILDREN.—After the painting at Aldworth by G. F. Watts, R.A.

nyson too was a true poet. Who that has ever read his sonnets will cease to love them? His brother loves and quotes them with affection. Coleridge loved them; James Spedding, wise critic, life-long friend, read them with unaltered delight from his youth to his much-honored age. In an introductory essay to a volume of the collected sonnets, published after Charles Turner's death,

though shorter in stature, gentle, spiritual, very noble, simple. I once saw him kneeling in a church, and only once again. He was like something out of another world, more holy, more silent than that in which most of us are living; there is a picture in the National Gallery of St. Jerome which always recalls him to me. The sons must have inherited their poetic gifts from their father, George Clayton Tennyson, LL.D., a tall, striking, and impressive man, full of accomplishments and parts, a strong nature, high-souled, high-tempered. He was the head of the old family; but his own elder-brother share of its good things had passed by will into the hands of another branch, which is still represented by the Tennysons d'Eyncourt. Perhaps before he died he may have realized that to one of his had come possessions greater than any ever yet entailed by lawyer's deeds—an inheritance, a priceless Benjamin's portion, not to be measured or defined.

II.

Alfred Tennyson, as he grew up toward manhood, found other and stronger inspirations than Thomson's gentle *Seasons*. Byron's spell had fallen on his generation, and for a boy of genius it must have been absolute and overmastering. Tennyson was soon to find his own voice, but meanwhile he began to write like Byron. He produced poems and verses in profusion and endless abundance; trying his wings, as people say, before starting on his own strong flight. One day the news came to the village—the dire news which spread across the land, filling men's hearts with consternation—that Byron was dead. Alfred was then a boy about fifteen.

"Byron was dead! I thought the whole world was at an end," he once said, speaking of these bygone days. "I thought everything was over and finished for every one—that nothing else mattered. I remember I walked out alone, and carved 'Byron is dead' into the sandstone."

I have spoken of Tennyson from the account of an old friend, whose recollections go back to those days, which seem perhaps more distant to us than others of earlier date and later fashion. Mrs. Tennyson, the mother of the family, so this same friend tells me, was a sweet and gentle and most imaginative woman; so kind-hearted that it had passed into a proverb, and the wicked inhabitants of a neighboring village used to bring their dogs to her windows and beat them in order to be bribed to leave off by the gentle lady, or to make advantageous bargains by selling her the worthless curs. She was intensely, fervently religious, as a poet's mother should be. After her husband's death (he had added to the rectory, and made it suitable for his large family) she still lived on at Somersby with her children and their friends. The daughters were growing up, the elder sons were going to college. Frederick, the eldest, went first to Trinity, Cambridge, and his brothers followed him there in turn. Life was opening for them, they were seeing new aspects and places, making new friends, and bringing them home to their Lincolnshire rectory.

"In Memoriam" gives many a glimpse of the old home, of which the echoes still reach us across half a century.

"O sound to rout the brood of cares,
  The sweep of scythe in morning dew,
  The gust that round the garden flew,
And tumbled half the mellowing pears!

"O bliss, when all in circle drawn
  About him, heart and ear were fed
  To hear him, as he lay and read
The Tuscan poet on the lawn:

"Or in the all-golden afternoon
  A guest, or happy sister, sung,
  Or here she brought the harp and flung
A ballad to the brightening moon."

Dean Garden was one of those friends sometimes spoken of who, with Arthur Hallam, the reader of the Tuscan poet, and James Spedding and others, used to gather upon the lawn at Somersby—the young men and women in the light of their youth and high spirits, the widowed mother leading her quiet life within the rectory walls. Was it not a happy sister herself who in afterdays once described how, on a lovely summer night, they had all sat up so late talking in the starlight that the dawn came shining unawares; but the young men, instead of going to bed, then and there set off for a long walk across the hills in the sunrise,

"And, suck'd from out the distant gloom,
  A breeze began to tremble o'er
  The large leaves of the sycamore,*
And fluctuate all the still perfume,

"And gathering freshlier overhead,
  Rock'd the full-foliaged elms, and swung
  The heavy-folded rose, and flung
The lilies to and fro, and said

"'The dawn, the dawn,' and died away;
  And East and West, without a breath,
  Mixt their dim lights, like life and death,
To broaden into boundless day."

III.

One thing which cannot fail to strike us when we are looking over the records of these earlier days is the remarkable influence which Alfred Tennyson seems to have had from the very first upon his contemporaries, even before his genius had been recognized by the rest of the world. Not only those of his own generation, but his elders and masters seem to have felt something of this. I remember long ago hearing one of Tennyson's oldest friends, who has the best right of any to recall the fact, say that "Whewell, who was a man himself, and who knew a man when he saw him," used to pass over in Alfred Tennyson certain informalities and forgetfulness of combinations as to gowns, and places, and times, which in another he would never have overlooked.

Whewell ruled a noble generation—a race of men born in the beginning of the century, whose praise and loyal friendship were indeed worth having, and whose good opinion

---

* The sycamore has been cut down, and the lawn is altered to another shape.

Tennyson himself may have been proud to possess. Wise, sincere, and witty, these contemporaries of his spoke with authority, with the modesty of conscious strength. Those of this race whom I have known in later days—for they were many of them my father's friends also—have all been men of unmistakable stamp, of great culture, of a certain dignified bearing, and of independence of mind and of character.

Most of them have succeeded in life as men do who are possessed of intellect and high character. Some have not made the less mark upon their time because their names are less widely known; but each name is a memorable chapter in life to one and another of us who have known them from our youth. One of those old friends, who also loved my father, and whom he loved, who has himself just passed away, one who saw life with his own eyes, described Alfred in his youth, in a pamphlet or book which has been privately printed, and which is a remembrance, a sort of waking dream, of some bygone days and talks. How many of us might have been glad to listen to our poet, and to the poet who has made the philosophy of Omar Khâyîm known to the world, as they discoursed together; of life, of boyish memories, of books, and again more books, of chivalry—mainly but another name for youth—of a possible old age, so thoroughly seasoned with its spirit that all the experience of the world should serve not to freeze but to direct the genial current of the soul! and who that has known them both will not recognize the truth of this description of Alfred in those early days—

"A man at all points, of grand proportion and feature, significant of that inward chivalry becoming his ancient and honorable race; when himself a 'Yonge Squire,' like him in Chaucer, 'of grete strength,' that could hurl the crowbar farther than any of the neighboring clowns, whose humors, as well as of their betters — knight, squire, landlord, and lieutenant — he took quiet note of, like Chaucer himself; like Wordsworth on the mountain, he too when a lad abroad on the world, sometimes of a night with the shepherd, watching not only the flock on the greensward, but also

'the fleecy star that bears
Andromeda far off Atlantic seas,'

along with those other Zodiacal constellations which Aries, I think, leads over the field of heaven."

Arthur Hallam has also written in some lines to R. J. Tennant of

"a friend, a rare one,
A noble being full of clearest insight,
. . . whose fame
Is couching now with pantherized intent,
As who shall say, I'll spring to him anon,
And have him for my own."

All these men could understand each other, although they had not then told the world their secrets. Poets, critics, men of learning—such names as Trench and Monckton Milnes, George Stovin Venables, the Lush-

ingtons and Kinglake, need no comment; many more there are, and deans and canons, and the Master of Trinity himself—

"a band
Of youthful friends, on mind and art,
And labor, and the changing mart,
And all the framework of the land;

"When one would aim an arrow fair,
But send it slackly from the string;
And one would pierce an outer ring,
And one an inner, here and there;

"And last the master-bowman, he,
Would cleave the mark."

The lines to J. S. were written to one of these earlier associates;

"And gently comes the world to those
That are cast in gentle mould."

It was the prophecy of a whole lifetime. There were but few signs of age in James Spedding's looks, none in his charming companionship, when the accident befell him which took him away from those who loved him. To another old companion, the Rev. W. H. Brookfield, is dedicated that sonnet which flows like an echo of Cambridge chimes on a Sabbath morning. It is in this sonnet that Tennyson speaks of "him the lost light of those dawn-golden times," who was himself one of that generation of which I have been writing.

IV.

Arthur Hallam was the same age as my own father, and born in 1811. When he died he was but twenty-three; but he had lived long enough to show what his life might have been.

In the preface to a little volume of his collected poems and essays, published some time after his death, there is a pathetic introduction. "He seemed to tread the earth as a spirit from some better world," writes his father; and a correspondent, who, I have been told, is Arthur Hallam's and Tennyson's common friend, Mr. Gladstone, and whose letter is quoted, says, with true feeling: "It has pleased God that in his death, as well as in his life and nature, he should be marked beyond ordinary men. When much time has elapsed, when most bereavements will be forgotten, he will still be remembered, and his place, I fear, will be felt to be still vacant; singularly as his mind was calculated by its native tendencies to work powerfully and for good, in an age full of import to the nature and destinies of man."

How completely these words have been carried out must strike us all now. The father lived to see the young man's unconscious influence working through his friend's genius, and reaching a whole generation unborn as yet on the day when he died. A lady, speaking of Arthur Hallam after his death, said to Mr. Tennyson, "I think he was perfect." "And so he was," said Mr. Tennyson, "as near perfection as a mortal

THE MEETING OF THE SEVERN AND WYE.

man can be." Arthur Hallam was a man of remarkable intellect. He could take in the most difficult and abstruse ideas with an extraordinary rapidity and insight. On one occasion he began to work one afternoon, and mastered a difficult book of Descartes at one single sitting. In the preface to the *Memorials* Mr. Hallam speaks of this peculiar clearness of perception and facility for acquiring knowledge; but, above all, the father dwells on his son's undeviating sweetness of disposition and adherence to his sense of what was right. In the quarterlies and reviews of the time his opinion is quoted here and there with a respect which shows in what esteem it was already held.

At the time Arthur Hallam died, he was engaged to be married to a sister of the poet's. She was scarcely seventeen at the time. One of the sonnets, addressed by Arthur Hallam to his betrothed, was written when he began to teach her Italian.

"Lady, I bid thee to a sunny dome,
  Ringing with echoes of Italian song;
  Henceforth to thee these magic halls belong,
  And all the pleasant place is like a home.
Hark, on the right, with full piano tone,
  Old Dante's voice encircles all the air;
  Hark yet again, like flute-tones mingling rare
Comes the keen sweetness of Petrarca's moan.
Pass thou the lintel freely; without fear
  Feast on the music. I do better know thee
Than to suspect this pleasure thou dost owe me
Will wrong thy gentle spirit, or make less dear
  That element whence thou must draw thy life—
  An English maiden and an English wife."

As we read the pages of this little book, we come upon more than one happy moment saved out of the past, hours of delight and peaceful friendship, saddened by no foreboding, and complete in themselves.

"Alfred, I would that you beheld me now,
  Sitting beneath an ivied, mossy wall.
        . . . . Above my head
  Dilates immeasurable a wild of leaves,
  Seeming received into the blue expanse
  That vaults the summer noon."

There is something touching in the tranquil ring of the voice calling out in the summer noontide with all a young man's expansion.

It seemed to be but the beginning of a beautiful happy life, when suddenly the end came. Arthur Hallam was travelling with his father in Austria when he died very suddenly, with scarce a warning sign of illness. Mr. Hallam had come home and found his son, as he supposed, sleeping upon a couch; but it was death, not sleep. "Those whose eyes must long be dim with tears"—so writes the heart-stricken father—"brought him home to rest among his kindred and in his own country." They chose his resting-place in a tranquil spot on a lone hill that overhangs the Bristol Channel. He was buried in the chancel of Clevedon Church, in Somerset, by Clevedon Court, which had been his mother's early home.

> "The Danube to the Severn gave
> The darken'd heart that beat no more:
> They laid him by the pleasant shore,
> And in the hearing of the wave.
>
> "There twice a day the Severn fills;
> The salt sea-water passes by,
> And hushes half the babbling Wye,
> And makes a silence in the hills."

In all England there was not a sweeter place than the sunny old Court upon the hill, with its wide prospects and grassy terraces, where Arthur Hallam must have played in his childhood, whence others of his kindred, touched with his own bright and beautiful spirit, have come forth. His brother Harry, a gentle and delightful person, used to be constantly at the house of their cousin, Mrs. Brookfield. He too was carried off in his youth of fullest promise. When Mr. Hallam, after a life of repeated sorrows, at last went to his rest with his wife and his children, it was Alfred Tennyson who wrote his epitaph, which may still be read in the chancel of the old church. The lovely old house was burned in 1883.

V.

Once in their early youth we hear of the two friends, Tennyson and Hallam, travelling in the Pyrenees. This was at the time of the war of early Spanish independence, when many generous young men went over with funds and good energies to help the cause of liberty. These two were taking money, and letters written in invisible ink, to certain conspirators who were then revolting against the intolerable tyranny of Ferdinand, and who were chiefly hiding in the Pyrenees. The young men met, among others, a Señor Ojeda, who confided to Alfred his intentions, which were to *couper la gorge à tous les curés.* Señor Ojeda could not talk English or fully explain all his aspirations. "*Mais vous connaissez mon cœur,*" said he, effusively; and a pretty black one it is, thought the poet. I have heard Alfred described in those days as "straight and with a broad breast," and when he had crossed over from the Continent and was coming back, walking through Wales, he went one day into a little way-side inn, where an old man sat by the fire, who looked up, and asked many questions. "Are you from the army? Not from the army? Then where do you come from?" said the old man. "I am just come from the Pyrenees," said Alfred. "Ah, I knew there was a something," said the wise old man.

John Kemble was among those who had gone over to Spain, and one day a rumor came to distant Somersby that he was to be tried for his life by the Spanish authorities. No one else knew much about him except Alfred Tennyson, who started before dawn to drive across the country in search of some person of authority who knew the consul at Cadiz, and who could send letters of protection to the poor prisoner.

CLEVEDON COURT.—After an unpublished sketch by W. M. Thackeray.

BURLEIGH HOUSE, BY STAMFORD TOWN.

It was a false alarm. John Kemble came home to make a name for himself in other fields. Meanwhile Alfred Tennyson's own reputation was growing, and when the first two volumes of his collected poems were published in 1842, followed by *The Princess* in 1847, his fame spread throughout the land.

Some of the reviews were violent and antagonistic at first. One in particular had tasted blood, and the "Hang, draw, and *Quarterly*," as it has been called, of those days, having lately cut up *Endymion*, now proceeded to demolish Tennyson.

But this was a passing phase. It is curious to note the sudden change in the tone of the criticisms—the absolute surrender of these knights of the pen to the irresistible and brilliant advance of the unknown and visored warrior. The visor is raised now, the face is familiar to us all, but the arms, though tested in a hundred fights, are shining and unconquered still.

William Howitt, whom we have already quoted, has written an article upon the Tennyson of these earlier days. It is fanciful, suggestive, full of interest, with a gentle mysterious play and tender appreciation. Speaking of the poet himself, he asks, with the rest of the world of that time: "You may hear his voice, but where is the man? He is wandering in some dream-land, beneath the shade of old and charmed forests, by far-off shores, where

'all night
The plunging seas draw backward from the land
Their moon-led waters white;'

by the old mill-dam, thinking of the merry miller and his pretty daughter; or wandering over the open wolds where

'Norland whirlwinds blow.'

From all these places—from the silent corridor of an ancient convent, from some shrine where a devoted knight recites his vows, from the drear monotony of 'the moated grange,' or the forest beneath the 'talking oak'—comes the voice of Tennyson, rich, dreamy, passionate, yet not impatient, musical with the airs of chivalrous ages, yet mingling in his song the theme and the spirit of those that are yet to come."

This article was written many years ago, when but the first chords had sounded, before the glorious Muse, passing beyond her morning joy, had met with the sorrow of life. But it is well that as we travel on through later, sadder scenes we should still carry in our hearts this joyous and romantic music. One must be English born, I think, to know how English is the spell which this great enchanter casts over us; the very spirit of the land upon us as the visions he evokes come closing round. Whether it is the moated grange that he shows us, or Locksley Hall that in the distance overlooks the sandy tracts, or Dora standing in the corn, or the sight of the brimming wave that swings through quiet meadows round the mill, it is all home in its broadest, sweetest aspect. Take the gallant wooing of the Lord of Burleigh:

"So she goes by him attended,
  Hears him lovingly converse,
Sees whatever fair and splendid
  Lay betwixt his home and hers:
Parks with oak and chestnut shady,
  Parks and order'd gardens great,
Ancient homes of lord and lady,
  Built for pleasure and for state.
All he shows her makes him dearer:
  Evermore she seems to gaze
On that cottage growing nearer,
  Where they twain will spend their days.
O but she will love him truly!
  He shall have a cheerful home;
She will order all things duly,
  When beneath his roof they come.
Thus her heart rejoices greatly,
  Till a gateway she discerns
With armorial bearings stately,
  And beneath the gate she turns;
Sees a mansion more majestic
  Than all those she saw before."

But one might go on quoting forever.

Another critic, writing even before this time, had said of Tennyson, "He imitates nobody; in him we recognize the spirit of his age." It would not be easy for a generation that has grown up to the music of Tennyson, that has in a manner beaten time to it with the pulse of its life, to imagine what the world would be without it. Even the most original amongst us must needs think of things more or less in the shape in which they come before us. The mystery of the charm of words is as great as that by which a wonder of natural beauty comes around us, and lays hold of our imagination. It may be fancy, but I for one feel as if summer-time could scarcely be summer without the song of the familiar green books.

VI.

In Memoriam, with music in its cantos, belonging to the school of all men's sad hearts, rings the awful *De Profundis* of death, faced and realized as far as may be by a human soul. It came striking suddenly into all the sweet ideal beauty and lovely wealth which had gone before, with a revelation of that secret of life which is told to each of us in turn by the sorrow of its own soul. Nothing can be more simple than the form of the poem as it flows.

"Short swallow-flights of song, that dip
Their wings in tears, and skim away,"

the poet says himself, but it is something else which we can all acknowledge—something which has given words and ease to many of those who in their lonely frozen grief perhaps felt that they are no longer quite alone, when such a voice as this can reach them:

"Peace: come away: the song of woe
Is after all an earthly song:
Peace: come away: we do him wrong
To sing so wildly: let us go."

And as the cry passes away, come signs of peace and dawning light:

"Be neither song, nor game, nor feast;
Nor harp be touch'd, nor flute be blown;
No dance, no motion, save alone
What lightens in the lucid east.

"Of rising worlds by yonder wood.
Long sleeps the summer in the seed;
Run out your measured arcs, and lead
The closing cycle rich in good."

And the teacher who can read the great book of nature interprets for us as he turns the page.

With *In Memoriam*, which was not published till 1850, Alfred Tennyson's fame was firmly established; and when Wordsworth died, April 23, its author was appointed by the Queen Poet Laureate. There is a story that at the time Sir Robert Peel was consulted he had never read any Tennyson, but he read "Ulysses" and warmed up, and acknowledged the right of this new-come poet to be England's Laureate.

The home at Somersby was broken up by this time, by marriages and other family events. Alfred Tennyson had come to live in London. He was poor; he had in turn to meet that struggle with wholesome poverty which brings the vagueness of genius into contact with reality, and teaches, better, perhaps, than any other science, the patience, the forbearance, and knowledge of life which belong to it.

CAERLEON UPON USK.

The Princess, with all her lovely court and glowing harmonies, was born in London, among the fogs and smuts of Lincoln's Inn, although, like all works of true art, this poem had grown by degrees in other times and places. The poet came and went, free, unshackled, meditating, inditing. One of my family remembers hearing Tennyson say that "Tears, idle Tears," was suggested by Tintern Abbey; who shall say by what mysterious wonder of beauty and regret, by what sense of the "transient with the abiding"?

In Memoriam was followed by the first part of the *Idylls*, and the record of the court King Arthur held at Camelot, and at "old Caerleon upon Usk" on that eventful Whitsuntide when Prince Geraint came quickly flashing through the shallow ford to the little knoll where the queen stood with her maiden, and

> .... "listen'd for the distant hunt,
> And chiefly for the baying of Cavall."

If *In Memoriam* is the record of a human soul, the *Idylls* mean the history, not of one man or of one generation, but of a whole cycle, of the faith of a nation failing and falling away into darkness. "It is the dream of man coming into practical life, and ruined by one sin." Birth is a mystery, and death is a mystery, and in the midst lies the table-land of life, and its struggle and performance.

The first "Idyll" and the last, I have heard Mr. Tennyson say, are intentionally more archaic than the others. He once told us that the song of the knights marching past the king at the marriage of Arthur was made one spring afternoon on Clapham Common as he walked along.

> "Blow trumpet, for the world is white with May;
> Blow trumpet, the long night hath roll'd away!
> Blow through the living world — 'Let the King reign.'"

So sang the young knights in the first bright days of early chivalry.

> "Clang battle-axe, and clash brand! Let the King reign.
> The King will follow Christ, and we the King."

And then when the doom of evil spread, bringing not sorrow alone, but destruction in its train, not death only, but hopelessness and consternation, the song is finally changed into an echo of strange woe; we hear no shout of triumph, but the dim shocks of battle,

> "the crash
> Of battle-axe on shatter'd helms, and shrieks
> After the Christ, of those who falling down
> Look'd up for heaven, and only saw the mist."

All is over with the fair court; Guinevere's golden head is low; she has fled to Almesbury—

> "Fled all night long by glimmering waste and weald,
> And heard the Spirits of the waste and weald
> Moan as she fled, or thought she heard them moan:
> And in herself she moan'd, 'Too late, too late!'
> Till in the cold wind that forerans the morn,
> A blot in heaven, the Raven, flying high,
> Croak'd, and she thought, 'He spies a field of death.'"

And finally comes the conclusion, and the "Passing of Arthur," and he vanishes as he came, in mystery, silently floating away

ALMESBURY.

FARRINGFORD HOUSE, ISLE OF WIGHT.

upon the barge toward the East, whence all religions are said to come.

I have heard them all speak of these London days when Alfred Tennyson lived in poverty with his friends and his golden dreams. He lived in the Temple, at 58 Lincoln's Inn Fields, and elsewhere.

It was about this time that Carlyle introduced Sir John Simeon to Tennyson one night at Bath House, and made the often-quoted speech, "There he sits upon a dung-heap surrounded by innumerable dead dogs;" by which dead dogs he meant "Œnone" and other Greek versions and adaptations. He had said the same thing of Landor and his Hellenics. "I was told of this," said Mr. Tennyson, "and some time afterward I repeated it to Carlyle: 'I'm told that is what you say of me.' He gave a kind of guffaw. 'Eh, that wasn't a very luminous description of you,' he answered."

The story is well worth retelling, so completely does it illustrate the grim humor and unaffected candor of a dyspeptic man of genius, who flung words and epithets without malice, who neither realized the pain his chance sallies might give, nor the indelible flash which branded them upon people's memories.

The world has pointed its moral finger of late at the old man in his great old age, accusing himself in the face of all, and confessing the overpowering irritations which the suffering of a lifetime had laid upon him and upon her he loved. That old caus-

tic man of deepest feeling, with an ill temper and a tender heart and a racking imagination, speaking from the grave, and bearing unto it that cross of passionate remorse which few among us dare to face, seems to some of us now a figure nobler and truer, a teacher greater far, than in the days when all his pain and love and remorse were still hidden from us all.

Carlyle and Mr. Fitzgerald used to be often with Tennyson at that time. They used to dine together at the "Cock" tavern in the Strand among other places; sometimes Tennyson and Carlyle took long solitary walks late into the night.

The other day a lady was describing a bygone feast given about this time by the poet to Lady Duff Gordon, and to another young and beautiful lady, a niece of Mr. Hallam's. Harry Hallam was also asked. Mr. Tennyson, in his hospitality, had sent for a carpenter to change the whole furniture of his bedroom in order to prepare a proper drawing-room for the ladies. Mr. Brookfield, coming in, was in time to suggest some compromise, to which the host reluctantly agreed. One can imagine that it was a delightful feast, but indeed it is always a feast-day when one breaks bread with those one loves, and the writer is glad to think that she too has been among those to sit at the kind board where the salt has not lost its savor in the years that have passed, and where the guests can say their grace not for bread and wine alone. May she add that the first occasion of her having the honor of breaking bread in company with Mr. Tennyson was in her father's house, when she was propped up in a tall chair between her parents.

VII.

Some of the writer's earliest recollections are of days now long gone by, when many of these young men of whom she has been speaking, grown to be middle-aged, used to come from time to time to her father's house, and smoke with him, and talk and laugh quietly, taking life seriously, but humorously too, with a certain loyalty to others and self-respect which was their characteristic. They were somewhat melancholy men at soul, but for that very reason, perhaps, the humors of life may have struck them more especially. It is no less possible that our children will think of us as cheerful folks upon the whole, with no little affectation of melancholy and all the graces.

I can remember on one occasion looking across a darkening room through a cloud of smoke at the noble, grave head of the Poet Laureate. He was sitting with my father in the twilight after some family meal in the old house in Kensington. It is Mr. Tennyson himself who has reminded me how upon this occasion, while my father was speaking to me, my little sister looked up suddenly from the book over which she had been absorbed, saying, in her sweet childish voice, "Papa, why do you not write books like *Nicholas Nickleby?*" Then again I seem to hear, across that same familiar table, voices without shape or name, talking and telling each other that Mr. Tennyson was married—that he and his wife had been met walking on the terrace

at Clevedon Court; and then the clouds descend again, except, indeed, that I still see my father riding off on his brown cob to Mr. and Mrs. Tennyson's house at Twickenham to attend the christening of Hallam, their eldest son. In after-years we were shown the old ivy-grown church and the rectory at Shiplake, by the deep bend of the Thames, where their marriage took place. One can not but believe that which one has seen and heard, and yet it is hard to realize that some homes were not always there, created in one breath, complete in themselves and in their blessings.

It was at Somersby that Alfred Tennyson first became acquainted with his wife. She was eldest daughter of Henry Sellwood, the last but one of a family of country gentlemen settled in Berkshire in the time of Charles I., and before that, in Saxon times, as it is said, more important people in the forest of their name. Her mother was a sister of Sir John Franklin.

Not many years after their marriage Mr. and Mrs. Tennyson settled at Freshwater, in the Isle of Wight. There is a photograph I have always liked, in which it seems to me the history of this home is written, in sunlight, in the flashing of a bright beam, in an instant, and forever. It was taken in the green glade at Farringford. Hallam and Lionel Tennyson stand on either side of their parents, the sun is shining, and no doubt the thrushes and robins are singing and fluttering in the wind-blown branches of the trees, as the father and mother and the children come advancing towards us. Who does not know the beautiful lines of the poet:

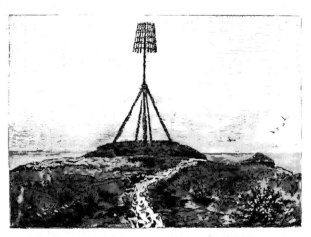

FARRINGFORD BEACON.—From an unpublished sketch by Frederick Walker.

IN THE NEW FOREST.

"Dear, near, and true—no truer Time himself
Can prove you, though he make you evermore
Dearer and nearer."

And though years have passed, and the children with their wind-blown locks are now men, and it is another generation—little golden-haired Ally and his brother Charlie babbling of life's new wine—who are now picking the daffodils under the Farringford hedge, yet the old picture remains, and shines through to the present.

As the writer notes down these various fragments of remembrance, and compiles this sketch of present things, she can not but feel how much of the past it all means to her, and how very much her own feeling is an inheritance which has gathered interest during a lifetime, so that the chief claim of her words to be regarded is that they are those of an old friend. Her father's warmth of admiration comes back vividly as she writes, all his pleasure when he secured "Tithonus" for one of the early numbers of the Cornhill Magazine, his immense and outspoken admiration for the Idylls of the King.

VIII.

One autumn, when everything seemed bright at home, Mrs. Cameron took me with her to Freshwater for a few happy weeks, and then, for the first time, I lived with them all, and with kind Mrs. Cameron, in the ivy-grown house near the gates of Farringford. For the first time I stayed in the island, and with the people who were dwelling there, and walked with Tennyson along

High Down, treading the turf, listening to his talk, while the gulls came sideways, flashing their white breasts against the edge of the cliffs, and the poet's cloak beat time to the gusts of the west wind.

The house at Farringford itself seemed like a charmed palace, with green walls without, and speaking walls within. There hung Dante with his solemn nose and wreath; Italy gleamed over the doorways; friends' faces lined the way; books filled the shelves, and a glow of crimson was everywhere; the great oriel drawing-room window was full of green and golden leaves, of the sound of birds and of the distant sea.

The very names of the people who have stood upon the lawn at Farringford would be an interesting study for some future biographer: Longfellow, Maurice, Kingsley, the Duke of Argyll, Locker, Dean Stanley, the Prince Consort. Good Garibaldi once planted a tree there, off which some too ardent republican broke a branch before twenty-four hours had passed. Here came Clough in the last year of his life. Here Mrs. Cameron fixed her lens, marking the well-known faces as they passed: Darwin and Henry Taylor, Watts and Aubrey de Vere, Leeky and Jowett, and a score of others.

I first knew the place in the autumn, but perhaps it is even more beautiful in spring-time, when all day the lark trills high over-head, and then when the lark has flown out of our hearing the thrushes begin, and the air is sweet with scents from the many fra-

1*

I hate the dreadful hollow behind the little wood

TENNYSON READING "MAUD."—From a sketch by Dante Gabriel Rossetti, 1855.

grant shrubs. The woods are full of ane-mones and primroses; narcissus grows wild in the lower fields; a lovely creamy stream of flowers flows along the lanes, and lies hidden in the levels; hyacinth pools of blue shine in the woods; and then with a later burst of glory comes the gorse, light-ing up the country round about, and blazing round about the beacon hill. The little sketch here given was made early one morn-ing by Frederick Walker, who had come over to see us at Freshwater. The beacon hill stands behind Farringford. If you cross the little wood of nightingales and thrushes, and follow the lane where the blackthorn hedges shine in spring-time (lovely dials that illuminate to show the hour), you come to the downs, and climbing their smooth steeps you reach "Mr. Tennyson's Down," where the beacon-staff stands firm upon the mound. Then, following the line of the coast, you come at last to the Needles, and may look down upon the ridge of rocks that rises, crisp, sharp, shining, out of the blue wash of fierce delicious waters.

The lovely places and sweet country all about Farringford are not among the least of its charms. Beyond the Primrose Island itself and the blue Solent, the New Forest spreads its shades, and the green depths reach to the very shores. Have we not all read of the forest where Merlin was be-charmed, where the winds were still in the wild woods of Broceliande? The forest of

Brockenhurst, in Hampshire, waves no less green, its ferns and depths are no less sweet and sylvan, than those of Brittany.

> "Before an oak, so hollow, huge, and old
> It look'd a tower of ruin'd mason-work,
> At Merlin's feet the wily Vivien lay."

I have heard of Mr. Tennyson wandering for days together in the glades round about Lyndhurst. Some people once told me of meeting a mysterious figure in a cloak coming out of a deep glade, passing straight on, looking neither to the right nor the left. "It was either a ghost or it was Mr. Tennyson," said they.

In Sir John Simeon's lifetime there was a constant intercourse between Farringford and Swainston. Sir John was one of Tennyson's most constant companions—a knight of courtesy he calls him in the sad lines written in the garden at Swainston.

Maud grew out of a remark of Sir John Simeon's, to whom Mr. Tennyson had read the lines,

> "O that 'twere possible
> After long grief and pain,"

which lines were, so to speak, the heart of *Maud*. Sir John said that it seemed to him as if something were wanting to explain the story of this poem, and so by degrees it all grew. One little story was told me on the authority of Mr. Henry Sidgwick, who was perhaps present on that occasion. Mr. Tennyson was reading the poem to a silent company assembled in the twilight, and when he got to the birds in the high hall garden calling Maud, Maud, Maud, Maud, he stopped short, and asked an authoress who happened to be present what birds these were. The authoress, much alarmed, and feeling that she must speak, and that the eyes of the whole company were upon her, faltered out, "Nightingales, sir." "Pooh," said Tennyson, "what a cockney you are! Nightingales don't say Maud. Rooks do, or something like it. Caw, caw, caw, caw, caw". Then he went on reading.

Reading, is it? One can hardly describe it. It is a sort of mystical incantation, a chant in which every note rises and falls and reverberates again. As we sit around the twilight room at Farringford, with its great oriel-window looking to the garden, across fields of hyacinth and self-sowed daffodils toward the sea, where the waves wash against the rock, we seem carried by a tide not unlike the ocean's sound; it fills the room, it ebbs and flows away; and when we leave, it is with a strange music in our ears, feeling that we have for the first time, perhaps, heard what we may have read a hundred times before.

More than once after a reading I can remember the whole party starting forth into the night to listen to the song of the nightingale coming across the field or the quiet park. The nightingales in the island do not sing with passion, but calmly and delightfully, to their mates as they sit upon their nests, singing and stopping, and singing again. Once when Mr. Tennyson was in Yorkshire, as he told me, as he was walking at night in a friend's garden, he heard a nightingale singing with such a frenzy of passion that it was unconscious of everything else, and not frightened though he came and stood quite close beside it; he could see its eye flashing, and feel the air bubble in his ear through the vibration. Our poet, with his short-sighted eyes, can see farther than most people. Almost the first time I ever walked out with him, he told me to look and tell him if the field-lark did not come down sideways upon its wing.

Like his friend Mr. Browning, he instinctively knows everything that is going on round about him, though at the time he

THE EDGE OF BLACKDOWN, SHOWING TENNYSON'S HOUSE.

may not always stop to note it. There is a tribute to this peculiar gift in Mrs. Gaskell's story of *Cranford;* it is from the old farmer who had lived so long before the young poet came who taught him that ash buds were black in May. Nature in its various aspects makes up a larger part of this man's life than it does for other people. He goes his way unconsciously absorbing life, and its lights and sounds, and teaching us to do the same as far as may be. There is an instance of this given in the pamphlet already

boatman, "When I last was here I heard eight echoes, and now I only hear one." To which the man, who had heard people quoting the Bugle Song, replied, "Why, you must be the gentleman that brought all the money to the place."

People have different ideas of poets. Mrs. B——, of Totland's Bay, once asked a Freshwater boy, who was driving her, if he knew Mr. Tennyson. "He makes poets for the Queen," said the boy. "What do you mean?" said the lady, amused. "I don't

THE OAK LAWN, ALDWORTH.

quoted from, where the two friends talk on of one theme and another from Kenelm Digby to Aristophanes, and the poet is described as saying, among other things, that he knows of no human outlook so solemn as that from an infant's eyes, and that it was from those of his own he learned that those of the Divine Child in Raffaello's Sistine Madonna were not overcharged with expression.

Here is a reminiscence of Tennyson's about the echo at Killarney, where he said to the

know what they means," said the boy, "but p'liceman often seen him walking about a-making of 'em under the stars." The author of *Euphranor* has his own definition of a poet:

"The only living—and like to live—poet I have known, when he found himself beside the 'bonnie Doon,' whether it were from recollection of poor Burns, or of 'the days that are no more' which haunt us all, I know not—I think he did not know—'broke into a passion of tears' (as he told me). Of tears, which during a pretty long and intimate intercourse

I had never seen glistening in his eyes but once, when reading Virgil—'dear old Virgil,' as he called him—together; and then—oh, not of Queen Dido, nor of young Marcellus even, but of the burning of Troy, in the second Æneid — whether moved by the catastrophe itself, or the majesty of the verse it is told in, or as before, scarce knowing why. For as King Arthur shall bear witness, no young Edwin he, though, as a great poet, comprehending all the softer stops of human emotion in that diapason where the intellectual, no less than what is called the poetical, faculty predominated."

TENNYSON'S HOME AT ALDWORTH, SURREY.

"You will last," Douglas Jerrold said. And there was Carlyle's "Eh! he has got the grip of it," when Tennyson read him the *Revenge*. But perhaps the best compliment Mr. Tennyson ever received was one day when walking in Covent Garden, when he was stopped by a rough-looking man, who held out his hand, and said: "You're Mr. Tennyson. Look here, sir, here am I. I've been drunk for six days out of the seven, but if you will shake me by the hand, I'm d——d if I ever get drunk again."

IX.

Aldworth was built some dozen years ago, when Mrs. Tennyson had been ordered change, and Freshwater was found to be unbearable and overcrowded during the summer months. It must be borne in mind that to hospitable people there are dangers from friendly inroads as well as from the attacks of enemies. The new house, where for many years past the family has spent its summers, stands on the summit of a high lonely hill in Surrey, and yet it is not quite out of reach of London life. It is a white stone house with many broad windows facing a great view and a long terrace, like some one of those at Siena or Perugia, with a low parapet of stone, where ivies and roses are trained, making a foreground to the lovely haze of the distance. Sometimes at Aldworth, when the summer days are at their brightest, and

high Blackdown top has been well warmed and sunned, I have seen a little procession coming along the terrace walk, and proceeding by its green boundary into a garden, where the sun shines its hottest upon a sheltered lawn, and where standard rose-trees burn their flames. Mr. Tennyson in his broad hat goes first, dragging the garden chair in which Mrs. Tennyson lies; perhaps one son is pushing from behind, while another follows with rugs and cushions for the rest of the party. If the little grandsons and their young mother are there, the family group is complete. One special day I remember when we all sat for an hour round about the homely chair and its gentle occupant. It seemed not unlike a realization of some Italian picture that I had somewhere seen, the tranquil eyes, the peaceful heights, the glorious summer day, some sense of lasting calm, of beauty beyond the present hour.

No impression of this life at Aldworth and Farringford would be complete if, beside the parents, the sons were not seen, adding each in his own measure to the grateful sight of a united household. Hallam, the eldest son, has been for years past the adviser, the friend, and companion of his father and mother at home; and Lionel, the younger, although living away in London in his own home, all the same holds fast to the family tradition of parents and children closely united through the chances and changes of life, and trusting and supporting one another.

Mr. Tennyson works alone in the early hours of the morning, and comes down long after his own frugal meal is over to find his guests assembling round the social breakfast-table. He generally goes out for a walk before luncheon, with a son and a friend, perhaps, and followed by a couple of dogs. All Londoners know the look of the stalwart figure and the fine face and broad-brimmed felt hat as he advances.

There is one little ceremony peculiar to the Tennyson family, and reminding one of some college custom, which is, that when dinner is over the guests are brought away into a second room, where stands a white table, upon which fruit and wine are set, and a fire burns bright, and a pleasant hour passes, while the master of the house sits in his carved chair and discourses upon any topic suggested by his guests, or brings forth reminiscences of early Lincolnshire days, or from the facts he remembers out of the lives of past men who have been his friends. There was Rogers, among the rest, for whom he had a great affection, with whom he constantly lived during that lonely time in London. "I have dined alone with him," I heard Mr. Tennyson say, "and we have talked about death till the tears rolled down his face."

Tennyson met Tom Moore at Rogers's, and there, too, he first met Mr. Gladstone. John Forster, Leigh Hunt, and Landor were also friends of that time. One of Tennyson's often companions in those days was Mr. Hallam, whose opinion he once asked of Carlyle's *French Revolution*. Mr. Hallam replied, in his quick, rapid way, "Upon my word, I once opened the book, and read four or five pages. The style is so abominable I could not get on with it." Whereas Carlyle's own criticism upon the *History of the Middle Ages* was, "Eh! the poor, miserable skeleton of a book!"

Was it not Charles Lamb who wanted to return grace after reading Shakspeare, little deeming in humble simplicity that many of us yet to come would be glad to return thanks for a jest of Charles Lamb's? The difference between those who speak with natural reality, and those who go through life fitting their second-hand ideas to other people's words, is one so marked that even a child may tell the difference. When the Laureate speaks, every word comes wise, racy, absolutely natural, and sincere; and how gladly do we listen to his delightful stories, full of odd humors and knowledge of men and women, or to his graver talk! When a man has read so much and thought so much, it is an epitome of the knowledge of to-day we find in him, touched by the solemn strain of the poet's own gift. I once heard Mr. Tennyson talking to some actors, to no less a person indeed than to Hamlet himself, for after the curtain fell the whole play seemed to flow from off the stage into the box where we had been sitting, and I could scarcely tell at last where reality began and Shakspeare ended. The play was over, and we ourselves seemed a part of it still; here were the players, and our own prince poet, in that familiar simple voice we all know, explaining the art, going straight to the point in his own downright fashion, criticising with delicate appreciation, by the simple force of truth and conviction carrying all before him. "You are a good actor lost," one of these real actors said to him.

It is a gain to the world when people are content to be themselves, not chipped to the smooth pattern of the times, but simple, original, and unaffected in ways and words. Here is a poet leading a poet's life; where he goes there goes the spirit of his home, whether in London among the crowds, or at Aldworth on the lonely height, or at Farringford in that beautiful bay. The last time I went to see him he was smoking in a top room in Eaton Square. It may interest an American public to be told that it was Durham tobacco from North Carolina, which Mr. Lowell had given him. I could not but feel how little even circumstance itself can contribute to that mysterious essence of individuality which we all recognize and love. In this commonplace London room, with all the stucco of Belgravia round about, I found the old dream realized, the old charm of youthful impression. There sat my friend as I had first seen him years ago among the clouds.

CONTENTS.

The present edition includes "Timbuctoo," the author's Cambridge University Prize Poem; Poems published in the London editions of 1830 and 1833, and omitted in later editions; "Poems by Two Brothers" (Charles and Alfred Tennyson); and a number of hitherto uncollected Poems from various sources.

CONTENTS.

CONTENTS.

A Tennyson

POEMS.

(PUBLISHED 1830.)

TO THE QUEEN.

REVERED, beloved—O you that hold
　A nobler office upon earth
　Than arms, or power of brain or birth
Could give the warrior kings of old,

Victoria,—since your Royal grace
　To one of less desert allows
　This laurel greener from the brows
Of him that uttered nothing base;

And should your greatness, and the care
　That yokes with empire, yield you time
　To make demand of modern rhyme
If aught of ancient worth be there;

Then—while a sweeter music wakes,
　And thro' wild March the throstle calls,
　• Where all about your palace-walls
The sunlit almond-blossom shakes—

Take, Madam, this poor book of song;
　For tho' the faults were thick as dust
　In vacant chambers, I could trust
Your kindness. May you rule us long,

And leave us rulers of your blood
　As noble till the latest day!
　May children of our children say,
"She wrought her people lasting good;

"Her court was pure; her life serene;
　God gave her peace; her land reposed;
　A thousand claims to reverence closed
In her as Mother, Wife, and Queen;

"And statesmen at her council met
　Who knew the seasons, when to take
　Occasion by the hand, and make
The bounds of freedom wider yet

"By shaping some august decree,
　Which kept her throne unshaken still,
　Broad based upon her people's will,
And compassed by the inviolate sea."
MARCH, 1851.

CLARIBEL.

A MELODY.

1.

WHERE Claribel low-lieth
　The breezes pause and die,
　　Letting the rose-leaves fall:
But the solemn oak-tree sigheth,

Thick-leaved, ambrosial,
　With an ancient melody
　Of an inward agony,
Where Claribel low-lieth.

2.

At eve the beetle boometh
Athwart the thicket lone:
At noon the wild bee hummeth
About the moss'd headstone:
At midnight the moon cometh,
　And looketh down alone.

3.

Her song the lintwhite swelleth,
The clear-voiced mavis dwelleth.
　The callow throstle lispeth,
The slumberous wave outwelleth
　The babbling runnel crispeth,
The hollow grot replieth
Where Claribel low-lieth.

LILIAN.

1.

AIRY, fairy Lilian,
　Flitting, fairy Lilian,
When I ask her if she love me,
Clasps her tiny hands above me,
　Laughing all she can;
She'll not tell me if she love me,
　Cruel little Lilian.

2.

When my passion seeks
　Pleasance in love-sighs
She, looking thro' and thro' me
Thoroughly to undo me,
　Smiling, never speaks:
So innocent-arch, so cunning-simple
From beneath her gather'd wimple
　Glancing with black-beaded eyes,
Till the lightning laughters dimple
　The baby-roses in her cheeks;
　Then away she flies.

3.

Prythee weep, May Lilian!
　Gayety without eclipse
Wearieth me, May Lilian:
Thro' my very heart it thrilleth
　When from crimson-threaded lips
Silver-treble laughter trilleth:
　Prythee weep, May Lilian.

4.

Praying all I can,
If prayers will not hush thee,
 Airy Lilian,
Like a rose-leaf I will crush thee,
 Fairy Lilian.

ISABEL.

1.

Eyes not down-dropped nor over-bright, but fed
 With the clear-pointed flame of chastity,
Clear, without heat, undying, tended by
 Pure vestal thoughts in the translucent fane
Of her still spirit; locks not wide dispread,
 Madonna-wise on either side her head:
 Sweet lips whereon perpetually did reign
The summer calm of golden charity,
Were fixed shadows of thy fixed mood,
 Revered Isabel, the crown and head,
The stately flower of female fortitude,
 Of perfect wifehood, and pure lowlihead.

2.

The intuitive decision of a bright
 And thorough-edged intellect to part
 Error from crime; a prudence to withhold;
 The laws of marriage character'd in gold
Upon the blanched tablets of her heart;
A love still burning upward, giving light
To read those laws; an accent very low
In blandishment, but a most silver flow
 Of subtle-paced counsel in distress,
Right to the heart and brain, tho' undescried,
 Winning its way with extreme gentleness
Thro' all the outworks of suspicious pride;

A courage to endure and to obey:
A hate of gossip parlance and of sway,
Crown'd Isabel, thro' all her placid life,
The queen of marriage, a most perfect wife.

3.

The mellowed reflex of a winter moon;
A clear stream flowing with a muddy one,
 Till in its onward current it absorbs
  With swifter movement and in purer light
  The vexed eddies of its wayward brother;
  A leaning and upbearing parasite,
 Clothing the stem, which else had fallen quite,
With cluster'd flower-bells and ambrosial orbs
  Of rich fruit-bunches leaning on each other—
  Shadow forth thee;—the world hath not another
(Though all her fairest forms are types of thee,
And thou of God in thy great charity)
Of such a finish'd chasten'd purity.

MARIANA.

"Mariana in the moated grange."
Measure for Measure.

With blackest moss the flower-plots
 Were thickly crusted, one and all:
The rusted nails fell from the knots
 That held the peach to the garden-wall.
The broken sheds look'd sad and strange:
 Unlifted was the clinking latch;
 Weeded and worn the ancient thatch
Upon the lonely moated grange.
  She only said, "My life is dreary.
  He cometh not," she said;
  She said, "I am aweary, aweary
  I would that I were dead!"

"Her tears fell with the dews at even,
Her tears fell ere the dews were dried."

Her tears fell with the dews at even·
Her tears fell ere the dews were dr'ed;
She could not look on the sweet heaven,
Either at morn or eventide.
After the flitting of the bats,
When thickest dark did trance the sky,
She drew her casement-curtain by,
And glanced athwart the glooming flats.
  She only said, "The night is dreary,
    He cometh not," she said;
  She said, "I am aweary, aweary,
    I would that I were dead!"

Upon the middle of the night,
  Waking she heard the night-fowl crow:
The cock sung out an hour ere light:
  From the dark fen the oxen's low
Came to her: without hope of change,
  In sleep she seemed to walk forlorn,
Till cold winds woke the gray-eyed morn
About the lonely moated grange.
  She only said, "The day is dreary,
    He cometh not," she said;
  She said, "I am aweary, aweary,
    I would that I were dead!"

About a stone-cast from the wall
  A sluice with blacken'd waters slept,
And o'er it many, round and small,
  The cluster'd marish-mosses crept.
Hard by a poplar shook alway,
  All silver-green with gnarled bark:
For leagues no other tree did mark
The level waste, the rounding gray.
  She only said, "My life is dreary.
    He cometh not," she said;
  She said, "I am aweary, aweary,
    I would that I were dead!"

And ever when the moon was low,
  And the shrill winds were up and away,
In the white curtain, to and fro,
  She saw the gusty shadow sway.
But when the moon was very low,
  And wild winds bound within their cell,
The shadow of the poplar fell
Upon her bed, across her brow.
  She only said, "The night is dreary,
    He cometh not," she said;
  She said, "I am aweary, aweary,
    I would that I were dead!"

All day within the dreamy house,
  The doors upon their hinges creak'd;
The blue fly sung in the pane; the mouse
  Behind the mouldering wainscot shriek'd,
Or from the crevice peered about.
  Old faces glimmered thro' the doors,
  Old footsteps trod the upper floors,
Old voices called her from without.
  She only said, "My life is dreary,
    He cometh not," she said;
  She said, "I am aweary, aweary,
    I would that I were dead!"

The sparrow's chirrup on the roof,
  The slow clock ticking, and the sound
Which to the wooing wind aloof
  The poplar made, did all confound
Her sense; but most she loathed the hour
  When the thick-moted sunbeam lay
  Athwart the chambers, and the day
Was sloping toward his western bower.
  Then said she, "I am very dreary,
    He will not come," she said;
  She wept, "I am aweary, aweary,
    O God, that I were dead!"

TO ———.

1.

CLEAR-HEADED friend, whose joyful scorn,
  Edged with sharp laughter, cuts atwain
  The knots that tangle human creeds,
  The wounding cords that bind and strain
  The heart until it bleeds,
Ray-fringed eyelids of the morn
  Roof not a glance so keen as thine:
  If aught of prophecy be mine,
  Thou wilt not live in vain.

2.

Low-cowering shall the Sophist sit,
  Falsehood shall bare her plaited brow:
  Fair-fronted Truth shall droop not now
With shrilling shafts of subtle wit.
Nor martyr-flames, nor trenchant swords
  Can do away that ancient lie;
  A gentler death shall Falsehood die,
Shot thro' and thro' with cunning words.

3.

Weak Truth a-leaning on her crutch,
  Wan, wasted Truth in her utmost need,
  Thy kingly intellect shall feed,
  Until she be an athlete bold,
And weary with a finger's touch
  Those writhed limbs of lightning speed;
  Like that strange angel which of old,
  Until the breaking of the light,
Wrestled with wandering Israel,
  Past Yabbok brook the livelong night,
And heaven's mazed signs stood still
In the dim tract of Penuel.

———

MADELINE.

1.

Thou art not steeped in golden langnors,
  No tranced summer calm is thine,
    Ever varying Madeline.
  Thro' light and shadow thou dost range,
  Sudden glances, sweet and strange,
  Delicious spites and darling angers,
    And airy forms of flitting change.

2.

Smiling, frowning, evermore,
  Thou art perfect in love-lore.
  Revealings deep and clear are thine
  Of wealthy smiles; but who may know
  Whether smile or frown be fleeter?
  Whether smile or frown be sweeter,
    Who may know?
  Frowns perfect-sweet along the brow
  Light-glooming over eyes divine,
  Like little clouds, sun-fringed, are thine,
    Ever varying Madeline.
  Thy smile and frown are not aloof
  From one another,
    Each to each is dearest brother:
  Hues of the silken sheeny woof
  Momently shot into each other.
    All the mystery is thine;
  Smiling, frowning, evermore,
  Thou art perfect in love-lore,
    Ever varying Madeline.

3.

A subtle, sudden flame,
  By veering passion fann'd,
    About thee breaks and dances
  When I would kiss thy hand,

The flush of anger'd shame
O'erflows thy calmer glances,
And o'er black brows drops down
A sudden-curved frown,
But when I turn away,
Thou, willing me to stay,
  Wooest not, nor vainly wranglest;
  But, looking fixedly the while,
  All my bounding heart entanglest
  In a golden-netted smile;
Then in madness and in bliss,
If my lips should dare to kiss
Thy taper fingers amorously,
Again thou blushest angerly;
And o'er black brows drops down
A sudden-curved frown.

———⟡———

SONG.—THE OWL.

1.

When cats run home and light is come,
  And dew is cold upon the ground,
And the far-off stream is dumb,
  And the whirring sail goes round,
  And the whirring sail goes round;
    Alone and warming his five wits,
    The white owl in the belfry sits.

2.

When merry milkmaids click the latch,
  And rarely smells the new-mown hay,
And the cock hath sung beneath the thatch
  Twice or thrice his roundelay,
  Twice or thrice his roundelay:
    Alone and warming his five wits,
    The white owl in the belfry sits.

———⟡———

SECOND SONG.

TO THE SAME.

1.

Thy tuwhits are lull'd I wot,
  Thy tuwhoos of yesternight,
Which upon the dark afloat,
  So took echo with delight,
  So took echo with delight,
    That her voice untuneful grown,
    Wears all day a fainter tone.

2.

I would mock thy chaunt anew,
  But I cannot mimic it:
Not a whit of thy tuwhoo,
  Thee to woo to thy tuwhit,
  Thee to woo to thy tuwhit,
    With a lengthen'd loud halloo,
    Tuwhoo, tuwhit, tuwhit, tuwhoo-o-o.

———⟡———

RECOLLECTIONS OF THE ARABIAN NIGHTS.

When the breeze of a joyful dawn blew free
In the silken sail of infancy,
The tide of time flow'd back with me,
  The forward-flowing tide of time;
And many a sheeny summer morn,
Adown the Tigris I was borne,
By Bagdat's shrines of fretted gold,
High-walled gardens green and old;
True Mussulman was I and sworn,
  For it was in the golden prime
    Of good Haroun Alraschid.

Anight my shallop, rustling thro'
The low and bloomed foliage, drove
The fragrant, glistening deeps, and clove
The citron-shadows in the blue:
By garden porches on the brim,
The costly doors flung open wide,
Gold glittering thro' lamplight dim,
And broider'd sofas on each side:
  In sooth it was a goodly time,
  For it was in the golden prime
    Of good Haroun Alraschid,

Often, where clear-stemm'd platans guard
The outlet, did I turn away
The boat-head down a broad canal
From the main river sluiced, where all
The sloping of the moon-lit sward
Was damask-work, and deep inlay
Of braided blooms unmown, which crept
Adown to where the water slept.
  A goodly place, a goodly time,
  For it was in the golden prime
    Of good Haroun Alraschid.

A motion from the river won
Ridged the smooth level, bearing on
My shallop thro' the star-strown calm,
Until another night in night
I enter'd, from the clearer light,
Imbower'd vaults of pillar'd palm,
Imprisoning sweets, which as they clomb
Heavenward, were stay'd beneath the dome
  Of hollow boughs.—A goodly time,
  For it was in the golden prime
    Of good Haroun Alraschid.

Still onward; and the clear canal
Is rounded to as clear a lake.
From the green rivage many a fall
Of diamond rillets musical,
Thro' little crystal arches low
Down from the central fountain's flow
Fall'n silver-chiming, seem'd to shake
The sparkling flints beneath the prow.
  A goodly place, a goodly time,
  For it was in the golden prime
    Of good Haroun Alraschid.

Above thro' many a bowery turn
A walk with vary-color'd shells
Wander'd engrain'd. On either side
All round about the fragrant marge
From fluted vase, and brazen urn
In order, eastern flowers large,
Some dropping low their crimson bells
Half-closed, and others studded wide
  With disks and tiars, fed the time
  With odor in the golden prime
    Of good Haroun Alraschid.

Far off, and where the lemon-grove
In closest coverture upsprung,
The living airs of middle night
Died round the bulbul as he sung;
Not he: but something which possess'd
The darkness of the world, delight,
Life, anguish, death, immortal love,
Ceasing not, mingled, unrepress'd,
  Apart from place, withholding time,
  But flattering the golden prime
    Of good Haroun Alraschid.

Black the garden-bowers and grots
Slumber'd: the solemn palms were ranged
Above, unwoo'd of summer wind:
A sudden splendor from behind
Flush'd all the leaves with rich gold-green,
And, flowing rapidly between

Their interspaces. counterchanged
The level lake with diamond-plots
 Of dark and bright. A lovely time,
 For it was in the golden prime
 Of good Haroun Alraschid.

Dark-blue the deep sphere overhead,
Distinct with vivid stars inlaid.
Grew darker from that under-flame:
So, leaping lightly from the boat,
With silver anchor left afloat,
In marvel whence that glory came
Upon me, as in sleep I sank
In cool soft turf upon the bank,
 Entranced with that place and time,
 So worthy of the golden prime
 Of good Haroun Alraschid.

Thence thro' the garden I was drawn—
A realm of pleasance, many a mound,
And many a shadow-chequer'd lawn
Full of the city's stilly sound,
And deep myrrh-thickets blowing round
The stately cedar, tamarisks,
Thick rosaries of scented thorn,
Tall orient shrubs, and obelisks
 Graven with emblems of the time,
 In honor of the golden prime
 Of good Haroun Alraschid.

With dazed vision unawares
From the long alley's latticed shade
Emerged, I came upon the great
Pavilion of the Caliphat.
Right to the carven cedarn doors,
Flung inward over spangled floors,
Broad-based flights of marble stairs
Ran up with golden balustrade,
 After the fashion of the time,
 And humor of the golden prime
 Of good Haroun Alraschid.

The fourscore windows all alight
As with the quintessence of flame,
A million tapers flaring bright
From twisted silvers look'd to shame
The hollow-vaulted dark, and stream'd
Upon the mooned domes aloof
In inmost Bagdat, till there seem'd
Hundreds of crescents on the roof
 Of night new-risen, that marvellous time,
 To celebrate the golden prime
 Of good Haroun Alraschid.

Then stole I up, and trancedly
Gazed on the Persian girl alone,
Serene with argent-lidded eyes
Amorous, and lashes like to rays
Of darkness, and a brow of pearl
Tressed with redolent ebony.
In many a dark delicious curl,
 Flowing beneath her rose-hued zone:
 The sweetest lady of the time,
 Well worthy of the golden prime
 Of good Haroun Alraschid.

Six columns, three on either side,
Pure silver, underpropt a rich
Throne of the massive ore, from which
Down-droop'd in many a floating fold,
Engarlanded and diaper'd
With inwrought flowers, a cloth of gold.
Thereon, his deep eye laughter-stirr'd
With merriment of kingly pride,
 Sole star of all that place and time,
 I saw him—in his golden prime,
 THE GOOD HAROUN ALRASCHID!

ODE TO MEMORY.

1.

Thou who stealest fire,
 From the fountains of the past,
 To glorify the present; oh, haste,
  Visit my low desire!
 Strengthen me, enlighten me!
 I faint in this obscurity,
 Thou dewy dawn of memory.

2.

Come not as thou camest of late,
Flinging the gloom of yesternight
On the white day; but robed in soften'd light
 Of orient state.
Whilome thou camest with the morning mist,
 Even as a maid, whose stately brow
The dew-impearled winds of dawn have kiss'd,
  When she, as thou,
Stays on her floating locks the lovely freight
Of overflowing blooms, and earliest shoots
Of orient green, giving safe pledge of fruits,
Which in wintertide shall star
The black earth with brilliance rare.

3.

Whilome thou camest with the morning mist,
 And with the evening cloud,
Showering thy gleamed wealth into my open breast,
(Those peerless flowers which in the rudest wind
  Never grow sere,
When rooted in the garden of the mind.
 Because they are the earliest of the year).
 Nor was the night thy shroud.
In sweet dreams softer than unbroken rest
Thou leddest by the hand thine infant Hope.
The eddying of her garments caught from thee
The light of thy great presence; and the cope
 Of the half-attain'd futurity,
 Though deep not fathomless,
Was cloven with the million stars which tremble
O'er the deep mind of dauntless infancy.
Small thought was there of life's distress:
For sure she deem'd no mist of earth could dull
Those spirit-thrilling eyes so keen and beautiful
Sure she was nigher to heaven's spheres,
Listening the lordly music flowing from
  The illimitable years.
O strengthen me, enlighten me!
I faint in this obscurity,
Thou dewy dawn of memory.

4.

Come forth I charge thee, arise,
Thou of the many tongues, the myriad eyes!
Thou comest not with shows of flaunting vines
 Unto mine inner eye,
 Divinest Memory!
Thou wert not nursed by the waterfall
Which ever sounds and shines
 A pillar of white light upon the wall
Of purple cliffs, aloof descried:
Come from the woods that belt the gray hillside,
The seven elms, the poplars four
That stand beside my father's door,
And chiefly from the brook that loves
To purl o'er matted cress and ribbed sand,
Or dimple in the dark of rushy coves,
Drawing into his narrow earthen urn,
 In every elbow and turn,
The filter'd tribute of the rough woodland.
 O! hither lead thy feet!
Pour round mine ears the livelong bleat
Of the thick-fleeced sheep from wattled folds,
 Upon the ridged wolds,

When the first matin-song hath waken'd loud
Over the dark dewy earth forlorn,
What time the amber morn
Forth gushes from beneath a low-hung cloud.

5.

Large dowries doth the raptured eye
    To the young spirit present
        When first she is wed ;
        And like a bride of old
    In triumph led,
        With music and sweet showers
        Of festal flowers,
    Unto the dwelling she must sway.
Well hast thou done, great artist Memory,
    In setting round thy first experiment
    With royal frame-work of wrought gold ;
Needs must thou dearly love thy first essay,
And foremost in thy various gallery
    Place it, where sweetest sunlight falls
    Upon the storied walls ;
        For the discovery
And newness of thine art so pleased thee,
That all which thou hast drawn of fairest
Or boldest since, but lightly weighs
With thee unto the love thou bearest
The first-born of thy genius. Artist-like,
Ever retiring thou dost gaze
On the prime labor of thine early days ;
No matter what the sketch might be ;
Whether the high field on the bushless Pike,
Or even a sand-built ridge
Of heaped hills that mound the sea,
Overblown with murmurs harsh,
Or even a lowly cottage whence we see
Stretch'd wide and wild the waste enormous marsh,
Where from the frequent bridge,
Like emblems of infinity,
The trenched waters run from sky to sky ;
Or a garden bower'd close
With plaited alleys of the trailing rose,
Long alleys falling down to twilight grots,
Or opening upon level plots
Of crowned lilies, standing near
Purple-spiked lavender ;
Whither in after life retired
From brawling storms,
From weary wind,
With youthful fancy reinspired,
We may hold converse with all forms
Of the many-sided mind,
And those whom passion hath not blinded,
Subtle-thoughted, myriad-minded,
My friend, with you to live alone,
Were how much better than to own
A crown, a sceptre, and a throne !
O strengthen me, enlighten me !
I faint in this obscurity,
Thou dewy dawn of memory.

———◁◦▷———

SONG.

1

A spirit haunts the year's last hours
Dwelling amid these yellowing bowers:
    To himself he talks ;
For at eventide, listening earnestly,
At his work you may hear him sob and sigh
    In the walks ;
Earthward he boweth the heavy stalks
Of the mouldering flowers:
    Heavily hangs the broad sunflower
        Over its grave i' the earth so chilly ;
    Heavily hangs the hollyhock,
        Heavily hangs the tiger-lily.

2.

The air is damp, and hush'd, and close,
As a sick man's room when he taketh repose
    An hour before death ;
My very heart faints and my whole soul grieve
At the moist rich smell of the rotting leaves,
    And the breath
    Of the fading edges of box beneath,
And the year's last rose.
    Heavily hangs the broad sunflower
        Over its grave i' the earth so chilly,
    Heavily hangs the hollyhock,
        Heavily hangs the tiger-lily.

———◁◦▷———

ADELINE.

1.

Mystery of mysteries,
    Faintly smiling Adeline,
Scarce of earth nor all divine,
    Nor unhappy, nor at rest,
        But beyond expression fair
        With thy floating flaxen hair:
Thy rose-lips and full blue eyes
    Take the heart from out my breast.
Wherefore those dim looks of thine,
Shadowy, dreaming Adeline ?

2.

Whence that aery bloom of thine,
    Like a lily which the sun
Looks thro' in his sad decline,
    And a rose-bush leans upon,
Thou that faintly smilest still,
    As a Naiad in a well,
    Looking at the set of day,
Or a phantom two hours old
    Of a maiden past away,
Ere the placid lips be cold ?
Wherefore those faint smiles of thine,
    Spiritual Adeline ?

3.

What hope or fear or joy is thine?
Who talketh with thee, Adeline?
    For sure thou art not all alone:
    Do beating hearts of salient springs
Keep measure with thine own?
    Hast thou heard the butterflies,
    What they say betwixt their wings?
    Or in stillest evenings
With what voice the violet woos
To his heart the silver dews?
    Or when little airs arise,
    How the merry bluebell rings
        To the mosses underneath?
    Hast thou look'd upon the breath
Of the lilies at sunrise?
Wherefore that faint smile of thine,
Shadowy, dreaming Adeline ?

4.

Some honey-converse feeds thy mind,
    Some spirit of a crimson rose
In love with thee forgets to close
His curtains, wasting odorous sighs
All night long on darkness blind.
What aileth thee? whom waitest thou
With thy soften'd, shadow'd brow,
    And those dew-lit eyes of thine,
    Thou faint smiler, Adeline ?

5.

Lovest thou the doleful wind
    When thou gazest at the skies ?

Doth the low-tongued Orient
   Wander from the side of the morn,
Dripping with Sabean spice
On thy pillow, lowly bent
With melodious airs lovelorn,
Breathing Light against thy face,
While his locks a-dropping twined
   Round thy neck in subtle ring
Make a carcanet of rays,
   And ye talk together still,
In the language wherewith Spring
   Letters cowslips on the hill?
Hence that look and smile of thine,
   Spiritual Adeline.

———————

A CHARACTER.

With a half-glance upon the sky
At night he said, "The wanderings
Of this most intricate Universe
Teach me the nothingness of things."
Yet could not all creation pierce
Beyond the bottom of his eye.

He spake of beauty: that the dull
Saw no divinity in grass,
Life in dead stones, or spirit in air;
Then looking as 't were in a glass,
He smooth'd his chin and sleek'd his hair,
And said the earth was beautiful.

He spake of virtue: not the gods
More purely, when they wish to charm
Pallas and Juno sitting by:
And with a sweeping of the arm,
And a lack-lustre dead-blue eye,
Devolved his rounded periods.

Most delicately hour by hour
He canvassed human mysteries,
And trod on silk, as if the winds
Blew his own praises in his eyes,
And stood aloof from other minds
In impotence of fancied power.

With lips depress'd as he were meek,
Himself unto himself he sold:
Upon himself himself did feed:
Quiet, dispassionate, and cold,
And other than his form of creed,
With chisell'd features clear and sleek.

———————

THE POET.

The poet in a golden clime was born,
   With golden stars above;
Dower'd with the hate of hate, the scorn of scorn,
   The love of love.

He saw thro' life and death, thro' good and ill
   He saw thro' his own soul.
The marvel of the everlasting will,
   An open scroll,

Before him lay: with echoing feet he threaded
   The secretest walks of fame:
The viewless arrows of his thoughts were headed
   And wing'd with flame,

Like Indian reeds blown from his silver tongue,
   And of so fierce a flight,
From Calpe unto Caucasus they sung,
   Filling with light

2

And vagrant melodies the winds which bore
   Them earthward till they lit;
Then, like the arrow-seeds of the field flower,
   The fruitful wit

Cleaving, took root, and springing forth anew,
   Where'er they fell, behold,
Like to the mother plant in semblance, grew
   A flower all gold,

And bravely furnish'd all abroad to fling
   The winged shafts of truth,
To throng with stately blooms the breathing spring
   Of Hope and Youth.

So many minds did gird their orbs with beams,
   Tho' one did fling the fire.
Heaven flow'd upon the soul in many dreams
   Of high desire.

Thus truth was multiplied on truth, the world
   Like one great garden show'd,
And thro' the wreaths of floating dark upcurl'd,
   Rare sunrise flow'd.

And Freedom rear'd in that august sunrise
   Her beautiful bold brow,
When rites and forms before his burning eyes
   Melted like snow.

There was no blood upon her maiden robes
   Sunn'd by those orient skies:
But round about the circles of the globes
   Of her keen eyes

And in her raiment's hem was traced in flame
   Wisdom, a name to shake
All evil dreams of power—a sacred name
   And when she spake,

Her words did gather thunder as they ran,
   And as the lightning to the thunder
Which follows it, riving the spirit of man,
   Making earth wonder,

So was their meaning to her words. No sword
   Of wrath her right arm whirl'd,
But one poor poet's scroll, and with *his* word
   She shook the world.

———————

THE POET'S MIND.

1.

Vex not thou the poet's mind
   With thy shallow wit:
Vex not thou the poet's mind;
   For thou canst not fathom it.
Clear and bright it should be ever,
   Flowing like a crystal river;
Bright as light, and clear as wind.

2.

Dark-brow'd sophist, come not anear;
   All the place is holy ground;
Hollow smile and frozen sneer
   Come not here.
Holy water will I pour
Into every spicy flower
Of the laurel-shrubs that hedge it around.
The flowers would faint at your cruel cheer
In your eye there is death,
There is frost in your breath
Which would blight the plants.
   Where you stand you cannot hear
      From the groves within
      The wild-bird's din.

In the heart of the garden the merry bird chants,
It would fall to the ground if you came in.
　In the middle leaps a fountain
　　Like sheet lightning,
　　Ever brightening
　With a low melodious thunder;
All day and all night it is ever drawn
　From the brain of the purple mountain
　Which stands in the distance yonder:
It springs on a level of bowery lawn,
And the mountain draws it from Heaven above,
And it sings a song of undying love;
And yet, tho' its voice be so clear and full,
You never would hear it: your ears are so dull;
So keep where you are: you are foul with sin;
It would shrink to the earth if you came in.

THE SEA-FAIRIES.

Slow sail'd the weary mariners and saw,
Betwixt the green brink and the running foam,
Sweet faces, rounded arms, and bosoms prest
To little harps of gold; and while they mused,
Whispering to each other half in fear,
Shrill music reach'd them on the middle sea.

Whither away, whither away, whither away? fly no
　more.
Whither away from the high green field, and the
　happy blossoming shore?
Day and night to the billow the fountain calls;
Down shower the gambolling waterfalls
From wandering over the lea:
Out of the live-green heart of the dells
They freshen the silvery-crimson shells,
And thick with white bells the clover-hill swells
High over the full-toned sea:
O hither, come hither and furl your sails,
Come hither to me and to me:
Hither, come hither and frolic and play;
Here it is only the mew that wails;
We will sing to you all the day:
Mariner, mariner, furl your sails,

For here are the blissful downs and dales,
And merrily merrily carol the gales,
And the spangle dances in bight and bay,
And the rainbow forms and flies on the land
Over the islands free;
And the rainbow lives in the curve of the sand;
Hither, come hither and see;
And the rainbow hangs on the poising wave,
And sweet is the color of cove and cave,
And sweet shall your welcome be:
O hither, come hither, and be our lords,
For merry brides are we:
We will kiss sweet kisses, and speak sweet words:
O listen, listen, your eyes shall glisten
With pleasure and love and jubilee:
O listen, listen, your eyes shall glisten
When the sharp clear twang of the golden chords
Runs up the ridged sea.
Who can light on as happy a shore
All the world o'er, all the world o'er?
Whither away? listen and stay: mariner, mariner
　fly no more.

THE DESERTED HOUSE.

1.

Life and Thought have gone away
　　Side by side,
　Leaving door and windows wide.
Careless tenants they!

2.

All within is dark as night:
In the windows is no light:
And no murmur at the door,
So frequent on its hinge before.

3.

Close the door, the shutters close,
　Or thro' the windows we shall see
　The nakedness and vacancy
Of the dark deserted house.

" Life and Thought have gone away
Side by side."

4.

Come away: no more of mirth
  Is here or merry-making sound.
The house was builded of the earth,
  And shall fall again to ground.

5.

Come away: for Life and Thought
  Here no longer dwell;
  But in a city glorious—
A great and distant city—have bought
  A mansion incorruptible.
  Would they could have stayed with us!

———⟡———

THE DYING SWAN.

1.

The plain was grassy, wild and bare,
  Wide, wild, and open to the air,
Which had built up everywhere
  An under-roof of doleful gray.
With an inner voice the river ran,
Adown it floated a dying swan,
  And loudly did lament.
It was the middle of the day.
Ever the weary wind went on,
  And took the reed-tops as it went.

2.

Some blue peaks in the distance rose,
And white against the cold-white sky,
Shone out their crowning snows.
  One willow over the river wept,
And shook the wave as the wind did sigh;
Above in the wind was the swallow,
Chasing itself at its own wild will,
And far thro' the marish green and still
  The tangled water-courses slept,
Shot over with purple, and green, and yellow.

3.

The wild swan's death-hymn took the soul
Of that waste place with joy
Hidden in sorrow: at first to the ear
The warble was low, and full and clear;
And floating about the under-sky,
Prevailing in weakness, the coronach stole;
Sometimes afar, and sometimes anear,
But anon her awful, jubilant voice,
With a music strange and manifold,
Flow'd forth on a carol free and bold;
As when a mighty people rejoice,
With shawms, and with cymbals, and harps of gold,
And the tumult of their acclaim is roll'd
Thro' the open gates of the city afar,
To the shepherd who watcheth the evening star.
And the creeping mosses and clambering weeds,
And the willow-branches hoar and dank,
And the wavy swell of the soughing reeds,
And the wave-worn horns of the echoing bank,
And the silvery marish-flowers that throng
The desolate creeks and pools among,
Were flooded over with eddying song.

———⟡———

A DIRGE.

1.

Now is done thy long day's work:
  Fold thy palms across thy breast,
  Fold thine arms, turn to thy rest.
    Let them rave.

Shadows of the silver birk
Sweep the green that folds thy grave.
  Let them rave.

2.

Thee nor careth care nor slander;
Nothing but the small cold worm
Fretteth thine enshrouded form.
  Let them rave.
Light and shadow ever wander
O'er the green that folds thy grave.
  Let them rave.

3.

Thou wilt not turn upon thy bed;
Chanteth not the brooding bee
Sweeter tones than calumny?
  Let them rave.
Thou wilt never raise thine head
From the green that folds thy grave.
  Let them rave.

4.

Crocodiles wept tears for thee;
The woodbine and eglatere
Drip sweeter dews than traitor's tear.
  Let them rave.
Rain makes music in the tree
O'er the green that folds thy grave.
  Let them rave.

5.

Round thee blow, self-pleached deep,
Bramble-roses, faint and pale,
And long purples of the dale.
  Let them rave.
These in every shower creep
Thro' the green that folds thy grave.
  Let them rave.

6.

The gold-eyed kingcups fine;
The frail bluebell peereth over
Rare broidry of the purple clover.
  Let them rave.
Kings have no such couch as thine,
As the green that folds thy grave.
  Let them rave.

7.

Wild words wander here and there;
God's great gift of speech abused
Makes thy memory confused:
  But let them rave.
The balm-cricket carols clear
In the green that folds thy grave.
  Let them rave.

———⟡———

LOVE AND DEATH.

What time the mighty moon was gathering light
Love paced the thymy plots of Paradise,
And all about him roll'd his lustrous eyes;
When, turning round a cassia, full in view
Death, walking all alone beneath a yew,
And talking to himself, first met his sight:
"You must begone," said Death, "these walks are
    mine."
Love wept and spread his sheeny vans for flight;
Yet ere he parted said, "This hour is thine:
Thou art the shadow of life, and as the tree
Stands in the sun and shadows all beneath,
So in the light of great eternity
Life eminent creates the shade of death;
The shadow passeth when the tree shall fall,
But I shall reign forever over all."

THE BALLAD OF ORIANA.

My heart is wasted with my woe,
    Oriana.
There is no rest for me below,
    Oriana.
When the long dun wolds are ribb'd with snow,
And loud the Norland whirlwinds blow,
    Oriana,
Alone I wander to and fro,
    Oriana.

Ere the light on dark was growing,
    Oriana,
At midnight the cock was crowing,
    Oriana:
Winds were blowing, waters flowing,
We heard the steeds to battle going,
    Oriana;
Aloud the hollow bugle blowing,
    Oriana.

In the yew-wood black as night,
    Oriana,
Ere I rode into the fight,
    Oriana,
While blissful tears blinded my sight
By star-shine and by moonlight,
    Oriana,
I to thee my troth did plight,
    Oriana.

She stood upon the castle wall,
    Oriana:
She watch'd my crest among them all,
    Oriana:
She saw me fight, she heard me call,
When forth there stept a foeman tall,
    Oriana,
Atween me and the castle wall,
    Oriana.

The bitter arrow went aside,
    Oriana:
The false, false arrow went aside,
    Oriana:
The damned arrow glanced aside,
And pierced thy heart, my love, my bride,
    Oriana!
Thy heart, my life, my love, my bride,
    Oriana!

Oh! narrow, narrow was the space,
    Oriana.
Loud, loud rung out the bugle's brays,
    Oriana.
Oh! deathful stabs were dealt apace,
The battle deepen'd in its place,
    Oriana;
But I was down upon my face,
    Oriana.

They should have stabb'd me where I lay,
    Oriana!
How could I rise and come away,
    Oriana?
How could I look upon the day?
They should have stabb'd me where I lay,
    Oriana—
They should have trod me into clay,
    Oriana.

O breaking heart that will not break,
    Oriana!
O pale, pale face so sweet and meek,
    Oriana!
Thou smilest, but thou dost not speak,
And then the tears run down my cheek,
    Oriana:

What wantest thou? whom dost thou seek,
    Oriana?

I cry aloud: none hear my cries,
    Oriana.
Thou comest atween me and the skies,
    Oriana.
I feel the tears of blood arise
Up from my heart unto my eyes,
    Oriana.
Within thy heart my arrow lies,
    Oriana.

O cursed hand! O cursed blow!
    Oriana!
O happy thou that liest low,
    Oriana!
All night the silence seems to flow
Beside me in my utter woe,
    Oriana.
A weary, weary way I go,
    Oriana.

When Norland winds pipe down the sea,
    Oriana,
I walk, I dare not think of thee.
    Oriana.
Thou liest beneath the greenwood tree,
I dare not die and come to thee,
    Oriana.
I hear the roaring of the sea,
    Oriana.

———

CIRCUMSTANCE.

Two children in two neighbor villages
Playing mad pranks along the healthy leas;
Two strangers meeting at a festival;
Two lovers whispering by an orchard wall;
Two lives bound fast in one with golden ease;
Two graves grass-green beside a gray church-tower
Wash'd with still rains and daisy-blossomed:
Two children in one hamlet born and bred;
So runs the round of life from hour to hour.

———

THE MERMAN.

1.

Who would be
A merman bold,
Sitting alone,
Singing alone
Under the sea,
With a crown of gold,
On a throne?

2.

I would be a merman bold;
I would sit and sing the whole of the day;
I would fill the sea-halls with a voice of power
But at night I would roam abroad and play
With the mermaids in and out of the rocks,
Dressing their hair with the white sea-flower;
And holding them back by their flowing locks
I would kiss them often under the sea,
And kiss them again till they kiss'd me
    Laughingly, laughingly;
And then we would wander away, away
To the pale-green sea-groves straight and high,
    Chasing each other merrily.

3.

There would be neither moon nor star·
But the wave would make music above us afar—
Low thunder and light in the magic night—
    Neither moon nor star.

We would call aloud in the dreamy dells,
  Call to each other and whoop and cry
    All night, merrily, merrily;
They would pelt me with starry spangles and shells,
  Laughing and clapping their hands between,
    All night, merrily, merrily:
But I would throw to them back in mine
Turkis and agate and almondine:
Then leaping out upon them unseen
I would kiss them often under the sea,
And kiss them again till they kiss'd me
    Laughingly, laughingly.
Oh! what a happy life were mine
Under the hollow-hung ocean green!
Soft are the moss-beds under the sea;
We would live merrily, merrily.

—◇—

THE MERMAID.

1.

Who would be
A mermaid fair,
Singing alone,
Combing her hair
Under the sea,
In a golden curl
With a comb of pearl,
On a throne?

2.

I would be a mermaid fair;
I would sing to myself the whole of the day;
With a comb of pearl I would comb my hair;
And still as I comb'd I would sing and say,
"Who is it loves me? who loves not me?"
I would comb my hair till my ringlets would fall,
    Low adown, low adown,
  From under my starry sea-bud crown
    Low adown and around,
  And I should look like a fountain of gold
      Springing alone
    With a shrill inner sound,
      Over the throne
In the midst of the hall:
Till that great sea-snake under the sea
From his coiled sleeps in the central deeps
Would slowly trail himself sevenfold
Round the hall where I sate, and look in at the gate

With his large calm eyes for the love of me.
And all the mermen under the sea
Would feel their immortality
Die in their hearts for the love of me.

3.

But at night I would wander away, away,
  I would fling on each side my low-flowing locks,
And lightly vault from the throne and play
  With the mermen in and out of the rocks;
We would run to and fro, and hide and seek,
  On the broad sea-wolds in the crimson shells,
  Whose silvery spikes are nighest the sea,
But if any came near I would call, and shriek,
And adown the steep like a wave I would leap
  From the diamond-ledges that jut from the dells;
For I would not be kiss'd by all who would list,
Of the bold merry mermen under the sea;
They would sue me, and woo me, and flatter me,
In the purple twilights under the sea;
But the king of them all would carry me,
Woo me, and win me, and marry me,
In the branching jaspers under the sea;
Then all the dry pied things that be
In the hueless mosses under the sea
Would curl round my silver feet silently.
All looking up for the love of me.
And if I should carol aloud, from aloft
All things that are forked, and horned, and soft
Would lean out from the hollow sphere of the sea,
All looking down for the love of me.

—◇—

SONNET TO J. M. K.

My hope and heart is with thee—thou wilt be
A latter Luther, and a soldier-priest
To scare church-harpies from the master's feast:
Our dusted velvets have much need of thee;
Thou art no Sabbath-drawler of old saws,
Distill'd from some worm-canker'd homily;
But spurr'd at heart with fiercest energy
To embattail and to wall about thy cause
With iron-worded proof, hating to hark
The humming of the drowsy pulpit-drone
Half God's good Sabbath, while the worn-out clerk
Brow-beats his desk below. Thou from a throne
Mounted in heaven wilt shoot into the dark
Arrows of lightnings. I will stand and mark.

————◇◇◇◇————

POEMS.

(Published 1832.)

[This division of this volume was published in the winter of 1832. Some of the poems have been considerably altered. Others have been added, which, with one exception, were written in 1833.]

THE LADY OF SHALOTT.

PART I.

On either side the river lie
Long fields of barley and of rye,
That clothe the wold and meet the sky;
And thro' the field the road runs by
    To many-towered Camelot;
And up and down the people go,
Gazing where the lilies blow
Round an island there below,
    The island of Shalott.

Willows whiten, aspens quiver,
Little breezes dusk and shiver

Thro' the wave that runs forever
By the island in the river
    Flowing down to Camelot.
Four gray walls, and four gray towers,
Overlook a space of flowers,
And the silent isle imbowers
    The Lady of Shalott.

By the margin, willow-veil'd,
Slide the heavy barges trail'd
By slow horses; and unhail'd
The shallop flitteth silken-sail'd
    Skimming down to Camelot:
But who hath seen her wave her hand?
Or at the casement seen her stand?
Or is she known in all the land,
    The Lady of Shalott?

" 'The curse is come upon me,' cried
The Lady of Shalott."

Only reapers, reaping early
In among the bearded barley,
Hear a song that echoes cheerly
From the river winding clearly,
    Down to tower'd Camelot:
And by the moon the reaper weary,
Piling sheaves in uplands airy,
Listening, whispers, "'Tis the fairy
    Lady of Shalott."

PART II.

THERE she weaves by night and day
A magic web with colors gay.
She has heard a whisper say,
A curse is on her if she stay
    To look down to Camelot.
She knows not what the curse may be,
And so she weaveth steadily,
And little other care hath she,
    The Lady of Shalott.

And moving thro' a mirror clear
That hangs before her all the year,
Shadows of the world appear.
There she sees the highway near
    Winding down to Camelot:
There the river eddy whirls,
And there the surly village-churls,
And the red cloaks of market girls,
    Pass onward from Shalott.

Sometimes a troop of damsels glad,
An abbot on an ambling pad,
Sometimes a curly shepherd-lad,
Or long-hair'd page in crimson clad,
    Goes by to tower'd Camelot:

And sometimes thro' the mirror blue
The knights come riding two and two:
She hath no loyal knight and true,
    The Lady of Shalott.

But in her web she still delights
To weave the mirror's magic sights,
For often thro' the silent nights
A funeral, with plumes and lights,
    And music, went to Camelot:
Or when the moon was overhead,
Came two young lovers lately wed;
"I am half-sick of shadows," said
    The Lady of Shalott.

PART III.

A BOW-SHOT from her bower-eaves,
He rode between the barley-sheaves,
The sun came dazzling thro' the leaves,
And flamed upon the brazen greaves
    Of bold Sir Lancelot.
A redcross knight forever kneeled
To a lady in his shield,
That sparkled on the yellow field,
    Beside remote Shalott.

The gemmy bridle glitter'd free,
Like to some branch of stars we see
Hung in the golden Galaxy.
The bridle bells rang merrily
    As he rode down to Camelot:
And from his blazon'd baldric slung
A mighty silver bugle hung,
And as he rode his armor rung,
    Beside remote Shalott.

All in the blue unclouded weather
Thick-jewell'd shone the saddle-leather,

The helmet and the helmet-feather
Burned like one burning flame together,
      As he rode down to Camelot.
As often thro' the purple night,
Below the starry clusters bright,
Some bearded meteor, trailing light,
      Moves over still Shalott.

His broad clear brow in sunlight glow'd;
On burnish'd hooves his war-horse trode;
From underneath his helmet flow'd
His coal-black curls as on he rode,
      As he rode down to Camelot.
From the bank and from the river
He flashed into the crystal mirror,
"Tirra lirra," by the river
      Sang Sir Lancelot.

She left the web, she left the loom,
She made three paces thro' the room,
She saw the water-lily bloom,
She saw the helmet and the plume,
      She look'd down to Camelot.
Out flew the web and floated wide;
The mirror crack'd from side to side;
"The curse is come upon me," cried
      The Lady of Shalott.

PART IV.

In the stormy east-wind straining,
The pale yellow woods were waning,
The broad stream in his banks complaining,
Heavily the low sky raining
      Over tower'd Camelot;
Down she came and found a boat
Beneath a willow left afloat,
And round about the prow she wrote
      The Lady of Shalott.

And down the river's dim expanse—
Like some bold seer in a trance,
Seeing all his own mischance—
With a glassy countenance
      Did she look to Camelot.
And at the closing of the day
She loosed the chain, and down she lay;
The broad stream bore her far away,
      The Lady of Shalott.

Lying, robed in snowy white
That loosely flew to left and right—
The leaves upon her falling light—
Thro' the noises of the night
      She floated down to Camelot:
And as the boat-head wound along
The willow hills and fields among,
They heard her singing her last song,
      The Lady of Shalott.

Heard a carol, mournful, holy,
Chanted loudly, chanted lowly,
Till her blood was frozen slowly,
And her eyes were darken'd wholly,
      Turn'd to tower'd Camelot;
For ere she reach'd upon the tide
The first house by the water-side,
Singing in her song she died,
      The Lady of Shalott.

Under tower and balcony,
By garden-wall and gallery,
A gleaming shape she floated by,
A corse between the houses high,
      Silent into Camelot.
Out upon the wharfs they came,
Knight and burgher, lord and dame,
And round the prow they read her name,
      The Lady of Shalott.

Who is this? and what is here?
And in the lighted palace near
Died the sound of royal cheer:
And they cross'd themselves for fear,
      All the knights at Camelot:
But Lancelot mused a little space.
He said, "She has a lovely face;
God in his mercy lend her grace,
      The Lady of Shalott."

———◇◇◇———

MARIANA IN THE SOUTH.

With one black shadow at its feet,
The house thro' all the level shines,
Close-latticed to the brooding heat,
And silent in its dusty vines:
A faint-blue ridge upon the right,
An empty river-bed before,
And shallows on a distant shore,
In glaring sand and inlets bright.
      But "Ave Mary," made she moan,
      And "Ave Mary," night and morn,
      And "Ah," she sang, "to be all alone,
      To live forgotten, and love forlorn."

She, as her carol sadder grew,
From brow and bosom slowly down
Thro' rosy taper fingers drew
Her streaming curls of deepest brown
To left and right, and made appear,
Still-lighted in a secret shrine,
Her melancholy eyes divine,
The home of woe without a tear.
      And "Ave Mary," was her moan,
      "Madonna, sad is night and morn;"
      And "Ah," she sang, "to be all alone,
      To live forgotten, and love forlorn."

Till all the crimson changed, and past
Into deep orange o'er the sea,
Low on her knees herself she cast,
Before Our Lady murmur'd she;
Complaining, "Mother, give me grace
To help me of my weary load,"
And on the liquid mirror glow'd
The clear perfection of her face.
      "Is this the form," she made her moan,
      "That won his praises night and morn?"
      And "Ah," she said, "but I wake alone,
      I sleep forgotten, I wake forlorn."

Nor bird would sing, nor lamb would bleat,
Nor any cloud would cross the vault,
But day increased from heat to heat,
On stony drought and steaming salt;
Till now at noon she slept again,
And seem'd knee-deep in mountain grass,
And heard her native breezes pass,
And runlets babbling down the glen.
      She breathed in sleep a lower moan,
      And murmuring, as at night and morn,
      She thought, "My spirit is here alone,
      Walks forgotten, and is forlorn."

Dreaming, she knew it was a dream:
She felt he was and was not there.
She woke: the babble of the stream
Fell, and without the steady glare
Shrank one sick willow sere and small.
The river-bed was dusty-white:
And all the furnace of the light
Struck up against the blinding wall.
      She whisper'd, with a stifled moan
      More inward than at night or morn,
      "Sweet Mother, let me not here alone
      Live forgotten and die forlorn."

And, rising, from her bosom drew
Old letters, breathing of her worth,
For "Love," they said, "must needs be true,
To what is loveliest upon earth."
An image seem'd to pass the door,
To look at her with slight, and say,
"But now thy beauty flows away,
So be alone forevermore."
   "O cruel heart," she changed her tone,
   "And cruel love, whose end is scorn,
   Is this the end to be left alone,
   To live forgotten, and die forlorn!"

But sometimes in the falling day
An image seem'd to pass the door,
To look into her eyes and say,
"But thou shalt be alone no more."
And flaming downward over all
From heat to heat the day decreased,
And slowly rounded to the east
The one black shadow from the wall.
   "The day to night," she made her moan,
   "The day to night, the night to morn,
   And day and night I am left alone
   To live forgotten, and love forlorn."

At eve a dry cicala sung,
There came a sound as of the sea;
Backward the latticed-blind she flung,
And lean'd upon the balcony.
There all in spaces rosy-bright
Large Hesper glitter'd on her tears,
And deepening through the silent spheres,
Heaven over Heaven rose the night.
   And weeping then she made her moan,
   "The night comes on that knows not morn,
   When I shall cease to be all alone,
   To live forgotten, and love forlorn."

ELEÄNORE.

1.

Thy dark eyes open'd not,
Nor first reveal'd themselves to English air,
   For there is nothing here,
Which, from the outward to the inward brought,
Moulded thy baby thought.
Far off from human neighborhood,
   Thou wert born, on a summer morn,
A mile beneath the cedar-wood.
Thy bounteous forehead was not fann'd
   With breezes from our oaken glades,
But thou wert nursed in some delicious land
Of lavish lights, and floating shades:
And flattering thy childish thought
   The oriental fairy brought,
   At the moment of thy birth,
From old well-heads of haunted rills,
And the hearts of purple hills,
   And shadow'd coves on a sunny shore,
   The choicest wealth of all the earth,
   Jewel or shell, or starry ore,
   To deck thy cradle, Eleänore.

2.

Or the yellow-banded bees,
Thro' half-open lattices
Coming in the scented breeze,
   Fed thee, a child, lying alone,
   With whitest honey in fairy gardens cull'd—
A glorious child, dreaming alone,
In silk-soft folds, upon yielding down,
With the hum of swarming bees
   Into dreamful slumber lull'd.

3.

Who may minister to thee?
Summer herself should minister
   To thee, with fruitage golden-rinded
   On golden salvers, or it may be,
Youngest Autumn, in a bower
Grape-thicken'd from the light, and blinded
   With many a deep-hued bell-like flower
Of fragrant trailers, when the air
   Sleepeth over all the heaven,
   And the crag that fronts the Even,
   All along the shadowing shore,
Crimsons over an inland mere,
   Eleänore!

4.

How may full-sail'd verse express,
How may measured words adore
   The full-flowing harmony
Of thy swan-like stateliness,
   Eleänore?
   The luxuriant symmetry
Of thy floating gracefulness,
   Eleänore?
   Every turn and glance of thine,
   Every lineament divine,
   Eleänore,
   And the steady sunset glow,
   That stays upon thee? For in thee
   Is nothing sudden, nothing single.
   Like two streams of incense free
   From one censer, in one shrine,
   Thought and motion mingle,
Mingle ever. Motions flow
To one another, even as tho'
They were modulated so
   To an unheard melody,
Which lives about thee, and a sweep
Of richest pauses, evermore
Drawn from each other mellow-deep;
   Who may express thee, Eleänore?

5.

I stand before thee, Eleänore;
   I see thy beauty gradually unfold,
Daily and hourly, more and more.
I muse, as in a trance, the while
   Slowly, as from a cloud of gold,
Comes out thy deep ambrosial smile.
I muse, as in a trance, whene'er
   The languors of thy love-deep eyes
Float on to me. I would I were
   So tranced, so rapt in ecstasies,
To stand apart, and to adore,
Gazing on thee forevermore,
Serene, imperial Eleänore!

6.

Sometimes, with most intensity
Gazing, I seem to see
Thought folded over thought, smiling asleep,
Slowly awaken'd, grow so full and deep
In thy large eyes, that, overpower'd quite,
I cannot veil, or droop my sight,
But am as nothing in its light:
As tho' a star, in inmost heaven set,
Ev'n while we gaze on it,
Should slowly round his orb, and slowly grow
To a full face, there like a sun remain
Fix'd—then as slowly fade again,
   And draw itself to what it was before;
   So full, so deep, so slow,
   Thought seems to come and go
   In thy large eyes, imperial Eleänore.

7.

As thunder-clouds, that, hung on high,
   Roof'd the world with doubt and fear,

Floating thro' an evening atmosphere,
Grow golden all about the sky;
In thee all passion becomes passionless,
Touch'd by thy spirit's mellowness,
Losing his fire and active might
  In a silent meditation,
Falling into a still delight,
  And luxury of contemplation:
As waves that up a quiet cove
  Rolling slide, and lying still
    Shadow forth the banks at will:
Or sometimes they swell and move,
  Pressing up against the land.
  With motions of the outer sea:
    And the self-same influence
    Controlleth all the soul and sense
Of Passion gazing upon thee.
His bow-string slacken'd, languid Love,
  Leaning his cheek upon his hand,
  Droops both his wings, regarding thee,
  And so would languish evermore,
  Serene, imperial Eleänore.

8.

But when I see thee roam, with tresses unconfined,
While the amorous, odorous wind
  Breathes low between the sunset and the moon;
  Or, in a shadowy saloon,
On silken curtains half reclined;
  I watch thy grace; and in its place
My heart a charmed slumber keeps,
  While I muse upon thy face;
And a languid fire creeps
  Thro' my veins to all my frame,
Dissolvingly and slowly; soon
  From thy rose-red lips my name
Floweth; and then, as in a swoon,
  With dinning sound my ears are rife,
  My tremulous tongue faltereth,
  I lose my color, I lose my breath,
  I drink the cup of a costly death,
Brimm'd with delirious draughts of warmest life.
  I die with my delight, before
    I hear what I would hear from thee;
    Yet tell my name again to me,
  I would be dying evermore,
  So dying ever, Eleänore.

———⋘⋙———

THE MILLER'S DAUGHTER.

I see the wealthy miller yet,
  His double chin, his portly size,
And who that knew him could forget
  The busy wrinkles round his eyes?
. The slow wise smile that, round about
  His dusty forehead dryly curl'd,
  Seem'd half-within and half-without,
  And full of dealings with the world?

In yonder chair I see him sit,
  Three fingers round the old silver cup—
I see his gray eyes twinkle yet
  At his own jest—gray eyes lit up
With summer lightnings of a soul
  So full of summer warmth, so glad,
  So healthy, sound, and clear and whole,
  His memory scarce can make me sad.

Yet fill my glass: give me one kiss:
  My own sweet Alice, we must die.
There's somewhat in this world amiss
  Shall be unriddled by-and-by.
There's somewhat flows to us in life,
  But more is taken quite away.
Pray, Alice, pray, my darling wife,
  That we may die the self-same day.

Have I not found a happy earth?
  I least should breathe a thought of pain.
Would God renew me from my birth
  I'd almost live my life again.
So sweet it seems with thee to walk,
  And once again to woo thee mine—
It seems in after-dinner talk
  Across the walnuts and the wine—

To be the long and listless boy
  Late-left an orphan of the squire,
Where this old mansion mounted high
  Looks down upon the village spire:
For even here, where I and you
  Have lived and loved alone so long,
Each morn my sleep was broken thro'
  By some wild skylark's matin-song.

And oft I heard the tender dove
  In firry woodlands making moan;
But ere I saw your eyes, my love,
  I had no motion of my own.
For scarce my life with fancy play'd
  Before I dream'd that pleasant dream—
Still hither thither idly sway'd
  Like those long mosses in the stream.

Or from the bridge I lean'd to hear
  The milldam rushing down with noise,
And see the minnows everywhere
  In crystal eddies glance and poise,
The tall flag-flowers when they sprung
  Below the range of stepping-stones,
Or those three chestnuts near, that hung
  In masses thick with milky cones.

But, Alice, what an hour was that,
  When after roving in the woods
('Twas April then), I came and sat
  Below the chestnuts, when their buds
Were glistening to the breezy blue;
  And on the slope, an absent fool,
I cast me down, nor thought of you,
  But angled in the higher pool.

A love-song I had somewhere read,
  An echo from a measured strain,
Beat time to nothing in my head
  From some odd corner of the brain.
It haunted me, the morning long,
  With weary sameness in the rhymes,
The phantom of a silent song,
  That went and came a thousand times.

Then leapt a trout. In lazy mood
  I watch'd the little circles die;
They past into the level flood,
  And there a vision caught my eye;
The reflex of a beauteous form,
  A glowing arm, a gleaming neck,
As when a sunbeam wavers warm
  Within the dark and dimpled beck.

For you remember, you had set,
  That morning, on the casement's edge
A long green box of mignonette,
  And you were leaning from the ledge:
And when I raised my eyes, above
  They met with two so full and bright—
Such eyes! I swear to you, my love,
  That these have never lost their light.

I loved, and love dispell'd the fear
  That I should die an early death;
For love possess'd the atmosphere,
  And fill'd the breast with purer breath
My mother thought, What ails the boy?
  For I was alter'd, and began

To move about the house with joy,
  And with the certain step of man.

I loved the brimming wave that swam
  Thro' quiet meadows round the mill,
The sleepy pool above the dam,
  The pool beneath it never still,
The meal-sacks on the whiten'd floor,
The dark round of the dripping wheel,
The very air about the door
  Made misty with the floating meal.

And oft in ramblings on the wold,
  When April nights began to blow,
And April's crescent glimmer'd cold,
  I saw the village lights below;
I knew your taper far away,
  And full at heart of trembling hope,
From off the wold I came, and lay
  Upon the freshly-flower'd slope.

The deep brook groan'd beneath the mill:
  And "by that lamp," I thought, "she sits!"
The white chalk-quarry from the hill
  Gleamed to the flying moon by fits.
"O that I were beside her now!
  O will she answer if I call?
O would she give me vow for vow,
  Sweet Alice, if I told her all?"

Sometimes I saw you sit and spin;
  And, in the pauses of the wind,
Sometimes I heard you sing within;
  Sometimes your shadow cross'd the blind.
At last you rose and moved the light,
  And the long shadow of the chair
Flitted across into the night,
  And all the casement darken'd there.

But when at last I dared to speak,
  The lanes, you know, were white with May,
Your ripe lips moved not, but your cheek
  Flush'd like the coming of the day;
And so it was—half-sly, half-shy,
  You would, and would not, little one!
Although I pleaded tenderly,
  And you and I were all alone.

And slowly was my mother brought
  To yield consent to my desire:
She wish'd me happy, but she thought
  I might have look'd a little higher;
And I was young—too young to wed:
  "Yet must I love her for your sake:
Go fetch your Alice here," she said:
  Her eyelid quiver'd as she spake.

And down I went to fetch my bride:
  But, Alice, you were ill at ease;
This dress and that by turns you tried,
  Too fearful that you should not please.
I loved you better for your fears,
  I knew you could not look but well;
And dews, that would have fall'n in tears,
  I kiss'd away before they fell.

I watch'd the little flutterings,
  The doubt my mother would not see;
She spoke at large of many things,
  And at the last she spoke of me;
And turning look'd upon your face,
  As near this door you sat apart,
And rose, and, with a silent grace
  Approaching, press'd you heart to heart.

Ah, well—but sing the foolish song
  I gave you, Alice, on the day

When, arm in arm, we went along,
  A pensive pair, and you were gay
With bridal flowers—that I may seem,
  As in the nights of old, to lie
Beside the mill-wheel in the stream,
  While those fall chestnuts whisper by.

It is the miller's daughter,
  And she is grown so dear, so dear,
That I would be the jewel
  That trembles at her ear:
For hid in ringlets day and night,
  I'd touch her neck so warm and white.

And I would be the girdle
  About her dainty dainty waist,
And her heart would beat against me,
  In sorrow and in rest:
And I should know if it beat right,
  I'd clasp it round so close and tight.

And I would be the necklace,
  And all day long to fall and rise
Upon her balmy bosom,
  With her laughter or her sighs,
And I would lie so light, so light,
  I scarce should be unclasp'd at night.

A trifle, sweet! which true love spells—
  True love interprets—right alone.
His light upon the letter dwells,
  For all the spirit is his own.
So, if I waste words now, in truth,
  You must blame Love. His early rage
Had force to make me rhyme in youth,
  And makes me talk too much in age.

And now those vivid hours are gone,
  Like mine own life to me thou art,
Where Past and Present, wound in one,
  Do make a garland for the heart:
So sing that other song I made,
  Half-anger'd with my happy lot,
The day, when in the chestnut-shade
  I found the blue Forget-me-not.

  Love that hath us in the net,
  Can he pass, and we forget?
  Many suns arise and set.
  Many a chance the years beget.
  Love the gift is Love the debt,
      Even so.

  Love is hurt with jar and fret.
  Love is made a vague regret.
  Eyes with idle tears are wet.
  Idle habit links us yet.
  What is love? for we forget:
      Ah, no! no!

Look thro' mine eyes with thine. True wife,
  Round my true heart thine arms entwine;
My other dearer life in life.
  Look thro' my very soul with thine!
Untouch'd with any shade of years,
  May those kind eyes forever dwell!
They have not shed a many tears,
  Dear eyes, since first I knew them well!

Yet tears they shed: they had their part
  Of sorrow: for when time was ripe,
The still affection of the heart
  Became an outward breathing type,
That into stillness past again,
  And left a want unknown before;
Although the loss that brought us pain,
  That loss but made us love the more,

With farther lookings on. The kiss,
The woven arms, seem but to be
Weak symbols of the settled bliss,
The comfort, I have found in thee:
But that God bless thee, dear—who wrought
Two spirits to one equal mind—
With blessings beyond hope or thought,
With blessings which no words can find.

Arise. and let us wander forth,
To yon old mill across the wolds:
For look, the sunset, south and north,
Winds all the vale in rosy folds,
And fires your narrow casement glass,
Touching the sullen pool below:
On the chalk-hill the bearded grass
Is dry and dewless. Let us go.

———<>———

FATIMA.

O Love, Love, Love! O withering might!
O sun, that from thy noonday height
Shudderest when I strain my sight,
Throbbing thro' all thy heat and light,
Lo, falling from my constant mind,
Lo, parch'd and wither'd, deaf and blind,
I whirl like leaves in roaring wind.

Last night I wasted hateful hours
Below the city's eastern towers:
I thirsted for the brooks, the showers:
I roll'd among the tender flowers ·
I crush'd them on my breast, my mouth :
I look'd athwart the burning drouth
Of that long desert to the south.

Last night, when some one spoke his name,
From my swift blood that went and came
A thousand little shafts of flame
Were shiver'd in my narrow frame.
O Love, O fire! once he drew
With one long kiss my whole soul thro'
My lips, as sunlight drinketh dew.

Before he mounts the hill, I know
He cometh quickly: from below
Sweet gales, as from deep gardens, blow
Before him, striking on my brow.
In my dry brain my spirit soon,
Down-deepening from swoon to swoon,
Faints like a dazzled morning moon.

The wind sounds like a silver wire,
And from beyond the noon a fire
Is pour'd upon the hills, and nigher
The skies stoop down in their desire;
And, isled in sudden seas of light,
My heart, pierced thro' with fierce delight,
Bursts into blossom in his sight.

My whole soul waiting silently,
All naked in a sultry sky,
Droops blinded with his shining eye:
I will possess him or will die.
I will grow round him in his place,
Grow, live, die looking on his face,
Die, dying clasp'd in his embrace.

———<>———

ŒNONE.

There lies a vale in Ida, lovelier
Than all the valleys of Ionian hills.
The swimming vapor slopes athwart the glen,
Puts forth an arm, and creeps from pine to pine,
And loiters, slowly drawn. On either hand
The lawns and meadow-ledges midway down

Hang rich in flowers, and far below them roars
The long brook falling thro' the clov'n ravine
In cataract after cataract to the sea.
Behind the valley topmost Gargarus
Stands up and takes the morning: but in front
The gorges, opening wide apart, reveal
Troas and Ilion's column'd citadel,
The crown of Troas.

          Hither came at noon
Mournful Œnone, wandering forlorn
Of Paris, once her playmate on the hills.
Her cheek had lost the rose, and round her neck
Floated her hair or seem'd to float in rest.
She, leaning on a fragment twined with vine,
Sang to the stillness, till the mountain-shade
Sloped downward to her seat in the upper cliff.

"O mother Ida, many-fountain'd Ida,
Dear mother Ida, hearken ere I die.
For now the noonday quiet holds the hill:
The grasshopper is silent in the grass:
The lizard, with his shadow on the stone,
Rests like a shadow, and the cicala sleeps.
The purple flowers droop: the golden bee
Is lily-cradled: I alone awake.
My eyes are full of tears, my heart of love,
My heart is breaking, and my eyes are dim,
And I am all aweary of my life.

"O mother Ida, many-fountain'd Ida,
Dear mother Ida, hearken ere I die.
Hear me O Earth, hear me O Hills, O Caves
That house the cold-crown'd snake! O mountain
      brooks,
I am the daughter of a River-God,
Hear me, for I will speak, and build up all
My sorrow with my song, as yonder walls
Rose slowly to a music slowly breathed,
A cloud that gather'd shape: for it may be
That, while I speak of it, a little while
My heart may wander from its deeper woe.

"O mother Ida, many-fountain'd Ida,
Dear mother Ida, hearken ere I die.
I waited underneath the dawning hills,
Aloft the mountain lawn was dewy-dark,
And dewy-dark aloft the mountain pine:
Beautiful Paris, evil-hearted Paris,
Leading a jet-black goat white-horn'd, white-hooved,
Came up from reedy Simois all alone.

"O mother Ida, hearken ere I die.
Far-off the torrent call'd me from the cleft:
Far up the solitary morning smote
The streaks of virgin snow. With down-dropt eyes
I sat alone: white-breasted like a star
Fronting the dawn he moved; a leopard skin
Droop'd from his shoulder, but his sunny hair
Cluster'd about his temples like a God's:
And his cheek brighten'd as the foam-bow brightens
When the wind blows the foam, and all my heart
Went forth to embrace him coming ere he came.

"Dear mother Ida, hearken ere I die.
He smiled, and opening out his milk-white palm
Disclosed a fruit of pure Hesperian gold,
That smelt ambrosially, and while I look'd
And listen'd, the full-flowing river of speech
Came down upon my heart.
                    "'My own Œnone,
Beautiful-brow'd Œnone, my own soul,
Behold this fruit, whose gleaming rind engrav'n
"For the most fair," would seem to award it thine,
As lovelier than whatever Oread haunt
The knolls of Ida, loveliest in all grace
Of movement, and the charm of married brows.'

"Dear mother Ida, hearken ere I die.
He prest the blossom of his lips to mine,

And added, 'This was cast upon the board,
When all the full-faced presence of the Gods
Ranged in the halls of Peleus; whereupon
Rose feud, with question unto whom 'twere due:
But light-foot Iris brought it yester-eve,
Delivering, that to me, by common voice
Elected umpire, Herè comes to-day,
Pallas and Aphrodite, claiming each
This meed of fairest. Thou, within the cave
Behind yon whispering tuft of oldest pine,
Mayst well behold them unbeheld, unheard
Hear all, and see thy Paris judge of Gods.'

"Dear mother Ida, hearken ere I die.
It was the deep midnoon: one silvery cloud
Had lost his way between the piny sides
Of this long glen. Then to the bower they came,
Naked they came to that smooth-swarded bower,
And at their feet the crocus brake like fire,
Violet, amaracus, and asphodel,
Lotos and lilies: and a wind arose,
And overhead the wandering ivy and vine,
This way and that, in many a wild festoon
Ran riot, garlanding the gnarled boughs
With bunch and berry and flower thro' and thro.'

"O mother Ida, hearken ere I die.
On the tree-tops a crested peacock lit,
And o'er him flow'd a golden cloud, and lean'd
Upon him, slowly dropping fragrant dew.
Then first I heard the voice of her, to whom
Coming thro' Heaven, like a light that grows
Larger and clearer, with one mind the Gods
Rise up for reverence. She to Paris made
Proffer of royal power, ample rule
Unquestion'd, overflowing revenue
Wherewith to embellish state, 'from many a vale
And river-sunder'd champaign clothed with corn,
Or labor'd mines undrainable of ore.
Honor,' she said, 'and homage, tax and toll,
From many an inland town and haven large,
Mast-throng'd beneath her shadowing citadel
In glassy bays among her tallest towers.'

"O mother Ida, hearken ere I die.
Still she spake on and still she spake of power,
'Which in all action is the end of all:
Power fitted to the season: wisdom-bred
And throned of wisdom—from all neighbor crowns
Alliance and allegiance, till thy hand
Fail from the sceptre-staff. Such boon from me,
From me, Heaven's Queen, Paris, to thee king-born,
A shepherd all thy life but yet king-born,
Should come most welcome, seeing men, in power
Only, are likest gods, who have attain'd
Rest in a happy place and quiet seats
Above the thunder, with undying bliss
In knowledge of their own supremacy.'

"Dear mother Ida, hearken ere I die.
She ceased, and Paris held the costly fruit
Out at arm's-length, so much the thought of power
Flatter'd his spirit; but Pallas where she stood
Somewhat apart, her clear and bared limbs
O'erthwarted with the brazen-headed spear
Upon her pearly shoulder leaning cold,
The while, above, her full and earnest eye
Over her snow-cold breast and angry cheek
Kept watch, waiting decision, made reply.

"'Self-reverence, self-knowledge, self-control,
These three alone lead life to sovereign power.
Yet not for power, (power of herself
Would come uncall'd for) but to live by law,
Acting the law we live by without fear;
And, because right is right, to follow right
Were wisdom in the scorn of consequence.'

"Dear mother Ida, hearken ere I die.
Again she said: 'I woo thee not with gifts.
Sequel of guerdon could not alter me
To fairer. Judge thou me by what I am,
So shalt thou find me fairest.

                          Yet, indeed,
If gazing on divinity disrobed
Thy mortal eyes are frail to judge of fair,
Unbiass'd by self-profit, oh! rest thee sure
That I shall love thee well and cleave to thee,
So that my vigor, wedded to thy blood,
Shall strike within thy pulses, like a God's,
To push thee forward thro' a life of shocks,
Dangers, and deeds, until endurance grow
Sinew'd with action, and the full-grown will,
Circled thro' all experiences, pure law,
Commeasure perfect freedom.'
                          "Here she ceased,
And Paris ponder'd, and I cried, 'O Paris,
Give it to Pallas!' but he heard me not,
Or hearing would not hear me, woe is me!

"O mother Ida, many-fountain'd Ida,
Dear mother Ida, hearken ere I die.
Idalian Aphrodite beautiful,
Fresh as the foam, new-bathed in Paphian wells,
With rosy slender fingers backward drew
From her warm brows and bosom her deep hair
Ambrosial, golden round her lucid throat
And shoulder: from the violets her light foot
Shone rosy-white, and o'er her rounded form
Between the shadows of the vine-bunches
Floated the glowing sunlights, as she moved.

"Dear mother Ida, hearken ere I die.
She with a subtle smile in her mild eyes,
The herald of her triumph, drawing nigh
Half-whisper'd in his ear, 'I promise thee
The fairest and most loving wife in Greece.'
She spoke and laughed: I shut my sight for fear
But when I look'd, Paris had raised his arm,
And I beheld great Herè's angry eyes,
As she withdrew into the golden cloud,
And I was left alone within the bower;
And from that time to this I am alone,
And I shall be alone until I die.

"Yet, mother Ida, hearken ere I die.
Fairest—why fairest wife? am I not fair?
My love hath told me so a thousand times.
Methinks I must be fair, for yesterday,
When I passed by, a wild and wanton bird,
Eyed like the evening star, with playful tail
Crouch'd fawning in the weed. Most loving is she?
Ah me, my mountain shepherd, that my arms
Were wound about thee, and my hot lips prest
Close, close to thine in that quick-falling dew
Of fruitful kisses, thick as Autumn rains
Flash in the pools of whirling Simois.

"O mother, hear me yet before I die.
They came, they cut away my tallest pines,
My dark tall pines, that plumed the craggy ledge
High over the blue gorge, and all between
The snowy peak and snow-white cataract
Foster'd the callow eaglet—from beneath
Whose thick mysterious boughs in the dark morn
The panther's roar came muffled, while I sat
Low in the valley. Never, never more
Shall lone Œnone see the morning mist
Sweep thro' them: never see them overlaid
With narrow moon-lit slips of silver cloud,
Between the loud stream and the trembling stars.

"O mother, hear me yet before I die.
I wish that somewhere in the ruin'd folds,
Among the fragments tumbled from the glens,
Or the dry thickets, I could meet with her,
The Abominable, that uninvited came

Into the fair Peleïan banquet-hall,
And cast the golden fruit upon the board,
And bred this change; that I might speak my mind,
And tell her to her face how much I hate
Her presence, hated both of Gods and men.

"O mother, hear me yet before I die.
Hath he not sworn his love a thousand times,
In this green valley, under this green hill,
Ev'n on this hand, and sitting on this stone?
Seal'd it with kisses? water'd it with tears?
O happy tears, and how unlike to these!
O happy Heaven, how canst thou see my face?
O happy earth, how canst thou bear my weight?
O death, death, death, thou ever-floating cloud,
There are enough unhappy on this earth,
Pass by the happy souls, that love to live:
I pray thee, pass before my light of life,
And shadow all my soul, that I may die.
Thou weighest heavy on the heart within,
Weigh heavy on my eyelids: let me die.

"O mother, hear me yet before I die.
I will not die alone, for fiery thoughts
Do shape themselves within me, more and more,
Whereof I catch the issue, as I hear
Dead sounds at night come from the inmost hills,
Like footsteps upon wool. I dimly see
My far-off doubtful purpose, as a mother
Conjectures of the features of her child
Ere it is born: her child! a shudder comes
Across me: never child be born of me,
Unblest, to vex me with his father's eyes!

"O mother, hear me yet before I die.
Hear me, O earth. I will not die alone,
Lest their shrill happy laughter come to me
Walking the cold and starless road of Death
Uncomforted, leaving my ancient love
With the Greek woman. I will rise and go
Down into Troy, and ere the stars come forth
Talk with the wild Cassandra, for she says
A fire dances before her, and a sound
Rings ever in her ears of armed men.
What this may be I know not, but I know
That, wheresoe'er I am by night and day,
All earth and air seem only burning fire."

———

THE SISTERS.

We were two daughters of one race:
She was the fairest in the face:
    The wind is blowing in turret and tree.
They were together, and she fell;
Therefore revenge became me well.
    O the Earl was fair to see!

She died: she went to burning flame:
She mix'd her ancient blood with shame.
    The wind is howling in turret and tree.
Whole weeks and months, and early and late,
To win his love I lay in wait:
    O the Earl was fair to see!

I made a feast; I bade him come;
I won his love, I brought him home.
    The wind is roaring in turret and tree.
And after supper, on a bed,
Upon my lap he laid his head:
    O the Earl was fair to see!

I kiss'd his eyelids into rest:
His ruddy cheek upon my breast.
    The wind is raging in turret and tree.
I hated him with the hate of hell,
But I loved his beauty passing well.
    O the Earl was fair to see!

I rose up in the silent night:
I made my dagger sharp and bright.
    The wind is raving in turret and tree.
As half-asleep his breath he drew,
Three times I stabb'd him thro' and thro'.
    O the Earl was fair to see!

I curl'd and comb'd his comely head,
He look'd so grand when he was dead.
    The wind is blowing in turret and tree.
I wrapt his body in the sheet,
And laid him at his mother's feet.
    O the Earl was fair to see!

———

TO ———.

WITH THE FOLLOWING POEM.

I send you here a sort of allegory,
(For you will understand it) of a soul,
A sinful soul possess'd of many gifts,
A spacious garden full of flowering weeds,
A glorious Devil, large in heart and brain,
That did love Beauty only, (Beauty seen
In all varieties of mould and mind,)
And Knowledge for its beauty; or if Good,
Good only for its beauty, seeing not
That Beauty, Good, and Knowledge are three sisters
That doat upon each other, friends to man,
Living together under the same roof,
And never can be sunder'd without tears,
And he that shuts Love out, in turn shall be
Shut out from Love, and on her threshold lie
Howling in outer darkness. Not for this
Was common clay ta'en from the common earth,
Moulded by God, and temper'd with the tears
Of angels to the perfect shape of man.

———

THE PALACE OF ART.

I built my soul a lordly pleasure-house,
    Wherein at ease for aye to dwell.
I said, "O Soul, make merry and carouse,
    Dear soul, for all is well."

A huge crag-platform, smooth as burnish'd brass,
    I chose. The ranged ramparts bright
From level meadow-bases of deep grass
    Suddenly scaled the light.

Thereon I built it firm. Of ledge or shelf
    The rock rose clear, or winding stair.
My soul would live alone unto herself
    In her high palace there.

And "while the world runs round and round," I said,
    "Reign thou apart, a quiet king,
Still as, while Saturn whirls, his steadfast shade
    Sleeps on his luminous ring."

To which my soul made answer readily:
    "Trust me, in bliss I shall abide
In this great mansion, that is built for me,
    So royal-rich and wide."

    *   *   *   *   *   *   *

    *   *   *   *   *   *   *

Four courts I made, East, West and South and North,
    In each a squared lawn, wherefrom
The golden gorge of dragons spouted forth
    A flood of fountain-foam.

And round the cool green courts there ran a row
    Of cloisters, branch'd like mighty woods,
Echoing all night to that sonorous flow
    Of spouted fountain-floods.

And round the roofs a gilded gallery
  That lent broad verge to distant lands,
Far as the wild swan wings, to where the sky
  Dipt down to sea and sands.

From those four jets four currents in one swell
  Across the mountain stream'd below
In misty folds, that floating as they fell
  Lit up a torrent-bow.

And high on every peak a statue seem'd
  To hang on tiptoe, tossing up
A cloud of incense of all odor steam'd
  From out a golden cup.

So that she thought, "And who shall gaze upon
  My palace with unblinded eyes,
While this great bow will waver in the sun,
  And that sweet incense rise?"

For that sweet incense rose and never fail'd,
  And, while day sank or mounted higher,
The light aërial gallery, golden-rail'd,
  Burnt like a fringe of fire.

Likewise the deep-set windows, stain'd and traced,
  Would seem slow-flaming crimson fires
From shadow'd grots of arches interlaced,
  And tipt with frost-like spires.

*   *   *   *   *   *   *

*   *   *   *   *   *   *

Full of long-sounding corridors it was,
  That over-vaulted grateful gloom,
Thro' which the live-long day my soul did pass,
  Well-pleased, from room to room.

Full of great rooms and small the palace stood,
  All various, each a perfect whole
From living Nature, fit for every mood
  And change of my still soul.

For some were hung with arras green and blue,
  Showing a gaudy summer-morn,
Where with puff'd cheek the belted hunter blew
  His wreathèd bugle-horn.

One seem'd all dark and red,—a tract of sand,
  And some one pacing there alone,
Who paced forever in a glimmering land,
  Lit with a low large moon.

One show'd an iron coast and angry waves.
  You seem'd to hear them climb and fall
And roar rock-thwarted under bellowing caves,
  Beneath the windy wall.

And one, a full-fed river winding slow
  By herds upon an endless plain,
The ragged rims of thunder brooding low,
  With shadow-streaks of rain.

And one, the reapers at their sultry toil,
  In front they bound the sheaves. Behind
Were realms of upland, prodigal in oil,
  And hoary to the wind.

And one, a foreground black with stones and slags,
  Beyond, a line of heights, and higher
All barr'd with long white cloud the scornful crags,
  And highest, snow and fire.

And one, an English home,—gray twilight pour'd
  On dewy pastures, dewy trees,
Softer than sleep,—all things in order stored,
  A haunt of ancient Peace.

Nor these alone, but every landscape fair,
  As fit for every mood of mind,
Or gay, or grave, or sweet, or stern, was there,
  Not less than truth design'd.

*   *   *   *   *   *

*   *   *   *   *   *   *

Or the maid-mother by a crucifix,
  In tracts of pasture sunny-warm,
Beneath branch-work of costly sardonyx
  Sat smiling, babe in arm.

Or in a clear-wall'd city on the sea,
  Near gilded organ-pipes, her hair
Wound with white roses, slept St. Cecily;
  An angel looked at her.

Or thronging all one porch of Paradise,
  A group of Houris bow'd to see
The dying Islamite, with hands and eyes
  That said, We wait for thee.

Or mythic Uther's deeply-wounded son
  In some fair space of sloping greens
Lay, dozing in the vale of Avalon,
  And watch'd by weeping queens.

Or hollowing one hand against his ear,
  To list a footfall, ere he saw
The wood-nymph, stay'd the Ausonian king to hear
  Of wisdom and of law.

Or over hills with peaky tops engrail'd,
  And many a tract of palm and rice,
The throne of Indian Cama slowly sail'd
  A summer fann'd with spice.

Or sweet Europa's mantle blew unclasp'd,
  From off her shoulder backward borne:
From one hand droop'd a crocus: one hand grasp'd
  The mild bull's golden horn.

Or else flushed Ganymede, his rosy thigh
  Half-buried in the Eagle's down,
Sole as a flying star shot thro' the sky
  Above the pillar'd town.

Nor these alone: but every legend fair
  Which the supreme Caucasian mind
Carved out of Nature for itself, was there,
  Not less than life, design'd.

*   *   *   *   *   *   *

*   *   *   *   *   *   *

Then in the towers I placed great bells that swung,
  . Moved of themselves, with silver sound;
And with choice paintings of wise men I hung
  The royal dais round.

For there was Milton like a seraph strong,
  Beside him Shakespeare bland and mild;
And there the world-worn Dante grasp'd his song,
  And somewhat grimly smiled.

And there the Ionian father of the rest;
  A million wrinkles carved his skin;
A hundred winters snow'd upon his breast,
  From cheek and throat and chin.

Above, the fair hall-ceiling stately-set
  Many an arch high up did lift,
And angels rising and descending met
  With interchange of gift.

Below was all mosaic choicely plann'd
  With cycles of the human tale

"Lay, dozing in the vale of Avalon,
And watch'd by weeping queens."

Of this wide world, the times of every land
　So wrought, they will not fail.

The people here, a beast of burden slow,
　Toil'd onward, prick'd with goads and stings;
Here play'd a tiger, rolling to and fro
　The heads and crowns of kings;

Here rose an athlete, strong to break or bind
　All force in bonds that might endure,
And here once more like some sick man declin'd,
　And trusted any cure.

But over these she trod: and those great bells
　Began to chime. She took her throne:
She sat betwixt the shining Oriels,
　To sing her songs alone.

And thro' the topmost Oriels' color'd flame
　Two godlike faces gazed below;
Plato the wise, and large-brow'd Verulam,
　The first of those who know.

And all those names, that in their motion were
　Full-welling fountain-heads of change,
Betwixt the slender shafts were blazon'd fair
　In diverse raiment strange:

Thro' which the lights, rose, amber, emerald, blue,
　Flush'd in her temples and her eyes,
And from her lips, as morn from Memnon, drew
　Rivers of melodies.

No nightingale delighteth to prolong
　Her low preamble all alone,
More than my soul to hear her echo'd song
　Throb thro' the ribbed stone;

Singing and murmuring in her feastful mirth,
　Joying to feel herself alive,
Lord over Nature, Lord of the visible earth,
　Lord of the senses five;

Communing with herself: "All these are mine,
　And let the world have peace or wars,
'Tis one to me." She—when young night divine
　Crown'd dying day with stars,

Making sweet close of his delicious toils—
　Lit light in wreaths and anadems,
And pure quintessences of precious oils
　In hollow'd moons of gems,

To mimic heaven; and clapt her hands and cried,
　"I marvel if my still delight
In this great house so royal-rich, and wide,
　Be flatter'd to the height.

"O all things fair to sate my various eyes!
　O shapes and hues that please me well!
O silent faces of the Great and Wise,
　My Gods, with whom I dwell!

"O God-like isolation which art mine,
　I can but count thee perfect gain,
What time I watch the darkening droves of swine
　That range on yonder plain.

"In filthy sloughs they roll a prurient skin,
　They graze and wallow, breed and sleep;
And oft some brainless devil enters in,
　And drives them to the deep."

Then of the moral instinct would she prate,
　And of the rising from the dead,
As hers by right of full-accomplish'd Fate;
　And at the last she said:

"I take possession of man's mind and deed.
　I care not what the sects may brawl.
I sit as God holding no form of creed,
　But contemplating all."

　＊　　＊　　＊　　＊　　＊　　＊　　＊

　＊　　＊　　＊　　＊　　＊　　＊　　＊

Full oft the riddle of the painful earth
 Flash'd thro' her as she sat alone,
Yet not the less held she her solemn mirth,
 And intellectual throne.

And so she throve and prosper'd: so three years
 She prosper'd: on the fourth she fell,
Like Herod, when the shout was in his ears,
 Struck thro' with pangs of hell.

Lest she should fail and perish utterly,
 God, before whom ever lie bare
The abysmal deeps of Personality,
 Plagued her with sore despair.

When she would think, where'er she turn'd her sight,
 The airy hand confusion wrought,
Wrote "Mene, mene," and divided quite
 The kingdom of her thought.

Deep dread and loathing of her solitude
 Fell on her, from which mood was born
Scorn of herself; again, from out that mood
 Laughter at her self-scorn.

"What! is not this my place of strength," she said,
 "My spacious mansion built for me,
Whereof the strong foundation-stones were laid
 Since my first memory?"

But in dark corners of her palace stood
 Uncertain shapes; and unawares
On white-eyed phantasms weeping tears of blood,
 And horrible nightmares,

And hollow shades enclosing hearts of flame,
 And, with dim fretted foreheads all,
On corpses three-months old at noon she came,
 That stood against the wall.

A spot of dull stagnation, without light
 Or power of movement, seem'd my soul,
'Mid onward-sloping motions infinite
 Making for one sure goal.

A still salt pool, lock'd in with bars of sand;
 Left on the shore; that hears all night
The plunging seas draw backward from the land
 Their moon-led waters white.

A star that with the choral starry dance
 Join'd not, but stood, and standing saw
The hollow orb of moving Circumstance
 Roll'd round by one fix'd law.

Back on herself her serpent pride had curl'd.
 "No voice," she shriek'd in that lone hall,
"No voice breaks thro' the stillness of this world:
 One deep, deep silence all!"

She, mouldering with the dull earth's mouldering sod,
 Inwrapt tenfold in slothful shame,
Lay there exiled from eternal God,
 Lost to her place and name;

And death and life she hated equally,
 And nothing saw, for her despair,
But dreadful time, dreadful eternity,
 No comfort anywhere;

Remaining utterly confused with fears,
 And ever worse with growing time,
And ever unrelieved by dismal tears,
 And all alone in crime:

Shut up as in a crumbling tomb, girt round
 With blackness as a solid wall,
Far off she seem'd to hear the dully sound
 Of human footsteps fall.

As in strange lands a traveller walking slow,
 In doubt and great perplexity,
A little before moon-rise hears the low
 Moan of an unknown sea;

And knows not if it be thunder or a sound
 Of rocks thrown down, or one deep cry
Of great wild beasts; then thinketh, "I have found
 A new land, but I die."

She howl'd aloud, "I am on fire within.
 There comes no murmur of reply.
What is it that will take away my sin,
 And save me lest I die?"

So when four years were wholly finished,
 She threw her royal robes away,
"Make me a cottage in the vale," she said,
 "Where I may mourn and pray.

"Yet pull not down my palace towers, that are
 So lightly, beautifully built:
Perchance I may return with others there
 When I have purged my guilt."

LADY CLARA VERE DE VERE.

Lady Clara Vere de Vere,
 Of me you shall not win renown:
You thought to break a country heart
 For pastime, ere you went to town.
At me you smiled, but unbeguiled
 I saw the snare, and I retired:
The daughter of a hundred Earls,
 You are not one to be desired.

Lady Clara Vere de Vere,
 I know you proud to bear your name,
Your pride is yet no mate for mine,
 Too proud to care from whence I came.
Nor would I break for your sweet sake
 A heart that doats on truer charms.
A simple maiden in her flower
 Is worth a hundred coats-of-arms.

Lady Clara Vere de Vere,
 Some meeker pupil you must find,
For were you queen of all that is,
 I could not stoop to such a mind.
You sought to prove how I could love,
 And my disdain is my reply.
The lion on your old stone gates
 Is not more cold to you than I.

Lady Clara Vere de Vere,
 You put strange memories in my head.
Not thrice your branching limes have blown
 Since I beheld young Laurence dead.
Oh your sweet eyes, your low replies:
 A great enchantress you may be;
But there was that across his throat
 Which you had hardly cared to see.

Lady Clara Vere de Vere,
 When thus he met his mother's view,
She had the passions of her kind,
 She spake some certain truths of you.
Indeed I heard one bitter word
 That scarce is fit for you to hear;
Her manners had not that repose
 Which stamps the caste of Vere de Vere.

Lady Clara Vere de Vere,
 There stands a spectre in your hall:
The guilt of blood is at your door:
 You changed a wholesome heart to gall.

You held your course without remorse,
    To make him trust his modest worth,
And, last, you fix'd a vacant stare,
    And slew him with your noble birth.

Trust me, Clara Vere de Vere,
    From yon blue heavens above us bent
The grand old gardener and his wife
    Smile at the claims of long descent.
Howe'er it be, it seems to me,
    'Tis only noble to be good.
Kind hearts are more than coronets,
    And simple faith than Norman blood.

I know you, Clara Vere de Vere:
    You pine among your halls and towers:

The languid light of your proud eyes
    Is wearied of the rolling hours.
In glowing health, with boundless wealth,
    But sickening of a vague disease,
You know so ill to deal with time,
    You needs must play such pranks as these.

Clara, Clara Vere de Vere,
    If Time be heavy on your hands,
Are there no beggars at your gate,
    Nor any poor about your lands?
Oh! teach the orphan-boy to read,
    Or teach the orphan-girl to sew,
Pray Heaven for a human heart,
    And let the foolish yeoman go.

THE MAY QUEEN.

"You must wake and call me early, call me early, mother dear."

You must wake and call me early, call me early, mother dear;
To-morrow 'ill be the happiest time of all the glad New-year;
Of all the glad New-year, mother, the maddest merriest day;
For I'm to be Queen o' the May, mother, I'm to be Queen o' the May.

There's many a black black eye, they say, but none so bright as mine;
There's Margaret and Mary, there's Kate and Caroline:
But none so fair as little Alice in all the land they say,
So I'm to be Queen o' the May, mother, I'm to be Queen o' the May.

I sleep so sound all night, mother, that I shall never wake,
If you do not call me loud when the day begins to break:
But I must gather knots of flowers, and buds and garlands gay,
For I'm to be Queen o' the May, mother, I'm to be Queen o' the May.

As I came up the valley whom think ye should I see,
But Robin leaning on the bridge beneath the hazel-tree?
He thought of that sharp look, mother, I gave him yesterday,—
But I'm to be Queen o' the May, mother, I'm to be Queen o' the May.

He thought I was a ghost, mother, for I was all in white,
And I ran by him without speaking, like a flash of light.
They call me cruel-hearted, but I care not what they say,
For I'm to be Queen o' the May, mother, I'm to be Queen o' the May.

They say he's dying all for love, but that can never be:
They say his heart is breaking, mother—what is that to me?
There's many a bolder lad 'ill woo me any summer day,
And I'm to be Queen o' the May, mother, I'm to be Queen o' the May.

Little Effie shall go with me to-morrow to the green,
And you'll be there, too, mother, to see me made the Queen;
For the shepherd lads on every side 'ill come from far away,
And I'm to be Queen o' the May, mother, I'm to be Queen o' the May.

The honeysuckle round the porch has wov'n its wavy bowers,
And by the meadow-trenches blow the faint sweet cuckoo-flowers;
And the wild marsh-marigold shines like fire in swamps and hollows gray,
And I'm to be Queen o' the May, mother, I'm to be Queen o' the May.

The night-winds come and go, mother, upon the meadow-grass,
And the happy stars above them seem to brighten as they pass;
There will not be a drop of rain the whole of the livelong day,
And I'm to be Queen o' the May, mother, I'm to be Queen o' the May.

All the valley, mother, 'ill be fresh and green and still,
And the cowslip and the crowfoot are over all the hill,
And the rivulet in the flowery dale 'ill merrily glance and play,
For I'm to be Queen o' the May, mother, I'm to be Queen o' the May.

So you must wake and call me early, call me early, mother dear,
To-morrow 'ill be the happiest time of all the glad New-year:
To-morrow 'ill be of all the year the maddest merriest day,
For I'm to be Queen o' the May, mother, I'm to be Queen o' the May.

NEW-YEAR'S EVE.

If you're waking, call me early, call me early, mother dear,
For I would see the sun rise upon the glad New-year.
It is the last New-year that I shall ever see,
Then you may lay me low i' the mould and think no more of me.

To-night I saw the sun set: he set and left behind
The good old year, the dear old time, and all my peace of mind;
And the New-year's coming up, mother, but I shall never see
The blossom on the blackthorn, the leaf upon the tree.

Last May we made a crown of flowers: we had a merry day;
Beneath the hawthorn on the green they made me Queen of May;
And we danced about the may-pole and in the hazel copse,
Till Charles's Wain came out above the tall white chimney-tops.

There's not a flower on all the hills; the frost is on the pane:
I only wish to live till the snowdrops come again:
I wish the snow would melt and the sun come out on high:
I long to see a flower so before the day I die.

The building rook 'ill caw from the windy tall elm-tree,
And the tufted plover pipe along the fallow lea,
And the swallow 'ill come back again with summer o'er the wave,
But I shall lie alone, mother, within the mouldering grave.

" Last May we made a crown of flowers, we had a merry day;
Beneath the hawthorn on the green they made me Queen of May."

Upon the chancel-casement, and upon that grave of mine,
In the early early morning the summer sun 'ill shine,
Before the red cock crows from the farm upon the hill,
When you are warm-asleep, mother, and all the world is still.

When the flowers come again, mother, beneath the waning light
You'll never see me more in the long gray fields at night;
When from the dry dark wold the summer airs blow cool
On the oat-grass and the sword-grass, and the bulrush in the pool.

You'll bury me, my mother, just beneath the hawthorn shade,
And you'll come sometimes and see me where I am lowly laid.
I shall not forget you, mother, I shall hear you when you pass,
With your feet above my head in the long and pleasant grass.

I have been wild and wayward, but you'll forgive me now;
You'll kiss me, my own mother, and forgive me ere I go;
Nay, nay, you must not weep, nor let your grief be wild,
You should not fret for me, mother, you have another child.

If I can I'll come again, mother, from out my resting-place;
Tho' you'll not see me, mother, I shall look upon your face;
Tho' I cannot speak a word, I shall hearken what you say,
And be often, often with you when you think I'm far away.

Good-night, good-night, when I have said good-night forevermore,
And you see me carried out from the threshold of the door;
Don't let Effie come to see me till my grave be growing green,
She'll be a better child to you than ever I have been.

She'll find my garden-tools upon the granary floor:
Let her take 'em: they are hers: I shall never garden more:
But tell her, when I'm gone, to train the rose-bush that I set
About the parlor-window and the box of mignonette.

Good-night, sweet mother: call me before the day is born,
All night I lie awake, but I fall asleep at morn;
But I would see the sun rise upon the glad New-year,
So, if you're waking, call me, call me early, mother dear.

CONCLUSION.

I thought to pass away before, and yet alive I am;
And in the fields all round I hear the bleating of the lamb.
How sadly, I remember, rose the morning of the year!
To die before the snowdrop came, and now the violet's here.

O sweet is the new violet, that comes beneath the skies,
And sweeter is the young lamb's voice to me that cannot rise,
And sweet is all the land about, and all the flowers that blow,
And sweeter far is death than life to me that long to go.

It seem'd so hard at first, mother, to leave the blessed sun,
And now it seems as hard to stay, and yet His will be done!
But still I think it can't be long before I find release;
And that good man, the clergyman, has told me words of peace.

O blessings on his kindly voice and on his silver hair!
And blessings on his whole life long, until he meet me there.
O blessings on his kindly heart and on his silver head!
A thousand times I bless him, as he knelt beside my bed.

He taught me all the mercy, for he show'd me all the sin.
Now, tho' my lamp was lighted late, there's One will let me in;
Nor would I now be well, mother, again, if that could be,
For my desire is but to pass to Him that died for me.

I did not hear the dog howl, mother, or the death-watch beat,
There came a sweeter token when the night and morning meet:
But sit beside my bed, mother, and put your hand in mine,
And Effie on the other side, and I will tell the sign.

All in the wild March-morning I heard the angels call:
It was when the moon was setting, and the dark was over all;
The trees began to whisper, and the wind began to roll,
And in the wild March-morning I heard them call my soul.

" But sit beside my bed, mother, and put your hand in mine,
And Effie on the other side, and I will tell the sign."

For lying broad awake I thought of you and Effie dear;
I saw you sitting in the house, and I no longer here;
With all my strength I pray'd for both, and so I felt resigned,
And up the valley came a swell of music on the wind.

I thought that it was fancy, and I listen'd in my bed,
And then did something speak to me—I know not what was said;
For great delight and shuddering took hold of all my mind,
And up the valley came again the music on the wind.

But you were sleeping: and I said, "It's not for them: it's mine."
And if it comes three times, I thought, I take it for a sign.
And once again it came, and close beside the window-bars,
Then seem'd to go right up to Heaven and die among the stars.

So now I think my time is near. I trust it is. I know
The blessed music went that way my soul will have to go.
And for myself, indeed, I care not if I go to-day.
But Effie, you must comfort her when I am past away.

" And say to Robin a kind word, and tell him not to fret ;
There's many worthier than I, would make him happy yet."

And say to Robin a kind word, and tell him not to fret;
There's many worthier than I, would make him happy yet.
If I had lived—I cannot tell—I might have been his wife;
But all these things have ceased to be, with my desire of life.

O look! the sun begins to rise, the heavens are in a glow;
He shines upon a hundred fields, and all of them I know.
And there I move no longer now, and there his light may shine—
Wild flowers in the valley for other hands than mine.

O sweet and strange it seems to me, that ere this day is done
The voice, that now is speaking, may be beyond the sun—
For ever and for ever with those just souls and true—
And what is life, that we should moan? why make we such ado?

For ever and for ever, all in a blessed home—
And there to wait a little while till you and Effie come—
To lie within the light of God, as I lie upon your breast—
And the wicked cease from troubling, and the weary are at rest.

THE LOTOS-EATERS.

"COURAGE!" he said, and pointed toward the land,
"This mounting wave will roll us shoreward soon."
In the afternoon they came unto a land,
In which it seemed always afternoon.
All round the coast the languid air did swoon,
Breathing like one that hath a weary dream.
Full-faced above the valley stood the moon;
And like a downward smoke, the slender stream
Along the cliff to fall and pause and fall did seem.

A land of streams! some, like a downward smoke,
Slow-dropping veils of thinnest lawn, did go;
And some thro' wavering lights and shadows broke,
Rolling a slumbrous sheet of foam below.
They saw the gleaming river seaward flow
From the inner land: far off, three mountain-tops,
Three silent pinnacles of aged snow,
Stood sunset-flushed: and, dew'd with showery drops,
Up-clomb the shadowy pine above the woven copse.

The charmed sunset linger'd low adown
In the red West: thro' mountain clefts the dale
Was seen far inland, and the yellow down
Border'd with palm, and many a winding vale
And meadow, set with slender galingale:
A land where all things always seem'd the same!
And round about the keel with faces pale,
Dark faces pale against that rosy flame,
The mild-eyed melancholy Lotos-eaters came.

Branches they bore of that enchanted stem,
Laden with flower and fruit, whereof they gave
To each, but whoso did receive of them,
And taste, to him the gushing of the wave
Far far away did seem to mourn and rave
On alien shores; and if his fellow spake,
His voice was thin, as voices from the grave;
And deep-asleep he seem'd, yet all awake,
And music in his ears his beating heart did make.

They sat them down upon the yellow sand,
Between the sun and moon upon the shore;
And sweet it was to dream of Fatherland,
Of child, and wife, and slave; but evermore
Most weary seem'd the sea, weary the oar,
Weary the wandering fields of barren foam.
Then some one said, "We will return no more;"
And all at once they sang, "Our Island home
Is far beyond the wave; we will no longer roam."

CHORIC SONG.

1.

THERE is sweet music here that softer falls
Than petals from blown roses on the grass,
Or night-dews on still waters between walls
Of shadowy granite, in a gleaming pass;
Music that gentlier on the spirit lies,
Than tir'd eyelids upon tir'd eyes;
Music that brings sweet sleep down from the bliss-
ful skies.
Here are cool mosses deep,
And thro' the moss the ivies creep,
And in the stream the long-leaved flowers weep,
And from the craggy ledge the poppy hangs in sleep.

2.

Why are we weigh'd upon with heaviness,
And utterly consumed with sharp distress,
While all things else have rest from weariness?
All things have rest: why should we toil alone,
We only toil, who are the first of things,
And make perpetual moan,
Still from one sorrow to another thrown:
Nor ever fold our wings,
And cease from wanderings,
Nor steep our brows in slumber's holy balm;
Nor hearken what the inner spirit sings,
"There is no joy but calm!"
Why should we only toil, the roof and crown of
things?

3.

Lo! in the middle of the wood,
The folded leaf is woo'd from out the bud
With winds upon the branch, and there
Grows green and broad, and takes no care,
Sun-steep'd at noon, and in the moon
Nightly dew-fed; and turning yellow
Falls, and floats adown the air.
Lo! sweeten'd with the summer light,
The full-juiced apple, waxing over-mellow,
Drops in a silent autumn night.
All its allotted length of days,
The flower ripens in its place,
Ripens and fades, and falls, and hath no toil,
Fast-rooted in the fruitful soil.

4.

Hateful is the dark-blue sky,
Vaulted o'er the dark-blue sea.
Death is the end of life; ah, why
Should life all labor be?
Let us alone. Time driveth onward fast,
And in a little while our lips are dumb.
Let us alone. What is it that will last?
All things are taken from us, and become
Portions and parcels of the dreadful Past.
Let us alone. What pleasure can we have
To war with evil? Is there any peace

In ever climbing up the climbing wave?
All things have rest, and ripen toward the grave
In silence; ripen, fall and cease:
Give us long rest or death, dark death, or dreamful
    ease.

5.

How sweet it were, hearing the downward stream,
With half-shut eyes ever to seem
Falling asleep in a half-dream!
To dream and dream, like yonder amber light,
Which will not leave the myrrh-bush on the height;
To hear each other's whisper'd speech;
Eating the Lotos day by day,
To watch the crisping ripples on the beach,
And tender curving lines of creamy spray:
To lend our hearts and spirits wholly
To the influence of mild-minded melancholy;
To muse and brood and live again in memory,
With those old faces of our infancy
Heap'd over with a mound of grass,
Two handfuls of white dust, shut in an urn of
    brass!

6.

Dear is the memory of our wedded lives,
And dear the last embraces of our wives
And their warm tears: but all hath suffer'd change:
For surely now our household hearths are cold:
Our sons inherit us: our looks are strange:
And we should come like ghosts to trouble joy.
Or else the island princes over-bold
Have eat our substance, and the minstrel sings
Before them of the ten-years' war in Troy,
And our great deeds, as half-forgotten things.
Is there confusion in the little isle?
Let what is broken so remain.
The Gods are hard to reconcile:
'Tis hard to settle order once again.
There is confusion worse than death,
Trouble on trouble, pain on pain,
Long labor unto aged breath,
Sore task to hearts worn out with many wars,
And eyes grown dim with gazing on the pilot-stars.

7.

But, propt on beds of amaranth and moly,
How sweet (while warm airs lull us, blowing lowly)
With half-dropt eyelids still,
Beneath a heaven dark and holy,
To watch the long bright river drawing slowly
His waters from the purple hill—
To hear the dewy echoes calling
From cave to cave thro' the thick-twined vine—
To watch the emerald-color'd water falling
Thro' many a wov'n acanthus-wreath divine!
Only to hear and see the far-off sparkling brine,
Only to hear were sweet, stretch'd out beneath the
    pine.

8.

The Lotos blooms below the barren peak:
The Lotos blows by every winding creek:
All day the wind breathes low with mellower tone:
Thro' every hollow cave and alley lone
Round and round the spicy downs the yellow Lotos-
    dust is blown.
We have had enough of action, and of motion we,
Roll'd to starboard, roll'd to larboard, when the
    surge was seething free,
Where the wallowing monster spouted his foam-
    fountains in the sea.
Let us swear an oath, and keep it with an equal
    mind,
In the hollow Lotos-land to live and lie reclined
On the hills like Gods together, careless of man-
    kind.

For they lie beside their nectar, and the bolts are
    hurl'd
Far below them in the valleys, and the clouds are
    lightly curl'd
Round their golden houses, girdled with the gleam-
    ing world:
Where they smile in secret, looking over wasted
    lands,
Blight and famine, plague and earthquake, roaring
    deeps and fiery sands,
Clanging fights, and flaming towns, and sinking
    ships, and praying hands.
But they smile, they find a music centred in a dole-
    ful song
Steaming up, a lamentation and an ancient tale of
    wrong,
Like a tale of little meaning tho' the words are
    strong;
Chanted from an ill-used race of men that cleave
    the soil,
Sow the seed, and reap the harvest with enduring
    toil,
Storing yearly little dues of wheat, and wine, and oil;
Till they perish and they suffer—some, 'tis whis-
    pered—down in hell
Suffer endless anguish, others in Elysian valleys
    dwell,
Resting weary limbs at last on beds of asphodel.
Surely, surely, slumber is more sweet than toil, the
    shore
Than labor in the deep mid-ocean, wind and wave
    and oar:
O rest ye, brother mariners, we will not wander
    more.

———❦———

A DREAM OF FAIR WOMEN.

I READ, before my eyelids dropt their shade,
  " The Legend of Good Women," long ago
Sung by the morning star of song, who made
  His music heard below;

Dan Chaucer, the first warbler, whose sweet breath
  Preluded those melodious bursts that fill
The spacious times of great Elizabeth
  With sounds that echo still.

And, for a while, the knowledge of his art
  Held me above the subject, as strong gales
Hold swollen clouds from raining, tho' my heart,
  Brimful of those wild tales,

Charged both mine eyes with tears. In every land
  I saw, wherever light illumineth,
Beauty and anguish walking hand in hand
  The downward slope to death.

Those far-renowned brides of ancient song
  Peopled the hollow dark, like burning stars,
And I heard sounds of insult, shame, and wrong,
  And trumpets blown for wars;

And clattering flints batter'd with clanging hoofs:
  And I saw crowds in column'd sanctuaries;
And forms that pass'd at windows and on roofs
  Of marble palaces;

Corpses across the threshold; heroes tall
  Dislodging pinnacle and parapet
Upon the tortoise creeping to the wall;
  Lances in ambush set;

And high shrine-doors burst thro' with heated
    blasts
  That run before the fluttering tongues of fire:
White surf wind-scatter'd over sails and masts,
  And ever climbing higher;

Squadrons and squares of men in brazen plates,
    Scaffolds, still sheets of water, divers woes,
Ranges of glimmering vaults with iron grates,
    And hush'd seraglios.

So shape chased shape as swift as, when to land
    Bluster the winds and tides the self-same way,
Crisp foam-flakes scud along the level sand,
    Torn from the fringe of spray.

I started once, or seem'd to start in pain,
    Resolved on noble things, and strove to speak,
As when a great thought strikes along the brain,
    And flushes all the cheek.

And once my arm was lifted to hew down
    A cavalier from off his saddle-bow,
That bore a lady from a leaguer'd town;
    And then, I know not how,

All those sharp fancies by down-lapsing thought
    Stream'd onward, lost their edges, and did creep
Roll'd on each other, rounded, smooth'd, and brought
    Into the gulfs of sleep.

At last methought that I had wandered far
    In an old wood: fresh-wash'd in coolest dew,
The maiden splendors of the morning star
    Shook in the steadfast blue.

Enormous elm-tree boles did stoop and lean
    Upon the dusky brushwood underneath
Their broad curved branches, fledged with clearest
      green,
    New from its silken sheath.

The dim red morn had died, her journey done,
    And with dead lips smiled at the twilight plain,
Half-fall'n across the threshold of the sun,
    Never to rise again.

There was no motion in the dumb dead air,
    Not any song of bird or sound of rill:
Gross darkness of the inner sepulchre
    Is not so deadly still

As that wide forest. Growths of jasmine turn'd
    Their humid arms festooning tree to tree,
And at the root thro' lush green grasses burn'd
    The red anemone.

I knew the flowers, I knew the leaves, I knew
    The tearful glimmer of the languid dawn
On those long, rank, dark wood-walks drench'd in
      dew,
    Leading from lawn to lawn.

The smell of violets, hidden in the green,
    Pour'd back into my empty soul and frame
The times when I remember to have been
    Joyful and free from blame.

And from within me a clear under-tone
    Thrill'd thro' mine ears in that unblissful clime,
"Pass freely thro': the wood is all thine own,
    Until the eud of time."

At length I saw a lady within call,
    Stiller than chisell'd marble, standing there;
A daughter of the gods, divinely tall,
    And most divinely fair.

Her loveliness with shame and with surprise
    Froze my swift speech; she turning on my face
The star-like sorrows of immortal eyes,
    Spoke slowly in her place.

"I had great beauty; ask thou not my name:
    No one can be more wise than destiny.

Many drew swords and died. Where'er I came
    I brought calamity."

"No marvel, sovereign lady: in fair field
    Myself for such a face had boldly died."
I answer'd free; and turning I appeal'd
    To one that stood beside.

But she, with sick and scornful looks averse,
    To her full height her stately stature draws;
"My youth," she said, "was blasted with a curse:
    This woman was the cause.

"I was cut off from hope in that sad place,
    Which yet to name my spirit loathes and fears·
My father held his hand upon his face:
    I, blinded with my tears,

"Still strove to speak: my voice was thick with
      sighs
    As in a dream. Dimly I could descry
The stern black-bearded kings with wolfish eyes,
    Waiting to see me die.

"The high masts flicker'd as they lay afloat;
    The crowds, the temples, waver'd, and the shore;
The bright death quiver'd at the victim's throat;
    Touch'd; and I knew no more."

Whereto the other with a downward brow:
    "I would the white cold heavy-plunging foam,
Whirl'd by the wind, had roll'd me deep below,
    Then when I left my home."

Her slow full words sank thro' the silence drear,
    As thunder-drops fall on a sleeping sea:
Sudden I heard a voice that cried, "Come here,
    That I may look on thee."

I turning saw, throned on a flowery rise,
    One sitting on a crimson scarf unroll'd;
A queen, with swarthy cheeks and bold black eyes,
    Brow-bound with burning gold.

She, flashing forth a haughty smile, began:
    "I govern'd men by change, and so I sway'd
All moods. 'Tis long since I have seen a man
    Once, like the moon, I made

"The ever-shifting currents of the blood
    According to my humor ebb and flow.
I have no men to govern in this wood:
    That makes my only woe.

"Nay—yet it chafes me that I could not bend
    One will; nor tame and tutor with mine eye
That dull cold-blooded Cæsar. Prythee, friend,
    Where is Mark Antony?

"The man, my lover, with whom I rode sublime
    On Fortune's neck: we sat as God by God:
The Nilus would have risen before his time
    And flooded at our nod.

"We drank the Libyan Sun to sleep, and lit
    Lamps which outburn'd Canopus. O my life
In Egypt! O the dalliance and the wit,
    The flattery and the strife,

"And the wild kiss, when fresh from war's alarms,
    My Hercules, my Roman Antony,
My mailed Bacchus leapt into my arms,
    Contented there to die!

"And there he died: and when I heard my name
    Sigh'd forth with life I would not brook my fear
Of the other: with a worm I balk'd his fame.
    What else was left? look here!"

(With that she tore her robe apart, and half
   The polish'd argent of her breast to sight
Laid bare. Thereto she pointed with a laugh,
   Showing the aspic's bite.)

"I died a Queen. The Roman soldier found
   Me lying dead, my crown about my brows,
A name forever!—lying robed and crown'd,
   Worthy a Roman spouse."

Her warbling voice, a lyre of widest range
   Struck by all passion, did fall down and glance
From tone to tone, and glided thro' all change
   Of liveliest utterance.

When she made pause I knew not for delight·
   Because with sudden motion from the ground
She raised her piercing orbs, and fill'd with light
   The interval of sound.

Still with their fires Love tipt his keenest darts;
   As once they drew into two burning rings
All beams of Love, melting the mighty hearts
   Of captains and of kings.

Slowly my sense undazzled. Then I heard
   A noise of some one coming thro' the lawn,
And singing clearer than the crested bird,
   That claps his wings at dawn.

"The torrent brooks of hallow'd Israel
   From craggy hollows pouring, late and soon,
Sound all night long, in falling thro' the dell,
   Far-heard beneath the moon.

"The balmy moon of blessed Israel
   Floods all the deep-blue gloom with beams di-
    vine:
All night the splinter'd crags that wall the dell
   With spires of silver shine."

As one that museth where broad sunshine laves
   The lawn of some cathedral, thro' the door
Hearing the holy organ rolling waves
   Of sound on roof and floor

Within, and anthem sung, is charm'd and tied
   To where he stands,—so stood I, when that flow
Of music left the lips of her that died
   To save her father's vow;

The daughter of the warrior Gileadite,
   A maiden pure: as when she went along
From Mizpeh's tower'd gate with welcome light,
   With timbrel and with song.

My words leapt forth: "Heaven heads the count of
    crimes
   With that wild oath." She render'd answer high:
"Not so, nor once alone; a thousand times
   I would be born and die.

"Single I grew, like some green plant, whose root
   Creeps to the garden water-pipes beneath,
Feeding the flower: but ere my flower to fruit
   Changed, I was ripe for death.

"My God, my land, my father,—these did move
   Me from my bliss of life, that Nature gave,
Lower'd softly with a threefold cord of love
   Down to a silent grave.

"And I went mourning, 'No fair Hebrew boy
   Shall smile away my maiden blame among
The Hebrew mothers' —emptied of all joy
   Leaving the dance and song,

"Leaving the olive-gardens far below,
   Leaving the promise of my bridal bower,

The valleys of grape-loaded vines that glow
   Beneath the battled tower.

"The light white cloud swam over us. Anon
   We heard the lion roaring from his den;
We saw the large white stars rise one by one,
   Or, from the darken'd glen,

"Saw God divide the night with flying flame,
   And thunder on the everlasting hills.
I heard Him, for He spake, and grief became
   A solemn scorn of ills.

"When the next moon was roll'd into the sky,
   Strength came to me that equall'd my desire.
How beautiful a thing it was to die
   For God and for my sire!

"It comforts me in this one thought to dwell,
   That I subdued me to my father's will;
Because the kiss he gave me, ere I fell,
   Sweetens the spirit still.

"Moreover it is written that my race
   Hew'd Ammon, hip and thigh, from Aroer
On Arnon unto Minneth." Here her face
   Glow'd, as I look'd at her.

She lock'd her lips; she left me where I stood:
   "Glory to God," she sang, and past afar,
Thridding the sombre boskage of the wood,
   Toward the morning-star.

Losing her carol I stood pensively,
   As one that from a casement leans his head,
When midnight bells cease ringing suddenly,
   And the old year is dead.

"Alas! alas!" a low voice, full of care,
   Murmur'd beside me: "Turn and look on me:
I am that Rosamond, whom men call fair,
   If what I was I be.

"Would I had been some maiden coarse and poor
   O me, that I should ever see the light!
Those dragon eyes of anger'd Eleanor
   Do hunt me, day and night."

She ceased in tears, fallen from hope and trust:
   To whom the Egyptian: "O, you tamely died!
You should have clung to Fulvia's waist, and thrust
   The dagger thro' her side."

With that sharp sound the white dawn's creeping
    beams,
   Stol'n to my brain, dissolved the mystery
Of folded sleep. The captain of my dreams
   Ruled in the eastern sky.

Morn broaden'd on the borders of the dark,
   Ere I saw her, who clasp'd in her last trance
Her murder'd father's head, or Joan of Arc,
   A light of ancient France;

Or her, who knew that Love can vanquish Death,
   Who kneeling, with one arm about her king,
Drew forth the poison with her balmy breath,
   Sweet as new buds in Spring.

No memory labors longer from the deep
   Gold-mines of thought to lift the hidden ore
That glimpses, moving up, than I from sleep
   To gather and tell o'er

Each little sound and sight. With what dull pain
   Compass'd, how eagerly I sought to strike
Into that wondrous track of dreams again!
   But no two dreams are like.

As when a soul laments, which hath been blest,
　　Desiring what is mingled with past years,
In yearnings that can never be exprest
　　By signs or groans or tears:

Because all words, tho' cull'd with choicest art,
　　Failing to give the bitter of the sweet,
Wither beneath the palate, and the heart
　　Faints, faded by its heat.

—⟡—

MARGARET.

1.

O sweet pale Margaret,
　　O rare pale Margaret,
What lit your eyes with tearful power,
Like moonlight on a falling shower?
Who lent you, love, your mortal dower
　　Of pensive thought and aspect pale,
　　Your melancholy sweet and frail
As perfume of the cuckoo-flower?
From the westward-winding flood,
From the evening-lighted wood,
　　From all things outward you have won
A tearful grace, as tho' you stood
　　Between the rainbow and the sun.
The very smile before you speak,
That dimples your transparent cheek,
　　Encircles all the heart and feedeth
The senses with a still delight
　　Of dainty sorrow without sound,
　　Like the tender amber round,
Which the moon about her spreadeth,
Moving thro' a fleecy night.

2.

You love, remaining peacefully,
　　To hear the murmur of the strife,
But enter not the toil of life.
Your spirit is the calmed sea,
　　Laid by the tumult of the fight.
You are the evening star, alway
　　Remaining betwixt dark and bright:
Lull'd echoes of laborious day
　　Come to you, gleams of mellow light
Float by you on the verge of night.

3.

What can it matter, Margaret,
　　What songs below the waning stars
The lion-heart, Plantagenet,
　　Sang looking thro' his prison bars?
　　Exquisite Margaret, who can tell
The last wild thought of Chatelet,
　　Just ere the fallen axe did part
　　The burning brain from the true heart,
Even in her sight he loved so well?

4.

A fairy shield your Genius made
　　And gave you on your natal day.
Your sorrow, only sorrow's shade,
　　Keeps real sorrow far away.
You move not in such solitudes,
　　You are not less divine,
But more human in your moods,
　　Than your twin-sister, Adeline.
Your hair is darker, and your eyes
　　Touch'd with a somewhat darker hue,
　　And less aërially blue
But ever trembling thro' the dew
Of dainty-woful sympathies.

5.

O sweet pale Margaret,
　　O rare pale Margaret,

Come down, come down, and hear me speak:
Tie up the ringlets on your cheek:
　　The sun is just about to set.
The arching limes are tall and shady,
　　And faint, rainy lights are seen,
　　Moving in the leafy beech.
Rise from the feast of sorrow, lady,
　　Where all day long you sit between
　　Joy and woe, and whisper each.
Or only look across the lawn,
　　Look out below your bower-eaves,
Look down, and let your blue eyes dawn
Upon me thro' the jasmine-leaves.

—⟡—

THE BLACKBIRD.

O Blackbird! sing me something well:
　　While all the neighbors shoot thee round,
　　I keep smooth plats of fruitful ground,
Where thou may'st warble, eat and dwell.

The espaliers and the standards all
　　Are thine: the range of lawn and park:
　　The unnetted black-hearts ripen dark,
All thine, against the garden wall.

Yet, tho' I spared thee all the Spring,
　　Thy sole delight is, sitting still,
　　With that gold dagger of thy bill
To fret the Summer jennetiug.

A golden bill! the silver tongue,
　　Cold February loved, is dry:
　　Plenty corrupts the melody
That made thee famous once, when young:

And in the sultry garden-squares,
　　Now thy flute-notes are changed to coarse,
　　I hear thee not at all, or hoarse
As when a hawker hawks his wares.

Take warning! he that will not sing
　　While yon sun prospers in the blue,
　　Shall sing for want, ere leaves are new,
Caught in the frozen palms of Spring.

—⟡—

THE DEATH OF THE OLD YEAR.

Full knee-deep lies the winter snow,
And the winter winds are wearily sighing:
Toll ye the church-bell sad and slow,
And tread softly and speak low,
For the old year lies a-dying.
　　Old year, you must not die:
　　You came to us so readily,
　　You lived with us so steadily,
　　Old year, you shall not die.

He lieth still: he doth not move:
He will not see the dawn of day.
He hath no other life above.
He gave me a friend, and a true, true-love,
And the New-year will take 'em away.
　　Old year, you must not go;
　　So long as you have been with us,
　　Such joy as you have seen with us,
　　Old year, you shall not go.

He froth'd his bumpers to the brim;
A jollier year we shall not see.
But tho' his eyes are waxing dim,
And tho' his foes speak ill of him,
He was a friend to me.

"Toll ye the church-bell sad and slow,
And tread softly and speak low,
For the old year lies a-dying."

Old year, you shall not die;
We did so laugh and cry with you,
I've half a mind to die with you,
Old year, if you must die.

He was full of joke and jest,
But all his merry qnips are o'er.
To see him die across the waste
His son and heir doth ride post-haste,
But he'll be dead before.
     Every one for his own.
The night is starry and cold, my friend,
And the New-year blithe and bold, my friend,
Comes up to take his own.

How hard he breathes! over the snow
I heard just now the crowing cock.
The shadows flicker to and fro:
The cricket chirps: the light burns low:
'Tis nearly twelve o'clock.
     Shake hands, before you die.
Old year, we'll dearly rue for you:
What is it we can do for you?
Speak out before you die.

His face is growing sharp and thin.
Alack! our friend is gone,
Close up his eyes: tie up his chin:
Step from the corpse, and let him in
That standeth there alone,
     And waiteth at the door.
There's a new foot on the floor, my friend,
And a new face at the door, my friend,
A new face at the door.

TO J. S.

The wind, that beats the mountain, blows
     More softly round the open wold,
And gently comes the world to those
     That are cast in gentle mould.

And me this knowledge bolder made,
     Or else I had not dare to flow
In these words toward you, and invade
     Even with a verse your holy woe.

'Tis strange that those we lean on most,
     Those in whose laps our limbs are nursed,
Fall into shadow, soonest lost:
     Those we love first are taken first.

God gives us love. Something to love
     He lends us; but, when love is grown
To ripeness, that on which it throve
     Falls off, and love is left alone.

This is the curse of time. Alas!
     In grief I am not all unlearn'd;
Once thro' mine own doors Death did pass;
     One went, who never hath return'd.

He will not smile—nor speak to me
     Once more. Two years his chair is seen
Empty before us. That was he
     Without whose life I had not been.

Your loss is rarer; for this star
     Rose with you thro' a little arc

Of heaven, nor having wander'd far
  Shot on the sudden into dark.

I knew your brother: his mute dust
  I honor and his living worth:
A man more pure and bold and just
  Was never born into the earth.

I have not look'd upon you nigh,
  Since that dear soul hath fall'n asleep.
Great Nature is more wise than I:
  I will not tell you not to weep.

And tho' mine own eyes fill with dew,
  Drawn from the spirit thro' the brain,
I will not even preach to you,
  "Weep, weeping dulls the inward pain."

Let Grief be her own mistress still.
  She loveth her own anguish deep
More than much pleasure. Let her will
  Be done—to weep or not to weep.

I will not say "God's ordinance
  Of death is blown in every wind;"
For that is not a common chance
  That takes away a noble mind.

His memory long will live alone
  In all our hearts, as mournful light
That broods above the fallen sun,
  And dwells in heaven half the night.

Vain solace! Memory standing near
  Cast down her eyes, and in her throat
Her voice seem'd distant, and a tear
  Dropt on the letters as I wrote.

I wrote I know not what. In truth,
  How *should* I soothe you anyway,
Who miss the brother of your youth?
  Yet something I did wish to say:

For he too was a friend to me:
  Both are my friends, and my true breast
Bleedeth for both: yet it may be
  That only silence suiteth best.

Words weaker than your grief would make
  Grief more. 'Twere better I should cease;
Although myself could almost take
  The place of him that sleeps in peace.

Sleep sweetly, tender heart, in peace;
  Sleep, holy spirit, blessed soul,
While the stars burn, the moons increase,
  And the great ages onward roll.

Sleep till the end, true soul and sweet.
  Nothing comes to thee new or strange,
Sleep full of rest from head to feet;
  Lie still, dry dust, secure of change.

———◇◇———

You ask me, why, tho' ill at ease,
  Within this region I subsist,
  Whose spirits falter in the mist,
And languish for the purple seas?

It is the land that freemen till,
  That sober-suited Freedom chose,
  The land, where girt with friends or foes
A man may speak the thing he will;

A land of settled government,
  A land of just and old renown,
  Where freedom broadens slowly down
From precedent to precedent:

Where faction seldom gathers head,
  But by degrees to fulness wrought,
  The strength of some diffusive thought
Hath time and space to work and spread.

Should banded unions persecute
  Opinion, and induce a time
  When single thought is civil crime,
And individual freedom mute;

Tho' Power should make from land to land
  The name of Britain trebly great—
  Tho' every channel of the State
Should almost choke with golden sand—

Yet waft me from the harbor-mouth,
  Wild wind! I seek a warmer sky,
  And I will see before I die
The palms and temples of the South.

———◇◇———

Of old sat Freedom on the heights,
  The thunders breaking at her feet:
Above her shook the starry lights:
  She heard the torrents meet.

There in her place she did rejoice,
  Self-gather'd in her prophet-mind,
But fragments of her mighty voice
  Come rolling on the wind.

Then stept she down thro' town and field
  To mingle with the human race,
And part by part to men reveal'd
  The fulness of her face—

Grave mother of majestic works,
  From her isle-altar gazing down,
Who, God-like, grasps the triple forks,
  And, King-like, wears the crown:

Her open eyes desire the truth.
  The wisdom of a thousand years
Is in them. May perpetual youth
  Keep dry their light from tears;

That her fair form may stand and shine,
  Make bright our days and light our dreams
Turning to scorn with lips divine
  The falsehood of extremes!

———◇◇———

Love thou thy land, with love far-brought
  From out the storied Past, and used
  Within the Present, but transfused
Thro' future time by power of thought.

True love turn'd round on fixed poles,
  Love, that endures not sordid ends,
  For English natures, freemen, friends,
Thy brothers and immortal souls.

But pamper not a hasty time,
  Nor feed with crude imaginings
  The herd, wild hearts and feeble wings,
That every sophister can lime.

Deliver not the tasks of might
  To weakness, neither hide the ray
  From those, not blind, who wait for day.
Tho' sitting girt with doubtful light.

Make knowledge circle with the winds:
But let her herald, Reverence, fly
Before her to whatever sky
Bear seed of men and growth of minds.

Watch what main-currents draw the years:
Cut Prejudice against the grain:
But gentle words are always gain:
Regard the weakness of thy peers:

Nor toil for title, place, or touch
Of pension, neither count on praise:
It grows to guerdon after-days:
Nor deal in watch-words over-much;

Not clinging to some ancient saw;
Not master'd by some modern term;
Not swift or slow to change, but firm;
And in its season bring the law;

That from Discussion's lip may fall
With Life, that, working strongly, binds—
Set in all lights by many minds,
To close the interests of all.

For Nature, also, cold and warm,
And moist and dry, devising long,
Thro' many agents making strong,
Matures the individual form.

Meet is it changes should control
Our being, lest we rust in ease.
We all are changed by still degrees,
All but the basis of the soul.

So let the change which comes be free
To ingroove itself with that, which flies,
And work, a joint of state, that plies
Its office, moved with sympathy.

A saying, hard to shape in act;
For all the past of Time reveals
A bridal dawn of thunder-peals,
Wherever Thought hath wedded Fact.

Ev'n now we hear with inward strife
A motion toiling in the gloom—
The Spirit of the years to come
Yearning to mix himself with Life.

A slow-develop'd strength awaits
Completion in a painful school;
Phantoms of other forms of rule,
New Majesties of mighty States—

The warders of the growing hour,
But vague in vapor, hard to mark;
And round them sea and air are dark
With great contrivances of Power.

Of many changes, aptly join'd,
Is bodied forth the second whole.
Regard gradation, lest the soul
Of Discord race the rising wind;

A wind to puff your idol-fires,
And heap their ashes on the head;
To shame the boast so often made,
That we are wiser than our sires.

O yet, if Nature's evil star
Drive men in manhood, as in youth,
To follow flying steps of Truth
Across the brazen bridge of war—

If New and Old, disastrous feud,
Must ever shock, like armed foes,
And this be true, till Time shall close,
That Principles are rain'd in blood;

Not yet the wise of heart would cease
To hold his hope thro' shame and guilt,
But with his hand against the hilt,
Would pace the troubled land, like Peace

Not less, tho' dogs of Faction bay,
Would serve his kind in deed and word,
Certain, if knowledge bring the sword,
That knowledge takes the sword away—

Would love the gleams of good that broke
From either side, nor veil his eyes:
And if some dreadful need should rise
Would strike, and firmly, and one stroke

To-morrow yet would reap to-day.
As we bear blossom of the dead;
Earn well the thrifty months, nor wed
Raw Haste, half-sister to Delay.

—◇◇—

THE GOOSE.

I KNEW an old wife lean and poor,
Her rags scarce held together;
There strode a stranger to the door,
And it was windy weather.

He held a goose upon his arm,
He utter'd rhyme and reason,
"Here, take the goose, and keep you warm,
It is a stormy season."

She caught the white goose by the leg.
A goose—'twas no great matter.
The goose let fall a golden egg
With cackle and with clatter.

She dropt the goose, and caught the pelf,
And ran to tell her neighbors;
And bless'd herself, and cursed herself,
And rested from her labors.

And feeding high, and living soft,
Grew plump and able-bodied;
Until the grave churchwarden doff'd,
The parson smirk'd and nodded.

So sitting, served by man and maid,
She felt her heart grow prouder:
But ah! the more the white goose laid
It clack'd and cackled louder.

It clutter'd here, it chuckled there;
It stirr'd the old wife's mettle:
She shifted in her elbow-chair,
And hurl'd the pan and kettle.

"A quinsy choke thy cursed note!"
Then wax'd her anger stronger.
"Go, take the goose, and wring her throat,
I will not bear it longer."

Then yelp'd the cur, and yawl'd the cat;
Ran Gaffer, stumbled Gammer,
The goose flew this way and flew that,
And fill'd the house with clamor.

As head and heels upon the floor
They floundered all together,
There strode a stranger to the door,
And it was windy weather:

He took the goose upon his arm,
He utter'd words of scorning;
"So keep you cold, or keep you warm,
It is a stormy morning."

"As head and heels upon the floor
They floundered all together,
There strode a stranger to the door."

The wild wind rang from park and plain,
　And round the attics rumbled,
Till all the tables danced again,
　And half the chimneys tumbled.

The glass blew in, the fire blew out,
　The blast was hard and harder.

Her cap blew off, her gown blew up,
　And a whirlwind clear'd the larder:

And while on all sides breaking loose
　Her household fled the danger,
Quoth she, "The Devil take the goose,
　And God forget the stranger!"

ENGLISH IDYLS AND OTHER POEMS.

(Published 1842.)

[A few poems in this division were inserted later.]

THE EPIC.

At Francis Allen's on the Christmas-eve,—
The game of forfeits done—the girls all kiss'd
Beneath the sacred bush and past away—
The parson Holmes, the poet Everard Hall,
The host, and I sat round the wassail-bowl,
Then half-way ebb'd: and there we held a talk,
How all the old honor had from Christmas gone,
Or gone, or dwindled down to some odd games
In some odd nooks like this; till I, tired out
With cutting eights that day upon the pond,
Where, three times slipping from the outer edge,
I bump'd the ice into three several stars,
Fell in a doze; and half-awake I heard
The parson taking wide and wider sweeps,
Now harping on the church-commissioners,
Now hawking at Geology and schism:
Until I woke, and found him settled down
Upon the general decay of faith
Right thro' the world, "at home was little left,
And none abroad: there was no anchor, none,
To hold by." Francis, laughing, clapt his hand
On Everard's shoulder, with "I hold by him."

"And I," quoth Everard, "by the wassail-bowl."
"Why yes," I said, "we knew your gift that way
At college: but another which you had—
I mean of verse (for so we held it then,)
What came of that?" "You know," said Frank,
　　　"he burnt
His epic, his King Arthur, some twelve books"—
And then to me demanding why? "O, sir,
He thought that nothing new was said, or else
Something so said 'twas nothing—that a truth
Looks freshest in the fashion of the day:
God knows: he has a mint of reasons: ask.
It pleased me well enough." "Nay, nay," said Hall,
"Why take the style of those heroic times?
For nature brings not back the Mastodon,
Nor we those times; and why should any man
Remodel models? these twelve books of mine
Were faint Homeric echoes, nothing-worth,
Mere chaff and draff, much better burnt." "But I,"
Said Francis, "pick'd the eleventh from this hearth,
And have it: keep a thing, its use will come.
I hoard it as a sugar-plum for Holmes."
He laugh'd, and I, though sleepy, like a horse
That hears the corn-bin open, prick'd my ears;

For I remember'd Everard's college fame
When we were Freshmen: then at my request
He brought it; and the poet, little urged,
But with some prelude of disparagement,
Read, mouthing out his hollow oes and aes,
Deep-chested music, and to this result.

MORTE D'ARTHUR.

So all day long the noise of battle roll'd
Among the mountains by the winter sea;
Until King Arthur's table, man by man,
Had fall'n in Lyonness about their Lord,
King Arthur: then, because his wound was deep,
The bold Sir Bedivere uplifted him,
Sir Bedivere, the last of all his knights,
And bore him to a chapel nigh the field,
A broken chancel with a broken cross,
That stood on a dark strait of barren land.
On one side lay the Ocean, and on one
Lay a great water, and the moon was full.
    Then spake King Arthur to Sir Bedivere:
"The sequel of to-day unsolders all
The goodliest fellowship of famous knights
Whereof this world holds record. Such a sleep
They sleep—the men I loved. I think that we
Shall never more, at any future time,

Delight our souls with talk of knightly deeds,
Walking about the gardens and the halls
Of Camelot, as in the days that were.
I perish by this people which I made,—
Tho' Merlin sware that I should come again
To rule once more—but let what will be, be,
I am so deeply smitten thro' the helm
That without help I cannot last till morn.
Thou therefore take my brand Excalibur,
Which was my pride: for thou rememberest how
In those old days, one summer noon, an arm
Rose up from out the bosom of the lake,
Clothed in white samite, mystic, wonderful,
Holding the sword—and how I rowed across
And took it, and have worn it, like a king:
And, wheresoever I am sung or told
In aftertime, this also shall be known:
But now delay not: take Excalibur,
And fling him far into the middle mere:
Watch what thou seëst, and lightly bring me word."
    To him replied the bold Sir Bedivere:
"It is not meet, Sir King, to leave thee thus,
Aidless, alone, and smitten thro' the helm.
A little thing may harm a wounded man.
Yet I thy hest will all perform at full,
Watch what I see, and lightly bring thee word."
    So saying, from the ruined shrine he stept
And in the moon athwart the place of tombs,
Where lay the mighty bones of ancient men,

"An arm
Rose up from out the bosom of the lake,
Clothed in white samite."

Old knights, and over them the sea-wind sang
Shrill, chill, with flakes of foam. He, stepping down
By zig-zag paths, and juts of pointed rock,
Came on the shining levels of the lake.

There drew he forth the brand Excalibur,
And o'er him, drawing it, the winter moon,
Brightening the skirts of a long cloud, ran forth
And sparkled keen with frost against the hilt:
For all the haft twinkled with diamond studs,
Myriads of topaz-lights, and jacinth-work
Of subtlest jewellery. He gazed so long
That both his eyes were dazzled, as he stood,
This way and that dividing the swift mind,
In act to throw: but at the last it seem'd
Better to leave Excalibur conceal'd
There in the many-knotted waterflags,
That whistled stiff and dry about the marge.
So strode he back slow to the wounded king.

Then spake King Arthur to Sir Bedivere:
"Hast thou performed my mission which I gave?
What is it thou hast seen or what hast heard?"

And answer made the bold Sir Bedivere:
"I heard the ripple washing in the reeds,
And the wild water lapping on the crag."

To whom replied King Arthur, faint and pale:
"Thou hast betray'd thy nature and thy name,
Not rendering true answer, as beseem'd
Thy fealty, nor like a noble knight:
For surer sign had follow'd, either hand,
Or voice, or else a motion of the mere.
This is a shameful thing for men to lie.
Yet now, I charge thee, quickly go again
As thou art lief and dear, and do the thing
I bade thee, watch, and lightly bring me word."

Then went Sir Bedivere the second time
Across the ridge, and paced beside the mere,
Counting the dewy pebbles, fix'd in thought;
But when he saw the wonder of the hilt,
How curiously and strangely chased, he smote
His palms together, and he cried aloud,

"And if indeed I cast the brand away,
Surely a precious thing, one worthy note,
Should thus be lost forever from the earth,
Which might have pleased the eyes of many men.
What good should follow this, if this were done?
What harm, undone? deep harm to disobey,
Seeing obedience is the bond of rule.
Were it well to obey then, if a king demand
An act unprofitable, against himself?
The King is sick, and knows not what he does.
What record, or what relic of my lord
Should be to aftertime, but empty breath
And rumors of a doubt? but were this kept,
Stored in some treasure-house of mighty kings,
Some one might show it at a joust of arms,
Saying, 'King Arthur's sword, Excalibur,
Wrought by the lonely maiden of the Lake.
Nine years she wrought it, sitting in the deeps
Upon the hidden bases of the hills.'
So might some old man speak in the aftertime
To all the people, winning reverence.
But now much honor and much fame were lost."

So spake he, clouded with his own conceit,
And hid Excalibur the second time,
And so strode back slow to the wounded King.

Then spoke King Arthur, breathing heavily:
"What is it thou hast seen? or what hast heard?"

And answer made the bold Sir Bedivere:
"I heard the water lapping on the crag,
And the long ripple washing in the reeds."

To whom replied King Arthur, much in wrath:
"Ah, miserable and unkind, untrue,
Unknightly, traitor-hearted! Woe is me!
Authority forgets a dying king,
Laid widow'd of the power in his eye
That bow'd the will. I see thee what thou art,
For thou, the latest left of all my knights,
In whom should meet the offices of all.

Thou wouldst betray me for the precious hilt;
Either from lust of gold, or like a girl
Valuing the giddy pleasure of the eyes
Yet, for a man may fail in duty twice,
And the third time may prosper, get thee hence:
But, if thou spare to fling Excalibur,
I will arise and slay thee with my hands."

Then quickly rose Sir Bedivere, and ran,
And, leaping down the ridges lightly, plunged
Among the bulrush-beds, and clutch'd the sword,
And strongly wheel'd and threw it. The great brand
Made lightnings in the splendor of the moon,
And flashing round and round, and whirl'd in an
    arch,
Shot like a streamer of the northern morn,
Seen where the moving isles of winter shock
By night, with noises of the northern sea.
So flash'd and fell the brand Excalibur:
But ere he dipt the surface, rose an arm
Cloth'd in white samite, mystic, wonderful,
And caught him by the hilt, and brandish'd him
Three times, and drew him under in the mere.
And lightly went the other to the King.

Then spoke King Arthur, drawing thicker breath:
"Now see I by thine eyes that this is done.
Speak out: what is it thou hast heard, or seen?"

And answer made the bold Sir Bedivere:
"Sir King, I closed mine eyelids, lest the gems
Should blind my purpose, for I never saw,
Nor shall see, here or elsewhere, till I die,
Not tho' I live three lives of mortal men,
So great a miracle as yonder hilt.
Then with both hands I flung him, wheeling him;
But when I look'd again, behold an arm,
Clothed in white samite, mystic, wonderful,
That caught him by the hilt, and brandish'd him
Three times, and drew him under in the mere."

And answer made King Arthur, breathing hard:
"My end draws nigh; 'tis time that I were gone,
Make broad thy shoulders to receive my weight,
And bear me to the margin: yet I fear
My wound hath taken cold, and I shall die."

So saying, from the pavement he half rose,
Slowly, with pain, reclining on his arm,
And looking wistfully with wide blue eyes
As in a picture. Him Sir Bedivere
Remorsefully regarded thro' his tears,
And would have spoken, but he found not words,
Then took with care, and kneeling on one knee,
O'er both his shoulders drew the languid hands,
And rising bore him thro' the place of tombs.

But, as he walk'd, King Arthur panted hard,
Like one that feels a nightmare on his bed
When all the house is mute. So sigh'd the King,
Muttering and murmuring at his ear "Quick, quick!
I fear it is too late, and I shall die."
But the other swiftly strode from ridge to ridge,
Clothed with his breath, and looking, as he walk'd,
Larger than human on the frozen hills.
He heard the deep behind him, and a cry
Before. His own thought drove him like a goad.
Dry clash'd his harness in the icy caves
And barren chasms, and all to left and right
The bare black cliff clang'd round him, as he based
His feet on juts of slippery crag that rang
Sharp-smitten with the dint of armed heels—
And on a sudden, lo! the level lake,
And the long glories of the winter moon.

Then saw they how there hove a dusky barge,
Dark as a funeral scarf from stem to stern,
Beneath them; and descending they were ware
That all the decks were dense with stately forms
Black-stoled, black-hooded, like a dream—by these
Three Queens with crowns of gold—and from them
    rose
A cry that shiver'd to the tingling stars,
And, as it were one voice, an agony
Of lamentation, like a wind, that shrills

All night in a waste land, where no one comes,
Or hath come, since the making of the world.
   Then murmur'd Arthur, "Place me in the barge,"
And to the barge they came. There those three
    Queens
Put forth their hands, and took the King, and wept.
But she that rose the tallest of them all
And fairest, laid his head upon her lap,
And loosed the shatter'd casque, and chafed his hands,
And call'd him by his name, complaining loud,
And dropping bitter tears against his brow
Striped with dark blood: for all his face was white
And colorless, and like the wither'd moon
Smote by the fresh beam of the springing east;

"Ah! my Lord Arthur, whither shall I go?
Where shall I hide my forehead and my eyes?
For now I see the true old times are dead,
When every morning brought a noble chance,
And every chance brought out a noble knight.
Such times have been not since the light hath led
The holy Elders with the gift of myrrh.
But now the whole ROUND TABLE is dissolved
Which was an image of the mighty world;
And I, the last, go forth companionless,
And the days darken round me, and the years,
Among new men, strange faces, other minds."
   And slowly answer'd Arthur from the barge;
"The old order changeth, yielding place to new,

"Laid his head upon her lap,
And loosed the shatter'd casque, and chafed his hands,
And called him by his name."

And all his greaves and cuisses dash'd with drops
Of onset; and the light and lustrous curls—
That made his forehead like a rising sun
High from the dais-throne—were parch'd with dust;
Or, clotted into points and hanging loose,
Mix'd with the knightly growth that fringed his lips.
So like a shatter'd column lay the King;
Not like that Arthur who, with lance in rest,
From spur to plume a star of tournament,
Shot thro' the lists at Camelot, and charged
Before the eyes of ladies and of kings.
   Then loudly cried the bold Sir Bedivere,

And God fulfils himself in many ways,
Lest one good custom should corrupt the world.
Comfort thyself: what comfort is in me?
I have lived my life, and that which I have done
May He within himself make pure! but thou,
If thou shouldst never see my face again,
Pray for my soul. More things are wrought by prayer
Than this world dreams of. Wherefore, let thy voice
Rise like a fountain for me night and day.
For what are men better than sheep or goats
That nourish a blind life within the brain,
If, knowing God, they lift not hands of prayer

Both for themselves and those who call them friend?
For so the whole round earth is every way
Bound by gold chains about the feet of God.
But now farewell. I am going a long way
With these thou seest—if indeed I go—
(For all my mind is clouded with a doubt)
To the island-valley of Avilion;
Where falls not hail, or rain, or any snow,
Nor ever wind blows loudly; but it lies
Deep-meadow'd, happy, fair with orchard lawns
And bowery hollows crown'd with summer sea,
Where I will heal me of my grievous wound."

    So said he, and the barge with oar and sail
Moved from the brink, like some full-breasted swan—
That, fluting a wild carol ere her death,
Ruffles her pure cold plume, and takes the flood
With swarthy webs. Long stood Sir Bedivere
Revolving many memories, till the hull
Look'd one black dot against the verge of dawn,
And on the mere the wailing died away.

    Here ended Hall, and our last light, that long
Had wink'd and threaten'd darkness, flared and fell:
At which the Parson, sent to sleep with sound,
And waked with silence, granted "Good!" but we
Sat rapt: it was the tone with which he read—
Perhaps some modern touches here and there
Redeem'd it from the charge of nothingness—
Or else we loved the man, and prized his work;
I know not: but we sitting, as I said,
The cock crew loud; as at that time of year
The lusty bird takes every hour for dawn:
Then Francis, muttering, like a man ill-used,
"There now—that's nothing!" drew a little back,
And drove his heel into the smoulder'd log,
That sent a blast of sparkles up the flue:
And so to bed; where yet in sleep I seem'd
To sail with Arthur under looming shores,
Point after point; till on to dawn, when dreams
Begin to feel the truth and stir of day,
To me, methought, who waited with a crowd,
There came a bark that, blowing forward, bore
King Arthur, like a modern gentleman
Of stateliest port; and all the people cried,
"Arthur is come again: he cannot die."
Then those that stood upon the hills behind
Repeated—"Come again, and thrice as fair;"
And, further inland, voices echoed—"Come
With all good things, and war shall be no more."
At this a hundred bells began to peal,
That with the sound I woke, and heard indeed
The clear church-bells ring in the Christmas morn.

~∞~

THE GARDENER'S DAUGHTER; OR, THE PICTURES.

This morning is the morning of the day,
When I and Eustace from the city went
To see the Gardener's Daughter; I and he,
Brothers in Art; a friendship so complete
Portion'd in halves between us, that we grew
The fable of the city where we dwelt.

    My Eustace might have sat for Hercules;
So muscular he spread, so broad of breast.
He, by some law that holds in love, and draws
The greater to the lesser, long desired
A certain miracle of symmetry,
A miniature of loveliness, all grace
Summ'd up and closed in little;—Juliet, she
So light of foot, so light of spirit—oh, she
To me myself, for some three careless moons,
The summer pilot of an empty heart
Unto the shores of nothing! Know you not
Such touches are but embassies of love,
To tamper with the feelings, ere he found

Empire for life? but Eustace painted her,
And said to me, she sitting with us then,
"When will you paint like this?" and I replied,
(My words were half in earnest, half in jest,)
"'Tis not your work, but Love's. Love, unperceived,
A more ideal Artist he than all,
Came, drew your pencil from you, made those eyes
Darker than darkest pansies, and that hair
More black than ashbuds in the front of March."
And Juliet answer'd laughing, "Go and see
The Gardener's daughter: trust me, after that,
You scarce can fail to match his masterpiece."
And up we rose, and on the spur we went.

    Not wholly in the busy world, nor quite
Beyond it, blooms the garden that I love.
News from the humming city comes to it
In sound of funeral or of marriage bells;
And, sitting muffled in dark leaves, you hear
The windy clanging of the minster clock;
Although between it and the garden lies
A league of grass, wash'd by a slow broad stream,
That, stirr'd with languid pulses of the oar,
Waves all its lazy lilies, and creeps on,
Barge-laden, to three arches of a bridge
Crown'd with the minster towers.
                The fields between
Are dewy-fresh, browsed by deep-udder'd kine,
And all about the large lime feathers low,
The lime a summer home of murmurous wings.

    In that still place she, hoarded in herself,
Grew, seldom seen: not less among us lives
Her fame from lip to lip. Who had not heard
Of Rose, the Gardener's daughter? Where was he,
So blunt in memory, so old at heart,
At such a distance from his youth in grief,
That, having seen, forgot? The common mouth
So gross to express delight, in praise of her
Grew oratory. Such a lord is Love,
And Beauty such a mistress of the world.

    And if I said that Fancy, led by Love,
Would play with flying forms and images,
Yet this is also true, that, long before
I look'd upon her, when I heard her name
My heart was like a prophet to my heart
And told me I should love. A crowd of hopes,
That sought to sow themselves like winged seeds,
Born out of everything I heard and saw,
Flutter'd about my senses and my soul;
And vague desires, like fitful blasts of balm
To one that travels quickly, made the air
Of Life delicious, and all kinds of thought,
That verged upon them, sweeter than the dream
Dream'd by a happy man, when the dark East,
Unseen, is brightening to his bridal morn.

    And sure this orbit of the memory folds
Forever in itself the day we went
To see her. All the land in flowery squares
Beneath a broad and equal-blowing wind,
Smelt of the coming summer, as one large cloud
Drew downward; but all else of Heaven was pure
Up to the Sun, and May from verge to verge,
And May with me from head to heel. And now,
As tho' 't were yesterday, as tho' it were
The hour just flown, that morn with all its sound,
(For those old Mays had thrice the life of these,)
Rings in mine ears. The steer forgot to graze,
And, where the hedge-row cuts the pathway, stood
Leaning his horns into the neighbor field,
And lowing to his fellows. From the woods
Came voices of the well-contented doves.
The lark could scarce get out his notes for joy,
But shook his song together as he near'd
His happy home, the ground. To left and right,
The cuckoo told his name to all the hills;
The mellow ouzel fluted in the elm;
The redcap whistled; and the nightingale
Sang loud, as tho' he were the bird of day.

    And Eustace turn'd, and smiling said to me.

4

"Hear how the bushes echo! by my life.
These birds have joyful thoughts. Think you they
　　sing
Like poets, from the vanity of song?
Or have they any sense of why they sing?
And would they praise the heavens for what they
　　have?"
And I made answer, "Were there nothing else
For which to praise the heavens but only love,
That only love were cause enough for praise."
　　Lightly he laugh'd, as one that read my thought,
And on we went; but ere an hour had pass'd,
We reach'd a meadow slanting to the North;
Down which a well-worn pathway courted us
To one green wicket in a privet hedge;
This, yielding, gave into a grassy walk
Thro' crowded lilac-ambush trimly pruned:
And one warm gust, full-fed with perfume, blew
Beyond us, as we enter'd in the cool.
The garden stretches southward. In the midst
A cedar spread his dark-green layers of shade.
The garden-glasses shone, and momently
The twinkling laurel scatter'd silver lights.
　　"Eustace," I said, "this wonder keeps the house."
He nodded, but a moment afterwards
He cried, "Look! look!" Before he ceased I turn'd,
And, ere a star can wink, beheld her there.
　　For up the porch there grew an Eastern rose,
That, flowering high, the last night's gale had caught,
And blown across the walk. One arm aloft—
Gown'd in pure white, that fitted to the shape—
Holding the bush, to fix it back, she stood.
A single stream of all her soft brown hair
Pour'd on one side: the shadow of the flowers
Stole all the golden gloss, and, wavering
Lovingly lower, trembled on her waist—
Ah, happy shade—and still went wavering down,
But, ere it touch'd a foot, that might have danced
The greensward into greener circles, dipt,
And mix'd with shadows of the common ground!
But the full day dwelt on her brows, and sunn'd
Her violet eyes, and all her Hebe-bloom,
And doubled his own warmth against her lips,
And on the bounteous wave of such a breast
As never pencil drew. Half light, half shade,
She stood, a sight to make an old man young.
　　So rapt, we near'd the house; but she, a Rose
In roses, mingled with her fragrant toil,
Nor heard us come, nor from her tendance turn'd
Into the world without; till close at hand,
And almost ere I knew mine own intent,
This murmur broke the stillness of that air
Which brooded round about her:
　　　　　　　　　　"Ah, one rose,
One rose, but one, by those fair fingers cull'd,
Were worth a hundred kisses press'd on lips
Less exquisite than thine."
　　　　　　　　　She look'd: but all
Suffused with blushes—neither self-possess'd
Nor startled, but betwixt this mood and that,
Divided in a graceful quiet—paused,
And dropt the branch she held, and turning, wound
Her looser hair in braid, and stirr'd her lips
For some sweet answer, tho' no answer came,
Nor yet refused the rose, but granted it,
And moved away, and left me, statue-like,
In act to render thanks.
　　　　　　　　　I, that whole day,
Saw her no more, altho' I linger'd there
Till every daisy slept, and Love's white star
Beam'd thro' the thicken'd cedar in the dusk.
　　So home we went, and all the livelong way
With solemn gibe did Eustace banter me.
"Now," said he, "will you climb the top of Art.
You cannot fail but work in hues to dim
The Titianic Flora. Will you match
My Juliet? you, not you,—the Master, Love,
A more ideal Artist he than all."

　　So home I went, but could not sleep for joy,
Reading her perfect features in the gloom,
Kissing the rose she gave me o'er and o'er,
And shaping faithful record of the glance
That graced the giving—such a noise of life
Swarm'd in the golden present, such a voice
Call'd to me from the years to come, and such
A length of bright horizon rimm'd the dark.
And all that night I heard the watchmen peal
The sliding season: all that night I heard
The heavy clocks knolling the drowsy hours.
The drowsy hours, dispensers of all good,
O'er the mute city stole with folded wings,
Distilling odors on me as they went
To greet their fairer sisters of the East.
　　Love at first sight, first-born, and heir to all,
Made this night thus. Henceforward squall nor storm
Could keep me from that Eden where she dwelt.
Light pretexts drew me: sometimes a Dutch love
For tulips: then for roses, moss or musk,
To grace my city-rooms: or fruits and cream
Served in the weeping elm; and more and more
A word could bring the color to my cheek;
A thought would fill my eyes with happy dew;
Love trebled life within me, and with each
The year increased.
　　　　　　　　The daughters of the year,
One after one, thro' that still garden pass'd:
Each garlanded with her peculiar flower
Danced into light, and died into the shade:
And each in passing touch'd with some new grace
Or seem'd to touch her, so that day by day.
Like one that never can be wholly known,
Her beauty grew; till Autumn brought an hour
For Eustace, when I heard his deep "I will,"
Breathed, like the covenant of a God, to hold
From thence thro' all the worlds; but I rose up
Full of his bliss, and following her dark eyes
Felt earth as air beneath me, till I reach'd
The wicket-gate, and found her standing there.
　　There sat we down upon a garden mound,
Two mutually enfolded; Love, the third,
Between us, in the circle of his arms
Enwound us both; and over many a range
Of waning lime the gray cathedral towers,
Across a hazy glimmer of the west,
Reveal'd their shining windows: from them clash'd
The bells; we listen'd; with the time we play'd;
We spoke of other things; we coursed about
The subject most at heart, more near and near,
Like doves about a dovecote, wheeling round
The central wish, until we settled there.
　　Then, in that time and place, I spoke to her,
Requiring, tho' I knew it was mine own,
Yet for the pleasure that I took to hear,
Requiring at her hand the greatest gift,
A woman's heart, the heart of her I loved:
And in that time and place she answer'd me,
And in the compass of three little words,
More musical than ever came in one,
The silver fragments of a broken voice,
Made me most happy, faltering "I am thine."
　　Shall I cease here? Is this enough to say
That my desire, like all strongest hopes,
By its own energy fulfill'd itself,
Merged in completion? Would you learn at full
How passion rose thro' circumstantial grades
Beyond all grades develop'd? and indeed
I had not stayed so long to tell you all,
But while I mused came Memory with sad eyes,
Holding the folded annals of my youth;
And while I mused, Love with knit brows went by,
And with a flying finger swept my lips,
And spake, "Be wise: not easily forgiven
Are those, who, setting wide the doors that bar
The secret bridal chambers of the heart,
Let in the day." Here, then, my words have end.
　　Yet might I tell of meetings, of farewells—

Of that which came between, more sweet than each,
In whispers, like the whispers of the leaves
That tremble round a nightingale—in sighs
Which perfect Joy, perplex'd for utterance,
Stole from her sister Sorrow. Might I not tell
Of difference, reconcilement, pledges given,
And vows, where there was never need of vows,
And kisses, where the heart on one wild leap
Hung tranced from all pulsation, as above
The heavens between their fairy fleeces pale
Sow'd all their mystic gulfs with fleeting stars;
Or while the balmy glooming, crescent-lit,
Spread the light haze along the river-shores,
And in the hollows; or as once we met
Unheedful, tho' beneath a whispering rain
Night slid down one long stream of sighing wind,
And in her bosom bore the baby, Sleep.

But this whole hour your eyes have been intent
On that veil'd picture—veil'd, for what it holds
May not be dwelt on by the common day.
This prelude has prepared thee. Raise thy soul;
Make thine heart ready with thine eyes; the time
Is come to raise the veil.

            Behold her there,
As I beheld her ere she knew my heart,
My first, last love; the idol of my youth,
The darling of my manhood, and, alas!
Now the most blessed memory of mine age.

DORA.

With farmer Allan at the farm abode
William and Dora. William was his son,
And she his niece. He often look'd at them,
And often thought "I'll make them man and wife."
Now Dora felt her uncle's will in all,
And yearn'd towards William; but the youth, because
He had been always with her in the house,
Thought not of Dora.

            Then there came a day
When Allan call'd his son, and said, "My son:
I married late, but I would wish to see
My grandchild on my knees before I die:
And I have set my heart upon a match.
Now therefore look to Dora; she is well
To look to; thrifty too beyond her age.
She is my brother's daughter: he and I
Had once hard words, and parted, and he died
In foreign lands; but for his sake I bred
His daughter Dora: take her for your wife;
For I have wish'd this marriage, night and day,
For many years." But William answer'd short:
"I cannot marry Dora; by my life,
I will not marry Dora." Then the old man
Was wroth, and doubled up his hands, and said:
"You will not, boy! you dare to answer thus!
But in my time a father's word was law,
And so it shall be now for me. Look to it:
Consider, William: take a month to think,
And let me have an answer to my wish;
Or, by the Lord that made me, you shall pack,
And never more darken my doors again."
But William answer'd madly; bit his lips,
And broke away. The more he look'd at her
The less he liked her; and his ways were harsh;
But Dora bore them meekly. Then before
The month was out he left his father's house,
And hired himself to work within the fields;
And half in love, half spite, he woo'd and wed
A laborer's daughter, Mary Morrison.

Then when the bells were ringing, Allan call'd
His niece and said: "My girl, I love you well;
But if you speak with him that was my son,
Or change a word with her he calls his wife,
My home is none of yours. My will is law."

And Dora promised, being meek. She thought,
"It cannot be: my uncle's mind will change!"
And days went on, and there was born a boy
To William; then distresses came on him;
And day by day he pass'd his father's gate,
Heart-broken, and his father help'd him not,
But Dora stored what little she could save,
And sent it them by stealth, nor did they know
Who sent it; till at last a fever seized
On William, and in harvest time he died.

Then Dora went to Mary. Mary sat
And look'd with tears upon her boy, and thought
Hard things of Dora. Dora came and said:
"I have obey'd my uncle until now,
And I have sinn'd, for it was all thro' me
This evil came on William at the first.
But, Mary, for the sake of him that's gone,
And for your sake, the woman that he chose,
And for this orphan, I am come to you:
You know there has not been for these five years
So full a harvest: let me take the boy,
And I will set him in my uncle's eye
Among the wheat; that when his heart is glad
Of the full harvest, he may see the boy,
And bless him for the sake of him that's gone."

And Dora took the child, and went her way
Across the wheat, and sat upon a mound
That was unsown, where many poppies grew.
Far off the farmer came into the field
And spied her not; but none of all his men
Dare tell him Dora waited with the child;
And Dora would have risen and gone to him,
But her heart fail'd her; and the reapers reap'd,
And the sun fell, and all the land was dark.

But when the morrow came, she rose and took
The child once more, and sat upon the mound;
And made a little wreath of all the flowers
That grew about, and tied it round his hat
To make him pleasing in her uncle's eye.
Then when the farmer pass'd into the field
He spied her, and he left his men at work,
And came and said: "Where were you yesterday?
Whose child is that? What are you doing here?"
So Dora cast her eyes upon the ground,
And answer'd softly, "This is William's child!"
"And did I not," said Allan, "did I not
Forbid you, Dora?" Dora said again,
"Do with me as you will, but take the child
And bless him for the sake of him that's gone!"
And Allan said, "I see it is a trick
Got up betwixt you and the woman there.
I must be taught my duty, and by you!
You knew my word was law, and yet you dared
To slight it. Well—for I will take the boy:
But go you hence, and never see me more."

So saying, he took the boy, that cried aloud
And struggled hard. The wreath of flowers fell
At Dora's feet. She bow'd upon her hands,
And the boy's cry came to her from the field,
More and more distant. She bow'd down her head,
Remembering the day when first she came,
And all the things that had been. She bow'd down
And wept in secret; and the reapers reap'd,
And the sun fell, and all the land was dark.

Then Dora went to Mary's house, and stood
Upon the threshold. Mary saw the boy
Was not with Dora. She broke out in praise
To God, that help'd her in her widowhood.
And Dora said, "My uncle took the boy;
But, Mary, let me live and work with you:
He says that he will never see me more."
Then answer'd Mary, "This shall never be,
That thou shouldst take my trouble on thyself:
And now I think, he shall not have the boy,
For he will teach him hardness, and to slight
His mother; therefore thou and I will go,
And I will have my boy, and bring him home;
And I will beg of him to take thee back:

B... if he w... not take thee back again.
Then ... I w... live within, one h...se,
Ar.. .... William's child, until he grows
Of age ... keep us."

So the women kiss'd

E...... ..... set out, and ...
T... ....ff the latch: th. ...
T.... ...... betwixt ...
W... ....in the b.... ....
An... .....la on the ha........
Lik... ...at I will him...
An... ..... for the g.... ...
Fio..a A...s w........
Then ...ev came ... ...
His ....
An... A....... ...
"O F....... if........
I ne......
Or W.......
For D.... ....k....
O S... ... W....
W... ...... I ....
He .... his ....rrying me—
I l.... n...... .....v ..... Sir, he sat
Th.... was w....g... ...ss his fr..r th...:
'G.... ss him ... s... ... m... t.. er kn....
T.... .. s I b... g a.. th... T..... ....
Hi... ... l passi—n..... ... he. I a!
Bu... Sir, ... he... my ...v.fr y..
W... use...... ..n.... ....v...... t.. sl...
His fa... er's me...... a...k D... ....
An... ..... th... ... ... s s... f ...
S... M. y... l.... ...
By M.... ... .:
And ... n.... ....:
"I l... ....— ... I we kl...
r......
I have .... I ...v l ...n—my ...
May ... r g... me —I h..ve been to ...
Kiss ... ...ed."

Then they ... .
The ... mention.. k. and kiss ...
Ar... the ... .. was ... ken w........
A... .... a g a l.......
A... .. th... ...... s ... ... W... n's
Think ..... W.... ....

So ... se f... a... ...e
Within .... ge... r... l.. y .. s
We .. f..... M...y ... k a.... D .. ...;
But D........ ..nman.. l t... .....

<hr>

AUDLEY COURT.

"The B..." t... F...ce are c... mm'd. an ln ... ..om
For l.... .... Let ...s pi.. .. there
At A........
I s... k... while An..ay feast
Hamm.... l....... ... l ... n... w ...
To Fr....s, ... k ... his ....rm.
To Fr... ... ...t... a... t....
An... n..... ..... W.... my h..."
S.. l Fr.. ..s. T.... ... t.. s.. rm.
A... r..... ... f ... ...
To w...... y ....
We .. f. th....... f.
The .. .. t ...
Of m....... f... 1
The ....ff...g ... ...
The ....r... ...f..... ... .. r..
An... ...se. l ...
With .. its .....
An... chimneys mu...." l ... f......
Th...e n a s... ..e ....
A d...sk napkin w... ... wh.. h ... ...
Br... ... out a du...ky ... if that sm...
A..., h..lf-eat-down, a pasty costly ma..

Where ... .. and pigeon, lark and leveret lay,
Like fossils of the r..k, with g..den yolks
Im...led a... l injelle...d: last, with these,
A fl..k of ..r f.. m his father's vats,
Prim... w... I kn..w; and so we sat and eat
An... talk.. 'd matters over: who was dead,
Who mar.i.. who was like to be, and h..w
The ... es v... ... l who w... l read the ball.
Then r .. l.. ip .. the game, Low s... it was
Th s s... .. .... g these .. ms ... farm,
A... f... ..r syste... and the ......
A... st... d g..t.. th ..ck.. was... m... ...split,
A.. ... m.. ag... t g...uer on the king
W .... t.. es.. t.. he ......
A... wal.. the ..ck h.. l.. ...the ......g
T.. .ear him. cl... his ha... in m......l song:
... O... wh... wo..ld fight and m.. ... and counter.
...arth.

lie sh.. for sixpence in a h..t..e..
A... su voll.. t... ... u h.. .... h
Wei e ... k... x...l.. la... e my life.
"...w ..r ... st ... t a desk.
Per ...ums e..r ... k.. ... e....g'd stool,
Th... his ji... es ...t.. bi... iats
A... .. t.. e..k.. ...t ... e my ..fe.
"Wa... scive ti. ..n'es.. ..I .. .re l my name
...pu.. t.. .ffe sh..r .. ..i n.. m.......
I u..di..s w.... ...el..in te... so..i;
T.. s... w.r s... ...... me ...e my ..fe.
"O.w... w.... .. f I w.... ..w m..n once,
Br s..... .... ba..u ... st.. wi..l
A l.. ...ny e.. t... .. thon.. l.. sa..ti..n
T...s l ... se ... . r ..e my ...fe."
H st... ... ss... .I .... with m..ne:
I f.... ... ...fs.. gs.
K... X... w.. t... s w... .. Si. R..ert's pride,
H... ks... e.... r.. e .. I s....—
l...... t.. e ... M..... nd this—
I se.. ... s... ... n.mes I k..w.
"S..... E... A.. y. s... ..a... lv m of me:
S.. E... f .... thy sis ..s ...n
A.... .... is mine.
"S... E... f .... Ei.... .. a.m;
Emilia false .... e..h... t,
F... ... art f... ...... is.
"S... .. rea...g l... ... .. l.. .re upon her
...est.
S..ep. .... ..ng .ove and t..ust against her lip:
I g.. .... I... .. l ... m w m...
"I... .. I re.. ... I w... l w..te
The p... f the .rkne.. a... the Ge.n.
S...p, E.. A... y, l..e, and dream ..me."
S... ng we ....e'ber, F..n.. H..e,
T.. farmer's s.. wl. ... ...er ss the ...y,
My ...fe ..: ard l th.. b... ng wherewith..l,
A.. l..e be f... w. l..re of my l..l
D.. w.. I w.... ..: .. t e.. the n... ... we rose
A .. u...ter'h .. ..b a m... in that, ast
I.. ...e o.. th... ... l about th.. f
Tw... g.. .. t .ry .... ..n.. .i av e r... ..
Th... r.... f the ... ...r ... is we.. k
F... n r.. k t.. r.. k upon the g... ...lg c... ..
T.. l r... was l ..l .. e rath ..: l... d...wn
The.. ..y w..s ofilc... ...... l ha... r.. l.. y
With .. e gre... sp..k.e .. ... r...
Dipt by itself, and we w... l... . heart.

<hr>

WALKING TO THE MAIL.

J..hn.　I'm glad I walk'd.　How fresh the mead
　　　ws l..k
A..ov the river. and, but a month ago,
The whole hillside was redder than a fox.
Is yon plantation where this byway joins
The turnpike?
James.　　Yes.

John. And when does this come by?
James. The mail? At one o'clock.
John. What is it now?
James. A quarter to.
John. Whose house is that I see?
No, not the County Member's with the vane:
Up higher with the yewtree by it, and half
A score of gables.
James. That? Sir Edward Head's:
But he 's abroad: the place is to be sold.
John. O, his. He was not broken.
James. No, sir, he,
Vex'd with a morbid devil in his blood
That veil'd the world with jaundice, hid his face
From all men, and commercing with himself,
He lost the sense that handles daily life—
That keeps us all in order more or less—
And sick of home went oversea for change.
John. And whither?
James. Nay, who knows? he's here and there.
But let him go; his devil goes with him,
As well as with his tenant, Jocky Dawes.
John. What 's that?
James. You saw the man—on Monday, was it?—
There by the humpback'd willow; half stands up
And bristles; half has fall'n and made a bridge;
And there he caught the younker tickling trout—
Caught in *flagrante*—what's the Latin word?—
Delicto: but his house, for so they say,
Was haunted with a jolly ghost, that shook
The curtains, whined in lobbies, tapt at doors,
And rummaged like a rat: no servants stay'd:
The farmer vext packs up his beds and chairs,
And all his household stuff: and with this boy
Betwixt his knees, his wife upon the tilt,
Sets out, and meets a friend who hails him, "What!
You 're flitting!" "Yes, we 're flitting," says the
ghost,
(For they had pack'd the thing among the beds,)
"O well," says he, "you flitting with us too—
Jack, turn the horses' heads and home again."
John. He left *his* wife behind: for so I heard.
James. He left her, yes. I met my lady once:
A woman like a butt, and harsh as crabs.
John. O yet but I remember, ten years back—
'T is now at least ten years—and then she was—
You could not light upon a sweeter thing:
A body slight and round, and like a pear
In growing, modest eyes, a hand, a foot
Lessening in perfect cadence, and a skin
As clean and white as privet when it flowers.
James. Ay, ay, the blossom fades, and they that
loved
At first like dove and dove were cat and dog.
She was the daughter of a cottager,
Out of her sphere. What betwixt shame and pride,
New things and old, himself and her, she sour'd
To what she is: a nature never kind!
Like men, like manners: like breeds like, they say.
Kind nature is the best: those manners next
That fit us like a nature second-hand;
Which are indeed the manners of the great.
John. But I had heard it was this bill that past.
And fear of change at home, that drove him hence.
James. That was the last drop in his cup of gall.
I once was near him, when his bailiff brought
A Chartist pike. You should have seen him wince
As from a venomous thing: he thought himself
A mark for all, and shudder'd, lest a cry
Should break his sleep by night, and his nice eyes
Should see the raw mechanic's bloody thumbs
Sweat on his blazon'd chairs: but, sir, you know
That these two parties still divide the world—
Of those that want, and those that have: and still
The same old sore breaks out from age to age
With much the same result. Now I myself,
A Tory to the quick, was as a boy
Destructive, when I had not what I would.

I was at school—a college in the South:
There lived a flayflint near: we stole his fruit,
His hens, his eggs: but there was law for us;
We paid in person. He had a sow, sir. She,
With meditative grunts of much content,
Lay great with pig, wallowing in sun and mud.
By night we dragg'd her to the college tower
From her warm bed, and up the corkscrew stair
With hand and rope we haled the groaning sow,
And on the leads we kept her till she pigg'd.
Large range of prospect had the mother sow,
And but for daily loss of one she loved,
As one by one we took them—but for this—
As never sow was higher in this world—
Might have been happy: but what lot is pure?
We took them all, till she was left alone
Upon her tower, the Niobe of swine,
And so return'd unfarrow'd to her sty.
John. They found you out?
James. Not they.
John. Well—after all—
What know we of the secret of a man?
His nerves were wrong. What ails us, who are
sound,
That we should mimic this raw fool the world,
Which charts us all in its coarse blacks or whites,
As ruthless as a baby with a worm,
As cruel as a schoolboy ere he grows
To Pity—more from ignorance than will.
But put your best foot forward, or I fear
That we shall miss the mail: and here it comes
With five at top: as quaint a four-in-hand
As you shall see—three piebalds and a roan.

EDWIN MORRIS; OR, THE LAKE.

O ME, my pleasant rambles by the lake.
My sweet, wild, fresh three quarters of a year,
My one Oasis in the dust and drouth
Of city life; I was a sketcher then:
See here, my doing: curves of mountain, bridge,
Boat, island, ruins of a castle, built
When men knew how to build, upon a rock,
With turrets lichen-gilded like a rock:
And here, new-comers in an ancient hold,
New-comers from the Mersey, millionnaires,
Here lived the Hills—a Tudor-chimneyed bulk
Of mellow brickwork on an isle of bowers.

O me, my pleasant rambles by the lake
With Edwin Morris and with Edward Bull
The curate; he was fatter than his cure.

But Edwin Morris, he that knew the names,
Long learned names of agaric, moss, and fern,
Who forged a thousand theories of the rocks,
Who taught me how to skate, to row, to swim,
Who read me rhymes elaborately good,
His own—I call'd him Crichton, for he seem'd
All-perfect, finish'd to the finger nail.

And once I ask'd him of his early life,
And his first passion; and he answer'd me;
And well his words became him: was he not
A full-cell'd honeycomb of eloquence
Stored from all flowers? Poet-like he spoke.

"My love for Nature is as old as I;
But thirty moons, one honeymoon to that,
And three rich sennights more, my love for her.
My love for Nature and my love for her,
Of different ages, like twin-sisters grew,
Twin-sisters differently beautiful.
To some full music rose and sank the sun.
And some full music seem'd to move and change

With all the varied changes of the dark,
And either twilight and the day between;
For daily hope fulfill'd, to rise again
Revolving toward fulfilment, made it sweet
To walk, to sit, to sleep, to breathe, to wake."

Or this or something like to this he spoke.
Then said the fat-faced curate, Edward Bull:

"I take it, God made the woman for the man,
And for the good and increase of the world.
A pretty face is well, and this is well,
To have a dame indoors, that trims us up,
And keeps us tight; but these unreal ways
Seem but the theme of writers, and indeed
Worn threadbare. Man is made of solid stuff.
I say, God made the woman for the man,
And for the good and increase of the world."

"Parson," said I, "you pitch the pipe too low:
But I have sudden touches, and can run
My faith beyond my practice into his:
Tho' if, in dancing after Letty Hill,
I do not hear the bells upon my cap,
I scarce hear other music: yet say on.
What should one give to light on such a dream?"
I ask'd him half-sardonically.

                              "Give?
Give all thou art," he answer'd, and a light
Of laughter dimpled in his swarthy cheek;
"I would have hid her needle in my heart,
To save her little finger from a scratch
No deeper than the skin: my ears could hear
Her lightest breaths: her least remark was worth
The experience of the wise. I went and came;
Her voice fled always thro' the summer land;
I spoke her name alone. Thrice-happy days!
The flower of each, those moments when we met,
The crown of all, we met to part no more."

Were not his words delicious, I a beast
To take them as I did? but something jarr'd;
Whether he spoke too largely; that there seem'd
A touch of something false, some self-conceit,
Or over-smoothness: howso'er it was,
He scarcely hit my humor, and I said:

"Friend Edwin, do not think yourself alone
Of all men happy. Shall not Love to me,
As in the Latin song I learnt at school,
Sneeze out a full God-bless-you right and left?
But you can talk: yours is a kindly vein:
I have, I think,—Heaven knows—as much within:
Have, or should have, but for a thought or two,
That like a purple beech among the greens
Looks out of place: 't is from no want in her:
It is my shyness, or my self-distrust,
Or something of a wayward modern mind
Dissecting passion. Time will set me right."

So spoke I knowing not the things that were.
Then said the fat-faced curate, Edward Bull
"God made the woman for the use of man,
And for the good and increase of the world."
And I and Edwin laugh'd; and now we paused
About the windings of the marge to hear
The soft wind blowing over meadowy holms
And alders, garden-isles; and now we left
The clerk behind us, I and he, and ran
By ripply shallows of the lisping lake,
Delighted with the freshness and the sound.

But, when the bracken rusted on their crags,
My suit had wither'd, nipt to death by him
That was a God, and is a lawyer's clerk,
The rentroll Cupid of our rainy isles.
'Tis true, we met; one hour I had, no more:
She sent a note, the seal an *Elle vous suit*,

The close "Your Letty, only yours;" and this
Thrice underscored. The friendly mist of morn
Clung to the lake. I boated over, ran
My craft aground, and heard with beating heart
The Sweet-Gale rustle round the shelving keel:
And out I stept, and up I crept; she moved,
Like Proserpine in Enna, gathering flowers:
Then low and sweet I whistled thrice; and she,
She turn'd, we closed, we kiss'd, swore faith, I
                  breathed
In some new planet: a silent cousin stole
Upon us and departed: "Leave," she cried,
"O leave me!" "Never, dearest, never: here
I brave the worst:" and while we stood like fools
Embracing, all at once a score of pugs
And poodles yell'd within, and out they came
Trustees and Aunts and Uncles. "What, with him!"
"Go," (shrill'd the cottonspinning chorus) "him!"
I choked. Again they shriek'd the burthen "Him!"
Again with hands of wild rejection "Go!—
Girl, get you in!" She went—and in one month
They wedded her to sixty thousand pounds,
To lands in Kent and messuages in York,
And slight Sir Robert with his watery smile
And educated whisker. But for me,
They set an ancient creditor to work:
It seems I broke a close with force and arms:
There came a mystic token from the king
To greet the sheriff, needless courtesy!
I read, and fled by night, and flying turn'd:
Her taper glimmer'd in the lake below:
I turn'd once more, close button'd to the storm;
So left the place, left Edwin, nor have seen
Him since, nor heard of her, nor cared to hear.
  Nor cared to hear? perhaps: yet long ago
I have pardon'd little Letty: not indeed,
It may be, for her own dear sake but this,
She seems a part of those fresh days to me;
For in the dust and drouth of London life
She moves among my visions of the lake,
While the prime swallow dips his wing, or then
While the gold-lily blows, and overhead
The light cloud smoulders on the summer crag.

————◇◇————

ST. SIMEON STYLITES.

Altho' I be the basest of mankind,
From scalp to sole one slough and crust of sin,
Unfit for earth, unfit for heaven, scarce meet
For troops of devils, mad with blasphemy,
I will not cease to grasp the hope I hold
Of saintdom, and to clamor, mourn, and sob,
Battering the gates of heaven with storms of prayer.
Have mercy, Lord, and take away my sin.
  Let this avail, just, dreadful, mighty God,
This not be all in vain, that thrice ten years,
Thrice multiplied by superhuman pangs,
In hungers and in thirsts, fevers and cold,
In coughs, aches, stitches, ulcerous throes and
                  cramps,
A sign betwixt the meadow and the cloud,
Patient on this tall pillar I have borne
Rain, wind, frost, heat, hail, damp, and sleet, and
                  snow;
And I had hoped that ere this period closed
Thou wouldst have caught me up into thy rest,
Denying not these weather-beaten limbs
The meed of saints, the white robe and the palm.
  O take the meaning, Lord: I do not breathe,
Not whisper any murmur of complaint,
Pain heap'd ten-hundred-fold to this, were still
Less burthen, by ten-hundred-fold, to bear,
Than were those lead-like tons of sin, that crush'd
My spirit flat before thee.
                              O Lord, Lord,
Thou knowest I bore this better at the first,

For I was strong and hale of body then :
And tho' my teeth, which now are dropt away,
Would chatter with the cold, and all my beard
Was tagg'd with icy fringes in the moon,
I drown'd the whoopings of the owl with sound
Of pious hymns and psalms, and sometimes saw
An angel stand and watch me, as I sang.
Now am I feeble grown; my end draws nigh;
I hope my end draws nigh: half deaf I am,
So that I scarce can hear the people hum
About the column's base, and almost blind,
And scarce can recognize the fields I know;
And both my thighs are rotted with the dew;
Yet cease I not to clamor and to cry,
While my stiff spine can hold my weary head,
Till all my limbs drop piecemeal from the stone,
Have mercy, mercy : take away my sin.

O Jesus, if thou wilt not save my soul,
Who may be saved? who is it may be saved?
Who may be made a saint, if I fail here?
Show me the man hath suffer'd more than I.
For did not all thy martyrs die one death?
For either they were stoned, or crucified,
Or burn'd in fire, or boil'd in oil, or sawn
In twain beneath the ribs; but I die here
To-day, and whole years long, a life of death.
Bear witness, if I could have found a way
(And heedfully I sifted all my thought)
More slowly-painful to subdue this home
Of sin, my flesh, which I despise and hate,
I had not stinted practice, O my God.

For not alone this pillar-punishment,
Not this alone I bore: but while I lived
In the white convent down the valley there,
For many weeks about my loins I wore
The rope that haled the buckets from the well,
Twisted as tight as I could knot the noose;
And spake not of it to a single soul,
Until the ulcer, eating thro' my skin,
Betray'd my secret penance, so that all
My brethren marvell'd greatly. More than this
I bore, whereof, O God, thou knowest all.

Three winters, that my soul might grow to thee,
I lived up there on yonder mountain side.
My right leg chain'd into the crag, I lay
Pent in a roofless close of ragged stones;
Inswathed sometimes in wandering mist, and twice
Black'd with thy branding thunder, and sometimes
Sucking the damps for drink, and eating not,
Except the spare chance-gift of those that came
To touch my body and be heal'd, and live:
And they say then that I work'd miracles,
Whereof my fame is loud amongst mankind,
Cured lameness, palsies, cancers. Thou, O God,
Knowest alone whether this was or no.
Have mercy, mercy; cover all my sin.

Then, that I might be more alone with thee,
Three years I lived upon a pillar, high
Six cubits, and three years on one of twelve;
And twice three years I cronch'd on one that rose
Twenty by measure; last of all, I grew,
Twice ten long weary weary years to this,
That numbers forty cubits from the soil.

I think that I have borne as much as this—
Or else I dream—and for so long a time.
If I may measure time by yon slow light,
And this high dial, which my sorrow crowns—
So much—even so.

　　　　　　And yet I know not well,
For that the evil ones come here, and say,
"Fall down, O Simeon: thou hast suffer'd long
For ages and for ages!" then they prate
Of penances I cannot have gone thro'.
Perplexing me with lies; and oft I fall,
Maybe for months, in such blind lethargies,
That Heaven, and Earth, and Time are choked.
　　　　　　　　　　　　　　　　But yet
Bethink thee, Lord, while thou and all the saints

Enjoy themselves in heaven, and men on earth
House in the shade of comfortable roofs,
Sit with their wives by fires, eat wholesome food,
And wear warm clothes, and even beasts have stalls
I, 'tween the spring and downfall of the light,
Bow down one thousand and two hundred times,
To Christ, the Virgin Mother, and the Saints;
Or in the night, after a little sleep,
I wake : the chill stars sparkle; I am wet
With drenching dews, or stiff with crackling frost.
I wear an undress'd goatskin on my back;
A grazing iron collar grinds my neck;
And in my weak, lean arms I lift the cross,
And strive and wrestle with thee till I die:
O mercy, mercy! wash away my sin.

O Lord, thou knowest what a man I am;
A sinful man, conceived and born in sin :
'Tis their own doing; this is none of mine;
Lay it not to me. Am I to blame for this,
That here come those that worship me? Ha! ha!
They think that I am somewhat. What am I?
The silly people take me for a saint,
And bring me offerings of fruit and flowers:
And I, in truth (thou wilt bear witness here)
Have all in all endured as much, and more
Than many just and holy men, whose names
Are register'd and calendar'd for saints.

Good people, you do ill to kneel to me.
What is it I can have done to merit this!
I am a sinner viler than you all.
It may be I have wrought some miracles,
And cured some halt and maim'd; but what of that!
It may be, no one, even among the saints,
May match his pains with mine; but what of that?
Yet do not rise: for you may look on me,
And in your looking you may kneel to God.
Speak! is there any of you halt or maim'd?
I think you know I have some power with Heaven
From my long penance: let him speak his wish.

Yes, I can heal him. Power goes forth from me.
They say that they are heal'd. Ah, hark! they
　　　　shout

"St. Simeon Stylites." Why, if so,
God reaps a harvest in me. O my soul,
God reaps a harvest in thee. If this be,
Can I work miracles and not be saved?
This is not told of any. They were saints.
It cannot be but that I shall be saved;
Yea, crown'd a saint. They shout, "Behold a saint!"
And lower voices saint me from above.
Courage, St. Simeon! This dull chrysalis
Cracks into shining wings, and hope ere death
Spreads more and more and more, that God hath now
Sponged and made blank of crimeful record all
My mortal archives.

　　　　　　O my sons, my sons,
I, Simeon of the pillar, by surname
Stylites, among men; I, Simeon,
The watcher on the column till the end;
I, Simeon, whose brain the sunshine bakes;
I, whose bald brows in silent hours become
Unnaturally hoar with rime, do now
From my high nest of penance here proclaim
That Pontius and Iscariot by my side
Show'd like fair seraphs. On the coals I lay,
A vessel full of sin: all hell beneath
Made me boil over. Devils pluck'd my sleeve;
Abaddon and Asmodeus caught at me.
I smote them with the cross; they swarm'd again.
In bed like monstrous apes they crush'd my chest.
They flapp'd my light out as I read: I saw
Their faces grow between me and my book:
With colt-like whinny and with hoggish whine
They burst my prayer. Yet this way was left,
And by this way I 'scaped them. Mortify
Your flesh, like me, with scourges and with thorns;
Smite, shrink not, spare not. If it may be, fast
Whole Lents, and pray. I hardly, with slow steps,

With slow, faint steps, and much exceeding pain,
Have scrambled past those pits of fire, that still
Sing in mine ears. But yield not me the praise:
God only thro' his bounty hath thought fit,
Among the powers and princes of this world,
To make me an example to mankind,
Which few can reach to. Yet I do not say
But that a time may come—yea, even now,
Now, now, his footsteps smite the threshold stairs
Of life—I say, that time is at the doors
When you may worship me without reproach;
For I will leave my relics in your land,
And you may carve a shrine about my dust,
And burn a fragrant lamp before my bones,
When I am gather'd to the glorious saints.

While I spake then, a sting of shrewdest pain
Ran shrivelling thro' me, and a cloud-like change,
In passing, with a grosser film made thick
These heavy, horny eyes. The end! the end!
Surely the end! What's here? a shape, a shade,
A flash of light. Is that the angel there
That holds a crown? Come, blessed brother, come,
I know thy glittering face. I waited long;
My brows are ready. What! deny it now?
Nay, draw, draw, draw nigh. So I clutch it. Christ!
'Tis gone: 'tis here again: the crown! the crown!
So now 'tis fitted on and grows to me.
And from it melt the dews of Paradise,
Sweet! sweet! spikenard, and balm, and frankincense.

Ah! let me not be fool'd, sweet saints: I trust
That I am whole, and clean, and meet for Heaven.

Speak, if there be a priest, a man of God,
Among you there, and let him presently
Approach, and lean a ladder on the shaft,
And climbing up into my airy home,
Deliver me the blessed sacrament:
For by the warning of the Holy Ghost,
I prophesy that I shall die to-night,
A quarter before twelve.

         But thou, O Lord,
Aid all this foolish people; let them take
Example, pattern: lead them to thy light.

THE TALKING OAK.

Once more the gate behind me falls;
  Once more before my face
I see the moulder'd Abbey-walls,
  That stand within the chace.

Beyond the lodge the city lies,
  Beneath its drift of smoke;
And ah! with what delighted eyes
  I turn to yonder oak.

For when my passion first began,
  Ere that, which in me burn'd,
The love, that makes me thrice a man,
  Could hope itself return'd:

To yonder oak within the field
  I spoke without restraint,
And with a larger faith appeal'd
  Than Papist unto Saint.

For oft I talk'd with him apart,
  And told him of my choice,
Until he plagiarized a heart,
  And answer'd with a voice.

Tho' what he whisper'd, under Heaven
  None else could understand;
I found him garrulously given,
  A babbler in the land.

But since I heard him make reply
  Is many a weary hour;

'Twere well to question him, and try
  If yet he keeps the power.

Hail, hidden to the knees in fern,
  Broad Oak of Sumner-chace,
Whose topmost branches can discern
  The roofs of Sumner-place!

Say thou, whereon I carved her name,
  If ever maid or spouse,
As fair as my Olivia, came
  To rest beneath thy boughs.—

"O Walter, I have shelter'd here
  Whatever maiden grace
The good old Summers, year by year,
  Made ripe in Sumner-chace:

"Old Summers, when the monk was fat,
  And, issuing shorn and sleek,
Would twist his girdle tight, and pat
  The girls upon the cheek,

"Ere yet, in scorn of Peter's-pence,
  And number'd bead and shrift,
Bluff Harry broke into the spence,
  And turn'd the cowls adrift:

"And I have seen some score of those
  Fresh faces that would thrive
When his man-minded offset rose
  To chase the deer at five;

"And all that from the town would stroll,
  Till that wild wind made work
In which the gloomy brewer's soul
  Went by me, like a stork:

"The slight she-slips of loyal blood,
  And others, passing praise,
Strait-laced, but all-too-full in bud
  For puritanic stays:

"And I have shadow'd many a group
  Of beauties that were born
In teacup-times of hood and hoop,
  Or while the patch was worn;

"And, leg and arm with love-knots gay,
  About me leap'd and laugh'd
The modish Cupid of the day,
  And shrill'd his tinsel shaft.

"I swear (and else may insects prick
  Each leaf into a gall)
This girl, for whom your heart is sick,
  Is three times worth them all;

"For those and theirs, by Nature's law,
  Have faded long ago;
But in these latter springs I saw
  Your own Olivia blow,

"From when she gamboll'd on the greens,
  A baby-germ, to when
The maiden blossoms of her teens
  Could number five from ten.

"I swear, by leaf, and wind, and rain,
  (And hear me with thine ears,)
That, tho' I circle in the grain
  Five hundred rings of years—

"Yet, since I first could cast a shade,
  Did never creature pass
So slightly, musically made,
  So light upon the grass:

"For as to fairies, that will flit
  To make the greensward fresh,

I hold them exquisitely knit,
  But far too spare of flesh."

O, hide thy knotted knees in fern,
  And overlook the chace;
And from thy topmost branch discern
  The roofs of Sumner-place.

But thou, whereon I carved her name,
  That oft hast heard my vows,
Declare when last Olivia came
  To sport beneath thy boughs.

"O yesterday, you know, the fair
  Was holden at the town:
Her father left his good arm-chair,
  And rode his hunter down.

"And with him Albert came on his,
  I look'd at him with joy:
As cowslip unto oxlip is,
  So seems she to the boy.

"An hour had past—and, sitting straight
  Within the low-wheel'd chaise,
Her mother trundled to the gate
  Behind the dappled grays.

"But, as for her, she stay'd at home,
  And on the roof she went,
And down the way you use to come
  She look'd with discontent.

"She left the novel half-uncut
  Upon the rosewood shelf;
She left the new piano shut:
  She could not please herself.

"Then ran she, gamesome as the colt,
  And livelier than a lark
She sent her voice thro' all the holt
  Before her, and the park.

"A light wind chased her on the wing,
  And in the chase grew wild,
As close as might be would he cling
  About the darling child:

"But light as any wind that blows
  So fleetly did she stir,
The flower, she touch'd on, dipt and rose,
  And turn'd to look at her.

"And here she came, and round me play'd,
  And sang to me the whole
Of those three stanzas that you made
  About my 'giant bole;'

"And in a fit of frolic mirth
  She strove to span my waist;
Alas, I was so broad of girth,
  I could not be embraced.

"I wish'd myself the fair young beech
  That here beside me stands,
That round me, clasping each in each,
  She might have lock'd her hands.

"Yet seem'd the pressure thrice as sweet
  As woodbine's fragile hold,
Or when I feel about my feet
  The berried briony fold."

O muffle round thy knees with fern,
  And shadow Sumner-chace!
Long may thy topmost branch discern
  The roofs of Sumner-place!

But tell me, did she read the name
  I carved with many vows
When last with throbbing heart I came
  To rest beneath thy boughs?

"O yes, she wander'd round and round
  These knotted knees of mine,
And found, and kiss'd the name she found,
  And sweetly murmur'd thine.

"A teardrop trembled from its source,
  And down my surface crept.
My sense of touch is something coarse,
  But I believe she wept.

"Then flush'd her cheek with rosy light,
  She glanced across the plain;
But not a creature was in sight;
  She kiss'd me once again.

"Her kisses were so close and kind,
  That, trust me on my word,
Hard wood I am, and wrinkled rind,
  But yet my sap was stirr'd:

"And even into my inmost ring
  A pleasure I discern'd,
Like those blind motions of the Spring,
  That show the year is turn'd.

"Thrice-happy he that may caress
  The ringlet's waving balm—
The cushions of whose touch may press
  The maiden's tender palm.

"I, rooted here among the groves,
  But languidly adjust
My vapid vegetable loves
  With anthers and with dust:

"For ah! my friend, the days were brief
  Whereof the poets talk,
When that, which breathes within the leaf,
  Could slip its bark and walk.

"But could I, as in times foregone,
  From spray, and branch, and stem,
Have suck'd and gather'd into one
  The life that spreads in them,

"She had not found me so remiss;
  But lightly issuing thro',
I would have paid her kiss for kiss
  With usury thereto."

O flourish high, with leafy towers,
  And overlook the lea,
Pursue thy loves among the bowers,
  But leave thou mine to me.

O flourish, hidden deep in fern,
  Old oak, I love thee well;
A thousand thanks for what I learn
  And what remains to tell.

"'T is little more; the day was warm;
  At last, tired out with play,
She sank her head upon her arm,
  And at my feet she lay.

"Her eyelids dropp'd their silken eaves
  I breathed upon her eyes
Thro' all the summer of my leaves
  A welcome mix'd with sighs.

"I took the swarming sound of life—
  The music from the town—

The murmurs of the drum and fife,
 And lull'd them in my own.

"Sometimes I let a sunbeam slip,
 To light her shaded eye;
A second flutter'd round her lip
 Like a golden butterfly;

"A third would glimmer on her neck
 To make the necklace shine;
Another slid, a sunny fleck,
 From head to ankle fine.

"Then close and dark my arms I spread,
 And shadow'd all her rest —
Dropt dews upon her golden head,
 An acorn in her breast.

"But in a pet she started up,
 And pluck'd it out, and drew
My little oakling from the cup,
 And flung him in the dew.

"And yet it was a graceful gift—
 I felt a pang within
As when I see the woodman lift
 His axe to slay my kin.

"I shook him down because he was
 The finest on the tree.
He lies beside thee on the grass.
 O kiss him once for me.

"O kiss him twice and thrice for me,
 That have no lips to kiss,
For never yet was oak on lea
 Shall grow so fair as this."

Step deeper yet in herb and fern,
 Look further thro' the chace,
Spread upward till thy boughs discern
 The front of Sumner-place.

This fruit of thine by Love is blest,
 That but a moment lay
Where fairer fruit of Love may rest
 Some happy future day.

I kiss it twice, I kiss it thrice,
 The warmth it thence shall win
To riper life may magnetize
 The baby-oak within.

But thou, while kingdoms overset
 Or lapse from hand to hand,
Thy leaf shall never fail, nor yet
 Thine acorn in the land.

May never saw dismember thee,
 Nor wielded axe disjoint,
That art the fairest-spoken tree
 From here to Lizard-point.

O rock upon thy towery top
 All throats that gurgle sweet!
All starry culmination drop
 Balm-dews to bathe thy feet!

All grass of silky feather grow—
 And while he sinks or swells
The full south-breeze around thee blow
 The sound of minster bells.

The fat earth feed thy branchy root,
 That under deeply strikes!
The northern morning o'er thee shoot,
 High up, in silver spikes!

Nor ever lightning char thy grain,
 But, rolling as in sleep,
Low thunders bring the mellow rain,
 That makes thee broad and deep!

And hear me swear a solemn oath,
 That only by thy side
Will I to Olive plight my troth,
 And gain her for my bride.

And when my marriage morn may fall,
 She, Dryad-like, shall wear
Alternate leaf and acorn-ball
 In wreath about her hair.

And I will work in prose and rhyme,
 And praise thee more in both
Than bard has honor'd beech or lime,
 Or that Thessalian growth,

In which the swarthy ringdoves sat,
 And mystic sentence spoke:
And more than England honors that,
 Thy famous brother-oak,

Wherein the younger Charles abode
 Till all the paths were dim,
And far below the Roundhead rode,
 And humm'd a surly hymn.

———⊲⊳———

LOVE AND DUTY.

Of love that never found his earthly close,
What sequel? Streaming eyes and breaking hearts?
Or all the same as if he had not been?
 Not so. Shall Error in the round of time
Still father Truth? O shall the braggart shout
For some blind glimpse of freedom work itself
Thro' madness, hated by the wise, to law
System and empire? Sin itself be found
The cloudy porch oft opening on the Sun?
And only he, this wonder, dead, become
Mere highway dust! or year by year alone
Sit brooding in the ruins of a life,
Nightmare of youth, the spectre of himself?
If this were thus, if this, indeed, were all,
Better the narrow brain, the stony heart,
The staring eye glazed o'er with sapless days,
The long mechanic pacings to and fro,
The set gray life, and apathetic end.
But am I not the nobler thro' thy love?
O three times less unworthy! likewise thou
Art more thro' Love, and greater than thy years.
The Sun will run his orbit, and the Moon
Her circle. Wait, and Love himself will bring
The drooping flower of knowledge changed to fruit
Of wisdom. Wait: my faith is large in Time,
And that which shapes it to some perfect end.
 Will some one say, then why not ill for good
Why took ye not your pastime? To that man
My work shall answer, since I knew the right
And did it: for a man is not as God,
But then most Godlike being most a man.
 —So let me think 't is well for thee and me—
Ill-fated that I am, what lot is mine
Whose foresight preaches peace, my heart so slow
To feel it? For how hard it seem'd to me,
When eyes, love-languid thro' half-tears, would dwel
One earnest, earnest moment upon mine,
Then not to dare to see! when thy low voice,
Faltering, would break its syllables, to keep
My own full-tuned,—hold passion in a leash,
And not leap forth and fall about thy neck,
And on thy bosom, (deep-desired relief!)
Rain out the heavy mist of tears, that weigh'd
Upon my brain, my senses, and my soul!

For Love himself took part against himself
To warn us off. and Duty loved of Love—
O this world's curse,—beloved but hated—came
Like Death betwixt thy dear embrace and mine,
And crying, Who is this? behold thy bride,"
She push'd me from thee.
           If the sense is hard
To alien ears, I did not speak to these—
No, not to thee, but to myself in thee:
Hard is my doom and thine: thou knowest it all.
Could Love part thus? was it not well to speak,
To have spoken once? It could not but be well.
The slow sweet hours that bring us all things good,
The slow sad hours that bring us all things ill,
And all good things from evil, brought the night
In which we sat together and alone,
And to the want. that hollow'd all the heart,
Gave utterance by the yearning of an eye,
That burn'd upon its object thro' such tears
As flow but once a life.
           The trance gave way
To those caresses, when a hundred times
In that last kiss, which never was the last,
Farewell. like endless welcome, lived and died.
Then follow'd counsel, comfort, and the words
That make a man feel strong in speaking truth;
Till now the dark was worn, and overhead
The lights of sunset and of sunrise mix'd
In that brief night; the summer night, that passed
Among her stars to hear us; stars that hung
Love-charm'd to listen: all the wheels of Time
Spun round in station, but the end had come.
O then like those, who clench their nerves to rush
Upon their dissolution, we two rose,
There—closing like an individual life—
In one blind cry of passion and of pain,
Like bitter accusation ev'n to death,
Caught up the whole of love and utter'd it,
And bade adieu forever.
           Live—yet live—
Shall sharpest pathos blight us, knowing all
Life needs for life is possible to will—
Live happy; tend thy flowers; be tended by
My blessing! Should my Shadow cross thy thoughts
Too sadly for their peace, remand it thou
For calmer hours to Memory's darkest hold,
If not to be forgotten—not at once—
Not all forgotten. Should it cross thy dreams,
O might it come like one that looks content,
With quiet eyes unfaithful to the truth,
And point thee forward to a distant light,
Or seem to lift a burthen from thy heart
And leave thee freër, till thou wake refresh'd,
Then when the low matin-chirp hath grown
Full choir, and morning driv'n her plough of pearl
Far furrowing into light the mounded rack,
Beyond the fair green field and eastern sea.

THE GOLDEN YEAR.

WELL, you shall have that song which Leonard
    wrote:
It was last summer on a tour in Wales:
Old James was with me: we that day had been
Up Snowdon; and I wish'd for Leonard there,
And found him in Llanberis: then we crost
Between the lakes, and clamber'd half way up
The counter side; and that same song of his
He told me; for I banter'd him, and swore
They said he lived shut up within himself,
A tongue-tied Poet in the feverous days,
That, setting the *how much* before the *how*,
Cry, like the daughters of the horse-leech, "Give,
Cram us with all," but count not me the herd!
  To which "They call me what they will," he said:
"But I was born too late: the fair new forms,

That float about the threshold of an age,
Like truths of Science waiting to be caught—
Catch me who can, and make the catcher crown'd—
Are taken by the forelock. Let it be.
But if you care indeed to listen, hear
These measured words, my work of yestermorn.
  "We sleep and wake and sleep, but all things
    move:
The Sun flies forward to his brother Sun;
The dark Earth follows wheel'd in her ellipse;
And human things returning on themselves
Move onward, leading up the golden year.
  "Ah, tho' the times, when some new thought can
    bud,
Are but as poets' seasons when they flower,
Yet seas, that daily gain upon the shore,
Have ebb and flow conditioning their march,
And slow and sure comes up the golden year.
  "When wealth no more shall rest in mounded
    heaps,
But smit with freër light shall slowly melt
In many streams to fatten lower lands,
And light shall spread, and man be liker man
Thro' all the season of the golden year.
  "Shall eagles not be eagles? wrens be wrens?
If all the world were falcons, what of that?
The wonder of the eagle were the less,
But he not less the eagle. Happy days
Roll onward, leading up the golden year.
  "Fly, happy happy sails and bear the Press;
Fly, happy with the mission of the Cross;
Knit land to land, and blowing havenward
With silks, and fruits, and spices, clear of toil.
Enrich the markets of the golden year.
  "But we grow old. Ah! when shall all men's
    good
Be each man's rule, and universal Peace
Lie like a shaft of light across the land,
And like a lane of beams athwart the sea,
Thro' all the circle of the golden year?"
  Thus far he flowed, and ended; whereupon
"Ah, folly!" in mimic cadence answer'd James—
"Ah, folly! for it lies so far away,
Not in our time, nor in our children's time,
'T is like the second world to us that live:
'T were all as one to fix our hopes on Heaven
As on this vision of the golden year."
  With that he struck his staff against the rocks
And broke it,—James,—you know him,—old, but full
Of force and choler, and firm upon his feet,
And like an oaken stock in winter woods,
O'erflourish'd with the hoary clematis:
Then added, all in heat:
           "What stuff is this!
Old writers push'd the happy season back,—
The more fools they,—we forward: dreamers both:
You most, that in an age, when every hour
Must sweat her sixty minutes to the death,
Live on, God love us, as if the seedsman, rapt
Upon the teeming harvest, should not dip
His hand into the bag: but well I know
That unto him who works, and feels he works,
This same grand year is ever at the doors."
  He spoke; and, high above, I heard them blast
The steep slate-quarry, and the great echo flap
And buffet round the hills from bluff to bluff.

ULYSSES.

IT little profits that an idle king,
By this still hearth, among these barren crags,
Match'd with an aged wife. I mete and dole
Unequal laws unto a savage race,
That hoard, and sleep, and feed, and know not me.
I cannot rest from travel: I will drink
Life to the lees: all times I have enjoy'd

Greatly, have suffer'd greatly, both with those
That loved me, and alone ; on shore, and when
Thro' scudding drifts the rainy Hyades
Vext the dim sea : I am become a name ;
For always roaming with a hungry heart
Much have I seen and known ; cities of men
And manners, climates, councils, governments,
Myself not least, but honor'd of them all ;
And drunk delight of battle with my peers,
Far on the ringing plains of windy Troy.
I am a part of all that I have met ;
Yet all experience is an arch wherethro'
Gleams that untravell'd world, whose margin fades
Forever and forever when I move.
How dull it is to pause, to make an end,
To rust unburnish'd, not to shine in use !
As tho' to breathe were life. Life piled on life
Were all too little, and of one to me
Little remains : but every hour is saved
From that eternal silence, something more,
A bringer of new things ; and vile it were
For some three suns to store and hoard myself,
And this gray spirit yearning in desire
To follow knowledge, like a sinking star,
Beyond the utmost bound of human thought.

This is my son, mine own Telemachus,
To whom I leave the sceptre and the isle—
Well-loved of me, discerning to fulfil
This labor, by slow prudence to make mild
A rugged people, and thro' soft degrees
Subdue them to the useful and the good.
Most blameless is he, centred in the sphere
Of common duties, decent not to fail

In offices of tenderness, and pay
Meet adoration to my household gods,
When I am gone. He works his work, I mine.
There lies the port : the vessel puffs her sail :
There gloom the dark broad seas. My mariners,
Souls that have toil'd, and wrought, and thought
     with me—
That ever with a frolic welcome took
The thunder and the sunshine, and opposed
Free hearts, free foreheads—you and I are old ;
Old age hath yet his honor and his toil :
Death closes all : but something ere the end,
Some work of noble note, may yet be done,
Not unbecoming men that strove with Gods.
The lights begin to twinkle from the rocks :
The long day wanes : the slow moon climbs : the
     deep
Moans round with many voices. Come, my friends,
'T is not too late to seek a newer world.
Push off, and sitting well in order smite
The sounding furrows ; for my purpose holds
To sail beyond the sunset, and the baths
Of all the western stars, until I die.
It may be that the gulfs will wash us down :
It may be we shall touch the Happy Isles,
And see the great Achilles, whom we knew.
Tho' much is taken, much abides ; and tho'
We are not now that strength which in old days
Moved earth and heaven ; that which we are, we
     are ;
One equal temper of heroic hearts,
Made weak by time and fate, but strong in will
To strive, to seek, to find, and not to yield.

" There lies the port : the vessel puffs her sail :
     There gloom the dark broad seas."

LOCKSLEY HALL.

COMRADES, leave me here a little, while as yet 't is early morn ·
Leave me here, and when you want me, sound upon the bugle norn.

'T is the place, and all around it, as of old, the curlews call,
Dreary gleams about the moorland flying over Locksley Hall;

Locksley Hall, that in the distance overlooks the sandy tracts,
And the hollow ocean-ridges roaring into cataracts.

Many a night from yonder ivied casement, ere I went to rest,
Did I look on great Orion sloping slowly to the West.

Many a night I saw the Pleiads, rising thro' the mellow shade,
Glitter like a swarm of fire-flies tangled in a silver braid.

Here about the beach I wander'd, nourishing a youth sublime
With the fairy tales of science, and the long result of Time;

When the centuries behind me like a fruitful land reposed;
When I clung to all the present for the promise that it closed:

When I dipt into the future far as human eye could see;
Saw the Vision of the world, and all the wonder that would be.—

In the Spring a fuller crimson comes upon the robin's breast;
In the Spring the wanton lapwing gets himself another crest;

In the Spring a livelier iris changes on the burnish'd dove;
In the Spring a young man's fancy lightly turns to thoughts of love.

Then her cheek was pale and thinner than should be for one so young,
And her eyes on all my motions with a mute observance hung.

And I said, "My cousin Amy, speak, and speak the truth to me,
Trust me, cousin, all the current of my being sets to thee."

On her pallid cheek and forehead came a color and a light,
As I have seen the rosy red flushing in the northern night.

And she turn'd—her bosom shaken with a sudden storm of sighs—
All the spirit deeply dawning in the dark of hazel eyes—

Saying, "I have hid my feelings, fearing they should do me wrong;"
Saying, "Dost thou love me, cousin?" weeping, "I have loved thee long."

Love took up the glass of Time, and turn'd it in his glowing hands;
Every moment, lightly shaken, ran itself in golden sands.

Love took up the harp of Life, and smote on all the chords with might;
Smote the chord of Self, that, trembling, pass'd in music out of sight.

Many a morning on the moorland did we hear the copses ring,
And her whisper throng'd my pulses with the fulness of the Spring.

Many an evening by the waters did we watch the stately ships,
And our spirits rush'd together at the touching of the lips.

O my cousin, shallow-hearted! O my Amy, mine no more!
O the dreary, dreary moorland! O the barren, barren shore!

Falser than all fancy fathoms, falser than all songs have sung,
Puppet to a father's threat, and servile to a shrewish tongue!

Is it well to wish thee happy?—having known me—to decline
On a range of lower feelings and a narrower heart than mine!

"Many an evening by the waters did we watch the stately ships,
And our spirits rushed together at the touching of the lips."

Yet it shall be: thou shalt lower to his level day by day,
What is fine within thee growing coarse to sympathize with clay.

As the husband is, the wife is: thou art mated with a clown,
And the grossness of his nature will have weight to drag thee down.

He will hold thee, when his passion shall have spent its novel force,
Something better than his dog, a little dearer than his horse.

What is this? his eyes are heavy: think not they are glazed with wine.
Go to him: it is thy duty: kiss him: take his hand in thine.

It may be my lord is weary, that his brain is overwrought:
Soothe him with thy finer fancies, touch him with thy lighter thought.

He will answer to the purpose, easy things to understand—
Better thou wert dead before me, tho' I slew thee with my hand!

Better thou and I were lying, hidden from the heart's disgrace,
Roll'd in one another's arms, and silent in a last embrace.

Cursed be the social wants that sin against the strength of youth!
Cursed be the social lies that warp us from the living truth!

Cursed be the sickly forms that err from honest Nature's rule!
Cursed be the gold that gilds the straiten'd forehead of the fool!

Well—'tis well that I should bluster!—Hadst thou less unworthy proved—
Would to God—for I had loved thee more than ever wife was loved.

Am I mad, that I should cherish that which bears but bitter fruit?
I will pluck it from my bosom, tho' my heart be at the root.

Never, tho' my mortal summers to such length of years should come
As the many-winter'd crow that leads the clanging rookery home.

Where is comfort? in division of the records of the mind?
Can I part her from herself, and love her, as I knew her, kind?

I remember one that perish'd: sweetly did she speak and move:
Such a one do I remember, whom to look at was to love.

Can I think of her as dead, and love her for the love she bore?
No—she never loved me truly: love is love forevermore.

Comfort? comfort scorn'd of devils! this is truth the poet sings,
That a sorrow's crown of sorrow is remembering happier things.

Drug thy memories, lest thou learn it, lest thy heart be put to proof,
In the dead unhappy night, when the rain is on the roof.

Like a dog, he hunts in dreams, and thou art staring at the wall,
Where the dying night-lamp flickers, and the shadows rise and fall.

Then a hand shall pass before thee, pointing to his drunken sleep,
To thy widow'd marriage pillows, to the tears that thou wilt weep.

Thou shalt hear the "Never, never," whisper'd by the phantom years,
And a song from out the distance in the ringing of thine ears;

And an eye shall vex thee, looking ancient kindness on thy pain.
Turn thee, turn thee on thy pillow: get thee to thy rest again.

Nay, but Nature brings thee solace; for a tender voice will cry.
'Tis a purer life than thine; a lip to drain thy trouble dry.

Baby lips will laugh me down: my latest rival brings thee rest.
Baby fingers, waxen touches, press me from the mother's breast.

O, the child too clothes the father with a dearness not his due.
Half is thine and half is his: it will be worthy of the two.

O, I see thee old and formal, fitted to thy petty part,
With a little hoard of maxims preaching down a daughter's heart.

"They were dangerous guides the feelings—she herself was not exempt—
Truly, she herself had suffer'd"—Perish in thy self-contempt!

Overlive it—lower yet—be happy! wherefore should I care?
I myself must mix with action, lest I wither by despair.

What is that which I should turn to, lighting upon days like these?
Every door is barr'd with gold, and opens but to golden keys.

Every gate is throng'd with suitors, all the markets overflow.
I have but an angry fancy: what is that which I should do?

I had been content to perish, falling on the foeman's ground,
When the ranks are roll'd in vapor, and the winds are laid with sound.

But the jingling of the guinea helps the hurt that Honor feels,
And the nations do but murmur, snarling at each other's heels.

Can I but relive in sadness? I will turn that earlier page.
Hide me from my deep emotion, O thou wondrous Mother-Age!

Make me feel the wild pulsation that I felt before the strife,
When I heard my days before me, and the tumult of my life.

Yearning for the large excitement that the coming years would yield,
Eager-hearted as a boy when first he leaves his father's field,

And at night along the dusky highway, near and nearer drawn,
Sees in heaven the light of London flaring like a dreary dawn;

And his spirit leaps within him to be gone before him then,
Underneath the light he looks at, in among the throngs of men;

Men, my brothers, men the workers, ever reaping something new:
That which they have done but earnest of the things that they shall do:

For I dipt into the future, far as human eye could see,
Saw the Vision of the world, and all the wonder that would be;

Saw the heavens fill with commerce, argosies of magic sails,
Pilots of the purple twilight, dropping down with costly bales;

Heard the heavens fill with shouting, and there rain'd a ghastly dew
From the nations' airy navies grappling in the central blue;

Far along the world-wide whisper of the south-wind rushing warm,
With the standards of the peoples plunging thro' the thunder-storm;

Till the war-drum throbb'd no longer, and the battle-flags were furl'd
In the Parliament of man, the Federation of the world.

There the common sense of most shall hold a fretful realm in awe,
And the kindly earth shall slumber, lapt in universal law.

So I triumph'd, ere my passion sweeping thro' me left me dry,
Left me with the palsied heart, and left me with the jaundiced eye;

Eye, to which all order festers, all things here are out of joint,
Science moves, but slowly slowly, creeping on from point to point:

Slowly comes a hungry people, as a lion, creeping nigher,
Glares at one that nods and winks behind a slowly-dying fire.

Yet I doubt not thro' the ages one increasing purpose runs,
And the thoughts of men are widen'd with the process of the suns.

What is that to him that reaps not harvest of his youthful joys,
Tho' the deep heart of existence beat forever like a boy's?

Knowledge comes, but wisdom lingers, and I linger on the shore,
And the individual withers, and the world is more and more.

Knowledge comes, but wisdom lingers, and he bears a laden breast,
Full of sad experience, moving toward the stillness of his rest.

Hark, my merry comrades call me, sounding on the bugle-horn,
They to whom my foolish passion were a target for their scorn:

Shall it not be scorn to me to harp on such a moulder'd string?
I am shamed thro' all my nature to have loved so slight a thing.

Weakness to be wroth with weakness! woman's pleasure, woman's pain—
Nature made them blinder motions bounded in a shallower brain:

Woman is the lesser man, and all thy passions, match'd with mine,
Are as moonlight unto sunlight, and as water unto wine—

Here at least, where nature sickens, nothing. Ah, for some retreat
Deep in yonder shining Orient, where my life began to beat;

Where in wild Mahratta-battle fell my father evil-starr'd;—
I was left a trampled orphan, and a selfish uncle's ward.

Or to burst all links of habit—there to wander far away,
On from island unto island at the gateways of the day.

Larger constellations burning, mellow moons and happy skies,
Breadths of tropic shade and palms in cluster, knots of Paradise.

Never comes the trader, never floats an European flag,
Slides the bird o'er lustrous woodland, swings the trailer from the crag;

Droops the heavy-blossom'd bower, hangs the heavy-fruited tree—
Summer isles of Eden lying in dark-purple spheres of sea.

There methinks would be enjoyment more than in this march of mind,
In the steamship, in the railway, in the thoughts that shake mankind.

There the passions cramp'd no longer shall have scope and breathing-space;
I will take some savage woman, she shall rear my dusky race.

Iron-jointed, supple-sinew'd, they shall dive, and they shall run,
Catch the wild goat by the hair, and hurl their lances in the sun;

Whistle back the parrot's call, and leap the rainbows of the brooks,
Not with blinded eyesight poring over miserable books—

Fool, again the dream, the fancy! but I *know* my words are wild,
But I count the gray barbarian lower than the Christian child.

I, to herd with narrow foreheads, vacant of our glorious gains,
Like a beast with lower pleasures, like a beast with lower pains!

Mated with a squalid savage—what to me were sun or clime?
I the heir of all the ages, in the foremost files of time—

I that rather held it better men should perish one by one,
Than that earth should stand at gaze like Joshua's moon in Ajalon!

Not in vain the distance beacons. Forward, forward let us range.
Let the great world spin forever down the ringing grooves of change.

Thro' the shadow of the globe we sweep into the younger day:
Better fifty years of Europe than a cycle of Cathay.

Mother-Age (for mine I knew not) help me as when life begun:
Rift the hills, and roll the waters, flash the lightnings, weigh the Sun—

O, I see the crescent promise of my spirit hath not set.
Ancient founts of inspiration well thro' all my fancy yet.

Howsoever these things be, a long farewell to Locksley Hall!
Now for me the woods may wither, now for me the roof-tree fall.

Comes a vapor from the margin, blackening over heath and holt,
Cramming all the blast before it, in its breast a thunderbolt.

Let it fall on Locksley Hall, with rain or hail, or fire or snow;
For the mighty wind arises, roaring seaward, and I go.

GODIVA.

I waited for the train at Coventry;
I hung with grooms and porters on the bridge,
To watch the three tall spires; and there I shaped
The city's ancient legend into this:

Not only we, the latest seed of Time,
New men, that in the flying of a wheel
Cry down the past, not only we, that prate
Of rights and wrongs, have loved the people we..
And loathed to see them overtax'd: but she
Did more, and underwent, and overcame,

"Then fled she to her inmost bower, and there
Unclasp'd the wedded eagles of her belt."

The woman of a thousand summers back,
Godiva, wife to that grim Earl, who ruled
In Coventry: for when he laid a tax
Upon his town, and all the mothers brought
Their children, clamoring, "If we pay, we starve!"
She sought her lord, and found him, where he strode
About the hall, among his dogs, alone,
His beard a foot before him, and his hair
A yard behind. She told him of their tears,
And pray'd him, "If they pay this tax, they starve."
Whereat he stared, replying, half-amazed,
"You would not let your little finger ache
For such as these?"—"But I would die," said she.
He laugh'd, and swore by Peter and by Paul:
Then fillip'd at the diamond in her ear;
"O ay, ay, ay, you talk!"—"Alas!" she said,
"But prove me what it is I would not do."
And from a heart as rough as Esau's hand,
He answer'd, "Ride you naked thro' the town,
And I repeal it;" and nodding, as in scorn,
He parted, with great strides among his dogs.

So left alone, the passions of her mind,
As winds from all the compass shift and blow,
Made war upon each other for an hour,
Till pity won. She sent a herald forth,
And bade him cry, with sound of trumpet, all
The hard condition; but that she would loose
The people: therefore, as they loved her well,
From then till noon no foot should pace the street,
No eye look down, she passing; but that all
Should keep within, door shut, and window barr'd.

Then fled she to her inmost bower, and there
Unclasp'd the wedded eagles of her belt,
The grim Earl's gift; but ever at a breath
She linger'd, looking like a summer moon
Half-dipt in cloud: anon she shook her head,
And shower'd the rippled ringlets to her knee;
Unclad herself in haste; adown the stair
Stole on; and, like a creeping sunbeam, slid
From pillar unto pillar, until she reach'd
The gateway; there she found her palfrey trapt
In purple blazon'd with armorial gold.

Then she rode forth, clothed on with chastity:
The deep air listen'd round her as she rode,
And all the low wind hardly breathed for fear.
The little wide-mouth'd heads upon the spout
Had cunning eyes to see: the barking cur
Made her cheek flame: her palfrey's footfall shot
Light horrors thro' her pulses: the blind walls
Were full of chinks and holes; and overhead
Fantastic gables, crowding, stared: but she
Not less thro' all bore up, till, last, she saw
The white-flower'd elder-thicket from the field
Gleam thro' the Gothic archways in the wall.

Then she rode back, clothed on with chastity:
And one low churl, compact of thankless earth,
The fatal byword of all years to come,
Boring a little auger-hole in fear,
Peep'd—but his eyes, before they had their will,
Were shrivell'd into darkness in his head,
And dropt before him. So the Powers, who wait
On noble deeds, cancell'd a sense misused;
And she, that knew not, pass'd: and all at once,
With twelve great shocks of sound, the shameless noon
Was clash'd and hammer'd from a hundred towers,
One after one: but even then she gain'd
Her bower; whence reissuing, robed and crown'd,
To meet her lord, she took the tax away,
And built herself an everlasting name.

———&c;———

THE TWO VOICES.

A STILL small voice spake unto me,
"Thou art so full of misery,
Were it not better not to be?"

Then to the still small voice I said:
"Let me not cast in endless shade
What is so wonderfully made."

To which the voice did urge reply:
"To-day I saw the dragon-fly
Come from the wells where he did lie.

"An inner impulse rent the veil
Of his old husk: from head to tail
Came out clear plates of sapphire mail.

"He dried his wings: like gauze they grew:
Thro' crofts and pastures wet with dew
A living flash of light he flew."

I said, "When first the world began,
Young Nature thro' five cycles ran,
And in the sixth she moulded man.

"She gave him mind, the lordliest
Proportion, and, above the rest,
Dominion in the head and breast."

Thereto the silent voice replied:
"Self-blinded are you by your pride,
Look up thro' night: the world is wide.

"This truth within thy mind rehearse,
That in a boundless universe
Is boundless better, boundless worse.

"Think you this mould of hopes and fears
Could find no statelier than his peers
In yonder hundred million spheres?"

It spake, moreover, in my mind:
"Tho' thou wert scatter'd to the wind,
Yet is there plenty of the kind."

Then did my response clearer fall:
"No compound of this earthly ball
Is like another, all in all."

To which he answer'd scoffingly:
"Good soul! suppose I grant it thee,
Who 'll weep for thy deficiency?

"Or will one beam be less intense,
When thy peculiar difference
Is cancell'd in the world of sense?"

I would have said, "Thou canst not know,"
But my full heart, that work'd below,
Rain'd thro' my sight its overflow.

Again the voice spake unto me:
"Thou art so steep'd in misery,
Surely, 't were better not to be.

"Thine anguish will not let thee sleep,
Nor any train of reason keep:
Thou canst not think but thou wilt weep."

I said, "The years with change advance:
If I make dark my countenance,
I shut my life from happier chance.

"Some turn this sickness yet might take.
Ev'n yet." But he: "What drug can make
A wither'd palsy cease to shake?"

I wept, "Tho' I should die, I know
That all about the thorn will blow
In tufts of rosy-tinted snow;

"And men, thro' novel spheres of thought
Still moving after truth long sought,
Will learn new things when I am not."

"Yet," said the secret voice, "some time
Sooner or later, will gray prime
Make thy grass hoar with early rime.

"Not less swift souls that yearn for light,
Rapt after heaven's starry flight,
Would sweep the tracts of day and night.

"Not less the bee would range her cells,
The furzy prickle fire the dells,
The foxglove cluster dappled bells."

I said that "all the years invent·
Each month is various to present
The world with some development.

"Were this not well, to bide mine hour,
Tho' watching from a ruin'd tower
How grows the day of human power?"

"The highest-mounted mind," he said,
"Still sees the sacred morning spread
The silent summit overhead.

"Will thirty seasons render plain
Those lonely lights that still remain,
Just breaking over land and main?

"Or make that morn, from his cold crown
And crystal silence creeping down,
Flood with full daylight glebe and town?

"Forerun thy peers, thy time, and let
Thy feet, millenniums hence, be set
In midst of knowledge, dream'd not yet.

"Thou hast not gained a real height,
Nor art thou nearer to the light,
Because the scale is infinite.

"'T were better not to breathe or speak,
Than cry for strength, remaining weak,
And seem to find, but still to seek.

"Moreover, but to seem to find
Asks what thou lackest, thought resign'd,
A healthy frame, a quiet mind."

I said, "When I am gone away,
'He dared not tarry,' men will say,
Doing dishonor to my clay."

"This is more vile," he made reply,
"To breathe and loathe, to live and sigh,
Than once from dread of pain to die.

"Sick art thou—a divided will
Still heaping on the fear of ill
The fear of men, a coward still.

"Do men love thee? Art thou so bound
To men, that how thy name may sound
Will vex thee lying underground?

"The memory of the wither'd leaf
In endless time is scarce more brief
Than of the garner'd Autumn-sheaf.

"Go, vexed Spirit, sleep in trust:
The right ear, that is fill'd with dust,
Hears little of the false or just."

"Hard task, to pluck resolve," I cried,
"From emptiness and the waste wide
Of that abyss, or scornful pride!

"Nay—rather yet that I could raise
One hope that warm'd me in the days
While still I yearn'd for human praise.

"When, wide in soul and bold of tongue,
Among the tents I paused and sung,
The distant battle flash'd and rung.

"I sung the joyful Pæan clear,
And, sitting, burnish'd without fear
The brand, the buckler, and the spear—

"Waiting to strive a happy strife,
To war with falsehood to the knife,
And not to lose the good of life—

"Some hidden principle to move,
To put together, part and prove,
And mete the bounds of hate and love—

"As far as might be, to carve out
Free space for every human doubt,
That the whole mind might orb about—

"To search thro' all I felt or saw,
The springs of life, the depths of awe,
And reach the law within the law:

"At least, not rotting like a weed,
But, having sown some generous seed,
Fruitful of further thought and deed,

"To pass, when Life her light withdraws,
Not void of righteous self-applause,
Nor in a merely selfish cause—

"In some good cause, not in mine own,
To perish, wept for, honor'd, known,
And like a warrior overthrown:

"Whose eyes are dim with glorious tears,
When, soil'd with noble dust, he hears
His country's war-song thrill his ears:

"Then dying of a mortal stroke,
What time the foeman's line is broke,
And all the war is roll'd in smoke."

"Yea!" said the voice, "thy dream was good,
While thou abodest in the bud.
It was the stirring of the blood.

"If Nature put not forth her power
About the opening of the flower,
Who is it that could live an hour?

"Then comes the check, the change, the fall.
Pain rises up, old pleasures pall.
There is one remedy for all.

"Yet hadst thou, thro' enduring pain,
Link'd month to month with such a chain
Of knitted purport, all were vain.

"Thou hadst not between death and birth
Dissolved the riddle of the earth.
So were thy labor little-worth.

"That men with knowledge merely play'd,
I told thee—hardly nigher made,
Tho' scaling slow from grade to grade;

"Much less this dreamer, deaf and blind,
Named man, may hope some truth to find,
That bears relation to the mind.

"For every worm beneath the moon
Draws different threads, and late and soon
Spins, toiling out his own cocoon.

"Cry, faint not: either Truth is born
Beyond the polar gleam forlorn,
Or in the gateways of the morn.

"Cry, faint not, climb: the summits slope
Beyond the furthest flights of hope,
Wrapt in dense cloud from base to cope.

"Sometimes a little corner shines,
As over rainy mist inclines
A gleaming crag with belts of pines.

"I will go forward, sayest thou,
I shall not fail to find her now.
Look up, the fold is on her brow.

"If straight thy tract, or if oblique,
Thou know'st not. Shadows thou dost strike,
Embracing cloud, Ixion-like;

"And owning but a little more
Than beasts, abidest lame and poor,
Calling thyself a little lower

"Than angels. Cease to wail and brawl!
Why inch by inch to darkness crawl?
There is one remedy for all."

"O dull, one-sided voice," said I,
"Wilt thou make everything a lie,
To flatter me that I may die?

"I know that age to age succeeds,
Blowing a noise of tongues and deeds,
A dust of systems and of creeds.

"I cannot hide that some have striven,
Achieving calm, to whom was given
The joy that mixes man with Heaven:

"Who, rowing hard against the stream,
Saw distant gates of Eden gleam,
And did not dream it was a dream;

"But heard, by secret transport led,
Ev'n in the charnels of the dead,
The murmur of the fountain-head—

"Which did accomplish their desire,
Bore and forbore, and did not tire,
Like Stephen, an unquenched fire.

"He heeded not reviling tones,
Nor sold his heart to idle moans,
Tho' curs'd and scorn'd, and bruised with stones:

"But looking upward, full of grace,
He pray'd, and from a happy place
God's glory smote him on the face."

The sullen answer slid betwixt:
"Not that the grounds of hope were fix'd,
The elements were kindlier mix'd."

I said, "I toil beneath the curse,
But, knowing not the universe,
I fear to slide from bad to worse.

"And that, in seeking to undo
One riddle, and to find the true,
I knit a hundred others new:

"Or that this anguish fleeting hence,
Unmanacled from bonds of sense,
Be fix'd and froz'n to permanence:

"For I go, weak from suffering here;
Naked I go, and void of cheer:
What is it that I may not fear?"

"Consider well," the voice replied,
"His face, that two hours since hath died;
Wilt thou find passion, pain, or pride?

"Will he obey when one commands?
Or answer should one press his hands?
He answers not, nor understands.

"His palms are folded on his breast:
There is no other thing express'd
But long disquiet merged in rest.

"His lips are very mild and meek:
Tho' one should smite him on the cheek,
And on the mouth, he will not speak.

"His little daughter, whose sweet face
He kiss'd, taking his last embrace,
Becomes dishonor to her race—

"His sons grow up that bear his name,
Some grow to honor, some to shame,—
But he is chill to praise or blame.

"He will not hear the north-wind rave,
Nor, moaning, household shelter crave
From winter rains that beat his grave.

"High up the vapors fold and swim:
About him broods the twilight dim:
The place he knew forgetteth him."

"If all be dark, vague voice," I said,
"These things are wrapt in doubt and dread,
Nor canst thou show the dead are dead.

"The sap dries up: the plant declines.
A deeper tale my heart divines.
Know I not Death? the outward signs?

"I found him when my years were few;
A shadow on the graves I knew,
And darkness in the village yew.

"From grave to grave the shadow crept:
In her still place the morning wept:
Touch'd by his feet the daisy slept.

"The simple senses crown'd his head:
'Omega! thou art Lord,' they said,
'We find no motion in the dead.'

"Why, if man rot in dreamless ease,
Should that plain fact, as taught by these,
Not make him sure that he shall cease?

"Who forged that other influence,
That heat of inward evidence,
By which he doubts against the sense?

"He owns the fatal gift of eyes,
That read his spirit blindly wise,
Not simple as a thing that dies.

"Here sits he shaping wings to fly:
His heart forebodes a mystery:
He names the name Eternity.

"That type of Perfect in his mind
In Nature can he nowhere find.
He sows himself on every wind.

"He seems to hear a Heavenly Friend,
And thro' thick veils to apprehend
A labor working to an end.

"The end and the beginning vex
His reason: many things perplex,
With motions, checks, and counter-checks.

"He knows a baseness in his blood
At such strange war with something good,
He may not do the thing he would.

"Heaven opens inward, chasms yawn,
Vast images in glimmering dawn,
Half-shown, are broken and withdrawn.

"Ah! sure within him and without,
Could his dark wisdom find it out,
There must be answer to his doubt.

"But thou canst answer not again.
With thine own weapon art thou slain,
Or thou wilt answer but in vain.

"The doubt would rest, I dare not solve.
In the same circle we revolve.
Assurance only breeds resolve."

As when a billow, blown against,
Falls back, the voice with which I fenced
A little ceased, but recommenced:

"Where wert thou when thy father play'd
In his free field, and pastime made,
A merry boy in sun and shade?

"A merry boy they called him then.
He sat upon the knees of men
In days that never come again.

"Before the little ducts began
To feed thy bones with lime, and ran
Their course, till thou wert also man:

"Who took a wife, who rear'd his race,
Whose wrinkles gather'd on his face,
Whose troubles number with his days:

"A life of nothings, nothing-worth.
From that first nothing ere his birth
To that last nothing under earth!"

"These words," I said, "are like the rest,
No certain clearness, but at best
A vague suspicion of the breast:

"But if I grant, thou might'st defend
The thesis which thy words intend—
That to begin implies to end;

"Yet how should I for certain hold,
Because my memory is so cold,
That I first was in human mould?

"I cannot make this matter plain,
But I would shoot, howe'er in vain,
A random arrow from the brain.

"It may be that no life is found,
Which only to one engine bound
Falls off, but cycles always round.

"As old mythologies relate,
Some draught of Lethe might await
The slipping thro' from state to state.

"As here we find in trances, men
Forget the dream that happens then,
Until they fall in trance again.

"So might we, if our state were such
As one before, remember much,
For those two likes might meet and touch.

"But, if I lapsed from nobler place,
Some legend of a fallen race
Alone might hint of my disgrace;

"Some vague emotion of delight
In gazing up an Alpine height,
Some yearning toward the lamps of night.

"Or if thro' lower lives I came—
Tho' all experience past became
Consolidate in mind and frame—

"I might forget my weaker lot;
For is not our first year forgot?
The haunts of memory echo not.

"And men, whose reason long was blind,
From cells of madness unconfined,
Oft lose whole years of darker mind.

"Much more, if first I floated free,
As naked essence, must I be
Incompetent of memory:

"For memory dealing but with time,
And he with matter, could she climb
Beyond her own material prime?

"Moreover, something is or seems,
That touches me with mystic gleams,
Like glimpses of forgotten dreams—

"Of something felt, like something here.
Of something done, I know not where;
Such as no language may declare.'

The still voice laugh'd. "I talk," said he,
"Not with thy dreams. Suffice it thee
Thy pain is a reality."

"But thou," said I, "hast miss'd thy mark,
Who sought'st to wreck my mortal ark,
By making all the horizon dark.

"Why not set forth, if I should do
This rashness, that which might ensue
With this old soul in organs new?

"Whatever crazy sorrow saith,
No life that breathes with human breath
Has ever truly long'd for death.

"'T is life, whereof our nerves are scant,
O life, not death, for which we pant;
More life, and fuller, that I want."

I ceased, and sat as one forlorn.
Then said the voice, in quiet scorn:
"Behold, it is the Sabbath morn."

And I arose, and I released
The casement, and the light increased
With freshness in the dawning east.

Like soften'd airs that blowing steal,
When meres begin to uncongeal,
The sweet church bells began to peal.

On to God's house the people prest:
Passing the place where each must rest,
Each enter'd like a welcome guest.

One walk'd between his wife and child,
With measur'd footfall firm and mild,
And now and then he gravely smiled.

The prudent partner of his blood
Lean'd on him, faithful, gentle, good,
Wearing the rose of womanhood.

And in their double love secure,
The little maiden walk'd demure,
Pacing with downward eyelids pure.

These three made unity so sweet,
My frozen heart began to beat,
Remembering its ancient heat.

I blest them, and they wander'd on:
I spoke, but answer came there none:
The dull and bitter voice was gone.

A second voice was at mine ear,
A little whisper silver-clear,
A murmur, "Be of better cheer."

As from some blissful neighborhood,
A notice faintly understood,
"I see the end, and know the good."

A little hint to solace woe,
A hint, a whisper breathing low,
"I may not speak of what I know."

Like an Æolian harp that wakes
No certain air, but overtakes
Far thought with music that it makes.

Such seem'd the whisper at my side:
"What is it thou knowest, sweet voice?" I cried.
"A hidden hope," the voice replied:

So heavenly-toned, that in that hour
From out my sullen heart a power
Broke, like the rainbow from the shower,

To feel, altho' no tongue can prove,
That every cloud, that spreads above
And veileth love, itself is love.

And forth into the fields I went,
And Nature's living motion lent
The pulse of hope to discontent.

I wonder'd at the bounteous hours,
The slow result of winter-showers:
You scarce could see the grass for flowers.

I wonder'd, while I paced along:
The woods were fill'd so full with song,
There seem'd no room for sense of wrong.

So variously seem'd all things wrought,
I marvell'd how the mind was brought
To anchor by one gloomy thought;

And wherefore rather I made choice
To commune with that barren voice.
Than him that said, "Rejoice! rejoice!"

———❖———

THE DAY-DREAM.

PROLOGUE.

O Lady Flora, let me speak:
A pleasant hour has past away
While, dreaming on your damask cheek,
The dewy sister-eyelids lay.
As by the lattice you reclined,
I went thro' many wayward moods
To see you dreaming—and, behind,
A summer crisp with shining woods.
And I too dream'd, until at last
Across my fancy, brooding warm,
The reflex of a legend past,
And loosely settled into form.
And would you have the thought I had,
And see the vision that I saw,
Then take the broidery-frame, and add
A crimson to the quaint Macaw,
And I will tell it. Turn your face,
Nor look with that too-earnest eye—
The rhymes are dazzled from their place,
And order'd words asunder fly.

THE SLEEPING PALACE.

1.

The varying year with blade and sheaf
Clothes and reclothes the happy plains:
Here rests the sap within the leaf,
Here stays the blood along the veins.
Faint shadows, vapors lightly curl'd,
Faint murmurs from the meadows come,
Like hints and echoes of the world
To spirits folded in the womb.

2.

Soft lustre bathes the range of urns
On every slanting terrace-lawn.
The fountain to his place returns,
Deep in the garden lake withdrawn.
Here droops the banner on the tower,
On the hall-hearths the festal fires,
The peacock in his laurel bower,
The parrot in his gilded wires.

3.

Roof-haunting martins warm their eggs:
In these, in those the life is stay'd,
The mantles from the golden pegs
Droop sleepily: no sound is made,
Not even of a gnat that sings.
More like a picture seemeth all
Than those old portraits of old kings,
That watch the sleepers from the wall.

4.

Here sits the butler with a flask
Between his knees half-drained; and there,
The wrinkled steward at his task,
The maid-of-honor blooming fair:
The page has caught her hand in his:
Her lips are sever'd as to speak:
His own are pouted to a kiss:
The blush is fix'd upon her cheek.

5.

Till all the hundred summers pass,
The beams, that through the oriel shine,
Make prisms in every carven glass,
And beaker brimm'd with noble wine.
Each baron at the banquet sleeps,
Grave faces gather'd in a ring.
His state the king reposing keeps.
He must have been a jovial king.

6.

All round a hedge upshoots, and shows
At distance like a little wood;
Thorns, ivies, woodbine, mistletoes,
And grapes with bunches red as blood;
All creeping plants, a wall of green
Close-matted, bur and brake and brier,
And glimpsing over these, just seen,
High up the topmost palace-spire.

7.

When will the hundred summers die,
And thought and time be born again,
And newer knowledge, drawing nigh,
Bring truth that sways the soul of men?
Here all things in their place remain,
As all were order'd, ages since.
Come, Care and Pleasure, Hope and Pain,
And bring the fated fairy Prince.

THE SLEEPING BEAUTY.

1.

Year after year unto her feet,
She lying on her conch alone,
Across the purpled coverlet,
The maiden's jet-black hair has grown,
On either side her tranced form
Forth streaming from a braid of pearl
The slumbrous light is rich and warm,
And moves not on the rounded curl.

2.

The silk star-broider'd coverlid
Unto her limbs itself doth mould
Languidly ever; and, amid
Her full black ringlets downward roll'd,

Glows forth each softly-shadowed arm
  With bracelets of the diamond bright:
Her constant beauty doth inform
  Stillness with love, and day with light.

3.

She sleeps: her breathings are not heard
  In palace chambers far apart.
The fragrant tresses are not stirr'd
  That lie upon her charmed heart.
She sleeps: on either hand upswells
  The gold-fringed pillow lightly prest:
She sleeps, nor dreams, but ever dwells
  A perfect form in perfect rest.

THE ARRIVAL.

1.

All precious things, discover'd late,
  To those that seek them issue forth:
For love in sequel works with fate,
  And draws the veil from hidden worth.
He travels far from other skies—
  His mantle glitters on the rocks—
A fairy Prince, with joyful eyes,
  And lighter-footed than the fox.

2.

The bodies and the bones of those
  That strove in other days to pass,
Are wither'd in the thorny close,
  Or scattered blanching on the grass.
He gazes on the silent dead,
  "They perish'd in their daring deeds."
This proverb flashes thro' his head,
  "The many fail: the one succeeds."

3.

He comes, scarce knowing what he seeks:
  He breaks the hedge: he enters there:
The color flies into his cheeks:
  He trusts to light on something fair;
For all his life the charm did talk
  About his path, and hover near
With words of promise in his walk,
  And whisper'd voices at his ear.

4.

More close and close his footsteps wind;
  The Magic Music in his heart
Beats quick and quicker, till he find
  The quiet chamber far apart.
His spirit flutters like a lark,
  He stoops—to kiss her—on his knee.
"Love, if thy tresses be so dark,
  How dark those hidden eyes must be!"

THE REVIVAL.

1.

A touch, a kiss! the charm was snapt.
  There rose a noise of striking clocks,
And feet that ran, and doors that clapt,
  And barking dogs, and crowing cocks;
A fuller light illumined all,
  A breeze thro' all the garden swept,
A sudden hubbub shook the hall,
  And sixty feet the fountain leapt.

2.

The hedge broke in, the banner blew,
  The butler drank, the steward scrawl'd,
The fire shot up, the martin flew,
  The parrot scream'd, the peacock squall'd,
The maid and page renew'd their strife,
  The palace bang'd, and buzz'd, and clackt,
And all the long-pent stream of life
  Dash'd downward in a cataract.

3.

And last with these the king awoke,
  And in his chair himself uprear'd,
And yawn'd, and rubb'd his face, and spoke,
  "By holy rood, a royal beard!
How say you? we have slept, my lords.
  My beard has grown into my lap."
The barons swore, with many words,
  'T was but an after-dinner's nap.

4.

"Pardy," return'd the king, "but still
  My joints are something stiff or so.
My lord. and shall we pass the bill
  I mention'd half an hour ago?"
The chancellor, sedate and vain,
  In courteous words return'd reply,
But dallied with his golden chain,
  And, smiling, put the question by.

THE DEPARTURE.

1.

And on her lover's arm she leant,
  And round her waist she felt it fold,
And far across the hills they went
  In that new world which is the old.
Across the hills, and far away
  Beyond their utmost purple rim,
And deep into the dying day
  The happy princess follow'd him.

2.

"I'd sleep another hundred years,
  O love, for such another kiss;"
"O wake forever, love," she hears,
  "O love, 't was such as this and this."
And o'er them many a sliding star,
  And many a merry wind was borne,
And, stream'd thro' many a golden bar,
  The twilight melted into morn.

3.

"O eyes long laid in happy sleep!"
  "O happy sleep, that lightly fled!"
"O happy kiss, that woke thy sleep!"
  "O love, thy kiss would wake the dead!"
And o'er them many a flowing range
  Of vapor buoy'd the crescent-bark,
And, rapt thro' many a rosy change,
  The twilight died into the dark.

4.

"A hundred summers! can it be?
  And whither goest thou, tell me where?"
"O seek my father's court with me,
  For there are greater wonders there."
And o'er the hills, and far away
  Beyond their utmost purple rim,
Beyond the night, across the day,
  Thro' all the world she follow'd him.

MORAL.

1.

So, Lady Flora, take my lay,
  And if you find no moral there,
Go, look in any glass and say,
  What moral is in being fair.
O, to what uses shall we put
  The wildweed flower that simply blows?
And is there any moral shut
  Within the bosom of the rose?

2.

But any man that walks the mead,
  In bud or blade, or bloom, may find,
According as his humors lead,
  A meaning suited to his mind

And liberal applications lie
  In Art like Nature, dearest friend;
So 't were to cramp its use, if I
  Should hook it to some useful end.

L'ENVOI.

1.

You shake your head. A random string
  Your finer female sense offends.
Well—were it not a pleasant thing
  To fall asleep with all one's friends;
To pass with all our social ties
  'To silence from the paths of men;
And every hundred years to rise
  And learn the world, and sleep again;
To sleep thro' terms of mighty wars,
  And wake on science grown to more,
On secrets of the brain, the stars,
  As wild as aught of fairy lore;
And all that else the years will show,
  The Poet-forms of stronger hours,
The vast Republics that may grow,
  The Federations and the Powers;
Titanic forces taking birth
  In divers seasons, divers climes;
For we are Ancients of the earth,
  And in the morning of the times.

2.

So sleeping, so aroused from sleep
Thro' sunny decades new and strange,
Or gay quinquenniads would we reap
  The flower and quintessence of change.

3.

Ah, yet would I—and would I might!
  So much your eyes my fancy take—
Be still the first to leap to light
  That I might kiss those eyes awake!
For, am I right or am I wrong,
  To choose your own you did not care;
You'd have *my* moral from the song,
  And I will take my pleasure there:
And, am I right or am I wrong,
  My fancy, ranging thro' and thro',
To search a meaning for the song,
  Perforce will still revert to you;
Nor finds a closer truth than this
  All-graceful head, so richly curl'd,
And evermore a costly kiss
  The prelude to some brighter world.

4.

For since the time when Adam first
  Embraced his Eve in happy hour,
And every bird of Eden burst
  In carol, every bud to flower,
What eyes, like thine, have waken'd hopes?
  What lips, like thine, so sweetly join'd?
Where on the double rosebud droops
  The fulness of the pensive mind;
Which all too dearly self-involved.
  Yet sleeps a dreamless sleep to me;
A sleep by kisses undissolved,
  That lets thee neither hear nor see:
But break it. In the name of wife,
  And in the rights that name may give,
Are clasp'd the moral of thy life,
  And that for which I care to live.

EPILOGUE.

So, Lady Flora, take my lay,
  And, if you find a meaning there,
O whisper to your glass, and say,
  "What wonder, if he thinks me fair?"
What wonder I was all unwise,
  To shape the song for your delight,

Like long-tail'd birds of Paradise,
  That float thro' Heaven, and cannot light?
Or old-world trains, upheld at court
  By Cupid-boys of blooming hue—
But take it—earnest wed with sport,
  And either sacred unto you.

AMPHION.

My father left a park to me,
  But it is wild and barren,
A garden too with scarce a tree
  And waster than a warren:
Yet say the neighbors when they call,
  It is not bad but good land,
And in it is the germ of all
  That grows within the woodland.

O had I lived when song was great,
  In days of old Amphion,
And ta'en my fiddle to the gate,
  Nor cared for seed or scion!
And had I lived when song was great,
  And legs of trees were limber,
And ta'en my fiddle to the gate,
  And fiddled in the timber!

'T is said he had a tuneful tongue,
  Such happy intonation,
Wherever he sat down and sung
  He left a small plantation;
Wherever in a lonely grove
  He set up his forlorn pipes,
The gouty oak began to move,
  And flounder into hornpipes.

The mountain stirr'd its bushy crown,
  And, as tradition teaches,
Young ashes pirouetted down
  Coquetting with young beeches:
And briony-vine and ivy-wreath
  Ran forward to his rhyming,
And from the valleys underneath
  Came little copses climbing.

The birch-tree swang her fragrant hair,
  The bramble cast her berry,
The gin within the juniper
  Began to make him merry,
The poplars, in long order due,
  With cypress promenaded,
The shock-head willows two and two
  By rivers gallopaded.

Came wet-shot alder from the wave,
  Came yews, a dismal coterie,
Each pluck'd his one foot from the grave,
  Poussetting with a sloe-tree:
Old elms came breaking from the vine,
  The vine stream'd out to follow,
And, sweating rosin, plump'd the pine
  From many a cloudy hollow.

And was n't it a sight to see,
  When, ere his song was ended,
Like some great landslip, tree by tree,
  The country-side descended;
And shepherds from the mountain-eaves
  Look'd down, half-pleased, half-frighten'd
As dash'd about the drunken leaves
  The random sunshine lighten'd!

O, nature first was fresh to men,
  And wanton without measure;
So youthful and so flexile then,
  You moved her at your pleasure.

Twang out, my fiddle! shake the twigs!
  And make her dance attendance;
Blow, flute, and stir the stiff-set sprigs,
  And scirrhous roots and tendons.

'T is vain! in such a brassy age
  I could not move a thistle;
The very sparrows in the hedge
  Scarce answer to my whistle;
Or at the most, when three-parts-sick
  With strumming and with scraping,
A jackass heehaws from the rick,
  The passive oxen gaping.

But what is that I hear? a sound
  Like sleepy counsel pleading:
O Lord!—'t is in my neighbor's ground,
  The modern Muses reading.
They read Botanic Treatises,
  And Works on Gardening through there,
And Methods of transplanting trees,
  To look as if they grew there.

The wither'd Misses! how they prose
  O'er books of travell'd seamen,
And show you slips of all that grows
  From England to Van Diemen.
They read in arbors clipt and cut,
  And alleys, faded places,
By squares of tropic summer shut
  And warm'd in crystal cases.

But these, tho' fed with careful dirt,
  Are neither green nor sappy;
Half-conscious of the garden-squirt,
  The spindlings look unhappy.
Better to me the meanest weed
  That blows upon its mountain,
The vilest herb that runs to seed
  Beside its native fountain.

And I must work thro' months of toil,
  And years of cultivation,
Upon my proper patch of soil
  To grow my own plantation.
I'll take the showers as they fall,
  I will not vex my bosom:
Enough if at the end of all
  A little garden blossom.

———◇———

WILL WATERPROOF'S LYRICAL MON-OLOGUE.

MADE AT THE COCK.

O PLUMP head-waiter at The Cock,
  To which I most resort,
How goes the time? 'T is five o'clock.
  Go fetch a pint of port:
But let it not be such as that
  You set before chance-comers,
But such whose father-grape grew fat
  On Lusitanian summers.

No vain libation to the Muse,
  But may she still be kind,
And whisper lovely words, and use
  Her influence on the mind,
To make me write my random rhymes,
  Ere they be half-forgotten;
Nor add and alter, many times,
  Till all be ripe and rotten.

I pledge her, and she comes and dips
  Her laurel in the wine,
And lays it thrice upon my lips,
  These favor'd lips of mine;

Until the charm have power to make
  New lifeblood warm the bosom,
And barren commonplaces break
  In full and kindly blossom.

I pledge her silent at the board;
  Her gradual fingers steal
And touch upon the master-chord
  Of all I felt and feel.
Old wishes, ghosts of broken plans,
  And phantom hopes assemble;
And that child's heart within the man's
  Begins to move and tremble.

Thro' many an hour of summer suns
  By many pleasant ways,
Against its fountain upward runs
  The current of my days.
I kiss the lips I once have kiss'd;
  The gas-light wavers dimmer;
And softly, thro' a vinous mist,
  My college friendships glimmer.

I grow in worth, and wit, and sense,
  Unboding critic-pen,
Or that eternal want of pence,
  Which vexes public men,
Who hold their hands to all, and cry
  For that which all deny them,—
Who sweep the crossings, wet or dry,
  And all the world go by them.

Ah yet, tho' all the world forsake,
  Tho' fortune clip my wings,
I will not cramp my heart, nor take
  Half-views of men and things.
Let Whig and Tory stir their blood;
  There must be stormy weather:
But for some true result of good
  All parties work together.

Let there be thistles, there are grapes·
  If old things, there are new;
Ten thousand broken lights and shapes,
  Yet glimpses of the true.
Let raffs be rife in prose and rhyme,
  We lack not rhymes and reasons,
As on this whirligig of Time
  We circle with the seasons.

This earth is rich in man and maid;
  With fair horizons bound!
This whole wide earth of light and shade
  Comes out, a perfect round.
High over roaring Temple-bar,
  And, set in Heaven's third story,
I look at all things as they are,
  But thro' a kind of glory.

Head-waiter, honor'd by the guest
  Half-mused, or reeling-ripe,
The pint, you brought me, was the best
  That ever came from pipe.
But tho' the port surpasses praise,
  My nerves have dealt with stiffer.
Is there some magic in the place?
  Or do my peptics differ?

For since I came to live and learn,
  No pint of white or red
Had ever half the power to turn
  This wheel within my head,
Which bears a season'd brain about,
  Unsubject to confusion,
Tho' soak'd and saturate, out and out,
  Thro' every convolution.

For I am of a numerous house,
  With many kinsmen gay,

Where long and largely we carouse,
  As who shall say me nay:
Each month, a birthday coming on,
  We drink defying trouble,
Or sometimes two would meet in one,
  And then we drank it double,

Whether the vintage, yet unkept,
  Had relish fiery-new,
Or, elbow-deep in sawdust, slept,
  As old as Waterloo:
Or stow'd (when classic Canning died)
  In musty bins and chambers,
Had cast upon its crusty side
  The gloom of ten Decembers.

The Muse, the jolly Muse, it is!
  She answer'd to my call,
She changes with that mood or this,
  Is all-in-all to all:
She lit the spark within my throat,
  To make my blood run quicker,
Used all her fiery will, and smote
  Her life into the liquor.

And hence this halo lives about
  The waiter's hands, that reach
To each his perfect pint of stout,
  His proper chop to each.
He looks not like the common breed
  That with the napkin dally;
I think he came like Ganymede,
  From some delightful valley.

The Cock was of a larger egg
  Than modern poultry drop,
Stept forward on a firmer leg,
  And cramm'd a plumper crop;
Upon an ampler dunghill trod,
  Crow'd lustier late and early,
Sipt wine from silver, praising God,
  And raked in golden barley.

A private life was all his joy,
  Till in a court he saw
A something-pottle-bodied boy
  That knuckled at the taw:
He stoop'd and clutch'd him, fair and good,
  Flew over roof and casement:
His brothers of the weather stood
  Stock-still for sheer amazement.

But he, by farmstead, thorpe, and spire,
  And follow'd with acclaims,
A sign to many a staring shire,
  Came crowing over Thames.
Right down by smoky Paul's they bore,
  Till, where the street grows straiter,
One fix'd forever at the door,
  And one became head-waiter.

But whither would my fancy go?
  How out of place she makes
The violet of a legend blow
  Among the chops and steaks!
'Tis but a steward of the can,
  One shade more plump than common;
As just and mere a serving-man
  As any, born of woman.

I ranged too high: what draws me down
  Into the common day?
Is it the weight of that half-crown,
  Which I shall have to pay?
For, something duller than at first,
  Nor wholly comfortable,
I sit (my empty glass reversed),
  And thrumming on the table:

Half fearful that, with self at strife,
  I take myself to task;
Lest of the fulness of my life
  I leave an empty flask:
For I had hope, by something rare,
  To prove myself a poet;
But, while I plan and plan, my hair
  Is gray before I know it.

So fares it since the years began,
  Till they be gather'd up;
The truth, that flies the flowing can,
  Will haunt the vacant cup:
And others' follies teach us not,
  Nor much their wisdom teaches;
And most, of sterling worth, is what
  Our own experience preaches.

Ah, let the rusty theme alone!
  We know not what we know.
But for my pleasant hour, 'tis gone,
  'Tis gone, and let it go.
'Tis gone: a thousand such have slipt
  Away from my embraces,
And fall'n into the dusty crypt
  Of darken'd forms and faces.

Go, therefore, thou! thy betters went
  Long since, and came no more:
With peals of genial clamor sent
  From many a tavern-door,
With twisted quirks and happy hits,
  From misty men of letters;
The tavern-hours of mighty wits,—
  Thine elders and thy betters.

Hours, when the Poet's words and looks
  Had yet their native glow,
Not yet the fear of little books
  Had made him talk for show;
But, all his vast heart sherris-warm'd
  He flash'd his random speeches;
Ere days, that deal in ana, swarm'd
  His literary leeches.

So mix forever with the past,
  Like all good things on earth!
For should I prize thee, could'st thou last,
  At half thy real worth?
I hold it good, good things should pass.
  With time I will not quarrel:
It is but yonder empty glass
  That makes me maudlin-moral.

Head-waiter of the chop-house here,
  To which I most resort,
I too must part: I hold thee dear
  For this good pint of port.
For this, thou shalt from all things suck
  Marrow of mirth and laughter;
And, wheresoe'er thou move, good luck
  Shall fling her old shoe after.

But thou wilt never move from hence,
  The sphere thy fate allots:
Thy latter days increased with pence
  Go down among the pots:
Thou batten est by the greasy gleam
  In haunts of hungry sinners,
Old boxes, larded with the steam
  Of thirty thousand dinners.

We fret, we fume, would shift our skins,
  Would quarrel with our lot;
Thy care is, under polish'd tins,
  To serve the hot-and-hot;
To come and go, and come again,
  Returning like the pewit,
And watch'd by silent gentlemen,
  That trifle with the cruet.

Live long, ere from thy topmost head
  The thick-set hazel dies;
Long, ere the hateful crow shall tread
  The corners of thine eyes:
Live long, nor feel in head or chest
  Our changeful equinoxes,
Till mellow Death, like some late guest,
  Shall call thee from the boxes.

But when he calls, and thou shalt cease
  To pace the gritted floor,
And, laying down an unctuous lease
  Of life, shalt earn no more:
No carved cross-bones, the types of Death,
  Shall show thee past to Heaven:
But carved cross-pipes, and, underneath,
  A pint-pot, neatly graven.

———<>———

TO ———.

AFTER READING A LIFE AND LETTERS.

"Cursed be he that moves my bones."
                    Shakespeare's Epitaph.

You might have won the Poet's name,
  If such be worth the winning now,
  And gain'd a laurel for your brow
Of sounder leaf than I can claim;

But you have made the wiser choice,
  A life that moves to gracious ends
  Thro' troops of unrecording friends,
A deedful life, a silent voice:

And you have miss'd the irreverent doom
  Of those that wear the Poet's crown:
  Hereafter, neither knave nor clown
Shall hold their orgies at your tomb.

For now the Poet cannot die
  Nor leave his music as of old,
  But round him ere he scarce be cold
Begins the scandal and the cry:

"Proclaim the faults he would not show:
  Break lock and seal: betray the trust:
  Keep nothing sacred: 't is but just
The many-headed beast should know."

Ah shameless! for he did but sing
  A song that pleased us from its worth;
  No public life was his on earth,
No blazon'd statesman he, nor king.

He gave the people of his best:
  His worst he kept, his best he gave.
  My Shakespeare's curse on clown and knave
Who will not let his ashes rest!

Who make it seem more sweet to be
  The little life of bank and brier,
  The bird that pipes his lone desire
And dies unheard within his tree,

Than he that warbles long and loud
  And drops at Glory's temple-gates,
  For whom the carrion vulture waits
To tear his heart before the crowd!

———<>———

LADY CLARE.

It was the time when lilies blow,
  And clouds are highest up in air,
Lord Ronald brought a lily-white doe
  To give his cousin, Lady Clare.

I trow they did not part in scorn:
  Lovers long-betroth'd were they:

They two will wed the morrow morn:
  God's blessing on the day!

"He does not love me for my birth,
  Nor for my lands so broad and fair:
He loves me for my own true worth,
  And that is well," said Lady Clare.

In there came old Alice the nurse,
  Said, "Who was this that went from thee?"
"It was my cousin," said Lady Clare
  "To-morrow he weds with me."

"O God be thank'd!" said Alice the nurse,
  "That all comes round so just and fair:
Lord Ronald is heir of all your lands,
  And you are not the Lady Clare."

"Are ye out of your mind, my nurse, my nurse?"
  Said Lady Clare, "that ye speak so wild?"
"As God 's above," said Alice the nurse,
  "I speak the truth: you are my child.

"The old Earl's daughter died at my breast;
  I speak the truth, as I live by bread!
I buried her like my own sweet child,
  And put my child in her stead."

"Falsely, falsely have ye done,
  O mother," she said, "if this be true,
To keep the best man under the sun
  So many years from his due."

"Nay now, my child," said Alice the nurse,
  "But keep the secret for your life,
And all you have will be Lord Ronald's,
  When you are man and wife."

"If I'm a beggar born," she said,
  "I will speak out, for I dare not lie.
Pull off, pull off, the broach of gold,
  And fling the diamond necklace by."

"Nay now, my child," said Alice the nurse.
  "But keep the secret all ye can."
She said "Not so: but I will know
  If there be any faith in man."

"Nay now, what faith?" said Alice the nurse,
  "The man will cleave unto his right."
"And he shall have it," the lady replied,
  "Tho' I should die to-night."

"Yet give one kiss to your mother dear!
  Alas, my child, I sinn'd for thee."
"O mother, mother, mother," she said,
  "So strange it seems to me.

"Yet here's a kiss for my mother dear,
  My mother dear, if this be so,
And lay your hand upon my head,
  And bless me, mother, ere I go."

She clad herself in a russet gown,
  She was no longer Lady Clare:
She went by dale, and she went by down
  With a single rose in her hair.

The lily-white doe Lord Ronald had brought
  Leapt up from where she lay,
Dropt her head in the maiden's hand,
  And followed her all the way.

Down stept Lord Ronald from his tower:
  "O Lady Clare, you shame your worth!
Why come you drest like a village maid,
  That are the flower of the earth?"

"If I come drest like a village maid,
  I am but as my fortunes are:
I am a beggar born," she said,
  "And not the Lady Clare."

"Play me no tricks," said Lord Ronald,
 "For I am yours in word and in deed,
Play me no tricks," said Lord Ronald,
 "Your riddle is hard to read."

O and proudly stood she up!
 Her heart within her did not fail:
She look'd into Lord Ronald's eyes,
 And told him all her nurse's tale.

He laugh'd a laugh of merry scorn:
 He turn'd, and kiss'd her where she stood:
"If you are not the heiress born,
 And I," said he, " the next in blood—

"If you are not the heiress born,
 And I," said he, "the lawful heir,
We two will wed to-morrow morn,
 And you shall still be Lady Clare."

※

ST. AGNES.

DEEP on the convent-roof the snows
 Are sparkling to the moon:
My breath to heaven like vapor goes:
 May my soul follow soon!
The shadows of the convent-towers
 Slant down the snowy sward,
Still creeping with the creeping hours
 That lead me to my Lord:

Make Thou my spirit pure and clear
 As are the frosty skies,
Or this first snowdrop of the year
 That in my bosom lies.

As these white robes are soiled and dark,
 To yonder shining ground;
As this pale taper's earthly spark,
 To yonder argent round;
So shows my soul before the Lamb,
 My spirit before Thee;
So in mine earthly house I am,
 To that I hope to be.
Break up the heavens, O Lord! and far,
 Thro' all yon starlight keen,
Draw me, thy bride, a glittering star,
 In raiment white and clean.

He lifts me to the golden doors;
 The flashes come and go;
All heaven bursts her starry floors,
 And strews her lights below,
And deepens on and up! the gates
 Roll back, and far within
For me the Heavenly Bridegroom waits,
 To make me pure of sin.
The sabbaths of Eternity,
 One sabbath deep and wide—
A light upon the shining sea—
 The Bridegroom with his bride!

"Deep on the convent-roof the snows
Are sparkling to the moon,"

" The stalls are void, the doors are wide,
The tapers burning fair."

SIR GALAHAD.

My good blade carves the casques of men,
  My tough lance thrusteth sure,
My strength is as the strength of ten,
  Because my heart is pure.
The shattering trumpet shrilleth high,
  The hard brands shiver on the steel,
The splinter'd spear-shafts crack and fly,
  The horse and rider reel:
They reel, they roll in clanging lists,
  And when the tide of combat stands,
Perfume and flowers fall in showers,
  That lightly rain from ladies' hands.

How sweet are looks that ladies bend
  On whom their favors fall!
For them I battle to the end,
  To save from shame and thrall:
But all my heart is drawn above,
  My knees are bow'd in crypt and shrine:
I never felt the kiss of love,
  Nor maiden's hand in mine.
More bounteous aspects on me beam,
  Me mightier transports move and thrill;
So keep I fair thro' faith and prayer
  A virgin heart in work and will.

When down the stormy crescent goes,
  A light before me swims,
Between dark stems the forest glows,
  I hear a noise of hymns:
Then by some secret shrine I ride;
  I hear a voice, but none are there:
The stalls are void, the doors are wide,
  The tapers burning fair.
Fair gleams the snowy altar-cloth,
  The silver vessels sparkle clean,

The shrill bell rings, the censer swings,
  And solemn chants resound between.

Sometimes on lonely mountain-meres
  I find a magic bark;
I leap on board: no helmsman steers:
  I float till all is dark.
A gentle sound, an awful light!
  Three angels bear the holy Grail:
With folded feet, in stoles of white,
  On sleeping wings they sail.
Ah, blessed vision! blood of God!
  My spirit beats her mortal bars,
As down dark tides the glory slides,
  And star-like mingles with the stars.

When on my goodly charger borne
  Thro' dreaming towns I go,
The cock crows ere the Christmas morn,
  The streets are dumb with snow.
The tempest crackles on the leads,
  And, ringing, spins from brand and mail;
But o'er the dark a glory spreads,
  And gilds the driving hail.
I leave the plain, I climb the height;
  No branchy thicket shelter yields:
But blessed forms in whistling storms
  Fly o'er waste fens and windy fields.

A maiden knight—to me is given
  Such hope, I know not fear;
I yearn to breathe the airs of heaven
  That often meet me here.
I muse on joy that will not cease,
  Pure spaces clothed in living beams,
Pure lilies of eternal peace,
  Whose odors haunt my dreams;

And, stricken by an angel's hand,
  This mortal armor that I wear,
This weight and size, this heart and eyes,
  Are touch'd, are turn'd to finest air.

The clouds are broken in the sky,
  And thro' the mountain-walls
A rolling organ-harmony
  Swells up, and shakes and falls.
Then move the trees, the copses nod,
  Wings flutter, voices hover clear:
"O just and faithful knight of God!
  Ride on! the prize is near."
So pass I hostel, hall, and grange:
  By bridge and ford, by park and pale,
All-arm'd I ride, whate'er betide,
  Until I find the holy Grail.

TO E. L., ON HIS TRAVELS IN GREECE.

ILLYRIAN woodlands, echoing falls
  Of water, sheets of summer glass,
  The long divine Peneian pass,
The vast Akrokeraunian walls,

Tomohrit, Athos, all things fair,
  With such a pencil, such a pen,
  You shadow forth to distant men,
I read and felt that I was there:

And trust me while I turn'd the page,
  And track'd you still on classic ground,
  I grew in gladness till I found
My spirits in the golden age.

For me the torrent ever pour'd
  And glisten'd—here and there alone
  The broad-limb'd Gods at random thrown
By fountain-urns;—and Naiads oar'd

A glimmering shoulder under gloom
  Of cavern pillars; on the swell
  The silver lily heaved and fell;
And many a slope was rich in bloom

From him that on the mountain lea
  By dancing rivulets fed his flocks,
  To him who sat upon the rocks,
And fluted to the morning sea.

THE LORD OF BURLEIGH.

IN her ear he whispers gayly,
  "If my heart by signs can tell,
Maiden, I have watch'd thee daily,
  And I think thou lov'st me well."
She replies, in accents fainter,
  "There is none I love like thee."
He is but a landscape-painter,
  And a village maiden she.
He to lips, that fondly falter,
  Presses his without reproof:
Leads her to the village altar,
  And they leave her father's roof.
"I can make no marriage present:
  Little can I give my wife.
Love will make our cottage pleasant,
  And I love thee more than life."
They by parks and lodges going
  See the lordly castles stand:
Summer woods, about them blowing,
  Made a murmur in the land.
From deep thought himself he rouses,
  Says to her that loves him well,

"Let us see these handsome houses
  Where the wealthy nobles dwell."
So she goes by him attended,
  Hears him lovingly converse,
Sees whatever fair and splendid
  Lay betwixt his home and hers;
Parks with oak and chestnut shady,
  Parks and order'd gardens great,
Ancient homes of lord and lady,
  Built for pleasure and for state.
All he shows her makes him dearer:
  Evermore she seems to gaze
On that cottage growing nearer,
  Where they twain will spend their days.
O but she will love him truly!
  He shall have a cheerful home:
She will order all things duly,
  When beneath his roof they come.
Thus her heart rejoices greatly,
  Till a gateway she discerns
With armorial bearings stately,
  And beneath the gate she turns;
Sees a mansion more majestic
  Than all those she saw before:
Many a gallant gay domestic
  Bows before him at the door.
And they speak in gentle murmur,
  When they answer to his call,
While he treads with footstep firmer,
  Leading on from hall to hall.
And, while now she wonders blindly,
  Nor the meaning can divine,
Proudly turns he round and kindly,
  "All of this is mine and thine."
Here he lives in state and bounty,
  Lord of Burleigh, fair and free,
Not a lord in all the county
  Is so great a lord as he.
All at once the color flushes
  Her sweet face from brow to chin:
As it were with shame she blushes,
  And her spirit changed within.
Then her countenance all over
  Pale again as death did prove:
But he clasp'd her like a lover,
  And he cheer'd her soul with love.
So she strove against her weakness,
  Tho' at times her spirits sank:
Shaped her heart with woman's meekness
  To all duties of her rank:
And a gentle consort made he,
  And her gentle mind was such
That she grew a noble lady,
  And the people loved her much.
But a trouble weigh'd upon her,
  And perplex'd her, night and morn,
With the burden of an honor
  Unto which she was not born.
Faint she grew, and ever fainter,
  As she murmur'd, "O, that he
Were once more that landscape-painter,
  Which did win my heart from me!"
So she droop'd and droop'd before him,
  Fading slowly from his side:
Three fair children first she bore him,
  Then before her time she died.
Weeping, weeping late and early,
  Walking up and pacing down,
Deeply mourn'd the Lord of Burleigh,
  Burleigh-house by Stamford-town.
And he came to look upon her,
  And he look'd at her and said,
"Bring the dress and put it on her,
  That she wore when she was wed."
Then her people, softly treading,
  Bore to earth her body, drest
In the dress that she was wed in,
  That her spirit might have rest.

EDWARD GRAY.

Sweet Emma Moreland of yonder town
Met me walking on yonder way,
"And have you lost your heart?" she said;
"And are you married yet, Edward Gray?"

Sweet Emma Moreland spoke to me:
Bitterly weeping I turn'd away:
"Sweet Emma Moreland, love no more
Can touch the heart of Edward Gray.

"Ellen Adair she loved me well,
Against her father's and mother's will:
To-day I sat for an hour and wept,
By Ellen's grave, on the windy hill.

"Shy she was, and I thought her cold;
Thought her proud, and fled over the sea;
Fill'd I was with folly and spite,
When Ellen Adair was dying for me.

"Cruel, cruel the words I said!
Cruelly came they back to-day:

'You 're too slight and fickle,' I said,
'To trouble the heart of Edward Gray.'

"There I put my face in the grass—
Whisper'd, 'Listen to my despair:
I repent me of all I did:
Speak a little, Ellen Adair!'

"Then I took a pencil and wrote
On the mossy stone, as I lay,
'Here lies the body of Ellen Adair;
And here the heart of Edward Gray!'

"Love may come, and love may go,
And fly, like a bird, from tree to tree:
But I will love no more, no more,
Till Ellen Adair come back to me.

"Bitterly wept I over the stone:
Bitterly weeping I turn'd away:
There lies the body of Ellen Adair!
And there the heart of Edward Gray!"

"Sweet Emma Moreland spoke to me:
Bitterly weeping I turn'd away."

SIR LAUNCELOT AND QUEEN GUINE-VERE.

A FRAGMENT.

Like souls that balance joy and pain,
With tears and smiles from heaven again
The maiden Spring upon the plain
Came in a sunlit fall of rain.
    In crystal vapor everywhere
Blue isles of heaven laugh'd between,
And, far in forest-deeps unseen,
The topmost elm-tree gather'd green
    From draughts of balmy air.

Sometimes the linnet piped his song:
Sometimes the throstle whistled strong:
Sometimes the sparhawk, wheel'd along,
Hush'd all the groves from fear of wrong:
    By grassy capes with fuller sound
In curves the yellowing river ran,
And drooping chestnut-buds began
To spread into the perfect fan,
    Above the teeming ground.

Then, in the boyhood of the year,
Sir Launcelot and Queen Guinevere
Rode thro' the coverts of the deer,
With blissful treble ringing clear.

She seem'd a part of joyous Spring;
A gown of grass-green silk she wore,
Buckled with golden clasps before;
A light-green tuft of plumes she bore
    Closed in a golden ring.

Now on some twisted ivy-net,
Now by some tinkling rivulet,
In mosses mixt with violet
Her cream-white mule his pastern set;
    And fleeter now she skimm'd the plains
Than she whose elfin prancer springs
By night to eery warblings,
When all the glimmering moorland rings
    With jingling bridle-reins.

As she fled fast thro' sun and shade,
The happy winds upon her play'd,
Blowing the ringlet from the braid:
She look'd so lovely, as she sway'd
    The rein with dainty finger-tips,
A man had given all other bliss,
And all his worldly worth for this,
To waste his whole heart in one kiss
    Upon her perfect lips.

———⟨⟩———

A FAREWELL.

Flow down, cold rivulet, to the sea,
    Thy tribute wave deliver:
No more by thee my steps shall be,
    Forever and forever.

Flow, softly flow, by lawn and lea,
    A rivulet then a river:
Nowhere by thee my steps shall be,
    Forever and forever.

But here will sigh thine alder tree,
    And here thine aspen shiver;
And here by thee will hum the bee,
    Forever and forever.

A thousand suns will stream on thee,
    A thousand moons will quiver;
But not by thee my steps shall be,
    Forever and forever.

———⟨⟩———

THE VISION OF SIN.

1.

I had a vision when the night was late:
A youth came riding toward a palace-gate.
He rode a horse with wings, that would have flown,
But that his heavy rider kept him down.
And from the palace came a child of sin,
And took him by the curls, and led him in,
Where sat a company with heated eyes,
Expecting when a fountain should arise:
A sleepy light upon their brows and lips—
As when the sun, a crescent of eclipse,
Dreams over lake and lawn, and isles and capes—
Suffused them, sitting, lying, languid shapes,
By heaps of gourds, and skins of wine, and piles of
    grapes.

2.

Then methought I heard a mellow sound,
Gathering up from all the lower ground;
Narrowing in to where they sat assembled
Low voluptuous music winding trembled,
Wov'n in circles: they that heard it sigh'd,
Panted hand in hand with faces pale,
Swung themselves, and in low tones replied.
Till the fountain spouted, showering wide
Sleet of diamond-drift and pearly hail:
Then the music touch'd the gates and died.
Rose again from where it seem'd to fail,
Storm'd in orbs of song, a growing gale;
Till thronging in and in, to where they waited,
As 't were a hundred-throated nightingale,
The strong tempestuous treble throbb'd and palpi
    tated;
Ran into its giddiest whirl of sound,
Caught the sparkles, and in circles,
Purple gauzes, golden hazes, liquid mazes,
Flung the torrent rainbow round:
Then they started from their places,
Moved with violence, changed in hue,
Caught each other with wild grimaces,
Half-invisible to the view,
Wheeling with precipitate paces
To the melody, till they flew,
Hair, and eyes, and limbs, and faces,
Twisted hard in fierce embraces,
Like to Furies, like to Graces,
Dash'd together in blinding dew:
Till, kill'd with some luxurious agony,
The nerve-dissolving melody
Flutter'd headlong from the sky.

3.

And then I look'd up toward a mountain-tract,
That girt the region with high cliff and lawn:
I saw that every morning, far withdrawn
Beyond the darkness and the cataract,
God made himself an awful rose of dawn,
Unheeded: and detaching, fold by fold,
From those still heights, and, slowly drawing near
A vapor heavy, hueless, formless, cold,
Came floating on for many a month and year,
Unheeded: and I thought I would have spoken,
And warned that madman ere it grew too late:
But, as in dreams, I could not. Mine was broken,
When that cold vapor touch'd the palace gate,
And link'd again. I saw within my head
A gray and gap-tooth'd man as lean as death,
Who slowly rode across a wither'd heath,
And lighted at a ruin'd inn, and said:

4.

"Wrinkled hostler, grim and thin!
    Here is custom come your way;
Take my brute, and lead him in,
    Stuff his ribs with mouldy hay.

"Bitter barmaid, waning fast!
    See that sheets are on my bed;
What! the flower of life is past:
    It is long before you wed.

"Slip-shod waiter, lank and sour,
    At the Dragon on the heath!
Let us have a quiet hour,
    Let us hob-and-nob with Death.

"I am old, but let me drink;
    Bring me spices, bring me wine;
I remember, when I think,
    That my youth was half divine.

"Wine is good for shrivell'd lips,
    When a blanket wraps the day,
When the rotten woodland drips,
    And the leaf is stamp'd in clay.

"Sit thee down, and have no shame,
    Cheek by jowl, and knee by knee:
What care I for any name?
    What for order or degree?

"Let me screw thee up a peg:
Let me loose thy tongue with wine:
Callest thou that thing a leg?
Which is thinnest? thine or mine?

"Thou shalt not be saved by works:
Thou hast been a sinner too:
Ruin'd trunks on wither'd forks,
Empty scarecrows, I and you!

"Fill the cup, and fill the can:
Have a rouse before the morn:
Every moment dies a man,
Every moment one is born.

"We are men of ruin'd blood;
Therefore comes it we are wise.
Fish are we that love the mud,
Rising to no fancy-flies.

"Name and fame! to fly sublime
Through the courts, the camps, the schools,
Is to be the ball of Time,
Bandied in the hands of fools.

"Friendship!—to be two in one—
Let the canting liar pack!
Well I know, when I am gone.
How she mouths behind my back.

"Virtue!—to be good and just—
Every heart, when sifted well,
Is a clot of warmer dust,
Mix'd with cunning sparks of hell.

"O! we two as well can look
Whited thought and cleanly life
As the priest, above his book
Leering at his neighbor's wife.

"Fill the cup, and fill the can:
Have a rouse before the morn:
Every moment dies a man,
Every moment one is born.

"Drink, and let the parties rave:
They are fill'd with idle spleen;
Rising, falling, like a wave,
For they know not what they mean.

"He that roars for liberty
Faster binds a tyrant's power;
And the tyrant's cruel glee
Forces on the freer hour.

"Fill the can, and fill the cup:
All the windy ways of men
Are but dust that rises up,
And is lightly laid again.

"Greet her with applausive breath,
Freedom, gayly doth she tread;
In her right a civic wreath,
In her left a human head

"No, I love not what is new;
She is of an ancient house:
And I think we know the hue
Of that cap upon her brows.

"Let her go! her thirst she slakes
Where the bloody conduit runs.
Then her sweetest meal she makes
On the first-born of her sons.

"Drink to lofty hopes that cool—
Visions of a perfect State:
Drink we, last, the public fool,
Frantic love and frantic hate.

"Chant me now some wicked stave,
Till thy drooping courage rise,

6

And the glow-worm of the grave
Glimmer in thy rheumy eyes.

"Fear not thou to loose thy tongue;
Set thy hoary fancies free;
What is loathsome to the young
Savors well to thee and me.

"Change, reverting to the years,
When thy nerves could understand
What there is in loving tears,
And the warmth of hand in hand.

"Tell me tales of thy first love—
April hopes, the fools of chance;
Till the graves begin to move,
And the dead begin to dance.

"Fill the can, and fill the cup:
All the windy ways of men
Are but dust that rises up,
And is lightly laid again.

"Trooping from their mouldy dens
The chap-fallen circle spreads:
Welcome, fellow-citizens,
Hollow hearts and empty heads!

"You are bones, and what of that?
Every face, however full,
Padded round with flesh and fat,
Is but modell'd on a skull.

"Death is king, and Vivat Rex!
Tread a measure on the stones,
Madam—if I know your sex,
From the fashion of your bones.

"No, I cannot praise the fire
In your eye—nor yet your lip:
All the more do I admire
Joints of cunning workmanship.

"Lo! God's likeness—the ground-plan—
Neither modell'd, glazed, or framed,
Buss me, thou rough sketch of man,
Far too naked to be shamed!

"Drink to Fortune, drink to Chance,
While we keep a little breath!
Drink to heavy Ignorance!
Hob-and-nob with brother Death!

"Thou art mazed, the night is long,
And the longer night is near:
What! I am not all as wrong
As a bitter jest is dear.

"Youthful hopes, by scores, to all,
When the locks are crisp and curl'd;
Unto me my maudlin gall
And my mockeries of the world.

"Fill the cup, and fill the can!
Mingle madness, mingle scorn!
Dregs of life, and lees of man:
Yet we will not die forlorn."

5.

The voice grew faint: there came a further change:
Once more uprose the mystic mountain-range:
Below were men and horses pierced with worms,
And slowly quickening into lower forms;
By shards and scurf of salt, and scum of dross,
Old plash of rains, and refuse patch'd with moss.
Then some one spake: "Behold! it was a crime
Of sense avenged by sense that wore with time."
Another said: "The crime of sense became
The crime of malice, and is equal blame."

And one: "He had not wholly quench'd his power;
A little grain of conscience made him sour."
At last I heard a voice upon the slope
Cry to the summit, "Is there any hope?"
To which an answer peal'd from that high land,
But in a tongue no man could understand;
And on the glimmering limit far withdrawn
God made Himself an awful rose of dawn.

———◇———

Come not, when I am dead,
  To drop thy foolish tears upon my grave,
To trample round my fallen head,
  And vex the unhappy dust thou wouldst not save.
There let the wind sweep and the plover cry;
  But thou, go by.

Child, if it were thine error or thy crime
  I care no longer, being all unblest:
Wed whom thou wilt, but I am sick of Time,
  And I desire to rest.
Pass on, weak heart, and leave me where I lie:
  Go by, go by.

———◇———

THE EAGLE.

FRAGMENT.

He clasps the crag with hooked hands;
Close to the sun in lonely lands,
Ring'd with the azure world, he stands.

The wrinkled sea beneath him crawls;
He watches from his mountain walls,
And like a thunderbolt he falls.

———◇———

Move eastward, happy earth, and leave
  Yon orange sunset waning slow;
From fringes of the faded eve,
  O, happy planet, eastward go·
Till over thy dark shoulder glow
  Thy silver sister-world, and rise
To glass herself in dewy eyes
  That watch me from the glen below.

Ah, bear me with thee, lightly borne,
  Dip forward under starry light,
And move me to my marriage-morn,
  And round again to happy night.

———◇———

Break, break, break,
  On thy cold gray stones, O Sea!
And I would that my tongue could utter
  The thoughts that arise in me.

O well for the fisherman's boy,
  That he shouts with his sister at play!
O well for the sailor lad,
  That he sings in his boat on the bay!

"Break, break, break,
On thy cold gray stones, O Sea!"

And the stately ships go on
  To their haven under the hill;
But O for the touch of a vanish'd hand,
  And the sound of a voice that is still!

Break, break, break,
  At the foot of thy crags, O Sea!
But the tender grace of a day that is dead
  Will never come back to me.

THE BEGGAR MAID.

Her arms across her breast she laid;
  She was more fair than words can say:
Barefooted came the beggar maid
  Before the king Cophetua.
In robe and crown the king stept down,
  To meet and greet her on her way;
"It is no wonder," said the lords,
  "She is more beautiful than day."

As shines the moon in clouded skies,
  She in her poor attire was seen:
One praised her ankles, one her eyes,
  One her dark hair and lovesome mien.

So sweet a face, such angel grace,
  In all that land had never been:
Cophetua sware a royal oath:
  "This beggar maid shall be my queen!"

THE POET'S SONG.

The rain had fallen, the Poet arose,
  He pass'd by the town and out of the street,
A light wind blew from the gates of the sun,
  And waves of shadow went over the wheat,
And he sat him down in a lonely place,
  And chanted a melody loud and sweet,
That made the wild-swan pause in her cloud,
  And the lark drop down at his feet.

The swallow stopt as he hunted the bee,
  The snake slipt under a spray,
The wild hawk stood with the down on his beak,
  And stared, with his foot on the prey,
And the nightingale thought, "I have sung many
      songs,
  But never a one so gay,
For he sings of what the world will be
  When the years have died away."

"In robe and crown the king stept down,
  To meet and greet her on her way."

THE PRINCESS:

A MEDLEY.

TO

HENRY LUSHINGTON

THIS VOLUME IS INSCRIBED BY HIS FRIEND

A. TENNYSON.

PROLOGUE.

Sir WALTER VIVIAN all a summer's day
Gave his broad lawns until the set of sun
Up to the people: thither flock'd at noon
His tenants, wife and child, and thither half
The neighboring borough with their Institute
Of which he was the patron. I was there
From college, visiting the son,—the son
A Walter too,—with others of our set,
Five others: we were seven at Vivian-place.

And me that morning Walter show'd the house,
Greek, set with busts: from vases in the hall
Flowers of all heavens, and lovelier than their names,
Grew side by side; and on the pavement lay
Carved stones of the Abbey-ruin in the park,
Huge Ammonites, and the first bones of Time;
And on the tables every clime and age
Jumbled together: celts and calumets,
Claymore and snow-shoe, toys in lava, fans
Of sandal, amber, ancient rosaries,
Laborious orient ivory sphere in sphere,
The cursed Malayan crease, and battle-clubs
From the isles of palm: and higher on the walls,
Betwixt the monstrous horns of elk and deer,
His own forefathers' arms and armor hung.

And "this," he said, "was Hugh's at Agincourt;
And that was old Sir Ralph's at Ascalon:
A good knight he! we keep a chronicle
With all about him,"—which he brought, and I
Dived in a hoard of tales that dealt with knights
Half-legend, half-historic, counts and kings
Who laid about them at their wills and died;
And mixt with these, a lady, one that arm'd
Her own fair head, and sallying thro' the gate,
Had beat her foes with slaughter from her walls.

"O miracle of women," said the book,
"O noble heart who, being strait-besieged
By this wild king to force her to his wish,
Nor bent, nor broke, nor shunn'd a soldier's death,
But now when all was lost or seem'd as lost—
Her stature more than mortal in the burst
Of sunrise, her arm lifted, eyes on fire—
Brake with a blast of trumpets from the gate,
And, falling on them like a thunderbolt,
She trampled some beneath her horses' heels,
And some were whelm'd with missiles of the wall,
And some were push'd with lances from the rock,
And part were drown'd within the whirling brook:
O miracle of noble womanhood!"

So sang the gallant glorious chronicle;
And, I all rapt in this, "Come out," he said,
"To the Abbey: there is Aunt Elizabeth

And sister Lilia with the rest." We went
(I kept the book and had my finger in it)
Down thro' the park: strange was the sight to me;
For all the sloping pasture murmur'd, sown
With happy faces and with holiday.
There moved the multitude, a thousand heads;
The patient leaders of their Institute
Taught them with facts. One rear'd a font of stone
And drew from butts of water on the slope,
The fountain of the moment, playing now
A twisted snake, and now a rain of pearls,
Or steep-up spout whereon the gilded ball
Danced like a wisp: and somewhat lower down
A man with knobs and wires and vials fired
A cannon: Echo answer'd in her sleep
From hollow fields: and here were telescopes
For azure views; and there a group of girls
In circle waited, whom the electric shock
Dislink'd with shrieks and laughter: round the lake
A little clock-work steamer paddling plied
And shook the lilies: perch'd about the knolls
A dozen angry models jetted steam:
A petty railway ran: a fire-balloon
Rose gem-like up before the dusky groves
And dropt a fairy parachute and past:
And there thro' twenty posts of telegraph
They flash'd a saucy message to and fro
Between the mimic stations; so that sport
Went hand in hand with Science; otherwhere
Pure sport: a herd of boys with clamor bowl'd
And stump'd the wicket; babies roll'd about
Like tumbled fruit in grass; and men and maids
Arranged a country dance, and flew thro' light
And shadow, while the twangling violin
Struck up with Soldier-laddie, and overhead
The broad ambrosial aisles of lofty lime
Made noise with bees and breeze from end to end.

Strange was the sight and smacking of the time;
And long we gazed, but satiated at length
Came to the ruins. High-arch'd and ivy-claspt,
Of finest Gothic lighter than a fire,
Thro' one wide chasm of time and frost they gave
The park, the crowd, the house; but all within
The sward was trim as any garden lawn:
And here we lit on Aunt Elizabeth,
And Lilia with the rest, and lady friends
From neighbor seats: and there was Ralph himself,
A broken statue propt against the wall,
As gay as any. Lilia, wild with sport,
Half child, half woman as she was, had wound
A scarf of orange round the stony helm,
And robed the shoulders in a rosy silk,
That made the old warrior from his ivied nook
Glow like a sunbeam: near his tomb a feast
Shone, silver-set; about it lay the guests,
And there we joined them: then the maiden Aunt

Took this fair day for text, and from it preach'd
An universal culture for the crowd,
And all things great; but we, unworthier, told
Of College: he had climb'd across the spikes,
And he had squeezed himself betwixt the bars,
And he had breathed the Proctor's dogs: and one
Discuss'd his tutor, rough to common men,
But honeying at the whisper of a lord;
And one the Master, as a rogue in grain
Veneer'd with sanctimonious theory.

But while they talk'd, above their heads I saw
The feudal warrior lady-clad; which brought
My book to mind: and opening this I read
Of old Sir Ralph a page or two that rang
With tilt and tourney; then the tale of her
That drove her foes with slaughter from her walls,
And much I praised her nobleness, and "Where,"
Ask'd Walter, patting Lilia's head (she lay
Beside him) "lives there such a woman now?"

Quick answer'd Lilia, "There are thousands now
Such women, but convention beats them down:
It is but bringing up; no more than that:
You men have done it: how I hate you all!
Ah, were I something great! I wish I were
Some mighty poetess, I would shame you then,
That love to keep us children! O I wish
That I were some great Princess, I would build
Far off from men a college like a man's,
And I would teach them all that men are taught;
We are twice as quick!" And here she shook aside
The hand that play'd the patron with her curls.

And one said smiling, "Pretty were the sight
If our old halls could change their sex, and flaunt
With prudes for proctors, dowagers for deans,
And sweet girl-graduates in their golden hair.
I think they should not wear our rusty gowns,
But move as rich as Emperor-moths or Ralph
Who shines so in the corner; yet I fear,
If there were many Lilias in the brood,
However deep you might embower the nest,
Some boy would spy it."

                    At this upon the sward
She tapt her tiny silken-sandal'd foot:
"That's your light way: but I would make it death
For any male thing but to peep at us."

Petulant she spoke, and at herself she laugh'd;
A rose-bud set with little wilful thorns,
And sweet as English air could make her, she:
But Walter hail'd a score of names upon her,
And "petty Ogress," and "ungrateful Puss,"
And swore he long'd at College, only long'd,
All else was well, for she-society.
They boated and they cricketed; they talk'd
At wine, in clubs, of art, of politics;
They lost their weeks; they vext the souls of deans;
They rode; they betted; made a hundred friends,
And caught the blossom of the flying terms,
But miss'd the mignonette of Vivian-place,
The little hearth-flower Lilia. Thus he spoke,
Part banter, part affection.

                    "True," she said,
"We doubt not that. O yes, you miss'd us much.
I'll stake my ruby ring upon it you did."

She held it out; and as a parrot turns
Up thro' gilt wires a crafty loving eye,
And takes a lady's finger with all care,
And bites it for true heart and not for harm,
So he with Lilia's. Daintily she shriek'd
And wrung it. "Doubt my word again!" he said.
"Come, listen! here is proof that you were miss'd:
We seven stay'd at Christmas up to read,
And there we took one tutor as to read:
The hard-grain'd Muses of the cube and square
Were out of season: never man, I think,

So moulder'd in a sinecure as he:
For while our cloisters echo'd frosty feet,
And our long walks were stript as bare as brooms,
We did but talk you over, pledge you all
In wassail: often, like as many girls—
Sick for the hollies and the yews of home—
As many little trifling Lilias—play'd
Charades and riddles as at Christmas here,
And what's my thought and when and where and how
And often told a tale from mouth to mouth
As here at Christmas."

                    She remember'd that:
A pleasant game, she thought: she liked it more
Than magic music, forfeits, all the rest.
But these—what kind of tales did men tell men,
She wonder'd, by themselves?

                    A half-disdain
Perch'd on the pouted blossom of her lips:
And Walter nodded at me; "He began,
The rest would follow, each in turn: and so
We forged a sevenfold story. Kind? what kind?
Chimeras, crotchets, Christmas solecisms,
Seven-headed monsters only made to kill
Time by the fire in winter."

                    "Kill him now,
The tyrant! kill him in the summer too,"
Said Lilia; "Why not now," the maiden Aunt.
"Why not a summer's as a winter's tale?
A tale for summer as befits the time,
And something it should be to suit the place,
Heroic, for a hero lies beneath,
Grave, solemn!"

                    Walter warp'd his mouth at this
To something so mock-solemn, that I laugh'd
And Lilia woke with sudden-shrilling mirth
An echo like a ghostly woodpecker,
Hid in the ruins; till the maiden Aunt
(A little sense of wrong had touch'd her face
With color) turn'd to me with "As you will;
Heroic if you will, or what you will,
Or be yourself your hero if you will."

"Take Lilia, then, for heroine," clamor'd he,
"And make her some great Princess, six feet high,
Grand, epic, homicidal; and be you
The Prince to win her!"

                    "Then follow me, the Prince,"
I answer'd, "each be hero in his turn!
Seven and yet one, like shadows in a dream.—
Heroic seems our Princess as required.—
But something made to suit with Time and place,
A Gothic ruin and a Grecian house,
A talk of college and of ladies' rights,
A feudal knight in silken masquerade,
And, yonder, shrieks and strange experiments
For which the good Sir Ralph had burnt them all—
This were a medley! we should have him back
Who told the 'Winter's tale' to do it for us.
No matter: we will say whatever comes.
And let the ladies sing us, if they will,
From time to time, some ballad or a song
To give us breathing-space."

                    So I began,
And the rest follow'd: and the women sang
Between the rougher voices of the men,
Like linnets in the pauses of the wind:
And here I give the story and the songs.

I.

A Prince I was, blue-eyed, and fair in face,
Of temper amorous, as the first of May,
With lengths of yellow ringlet, like a girl,
For on my cradle shone the Northern star.

There lived an ancient legend in our house.
Some sorcerer, whom a far-off grandsire burnt
Because he cast no shadow, had foretold,
Dying, that none of all our blood should know

The shadow from the substance, and that one
Should come to fight with shadows and to fall.
For so, my mother said, the story ran.
And, truly, waking dreams were, more or less,
An old and strange affection of the house.
Myself too had weird seizures, Heaven knows what:
On a sudden in the midst of men and day,
And while I walk'd and talk'd as heretofore,
I seem'd to move among a world of ghosts,
And feel myself the shadow of a dream.
Our great court-Galen poised his gilt-head cane,
And paw'd his beard, and mutter'd "catalepsy."
My mother pitying made a thousand prayers;
My mother was as mild as any saint,
Half-canonized by all that look'd on her,
So gracious was her tact and tenderness:
But my good father thought a king a king;
He cared not for the affection of the house;
He held his sceptre like a pedant's wand
To lash offence, and with long arms and hands
Reach'd out, and pick'd offenders from the mass
For judgment.
      Now it chanced that I had been,
While life was yet in bud and blade, betroth'd
To one, a neighboring Princess: she to me
Was proxy-wedded with a bootless calf
At eight years old; and still from time to time
Came murmurs of her beauty from the South,
And of her brethren, youths of puissance;
And still I wore her picture by my heart,
And one dark tress; and all around them both
Sweet thoughts would swarm as bees about their
queen.

But when the days drew nigh that I should wed,
My father sent ambassadors with furs
And jewels, gifts, to fetch her: these brought back
A present, a great labor of the loom:
And therewithal an answer vague as wind:
Besides, they saw the king; he took the gifts,
He said there was a compact; that was true:
But then she had a will; was he to blame?
And maiden fancies; loved to live alone
Among her women; certain, would not wed.

That morning in the presence-room I stood
With Cyril and with Florian, my two friends:
The first, a gentleman of broken means
(His father's fault) but given to starts and bursts
Of revel; and the last, my other heart,
And almost my half-self, for still we moved
Together, twinn'd as horse's ear and eye.

Now, while they spake, I saw my father's face
Grow long and troubled like a rising moon,
Inflamed with wrath: he started on his feet,
Tore the king's letter, snow'd it down, and rent
The wonder of the loom thro' warp and woof
From skirt to skirt; and at the last he sware
That he would send a hundred thousand men,
And bring her in a whirlwind: then he chew'd
The thrice-turn'd cud of wrath, and cook'd his spleen,
Communing with his captains of the war.

At last I spoke. "My father, let me go.
It cannot be but some gross error lies
In this report, this answer of a king,
Whom all men rate as kind and hospitable:
Or, maybe, I myself, my bride once seen,
Whate'er my grief to find her less than fame,
May rue the bargain made." And Florian said:
"I have a sister at the foreign court,
Who moves about the Princess; she, you know,
Who wedded with a nobleman from thence:
He, dying lately, left her, as I hear,
The lady of three castles in that land:
Thro' her this matter might be sifted clean."
And Cyril whisper'd: "Take me with you too."

Then laughing "what, if these weird seizures come
Upon you in those lands, and no one near
To point you out the shadow from the truth!
Take me: I'll serve you better in a strait;
I grate on rusty hinges here:" but "No!"
Roar'd the rough king, "you shall not; we ourself
Will crush her pretty maiden fancies dead
In iron gauntlets: break the council up."

But when the council broke, I rose and past
Thro' the wild woods that hung about the town,
Found a still place, and pluck'd her likeness out;
Laid it on flowers, and watch'd it lying bathed
In the green gleam of dewy-tassell'd trees:
What were those fancies? wherefore break her troth?
Proud look'd the lips: but while I meditated
A wind arose and rush'd upon the South,
And shook the songs, the whispers, and the shrieks
Of the wild woods together; and a Voice
Went with it, "Follow, follow, thou shalt win."

Then, ere the silver sickle of that month
Became her golden shield, I stole from court
With Cyril and with Florian, unperceived,
Cat-footed thro' the town and half in dread
To hear my father's clamor at our backs
With Ho! from some bay-window shake the night:
But all was quiet. from the bastion'd walls
Like threaded spiders, one by one, we dropt,
And flying reach'd the frontier: then we crost
To a livelier land; and so by tilth and grange,
And vines, and blowing bosks of wilderness,
We gain'd the mother-city thick with towers,
And in the imperial palace found the king.

His name was Gama; crack'd and small his voice,
But bland the smile that like a wrinkling wind
On glassy water drove his cheek in lines;
A little dry old man, without a star,
Not like a king: three days he feasted us,
And on the fourth I spake of why we came,
And my betroth'd. "You do us, Prince," he said,
Airing a snowy hand and signet gem,
"All honor. We remember love ourselves
In our sweet youth: there did a compact pass
Long summers back, a kind of ceremony—
I think the year in which our olives fail'd.
I would you had her, Prince, with all my heart,
With my full heart: but there were widows here,
Two widows, Lady Psyche, Lady Blanche,
They fed her theories, in and out of place
Maintaining that with equal husbandry
The woman were an equal to the man.
They harp'd on this; with this our banquets rang;
Our dances broke and buzz'd in knots of talk;
Nothing but this; my very ears were hot
To hear them: knowledge, so my daughter held,
Was all in all; they had but been, she thought,
As children; they must lose the child, assume
The woman: then, Sir, awful odes she wrote,
Too awful, sure, for what they treated of,
But all she is and does is awful; odes
About this losing of the child; and rhymes
And dismal lyrics, prophesying change
Beyond all reason: these the women sang;
And they that know such things—I sought but peace;
No critic I—would call them masterpieces;
They master'd me. At last she begg'd a boon
A certain summer-palace which I have
Hard by your father's frontier: I said no,
Yet being an easy man, gave it; and there,
All wild to found an University
For maidens, on the spur she fled; and more
We know not,—only this: they see no men,
Not ev'n her brother Arac, nor the twins
Her brethren, tho' they love her, look upon her
As on a kind of paragon; and I
(Pardon me saying it) were much loath to breed

Dispute betwixt myself and mine: but since
(And I confess with right) you think me bound
In some sort, I can give you letters to her;
And, yet, to speak the truth, I rate your chance
Almost at naked nothing."

             Thus the king;
And I, tho' nettled that he seem'd to slur
With garrulous ease and oily courtesies
Our formal compact, yet, not less (all frets
But chafing me on fire to find my bride)
Went forth again with both my friends. We rode
Many a long league back to the North. At last
From hills, that look'd across a land of hope,
We dropt with evening on a rustic town
Set in a gleaming river's crescent-curve,
Close at the boundary of the liberties:
There enter'd an old hostel, call'd mine host
To council, plied him with his richest wines,
And show'd the late-writ letters of the king.

He with a long low sibilation, stared
As blank as death in marble; then exclaim'd
Averring it was clear against all rules
For any man to go: but as his brain
Began to mellow, "If the king," he said,
"Had given us letters, was he bound to speak?
The king would bear him out;" and at the last—
The summer of the vine in all his veins—
"No doubt that we might make it worth his while.
She once had past that way: he heard her speak;
She scared him; life! he never saw the like;
She look'd as grand as doomsday and as grave:
And he, reverenced his liege-lady there;
He always made a point to post with mares;
His daughter and his housemaid were the boys;
The land he understood for miles about
Was till'd by women; all the swine were sows,
And all the dogs—"

           But while he jested thus
A thought flash'd thro' me which I cloth'd in act,
Remembering how we three presented Maid
Or Nymph, or Goddess, at high tide of feast,
In masque or pageant at my father's court.
We sent mine host to purchase female gear;
He brought it, and himself, a sight to shake
The midriff of despair with laughter, holp
To lace us up, till each, in maiden plumes
We rustled: him we gave a costly bribe
To guerdon silence, mounted our good steeds,
And boldly ventured on the liberties.

We follow'd up the river as we rode,
And rode till midnight when the college lights
Began to glitter firefly-like in copse
And linden alley: then we past an arch,
Whereon a woman-statue rose with wings
From four wing'd horses dark against the stars;
And some inscription ran along the front,
But deep in shadow: further on we gain'd
A little street half garden and half house;
But scarce could hear each other speak for noise
Of clocks and chimes, like silver hammers falling
On silver anvils, and the splash and stir
Of fountains spouted up and showering down
In meshes of the jasmine and the rose:
And all about us peal'd the nightingale,
Rapt in her song, and careless of the snare.

There stood a bust of Pallas for a sign,
By two sphere lamps blazon'd like Heaven and
    Earth
With constellation and with continent,
Above an entry: riding in, we call'd;
A plump-arm'd Ostleress and a stable wench
Came running at the call, and help'd us down.
Then stept a buxom hostess forth, and sail'd,
Full blown, before us into rooms which gave
Upon a pillar'd porch, the bases lost
In laurel: her we ask'd of that and this,
And who were tutors. "Lady Blanche," she said,

"And Lady Psyche." "Which was prettiest,
Best-natured?" "Lady Psyche." "Hers are we,"
One voice, we cried; and I sat down and wrote,
In such a hand as when a field of corn
Bows all its ears before the roaring East:

"Three ladies of the Northern empire pray
Your Highness would enroll them with your own,
As Lady Psyche's pupils."

            This I seal'd:
The seal was Cupid bent above a scroll,
And o'er his head Uranian Venus hung,
And raised the blinding bandage from his eyes:
I gave the letter to be sent with dawn:
And then to bed, where half in doze I seem'd
To float about a glimmering night, and watch
A full sea glazed with muffled moonlight, swell
On some dark shore just seen that it was rich.

     As thro' the land at eve we went,
      And pluck'd the ripen'd ears,
    We fell out, my wife and I,
     O we fell out I know not why,
      And kiss'd again with tears.
    And blessings on the falling out
      That all the more endears,
    When we fall out with those we love
      And kiss again with tears!
    For when we came where lies the child
      We lost in other years,
    There above the little grave,
     O there above the little grave,
      We kiss'd again with tears

           II.

At break of day the College Portress came:
She brought us Academic silks, in hue
The lilac, with a silken hood to each,
And zoned with gold; and now when these were on
And we as rich as moths from dusk cocoons,
She, curtseying her obeisance, let us know
The Princess Ida waited: out we paced,
I first, and following thro' the porch that sang
All round with laurel, issued in a court
Compact of lucid marbles, boss'd with lengths
Of classic frieze, with ample awnings gay
Betwixt the pillars, and with great urns of flowers.
The Muses and the Graces, group'd in threes,
Enring'd a billowing fountain in the midst;
And here and there on lattice edges lay
Or book or lute; but hastily we past,
And up a flight of stairs into the hall.

There at a board by tome and paper sat,
With two tame leopards couch'd beside her throne,
All beauty compass'd in a female form,
The Princess; liker to the inhabitant
Of some clear planet close upon the Sun,
Than our man's earth; such eyes were in her head,
And so much grace and power, breathing down
From over her arch'd brows, with every turn
Lived thro' her to the tips of her long hands,
And to her feet. She rose her height, and said:

"We give you welcome: not without rebound
Of use and glory to yourselves ye come,
The first-fruits of the stranger: aftertime,
And that full voice which circles round the grave
Will rank you nobly, mingled up with me.
What! are the ladies of your land so tall?"
"We of the court," said Cyril. "From the court,"
She answer'd, "then ye know the Prince?" and he:
"The climax of his age! as tho' there were
One rose in all the world, your Highness that,
He worships your ideal." She replied:
"We scarcely thought in our own hall to hear
This barren verbiage, current among men,
Like coin, the tinsel clink of compliment.
Your flight from out your bookless wilds would seem
As arguing love of knowledge and of power;

Your language proves you still the child. Indeed,
We dream not of him: when we set our hand
To this great work, we purposed with ourself
Never to wed. You likewise will do well,
Ladies, in entering here, to cast and fling
The tricks, which make us toys of men, that so,
Some future time, if so indeed you will,
You may with those self-styled our lords ally
Your fortunes, justlier balanced, scale with scale."

At those high words, we, conscious of ourselves,
Perused the matting; then an officer
Rose up, and read the statutes, such as these:
Not for three years to correspond with home;
Not for three years to cross the liberties:
Not for three years to speak with any men;
And many more, which hastily subscribed,
We enter'd on the boards: and "Now," she cried,
"Ye are green wood, see ye warp not. Look, our
    hall!
Our statues!—not of those that men desire,
Sleek Odalisques, or oracles of mode,
Nor stunted squaws of West or East; but she
That taught the Sabine how to rule, and she
The foundress of the Babylonian wall,
The Carian Artemisia strong in war,
The Rhodope, that built the pyramid,
Clelia, Cornelia, with the Palmyrene
That fought Aurelian, and the Roman brows
Of Agrippina. Dwell with these and lose
Convention, since to look on noble forms
Makes noble thro' the sensuous organism
That which is higher. O lift your natures up:
Embrace our aims: work out your freedom. Girls,
Knowledge is now no more a fountain seal'd:
Drink deep, until the habits of the slave,
The sins of emptiness, gossip and spite
And slander, die. Better not be at all
Than not be noble. Leave us: you may go:
To-day the Lady Psyche will harangue
The fresh arrivals of the week before;
For they press in from all the provinces,
And fill the hive."

                    She spoke, and bowing waved
Dismissal: back again we crost the court
To Lady Psyche's: as we enter'd in,
There sat along the forms, like morning doves
That sun their milky bosoms on the thatch,
A patient range of pupils: she herself
Erect behind a desk of satin-wood,
A quick brunette, well-moulded, falcon-eyed,
And on the hither side, or so she look'd,
Of twenty summers. At her left, a child,
In shining draperies, headed like a star,
Her maiden babe, a double April old,
Aglaïa slept. We sat: the Lady glanced:
Then Florian, but no livelier than the dame
That whisper'd "Asses' ears" among the sedge,
"My sister." "Comely too by all that's fair,"
Said Cyril. "O hush, hush!" and she began.

"This world was once a fluid haze of light,
Till toward the centre set the starry tides,
And eddied into suns, that wheeling cast
The planets: then the monster, then the man;
Tattoo'd or woaded, winter-clad in skins,
Raw from the prime, and crushing down his mate:
As yet we find in barbarous isles, and here
Among the lowest."

                    Thereupon she took
A bird's-eye view of all the ungracious past;
Glanced at the legendary Amazon
As emblematic of a nobler age;
Appraised the Lycian custom, spoke of those
That lay at wine with Lar and Lucumo;
Ran down the Persian, Grecian, Roman lines
Of empire, and the woman's state in each,
How far from just; till, warming with her theme,

She fulmined out her scorn of laws Salique
And little-footed China, touch'd on Mahomet
With much contempt, and came to chivalry:
When some respect, however slight, was paid
To woman, superstition all awry:
However then commenced the dawn: a beam
Had slanted forward, falling in a land
Of promise; fruit would follow. Deep, indeed,
Their debt of thanks to her who first had dared
To leap the rotten pales of prejudice,
Disyoke their necks from custom, and assert
None lordlier than themselves but that which made
Woman and man. She had founded; they must build.
Here might they learn whatever men were taught;
Let them not fear: some said their heads were less:
Some men's were small; not they the least of men;
For often fineness compensated size:
Besides the brain was like the hand, and grew
With using; thence the man's, if more, was more:
He took advantage of his strength to be
First in the field: some ages had been lost;
But woman ripen'd earlier, and her life
Was longer; and albeit their glorious names
Were fewer, scatter'd stars, yet since in truth
The highest is the measure of the man,
And not the Kaffir, Hottentot, Malay,
Nor those horn-handed breakers of the glebe,
But Homer, Plato, Verulam; even so
With woman: and in arts of government
Elizabeth and others; arts of war
The peasant Joan and others; arts of grace
Sappho and others vied with any man:
And, last not least, she who had left her place,
And bow'd her state to them, that they might grow
To use and power on this Oasis, lapt
In the arms of leisure, sacred from the blight
Of ancient influence and scorn."

                                At last
She rose upon a wind of prophecy
Dilating on the future; "everywhere
Two heads in council, two beside the hearth,
Two in the tangled business of the world,
Two in the liberal offices of life,
Two plummets dropt for one to sound the abyss
Of science, and the secrets of the mind:
Musician, painter, sculptor, critic, more:
And everywhere the broad and bounteous Earth
Should bear a double growth of those rare souls,
Poets, whose thoughts enrich the blood of the world."

She ended here, and beckon'd us: the rest
Parted: and, glowing full-faced welcome, she
Began to address us, and was moving on
In gratulation, till as when a boat
Tacks, and the slacken'd sail flaps, all her voice
Faltering and fluttering in her throat, she cried,
"My brother!" "Well, my sister." "O," she said,
"What do you here? and in this dress? and these?
Why who are these? a wolf within the fold!
A pack of wolves! the Lord be gracious to me!
A plot, a plot, a plot to ruin all!"
"No plot, no plot," he answer'd. "Wretched boy,
How saw you not the inscription on the gate,
LET NO MAN ENTER IN ON PAIN OF DEATH?"
"And if I had," he answer'd, "who could think
The softer Adams of your Academe,
O sister, Sirens tho' they be, were such
As chanted on the blanching bones of men?"
"But you will find it otherwise," she said.
"You jest: ill jesting with edge-tools! my vow
Binds me to speak, and O that iron will,
That axelike edge unturnable, our Head,
The Princess." "Well then, Psyche, take my life,
And nail me like a weasel on a grange
For warning: bury me beside the gate,
And cut this epitaph above my bones;
Here lies a brother by a sister slain,
All for the common good of womankind."

"Let me die too," said Cyril, "having seen
And heard the Lady Psyche."

                I struck in:
"Albeit so mask'd, Madam, I love the truth;
Receive it; and in me behold the Prince
Your countryman, affianced years ago
To the Lady Ida: here, for here she was,
And thus (what other way was left?) I came."
"O Sir, O Prince, I have no country; none;
If any, this; but none. Whate'er I was
Disrooted, what I am is grafted here.
Affianced, Sir? love-whispers may not breathe
Within this vestal limit, and how should I,
Who am not mine, say, live: the thunderbolt
Hangs silent; but prepare: I speak; it falls."
"Yet pause," I said: "for that inscription there,
I think no more of deadly lurks therein,
Than in a clapper clapping in a garth,
To scare the fowl from fruit: if more there be,
If more and acted on, what follows? war;
Your own work marr'd: for this your Academe,
Whichever side be Victor, in the halloo
Will topple to the trumpet down, and pass
With all fair theories only made to gild
A stormless summer." "Let the Princess judge
Of that," she said: "farewell, Sir—and to you.
I shudder at the sequel, but I go."

"Are you that Lady Psyche," I rejoin'd,
"The fifth in line from that old Florian,
Yet hangs his portrait in my father's hall
(The gaunt old Baron with his beetle brow
Sun-shaded in the heat of dusty fights)
As he bestrode my Grandsire, when he fell,
And all else fled: we point to it, and we say,
The loyal warmth of Florian is not cold,
But branches current yet in kindred veins."
"Are you that Psyche," Florian added, "she
With whom I sang about the morning hills,
Flung ball, flew kite, and raced the purple fly,
And snared the squirrel of the glen? are you
That Psyche, wont to bind my throbbing brow,
To smooth my pillow, mix the foaming draught
Of fever, tell me pleasant tales, and read
My sickness down to happy dreams? are you
That brother-sister Psyche, both in one?
You were that Psyche, but what are you now?"
"You are that Psyche," Cyril said, "for whom
I would be that forever which I seem,
Woman, if I might sit beside your feet,
And glean your scatter'd sapience."

                Then once more,
"Are you that Lady Psyche," I began,
"That on her bridal morn before she past
From all her old companions, when the king
Kiss'd her pale cheek, declared that ancient ties
Would still be dear beyond the southern hills;
That were there any of our people there
In want or peril, there was one to hear
And help them: look! for such are these and I."
"Are you that Psyche," Florian ask'd, "to whom,
In gentler days, your arrow-wounded fawn
Came flying while you sat beside the well?
The creature laid his muzzle on your lap,
And sobb'd, and you sobb'd with it, and the blood
Was sprinkled on your kirtle, and you wept.
That was fawn's blood, not brother's, yet you wept.
O by the bright head of my little niece,
You were that Psyche, and what are you now?"
"You are that Psyche," Cyril said again,
"The mother of the sweetest little maid,
That ever crow'd for kisses."

                "Out upon it!"
She answer'd, "peace! and why should I not play
The Spartan Mother with emotion, be
The Lucius Junius Brutus of my kind?
Him you call great: he for the common weal,
The fading politics of mortal Rome,

As I might slay this child, if good need were,
Slew both his sons: and I, shall I, on whom
The secular emancipation turns
Of half this world, be swerved from right to save
A prince, a brother? a little will I yield.
Best so, perchance, for us, and well for you.
O hard, when love and duty clash! I fear
My conscience will not count me fleckless; yet—
Hear my conditions: promise (otherwise
You perish) as you came to slip away,
To-day, to-morrow, soon: it shall be said,
These women are too barbarous, would not learn;
They fled, who might have shamed us: promise, all."

What could we else, we promised each; and she.
Like some wild creature newly caged, commenced
A to-and-fro, so pacing till she paused
By Florian; holding out her lily arms
Took both his hands, and smiling faintly said:
"I knew you at the first; tho' you have grown
You scarce have alter'd: I am sad and glad
To see you, Florian. I give thee to death,
My brother! it was duty spoke, not I.
My needful seeming harshness, pardon it.
Our mother, is she well?"

                With that she kiss'd
His forehead, then, a moment after, clung
About him, and betwixt them blossom'd up
From out a common vein of memory
Sweet household talk, and phrases of the hearth,
And far allusion, till the gracious dews
Began to glisten and to fall: and while
They stood, so rapt, we gazing, came a voice.
"I brought a message here from Lady Blanche."
Back started she, and turning round we saw
The Lady Blanche's daughter where she stood,
Melissa, with her hand upon the lock.
A rosy blonde, and in a college gown,
That clad her like an April daffodilly
(Her mother's color) with her lips apart,
And all her thoughts as fair within her eyes,
As bottom agates seen to wave and float
In crystal currents of clear morning seas.

So stood that same fair creature at the door.
Then Lady Psyche, "Ah—Melissa—you!
You heard us?" and Melissa, "O pardon me!
I heard, I could not help it, did not wish:
But, dearest Lady, pray you fear me not,
Nor think I bear that heart within my breast,
To give three gallant gentlemen to death."
"I trust you," said the other, "for we two
Were always friends, none closer, elm and vine:
But yet your mother's jealous temperament—
Let not your prudence, dearest, drowse, or prove
The Danaid of a leaky vase, for fear
This whole foundation ruin, and I lose
My honor, these their lives." "Ah, fear me not,"
Replied Melissa; "no—I would not tell,
No, not for all Aspasia's cleverness,
No, not to answer, Madam, all those hard things
That Sheba came to ask of Solomon."
"Be it so," the other, "that we still may lead
The new light up, and culminate in peace,
For Solomon may come to Sheba yet."
Said Cyril, "Madam, he the wisest man
Feasted the woman wisest then, in halls
Of Lebanonian cedar: nor should you
(Tho' Madam you should answer, we would ask)
Less welcome find among us, if you came
Among us, debtors for our lives to you,
Myself for something more." He said not what,
But "Thanks," she answer'd, "go: we have been
too long
Together: keep your hoods about the face;
They do so that affect abstraction here.
Speak little: mix not with the rest; and hold
Your promise: all, I trust, may yet be well."

We turn'd to go, but Cyril took the child,
And held her round the knees against his waist,
And blew the swoll'n cheek of a trumpeter,
While Psyche watch'd them, smiling, and the child
Push'd her flat hand against his face and laugh'd;
And thus our conference closed.   •
                    And then we strolled
For half the day thro' stately theatres
Bench'd crescent-wise. In each we sat, we heard
The grave Professor. On the lecture slate
The circle rounded under female hands
With flawless demonstration: follow'd then
A classic lecture, rich in sentiment,
With scraps of thunderous Epic lilted out
By violet-hooded Doctors, elegies
And quoted odes, and jewels five-words-long
That on the stretch'd forefinger of all Time
Sparkle forever: then we dipt in all
That treats of whatsoever is, the state,
The total chronicles of man, the mind,
The morals, something of the frame, the rock,
The star, the bird, the fish, the shell, the flower,
Electric, chemic laws, and all the rest,
And whatsoever can be taught and known;
Till like three horses that have broken fence,
And glutted all night long breast-deep in corn,
We issued gorged with knowledge, and I spoke:
"Why, Sirs, they do all this as well as we."
"They hunt old trails," said Cyril, "very well;
But when did woman ever yet invent?"
"Ungracious!" answer'd Florian, "have you learnt
No more from Psyche's lecture, you that talk'd
The trash that made me sick, and almost sad?"
"O trash," he said, "but with a kernel in it.
Should I not call her wise, who made me wise?
And learnt? I learnt more from her in a flash,
Than if my brainpan were an empty hull,
And every Muse tumbled a science in.
A thousand hearts lie fallow in these halls,
And round these halls a thousand baby loves
Fly twanging headless arrows at the hearts,
Whence follows many a vacant pang: but O
With me, Sir, enter'd in the bigger boy,
The Head of all the golden-shafted firm,
The long-limb'd lad that had a Psyche too;
He cleft me thro' the stomacher: and now
What think you of it, Florian? do I chase
The substance or the shadow? will it hold?
I have no sorcerer's malison on me,
No ghostly hauntings like his Highness. I
Flatter myself that always everywhere
I know the substance when I see it. Well,
Are castles shadows? Three of them? Is she
The sweet proprietress a shadow? If not,
Shall those three castles patch my tatter'd coat?
For dear are those three castles to my wants,
And dear is sister Psyche to my heart,
And two dear things are one of double worth,
And much I might have said, but that my zone
Unmann'd me: then the Doctors! O to hear
The Doctors! O to watch the thirsty plants
Imbibing! once or twice I thought to roar,
To break my chain, to shake my mane: but thou,
Modulate me, Soul of mincing mimicry!
Make liquid treble of that bassoon, my throat;
Abase those eyes that ever loved to meet
Star-sisters answering under crescent brows;
Abate the stride, which speaks of man, and loose
A flying charm of blushes o'er this cheek,
Where they like swallows coming out of time
Will wonder why they came; but hark the bell
For dinner, let us go!"
                    And in we stream'd
Among the columns, pacing staid and still
By twos and threes, till all from end to end
With beauties every shade of brown and fair,
In colors gayer than the morning mist,
The long hall glitter'd like a bed of flowers.

How might a man not wander from his wits
Pierced thro' with eyes, but that I kept mine own
Intent on her, who past in glorious dreams,
The second-sight of some Astræan age,
Sat compass'd with professors: they, the while,
Discuss'd a doubt and tost it to and fro:
A clamor thicken'd, mixt with inmost terms
Of art and science: Lady Blanche alone
Of faded form and haughtiest lineaments,
With all her Autumn tresses falsely brown,
Shot sidelong daggers at us, a tiger-cat
In act to spring.
                    At last a solemn grace
Concluded, and we sought the gardens: there
One walk'd reciting by herself, and one
In this hand held a volume as to read,
And smoothed a petted peacock down with that:
Some to a low song oar'd a shallop by,
Or under arches of the marble bridge
Hung, shadow'd from the heat: some hid and sought
In the orange thickets: others tost a ball
Above the fountain-jets, and back again
With laughter: others lay about the lawns,
Of the older sort, and murmur'd that their May
Was passing: what was learning unto them?
They wish'd to marry; they could rule a house;
Men hated learned women: but we three
Sat muffled like the Fates; and often came
Melissa hitting all we saw with shafts
Of gentle satire, kin to charity,
That harm'd not: then day droopt; the chapel bells
Call'd us: we left the walks; we mixt with those
Six hundred maidens clad in purest white,
Before two streams of light from wall to wall,
While the great organ almost burst his pipes,
Groaning for power, and rolling thro' the court
A long melodious thunder to the sound
Of solemn psalms, and silver litanies,
The work of Ida, to call down from Heaven
A blessing on her labors for the world.

————

Sweet and low, sweet and low,
    Wind of the western sea,
Low, low, breathe and blow,
    Wind of the western sea!
Over the rolling waters go,
Come from the dying moon, and blow,
    Blow him again to me:
While my little one, while my pretty one, sleeps.

Sleep and rest, sleep and rest,
    Father will come to thee soon;
Rest, rest, on mother's breast,
    Father will come to thee soon;
Father will come to his babe in the nest,
Silver sails all out of the west
    Under the silver moon:
Sleep, my little one, sleep, my pretty one, sleep.

III.

Morn in the white wake of the morning star
Came furrowing all the orient into gold.
We rose, and each by other drest with care
Descended to the court that lay three parts
In shadow, but the Muses' heads were touch'd
Above the darkness from their native East.

There while we stood beside the fount, and watch'd
Or seem'd to watch the dancing bubble, approach'd
Melissa, tinged with wan from lack of sleep,
Or grief, and glowing round her dewy eyes
The circled Iris of a night of tears;
"And fly," she cried, "O fly, while yet you may!
My mother knows:" and when I ask'd her "how,"
"My fault," she wept, "my fault! and yet not mine;
Yet mine in part. O hear me, pardon me.
My mother, 't is her wont from night to night

To rail at Lady Psyche and her side.
She says the Princess should have been the Head,
Herself and Lady Psyche the two arms;
And so it was agreed when first they came;
But Lady Psyche was the right hand now,
And she the left, or not, or seldom used;
Hers more than half the students, all the love.
And so last night she fell to canvass you:
'Her countrywomen! she did not envy her.
Who ever saw such wild barbarians?
Girls?—more like men!' and at these words the
            snake,
My secret, seem'd to stir within my breast;
And O, Sirs, could I help it, but my cheek
Began to burn and burn, and her lynx eye
To fix and make me hotter, till she laugh'd:
'O marvellously modest maiden, you!
Men! girls, like men! why, if they had been men
You need not set your thoughts in rubric thus
For wholesale comment.' Pardon, I am shamed
That I must needs repeat for my excuse
What looks so little graceful: 'men' (for still
My mother went revolving on the word)
'And so they are,—very like men indeed—
And with that woman closeted for hours!'
'Why—these—are—men?' I shudder'd: 'and you
            know it.'
Then came these dreadful words out one by one,
'O ask me nothing,' I said: 'And she knows too,
And she conceals it.' So my mother clutch'd
The truth at once, but with no word from me;
And now thus early risen she goes to inform
The Princess: Lady Psyche will be crush'd;
But you may yet be saved, and therefore fly;
But heal me with your pardon ere you go."

   "What pardon, sweet Melissa, for a blush?"
Said Cyril: "Pale one, blush again: than wear
Those lilies, better blush our lives away.
Yet let us breathe for one hour more in Heaven,"
He added, "lest some classic Angel speak
In scorn of us, 'they mounted, Ganymedes,
To tumble, Vulcans, on the second morn.'
But I will melt this marble into wax
To yield us farther furlough:" and he went.

   Melissa shook her doubtful curls, and thought
He scarce would prosper. "Tell us," Florian ask'd,
"How grew this feud betwixt the right and left."
"O long ago," she said, "betwixt these two
Division smoulders hidden: 't is my mother,
Too jealous, often fitful as the wind
Pent in a crevice: much I bear with her:
I never knew my father, but she says
(God help her) she was wedded to a fool;
And still she rail'd against the state of things.
She had the care of Lady Ida's youth,
And from the Queen's decease she brought her up.
But when your sister came she won the heart
Of Ida: they were still together, grew
(For so they said themselves) inosculated;
Consonant chords that shiver to one note:
One mind in all things: yet my mother still
Affirms your Psyche thieved her theories,
And angled with them for her pupil's love:
She calls her plagiarist; I know not what:
But I must go: I dare not tarry," and light,
As flies the shadow of a bird, she fled.

   Then murmur'd Florian, gazing after her:
"An open-hearted maiden, true and pure.
If I could love, why this were she: how pretty
Her blushing was, and how she blush'd again,
As if to close with Cyril's random wish:
Not like your Princess cramm'd with erring pride,
Nor like poor Psyche whom she drags in tow."

   "The crane," I said, "may chatter of the crane,
The dove may murmur of the dove, but I

An eagle clang an eagle to the sphere.
My princess, O my princess! true she errs,
But in her own grand way; being herself
Three times more noble than three-score of men,
She sees herself in every woman else,
And so she wears her error like a crown
To blind the truth and me: for her, and her,
Hebes are they to hand ambrosia, mix
The nectar; but—ah she—whene'er she moves
The Samian Here rises and she speaks
A Memnon smitten with the morning Sun."

   So saying, from the court we paced, and gain'd
The terrace ranged along the Northern front,
And leaning there on those balusters, high
Above the empurpled champaign, drank the gale
That blown about the foliage underneath,
And sated with the innumerable rose,
Beat balm upon our eyelids. Hither came
Cyril, and yawning "O hard task," he cried:
"No fighting shadows here! I forced a way
Thro' solid opposition crabb'd and gnarl'd.
Better to clear prime forests, heave and thump
A league of street in summer solstice down,
Than hammer at this reverend gentlewoman.
I knock'd and, bidden, enter'd; found her there
At point to move, and settled in her eyes
The green malignant light of coming storm.
Sir, I was courteous, every phrase well-oil'd,
As man's could be; yet maiden-meek I pray'd
Concealment: she demanded who we were,
And why we came? I fabled nothing fair,
But, your example pilot, told her all.
Up went the hush'd amaze of hand and eye,
But when I dwelt upon your old affiance,
She answer'd sharply that I talk'd astray.
I urged the fierce inscription on the gate,
And our three lives. True—we had limed ourselves,
With open eyes, and we must take the chance.
But such extremes, I told her, well might harm
The woman's cause. 'Not more than now,' she
            said,
'So puddled as it is with favoritism.'
I tried the mother's heart. Shame might befall
Melissa, knowing, saying not she knew:
Her answer was, 'Leave me to deal with that.'
I spoke of war to come and many deaths,
And she replied, her duty was to speak,
And duty duty, clear of consequences.
I grew discouraged, Sir, but since I knew
No rock so hard but that a little wave
May beat admission in a thousand years,
I recommenced: 'Decide not ere you pause.
I find you here but in the second place,
Some say the third—the authentic foundress you.
I offer boldly: we will seat you highest:
Wink at our advent: help my prince to gain
His rightful bride, and here I promise you
Some palace in our land, where you shall reign
The head and heart of all our fair she-world,
And your great name flow on with broadening time
Forever.' Well, she balanced this a little,
And told me she would answer us to-day,
Meantime be mute: thus much, nor more I gain'd."

   He ceasing, came a message from the Head.
"That afternoon the Princess rode to take
The dip of certain strata to the North.
Would we go with her? we should find the land
Worth seeing; and the river made a fall
Out yonder;" then she pointed on to where
A double hill ran up his furrowy forks
Beyond the thick-leaved platans of the vale.

   Agreed to, this, the day fled on thro' all
Its range of duties to the appointed hour.
Then summon'd to the porch we went. She stood
Among her maidens, higher by the head,

Her back against a pillar, her foot on one
Of those tame leopards. Kittenlike he roll'd
And paw'd about her sandal. I drew near;
I gazed. On a sudden my strange seizure came
Upon me, the weird vision of our house:
The Princess Ida seem'd a hollow show,
Her gay-furr'd cats a painted fantasy,
Her college and her maidens, empty masks,
And I myself the shadow of a dream,
For all things were and were not. Yet I felt
My heart beat thick with passion and with awe;
Then from my breast the involuntary sigh
Brake, as she smote me with the light of eyes
That lent my knee desire to kneel, and shook
My pulses, till to horse we got, and so
Went forth in long retinue following up
The river as it narrow'd to the hills.

I rode beside her and to me she said:
"O friend, we trust that you esteem'd us not
Too harsh to your companion yester-morn;
Unwillingly we spake." "No—not to her,"
I answer'd, "but to one of whom we spake
Your Highness might have seem'd the thing you say."
"Again?" she cried, "are you ambassadresses
From him to me? we give you, being strange,
A license: speak, and let the topic die."

I stammer'd that I knew him—could have wish'd—
"Our king expects—was there no precontract?
There is no truer-hearted—ah, you seem
All he prefigured, and he could not see
The bird of passage flying south but long'd
To follow: surely, if your Highness keep
Your purport, you will shock him ev'n to death,
Or baser courses, children of despair."

"Poor boy," she said, "can he not read — no
     books?
Quoit, tennis, ball—no games? nor deals in that
Which men delight in, martial exercise?
To nurse a blind ideal like a girl,
Methinks he seems no better than a girl;
As girls were once, as we ourself have been:
We had our dreams—perhaps he mixt with them:
We touch on our dead self, nor shun to do it,
Being other—since we learnt our meaning here,
To lift the woman's fall'n divinity,
Upon an even pedestal with man."

She paused, and added with a haughtier smile:
"And as to precontracts, we move, my friend,
At no man's beck, but know ourself and thee,
O Vashti, noble Vashti! Summon'd out
She kept her state, and left the drunken king
To brawl at Shushan underneath the palms."

"Alas your Highness breathes full East," I said,
"On that which leans to you. I know the Prince,
I prize his truth: and then how vast a work
To assail this gray pre-eminence of man!
You grant me license; might I use it? think,
Ere half be done perchance your life may fail;
Then comes the feebler heiress of your plan,
And takes and ruins all; and thus your pains
May only make that footprint upon sand
Which old-recurring waves of prejudice
Resmooth to nothing: might I dread that you,
With only Fame for spouse and your great deeds
For issue, yet may live in vain, and miss,
Meanwhile, what every woman counts her due,
Love, children, happiness?"
             And she exclaim'd,
"Peace, you young savage of the Northern wild!
What! tho' your Prince's love were like a God's,
Have we not made ourself the sacrifice?
You are bold indeed: we are not talk'd to thus:
Yet will we say for children, would they grew,

Like field-flowers everywhere! we like them well:
But children die; and let me tell you, girl,
Howe'er you babble, great deeds cannot die:
They with the sun and moon renew their light
Forever, blessing those that look on them.
Children—that men may pluck them from our hearts,
Kill us with pity, break us with ourselves—
O—children—there is nothing upon earth
More miserable than she that has a son
And sees him err: nor would we work for fame:
Tho' she perhaps might reap the applause of Great,
Who learns the one roû sto whence afterhands
May move the world, tho' she herself effect
But little: wherefore up and act, nor shrink
For fear our solid aim be dissipated
By frail successors. Would, indeed, we had been,
In lieu of many mortal flies, a race
Of giants living, each, a thousand years,
That we might see our own work out, and watch
The sandy footprint harden into stone."

I answer'd nothing, doubtful in myself
If that strange Poet-princess with her grand
Imaginations might at all be won.
And she broke out interpreting my thoughts:

"No doubt we seem a kind of monster to you;
We are used to that: for women, up till this
Cramp'd under worse than South-sea-isle taboo,
Dwarfs of the gynæceum, fail so far
In high desire, they know not, cannot guess
How much their welfare is a passion to us.
If we could give them surer, quicker proof—
O if our end were less achievable
By slow approaches, than by single act
Of immolation, any phase of death,
We were as prompt to spring against the pikes,
Or down the fiery gulf as talk of it,
To compass our dear sisters' liberties."

She bow'd as if to veil a noble tear;
And up we came to where the river sloped
To plunge in cataract, shattering on black blocks
A breath of thunder. O'er it shook the woods,
And danced the color, and, below, stuck out
The bones of some vast bulk that lived and roar'd
Before man was. She gazed awhile and said,
"As these rude bones to us, are we to her
That will be." "Dare we dream of that," I ask'd,
"Which wrought us, as the workman and his work,
That practice betters?" "How," she cried, "you love
The metaphysics! read and earn our prize,
A golden broach: beneath an emerald plane
Sits Diotima, teaching him that died
Of hemlock; our device; wrought to the life;
She rapt upon her subject, he on her:
For there are schools for all." "And yet," I said,
"Methinks I have not found among them all
One anatomic." "Nay, we thought of that,"
She answer'd, "but it pleased us not: in truth
We shudder but to dream our maids should ape
Those monstrous males that carve the living hound,
And cram him with the fragments of the grave,
Or in the dark dissolving human heart,
And holy secrets of this microcosm,
Dabbling a shameless hand with shameful jest,
Encarnalize their spirits: yet we know
Knowledge is knowledge, and this matter hangs:
Howbeit ourself, foreseeing casualty,
Nor willing men should come among us, learnt,
For many weary moons before we came,
This craft of healing. Were you sick, ourself
Would tend upon you. To your question now,
Which touches on the workman and his work.
Let there be light and there was light: 't is so:
For was, and is, and will be, are but is;
And all creation is one act at once,
The birth of light: but we that are not all,

As parts, can see but parts, now this, now that,
And live, perforce, from thought to thought, and
make
One act a phantom of succession: thus
Our weakness somehow shapes the shadow, Time;
But in the shadow will we work, and mould
The woman to the fuller day."
                                        She spake
With kindled eyes: we rode a league beyond,
And, o'er a bridge of pinewood crossing, came
On flowery levels underneath the crag,
Full of all beauty. "O how sweet," I said,
(For I was half-oblivious of my mask,)
"To linger here with one that loved us." "Yea,"
She answer'd, "or with fair philosophies
That lift the fancy; for indeed these fields
Are lovely, lovelier not the Elysian lawns,
Where paced the Demigods of old, and saw
The soft white vapor streak the crowned towers
Built to the Sun:" then, turning to her maids,
"Pitch our pavilion here upon the sward;
Lay out the viands." At the word, they raised
A tent of satin, elaborately wrought
With fair Corinna's triumph: here she stood.
Engirt with many a florid maiden-cheek.
The woman-conqueror: woman-conquer'd there
The bearded Victor of ten-thousand hymns,
And all the men mourn'd at his side: but we
Set forth to climb; then, climbing, Cyril kept
With Psyche, with Melissa Florian. I
With mine affianced. Many a little hand
Glanced like a touch of sunshine on the rocks,
Many a light foot shone like a jewel set
In the dark crag: and then we turn'd, we wound
About the cliffs, the copses, out and in,
Hammering and clinking, chattering stony names
Of shale and hornblende, rag and trap and tuff,
Amygdaloid and trachyte, till the Sun
Grew broader toward his death and fell, and all
The rosy heights came out above the lawns.

　　　The splendor falls on castle walls
　　　　And snowy summits old in story:
　　　The long light shakes across the lakes
　　　　And the wild cataract leaps in glory.
Blow, bugle, blow, set the wild echoes flying,
Blow, bugle; answer, echoes, dying, dying, dying.

　　　O hark, O hear! how thin and clear,
　　　　And thinner, clearer, farther going!
　　　O sweet and far from cliff and scar
　　　　The horns of Elfland faintly blowing!
Blow, let us hear the purple glens replying:
Blow, bugle; answer, echoes, dying, dying, dying.

　　　O love, they die in yon rich sky,
　　　　They faint on hill or field or river:
　　　Our echoes roll from soul to soul,
　　　　And grow forever and forever.
Blow, bugle, blow, set the wild echoes flying,
And answer, echoes, answer, dying, dying, dying.

IV.

"THERE sinks the nebulous star we call the Sun,
If that hypothesis of theirs be sound,"
Said Ida; "let us down and rest:" and we
Down from the lean and wrinkled precipices,
By every coppice-feather'd chasm and cleft,
Dropt thro' the ambrosial gloom to where below
No bigger than a glow-worm shone the tent
Lamp-lit from the inner. Once she lean'd on me,
Descending; once or twice she lent her hand,
And blissful palpitations in the blood,
Stirring a sudden transport rose and fell.

But when we planted level feet, and dipt
Beneath the satin dome and enter'd in,

There leaning deep in broider'd down we sank
Our elbows: on a tripod in the midst
A fragrant flame rose, and before us glow'd
Fruit, blossom, viand, amber wine, and gold.

Then she, "Let some one sing to us: lightlier
move
The minutes fledged with music:" and a maid,
Of those beside her, smote her harp, and sang.

"Tears, idle tears, I know not what they mean,
Tears from the depth of some divine despair
Rise in the heart, and gather to the eyes,
In looking on the happy Autumn-fields,
And thinking of the days that are no more.

"Fresh as the first beam glittering on a sail,
That brings our friends up from the underworld,
Sad as the last which reddens over one
That sinks with all we love below the verge:
So sad, so fresh, the days that are no more.

"Ah, sad and strange as in dark summer dawns
The earliest pipe of half-awaken'd birds
To dying ears, when unto dying eyes
The casement slowly grows a glimmering square;
So sad, so strange, the days that are no more.

"Dear as remember'd kisses after death,
And sweet as those by hopeless fancy feign'd
On lips that are for others: deep as love,
Deep as first love, and wild with all regret;
O Death in Life, the days that are no more."

She ended with such passion that the tear,
She sang of, shook and fell, an erring pearl
Lost in her bosom: but with some disdain
Answer'd the Princess: "If indeed there haunt
About the moulder'd lodges of the Past
So sweet a voice and vague, fatal to men,
Well needs it we should cram our ears with wool
And so pace by: but thine are fancies hatch'd
In silken-folded idleness; nor is it
Wiser to weep a true occasion lost,
But trim our sails, and let old bygones be,
While down the streams that float us each and all
To the issue, goes, like glittering bergs of ice,
Throne after throne, and molten on the waste
Becomes a cloud: for all things serve their time
Toward that great year of equal mights and rights,
Nor would I fight with iron laws, in the end
Found golden: let the past be past; let be
Their cancell'd Babels: tho' the rough kex break
The starr'd mosaic, and the wild goat hang
Upon the shaft, and the wild fig-tree split
Their monstrous idols, care not while we hear
A trumpet in the distance pealing news
Of better, and Hope, a poising eagle, burns
Above the unrisen morrow:" then to me,
"Know you no song of your own land," she said,
"Not such as moans about the retrospect,
But deals with the other distance and the lines
Of promise; not a death's-head at the wine."

Then I remember'd one myself had made,
What time I watch'd the swallow winging south
From mine own land, part made long since, and
part
Now while I sang, and maidenlike as far
As I could ape their treble, did I sing.

"O Swallow, Swallow, flying, flying South,
Fly to her, and fall upon her gilded eaves,
And tell her, tell her what I tell to thee.

"O tell her, Swallow, thou that knowest each,
That bright and fierce and fickle is the South,
And dark and true and tender is the North.

"O Swallow, Swallow, if I could follow and light
Upon her lattice, I would pipe and trill,
And cheep and twitter twenty million loves.

"O were I thou that she might take me in,
And lay me on her bosom, and her heart
Would rock the snowy cradle till I died.

"Why lingereth she to clothe her heart with love,
Delaying as the tender ash delays
To clothe herself, when all the woods are green?

"O tell her, Swallow, that thy brood is flown:
Say to her, I do but wanton in the South,
But in the North long since my nest is made.

"O tell her, brief is life, but love is long,
And brief the sun of summer in the North,
And brief the moon of beauty in the South.

"O Swallow, flying from the golden woods,
Fly to her, and pipe and woo her, and make her
    mine,
And tell her, tell her, that I follow thee."

    I ceased, and all the ladies, each at each,
Like the Ithacensian suitors in old time,
Stared with great eyes, and laugh'd with alien lips,
And knew not what they meant; for still my voice
Rang false: but smiling, "Not for thee," she said.
"O Bulbul, any rose of Gulistan
Shall burst her veil: marsh-divers, rather, maid,
Shall croak thee sister, or the meadow-crake
Grate her harsh kindred in the grass: and this
A mere love poem! O for such, my friend,
We hold them slight: they mind us of the time
When we made bricks in Egypt. Knaves are men,
That lute and flute fantastic tenderness,
And dress the victim to the offering up,
And paint the gates of Hell with Paradise,
And play the slave to gain the tyranny.
Poor soul! I had a maid of honor once:
She wept her true eyes blind for such a one,
A rogue of canzonets and serenades. ·
I loved her. Peace be with her. She is dead.
So they blaspheme the muse! but great is song
Used to great ends: ourself have often tried
Valkyrian hymns, or into rhythm have dash'd
The passion of the prophetess; for song
Is duer unto freedom, force and growth
Of spirit, than to junketing and love.
Love is it? Would this same mock-love, and this
Mock-Hymen were laid up like winter bats,
Till all men grew to rate us at our worth,
Not vassals to be beat, nor pretty babes
To be dandled, no, but living wills, and sphered
Whole in ourselves and owed to none. Enough!
But now to leaven play with profit, you,
Know you no song, the true growth of your soil,
That gives the manners of your countrywomen?"

    She spoke and turn'd her sumptuous head with
    eyes
Of shining expectation fixt on mine.
Then while I dragg'd my brains for such a song,
Cyril, with whom the bell-mouth'd flask had wrought,
Or master'd by the sense of sport, began
To troll a careless, careless tavern-catch
Of Moll and Meg, and strange experiences
Unmeet for ladies. Florian nodded at him,
I frowning; Psyche flush'd and wann'd and shook;
The lilylike Melissa droop'd her brows;
"Forbear." the Princess cried; "Forbear, Sir," I:
And heated thro' and thro' with wrath and love,
I smote him on the breast; he started up;
There rose a shriek as of a city sack'd;
Melissa clamor'd, "Flee the death;" "To horse,"
Said Ida; "home! to horse!" and fled, as flies

A troop of snowy doves athwart the dusk,
When some one batters at the dovecote doors,
Disorderly the women. Alone I stood
With Florian, cursing Cyril, vext at heart,
In the pavilion: there like parting hopes
I heard them passing from me: hoof by hoof,
And every hoof a knell to my desires,
Clang'd on the bridge; and then another shriek,
"The Head, the Head, the Princess, O the Head!"
For blind with rage she miss'd the plank, and roll'd
In the river. Out I sprang from glow to gloom:
There whirl'd her white robe like a blossom'd branch
Rapt to the horrible fall: a glance I gave,
No more; but woman-vested as I was
Plunged; and the flood drew; yet I caught her;
    then
Oaring one arm, and bearing in my left
The weight of all the hopes of half the world,
Strove to buffet to land in vain. A tree
Was half-disrooted from his place and stoop'd
To drench his dark locks in the gurgling wave
Mid-channel. Right on this we drove and caught,
And grasping down the boughs I gain'd the shore.

    There stood her maidens glimmeringly group'd
In the hollow bank. One reaching forward drew
My burthen from mine arms; they cried, "She
    lives!"
They bore her back into the tent; but I,
So much a kind of shame within me wrought,
Not yet endured to meet her opening eyes,
Nor found my friends; but push'd alone on foot
(For since her horse was lost I left her mine)
Across the woods, and less from Indian craft
Than beelike instinct hiveward, found at length
The garden portals. Two great statues, Art
And Science, Caryatids. lifted up
A weight of emblem, and betwixt were valves
Of open-work in which the hunter rued
His rash intrusion, manlike, but his brows
Had sprouced. and the branches thereupon
Spread out at top, and grimly spiked the gates.

    A little space was left between the horns.
Thro' which I clamber'd o'er at top with pain,
Dropt on the sward, and up the linden walks,
And, tost on thoughts that changed from hue to hue,
Now poring on the glow-worm, now the star,
I paced the terrace till the bear had wheel'd
Thro' a great arc his seven slow suns.

.   A step
Of lightest echo, then a loftier form
Than female, moving thro' the uncertain gloom,
Disturb'd me with the doubt "if this were she,"
But it was Florian. "Hist, O hist," he said,
"They seek us: out so late is out of rules.
Moreover 'Seize the strangers' is the cry.
How came you here?" I told him: "I," said he,
"Last of the train, a moral leper, I,
To whom none spake, half-sick at heart, return'd,
Arriving all confused among the rest
With hooded brows I crept into the hall,
And, couch'd behind a Judith, underneath
The head of Holofernes peep'd and saw.
Girl after girl was call'd to trial: each
Disclaim'd all knowledge of us: last of all,
Melissa: trust me, Sir. I pitied her.
She, question'd if she knew us men, at first
Was silent; closer prest, denied it not:
And then, demanded if her mother knew,
Or Psyche, she affirm'd not, or denied:
From whence the Royal mind, familiar with her,
Easily gather'd either guilt. She sent
For Psyche, but she was not there: she call'd
For Psyche's child to cast it from the doors;
She sent for Blanche to accuse her face to face,
And I slipt out: but whither will you now?
And where are Psyche, Cyril? both are fled:

What, if together? that were not so well.
Would rather we had never come! I dread
His wildness, and the chances of the dark."

"And yet," I said, "you wrong him more than I
That struck him: this is proper to the clown,
Tho' smock'd, or furr'd and purpled, still the clown,
To harm the thing that trusts him, and to shame
That which he says he loves: for Cyril, howe'er
He deal in frolic, as to-night—the song
Might have been worse and sinn'd in grosser lips
Beyond all pardon—as it is, I hold
These flashes on the surface are not he.
He has a solid base of temperament:
But as the water-lily starts and slides
Upon the level in little puffs of wind,
Tho' anchor'd to the bottom, such is he."

Scarce had I ceased when from a tamarisk near
Two Proctors leapt upon us, crying, "Names,"
He, standing still, was clutch'd; but I began
To thrid the musky-circled mazes, wind
And double in and out the boles, and race
By all the fountains: fleet I was of foot:
Before me shower'd the rose in flakes; behind
I heard the puff'd pursuer; at mine ear
Bubbled the nightingale and heeded not,
And secret laughter tickled all my soul.
At last I hook'd my ankle in a vine,
That claspt the feet of a Mnemosyne,
And falling on my face was caught and known.

They haled us to the Princess where she sat
High in the hall: above her droop'd a lamp,
And made the single jewel on her brow
Burn like the mystic fire on a mast-head,
Prophet of storm: a handmaid on each side
Bow'd toward her, combing out her long black hair
Damp from the river: and close behind her stood
Eight daughters of the plough, stronger than men,
Huge women blowzed with health, and wind, and rain,
And labor. Each was like a Druid rock;
Or like a spire of land that stands apart
Cleft from the main, and wail'd about with mews.

Then, as we came, the crowd dividing clove
An advent to the throne; and there-beside,
Half-naked, as if caught at once from bed
And tumbled on the purple footcloth, lay
The lily-shining child; and on the left,
Bow'd on her palms and folded up from wrong,
Her round white shoulder shaken with her sobs,
Melissa knelt; but Lady Blanche erect
Stood up and spake, an affluent orator.

"It was not thus, O Princess, in old days:
You prized my counsel, lived upon my lips: ·
I led you then to all the Castalies;
I fed you with the milk of every Muse;
I loved you like this kneeler, and you me
Your second mother: those were gracious times.
Then came your new friend: you began to change—
I saw it and grieved—to slacken and to cool;
Till taken with her seeming openness
You turned your warmer currents all to her,
To me you froze: this was my meed for all.
Yet I bore up in part from ancient love,
And partly that I hoped to win you back,
And partly conscious of my own deserts,
And partly that you were my civil head,
And chiefly you were born for something great,
In which I might your fellow-worker be,
When time should serve; and thus a noble scheme
Grew up from seed we two long since had sown;
In us true growth, in her a Jonah's gourd,
Up in one night and due to sudden sun:
We took this palace; but even from the first

You stood in your own light and darken'd mine.
What student came but that you planed her path
To Lady Psyche, younger, not so wise,
A foreigner, and I your countrywoman,
I your old friend and tried, she new in all?
But still her lists were swell'd and mine were lean:
Yet I bore up in hope she would be known:
Then came these wolves: they knew her: they endured,
Long-closeted with her the yester-morn,
To tell her what they were, and she to hear:
And me none told: not less to an eye like mine,
A lidless watcher of the public weal,
Last night, their mask was patent, and my foot
Was to you: but I thought again: I fear'd
To meet a cold 'We thank you, we shall hear of it
From Lady Psyche:' you had gone to her,
She told, perforce: and winning easy grace,
No doubt, for slight delay, remain'd among us
In our young nursery still unknown, the stem
Less grain than touchwood, while my honest heat
Were all miscounted as malignant haste
To push my rival out of place and power.
But public use required she should be known;
And since my oath was ta'en for public use,
I broke the letter of it to keep the sense.
I spoke not then at first, but watch'd them well,
Saw that they kept apart, no mischief done;
And yet this day (tho' you should hate me for it)
I came to tell you: found that you had gone,
Ridd'n to the hills, she likewise: now, I thought,
That surely she will speak; if not, then I:
Did she? These monsters blazon'd what they were,
According to the coarseness of their kind,
For thus I hear; and known at last (my work)
And full of cowardice and guilty shame,
I grant in her some sense of shame, she flies;
And I remain on whom to wreak your rage,
I, that have lent my life to build up yours,
I that have wasted here health, wealth, and time, ·
And talents, I—you know it—I will not boast·
Dismiss me, and I prophesy your plan,
Divorced from my experience, will be chaff
For every gust of chance, and men will say
We did not know the real light, but chased
The wisp that flickers where no foot can tread."

She ceased: the Princess answer'd coldly "Good:
Your oath is broken: we dismiss you: go.
For this lost lamb (she pointed to the child)
Our mind is changed: we take it to ourself."

Therent the Lady stretch'd a vulture throat,
And shot from crooked lips a haggard smile.
"The plan was mine. I built the nest," she said,
"To hatch the cuckoo. Rise!" and stoop'd to updrag
Melissa: she, half on her mother prept,
Half-drooping from her, turn'd her face, and cast
A liquid look on Ida, full of prayer,
Which melted Florian's fancy as she hung,
A Niobëan daughter, one arm out,
Appealing to the bolts of Heaven; and while
We gazed upon her came a little stir
About the doors, and on a sudden rush'd
Among us, out of breath, as one pursued,
A woman-post in flying raiment. Fear
Stared in her eyes, and chalk'd her face, and wing'd
Her transit to the throne, whereby she fell
Delivering seal'd despatches which the Head
Took half-amazed, and in her lion's mood
Tore open, silent we with blind surmise
Regarding, while she read, till over brow
And cheek and bosom brake the wrathful bloom
As of some fire against a stormy cloud,
When the wild peasant rights himself, the rick
Flames, and his anger reddens in the heavens;
For anger most it seem'd, while now her breast,
Beaten with some great passion at her heart.

Palpitated, her hand shook, and we heard
In the dead hush the papers that she held
Rustle: at once the lost lamb at her feet
Sent out a bitter bleating for its dam;
The plaintive cry jarr'd on her ire: she crush'd
The scrolls together, made a sudden turn
As if to speak, but, utterance failing her,
She whirl'd them on to me, as who should say
"Read," and I read—two letters—one her sire's.

"Fair daughter, when we sent the Prince your way
We knew not your ungracious laws, which learnt,
We, conscious of your temper you are built,
Came all in haste to hinder wrong, but fell
Into his father's hands, who has this night,
You lying close upon his territory,
Slipt round and in the dark invested you,
And here he keeps me hostage for his son."

The second was my father's, running thus:
"You have our son: touch not a hair of his head:
Render him up unscathed: give him your hand:
Cleave to your contract: tho' indeed we hear
You hold the woman is the better man;
A rampant heresy, such as if it spread
Would make all women kick against their lords
Thro' all the world, and which might well deserve
That we this night should pluck your palace down;
And we will do it, unless you send us back
Our son, on the instant, whole."

                          So far I read;
And then stood up and spoke impetuously.

"O not to pry and peer on your reserve,
But led by golden wishes, and a hope
The child of regal compact, did I break
Your precinct: not a scorner of your sex
But venerator, zealous it should be
All that it might be; hear me, for I bear,
Tho' man, yet human, whatsoe'er your wrongs,
From the flaxen curl to the gray lock a life
Less mine than yours: my nurse would tell me of
    you:
I babbled for you, as babies for the moon,
Vague brightness; when a boy, you stoop'd to me
From all high places, lived in all fair lights,
Came in long breezes rapt from inmost south
And blown to inmost north; at eve and dawn
With Ida, Ida, Ida, rang the woods;
The leader wildswan in among the stars
Would clang it, and lapt in wreaths of glow-worm
    light
The mellow breaker murmur'd Ida. Now,
Because I would have reach'd you, had you been
Sphered up with Cassiopëia, or the enthroned
Persephone in Hades, now at length,
Those winters of abeyance all worn out,
A man I came to see you: but, indeed,
Not in this frequence can I lend full tongue,
O noble Ida, to those thoughts that wait
On you, their centre: let me say but this,
That many a famous man and woman, town
And landskip, have I heard of, after seen
The dwarfs of prestige; tho' when known, there grew
Another kind of beauty in detail
Made them worth knowing; but in you I found
My boyish dream involved and dazzled down
And master'd, while that after-beauty makes
Such head from act to act, from hour to hour,
Within me, that except you slay me here,
According to your bitter statute-book,
I can not cease to follow you, as they say
The seal does music; who desire you more
Than growing boys their manhood; dying lips,
With many thousand matters left to do,
The breath of life; O more than poor men wealth,
Than sick men health—yours, yours, not mine—but
    half

Without you, with you, whole; and of those halves
You worthiest; and howe'er you block and bar
Your heart with system out from mine, I hold
That it becomes no man to nurse despair,
But in the teeth of clench'd antagonisms
To follow up the worthiest till he die:
Yet that I came not all unauthorized
Behold your father's letter."

                          On one knee
Kneeling, I gave it, which she caught, and dash'd
Unopen'd at her feet: a tide of fierce
Invective seem'd to wait behind her lips,
As waits a river level with the dam
Ready to burst and flood the world with foam;
And so she would have spoken, but there rose
A hubbub in the court of half the maids
Gather'd together: from the illumined hall
Long lanes of splendor slanted o'er a press
Of snowy shoulders, thick as herded ewes,
And rainbow robes, and gems and gem-like eyes,
And gold and golden heads; they to and fro
Fluctuated, as flowers in storm, some red, some pale,
All open-mouth'd, all gazing to the light,
Some crying there was an army in the land,
And some that men were in the very walls,
And some they cared not; till a clamor grew
As of a new-world Babel, woman-built,
And worse confounded: high above them stood
The placid marble Muses, looking peace.

Not peace she look'd, the Head: but rising up
Robed in the long night of her deep hair, so
To the open window moved, remaining there
Fixt like a beacon-tower above the waves
Of tempest, when the crimson-rolling eye
Glares ruin, and the wild birds on the light
Dash themselves dead. She stretch'd her arms and
    call'd
Across the tumult and the tumult fell.

"What fear ye brawlers? am not I your Head?
On me, me, me, the storm first breaks: I dare
All these male thunderbolts: what is it ye fear?
Peace! there are those to avenge us and they come:
If not,—myself were like enough, O girls,
To unfurl the maiden banner of our rights,
And clad in iron burst the ranks of war,
Or, falling, protomartyr of our cause,
Die: yet I blame ye not so much for fear;
Six thousand years of fear have made ye that
From which I would redeem ye: but for those
That stir this hubbub—you and you—I know
Your faces there in the crowd—to-morrow morn
We hold a great convention: then shall they
That love their voices more than duty, learn
With whom they deal, dismiss'd in shame to live
No wiser than their mothers, household stuff,
Live chattels, mincers of each other's fame,
Full of weak poison, turnspits for the clown,
The drunkard's football, laughing-stocks of Time,
Whose brains are in their hands and in their heels,
But fit to flaunt, to dress, to dance, to thrum,
To tramp, to scream, to burnish, and to scour,
Forever slaves at home and fools abroad."

She, ending, waved her hands: thereat the crowd
Muttering dissolved: then with a smile, that look'd
A stroke of cruel sunshine on the cliff,
When all the glens are drown'd in azure gloom
Of thunder-shower, she floated to us and said:

"You have done well and like a gentleman,
And like a prince: you have our thanks for all:
And you look well too in your woman's dress:
Well have you done and like a gentleman.
You saved our life: we owe you bitter thanks:
Better have died and spilt our bones in the flood—
Then men had said—but now—What hinders me

To take such bloody vengeance on you both?—
Yet since our father—Wasps in our good hive,
You would-be quenchers of the light to be,
Barbarians, grosser than your native bears—
O would I had his sceptre for one hour!
You that have dared to break our bound, and gull'd
Our servants, wrong'd and lied and thwarted us—
I wed with thee! *I* bound by precontract
Your bride, your bondslave! not tho' all the gold
That veins the world were pack'd to make your
crown,
And every spoken tongue should lord you. Sir,
Your falsehood and yourself are hateful to us:
I trample on your offers and on you:
Begone: we will not look upon you more.
Here, push them out at gates."
                                In wrath she spake.
Then those eight mighty daughters of the plough
Bent their broad faces toward us and address'd
Their motion: twice I sought to plead my cause,
But on my shoulder hung their heavy hands,
The weight of destiny: so from her face
They push'd us, down the steps, and thro' the court,
And with grim laughter thrust us out at gates.

We cross'd the street and gain'd a petty mound
Beyond it, whence we saw the lights and heard
The voices murmuring. While I listen'd, came
On a sudden the weird seizure and the doubt:
I seem'd to move among a world of ghosts;
The Princess with her monstrous woman-guard,
The jest and earnest working side by side,
The cataract and the tumult and the kings
Were shadows; and the long fantastic night
With all its doings had and had not been,
And all things were and were not.
                                This went by
As strangely as it came, and on my spirits
Settled a gentle cloud of melancholy;
Not long; I shook it off; for spite of doubts
And sudden ghostly shadowings I was one
To whom the touch of all mischance but came
As night to him that sitting on a hill
Sees the midsummer, midnight, Norway sun
Set into sunrise: then we moved away.

Thy voice is heard thro' rolling drums,
    That beat to battle where he stands;
Thy face across his fancy comes,
    And gives the battle to his hands:
A moment, while the trumpets blow,
    He sees his brood about thy knee;
The next, like fire he meets the foe,
    And strikes him dead for thine and thee.

So Lilia sang: we thought her half-possess'd,
She struck such warbling fury thro' the words;
And, after, feigning pique at what she call'd
The raillery, or grotesque, or false sublime—
Like one that wishes at a dance to change
The music—clapt her hands and cried for war,
Or some grand fight to kill and make an end:
And he that next inherited the tale
Half turning to the broken statue said,
"Sir Ralph has got your colors: if I prove
Your knight, and fight your battle, what for me?"
It chanced, her empty glove upon the tomb
Lay by her like a model of her hand.
She took it and she flung it. "Fight," she said,
"And make us all we would be, great and good."
He knightlike in his cap instead of casque,
A cap of Tyrol borrow'd from the hall,
Arranged the favor, and assumed the Prince.

V.

Now, scarce three paces measured from the mound,
We stumbled on a stationary voice,
And "Stand, who goes?" "Two from the palace," I.
                        7

"The second two: they wait," he said, "pass on:
His Highness wakes:" and one, that clash'd in arms,
By glimmering lanes and walls of canvas, led
Threading the soldier-city, till we heard
The drowsy folds of our great ensign shake
From blazon'd lions o'er the imperial tent
Whispers of war.

Entering, the sudden light
Dazed me half-blind: I stood and seem'd to hear,
As in a poplar grove when a light wind wakes
A lisping of the innumerous leaf and dies,
Each hissing in his neighbor's ear; and then
A strangled titter, out of which there brake
On all sides, clamoring etiquette to death,
Unmeasured mirth; while now the two old kings
Began to wag their baldness up and down,
The fresh young captains flash'd their glittering teeth
The huge bush-bearded Barons heaved and blew,
And slain with laughter roll'd the gilded Squire.

At length my Sire, his rough cheek wet with tears,
Panted from weary sides, "King, you are free!
We did but keep you surety for our son,
If this be he,—or a draggled mawkin, thou,
That tends her bristled grunters in the sludge:"
For I was drench'd with ooze, and torn with briers
More crumpled than a poppy from the sheath,
And all one rag, disprinced from head to heel.
Then some one sent beneath his vaulted palm
A whisper'd jest to some one near him "Look,
He has been among his shadows." "Satan take
The old woman and their shadows! (thus the King
Roar'd) make yourself a man to fight with men.
Go: Cyril told us all."

As boys that slink
From ferule and the trespass-chiding eye,
Away we stole, and transient in a trice
From what was left of faded woman-slough
To sheathing splendors and the golden scale
Of harness, issued in the sun, that now
Leapt from the dewy shoulders of the Earth,
And hit the northern hills. Here Cyril met us,
A little shy at first, but by and by
We twain, with mutual pardon ask'd and given
For stroke and song, resolder'd peace, whereon
Follow'd his tale. Amazed he fled away
Thro' the dark land, and later in the night
Had come on Psyche weeping: "then we fell
Into each other's hand, and there she lies,
But will not speak, nor stir."
                        He show'd a tent
A stone-shot off: we enter'd in, and there
Among piled arms and rough accoutrements,
Pitiful sight, wrapt in a soldier's cloak,
Like some sweet sculpture draped from head to foot,
And push'd by rude hands from its pedestal,
All her fair length upon the ground she lay:
And at her head a follower of the camp,
A charr'd and wrinkled piece of womanhood,
Sat watching like a watcher for the dead.

Then Florian knelt, and "Come," he whisper'd to
her,
"Lift up your head, sweet sister: lie not thus.
What have you done, but right? you could not slay
Me, nor your prince: look up: be comforted:
Sweet is it to have done the thing one ought,
When fall'n in darker ways." And likewise I:
"Be comforted: have I not lost her too,
In whose least act abides the nameless charm
That none has else for me?" She heard, she moved,
She moan'd, a folded voice; and up she sat,
And raised the cloak from brows as pale and smooth
As those that mourn half-shrouded over death
In deathless marble. "Her," she said, "my friend—
Parted from her—betray'd her cause and mine—
Where shall I breathe? why kept ye not your faith?
O base and bad! what comfort? none for me:"
To whom remorseful Cyril, "Yet I pray

Take comfort: live, dear lady, for your child !"
At which she lifted up her voice and cried.

"Ah me, my babe, my blossom, ah my child,
My one sweet child, whom I shall see no more !
For now will cruel Ida keep her back ;
And either she will die for want of care,
Or sicken with ill usage, when they say
The child is hers—for every little fault,
The child is hers ; and they will beat my girl
Remembering her mother: O my flower !
Or they will take her, they will make her hard,
And she will pass me by in after-life
With some cold reverence worse than were she dead.
Ill mother that I was to leave her there,
To lag behind, scared by the cry they made,
The horror of the shame among them all :
But I will go and sit beside the doors,
And make a wild petition night and day,
Until they hate to hear me like a wind
Wailing forever, till they open to me,
And lay my little blossom at my feet,
My babe, my sweet Aglaia, my one child :
And I will take her up and go my way,
And satisfy my soul with kissing her :
Ah ! what might that man not deserve of me,
Who gave me back my child ?" "Be comforted,"
Said Cyril. "you shall have it," but again
She veil'd her brows, and prone she sank, and so
Like tender things that being caught feign death,
Spoke not, nor stirr'd.

                     By this a murmur ran
Thro' all the camp and inward raced the scouts
With rumor of Prince Arac hard at hand.
We left her by the woman, and without
Found the gray kings at parle: and "Look you,"
cried
My father, "that our compact be fulfill'd
You have spoilt this child ; she laughs at you and
man :
She wrongs herself, her sex, and me, and him :
But red-faced war has rods of steel and fire ;
She yields, or war."
               Then Gama turn'd to me:
"We fear, indeed, you spent a stormy time
With our strange girl : and yet they say that still
You love her. Give us, then, your mind at large :
How say you, war or not ?"
                       "Not war, if possible,
O king," I said, "lest from the abuse of war,
The desecrated shrine, the trampled year,
The smouldering homestead, and the household flower
Torn from the lintel—all the common wrong—
A smoke go up thro' which I loom to her
Three times a monster: now she lightens scorn
At him that mars her plan, but then would hate
(And every voice she talk'd with ratify it,
And every face she look'd on justify it)
The general foe. More soluble is this knot,
By gentleness than war. I want her love.
What were I nigher this altho' we dash'd
Your cities into shards with catapults,
She would not love ;—or brought her chain'd, a slave,
The lifting of whose eyelash is my lord,
Not ever would she love ; but brooding turn
The book of scorn till all my little chance
Were caught within the record of her wrongs,
And crush'd to death : and rather, Sire, than this
I would the old god of war himself were dead,
Forgotten, rusting on his iron hills,
Rotting on some wild shore with ribs of wreck,
Or like an old-world mammoth bulk'd in ice,
Not to be molten out."
                  And roughly spake
My father, "Tut, you know them not, the girls.
Boy, when I hear you prate I almost think
That idiot legend credible. Look you, Sir !
Man is the hunter ; woman is his game :

The sleek and shining creatures of the chase,
We hunt them for the beauty of their skins ;
They love us for it, and we ride them down.
Wheedling and siding with them ! Out ! for shame !
Boy, there's no rose that's half so dear to them
As he that does the thing they dare not do,
Breathing and sounding beauteous battle, comes
With the air of the trumpet round him, and leaps in
Among the women, snares them by the score
Flatter'd and fluster'd, wins, though dash'd with death
He reddens what he kisses: thus I won
Your mother, a good mother, a good wife,
Worth winning ; but this firebrand—gentleness
To such as her ! if Cyril spake her true,
To catch a dragon in a cherry net,
To trip a tigress with a gossamer,
Were wisdom to it."
                  "Yea, but Sire," I cried,
"Wild natures need wise curbs. The soldier ? No :
What dares not Ida do that she should prize
The soldier ? I beheld her, when she rose
The yester-night, and storming in extremes
Stood for her cause, and fling defiance down
Gagelike to man, and had not shunn'd the death,
No, not the soldier's: yet I hold her, king,
True woman: but you clash them all in one,
That have as many differences as we.
The violet varies from the lily as far
As oak from elm: one loves the soldier, one
The silken priest of peace, one this, one that,
And some unworthily ; their sinless faith,
A maiden moon that sparkles on a sty,
Glorifying clown and satyr ; whence they need
More breadth of culture: is not Ida right ?
They worth it ? truer to the law within ?
Severer in the logic of a life ?
Twice as magnetic to sweet influences
Of earth and heaven ? and she of whom you speak,
My mother, looks as whole as some serene
Creation minted in the golden moods
Of sovereign artists : not a thought, a touch,
But pure as lines of green that streak the white
Of the first snowdrop's inner leaves ; I say,
Not like the piebald miscellany, man,
Bursts of great heart and slips in sensual mire,
But whole and one : and take them all-in-all,
Were we ourselves but half as good, as kind,
As truthful, much that Ida claims as right
Had ne'er been mooted, but as frankly theirs
As dues of Nature. To our point: not war:
Least I lose all."
                  "Nay, nay, you spake but sense,"
Said Gama. "We remember love ourselves
In our sweet youth ; we did not rate him then
This red-hot iron to be shaped with blows.
You talk almost like Ida: she can talk ;
And there is something in it as you say :
But you talk kindlier: we esteem you for it.—
He seems a gracious and a gallant Prince,
I would he had our daughter: for the rest,
Our own detention, why the causes weigh'd,
Fatherly fears—you used us courteously—
We would do much to gratify your Prince—
We pardon it ; and for your ingress here
Upon the skirt and fringe of our fair land,
You did but come as goblins in the night,
Nor in the furrow broke the ploughman's head,
Nor burnt the grange, nor buss'd the milkingmaid,
Nor robb'd the farmer of his bowl of cream:
But let your Prince (our royal word upon it,
He comes back safe) ride with us to our lines,
And speak with Arac: Arac's word is thrice
As ours with Ida: something may be done—
I know not what—and ours shall see us friends.
You, likewise, our late guests, if so you will,
Follow us : who knows ? we four may build some
plan
Foursquare to opposition."

Here he reach'd
White hands of farewell to my sire, who growl'd
An answer which, half-muffled in his beard,
Let so much out as gave us leave to go.

Then rode we with the old king across the lawns
Beneath huge trees, a thousand rings of Spring
In every bole, a song on every spray
Of birds that piped their Valentines, and woke
Desire in me to infuse my tale of love
In the old king's ear, who promised help,'and cozed
All o'er with honey'd answer as we rode;
And blossom-fragrant slipt the heavy dews
Gather'd by night and peace. with each light air
On our mail'd heads: but other thoughts than Peace
Burnt in us, when we saw the embattled squares,
And squadrons of the Prince, trampling the flowers
With clamor: for among them rose a cry
As if to greet the king: they made a halt;
The horses yell'd; they clash'd their arms; the drum
Beat; merrily-blowing shrill'd the martial fife;
And in the blast and bray of the long horn
And serpent-throated bugle, undulated
The banner: anon to meet us lightly pranced
Three captains out; nor ever had I seen
Such thews of men: the midmost and the highest
Was Arac: all about his motion clung
The shadow of his sister, as the bean
Of the East, that play'd upon them, made them glance
Like those three stars of the airy Giant's zone,
That glitter burnish'd by the frosty dark;
And as the fiery Sirius alters hue,
And bickers into red and emerald, shone
Their morions, wash'd with morning, as they came.

And I that prated peace, when first I heard
War-music, felt the blind wildbeast of force,
Whose home is in the sinews of a man,
Stir in me as to strike: then took the king
His three broad sons; with now a wandering hand
And now a pointed finger, told them all:
A common light of smiles at our disguise
Broke from their lips, and, ere the windy jest
Had labor'd down within his ample lungs,
The genial giant, Arac, roll'd himself
Thrice in the saddle, then burst out in words.

"Our land invaded, 'sdeath! and he himself
Your captive, yet my father wills not war:
And, 'sdeath! myself, what care I, war or no?
But then this question of your troth remains:
And there 's a downright honest meaning in her;
She flies too high, she flies too high! and yet
She ask'd but space and fairplay for her scheme:
She prest and prest it on me—I myself,
What know I of these things? but, life and soul!
I thought her half-right talking of her wrongs:
I say she flies too high, 'sdeath! what of that?
I take her for the flower of womankind,
And so I often told her, right or wrong,
And, Prince, she can be sweet to those she loves,
And, right or wrong, I care not: this is all,
I stand upon her side: she made me swear it—
Sdeath,—and with solemn rites by candlelight—
Swear by St. something—I forget her name:
Her that talk'd down the fifty wisest men:
She was a princess too; and so I swore.
Come, this is all; she will not: waive your claim,
If not, the foughten field, what else, at once
Decides it, 'sdeath! against my father's will."

I lagg'd in answer loath to render up
My precontract, and loath by brainless war
To cleave the rift of difference deeper yet;
Till one of those two brothers, half aside
And fingering at the hair about his lip,
To prick us on to combat "Like to like!
The woman's garment hid the woman's heart."

A taunt that clench'd his purpose like a blow!
For fiery-short was Cyril's counter-scoff,
And sharp I answer'd, touch'd upon the point
Where idle boys are cowards to their shame,
"Decide it here: why not? we are three to three."

Then spoke the third, "But three to three? no
more?
No more, and in our noble sister's cause?
More, more, for honor: every captain waits
Hungry for honor, angry for his king.
More, more, some fifty on a side, that each
May breathe himself, and quick! by overthrow
Of these or those, the question settled die."

"Yea," answer'd I, "for this wild wreath of air,
This flake of rainbow flying on the highest
Foam of men's deeds—this honor, if ye will.
It needs must be for honor if at all:
Since, what decision? if we fail, we fail,
And if we win, we fail: she would not keep
Her compact." "'Sdeath! but we will send to her,'
Said Arac, "worthy reasons why she should
Bide by this issue: let our missive thro',
And you shall have her answer by the word.'

"Boys!" shriek'd the old king, but vainlier than
a hen
To her false daughters in the pool; for none
Regarded; neither seem'd there more to say:
Back rode we to my father's camp, and found
He thrice had sent a herald to the gates,
To learn if Ida yet would cede our claim,
Or by denial flush her babbling wells
With her own people's life: three times he went:
The first, he blew and blew, but none appear'd:
He batter'd at the doors: none came: the next,
An awful voice within had warn'd him thence:
The third, and those eight daughters of the plough
Came sallying thro' the gates, and caught his hair,
And so belabor'd him on rib and cheek
They made him wild: not less one glance he caught
Thro' open doors of Ida station'd there
Unshaken, clinging to her purpose, firm
Tho' compass'd by two armies and the noise
Of arms; and standing like a stately Pine
Set in a cataract on an island-crag,
When storm is on the heights, and right and left
Suck'd from the dark heart of the long hills roll
The torrents, dash'd to the vale: and yet her will
Bred will in me to overcome it or fall.

But when I told the king that I was pledged
To fight in tourney for my bride, he clash'd
His iron palms together with a cry;
Himself would tilt it out among the lads:
But overborne by all his bearded lords
With reasons drawn from age and state, perforce
He yielded, wroth and red, with fierce demur:
And many a bold knight started up in heat,
And sware to combat for my claim till death.

All on this side the palace ran the field
Flat to the garden wall: and likewise here,
Above the garden's glowing blossom-belts,
A column'd entry shone and marble stairs,
And great bronze valves, emboss'd with Tomyris
And what she did to Cyrus after fight,
But now fast barr'd: so here upon the flat
All that long morn the lists were hammer'd up,
And all that morn the heralds to and fro,
With message and defiance, went and came;
Last, Ida's answer, in a royal hand,
But shaken here and there, and rolling words
Oration-like. I kiss'd it and I read.

"O brother, you have known the pangs we felt,
What heats of indignation when we heard

Of those that iron-cramp'd their women's feet;
Of lands in which at the altar the poor bride
Gives her harsh groom for bridal-gift a scourge;
Of living hearts that crack within the fire
Where smoulder their dead despots; and of those,—
Mothers,—that, all prophetic pity, fling
Their pretty maids in the running flood, and swoops
The vulture, beak and talon, at the heart
Made for all noble motion: and I saw
That equal baseness lived in sleeker times
With smoother men: the old leaven leaven'd all:
Millions of throats would bawl for civil rights,
No woman named: therefore I set my face
Against all men, and lived but for mine own.
Far off from men I built a fold for them:
I stored it full of rich memorial:
I fenced it round with gallant institutes,
And biting laws to scare the beasts of prey,
And prosper'd; till a rout of saucy boys
Brake on us at our books, and marr'd our peace,
Mask'd like our maids, blustering I know not what
Of insolence and love, some pretext held
Of baby troth, invalid, since my will
Seal'd not the bond—the striplings!—for their sport!—
I tamed my leopards: shall I not tame these?
Or you? or I? for since you think me touch'd
In honor—what, I would not aught of false—
Is not our cause pure? and whereas I know
Your prowess, Arac, and what mother's blood
You draw from, fight; you failing, I abide
What end soever: fail you will not. Still
Take not his life: he risk'd it for my own;
His mother lives: yet whatsoe'er you do,
Fight and fight well; strike and strike home. O dear
Brothers, the woman's Angel guards you, you
The sole men to be mingled with our cause,
The sole men we shall prize in the after-time,
Your very armor hallow'd, and your statues
Rear'd, sung to, when this gad-fly brush'd aside,
We plant a solid foot into the Time,
And mould a generation strong to move
With claim on claim from right to right, till she
Whose name is yoked with children's, know herself;
And Knowledge in our own land make her free,
And, ever following those two crowned twins,
Commerce and conquest, shower the fiery grain
Of freedom broadcast over all that orbs
Between the Northern and the Southern morn."

   Then came a postscript dash'd across the rest.
"See that there be no traitors in your camp:
We seem a nest of traitors—none to trust:
Since our arms fail'd—this Egypt plague of men!
Almost our maids were better at their homes,
Than thus man-girdled here: indeed I think
Our chiefest comfort is the little child
Of one unworthy mother; which she left:
She shall not have it back: the child shall grow
To prize the authentic mother of her mind.
I took it for an hour in mine own bed
This morning: there the tender orphan hands
Felt at my heart, and seem'd to charm from thence
The wrath I nursed against the world: farewell."

   I ceased; he said: "Stubborn, but she may sit
Upon a king's right hand in thunder-storms,
And breed up warriors! See now, tho' yourself
Be dazzled by the wildfire Love to sloughs
That swallow common sense, the spindling king,
This Gama swamp'd in lazy tolerance.
When the man wants weight, the woman takes it up,
And topples down the scales; but this is fixt
As are the roots of earth and base of all;
Man for the field and woman for the hearth;
Man for the sword and for the needle she:
Man with the head and woman with the heart:
Man to command and woman to obey ·

All else confusion. Look you! the gray mare
Is ill to live with, when her whinny shrills
From tile to scullery, and her small goodman
Shrinks in his arm-chair while the fires of Hell
Mix with his hearth: but you—she's yet a colt—
Take, break her: strongly groom'd and straitly curb'd
She might not rank with those detestable
That let the bantling scald at home, and brawl
Their rights or wrongs like potherbs in the street.
They say she's comely; there's the fairer chance:
I like her none the less for rating at her!
Besides, the woman wed is not as we,
But suffers change of frame. A lusty brace
Of twins may weed her of her folly. Boy,
The bearing and the training of a child
Is woman's wisdom."
                          Thus the hard old king:
I took my leave, for it was nearly noon:
I pored upon her letter which I held,
And on the little clause "take not his life:"
I mused on that wild morning in the woods,
And on the "Follow, follow, thou shalt win:"
I thought on all the wrathful king had said,
And how the strange betrothment was to end:
Then I remember'd that burnt sorcerer's curse
That one should fight with shadows and should fall;
And like a flash the weird affection came:
King, camp and college turn'd to hollow shows:
I seem'd to move in old memorial tilts,
And doing battle with forgotten ghosts,
To dream myself the shadow of a dream:
And ere I woke it was the point of noon,
The lists were ready. Empanoplied and plumed
We enter'd in, and waited, fifty there
Opposed to fifty, till the trumpet blared
At the barrier like a wild horn in a land
Of echoes, and a moment, and once more
The trumpet, and again: at which the storm
Of galloping hoofs bare on the ridge of spears
And riders front to front, until they closed
In conflict with the crash of shivering points.
And thunder. Yet it seem'd a dream; I dream'd
Of fighting. On his haunches rose the steed,
And into fiery splinters leapt the lance,
And out of stricken helmets sprang the fire.
A noble dream! what was it else I saw?
Part sat like rocks; part reel'd but kept their seats
Part roll'd on the earth and rose again and drew:
Part stumbled mixt with floundering horses. Down
From those two bulks at Arac's side, and down
From Arac's arm, as from a giant's flail,
The large blows rain'd, as here and everywhere
He rode the mellay, lord of the ringing lists,
And all the plain—brand, mace, and shaft, and
        shield—
Shock'd, like an iron-clanging anvil bang'd
With hammers; till I thought, can this be he
From Gama's dwarfish loins? if this be so,
The mother makes us most—and in my dream
I glanced aside, and saw the palace-front
Alive with fluttering scarfs and ladies' eyes,
And highest, among the statues, statue-like,
Between a cymbal'd Miriam and a Jael,
With Psyche's babe, was Ida watching us,
A single band of gold about her hair,
Like a Saint's glory up in heaven: but she
No saint—inexorable—no tenderness—
Too hard, too cruel: yet she sees me fight,
Yea, let her see me fall! with that I drave
Among the thickest and bore down a Prince,
And Cyril, one. Yea, let me make my dream
All that I would. But that large-moulded man,
His visage all agrin as at a wake,
Made at me thro' the press, and, staggering back
With stroke on stroke the horse and horseman, came
As comes a pillar of electric cloud,
Flaying the roofs and sucking up the drains,
And shadowing down the champaign till it strikes

On a wood, and takes, and breaks, and cracks, and
      splits,
And twists the grain with such a roar that Earth
Reels, and the herdsmen cry; for everything
Gave way before him: only Florian, he
That loved me closer than his own right eye,
Thrust in between; but Arac rode him down:
And Cyril seeing it, push'd against the Prince.
With Psyche's color round his helmet, tough,
Strong, supple, sinew-corded, apt at arms;
But tougher, heavier, stronger, he that smote
And threw him: last I spurr'd; I felt my veins
Stretch with fierce heat; a moment hand to hand,
And sword to sword, and horse to horse we hung,
Till I struck out and shouted; the blade glanced;
I did but shear a feather, and dream and truth
Flow'd from me; darkness closed me; and I fell.

Home they brought her warrior dead:
  She nor swoon'd, nor utter'd cry:
All her maidens, watching, said,
  "She must weep or she will die."

Then they praised him, soft and low,
  Call'd him worthy to be loved,
Truest friend and noblest foe;
  Yet she neither spoke nor moved.

Stole a maiden from her place,
  Lightly to the warrior stept,
Took the face-cloth from the face;
  Yet she neither moved nor wept.

Rose a nurse of ninety years,
  Set his child upon her knee—
Like summer tempest came her tears—
  "Sweet my child, I live for thee."

VI.

My dream had never died or lived again.
As in some mystic middle state I lay
Seeing I saw not, hearing not I heard:
Tho', if I saw not, yet they told me all
So often that I spake as having seen.

For so it seem'd, or so they said to me,
That all things grew more tragic and more strange;
That when our side was vanquish'd and my cause
Forever lost, there went up a great cry,
The Prince is slain. My father heard and ran
In on the lists, and there unlaced my casque
And grovell'd on my body, and after him
Came Psyche, sorrowing for Aglaïa.

But high upon the palace Ida stood
With Psyche's babe in arm: there on the roofs
Like that great dame of Lapidoth she sang.

"Our enemies have fall'n, have fall'n: the seed
The little seed they laugh'd at in the dark,
Has risen and cleft the soil, and grown a bulk
Of spanless girth, that lays on every side
A thousand arms and rushes to the Sun.

"Our enemies have fall'n, have fall'n: they came:
The leaves were wet with women's tears: they heard
A noise of songs they would not understand:
They mark'd it with the red cross to the fall,
And would have strown it, and are fall'n themselves.

"Our enemies have fall'n, have fall'n: they came,
The woodmen with their axes: lo the tree!
But we will make it fagots for the hearth,
And shape it plank and beam for roof and floor,
And boats and bridges for the use of men.

"Our enemies have fall'n, have fall'n: they struck;
  With their own blows they hurt themselves, nor
      knew

There dwelt an iron nature in the grain:
The glittering axe was broken in their arms.
Their arms were shatter'd to the shoulder blade.

"Our enemies have fall'n, but this shall grow
A night of Summer from the heat, a breadth
Of Autumn, dropping fruits of power; and roll'd
With music in the growing breeze of Time,
The tops shall strike from star to star, the fangs
Shall move the stony bases of the world.

"And now, O maids, behold our sanctuary
Is violate, our laws broken: fear we not
To break them more in their behoof, whose arms
Champion'd our cause and won it with a day
Blanch'd in our annals, and perpetual feast,
When dames and heroines of the golden year
Shall strip a hundred hollows bare of Spring,
To rain an April of ovation round
Their statues, borne aloft, the three: but come,
We will be liberal, since our rights are won.
Let them not lie in the tents with coarse mankind.
Ill nurses; but descend, and proffer these
The brethren of our blood and cause, that there
Lie bruised and maim'd, the tender ministries
Of female hands and hospitality."

She spoke, and with the babe yet in her arms,
Descending, burst the great bronze valves, and led
A hundred maids in train across the Park.
Some cowl'd, and some bare-headed, on they came,
Their feet in flowers, her loveliest: by them went
The enamor'd air sighing, and on their curls
From the high tree the blossom wavering fell,
And over them the tremulous isles of light,
Slided, they moving under shade: but Blanche
At distance follow'd: so they came: anon
Thro' open field into the lists they wound
Timorously; and as the leader of the herd
That holds a stately fretwork to the Sun,
And follow'd up by a hundred airy does,
Steps with a tender foot, light as on air,
The lovely, lordly creature floated on
To where her wounded brethren lay; there stay'd;
Knelt on one knee,—the child on one,—and prest
Their hands, and call'd them dear deliverers,
And happy warriors and immortal names,
And said, "You shall not lie in the tents but here,
And nursed by those for whom you fought, and
      served
With female hands and hospitality."

Then, whether moved by this, or was it chance,
She past my way. Up started from my side
The old lion, glaring with his whelpless eye,
Silent; but when she saw me lying stark,
Dishelm'd and mute, and motionlessly pale,
Cold ev'n to her, she sigh'd; and when she saw
The haggard father's face and reverend beard
Of grisly twine, all dabbled with the blood
Of his own son, shudder'd, a twitch of pain
Tortured her mouth, and o'er her forehead past
A shadow, and her hue changed, and she said:
"He saved my life: my brother slew him for it."
No more: at which the king in bitter scorn
Drew from my neck the painting and the tress,
And held them up: she saw them, and a day
Rose from the distance on her memory,
When the good Queen, her mother, shore the tress
With kisses, ere the days of Lady Blanche:
And then once more she look'd at my pale face:
Till understanding all the foolish work
Of Fancy, and the bitter close of all,
Her iron will was broken in her mind;
Her noble heart was molten in her breast;
She bow'd, she set the child on the earth: she laid
A feeling finger on my brows, and presently

"O Sire." she said, "he lives: he is not dead:
O let me have him with my brethren here
In our own palace: we will tend on him
Like one of these: if so, by any means,
To lighten this great clog of thanks, that make
Our progress falter to the woman's goal."

She said: but at the happy word "he lives,"
My father stoop'd, re-father'd o'er my wounds.
So those two foes above my fallen life,
With brow to brow like night and evening mixt
Their dark and gray, while Psyche ever stole
A little nearer, till the babe that by us,
Half-lapt in glowing gauze and golden brede,
Lay like a new-fall'n meteor on the grass,
Uncared for, spied its mother and began
A blind and babbling laughter, and to dance
Its body, and reach its fatling innocent arms
And lazy lingering fingers. She the appeal
Brook'd not, but clamoring out "Mine—mine—not
      yours,
It is not yours, but mine: give me the child,"
Ceased all on tremble: piteous was the cry:
So stood the unhappy mother open-mouth'd,
And turn'd each face her way: wan was her cheek
With hollow watch, her blooming mantle torn,
Red grief and mother's hunger in her eye,
And down dead-heavy sank her curls, and half
The sacred mother's bosom, panting, burst
The laces toward her babe; but she nor cared
Nor knew it, clamoring on, till Ida heard,
Look'd up, and rising slowly from me, stood
Erect and silent, striking with her glance
The mother, me, the child; but he that lay
Beside us, Cyril, batter'd as he was,
Trail'd himself up on one knee: then he drew
Her robe to meet his lips, and down she look'd
At the arm'd man sideways, pitying, as it seem'd,
Or self-involved; but when she learnt his face,
Remembering his ill-omen'd song, arose
Once more thro' all her height, and o'er him grew
Tall as a figure lengthen'd on the sand
When the tide ebbs in sunshine, and he said:

"O fair and strong and terrible! Lioness
That with your long locks play the Lion's mane!
But Love and Nature, these are two more terrible
And stronger. See, your foot is on our necks,
We vanquish'd, you the Victor of your will.
What would you more? give her the child! remain
Orb'd in your isolation: he is dead,
Or all as dead: henceforth we let you be:
Win you the hearts of women; and beware
Lest, where you seek the common love of these,
The common hate with the revolving wheel
Should drag you down, and some great Nemesis
Break from a darken'd future, crown'd with fire,
And tread you out forever: but howsoe'er
Fix'd in yourself, never in your own arms
To hold your own, deny not hers to her,
Give her the child! O if, I say, you keep
One pulse that beats true woman, if you loved
The breast that fed or arm that dandled you,
Or own one part of sense not flint to prayer,
Give her the child! or if you scorn to lay it,
Yourself, in hands so lately claspt with yours,
Or speak to her, your dearest, her one fault
The tenderness, not yours, that could not kill,
Give me it; I will give it her."
                                He said:
At first her eye with slow dilation roll'd
Dry flame, she listening: after sank and sank
And, into mournful twilight mellowing, dwelt
Full on the child; she took it: "Pretty bud!
Lily of the vale: half-open'd bell of the woods!
Sole comfort of my dark hour, when a world
Of traitorous friend and broken system made
No purple in the distance, mystery,

Pledge of a love not to be mine, farewell;
These men are hard upon us as of old,
We two must part: and yet how fain was I
To dream thy cause embraced in mine, to think
I might be something to thee, when I felt
Thy helpless warmth about my barren breast
In the dead prime: but may thy mother prove
As true to thee as false, false, false to me!
And, if thou needs must bear the yoke, I wish it
Gentle as freedom"—here she kissed it: then—
"All good go with thee! take it, Sir," and so
Laid the soft babe in his hard-mailed hands,
Who turn'd half-round to Psyche as she sprang
To meet it, with an eye that swum in thanks;
Then felt it sound and whole from head to foot,
And hugg'd and never hugg'd it close enough,
And in her hunger mouth'd and mumbled it,
And hid her bosom with it; after that
Put on more calm and added suppliantly:

"We two were friends: I go to mine own land
Forever: find some other: as for me
I scarce am fit for your great plans: yet speak
      to me,
Say one soft word and let me part forgiven."

But Ida spoke not, rapt upon the child.
Then Arac. "Ida—'sdeath! you blame the man;
You wrong yourselves—the woman is so hard
Upon the woman. Come, a grace to me!
I am your warrior; I and mine have fought
Your battle: kiss her; take her hand, she weeps:
'Sdeath! I would sooner fight thrice o'er than see it."

But Ida spoke not, gazing on the ground,
And reddening in the furrows of his chin,
And moved beyond his custom, Gama said:

"I've heard that there is iron in the blood,
And I believe it. Not one word? not one?
Whence drew you this steel temper? not from me,
Not from your mother now a saint with saints.
She said you had a heart—I heard her say it—
'Our Ida has a heart'—just ere she died—
'But see that some one with authority
Be near her still,' and I—I sought for one—
All people said she had authority—
The Lady Blanche: much profit! Not one word;
No! tho' your father sues: see how you stand
Stiff as Lot's wife, and all the good knights maim'd,
I trust that there is no one hurt to death,
For your wild whim: and was it then for this,
Was it for this we gave our palace up,
Where we withdrew from summer heats and state,
And had our wine and chess beneath the planes,
And many a pleasant hour with her that's gone,
Ere you were born to vex us? Is it kind?
Speak to her I say: is this not she of whom,
When first she came, all flush'd you said to me
Now had you got a friend of your own age,
Now could you share your thought; now should
      men see
Two women faster welded in one love
Than pairs of wedlock; she you walk'd with, she
You talk'd with, whole nights long, up in the tower,
Of slue and arc, spheroid and azimuth,
And right ascension, Heaven knows what; and now
A word, but one, one little kindly word,
Not one to spare her: out upon you, flint!
You love nor her, nor me, nor any; nay,
You shame your mother's judgment too. Not one?
You will not? well—no heart have you, or such
As fancies like the vermin in a nut
Have fretted all to dust and bitterness."
So said the small king moved beyond his wont.

But Ida stood nor spoke, drain'd of her force
By many a varying influence and so long.

Down thro' her limbs a drooping languor wept:
Her head a little bent; and on her mouth
A doubtful smile dwelt like a clouded moon
In a still water: then brake out my sire
Lifting his grim head from my wounds. "O you,
Woman, whom we thought woman even now,
And were half fool'd to let you tend our son,
Because he might have wish'd it—but we see
The accomplice of your madness unforgiven,
And think that you might mix his draught with
      death,
When your skies change again: the rougher hand
Is safer: on to the tents: take up the Prince."

   He rose, and while each ear was prick'd to attend
A tempest, thro' the cloud that dimm'd her broke
A genial warmth and light once more, and shone
Thro' glittering drops on her sad friend.
                           "Come hither,
O Psyche," she cried out, "embrace me, come,
Quick while I melt; make a reconcilement sure
With one that cannot keep her mind an hour:
Come to the hollow heart they slander so!
Kiss and be friends, like children being chid!
I seem no more· *I* want forgiveness too:
I should have had to do with none but maids,
That have no links with men. Ah false but dear,
Dear traitor, too much loved, why?—why? Yet see
Before these kings we embrace you yet once more
With all forgiveness, all oblivion,
And trust, not love, you less.
                    And now, O Sire,
Grant me your son, to nurse, to wait upon him,
Like mine own brother. For my debt to him,
This nightmare weight of gratitude, I know it;
Taunt me no more: yourself and yours shall have
Free adit; we will scatter all our maids
Till happier times each to her proper hearth:
What use to keep them here now? grant my prayer.
Help, father, brother, help; speak to the king:
Thaw this male nature to some touch of that
Which kills me with myself, and drags me down
From my fixt height to mob me up with all
The soft and milky rabble of womankind,
Poor weakling ev'n as they are."
                       Passionate tears
Follow'd: the king replied not: Cyril said:
"Your brother, Lady,—Florian,—ask for him
Of your great head—for he is wounded too—
That you may tend upon him with the prince."
"Ay so," said Ida with a bitter smile,
"Our laws are broken: let him enter too."
Then Violet, she that sang the mournful song,
And had a cousin tumbled on the plain,
Petition'd too for him. "Ay so," she said,
"I stagger in the stream: I cannot keep
My heart an eddy from the brawling hour:
We break our laws with ease, but let it be."
"Ay so?" said Blanche: "Amazed am I to hear
Your Highness: but your Highness breaks with ease
The law your Highness did not make: 'twas I.
I had been wedded wife, I knew mankind,
And block'd them out; but these men came to woo
Your Highness—verily I think to win."

   So she, and turn'd askance a wintry eye:
But Ida with a voice, that like a bell
Toll'd by an earthquake in a trembling tower,
Rang ruin, answer'd full of grief and scorn.

   ' "Fling our doors wide! all, all, not one, but all,
Not only he, but by my mother's soul,
Whatever man lies wounded, friend or foe,
Shall enter, if he will. Let our girls flit,
Till the storm die! but had ye not stood by us,
The roar that breaks the Pharos from his base
Had left us rock. She fain would sting us too,

But shall not. Pass, and mingle with your likes.
We brook no further insult but are gone."

   She turn'd; the very nape of her white neck
Was rosed with indignation: but the Prince
Her brother came; the king her father charm'd
Her wounded soul with words: nor did mine own
Refuse her proffer, lastly gave his hand.

   Then us they lifted up, dead weights, and bare
Straight to the doors: to them the doors gave way;
Groaning, and in the Vestal entry shriek'd
The virgin marble under iron heels:
And on they moved and gain'd the hall, and there
Rested: but great the crush was, and each base,
To left and right, of those tall columns drown'd
In silken fluctuation and the swarm
Of female whisperers: at the further end
Was Ida by the throne, the two great cats
Close by her, like supporters on a shield,
Bow-back'd with fear: but in the centre stood
The common men with rolling eyes; amazed
They glared upon the women, and aghast
The women stared at these, all silent, save
When armor clash'd or jingled, while the day,
Descending, struck athwart the hall, and shot
A flying splendor out of brass and steel,
That o'er the statues leapt from head to head,
Now fired an angry Pallas on the helm,
Now set a wrathful Dian's moon on flame,
And now and then an echo started up,
And shuddering fled from room to room, and died
Of fright in far apartments.
                      Then the voice
Of Ida sounded, issuing ordinance:
And me they bore up the broad stairs, and thro'
The long-laid galleries past a hundred doors
To one deep chamber shut from sound, and due
To languid limbs and sickness; left me in it;
And others otherwhere they laid; and all
That afternoon a sound arose of hoof
And chariot, many a maiden passing home
Till happier times; but some were left of those
Held sagest, and the great lords out and in,
From those two hosts that lay beside the walls,
Walk'd at their will, and everything was changed.

   Ask me no more: the moon may draw the sea;
   The cloud may stoop from heaven and take the
      shape,
   With fold to fold, of mountain or of cape;
But O too fond, when have I answer'd thee?
      Ask me no more.

   Ask me no more: what answer should I give?
   I love not hollow cheek or faded eye:
   Yet, O my friend, I will not have thee die!
Ask me no more, lest I should bid thee live;
      Ask me no more.

   Ask me no more: thy fate and mine are seal'd:
   I strove against the stream and all in vain:
   Let the great river take me to the main:
No more, dear love, for at a touch I yield;
      Ask me no more.

VII.

So was their sanctuary violated,
So their fair college turn'd to hospital;
At first with all confusion: by and by
Sweet order lived again with other laws:
A kindlier influence reign'd; and everywhere
Low voices with the ministering hand
Hung round the sick: the maidens came, they talk'd,
They sang, they read: till she not fair, began
To gather light, and she that was, became
Her former beauty treble; and to and fro

With books, with flowers, with Angel offices,
Like creatures native unto gracious act,
And in their own clear element, they moved.

But sadness on the soul of Ida fell,
And hatred of her weakness, blent with shame.
Old studies fail'd; seldom she spoke; but oft
Clomb to the roofs, and gazed alone for hours
On that disastrous leaguer, swarms of men
Darkening her female field: void was her use;
And she as one that climbs a peak to gaze
O'er land and main, and sees a great black cloud
Drag inward from the deeps, a wall of night,
Blot out the slope of sea from verge to shore,
And suck the blinding splendor from the sand,
And quenching lake by lake and tarn by tarn
Expunge the world: so fared she gazing there;
So blacken'd all her world in secret, blank
And waste it seem'd and vain; till down she came,
And found fair peace once more among the sick.

And twilight dawn'd; and morn by morn the lark
Shot up and shrill'd in flickering gyres, but I
Lay silent in the muffled cage of life:
And twilight gloom'd; and broader-grown the bowers
Drew the great night into themselves, and Heaven,
Star after star, arose and fell; but I,
Deeper than those weird doubts could reach me, lay
Quite sunder'd from the moving Universe,
Nor knew what eye was on me, nor the hand
That nursed me, more than infants in their sleep.

But Psyche tended Florian: with her oft
Melissa came; for Blanche had gone, but left
Her child among us, willing she should keep
Court-favor; here and there the small bright head,
A light of healing glanced about the couch,
Or thro' the parted silks the tender face
Peep'd, shining in upon the wounded man
With blush and smile, a medicine in themselves
To wile the length from languorous hours, and draw
The sting from pain; nor seem'd it strange that soon
He rose up whole, and those fair charities
Join'd at her side; nor stranger seem'd that hearts
So gentle, so employ'd, should close in love,
Than when two dew-drops on the petal shake
To the same sweet air, and tremble deeper down,
And slip at once all-fragrant into one.

Less prosperously the second suit obtain'd
At first with Psyche. Not though Blanche had sworn
That after that dark night among the fields,
She needs must wed him for her own good name;
Not tho' he built upon the babe restored;
Nor tho' she liked him, yielded she, but fear'd
To incense the Head once more; till on a day
When Cyril pleaded, Ida came behind
Seen but of Psyche: on her foot she hung
A moment, and she heard, at which her face
A little flush'd, and she past on; but each
Assumed from thence, a half-consent involved
In stillness, plighted troth, and were at peace.

Nor only these: Love in the sacred halls
Held carnival at will, and flying struck
With showers of random sweet on maid and man.
Nor did her father cease to press my claim.
Nor did mine own now reconciled: nor yet
Did those twin brothers, risen again and whole;
Nor Arac, satiate with his victory.

But I lay still, and with me oft she sat:
Then came a change; for sometimes I would catch
Her hand in wild delirium, gripe it hard,
And fling it like a viper off, and shriek
"You are not Ida;" clasp it once again,
And call her Ida, tho' I knew her not,
And call her sweet, as if in irony,

And call her hard and cold which seem'd a truth:
And still she fear'd that I should lose my mind,
And often she believed that I should die:
Till out of long frustration of her care,
And pensive tendance in the all-weary noons,
And watches in the dead, the dark, when clocks
Throbb'd thunder thro' the palace floors, or call'd
On flying Time from all their silver tongues—
And out of memories of her kindlier days,
And sidelong glances at my father's grief,
And at the happy lovers heart in heart—
And out of hauntings of my spoken love,
And lonely listenings to my mutter'd dream,
And often feeling of the helpless hands,
And wordless broodings on the wasted cheek—
From all a closer interest flourish'd up,
Tenderness touch by touch, and last, to these,
Love, like an Alpine harebell hung with tears
By some cold morning glacier; frail at first
And feeble, all unconscious of itself,
But such as gather'd color day by day.

Last I woke sane, but wellnigh close to death
For weakness: it was evening: silent light
Slept on the painted walls, wherein were wrought
Two grand designs: for on one side arose
The women up in wild revolt, and storm'd
At the Oppian law. Titanic shapes, they cramm'd
The forum, and half-crush'd among the rest
A dwarflike Cato cower'd. On the other side
Hortensia spoke against the tax; behind,
A train of dames: by axe and eagle sat,
With all their foreheads drawn in Roman scowls,
And half the wolfs-milk curdled in their veins,
The fierce triumvirs; and before them paused
Hortensia, pleading: angry was her face.

I saw the forms: I knew not where I was:
They did but seem as hollow shows; nor more
Sweet Ida: palm to palm she sat: the dew
Dwelt in her eyes, and softer all her shape
And rounder show'd: I moved: I sigh'd: a touch
Came round my wrist, and tears upon my hand:
Then all for languor and self-pity ran
Mine down my face, and with what life I had,
And like a flower that cannot all unfold,
So drench'd it is with tempest, to the sun,
Yet, as it may, turns toward him, I on her
Fixt my faint eyes, and utter'd whisperingly:

"If you be, what I think you, some sweet dream,
I would but ask you to fulfil yourself:
But if you be that Ida whom I knew,
I ask you nothing: only, if a dream,
Sweet dream, be perfect. I shall die to-night.
Stoop down and seem to kiss me ere I die."

I could no more, but lay like one in trance,
That hears his burial talk'd of by his friends,
And cannot speak, nor move, nor make one sign,
But lies and dreads his doom. She turn'd; she
        paused;
She stoop'd; and out of languor leapt a cry;
Leapt fiery Passion from the brinks of death;
And I believed that in the living world
My spirit closed with Ida's at the lips;
Till back I fell, and from mine arms she rose
Glowing all over noble shame; and all
Her falser self slipt from her like a robe,
And left her woman, lovelier in her mood
Than in her mould that other, when she came
From barren deeps to conquer all with love;
And down the streaming crystal dropt; and she
Far-fleeted by the purple island-sides,
Naked, a double light in air and wave,
To meet her Graces, where they deck'd her out
For worship without end; nor end of mine,
Stateliest, for thee! but mute she glided forth,

Nor glanced behind her, and I sank and slept,
Fill'd thro' and thro' with Love, a happy sleep.

Deep in the night I woke: she, near me, held
A volume of the Poets of her land:
There to herself, all in low tones, she read.

' "Now sleeps the crimson petal, now the white;
Nor waves the cypress in the palace walk;
Nor winks the gold fin in the porphyry font:
The firefly wakens: waken thou with me.

"Now droops the milkwhite peacock like a ghost,
And like a ghost she glimmers on to me.

"Now lies the Earth all Danaë to the stars,
And all thy heart lies open unto me.

"Now slides the silent meteor on, and leaves
A shining furrow, as thy thoughts in me.

"Now folds the lily all her sweetness up,
And slips into the bosom of the lake:
So fold thyself, my dearest, thou, and slip
Into my bosom and be lost in me."

I heard her turn the page; she found a small
Sweet Idyl, and once more, as low, she read:

"Come down, O maid, from yonder mountain
    height:
What pleasure lives in height (the shepherd sang),
In height and cold, the splendor of the hills?
But cease to move so near the Heavens, and cease
To glide a sunbeam by the blasted Pine,
To sit a star upon the sparkling spire;
And come, for Love is of the valley, come,
For Love is of the valley, come thou down
And find him; by the happy threshold, he,
Or hand in hand with Plenty in the maize,
Or red with spirted purple of the vats,
Or foxlike in the vine; nor cares to walk
With Death and Morning on the Silver Horns,
Nor wilt thou snare him in the white ravine,
Nor find him dropt upon the firths of ice,
That huddling slant in furrow-cloven falls
To roll the torrent out of dusky doors:
But follow; let the torrent dance thee down
To find him in the valley; let the wild
Lean-headed Eagles yelp alone, and leave
The monstrous ledges there to slope, and spill
Their thousand wreaths of dangling water-smoke,
That like a broken purpose waste in air:
So waste not thou; but come; for all the vales
Await thee; azure pillars of the hearth
Arise to thee; the children call, and I
Thy shepherd pipe, and sweet is every sound,
Sweeter thy voice, but every sound is sweet;
Myriads of rivulets hurrying thro' the lawn,
The moan of doves in immemorial elms,
And murmuring of innumerable bees."

So she low-toned; while with shut eyes I lay
Listening; then look'd. Pale was the perfect face;
The bosom with long sighs labor'd, and meek
Seem'd the full lips, and mild the luminous eyes,
And the voice trembled and the hand. She said
Brokenly, that she knew it, she had fail'd
In sweet humility; had fail'd in all;
That all her labor was but as a block
Left in the quarry; but she still were loath,
She still were loath to yield herself to one,
That wholly scorn'd to help their equal rights
Against the sons of men, and barbarous laws.
She pray'd me not to judge their cause from her
That wrong'd it, sought far less for truth than
    power
In knowledge: something wild within her breast,

A greater than all knowledge, beat her down.
And she had nurs'd me there from week to week:
Much had she learnt in little time. In part
It was ill counsel had misled the girl
To vex true hearts: yet was she but a girl—
"Ah fool, and made myself a Queen of farce!
When comes another such? never, I think
Till the Sun drop dead from the signs."

                        Her voice
Choked, and her forehead sank upon her hands,
And her great heart through all the faultful Past
Went sorrowing in a pause I dared not break;
Till slowly, as a change in the dark world
Was lisp'd about the acacias, and a bird,
That early woke to feed her little ones,
Sent from a dewy breast a cry for light:
She moved, and at her feet the volume fell.

"Blame not thyself too much," I said, "nor blame
Too much the sons of men and barbarous laws;
These were the rough ways of the world till now.
Henceforth thou hast a helper, me, that know
The woman's cause is man's: they rise or sink
Together, dwarf'd or godlike, bond or free:
For she that out of Lethe scales with man
The shining steps of Nature, shares with man
His nights, his days, moves with him to one goal,
Stays all the fair young planet in her hands—
If she be small, slight-natured, miserable,
How shall men grow? but work no more alone!
Our place is much: as far as in us lies
We two will serve them both in aiding her—
Will clear away the parasitic forms
That seem to keep her up but drag her down—
Will leave her space to burgeon out of all
Within her—let her make herself her own
To give or keep, to live and learn and be
All that not harms distinctive womanhood.
For woman is not undevelopt man,
But diverse: could we make her as the man,
Sweet love were slain: his dearest bond is this,
Not like to like, but like in difference.
Yet in the long years liker must they grow;
The man be more of woman, she of man;
He gain in sweetness and in moral height,
Nor lose the wrestling thews that throw the world;
She mental breadth, nor fail in childward care,
Nor lose the childlike in the larger mind;
Till at the last she set herself to man,
Like perfect music unto noble words;
And so these twain, upon the skirts of Time,
Sit side by side, full-summ'd in all their powers,
Dispensing harvest, sowing the To-be,
Self-reverent each and reverencing each,
Distinct in individualities,
But like each other ev'n as those who love.
Then comes the statelier Eden back to men:
Then reign the world's great bridals, chaste and
    calm:
Then springs the crowning race of humankind.
May these things be!"

                    Sighing she spoke, "I fear
They will not."

            "Dear, but let us type them now
In our own lives, and this proud watchword rest
Of equal; seeing either sex alone
Is half itself, and in true marriage lies
Nor equal, nor unequal: each fulfils
Defect in each, and always thought in thought,
Purpose in purpose, will in will, they grow,
The single pure and perfect animal,
The two-cell'd heart beating, with one full stroke,
Life."

            And again sighing she spoke: "A dream
That once was mine! what woman taught you this?"

"Alone," I said, "from earlier than I know,
Immersed in rich foreshadowings of the world,

I, loved the woman: he, that doth not, lives
A drowning life, besotted in sweet self,
Or pines in sad experience worse than death,
Or keeps his wing'd affections clipt with crime:
Yet was there one thro' whom I loved her, one
Not learned, save in gracious household ways,
Not perfect, nay, but full of tender wants.
No Angel, but a dearer being, all dipt
In Angel instincts, breathing Paradise,
Interpreter between the Gods and men,
Who look'd all native to her place, and yet
On tiptoe seem'd to touch upon a sphere
Too gross to tread, and all male minds perforce
Sway'd to her from their orbits as they moved,
And girded her with music. Happy he
With such a mother! faith in womankind
Beats with his blood, and trust in all things high
Comes easy to him, and tho' he trip and fall
He shall not blind his soul with clay."

                                        "But I,"
Said Ida, tremulously, "so all unlike—
It seems you love to cheat yourself with words:
This mother is your model. I have heard
Of your strange doubts: they well might be: I
          seem
A mockery to my own self. Never, Prince;
You cannot love me."

                    "Nay but thee," I said,
"From yearlong poring on thy pictured eyes,
Ere seen I loved, and loved thee seen, and saw
Thee woman thro' the crust of iron moods
That mask'd thee from men's reverence up, and
          forced
Sweet love on pranks of saucy boyhood: now,
Giv'n back to life, to life indeed, thro' thee,
Indeed I love: the new day comes, the light
Dearer for night, as dearer thou for faults
Lived over: lift thine eyes, my doubts are dead,
My haunting sense of hollow shows: the change,
This truthful change in thee has kill'd it. Dear,
Look up, and let thy nature strike on mine,
Like yonder morning on the blind half-world;
Approach and fear not; breathe upon my brows;
In that fine air I tremble, all the past
Melts mist-like into this bright hour, and this
Is morn to more, and all the rich to-come
Reels, as the golden Autumn woodland reels
Athwart the smoke of burning weeds. Forgive me,
I waste my heart in signs: let be. My bride,
My wife, my life. O we will walk this world,
Yoked in all exercise of noble end.
And so thro those dark gates across the wild
That no man knows. Indeed I love thee: come,
Yield thyself up: my hopes and thine are one:
Accomplish thou my manhood and thyself;
Lay thy sweet hands in mine and trust to me."

CONCLUSION.

So closed our tale, of which I give you all
The random scheme as wildly as it rose:
The words are mostly mine; for when we ceased
There came à minute's pause, and Walter said,
"I wish she had not yielded!" then to me,
"What, if you drest it up poetically?"
So pray'd the men, the women: I gave assent:
Yet how to bind the scatter'd scheme of seven
Together in one sheaf? What style could suit?
The men required that I should give throughout
The sort of mock-heroic gigantesque,
With which we banter'd little Lilia first:
The women—and perhaps they felt their power,
For something in the ballads which they sang,
Or in their silent influence as they sat,
Had ever seem'd to wrestle with burlesque,
And drove us, last, to quite a solemn close—
They hated banter, wish'd for something real,

A gallant fight, a noble princess—why
Not make her true-heroic—true-sublime?
Or all, they said, as earnest as the close?
Which yet with such a framework scarce could be
Then rose a little feud betwixt the two,
Betwixt the mockers and the realists:
And I, betwixt them both, to please them both,
And yet to give the story as it rose,
I moved as in a strange diagonal,
And maybe neither pleased myself nor them.

But Lilia pleased me, for she took no part
In our dispute: the sequel of the tale
Had touch'd her; and she sat, she pluck'd the grass,
She flung it from her, thinking: last, she fixt
A showery glance upon her aunt, and said,
"You—tell us what we are" who might have told,
For she was cramm'd with theories out of books,
But that there rose a shout: the gates were closed
At sunset, and the crowd were swarming now,
To take their leave, about the garden rails.

So I and some went out to these: we climb'd
The slope to Vivian-place, and turning saw
The happy valleys, half in light, and half
Far-shadowing from the west, a land of peace;
Gray halls alone among the massive groves;
Trim hamlets; here and there a rustic tower
Half-lost in belts of hop and breadths of wheat;
The shimmering glimpses of a stream; the seas;
A red sail, or a white; and far beyond,
Imagined more than seen, the skirts of France.

"Look there, a garden!" said my college friend,
The Tory member's elder son, "and there!
God bless the narrow sea which keeps her off,
And keeps our Britain, whole within herself,
A nation yet, the rulers and the ruled—
Some sense of duty, something of a faith,
Some reverence for the laws ourselves have made,
Some patient force to change them when we will,
Some civic manhood firm against the crowd—
But yonder, whiff! there comes a sudden heat,
The gravest citizen seems to lose his head,
The king is scared, the soldier will not fight,
The little boys begin to shoot and stab,
A kingdom topples over with a shriek
Like an old woman, and down rolls the world
In mock heroics stranger than our own;
Revolts, republics, revolutions, most
No graver than a school-boys' barring out;
Too comic for the solemn things they are,
Too solemn for the comic touches in them,
Like our wild Princess with as wise a dream
As some of theirs—God bless the narrow seas!
I wish they were a whole Atlantic broad."

"Have patience," I replied, "ourselves are full
Of social wrong: and maybe wildest dreams
Are but the needful preludes of the truth:
For me, the genial day, the happy crowd,
The sport half-science, fill me with a faith.
This fine old world of ours is but a child
Yet in the go-cart. Patience! Give it time
To learn its limbs: there is a hand that guides."

In such discourse we gain'd the garden rails,
And there we saw Sir Walter where he stood,
Before a tower of crimson holly-oaks,
Among six boys, head under head, and look'd
No little lily-handed Baronet he,
A great broad-shoulder'd genial Englishman,
A lord of fat prize-oxen and of sheep,
A raiser of huge melons and of pine,
A patron of some thirty charities,
A pamphleteer on guano and on grain,
A quarter-sessions chairman, abler none:

Fair-hair'd and redder than a windy morn:
Now shaking hands with him, now him, of those
That stood the nearest—now address'd to speech—
Who spoke few words and pithy, such as closed
Welcome, farewell, and welcome for the year
To follow: a shout rose again, and made
The long line of the approaching rookery swerve
From the elms, and shook the branches of the deer
From slope to slope thro' distant ferns, and rang
Beyond the bourn of sunset; O, a shout
More joyful than the city-roar that halls
Premier or king! Why should not these great Sirs
Give up their parks some dozen times a year
To let the people breathe? So thrice they cried,
I likewise, and in groups they stream'd away.

But we went back to the Abbey, and sat on,
So much the gathering darkness charm'd: we sat
But spoke not, rapt in nameless reverie,
Perchance upon the future man: the walls
Blacken'd about us, bats wheel'd, and owls whoop'd.
And gradually the powers of the night,
That range above the region of the wind,
Deepening the courts of twilight broke them up
Thro' all the silent spaces of the worlds,
Beyond all thought into the Heaven of Heavens.

Last little Lilia, rising quietly,
Disrobed the glimmering statue of Sir Ralph
From those rich silks, and home well-pleased we
went.

IN MEMORIAM.

Strong Son of God, immortal Love,
  Whom we, that have not seen thy face,
  By faith, and faith alone, embrace,
Believing where we cannot prove;

Thine are these orbs of light and shade;
  Thou madest life in man and brute;
  Thou madest Death; and lo, thy foot
Is on the skull which thou hast made.

Thou wilt not leave us in the dust:
  Thou madest man, he knows not why;
  He thinks he was not made to die;
And thou hast made him: thou art just.

Thou seemest human and divine,
  The highest, holiest manhood, thou:
  Our wills are ours, we know not how;
Our wills are ours, to make them thine.

Our little systems have their day;
  They have their day and cease to be:
  They are but broken lights of thee,
And thou, O Lord, art more than they.

We have but faith: we cannot know;
  For knowledge is of things we see;
  And yet we trust it comes from thee,
A beam in darkness: let it grow.

Let knowledge grow from more to more,
  But more of reverence in us dwell;
  That mind and soul according well,
May make one music as before,

But vaster. We are fools and slight;
  We mock thee when we do not fear:
  But help thy foolish ones to bear;
Help thy vain worlds to bear thy light.

Forgive what seem'd my sin in me;
  What seem'd my worth since I began;
  For merit lives from man to man,
And not from man, O Lord, to thee.

Forgive my grief for one removed,
  Thy creature, whom I found so fair.
  I trust he lives in thee, and there
I find him worthier to be loved.

Forgive these wild and wandering cries,
  Confusions of a wasted youth;
  Forgive them where they fail in truth,
And in thy wisdom make me wise.
1849.

IN MEMORIAM.

A. H. H.

OBIIT MDCCCXXXIII.

I.

I held it truth, with him who sings
  To one clear harp in divers tones,
  That men may rise on stepping-stones
Of their dead selves to higher things.

But who shall so forecast the years,
  And find in loss a gain to match?
  Or reach a hand thro' time to catch
The far-off interest of tears?

Let Love clasp Grief lest both be drown'd,
  Let darkness keep her raven gloss:
  Ah, sweeter to be drunk with loss,
To dance with death, to beat the ground,

Than that the victor Hours should scorn
  The long result of love, and boast,
  "Behold the man that loved and lost
But all he was is overworn."

II.

Old Yew, which graspest at the stones
  That name the underlying dead,
  Thy fibres net the dreamless head,
Thy roots are wrapt about the bones.

The seasons bring the flower again,
  And bring the firstling to the flock;
  And in the dusk of thee, the clock
Beats out the little lives of men.

O not for thee the glow, the bloom,
  Who changest not in any gale,
  Nor branding summer suns avail
To touch thy thousand years of gloom:

And gazing on thee, sullen tree,
  Sick for thy stubborn hardihood,
  I seem to fail from out my blood
And grow incorporate into thee.

III.

O sorrow, cruel fellowship,
  O Priestess in the vaults of Death,
  O sweet and bitter in a breath,
What whispers from thy lying lip?

"The stars," she whispers, "blindly run;
A web is wov'n across the sky;
From out waste places comes a cry,
And murmurs from the dying sun:

"And all the phantom, Nature, stands,—
With all the music in her tone,
A hollow echo of my own,—
A hollow form with empty hands."

And shall I take a thing so blind,
Embrace her as my natural good;
Or crush her, like a vice of blood,
Upon the threshold of the mind?

IV.

To Sleep I give my powers away;
My will is bondsman to the dark;
I sit within a helmless bark,
And with my heart I muse and say:

O heart, how fares it with thee now,
That thou shouldst fail from thy desire,
Who scarcely darest to inquire
"What is it makes me beat so low?"

Something it is which thou hast lost,
Some pleasure from thine early years.
Break, thou deep vase of chilling tears,
That grief hath shaken into frost!

Such clouds of nameless trouble cross
All night below the darken'd eyes;
With morning wakes the will, and cries,
"Thou shalt not be the fool of loss."

V.

I SOMETIMES hold it half a sin
To put in words the grief I feel;
For words, like Nature, half reveal
And half conceal the Soul within.

But, for the unquiet heart and brain,
A use in measured language lies;
The sad mechanic exercise,
Like dull narcotics, numbing pain.

In words, like weeds, I'll wrap me o'er,
Like coarsest clothes against the cold,
But that large grief which these enfold
Is given in outline and no more.

VI.

ONE writes, that "Other friends remain,"
That "Loss is common to the race,"—
And common is the commonplace,
And vacant chaff well meant for grain.

That loss is common would not make
My own less bitter, rather more:
Too common! Never morning wore
To evening, but some heart did break.

O father, wheresoe'er thou be,
Who pledgest now thy gallant son;
A shot, ere half thy draught be done,
Hath still'd the life that beat from thee.

O mother, praying God will save
Thy sailor,—while thy head is bow'd,
His heavy-shotted hammock-shroud
Drops in his vast and wandering grave.

Ye know no more than I who wrought
At that last hour to please him well;
Who mused on all I had to tell,
And something written, something thought;

Expecting still his advent home;
And ever met him on his way
With wishes, thinking, here to-day,
Or here to-morrow will he come.

O somewhere, meek unconscious dove,
That sittest ranging golden hair;
And glad to find thyself so fair,
Poor child, that waitest for thy love!

For now her father's chimney glows
In expectation of a guest;
And thinking "This will please him best,"
She takes a riband or a rose;

For he will see them on to-night;
And with the thought her color burns;
And, having left the glass, she turns
Once more to set a ringlet right;

And, ev'n when she turn'd, the curse
Had fallen, and her future lord
Was drown'd in passing thro' the ford,
Or kill'd in falling from his horse.

O what to her shall be the end?
And what to me remains of good?
To her, perpetual maidenhood,
And unto me no second friend.

VII.

DARK house, by which once more I stand
Here in the long unlovely street,
Doors, where my heart was used to beat
So quickly, waiting for a hand,

A hand that can be clasp'd no more,—
Behold me, for I cannot sleep,
And like a guilty thing I creep
At earliest morning to the door.

He is not here; but far away
The noise of life begins again,
And ghastly thro' the drizzling rain
On the bald street breaks the blank day.

VIII.

A HAPPY lover who has come
To look on her that loves him well,
Who 'lights and rings the gateway bell,
And learns her gone and far from home;

He saddens, all the magic light
Dies off at once from bower and hall,
And all the place is dark, and all
The chambers emptied of delight:

So find I every pleasant spot
In which we two were wont to meet,
The field, the chamber, and the street,
For all is dark where thou art not.

Yet as that other, wandering there
In those deserted walks, may find
A flower beat with rain and wind,
Which once she foster'd up with care;

So seems it in my deep regret,
O my forsaken heart, with thee
And this poor flower of poesy
Which little cared for fades not yet.

But since it pleased a vanish'd eye,
I go to plant it on his tomb,
That if it can it there may bloom,
Or dying, there at least may die.

IX.

Fair ship, that from the Italian shore
Sailest the placid ocean-plains
With my lost Arthur's loved remains,
Spread thy full wings, and waft him o'er.

So draw him home to those that mourn
In vain; a favorable speed
Ruffle thy mirror'd mast, and lead
Thro' prosperous floods his holy urn.

All night no ruder air perplex
Thy sliding keel, till Phosphor, bright
As our pure love, thro' early light
Shall glimmer on the dewy decks.

Sphere all your lights around, above;
Sleep, gentle heavens, before the prow;
Sleep, gentle winds, as he sleeps now,
My friend, the brother of my love;

My Arthur, whom I shall not see
Till all my widow'd race be run;
Dear as the mother to the son,
More than my brothers are to me.

X.

I hear the noise about thy keel;
I hear the bell struck in the night;
I see the cabin-window bright;
I see the sailor at the wheel.

Thou bringest the sailor to his wife,
And travell'd men from foreign lands;
And letters unto trembling hands;
And, thy dark freight, a vanish'd life.

So bring him: we have idle dreams:
This look of quiet flatters thus
Our home-bred fancies: O to us,
The fools of habit, sweeter seems

To rest beneath the clover sod,
That takes the sunshine and the rains,
Or where the kneeling hamlet drains
The chalice of the grapes of God;

Than if with thee the roaring wells
Should gulf him fathom-deep in brine;
And hands so often clasp'd in mine
Should toss with tangle and with shells.

XI.

Calm is the morn without a sound,
Calm as to suit a calmer grief,
And only thro' the faded leaf
The chestnut pattering to the ground:

Calm and deep peace on this high wold
And on these dews that drench the furze,
And all the silvery gossamers
That twinkle into green and gold:

Calm and still light on yon great plain
That sweeps with all its autumn bowers,
And crowded farms and lessening towers,
To mingle with the bounding main:

Calm and deep peace in this wide air,
These leaves that redden to the fall;
And in my heart, if calm at all,
If any calm, a calm despair:

Calm on the seas, and silver sleep,
And waves that sway themselves in rest,
And dead calm in that noble breast
Which heaves but with the heaving deep.

XII.

Lo, as a dove when up she springs
To bear thro' Heaven a tale of woe,
Some dolorous message knit below
The wild pulsation of her wings;

Like her I go; I cannot stay;
I leave this mortal ark behind,
A weight of nerves without a mind,
And leave the cliffs, and haste away.

O'er ocean-mirrors rounded large,
And reach the glow of southern skies,
And see the sails at distance rise,
And linger weeping on the marge,

And saying, "Comes he thus, my friend?
Is this the end of all my care?"
And circle moaning in the air:
"Is this the end? Is this the end?"

And forward dart again, and play
About the prow, and back return
To where the body sits, and learn,
That I have been an hour away.

XIII.

Tears of the widower, when he sees
A late-lost form that sleep reveals,
And moves his doubtful arms, and feels
Her place is empty, fall like these ·

Which weep a loss forever new,
A void where heart on heart reposed;
And, where warm hands have prest and clos'd
Silence, till I be silent too.

Which weep the comrade of my choice,'
An awful thought, a life removed,
The human-hearted man I loved,
A Spirit, not a breathing voice.

Come Time, and teach me, many years,
I do not suffer in a dream;
For now so strange do these things seem,
Mine eyes have leisure for their tears;

My fancies time to rise on wing,
And glance about the approaching sails,
As tho' they brought but merchants' bales,
And not the burthen that they bring.

XIV.

If one should bring me this report,
That thou hadst touch'd the land to-day,
And I went down unto the quay,
And found thee lying in the port;

And standing, muffled round with woe,
Should see thy passengers in rank
Come stepping lightly down the plank,
And beckoning unto those they know;

And if along with these should come
The man I held as half-divine;
Should strike a sudden hand in mine,
And ask a thousand things of home;

And I should tell him all my pain,
And how my life had droop'd of late,
And he should sorrow o'er my state
And marvel what possess'd my brain;

And I perceived no touch of change,
No hint of death in all his frame,
But found him all in all the same,
I should not feel it to be strange.

XV.

To-night the winds begin to rise
  And roar from yonder dropping day:
  The last red leaf is whirl'd away,
The rooks are blown about the skies;

The forest crack'd, the waters curl'd,
  The cattle huddled on the lea;
  And wildly dash'd on tower and tree
The sunbeam strikes along the world:

And but for fancies, which aver
  That all thy motions gently pass
  Athwart a plane of molten glass,
I scarce could brook the strain and stir

That makes the barren branches loud;
  And but for fear it is not so,
  The wild unrest that lives in woe
Would dote and pore on yonder cloud

That rises upward always higher,
  And onward drags a laboring breast,
  And topples round the dreary west,
A looming bastion fringed with fire.

XVI.

What words are these have fall'n from me?
  Can calm despair and wild unrest
  Be tenants of a single breast,
Or sorrow such a changeling be?

Or doth she only seem to take
  The touch of change in calm or storm;
  But knows no more of transient form
In her deep self, than some dead lake

That holds the shadow of a lark
  Hung in the shadow of a heaven?
  Or has the shock, so harshly given,
Confused me like the unhappy bark

That strikes by night a craggy shelf,
  And staggers blindly ere she sink?
  And stunn'd me from my power to think
And all my knowledge of myself;

And made me that delirious man
  Whose fancy fuses old and new,
  And flashes into false and true,
And mingles all without a plan?

XVII.

Thou comest, much wept for: such a breeze
  Compell'd thy canvas, and my prayer
  Was as the whisper of an air
To breathe thee over lonely seas.

For I in spirit saw thee move
  Thro' circles of the bounding sky,
  Week after week: the days go by:
Come quick, thou bringest all I love.

Henceforth, wherever thou may'st roam,
  My blessing, like a line of light,
  Is on the waters day and night,
And like a beacon guards thee home.

So may whatever tempest mars
  Mid-ocean spare thee, sacred bark;
  And balmy drops in summer dark
Glide from the bosom of the stars.

So kind an office hath been done,
  Such precious relics brought by thee;
  The dust of him I shall not see
Till all my widow'd race be run.

XVIII.

'T is well; 't is something: we may stand
  Where he in English earth is laid,
  And from his ashes may be made
The violet of his native land.

'T is little: but it looks in truth
  As if the quiet bones were blest
  Among familiar names to rest
And in the places of his youth.

Come then, pure hands, and bear the head
  That sleeps or wears the mask of sleep,
  And come, whatever loves to weep,
And hear the ritual of the dead.

Ah yet, ev'n yet, if this might be,
  I, falling on his faithful heart,
  Would breathing through his lips impart
The life that almost dies in me;

That dies not, but endures with pain,
  And slowly forms the firmer mind,
  Treasuring the look it cannot find,
The words that are not heard again.

XIX.

The Danube to the Severn gave
  The darken'd heart that beat no more:
  They laid him by the pleasant shore,
And in the hearing of the wave.

There twice a day the Severn fills;
  The salt sea-water passes by,
  And hushes half the babbling Wye,
And makes a silence in the hills.

The Wye is hush'd nor moved along,
  And hush'd my deepest grief of all,
  When fill'd with tears that cannot fall,
I brim with sorrow drowning song.

The tide flows down, the wave again
  Is vocal in its wooded walls;
  My deeper anguish also falls,
And I can speak a little then.

XX.

The lesser griefs that may be said,
  That breathe a thousand tender vows,
  Are but as servants in a house
Where lies the master newly dead;

Who speak their feeling as it is,
  And weep the fulness from the mind:
  "It will be hard," they say, "to find
Another service such as this."

My lighter moods are like to these,
  That out of words a comfort win;
  But there are other griefs within,
And tears that at their fountain freeze:

For by the hearth the children sit
  Cold in that atmosphere of Death,
  And scarce endure to draw the breath,
Or like to noiseless phantoms flit:

But open converse is there none,
  So much the vital spirits sink
  To see the vacant chair, and think,
"How good! how kind! and he is gone."

XXI.

I sing to him that rests below,
  And, since the grasses round me wave,
  I take the grasses of the grave,
And make them pipes whereon to blow.

The traveller hears me now and then,
And sometimes harshly will he speak:
"This fellow would make weakness weak,
And melt the waxen hearts of men."

Another answers, "Let him be,
He loves to make parade of pain,
That with his piping he may gain
The praise that comes to constancy."

A third is wroth, "Is this an hour
For private sorrow's barren song,
When more 'and more the people throng
The chairs and thrones of civil power?

"A time to sicken and to swoon,
When Science reaches forth her arms
To feel from world to world, and charms
Her secret from the latest moon?"

Behold, ye speak an idle thing:
Ye never knew the sacred dust:
I do but sing because I must,
And pipe but as the linnets sing:

And one is glad: her note is gay,
For now her little ones have ranged;
And one is sad: her note is changed,
Because her brood is stol'n away.

XXII.

The path by which we twain did go,
Which led by tracts that pleased us well,
Thro' four sweet years arose and fell,
From flower to flower, from snow to snow:

And we with singing cheer'd the way,
And crown'd with all the season lent,
From April on to April went,
And glad at heart from May to May:

But where the path we walk'd began
To slant the fifth autumnal slope,
As we descended, following Hope,
There sat the Shadow fear'd of man;

Who broke our fair companionship,
And spread his mantle dark and cold,
And wrapt thee formless in the fold,
And dull'd the murmur on thy lip,

And bore thee where I could not see
Nor follow, tho' I walk in haste,
And think that somewhere in the waste
The Shadow sits and waits for me.

XXIII.

Now, sometimes in my sorrow shut,
Or breaking into song by fits,
Alone, alone, to where he sits,
The Shadow cloak'd from head to foot,

Who keeps the keys of all the creeds,
I wander, often falling lame,
And looking back to whence I came,
Or on to where the pathway leads;

And crying, "How changed from where it ran
Thro' lands where not a leaf was dumb;
But all the lavish hills would hum
The murmur of a happy Pan:

"When each by turns was guide to each,
And Fancy light from Fancy caught,
And Thought leapt out to wed with Thought
Ere Thought could wed itself with Speech;

"And all we met was fair and good,
And all was good that Time could bring,
And all the secret of the Spring
Moved in the chambers of the blood;

"And many an old philosophy
On Argive heights divinely sang,
And round us all the thicket rang
To many a flute of Arcady."

XXIV.

And was the day of my delight
As sure and perfect as I say?
The very source and font of Day
Is dash'd with wandering isles of night.

If all was good and fair we met,
This earth had been the Paradise
It never look'd to human eyes
Since Adam left his garden yet.

And is it that the haze of grief
Makes former gladness loom so great?
The lowness of the present state,
That sets the past in this relief?

Or that the past will always win
A glory from its being far;
And orb into the perfect star
We saw not, when we moved therein?

XXV.

I know that this was Life,—the track
Whereon with equal feet we fared;
And then, as now, the day prepared
The daily burden for the back.

But this it was that made me move
As light as carrier-birds in air;
I loved the weight I had to bear,
Because it needed help of love:

Nor could I weary, heart or limb,
When mighty Love would cleave in twain
The lading of a single pain,
And part it, giving half to him.

XXVI.

Still, onward winds the dreary way;
I with it: for I long to prove
No lapse of moons can canker Love,
Whatever fickle tongues may say.

And if that eye which watches guilt
And goodness, and hath power to see
Within the green the moulder'd tree,
And towers fall'n as soon as built,—

O, if indeed that eye foresee
Or see (in Him is no before)
In more of life true life no more,
And Love the indifference to be,

Then might I find, ere yet the morn
Breaks hither over Indian seas,
That Shadow waiting with the keys,
To shroud me from my proper scorn.

XXVII.

I envy not in any moods
The captive void of noble rage,
The linnet born within the cage,
That never knew the summer woods;

I envy not the beast that takes
His license in the field of time,
Unfetter'd by the sense of crime,
To whom a conscience never wakes;

Nor, what may count itself as blest,
  The heart that never plighted troth,
  But stagnates in the weeds of sloth ;
Nor any want-begotten rest.

I hold it true, whate'er befall ;
  I feel it, when I sorrow most ;
  'T is better to have loved and lost
Than never to have loved at all.

XXVIII.

The time draws near the birth of Christ :
  The moon is hid ; the night is still ;
  The Christmas bells from hill to hill
Answer each other in the mist.

Four voices of four hamlets round,
  From far and near, on mead and moor,
  Swell out and fail, as if a door
Were shut between me and the sound :

Each voice four changes on the wind,
  That now dilate, and now decrease,
  Peace and good-will, good-will and peace,
Peace and good-will, to all mankind.

This year I slept and woke with pain,
  I almost wish'd no more to wake,
  And that my hold on life would break
Before I heard those bells again :

But they my troubled spirit rule,
  For they controll'd me when a boy ;
  They bring me sorrow touch'd with joy,
The merry, merry bells of Yule.

XXIX.

With such compelling cause to grieve
  As daily vexes household peace,
  And chains regret to his decease,
How dare we keep our Christmas-eve ;

Which brings no more a welcome guest
  To enrich the threshold of the night
  With shower'd largess of delight,
In dance and song and game and jest.

Yet go, and while the holly-boughs
  Entwine the cold baptismal font,
  Make one wreath more for Use and Wont
That guard the portals of the house ;

Old sisters of a day gone by,
  Gray nurses, loving nothing new ;
  Why should they miss their yearly due
Before their time ? They too will die.

XXX.

With trembling fingers did we weave
  The holly round the Christmas hearth ;
  A rainy cloud possess'd the earth,
And sadly fell our Christmas-eve.

At our old pastimes in the hall
  We gamboll'd, making vain pretence
  Of gladness, with an awful sense
Of one mute Shadow watching all.

We paused : the winds were in the beech :
  We heard them sweep the winter land ;
  And in a circle hand-in-hand
Sat silent, looking each at each.

Then echo-like our voices rang ;
  We sung, tho' every eye was dim,
  A merry song we sang with him
Last year : impetuously we sang :

We ceased : a gentler feeling crept
  Upon us : surely rest is meet :
  "They rest," we said, "their sleep is sweet,"
And silence follow'd, and we wept.

Our voices took a higher range ;
  Once more we sung : "They do not die
  Nor lose their mortal sympathy,
Nor change to us, although they change ;

"Rapt from the fickle and the frail
  With gather'd power, yet the same,
  Pierces the keen seraphic flame
From orb to orb, from veil to veil."

Rise, happy morn, rise, holy morn,
  Draw forth the cheerful day from night :
  O Father, touch the east, and light
The light that shone when Hope was born.

XXXI.

When Lazarus left his charnel-cave,
  And home to Mary's house return'd,
  Was this demanded,—if he yearn'd
To hear her weeping by his grave ?

"Where wert thou, brother, those four days ?"
  There lives no record of reply,
  Which telling what it is to die
Had surely added praise to praise.

From every house the neighbors met,
  The streets were fill'd with joyful sound,
  A solemn gladness even crown'd
The purple brows of Olivet.

Behold a man raised up by Christ !
  The rest remaineth unreveal'd ;
  He told it not ; or something seal'd
The lips of that Evangelist.

XXXII.

Her eyes are homes of silent prayer,
  Nor other thought her mind admits
  But, he was dead, and there he sits,
And he that brought him back is there.

Then one deep love doth supersede
  All other, when her ardent gaze
  Roves from the living brother's face,
And rests upon the Life indeed.

All subtle thought, all curious fears,
  Borne down by gladness so complete,
  She bows, she bathes the Saviour's feet
With costly spikenard and with tears.

Thrice blest whose lives are faithful prayers,
  Whose loves in higher love endure ;
  What souls possess themselves so pure,
Or is there blessedness like theirs ?

XXXIII.

O thou that after toil and storm
  Mayst seem to have reach'd a purer air,
  Whose faith has centre everywhere,
Nor cares to fix itself to form,

Leave thou thy sister, when she prays,
  Her early Heaven, her happy views ;
  Nor thou with shadow'd hint confuse
A life that leads melodious days.

Her faith thro' form is pure as thine,
  Her hands are quicker unto good :
  O, sacred be the flesh and blood
To which she links a truth divine !

See thou, that countest reason ripe
  In holding by the law within,
  Thou fail not in a world of sin,
And ev'n for want of such a type.

XXXIV.

My own dim life should teach me this,
  That life shall live forevermore,
  Else earth is darkness at the core,
And dust and ashes all that is;

This round of green, this orb of flame,
  Fantastic beauty; such as lurks
  In some wild Poet, when he works
Without a conscience or an aim.

What then were God to such as I?
  'T were hardly worth my while to choose
  Of things all mortal, or to use
A little patience ere I die;

'T were best at once to sink to peace,
  Like birds the charming serpent draws,
  To drop head-foremost in the jaws
Of vacant darkness, and to cease.

XXXV.

Yet if some voice that man could trust
  Should murmur from the narrow house,
  "The cheeks drop in; the body bows;
Man dies: nor is there hope in dust:"

Might I not say, "Yet even here,
  But for one hour, O Love, I strive
  To keep so sweet a thing alive?"
But I should turn mine ears and hear

The moanings of the homeless sea,
  The sound of streams that swift or slow
  Draw down Æolian hills, and sow
The dust of continents to be;

And Love would answer with a sigh,
  "The sound of that forgetful shore
  Will change my sweetness more and more,
Half-dead to know that I shall die."

O me! what profits it to put
  An idle case? If Death were seen
  At first as Death, Love had not been,
Or been in narrowest working shut,

Mere fellowship of sluggish moods,
  Or in his coarsest Satyr-shape
  Had bruised the herb and crush'd the grape,
And bask'd and batten'd in the woods.

XXXVI.

Tho' truths in manhood darkly join,
  Deep-seated in our mystic frame,
  We yield all blessing to the name
Of Him that made them current coin;

For Wisdom dealt with mortal powers,
  Where Truth in closest words shall fail,
  When Truth embodied in a tale
Shall enter in at lowly doors.

And so the Word had breath, and wrought
  With human hands the creed of creeds
  In loveliness of perfect deeds,
More strong than all poetic thought;

Which he may read that binds the sheaf,
  Or builds the house, or digs the grave,
  And those wild eyes that watch the wave
In roarings round the coral reef.

XXXVII.

Urania speaks with darken'd brow:
  "Thou pratest here where thou art least;
  This faith has many a purer priest,
And many an abler voice than thou.

"Go down beside thy native rill,
  On thy Parnassus set thy feet,
  And hear thy laurel whisper sweet
About the ledges of the hill."

And my Melpomene replies,
  A touch of shame upon her cheek:
  "I am not worthy ev'n to speak
Of thy prevailing mysteries:

"For I am but an earthly Muse,
  And owning but a little art
  To lull with song an aching heart,
And render human love his dues;

"But brooding on the dear one dead,
  And all be said of things divine,
  (And dear to me as sacred wine
To dying lips is all he said,)

"I murmur'd, as I came along,
  Of comfort clasp'd in truth reveal'd;
  And loiter'd in the Master's field,
And darken'd sanctities with song."

XXXVIII.

With weary steps I loiter on,
  Tho' always under alter'd skies
  The purple from the distance dies,
My prospect and horizon gone.

No joy the blowing season gives,
  The herald melodies of spring,
  But in the songs I love to sing
A doubtful gleam of solace lives,

If any care for what is here
  Survive in spirits render'd free,
  Then are these songs I sing of thee
Not all ungrateful to thine ear.

XXXIX.

Old warder of these buried bones,
  And answering now my random stroke
  With fruitful cloud and living smoke,
Dark yew, that graspest at the stones

And dippest toward the dreamless head,
  To thee too comes the golden hour
  When flower is feeling after flower;
But Sorrow—fixt upon the dead,

And darkening the dark graves of men,—
  What whisper'd from her lying lips?
  Thy gloom is kindled at the tips,
And passes into gloom again.

XL.

Could we forget the widow'd hour,
  And look on Spirits breathed away,
  As on a maiden in the day
When first she wears her orange-flower!

When crown'd with blessing she doth rise
  To take her latest leave of home,
  And hopes and light regrets that come
Make April of her tender eyes:

And doubtful joys the father move,
  And tears are on the mother's face,
  As parting with a long embrace
She enters other realms of love:

Her office there to rear, to teach,
  Becoming, as is meet and fit,
  A link among the days, to knit
The generations each with each;

And, doubtless, unto thee is given
  A life that bears immortal fruit
  In such great offices as suit
The full-grown energies of heaven.

8

Ay me, the difference I discern!
    How often shall her old fireside
    Be cheer'd with tidings of the bride,
How often she herself return,

And tell them all they would have told,
    And bring her babe, and make her boast,
    Till even those that miss'd her most
Shall count new things as dear as old:

But thou and I have shaken hands,
    Till growing winters lay me low;
    My paths are in the fields I know,
And thine in undiscover'd lands.

XLI.

Thy spirit ere our fatal loss
    Did ever rise from high to higher;
    As mounts the heavenward altar-fire,
As flies the lighter thro' the gross.

But thou art turn'd to something strange,
    And I have lost the links that bound
    Thy changes; here upon the ground,
No more partaker of thy change.

Deep folly! yet that this could be,—
    That I could wing my will with might
    To leap the grades of life and light,
And flash at once, my friend, to thee:

For tho' my nature rarely yields
    To that vague fear implied in death;
    Nor shudders at the gulfs beneath,
The howlings from forgotten fields:

Yet oft when sundown skirts the moor
    An inner trouble I behold,
    A spectral doubt which makes me cold,
That I shall be thy mate no more,

Tho' following with an upward mind
    The wonders that have come to thee,
    Thro' all the secular to-be,
But evermore a life behind.

XLII.

I vex my heart with fancies dim:
    He still outstript me in the race;
    It was but unity of place
That made me dream I rank'd with him.

And so may Place retain us still,
    And he the much-beloved again,
    A lord of large experience, train
To riper growth the mind and will:

And what delights can equal those
    That stir the spirit's inner deeps,
    When one that loves, but knows not, reaps
A truth from one that loves and knows?

XLIII.

If Sleep and Death be truly one,
    And every spirit's folded bloom
    Thro' all its intervital gloom
In some long trance should slumber on;

Unconscious of the sliding hour,
    Bare of the body, might it last,
    And silent traces of the past
Be all the color of the flower:

So then were nothing lost to man;
    So that still garden of the souls
    In many a figured leaf enrolls
The total world since life began;

And Love will last as pure and whole
    As when he loved me here in Time,
    And at the spiritual prime
Rewaken with the dawning soul.

XLIV.

How fares it with the happy dead?
    For here the man is more and more;
    But he forgets the days before
God shut the doorways of his head.

The days have vanish'd, tone and tint,
    And yet perhaps the hoarding sense
    Gives out at times (he knows not whence)
A little flash, a mystic hint;

And in the long harmonious years
    (If Death so taste Lethean springs)
    May some dim touch of earthly things
Surprise thee ranging with thy peers.

If such a dreamy touch should fall,
    O turn thee round, resolve the doubt;
    My guardian angel will speak out
In that high place, and tell thee all.

XLV.

The baby new to earth and sky,
    What time his tender palm is prest
    Against the circle of the breast,
Has never thought that "this is I:"

But as he grows he gathers much,
    And learns the use of "I," and "me,"
    And finds "I am not what I see,
And other than the things I touch."

So rounds he to a separate mind
    From whence clear memory may begin,
    As thro' the frame that binds him in
His isolation grows defined.

This use may lie in blood and breath,
    Which else were fruitless of their due,
    Had man to learn himself anew
Beyond the second birth of Death.

XLVI.

We ranging down this lower track,
    The path we came by, thorn and flower,
    Is shadow'd by the growing hour,
Lest life should fail in looking back.

So be it: there no shade can last
    In that deep dawn behind the tomb,
    But clear from marge to marge shall bloom
The eternal landscape of the past:

A lifelong tract of time reveal'd;
    The fruitful hours of still increase;
    Days order'd in a wealthy peace,
And those five years its richest field.

O Love, thy province were not large,
    A bounded field, nor stretching far;
    Look also, Love, a brooding star,
A rosy warmth from marge to marge.

XLVII.

That each, who seems a separate whole,
    Should move his rounds, and fusing all
    The skirts of self again, should fall
Remerging in the general Soul,

Is faith as vague as all unsweet:
    Eternal form shall still divide
    The eternal soul from all beside;
And I shall know him when we meet;

And we shall sit at endless feast,
    Enjoying each the other's good:
    What vaster dream can hit the mood
Of Love on earth? He seeks at least

Upon the last and sharpest height,
　Before the spirits fade away,
　Some landing-place to clasp and say,
"Farewell! We lose ourselves in light."

XLVIII.

IF these brief lays of Sorrow born,
　Were taken to be such as closed
　Grave doubts and answers here proposed,
Then these were such as men might scorn:

Her care is not to part and prove;
　She takes, when harsher moods remit,
　What slender shade of doubt may flit,
And makes it vassal unto love:

And hence, indeed, she sports with words,
　But better serves a wholesome law,
　And holds it sin and shame to draw
The deepest measure from the chords:

Nor dare she trust a larger lay,
　But rather loosens from the lip
　Short swallow-flights of song, that dip
Their wings in tears, and skim away.

XLIX.

FROM art, from nature, from the schools,
　Let random influences glance,
　Like light in many a shiver'd lance
That breaks about the dappled pools:

The lightest wave of thought shall lisp,
　The fancy's tenderest eddy wreathe,
　The slightest air of song shall breathe
To make the sullen surface crisp.

And look thy look, and go thy way,
　But blame not thou the winds that make
　The seeming-wanton ripple break,
The tender-pencil'd shadow play.

Beneath all fancied hopes and fears,
　Ay me! the sorrow deepens down,
　Whose muffled motions blindly drown
The bases of my life in tears.

L.

BE near me when my light is low,
　When the blood creeps, and the nerves prick
　And tingle; and the heart is sick,
And all the wheels of Being slow.

Be near me when the sensuous frame
　Is rack'd with pangs that conquer trust:
　And Time, a maniac scattering dust,
And Life, a Fury slinging flame.

Be near me when my faith is dry,
　And men the flies of latter spring.
　That lay their eggs, and sting and sing,
And weave their petty cells and die.

Be near me when I fade away,
　To point the term of human strife,
　And on the low dark verge of life
The twilight of eternal day.

LI.

Do we indeed desire the dead
　Should still be near us at our side?
　Is there no baseness we would hide?
No inner vileness that we dread?

Shall he for whose applause I strove,
　I had such reverence for his blame,
　See with clear eye some hidden shame,
And I be lessen'd in his love?

I wrong the grave with fears untrue:
　Shall love be blamed for want of faith?
　There must be wisdom with great Death
The dead shall look me thro' and thro'.

Be near us when we climb or fall:
　Ye watch, like God, the rolling hours
　With larger other eyes than ours,
To make allowance for us all.

LII.

I CANNOT love thee as I ought,
　For love reflects the thing beloved;
　My words are only words, and moved
Upon the topmost froth of thought.

"Yet blame not thou thy plaintive song,"
　The Spirit of true love replied;
　"Thou canst not move me from thy side,
Nor human frailty do me wrong.

"What keeps a spirit wholly true
　To that ideal which he bears?
　What record? not the sinless years
That breathed beneath the Syrian blue:

"So fret not, like an idle girl,
　That life is dash'd with flecks of sin.
　Abide: thy wealth is gather'd in,
When Time hath sunder'd shell from pearl.'

LIII.

HOW many a father have I seen,
　A sober man among his boys,
　Whose youth was full of foolish noise,
Who wears his manhood hale and green:

And dare we to this fancy give,
　That had the wild-oat not been sown,
　The soil, left barren, scarce had grown
The grain by which a man may live?

O, if we held the doctrine sound
　For life outliving heats of youth,
　Yet who would preach it as a truth
To those that eddy round and round?

Hold thou the good: define it well:
　For fear divine Philosophy
　Should push beyond her mark, and be
Procuress to the Lords of Hell.

LIV.

O YET we trust that somehow good
　Will be the final goal of ill,
　To pangs of nature, sins of will,
Defects of doubt, and taints of blood;

That nothing walks with aimless feet;
　That not one life shall be destroy'd,
　Or cast as rubbish to the void,
When God hath made the pile complete;

That not a worm is cloven in vain;
　That not a moth with vain desire
　Is shrivell'd in a fruitless fire,
Or but subserves another's gain.

Behold we know not anything;
　I can but trust that good shall fall
　At last—far off—at last, to all,
And every winter change to spring.

So runs my dream: but what am I?
　An infant crying in the night:
　An infant crying for the light:
And with no language but a cry.

LV.

Thr wish, that of the living whole
  No life may fail beyond the grave,
  Derives it not from what we have
The likest God within the soul?

Are God and Nature then at strife,
  That Nature lends such evil dreams?
  So careful of the type she seems,
So careless of the single life;

That I, considering everywhere
  Her secret meaning in her deeds,
  And finding that of fifty seeds
She often brings but one to bear,

I falter where I firmly trod,
  And falling with my weight of cares
  Upon the great world's altar-stairs
That slope thro' darkness up to God,

I stretch lame hands of faith, and grope,
  And gather dust and chaff, and call
  To what I feel is Lord of all,
And faintly trust the larger hope.

LVI.

"So careful of the type?" but no.
  From scarped cliff and quarried stone
  She cries, "A thousand types are gone:
I care for nothing, all shall go.

"Thou makest thine appeal to me:
  I bring to life, I bring to death:
  The spirit does but mean the breath:
I know no more." And he, shall he,

Man, her last work, who seem'd so fair,
  Such splendid purpose in his eyes,
  Who roll'd the psalm to wintry skies,
Who built him fanes of fruitless prayer,

Who trusted God was love indeed,
  And love Creation's final law,—
  Tho' Nature, red in tooth and claw
With ravin, shriek'd against his creed,—

Who loved, who suffer'd countless ills,
  Who battled for the True, the Just,
  Be blown about the desert dust,
Or seal'd within the iron hills?

No more? A monster then, a dream,
  A discord. Dragons of the prime,
  That tare each other in their slime,
Were mellow music match'd with him.

O life as futile, then, as frail!
  O for thy voice to soothe and bless!
  What hope of answer, or redress?
Behind the veil, behind the veil.

LVII.

Peace; come away: the song of woe
  Is after all an earthly song:
  Peace; come away: we do him wrong
To sing so wildly: let us go.

Come; let us go: your cheeks are pale;
  But half my life I leave behind:
  Methinks my friend is richly shrined:
But I shall pass; my work will fail.

Yet in these ears, till hearing dies,
  One set slow bell will seem to toll
  The passing of the sweetest soul
That ever look'd with human eyes.

I hear it now, and o'er and o'er,
  Eternal greetings to the dead;
  And "Ave, Ave, Ave," said,
"Adieu, adieu," forevermore.

LVIII.

In those sad words I took farewell:
  Like echoes in sepulchral halls,
  As drop by drop the water falls
In vaults and catacombs, they fell;

And, falling, idly broke the peace
  Of hearts that beat from day to day,
  Half conscious of their dying clay,
And those cold crypts where they shall cease.

The high Muse answer'd: "Wherefore grieve
  Thy brethren with a fruitless tear?
  Abide a little longer here,
And thou shalt take a nobler leave."

LIX.

O Sorrow, wilt thou live with me,
  No casual mistress, but a wife,
  My bosom-friend and half of life;
As I confess it needs must be;

O Sorrow, wilt thou rule my blood,
  Be sometimes lovely like a bride,
  And put thy harsher moods aside,
If thou wilt have me wise and good.

My centred passion cannot move,
  Nor will it lessen from to-day;
  But I'll have leave at times to play
As with the creature of my love;

And set thee forth, for thou art mine,
  With so much hope for years to come,
  That, howsoe'er I know thee, some
Could hardly tell what name were thine.

LX.

He past; a soul of nobler tone:
  My spirit loved and loves him yet,
  Like some poor girl whose heart is set
On one whose rank exceeds her own.

He mixing with his proper sphere,
  She finds the baseness of her lot,
  Half jealous of she knows not what,
And envying all that meet him there.

The little village looks forlorn;
  She sighs amid her narrow days,
  Moving about the household ways,
In that dark house where she was born.

The foolish neighbors come and go,
  And tease her till the day draws by;
  At night she weeps, "How vain am I!
How should he love a thing so low?"

LXI.

If, in thy second state sublime,
  Thy ransom'd reason change replies
  With all the circle of the wise,
The perfect flower of human time;

And if thou cast thine eyes below,
  How dimly character'd and slight,
  How dwarf'd a growth of cold and night,
How blanch'd with darkness must I grow!

Yet turn thee to the doubtful shore,
  Where thy first form was made a man;
  I loved thee, Spirit, and love, nor can
The soul of Shakespeare love thee more.

LXII.

Tho' if an eye that 's downward cast
  Could make thee somewhat bleuch or fail,
  Then be my love an idle tale,
And fading legend of the past;

And thou, as one that once declined
  When he was little more than boy,
  On some unworthy heart with joy,
But lives to wed an equal mind;

And breathes a novel world, the while
  His other passion wholly dies,
  Or in the light of deeper eyes
Is matter for a flying smile.

LXIII.

Yet pity for a horse o'er-driven,
  And love in which my hound has part,
  Can hang no weight upon my heart
In its assumptions up to heaven;

And I am so much more than these,
  As thou, perchance, art more than I,
  And yet I spare them sympathy,
And I would set their pains at ease.

So mayst thou watch me where I weep,
  As, unto vaster motions bound,
  The circuits of thine orbit round
A higher height, a deeper deep.

LXIV.

Dost thou look back on what hath been,
  As some divinely gifted man,
  Whose life in low estate began
And on a simple village green;

Who breaks his birth's invidious bar,
  And grasps the skirts of happy chance,
  And breasts the blows of circumstance,
And grapples with his evil star;

Who makes by force his merit known,
  And lives to clutch the golden keys,
  To mould a mighty state's decrees,
And shape the whisper of the throne;

And moving up from high to higher,
  Becomes on Fortune's crowning slope
  The pillar of a people's hope,
The centre of a world's desire;

Yet feels, as in a pensive dream,
  When all his active powers are still,
  A distant dearness in the hill,
A secret sweetness in the stream,

The limit of his narrower fate,
  While yet beside its vocal springs
  He play'd at counsellors and kings,
With one that was his earliest mate;

Who ploughs with pain his native lea
  And reaps the labor of his hands,
  Or in the furrow musing stands:
"Does my old friend remember me?"

LXV.

Sweet soul, do with me as thou wilt;
  I lull a fancy trouble-tost
  With "Love's too precious to be lost,
A little grain shalt not be spilt."

And in that solace can I sing,
  Till out of painful phases wrought
  There flutters up a happy thought,
Self-balanced on a lightsome wing:

Since we deserved the name of friends,
  And thine effect so lives in me,
  A part of mine may live in thee,
And move thee on to noble ends.

LXVI.

You thought my heart too far diseased;
  You wonder when my fancies play
  To find me gay among the gay,
Like one with any trifle pleased.

The shade by which my life was crost,
  Which makes a desert in the mind,
  Has made me kindly with my kind,
And like to him whose sight is lost;

Whose feet are guided thro' the land,
  Whose jest among his friends is free,
  Who takes the children on his knee,
And winds their curls about his hand:

He plays with threads, he beats his chair
  For pastime, dreaming of the sky;
  His inner day can never die,
His night of loss is always there."

LXVII.

When on my bed the moonlight falls,
  I know that in thy place of rest,
  By that broad water of the west,
There comes a glory on the walls:

Thy marble bright in dark appears,
  As slowly steals a silver flame
  Along the letters of thy name,
And o'er the number of thy years.

The mystic glory swims away:
  From off my bed the moonlight dies;
  And, closing eaves of wearied eyes,
I sleep till dusk is dipt in gray:

And then I know the mist is drawn
  A lucid veil from coast to coast,
  And in the dark church, like a ghost,
Thy tablet glimmers to the dawn.

LXVIII.

When in the down I sink my head,
  Sleep, Death's twin-brother, times my breath,
  Sleep, Death's twin-brother, knows not Death,
Nor can I dream of thee as dead:

I walk as ere I walk'd forlorn,
  When all our path was fresh with dew,
  And all the bugle breezes blew
Reveillée to the breaking morn.

But what is this? I turn about,
  I find a trouble in thine eye,
  Which makes me sad, I know not why,
Nor can my dream resolve the doubt:

But ere the lark hath left the lea
  I wake, and I discern the truth;
  It is the trouble of my youth
That foolish sleep transfers to thee.

LXIX.

I dream'd there would be Spring no more,
  That Nature's ancient power was lost:
  The streets were black with smoke and frost,
They chatter'd trifles at the door:

I wander'd from the noisy town,
  I found a wood with thorny boughs:
  I took the thorns to bind my brows,
I wore them like a civic crown:

I met with scoffs, I met with scorns
    From youth and babe and hoary hairs:
    They call'd me in the public squares
The fool that wears a crown of thorns:

They call'd me fool, they call'd me child:
    I found an angel of the night:
    The voice was low, the look was bright;
He look'd upon my crown and smiled:

He reach'd the glory of a hand,
    That seem'd to touch it into leaf:
    The voice was not the voice of grief;
The words were hard to understand.

LXX.

I cannot see the features right,
    When on the gloom I strive to paint
    The face I know; the hues are faint
And mix with hollow masks of night;

Cloud-towers by ghostly masons wrought,
    A gulf that ever shuts and gapes,
    A hand that points, and palled shapes
In shadowy thoroughfares of thought;

And crowds that stream from yawning doors,
    And shoals of pucker'd faces drive;
    Dark bulks that tumble half alive,
And lazy lengths on boundless shores:

Till all at once beyond the will
    I hear a wizard music roll,
    And thro' a lattice on the soul
Looks thy fair face and makes it still.

LXXI.

Sleep, kinsman thou to death and trance
    And madness, thou hast forged at last
    A night-long Present of the Past
In which we went thro' summer France.

Hadst thou such credit with the soul?
    Then bring an opiate trebly strong,
    Drug down the blindfold sense of wrong
That so my pleasure may be whole;

While now we talk as once we talk'd
    Of men and minds, the dust of change,
    The days that grow to something strange,
In walking as of old we walk'd

Beside the river's wooded reach,
    The fortress, and the mountain ridge,
    The cataract flashing from the bridge,
The breaker breaking on the beach.

LXXII.

Risest thou thus, dim dawn, again,
    And howlest, issuing out of night,
    With blasts that blow the poplar white,
And lash with storm the streaming pane?

Day, when my crown'd estate begun
    To pine in that reverse of doom,
    Which sicken'd every living bloom,
And blurr'd the splendor of the sun;

Who usherest in the dolorous hour
    With thy quick tears that make the rose
    Pull sideways, and the daisy close
Her crimson fringes to the shower;

Who might'st have heaved a windless flame
    Up the deep East, or, whispering, play'd
    A chequer-work of beam and shade
Along the hills, yet looked the same.

As wan, as chill, as wild as now;
    Day, mark'd as with some hideous crime
    When the dark hand struck down thro' time,
And cancell'd nature's best: but thou,

Lift as thou mayst thy burthen'd brows
    Thro' clouds that drench the morning star,
    And whirl the ungarner'd sheaf afar,
And sow the sky with flying boughs,

And up thy vault with roaring sound
    Climb thy thick noon, disastrous day,
    Touch thy dull goal of joyless gray.
And hide thy shame beneath the ground.

LXXIII.

So many worlds, so much to do,
    So little done, such things to be,
    How know I what had need of thee,
For thou wert strong as thou wert true?

The fame is quench'd that I foresaw,
    The head hath miss'd an earthly wreath
    I curse not nature, no, nor death;
For nothing is that errs from law.

We pass; the path that each man trod
    Is dim, or will be dim, with weeds:
    What fame is left for human deeds
In endless age? It rests with God.

O hollow wraith of dying fame,
    Fade wholly, while the soul exults,
    And self-infolds the large results
Of force that would have forged a name.

LXXIV.

As sometimes in a dead man's face,
    To those that watch it more and more,
    A likeness, hardly seen before,
Comes out—to some one of his race:

So, dearest, now thy brows are cold,
    I see thee what thou art, and know
    Thy likeness to the wise below,
Thy kindred with the great of old.

But there is more than I can see,
    And what I see I leave unsaid,
    Nor speak it, knowing Death has made
His darkness beautiful with thee.

LXXV.

I leave thy praises unexpress'd
    In verse that brings myself relief,
    And by the measure of my grief
I leave thy greatness to be guess'd;

What practice howsoe'er expert
    In fitting aptest words to things,
    Or voice the richest-toned that sings
Hath power to give thee as thou wert?

I care not in these fading days
    To raise a cry that lasts not long,
    And round thee with the breeze of song
To stir a little dust of praise.

Thy leaf has perish'd in the green,
    And, while we breathe beneath the sun,
    The world which credits what is done
Is cold to all that might have been.

So here shall silence guard thy fame;
    But somewhere, out of human view,
    Whate'er thy hands are set to do
Is wrought with tumult of acclaim.

LXXVI.

TAKE wings of fancy, and ascend,
    And in a moment set thy face
Where all the starry heavens of space
Are sharpen'd to a needle's end;

Take wings of foresight; lighten thro'
    The secular abyss to come,
    And lo, thy deepest lays are dumb
Before the mouldering of a yew;

And if the matin songs, that woke
    The darkness of our planet, last,
    Thine own shall wither in the vast,
Ere half the lifetime of an oak.

Ere these have clothed their branchy bowers
    With fifty Mays, thy songs are vain;
    And what are they when these remain
The ruin'd shells of hollow towers?

LXXVII.

WHAT hope is here for modern rhyme
    To him who turns a musing eye
    On songs, and deeds, and lives, that lie
Foreshorten'd in the tract of time?

These mortal lullabies of pain
    May bind a book, may line a box,
    May serve to curl a maiden's locks;
Or when a thousand moons shall wane

A man upon a stall may find,
    And, passing, turn the page that tells
    A grief, then changed to something else,
Sung by a long-forgotten mind.

But what of that? My darken'd ways
    Shall ring with music all the same;
    To breathe my loss is more than fame,
To utter love more sweet than praise.

LXXVIII.

AGAIN at Christmas did we weave
    The holly round the Christmas hearth;
    The silent snow possess'd the earth,
And calmly fell our Christmas-eve:

The yule-clog sparkled keen with frost,
    No wing of wind the region swept,
    But over all things brooding slept
The quiet sense of something lost.

As in the winters left behind,
    Again our ancient games had place,
    The mimic picture's breathing grace,
And dance and song and hoodman-blind.

Who show'd a token of distress?
    No single tear, no mark of pain:
    O sorrow, then can sorrow wane?
O grief, can grief be changed to less?

O last regret, regret can die!
    No,—mixt with all this mystic frame,
    Her deep relations are the same,
But with long use her tears are dry.

LXXIX.

"MORE than my brothers are to me,"
    Let this not vex thee, noble heart.
    I know thee of what force thou art
To hold the costliest love in fee.

But thou and I are one in kind,
    As moulded like in nature's mint;
    And hill and wood and field did print
The same sweet forms in either mind.

For us the same cold streamlet curl'd
    Thro' all his eddying coves; the same
    All winds that roam the twilight came
In whispers of the beauteous world.

At one dear knee we proffer'd vows,
    One lesson from one book we learn'd,
    Ere childhood's flaxen ringlet turn'd
To black and brown on kindred brows.

And so my wealth resembles thine,
    But he was rich where I was poor,
    And he supplied my want the more
As his unlikeness fitted mine.

LXXX.

IF any vague desire should rise,
    That holy Death ere Arthur died
    Had moved me kindly from his side,
And dropt the dust on tearless eyes;

Then fancy shapes, as fancy can,
    The grief my loss in him had wrought,
    A grief as deep as life or thought,
But stay'd in peace with God and man.

I make a picture in the brain;
    I hear the sentence that he speaks;
    He bears the burthen of the weeks;
But turns his burthen into gain.

His credit thus shall set me free;
    And, influence-rich to soothe and save,
    Unused example from the grave
Reach out dead hands to comfort me.

LXXXI.

COULD I have said while he was here,
    "My love shall now no further range;
    There cannot come a mellower change,
For now is love mature in ear."

Love, then, had hope of richer store:
    What end is here to my complaint?
    This haunting whisper makes me faint,
"More years had made me love thee more.'

But Death returns an answer sweet:
    "My sudden frost was sudden gain,
    And gave all ripeness to the grain
It might have drawn from after-heat."

LXXXII.

I WAGE not any feud with Death
    For changes wrought on form and face;
    No lower life that earth's embrace
May breed with him can fright my faith.

Eternal process moving on,
    From state to state the spirit walks;
    And these are but the shatter'd stalks,
Or ruin'd chrysalis of one.

Nor blame I Death, because he bare
    The use of virtue out of earth:
    I know transplanted human worth
Will bloom to profit, otherwhere.

For this alone on Death I wreak
    The wrath that garners in my heart ·
    He put our lives so far apart
We cannot hear each other speak

LXXXIII.

DIP down upon the northern shore,
    O sweet new-year, delaying long:
    Thou doest expectant nature wrong;
Delaying long, delay no more.

What stays thee from the clouded noons,
　Thy sweetness from its proper place?
　Can trouble live with April days,
Or sadness in the summer moons?

Bring orchis, bring the foxglove spire,
　The little speedwell's darling blue,
　Deep tulips dash'd with fiery dew,
Laburnums, dropping-wells of fire.

O thou, new-year. delaying long,
　Delayest the sorrow in my blood,
　That longs to burst a frozen bud,
And flood a fresher throat with song.

LXXXIV.

When I contemplate all alone
　The life that had been thine below,
　And fix my thoughts on all the glow
To which thy crescent would have grown;

I see thee sitting crown'd with good,
　A central warmth diffusing bliss
　In glance and smile, and clasp and kiss,
On all the branches of thy blood;

Thy blood, my friend, and partly mine;
　For now the day was drawing on
　When thou shouldst link thy life with one
Of mine own house, and boys of thine

Had babbled "Uncle" on my knee;
　But that remorseless iron hour
　Made cypress of her orange-flower,
Despair of Hope, and earth of thee.

I seem to meet their least desire,
　To clap their cheeks, to call them mine.
　I see their unborn faces shine
Beside the never-lighted fire.

I see myself an honor'd guest,
　Thy partner in the flowery walk
　Of letters, genial table-talk,
Or deep dispute, and graceful jest;

While now thy prosperous labor fills
　The lips of men with honest praise,
　And sun by sun the happy days
Descend below the golden hills

With promise of a morn as fair;
　And all the train of bounteous hours
　Conduct by paths of growing powers
To reverence and the silver hair;

Till slowly worn her earthly robe,
　Her lavish mission richly wrought,
　Leaving great legacies of thought,
Thy spirit should fail from off the globe;

What time mine own might also flee,
　As link'd with thine in love and fate,
　And, hovering o'er the dolorous strait
To the other shore, involved in thee,

Arrive at last the blessed goal,
　And He that died in Holy Land
　Would reach us out the shining hand,
And take us as a single soul.

What reed was that on which I leant?
　Ah, backward fancy, wherefore wake
　The old bitterness again, and break
The low beginnings of content?

LXXXV.

This truth came borne with bier and pall,
　I felt it, when I sorrow'd most,
　'T is better to have loved and lost,
Than never to have loved at all——

O true in word, and tried in deed,
　Demanding so to bring relief
　To this which is our common grief,
What kind of life is that I lead;

And whether trust in things above
　Be dimm'd of sorrow or sustain'd;
　And whether love for him have drain'd
My capabilities of love;

Your words have virtue such as draws
　A faithful answer from the breast,
　Thro' light reproaches, half exprest,
And loyal unto kindly laws.

My blood an even tenor kept,
　Till on mine ear this message falls,
　That in Vienna's fatal walls
God's finger touch'd him, and he slept.

The great Intelligences fair
　That range above our mortal state,
　In circle round the blessed gate,
Received and gave him welcome there.

And led him thro' the blissful climes,
　And show'd him in the fountain fresh
　All knowledge that the sons of flesh
Shall gather in the cycled times.

But I remain'd, whose hopes were dim,
　Whose life, whose thoughts were little worth,
　To wander on a darken'd earth,
Where all things round me breathed of him.

O friendship, equal-poised control,
　O heart, with kindliest motion warm,
　O sacred essence, other form,
O solemn ghost, O crowned soul!

Yet none could better know than I,
　How much of act at human hands
　The sense of human will demands,
By which we dare to live or die.

Whatever way my days decline,
　I felt and feel, tho' left alone,
　His being working in mine own,
The footsteps of his life in mine;

A life that all the Muses deck'd
　With gifts of grace, that might express
　All-comprehensive tenderness,
All-subtilizing intellect:

And so my passion hath not swerved
　To works of weakness, but I find
　An image comforting the mind,
And in my grief a strength reserved.

Likewise the imaginative woe,
　That loved to handle spiritual strife,
　Diffused the shock thro' all my life,
But in the present broke the blow.

My pulses therefore beat again
　For other friends that once I met;
　Nor can it suit me to forget
The mighty hopes that make us men.

I wo'd your love: I count it crime
To mourn for any overmuch;
I, the divided half of such
A friendship as had master'd Time:

Which masters Time indeed, and is
Eternal, separate from fears:
The all-assuming months and years
Can take no part away from this:

But Summer on the steaming floods,
And Spring that swells the narrow brooks,
And Autumn, with a noise of rooks,
That gather in the waning woods,

And every pulse of wind and wave
Recalls, in change of light or gloom,
My old affection of the tomb,
And my prime passion in the grave:

My old affection of the tomb,
A part of stillness, yearns to speak:
"Arise, and get thee forth and seek
A friendship for the years to come.

"I watch thee from the quiet shore;
Thy spirit up to mine can reach;
But in dear words of human speech
We two communicate no more."

And I, "Can clouds of nature stain
The starry clearness of the free?
How is it? Canst thou feel for me
Some painless sympathy with pain?"

And lightly does the whisper fall:
"'T is hard for thee to fathom this:
I triumph in conclusive bliss,
And that serene result of all."

So hold I commerce with the dead;
Or so methinks the dead would say;
Or so shall grief with symbols play,
And pining life be fancy-fed.

Now looking to some settled end,
That these things pass, and I shall prove
A meeting somewhere, love with love,
I crave your pardon, O my friend;

If not so fresh, with love as true,
I, clasping brother-hands, aver
I could not, if I would, transfer
The whole I felt for him to you.

For which he they that hold apart
The promise of the golden hours?
First love, first friendship, equal powers,
That marry with the virgin heart.

Still mine, that cannot but deplore,
That beats within a lonely place,
That yet remembers his embrace,
But at his footstep leaps no more,

My heart, tho' widow'd, may not rest
Quite in the love of what is gone,
But seeks to beat in time with one
That warms another living breast.

Ah, take the imperfect gift I bring,
Knowing the primrose yet is dear,
The primrose of the later year,
As not unlike to that of Spring.

LXXXVI.

SWEET after showers, ambrosial air,
That rollest from the gorgeous gloom
Of evening over brake and bloom
And meadow, slowly breathing bare

The round of space, and rapt below
Thro' all the dewy-tassell'd wood,
And shadowing down the horned flood
In ripples, fan my brows and blow

The fever from my cheek, and sigh
The full new life that feeds thy breath
Throughout my frame, till Doubt and Death,
Ill brethren let the fancy fly

From belt to belt of crimson seas
On leagues of odor streaming far,
To where in yonder orient star
A hundred spirits whisper "Peace."

LXXXVII.

I PAST beside the reverend walls
In which of old I wore the gown;
I roved at random thro' the town,
And saw the tumult of the halls;

And heard once more in college fanes
The storm their high-built organs make,
And thunder-music, rolling, shake
The prophets blazon'd on the panes;

And caught once more the distant shout,
The measured pulse of racing oars
Among the willows; paced the shores
And many a bridge, and all about

The same gray flats again, and felt
The same, but not the same: and last
Up that long walk of limes I past
To see the rooms in which he dwelt.

Another name was on the door:
I linger'd; all within was noise
Of songs, and clapping hands, and boys
That crash'd the glass and beat the floor;

Where once we held debate, a band
Of youthful friends, on mind and art,
And labor, and the changing mart,
And all the framework of the land;

When one would aim an arrow fair,
But send it slackly from the string;
And one would pierce an outer ring,
And one an inner, here and there;

And last the master-bowman, he
Would cleave the mark. A willing ear
We lent him. Who, but hung to hear
The rapt oration flowing free

From point to point, with power and grace
And music in the bounds of law,
To those conclusions when we saw
The God within him light his face.

And seem to lift the form, and glow
In azure orbits heavenly-wise;
And over those ethereal eyes
The bar of Michael Angelo.

LXXXVIII.

WILD bird, whose warble, liquid sweet,
Rings Eden thro' the budded quicks,
O tell me where the senses mix,
O tell me where the passions meet,

Whence radiate: fierce extremes employ
Thy spirits in the darkening leaf,
And in the midmost heart of grief
Thy passion clasps a secret joy:

And I—my harp would prelude woe—
I cannot all command the strings:
The glory of the sum of things
Will flash along the chords and go.

LXXXIX.

WITCH-ELMS that counterchange the floor
Of this flat lawn with dusk and bright;
And thou, with all thy breadth and height
Of foliage, towering sycamore;

How often, hither wandering down,
My Arthur found your shadows fair,
And shook to all the liberal air
The dust and din and steam of town:

He brought an eye for all he saw;
He mixt in all our simple sports;
They pleased him, fresh from broiling courts
And dusty purlieus of the law.

O joy to him in this retreat,
Immantled in ambrosial dark,
To drink the cooler air, and mark
The landscape winking thro' the heat:

O sound to rout the brood of cares,
The sweep of scythe in morning dew,
The gust that round the garden flew,
And tumbled half the mellowing pears!

O bliss, when all in circle drawn
About him, heart and ear were fed
To hear him, as he lay and read
The Tuscan poet on the lawn:

Or in the all-golden afternoon
A guest, or happy sister, sung,
Or here she brought the harp and flung
A ballad to the brightening moon:

Nor less it pleased in livelier moods,
Beyond the bounding hill to stray,
And break the livelong summer day
With banquet in the distant woods;

Whereat we glanced from theme to theme,
Discuss'd the books to love or hate,
Or touch'd the changes of the state,
Or threaded some Socratic dream;

But if I praised the busy town,
He loved to rail against it still,
For "ground in yonder social mill,
We rub each other's angles down,

"And merge," he said, "in form and gloss
The picturesque of man and man."
We talk'd: the stream beneath us ran,
The wine-flask lying couch'd in moss,

Or cool'd within the gloomixg wave;
And last, returning from afar,
Before the crimson-circled star
Had fall'n into her father's grave,

And brushing ankle-deep in flowers,
We heard behind the woodbine veil
The milk that bubbled in the pail,
And buzzings of the honeyed hours.

XC.

HE tasted love with half his mind,
Nor ever drank the inviolate spring
Where nighest heaven, who first could fling
This bitter seed among mankind:

That could the dead, whose dying eyes
Were closed with wail, resume their life,
They would but find in child and wife
An iron welcome when they rise:

'T was well, indeed, when warm with wine,
To pledge them with a kindly tear,
To talk them o'er, to wish them here,
To count their memories half divine;

But if they came who passed away,
Behold their brides in other hands;
The hard heir strides about their lands,
And will not yield them for a day.

Yea, tho' their sons were none of these,
Not less the yet-loved sire would make
Confusion worse than death, and shake
The pillars of domestic peace.

Ah dear, but come thou back to me:
Whatever change the years have wrought,
I find not yet one lonely thought
That cries against my wish for thee.

XCI.

WHEN rosy plumelets tuft the larch,
And rarely pipes the mounted thrush;
Or underneath the barren bush
Flits by the sea-blue bird of March:

Come, wear the form by which I know
Thy spirit in time among thy peers;
The hope of unaccomplish'd years
Be large and lucid round thy brow.

When summer's hourly-mellowing change
May breathe, with many roses sweet,
Upon the thousand waves of wheat,
That ripple round the lonely grange;

Come: not in watches of the night,
But where the sunbeam broodeth warm,
Come, beauteons in thine after form,
And like a finer light in light.

XCII.

IF any vision should reveal
Thy likeness, I might count it vain,
As but the canker of the brain:
Yea, tho' it spake and made appeal

To chances where our lots were cast
Together in the days behind.
I might but say, I hear a wind
Of memory murmuring the past.

Yea, tho' it spake and bared to view
A fact within the coming year;
And tho' the months, revolving near,
Should prove the phantom-warning true,

They might not seem thy prophecies,
But spiritual presentiments,
And such refraction of events
As often rises ere they rise.

XCIII.

I SHALL not see thee. Dare I say
No spirit ever brake the band
That stays him from the native land,
Where first he walk'd when claspt in clay?

No visual shade of some one lost,
But he, the Spirit himself, may come
Where all the nerve of sense is numb
Spirit to Spirit, Ghost to Ghost.

O, therefore from thy sightless range
With gods in unconjectured bliss,
O, from the distance of the abyss
Of tenfold-complicated change,

Descend, and touch, and enter; hear
The wish too strong for words to name;
That in this blindness of the frame
My Ghost may feel that thine is near.

XCIV.

How pure at heart and sound in head,
With what divine affections bold,
Should be the man whose thought would hold
An hour's communion with the dead.

In vain shalt thou, or any, call
The spirits from their golden day,
Except, like them, thou too canst say,
My spirit is at peace with all.

They haunt the silence of the breast,
Imaginations calm and fair,
The memory like a cloudless air,
The conscience as a sea at rest:

But when the heart is full of din,
And doubt beside the portal waits,
They can but listen at the gates,
And hear the household jar within.

XCV.

By night we linger'd on the lawn,
For underfoot the herb was dry;
And genial warmth; and o'er the sky
The silvery haze of summer drawn;

And calm that let the tapers burn
Unwavering: not a cricket chirr'd:
The brook alone far-off was heard,
And on the board the fluttering urn:

And bats went round in fragrant skies,
And wheel'd or lit the filmy shapes
That haunt the dusk, with ermine capes
And woolly breasts and beaded eyes;

While now we sang old songs that peal'd
From knoll to knoll, where, couch'd at ease,
The white kine glimmer'd, and the trees
Laid their dark arms about the field.

But when those others, one by one,
Withdrew themselves from me and night,
And in the house light after light
Went out, and I was all alone,

A hunger seized my heart; I read
Of that glad year that once had been,
In those fall'n leaves which kept their green,
The noble letters of the dead:

And strangely on the silence broke
The silent-speaking words, and strange
Was love's dumb cry defying change
To test his worth; and strangely spoke

The faith, the vigor, bold to dwell
On doubts that drive the coward back,
And keen thro' wordy snares to track
Suggestion to her inmost cell.

So word by word, and line by line,
The dead man touch'd me from the past,
And all at once it seem'd at last
His living soul was flash'd on mine,

And mine in his was wound, and whirl'd
About empyreal heights of thought,
And came on that which is, and caught
The deep pulsations of the world,

Æonian music measuring out
The steps of Time, the shocks of Chance,
The blows of Death. At length my trance
Was cancell'd, stricken thro' with doubt.

Vague words! but ah, how hard to frame
In matter-moulded forms of speech,
Or ev'n for intellect to reach
Thro' memory that which I became:

Till now the doubtful dusk reveal'd
The knoll once more where, couch'd at ease,
The white kine glimmer'd, and the trees
Laid their dark arms about the field:

And, suck'd from out the distant gloom,
A breeze began to tremble o'er
The large leaves of the sycamore,
And fluctuate all the still perfume,

And gathering freshlier overhead,
Rock'd the full-foliaged elms, and swung
The heavy-folded rose, and flung
The lilies to and fro, and said,

"The dawn, the dawn," and died away;
And East and West, without a breath,
Mixt their dim lights, like life and death,
To broaden into boundless day.

XCVI.

You say, but with no touch of scorn,
Sweet-hearted, you, whose light-blue eyes
Are tender over drowning flies,
You tell me, doubt is Devil-born.

I know not: one indeed I knew
In many a subtle question versed,
Who touch'd a jarring lyre at first,
But ever strove to make it true:

Perplext in faith, but pure in deeds,
At last he beat his music out.
There lives more faith in honest doubt,
Believe me, than in half the creeds.

He fought his doubts and gather'd strength,
He would not make his judgment blind,
He faced the spectres of the mind
And laid them: thus he came at length

To find a stronger faith his own;
And Power was with him in the night,
Which makes the darkness and the light,
And dwells not in the light alone,

But in the darkness and the cloud,
As over Sinai's peaks of old,
While Israel made their gods of gold,
Altho' the trumpet blew so loud.

XCVII.

My love has talk'd with rocks and trees;
He finds on misty mountain-ground
His own vast shadow glory-crown'd;
He sees himself in all he sees.

Two partners of a married life,—
I look'd on these, and thought of thee
In vastness and in mystery,
And of my spirit as of a wife.

These two—they dwelt with eye on eye,
 Their hearts of old have beat in tune,
 Their meetings made December June,
Their every parting was to die.

Their love has never past away;
 The days she never can forget
 Are earnest that he loves her yet,
Whate'er the faithless people say.

Her life is lone, he sits apart,
 He loves her yet, she will not weep,
 Tho' rapt in matters dark and deep
He seems to slight her simple heart.

He thrids the labyrinth of the mind,
 He reads the secret of the star,
 He seems so near and yet so far,
He looks so cold: she thinks him kind.

She keeps the gift of years before,
 A wither'd violet is her bliss:
 She knows not what his greatness is:
For that, for all, she loves him more.

For him she plays, to him she sings
 Of early faith and plighted vows;
 She knows but matters of the house,
And he, he knows a thousand things.

Her faith is fixt and cannot move,
 She darkly feels him great and wise,
 She dwells on him with faithful eyes,
"I cannot understand: I love."

XCVIII.

You leave us: you will see the Rhine,
 And those fair hills I sail'd below,
 When I was there with him; and go
By summer belts of wheat and vine

To where he breathed his latest breath,
 That City. All her splendor seems
 No livelier than the wisp that gleams
On Lethe in the eyes of Death.

Let her great Danube rolling fair
 Enwind her isles, unmark'd of me:
 I have not seen, I will not see
Vienna: rather dream that there,

A treble darkness, Evil haunts
 The birth, the bridal; friend from friend
 Is oftener parted, fathers bend
Above more graves, a thousand wants

Gnarr at the heels of men, and prey
 By each cold hearth, and sadness flings
 Her shadow on the blaze of kings:
And yet myself have heard him say,

That not in any mother town
 With statelier progress to and fro
 The double tides of chariots flow
By park and suburb under brown

Of lustier leaves; nor more content,
 He told me, lives in any crowd,
 When all is gay with lamps, and loud
With sport and song, in booth and tent,

Imperial halls, or open plain;
 And wheels the circled dance, and breaks
 The rocket molten into flakes
Of crimson or in emerald rain.

XCIX.

RISEST thou thus, dim dawn, again,
 So loud with voices of the birds,
 So thick with lowings of the herds,
Day, when I lost the flower of men;

Who tremblest thro' thy darkling red
 On yon swoll'n brook that bubbles fast,
 By meadows breathing of the past,
And woodlands holy to the dead;

Who murmurest in the foliaged eaves
 A song that slights the coming care,
 And Autumn laying here and there
A fiery finger on the leaves;

Who wakenest with thy balmy breath,
 To myriads on the genial earth,
 Memories of bridal, or of birth,
And unto myriads more, of death

O, wheresoever those may be,
 Betwixt the slumber of the poles,
 To-day they count as kindred souls;
They know me not, but mourn with me.

C.

I CLIMB the hill: from end to end
 Of all the landscape underneath,
 I find no place that does not breathe
Some gracious memory of my friend;

No gray old grange, or lonely fold,
 Or low morass and whispering reed,
 Or simple stile from mead to mead,
Or sheepwalk up the windy wold;

No hoary knoll of ash and haw
 That hears the latest linnet trill,
 Nor quarry trench'd along the hill,
And haunted by the wrangling daw;

Nor runlet tinkling from the rock;
 Nor pastoral rivulet that swerves
 To left and right thro' meadowy curves,
That feed the mothers of the flock;

But each has pleased a kindred eye,
 And each reflects a kindlier day;
 And, leaving these, to pass away,
I think once more he seems to die.

CI.

UNWATCH'D, the garden bough shall sway,
 The tender blossom flutter down,
 Unloved, that beech will gather brown,
This maple burn itself away;

Unloved, the sun-flower, shining fair,
 Ray round with flames her disk of seed,
 And many a rose-carnation feed
With summer spice the humming air;

Unloved, by many a sandy bar,
 The brook shall babble down the plain,
 At noon, or when the lesser wain
Is twisting round the polar star;

Uncared for, gird the windy grove,
 And flood the haunts of hern and crake;
 Or into silver arrows break
The sailing moon in creek and cove;

Till from the garden and the wild
 A fresh association blow,
 And year by year the landscape grow
Familiar to the stranger's child:

As year by year the laborer tills
His wonted glebe, or lops the glades:
And year by year our memory fades
From all the circle of the hills.

CII.

WE leave the well-beloved place
Where first we gazed upon the sky;
The roofs, that heard our earliest cry,
Will shelter one of stranger race.

We go, but ere we go from home,
As down the garden-walks I move,
Two spirits of a diverse love
Contend for loving masterdom.

One whispers, here thy boyhood sung
Long since its matin song, and heard
The low love-language of the bird
In native hazels tassel-hung.

The other answers, "Yea, but here
Thy feet have strayed in after hours
With thy lost friend among the bowers,
And this hath made them trebly dear."

These two have striven half the day,
And each prefers his separate claim,
Poor rivals in a losing game,
That will not yield each other way.

I turn to go: my feet are set
To leave the pleasant fields and farms;
They mix in one another's arms
To one pure image of regret.

CIII.

On that last night before we went
From out the doors where I was bred,
I dream'd a vision of the dead,
Which left my after-morn content.

Methought I dwelt within a hall,
And maidens with me: distant hills
From hidden summits fed with rills
A river sliding by the wall.

The hall with harp and carol rang.
They sang of what is wise and good
And graceful. In the centre stood
A statue veil'd, to which they sang;

And which, tho' veil'd, was known to me,
The shape of him I loved, and love
Forever: then flew in a dove
And brought a summons from the sea:

And when they learnt that I must go,
They wept and wail'd, but led the way
To where a little shallop lay
At anchor in the flood below;

And on by many a level mead,
And shadowing bluff that made the banks,
We glided winding under ranks
Of iris, and the golden reed;

And still as vaster grew the shore,
And roll'd the floods in grander space,
The maidens gather'd strength and grace
And presence, lordlier than before;

And I myself, who sat apart
And watch'd them, wax'd in every limb;
I felt the thews of Anakim,
The pulses of a Titan's heart;

As one would sing the death of war,
And one would chant the history
Of that great race, which is to be,
And one the shaping of a star;

Until the forward-creeping tides
Began to foam, and we to draw,
From deep to deep, to where we saw
A great ship lift her shining sides.

The man we loved was there on deck,
But thrice as large as man he bent
To greet us. Up the side I went,
And fell in silence on his neck:

Whereat those maidens with one mind
Bewail'd their lot; I did them wrong:
"We served thee here," they said, "so long,
And wilt thou leave us now behind?"

So rapt I was, they could not win
An answer from my lips, but he
Replying, "Enter likewise ye
And go with us:" they enter'd in.

And while the wind began to sweep
A music out of sheet and shroud,
We steer'd her toward a crimson cloud
That landlike slept along the deep.

CIV.

THE time draws near the birth of Christ:
The moon is hid, the night is still;
A single church below the hill
Is pealing, folded in the mist.

A single peal of bells below,
That wakens at this hour of rest
A single murmur in the breast,
That these are not the bells I know.

Like strangers' voices here they sound,
In lands where not a memory strays,
Nor landmark breathes of other days,
But all is new unhallow'd ground.

CV.

THIS holly by the cottage-eave,
To-night, ungather'd, shall it stand:
We live within the stranger's land,
And strangely falls our Christmas-eve.

Our father's dust is left alone
And silent under other snows;
There in due time the woodbine blows,
The violet comes, but we are gone.

No more shall wayward grief abuse
The genial hour with mask and mime;
For change of place, like growth of time,
Has broke the bond of dying use.

Let cares that petty shadows cast,
By which our lives are chiefly proved,
A little spare the night I loved,
And hold it solemn to the past.

But let no footstep beat the floor,
Nor bowl of wassail mantle warm;
For who would keep an ancient form
Thro' which the spirit breathes no more?

Be neither song, nor game, nor feast;
Nor harp be touch'd, nor flute be blown;
No dance, no motion, save alone
What lightens in the lucid east

Of rising worlds by yonder wood.
Long sleeps the summer in the seed;
Run out your measured arcs, and lead
The closing cycle rich in good.

CVI.

Ring out wild bells to the wild sky,
The flying cloud, the frosty light:
The year is dying in the night;
Ring out, wild bells, and let him die.

Ring out the old, ring in the new,
Ring, happy bells, across the snow:
The year is going, let him go;
Ring out the false, ring in the true.

Ring out the grief that saps the mind,
For those that here we see no more;
Ring out the feud of rich and poor,
Ring in redress to all mankind.

Ring out a slowly dying cause.
And ancient forms of party strife;
Ring in the nobler modes of life,
With sweeter manners, purer laws.

Ring out the want, the care, the sin,
The faithless coldness of the times;
Ring out, ring out my mournful rhymes,
But ring the fuller minstrel in.

Ring out false pride in place and blood,
The civic slander and the spite;
Ring in the love of truth and right,
Ring in the common love of good.

Ring out old shapes of foul disease;
Ring out the narrowing lust of gold;
Ring out the thousand wars of old,
Ring in the thousand years of peace.

Ring in the valiant man and free,
The larger heart, the kindlier hand;
Ring out the darkness of the land,
Ring in the Christ that is to be.

CVII.

It is the day when he was born,
A bitter day that early sank
Behind a purple-frosty bank
Of vapor, leaving night forlorn.

The time admits not flowers or leaves
To deck the banquet. Fiercely flies
The blast of North and East, and ice
Makes daggers at the sharpen'd eaves,

And bristles all the brakes and thorns
To yon hard crescent, as she hangs
Above the wood which grides and clangs
Its leafless ribs and iron horns

Together, in the drifts that pass
To darken on the rolling brine
That breaks the coast. But fetch the wine,
Arrange the board and brim the glass;

Bring in great logs and let them lie,
To make a solid core of heat;
Be cheerful-minded, talk and treat
Of all things ev'n as he were by;

We keep the day. With festal cheer,
With books and music, surely we
Will drink to him whate'er he be,
And sing the songs he loved to hear.

CVIII.

I will not shut me from my kind,
And, lest I stiffen into stone,
I will not eat my heart alone,
Nor feed with sighs a passing wind:

What profit lies in barren faith,
And vacant yearning, tho' with might
To scale the heaven's highest height,
Or dive below the wells of Death?

What find I in the highest place,
But mine own phantom chanting hymns?
And on the depths of death there swims
The reflex of a human face.

I 'll rather take what fruit may be
Of sorrow under human skies:
'T is held that sorrow makes us wise,
Whatever wisdom sleep with thee.

CIX.

Heart-affluence in discursive talk
From household fountains never dry;
The critic clearness of an eye,
That saw thro' all the Muses' walk;

Seraphic intellect and force
To seize and throw the doubts of man;
Impassion'd logic, which outran
The hearer in its fiery course;

High nature amorous of the good,
But touch'd with no ascetic gloom;
And passion pure in snowy bloom
Thro' all the years of April blood;

A love of freedom rarely felt,
Of freedom in her regal seat
Of England; not the school-boy heat,
The blind hysterics of the Celt;

And manhood fused with female grace
In such a sort, the child would twine
A trustful hand, unask'd, in thine,
And find his comfort in thy face;

All these have been, and thee mine eyes
Have look'd on: if they look'd in vain,
My shame is greater who remain,
Nor let thy wisdom make me wise.

CX.

Thy converse drew us with delight,
The men of rathe and riper years;
The feeble soul, a haunt of fears,
Forgot his weakness in thy sight.

On thee the loyal-hearted hung,
The proud was half disarm'd of pride,
Nor cared the serpent at thy side
To flicker with his double tongue.

The stern were mild when thou wert by,
The flippant put himself to school
And heard thee, and the brazen fool
Was soften'd, and he knew not why;

While I, thy dearest, sat apart,
And felt thy triumph was as mine;
And loved them more, that they were thine,
The graceful tact, the Christian art;

Not mine the sweetness or the skill
But mine the love that will not tire,
And, born of love, the vague desire
That spurs an imitative will.

CXI.

Tue churl in spirit, up or down
  Along the scale of ranks, thro' all,
  To him who grasps a golden ball,
By blood a king, at heart a clown;

The churl in spirit, howe'er he veil
  His want in forms for fashion's sake,
  Will let his coltish nature break
At seasons thro' the gilded pale:

For who can always act? but he,
  To whom a thousand memories call,
  Not being less but more than all
The gentleness he seem'd to be,

Best seem'd the thing he was, and join'd
  Each office of the social hour
  To noble manners, as the flower
And native growth of noble mind;

Nor ever narrowness or spite,
  Or villain fancy fleeting by,
  Drew in the expression of an eye,
Where God and Nature met in light;

And thus he bore without abuse
  The grand old name of gentleman,
  Defamed by every charlatan,
And soil'd with all ignoble use.

CXII.

High wisdom holds my wisdom less,
  That I, who gaze with temperate eyes
  On glorious insufficiencies,
Set light by narrower perfectness.

But thou, that fillest all the room
  Of all my love, art reason why
  I seem to cast a careless eye
On souls, the lesser lords of doom.

For what wert thou? some novel power
  Sprang up forever at a touch,
  And hope could never hope too much,
In watching thee from hour to hour,

Large elements in order brought,
  And tracts of calm from tempest made,
  And world-wide fluctuation sway'd
In vassal tides that follow'd thought.

CXIII.

'T is held that sorrow makes us wise;
  Yet how much wisdom sleeps with thee
  Which not alone had guided me,
But served the seasons that may rise;

For can I doubt who knew thee keen
  In intellect, with force and skill
  To strive, to fashion, to fulfil—
I doubt not what thou wouldst have been:

A life in civic action warm,
  A soul on highest mission sent,
  A potent voice of Parliament,
A pillar steadfast in the storm,

Should licensed boldness gather force,
  Becoming, when the time has birth,
  A lever to uplift the earth
And roll it in another course,

With thousand shocks that come and go,
  With agonies, with energies,
  With overthrowings, and with cries,
And undulations to and fro.

CXIV.

Who loves not Knowledge? Who shall rail
  Against her beauty? May she mix
  With men and prosper! Who shall fix
Her pillars? Let her work prevail.

But on her forehead sits a fire:
  She sets her forward countenance
  And leaps into the future chance,
Submitting all things to desire.

Half-grown as yet, a child, and vain,
  She cannot fight the fear of death.
  What is she, cut from love and faith,
But some wild Pallas from the brain

Of Demons? fiery-hot to burst
  All barriers in her onward race
  For power. Let her know her place;
She is the second, not the first.

A higher hand must make her mild,
  If all be not in vain; and guide
  Her footsteps, moving side by side
With wisdom, like the younger child:

For she is earthly of the mind,
  But Wisdom heavenly of the soul.
  O friend, who camest to thy goal
So early, leaving me behind,

I would the great world grew like thee,
  Who grewest not alone in power
  And knowledge, but by year and hour
In reverence and in charity.

CXV.

Now fades the last long streak of snow,
  Now bourgeons every maze of quick
  About the flowering squares, and thick
By ashen roots the violets blow.

Now rings the woodland loud and long,
  The distance takes a lovelier hue,
  And drown'd in yonder living blue
The lark becomes a sightless song.

Now dance the lights on lawn and lea,
  The flocks are whiter down the vale,
  And milkier every milky sail
On winding stream or distant sea;

Where now the seamew pipes, or dives
  In yonder gleaming green, and fly
  The happy birds, that change their sky
To build and brood; that live their lives

From land to land; and in my breast
  Spring wakens too: and my regret
  Becomes an April violet,
And buds and blossoms like the rest.

CXVI.

Is it, then, regret for buried time
  That keenlier in sweet April wakes,
  And meets the year, and gives and takes
The colors of the crescent prime?

Not all: the songs, the stirring air,
  The life re-orient out of dust,
  Cry thro' the sense to hearten trust
In that which made the world so fair.

Not all regret: the face will shine
  Upon me, while I muse alone;
  And that dear voice I once have known
Still speak to me of me and mine:

Yet less of sorrow lives in me
  For days of happy commune dead ;
  Less yearning for the friendship fled,
Than some strong bond which is to be.

CXVII.

O DAYS and hours, your work is this,
  To hold me from my proper place,
  A little while from his embrace,
For fuller gain of after bliss ;

That out of distance might ensue
  Desire of nearness doubly sweet :
  And unto meeting when we meet,
Delight a hundred-fold accrue,

For every grain of sand that runs,
  And every span of shade that steals,
  And every kiss of toothed wheels,
And all the courses of the suns.

CXVIII.

CONTEMPLATE all this work of Time,
  The giant laboring in his youth ;
  Nor dream of human love and truth,
As dying Nature's earth and lime ;

But trust that those we call the dead
  Are breathers of an ampler day,
  Forever nobler ends. They say,
The solid earth whereon we tread

In tracts of fluent heat began,
  And grew to seeming-random forms,
  The seeming prey of cyclic storms,
Till at the last arose the man ;

Who throve and branch'd from clime to clime
  The herald of a higher race,
  And of himself in higher place
If so he type this work of time

Within himself, from more to more ·
  Or, crown'd with attributes of woe
  Like glories, move his course, and show
That life is not as idle ore,

But iron dug from central gloom,
  And heated hot with burning fears,
  And dipt in baths of hissing tears,
And batter'd with the shocks of doom

To shape and use. Arise and fly
  The reeling Faun, the sensual feast ;
  Move upward, working out the beast,
And let the ape and tiger die.

CXIX.

Doors, where my heart was used to beat
  So quickly, not as one that weeps
  I come once more ; the city sleeps ;
I smell the meadow in the street ;

I hear a chirp of birds ; I see
  Betwixt the black fronts long-withdrawn
  A light-blue lane of early dawn,
And think of early days and thee,

And bless thee, for thy lips are bland,
  And bright the friendship of thine eye :
  And in my thoughts with scarce a sigh
I take the pressure of thine hand.

CXX.

I TRUST I have not wasted breath ;
  I think we are not wholly brain,
  Magnetic mockeries ; not in vain,
Like Paul with beasts, I fought with Death ;

Not only cunning casts in clay :
  Let Science prove we are, and then
  What matters Science unto men,
At least to me ? I would not stay.

Let him, the wiser man who springs
  Hereafter, up from childhood shape
  His action, like the greater ape,
But I was born to other things.

CXXI.

SAD Hesper o'er the buried sun,
  And ready, thou, to die with him,
  Thou watchest all things ever dim
And dimmer, and a glory done :

The team is loosen'd from the wain,
  The boat is drawn upon the shore ;
  Thou listenest to the closing door,
And life is darken'd in the brain.

Bright Phosphor, fresher for the night,
  By thee the world's great work is heard
  Beginning, and the wakeful bird :
Behind thee comes the greater light :

The market boat is on the stream,
  And voices hail it from the brink ;
  Thou hear'st the village hammer clink,
And see'st the moving of the team.

Sweet Hesper-Phosphor, double name
  For what is one, the first, the last,
  Thou, like my present and my past,
Thy place is changed , thou art the same.

CXXII.

O, WAST thou with me, dearest, then,
  While I rose up against my doom,
  And yearn'd to burst the folded gloom,
To bare the eternal Heavens again,

To feel once more, in placid awe,
  The strong imagination roll
  A sphere of stars about my soul,
In all her motion one with law.

If thou wert with me, and the grave
  Divide us not, be with me now,
  And enter in at breast and brow,
Till all my blood, a fuller wave,

Be quicken'd with a livelier breath,
  And like an inconsiderate boy,
  As in the former flash of joy,
I slip the thoughts of life and death ;

And all the breeze of Fancy blows,
  And every dew-drop paints a bow,
  The wizard lightnings deeply glow,
And every thought breaks out a rose.

CXXIII.

THERE rolls the deep where grew the tree.
  O earth, what changes thou hast seen !
  There where the long street roars, hath been
The stillness of the central sea.

The hills are shadows, and they flow
  From form to form, and nothing stands ;
  They melt like mist, the solid lands,
Like clouds they shape themselves and go.

But in my spirit will I dwell,
  And dream my dream, and hold it true ;
  For tho' my lips may breathe adieu,
I cannot think the thing farewell.

CXXIV.

That which we dare invoke to bless;
  Our dearest faith; our ghastliest doubt;
  He, They, One, All; within, without;
The Power in darkness whom we guess;

I found Him not in world or sun,
  Or eagle's wing, or insect's eye:
  Nor thro' the questions men may try,
The petty cobwebs we have spun:

If e'er, when faith had fall'n asleep,
  I heard a voice, "Believe no more,"
  And heard an ever-breaking shore
That tumbled in the Godless deep;

A warmth within the breast would melt
  The freezing reason's colder part.
  And like a man in wrath the heart
Stood up and answer'd, "I have felt."

No, like a child in doubt and fear:
  But that blind clamor made me wise:
  Then was I as a child that cries,
But, crying, knows his father near;

And what I am beheld again
  What is, and no man understands;
  And out of darkness came the hands
That reach thro' nature, moulding men.

CXXV.

Whatever I have said or sung,
  Some bitter notes my harp would give,
  Yea, tho' there often seem'd to live
A contradiction on the tongue,

Yet Hope had never lost her youth;
  She did but look thro' dimmer eyes;
  Or Love but play'd with gracious lies
Because he felt so fix'd in truth:

And if the song were full of care,
  He breathed the spirit of the song;
  And if the words were sweet and strong,
He set his royal signet there;

Abiding with me till I sail
  To seek thee on the mystic deeps,
  And this electric force, that keeps
A thousand pulses dancing, fail.

CXXVI.

Love is and was my Lord and King,
  And in his presence I attend
  To hear the tidings of my friend,
Which every hour his couriers bring.

Love is and was my King and Lord,
  And will be, tho' as yet I keep
  Within his court on earth, and sleep
Encompass'd by his faithful guard,

And hear at times a sentinel
  Who moves about from place to place,
  And whispers to the worlds of space,
In the deep night, that all is well.

CXXVII.

And all is well, tho' faith and form
  Be sunder'd in the night of fear;
  Well roars the storm to those that hear
A deeper voice across the storm,

Proclaiming social truth shall spread,
  And justice, ev'n tho' thrice again
  The red fool-fury of the Seine
Should pile her barricades with dead.

But ill for him that wears a crown,
  And him, the lazar, in his rags:
  They tremble, the sustaining crags;
The spires of ice are toppled down,

And molten up, and roar in flood;
  The fortress crashes from on high,
  The brute earth lightens to the sky,
And the great Æon sinks in blood,

And compass'd by the fires of Hell;
  While thou, dear spirit, happy star,
  O'erlook'st the tumult from afar,
And smilest, knowing all is well.

CXXVIII.

The love that rose on stronger wings,
  Unpalsied when we met with Death,
  Is comrade of the lesser faith
That sees the course of human things.

No doubt vast eddies in the flood
  Of onward time shall yet be made,
  And throned races may degrade;
Yet, O ye mysteries of good,

Wild Hours that fly with Hope and Fear.
  If all your office had to do
  With old results that look like new;
If this were all your mission here,

To draw, to sheathe a useless sword,
  To fool the crowd with glorious lies,
  To cleave a creed in sects and cries,
To change the bearing of a word,

To shift an arbitrary power,
  To cramp the student at his desk,
  To make old bareness picturesque
And tuft with grass a feudal tower;

Why then my scorn might well descend
  On you and yours. I see in part
  That all, as in some piece of art,
Is toil coöperant to an end.

CXXIX.

Dear friend, far off, my lost desire,
  So far, so near in woe and weal;
  O loved the most, when most I feel
There is a lower and a higher;

Known and unknown; human, divine;
  Sweet human hand and lips and eye;
  Dear heavenly friend that canst not die
Mine, mine, forever, ever mine;

Strange friend, past, present, and to be;
  Love deeplier, darklier understood;
  Behold, I dream a dream of good,
And mingle all the world with thee.

CXXX.

Thy voice is on the rolling air;
  I hear thee where the waters run;
  Thou standest in the rising sun,
And in the setting thou art fair.

What art thou then? I cannot guess;
  But tho' I seem in star and flower
  To feel thee some diffusive power,
I do not therefore love thee less:

My love involves the love before;
  My love is vaster passion now;
  Tho' mix'd with God and Nature thou,
I seem to love thee more and more.

9

Far off thou art, but ever nigh;
I have thee still, and I rejoice;
I prosper, circled with thy voice;
I shall not lose thee tho' I die.

CXXXI.

O LIVING will that shalt endure
When all that seems shall suffer shock,
Rise in the spiritual rock,
Flow thro' our deeds and make them pure,

That we may lift from out of dust
A voice as unto him that hears,
A cry above the conquer'd years
To one that with us works, and trusts,

With faith that comes of self-control,
The truths that never can be proved
Until we close with all we loved,
And all we flow from, soul in soul.

O TRUE and tried, so well and long,
Demand not thou a marriage lay;
In that it is thy marriage day
Is music more than any song.

Nor have I felt so much of bliss
Since first he told me that he loved
A daughter of our house; nor proved
Since that dark day a day like this;

Tho' I since then have number'd o'er
Some thrice three years: they went and came,
Remade the blood and changed the frame,
And yet is love not less, but more;

No longer caring to embalm
In dying songs a dead regret,
But like a statue solid-set,
And moulded in colossal calm.

Regret is dead, but love is more
Than in the summers that are flown,
For I myself with these have grown
To something greater than before;

Which makes appear the songs I made
As echoes out of weaker times,
As half but idle brawling rhymes,
The sport of random sun and shade.

But where is she, the bridal flower,
That must be made a wife ere noon?
She enters, glowing like the moon
Of Eden on its bridal bower:

On me she bends her blissful eyes,
And then on thee; they meet thy look
And brighten like the star that shook
Betwixt the palms of paradise.

O when her life was yet in bud,
He too foretold the perfect rose.
For thee she grew, for thee she grows
Forever, and as fair as good.

And thou art worthy; full of power;
As gentle; liberal-minded, great,
Consistent; wearing all that weight
Of learning lightly like a flower.

But now set out: the noon is near,
And I must give away the bride;
She fears not, or with thee beside
And me behind her, will not fear:

For I that danced her on my knee,
That watch'd her on her nurse's arm,
That shielded all her life from harm,
At last must part with her to thee;

Now waiting to be made a wife,
Her feet, my darling, on the dead;
Their pensive tablets round her head,
And the most living words of life

Breathed in her ear. The ring is on,
The "wilt thou," answer'd, and again
The "wilt thou" ask'd till out of twain
Her sweet "I will" has made ye one.

Now sign your names, which shall be read,
Mute symbols of a joyful morn,
By village eyes as yet unborn;
The names are sign'd, and overhead

Begins the clash and clang that tells
The joy to every wandering breeze;
The blind wall rocks, and on the trees
The dead leaf trembles to the bells.

O happy hour, and happier hours
Await them. Many a merry face
Salutes them—maidens of the place,
That pelt us in the porch with flowers.

O happy hour, behold the bride
With him to whom her hand I gave.
They leave the porch, they pass the grave
That has to-day its sunny side.

To-day the grave is bright for me,
For them the light of life increased,
Who stay to share the morning feast,
Who rest to-night beside the sea.

Let all my genial spirits advance
To meet and greet a whiter sun;
My drooping memory will not shun
The foaming grape of eastern France.

It circles round, and fancy plays,
And hearts are warm'd, and faces bloom
As drinking health to bride and groom
We wish them store of happy days.

Nor count me all to blame if I
Conjecture of a stiller guest,
Perchance, perchance, among the rest,
And, tho' in silence, wishing joy.

But they must go, the time draws on,
And those white-favor'd horses wait;
They rise, but linger; it is late;
Farewell, we kiss, and they are gone.

A shade falls on us like the dark
From little cloudlets on the grass,
But sweeps away as out we pass
To range the woods, to roam the park,

Discussing how their courtship grew,
And talk of others that are wed,
And how she look'd, and what he said,
And back we come at fall of dew.

Again the feast, the speech, the glee,
The shade of passing thought, the wealth
Of words and wit, the double health,
The crowning cup, the three-times-three,

And last the dance;—till I retire:
  Dumb is that tower which spake so loud,
  And high in heaven the streaming cloud,
And on the downs a rising fire;

And rise, O moon, from yonder down,
  Till over down and over dale
  All night the shining vapor sail
And pass the silent-lighted town,

The white-faced halls, the glancing rills,
  And catch at every mountain head,
  And o'er the friths that branch and spread
Their sleeping silver thro' the hills;

And touch with shade the bridal doors,
  With tender gloom the roof, the wall;
  And breaking let the splendor fall
To spangle all the happy shores

By which they rest, and ocean sounds,
  And, star and system rolling past,
  A soul shall draw from out the vast
And strike his being into bounds,

And, moved thro' life of lower phase,
  Result in man, be born and think,
  And act and love, a closer link
Betwixt us and the crowning race

Of those that, eye to eye, shall look
  On knowledge: under whose command
  Is Earth and Earth's, and in their hand
Is Nature like an open book;

No longer half-akin to brute,
  For all we thought and loved and did,
  And hoped, and suffer'd, is but seed
Of what in them is flower and fruit;

Whereof the man, that with me trod
  This planet, was a noble type
  Appearing ere the times were ripe,
That friend of mine who lives in God,

That God, which ever lives and loves,
  One God, one law, one element,
  And one far-off divine event,
To which the whole creation moves.

MAUD, AND OTHER POEMS.

MAUD.

I.

1.

I HATE the dreadful hollow behind the little wood,
Its lips in the field above are dabbled with blood-red heath,
The red-ribb'd ledges drip with a silent horror of blood,
And Echo there, whatever is ask'd her, answers "Death."

2.

For there in the ghastly pit long since a body was found,
His who had given me life—O father! O God! was it well?—
Mangled, and flatten'd, and crush'd, and dinted into the ground:
There yet lies the rock that fell with him when he fell.

3.

Did he fling himself down? who knows? for a vast speculation had fail'd,
And ever he mutter'd and madden'd, and ever wann'd with despair,
And out he walk'd when the wind like a broken worldling wail'd,
And the flying gold of the ruin'd woodlands drove thro' the air.

4.

I remember the time, for the roots of my hair were stirr'd
By a shuffled step, by a dead weight trail'd, by a whisper'd fright,
And my pulses closed their gates with a shock on my heart as I heard
The shrill-edged shriek of a mother divide the shuddering night.

5.

Villany somewhere! whose? One says, we are villains all.
Not he: his honest fame should at least by me be maintain'd:
But that old man, now lord of the broad estate and the Hall,
Dropt off gorged from a scheme that had left us flaccid and drain'd.

6.

Why do they prate of the blessings of Peace? we have made them a curse,
Pickpockets, each hand lusting for all that is not its own;
And lust of gain, in the spirit of Cain, is it better or worse
Than the heart of the citizen hissing in war on his own hearthstone?

7.

But these are the days of advance, the works of the men of mind,
When who but a fool would have faith in a tradesman's ware or his word?
Is it peace or war? Civil war, as I think, and that of a kind
The viler, as underhand, not openly bearing the sword.

8.

Sooner or later I too may passively take the print
Of the golden age—why not? I have neither hope nor trust,
May make my heart as a millstone, set my face as a flint,
Cheat and be cheated, and die: who knows? we are ashes and dust.

9.

Peace sitting under her olive, and slurring the days gone by,
When the poor are hovell'd and hustled together, each sex, like swine,
When only the ledger lives, and when only not all men lie:
Peace in her vineyard—yes!—but a company forges the wine.

10.

And the vitriol madness flushes up in the ruffian's head,
Till the filthy by-lane rings to the yell of the trampled wife,
While chalk and alum and plaster are sold to the poor for bread,
And the spirit of murder works in the very means of life.

11.

And Sleep must lie down arm'd, for the villanous centre-bits
Grind on the wakeful ear in the hush of the moonless nights,
While another is cheating the sick of a few last gasps, as he sits
To pestle a poison'd poison behind his crimson lights.

12.

When a Mammonite mother kills her babe for a burial fee,
And Timour-Mammon grins on a pile of children's bones,
Is it peace or war? better, war! loud war by land and by sea,
War with a thousand battles, and shaking a hundred thrones.

13.

For I trust if an enemy's fleet came yonder round by the hill,
And the rushing battle-bolt sang from the three-decker out of the foam,
That the smooth-faced snub-nosed rogue would leap from his counter and till,
And strike, if he could, were it but with his cheating yardwand, home.—

14.

What! am I raging alone as my father raged in his mood?
Must *I* too creep to the hollow and dash myself down and die
Rather than hold by the law that I made, nevermore to brood
On a horror of shatter'd limbs and a wretched swindler's lie?

15.

Would there be sorrow for *me?* there was *love* in the passionate shriek,
Love for the silent thing that had made false haste to the grave—
Wrapt in a cloak, as I saw him, and thought he would rise and speak
And rave at the lie and the liar, ah God, as he used to rave.

16.

I am sick of the Hall and the hill, I am sick of the moor and the main.
Why should I stay? can a sweeter chance ever come to me here?
O, having the nerves of motion as well as the nerves of pain,
Were it not wise if I fled from the place and the pit and the fear?

17.

There are workmen up at the Hall: they are coming back from abroad;
The dark old place will be gilt by the touch of a millionnaire:
I have heard, I know not whence, of the singular beauty of Maud;
I play'd with the girl when a child; she promised then to be fair.

18.

Maud with her venturous climbings and tumbles and childish escapes,
Maud the delight of the village, the ringing joy of the Hall,
Maud with her sweet purse-mouth when my father dangled the grapes,
Maud the beloved of my mother, the moon-faced darling of all,—

19.

What is she now? My dreams are bad. She may bring me a curse.
No, there is fatter game on the moor; she will let me alone.
Thanks, for the fiend best knows whether woman or man be the worse
I will bury myself in my books, and the Devil may pipe to his own.

II.

Long have I sigh'd for a calm: God grant I may find it at last!
It will never be broken by Maud, she has neither savor nor salt,
But a cold and clear-cut face, as I found when her carriage past,
Perfectly beautiful: let it be granted her: where is the fault?
All that I saw (for her eyes were downcast, not to be seen)
Faultily faultless, icily regular, splendidly null,
Dead perfection, no more; nothing more, if it had not been
For a chance of travel, a paleness, an hour's defect of the rose,
Or an underlip, you may call it a little too ripe, too full,
Or the least little delicate aquiline curve in a sensitive nose,
From which I escaped heart-free, with the least little touch of spleen.

III.

Cold and clear-cut face, why come you so cruelly meek,
Breaking a slumber in which all spleenful folly was drown'd,
Pale with the golden beam of an eyelash dead on the cheek,
Passionless, pale, cold face, star-sweet on a gloom profound;
Womanlike, taking revenge too deep for a transient wrong
Done but in thought to your beauty, and ever as pale as before
Growing and fading and growing upon me without a sound,
Luminous, gemlike, ghostlike, deathlike, half the night long
Growing and fading and growing, till I could bear it no more,
But arose, and all by myself in my own dark garden ground,
Listening now to the tide in its broad-flung shipwrecking roar,
Now to the scream of a madden'd beach dragg'd down by the wave,
Walk'd in a wintry wind by a ghastly glimmer, and found
The shining daffodil dead, and Orion low in his grave.

IV.

1.

A MILLION emeralds break from the ruby-budded lime
In the little grove where I sit—ah, wherefore cannot I be
Like things of the season gay, like the bountiful season bland,
When the far-off sail is blown by the breeze of a softer clime,
Half-lost in the liquid azure bloom of a crescent of sea,
The silent sapphire-spangled marriage ring of the land?

2.

Below me, there, is the village, and looks how quiet and small!
And yet bubbles o'er like a city, with gossip, scandal, and spite;
And Jack on his alehouse bench has as many lies as a Czar;
And here on the landward side, by a red rock, glimmers the Hall;
And up in the high Hall-garden I see her pass like a light;
But sorrow seize me if ever that light be my leading star!

3.

When have I bow'd to her father, the wrinkled head of the race?
I met her to-day with her brother, but not to her brother I bow'd;
I bow'd to his lady-sister as she rode by on the moor;
But the fire of a foolish pride flash'd over her beautiful face.
O child, you wrong your beauty, believe it, in being so proud;
Your father has wealth well-gotten, and I am nameless and poor.

4.

I keep but a man and a maid, ever ready to slander and steal;
I know it, and smile a hard-set smile, like a stoic, or like
A wiser epicurean, and let the world have its way:
For nature is one with rapine, a harm no preacher can heal:
The Mayfly is torn by the swallow, the sparrow spear'd by the shrike,
And the whole little wood where I sit is a world of plunder and prey.

5.

We are puppets, Man in his pride, and Beauty fair in her flower;
Do we move ourselves, or are moved by an unseen hand at a game
That pushes us off from the board, and others ever succeed?
Ah yet, we cannot be kind to each other here for an hour;
We whisper, and hint, and chuckle, and grin at a brother's shame;
However we brave 't out, we men are a little breed.

6.

A monstrous eft was of old the Lord and Master of Earth,
For him did his high sun flame, and his river billowing ran,
And he felt himself in his force to be Nature's crowning race.
As nine months go to the shaping an infant ripe for his birth,
So many a million of ages have gone to the making of man:
He now is first, but is he the last? is he not too base?

7.

The man of science him-elf is fonder of glory, and vain,
An eye well-practised in nature, a spirit bounded and poor;
The passionate heart of the poet is whirl'd into folly and vice.
I would not marvel at either, but keep a temperate brain;
For not to desire or admire, if a man could learn it, were more
Than to walk all day like the sultan of old in a garden of spice.

8.

For the drift of the Maker is dark, an Isis hid by the veil.
Who knows the ways of the world, how God will bring them about?
Our planet is one, the suns are many, the world is wide.
Shall I weep if a Poland fall? shall I shriek if a Hungary fail?
Or an infant civilization be ruled with rod or with knout?
I have not made the world, and He that made it will guide.

9.

Be mine a philosopher's life in the quiet woodland ways,
Where if I cannot be gay let a passionless peace be my lot,
Far-off from the clamor of liars belied in the hubbub of lies;
From the long-neck'd geese of the world that are ever hissing dispraise,
Because their natures are little, and, whether he heed it or not,
Where each man walks with his head in a cloud of poisonous flies.

10.

And most of all would I flee from the cruel madness of love,
The honey of poison-flowers and all the measureless ill.
Ah Maud, you milk-white fawn, you are all unmeet for a wife.
Your mother is mute in her grave as her image in marble above;
Your father is ever in London, you wander about at your will;
You have but fed on the roses, and lain in the lilies of life.

V.

1.

A VOICE by the cedar-tree,
In the meadow under the Hall!
She is singing an air that is known to me,
A passionate ballad gallant and gay,
A martial song like a trumpet's call!
Singing alone in the morning of life.
In the happy morning of life and of May,
Singing of men that in battle array,
Ready in heart and ready in hand,
March with banner and bugle and fife
To the death, for their native land.

2.

Maud with her exquisite face,
And wild voice pealing up to the sunny sky,
And feet like sunny gems on an English green,
Maud in the light of her youth and her grace,
Singing of Death, and of Honor that cannot die,
Till I well could weep for a time so sordid and mean,
And myself so languid and base.

3.

Silence, beautiful voice!
Be still, for you only trouble the mind
With a joy in which I cannot rejoice,
A glory I shall not find.
Still I I will hear you no more,
For your sweetness hardly leaves me a choice
But to move to the meadow and fall before
Her feet on the meadow grass, and adore,
Not her, who is neither courtly nor kind,
Not her, not her, but a voice.

VI.

1.

MORNING arises stormy and pale,
No sun, but a wannish glare
In fold upon fold of hueless cloud,
And the budded peaks of the wood are bow'd
Caught and cuff'd by the gale:
I had fancied it would be fair.

2.

Whom but Maud should I meet
Last night, when the sunset burn'd
On the blossom'd gable-ends
At the head of the village street,
Whom but Maud should I meet?
And she touch'd my hand with a smile so sweet
She made me divine amends
For a courtesy not return'd.

3.

And thus a delicate spark
Of glowing and growing light
Thro' the livelong hours of the dark
Kept itself warm in the heart of my dreams,
Ready to burst in a color'd flame;
Till at last, when the morning came
In a cloud, it faded, and seems
But an ashen-gray delight.

4.

What if with her sunny hair,
And smile as sunny as cold,
She meant to weave me a snare
Of some coquettish deceit.

Cleopatra-like as of old
To entangle me when we met,
To have her lion roll in a silken net,
And fawn at a victor's feet.

5.

Ah, what shall I be at fifty
Should Nature keep me alive,
If I find the world so bitter
When I am but twenty-five?
Yet, if she were not a cheat,
If Maud were all that she seem'd,
And her smile were all that I dream'd,
Then the world were not so bitter
But a smile could make it sweet.

6.

What if tho' her eye seem'd full
Of a kind intent to me,
What if that dandy-despot, he,
That jewell'd mass of millinery,
That oil'd and curl'd Assyrian Bull
Smelling of musk and of insolence,
Her brother, from whom I keep aloof,
Who wants the finer politic sense
To mask, tho' but in his own behoof,
With a glassy smile his brutal scorn,—
What if he had told her yestermorn
How prettily for his own sweet sake
A face of tenderness might be feign'd,
And a moist mirage in desert eyes,
That so, when the rotten hustings shake
In another month to his brazen lies,
A wretched vote may be gain'd.

7.

For a raven ever croaks, at my side,
Keep watch and ward, keep watch and ward,
Or thou wilt prove their tool.
Yea too, myself from myself I guard,
For often a man's own angry pride
Is cap and bells for a fool.

8.

Perhaps the smile and tender tone
Came out of her pitying womanhood,
For am I not, am I not, here alone
So many a summer since she died,
My mother, who was so gentle and good?
Living alone in an empty house,
Here half-hid in the gleaming wood,
Where I hear the dead at midday moan,
And the shrieking rush of the wainscot mouse,
And my own sad name in corners cried,
When the shiver of dancing leaves is thrown
About its echoing chambers wide,
Till a morbid hate and horror have grown
Of a world in which I have hardly mixt,
And a morbid eating lichen fixt
On a heart half-turn'd to stone.

9.

O heart of stone, are you flesh, and caught
By that you swore to withstand?
For what was it else within me wrought
But, I fear, the new strong wine of love,
That made my tongue so stammer and trip
When I saw the treasured splendor, her hand,
Come sliding out of her sacred glove,
And the sunlight broke from her lip?

10.

I have play'd with her when a child;
She remembers it now we meet.
Ah well, well, well, I may be beguiled
By some coquettish deceit.
Yet, if she were not a cheat,

If Maud were all that she seem'd,
And her smile had all that I dream'd,
Then the world were not so bitter
But a smile could make it sweet.

VII.

1.

Did I hear it half in a doze
Long since. I know not where?
Did I dream it an hour ago,
When asleep in this arm-chair?

2.

Men were drinking together,
Drinking and talking of me;
"Well, if it prove a girl, the boy
Will have plenty: so let it be."

3.

Is it an echo of something
Read with a boy's delight,
Viziers nodding together
In some Arabian night?

4.

Strange, that I hear two men,
Somewhere, talking of me;
"Well, if it prove a girl, my boy
Will have plenty: so let it be."

VIII.

She came to the village church,
And sat by a pillar alone;
An angel watching an urn
Wept over her, carved in stone;
And once, but once, she lifted her eyes,
And suddenly, sweetly, strangely blush'd
To find they were met by my own;
And suddenly, sweetly, my heart beat stronger
And thicker, until I heard no longer
The snowy-banded, dilettante,
Delicate-handed priest intone;
And thought, is it pride, and mused and sigh'd
"No surely, now it cannot be pride."

IX.

I was walking a mile,
More than a mile from the shore,
The sun look'd out with a smile
Betwixt the cloud and the moor,
And riding at set of day
Over the dark moor land,
Rapidly riding far away,
She waved to me with her hand.
There were two at her side,
Something flash'd in the sun,
Down by the hill I saw them ride,
In a moment they were gone:
Like a sudden spark
Struck vainly in the night,
And back returns the dark
With no more hope of light.

X.

1.

Sick, am I sick of a jealous dread?
Was not one of the two at her side
This new-made lord, whose splendor plucks
The slavish hat from the villager's head?
Whose old grandfather has lately died,
Gone to a blacker pit, for whom
Grimy nakedness dragging his trucks
And laving his trams in a poison'd gloom
Wrought, till he crept from a gutted mine
Master of half a servile shire,

And left his coal all turn'd into gold
To a grandson, first of his noble line,
Rich in the grace all women desire,
Strong in the power that all men adore,
And simper and set their voices lower,
And soften as if to a girl, and hold
Awe-stricken breaths at a work divine,
Seeing his gewgaw castle shine,
New as his title, built last year,
There amid perky larches and pine,
And over the sullen-purple moor
(Look at it) pricking a cockney ear.

2.

What, has he found my jewel out?
For one of the two that rode at her side
Bound for the Hall, I am sure was he:
Bound for the Hall, and I think for a bride.
Blithe would her brother's acceptance be.
Maud could be gracious too, no doubt,
To a lord, a captain, a padded shape,
A bought commission, a waxen face,
A rabbit mouth that is ever agape—
Bought? what is it he cannot buy?
And therefore splenetic, personal, base,
A wounded thing with a rancorous cry,
At war with myself and a wretched race,
Sick, sick to the heart of life, am I.

3.

Last week came one to the county town,
To preach our poor little army down,
And play the game of the despot kings,
Tho' the state has done it and thrice as well:
This broad-brim'd hawker of holy things,
Whose ear is stuff'd with his cotton, and rings
Even in dreams to the chink of his pence,
This huckster put down war! can he tell
Whether war be a cause or a consequence?
Put down the passions that make earth Hell!
Down with ambition, avarice, pride,
Jealousy, down! cut off from the mind
The bitter springs of anger and fear;
Down too, down at your own fireside,
With the evil tongue and the evil ear,
For each is at war with mankind.

4.

I wish I could hear again
The chivalrous battle-song
That she warbled alone in her joy!
I might persuade myself then
She would not do herself this great wrong
To take a wanton, dissolute boy
For a man and leader of men.

5.

Ah God, for a man with heart, head, hand,
Like some of the simple great ones gone
For ever and ever by,
One still strong man in a blatant land,
Whatever they call him, what care I,
Aristocrat, democrat, autocrat.—one
Who can rule and dare not lie.

6.

And ah for a man to arise in me,
That the man I am may cease to be!

XI.

1.

O LET the solid ground
    Not fail beneath my feet
Before my life has found
    What some have found so sweet;

Then let come what come may,
What matter if I go mad,
I shall have had my day.

2.

Let the sweet heavens endure,
    Not close and darken above me
Before I am quite quite sure
    That there is one to love me;
Then let come what come may
To a life that has been so sad,
I shall have had my day.

XII.

1.

Birds in the high Hall-garden
    When twilight was falling,
Maud, Maud, Maud, Maud,
    They were crying and calling.

2.

Where was Maud? in our wood;
    And I, who else, was with her,
Gathering woodland lilies,
    Myriads blow together.

3.

Birds in our woods sang
    Ringing thro' the valleys,
Maud is here, here, here
    In among the lilies.

4.

I kiss'd her slender hand,
    She took the kiss sedately
Maud is not seventeen,
    But she is tall and stately

5.

I to cry out on pride
    Who have won her favor!
O Maud were sure of Heaven
    If lowliness could save her.

6.

I know the way she went
    Home with her maiden posy,
For her feet have touch'd the meadows
    And left the daisies rosy.

7.

Birds in the high Hall-garden
    Were crying and calling to her,
Where is Maud, Maud, Maud,
    One is come to woo her.

8.

Look, a horse at the door,
    And little King Charles is snarling,
Go back, my lord, across the moor,
    You are not her darling.

XIII.

1.

SCORN'D, to be scorn'd by one that I scorn,
Is that a matter to make me fret?
That a calamity hard to be borne?
Well, he may live to hate me yet.
Fool that I am to be vext with his pride!
I past him, I was crossing his lands;
He stood on the path a little aside;
His face, as I grant, in spite of spite,
Has a broad-blown comeliness, red and white

And six feet two, as I think, he stands;
But his essences turn'd the live air sick,
And barbarous opulence jewel-thick
Sunn'd itself on his breast and his hands.

2.

Who shall call me ungentle, unfair,
I long'd so heartily then and there
To give him the grasp of fellowship;
But while I past he was humming an air,
Stopt, and then with a riding whip
Leisurely tapping a glossy boot,
And curving a contumelious lip,
Gorgonized me from head to foot
With a stony British stare.

3.

Why sits he here in his father's chair?
That old man never comes to his place:
Shall I believe him ashamed to be seen?
For only once, in the village street,
Last year, I caught a glimpse of his face,
A gray old wolf and a lean.
Scarcely, now, would I call him a cheat;
For then, perhaps, as a child of deceit,
She might by a true descent be untrue;
And Maud is as true as Maud is sweet;
Tho' I fancy her sweetness only due
To the sweeter blood by the other side;
Her mother has been a thing complete,
However she came to be so allied.
And fair without, faithful within,
Maud to him is nothing akin:
Some peculiar mystic grace
Made her only the child of her mother,
And heap'd the whole inherited sin
On that huge scapegoat of the race,
All, all upon the brother.

4.

Peace, angry spirit, and let him be!
Has not his sister smiled on me?

XIV.

1.

MAUD has a garden of roses
And lilies fair on a lawn;
There she walks in her state
And tends upon bed and bower
And thither I climb'd at dawn
And stood by her garden gate;
A lion ramps at the top,
He is claspt by a passion-flower.

2.

Maud's own little oak-room
(Which Maud, like a precious stone
Set in the heart of the carven gloom,
Lights with herself, when alone
She sits by her music and books,
And her brother lingers late
With a roystering company) looks
Upon Maud's own garden gate:
And I thought as I stood, if a hand, as white
As ocean-foam in the moon, were laid
On the hasp of the window, and my Delight
Had a sudden desire, like a glorious ghost, to glide,
Like a beam of the seventh Heaven, down to my side,
There were but a step to be made.

3.

The fancy flatter'd my mind,
And again seem'd overbold;
Now I thought that she cared for me,
Now I thought she was kind
Only because she was cold.

4.

I heard no sound where I stood
But the rivulet on from the lawn
Running down to my own dark wood;
Or the voice of the long sea-wave as it swell'd
Now and then in the dim-gray dawn;
But I look'd, and round, all round the house I be
held
The death-white curtain drawn;
Felt a horror over me creep,
Prickle my skin and catch my breath,
Knew that the death-white curtain meant but sleep,
Yet I shudder'd and thought like a fool of the sleep
of death.

XV.

So dark a mind within me dwells,
And I make myself such evil cheer,
That if I be dear to some one else,
Then some one else may have much to fear;
But if I be dear to some one else,
Then I should be to myself more dear.
Shall I not take care of all that I think,
Yea ev'n of wretched meat and drink,
If I be dear,
If I be dear to some one else?

XVI.

1.

THIS lump of earth has left his estate
The lighter by the loss of his weight;
And so that he find what he went to seek,
And fulsome Pleasure clog him, and drown
His heart in the gross mud-honey of town,
He may stay for a year who has gone for a week
But this is the day when I must speak,
And I see my Oread coming down,
O this is the day!
O beautiful creature, what am I
That I dare to look her way;
Think I may hold dominion sweet,
Lord of the pulse that is lord of her breast,
And dream of her beauty with tender dread,
From the delicate Arab arch of her feet
To the grace that, bright and light as the crest
Of a peacock, sits on her shining head,
And she knows it not: O, if she knew it,
To know her beauty might half undo it.
I know it the one bright thing to save
My yet young life in the wilds of Time,
Perhaps from madness, perhaps from crime
Perhaps from a selfish grave.

2.

What, if she were fasten'd to this fool lord,
Dare I bid her abide by her word?
Should I love her so well if she
Had given her word to a thing so low?
Shall I love her as well if she
Can break her word were it even for me?
I trust that it is not so.

3.

Catch not my breath, O clamorous heart,
Let not my tongue be a thrall to my eye,
For I must tell her before we part,
I must tell her, or die.

XVII.

Go not, happy day,
From the shining fields,
Go not, happy day,
Till the maiden yields.

Rosy is the West,
  Rosy is the South,
Roses are her cheeks,
  And a rose her mouth.
When the happy Yes
  Falters from her lips,
Pass and blush the news
  O'er the blowing ships,
Over blowing seas,
  Over seas at rest,
Pass the happy news,
  Blush it thro' the West,
Till the red man dance
  By his red cedar-tree,
And the red man's babe
  Leap, beyond the sea.
Blush from West to East,
  Blush from East to West,
Till the West is East,
  Blush it thro' the West.
Rosy is the West,
  Rosy is the South,
Roses are her cheeks,
  And a rose her mouth.

XVIII.

1.

I HAVE led her home, my love, my only friend.
There is none like her, none,
And never yet so warmly ran my blood
And sweetly, on and on
Calming itself to the long-wish'd-for end,
Full to the banks, close on the promised good.

2.

None like her, none.
Just now the dry-tongued laurel's pattering talk
Seem'd her light foot along the garden walk,
And shook my heart to think she comes once more;
But even then I heard her close the door,
The gates of heaven are closed, and she is gone.

3.

There is none like her, none.
Nor will be when our summers have deceased.
O, art thou sighing for Lebanon
In the long breeze that streams to thy delicious
  East,
Sighing for Lebanon,
Dark cedar, tho' thy limbs have here increased,
Upon a pastoral slope as fair,
And looking to the South, and fed
With honey'd rain and delicate air,
And haunted by the starry head
Of her whose gentle will has changed my fate,
And made my life a perfumed altar-flame;
And over whom thy darkness must have spread
With such delight as theirs of old, thy great
Forefathers of the thornless garden, there
Shadowing the snow-limb'd Eve from whom she
  came.

4.

Here will I lie, while these long branches sway,
And you fair stars that crown a happy day
Go in and out as if at merry play,
Who am no more so all forlorn,
As when it seem'd far better to be born
To labor and the mattock-harden'd hand,
Than nursed at ease and brought to understand
A sad astrology, the boundless plan
That makes you tyrants in your iron skies,
Innumerable, pitiless, passionless eyes,
Cold fires, yet with power to burn and brand
His nothingness into man.

5.

But now shine on, and what care I,
Who in this stormy gulf have found a pearl
The countercharm of space and hollow sky,
And do accept my madness and would die
To save from some slight shame one simple girl.

6.

Would die; for sullen-seeming Death may give
More life to Love than is or ever was
In our low world, where yet 't is sweet to live.
Let no one ask me how it came to pass;
It seems that I am happy, that to me
A livelier emerald twinkles in the grass,
A purer sapphire melts into the sea.

7.

Not die; but live a life of truest breath,
And teach true life to fight with mortal wrongs.
O, why should Love, like men in drinking-songs,
Spice his fair banquet with the dust of death?
Make answer, Maud my bliss,
Maud made my Maud by that long lover's kiss,
Life of my life, wilt thou not answer this?
"The dusky strand of Death inwoven here
With dear Love's tie, makes Love himself more dear.

8.

Is that enchanted moan only the swell
Of the long waves that roll in yonder bay?
And hark the clock within, the silver knell
Of twelve sweet hours that past in bridal white,
And died to live, long as my pulses play;
But now by this my love has closed her sight
And given false death her hand, and stol'n away
To dreamful wastes where footless fancies dwell
Among the fancies of the golden day.
May nothing there her maiden grace affright!
Dear heart, I feel with thee the drowsy spell.
My bride to be, my evermore delight,
My own heart's heart and ownest own farewell;
It is but for a little space I go
And ye meanwhile far over moor and fell
Beat to the noiseless music of the night!
Has our whole earth gone nearer to the glow
Of your soft splendors that you look so bright?
I have climb'd nearer out of lonely Hell.
Beat, happy stars, timing with things below,
Beat with my heart more blest than heart can tell
Blest, but for some dark undercurrent woe
That seems to draw—but it shall not be so·
Let all be well, be well.

XIX.

1.

Her brother is coming back to-night,
Breaking up my dream of delight.

2.

My dream? do I dream of bliss?
I have walk'd awake with Truth.
O when did a morning shine
So rich in atonement as this
For my dark dawning youth,
Darken'd watching a mother decline
And that dead man at her heart and mine:
For who was left to watch her but I?
Yet so did I let my freshness die.

3.

I trust that I did not talk
To gentle Maud in our walk
(For often in lonely wanderings
I have cursed him even to lifeless things)

But I trust that I did not talk,
Not touch on her father's sin;
I am sure I did but speak
Of my mother's faded cheek
When it slowly grew so thin,
That I felt she was slowly dying
Vext with lawyers and harass'd with debt:
For how often I caught her with eyes all wet,
Shaking her head at her son and sighing
A world of trouble within!

4.

And Maud too, Maud was moved
To speak of the mother she loved
As one scarce less forlorn,
Dying abroad and it seems apart
From him who had ceased to share her heart,
And ever mourning over the feud,
The household Fury sprinkled with blood
By which our houses are torn;
How strange was what she said,
When only Maud and the brother
Hung over her dying bed,—
That Maud's dark father and mine
Had bound us one to the other,
Betrothed us over their wine
On the day when Maud was born;
Seal'd her mine from her first sweet breath.
Mine, mine by a right, from birth till death,
Mine, mine—our fathers have sworn.

5.

But the true blood spilt had in it a heat
To dissolve the precious seal on a bond,
That, if left uncancell'd, had been so sweet:
And none of us thought of a something beyond,
A desire that awoke in the heart of the child,
As it were a duty done to the tomb,
To be friends for her sake, to be reconciled;
And I was cursing them and my doom,
And letting a dangerous thought run wild
While often abroad in the fragrant gloom
Of foreign churches,—I see her there,
Bright English lily, breathing a prayer
To be friends, to be reconciled!

6.

But then what a flint is he!
Abroad, at Florence, at Rome,
I find whenever she touch'd on me
This brother had laugh'd her down,
And at last, when each came home,
He had darken'd into a frown,
Chid her, and forbid her to speak
To me, her friend of the years before;
And this was what had redden'd her cheek,
When I bow'd to her on the moor.

7.

Yet Maud, altho' not blind
To the faults of his heart and mind,
I see she cannot but love him,
And says he is rough but kind,
And wishes me to approve him,
And tells me, when she lay
Sick once, with a fear of worse,
That he left his wine and horses and play,
Sat with her, read to her, night and day,
And tended her like a nurse.

8.

Kind? but the death-bed desire
Spurn'd by this heir of the liar—
Rough but kind? yet I know
He has plotted against me in this,

That he plots against me still.
Kind to Maud? that were not amiss.
Well, rough but kind; why, let it be so:
For shall not Maud have her will?

9.

For, Maud, so tender and true,
As long as my life endures
I feel I shall owe you a debt,
That I never can hope to pay;
And if ever I should forget
That I owe this debt to you
And for your sweet sake to yours;
O then, what then shall I say?—
If ever I *should* forget,
May God make me more wretched
Than ever I have been yet!

10.

So now I have sworn to bury
All this dead body of hate,
I feel so free and so clear
By the loss of that dead weight,
That I should grow light-headed, I fear,
Fantastically merry;
But that her brother comes, like a blight
On my fresh hope, to the Hall to-night.

XX.

1.

Strange, that I felt so gay,
Strange that I tried to-day
To beguile her melancholy;
The Sultan, as we name him,—
She did not wish to blame him—
But he vext her and perplext her
With his worldly talk and folly:
Was it gentle to reprove her
For stealing out of view
From a little lazy lover
Who but claims her as his due?
Or for chilling his caresses
By the coldness of her manners,
Nay, the plainness of her dresses?
Now I know her but in two,
Nor can pronounce upon it
If one should ask me whether
The habit, hat, and feather,
Or the frock and gypsy bonnet
Be the neater and completer;
For nothing can be sweeter
Than maiden Maud in either.

2.

But to-morrow, if we live,
Our ponderous squire will give
A grand political dinner
To half the squirelings near;
And Maud will wear her jewels,
And the bird of prey will hover,
And the titmouse hope to win her
With his chirrup at her ear.

3.

A grand political dinner
To the men of many acres,
A gathering of the Tory,
A dinner and then a dance
For the maids and marriage-makers,
And every eye but mine will glance
At Maud in all her glory.

4.

For I am not invited,
But, with the Sultan's pardon
I am all as well delighted,
For I know her own rose-garden,

And mean to linger in it
Till the dancing will be over;
And then, O then, come out to me
For a minute, but for a minute,
Come out to your own true lover,
That your true lover may see
Your glory also, and render
All homage to his own darling,
Queen Maud in all her splendor.

XXI.

RIVULET crossing my ground,
And bringing me down from the Hall
This garden-rose that I found,
Forgetful of Maud and me,
And lost in trouble and moving round
Here at the head of a tinkling fall,
And trying to pass to the sea;
O Rivulet, born at the Hall,
My Maud has sent it by thee
(If I read her sweet will right)
On a blushing mission to me,
Saying in odor and color, "Ah, be
Among the roses to-night."

XXII.

1.

COME into the garden, Maud.
For the black bat, night, has flown,
Come into the garden, Maud,
I am here at the gate alone;
And the woodbine spices are wafted abroad,
And the musk of the roses blown.

2.

For a breeze of morning moves,
And the planet of Love is on high,
Beginning to faint in the light that she loves
On a bed of daffodil sky,
To faint in the light of the sun that she loves,
To faint in his light, and to die.

3.

All night have the roses heard
The flute, violin, bassoon;
All night has the casement jessamine stirr'd
To the dancers dancing in tune;
Till a silence fell with the waking bird,
And a hush with the setting moon.

4.

I said to the lily, "There is but one
With whom she has heart to be gay.
When will the dancers leave her alone?
She is weary of dance and play."
Now half to the setting moon are gone,
And half to the rising day;
Low on the sand and loud on the stone
The last wheel echoes away.

5.

I said to the rose, "The brief night goes
In babble and revel and wine.
O young lord-lover, what sighs are those,
For one that will never be thine?
But mine, but mine," so I sware to the rose,
"For ever and ever, mine."

6.

And the soul of the rose went into my blood,
As the music clash'd in the hall;
And long by the garden lake I stood,
For I heard your rivulet fall
From the lake to the meadow and on to the wood,
Our wood, that is dearer than all;

7.

From the meadow your walks have left so sweet
That whenever a March-wind sighs
He sets the jewel-print of your feet,
In violets blue as your eyes,
To the woody hollows in which we meet
And the valleys of Paradise.

8.

The slender acacia would not shake
One long milk-bloom on the tree;
The white lake-blossom fell into the lake,
As the pimpernel dozed on the lee;
But the rose was awake all night for your sake,
Knowing your promise to me;
The lilies and roses were all awake,
They sigh'd for the dawn and thee.

9.

Queen rose of the rosebud garden of girls,
Come hither, the dances are done,
In gloss of satin and glimmer of pearls,
Queen lily and rose in one:
Shine, out, little head, sunning over with curls,
To the flowers, and be their sun.

10.

There has fallen a splendid tear
From the passion-flower at the gate.
She is coming, my dove, my dear;
She is coming, my life, my fate;
The red rose cries, "She is near, she is near;"
And the white rose weeps, "She is late;"
The larkspur listens, "I hear, I hear;"
And the lily whispers, "I wait."

11.

She is coming, my own, my sweet,
Were it ever so airy a tread,
My heart would hear her and beat,
Were it earth in an earthy bed;
My dust would hear her and beat,
Had I lain for a century dead;
Would start and tremble under her feet,
And blossom in purple and red.

XXIII.

1.

"The fault was mine, the fault was mine'—
Why am I sitting here so stunn'd and still,
Plucking the harmless wild-flower on the hill?—
It is this guilty hand!—
And there rises ever a passionate cry
From underneath in the darkening land—
What is it, that has been done?
O dawn of Eden bright over earth and sky,
The fires of Hell brake out of thy rising sun,
The fires of Hell and of Hate;
For she, sweet soul, had hardly spoken a word,
When her brother ran in his rage to the gate,
He came with the babe-faced lord;
Heap'd on her terms of disgrace,
And while she wept, and I strove to be cool,
He fiercely gave me the lie,
Till I with as fierce an anger spoke,
And he struck me, madman, over the face,
Struck me before the languid fool,
Who was gaping and grinning by:
Struck for himself an evil stroke;
Wrought for his house an irredeemable woe;
For front to front in an hour we stood,
And a million horrible bellowing echoes broke
From the red-ribb'd hollow behind the wood,
And thunder'd up into Heaven the Christless code
That must have life for a blow.

Ever and ever afresh they seem'd to grow.
Was it he lay there with a fading eye?
"The fault was mine," he whisper'd, "fly!"
Then glided out of the joyous wood
The ghastly Wraith of one that I know;
And there rang on a sudden a passionate cry,
A cry for a brother's blood:
It will ring in my heart and my ears, till I die, till
   I die.

2.

Is it gone? my pulses beat—
What was it? a lying trick of the brain?
Yet I thought I saw her stand,
A shadow there at my feet,
High over the shadowy land.
It is gone: and the heavens fall in a gentle rain,
When they should burst and drown with deluging
   storms
The feeble vassals of wine and anger and lust,
The little hearts that know not how to forgive:
Arise, my God, and strike, for we hold Thee just,
Strike dead the whole weak race of venomous worms,
That sting each other here in the dust:
We are not worthy to live.

XXIV.

1.

SEE what a lovely shell,
Small and pure as a pearl,
Lying close to my foot,
Frail, but a work divine,
Made so fairily well
With delicate spire and whorl,
How exquisitely minute,
A miracle of design!

2.

What is it? a learned man
Could give it a clumsy name.
Let him name it who can,
The beauty would be the same.

3.

The tiny cell is forlorn,
Void of the little living will
That made it stir on the shore.
Did he stand at the diamond door
Of his house in a rainbow frill?
Did he push, when he was uncurl'd,
A golden foot or a fairy horn
Thro' his dim water-world?

4.

Slight, to be crush'd with a tap
Of my finger-nail on the sand,
Small, but a work divine,
Frail, but of force to withstand,
Year upon year, the shock
Of cataract seas that snap
The three-decker's oaken spine
Athwart the ledges of rock,
Here on the Breton strand!

5.

Breton, not Briton; here
Like a shipwreck'd man on a coast
Of ancient fable and fear,—
Plagued with a flitting to and fro,
A disease, a hard mechanic ghost
That never came from on high
Nor ever arose from below,
But only moves with the moving eye,
Flying along the land and the main,—

Why should it look like Maud?
Am I to be overawed
By what I cannot but know
Is a juggle born of the brain?

6.

Back from the Breton coast,
Sick of a nameless fear,
Back to the dark sea-line
Looking, thinking of all I have lost;
An old song vexes my ear;
But that of Lamech is mine.

7.

For years, a measureless ill,
For years, forever, to part,—
But she, she would love me still;
And as long, O God, as she
Have a grain of love for me,
So long, no doubt, no doubt,
Shall I nurse in my dark heart,
However weary, a spark of will
Not to be trampled out.

8.

Strange, that the mind, when fraught
With a passion so intense
One would think that it well
Might drown all life in the eye,—
That it should, by being so overwrought,
Suddenly strike on a sharper sense
For a shell, or a flower, little things
Which else would have been past by!
And now I remember, I,
When he lay dying there,
I noticed one of his many rings
(For he had many, poor worm) and thought
It is his mother's hair.

9.

Who knows if he be dead?
Whether I need have fled?
Am I guilty of blood?
However this may be,
Comfort her, comfort her, all things good,
While I am over the sea!
Let me and my passionate love go by,
But speak to her all things holy and high,
Whatever happen to me!
Me and my harmful love go by;
But come to her waking, find her asleep,
Powers of the height, Powers of the deep,
And comfort her tho' I die.

XXV.

COURAGE, poor heart of stone!
I will not ask thee why
Thou canst not understand
That thou art left forever alone:
Courage, poor stupid heart of stone.—
Or if I ask thee why,
Care not thou to reply:
She is but dead, and the time is at hand
When thou shalt more than die.

XXVI.

1.

O THAT 't were possible
After long grief and pain
To find the arms of my true love
Round me once again!

2.

When I was wont to meet her
In the silent woody places

By the home that gave me birth.
We stood tranced in long embraces
Mixt with kisses sweeter sweeter
Than anything on earth.

3.

A shadow flits before me,
Not thou, but like to thee;
Ah Christ, that it were possible
For one short hour to see
The souls we loved, that they might tell us
What and where they be.

4.

It leads me forth at evening,
It lightly winds and steals
In a cold white robe before me,
When all my spirit reels
At the shouts, the leagues of lights,
And the roaring of the wheels.

5.

Half the night I waste in sighs,
Half in dreams I sorrow after
The delight of early skies;
In a wakeful doze I sorrow
For the hand, the lips, the eyes,
For the meeting of the morrow,
The delight of happy laughter,
The delight of low replies.

6.

'T is a morning pure and sweet,
And a dewy splendor falls
On the little flower that clings
To the turrets and the walls;
'T is a morning pure and sweet,
And the light and shadow fleet;
She is walking in the meadow,
And the woodland echo rings;
In a moment we shall meet;
She is singing in the meadow,
And the rivulet at her feet
Ripples on in light and shadow
To the ballad that she sings.

7.

Do I hear her sing as of old,
My bird with the shining head,
My own dove with the tender eye?
But there rings on a sudden a passionate cry,
There is some one dying or dead,
And a sullen thunder is roll'd;
For a tumult shakes the city,
And I wake, my dream is fled;
In the shuddering dawn, behold,
Without knowledge, without pity,
By the curtains of my bed
That abiding phantom cold.

8.

Get thee hence, nor come again,
Mix not memory with doubt,
Pass, thou deathlike type of pain,
Pass and cease to move about,
'T is the blot upon the brain
That *will* show itself without.

9.

Then I rise, the eavedrops fall,
And the yellow vapors choke
The great city sounding wide;
The day comes, a dull red ball
Wrapt in drifts of lurid smoke
On the misty river-tide.

10.

Thro' the hubbub of the market
I steal, a wasted frame,
It crosses here, it crosses there,
Thro' all that crowd confused and loud,
The shadow still the same;
And on my heavy eyelids
My anguish hangs like shame.

11.

Alas for her that met me,
That heard me softly call,
Came glimmering thro' the laurels
At the quiet evenfall,
In the garden by the turrets
Of the old manorial hall.

12.

Would the happy spirit descend,
From the realms of light and song,
In the chamber or the street,
As she looks among the blest,
Should I fear to greet my friend
Or to say "forgive the wrong,"
Or to ask her, "take me sweet,
To the regions of thy rest?"

13.

But the broad light glares and beats,
And the shadow flits and fleets
And will not let me be;
And I loathe the squares and streets,
And the faces that one meets,
Hearts with no love for me:
Always I long to creep
Into some still cavern deep,
There to weep, and weep, and weep
My whole soul out to thee.

XXVII.

1.

DEAD, long dead,
Long dead!
And my heart is a handful of dust,
And the wheels go over my head,
And my bones are shaken with pain,
For into a shallow grave they are thrust,
Only a yard beneath the street,
And the hoofs of the horses beat, beat,
The hoofs of the horses beat,
Beat into my scalp and my brain,
With never an end to the stream of passing feet,
Driving, hurrying, marrying, burying,
Clamor and rumble, and ringing and clatter,
And here beneath it is all as bad,
For I thought the dead had peace, but it is not so;
To have no peace in the grave, is that not sad?
But up and down and to and fro,
Ever about me the dead men go;
And then to hear a dead man chatter
Is enough to drive one mad.

2.

Wretchedest age, since Time began,
They cannot even bury a man;
And tho' we paid our tithes in the days that are gone,
Not a bell was rung, not a prayer was read;
It is that which makes us loud in the world of the
    dead;
There is none that does his work, not one;
A touch of their office might have sufficed,
But the churchmen fain would kill their church,
As the churches have kill'd their Christ.

3.

See, there is one of us sobbing,
No limit to his distress;
And another, a lord of all things, praying
To his own great self, as I guess;
And another, a statesman there, betraying ,
His party-secret, fool, to the press;
And yonder a vile physician, blabbing
The case of his patient,—all for what?
To tickle the maggot born in an empty head,
And wheedle a world that loves him not,
For it is but a world of the dead.

4.

Nothing but idiot gabble!
For the prophecy given of old
And then not understood,
Has come to pass as foretold;
Not let any man think for the public good,
But babble, merely for babble.
For I never whisper'd a private affair
Within the hearing of cat or mouse,
No, not to myself in the closet alone,
But I heard it shouted at once from the top of the
house;
Everything came to be known:
Who told *him* we were there?

5.

Not that gray old wolf, for he came not back
From the wilderness, full of wolves, where he used
to lie:
He has gather'd the bones for his o'ergrown whelp
to crack;
Crack them now for yourself, and howl, and die.

6.

Prophet, curse me the blabbing lip,
And curse me the British vermin, the rat:
I know not whether he came in the Hanover ship,
But I know that he lies and listens mute
In an ancient mansion's crannies and holes:
Arsenic, arsenic, sure, would do it,
Except that now we poison our babes, poor souls?
It is all used up for that.

7.

Tell him now: she is standing here at my head;
Not beautiful now, not even kind;
He may take her now; for she never speaks her
mind,
But is ever the one thing silent here.
She is not of us, as I divine;
She comes from another stiller world of the dead,
Stiller, not fairer than mine.

8.

But I know where a garden grows,
Fairer than aught in the world beside,
All made up of the lily and rose
That blow by night, when the season is good,
To the sound of dancing music and flutes:
It is only flowers, they had no fruits,
And I almost fear they are not roses, but blood;
For the keeper was one, so full of pride,
He linkt a dead man there to a spectral bride;
For he, if he had not been a Sultan of brutes,
Would he have that hole in his side?

9.

But what will the old man say?
He laid a cruel snare in a pit
To catch a friend of mine one stormy day;
Yet now I could even weep to think of it;
For what will the old man say
When he comes to the second corpse in the pit?

10.

Friend, to be struck by the public foe,
Then to strike him and lay him low,
That were a public merit, far,
Whatever the Quaker holds, from sin;
But the red life spilt for a private blow—
I swear to you, lawful and lawless war
Are scarcely even akin.

11.

O me, why have they not buried me deep enough?
Is it kind to have made me a grave so rough,
Me, that was never a quiet sleeper?
Maybe still I am but half-dead;
Then I cannot be wholly dumb;
I will cry to the steps above my head,
And somebody, surely, some kind heart will come
To bury me, bury me
Deeper, ever so little deeper.

XXVIII.

1.

My life has crept so long on a broken wing
Thro' cells of madness, haunts of horror and fear,
That I come to be grateful at last for a little thing:
My mood is changed, for it fell at a time of year
When the face of night is fair on the dewy downs,
And the shining daffodil dies, and the Charioteer
And starry Gemini hang like glorious crowns
Over Orion's grave low down in the west,
That like a silent lightning under the stars
She seem'd to divide in a dream from a band of the
blest,
And spoke of a hope for the world in the coming
wars—
"And in that hope, dear soul, let trouble have rest,
Knowing I tarry for thee," and pointed to Mars
As he glow'd like a ruddy shield on the Lion's
breast.

2.

And it was but a dream, yet it yielded a dear de-
light
To have look'd, tho' but in a dream, upon eyes so
fair,
That had been in a weary world my one thing bright;
And it was but a dream, yet it lighten'd my despair
When I thought that a war would arise in defence
of the right,
That an iron tyranny now should bend or cease,
The glory of manhood stand on his ancient height,
Nor Britain's one sole God be the millionnaire:
No more shall commerce be all in all, and Peace
Pipe on her pastoral hillock a languid note,
And watch her harvest ripen, her herd increase,
Nor the cannon-bullet rust on a slothful shore,
And the cobweb woven across the cannon's throat
Shall shake its threaded tears in the wind no more.

3.

And as months ran on and rumor of battle grew,
"It is time, it is time, O passionate heart," said I
(For I cleaved to a cause that I felt to be pure and
true),
"It is time, O passionate heart and morbid eye,
That old hysterical mock-disease should die."
And I stood on a giant deck and mix'd my breath
With a loyal people shouting a battle cry,
Till I saw the dreary phantom arise and fly
Far into the North, and battle, and seas of death .

4.

Let it go or stay, so I wake to the higher aims
Of a land that has lost for a little her lust of gold,
And love of a peace that was full of wrongs and
shames,

Horrible, hateful, monstrous, not to be told;
And hail once more to the banner of battle unroll'd!
Tho' many a light shall darken, and many shall weep
For those that are crush'd in the clash of jarring
claims,
Yet God's just wrath shall be wreak'd on a giant
liar;
And many a darkness into the light shall leap
And shine in the sudden making of splendid names,
And noble thought be freer under the sun,
And the heart of a people beat with one desire;
For the peace, that I deem'd no peace, is over and
done,
And now by the side of the Black and the Baltic
deep,
And deathful-grinning mouths of the fortress, flames
The blood-red blossom of war with a heart of fire.

5.

Let it flame or fade, and the war roll down like a
wind,
We have proved we have hearts in a cause, we are
noble still,
And myself have awaked, as it seems, to the better
mind;
It is better to fight for the good, than to rail at the
ill;
I have felt with my native land, I am one with my
kind,
I embrace the purpose of God, and the doom assign'd.

———⟨⟩———

THE BROOK;

AN IDYL.

'HERE, by this brook, we parted; I to the East
And he for Italy—too late—too late:
One whom the strong sons of the world despise;
For lucky rhymes to him were scrip and share,
And mellow metres more than cent for cent;
Nor could he understand how money breeds,
Thought it a dead thing; yet himself could make
The thing that is not as the thing that is.
O had he lived! In our school-books we say,
Of those that held their heads above the crowd,
They flourish'd then or then; but life in him
Could scarce be said to flourish, only touch'd
On such a time as goes before the leaf.
When all the wood stands in a mist of green,
And nothing perfect: yet the brook he loved,
For which, in branding summers of Bengal,
Or ev'n the sweet half-English Neilgherry air,
I panted. seems, as I re-listen to it,
Prattling the primrose fancies of the boy,
To me that loved him; for 'O brook,' he says,
'O babbling brook,' says Edmund in his rhyme,
'Whence come you?' and the brook, why not? re-
plies.

I come from haunts of coot and hern,
I make a sudden sally
And sparkle out among the fern,
To bicker down a valley.

By thirty hills I hurry down,
Or slip between the ridges,
By twenty thorps, a little town,
And half a hundred bridges.

Till last by Philip's farm I flow
To join the brimming river,
For men may come and men may go,
But I go on forever.

"Poor lad, he died at Florence, quite worn out,
Travelling to Naples. There is Darnley bridge,
It has more ivy; there the river; and there
Stands Philip's farm where brook and river meet.

I chatter over stony ways,
In little sharps and trebles,
I bubble into eddying bays,
I babble on the pebbles.

With many a curve my banks I fret
By many a field and fallow,
And many a fairy foreland set
With willow-weed and mallow.

I chatter, chatter, as I flow
To join the brimming river,
For men may come and men may go,
But I go on forever.

"But Philip chatter'd more than brook or bird;
Old Philip; all about the fields you caught
His weary daylong chirping, like the dry
High-elbow'd grigs that leap in summer grass.

I wind about, and in and out,
With here a blossom sailing,
And here and there a lusty trout,
And here and there a grayling,

And here and there a foamy flake
Upon me, as I travel ·
With many a silvery waterbreak
Above the golden gravel,

And draw them all along, and flow
To join the brimming river,
For men may come and men may go,
But I go on forever.

"O darling Katie Willows, his one child!
A maiden of our century, yet most meek;
A daughter of our meadows, yet not coarse
Straight, but as lissome as a hazel wand;
Her eyes a bashful azure, and her hair
In gloss and hue the chestnut, when the shell
Divides threefold to show the fruit within.

"Sweet Katie, once I did her a good turn,
Her and her far-off cousin and betrothed,
James Willows, of one name and heart with her.
For here I came, twenty years back,—the week
Before I parted with poor Edmund; crost
By that old bridge which, half in ruins then,
Still makes a hoary eyebrow for the gleam
Beyond it, where the waters marry—crost,
Whistling a random bar of Bonny Doon,
And push'd at Philip's garden-gate. The gate,
Half-parted from a weak and scolding hinge,
Stuck; and he clamor'd from a casement, 'run'
To Katie somewhere in the walks below,
'Run, Katie!' Katie never ran: she moved
To meet me, winding under woodbine bowers,
A little flutter'd with her eyelids down,
Fresh apple-blossom, blushing for a boon.

"What was it? less of sentiment than sense
Had Katie; not illiterate; neither one
Who babbling in the fount of fictive tears,
And nursed by mealy-mouthed philanthropies,
Divorce the Feeling from her mate the Deed.

"She told me. She and James had quarrell'd.
Why?
What cause of quarrel? None, she said, no cause;
James had no cause: but when I prest the cause,
I learnt that James had flickering jealousies
Which anger'd her. Who anger'd James? I said.
But Katie snatch'd her eyes at once from mine,
And sketching with her slender-pointed foot
Some figure like a wizard's pentagram
On garden gravel, let my query pass
Unclaim'd, in flushing silence, till I ask'd

If James were coming. 'Coming every day,'
She answer'd, 'ever longing to explain,
But evermore her father came across
With some long-winded tale, and broke him short;
And James departed vext with him and her.'
How could I help her? 'Would I—was it wrong?'
(Claspt hands and that petitionary grace
Of sweet seventeen subdued me ere she spoke)
'O would I take her father for one hour,
'For one half-hour, and let him talk to me!'
And even while she spoke, I saw where James
Made towards us, like a wader in the surf,
Beyond the brook, waist-deep in meadow-sweet.

"O Katie, what I suffer'd for your sake!
For in I went and call'd old Philip out
To show the farm: full willingly he rose:
He led me thro' the short sweet-smelling lanes
Of his wheat suburb, babbling as he went.
He praised his land, his horses, his machines;
He praised his ploughs, his cows, his hogs, his dogs;
He praised his hens, his geese, his guinea-hens;
His pigeons, who in session on their roofs
Approved him, bowing at their own deserts:
Then from the plaintive mother's teat, he took
Her blind and shuddering puppies, naming each,
And naming those, his friends, for whom they were:
Then crost the common into Darnley chase
To show Sir Arthur's deer. In copse and fern
Twinkled the innumerable ear and tail.
Then, seated on a serpent-rooted beech,
He pointed out a pasturing colt, and said:
'That was the four-year-old I sold the squire.'
And there he told a long, long-winded tale
Of how the squire had seen the colt at grass,
And how it was the thing his daughter wish'd,
And how he sent the bailiff to the farm
To learn the price, and what the price he ask'd,
And how the bailiff swore that he was mad,
But he stood firm; and so the matter hung;
He gave them line: and five days after that
He met the bailiff at the Golden Fleece,
Who then and there had offer'd something more,
But he stood firm; and so the matter hung;
He knew the man; the colt would fetch its price;
He gave them line: and how by chance at last
(It might be May or April, he forgot,
The last of April or the first of May)
He found the bailiff riding by the farm,
And, talking from the point, he drew him in,
And there he mellow'd all his heart with ale,
Until they closed a bargain, hand in hand.

"Then, while I breathed in sight of haven, he,
Poor fellow, could he help it? recommenced,
And ran thro' all the coltish chronicle,
Wild Will, Black Bess, Tantivy, Tallyho,
Reform, White Rose, Bellerophon, and the rest,
Till, not to die a listener, I arose,
And with me Philip, talking still; and so
We turn'd our foreheads from the falling sun,
And following our own shadows thrice as long
As when they follow'd us from Philip's door,
Arrived, and found the sun of sweet content
Re-risen in Katie's eyes, and all things well.

I steal by lawns and grassy plots,
    I slide by hazel covers;
I move the sweet forget-me-nots
    That grow for happy lovers.

I slip, I slide, I gloom, I glance,
    Among my skimming swallows;
I make the netted sunbeam dance
    Against my sandy shallows.

I murmur under moon and stars
    In brambly wildernesses;

10

I linger by my shingly bars;
    I loiter round my cresses;

And out again I curve and flow
    To join the brimming river,
For men may come and men may go,
    But I go on forever.

Yes, men may come and go; and these are gone.
All gone. My dearest brother, Edmund, sleeps,
Not by the well-known stream and rustic spire,
But unfamiliar Arno, and the dome
Of Brunelleschi; sleeps in peace: and he,
Poor Philip, of all his lavish waste of words
Remains the lean P. W. on his tomb:
I scraped the lichen from it: Katie walks
By the long wash of Australasian seas
Far off, and holds her head to other stars,
And breathes in converse seasons. All are gone."

So Lawrence Aylmer, seated on a stile
In the long hedge, and rolling in his mind
Old waifs of rhyme, and bowing o'er the brook
A tonsured head in middle age forlorn,
Mused, and was mute. On a sudden a low breath
Of tender air made tremble in the hedge
The fragile bindweed-bells and briony rings;
And he look'd up. There stood a maiden near,
Waiting to pass. In much amaze he stared
On eyes a bashful azure, and on hair
In gloss and hue the chestnut, when the shell
Divides threefold to show the fruit within:
Then, wondering, ask'd her, "Are you from the
    farm?"
"Yes," answer'd she. "Pray stay a little: pardon
    me;
What do they call you?" "Katie." "That were
    strange.
What surname?" "Willows." "No I" "That is
    my name."
"Indeed!" and here he look'd so self-perplext,
That Katie laugh'd, and laughing blush'd, till he
Laugh'd also, but as one before he wakes,
Who feels a glimmering strangeness in his dream.
Then looking at her; "Too happy, fresh and fair,
Too fresh and fair in our sad world's best bloom,
To be the ghost of one who bore your name
About these meadows, twenty years ago."

"Have you not heard?" said Katie, "we came
    back.
We bought the farm we tenanted before.
Am I so like her? so they said on board.
Sir, if you knew her in her English days,
My mother, as it seems you did, the days
That most she loves to talk of, come with me.
My brother James is in the harvest-field:
But she—you will be welcome—O, come in!"

⊹≺⊙≻⊹

THE LETTERS.

1.

Still on the tower stood the vane,
    A black yew gloom'd the stagnant air,
I peer'd athwart the chancel pane
    And saw the altar cold and bare.
A clog of lead was round my feet,
    A band of pain across my brow;
"Cold altar, Heaven and earth shall meet
    Before you hear my marriage vow."

2.

I turn'd and humm'd a bitter song
    That mock'd the wholesome human heart,
And then we met in wrath and wrong,
    We met, but only meant to part.

Full cold my greeting was and dry;
  She faintly smiled, she hardly moved;
I saw with half-unconscious eye
  She wore the colors I approved.

3.

She took the little ivory chest,
  With half a sigh she turn'd the key,
Then raised her head with lips comprest,
  And gave my letters back to me.
And gave the trinkets and the rings,
  My gifts, when gifts of mine could please;
As looks a father on the things
  Of his dead son, I look'd on these.

4.

She told me all her friends had said;
  I raged against the public liar;
She talk'd as if her love were dead,
  But in my words were seeds of fire.
"No more of love; your sex is known:
  I never will be twice deceived.
Henceforth I trust the man alone,
  The woman cannot be believed.

5.

"Thro' slander, meanest spawn of Hell
  (And women's slander is the worst),
And you, whom once I lov'd so well,
  Thro' you, my life will be accurst."
I spoke with heart, and heat and force,
  I shook her breast with vague alarms—
Like torrents from a mountain source
  We rush'd into each other's arms.

6.

We parted: sweetly gleam'd the stars,
  And sweet the vapor-braided blue,
Low breezes faun'd the belfry bars,
  As homeward by the church I drew.
The very graves appear'd to smile,
  So fresh they rose in shadow'd swells;
"Dark porch," I said, "and silent aisle,
  There comes a sound of marriage bells."

—— ⌇ ——

ODE ON THE DEATH OF THE DUKE OF WELLINGTON.

1.

Bury the Great Duke
  With an empire's lamentation,
Let us bury the Great Duke
  To the noise of the mourning of a mighty nation,
Mourning when their leaders fall,
Warriors carry the warrior's pall,
And sorrow darkens hamlet and hall.

2.

Where shall we lay the man whom we deplore?
Here, in streaming London's central roar.
Let the sound of those he wrought for,
And the feet of those he fought for,
Echo round his bones forevermore.

3.

Lead out the pageant: sad and slow,
As fits an universal woe,
Let the long long procession go,
And let the sorrowing crowd about it grow,
And let the mournful martial music blow;
The last great Englishman is low.

4.

Mourn, for to us he seems the last,
Remembering all his greatness in the Past.
No more in soldier fashion will he greet
With lifted hand the gazer in the street.
O friends, our chief state-oracle is dead:
Mourn for the man of long-enduring blood,
The statesman-warrior, moderate, resolute,
Whole in himself, a common good.
Mourn for the man of amplest influence,
Yet clearest of ambitious crime,
Our greatest yet with least pretence,
Great in council and great in war,
Foremost captain of his time,
Rich in saving common-sense,
And, as the greatest only are,
In his simplicity sublime.
O good gray head which all men knew,
O voice from which their omens all men drew,
O iron nerve to true occasion true,
O fall'n at length that tower of strength
Which stood four-square to all the winds that blew!
Such was he whom we deplore.
The long self-sacrifice of life is o'er.
The great World-victor's victor will be seen no more.

5.

All is over and done:
Render thanks to the Giver,
England, for thy son.
Let the bell be toll'd.
Render thanks to the Giver,
And render him to the mould.
Under the cross of gold
That shines over city and river,
There he shall rest forever
Among the wise and the bold.
Let the bell be toll'd:
And a reverent people behold
The towering car, the sable steeds:
Bright let it be with his blazon'd deeds,
Dark in its funeral fold.
Let the bell be tolled:
And a deeper knell in the heart be knoll'd;
And the sound of the sorrowing anthem roll'd
Thro' the dome of the golden cross;
And the volleying cannon thunder his loss;
He knew their voices of old.
For many a time in many a clime
His captain's-ear has heard them boom
Bellowing victory, bellowing doom:
When he with those deep voices wrought,
Guarding realms and kings from shame;
With those deep voices our dead captain taught
The tyrant, and asserts his claim
In that dread sound to the great name,
Which he has worn so pure of blame,
In praise and in dispraise the same,
A man of well-attemper'd frame.
O civic muse, to such a name,
To such a name for ages long,
To such a name,
Preserve a broad approach of fame,
And ever-ringing avenues of song.

6.

Who is he that cometh, like an honor'd guest,
With banner and with music, with soldier and with
      priest,
With a nation weeping, and breaking on my rest?
Mighty seaman, this is he
Was great by land as thou by sea.
Thine Island loves thee well, thou famous man,
The greatest sailor since our world began.
Now, to the roll of muffled drums,
To thee the greatest soldier comes;
For this is he

Was great by land as thou by sea:
His foes were thine; he kept us free
O give him welcome, this is he,
Worthy of our gorgeous rites,
And worthy to be laid by thee;
For this is England's greatest son,
He that gain'd a hundred fights,
Nor ever lost an English gun;
This is he that far away
Against the myriads of Assaye
Clash'd with his fiery few and won;
And underneath another sun,
Warring on a later day,
Round affrighted Lisbon drew
The treble works, the vast designs
Of his labor'd rampart-lines,
Where he greatly stood at bay,
Whence he issued forth anew,
And ever great and greater grew,
Beating from the wasted vines
Back to France her banded swarms,
Back to France with countless blows,
Till o'er the hills her eagles flew
Past the Pyrenean pines,
Follow'd up in valley and glen
With blare of bugle, clamor of men,
Roll of cannon and clash of arms,
And England pouring on her foes.
Such a war had such a close.
Again their ravening eagle rose
In anger, wheel'd on Europe-shadowing wings,
And barking for the thrones of kings;
Till, one that sought but Duty's iron crown
On that loud sabbath shook the spoiler down:
A day of onsets of despair!
Dash'd on every rocky square
Their surging charges foam'd themselves away;
Last, the Prussian trumpet blew;
Thro the long-tormented air
Heaven flash'd a sudden jubilant ray.
And down we swept and charged and overthrew.
So great a soldier taught us there,
What long-enduring hearts could do
In that world's-earthquake, Waterloo!
Mighty seaman, tender and true,
And pure as he from taint of craven guile,
O saviour of the silver-coasted isle,
O shaker of the Baltic and the Nile,
If aught of things that here befall
Touch a spirit among things divine,
If love of country move thee there at all,
Be glad, because his bones are laid by thine!
And thro' the centuries let a people's voice
In full acclaim,
A people's voice,
The proof and echo of all human fame,
A people's voice, when they rejoice
At civic revel and pomp and game,
Attest their great commander's claim
With honor, honor, honor to him,
Eternal honor to his name.

7.

A people's voice! we are a people yet.
Tho' all men else their nobler dreams forget
Confused by brainless mobs and lawless Powers;
Thank Him who isled us here, and roughly set
His Saxon in blown seas and storming showers.
We have a voice, with which to pay the debt
Of boundless love and reverence and regret
To those great men who fought, and kept it ours.
And keep it ours, O God, from brute control;
O Statesmen, guard us, guard the eye, the soul
Of Europe, keep our noble England whole,
And save the one true seed of freedom sown
Betwixt a people and their ancient throne,
That sober freedom out of which there springs
Our loyal passion for our temperate kings;

For, saving that, ye help to save mankind
Till public wrong be crumbled into dust,
And drill the raw world for the march of mind,
Till crowds at length be sane and crowns be just.
But wink no more in slothful overtrust.
Remember him who led your hosts;
He bade you guard the sacred coasts.
Your cannons moulder on the seaward wall;
His voice is silent in your council-hall
Forever; and whatever tempests lower
Forever silent; even if they broke
In thunder, silent; yet remember all
He spoke among you, and the Man who spoke;
Who never sold the truth to serve the hour,
Nor palter'd with Eternal God for power;
Who let the turbid streams of rumor flow
Thro' either babbling world of high and low;
Whose life was work, whose language rife
With rugged maxims hewn from life;
Who never spoke against a foe:
Whose eighty winters freeze with one rebuke
All great self-seekers trampling on the right:
Truth-teller was our England's Alfred named:
Truth-lover was our English Duke,
Whatever record leap to light
He never shall be shamed.

8.

Lo, the leader in these glorious wars
Now to glorious burial slowly borne,
Follow'd by the brave of other lands,
He, on whom from both her open hands
Lavish Honor shower'd all her stars,
And affluent Fortune emptied all her horn.
Yea, let all good things await
Him who cares not to be great,
But as he saves or serves the state.
Not once or twice in our rough island-story,
The path of duty was the way to glory:
He that walks it, only thirsting
For the right, and learns to deaden
Love of self, before his journey closes,
He shall find the stubborn thistle bursting
Into glossy purples, which outredden
All voluptuous garden-roses.
Not once or twice in our fair island-story,
The path of duty was the way to glory:
He, that ever following her commands,
On with toil of heart and knees and hands,
Thro' the long gorge to the far light has won
His path upward, and prevail'd.
Shall find the toppling crags of Duty scaled
Are close upon the shining table-lands
To which our God Himself is moon and sun.
Such was he; his work is done.
But while the races of mankind endure,
Let his great example stand
Colossal, seen of every land,
And keep the soldier firm, the statesman pure;
Till in all lands and thro' all human story
The path of duty be the way to glory:
And let the land whose hearths he saved from shame
For many and many an age proclaim
At civic revel and pomp and game,
And when the long-illumined cities flame,
Their ever-loyal iron leader's fame,
With honor, honor, honor, honor to him,
Eternal honor to his name.

9.

Peace, his triumph will be sung
By some yet unmoulded tongue
Far on in summers that we shall not see.
Peace, it is a day of pain
For one about whose patriarchal knee
Late the little children clung:
O peace, it is a day of pain

For one upon whose hand and heart and brain
Once the weight and fate of Europe hung.
Ours the pain, be his the gain !
More than is of man's degree
Must be with us, watching here
At this, our great solemnity,
Whom we see not we revere.
We revere, and we refrain
From talk of battles loud and vain,
And brawling memories all too free
For such a wise humility
As befits a solemn fane:
We revere, and while we hear
The tides of Music's golden sea
Setting toward eternity,
Uplifted high in heart and hope are we,
Until we doubt not that for one so true
There must be other nobler work to do
Than when he fought at Waterloo,
And Victor he must ever be.
For tho' the Giant Ages heave the hill
And break the shore, and evermore
Make and break, and work their will ;
Tho' world on world in myriad myriads roll
Round us, each with different powers,
And other forms of life than ours,
What know we greater than the soul?
On God and Godlike men we build our trust.
Hush, the Dead March wails in the people's ears:
The dark crowd moves, and there are sobs and tears:
The black earth yawns· the mortal disappears ;
Ashes to ashes, dust to dust :
He is gone who seem'd so great.—
Gone ; but nothing can bereave him
Of the force he made his own
Being here, and we believe him
Something far advanced in state,
And that he wears a truer crown
Than any wreath that man can weave him.
But speak no more of his renown,
Lay your earthly fancies down,
And in the vast cathedral leave him.
God accept him, Christ receive him.

1852.

THE DAISY.

WRITTEN AT EDINBURGH.

O LOVE, what hours were thine and mine,
In lands of palm and southern pine;
   In lands of palm, of orange-blossom,
Of olive, aloe, and maize and vine.

What Roman strength Turbia show'd
In ruin, by the mountain road;
   How like a gem, beneath, the city
Of little Monaco, basking, glow'd.

How richly down the rocky dell
The torrent vineyard streaming fell
   To meet the sun and sunny waters,
That only heaved with a summer swell.

What slender campanili grew
By bays, the peacock's neck in hue;
   Where, here and there, on sandy beaches
A milky-bell'd amaryllis blew.

How young Columbus seem'd to rove,
Yet present in his natal grove,
   Now watching high on mountain cornice,
And steering, now, from a purple cove,

Now pacing mute by ocean's rim;
Till, in a narrow street and dim,
   I stay'd the wheels at Cogoletto,
And drank, and loyally drank to him.

Nor knew we well what pleased us most,
Not the clipt palm of which they boast;
   But distant color, happy hamlet,
A moulder'd citadel on the coast,

Or tower, or high hill-convent, seen
A light amid its olives green ;
   Or olive-hoary cape in ocean ,
Or rosy blossom in hot ravine,

Where oleanders flush'd the bed
Of silent torrents, gravel-spread ;
   And, crossing, oft we saw the glisten
Of ice, far up on a mountain head.

We loved that hall, tho' white and cold,
Those niched shapes of noble mould,
   A princely people's awful princes,
The grave, severe Genovese of old.

At Florence too what golden hours,
In those long galleries, were ours ;
   What drives about the fresh Cascinè,
Or walks in Boboli's ducal bowers.

In bright vignettes, and each complete,
Of tower or duomo, sunny-sweet,
   Or palace, how the city glitter'd,
Thro' cypress avenues, at our feet.

But when we crost the Lombard plain
Remember what a plague of rain;
   Of rain at Reggio, rain at Parma;
At Lodi, rain, Piacenza, rain.

And stern and sad (so rare the smiles
Of sunlight) look'd the Lombard piles,
   Porch-pillars on the lion resting,
And sombre, old, colonnaded aisles.

O Milan, O the chanting quires,
The giant windows' blazon'd fires,
   The height, the space, the gloom, the glory!
A mount of marble, a hundred spires!

I climb'd the roofs at break of day;
Sun-smitten Alps before me lay.
   I ·tood among the silent statues,
And statued pinnacles, mute as they.

How faintly-flush'd, how phantom-fair,
Was Monte Rosa, hanging there
   A thousand shadowy-pencill'd valleys
And snowy dells in a golden air.

Remember how we came at last
To Como; shower and storm and blast
   Had clown the lake beyond his limit,
And all was flooded; and how we past

From Como, when the light was gray,
And in my head, for half the day,
   The rich Virgilian rustic measure
Of Lari Maxume, all the way,

Like ballad-burthen music, kept,
As on the Lariano crept
   To that fair port below the castle
Of Queen Theodolind, where we slept;

Or hardly slept, but watch'd awake
A cypress in the moonlight shake,
   The moonlight touching o'er a terrace
One tall Agavè above the lake.

What more? we took our last adieu,
And up the snowy Splugen drew,
   But ere we reach'd the highest summit
I pluck'd a daisy, I gave it you.

It told of England then to me,
And now it tells of Italy.
O love, we two shall go no longer
To lands of summer across the sea;

So dear a life your arms enfold
Whose crying is a cry for gold:
Yet here to-night in this dark city,
When ill and weary, alone and cold,

I found, tho' crush'd to hard and dry,
This nurseling of another sky
Still in the little book you lent me,
And where you tenderly laid it by:

And I forgot the clouded Forth,
The gloom that saddens Heaven and Earth,
The bitter east, the misty summer
And gray metropolis of the North.

Perchance, to lull the throbs of pain,
Perchance, to charm a vacant brain,
Perchance, to dream you still beside me,
My fancy fled to the South again.

TO THE REV. F. D. MAURICE.

COME, when no graver cares employ,
God-father, come and see your boy:
Your presence will be sun in winter,
Making the little one leap for joy.

For, being of that honest few,
Who give the Fiend himself his due,
Should eighty thousand college councils
Thunder "Anathema," friend, at you:

Should all our churchmen foam in spite
At you, so careful of the right,
Yet one lay-hearth would give you welcome
(Take it and come) to the Isle of Wight;

Where, far from noise and smoke of town,
I watch the twilight falling brown
All round a careless-order'd garden
Close to the ridge of a noble down.

You'll have no scandal while you dine,
But honest talk and wholesome wine,
And only hear the magpie gossip
Garrulous under a roof of pine:

For groves of pine on either hand,
To break the blast of winter, stand;
And further on, the hoary Channel
Tumbles a breaker on chalk and sand;

Where, if below the milky steep
Some ship of battle slowly creep,
And on thro' zones of light and shadow
Glimmer away to the lonely deep,

We might discuss the Northern sin
Which made a selfish war begin;
Dispute the claims, arrange the chances;
Emperor, Ottoman, which shall win:

Or whether war's avenging rod
Shall lash all Europe into blood;
Till you should turn to dearer matters,
Dear to the man that is dear to God;

How best to help the slender store,
How mend the dwellings, of the poor;
How gain in life, as life advances,
Valor and charity more and more.

Come, Maurice, come: the lawn as yet
Is hoar with rime, or spongy-wet;
But when the wreath of March has blossom'd,
Crocus, anemone, violet,

Or later, pay one visit here,
For those are few we hold as dear;
Nor pay but one, but come for many,
Many and many a happy year.
        January, 1854.

WILL.

1.

O WELL for him whose will is strong!
He suffers, but he will not suffer long;
He suffers, but he cannot suffer wrong:
For him nor moves the loud world's random mock
Nor all Calamity's hugest waves confound,
Who seems a promontory of rock,
That, compass'd round with turbulent sound,
In middle ocean meets the surging shock,
Tempest-buffeted, citadel-crown'd.

2.

But ill for him who, bettering not with time,
Corrupts the strength of heaven-descended Will,
And ever weaker grows thro' acted crime,
Or seeming-genial venial fault,
Recurring and suggesting still!
He seems as one whose footsteps
Toiling in immeasurable sand,
And o'er a weary, sultry land,
Far beneath a blazing vault,
Sown in a wrinkle of the monstrous hill,
The city sparkles like a grain of salt.

THE CHARGE OF THE LIGHT BRIGADE

1.

HALF a league, half a league,
Half a league onward,
All in the valley of Death
    Rode the six hundred.
"Forward, the Light Brigade!
"Charge for the guns!" he said.
Into the valley of Death
    Rode the six hundred.

2.

"Forward, the Light Brigade!"
Was there a man dismay'd?
Not tho' the soldier knew
    Some one had blunder'd:
Theirs not to make reply,
Theirs not to reason why,
Theirs but to do and die,
Into the valley of Death
    Rode the six hundred.

3.

Cannon to right of them,
Cannon to left of them,
Cannon in front of them
    Volley'd and thunder'd;
Storm'd at with shot and shell,
Boldly they rode and well,
Into the jaws of Death,
Into the mouth of Hell
    Rode the six hundred.

4.

Flash'd all their sabres bare,
Flash'd as they turn'd in air,
Sabring the gunners there,
Charging an army, while
   All the world wonder'd:
Plunged in the battery-smoke,
Right thro' the line they broke;
Cossack and Russian
Reel'd from the sabre-stroke
   Shatter'd and sunder'd.
Then they rode back, but not,
   Not the six hundred.

5.

Cannon to right of them,
Cannon to left of them,

Cannon behind them
   Volley'd and thunder'd;
Storm'd at with shot and shell,
While horse and hero fell,
They that had fought so well
Came thro' the jaws of Death
Back from the mouth of Hell,
All that was left of them,
   Left of six hundred.

6.

When can their glory fade?
O the wild charge they made!
   All the world wonder'd.
Honor the charge they made!
Honor the Light Brigade!
   Noble six hundred!

IDYLS OF THE KING.

"Flos Regum Arthurus."
JOSEPH OF EXETER.

DEDICATION.

THESE to His Memory—since he held them dear,
Perchance as finding there unconsciously
Some image of himself—I dedicate,
I dedicate, I consecrate with tears—
These Idyls.

   And indeed He seems to me
Scarce other than my own ideal knight,
"Who reverenced his conscience as his king;
Whose glory was, redressing human wrong;
Who spake no slander, no, nor listen'd to it;
Who loved one only and who clave to her—"
Her—over all whose realms to their last isle,
Commingled with the gloom of imminent war,
The shadow of His loss drew like eclipse,
Darkening the world. We have lost him: he is gone:
We know him now: all narrow jealousies
Are silent; and we see him as he moved,
How modest, kindly, all-accomplish'd, wise,
With what sublime repression of himself,
And in what limits, and how tenderly;
Not swaying to this faction or to that;
Not making his high place the lawless perch
Of wing'd ambitions, nor a vantage-ground
For pleasure; but thro' all this tract of years
Wearing the white flower of a blameless life,
Before a thousand peering littlenesses,
In that fierce light which beats upon a throne,
And blackens every blot: for where is he,
Who dares foreshadow for an only son
-A lovelier life, a more unstain'd, than his?
Or how should England dreaming of *his* sons
Hope more for these than some inheritance
Of such a life, a heart, a mind as thine,
Thou noble Father of her Kings to be,
Laborious for her people and her poor—
Voice in the rich dawn of an ampler day—
Far-sighted summoner of War and Waste
To fruitful strifes and rivalries of peace—
Sweet nature gilded by the gracious gleam
Of letters, dear to Science, dear to Art,
Dear to thy land and ours, a Prince indeed,
Beyond all titles, and a household name,
Hereafter, thro' all times, Albert the Good.

   Break not, O woman's-heart, but still endure;
Break not, for thou art Royal, but endure,
Remembering all the beauty of that star
Which shone so close beside Thee, that ye made
One light together, but has past and leaves
The Crown a lonely splendor.

   May all love,
His love, unseen but felt, o'ershadow Thee,
The love of all Thy sons encompass Thee,
The love of all Thy daughters cherish Thee,
The love of all Thy people comfort Thee,
Till God's love set Thee at his side again!

THE COMING OF ARTHUR.

LEODOGRAN, the King of Cameliard,
Had one fair daughter, and none other child;
And she was fairest of all flesh on earth,
Guinevere, and in her his one delight.

   For many a petty king ere Arthur came
Ruled in this isle, and ever waging war
Each upon other, wasted all the land;
And still from time to time the heathen host
Swarm'd overseas, and harried what was left.
And so there grew great tracts of wilderness,
Wherein the beast was ever more and more,
But man was less and less, till Arthur came.
For first Aurelius lived and fought and died,
And after him King Uther fought and died,
But either fail'd to make the kingdom one.
And after these King Arthur for a space,
And thro' the puissance of his Table Round,
Drew all their petty princedoms under him,
Their king and head, and made a realm, and reign'd.

   And thus the land of Cameliard was waste,
Thick with wet woods, and many a beast therein,
And none or few to scare or chase the beast;
So that wild dog, and wolf and boar and bear
Came night and day, and rooted in the fields,
And wallow'd in the gardens of the King.
And ever and anon the wolf would steal
The children and devour, but now and then,
Her own brood lost or dead, lent her fierce teat
To human sucklings; and the children, housed
In her foul den, there at their meat would growl,
And mock their foster-mother on four feet,
Till, straighten'd, they grew up to wolf-like men,
Worse than the wolves. And King Leodogran
Groan'd for the Roman legions here again,
And Cæsar's eagle: then his brother king,
Urien, assail'd him: last a heathen horde,
Reddening the sun with smoke and earth with blood,
And on the spike that split the mother's heart
Spitting the child, brake on him, till, amazed,
He knew not whither he should turn for aid.

But—for he heard of Arthur newly crown'd,
Tho' not without an uproar made by those
Who cried, "He is not Uther's son"—the King
Sent to him, saying, "Arise, and help us, thou!
For here between the man and beast we die."

And Arthur yet had done no deed of arms,
But heard the call, and came; and Guinevere
Stood by the castle walls to watch him pass;
But since he neither wore on helm or shield
The golden symbol of his kinglihood,
But rode a simple knight among his knights,
And many of these in richer arms than he,
She saw him not, or mark'd not, if she saw,
One among many, tho' his face was bare.
But Arthur, looking downward as he past,
Felt the light of her eyes into his life
Smite on the sudden, yet rode on, and pitch'd
His tents beside the forest. Then he drave
The heathen, after slew the beast, and fell'd
The forest, letting in the sun, and made
Broad pathways for the hunter and the knight,
And so return'd.

      For while he linger'd there,
A doubt that ever smoulder'd in the hearts
Of those great lords and barons of his realm
Flash'd forth and into war: for most of these,
Colleaguing with a score of petty kings,
Made head against him, crying, "Who is he
That he should rule us? who hath proven him
King Uther's son? for lo! we look at him.
And find nor face nor bearing, limbs nor voice,
Are like to those of Uther whom we knew.
This is the son of Gorloïs, not the King;
This is the son of Anton, not the King."

And Arthur, passing thence to battle, felt
Travail, and throes and agonies of the life,
Desiring to be join'd with Guinevere;
And thinking as he rode, "Her father said
That there between the man and beast they die.
Shall I not lift her from this land of beasts
Up to my throne, and side by side with me?
What happiness to reign a lonely king,
Vext—O ye stars that shudder over me,
O earth that soundest hollow under me—
Vext with waste dreams? for saving I be join'd
To her that is the fairest under heaven,
I seem as nothing in the mighty world,
And cannot will my will, nor work my work
Wholly, nor make myself in mine own realm
Victor and lord. But were I join'd with her,
Then might we live together as one life,
And reigning with one will in everything
Have power on this dark land to lighten it,
And power on this dead world to make it live."

Thereafter—as he speaks who tells the tale—
When Arthur reach'd a field-of-battle bright
With pitch'd pavilions of his foe, the world
Was all so clear about him, that he saw
The smallest rock far on the faintest hill,
And even in high day the morning star.
So when the King had set his banner broad,
At once from either side, with trumpet-blast,
And shouts, and clarions shrilling unto blood,
The long-lanced battle let their horses run.
And now the barons and the kings prevail'd
And now the King, as here and there that war
Went swaying; but the Powers who walk the world
Made lightnings and great thunders over him,
And dazed all eyes, till Arthur by main might,
And mightier of his hands with every blow,
And leading all his knighthood threw the kings
Carádos, Urien, Cradlemont of Wales,
Claudias, and Clariance of Northumberland,
The King Brandagoras of Latangor,

With Anguisant of Erin, Morganore,
And Lot of Orkney. Then, before a voice
As dreadful as the shout of one who sees
To one who sins, and deems himself alone
And all the world asleep, they swerved and brake
Flying, and Arthur call'd to stay the brands
That hack'd among the flyers, "Ho! they yield!"
So like a painted battle the war stood
Silenced, the living quiet as the dead,
And in the heart of Arthur joy was lord.
He laugh'd upon his warrior whom he loved
And honor'd most. "Thou dost not doubt me King,
So well thine arm hath wrought for me to-day."
"Sir and my liege," he cried, "the fire of God
Descends upon thee in the battle-field:
I know thee for my King!" Whereat the two,
For each had warded either in the fight,
Sware on the field of death a deathless love.
And Arthur said, "Man's word is God in man:
Let chance what will, I trust thee to the death."

Then quickly from the foughten field he sent
Ulfius, and Brastias, and Bedivere,
His new-made knights, to King Leodogran,
Saying, "If I in aught have served thee well,
Give me thy daughter Guinevere to wife."

Whom when he heard, Leodogran in heart
Debating—"How should I that am a king,
However much he help me at my need,
Give my one daughter saving to a king,
And a king's son?"—lifted his voice, and call'd
A hoary man, his chamberlain, to whom
He trusted all things, and of him required
His counsel: "Knowest thou aught of Arthur's birth?"

Then spake the hoary chamberlain and said,
"Sir King, there be but two old men that know:
And each is twice as old as I; and one
Is Merlin, the wise man that ever served
King Uther thro' his magic art; and one
Is Merlin's master (so they call him) Bleys,
Who taught him magic; but the scholar ran
Before the master, and so far, that Bleys
Laid magic by, and sat him down, and wrote
All things and whatsoever Merlin did
In one great annal-book, where after-years
Will learn the secret of our Arthur's birth."

To whom the King Leodogran replied,
"O friend, had I been holpen half as well
By this King Arthur as by thee to-day,
Then beast and man had had their share of me;
But summon here before us yet once more
Ulfius, and Brastias, and Bedivere."

Then, when they came before him, the King said,
"I have seen the cuckoo chased by lesser fowl,
And reason in the chase: but wherefore now
Do these your lords stir up the heat of war,
Some calling Arthur born of Gorloïs,
Others of Anton? Tell me, ye yourselves,
Hold ye this Arthur for King Uther's son?"

And Ulfius and Brastias answer'd, "Ay."
Then Bedivere, the first of all his knights
Knighted by Arthur at his crowning, spake—
For bold in heart and act and word was he,
Whenever slander breathed against the King—

"Sir, there be many rumors on this head:
For there be those who hate him in their hearts,
Call him base-born, and, since his ways are sweet
And theirs are bestial, hold him less than man:
And there be those who deem him more than man,
And dream he dropt from heaven: but my belief
In all this matter—so ye care to learn—
Sir, for ye know that in King Uther's time

The prince and warrior Gorloïs, he that held
Tintagil castle by the Cornish sea,
Was wedded with a winsome wife, Ygerne:
And daughters had she borne him,—one whereof,
Lot's wife, the Queen of Orkney, Bellicent,
Hath ever like a loyal sister cleaved
To Arthur,—but a son she had not borne.
And Uther cast upon her eyes of love:
But she, a stainless wife to Gorloïs,
So loathed the bright dishonour of his love,
That Gorloïs and King Uther went to war:
And overthrown was Gorloïs and slain.
Then Uther in his wrath and heat besieged
Ygerne within Tintagil, where her men,
Seeing the mighty swarm about their walls,
Left her and fled, and Uther enter'd in,
And there was none to call to but himself.
So, compass'd by the power of the King,
Enforced she was to wed him in her tears,
And with a shameful swiftness: afterward,
Not many moons, King Uther died himself,
Moaning and wailing for an heir to rule
After him, lest the realm should go to wrack.
And that same night, the night of the new year,
By reason of the bitterness and grief
That vext his mother, all before his time
Was Arthur born, and all as soon as born
Deliver'd at a secret postern-gate
To Merlin, to be holden far apart
Until his hour should come; because the lords
Of that fierce day were as the lords of this,
Wild beasts, and surely would have torn the child
Piecemeal among them, had they known; for each
But sought to rule for his own self and hand,
And many hated Uther for the sake
Of Gorloïs. [Wherefore Merlin took the child,
And gave him to Sir Anton, an old knight
And ancient friend of Uther; and his wife
Nursed the young prince, and rear'd him with her
    own;
And no man knew. And ever since the lords
Have foughten like wild beasts among themselves,
So that the realm has gone to wrack: but now,
This year, when Merlin (for his hour had come)
Brought Arthur forth, and set him in the hall,
Proclaiming, 'Here is Uther's heir, your king,'
A hundred voices cried, 'Away with him!
No king of ours! a son of Gorloïs he,
Or else the child of Anton, and no king,
Or else base-born.' Yet Merlin thro' his craft,
And while the people clamor'd for a king,
Had Arthur crown'd; but after, the great lords
Banded, and so brake out in open war."

Then while the King debated with himself
If Arthur were the child of shamefulness,
Or born the son of Gorloïs, after death,
Or Uther's son, and born before his time,
Or whether there were truth in anything
Said by these three, then came to Cameliard,
With Gawain and young Modred, her two sons,
Lot's wife, the Queen of Orkney, Bellicent;
Whom as he could, not as he would, the King
Made feast for, saying, as they sat at meat,

"A doubtful throne is ice on summer seas.
Ye come from Arthur's court. Victor his men
Report him! Yea, but ye—think ye this king—
So many those that hate him, and so strong,
So few his knights, however brave they be—
Hath body enow to hold his foemen down?"

"O King," she cried, "and I will tell thee: few,
Few, but all brave, all of one mind with him;
For I was near him when the savage yells
Of Uther's peerage died, and Arthur sat
Crown'd on the daïs, and his warriors cried,
'Be thou the king, and we will work thy will

Who love thee.' Then the King, in low deep tones,
And simple words of great authority,
Bound them by so strait vows to his own self,
That when they rose, knighted from kneeling, some
Were pale as at the passing of a ghost,
Some flush'd, and others dazed, as one who wakes
Half-blinded at the coming of a light.

"But when he spake and cheer'd his Table Round
With large divine and comfortable words
Beyond my tongue to tell thee—I beheld
From eye to eye thro' all their Order flash
A momentary likeness of the King:
And ere it left their faces, thro' the cross
And those around it and the Crucified,
Down from the casement over Arthur, smote
Flame-color, vert and azure, in three rays,
One falling upon each of three fair queens,
Who stood in silence near his throne, the friends
Of Arthur, gazing on him, tall, with bright
Sweet faces, who will help him at his need.

"And there I saw mage Merlin, whose vast wit
And hundred winters are but as the hands
Of loyal vassals toiling for their liege.

"And near him stood the Lady of the Lake,
Who knows a subtler magic than his own—
Clothed in white samite, mystic, wonderful.
She gave the King his huge cross-hilted sword,
Whereby to drive the heathen out: a mist
Of incense curl'd about her, and her face
Wellnigh was hidden in the minster gloom;
But there was heard among the holy hymns
A voice as of the waters, for she dwells
Down in a deep, calm, whatsoever storms
May shake the world, and when the surface rolls,
Hath power to walk the waters like our Lord.

"There likewise I beheld Excalibur
Before him at his crowning borne, the sword
That rose from out the bosom of the lake,
And Arthur row'd across and took it—rich
With jewels, elfin Urim, on the hilt,
Bewildering heart and eye—the blade so bright
That men are blinded by it—on one side,
Graven in the oldest tongue of all this world,
'Take me,' but turn the blade and ye shall see,
And written in the speech ye speak yourself,
'Cast me away!' And sad was Arthur's face
Taking it, but old Merlin counsell'd him,
'Take thou and strike! the time to cast away
Is yet far-off.' So this great brand the King
Took, and by this will beat his foemen down."

Thereat Leodogran rejoiced, but thought
To sift his doubtings to the last, and ask'd,
Fixing full eyes of question on her face,
"The swallow and the swift are near akin,
But thou art closer to this noble prince,
Being his own dear sister;" and she said,
"Daughter of Gorloïs and Ygerne am I;"
"And therefore Arthur's sister," ask'd the King.
She answer'd, "These be secret things," and sign'd
To those two sons to pass and let them be.
And Gawain went, and breaking into song
Sprang out, and follow'd by his flying hair
Ran like a colt, and leapt at all he saw:
But Modred laid his ear beside the doors,
And there half heard; the same that afterward
Struck for the throne, and striking found his doom.

And then the Queen made answer. "What know I:
For dark my mother was in eyes and hair.
And dark in hair and eyes am I; and dark
Was Gorloïs, yea and dark was Uther too,
Wellnigh to blackness; but this King is fair
Beyond the race of Britons and of men.

Moreover, always in my mind I hear
A cry from out the dawning of my life,
A mother weeping. and I hear her say,
'O that ye had some brother, pretty one,
To guard thee on the rough ways of the world.'"

"Ay," said the King, "and hear ye such a cry?
But when did Arthur chance upon thee first?"

"O King!" she cried, "and I will tell thee true:
He found me first when yet a little maid.
Beaten I had been for a little fault
Whereof I was not guilty; and out I ran
And flung myself down on a bank of heath,
And hated this fair world and all therein,
And wept and wish'd that I were dead; and he—
I know not whether of himself he came,
Or brought by Merlin, who, they say, can walk
Unseen at pleasure—he was at my side,
And spake sweet words, and comforted my heart,
And dried my tears, being a child with me,
And many a time he came, and evermore
As I grew greater grew with me; and sad
At times he seem'd, and sad with him was I,
Stern too at times, and then I loved him not,
But sweet again, and then I loved him well.
And now of late I see him less and less,
But those first days had golden hours for me,
For then I surely thought he would be king.

"But let me tell thee now another tale:
For Bleys, our Merlin's master, as they say,
Died but of late, and sent his cry to me,
To hear him speak before he left his life.
Shrunk like a fairy changeling lay the mage:
And when I enter'd told me that himself
And Merlin ever served about the King,
Uther, before he died; and on the night
When Uther in Tintagil past away
Moaning and wailing for an heir, the two
Left the still King, and passing forth to breathe,
Then from the castle gateway by the chasm
Descending thro' the dismal night—a night
In which the bounds of heaven and earth were lost—
Beheld, so high upon the dreary deeps
It seem'd in heaven, a ship, the shape thereof
A dragon wing'd, and all from stem to stern
Bright with a shining people on the decks,
And gone as soon as seen. And then the two
Dropt to the cove, and watch'd the great sea fall,
Wave after wave, each mightier than the last,
Till last, a ninth one, gathering half the deep
And full of voices, slowly rose and plunged
Roaring, and all the wave was in a flame:
And down the wave and in the flame was borne
A naked babe, and rode to Merlin's feet,
Who stoopt and caught the babe, and cried, 'The
    King!
Here is an heir for Uther!' And the fringe
Of that great breaker, sweeping up the strand,
Lash'd at the wizard as he spake the word,
And all at once all round him rose in fire,
So that the child and he were clothed in fire.
And presently thereafter follow'd calm,
Free sky and stars: 'And this same child,' he said,
'Is he who reigns; nor could I part in peace
Till this were told.' And saying this the seer
Went thro' the strait and dreadful pass of death,
Not ever to be question'd any more
Save on the farther side; but when I met
Merlin, and ask'd him if these things were truth—
The shining dragon and the naked child
Descending in the glory of the seas—
He laugh'd as is his wont, and answer'd me
In riddling triplets of old time, and said:

"'Rain, rain, and sun! a rainbow in the sky!
A young man will be wiser by and by;

An old man's wit may wander ere he die.
Rain, rain, and sun! a rainbow on the lea!
And truth is this to me, and that to thee;
And truth or clothed or naked let it be.
Rain, sun, and rain! and the free blossom blows.
Sun, rain, and sun! and where is he who knows?
From the great deep to the great deep he goes.'

"So Merlin riddling anger'd me; but thou
Fear not to give this King thine only child,
Guinevere: so great bards of him will sing
Hereafter; and dark sayings from of old
Ranging and ringing thro' the minds of men,
And echo'd by old folk beside their fires
For comfort after their wage-work is done,
Speak of the King; and Merlin in our time
Hath spoken also, not in jest, and sworn
Tho' men may wound him that he will not die.
But pass, again to come; and then or now
Utterly smite the heathen underfoot,
Till these and all men hail him for their king."

She spake and King Leodogran rejoiced,
But musing "Shall I answer yea or nay?"
Doubted and drowsed, nodded and slept, and saw,
Dreaming, a slope of land that ever grew,
Field after field, up to a height, the peak
Haze-hidden, and thereon a phantom king,
Now looming, and now lost: and on the slope
The sword rose, the hind fell, the herd was driven,
Fire glimpsed; and all the land from roof and rick,
In drifts of smoke before a rolling wind,
Stream'd to the peak, and mingled with the haze
And made it thicker; while the phantom king
Sent out at times a voice; and here or there
Stood one who pointed toward the voice, the rest
Slew on and burnt, crying, "No king of ours,
No son of Uther, and no king of ours;"
Till with a wink his dream was changed, the haze
Descended, and the solid earth became
As nothing, but the king stood out in heaven,
Crown'd. And Leodogran awoke, and sent
Ulfius, and Brastias, and Bedivere,
Back to the court of Arthur answering yea.

Then Arthur charged his warrior whom he loved
And honor'd most, Sir Lancelot, to ride forth
And bring the Queen;—and watch'd him from the
    gates:
And Lancelot past away among the flowers
(For then was latter April) and return'd
Among the flowers, in May, with Guinevere.
To whom arrived, by Dubric the high saint,
Chief of the church in Britain, and before
The stateliest of her altar-shrines, the King
That morn was married, while in stainless white,
The fair beginners of a nobler time,
And glorying in their vows and him, his knights
Stood round him, and rejoicing in his joy.
Far shone the fields of May thro' open door,
The sacred altar blossom'd white with May,
The Sun of May descended on their King,
They gazed on all earth's beauty in their Queen,
Roll'd incense, and there past along the hymns
A voice as of the waters, while the two
Sware at the shrine of Christ a deathless love:
And Arthur said, "Behold, thy doom is mine.
Let chance what will, I love thee to the death!"
To whom the Queen replied with drooping eyes,
"King and my lord, I love thee to the death!"
And holy Dubric spread his hands and spake,
"Reign ye, and live and love, and make the world
Other, and may thy Queen be one with thee,
And all this Order of thy Table Round
Fulfil the boundless purpose of their King!"

So Dubric said: but when they left the shrine
Great lords from Rome before the portal stood,

In scornful stillness gazing as they past;
Then while they paced a city all on fire
With sun and cloth of gold, the trumpets blew,
And Arthur's knighthood sang before the King :—

"Blow trumpet, for the world is white with May;
Blow trumpet, the long night hath roll'd away!
Blow thro' the living world—'Let the King reign.'

"Shall Rome or heathen rule in Arthur's realm?
Flash brand and lance, fall battleaxe upon helm,
Fall battleaxe, and flash brand! Let the King reign.

"Strike for the King and live! his knights have
          heard
That God hath told the King a secret word.
Fall battleaxe, and flash brand! Let the King reign.

"Blow trumpet! he will lift us from the dust.
Blow trumpet! live the strength and die the lust!
Clang battleaxe, and clash brand! Let the King
          reign.

"Strike for the King and die! and if thou diest,
The King is King, and ever wills the highest.
Clang battleaxe, and clash brand! Let the King
          reign.

"Blow, for our Sun is mighty in his May!
Blow, for our Sun is mightier day by day!
Clang battleaxe, and clash brand! Let the King
          reign.

"The King will follow Christ, and we the King
In whom high God hath breathed a secret thing.
Fall battleaxe, and flash brand! Let the King reign."

So sang the knighthood, moving to their hall.
There at the banquet those great lords from Rome,
The slowly-fading mistress of the world,
Strode in, and claim'd their tribute as of yore.
But Arthur spake, "Behold, for these have sworn
To wage my wars, and worship me their King;
The old order changeth, yielding place to new;
And we that fight for our fair father Christ,
Seeing that ye be grown too weak and old
To drive the heathen from your Roman wall,
No tribute will we pay:" so those great lords
Drew back in wrath, and Arthur strove with Rome.

And Arthur and his knighthood for a space
Were all one will, and thro' that strength the King
Drew in the petty princedoms under him,
Fought, and in twelve great battles overcame
The heathen hordes, and made a realm and reign'd.

—————

GARETH AND LYNETTE.

The last tall son of Lot and Bellicent,
And tallest, Gareth, in a showerful spring
Stared at the spate. A slender-shafted Pine
Lost footing, fell, and so was whirl'd away.
"How he went down," said Gareth, "as a false knight
Or evil king before my lance if lance
Were mine to use—O senseless cataract,
Bearing all down in thy precipitancy—
And yet thou art but swollen with cold snows
And mine is living blood: thou dost His will,
The Maker's, and not knowest, and I that know,
Have strength and wit, in my good mother's hall
Linger with vacillating obedience,
Prison'd, and kept and coax'd and whistled to—
Since the good mother holds me still a child!
Good mother is bad mother unto me!
A worse were better; yet no worse would I.
Heaven yield her for it, but in me put force
To weary her ears with one continuous prayer,

Until she let me fly discaged to sweep
In ever-highering eagle-circles up
To the great Sun of Glory, and thence swoop
Down upon all things base, and dash them dead,
A knight of Arthur, working out his will,
To cleanse the world. Why, Gawain, when he came
With Modred hither in the summertime,
Ask'd me to tilt with him, the proven knight.
Modred for want of worthier was the judge.
Then I so shook him in the saddle, he said,
'Thou hast half prevail'd against me,' said so—he—
Tho' Modred biting his thin lips was mute,
For he is alway sullen: what care I?"

And Gareth went, and hovering round her chair
Ask'd, "Mother, tho' ye count me still the child,
Sweet mother, do ye love the child?" She laugh'd,
"Thou art but a wild-goose to question it."
"Then, mother, an ye love the child," he said,
"Being a goose and rather tame than wild,
Hear the child's story." "Yea, my well-beloved,
An 'twere but of the goose and golden eggs."

And Gareth answer'd her with kindling eyes,
"Nay, nay, good mother, but this egg of mine
Was finer gold than any goose can lay;
For this an Eagle, a royal Eagle, laid
Almost beyond eye-reach, on such a palm
As glitters gilded in thy Book of Hours.
And there was ever haunting round the palm
A lusty youth, but poor, who often saw
The splendor sparkling from aloft, and thought
'An I could climb and lay my hand upon it,
Then were I wealthier than a leash of kings.'
But ever when he reach'd a hand to climb,
One, that had loved him from his childhood, caught
And stay'd him, 'Climb not lest thou break thy neck,
I charge thee by my love,' and so the boy,
Sweet mother, neither clomb, nor brake his neck,
But brake his very heart in pining for it,
And past away."

          To whom the mother said,
"True love, sweet son, had risk'd himself and climb'd,
And handed down the golden treasure to him."

And Gareth answer'd her with kindling eyes,
"Gold?" said I gold?—ay then, why he, or she,
Or whosoe'er it was, or half the world
Had ventured—had the thing I spake of been
Mere gold—but this was all of that true steel
Whereof they forged the brand Excalibur,
And lightnings play'd about it in the storm,
And all the little fowl were flurried at it,
And there were cries and clashings in the nest,
That sent him from his senses: let me go."

Then Bellicent bemoan'd herself and said,
"Hast thou no pity upon my loneliness?
Lo, where thy father Lot beside the hearth
Lies like a log, and all but smoulder'd out!
For ever since when traitor to the King
He fought against him in the Barons' war,
And Arthur gave him back his territory,
His age hath slowly droopt, and now lies there
A yet-warm corpse, and yet unburiable,
No more: nor sees, nor hears, nor speaks, nor knows
And both thy brethren are in Arthur's hall,
Albeit neither loved with that full love
I feel for thee, nor worthy such a love:
Stay therefore thou; red berries charm the bird
And thee, mine innocent, the jousts, the wars,
Who never knewest finger-ache, nor pang
Of wrench'd or broken limb—an often chance
In those brain-stunning shocks, and tourney-falls,
Frights to my heart; but stay: follow the deer
By these tall firs and our fast-falling burns;
So make thy manhood mightier day by day;

Sweet is the chase: and I will seek thee out
Some comfortable bride and fair, to grace
Thy climbing life, and cherish my prone year,
Till falling into Lot's forgetfulness
I know not thee, myself, nor anything.
Stay, my best son! ye are yet more boy than man.''

Then Gareth, "An ye hold me yet for child,
Hear yet once more the story of the child.
For, mother, there was once a King, like ours;
The prince his heir, when tall and marriageable,
Ask'd for a bride; and thereupon the King
Set two before him. One was fair, strong, arm'd—
But to be won by force—and many men
Desired her; one, good luck, no man desired.
And these were the conditions of the King:
That save he won the first by force, he needs
Must wed that other, whom no man desired,
A red-faced bride who knew herself so vile,
That evermore she long'd to hide herself,
Nor fronted man or woman, eye to eye—
Yea—some she cleaved to, but they died of her.
And one—they call'd her Fame; and one,—O mother,
How can ye keep me tether'd to you—Shame!
Man am I grown, a man's work must I do.
Follow the deer? follow the Christ, the King,
Live pure, speak true, right wrong, follow the King—
Else, wherefore born?''

To whom the mother said,
"Sweet son, for there be many who deem him not,
Or will not deem him, wholly proven King—
Albeit in mine own heart I knew him King,
When I was frequent with him in my youth,
And heard him Kingly speak, and doubted him
No more than he, himself; but felt him mine,
Of closest kin to me: yet—wilt thou leave
Thine easeful biding here, and risk thine all,
Life, limbs, for one that is not proven King?
Stay, till the cloud that settles round his birth
Hath lifted but a little. Stay, sweet son.''

And Gareth answer'd quickly, "Not an hour,
So that ye yield me—I will walk thro' fire,
Mother, to gain it—your full leave to go.
Not proven, who swept the dust of ruin'd Rome
From off the threshold of the realm, and crush'd
The Idolaters, and made the people free?
Who should be King save him who makes us free?''

So when the Queen, who long had sought in vain
To break him from the intent to which he grew,
Found her son's will unwaveringly one,
She answer'd craftily, "Will ye walk thro' fire?
Who walks thro' fire will hardly heed the smoke.
Ay, go then, an ye must: only one proof,
Before thou ask the King to make thee knight,
Of thine obedience and thy love to me,
Thy mother,—I demand.''

And Gareth cried,
"A hard one, or a hundred, so I go.
Nay—quick! the proof to prove me to the quick!''

But slowly spake the mother, looking at him,
"Prince, thou shalt go disguised to Arthur's hall,
And hire thyself to serve for meats and drinks
Among the scullions and the kitchen-knaves,
And those that hand the dish across the bar.
Nor shalt thou tell thy name to anyone.
And thou shalt serve a twelvemonth and a day.''

For so the Queen believed that when her son
Beheld his only way to glory lead
Low down thro' villain kitchen-vassalage,
Her own true Gareth was too princely-proud
To pass thereby; so should he rest with her
Closed in her castle from the sound of arms.

Silent awhile was Gareth, then replied,
"The thrall in person may be free in soul,
And I shall see the jousts. Thy son am I,
And since thou art my mother, must obey.
I therefore yield me freely to thy will;
For hence will I, disguised, and hire myself
To serve with scullions and with kitchen-knaves;
Nor tell my name to any—no, not the King.''

Gareth awhile linger'd. The mother's eye
Full of the wistful fear that he would go,
And turning toward him wheresoe'er he turn'd,
Perplext his outward purpose, till an hour,
When waken'd by the wind which with full voice
Swept bellowing thro' the darkness on to dawn,
He rose, and out of slumber calling two
That still had tended on him from his birth,
Before the wakeful mother heard him, went.

The three were clad like tillers of the soil.
Southward they set their faces. The birds made
Melody on branch, and melody in mid-air.
The damp hill-slopes were quicken'd into green,
And the live green had kindled into flowers,
For it was past the time of Easterday.

So, when their feet were planted on the plain
That broaden'd toward the base of Camelot,
Far off they saw the silver-misty morn
Rolling her smoke about the royal mount,
That rose between the forest and the field.
At times the summit of the high city flash'd;
At times the spires and turrets half-way down
Prick'd thro' the mist: at times the great gate shone
Only, that open'd on the field below:
Anon, the whole fair city had disappear'd.

Then those who went with Gareth were amazed,
One crying, "Let us go no farther, lord.
Here is a city of Enchanters, built
By fairy kings.'' The second echo'd him,
"Lord, we have heard from our wise men at home
To Northward, that this King is not the King,
But only changeling out of Fairyland,
Who drave the heathen hence by sorcery
And Merlin's glamour.'' Then the first again,
"Lord, there is no such city anywhere,
But all a vision.''

Gareth answer'd them
With laughter, swearing he had glamour enow
In his own blood, his princedom, youth, and hopes,
To plunge old Merlin in the Arabian Sea;
So push'd them all unwilling toward the gate.
And there was no gate like it under heaven.
For barefoot on the key-stone, which was lined
And rippled like an ever-fleeting wave,
The Lady of the Lake stood: all her dress
Wept from her sides as water flowing away;
But like the cross her great and goodly arms
Stretch'd under all the cornice and upheld:
And drops of water fell from either hand;
And down from one a sword was hung, from one
A censer, either worn with wind and storm;
And o'er her breast floated the sacred fish;
And in the space to left of her, and right,
Were Arthur's wars in weird devices done,
New things and old co-twisted, as if Time
Were nothing, so inveterately, that men
Were giddy gazing there; and over all
High on the top were those three queens, the friends
Of Arthur, who should help him at his need.

Then those with Gareth for so long a space
Stared at the figures, that at last it seem'd
The dragon-boughts and elvish emblemings
Began to move, seethe, twine, and curl: they call'd
To Gareth, "Lord, the gateway is alive.''

And Gareth likewise on them fixt his eyes
So long, that ev'n to him they seem'd to move.
Out of the city a blast of music peal'd.
Back from the gate started the three, to whom
From out thereunder came an ancient man,
Long-bearded, saying, "Who be ye, my sons?"

Then Gareth, "We be tillers of the soil,
Who leaving share in furrow come to see
The glories of our King: but these, my men
(Your city moved so weirdly in the mist),
Doubt if the King be King at all, or come
From Fairyland; and whether this be built
By magic, and by fairy kings and queens;
Or whether there be any city at all,
Or all a vision: and this music now
Hath scared them both, but tell thou these the truth."

Then that old Seer made answer, playing on him,
And saying, "Son, I have seen the good ship sail
Keel upward and mast downward in the heavens,
And solid turrets topsy-turvy in air:
And here is truth; but an it please thee not,
Take thou the truth as thou hast told it me.
For truly, as thou sayest, a fairy king
And fairy queens have built the city, son;
They came from out a sacred mountain-cleft
Toward the sunrise, each with harp in hand,
And built it to the music of their harps.
And as thou sayest it is enchanted, son,
For there is nothing in it as it seems
Saving the King; tho' some there be that hold
The King a shadow, and the city real:
Yet take thou heed of him, for so thou pass
Beneath this archway, then wilt thou become
A thrall to his enchantments, for the King
Will bind thee by such vows, as is a shame
A man should not be bound by, yet the which
No man can keep; but, so thou dread to swear,
Pass not beneath this gateway, but abide
Without, among the cattle of the field.
For, an ye heard a music, like enow
They are building still, seeing the city is built
To music, therefore never built at all,
And therefore built for ever."

                    Gareth spake
Anger'd, "Old Master, reverence thine own beard
That looks as white as utter truth, and seems
Wellnigh as long as thou art statured tall!
Why mockest thou the stranger that hath been
To thee fair-spoken?"

                    But the Seer replied,
"Know ye not then the Riddling of the Bards?
'Confusion, and illusion, and relation,
Elusion, and occasion, and evasion?'
I mock thee not but as thou mockest me,
And all that see thee, for thou art not who
Thou seemest, but I know thee who thou art.
And now thou goest up to mock the King,
Who cannot brook the shadow of any lie."

Unmockingly the mocker ending here
Turn'd to the right, and past along the plain;
Whom Gareth looking after said, "My men,
Our one white lie sits like a little ghost
Here on the threshold of our enterprise.
Let love be blamed for it, not she, nor I:
Well, we will make amends."

                    With all good cheer
He spake and laugh'd, then enter'd with his twain
Camelot, a city of shadowy palaces
And stately, rich in emblem and the work
Of ancient kings who did their days in stone;
Which Merlin's hand, the Mage at Arthur's court,
Knowing all arts, had touch'd, and everywhere,

At Arthur's ordinance, tipt with lessening peak
And pinnacle, and had made it spire to heaven.
And ever and anon a knight would pass
Outward, or inward to the hall: his arms
Clash'd; and the sound was good to Gareth's ear.
And out of bower and casement shyly glanced
Eyes of pure women, wholesome stars of love;
And all about a healthful people stept
As in the presence of a gracious king.

Then into hall Gareth ascending heard
A voice, the voice of Arthur, and beheld
Far over heads in that long-vaulted hall
The splendor of the presence of the King
Throned, and delivering doom—and look'd no more—
But felt his young heart hammering in his ears,
And thought, "For this half-shadow of a lie
The truthful King will doom me when I speak."
Yet pressing on, tho' all in fear to find
Sir Gawain or Sir Modred, saw nor one
Nor other, but in all the listening eyes
Of those tall knights, that ranged about the throne,
Clear honor shining like the dewy star
Of dawn, and faith in their great King, with pure
Affection, and the light of victory,
And glory gain'd, and evermore to gain.

Then came a widow crying to the King,
"A boon, Sir King! Thy father, Uther, reft
From my dead lord a field with violence:
For howsoe'er at first he proffer'd gold,
Yet, for the field was pleasant in our eyes,
We yielded not; and then he reft us of it
Perforce, and left us neither gold nor field."

Said Arthur, "Whether would ye? gold or field?"
To whom the woman weeping, "Nay, my lord,
The field was pleasant in my husband's eye."

And Arthur, "Have thy pleasant field again,
And thrice the gold for Uther's use thereof,
According to the years. No boon is here,
But justice, so thy say be proven true.
Accursed, who from the wrongs his father did
Would shape himself a right!"

                    And while she past,
Came yet another widow crying to him,
"A boon, Sir King! Thine enemy, King, am I.
With thine own hand thou slewest my dear lord,
A knight of Uther in the Barons' war,
When Lot and many another rose and fought
Against thee, saying thou wert basely born.
I held with these, and loathe to ask thee aught.
Yet lo! my husband's brother had my son
Thrall'd in his castle, and hath starved him dead;
And standeth seized of that inheritance
Which thou that slewest the sire hast left the son.
So tho' I scarce can ask it thee for hate,
Grant me some knight to do the battle for me,
Kill the foul thief, and wreak me for my son."

Then strode a good knight forward, crying to him,
"A boon, Sir King! I am her kinsman, I.
Give me to right her wrong, and slay the man."

Then came Sir Kay, the seneschal, and cried,
"A boon, Sir King! ev'n that thou grant her none,
This railer, that hath mock'd thee in full hall—
None; or the wholesome boon of gyve and gag."

But Arthur, "We sit King, to help the wrong'd
Thro' all our realm. The woman loves her lord.
Peace to thee, woman, with thy loves and hates!
The kings of old had doom'd thee to the flames,
Aurelius Emrys would have scourged thee dead,
And Uther slit thy tongue: but get thee hence—
Lest that rough humor of the kings of old

Return upon me! Thou that art her kin,
Go likewise; lay him low and slay him not,
But bring him here, that I may judge the right,
According to the justice of the King:
Then, be he guilty, by that deathless King
Who lived and died for men, the man shall die."

Then came in hall the messenger of Mark,
A name of evil savor in the land,
The Cornish king. In either hand he bore
What dazzled all, and shone far-off as shines
A field of charlock in the sudden sun
Between two showers, a cloth of palest gold,
Which down he laid before the throne, and knelt,
Delivering, that his lord, the vassal king,
Was ev'n upon his way to Camelot;
For having heard that Arthur of his grace
Had made his goodly cousin, Tristram, knight,
And, for himself was of the greater state,
Being a king, he trusted his liege-lord
Would yield him this large honor all the more;
So pray'd him well to accept this cloth of gold,
In token of true heart and fealty.

Then Arthur cried to rend the cloth, to rend
In pieces, and so cast it on the hearth.
An oak-tree smoulder'd there. "The goodly knight!
What! shall the shield of Mark stand among these?"
For, midway down the side of that long hall
A stately pile—whereof along the front,
Some blazon'd, some but carven, and some blank,
There ran a treble range of stony shields—
Rose, and high-arching overbrow'd the hearth.
And under every shield a knight was named:
For this was Arthur's custom in his hall;
When some good knight had done one noble deed,
His arms were carven only; but if twain
His arms were blazon'd also; but if none
The shield was blank and bare, without a sign
Saving the name beneath; and Gareth saw
The shield of Gawain blazon'd rich and bright,
And Modred's blank as death; and Arthur cried
To rend the cloth and cast it on the hearth.

"More like are we to reave him of his crown
Than make him knight because men call him king.
The kings we found, ye know we stay'd their hands
From war among themselves, but left them kings;
Of whom were any bounteous, merciful,
Truth-speaking, brave, good livers, them we enroll'd
Among us, and they sit within our hall.
But Mark hath tarnish'd the great name of king,
As Mark would sully the low state of churl:
And, seeing he hath sent us cloth of gold,
Return, and meet, and hold him from our eyes,
Lest we should lap him up in cloth of lead,
Silenced for ever—craven—a man of plots,
Craft, poisonous counsels, wayside ambushings—
No fault of thine: let Kay, the seneschal,
Look to thy wants, and send thee satisfied—
Accursed, who strikes nor lets the hand be seen!"

And many another suppliant crying came
With noise of ravage wrought by beast and man,
And evermore a knight would ride away.

Last, Gareth leaning both hands heavily
Down on the shoulders of the twain, his men,
Approach'd between them toward the King, and ask'd,
"A boon, Sir King (his voice was all ashamed),
For see ye not how weak and hungerworn
I seem—leaning on these? grant me to serve
For meat and drink among thy kitchen-knaves
A twelvemonth and a day, nor seek my name.
Hereafter I will fight."

                    To him the King,
"A goodly youth and worth a goodlier boon!

But so thou wilt no goodlier, then must Kay,
The master of the meats and drinks, be thine."

He rose and past; then Kay, a man of mien
Wan-sallow as the plant that feels itself
Root-bitten by white lichen,

                         "Lo ye now!
This fellow hath broken from some abbey, where,
God wot, he had not beef and brewis enow,
However that might chance: but an he work,
Like any pigeon will I cram his crop,
And sleeker shall he shine than any hog."

Then Lancelot standing near, "Sir Seneschal,
Sleuth-hound thou knowest, and gray, and all the
       hounds;
A horse thou knowest, a man thou dost not know:
Broad brows and fair, a fluent hair and fine,
High nose, a nostril large and fine, and hands
Large, fair and fine!—Some young lad's mystery—
But, or from sheepcot or king's hall, the boy
Is noble-natured. Treat him with all grace,
Lest he should come to shame thy judging of him."

Then Kay, "What murmurest thou of mystery?
Think ye this fellow will poison the King's dish?
Nay, for he spake too fool-like: mystery!
Tut, an the lad were noble, he had ask'd
For horse and armor: fair and fine, forsooth!
Sir Fine-face, Sir Fair-hands? but see thou to it
That thine own fineness, Lancelot, some fine day
Undo thee not—and leave my man to me."

So Gareth all for glory underwent
The sooty yoke of kitchen-vassalage,
Ate with young lads his portion by the door,
And couch'd at night with grimy kitchen-knaves.
And Lancelot ever spake him pleasantly,
But Kay, the seneschal, who loved him not,
Would hustle and harry him, and labor him
Beyond his comrade of the hearth, and set
To turn the broach, draw water, or hew wood,
Or grosser tasks; and Gareth bow'd himself
With all obedience to the King, and wrought
All kind of service with a noble ease
That graced the lowliest act in doing it.
And when the thralls had talk among themselves,
And one would praise the love that linkt the King
And Lancelot—how the King had saved his life
In battle twice, and Lancelot once the King's—
For Lancelot was the first in tournament,
But Arthur mightiest on the battle-field—
Gareth was glad. Or if some other told,
How once the wandering forester at dawn,
Far over the blue tarns and hazy seas,
On Caer-Eryri's highest found the King,
A naked babe, of whom the Prophet spake,
"He passes to the Isle Avilion,
He passes and is heal'd and cannot die"—
Gareth was glad. But if their talk were foul,
Then would he whistle rapid as any lark,
Or carol some old roundelay, and so loud
That first they mock'd, but, after, reverenced him.
Or Gareth telling some prodigious tale
Of knights, who sliced a red life-bubbling way
Thro' twenty folds of twisted dragon, held
All in a gap-mouth'd circle his good mates
Lying or sitting round him, idle hands,
Charm'd; till Sir Kay, the seneschal, would come
Blustering upon them, like a sudden wind
Among dead leaves, and drive them all apart.
Or when the thralls had sport among themselves,
So there were any trial of mastery,
He, by two yards in casting bar or stone,
Was counted best; and if there chanced a joust,
So that Sir Kay nodded him leave to go,
Would hurry thither, and when he saw the knight's

Clash like the coming and retiring wave,
And the spear spring, and good horse reel, the boy
Was half beyond himself for ecstasy.

So for a month he wrought among the thralls;
But in the weeks that follow'd, the good Queen,
Repentant of the word she made him swear,
And saddening in her childless castle, sent,
Between the increscent and decrescent moon,
Arms for her son, and loosed him from his vow.

This, Gareth hearing from a squire of Lot
With whom he used to play at tourney once,
When both were children, and in lonely haunts
Would scratch a ragged oval on the sand,
And each at either dash from either end—
Shame never made girl redder than Gareth joy.
He laugh'd; he sprang. "Out of the smoke, at once
I leap from Satan's foot to Peter's knee—
These news be mine, none other's—nay, the King's—
Descend into the city:" whereon he sought
The King alone, and found, and told him all.

"I have stagger'd thy strong Gawain in a tilt
For pastime; yea, he said it: jonst can I.
Make me thy knight—in secret! let my name
Be hidd'n, and give me the first quest, I spring
Like flame from ashes."

        Here the King's calm eye
Fell on, and check'd, and made him flush, and bow
Lowly, to kiss his hand, who answer'd him,
"Son, the good mother let me know thee here,
And sent her wish that I would yield thee thine.
Make thee my knight? my knights are sworn to vows
Of utter hardihood, utter gentleness,
And, loving, utter faithfulness in love,
And uttermost obedience to the King."

Then Gareth, lightly springing from his knees,
"My King, for hardihood I can promise thee.
For uttermost obedience make demand
Of whom ye gave me to, the Seneschal.
No mellow master of the meats and drinks!
And as for love, God wot, I love not yet,
But love I shall, God willing."

                And the King—
"Make thee my knight in secret? yea, but he,
Our noblest brother, and our truest man,
And one with me in all, he needs must know."

"Let Lancelot know, my King, let Lancelot know,
Thy noblest and thy truest."

                And the King—
"But wherefore would ye men should wonder at you?
Nay, rather for the sake of me, their King,
And the deed's sake my knighthood do the deed,
Than to be noised of."

        Merrily Gareth ask'd,
"Have I not earn'd my cake in baking of it?
Let be my name until I make my name!
My deeds will speak: it is but for a day."
So with a kindly hand on Gareth's arm
Smiled the great King, and half-unwillingly,
Loving his lusty youthhood, yielded to him.
Then, after summoning Lancelot privily,
"I have given him the first quest: he is not proven.
Look therefore when he calls for this in hall,
Thou get to horse and follow him far away.
Cover the lions on thy shield, and see
Far as thou mayest, he be nor ta'en nor slain."

Then that same day there past into the hall
A damsel of high lineage, and a brow
May-blossom, and a cheek of apple-blossom,
Hawk-eyes; and lightly was her slender nose
Tip-tilted like the petal of a flower;
She into hall past with her page and cried,

"O King, for thou hast driven the foe without,
See to the foe within! bridge, ford, beset
By bandits, everyone that owns a tower
The Lord for half a league. Why sit ye there?
Rest would I not, Sir King, an I were king,
Till ev'n the lonest hold were all as free
From cursed bloodshed, as thine altar-cloth
From that blest blood it is a sin to spill."

"Comfort thyself," said Arthur, "I nor mine
Rest: so my knighthood keep the vows they sware,
The wastest moorland of our realm shall be
Safe, damsel, as the centre of this hall.
What is thy name? thy need?"

                "My name?" she said—
"Lynette my name; noble: my need, a knight
To combat for my sister, Lyonors,
A lady of high lineage, of great lands,
And comely, yea, and comelier than myself.
She lives in Castle Perilous: a river
Runs in three loops about her living-place;
And o'er it are three passings, and three knights
Defend the passings, brethren, and a fourth,
And of that four the mightiest, holds her stay'd
In her own castle, and so besieges her
To break her will, and make her wed with him:
And but delays his purport till thou send
To do the battle with him, thy chief man,
Sir Lancelot, whom he trusts to overthrow,
Then wed, with glory; but she will not wed
Save whom she loveth, or a holy life.
Now therefore have I come for Lancelot."

Then Arthur, mindful of Sir Gareth, ask'd,
"Damsel, ye know this Order lives to crush
All wrongers of the realm. But say, these four,
Who be they? What the fashion of the men?"

"They be of foolish fashion, O Sir King,
The fashion of that old knight-errantry
Who ride abroad and do but what they will;
Courteous or bestial from the moment, such
As have nor law nor king; and three of these,
Proud in their fantasy, call themselves the Day,
Morning-star, and Noon-sun, and Evening-star,
Being strong fools; and never a whit more wise
The fourth, who alway rideth arm'd in black,
A huge man-beast of boundless savagery.
He names himself the Night and oftener Death,
And wears a helmet mounted with a skull,
And bears a skeleton figured on his arms,
To show that who may slay or scape the three
Slain by himself shall enter endless night.
And all these four be fools, but mighty men,
And therefore am I come for Lancelot."

Hereat Sir Gareth call'd from where he rose,
A head with kindling eyes above the throng,
"A boon, Sir King—this quest!" then—for he mark'd
Kay near him groaning like a wounded bull—
"Yea, King, thou knowest thy kitchen-knave am I,
And mighty thro' thy meats and drinks am I,
And I can topple over a hundred such.
Thy promise, King," and Arthur glancing at him,
Brought down a momentary brow. "Rough, sudden,
And pardonable, worthy to be knight—
Go therefore," and all hearers were amazed.

But on the damsel's forehead shame, pride, wrath,
Slew the May-white; she lifted either arm,
"Fie on thee, King! I ask'd for thy chief knight,
And thou hast given me but a kitchen-knave."
Then, ere a man in hall could stay her, turn'd,

Fled down the lane of access to the King,
Took horse, descended the slope street, and past
The weird white gate, and paused without, beside
The field of tourney, murmuring "kitchen-knave."

Now two great entries open'd from the hall,
At one end one, that gave upon a range
Of level pavement where the King would pace
At sunrise, gazing over plain and wood :
And down from this a lordly stairway sloped
Till lost in blowing trees and tops of towers ;
And out by this main doorway past the King.
But one was counter to the hearth, and rose
High that the highest-crested helm could ride
Therethro' nor graze : and by this entry fled
The damsel in her wrath, and on to this
Sir Gareth strode, and saw without the door
King Arthur's gift, the worth of half a town,
A warhorse of the best, and near it stood
The two that out of north had follow'd him :
This bare a maiden shield, a casque ; that held
The horse, the spear ; whereat Sir Gareth loosed
A cloak that dropt from collar-bone to heel,
A cloth of roughest web, and cast it down,
And from it like a fuel-smother'd fire,
That lookt half dead, brake bright, and flash'd as
    those
Dull-coated things, that making slide apart
Their dusk wing-cases, all beneath there burns
A jewel'd harness, ere they pass and fly.
So Gareth ere he parted flash'd in arms.
Then, as he donn'd the helm, and took the shield
And mounted horse and graspt a spear, of grain
Storm-strengthen'd on a windy site, and tipt
With trenchant steel, around him slowly prest
The people, while from out of kitchen came
The thralls in throng, and seeing who had work'd
Lustier than any, and whom they could but love,
Mounted in arms, threw up their caps and cried,
"God bless the King, and all his fellowship !"
And on thro' lanes of shouting Gareth rode
Down the slope street, and past without the gate.

So Gareth past with joy ; but as the cur
Pluckt from the cur he fights with, ere his cause
Be cool'd by fighting, follows, being named,
His owner, but remembers all, and growls
Remembering, so Sir Kay beside the door
Mutter'd in scorn of Gareth whom he used
To harry and to hustle.

                    "Bound upon a quest
With horse and arms—the King hath past his time—
My scullion knave ! Thralls, to your work again,
For an your fire be low ye kindle mine !
Will there be dawn in West and eve in East ?
Begone !—my knave !—belike and like enow
Some old head-blow not heeded in his youth
So shook his wits they wander in his prime—
Crazed ! How the villain lifted up his voice,
Nor shamed to bawl himself a kitchen-knave.
Tut : he was tame and meek enow with me,
Till peacock'd up with Lancelot's noticing.
Well—I will after my loud knave, and learn
Whether he know me for his master yet.
Out of the smoke he came, and so my lance
Hold, by God's grace, he shall into the mire—
Thence, if the King awaken from his craze,
Into the smoke again."

                    But Lancelot said,
"Kay, wherefore wilt thou go against the King,
For that did never he whereon ye rail,
But ever meekly served the King in thee ?
Abide : take counsel ; for this lad is great
And lusty, and knowing both of lance and sword."
"Tut, tell me not," said Kay, "ye are overfine
To mar stout knaves with foolish courtesies."

Then mounted, on thro' silent faces rode
Down the slope city, and out beyond the gate.

But by the field of tourney lingering yet
Mutter'd the damsel, "Wherefore did the King
Scorn me ? for, were Sir Lancelot lackt, at least
He might have yielded to me one of those
Who tilt for lady's love and glory here.
Rather than—O sweet heaven ! O fie upon him !—
His kitchen-knave."

                    To whom Sir Gareth drew
(And there were none but few goodlier than he)
Shining in arms, "Damsel, the quest is mine.
Lead, and I follow." She thereat, as one
That smells a foul-flesh'd agaric in the holt,
And deems it carrion of some woodland thing,
Or shrew, or weasel, nipt her slender nose
With petulant thumb and finger, shrilling, "Hence !
Avoid, thou smellest all of kitchen-grease.
And look who comes behind," for there was Kay.
"Knowest thou not me ? thy master ? I am Kay,
We lack thee by the hearth."

                    And Gareth to him,
"Master no more ! too well I know thee, ay—
The most ungentle knight in Arthur's hall."
"Have at thee, then," said Kay : they shock'd, and
    Kay
Fell shoulder-slipt, and Gareth cried again,
"Lead, and I follow," and fast away she fled.

But after sod and shingle ceased to fly
Behind her, and the heart of her good horse
Was nigh to burst with violence of the beat,
Perforce she stay'd, and overtaken spoke.

"What doest thou, scullion, in my fellowship ?
Deem'st thou that I accept thee aught the more
Or love thee better, that by some device
Full cowardly, or by mere unhappiness,
Thou hast overthrown and slain thy master—thou !—
Dish-washer and broach-turner, loon !—to me
Thou smellest all of kitchen as before."

"Damsel," Sir Gareth answer'd gently, "say
Whate'er ye will, but whatsoe'er ye say,
I leave not till I finish this fair quest,
Or die therefore."

                    "Ay, wilt thou finish it ?
Sweet Lord, how like a noble knight he talks !
The listening rogue hath caught the manner of it.
But, knave, anon thou shalt be met with, knave,
And then by such a one that thou for all
The kitchen brewis that was ever supt
Shalt not once dare to look him in the face."

"I shall assay," said Gareth with a smile
That madden'd her, and away she flash'd again
Down the long avenues of a boundless wood,
And Gareth following was again beknaved.

"Sir Kitchen-knave, I have miss'd the only way
Where Arthur's men are set along the wood ;
The wood is nigh as full of thieves as leaves :
If both be slain, I am rid of thee ; but yet,
Sir Scullion, canst thou use that spit of thine ?
Fight, an thou canst : I have miss'd the only way."

So till the dusk that follow'd evensong
Rode on the two, reviler and reviled,
Then, after one long slope was mounted, saw,
Bowl-shaped, thro' tops of many thousand pines
A gloomy-gladed hollow slowly sink
To westward—in the deeps whereof a mere,
Round as the red eye of an eagle-owl,
Under the half-dead sunset glared ; and shouts

Ascended, and there brake a servingman
Flying from out of the black wood. and crying,
"They have bound my lord to cast him in the mere."

Then Gareth, "Bound am I to right the wrong'd,
But straitlier bound am I to bide with thee."
And when the damsel spake contemptuously,
"Lead, and I follow," Gareth cried again,
"Follow, I lead!" so down among the pines
He plunged; and there, blackshadow'd nigh the mere,
And mid-thigh-deep in bulrushes and reed,
Saw six tall men haling a seventh along,
A stone about his neck to drown him in it.
Three with good blows he quieted, but three
Fled thro' the pines; and Gareth loosed the stone
From off his neck, then in the mere beside
Tumbled it; olilly bubbled up the mere.
Last, Gareth loosed his bonds and on free feet
Set him, a stalwart Baron, Arthur's friend.

"Well that ye came, or else these caitiff rogues
Had wreak'd themselves on me; good cause is theirs
To hate me, for my wont hath ever been
To catch my thief, and then like vermin here
Drown him, and with a stone about his neck;
And under this wan water many of them
Lie rotting, but at night let go the stone,
And rise, and flickering in a grimly light,
Dance on the mere. Good now, ye have saved a life
Worth somewhat as the cleanser of this wood.
And fain would I reward thee worshipfully.
What guerdon will ye?"

              Gareth sharply spake,
"None! for the deed's sake have I done the deed,
In uttermost obedience to the King.
But wilt thou yield this damsel harborage?"

Whereat the Baron saying, "I well believe
You be of Arthur's Table," a light laugh
Broke from Lynette, "Ay, truly of a truth,
And in a sort, being Arthur's kitchen-knave!—
But deem not I accept thee aught the more,
Scullion, for running sharply with thy spit
Down on a rout of craven foresters.
A thresher with his flail had scatter'd them.
Nay—for thou smellest of the kitchen still.
But an this lord will yield us harborage,
Well."

        So she spake. A league beyond the wood,
All in a full-fair manor and a rich,
His towers where that day a feast had been
Held in high hall, and many a viand left,
And many a costly cate, received the three.
And there they placed a peacock in his pride
Before the damsel, and the Baron set
Gareth beside her, but at once she rose.

"Meseems, that here is much discourtesy,
Setting this knave, Lord Baron, at my side.
Hear me—this morn I stood in Arthur's hall,
And pray'd the King would grant me Lancelot
To fight the brotherhood of Day and Night—
The last a monster unsubduable
Of any save of him for whom I call'd—
Suddenly bawls this frontless kitchen-knave,
'The quest is mine; thy kitchen-knave am I,
And mighty thro' thy meats and drinks am I.'
Then Arthur all at once goue mad replies,
'Go therefore,' and so gives the quest to him—
Him—here—a villain fitter to stick swine
Than ride abroad redressing women's wrong,
Or sit beside a noble gentlewoman."

Then half-ashamed and part-amazed, the lord
Now look'd at one and now at other, left
The damsel by the peacock in his pride,

And, seating Gareth at another board,
Sat down beside him, ate and then began:

"Friend, whether thou be kitchen-knave, or not,
Or whether it be the maiden's fantasy,
And whether she be mad, or else the King,
Or both or neither, or thyself be mad,
I ask not: but thou strikest a strong stroke,
For strong thou art and goodly therewithal,
And saver of my life: and therefore now,
For here be mighty men to joust with, weigh
Whether thou wilt not with thy damsel back
To crave again Sir Lancelot of the King.
Thy pardon: I but speak for thine avail,
The saver of my life."

             And Gareth said,
"Full pardon, but I follow up the quest,
Despite of Day and Night, and Death and Hell."

So when, next morn, the lord whose life he saved
Had, some brief space, convey'd them on their way
And left them with God-speed, Sir Gareth spake,
"Lead, and I follow." Haughtily she replied,

"I fly no more: I allow thee for an hour.
Lion and stoat have isled together, knave,
In time of flood. Nay, furthermore, methinks
Some ruth is mine for thee. Back wilt thou, fool?
For hard by here is one will overthrow
And slay thee: then will I to court again,
And shame the King for only yielding me
My champion from the ashes of his hearth."

To whom Sir Gareth answer'd courteously,
"Say thou so, and I will do my deed.
Allow me for mine hour, and thou wilt find
My fortunes all as fair as hers, who lay
Among the ashes and wedded the King's son."

Then to the shore of one of those long loops
Wherethro' the serpent river coil'd, they came.
Rough-thicketed were the banks and steep; the
      stream
Full, narrow; this a bridge of single arc
Took at a leap; and on the further side
Arose a silk pavilion, gay with gold
In streaks and rays, and all Lent-lily in hue,
Save that the dome was purple, and above,
Crimson, a slender banneret fluttering.
And therebefore the lawless warrior paced
Unarm'd, and calling, "Damsel, is this he,
The champion thou hast brought from Arthur's
      hall,
For whom we let thee pass?" "Nay, nay," she
      said,
"Sir Morning-star. The King in utter scorn
Of thee and thy much folly hath sent thee here
His kitchen-knave: and look thou to thyself:
See that he fall not on thee suddenly,
And slay thee unarm'd: he is not knight but knave."

Then at his call, "O daughters of the Dawn,
And servants of the Morning-star, approach,
Arm me," from out the silken curtain-folds
Bare-footed and bare-headed three fair girls
In gilt and rosy raiment came: their feet
In dewy grasses glisten'd; and the hair
All over glanced with dewdrop or with gem
Like sparkles in the stone Avanturine.
These arm'd him in blue arms, and gave a shield
Blue also, and thereon the morning-star.
And Gareth silent gazed upon the knight,
Who stood a moment, ere his horse was brought,
Glorying; and in the stream beneath him, shone,
Immingled with Heaven's azure waveringly,
The gay pavilion and the naked feet,
His arms, the rosy raiment, and the star.

Then she that watch'd him, "Wherefore stare ye so?
Thou shakest in thy fear: there yet is time:
Flee down the valley before he get to horse.
Who will cry shame? Thou art not knight but
  knave."

Said Gareth, "Damsel, whether knave or knight,
Far liefer had I fight a score of times
Than hear thee so missay me and revile.
Fair words were best for him who fights for thee;
But truly foul are better, for they send
That strength of anger thro' mine arms, I know
That I shall overthrow him."

          And he that bore
The star, being mounted, cried from o'er the bridge,
"A kitchen-knave, and sent in scorn of me!
Such fight not I, but answer scorn with scorn.
For this were shame to do him further wrong
Than set him on his feet, and take his horse
And arms, and so return him to the King.
Come, therefore, leave thy lady lightly, knave.
Avoid: for it beseemeth not a knave
To ride with such a lady."

          "Dog, thou liest.
I spring from loftier lineage than thine own."
He spake; and all at fiery speed the two
Shock'd on the central bridge, and either spear
Bent but not brake, and either knight at once,
Hurl'd as a stone from out of a catapult
Beyond his horse's crupper and the bridge,
Fell, as if dead; but quickly rose and drew,
And Gareth lash'd so fiercely with his brand
He drave his enemy backward down the bridge,
The damsel crying, "Well-stricken, kitchen-knave!"
Till Gareth's shield was cloven; but one stroke
Laid him that clove it groveling on the ground.

Then cried the fall'n, "Take not my life: I yield."
And Gareth, "So this damsel ask it of me,
Good—I accord it easily as a grace."
She reddening, "Insolent scullion! I of thee?
I bound to thee for any favor ask'd!"
"Then shall he die." And Gareth there unlaced
His helmet as to slay him, but she shriek'd,
"Be not so hardy, scullion, as to slay
One nobler than thyself." "Damsel, thy charge
Is an abounding pleasure to me. Knight,
Thy life is thine at her command. Arise
And quickly pass to Arthur's hall, and say
His kitchen-knave hath sent thee. See thou crave
His pardon for the breaking of his laws.
Myself, when I return, will plead for thee.
Thy shield is mine—farewell; and, damsel, thou,
Lead, and I follow."

         And fast away she fled.
Then when he came upon her, spake, "Methought,
Knave, when I watch'd thee striking on the bridge,
The savor of thy kitchen came upon me
A little faintlier: but the wind hath changed:
I scent it twenty-fold." And then she sang,
"'O morning-star' (not that tall felon there
Whom thou by sorcery or unhappiness
Or some device, hast foully overthrown),
'O morning-star that smilest in the blue,
O star, my morning dream hath proven true,
Smile sweetly, thou! my love hath smiled on me.'

"But thou begone, take counsel, and away,
For hard by here is one that guards a ford—
The second brother in their fool's parable—
Will pay thee all thy wages, and to boot.
Care not for shame: thou art not knight but knave."

To whom Sir Gareth answer'd, laughingly,
"Parables? Hear a parable of the knave.

When I was kitchen-knave among the rest
Fierce was the hearth, and one of my co-mates
Own'd a rough dog, to whom he cast his coat,
'Guard it,' and there was none to meddle with it.
And such a coat art thou, and thee the King
Gave me to guard, and such a dog am I.
To worry, and not to flee—and—knight or knave—
The knave that doth thee service as full knight
Is all as good, meseems, as any knight
Toward thy sister's freeing."

         "Ay, Sir Knave!
Ay, knave, because thou strikest as a knight,
Being but knave, I hate thee all the more."

"Fair damsel, you should worship me the more,
That, being but knave, I throw thine enemies."

"Ay, ay," she said, "but thou shalt meet thy
  match."

So when they touch'd the second river-loop,
Huge on a huge red horse, and all in mail
Burnish'd to blinding, shone the Noonday Sun
Beyond a raging shallow. As if the flower,
That blows a globe of after arrowlets,
Ten thousand-fold had grown, flash'd the fierce
  shield,
All sun; and Gareth's eyes had flying blots
Before them when he turn'd from watching him.
He from beyond the roaring shallow roar'd,
"What doest thou, brother, in my marches here?"
And she athwart the shallow shrill'd again,
"Here is a kitchen-knave from Arthur's hall
Hath overthrown thy brother, and hath his arms."
"Ugh!" cried the Sun, and vizoring up a red
And cipher face of rounded foolishness,
Push'd horse across the foamings of the ford,
Whom Gareth met midstream: no room was there
For lance or tourney-skill: four strokes they struck
With sword, and these were mighty; the new knight
Had fear he might be shamed: but as the Sun
Heaved up a ponderous arm to strike the fifth,
The hoof of his horse slipt in the stream, the stream
Descended, and the Sun was wash'd away.

Then Gareth laid his lance athwart the ford:
So drew him home: but he that fought no more,
As being all bone-batter'd on the rock,
Yielded: and Gareth sent him to the King.
"Myself when I return will plead for thee.
Lead, and I follow." Quietly she led.
"Hath not the good wind, damsel, changed again?"
"Nay, not a point: nor art thou victor here.
There lies a ridge of slate across the ford;
His horse thereon stumbled—ay, for I saw it.

"'O sun' (not this strong fool whom thou, Sir
  Knave,
Hast overthrown thro' mere unhappiness),
'O sun, that wakenest all to bliss or pain,
O moon, that layest all to sleep again,
Shine sweetly: twice my love hath smiled on me.'

"What knowest thou of lovesong or of love?
Nay, nay, God wot, so thou wert nobly born,
Thou hast a pleasant presence. Yea, perchance,—

"'O dewy flowers that open to the sun,
O dewy flowers that close when day is done,
Blow sweetly: twice my love hath smiled on me.'

"What knowest thou of flowers, except, belike,
To garnish meats with? hath not our good King
Who lent me thee, the flower of kitchendom,
A foolish love for flowers? What stick ye round
The pasty? wherewithal deck the boar's head?
Flowers? nay, the boar hath rosemaries and bay,

          11

"'O birds, that warble to the morning sky,
O birds that warble as the day goes by,
Sing sweetly: twice my love hath smiled on me.'

"What knowest thou of birds, lark, mavis, merle,
Linnet? what dream ye when they utter forth
May-music growing with the growing light.
Their sweet sun-worship? these be for the snare
(So runs thy fancy), these be for the spit,
Larding and basting. See thou have not now
Larded thy last, except thou turn and fly.
There stands the third fool of their allegory."

For there beyond a bridge of treble bow,
All in a rose-red from the west, and all
Naked it seem'd, and glowing in the broad
Deep-dimpled current underneath, the knight,
That named himself the Star of Evening, stood.

And Gareth, "Wherefore waits the madman there
Naked in open dayshine?" "Nay," she cried,
"Not naked, only wrapt in harden'd skins
That fit him like his own; and so ye cleave
His armor off him, these will turn the blade."

Then the third brother shouted o'er the bridge,
"O brother-star, why shine ye here so low?
Thy ward is higher up: but have ye slain
The damsel's champion?" and the damsel cried,

"No star of thine, but shot from Arthur's heaven
With all disaster unto thine and thee!
For both thy younger brethren have gone down
Before this youth; and so wilt thou, Sir Star:
Art thou not old?"

         "Old, damsel, old and hard—
Old, with the might and breath of twenty boys."
Said Gareth, "Old, and over-bold in brag!
But that same strength which threw the Morning Star
Can throw the Evening."

         Then that other blew
A hard and deadly note upon the horn.
"Approach and arm me!" With slow steps from out
An old storm-beaten, russet, many-stain'd
Pavilion, forth a grizzled damsel came,
And arm'd him in old arms, and brought a helm
With but a drying evergreen for crest,
And gave a shield whereon the Star of Even
Half-tarnish'd and half-bright, his emblem, shone.
But when it glitter'd o'er the saddle-bow,
They madly hurl'd together on the bridge;
And Gareth overthrew him, lighted, drew,
There met him drawn, and overthrew him again,
But up like fire he started: and as oft
As Gareth brought him grovelling on his knees,
So many a time he vaulted up again;
Till Gareth panted hard, and his great heart,
Foredooming all his trouble was in vain,
Labor'd within him, for he seem'd as one
That all in later, sadder age begins
To war against ill uses of a life,
But these from all his life arise, and cry,
"Thou hast made us lords, and canst not put us down!"
He half despairs; so Gareth seem'd to strike
Vainly, the damsel clamoring all the while,
"Well done, knave-knight, well-stricken, O good knight-knave—
O knave, as noble as any of all the knights—
Shame me not, shame me not. I have prophesied—
Strike, thou art worthy of the Table Round—
His arms are old, he trusts the harden'd skin—
Strike—strike—the wind will never change again."
And Gareth hearing ever stronglier smote,
And hew'd great pieces of his armor off him,

But lash'd in vain against the harden'd skin,
And could not wholly bring him under, more
Than loud Southwesterns, rolling ridge on ridge,
The buoy that rides at sea, and dips and springs
For ever; till at length Sir Gareth's brand
Clash'd his, and brake it utterly to the hilt.
"I have thee now?" but forth that other sprang,
And, all unknightlike, writhed his wiry arms
Around him, till he felt, despite his mail,
Strangled, but straining ev'n his uttermost
Cast, and so hurl'd him headlong o'er the bridge
Down to the river, sink or swim, and cried,
"Lead, and I follow."

         But the damsel said,
"I lead no longer; ride thou at my side;
Thou art the kingliest of all kitchen-knaves.

"'O trefoil, sparkling on the rainy plain,
O rainbow with three colors after rain,
Shine sweetly: thrice my love hath smiled on me.'

"Sir,—and, good faith, I fain had added—Knight,
But that I heard thee call thyself a knave,—
Shamed am I that I so rebuked, reviled,
Missaid thee; noble I am; and thought the King
Scorn'd me and mine; and now thy pardon, friend,
For thou hast ever answer'd courteously,
And wholly bold thou art, and meek withal
As any of Arthur's best, but, being knave,
Hast mazed my wit: I marvel what thou art."

"Damsel," he said, "you be not all to blame,
Saving that you mistrusted our good King
Would handle scorn, or yield you, asking, one
Not fit to cope your quest. You said your say;
Mine answer was my deed. Good sooth! I hold
He scarce is knight, yea, but half-man, nor meet
To fight for gentle damsel, he who lets
His heart be stirr'd with any foolish heat
At any gentle damsel's waywardness.
Shamed? care not! thy foul sayings fought for me·
And seeing now thy words are fair, methinks
There rides no knight, not Lancelot, his great self,
Hath force to quell me."

         Nigh upon that hour
When the lone hern forgets his melancholy,
Lets down his other leg, and, stretching, dreams
Of goodly supper in the distant pool,
Then turn'd the noble damsel smiling at him,
And told him of a cavern hard at hand,
Where bread and baken meats and good red wine
Of Southland, which the Lady Lyonors
Had sent her coming champion, waited him.

Anon they past a narrow comb wherein
Were slabs of rock with figures, knights on horse
Sculptured, and deckt in slowly-waning hues.
"Sir Knave, my knight, a hermit once was here,
Whose holy hand hath fashion'd on the rock
The war of Time against the soul of man.
And you four fools have suck'd their allegory
From these damp walls, and taken but the form.
Know ye not these?" and Gareth lookt and read—
In letters like to those the vexillary
Hath left crag-carven o'er the streaming Gelt—
"PHOSPHORUS," then "MERIDIES"—"HESPERUS"—
"NOX"—"MORS," beneath five figures, armed men,
Slab after slab, their faces forward all,
And running down the Soul, a Shape that fled
With broken wings, torn raiment and loose hair,
For help and shelter to the hermit's cave.
"Follow the faces, and we find it. Look,
Who comes behind?"

         For one—delay'd at first
Thro' helping back the dislocated Kay

To Camelot, then by what thereafter chanced,
The damsel's headlong error thro' the wood—
Sir Lancelot, having swum the river-loops—
His blue shield-lions cover'd—softly drew
Behind the twain, and when he saw the star
Gleam, on Sir Gareth's turning to him, cried,
"Stay, felon knight, I avenge me for my friend."
And Gareth crying prick'd against the cry;
But when they closed—in a moment—at one touch
Of that skill'd spear, the wonder of the world—
We..t sliding down so easily, and fell,
That when he found the grass within his hands,
He laugh'd; the laughter jarr'd upon Lynette:
Harshly she ask'd him, "Shamed and overthrown,
And tumbled back into the kitchen-knave,
Why laugh ye? that ye blew your boast in vain?"
"Nay, noble damsel, but that I, the son
Of old King Lot and good Queen Bellicent,
And victor of the bridges and the ford,
And knight of Arthur, here lie thrown by whom
I know not, all thro' mere unhappiness—
Device and sorcery and unhappiness—
Out, sword; we are thrown!" And Lancelot answer'd, "Prince,
O Gareth—thro' the mere unhappiness
Of one who came to help thee, not to harm,
Lancelot, and all as glad to find thee whole,
As on the day when Arthur knighted him."

Then Gareth, "Thou—Lancelot!—thine the hand
That threw me? An some chance to mar the boast
Thy brethren of thee make—which could not chance—
Had sent thee down before a lesser spear,
Shamed had I been, and sad—O Lancelot—thou!"

Whereat the maiden, petulant, "Lancelot,
Why came ye not, when call'd? and wherefore now
Come ye, not call'd? I gloried in my knave,
Who being still rebuked, would answer still
Courteous as any knight—but now, if knight,
The marvel dies, and leaves me fool'd and trick'd,
And only wondering wherefore play'd upon:
And doubtful whether I and mine be scorn'd.
Where should be truth if not in Arthur's hall,
In Arthur's presence? Knight, knave, prince and fool,
I hate thee and for ever."

And Lancelot said,
"Blessed be thou, Sir Gareth! knight art thou
To the King's best wish. O damsel, be you wise
To call him shamed, who is but overthrown?
Thrown have I been, nor once, but many a time.
Victor from vanquish'd issues at the last,
And overthrower from being overthrown.
With sword we have not striven; and thy good horse
And thou are weary; yet not less I felt
Thy manhood thro' that wearied lance of thine.
Well hast thou done; for all the stream is freed,
And thou hast wreak'd his justice on his foes,
And when reviled, hast answer'd graciously,
And makest merry when overthrown. Prince, Knight,
Hail, Knight and Prince, and of our Table Round!"

And then when turning to Lynette he told
The tale of Gareth, petulantly she said,
"Ay well—ay well—for worse than being fool'd
Of others, is to fool one's self. A cave,
Sir Lancelot, is hard by. with meats and drinks
And forage for the horse, and flint for fire.
But all about it flies a honeysuckle.
Seek, till we find." And when they sought and found,
Sir Gareth drank and ate, and all his life
Past into sleep; on whom the maiden gazed.
* Sound sleep be thine! sound cause to sleep hast thou.
Wake lusty! Seem I not as tender to him
As any mother? Ay, but such a one

As all day long hath rated at her child,
And vext his day, but blesses him asleep—
Good lord, how sweetly smells the honeysuckle
In the hush'd night, as if the world were one
Of utter peace, and love, and gentleness!
O Lancelot, Lancelot"—and she clapt her hands—
"Full merry am I to find my goodly knave
Is knight and noble. See now, sworn have I,
Else yon black felon had not let me pass,
To bring thee back to do the battle with him.
Thus an thou goest, he will fight thee first;
Who doubts thee victor? so will my knight-knave
Miss the full flower of this accomplishment."

Said Lancelot, "Peradventure he you name
May know my shield. Let Gareth, an he will,
Change his for mine, and take my charger, fresh,
Not to be spurr'd, loving the battle as well
As he that rides him." "Lancelot-like," she said,
"Courteous in this, Lord Lancelot, as in all."

And Gareth, wakening, fiercely clutch'd the shield;
"Ramp, ye lance-splintering lions, on whom all spears
Are rotten sticks! ye seem agape to roar!
Yea, ramp and roar at leaving of your lord!—
Care not, good beasts, so well I care for you.
O noble Lancelot, from my hold on these
Streams virtue—fire—thro' one that will not shame
Even the shadow of Lancelot under shield.
Hence: let us go."

Silent the silent field
They traversed. Arthur's harp tho' summer-wan,
In counter motion to the clouds, allured
The glance of Gareth dreaming on his liege.
A star shot: "Lo," said Gareth, "the foe falls!"
An owl whoopt: "Hark the victor pealing there!"
Suddenly she that rode upon his left
Clung to the shield that Lancelot lent him, crying,
"Yield, yield him this again: 'tis he must fight:
I curse the tongue that all thro' yesterday
Reviled thee, and hath wrought on Lancelot now
To lend thee horse and shield: wonders ye have done:
Miracles ye cannot: here is glory enow
In having flung the three: I see thee maim'd,
Mangled: I swear thou canst not fling the fourth."

"And wherefore, damsel? tell me all ye know.
You cannot scare me; nor rough face, or voice,
Brute bulk of limb, or boundless savagery
Appal me from the quest."

"Nay, Prince," she cried,
"God wot, I never look'd upon the face,
Seeing he never rides abroad by day;
But watch'd him have I like a phantom pass
Chilling the night: nor have I heard the voice.
Always he made his mouthpiece of a page
Who came and went, and still reported him
As closing in himself the strength of ten,
And when his anger tare him, massacing
Man, woman, lad and girl—yea, the soft babe!
Some hold that he hath swallow'd infant flesh,
Monster! O Prince, I went for Lancelot first,
The quest is Lancelot's: give him back the shield."

Said Gareth, laughing, "An he fight for this,
Belike he wins it as the better man:
Thus—and not else!"

But Lancelot on him urged
All the devisings of their chivalry
When one might meet a mightier than himself;
How best to manage horse, lance, sword and shield,
And so fill up the gap where force might fail
With skill and fineness. Instant were his words.

Then Gareth, "Here be rules. I know but one—
To dash against mine enemy and to win.
Yet have I watch'd thee victor in the joust,
And seen thy way." "Heaven help thee!" sigh'd
            Lynette.

Then for a space, and under cloud that grew
To thunder-gloom palling all stars, they rode
In converse till she made her palfrey halt,
Lifted an arm, and softly whisper'd, "There."
And all the three were silent seeing, pitch'd
Beside the Castle Perilous on flat field,
A huge pavilion like a mountain peak
Sunder the glooming crimson on the marge,
Black, with black banner, and a long black horn
Beside it hanging; which Sir Gareth graspt,
And so, before the two could hinder him,
Sent all his heart and breath thro' all the horn.
Echo'd the walls; a light twinkled; anon
Came lights and lights, and once again he blew;
Whereon were hollow tramplings up and down,
And muffled voices heard, and shadows past;
Till high above him, circled with her maids,
The Lady Lyonors at a window stood,
Beautiful among lights, and waving to him
White hands, and courtesy; but when the Prince
Three times had blown—after long hush—at last—
The huge pavilion slowly yielded up,
Thro' those black foldings, that which housed therein.
High on a nightblack horse, in nightblack arms,
With white breast-bone, and barren ribs of Death,
And crown'd with fleshless laughter—some ten
            steps—
In the half-light—thro' the dim dawn—advanced
The monster, and then paused, and spake no word.

But Gareth spake and all indignantly,
"Fool, for thou hast, men say, the strength of ten.
Canst thou not trust the limbs thy God hath given,
But must, to make the terror of thee more,
Trick thyself out in ghastly imageries
Of that which Life hath done with, and the clod,
Less dull than thou, will hide with mantling flowers
As if for pity?" But he spake no word;
Which set the horror higher: a maiden swoon'd;
The Lady Lyonors wrung her hands and wept,
As doom'd to be the bride of Night and Death;
Sir Gareth's head prickled beneath his helm;
And ev'n Sir Lancelot thro' his warm blood felt
Ice strike, and all that mark'd him were aghast.

At once Sir Lancelot's charger fiercely neigh'd,
And Death's dark war-horse bounded forward with
            him.
Then those that did not blink the terror, saw
That Death was cast to ground, and slowly rose.
But with one stroke Sir Gareth split the skull.
Half fell to right and half to left and lay.
Then with a stronger buffet he clove the helm
As throughly as the skull; and out from this
Issued the bright face of a blooming boy
Fresh as a flower new-born, and crying, "Knight,
Slay me not: my three brethren bade me do it,
To make a horror all about the house,
And stay the world from Lady Lyonors."
They never dream'd the passes would be past."
Answer'd Sir Gareth graciously to one
Not many a moon his younger, "My fair child,
What madness made thee challenge the chief knight
Of Arthur's hall?" "Fair Sir, they bade me do it.
They hate the King, and Lancelot, the King's friend,
They hoped to slay him somewhere on the stream,
They never dream'd the passes could be past."

Then sprang the happier day from underground;
And Lady Lyonors and her house, with dance
And revel and song, made merry over Death,
As being after all their foolish fears

And horrors only proven a blooming boy.
So large mirth lived and Gareth won the quest.

And he that told the tale in older times
Says that Sir Gareth wedded Lyonors,
But he that told it later says Lynette.

———⊗———

GERAINT AND ENID.

I.

THE brave Geraint, a knight of Arthur's court,
A tributary prince of Devon, one
Of that great Order of the Table Round,
Had married Enid, Yniol's only child,
And loved her as he loved the light of heaven.
And as the light of heaven varies, now
At sunrise, now at sunset, now by night
With moon and trembling stars, so loved Geraint
To make her beauty vary day by day,
In crimsons and in purples and in gems.
And Enid, but to please her husband's eye,
Who first had found and loved her in a state
Of broken fortunes, daily fronted him
In some fresh splendor; and the Queen herself,
Grateful to Prince Geraint for service done,
Loved her, and often with her own white hands
Array'd and deck'd her, as the loveliest,
Next after her own self, in all the court.
And Enid loved the Queen, and with true heart
Adored her, as the stateliest and the best
And loveliest of all women upon earth.
And seeing them so tender and so close,
Long in their common love rejoiced Geraint.
But when a rumor rose about the Queen,
Touching her guilty love for Lancelot,
Tho' yet there lived no proof, nor yet was heard
The world's loud whisper breaking into storm,
Not less Geraint believed it; and there fell
A horror on him, lest his gentle wife,
Thro' that great tenderness for Guinevere,
Had suffer'd, or should suffer any taint
In nature: wherefore going to the King,
He made this pretext, that his princedom lay
Close on the borders of a territory,
Wherein were bandit earls, and caitiff knights,
Assassins, and all flyers from the hand
Of Justice, and whatever loathes a law:
And therefore, till the King himself should please
To cleanse this common sewer of all his realm,
He craved a fair permission to depart,
And there defend his marches; and the King
Mused for a little on his plea, but, last,
Allowing it, the Prince and Enid rode,
And fifty knights rode with them, to the shores
Of Severn, and they past to their own land;
Where, thinking, that if ever yet was wife
True to her lord, mine shall be so to me,
He compass'd her with sweet observances
And worship, never leaving her, and grew
Forgetful of his promise to the King,
Forgetful of the falcon and the hunt,
Forgetful of the tilt and tournament,
Forgetful of his glory and his name,
Forgetful of his princedom and its cares.
And this forgetfulness was hateful to her.
And by and by the people, when they met
In twos and threes, or fuller companies,
Began to scoff and jeer and babble of him
As of a prince whose manhood was all gone,
And molten down in mere uxoriousness.
And this she gather'd from the people's eyes:
This too the women who attired her head,
To please her, dwelling on his boundless love,
Told Enid, and they sadden'd her the more:
And day by day she thought to tell Geraint,

But could not out of bashful delicacy;
While he that watch'd her sadden, was the more
Suspicious that her nature had a taint.

At last, it chanced that on a summer morn
(They sleeping each by either) the new sun
Beat thro' the blindless casement of the room,
And heated the strong warrior in his dreams;
Who, moving, cast the coverlet aside,
And bared the knotted column of his throat,
The massive square of his heroic breast,
And arms on which the standing muscle sloped,
As slopes a wild brook o'er a little stone,
Running too vehemently to break upon it.
And Enid woke and sat beside the couch,
Admiring him, and thought within herself,
Was ever man so grandly made as he?
Then, like a shadow, past the people's talk
And accusation of uxoriousness
Across her mind, and bowing over him,
Low to her own heart piteously she said:

"O noble breast and all-puissant arms,
Am I the cause, I the poor cause that men
Reproach you, saying all your force is gone?
I am the cause, because I dare not speak
And tell him what I think and what they say.
And yet I hate that he should linger here;
I cannot love my lord and not his name.
Far liefer had I gird his harness on him,
And ride with him to battle and stand by,
And watch his mightful hand striking great blows
At caitiffs and at wrongers of the world.
Far better were I laid in the dark earth,
Not hearing any more his noble voice,
Not to be folded more in these dear arms,
And darken'd from the high light in his eyes,
Than that my lord thro' me should suffer shame.
Am I so bold, and could I so stand by,
And see my dear lord wounded in the strife,
Or maybe pierced to death before mine eyes,
And yet not dare to tell him what I think,
And how men slur him, saying all his force
Is melted into mere effeminacy?
O me, I fear that I am no true wife."

Half inwardly, half audibly she spoke,
And the strong passion in her made her weep
True tears upon his broad and naked breast,
And these awoke him, and by great mischance
He heard but fragments of her later words,
And that she fear'd she was not a true wife.
And then he thought, "In spite of all my care,
For all my pains, poor man, for all my pains,
She is not faithful to me, and I see her
Weeping for some gay knight in Arthur's hall."
Then, tho' he loved and reverenced her too much
To dream she could be guilty of foul act,
Right thro' his manful breast darted the pang
That makes a man, in the sweet face of her
Whom he loves most, lonely and miserable.
At this he hurl'd his huge limbs out of bed,
And shook his drowsy squire awake and cried,
"My charger and her palfrey;" then to her,
"I will ride forth into the wilderness;
For tho' it seems my spurs are yet to win,
I have not fall'n so low as some would wish.
And thou, put on thy worst and meanest dress
And ride with me." And Enid ask'd, amazed,
"If Enid errs, let Enid learn her fault."
But he, "I charge thee, ask not, but obey."
Then she bethought her of a faded silk,
A faded mantle and a faded veil,
And moving toward a cedarn cabinet,
Wherein she kept them folded reverently
With sprigs of summer laid between the folds,
She took them, and array'd herself therein,
Remembering when first he came on her

Drest in that dress, and how he loved her in it,
And all her foolish fears about the dress,
And all his journey to her, as himself
Had told her, and their coming to the court.

For Arthur on the Whitsuntide before
Held court at old Caerleon upon Usk.
There on a day he sitting high in hall,
Before him came a forester of Dean,
Wet from the woods, with notice of a hart
Taller than all his fellows, milky-white,
First seen that day: these things he told the King.
Then the good King gave order to let blow
His horns for hunting on the morrow morn.
And when the Queen petition'd for his leave
To see the hunt, allow'd it easily.
So with the morning all the court were gone.
But Guinevere lay late into the morn,
Lost in sweet dreams, and dreaming of her love
For Lancelot, and forgetful of the hunt;
But rose at last, a single maiden with her,
Took horse, and forded Usk, and gain'd the wood;
There, on a little knoll beside it, stay'd
Waiting to hear the hounds; but heard instead
A sudden sound of hoofs, for Prince Geraint,
Late also, wearing neither hunting-dress
Nor weapon, save a golden-hilted brand,
Came quickly flashing thro' the shallow ford
Behind them, and so gallop'd up the knoll.
A purple scarf, at either end whereof
There swung an apple of the purest gold,
Sway'd round about him, as he gallop'd up
To join them, glancing like a dragon-fly
In summer suit and silks of holiday.
Low bow'd the tributary Prince, and she,
Sweetly and statelily, and with all grace
Of womanhood and queenhood, answer'd him:
"Late, late, Sir Prince," she said, "later than we!"
"Yea, noble Queen," he answer'd, "and so late
That I but come like you to see the hunt,
Not join it." "Therefore wait with me," she said;
"For on this little knoll, if anywhere,
There is good chance that we shall hear the hounds:
Here often they break covert at our feet."

And while they listen'd for the distant hunt,
And chiefly for the baying of Cavall,
King Arthur's hound of deepest mouth, there rode
Full slowly by a knight, lady, and dwarf;
Whereof the dwarf lagg'd latest, and the knight
Had vizor up, and show'd a youthful face,
Imperious, and of haughtiest lineaments.
And Guinevere, not mindful of his face
In the King's hall, desired his name, and sent
Her maiden to demand it of the dwarf;
Who being vicious, old and irritable,
And doubling all his master's vice of pride,
Made answer sharply that she should not know.
"Then will I ask it of himself," she said.
"Nay, by my faith, thou shalt not," cried the dwarf;
"Thou art not worthy ev'n to speak of him;"
And when she put her horse toward the knight,
Struck at her with his whip, and she return'd
Indignant to the Queen; whereat Geraint
Exclaiming, "Surely I will learn the name,"
Made sharply to the dwarf, and ask'd it of him,
Who answer'd as before; and when the Prince
Had put his horse in motion toward the knight,
Struck at him with his whip, and cut his cheek.
The Prince's blood spirted upon the scarf,
Dyeing it; and his quick, instinctive hand
Caught at the hilt, as to abolish him:
But he, from his exceeding manfulness
And pure nobility of temperament,
Wroth to be wroth at such a worm, refrain'd
From ev'n a word, and so returning said:

"I will avenge this insult, noble Queen,

Done in your maiden's person to yourself:
And I will track this vermin to their earths:
For tho' I ride unarm'd, I do not doubt
To find, at some place I shall come at, arms
On loan, or else for pledge; and, being found,
Then will I fight him, and will break his pride,
And on the third day will again be here,
So that I be not fall'n in fight.   Farewell."

"Farewell, fair Prince," answer'd the stately Queen.
"Be prosperous in this journey, as in all;
And may you light on all things that you love,
And live to wed with her whom first you love:
But ere you wed with any, bring your bride,
And I, were she the daughter of a king,
Yea, tho' she were a beggar from the hedge,
Will clothe her for her bridals like the sun."

And Prince Geraint, now thinking that he heard
The noble hart at bay, now the far horn,
A little vext at losing of the hunt,
A little at the vile occasion, rode,
By ups and downs, thro' many a grassy glade
And valley, with fixt eye following the three.
At last they issued from the world of wood,
And climb'd upon a fair and even ridge,
And show'd themselves against the sky, and sank.
And thither came Geraint, and underneath
Beheld the long street of a little town
In a long valley, on one side whereof,
White from the mason's hand, a fortress rose;
And on one side a castle in decay,
Beyond a bridge that spann'd a dry ravine:
And out of town and valley came a noise
As of a broad brook o'er a shingly bed
Brawling, or like a clamor of the rooks
At distance, ere they settle for the night.

And onward to the fortress rode the three,
And enter'd, and were lost behind the walls.
"So," thought Geraint, "I have track'd him to his
        earth."
And down the long street riding wearily,
Found every hostel full, and everywhere
Was hammer laid to hoof, and the hot hiss
And bustling whistle of the youth who scour'd
His master's armor; and of such a one
He ask'd, "What means the tumult in the town?"
Who told him, scouring still, "The sparrow-hawk!"
Then riding close behind an ancient churl,
Who, smitten by the dusty sloping beam,
Went sweating underneath a sack of corn,
Ask'd yet once more what meant the hubbub here?
Who answer'd gruffly, "Ugh! the sparrow-hawk."
Then riding further past an armorer's,
Who, with back turn'd, and bow'd above his work,
Sat riveting a helmet on his knee,
He put the self-same query, but the man
Not turning round, nor looking at him, said:
"Friend, he that labors for the sparrow-hawk
Has little time for idle questioners."
Whereat Geraint flash'd into sudden spleen:
"A thousand pips eat up your sparrow-hawk!
Tits, wrens, and all wing'd nothings peck him dead!
Ye think the rustic cackle of your bourg
The murmur of the world!   What is it to me?
O wretched set of sparrows, one and all,
Who pipe of nothing but of sparrow-hawks!
Speak, if ye be not like the rest, hawk-mad,
Where can I get me harborage for the night?
And arms, arms, arms to fight my enemy?   Speak!"
Whereat the armorer turning all amazed
And seeing one so gay in purple silks,
Came forward with the helmet yet in hand
And answer'd, "Pardon me, O stranger knight;
We hold a tourney here to-morrow morn,
And there is scantly time for half the work.
Arms? truth! I know not: all are wanted here.

Harborage? truth, good truth, I know not, save,
It may be, at Earl Yniol's, o'er the bridge
Yonder."   He spoke and fell to work again.

Then rode Geraint, a little spleenful yet,
Across the bridge that spann'd the dry ravine.
There musing sat the hoary-headed Earl
(His dress a suit of fray'd magnificence,
Once fit for feasts of ceremony), and said:
"Whither, fair son?" to whom Geraint replied,
"O friend, I seek a harborage for the night."
Then Yniol, "Enter therefore and partake
The slender entertainment of a house
Once rich, now poor, but ever open-door'd."
"Thanks, venerable friend," replied Geraint:
"So that ye do not serve me sparrow-hawks
For supper, I will enter, I will eat
With all the passion of a twelve hours' fast."
Then sigh'd and smiled the hoary-headed Earl,
And answer'd, "Graver cause than yours is mine
To curse this hedgerow thief, the sparrow-hawk:
But in, go in; for save yourself desire it,
We will not touch upon him ev'n in jest."

Then rode Geraint into the castle court,
His charger trampling many a prickly star
Of sprouted thistle on the broken stones.
He look'd and saw that all was ruinous.
Here stood a shatter'd archway plumed with fern;
And here had fall'n a great part of a tower,
Whole, like a crag that tumbles from the cliff,
And like a crag was gay with wilding flowers:
And high above a piece of turret stair,
Worn by the feet that now were silent, wound
Bare to the sun, and monstrous ivy-stems
Claspt the gray walls with hairy-fibred arms,
And suck'd the joining of the stones, and look'd
A knot, beneath, of snakes, aloft, a grove.

And while he waited in the castle court,
The voice of Enid, Yniol's daughter, rang
Clear thro' the open casement of the hall,
Singing; and as the sweet voice of a bird,
Heard by the lander in a lonely isle,
Moves him to think what kind of bird it is
That sings so delicately clear, and make
Conjecture of the plumage and the form;
So the sweet voice of Enid moved Geraint;
And made him like a man abroad at morn
When first the liquid note beloved of men
Comes flying over many a windy wave
To Britain, and in April suddenly
Breaks from a coppice gemm'd with green and red,
And he suspends his converse with a friend,
Or it may be the labor of his hands,
To think or say, "There is the nightingale;"
So fared it with Geraint, who thought and said,
"Here, by God's grace, is the one voice for me."

It chanced the song that Enid sang was one
Of Fortune and her wheel, and Enid sang:

"Turn, Fortune, turn thy wheel and lower the
        proud;
Turn thy wild wheel thro' sunshine, storm, and
        cloud;
Thy wheel and thee we neither love nor hate.

"Turn, Fortune, turn thy wheel with smile or
        frown;
With that wild wheel we go not up or down;
Our hoard is little, but our hearts are great.

"Smile and we smile, the lords of many lands;
Frown and we smile, the lords of our own hands;
For man is man and master of his fate.

"Turn, turn thy wheel above the staring crowd;

Thy wheel and thou are shadows in the cloud;
Thy wheel and thee we neither love nor hate."

"Hark, by the bird's song ye may learn the nest,"
Said Yniol; "enter quickly." Entering then,
Right o'er a mount of newly-fallen stones,
The dusky-rafter'd many-cobwebb'd hall,
He found an ancient dame in dim brocade;
And near her, like a blossom vermeil-white,
That lightly breaks a faded flower-sheath,
Moved the fair Enid, all in faded silk,
Her daughter. In a moment thought Geraint,
"Here by God's rood is the one maid for me."
But none spake word except the hoary Earl:
"Enid, the good knight's horse stands in the court;
Take him to stall, and give him corn, and then
Go to the town and buy us flesh and wine;
And we will make us merry as we may.
Our board is little, but our hearts are great."

He spake: the Prince, as Enid past him, fain
To follow. strode a stride, but Yniol caught
His purple scarf, and held, and said, "Forbear!
Rest! the good house, tho' ruin'd, O my son,
Endures not that her guest should serve himself."
And reverencing the custom of the house,
Geraint, from utter courtesy, forbore.

So Enid took his charger to the stall;
And after went her way across the bridge,
And reach'd the town, and while the Prince and Earl
Yet spoke together. came again with one,
A youth, that following with a costrel bore
The means of goodly welcome, flesh and wine.
And Enid brought sweet cakes to make them cheer,
And in her veil enfolded, manchet bread.
And then, because their hall must also serve
For kitchen, boil'd the flesh, and spread the board,
And stood behind, and waited on the three.
And seeing her so sweet and serviceable,
Geraint had longing in him evermore
To stoop and kiss the tender little thumb,
That crost the trencher as she laid it down:
But after all had eaten, then Geraint,
For now the wine made summer in his veins,
Let his eye rove in following, or rest
On Enid at her lowly hand-maid-work,
Now here, now there, about the dusky hall;
Then suddenly addrest the hoary Earl:

"Fair host and earl, I pray your courtesy:
This sparrow-hawk, what is he? tell me of him.
His name? but no, good faith, I will not have it:
For if he be the knight whom late I saw
Ride into that new fortress by your town,
White from the mason's hand, then have I sworn
From his own lips to have it—I am Geraint
Of Devon—for this morning when the Queen
Sent her own maiden to demand the name,
His dwarf, a vicious under-shapen thing,
Struck at her with his whip, and she return'd
Indignant to the Queen; and then I swore
That I would track this caitiff to his hold,
And fight and break his pride, and have it of him.
And all unarm'd I rode, and thought to find
Arms in your town, where all the men are mad;
They take the rustic murmur of their bourg
For the great wave that echoes round the world;
They would not hear me speak: but if ye know
Where I can light on arms, or if yourself
Should have them, tell me, seeing I have sworn
That I will break his pride and learn his name,
Avenging this great insult done the Queen."

Then cried Earl Yniol, "Art thou he indeed,
Geraint, a name far-sounded among men
For noble deeds? and truly I, when first
I saw you moving by me on the bridge,

Felt ye were somewhat, yea, and by your state
And presence might have guess'd you one of those
That eat in Arthur's hall at Camelot.
Nor speak I now from foolish flattery;
For this dear child hath often heard me praise
Your feats of arms, and often when I paused
Hath ask'd again, and ever loved to hear;
So grateful is the noise of noble deeds
To noble hearts who see but acts of wrong:
O never yet had woman such a pair
Of suitors as this maiden; first Limours,
A creature wholly given to brawls and wine,
Drunk even when he woo'd; and be he dead
I know not, but he past to the wild land.
The second was your foe, the sparrow-hawk,
My curse, my nephew—I will not let his name
Slip from my lips if I can help it—he,
When I that knew him fierce and turbulent
Refused her to him, then his pride awoke;
And since the proud man often is the mean,
He sow'd a slander in the common ear,
Affirming that his father left me gold,
And in my charge, which was not render'd to him;
Bribed with large promises the men who served
About my person, the more easily
Because my means were somewhat broken into
Thro' open doors and hospitality;
Raised my own town against me in the night
Before my Enid's birthday, sack'd my house;
From mine own earldom foully ousted me;
Built that mine fort to overawe my friends,
For truly there are those who love me yet;
And keeps me in this ruinous castle here,
Where doubtless he would put me soon to death,
But that his pride too much despises me:
And I myself sometimes despise myself;
For I have let men be, and have their way;
Am much too gentle, have not used my power;
Nor know I whether I be very base
Or very manful, whether very wise
Or very foolish; only this I know,
That whatsoever evil happen to me,
I seem to suffer nothing heart or limb,
But can endure it all most patiently."

"Well said, true heart," replied Geraint, "but arms,
That if the sparrow-hawk, this nephew, fight
In next day's tourney I may break his pride."

And Yniol answer'd, "Arms, indeed, but old
And rusty, old and rusty, Prince Geraint,
Are mine, and therefore at thine asking, thine.
But in this tournament can no man tilt,
Except the lady he loves best be there.
Two forks are fixt into the meadow ground,
And over these is placed a silver wand,
And over that a golden sparrow-hawk,
The prize of beauty for the fairest there.
And this, what knight soever be in field
Lays claim to for the lady at his side,
And tilts with my good nephew thereupon,
Who being apt at arms and big of bone
Has ever won it for the lady with him,
And toppling over all antagonism
Has earn'd himself the name of sparrow-hawk.
But thou, that hast no lady, canst not fight."

To whom Geraint with eyes all bright replied,
Leaning a little toward him, "Thy leave!
Let me lay lance in rest, O noble host,
For this dear child, because I never saw,
Tho' having seen all beauties of our time,
Nor can see elsewhere, anything so fair.
And if I fall her name will yet remain
Untarnish'd as before; but if I live,
So aid me Heaven when at mine uttermost,
As I will make her truly my true wife."

Then, howsoever patient, Yniol's heart
Danced in his bosom, seeing better days.
And looking round he saw not Enid there
(Who hearing her own name had slipt away),
But that old dame, to whom full tenderly
And fondling all her hand in his he said,
"Mother, a maiden is a tender thing,
And best by her that bore her understood.
Go thou to rest, but ere thou go to rest
Tell her, and prove her heart toward the Prince."

So spake the kindly-hearted Earl, and she
With frequent smile and nod departing found,
Half disarray'd as to her rest, the girl;
Whom first she kiss'd on either cheek, and then
On either shining shoulder laid a hand,
And kept her off and gazed upon her face,
And told her all their converse in the hall,
Proving her heart: but never light and shade
Coursed one another more on open ground
Beneath a troubled heaven, than red and pale
Across the face of Enid hearing her;
While slowly falling as a scale that falls,
When weight is added only grain by grain,
Sank her sweet head upon her gentle breast;
Nor did she lift an eye nor speak a word,
Rapt in the fear and in the wonder of it;
So moving without answer to her rest
She found no rest, and ever fail'd to draw
The quiet night into her blood, but lay
Contemplating her own unworthiness:
And when the pale and bloodless east began
To quicken to the sun, arose, and raised
Her mother too, and hand in hand they moved
Down to the meadow where the jousts were held,
And waited there for Yniol and Geraint.

And thither came the twain, and when Geraint
Beheld her first in field, awaiting him,
He felt, were she the prize of bodily force,
Himself beyond the rest pushing could move
The chair of Idris. Yniol's rusted arms
Were on his princely person, but thro' these
Princelike his bearing shone; and errant knights
And ladies came, and by and by the crown
Flow'd in, and settling circled all the lists.
And there they fixt the forks into the ground,
And over these they placed the silver wand,
And over that the golden sparrow-hawk.
Then Yniol's nephew, after trumpet-blown,
Spake to the lady with him and proclaim'd,
"Advance and take as fairest of the fair,
For I these two years past have won it for thee,
The prize of beauty." Loudly spake the Prince,
"Forbear: there is a worthier," and the knight
With some surprise and thrice as much disdain
Turn'd, and beheld the four, and all his face
Glow'd like the heart of a great fire at Yule,
So burnt he was with passion, crying out,
"Do battle for it then," no more: and thrice
They clash'd together, and thrice they brake their
    spears.
Then each, dishorsed and drawing, lash'd at each
So often and with such blows, that all the crowd
Wonder'd, and now and then from distant walls
There came a clapping as of phantom hands.
So twice they fought, and twice they breathed, and
    still
The dew of their great labor, and the blood
Of their strong bodies, flowing, drain'd their force.
But either's force was match'd till Yniol's cry,
"Remember that great insult done the Queen,"
Increased Geraint's, who heaved his blade aloft,
And crack'd the helmet thro', and bit the bone,
And fell'd him, and set foot upon his breast,
And said, "Thy name?" To whom the fallen man
Made answer, groaning, "Edyrn, son of Nudd!
Ashamed am I that I should tell it thee.

My pride is broken: men have seen my fall."
"Then, Edyrn, son of Nudd," replied Geraint,
"These two things shalt thou do, or else thou diest.
First, thou thyself, with damsel and with dwarf,
Shalt ride to Arthur's court, and coming there,
Crave pardon for that insult done the Queen,
And shalt abide her judgment on it; next,
Thou shalt give back their earldom to thy kin.
These two things shalt thou do, or thou shalt die."
And Edyrn answer'd, "These things will I do,
For I have never yet been overthrown,
And thou hast overthrown me, and my pride
Is broken down, for Enid sees my fall!"
And rising up, he rode to Arthur's court,
And there the Queen forgave him easily.
And being young, he changed and came to loathe
His crime of traitor, slowly drew himself
Bright from his own dark life, and fell at last
In the great battle fighting for the King.

But when the third day from the hunting-morn
Made a low splendor in the world, and wings
Moved in her ivy, Enid, for she lay
With her fair head in the dim-yellow light,
Among the dancing shadows of the birds,
Woke and bethought her of her promise given
No later than last eve to Prince Geraint—
So bent he seem'd on going the third day,
He would not leave her, till her promise given—
To ride with him this morning to the court,
And there be made known to the stately Queen,
And there be wedded with all ceremony.
At this she cast her eyes upon her dress,
And thought it never yet had look'd so mean.
For as a leaf in mid-November is
To what it was in mid-October, seem'd
The dress that now she look'd on to the dress
She look'd on ere the coming of Geraint.
And still she look'd, and still the terror grew
Of that strange bright and dreadful thing, a court,
All staring at her in her faded silk:
And softly to her own sweet heart she said:

"This noble Prince who won our earldom back,
So splendid in his acts and his attire,
Sweet heaven, how much I shall discredit him!
Would he could tarry with us here awhile,
But being so beholden to the Prince,
It were but little grace in any of us,
Bent as he seem'd on going this third day,
To seek a second favor at his hands.
Yet if he could but tarry a day or two,
Myself would work eye dim, and finger lame,
Far liefer than so much discredit him."

And Enid fell in longing for a dress
All branch'd and flower'd with gold, a costly gift
Of her good mother, given her on the night
Before her birthday, three sad years ago,
That night of fire, when Edyrn sack'd their house,
And scatter'd all they had to all the winds:
For while the mother show'd it, and the two
Were turning and admiring it, the work
To both appear'd so costly, rose a cry
That Edyrn's men were on them, and they fled
With little save the jewels they had on,
Which being sold and sold had bought them bread.
And Edyrn's men had caught them in their flight,
And placed them in this ruin; and she wish'd
The Prince had found her in her ancient home;
Then let her fancy flit across the past,
And roam the goodly places that she knew;
And last bethought her how she used to watch,
Near that old home, a pool of golden carp;
And one was patch'd and blurr'd and lustreless
Among his burnish'd brethren of the pool;
And half asleep she made comparison
Of that and these to her own faded self

And the gay court, and fell asleep again:
And dreamt herself was such a faded form
Among her burnish'd sisters of the pool;
But this was in the garden of a king;
And tho' she lay dark in the pool, she knew
That all was bright; that all about were birds
Of sunny plume in gilded trellis-work;
That all the turf was rich in plots that look'd
Each like a garnet or a turkis in it;
And lords and ladies of the high court went
In silver tissue talking things of state;
And children of the King in cloth of gold
Glanced at the doors or gambol'd down the walks;
And while she thought "They will not see me,"
　　came
A stately queen whose name was Guinevere,
And all the children in their cloth of gold
Ran to her, crying, "If we have fish at all
Let them be gold; and charge the gardeners now
To pick the faded creature from the pool,
And cast it on the mixen that it die."
And therewithal one came and seized on her,
And Enid started waking, with her heart
All overshadow'd by the foolish dream,
And lo! it was her mother grasping her
To get her well awake; and in her hand
A suit of bright apparel, which she laid
Flat on the couch, and spoke exultingly:

"See here, my child, how fresh the colors look,
How fast they hold like colors of a shell
That keeps the wear and polish of the wave.
Why not? it never yet was worn, I trow:
Look on it, child, and tell me if ye know it."

And Enid look'd, but all confused at first,
Could scarce divide it from her foolish dream:
Then suddenly she knew it and rejoiced,
And answer'd, "Yea, I know it: your good gift,
So sadly lost on that unhappy night;
Your own good gift!" "Yea, surely," said the dame,
"And gladly given again this happy morn.
For when the jousts were ended yesterday,
Went Yniol through the town, and everywhere
He found the sack and plunder of our house
All scatter'd thro' the houses of the town;
And gave command that all which once was ours
Should now be ours again: and yester-eve,
While ye were talking sweetly with your Prince,
Came one with this and laid it in my hand,
For love or fear, or seeking favor of us,
Because we have our earldom back again.
And yester-eve I would not tell you of it,
But kept it for a sweet surprise at morn.
Yea, truly, is it not a sweet surprise?
For I myself unwillingly have worn
My faded suit, as you, my child, have yours,
And, howsoever patient, Yniol his.
Ah, dear, he took me from a goodly house,
With store of rich apparel, sumptuous fare,
And page, and maid, and squire, and seneschal,
And pastime both of hawk and hound, and all
That appertains to noble maintenance.
Yea, and he brought me to a goodly house;
But since our fortune slipt from sun to shade,
And all thro' that young traitor, cruel need
Constrain'd us, but a better time has come;
So clothe yourself in this, that better fits
Our mended fortunes and a Prince's bride:
For tho' ye won the prize of fairest fair,
And tho' I heard him call you fairest fair,
Let never maiden think, however fair,
She is not fairer in new clothes than old.
And should some great court-lady say, the Prince
Hath pick'd a ragged-robin from the hedge,
And like a madman brought her to the court,
Then were ye shamed, and, worse, might shame the
　　Prince

To whom we are beholden; but I know,
When my dear child is set forth at her best,
That neither court nor country, tho' they sought
Thro' all the provinces like those of old
That lighted on Queen Esther, has her match."

Here ceased the kindly mother out of breath;
And Enid listen'd brightening as she lay;
Then, as the white and glittering star of morn
Parts from a bank of snow, and by and by
Slips into golden cloud, the maiden rose,
And left her maiden couch, and robed herself,
Help'd by the mother's careful hand and eye,
Without a mirror, in the gorgeous gown;
Who, after, turn'd her daughter round, and said,
She never yet had seen her half so fair;
And call'd her like that maiden in the tale,
Whom Gwydion made by glamour out of flowers,
And sweeter than the bride of Cassivelaun,
Flur, for whose love the Roman Cæsar first
Invaded Britain, "but we beat him back,
As this great Prince invaded us, and we,
Not beat him back, but welcomed him with joy,
And I can scarcely ride with you to court,
For old am I, and rough the ways and wild;
But Yniol goes, and I full oft shall dream
I see my princess as I see her now,
Clothed with my gift, and gay among the gay."

But while the women thus rejoiced, Geraint
Woke where he slept in the high hall, and call'd
For Enid, and when Yniol made report
Of that good mother making Enid gay
In such apparel as might well beseem
His princess, or indeed the stately Queen,
He answer'd: "Earl, entreat her by my love,
Albeit I give no reason but my wish,
That she ride with me in her faded silk."
Yniol with that hard message went; it fell
Like flaws in summer laying lusty corn:
For Enid, all abash'd, she knew not why,
Dared not to glance at her good mother's face,
But silently, in all obedience,
Her mother silent too, nor helping her,
Laid from her limbs the costly-broider'd gift,
And robed them in her ancient suit again,
And so descended. Never man rejoiced
More than Geraint to greet her thus attired;
And glancing all at once as keenly at her
As careful robins eye the delver's toil,
Made her cheek burn and either eyelid fall,
But rested, with her sweet face satisfied;
Then seeing cloud upon the mother's brow,
Her by both hands he caught, and sweetly said,

"O my new mother, be not wroth or grieved
At thy new son, for my petition to her.
When late I left Caerleon, our great Queen,
In words whose echo lasts, they were so sweet,
Made promise, that whatever bride I brought,
Herself would clothe her like the sun in heaven.
Thereafter, when I reach'd this ruin'd hall,
Beholding one so bright in dark estate,
I vow'd that, could I gain her, our fair Queen,
No hand but hers, should make your Enid burst,
Sunlike, from cloud—and likewise thought, perhaps,
That service done so graciously would bind
The two together; fain I would the two
Should love each other: how can Enid find
A nobler friend? Another thought was mine;
I came among you here so suddenly,
That tho' her gentle presence at the lists
Might well have served for proof that I was loved,
I doubted whether daughter's tenderness,
Or easy nature, might not let itself
Be moulded by your wishes for her weal;
Or whether some false sense in her own self
Of my contrasting brightness, overbore

Her fancy dwelling in this dusky hall;
And such a sense might make her long for court
And all its perilous glories: and I thought,
That could I someway prove such force in her,
Link'd with such love for me, that at a word
(No reason given her) she could cast aside
A splendor dear to women, new to her,
And therefore dearer; or, if not so new,
Yet therefore tenfold dearer by the power
Of intermitted usage; then I felt
That I could rest, a rock in ebbs and flows,
Fixt on her faith. Now, therefore, I do rest,
A prophet certain of my prophecy,
That never shadow of mistrust can cross
Between us. Grant me pardon for my thoughts:
And for my strange petition I will make
Amends hereafter by some gaudy-day,
When your fair child shall wear your costly gift
Beside your own warm hearth, with, on her knees,
Who knows? another gift of the high God,
Which, maybe, shall have learn'd to lisp you thanks."

He spoke: the mother smiled, but half in tears,
Then brought a mantle down and wrapt her in it,
And claspt and kiss'd her, and they rode away.

Now thrice that morning Guinevere had climb'd
The giant tower, from whose high crest, they say,
Men saw the goodly hills of Somerset,
And white sails flying on the yellow sea;
But not to goodly hill or yellow sea
Look'd the fair Queen, but up the vale of Usk,
By the flat meadow, till she saw them come;
And then descending, met them at the gates,
Embraced her with all welcome as a friend,
And did her honor as the Prince's bride,
And clothed her for her bridals like the sun;
And all that week was old Caerleon gay,
For by the hands of Dubric, the high saint,
They twain were wedded with all ceremony.

And this was on the last year's Whitsuntide.
But Enid ever kept the faded silk,
Remembering how first he came on her,
Drest in that dress, and how he loved her in it,
And all her foolish fears about the dress,
And all his journey toward her, as himself
Had told her, and their coming to the court.

And now this morning, when he said to her,
"Put on your worst and meanest dress," she found
And took it, and array'd herself therein.

II.

O PURBLIND race of miserable men,
How many among us at this very hour
Do forge a life-long trouble for ourselves,
By taking true for false, or false for true;
Here, thro' the feeble twilight of this world
Groping, how many, until we pass and reach
That other, where we see as we are seen!

So fared it with Geraint, who, issuing forth
That morning, when they both had got to horse,
Perhaps because he loved her passionately,
And felt that tempest brooding round his heart,
Which, if he spoke at all, would break perforce
Upon a head so dear in thunder, said:
"Not at my side. I charge thee ride before,
Ever a good way on before; and this
I charge thee, on thy duty as a wife,
Whatever happens, not to speak to me,
No, not a word!" and Enid was aghast;
And forth they rode, but scarce three paces on,
When crying out, "Effeminate as I am,
I will not fight my way with gilded arms,
All shall be iron;" he loosed a mighty purse,

Hung at his belt, and hurl'd it toward the squire.
So the last sight that Enid had of home
Was all the marble threshold flashing, strown
With gold and scatter'd coinage, and the squire
Chafing his shoulder: then he cried again,
"To the wilds!" and Enid leading down the tracks
Thro' which he bade her lead him on, they past
The marches, and by bandit-haunted holds,
Gray swamps and pools, waste places of the hern,
And wildernesses, perilous paths, they rode:
Round was their pace at first, but slacken'd soon:
A stranger meeting them had surely thought,
They rode so slowly and they look'd so pale,
That each had suffer'd some exceeding wrong.
For he was ever saying to himself,
"O I that wasted time to tend upon her,
To compass her with sweet observances,
To dress her beautifully and keep her true"—
And there he broke the sentence in his heart
Abruptly, as a man upon his tongue
May break it, when his passion masters him.
And she was ever praying the sweet heavens
To save her dear lord whole from any wound.
And ever in her mind she cast about
For that unnoticed failing in herself,
Which made him look so cloudy and so cold;
Till the great plover's human whistle amazed
Her heart, and glancing around the waste, she fear'd
In every wavering brake an ambuscade.
Then thought again, "If there be such in me,
I might amend it by the grace of Heaven,
If he would only speak and tell me of it."

But when the fourth part of the day was gone,
Then Enid was aware of three tall knights
On horseback, wholly arm'd, behind a rock
In shadow, waiting for them, caitiffs all;
And heard one crying to his fellow, "Look,
Here comes a laggard hanging down his head,
Who seems no bolder than a beaten hound;
Come, we will slay him and will have his horse
And armor, and his damsel shall be ours."

Then Enid ponder'd in her heart, and said:
"I will go back a little to my lord,
And I will tell him all their caitiff talk;
For, be he wroth even to slaying me,
Far liefer by his dear hand had I die,
Than that my lord should suffer loss or shame."

Then she went back some paces of return,
Met his full frown timidly firm, and said:
"My lord, I saw three bandits by the rock
Waiting to fall on you, and heard them boast
That they would slay you, and possess your horse
And armor, and your damsel should be theirs."

He made a wrathful answer: "Did I wish
Your warning or your silence? one command
I laid upon you, not to speak to me,
And thus ye keep it! Well then, look—for now,
Whether ye wish me victory or defeat,
Long for my life, or hunger for my death,
Yourself shall see my vigor is not lost."

Then Enid waited pale and sorrowful,
And down upon him bare the bandit three.
And at the midmost charging, Prince Geraint
Drave the long spear a cubit thro' his breast,
And out beyond; and then against his brace
Of comrades, each of whom had broken on him
A lance that splinter'd like an icicle,
Swung from his brand a windy buffet out
Once, twice, to right, to left, and stunn'd the twain,
Or slew them, and dismounting like a man
That skins the wild beast after slaying him,
Stript from the three dead wolves of woman born
The three gay suits of armor which they wore,

And let the bodies lie, but bound the suits
Of armor on their horses, each on each.
And tied the bridle-reins of all the three
Together, and said to her, "Drive them on
Before you;" and she drove them thro' the waste.

He follow'd nearer: ruth began to work
Against his anger in him, while he watch'd
The being he loved best in all the world,
With difficulty in mild obedience
Driving them on: he fain had spoken to her,
And loosed in words of sudden fire the wrath
And smoulder'd wrong that burnt him all within;
But evermore it seem'd an easier thing
At once without remorse to strike her dead,
Than to cry "Halt," and to her own bright face
Accuse her of the least immodesty:
And thus tongue-tied, it made him wroth the more
That she *could* speak whom his own ear had heard
Call herself false: and suffering thus he made
Minutes an age: but in scarce longer time
Than at Caerleon the full-tided Usk,
Before he turn to fall seaward again,
Pauses, did Enid, keeping watch, behold
In the first shallow shade of a deep wood,
Before a gloom of stubborn-shafted oaks,
Three other horsemen waiting, wholly arm'd,
Whereof one seem'd far larger than her lord,
And shook her pulses, crying, "Look, a prize!
Three horses and three goodly suits of arms,
And all in charge of whom? a girl: set on."
"Nay," said the second, "yonder comes a knight."
The third, "A craven; how he hangs his head."
The giant answer'd merrily, "Yea, but one?
Wait here, and when he passes fall upon him."

And Enid ponder'd in her heart, and said,
"I will abide the coming of my lord,
And I will tell him all their villainy.
My lord is weary with the fight before,
And they will fall upon him unawares.
I needs must disobey him for his good;
How should I dare obey him to his harm?
Needs must I speak, and tho' he kill me for it,
I save a life dearer to me than mine."

And she abode his coming, and said to him,
With timid firmness, "Have I leave to speak?"
He said, "Ye take it, speaking," and she spoke.

"There lurk three villains yonder in the wood,
And each of them is wholly arm'd, and one
Is larger-limb'd than you are, and they say
That they will fall upon you while ye pass."

To which he flung a wrathful answer back:
"And if there were an hundred in the wood,
And every man were larger-limb'd than I,
And all at once should sally out upon me,
I swear it would not ruffle me so much
As you that not obey me. Stand aside,
And if I fall, cleave to the better man."

And Enid stood aside to wait the event,
Not dare to watch the combat, only breathe
Short fits of prayer, at every stroke a breath.
And he she dreaded most, bare down upon him.
Aim'd at the helm, his lance err'd; but Geraint's,
A little in the late encounter strain'd,
Struck thro' the bulky bandit's corselet home,
And then brake short, and down his enemy roll'd,
And there lay still: as he that tells the tale
Saw once a great piece of a promontory,
That had a sapling growing on it, slide
From the long shore-cliff's windy walls to the beach,
And there lie still, and yet the sapling grew:
So lay the man transfixt. His craven pair
Of comrades, making slowlier at the Prince,

When now they saw their bulwark fallen, stood;
On whom the victor, to confound them more,
Spurr'd with his terrible war-cry; for as one,
That listens near a torrent mountain-brook,
All thro' the crash of the near cataract hears
The drumming thunder of the huger fall
At distance, were the soldiers wont to hear
His voice in battle, and be kindled by it,
And foemen scared, like that false pair who turn'd
Flying, but, overtaken, died the death
Themselves had wrought on many an innocent.

Thereon Geraint, dismounting, pick'd the lance
That pleased him best, and drew from those dead wolves
Their three gay suits of armor, each from each,
And bound them on their horses, each on each,
And tied the bridle-reins of all the three
Together, and said to her, "Drive them on
Before you," and she drove them thro' the wood.

He follow'd nearer still; the pain she had
To keep them in the wild ways of the wood,
Two sets of three laden with jingling arms,
Together, served a little to disedge
The sharpness of that pain about her heart:
And they themselves, like creatures gently born,
But into bad hands fall'n, and now so long
By bandits groom'd, prick'd their light ears, and felt
Her low firm voice and tender government.

So thro' the green gloom of the wood they past,
And issuing under open heavens, beheld
A little town with towers, upon a rock,
And close beneath, a meadow, gemlike, chased
In the brown wild, and mowers mowing in it:
And down a rocky pathway from the place
There came a fair-hair'd youth, that in his hand
Bare victual for the mowers: and Geraint
Had ruth again on Enid looking pale:
Then, moving downward to the meadow ground,
He, when the fair-hair'd youth came by him, said,
"Friend, let her eat; the damsel is so faint."
"Yea, willingly," replied the youth; "and thou,
My lord, eat also, tho' the fare is coarse,
And only meet for mowers;" then set down
His basket, and dismounting on the sward,
They let the horses graze, and ate themselves.
And Enid took a little delicately,
Less having stomach for it than desire
To close with her lord's pleasure; but Geraint
Ate all the mowers' victual unawares,
And when he found it all empty, was amazed;
And, "Boy," said he, "I have eaten all, but take
A horse and arms for guerdon: choose the best."
He, reddening in extremity of delight,
"My lord, you overpay me fifty-fold."
"Ye will be all the wealthier," cried the Prince.
"I take it as free gift, then," said the boy,
"Not guerdon; for myself can easily,
While your good damsel rests, return, and fetch
Fresh victual for these mowers of our Earl:
For these are his, and all the field is his,
And I myself am his; and I will tell him
How great a man thou art; he loves to know
When men of mark are in his territory;
And he will have thee to his palace here,
And serve thee costlier than with mowers' fare."

Then said Geraint, "I wish no better fare:
I never ate with angrier appetite
Than when I left your mowers dinnerless,
And into no Earl's palace will I go.
I know, God knows, too much of palaces!
And if he want me, let him come to me.
But hire us some fair chamber for the night,
And stalling for the horses, and return
With victual for these men, and let us know."

"Yea, my kind lord," said the glad youth, and
			went,
Held his head high, and thought himself a knight,
And up the rocky pathway disappear'd,
Leading the horse, and they were left alone.

But when the Prince had brought his errant eyes
Home from the rock, sideways he let them glance
At Enid, where she droopt: his own false doom,
That shadow of mistrust should never cross
Betwixt them, came upon him, and he sigh'd;
Then with another humorous ruth remark'd
The lusty mowers laboring dinnerless,
And watch'd the sun blaze on the turning scythe,
And after nodded sleepily in the heat.
But she, remembering her old ruin'd hall,
And all the windy clamor of the daws
Above her hollow turret, pluck'd the grass,
There growing longest by the meadow's edge,
And into many a listless annulet,
Now over, now beneath her marriage ring,
Wove and unwove it, till the boy return'd,
And told them of a chamber, and they went;
Where, after saying to her, "If ye will,
Call for the woman of the house," to which
She answer'd, "Thanks, my lord;" the two remain'd
Apart by all the chamber's width, and mute
As creatures voiceless thro' the fault of birth,
Or two wild men, supporters of a shield,
Painted, who stare at open space, nor glance
The one at other, parted by the shield.

On a sudden, many a voice along the street,
And heel against the pavement echoing, burst
Their drowse; and either started while the door,
Push'd from without, drave backward to the wall,
And midmost of a rout of roisterers,
Femininely fair and dissolutely pale,
Her suitor in old years before Geraint,
Enter'd, the wild lord of the place, Limours.
He, moving up with pliant courtliness,
Greeted Geraint full face, but stealthily,
In the mid-warmth of welcome and graspt hand,
Found Enid with the corner of his eye,
And knew her sitting sad and solitary.
Then cried Geraint for wine and goodly cheer
To feed the sudden guest, and sumptuously,
According to his fashion, bade the host
Call in what men soever were his friends,
And feast with these in honor of their Earl;
"And care not for the cost; the cost is mine."

And wine and food were brought, and Earl Li-
			mours
Drank till he jested with all ease, and told
Free tales, and took the word and play'd upon it,
And made it of two colors; for his talk,
When wine and free companions kindled him,
Was wont to glance and sparkle like a gem
Of fifty facets; thus he moved the Prince
To laughter and his comrades to applause.
Then, when the Prince was merry, ask'd Limours,
"Your leave, my lord, to cross the room, and speak
To your good damsel there who sits apart,
And seems so lonely?" "My free leave," he said;
"Get her to speak: she doth not speak to me."
Then rose Limours, and looking at his feet,
Like him who tries the bridge he fears may fail,
Crost and came near, lifted adoring eyes,
Bow'd at her side and utter'd whisperingly:

"Enid, the pilot star of my lone life;
Enid, my early and my only love;
Enid, the loss of whom hath turn'd me wild—
What chance is this? how is it I see you here?
Ye are in my power at last, are in my power.
Yet fear me not: I call mine own self wild,
But keep a touch of sweet civility

Here in the heart of waste and wilderness.
I thought, but that your father came between,
In former days you saw me favorably.
And if it were so, do not keep it back:
Make me a little happier: let me know it:
Owe you me nothing for a life half-lost?
Yea, yea, the whole dear debt of all you are.
And, Enid, you and he, I see with joy,
Ye sit apart, you do not speak to him,
You come with no attendance, page or maid,
To serve you—doth he love you as of old?
For, call it lovers' quarrels, yet I know
Tho' men may bicker with the things they love,
They would not make them laughable in all eyes,
Not while they loved them; and your wretched
			dress,
A wretched insult on you, dumbly speaks
Your story, that this man loves you no more.
Your beauty is no beauty to him now:
A common chance—right well I know it—pall'd—
For I know men: nor will ye win him back,
For the man's love once gone never returns.
But here is one who loves you as of old;
With more exceeding passion than of old:
Good, speak the word: my followers ring him round
He sits unarm'd; I hold a finger up;
They understand: nay; I do not mean blood:
Nor need ye look so scared at what I say:
My malice is no deeper than a moat,
No stronger than a wall: there is the keep;
He shall not cross us more; speak but the word:
Or speak it not; but then, by Him that made me,
The one true lover whom you ever own'd,
I will make use of all the power I have.
Oh, pardon me! the madness of that hour,
When first I parted from thee, moves me yet."

At this the tender sound of his own voice
And sweet self-pity, or the fancy of it,
Made his eye moist; but Enid fear'd his eyes,
Moist as they were, wine-heated from the feast;
And answer'd with such craft as women use,
Guilty or guiltless, to stave off a chance
That breaks upon them perilously, and said:

"Earl, if you love me as in former years,
And do not practise on me, come with morn,
And snatch me from him by violence;
Leave me to-night: I am weary to the death."

Low at leave-taking, with his brandish'd plume
Brushing his instep, bow'd the all-amorous Earl,
And the stout Prince bade him a loud good-night.
He, moving homeward, babbled to his men,
How Enid never loved a man but him,
Nor cared a broken egg-shell for her lord.

But Enid, left alone with Prince Geraint,
Debating his command of silence given,
And that she now perforce must violate it,
Held commune with herself, and while she held
He fell asleep, and Enid had no heart
To wake him, but hung o'er him, wholly pleased
To find him yet unwounded after fight,
And hear him breathing low and equally.
Anon she rose, and stepping lightly, heap'd
The pieces of his armor in one place,
All to be there against a sudden need:
Then dozed awhile herself, but overtoil'd
By that day's grief and travel, evermore
Seem'd catching at a rootless thorn, and then
Went slipping down horrible precipices,
And strongly striking out her limbs, awoke;
Then thought she heard the wild Earl at the door,
With all his rout of random followers,
Sound on a dreadful trumpet, summoning her;
Which was the red cock shouting to the light,
As the gray dawn stole o'er the dewy world.

And glimmer'd on his armor in the room.
And once again she rose to look at it,
But touch'd it unawares: jangling, the casque
Fell, and he started up and stared at her.
Then breaking his command of silence given,
She told him all that Earl Limours had said,
Except the passage that he loved her not;
Nor left untold the craft herself had used;
But ended with apology so sweet,
Low-spoken, and of so few words, and seem'd
So justified by that necessity,
That tho' he thought "was it for him she wept
In Devon?" he but gave a wrathful groan,
Saying, "Your sweet faces make good fellows fools
And traitors. Call the host and bid him bring
Charger and palfrey." So she glided out
Among the heavy breathings of the house,
And like a household Spirit at the walls
Beat, till she woke the sleepers, and return'd:
Then tending her rough lord, tho' all unask'd,
In silence, did him service as a squire;
Till issuing arm'd, he found the host and cried,
"Thy reckoning, friend?" and ere he learnt it, "Take
Five horses and their armors;" and the host,
Suddenly honest, answer'd in amaze,
"My lord, I scarce have spent the worth of one!"
"Ye will be all the wealthier," said the Prince,
And then to Enid, "Forward! and to-day
I charge you, Enid, more especially,
What thing soever ye may hear, or see,
Or fancy (tho' I count it of small use
To charge you) that ye speak not, but obey."

And Enid answer'd, "Yea, my lord, I know
Your wish, and would obey; but riding first,
I hear the violent threats you do not hear,
I see the danger which you cannot see:
Then not to give you warning, that seems hard;
Almost beyond me; yet I would obey."

"Yea so," said he, "do it: be not too wise;
Seeing that ye are wedded to a man,
Not all mismated with a yawning clown,
But one with arms to guard his head and yours,
With eyes to find you out, however far,
And ears to hear you, even in his dreams."

With that he turn'd and look'd as keenly at her
As careful robins eye the delver's toil;
And that within her, which a wanton fool
Or hasty judger would have call'd her guilt,
Made her cheek burn and either eyelid fall.
And Geraint look'd and was not satisfied.

Then forward by a way which, beaten broad,
Led from the territory of false Limours
To the waste earldom of another earl,
Doorm, whom his shaking vassals call'd the Bull,
Went Enid with her sullen follower on.
Once she look'd back, and when she saw him ride
More near by many a rood than yester-morn,
It wellnigh made her cheerful; till Geraint
Waving an angry hand, as who should say,
"Ye watch me," sadden'd all her heart again.
But while the sun yet beat a dewy blade,
The sound of many a heavily-galloping hoof
Smote on her ear, and turning round, she saw
Dust, and the points of lances bicker in it.
Then, not to disobey her lord's behest,
And yet to give him warning, for he rode
As if he heard not, moving back, she held
Her finger up, and pointed to the dust.
At which the warrior in his obstinacy,
Because she kept the letter of his word,
Was in a manner pleased, and turning, stood.
And in a moment after, wild Limours,
Borne on a black horse, like a thunder-cloud
Whose skirts are loosen'd by the breaking storm,

Half ridden off with by the thing he rode,
And all in passion uttering a dry shriek,
Dash'd on Geraint, who closed with him, and bore
Down by the length of lance and arm beyond
The crupper, and so left him stunn'd or dead,
And overthrew the next that follow'd him,
And blindly rush'd on all the rout behind.
But at the flash and motion of the man
They vanish'd, panic-stricken, like a shoal
Of darting fish, that on a summer morn
Adown the crystal dykes at Camelot
Come slipping o'er their shadows on the sand,
But if a man who stands upon the brink
But lift a shining hand against the sun,
There is not left the twinkle of a fin
Betwixt the cressy islets white in flower;
So, scared but at the motion of the man,
Fled all the boon companions of the Earl,
And left him lying in the public way;
So vanish friendships only made in wine.

Then like a stormy sunlight smiled Geraint,
Who saw the chargers of the two that fell
Start from their fallen lords, and wildly fly,
Mixt with the flyers. "Horse and man," he said,
"All of one mind and all right honest friends!
Not a hoof left: and I, methinks, till now
Was honest—paid with horses and with arms;
I cannot steal or plunder, no, nor beg:
And so what say ye, shall we strip him there,
Your lover? has your palfrey heart enough
To bear his armor? shall we fast, or dine?
No?—then do thou, being right honest, pray
That we may meet the horsemen of Earl Doorm.
I too would still be honest." Thus he said:
And sadly gazing on her bridle-reins,
And answering not one word, she led the way.

But as a man to whom a dreadful loss
Falls in a far land, and he knows it not,
But coming back, he learns it, and the loss
So pains him that he sickens nigh to death;
So fared it with Geraint, who being prick'd
In combat with the follower of Limours,
Bled underneath his armor secretly,
And so rode on, nor told his gentle wife,
What ail'd him, hardly knowing it himself,
Till his eye darken'd and his helmet wagg'd;
And at a sudden swerving of the road,
Tho' happily down on a bank of grass,
The Prince, without a word, from his horse fell.

And Enid heard the clashing of his fall,
Suddenly came, and at his side all pale
Dismounting, loosed the fastenings of his arms.
Nor let her true hand falter, nor blue eye
Moisten, till she had lighted on his wound,
And tearing off her veil of faded silk,
Had bared her forehead to the blistering sun,
And swath'd the hurt that drain'd her dear lord's
    life.
Then after all was done that hand could do,
She rested, and her desolation came
Upon her, and she wept beside the way.

And many past, but none regarded her,
For in that realm of lawless turbulence,
A woman weeping for her murder'd mate
Was cared as much for as a summer shower:
One took him for a victim of Earl Doorm,
Nor dared to waste a perilous pity on him:
Another hurrying past, a man-at-arms,
Rode on a mission to the bandit Earl:
Half whistling and half singing a coarse song,
He drove the dust against her veilless eyes:
Another, flying from the wrath of Doorm,
Before an ever-fancied arrow, made
The long way smoke beneath him in his fear;

At which her palfrey, whinnying, lifted heel,
And scour'd into the coppices and was lost,
While the great charger stood, grieved like a man.

But at the point of noon the huge Earl Doorm,
Broad-faced, with under-fringe of russet beard,
Bound on a foray, rolling eyes of prey,
Came riding with a hundred lances up;
But ere he came, like one that hails a ship,
Cried out with a big voice, "What, is he dead?"
"No, no, not dead!" she answer'd in all haste.
"Would some of your kind people take him up,
And bear him hence out of this cruel sun?
Most sure am I, quite sure, he is not dead."

Then said Earl Doorm: "Well, if he be not dead,
Why wail ye for him thus? ye seem a child.
And be he dead, I count you for a fool;
Your wailing will not quicken him: dead or not,
Ye mar a comely face with idiot tears.
Yet, since the face *is* comely—some of you,
Here, take him up, and bear him to our hall:
And if he live, we will have him of our band;
And if he die, why earth has earth enough
To hide him. See ye take the charger too,
A noble one."

       He spake, and past away,
But left two brawny spearmen, who advanced,
Each growling like a dog, when his good bone
Seems to be pluck'd at by the village boys,
Who love to vex him eating, and he fears
To lose his bone, and lays his foot upon it,
Gnawing and growling: so the ruffians growl'd,
Fearing to lose, and all for a dead man,
Their chance of booty from the morning's raid;
Yet raised and laid him on a litter-bier,
Such as they brought upon their forays out
For those that might be wounded; laid him on it
All in the hollow of his shield, and took
And bore him to the naked hall of Doorm
(His gentle charger following him unled),
And cast him and the bier on which he lay
Down on an oaken settle in the hall,
And then departed, hot in haste to join
Their luckier mates, but growling as before,
And cursing their lost time, and the dead man,
And their own Earl, and their own souls, and her.
They might as well have blest her: she was deaf
To blessing or to cursing save from one.

So for long hours sat Enid by her lord,
There in the naked hall, propping his head,
And chafing his pale hands, and calling to him.
Till at the last he waken'd from his swoon,
And found his own dear bride propping his head,
And chafing his faint hands, and calling to him;
And felt the warm tears falling on his face;
And said to his own heart, "She weeps for me:"
And yet lay still, and feign'd himself as dead,
That he might prove her to the uttermost,
And say to his own heart, "She weeps for me."

But in the falling afternoon return'd
The huge Earl Doorm with plunder to the hall.
His lusty spearmen follow'd him with noise:
Each hurling down a heap of things that rang
Against the pavement, cast his lance aside,
And doff'd his helm: and then there flutter'd in,
Half-bold, half-frighted, with dilated eyes,
A tribe of women, dress'd in many hues.
And mingled with the spearmen: and Earl Doorm
Struck with a knife's haft hard against the board,
And call'd for flesh and wine to feed his spears.
And men brought in whole hogs and quarter beeves,
And all the hall was dim with steam of flesh:
And none spake word, but all sat down at once,
And ate with tumult in the naked hall,

Feeding like horses when you hear them feed;
Till Enid shrank far back into herself,
To shun the wild ways of the lawless tribe.
But when Earl Doorm had eaten all he would,
He roll'd his eyes about the hall, and found
A damsel drooping in a corner of it.
Then he remember'd her, and how she wept;
And out of her there came a power upon him;
And rising on the sudden, he said, "Eat!
I never yet beheld a thing so pale.
God's curse, it makes me mad to see you weep.
Eat! Look yourself. Good luck had your good man
For were I dead, who is it would weep for me?
Sweet lady, never since I first drew breath
Have I beheld a lily like yourself.
And so there lived some color in your cheek,
There is not one among my gentlewomen
Were fit to wear your slipper for a glove.
But listen to me. and by me be ruled,
And I will do the thing I have not done,
For ye shall share my earldom with me, girl,
And we will live like two birds in one nest,
And I will fetch you forage from all fields,
For I compel all creatures to my will."

He spoke: the brawny spearman let his cheek
Bulge with the unswallow'd piece, and turning
       stared;
While some, whose souls the old serpent long had
       drawn
Down, as the worm draws in the wither'd leaf
And makes it earth, hiss'd each at other's ear
What shall not be recorded—women they,
Women, or what had been those gracious things,
But now desired the humbling of their best,
Yea, would have help'd him to it: and all at once
They hated her, who took no thought of them,
But answer'd in low voice, her meek head yet
Drooping, "I pray you of your courtesy,
He being as he is, to let me be."

She spake so low he hardly heard her speak,
But like a mighty patron, satisfied
With what himself had done so graciously,
Assumed that she had thank'd him, adding, "Yea,
Eat and be glad, for I account you mine."

She answer'd meekly, "How should I be glad
Henceforth in all the world at anything,
Until my lord arise and look upon me?"

Here the huge Earl cried out upon her talk,
As all but empty heart and weariness
And sickly nothing; suddenly seized on her,
And bare her by main violence to the board,
And thrust the dish before her, crying, "Eat."

"No, no," said Enid, vext, "I will not eat
Till yonder man upon the bier arise,
And eat with me." "Drink, then," he answer'd.
       "Here!"
(And fill'd a horn with wine and held it to her,)
"Lo! I, myself, when flush'd with fight, or hot,
God's curse, with anger—often I myself,
Before I well have drunken, scarce can eat:
Drink therefore, and the wine will change your will."

"Not so," she cried, "by Heaven, I will not drink
Till my dear lord arise and bid me do it,
And drink with me; and if he rise no more,
I will not look at wine until I die."

At this he turn'd all red and paced his hall,
Now gnaw'd his under, now his upper lip.
And coming up close to her, said at last:
"Girl, for I see ye scorn my courtesies,
Take warning: yonder man is surely dead;
And I compel all creatures to my will.

Not eat nor drink? And wherefore wail for one,
Who put your beauty to this flout and scorn
By dressing it in rags? Amazed am I,
Beholding how ye butt against my wish,
That I forbear you thus: cross me no more.
At least put off to please me this poor gown,
This silken rag, this beggar-woman's weed:
I love that beauty should go beautifully:
For see ye not my gentlewomen here,
How gay, how suited to the house of one,
Who loves that beauty should go beautifully?
Rise therefore; robe yourself in this: obey."

He spoke, and one among his gentlewomen
Display'd a splendid silk of foreign loom,
Where like a shoaling sea the lovely blue
Play'd into green, and thicker down the front
With jewels than the swarth with drops of dew,
When all night long a cloud clings to the hill,
And with the dawn ascending lets the day
Strike where it clung: so thickly shone the gems.

But Enid answer'd, harder to be moved
Than hardest tyrants in their day of power,
With life-long injuries burning unavenged,
And now their hour has come; and Enid said:

"In this poor gown my dear lord found me first,
And loved me serving in my father's hall:
In this poor gown I rode with him to court,
And there the Queen array'd me like the sun:
In this poor gown he bade me clothe myself,
When now we rode upon this fatal quest
Of honor, where no honor can be gain'd:
And this poor gown I will not cast aside
Until himself arise a living man,
And bid me cast it. I have griefs enough:
Pray you be gentle, pray you let me be:
I never loved, can never love but him:
Yea, God, I pray you of your gentleness,
He being as he is, to let me be."

Then strode the brute Earl up and down his hall,
And took his russet beard between his teeth;
Last, coming up quite close, and in his mood
Crying, "I count it of no more avail,
Dame, to be gentle than ungentle with you;
Take my salute," unknightly with flat hand,
However lightly, smote her on the cheek.

Then Enid, in her utter helplessness,
And since she thought, "He had not dared to do it,
Except he surely knew my lord was dead,"
Sent forth a sudden sharp and bitter cry,
As of a wild thing taken in the trap,
Which sees the trapper coming thro' the wood.

This heard Geraint, and grasping at his sword
(It lay beside him in the hollow shield),
Made but a single bound, and with a sweep of it
Shore thro' the swarthy neck, and like a ball
The russet-bearded head roll'd on the floor.
So died Earl Doorm by him he counted dead.
And all the men and women in the hall
Rose when they saw the dead man rise, and fled
Yelling as from a spectre, and the two
Were left alone together, and he said:

"Enid, I have used you worse than that dead
man;
Done you more wrong: we both have undergone
That trouble which has left me thrice your own:
Henceforward I will rather die than doubt.
And here I lay this penance on myself,
Not, tho' mine own ears heard you yester-morn—
You thought me sleeping, but I heard you say,
I heard you say, that you were no true wife:
I swear I will not ask your meaning in it:

I do believe yourself against yourself,
And will henceforward rather die than doubt."

And Enid could not say one tender word,
She felt so blunt and stupid at the heart:
She only pray'd him, "Fly, they will return
And slay you; fly, your charger is without,
My palfrey lost." "Then, Enid, shall you ride
Behind me." "Yea," said Enid, "let us go."
And moving out they found the stately horse,
Who now no more a vassal to the thief,
But free to stretch his limbs in lawful fight,
Neigh'd with all gladness as they came, and stoop'd
With a low whinny toward the pair: and she
Kiss'd the white star upon his noble front,
Glad also; then Geraint, upon the horse
Mounted, and reach'd a hand and on his foot
She set her own and climb'd; he turn'd his face
And kiss'd her climbing, and she cast her arms
About him, and at once they rode away.

And never yet, since high in Paradise
O'er the four rivers the first roses blew,
Came purer pleasure unto mortal kind
Than lived thro' her, who in that perilous hour
Put hand to hand beneath her husband's heart,
And felt him hers again: she did not weep,
But o'er her meek eyes came a happy mist
Like that which kept the heart of Eden green
Before the useful trouble of the rain:
Yet not so misty were her meek blue eyes
As not to see before them on the path,
Right in the gateway of the bandit hold,
A knight of Arthur's court, who laid his lance
In rest, and made as if to fall upon him.
Then, fearing for his hurt and loss of blood,
She, with her mind all full of what had chanced,
Shriek'd to the stranger, "Slay not a dead man!"
"The voice of Enid," said the knight; but she,
Beholding it was Edyrn son of Nudd,
Was moved so much the more, and shriek'd again,
"O cousin, slay not him who gave you life."
And Edyrn, moving frankly forward, spake:
"My lord Geraint, I greet you with all love;
I took you for a bandit knight of Doorm;
And fear not, Enid, I should fall upon him,
Who love you, Prince, with something of the love
Wherewith we love the Heaven that chastens us.
For once, when I was up so high in pride
That I was halfway down the slope to Hell,
By overthrowing me you threw me higher.
Now, made a knight of Arthur's Table Round,
And since I knew this Earl, when I myself
Was half a bandit in my lawless hour,
I come, the mouthpiece of our King to Doorm
(The King is close behind me), bidding him
Disband himself, and scatter all his powers,
Submit, and hear the judgment of the King."

"He hears the judgment of the King of kings,"
Cried the wan Prince; "and lo, the powers of Doorm
Are scatter'd," and he pointed to the field,
Where, huddled here and there on mound and knoll,
Were men and women, staring and aghast,
While some yet fled; and then he plainlier told
How the huge Earl lay slain within his hall.
But when the knight besought him, "Follow me,
Prince, to the camp, and in the King's own ear
Speak what has chanced; ye surely have endured
Strange chances here alone;" that other flush'd,
And hung his head, and halted in reply,
Fearing the mild face of the blameless King,
And after madness acted question ask'd:
Till Edyrn crying, "If ye will not go
To Arthur, then will Arthur come to you,"
"Enough," he said, "I follow," and they went.
But Enid in their going had two fears,
One from the bandit scatter'd in the field,

"He turn'd his face,
And kiss'd her climbing, and she cast her arms
About him, and at once they rode away."

And one from Edyrn. Every now and then,
When Edyrn rein'd his charger at her side,
She shrank a little. In a hollow land,
From which old fires have broken, men may fear
Fresh fire and ruin. He, perceiving, said:

"Fair and dear cousin, you that most had cause
To fear me, fear no longer, I am changed.
Yourself were first the blameless cause to make
My nature's prideful sparkle in the blood
Break into furious flame; being repulsed
By Yniol and yourself, I schemed and wrought
Until I overturn'd him; then set up
(With one main purpose ever at my heart)
My haughty jousts, and took a paramour;
Did her mock-honor as the fairest fair,
And, toppling over all antagonism,
So wax'd in pride, that I believed myself
Unconquerable, for I was wellnigh mad:
And, but for my main purpose in these jousts,
I should have slain your father, seized yourself.
I lived in hope that sometime you would come
To these my lists with him whom best you loved;
And there, poor cousin, with your meek blue
    eyes,
The truest eyes that ever answer'd Heaven,
Behold me overturn and trample on him.
Then, had you cried, or knelt, or pray'd to me,
I should not less have kill'd him. And you came—
But once you came—and with your own true eyes
Beheld the man you loved (I speak as one
Speaks of a service done him) overthrow
My proud self, and my purpose, three years old,
And set his foot upon me, and give me life.
There was I broken down; there was I saved:
Tho' thence I rode all-shamed, hating the life
He gave me, meaning to be rid of it.
And all the penance the Queen laid upon me
Was but to rest awhile within her court;
Where first as sullen as a beast new-caged,
And waiting to be treated like a wolf,

Because I knew my deeds were known, I found,
Instead of scornful pity or pure scorn,
Such fine reserve and noble reticence,
Manners so kind, yet stately, such a grace
Of tenderest courtesy, that I began
To glance behind me at my former life,
And find that it had been the wolf's indeed:
And oft I talk'd with Dubric, the high saint,
Who, with mild heat of holy oratory,
Subdued me somewhat to that gentleness,
Which, when it weds with manhood, makes a man.
And you were often there about the Queen,
But saw me not, or mark'd not if you saw;
Nor did I care or dare to speak with you,
But kept myself aloof till I was changed;
And fear not, cousin; I am changed indeed."

He spoke, and Enid easily believed,
Like simple noble natures, credulous
Of what they long for, good in friend or foe,
There most in those who most have done them ill.
And when they reach'd the camp the King himself
Advanced to greet them, and beholding her,
Tho' pale, yet happy, ask'd her not a word,
But when apart with Edyrn, whom he held
In converse for a little, and return'd,
And gravely smiling, lifted her from horse,
And kiss'd her with all pureness, brother-like,
And show'd an empty tent allotted her,
And glancing for a minute, till he saw her
Pass into it, turn'd to the Prince, and said:

"Prince, when of late ye pray'd me for my leave
To move to your own land, and there defend
Your marches, I was prick'd with some reproof,
As one that let foul wrong stagnate and be,
By having look'd too much thro' alien eyes,
And wrought too long with delegated hands,
Not used mine own: but now behold me come
To cleanse this common sewer of all my realm,
With Edyrn and with others: have ye look'd

At Edyrn? have ye seen how nobly changed?
This work of his is great and wonderful.
His very face with change of heart is changed.
The world will not believe a man repents;
And this wise world of ours is mainly right.
Full seldom doth a man repent, or use
Both grace and will to pick the vicious quitch
Of blood and custom wholly out of him,
And make all clean, and plant himself afresh.
Edyrn has done it, weeding all his heart,
As I will weed this land before I go.
I, therefore, made him of our Table Round,
Not rashly, but have proved him everyway
One of our noblest, our most valorous,
Sanest, and most obedient: and indeed
This work of Edyrn, wrought upon himself
After a life of violence, seems to me
A thousand-fold more great and wonderful
Than if some knight of mine, risking his life,
My subject with my subjects under him,
Should make an onslaught single on a realm
Of robbers, tho' he slew them one by one,
And were himself nigh wounded to the death."

So spake the King; low bow'd the Prince, and felt
His work was neither great nor wonderful,
And past to Enid's tent; and thither came
The King's own leech to look into his hurt;
And Enid tended on him there; and there
Her constant motion round him, and the breath
Of her sweet tendance hovering over him,
Fill'd all the genial courses of his blood
With deeper and with ever deeper love,
As the southwest that, blowing Bala lake,
Fills all the sacred Dee. So past the days.

But while Geraint lay healing of his hurt,
The blameless King went forth and cast his eyes
On each of all whom Uther left in charge
Long since, to guard the justice of the King:
He look'd and found them wanting: and as now
Men weed the white horse on the Berkshire hills,
To keep him bright and clean as heretofore,
He rooted out the slothful officer
Or guilty, which for bribe had wink'd at wrong,
And in their chairs set up a stronger race,
With hearts and hands, and sent a thousand men
To till the wastes, and moving everywhere,
Clear'd the dark places and let in the law,
And broke the bandit holds and cleansed the land.

Then, when Geraint was whole again, they past
With Arthur to Caerleon upon Usk.
There the great Queen once more embraced her
          friend,
And clothed her in apparel like the day.
And tho' Geraint could never take again
That comfort from their converse which he took
Before the Queen's fair name was breathed upon,
He rested well content that all was well.
Thence, after tarrying for a space, they rode,
And fifty knights rode with them to the shores
Of Severn, and they past to their own land.
And there he kept the justice of the King
So vigorously yet mildly, that all hearts
Applauded, and the spiteful whisper died:
And being ever foremost in the chase,
And victor at the tilt and tournament,
They call'd him the great Prince and man of men.
But Enid, whom her ladies loved to call
Enid the Fair, a grateful people named
Enid the Good; and in their halls arose
The cry of children, Enids and Geraints
Of times to be; nor did he doubt her more,
But rested in her fealty, till he crown'd
A happy life with a fair death, and fell
Against the heathen of the Northern Sea
In battle, fighting for the blameless King.

          12

MERLIN AND VIVIEN.

A storm was coming, but the winds were still,
And in the wild woods of Broceliande,
Before an oak, so hollow, huge, and old,
It look'd a tower of ruin'd masonwork,
At Merlin's feet the wily Vivien lay.

Whence came she? One that bare in bitter grudge
The scorn of Arthur and his Table, Mark
The Cornish king, had heard a wandering voice,
A minstrel of Caerleon by strong storm
Blown into shelter at Tintagil, say
That out of naked knightlike purity
Sir Lancelot worshipt no unmarried girl
But the great Queen herself, fought in her name,
Sware by her—vows like theirs, that high in heaven
Love most, but neither marry, nor are given
In marriage, angels of our Lord's report.

He ceased, and then—for Vivien sweetly said
(She sat beside the banquet nearest Mark),
"And is the fair example follow'd, Sir,
In Arthur's household?"—answer'd innocently:

"Ay, by some few—ay, truly—youths that hold
It more beseems the perfect virgin knight
To worship woman as true wife beyond
All hopes of gaining, than as maiden girl.
They place their pride in Lancelot and the Queen.
So passionate for an utter purity
Beyond the limit of their bond, are these,
For Arthur bound them not to singleness.
Brave hearts and clean! and yet—God guide them—
          young."

Then Mark was half in heart to hurl his cup
Straight at the speaker, but forbore: he rose
To leave the hall, and, Vivien following him,
Turn'd to her: "Here are snakes within the grass;
And you methinks, O Vivien, save ye fear
The monkish manhood, and the mask of pure
Worn by this court, can stir them till they sting."

And Vivien answer'd, smiling scornfully,
'Why fear? because that foster'd at thy court
I savor of thy—virtues? fear them? no.
As Love, if Love be perfect, casts out fear,
So Hate, if Hate be perfect, casts out fear.
My father died in battle against the King,
My mother on his corpse in open field;
She bore me there, for born from death was I
Among the dead and sown upon the wind—
And then on thee! and shown the truth betimes,
That old true filth, and bottom of the well,
Where Truth is hidden. Gracious lessons thine
And maxims of the mud! 'This Arthur pure!
Great Nature thro' the flesh herself hath made
Gives him the lie! There is no being pure,
My cherub; saith not Holy Writ the same?'—
If I were Arthur, I would have thy blood.
Thy blessing, stainless King! I bring thee back,
When I have ferreted out their burrowings,
The hearts of all this Order in mine hand—
Ay—so that fate and craft and folly close,
Perchance, one curl of Arthur's golden beard.
To me this narrow grizzled fork of thine
Is cleaner-fashion'd—Well, I loved thee first,
That warps the wit."

          Loud laugh'd the graceless Mark.
But Vivien, into Camelot stealing, lodged
Low in the city, and on a festal day
When Guinevere was crossing the great hall
Cast herself down, knelt to the Queen, and wail'd.

"Why kneel ye there? What evil have ye wrought?
Rise!" and the damsel bidden rise arose
And stood with folded hands and downward eyes
Of glancing corner, and all meekly said,
"None wrought, but suffer'd much, an orphan maid!
My father died in battle for thy King,
My mother on his corpse—in open field,
The sad sea-sounding wastes of Lyonnesse—
Poor wretch—no friend!—and now by Mark the king
For that small charm of feature mine, pursued—
If any such be mine—I fly to thee.
Save, save me thou—Woman of women—thine
The wreath of beauty, thine the crown of power,
Be thine the balm of pity, O Heaven's own white
Earth-angel, stainless bride of stainless King—
Help, for he follows! take me to thyself!
O yield me shelter for mine innocency
Among thy maidens!"

          Here her slow sweet eyes
Fear-tremulous, but humbly hopeful, rose
Fixt on her hearer's, while the Queen who stood
All glittering like May sunshine on May leaves
In green and gold, and plumed with green, replied,
"Peace, child! of overpraise and overblame
We choose the last. Our noble Arthur, him
Ye scarce can overpraise, will hear and know.
Nay—we believe all evil of thy Mark—
Well, we shall test thee farther; but this hour
We ride a-hawking with Sir Lancelot.
He hath given us a fair falcon which he train'd;
We go to prove it. Bide ye here the while."

She past; and Vivien murmur'd after "Go!
I bide the while." Then thro' the portal-arch
Peering askance, and muttering broken-wise,
As one that labors with an evil dream,
Beheld the Queen and Lancelot get to horse.

"Is that the Lancelot? good'y—ay, but gaunt:
Courteous—amends for gauntness—takes her hand—
That glance of theirs, but for the street, had been
A clinging kiss—how hand lingers in hand!
Let go at last!—they ride away—to hawk
For waterfowl. Royaller game is mine.
For such a supersensual sensual bond
As that gray cricket chirpt of at our hearth—
Touch flax with flame—a glance will serve—the liars!
Ah little rat that borest in the dyke
Thy hole by night to let the boundless deep
Down upon far-off cities while they dance—
Or dream—of thee they dream'd not—nor of me
These—ay, but each of either: ride, and dream
The mortal dream that never yet was mine—
Ride, ride and dream until ye wake—to me!
Then, narrow court and lubber King, farewell!
For Lancelot will be gracious to the rat,
And our wise Queen, if knowing that I know,
Will hate, loathe, fear—but honor me the more."

Yet while they rode together down the plain,
Their talk was all of training, terms of art,
Diet and seeling, jesses, leash, and lure.
"She is too noble," he said, "to check at pies,
Nor will she rake: there is no baseness in her."
Here when the Queen demanded as by chance,
"Know ye the stranger woman?" "Let her be,"
Said Lancelot and unhooded casting off
The goodly falcon free; she tower'd; her bells,
Tone under tone, shrill'd; and they lifted up
Their eager faces, wondering at the strength,
Boldness and royal knighthood of the bird
Who pounced her quarry and slew it. Many a time
As once—of old—among the flowers they rode.

But Vivien half-forgotten of the Queen
Among her damsels broidering sat, heard, watch'd
And whisper'd: thro' the peaceful court she crept

And whisper'd: then as Arthur in the highest
Leaven'd the world, so Vivien in the lowest,
Arriving at a time of golden rest,
And sowing one ill hint from ear to ear,
While all the heathen lay at Arthur's feet,
And no quest came, but all was joust and play,
Leaven'd his hall. They heard and let her be.

Thereafter as an enemy that has left
Death in the living waters, and withdrawn,
The wily Vivien stole from Arthur's court.

She hated all the knights, and heard in thought
Their lavish comment when her name was named.
For once, when Arthur, walking all alone,
Vext at a rumor issued from herself
Of some corruption crept among his knights,
Had met her, Vivien, being greeted fair,
Would fain have wrought upon his cloudy mood
With reverent eyes mock-loyal, shaken voice,
And flutter'd adoration, and at last
With dark sweet hints of some who prized him more
Than who should prize him most; at which the King
Had gazed upon her blankly and gone by:
But one had watch'd, and had not held his peace:
It made the laughter of an afternoon
That Vivien should attempt the blameless King.
And after that she set herself to gain
Him, the most famous man of all those times,
Merlin, who knew the range of all their arts,
Had built the King his havens, ships, and halls,
Was also Bard, and knew the starry heavens:
The people call'd him Wizard; whom at first
She play'd about with slight and sprightly talk,
And vivid smiles, and faintly venom'd points
Of slander, glancing here and grazing there;
And yielding to his kindlier moods, the Seer
Would watch her at her petulance, and play,
Ev'n when they seem'd unlovable, and laugh
As those that watch a kitten; thus he grew
Tolerant of what she half disdain'd, and she,
Perceiving that she was but half disdain'd,
Began to break her sports with graver fits,
Turn red or pale, would often when they met
Sigh fully, or all-silent gaze upon him
With such a fixt devotion, that the old man,
Tho' doubtful, felt the flattery, and at times
Would flatter his own wish in age for love,
And half believe her true: for thus at times
He waver'd: but that other clung to him,
Fixt in her will, and so the seasons went.

Then fell on Merlin a great melancholy;
He walk'd with dreams and darkness, and he found
A doom that ever poised itself to fall,
An ever-moaning battle in the mist,
World-war of dying flesh against the life,
Death in all life and lying in all love,
The meanest having power upon the highest,
And the high purpose broken by the worm.

So leaving Arthur's court he gain'd the beach;
There found a little boat, and stept into it;
And Vivien follow'd, but he mark'd her not.
She took the helm and he the sail; the boat
Drave with a sudden wind across the deeps,
And touching Breton sands, they disembark'd.
And then she follow'd Merlin all the way,
Ev'n to the wild woods of Broceliande.
For Merlin once had told her of a charm,
The which if any wrought on anyone
With woven paces and with waving arms,
The man so wrought on ever seem'd to lie
Closed in the four walls of a hollow tower,
From which was no escape for evermore;
And none could find that man for evermore,
Nor could he see but him who wrought the charm
Coming and going, and he lay as dead

And lost to life and use and name and fame.
And Vivien ever sought to work the charm
Upon the great Enchanter of the Time,
As fancying that her glory would be great
According to his greatness whom she quench'd.

There lay she all her length and kiss'd his feet,
As if in deepest reverence and in love.
A twist of gold was round her hair; a robe
Of samite without price, that more exprest
Than hid her, clung about her lissome limbs,
In color like the satin-shining palm
On sallows in the windy gleams of March:
And while she kiss'd them, crying, "Trample me,
Dear feet, that I have follow'd thro' the world,
And I will pay you worship; tread me down
And I will kiss you for it;" he was mute:
So dark a forethought roll'd about his brain,
As on a dull day in an ocean cave
The blind wave feeling round his long sea-hall
In silence: wherefore, when she lifted up
A face of sad appeal, and spake and said,
"O Merlin, do ye love me?" and again,
"O Merlin, do ye love me?" and once more,
"Great Master, do ye love me?" he was mute.
And lissome Vivien, holding by his heel,
Writhed toward him, slided up his knee and sat,
Behind his ankle twined his hollow feet
Together, curved an arm about his neck,
Clung like a snake; and letting her left hand
Droop from his mighty shoulder, as a leaf,
Made with her right a comb of pearl to part
The lists of such a beard as youth gone out
Had left in ashes: then he spoke and said,
Not looking at her, "Who are wise in love
Love most, say least," and Vivien answer'd quick,
"I saw the little elf-god eyeless once
In Arthur's arras hall at Camelot:
But neither arms nor tongue—O stupid child!
Yet you are wise who say it; let me think
Silence is wisdom; I am silent then,
And ask no kiss;" then adding all at once,
"And lo! I clothe myself with wisdom," drew
The vast and shaggy mantle of his beard
Across her neck and bosom to her knee,
And call'd herself a gilded summer fly
Caught in a great old tyrant spider's web,
Who meant to eat her up in that wild wood
Without one word. So Vivien call'd herself,
But rather seem'd a lovely baleful star
Veil'd in gray vapor; till he sadly smiled:
"To what request for what strange boon," he said,
"Are these your pretty tricks and fooleries,
O Vivien, the preamble? yet my thanks,
For these have broken up my melancholy."

And Vivien answered, smiling saucily,
"What, O my Master, have ye found your voice?
I bid the stranger welcome. Thanks at last!
But yesterday you never open'd lip,
Except indeed to drink: no cup had we:
In mine own lady palms I cull'd the spring
That gather'd trickling dropwise from the cleft,
And made a pretty cup of both my hands
And offer'd you it kneeling; then you drank
And knew no more, nor gave me one poor word;
Oh, no more thanks than might a goat have given
With no more sign of reverence than a beard.
And when we halted at that other well,
And I was faint to swooning, and you lay
Foot-gilt with all the blossom-dust of those
Deep meadows we had traversed, did you know
That Vivien bathed your feet before her own?
And yet no thanks: and all thro' this wild wood
And all this morning when I fondled you:
Boon, ay, there was a boon, one not so strange—
How had I wrong'd you? surely ye are wise,
But such a silence is more wise than kind."

And Merlin lock'd his hand in hers and said:
"Oh, did ye never lie upon the shore,
And watch the curl'd white of the coming wave
Glass'd in the slippery sand before it breaks?
Ev'n such a wave, but not so pleasurable,
Dark in the glass of some presageful mood,
Had I for three days seen, ready to fall.
And then I rose and fled from Arthur's court
To break the mood. You follow'd me unask'd:
And when I look'd, and saw you following still,
My mind involved yourself the nearest thing
In that mind-mist: for shall I tell you truth?
Yon seem'd that wave about to break upon me
And sweep me from my hold upon the world,
My use and name and fame. Your pardon, child.
Your pretty sports have brighten'd all again,
And ask your boon, for boon I owe you thrice,
Once for wrong done you by confusion, next
For thanks it seems till now neglected, last
For these your dainty gambols: wherefore ask;
And take this boon so strange and not so strange."

And Vivien answer'd, smiling mournfully:
"Oh, not so strange as my long asking it,
Nor yet so strange as you yourself are strange,
Nor half so strange as that dark mood of yours.
I ever fear'd ye were not wholly mine;
And see, yourself have own'd ye did me wrong.
The people call you prophet: let it be:
But not of those that can expound themselves.
Take Vivien for expounder; she will call
That three-days-long presageful gloom of yours
No presage, but the same mistrustful mood
That makes you seem less noble than yourself,
Whenever I have ask'd this very boon,
Now ask'd again: for see you not, dear love,
That such a mood as that, which lately gloom'd
Your fancy when ye saw me following you,
Must make me fear still more you are not mine,
Must make me yearn still more to prove you mine,
And make me wish still more to learn this charm
Of woven paces and of waving hands,
As proof of trust. O Merlin, teach it me.
The charm so taught will charm us both to rest.
For, grant me some slight power upon your fate,
I, feeling that you felt me worthy trust,
Should rest and let you rest, knowing you mine.
And therefore be as great as ye are named,
Not muffled round with selfish reticence.
How hard you look, and how denyingly!
Oh, if you think this wickedness in me,
That I should prove it on you unawares,
That makes me passing wrathful; then our bond
Had best be loosed for ever: but think or not,
By Heaven that hears I tell you the clean truth,
As clean as blood of babes, as white as milk:
O Merlin, may this earth, if ever I,
If these unwitty wandering wits of mine,
Ev'n in the jumbled rubbish of a dream,
Have tript on such conjectural treachery—
May this hard earth cleave to the Nadir hell,
Down, down, and close again, and nip me flat,
If I be such a traitress. Yield my boon,
Till which I scarce can yield you all I am;
And grant my re-reiterated wish,
The great proof of your love: because I think,
However wise, ye hardly know me yet."

And Merlin loosed his hand from hers and said,
"I never was less wise, however wise,
Too curious Vivien, tho' you talk of trust,
Than when I told you first of such a charm.
Yea, if ye talk of trust I tell you this,
Too much I trusted when I told you that,
And stirr'd this vice in you which mind'd man
Thro' woman the first hour; for howsoe'er
In children a great curiousness be well,
Who have to learn themselves and all the world,

Iu you, that are no child, for still I find
Your face is practised when I spell the lines
I call it—well, I will not call it vice:
But since you name yourself the summer fly,
I well could wish a cobweb for the gnat,
That settles beaten back, and beaten back
Settles, till one could yield for weariness:
But since I will not yield to give you power
Upon my life and use and name and fame,
Why will ye never ask some other boon?
Yea, by God's rood, I trusted you too much."

And Vivien, like the tenderest-hearted maid
That ever bided tryst at village stile,
Made answer, either eyelid wet with tears:
"Nay, Master, be not wrathful with your maid;
Caress her: let her feel herself forgiven
Who feels no heart to ask another boon.
I think ye hardly know the tender rhyme
Of 'trust me not at all or all in all.'
I heard the great Sir Lancelot sing it once,
And it shall answer for me. Listen to it.

"'In Love, if Love be Love, if Love be ours,
Faith and unfaith can ne'er be equal powers:
Unfaith in aught is want of faith in all.

"'It is the little rift within the lute,
That by and by will make the music mute,
And ever widening slowly silence all.

"'The little rift within the lover's lute
Or little pitted speck in garner'd fruit,
That rotting inward, slowly moulders all.

"'It is not worth the keeping: let it go:
But shall it? answer, darling, answer, no.
And trust me not at all or all in all.'

"O Master, do ye love my tender rhyme?"

And Merlin look'd and half believed her true,
So tender was her voice, so fair her face,
So sweetly gleam'd her eyes behind her tears
Like sunlight on the plain behind a shower:
And yet he answer'd half indignantly:

"Far other was the song that once I heard
By this huge oak, sung nearly where we sit:
For here we met, some ten or twelve of us,
To chase a creature that was current then
In these wild woods, the hart with golden horns.
It was the time when first the question rose
About the founding of a Table Round,
That was to be, for love of God and men
And noble deeds, the flower of all the world.
And each incited each to noble deeds.
And while we waited, one, the youngest of us,
We could not keep him silent, out he flash'd,
And into such a song, such fire for fame,
Such trumpet-blowings in it, coming down
To such a stern and iron-clashing close,
That when he stopt we long'd to hurl together,
And should have done it; but the beauteous beast,
Scared by the noise, upstarted at our feet,
And like a silver shadow slipt away
Thro' the dim land; and all day long we rode
Thro' the dim land against a rushing wind,
That glorious roundel echoing in our ears,
And chased the flashes of his golden horns
Until they vanish'd by the fairy well
That laughs at iron—as our warriors did—
Where children cast their pins and nails, and cry,
'Laugh, little well!' but touch it with a sword,
It buzzes fiercely round the point; and there
We lost him: such a noble song was that.
But, Vivien, when you sang me that sweet rhyme,
I felt as though you knew this cursed charm,

Were proving it on me, and that I lay
And felt them slowly ebbing name and fame."

And Vivien answer'd, smiling mournfully:
"Oh, mine have ebb'd away for evermore,
And all thro' following you to this wild wood,
Because I saw you sad, to comfort you.
Lo now, what hearts have men! they never mount
As high as woman in her selfless mood.
And touching fame, howe'er ye scorn my song,
Take one verse more—the lady speaks it—this:

"'My name, once mine, now thine, is closelier
  mine,
For fame, could fame be mine, that fame were thine,
And shame, could shame be thine, that shame were
  mine.
So trust me not at all or all in all.'

"Says she not well? and there is more—this rhyme
Is like the fair pearl-necklace of the Queen,
That burst in dancing, and the pearls were spilt;
Some lost, some stolen, some as relics kept.
But nevermore the same two sister pearls
Ran down the silken thread to kiss each other
On her white neck—so is it with this rhyme:
It lives dispersedly in many hands,
And every minstrel sings it differently;
Yet is there one true line, the pearl of pearls:
'Man dreams of Fame while woman wakes to love.'
Yea! Love, tho' Love were of the grossest, carves
A portion from the solid present, eats
And uses, careless of the rest; but Fame,
The Fame that follows death is nothing to us;
And what is Fame in life but half-disfame,
And counterchanged with darkness? ye yourself
Know well that Envy calls you Devil's son,
And since ye seem the Master of all Art,
They fain would make you Master of all vice."

And Merlin lock'd his hand in hers and said,
"I once was looking for a magic weed,
And found a fair young squire who sat alone,
Had carved himself a knightly shield of wood,
And then was painting on it fancied arms,
Azure, an Eagle rising, or the Sun
In dexter chief; the scroll, 'I follow fame.'
And speaking not, but leaning over him,
I took the brush and blotted out the bird,
And made a Gardener putting in a graff,
With this for motto, 'Rather use than fame.'
You should have seen him blush; but afterwards
He made a stalwart knight. Oh, Vivien,
For you, methinks you think you love me well;
For me, I love you somewhat; rest: and Love
Should have some rest and pleasure in himself,
Not ever be too curious for a boon,
Too prurient for a proof against the grain
Of him ye say ye love: but Fame with men,
Being but ampler means to serve mankind,
Should have small rest or pleasure in herself,
But work as vassal to the larger love,
That dwarfs the petty love of one to one.
Use gave me Fame at first, and Fame again
Increasing gave me use. Lo, there my boon!
What other? for men sought to prove me vile,
Because I fain had given them greater wits:
And then did Envy call me Devil's son:
The sick weak beast, seeking to help herself
By striking at her better, miss'd. and brought
Her own claw back, and wounded her own heart.
Sweet were the days when I was all unknown,
But when my name was lifted up, the storm
Brake on the mountain and I cared not for it.
Right well know I that fame is half-disfame,
Yet needs must work my work. That other fame,
To one at least, who hath not children, vague,
The cackle of the unborn about the grave,

I cared not for it: a single misty star,
Which is the second in a line of stars
That seem a sword beneath a belt of three,
I never gazed upon it but I dreamt
Of some vast charm concluded in that star
To make fame nothing. Wherefore, if I fear,
Giving you power upon me thro' this charm,
That you might play me falsely, having power,
However well ye think ye love me now
(As sons of kings loving in pupilage
Have turn'd to tyrants when they came to power),
I rather dread the loss of use than fame;
If you—and not so much from wickedness,
As some wild turn of anger, or a mood
Of overstrain'd affection, it may be,
To keep me all to your own self—or else
A sudden spurt of woman's jealousy—
Should try this charm on whom ye say ye love."

And Vivien answer'd, smiling as in wrath:
"Have I not sworn? I am not trusted. Good!
Well, hide it, hide it; I shall find it out;
And being found, take heed of Vivien.
A woman, and not trusted, doubtless I
Might feel some sudden turn of anger born
Of your misfaith; and your fine epithet
Is accurate too, for this full love of mine
Without the full heart back may merit well
Your term of overstrain'd. So used as I,
My daily wonder is, I love at all.
And as to woman's jealousy, oh, why not?
Oh, to what end, except a jealous one,
And one to make me jealous if I love,
Was this fair charm invented by yourself?
I well believe that all about this world
Ye cage a buxom captive here and there,
Closed in the four walls of a hollow tower
From which is no escape for evermore."

Then the great Master merrily answer'd her:
"Full many a love in loving youth was mine;
I needed then no charm to keep them mine
But youth and love; and that full heart of yours
Whereof ye prattle, may now assure you mine:
So live uncharm'd. For those who wrought it first,
The wrist is parted from the hand that waved,
The feet unmortised from their ankle-bones
Who paced it, ages back: but will ye hear
The legend as in guerdon for your rhyme?

"There lived a king in the most Eastern East,
Less old than I, yet older, for my blood
Hath earnest in it of far springs to be.
A tawny pirate anchor'd in his port,
Whose bark had plunder'd twenty nameless isles;
And passing one, at the high peep of dawn,
He saw two cities in a thousand boats
All fighting for a woman on the sea.
And pushing his black craft among them all,
He lightly scatter'd theirs and brought her off,
With loss of half his people arrow-slain;
A maid so smooth, so white, so wonderful,
They said a light came from her when she moved:
And since the pirate would not yield her up,
The King impaled him for his piracy;
Then made her Queen: but those isle-nurtured eyes
Waged such unwilling tho' successful war
On all the youth: they sicken'd; councils thinn'd,
And armies waned, for, magnet-like, she drew
The rustiest iron of old fighters' hearts;
And beasts themselves would worship; camels knelt
Unbidden, and the brutes of mountain back
That carry kings in castles, bow'd black knees
Of homage, ringing with their serpent hands,
To make her smile, her golden ankle-bells.
What wonder, being jealous, that he sent
His horns of proclamation out thro' all
The hundred under-kingdoms that he sway'd

To find a wizard who might teach the King
Some charm, which being wrought upon the Queen,
Might keep her all his own: to such a one
He promised more than ever king has given,
A league of mountain full of golden mines,
A province with a hundred miles of coast,
A palace and a princess, all for him:
But on all those who tried and fail'd, the King
Pronounced a dismal sentence, meaning by it
To keep the list low and pretenders back,
Or like a king, not to be trifled with—
Their heads should moulder on the city gates.
And many tried and fail'd, because the charm
Of nature in her overbore their own:
And many a wizard brow blench'd on the walls:
And many weeks a troop of carrion crows
Hung like a cloud above the gateway towers."

And Vivien, breaking in upon him, said:
"I sit and gather honey; yet, methinks,
Thy tongue has tript a little: ask thyself.
The lady never made *unwilling* war
With those fine eyes: she had her pleasure in it,
And made her good man jealous with good cause.
And lived there neither dame nor damsel then
Wroth at a lover's loss? were all as tame,
I mean, as noble, as their Queen was fair?
Not one to flirt a venom at her eyes,
Or pinch a murderous dust into her drink,
Or make her paler with a poison'd rose?
Well, those were not our days: but did they find
A wizard? Tell me, was he like to thee?"

She ceased, and made her lithe arm round his
    neck
Tighten, and then drew back, and let her eyes
Speak for her, glowing on him, like a bride's
On her new lord, her own, the first of men.

He answer'd, laughing, "Nay, not like to me.
At last they found—his foragers for charms—
A little glassy-headed, hairless man,
Who lived alone in a great wild on grass;
Read but one book, and ever reading, grew
So grated down and filed away with thought,
So lean his eyes were monstrous; while the skin
Clung but to crate and basket, ribs and spine.
And since he kept his mind on one sole aim,
Nor ever touch'd fierce wine, nor tasted flesh,
Nor own'd a sensual wish, to him the wall
That sunders ghosts and shadow-casting men
Became a crystal, and he saw them thro' it,
And heard their voices talk behind the wall,
And learnt their elemental secrets, powers,
And forces; often o'er the sun's bright eye
Drew the vast eyelid of an inky cloud,
And lash'd it at the base with slanting storm;
Or in the noon of mist and driving rain,
When the lake whiten'd and the pinewood roar'd,
And the cairn'd mountain was a shadow, sunn'd
The world to peace again: here was the man.
And so by force they dragg'd him to the King.
And then he taught the King to charm the Queen
In such-wise, that no man could see her more,
Nor saw she save the King, who wrought the
    charm
Coming and going, and she lay as dead,
And lost all use of life: but when the King .
Made proffer of the league of golden mines,
The province with a hundred miles of coast,
The palace and the princess, that old man
Went back to his old wild, and lived on grass,
And vanish'd, and his book came down to me."

And Vivien answer'd, smiling saucily:
"Ye have the book: the charm is written in it:
Good: take my counsel: let me know it at once:
For keep it like a puzzle, chest in chest,

With each chest lock'd and padlock'd thirty-fold,
And whelm all this beneath as vast a mound
As after furious battle turfs the slain
On some wild down above the windy deep,
I yet should strike upon a sudden means
To dig, pick, open, find, and read the charm:
Then, if I tried it, who should blame me then?"

And smiling, as a master smiles at one
That is not of his school, nor any school
But that where blind and naked Ignorance
Delivers brawling judgments, unashamed,
On all things all day long, he answer'd her:

"Thou read the book, my pretty Vivien!
Oh ay, it is but twenty pages long,
But every page having an ample marge,
And every marge enclosing in the midst
A square of text that looks a little blot,
The text no larger than the limbs of fleas;
And every square of text an awful charm,
Writ in a language that has long gone by.
So long, that mountains have arisen since
With cities on their flanks—thou read the book!
And every margin scribbled, crost, and cramm'd
With comment, densest condensation, hard
To mind and eye; but the long sleepless nights
Of my long life have made it easy to me.
And none can read the text, not even I;
And none can read the comment but myself;
And in the comment did I find the charm.
Oh, the results are simple; a mere child
Might use it to the harm of anyone,
And never could undo it: ask no more:
For tho' you should not prove it upon me,
But keep that oath ye sware, ye might, perchance,
Assay it on some one of the Table Round,
And all because ye dream they babble of you."

And Vivien, frowning in true anger, said:
"What dare the full-fed liars say of me?
They ride abroad redressing human wrongs!
They sit with knife in meat and wine in horn.
They bound to holy vows of chastity!
Were I not woman, I could tell a tale.
But you are man, you well can understand
The shame that cannot be explain'd for shame.
Not one of all the drove should touch me: swine!"

Then answer'd Merlin, careless of her words:
"You breathe but accusation vast and vague,
Spleen-born, I think, and proofless. If ye know,
Set up the charge ye know, to stand or fall!"

And Vivien answer'd, frowning wrathfully:
"Oh ay, what say ye to Sir Valence, him
Whose kinsman left him watcher o'er his wife
And two fair babes, and went to distant lands,
Was one year gone, and on returning found
Not two but three? there lay the reckling, one
But one hour old! What said the happy sire?
A seven-months' babe had been a truer gift.
Those twelve sweet moons confused his fatherhood."

Then answer'd Merlin, "Nay, I know the tale.
Sir Valence wedded with an outland dame:
Some cause had kept him sunder'd from his wife:
One child they had: it lived with her: she died:
His kinsman traveling on his own affair,
Was charged by Valence to bring home the child.
He brought, not found it therefore: take the truth."

"Oh ay," said Vivien, "overtrue a tale.
What say ye then to sweet Sir Sagramore,
That ardent man? 'to pluck the flower in season,'
So says the song, 'I trow it is no treason.'
O Master, shall we call him overquick
To crop his own sweet rose before the hour?"

And Merlin answer'd, "Overquick art thou
To catch a loathly plume fall'n from the wing
Of that foul bird of rapine whose whole prey
Is man's good name: he never wrong'd his bride.
I know the tale. An angry gust of wind
Puff'd out his torch among the myriad-room'd
And many-corridor'd complexities
Of Arthur's palace: then he found a door,
And darkling felt the sculptured ornament
That wreathen round it, made it seem his own;
And wearied out, made for the couch and slept,
A stainless man beside a stainless maid;
And either slept, nor knew of other there;
Till the high dawn, piercing the royal rose
In Arthur's casement, glimmer'd chastely down,
Blushing upon them blushing, and at once
He rose without a word and parted from her:
But when the thing was blazed about the court,
The brute world howling forced them into bonds,
And as it chanced, they are happy, being pure."

"Oh ay," said Vivien, "that were likely too.
What say ye then to fair Sir Percivale,
And of the horrid foulness that he wrought,
The saintly youth, the spotless lamb of Christ,
Or some black wether of St. Satan's fold.
What, in the precincts of the chapel-yard,
Among the knightly brasses of the graves,
And by the cold Hic Jacets of the dead!"

And Merlin answer'd, careless of her charge,
"A sober man is Percivale and pure;
But once in life was fluster'd with new wine,
Then paced for coolness in the chapel-yard;
Where one of Satan's shepherdesses caught
And meant to stamp him with her master's mark,
And that he sinn'd is not believable;
For, look upon his face!—but if he sinn'd,
The sin that practice burns into the blood,
And not the one dark hour which brings remorse,
Will brand us, after, of whose fold we be:
Or else were he, the holy king, whose hymns
Are chanted in the minster, worse than all.
But is your spleen froth'd out, or have ye more?"

And Vivien answer'd, frowning yet in wrath:
"Oh ay; what say ye to Sir Lancelot, friend?
Traitor or true? that commerce with the Queen,
I ask you, is it clamor'd by the child,
Or whisper'd in the corner? do ye know it?"

To which he answer'd sadly, "Yea, I know it.
Sir Lancelot went ambassador, at first,
To fetch her, and she watch'd him from her walls.
A rumor runs, she took him for the King,
So fixt her fancy on him: let them be.
But have ye no one word of loyal praise
For Arthur, blameless King and stainless man?"

She answer'd with a low and chuckling laugh:
"Man! is he man at all, who knows and winks?
Sees what his fair bride is and does, and winks?
By which the good King means to blind himself
And blinds himself and all the Table Round
To all the foulness that they work. Myself
Could call him (were it not for womanhood)
The pretty, popular name such manhood earns,
Could call him the main cause of all their crime:
Yea, were he not crown'd King, coward, and fool."

Then Merlin to his own heart, loathing, said:
"O true and tender! O my liege and King!
O selfless man and stainless gentleman,
Who wouldst against thine own eye-witness fain
Have all men true and leal, all women pure;
How, in the mouths of base interpreters,
From over-fineness not intelligible
To things with every sense as false and foul

As the poach'd filth that floods the middle street,
Is thy white blamelessness accounted blame!"

But Vivien, deeming Merlin overborne
By instance, recommenced, and let her tongue
Rage like a fire among the noblest names,
Polluting, and imputing her whole self,
Defaming and defacing, till she left
Not even Lancelot brave, nor Galahad clean.

Her words had issue other than she will'd.
He dragg'd his eyebrow bushes down, and made
A snowy penthouse for his hollow eyes,
And mutter'd in himself, "Tell *her* the charm!
So, if she had it, would she rail on me
To snare the next, and if she have it not,
So will she rail. What did the wanton say?
'Not mount as high:' we scarce can sink as low:
For men at most differ as heaven and earth,
But women, worst and best, as heaven and hell.
I know the Table Round, my friends of old;
All brave, and many generous, and some chaste.
She cloaks the scar of some repulse with lies;
I well believe she tempted them and fail'd,
Being so bitter: for fine plots may fail,
Tho' harlots paint their talk as well as face
With colors of the heart that are not theirs.
I will not let her know: nine tithes of times
Face-flatterer and backbiter are the same.
And they, sweet soul, that most impute a crime
Are pronest to it, and impute themselves,
Wanting the mental range; or low desire
Not to feel lowest makes them level all:
Yea, they would pare the mountain to the plain,
To leave an equal baseness; and in this
Are harlots like the crowd, that if they find
Some stain or blemish in a name of note,
Not grieving that their greatest are so small,
Inflate themselves with some insane delight,
And judge all nature from her feet of clay,
Without the will to lift her eyes, and see
Her godlike head crown'd with spiritual fire,
And touching other worlds. I am weary of her."

He spoke in words part heard, in whispers part,
Half-suffocated in the hoary fell
And many-winter'd fleece of throat and chin.
But Vivien, gathering somewhat of his mood,
And hearing "harlot" mutter'd twice or thrice,
Leapt from her session on his lap, and stood
Stiff as a viper frozen; loathsome sight,
How from the rosy lips of life and love,
Flash'd the bare-grinning skeleton of death!
White was her cheek; sharp breaths of anger puff'd
Her fairy nostril out; her hand, half-clench'd,
Went faltering sideways downward to her belt,
And feeling; had she found a dagger there
(For in a wink the false love turns to hate)
She would have stabb'd him; but she found it not:
His eye was calm. and suddenly she took
To bitter weeping like a beaten child,
A long, long weeping, not consolable,
Then her false voice made way, broken with sobs:

"O crueller than was ever told in tale,
Or sung in song! O vainly lavish'd love!
O cruel, there was nothing wild or strange,
Or seeming shameful—for what shame in love,
So love be true, and not as yours is—nothing
Poor Vivien had not done to win his trust
Who call'd her what he call'd her—all her crime,
All—all—the wish to prove him wholly hers."

She mused a little, and then clapt her hands
Together with a wailing shriek, and said:
"Stabb'd through the heart's affections to the heart!
Seethed like the kid in its own mother's milk!
Kill'd with a word worse than a life of blows!

I thought that he was gentle, being great:
O God, that I had loved a smaller man!
I should have found in him a greater heart.
Oh, I, that flattering my true passion, saw
The knights, the court, the King, dark in your light,
Who loved to make men darker than they are,
Because of that high pleasure which I had
To seat you sole upon my pedestal
Of worship—I am answer'd, and henceforth
The course of life that seem'd so flowery to me
With you for guide and master, only you,
Becomes the sea-cliff pathway broken short,
And ending in a ruin—nothing left,
But into some low cave to crawl, and there,
If the wolf spare me, weep my life away,
Kill'd with inutterable unkindliness."

She paused, she turn'd away, she hung her head.
The snake of gold slid from her hair, the braid
Slipt and uncoil'd itself, she wept afresh,
And the dark wood grew darker toward the storm
In silence, while his anger slowly died
Within him, till he let his wisdom go
For ease of heart, and half believed her true:
Call'd her to shelter in the hollow oak,
"Come from the storm," and having no reply,
Gazed at the heaving shoulder, and the face
Hand-hidden, as for utmost grief or shame;
Then thrice essay'd, by tenderest-touching terms,
To sleek her ruffled peace of mind, in vain.
At last she let herself be conquer'd by him,
And as the cageling, newly-flown, returns,
The seeming-injured, simple-hearted thing,
Came to her old perch back, and settled there.
There while she sat, half-falling from his knees,
Half-nestled at his heart, and since he saw
The slow tear creep from her closed eyelid yet,
About her, more in kindness than in love,
The gentle wizard cast a shielding arm.
But she dislink'd herself at once and rose,
Her arms upon her breast across, and stood,
A virtuous gentlewoman deeply wrong'd,
Upright and flush'd before him: then she said:

"There must be now no passages of love
Betwixt us twain henceforward evermore;
Since, if I be what I am grossly call'd,
What should be granted which your own gross heart
Would reckon worth the taking? I will go.
In truth, but one thing now—better have died
Thrice than have ask'd it once—could make me stay—
That proof of trust so often ask'd in vain!
How justly, after that vile term of yours,
I find with grief! I might believe you then,
Who knows? once more. Lo! what was once to me
Mere matter of the fancy, now hath grown
The vast necessity of heart and life.
Farewell; think gently of me, for I fear
My fate or folly, passing gayer youth
For one so old, must be to love thee still.
But ere I leave thee let me swear once more
That if I schemed against thy peace in this,
May you just heaven, that darkens o'er me, send
One flash, that, missing all things else, may make
My scheming brain a cinder, if I lie."

Scarce had she ceased, when out of heaven a bolt
(For now the storm was close above them) struck,
Furrowing a giant oak, and javelining
With darted spikes and splinters of the wood
The dark earth round. He raised his eyes and saw
The tree that shone, white-listed, thro' the gloom.
But Vivien, fearing heaven had heard her oath,
And dazzled by the livid-flickering fork,
And deafen'd with the stammering cracks and claps
That follow'd, flying back and crying out,
"O Merlin, tho' you do not love me, save,
Yet save me!" clung to him and hugg'd him close;

And call'd him dear protector in her fright,
Nor yet forgot her practice in her fright,
But wrought upon his mood and hugg'd him close.
The pale blood of the wizard at her touch
Took gayer colors, like an opal warm'd.
She blamed herself for telling hearsay tales:
She shook from fear. and for her fault she wept
Of petulancy; she call'd him lord and liege,
Her seer, her bard, her silver star of eve,
Her God, her Merlin, the one passionate love
Of her whole life; and ever overhead
I sllow'd the tempest, and the rotten branch
Snapt in the rushing of the river-rain
Above them; and in change of glare and gloom
Her eyes and neck, glittering, went and came;
Till now the storm, its burst of passion spent,
Moaning and calling out of other lands,
Had left the ravaged woodland yet once more
To peace; and what should not have been had been,
For Merlin, overtalk'd and overworn,
Had yielded, told her all the charm, and slept.

Then, in one moment, she put forth the charm
Of woven paces and of waving hands,
And in the hollow oak he lay as dead,
And lost to life and use and name and fame.

Then crying, "I have made his glory mine,"
And shrieking out, "O fool!" the harlot leapt
Adown the forest, and the thicket closed
Behind her, and the forest echoed, "fool."

LANCELOT AND ELAINE.

ELAINE the fair, Elaine the lovable,
Elaine, the lily maid of Astolat,
High in her chamber up a tower to the east
Guarded the sacred shield of Lancelot;
Which first she placed where morning's earliest ray
Might strike it, and awake her with the gleam;
Then fearing rust or soilure, fashion'd for it
A case of silk, and braided thereupon
All the devices blazon'd on the shield
In their own tinct, and added, of her wit,
A border fantasy of branch and flower,
And yellow-throated nestling in the nest.
Nor rested thus content, but day by day,
Leaving her household and good father, climb'd
That eastern tower, and entering, barr'd her door,
Stript off the case, and read the naked shield,
Now guess'd a hidden meaning in his arms,
Now made a pretty history to herself
Of every dint a sword had beaten in it,
And every scratch a lance had made upon it,
Conjecturing when and where: this cut is fresh;
That ten years back; this dealt him at Caerlyle;
That at Caerleon; this at Camelot:
And ah, God's mercy, what a stroke was there!
And here a thrust that might have kill'd, but God
Broke the strong lance, and roll'd his enemy down,
And saved him: so she lived in fantasy.

How came the lily maid by that good shield
Of Lancelot, she that knew not ev'n his name?
He left it with her, when he rode to tilt
For the great diamond in the diamond jousts,
Which Arthur had ordain'd, and by that name
Had named them, since a diamond was the prize.

For Arthur, long before they crown'd him King,
Roving the trackless realms of Lyonnesse,
Had found a glen, gray boulder, and black tarn.
A horror lived about the tarn, and clave
Like its own mists to all the mountain side:
For here two brothers, one a king, had met

And fought together; but their names were lost ·
And each had slain his brother at a blow;
And down they fell and made the glen abhorr'd:
And there they lay till all their bones were bleach'd,
And lichen'd into color with the crags:
And he that once was king had on a crown
Of diamonds, one in front, and four aside.
And Arthur came, and laboring up the pass,
All in a misty moonshine, unawares
Had trodden that crown'd skeleton, and the skull
Brake from the nape, and from the skull the crown
Roll'd into light, and turning on its rims,
Fled like a glittering rivulet to the tarn:
And down the shingly scaur he plunged, and caught,
And set it on his head, and in his heart
Heard murmurs, "Lo, thou likewise shalt be King."

Thereafter, when a King, he had the gems
Pluck'd from the crown, and show'd them to his knights,
Saying, "These jewels, whereupon I chanced
Divinely, are the kingdom's, not the King's—
For public use: henceforward let there be,
Once every year, a joust for one of these:
For so by nine years' proof we needs must learn
Which is our mightiest, and ourselves shall grow
In use of arms and manhood, till we drive
The heathen, who, some say, shall rule the land
Hereafter, which God hinder." Thus he spoke:
And eight years past, eight jousts had been, and still
Had Lancelot won the diamond of the year,
With purpose to present them to the Queen,
When all were won; but meaning all at once
To snare her royal fancy with a boon
Worth half her realm, had never spoken word.

Now for the central diamond and the last
And largest, Arthur, holding then his court
Hard on the river, nigh the place which now
Is this world's hugest, let proclaim a joust
At Camelot, and when the time drew nigh
Spake (for she had been sick) to Guinevere,
"Are you so sick, my Queen, you cannot move
To these fair jousts?" "Yea, lord," she said, "ye know it."
"Then will ye miss," he answer'd, "the great deeds
Of Lancelot, and his prowess in the lists,
A sight ye love to look on." And the Queen
Lifted her eyes, and they dwelt languidly
On Lancelot, where he stood beside the King.
He, thinking that he read her meaning there,
"Stay with me, I am sick; my love is more
Than many diamonds," yielded; and a heart
Love-loyal to the least wish of the Queen
(However much he yearn'd to make complete
The tale of diamonds for his destined boon)
Urged him to speak against the truth, and say,
"Sir King, mine ancient wound is hardly whole,
And lets me from the saddle;" and the King
Glanced first at him, then her, and went his way.
No sooner gone than suddenly she began:

"To blame, my lord Sir Lancelot, much to blame!
Why go ye not to these fair jousts? the knights
Are half of them our enemies, and the crowd
Will murmur, "Lo, the shameless ones, who take
Their pastime now the trustful King is gone!'"
Then Lancelot, vext at having lied in vain:
"Are ye so wise? ye were not once so wise,
My Queen, that summer, when ye loved me first.
Then of the crowd ye took no more account
Than of the myriad cricket of the mead,
When its own voice clings to each blade of grass,
And every voice is nothing. As to knights,
Them surely can I silence with all ease.
But now my loyal worship is allow'd
Of all men: many a bard, without offence,
Has link'd our names together in his lay,

Lancelot, the flower of bravery; Guinevere,
The pearl of beauty: and our knights at feast
Have pledged us in this union, while the King
Would listen smiling. How then? is there more?
Has Arthur spoken aught? or would yourself,
Now weary of my service and devoir,
Henceforth be truer to your faultless lord?"

She broke into a little scornful laugh:
"Arthur, my lord, Arthur, the faultless King,
That passionate perfection, my good lord—
But who can gaze upon the Sun in heaven?
He never spake word of reproach to me,
He never had a glimpse of mine untruth,
He cares not for me: only here to-day
There gleam'd a vague suspicion in his eyes:
Some meddling rogue has tamper'd with him—else
Rapt in this fancy of his Table Round,
And swearing men to vows impossible,
To make them like himself: but, friend, to me
He is all fault who has no fault at all:
For who loves me must have a touch of earth;
The low sun makes the color: I am yours.
Not Arthur's, as ye know, save by the bond.
And therefore hear my words: go to the jousts:
The tiny-trumpeting gnat can break our dream
When sweetest; and the vermin voices here
May buzz so loud—we scorn them, but they sting."

Then answer'd Lancelot, the chief of knights:
"And with what face, after my pretext made,
Shall I appear, O Queen, at Camelot, I
Before a King who honors his own word,
As if it were his God's?"

                          "Yea," said the Queen,
"A moral child without the craft to rule,
Else had he not lost me: but listen to me,
If I must find you wit: we hear it said
That men go down before your spear at a touch,
But knowing you are Lancelot; your great name,
This conquers: hide it, therefore; go unknown:
Win! by this kiss you will: and our true King
Will then allow your pretext, O my knight,
As all for glory; for to speak him true,
Ye know right well, how meek soe'er he seem,
No keener hunter after glory breathes.
He loves it in his knights more than himself:
They prove to him his work: win and return."

Then got Sir Lancelot suddenly to horse,
Wroth at himself. Not willing to be known,
He left the barren-beaten thoroughfare,
Chose the green path that show'd the rarer foot,
And there among the solitary downs,
Full often lost in fancy, lost his way;
Till as he traced a faintly-shadow'd track,
That all in loops and links among the dales
Ran to the castle of Astolat, he saw
Fired from the west, far on a hill, the towers.
Thither he made, and blew the gateway horn.
Then came an old, dumb, myriad-wrinkled man,
Who let him into lodging and disarm'd.
And Lancelot marvell'd at the wordless man;
And issuing, found the Lord of Astolat,
With two strong sons, Sir Torre and Sir Lavaine,
Moving to meet him in the castle court:
And close behind them stept the lily maid,
Elaine, his daughter: mother of the house
There was not: some light jest among them rose
With laughter dying down as the great knight
Approach'd them: then the Lord of Astolat:
"Whence comest thou, my guest, and by what name
Livest between the lips? for by thy state
And presence I might guess the chief of those
After the King, who eat in Arthur's halls.
Him have I seen: the rest, his Table Round,
Known as they are, to me they are unknown."

Then answer'd Lancelot, the chief of knights:
"Known am I, and of Arthur's hall, and known,
What I by mere mischance have brought, my shield.
But since I go to joust as one unknown
At Camelot for the diamond, ask me not,
Hereafter ye shall know me—and the shield—
I pray you lend me one, if such you have,
Blank, or at least with some device not mine."

Then said the Lord of Astolat, "Here is Torre's:
Hurt in his first tilt was my son, Sir Torre.
And so, God wot, his shield is blank enough.
His ye can have." Then added plain Sir Torre,
"Yea, since I cannot use it, ye may have it."
Here laugh'd the father, saying. "Fie, Sir Churl,
Is that an answer for a noble knight?
Allow him! but Lavaine, my younger here,
He is so full of lustihood, he will ride,
Joust for it, and win, and bring it in an hour,
And set it in this damsel's golden hair,
To make her thrice as willful as before."

"Nay, father, nay, good father, shame me not
Before this noble knight," said young Lavaine,
"For nothing. Surely I but play'd on Torre:
He seem'd so sullen, vext he could not go:
A jest, no more! for, knight, the maiden dreamt
That some one put this diamond in her hand,
And that it was too slippery to be held,
And slipt and fell into some pool or stream,
The castle-well, belike: and then I said
That if I went, and if I fought and won it
(But all was jest and joke among ourselves),
Then must she keep it safelier. All was jest.
But, father, give me leave, an if he will,
To ride to Camelot with this noble knight:
Win shall I not, but do my best to win:
Young as I am, yet would I do my best."

"So ye will grace me," answer'd Lancelot,
Smiling a moment, "with your fellowship
O'er these waste downs whereon I lost myself.
Then were I glad of you as guide and friend:
And you shall win this diamond—as I hear,
It is a fair large diamond—if ye may,
And yield it to this maiden, if ye will."
"A fair large diamond," added plain Sir Torre.
"Such be for queens, and not for simple maids."
Then she, who held her eyes upon the ground.
Elaine, and heard her name so tost about,
Flush'd slightly at the slight disparagement
Before the stranger knight, who, looking at her,
Full courtly, yet not falsely, thus return'd:
"If what is fair be but for what is fair,
And only queens are to be counted so,
Rash were my judgment then, who deem this maid
Might wear as fair a jewel as is on earth,
Not violating the bond of like to like."

He spoke and ceased: the lily maid Elaine,
Won by the mellow voice before she look'd,
Lifted her eyes, and read his lineaments.
The great and guilty love he bare the Queen,
In battle with the love he bare his lord,
Had marr'd his face, and mark'd it ere his time.
Another sinning on such heights with one,
The flower of all the west and all the world,
Had been the sleeker for it: but in him
His mood was often like a fiend, and rose
And drove him into wastes and solitudes
For agony, who was yet a living soul,
Marr'd as he was, he seem'd the goodliest man
That ever among ladies ate in hall,
And noblest, when she lifted up her eyes.
However marr'd, of more than twice her years,
Seam'd with an ancient swordcut on the cheek,
And bruised and bronzed, she lifted up her eyes
And loved him, with that love which was her doom.

Then the great knight, the darling of the court,
Loved of the loveliest, into that rude hall
Stept with all grace, and not with half disdain
Hid under grace, as in a smaller time,
But kindly man moving among his kind:
Whom they with meats and vintage of their best,
And talk and minstrel melody entertain'd.
And much they ask'd of court and Table Round,
And ever well and readily answer'd he:
But Lancelot, when they glanced at Guinevere,
Suddenly speaking of the wordless man,·
Heard from the Baron that, ten years before,
The heathen caught and reft him of his tongue.
"He learnt and warn'd me of their fierce design
Against my house, and him they caught and maim'd;
But I, my sons, and little daughter fled
From bonds or death, and dwelt among the woods
By the great river in a boatman's hut.
Dull days were those, till our good Arthur broke
The Pagan yet once more on Badon hill."

"Oh, there, great lord, doubtless," Lavaine said,
     rapt,
By all the sweet and sudden passion of youth
Toward greatness in its elder, "you have fought.
O tell us—for we live apart—you know
Of Arthur's glorious wars." And Lancelot spoke
And answer'd him at full, as having been
With Arthur in the fight which all day long
Rang by the white mouth of the violent Glem;
And in the four loud battles by the shore
Of Duglas; that on Bassa; then the war
That thunder'd in and out the gloomy skirts
Of Celidon the forest; and again
By castle Gurnion, where the glorious King
Had on his cuirass worn our Lady's Head,
Carved of one emerald centred in a sun
Of silver rays, that lighten'd as he breath'd;
And at Caerleon had he help'd his lord,
When the strong neighings of the wild white Horse
Set every gilded parapet shuddering;
And up in Agned-Cathregonion too,
And down the waste sand-shores of Trath Treroit,
Where many a heathen fell; "and on the mount
Of Badon I myself beheld the King
Charge at the head of all his Table Round,
And all his legions crying Christ and him,
And break them; and I saw him, after, stand
High on a heap of slain, from spur to plume
Red as the rising sun with heathen blood,
And seeing me, with a great voice he cried,
'They are broken, they are broken!' for the King,
However mild he seems at home, nor cares
For triumph in our mimic wars, the jousts—
For if his own knight cast him down, he laughs,
Saying, his knights are better men than he—
Yet in this heathen war the fire of God
Fills him: I never saw his like: there lives
No greater leader."

                    While he utter'd this,
Low to her own heart said the lily maid,
"Save your great self, fair lord;" and when he fell
From talk of war to traits of pleasantry—
Being mirthful he, but in a stately kind—
She still took note that when the living smile
Died from his lips, across him came a cloud
Of melancholy severe, from which again,
Whenever, in her hovering to and fro,
The lily maid had striven to make him cheer,
There brake a sudden-beaming tenderness
Of manners and of nature: and she thought
That all was nature, all, perchance, for her.
And all night long his face before her lived,
As when a painter, poring on a face,
Divinely thro' all hindrance finds the man
Behind it, and so paints him that his face,
The shape and color of a mind and life,

Lives for his children, ever at its best
And fullest;·so the face before her lived,
Dark-splendid, speaking in the silence, full
Of noble things, and held her from her sleep.
Till rathe she rose, half-cheated in the thought
She needs must bid farewell to sweet Lavaine.
First as in fear, step after step, she stole
Down the long tower-stairs, hesitating:
Anon, she heard Sir Lancelot cry in the court,
"This shield, my friend, where is it?" and Lavaine
Past inward, as she came from out the tower.
There to his proud horse Lancelot turn'd, and
     smooth'd
The glossy shoulder, humming to himself.
Half-envious of the flattering hand, she drew
Nearer and stood. He look'd, and more amazed
Than if seven men had set upon him, saw
The maiden standing in the dewy light.
He had not dream'd she was so beautiful.
Then came on him a sort of sacred fear,
For silent, tho' he greeted her, she stood
Rapt on his face as if it were a God's.
Suddenly flash'd on her a wild desire,
That he should wear her favor at the tilt.
She braved a riotous heart in asking for it.
"Fair lord, whose name I know not—noble it is,
I well believe, the noblest—will you wear
My favor at this tourney?" "Nay," said he,
"Fair lady, since I never yet have worn
Favor of any lady in the lists.
Such is my wont, as those who know me, know."
"Yea, so," she answer'd; "then in wearing mine
Needs must be lesser likelihood, noble lord,
That those who know should know you." And he
     turn'd
Her counsel up and down within his mind,
And found it true, and answer'd, "True, my child.
Well, I will wear it: fetch it out to me:
What is it?" and she told him, "A red sleeve
Broider'd with pearls," and brought it: then he
     bound
Her token on his helmet, with a smile
Saying, "I never yet have done so much
For any maiden living," and the blood
Sprang to her face and fill'd her with delight;
But left her all the paler, when Lavaine
Returning, brought the yet unblazon'd shield,
His brother's: which he gave to Lancelot,
Who parted with his own to fair Elaine:
"Do me this grace, my child, to have my shield
In keeping till I come." "A grace to me,"
She answer'd, "twice to-day. I am your squire!"
Whereat Lavaine said, laughing, "Lily maid,
For fear our people call you lily maid
In earnest, let me bring your color back:
Once, twice, and thrice: now get you hence to bed:"
So kiss'd her, and Sir Lancelot his own hand,
And thus they moved away: she stay'd a minute,
Then made a sudden step to the gate, and there—
Her bright hair blown about the serious face
Yet rosy-kindled with her brother's kiss—
Paused by the gateway, standing near the shield
In silence, while she watch'd their arms far-off
Sparkle, until they dipt below the downs.
Then to her tower she climb'd, and took the shield,
There kept it, and so lived in fantasy.

Meanwhile the new companions past away
Far o'er the long backs of the bushless downs,
To where Sir Lancelot knew there lived a knight
Not far from Camelot, now for forty years
A hermit, who had pray'd, labor'd, and pray'd,
And ever laboring, had scoop'd himself
In the white rock a chapel and a hall
On massive columns, like a shorecliff cave,
And cells and chambers: all were fair and dry;
The green light from the meadows underneath
Struck up and lived along the milky roofs;

And in the meadows tremulous aspen-trees
And poplars made a noise of falling showers,
And thither wending there that night they bode.

But when the next day broke from underground,
And shot red fire and shadows thro' the cave,
They rose, heard mass, broke fast, and rode away:
Then Lancelot saying, "Hear, but hold my name
Hidden, you ride with Lancelot of the Lake,"
Abash'd Lavaine, whose instant reverence,
Dearer to true young hearts than their own praise,
But left him leave to stammer, "Is it indeed?"
And after muttering, "The great Lancelot,"
At last he got his breath and answer'd. "One,
One have I seen—that other, our liege lord,
The dread Pendragon, Britain's King of kings,
Of whom the people talk mysteriously,
He will be there—then were I stricken blind
That minute, I might say that I had seen."

So spake Lavaine, and when they reach'd the lists
By Camelot in the meadow, let his eyes
Run thro' the peopled gallery which half round
Lay like a rainbow fall'n upon the grass,
Until they found the clear-faced King, who sat
Robed in red samite, easily to be known,
Since to his crown the golden dragon clung,
And down his robe the dragon writhed in gold,
And from the carven-work behind him crept
Two dragons gilded, sloping down to make
Arms for his chair, while all the rest of them
Thro' knots and loops and folds innumerable
Fled ever thro' the woodwork, till they found
The new design wherein they lost themselves,
Yet with all ease, so tender was the work:
And, in the costly canopy o'er him set,
Blazed the last diamond of the nameless king.

Then Lancelot answer'd young Lavaine and said,
"Me you call great: mine is the firmer seat,
The truer lance: but there is many a youth
Now crescent, who will come to all I am
And overcome it; and in me there dwells
No greatness, save it be some far-off touch
Of greatness to know well I am not great:
There is the man." And Lavaine gaped upon him
As on a thing miraculous, and anon
The trumpets blew; and then did either side,
They that assail'd, and they that held the lists,
Set lance in rest, strike spur, suddenly move,
Meet in the midst, and there so furiously
Shock, that a man far-off might well perceive,
If any man that day were left afield,
The hard earth shake, and a low thunder of arms.
And Lancelot bode a little, till he saw
Which were the weaker; then he hurl'd into it
Against the stronger: little need to speak
Of Lancelot in his glory! King, duke, earl,
Count, baron—whom he smote, he overthrew.

But in the field were Lancelot's kith and kin,
Ranged with the Table Round that held the lists,
Strong men, and wrathful that a stranger knight
Should do and almost overdo the deeds
Of Lancelot; and one said to the other, "Lo!
What is he? I do not mean the force alone—
The grace and versatility of the man!
Is it not Lancelot?" "When has Lancelot worn
Favor of any lady in the lists?
Not such his wont, as we, that know him, know."
"How then? who then?" a fury seized them all,
A fiery family passion for the name
Of Lancelot, and a glory one with theirs.
They couch'd their spears and prick'd their steeds,
        and thus,
Their plumes driv'n backward by the wind they made
In moving, all together down upon him
Bare, as a wild wave in the wide North-sea,

Green-glimmering toward the summit, bears, with all
Its stormy crests that smoke against the skies,
Down on a bark, and overbears the bark,
And him that helms it, so they overbore
Sir Lancelot and his charger, and a spear
Down-glancing lamed the charger, and a spear
Prick'd sharply his own cuirass, and the head
Pierced thro' his side, and there snapt, and remain'd.

Then Sir Lavaine did well and worshipfully;
He bore a knight of old repute to the earth,
And brought his horse to Lancelot where he lay.
He up the side, sweating with agony, got,
But thought to do while he might yet endure,
And being lustily holpen by the rest,
His party—tho' it seem'd half-miracle
To those he fought with—drave his kith and kin,
And all the Table Round that held the lists,
Back to the barrier; then the trumpets blew
Proclaiming his the prize, who wore the sleeve
Of scarlet, and the pearls; and all the knights,
His party, cried, "Advance and take thy prize,
The diamond;" but he answer'd, "Diamond me
No diamonds! for God's love, a little air!
Prize me no prizes, for my prize is death!
Hence will I, and I charge you, follow me not."

He spoke, and vanish'd suddenly from the field
With young Lavaine into the poplar grove.
There from his charger down he slid, and sat,
Gasping to Sir Lavaine, "Draw the lance-head:"
"Ah, my sweet lord Sir Lancelot," said Lavaine,
"I dread me, if I draw it, you will die."
But he, "I die already with it: draw—
Draw,"—and Lavaine drew, and Sir Lancelot gave
A marvelous great shriek and ghastly groan,
And half his blood burst forth, and down he sank
For the pure pain, and wholly swoon'd away.
Then came the hermit out and bare him in,
There stanch'd his wound; and there, in daily doubt
Whether to live or die, for many a week
Hid from the wide world's rumor by the grove
Of poplars with their noise of falling showers,
And ever-tremulous aspen-trees, he lay.

But on that day when Lancelot fled the lists,
His party, knights of utmost North and West,
Lords of waste marches, kings of desolate isles,
Came round their great Pendragon, saying to him,
"Lo, Sire, our knight, thro' whom we won the day,
Hath gone sore wounded, and hath left his prize
Untaken, crying that his prize is death."
"Heaven hinder," said the King, "that such an one,
So great a knight as we have seen to-day—
He seem'd to me another Lancelot—
Yea, twenty times I thought him Lancelot—
He must not pass uncared for. Wherefore, rise,
O Gawain, and ride forth and find the knight.
Wounded and wearied, needs must he be near.
I charge you that you get at once to horse.
And, knights and kings, there breathes not one of you
Will deem this prize of ours is rashly given:
His prowess was too wondrous. We will do him
No customary honor: since the knight
Came not to us, of us to claim the prize,
Ourselves will send it after. Rise and take
This diamond, and deliver it, and return,
And bring us where he is, and how he fares,
And cease not from your quest until ye find."

So saying, from the carven flower above,
To which it made a restless heart, he took,
And gave, the diamond: then from where he sat
At Arthur's right, with smiling face arose,
With smiling face and frowning heart, a Prince
In the mid might and flourish of his May,
Gawain, surnamed The Courteous, fair and strong,
And after Lancelot, Tristram, and Geraint

And Gareth, a good knight, but therewithal
Sir Modred's brother, and the child of Lot,
Nor often loyal to his word, and now
Wroth that the King's command to sally forth
In quest of whom he knew not, made him leave
The banquet and concourse of knights and kings.

So all in wrath he got to horse and went;
While Arthur to the banquet, dark in mood,
Past, thinking, "Is it Lancelot who hath come
Despite the wound he spake of, all for gain
Of glory, and hath added wound to wound,
And ridd'n away to die?" So fear'd the King,
And, after two days' tarriance there, return'd.
Then when he saw the Queen, embracing, ask'd,
"Love, are you yet so sick?" "Nay, lord," she said.
"And where is Lancelot?" Then the Queen, amazed,
"Was he not with you? won he not your prize?"
"Nay, but one like him." "Why, that like was he."
And when the King demanded how she knew,
Said, "Lord, no sooner had ye parted from us,
Than Lancelot told me of a common talk
That men went down before his spear at a touch,
But knowing he was Lancelot; his great name
Conquer'd; and therefore would he hide his name
From all men, ev'n the King, and to this end
Had made the pretext of a hindering wound,
That he might joust unknown of all, and learn
If his old prowess were in aught decay'd;
And added, 'Our true Arthur, when he learns,
Will well allow my pretext, as for gain
Of purer glory.'"

        Then replied the King:
"Far lovelier in our Lancelot had it been,
In lieu of idly dallying with the truth,
To have trusted me as he hath trusted thee.
Surely his King and most familiar friend
Might well have kept his secret. True, indeed,
Albeit I know my knights fantastical,
So fine a fear in our large Lancelot
Must needs have moved my laughter: now remains
But little cause for laughter: his own kin—
Ill news, my Queen, for all who love him, this !—
His kith and kin, not knowing, set upon him;
So that he went sore wounded from the field:
Yet good news too: for goodly hopes are mine
That Lancelot is no more a lonely heart.
He wore, against his wont, upon his helm
A sleeve of scarlet, broider'd with great pearls,
Some gentle maiden's gift."

        "Yea, lord," she said,
"Thy hopes are mine." and saying that, she choked,
And sharply turn'd about to hide her face,
Past to her chamber, and there flung herself
Down on the great King's couch, and writhed upon it,
And clench'd her fingers till they bit the palm,
And shriek'd out, "Traitor," to the unhearing wall,
Then flash'd into wild tears, and rose again,
And moved about her palace, proud and pale.

Gawain the while thro' all the region round
Rode with his diamond, wearied of the quest,
Touch'd at all points. except the poplar grove,
And came at last, tho' late, to Astolat:
Whom, glittering in enamell'd arms, the maid
Glanced at, and cried, "What news from Camelot,
        lord?
What of the knight with the red sleeve?"   "He
        won."
"I knew it," she said. "But parted from the jousts
Hurt in the side," whereat she caught her breath;
Thro' her own side she felt the sharp lance go;
Thereon she smote her hand: wellnigh she swoon'd:
And, while he gazed wonderingly at her, came
The Lord of Astolat out, to whom the Prince
Reported who he was, and on what quest

Sent, that he bore the prize and could not find
The victor, but had ridd'n a random round
To seek him, and had wearied of the search.
To whom the Lord of Astolat, "Bide with us,
And ride no more at random, noble Prince !
Here was the knight, and here he left a shield;
This will he send or come for: furthermore,
Our son is with him; we shall hear anon,
Needs must we hear." To this the courteous Prince
Accorded with his wonted courtesy,
Courtesy with a touch of traitor in it,
And stay'd: and cast his eyes on fair Elaine:
Where could be found face daintier? then her shape,
From forehead down to foot, perfect—again
From foot to forehead exquisitely turn'd:
"Well—if I bide, lo! this wild flower for me !"
And oft they met among the garden yews,
And there he set himself to play upon her
With sallying wit, free flashes from a height
Above her, graces of the court, and songs,
Sighs, and slow smiles, and golden eloquence
And amorous adulation, till the maid
Rebell'd against it, saying to him, "Prince,
O loyal nephew of our noble King,
Why ask you not to see the shield he left,
Whence you might learn his name? Why slight your
        King
And lose the quest he sent yon on, and prove
No surer than our falcon yesterday,
Who lost the hern we slipt him at, and went
To all the winds?" "Nay, by mine head," said he,
"I lose it, as we lose the lark in heaven,
O damsel, in the light of your blue eyes;
But an ye will it, let me see the shield."
And when the shield was brought, and Gawain saw
Sir Lancelot's azure lions, crown'd with gold,
Ramp in the field, he smote his thigh, and mock'd:
"Right was the King ! our Lancelot ! that true
        man !"
"And right was I," she answer'd merrily, "I,
Who dream'd my knight the greatest knight of all."
"And if I dream'd," said Gawain, "that yon love
This greatest knight, your pardon ! lo, ye know it,
Speak therefore: shall I waste myself in vain ?"
Full simple was her answer, "What know I ?
My brethren have been all my fellowship;
And I, when often they have talk'd of love,
Wish'd it had been my mother, for they talk'd,
Meseem'd, of what they knew not; so myself—
I know not if I know what true love is,
But if I know, then, if I love not him,
I know there is none other I can love."
"Yea, by God's death," said he, "ye love him well,
But would not, knew ye what all others know,
And whom he loves." "So be it," cried Elaine,
And lifted her fair face and moved away:
But he pursued her, calling, "Stay a little !
One golden minute's grace ! he wore your sleeve:
Would he break faith with one I may not name?
Must our true man change like a leaf at last?
Nay—like enow: why, then far be it from me
To cross our mighty Lancelot in his loves !
And, damsel, for I deem you know full well
Where your great knight is hidden. let me leave
My quest with you; the diamond also: here !
For if you love, it will be sweet to give it;
And if he love, it will be sweet to have it
From your own hand; and whether he love or not,
A diamond is a diamond. Fare you well
A thousand times !—a thousand times farewell !
Yet, if he love, and his love hold, we two
May meet at court hereafter: there, I think,
So ye will learn the courtesies of the court,
We two shall know each other."

                        Then he gave,
And slightly kiss'd the hand to which he gave,
The diamond, and all wearied of the quest,

Leapt on his horse, and carolling as he went
A true-love ballad, lightly rode away.

Thence to the court he past; there told the King
What the King knew, "Sir Lancelot is the knight."
And added, "Sire, my liege, so much I learnt;
But fail'd to find him, tho' I rode all round
The region : but I lighted on the maid
Whose sleeve he wore; she loves him: and to her,
Deeming our courtesy is the truest law,
I gave the diamond: she will render it;
For by mine head she knows his hiding-place."

The seldom-frowning King frown'd, and replied,
"Too courteous truly ! ye shall go no more
On quest of mine, seeing that ye forget
Obedience is the courtesy due to kings."

He spake and parted. Wroth, but all in awe,
For twenty strokes of the blood, without a word,
Linger'd that other, staring after him ;
Then shook his hair, strode off, and buzz'd abroad
About the maid of Astolat and her love.
All ears were prick'd at once, all tongues were loosed:
"The maid of Astolat loves Sir Lancelot,
Sir Lancelot loves the maid of Astolat."
Some read the King's face, some the Queen's, and all
Had marvel what the maid might be, but most
Predoom'd her as unworthy. One old dame
Came suddenly on the Queen with the sharp news.
She, that had heard the noise of it before,
But sorrowing Lancelot should have stoop'd so low,
Marr'd her friend's aim with pale tranquillity.
So ran the tale like fire about the court,
Fire in dry stubble a nine-days' wonder flared :
Till ev'n the knights at banquet twice or thrice
Forgot to drink to Lancelot and the Queen,
And pledging Lancelot and the lily maid
Smiled at each other, while the Queen, who sat
With lips severely placid, felt the knot
Climb in her throat, and with her feet unseen
Crush'd the wild passion out against the floor
Beneath the banquet, where the meats became
As wormwood, and she hated all who pledged.

But far away the maid in Astolat,
Her guiltless rival, she that ever kept
The one-day-seen Sir Lancelot in her heart,
Crept to her father, while he mused alone,
Sat on his knee, stroked his gray face and said,
"Father, you call me wilful, and the fault
Is yours who let me have my will, and now,
Sweet father, will you let me lose my wits?"
"Nay," said he, "surely." "Wherefore, let me hence,"
She answer'd, "and find out our dear Lavaine."
"Ye will not lose your wits for dear Lavaine:
Bide," answer'd he : "we needs must hear anon
Of him, and of that other." "Ay," she said,
"And of that other, for I needs must hence
And find that other, wheresoe'er he be,
And with mine own hand give his diamond to him,
Lest I be found as faithless in the quest
As you proud Prince who left the quest to me.
Sweet father, I behold him in my dreams
Gaunt as it were the skeleton of himself,
Death-pale, for lack of gentle maiden's aid.
The gentler born the maiden, the more bound,
My father, to be sweet and serviceable
To noble knights in sickness, as ye know,
When these have worn their tokens: let me hence,
I pray you." Then her father nodding said,
"Ay, ay, the diamond: wit ye well, my child,
Right fain were I to learn this knight were whole,
Being our greatest: yea, and you must give it—
And sure I think this fruit is hung too high
For any mouth to gape for save a queen's—
Nay, I mean nothing: so then, get you gone,
Being so very wilful, you must go."

Lightly, her suit allow'd, she slipt away,
And while she made her ready for her ride,
Her father's latest word humm'd in her ear,
"Being so very wilful you must go,"
And changed itself, and echo'd in her heart,
"Being so very wilful you must die."
But she was happy enough and shook it off,
As we shake off the bee that buzzes at us;
And in her heart she answer'd it and said,
"What matter, so I help him back to life?"
Then far away, with good Sir Torre for guide,
Rode o'er the long backs of the bushless downs
To Camelot, and before the city-gates
Came on her brother with a happy face
Making a roan horse caper and curvet
For pleasure all about a field of flowers,
Whom when she saw, "Lavaine," she cried, "Le
vaine,
How fares my lord Sir Lancelot?" He amazed,
"Torre and Elaine! why here? Sir Lancelot!
How know ye my lord's name is Lancelot?"
But when the maid had told him all her tale,
Then turn'd Sir Torre, and being in his moods
Left them, and under the strange-statued gate,
Where Arthur's wars were render'd mystically,
Past up the still rich city to his kin,
His own far blood, which dwelt at Camelot;
And her, Lavaine across the poplar grove
Led to the caves: there first she saw the casque
Of Lancelot on the wall: her scarlet sleeve,
Tho' carved and cut, and half the pearls away,
Stream'd from it still; and in her heart she laugh'd,
Because he had not loosed it from his helm,
But meant once more perchance to tourney in it.
And when they gain'd the cell wherein he slept,
His battle-writhen arms and mighty hands
Lay naked on the wolfskin, and a dream
Of dragging down his enemy made them move.
Then she that saw him lying unsleek, unshorn,
Gaunt as it were the skeleton of himself,
Uttered a little tender dolorous cry.
The sound not wonted in a place so still
Woke the sick knight, and while he roll'd his eyes
Yet blank from sleep, she started to him, saying,
"Your prize the diamond sent you by the King:"
His eyes glisten'd: she fancied "Is it for me?"
And when the maid had told him all the tale
Of King and Prince, the diamond sent, the quest
Assign'd to her not worthy of it, she knelt
Full lowly by the corners of his bed,
And laid the diamond in his open hand.
Her face was near, and as we kiss the child
That does the task assign'd, he kiss'd her face.
At once she slipt like water to the floor.
"Alas," he said, "your ride hath wearied you.
Rest must you have." "No rest for me," she said ;
"Nay, for near you, fair lord. I am at rest."
What might she mean by that ? his large, black eyes,
Yet larger thro' his leanness, dwelt upon her,
Till all her heart's sad secret blazed itself
In the heart's colors on her simple face ;
And Lancelot look'd and was perplext in mind,
And being weak in body said no more ;
But did not love the color ; woman's love,
Save one, he not regarded, and so turn'd,
Sighing, and feign'd a sleep until he slept.

Then rose Elaine and glided thro' the fields,
And past beneath the weirdly-sculptured gates
Far up the dim rich city to her kin ;
There bode the night : but woke with dawn, and past
Down thro' the dim rich city to the fields,
Thence to the cave: so day by day she past
In either twilight ghost-like to and fro
Gliding, and every day she tended him,
And likewise many a night : and Lancelot
Would, tho' he call'd his wound a little hurt
Whereof he should be quickly whole, at times

Brain-feverous in his heat and agony, seem
Uncourteous, even he: but the meek maid
Sweetly forbore him ever, being to him
Meeker than any child to a rough nurse,
Milder than any mother to a sick child,
And never woman yet, since man's first fall,
Did kindlier unto man, but her deep love
Upbore her; till the hermit, skill'd in all
The simples and the science of that time,
Told him that her fine care had saved his life.
And the sick man forgot her simple blush,
Would call her friend and sister, sweet Elaine,
Would listen for her coming and regret
Her parting step, and held her tenderly,
And loved her with all love except the love
Of man and woman when they love their best,
Closest and sweetest, and had died the death
In any knightly fashion for her sake.
And peradventure had he seen her first
She might have made this and that other world
Another world for the sick man; but now
The shackles of an old love straiten'd him,
His honor rooted in dishonor stood,
And faith unfaithful kept him falsely true.

Yet the great knight in his mid-sickness made
Full many a holy vow and pure resolve.
These, as but born of sickness, could not live:
For when the blood ran lustier in him again,
Full often the bright image of one face,
Making a treacherous quiet in his heart,
Dispersed his resolution like a cloud.
Then if the maiden, while that ghostly grace
Beam'd on his fancy, spoke, he answer'd not,
Or short and coldly, and she knew right well
What the rough sickness meant, but what this meant
She knew not, and the sorrow dimm'd her sight,
And drave her ere her time across the fields
Far into the rich city, where alone
She murmur'd, "Vain, in vain: it cannot be.
He will not love me: how then? must I die?"
Then as a little helpless innocent bird,
That has but one plain passage of few notes,
Will sing the simple passage o'er and o'er
For all an April morning, till the ear
Wearies to hear it, so the simple maid '
Went half the night repeating, "Must I die?"
And now to right she turn'd, and now to left,
And found no ease in turning or in rest;
And "Him or death," she mutter'd, "death or him,"
Again and like a burthen, "Him or death."

But when Sir Lancelot's deadly hurt was whole,
To Astolat returning rode the three.
There morn by morn, arraying her sweet self
In that wherein she deem'd she look'd her best,
She came before Sir Lancelot, for she thought,
"If I be loved, these are my festal robes,
If not, the victim's flowers before he fall."
And Lancelot ever prest upon the maid
That she should ask some goodly gift of him
For her own self or hers; "and do not shun
To speak the wish most near to your true heart;
Such service have ye done me, that I make
My will of yours, and Prince and Lord am I
In mine own land, and what I will I can."
Then like a ghost she lifted up her face,
But like a ghost without the power to speak.
And Lancelot saw that she withheld her wish,
And bode among them yet a little space
Till he should learn it; and one morn it chanced
He found her in among the garden yews,
And said, "Delay no longer, speak your wish,
Seeing I go to-day:" then out she brake:
"Going? and we shall never see you more.
And I must die for want of one bold word."
"Speak: that I live to hear," he said, "is yours."
Then suddenly and passionately she spoke:

"I have gone mad. I love you: let me die."
"Ah, sister," answer'd Lancelot, "what is this?"
And innocently extending her white arms,
"Your love," she said, "your love—to be your wife.'
And Lancelot answer'd, "Had I chosen to wed,
I had been wedded earlier, sweet Elaine:
But now there never will be wife of mine." '
"No, no," she cried, "I care not to be wife,
But to be with you still, to see your face,
To serve you, and to follow you thro' the world."
And Lancelot answer'd, "Nay, the world, the world,
All ear and eye, with such a stupid heart
To interpret ear and eye, and such a tongue
To blare its own interpretation—nay.
Full ill then should I quit your brother's love,
And your good father's kindness." And she said,
"Not to be with you, not to see your face—
Alas for me then, my good days are done."
"Nay, noble maid," he answer'd, "ten times nay!
This is not love: but love's first flash in youth,
Most common: yea, I know it of mine own self:
And you yourself will smile at your own self
Hereafter, when you yield your flower of life
To one more fitly yours, not thrice your age:
And then will I, for true you are and sweet
Beyond mine old belief in womanhood,
More specially should your good knight be poor,
Endow you with broad land and territory
Even to the half my realm beyond the seas,
So that would make you happy: furthermore,
Ev'n to the death, as tho' ye were my blood,
In all your quarrels will I be your knight,
This will I do, dear damsel, for your sake,
And more than this I cannot."

              While he spoke
She neither blush'd nor shook, but deathly-pale
Stood grasping what was nearest, then replied:
"Of all this will I nothing;" and so fell,
And thus they bore her swooning to her tower.

Then spake, to whom thro' those black walls of yew
Their talk had pierced, her father: "Ay, a flash,
I fear me, that will strike my blossom dead.
Too courteous are ye, fair Lord Lancelot.
I pray you, use some rough discourtesy
To blunt or break her passion."

              Lancelot said,
"That were against me: what I can I will;"
And there that day remain'd, and toward even
Sent for his shield: full meekly rose the maid,
Stript off the case, and gave the naked shield:
Then, when she heard his horse upon the stones,
Unclasping, flung the casement back, and look'd
Down on his helm, from which her sleeve had gone,
And Lancelot knew the little clinking sound;
And she by tact of love was well aware
That Lancelot knew that she was looking at him.
And yet he glanced not up, nor waved his hand,
Nor bade farewell, but sadly rode away.
This was the one discourtesy that he used.

So in her tower alone the maiden sat:
His very shield was gone; only the case,
Her own poor work, her empty labor, left.
But still she heard him, still his picture form'd
And grew between her and the pictured wall.
Then came her father, saying in low tones,
"Have comfort," whom she greeted quietly.
Then came her brethren, saying, "Peace to th' ,
Sweet sister," whom she answer'd with all calm.
But when they left her to herself again,
Death, like a friend's voice from a distant field
Approaching thro' the darkness, call'd; the owls
Wailing had power upon her, and she mixt
Her fancies with the sallow-rifted glooms
Of evening, and the moanings of the wind.

And in those days she made a little song,
And call'd her song "The Song of Love and Death,"
And sang it: sweetly could she make and sing.

"Sweet is true love, tho' given in vain, in vain;
And sweet is death who puts an end to pain:
I know not which is sweeter, no, not I.

"Love, art thou sweet? then bitter death must be:
Love, thou art bitter; sweet is death to me.
O Love, if death be sweeter, let me die.

"Sweet love, that seems not made to fade away,
Sweet death, that seems to make us loveless clay,
I know not which is sweeter, no, not I.

"I fain would follow love, if that could be;
I needs must follow death, who calls for me;
Call and I follow, I follow! let me die."

High with the last line scaled her voice, and this,
All in a fiery dawning wild with wind
That shook her tower, the brothers heard, and
    thought,
With shuddering, "Hark the Phantom of the house,
That ever shrieks before a death," and call'd
The father, and all three in hurry and fear
Ran to her, and lo! the blood-red light of dawn
Flared on her face, she shrilling, "Let me die!"

As when we dwell upon a word we know,
Repeating, till the word we know so well
Becomes a wonder, and we know not why,
So dwelt the father on her face, and thought,
"Is this Elaine?" till back the maiden fell,
Then gave a languid hand to each, and lay,
Speaking a still good-morrow with her eyes.
At last she said, "Sweet brothers, yesternight
I seem'd a curious little maid again,
As happy as when we dwelt among the woods,
And when ye used to take me with the flood
Up the great river in the boatman's boat.
Only ye would not pass beyond the cape
That has the poplar on it: there ye fixt
Your limit, oft returning with the tide.
And yet I cried because ye would not pass
Beyond it, and far up the shining flood
Until we found the palace of the King.
And yet ye would not; but this night I dream'd
That I was all alone upon the flood,
And then I said, 'Now shall I have my will:'
And there I woke, but still the wish remain'd.
So let me hence that I may pass at last
Beyond the poplar and far up the flood,
Until I find the palace of the King.
There will I enter in among them all,
And no man there will dare to mock at me;
But there the fine Gawain will wonder at me,
And there the great Sir Lancelot muse at me;
Gawain, who bade a thousand farewells to me,
Lancelot, who coldly went, nor bade me one:
And there the King will know me and my love,
And there the Queen herself will pity me,
And all the gentle court will welcome me,
And after my long voyage I shall rest!"

"Peace," said her father, "O my child, ye seem
Light-headed, for what force is yours to go
So far, being sick? and wherefore would ye look
On this proud fellow again, who scorns us all?"

Then the rough Torre began to heave and move,
And bluster into stormy sobs, and say,
"I never loved him: an I meet with him,
I care not howsoever great he be,
Then will I strike at him and strike him down,
Give me good fortune, I will strike him dead,
For this discomfort he hath done the house."

To whom the gentle sister made reply,
"Fret not yourself, dear brother, nor be wroth,
Seeing it is no more Sir Lancelot's fault
Not to love me, than it is mine to love
Him of all men who seems to me the highest."

"'Highest?'" the father answer'd, echoing, "high-
    est"
(He meant to break the passion in her), "nay,
Daughter, I know not what you call the highest;
But this I know, for all the people know it,
He loves the Queen, and in an open shame:
And she returns his love in open shame.
If this be high, what is it to be low?"

Then spake the lily maid of Astolat:
"Sweet father, all too faint and sick am I
For anger: these are slanders: never yet
Was noble man but made ignoble talk.
He makes no friend who never made a foe.
But now it is my glory to have loved
One peerless, without stain: so let me pass,
My father, howsoe'er I seem to you,
Not all unhappy, having loved God's best
And greatest, tho' my love had no return:
Yet, seeing you desire your child to live,
Thanks, but you work against your own desire;
For if I could believe the things you say
I should but die the sooner; wherefore cease,
Sweet father, and bid call the ghostly man
Hither, and let me shrive me clean, and die."

So when the ghostly man had come and gone.
She with a face bright, as for sin forgiven,
Besought Lavaine to write as she devised
A letter, word for word: and when he ask'd,
"Is it for Lancelot, is it for my dear lord?"
Then will I bear it gladly;" she replied,
"For Lancelot and the Queen and all the world,
But I myself must bear it." Then he wrote
The letter she devised; which being writ
And folded, "O sweet father, tender and true,
Deny me not," she said—"ye never yet
Denied my fancies—this, however strange,
My latest: lay the letter in my hand
A little ere I die, and close the hand
Upon it; I shall guard it even in death.
And when the heat is gone from out my heart,
Then take the little bed on which I died
For Lancelot's love, and deck it like the Queen's
For richness, and me also like the Queen
In all I have of rich, and lay me on it.
And let there be prepared a chariot-bier
To take me to the river, and a barge
Be ready on the river, clothed in black.
I go in state to court, to meet the Queen.
There surely I shall speak for mine own self,
And none of you can speak for me so well.
And therefore let our dumb old man alone
Go with me, he can steer and row, and he
Will guide me to that palace, to the doors."

She ceased: her father promised; whereupon
She grew so cheerful that they deem'd her death
Was rather in the fantasy than the blood.
But ten slow mornings past, and on the eleventh
Her father laid the letter in her hand,
And closed the hand upon it, and she died.
So that day there was dole in Astolat.

But when the next sun brake from underground,
Then, those two brethren slowly with bent brows
Accompanying, the sad chariot-bier
Past like a shadow thro' the field, that shone
Full-summer, to that stream whereon the barge,
Pall'd all its length in blackest samite, lay.
There sat the lifelong creature of the house
Loyal, the dumb old servitor, on deck,

Winking his eyes, and twisted all his face.
So those two brethren from the chariot took
And on the black decks laid her in her bed,
Set in her hand a lily, o'er her hung
The silken case with braided blazonings,
And kiss'd her quiet brows, and saying to her
"Sister, farewell for ever," and again
"Farewell, sweet sister," parted all in tears.
Then rose the dumb old servitor, and the dead,
Oar'd by the dumb, went upward with the flood—
In her right hand the lily, in her left
The letter—all her bright hair streaming down—
And all the coverlid was cloth of gold
Drawn to her waist, and she herself in white
All but her face, and that clear-featured face
Was lovely, for she did not seem as dead,
But fast asleep, and lay as tho' she smiled.

That day Sir Lancelot at the palace craved
Audience of Guinevere, to give at last
The price of half a realm, his costly gift,
Hard-won and hardly won with bruise and blow,
With deaths of others, and almost his own,
The nine-years-fought-for diamonds: for he saw
One of her house, and sent him to the Queen
Bearing his wish, whereto the Queen agreed
With such and so unmoved a majesty
She might have seem'd her statue, but that he,
Low-drooping till he wellnigh kiss'd her feet
For loyal awe, saw with a sidelong eye
The shadow of some piece of pointed lace,
In the Queen's shadow, vibrate on the walls,
And parted, laughing in his courtly heart.

All in an oriel on the summer side,
Vine-clad, of Arthur's palace toward the stream,
They met, and Lancelot kneeling utter'd, "Queen,
Lady, my liege, in whom I have my joy,
Take, what I had not won except for you,
These jewels, and make me happy, making them
An armlet for the roundest arm on earth,
Or necklace for a neck to which the swan's
Is tawnier than her cygnet's: these are words:
Your beauty is your beauty, and I sin
In speaking, yet, oh grant my worship of it
Words, as we grant grief tears. Such sin in words
Perchance, we both can pardon: but, my Queen,
I hear of rumors flying thro' your court.
Our bond, as not the bond of man and wife,
Should have in it an absoluter trust
To make up that defect: let rumors be:
When did not rumors fly? these, as I trust
That you trust me in your own nobleness,
I may not well believe that you believe."

While thus he spoke, half turn'd away, the Queen
Brake from the vast oriel-embowering vine
Leaf after leaf, and tore, and cast them off,
Till all the place whereon she stood was green;
Then, when he ceased, in one cold passive hand
Received at once and laid aside the gems
There on a table near her, and replied:

"It may be, I am quicker of belief
Than you believe me, Lancelot of the Lake.
Our bond is not the bond of man and wife.
This good is in it, whatsoe'er of ill,
It can be broken easier. I for you
This many a year have done despite and wrong
To one whom ever in my heart of hearts
I did acknowledge nobler. What are these?
Diamonds for me! they had been thrice their worth
Being your gift, had you not lost your own.
To loyal hearts the value of all gifts
Must vary as the giver's. Not for me!
For her! for your new fancy. Only this
Grant me, I pray you: have your joys apart.
I doubt not that however changed, you keep

So much of what is graceful: and myself
Would shun to break those bounds of courtesy
In which as Arthur's Queen I move and rule:
So cannot speak my mind. An end to this!
A strange one! yet I take it with Amen.
So pray you, add my diamonds to her pearls;
Deck her with these; tell her, she shines me down:
An armlet for an arm to which the Queen's
Is haggard, or a necklace for a neck
Oh, as much fairer—as a faith once fair
Was richer than these diamonds—hers, not mine—
Nay, by the mother of our Lord himself,
Or hers or mine, mine now to work my will—
She shall not have them."

               Saying which she seized,
And thro' the casement standing wide for heat,
Flung them, and down they flash'd, and smote the
    stream.
Then from the smitten surface flash'd, as it were,
Diamonds to meet them, and they past away.
Then while Sir Lancelot leant, in half disdain
At love, life, all things, on the window ledge,
Close underneath his eyes, and right across
Where these had fallen, slowly past the barge
Whereon the lily maid of Astolat
Lay smiling, like a star in blackest night.

But the wild Queen, who saw not, burst away
To weep and wail in secret; and the barge,
On to the palace-doorway sliding, paused.
There two stood arm'd, and kept the door; to
    whom,
All up the marble stair, tier over tier,
Were added mouths that gaped, and eyes that ask'd
"What is it?" but that oarsman's haggard face,
As hard and still as is the face that men
Shape to their fancy's eye from broken rocks
On some cliff-side, appall'd them, and they said,
"He is enchanted, cannot speak—and she,
Look how she sleeps—the Fairy Queen, so fair!
Yea, but how pale! what are they? flesh and blood?
Or come to take the King to Fairyland?
For some do hold our Arthur cannot die,
But that he passes into Fairyland."

While thus they babbled of the King, the King
Came girt with knights: then turn'd the tongueless
    man
From the half-face to the full eye, and rose
And pointed to the damsel, and the doors.
So Arthur bade the meek Sir Percivale
And pure Sir Galahad to uplift the maid;
And reverently they bore her into hall.
Then came the fine Gawain and wonder'd at her,
And Lancelot later came and mused at her,
And last the Queen herself, and pitied her:
But Arthur spied the letter in her hand,
Stoopt, took, brake seal, and read it; this was all:

"Most noble lord, Sir Lancelot of the Lake,
I, sometime call'd the maid of Astolat,
Come, for you left me taking no farewell,
Hither, to take my last farewell of you.
I loved you, and my love had no return,
And therefore my true love has been my death.
And therefore to our Lady Guinevere,
And to all other ladies, I make moan.
Pray for my soul, and yield me burial.
Pray for my soul thou too, Sir Lancelot,
As thou art a knight peerless."

               Thus he read,
And ever in the reading, lords and dames
Wept, looking often from his face who read
To hers which lay so silent, and at times,
So touch'd were they, half-thinking that her lips,
Who had devised the letter, moved again.

Then freely spoke Sir Lancelot to them all:
"My lord liege Arthur, and all ye that hear,
Know that for this most gentle maiden's death
Right heavy am I; for good she was and true,
But loved me with a love beyond all love
In woman, whomsoever I have known.
Yet to be loved makes not to love again;
Not at my years, however it hold in youth.
I swear by truth and knighthood that I gave
No cause, not willingly, for such a love:
To this I call my friends in testimony,
Her brethren, and her father, who himself
Besought me to be plain and blunt, and use,
To break her passion, some discourtesy
Against my nature: what I could, I did.
I left her, and I bade her no farewell:
Tho', had I dreamt the damsel would have died,
I might have put my wits to some rough use,
And help'd her from herself."

                    Then said the Queen
(Sea was her wrath, yet working after storm),
"Ye might at least have done her so much grace.
Fair lord, as would have help'd her from her death."
He raised his head, their eyes met and hers fell,
He adding,

          "Queen, she would not be content
Save that I wedded her, which could not be.
Then might she follow me thro' the world, she
          ask'd:
It could not be. I told her that her love
Was but the flash of youth, would darken down
To rise hereafter in a stiller flame
Toward one more worthy of her—then would I,
More specially were he, she wedded, poor,
Estate them with large land and territory
In mine own realm beyond the narrow seas,
To keep them in all joyance: more than this
I could not: this she would not, and she died."

He pausing, Arthur answer'd, "O my knight,
It will be to thy worship, as my knight,
And mine, as head of all our Table Round,
To see that she be buried worshipfully."

So toward that shrine which then in all the
          realm
Was richest, Arthur leading, slowly went
The marshall'd Order of their Table Round,
And Lancelot sad beyond his wont, to see
The maiden buried, not as one unknown,
Nor meanly, but with gorgeous obsequies,
And mass, and rolling music, like a queen.
And when the knights had laid her comely head
Low in the dust of half-forgotten kings,
Then Arthur spake among them, "Let her tomb
Be costly, and her image thereupon.
And let the shield of Lancelot at her feet
Be carven, and her lily in her hand.
And let the story of her dolorous voyage
For all true hearts be blazon'd on her tomb
In letters gold and azure!" which was wrought
Thereafter; but when now the lords and dames
And people from the high door streaming, brake
Disorderly, as homeward each, the Queen,
Who mark'd Sir Lancelot where he moved apart,
Drew near, and sigh'd in passing, "Lancelot,
Forgive me; mine was jealousy in love."
He answer'd with his eyes upon the ground,
"That is love's curse; pass on, my Queen, forgiv-
en."
But Arthur, who beheld his cloudy brows.
Approach'd him, and with full affection said,

"Lancelot, my Lancelot, thou in whom I have
Most joy and most affiance, for I know

13

What thou hast been in battle by my side,
And many a time have watch'd thee at the tilt
Strike down the lusty and long-practised knight,
And let the younger and unskill'd go by
To win his honor and to make his name,
And loved thy courtesies and thee, a man
Made to be loved; but now I would to God,
Seeing the homeless trouble in thine eyes,
Thou couldst have loved this maiden, shaped, it
          seems,
By God for thee alone, and from her face,
If one may judge the living by the dead,
Delicately pure and marvellously fair,
Who might have brought thee, now a lonely man,
Wifeless and heirless, noble issue, sons
Born to the glory of thy name and fame,
My knight, the great Sir Lancelot of the Lake."

Then answer'd Lancelot, "Fair she was, my King,
Pure, as you ever wish your knights to be.
To doubt her fairness were to want an eye,
To doubt her pureness were to want a heart—
Yea, to be loved, if what is worthy love
Could bind him, but free love will not be bound."

"Free love, so bound, were freest," said the King.
"Let love be free; free love is for the best:
And, after heaven, on our dull side of death,
What should be best, if not so pure a love
Clothed in so pure a loveliness? yet thee
She fail'd to bind, tho' being, as I think,
Unbound as yet, and gentle, as I know."

And Lancelot answer'd nothing, but he went,
And at the inrunning of a little brook
Sat by the river in a cove, and watch'd
The high reed wave, and lifted up his eyes
And saw the barge that brought her moving down,
Far-off, a blot upon the stream, and said
Low in himself, "Ah, simple heart and sweet,
Ye loved me, damsel, surely with a love
Far tenderer than my Queen's. Pray for thy soul?
Ay, that will I. Farewell too—now at last—
Farewell, fair lily. 'Jealousy in love?'
Not rather dead love's harsh heir, jealous pride?
Queen, if I grant the jealousy as of love,
May not your crescent fear for name and fame
Speak, as it waxes, of a love that wanes?
Why did the King dwell on my name to me?
Mine own name shames me, seeming a reproach,
Lancelot, whom the Lady of the Lake
Caught from his mother's arms—the wondrous one
Who passes thro' the vision of the night—
She chanted snatches of mysterious hymns
Heard on the winding waters, eve and morn
She kiss'd me, saying, 'Thou art fair, my child,
As a king's son,' and often in her arms
She bare me, pacing on the dusky mere.
Would she had drown'd me in it, where'er it be!
For what am I? what profits me my name
Of greatest knight? I fought for it, and have it:
Pleasure to have it, none; to lose it, pain:
Now grown a part of me: but what use in it?
To make men worse by making my sin known?
Or sin seem less, the sinner seeming great?
Alas for Arthur's greatest knight, a man
Not after Arthur's heart! I needs must break
These bonds that so defame me: not without
She wills it: would I, if she will'd it? nay,
Who knows? but if I would not, then may God,
I pray him, send a sudden Angel down
To seize me by the hair and bear me far,
And fling me deep in that forgotten mere,
Among the tumbled fragments of the hills."

So groan'd Sir Lancelot in remorseful pain,
Not knowing he should die a holy man.

THE HOLY GRAIL.

FROM noiseful arms, and acts of prowess done
In tournament or tilt, Sir Percivale,
Whom Arthur and his knighthood call'd The Pure,
Had pass'd into the silent life of prayer,
Praise, fast, and alms; and leaving for the cowl
The helmet in an abbey far away
From Camelot, there, and not long after, died.

And one, a fellow-monk among the rest,
Ambrosius, loved him much beyond the rest,
And honor'd him, and wrought into his heart
A way by love that waken'd love within,
To answer that which came: and as they sat
Beneath a world-old yew-tree, darkening half
The cloisters, on a gustful April morn
That puff'd the swaying branches into smoke
Above them, ere the summer when he died,
The monk Ambrosius question'd Percivale:

"O brother, I have seen this yew-tree smoke,
Spring after spring, for half a hundred years:
For never have I known the world without,
Nor ever stray'd beyond the pale: but thee,
When first thou camest—such a courtesy
Spake thro' the limbs and in the voice—I knew
For one of those who eat in Arthur's hall;
For good ye are and bad, and like to coins,
Some true, some light, but every one of you
Stamp'd with the image of the King; and now
Tell me, what drove thee from the Table Round,
My brother? was it earthly passion crost?"

"Nay," said the knight; "for no such passion
mine.
But the sweet vision of the Holy Grail
Drove me from all vainglories, rivalries,
And earthly heats that spring and sparkle out
Among us in the jousts, while women watch
Who wins, who falls; and waste the spiritual strength
Within us, better offer'd up to Heaven."

To whom the monk: "The Holy Grail!—I trust
We are green in Heaven's eyes; but here too much
We moulder—as to things without I mean—
Yet one of your own knights, a guest of ours,
Told us of this in our refectory,
But spake with such a sadness and so low
We heard not half of what he said. What is it?
The phantom of a cup that comes and goes?"

"Nay, monk! what phantom?" answer'd Percivale.
"The cup, the cup itself, from which our Lord
Drank at the last sad supper with his own.
This, from the blessed land of Aromat—
After the day of darkness, when the dead
Went wandering o'er Moriah—the good saint,
Arimathæan Joseph, journeying brought
To Glastonbury, where the winter thorn
Blossoms at Christmas, mindful of our Lord.
And there awhile it bode; and if a man
Could touch or see it, he was heal'd at once,
By faith, of all his ills. But then the times
Grew to such evil that the Holy Cup
Was caught away to Heaven, and disappear'd."

To whom the monk: "From our old books I know
That Joseph came of old to Glastonbury,
And there the heathen Prince, Arviragus,
Gave him an isle of marsh whereon to build;
And there he built with wattles from the marsh
A little lonely church in days of yore,
For so they say, these books of ours, but seem
Mute of this miracle, far as I have read.
But who first saw the Holy Thing to-day?"

"A woman," answer'd Percivale, "a nun,

And one no further off in blood from me
Than sister; and if ever holy maid
With knees of adoration wore the stone,
A holy maid; tho' never maiden glow'd,
But that was in her earlier maidenhood,
With such a fervent flame of human love,
Which being rudely blunted, glanced and shot
Only to holy things; to prayer and praise
She gave herself, to fast and alms. And yet,
Nun as she was, the scandal of the Court,
Sin against Arthur and the Table Round,
And the strange sound of an adulterous race,
Across the iron grating of her cell
Beat, and she pray'd and fasted all the more.

"And he to whom she told her sins, or what
Her all but utter whiteness held for sin,
A man wellnigh a hundred winters old,
Spake often with her of the Holy Grail,
A legend handed down thro' five or six,
And each of these a hundred winters old,
From our Lord's time. And when King Arthur made
His Table Round, and all men's hearts became
Clean for a season, surely he had thought
That now the Holy Grail would come again;
But sin broke out. Ah, Christ, that it would come,
And heal the world of all their wickedness!
'O Father!' ask'd the maiden, 'might it come
To me by prayer and fasting?' 'Nay,' said he,
'I know not, for thy heart is pure as snow.'
And so she pray'd and fasted, till the sun
Shone, and the wind blew, thro' her, and I thought
She might have risen and floated when I saw her.

"For on a day she sent to speak with me.
And when she came to speak, behold her eyes
Beyond my knowing of them, beautiful,
Beyond all knowing of them, wonderful,
Beautiful in the light of holiness,
And 'O my brother Percivale,' she said,
'Sweet brother, I have seen the Holy Grail:
For, waked at dead of night, I heard a sound
As of a silver horn from o'er the hills
Blown, and I thought, "It is not Arthur's use
To hunt by moonlight;" and the slender sound
As from a distance beyond distance grew
Coming upon me. Oh, never harp nor horn,
Nor aught we blow with breath or touch with hand,
Was like that music as it came; and then
Stream'd thro' my cell a cold and silver beam,
And down the long beam stole the Holy Grail,
Rose-red with beatings in it, as if alive,
Till all the white walls of my cell were dyed
With rosy colors leaping on the wall;
And then the music faded, and the Grail
Past, and the beam decay'd, and from the walls
The rosy quiverings died into the night.
So now the Holy Thing is here again
Among us, brother, fast thou too and pray,
And tell thy brother knights to fast and pray,
That so perchance the vision may be seen
By thee and those, and all the world be heal'd.'

"Then leaving the pale nun. I spake of this
To all men; and myself fasted and pray'd
Always, and many among us many a week
Fasted and pray'd even to the uttermost,
Expectant of the wonder that would be.

"And one there was among us, ever moved
Among us in white armor, Galahad.
'God make thee good as thou art beautiful,'
Said Arthur, when he dubb'd him knight; and none,
In so young youth, was ever made a knight
Till Galahad; and this Galahad, when he heard
My sister's vision, fill'd me with amaze;
His eyes became so like her own, they seem'd
Hers, and himself her brother more than I.

"Sister or brother none had he; but some
Call'd him a son of Lancelot, and some said
Begotten by euchantment—chatterers they,
(Like birds of passage piping up and down,)
That gape for flies—we know not whence they come;
For when was Lancelot wanderingly lewd?

"But she, the wan sweet maiden, shore away
Clean from her forehead all that wealth of hair
Which made a silken mat-work for her feet;
And out of this she plaited broad and long
A strong sword-belt, and wove with silver thread
And crimson in the belt a strange device,
A crimson grail within a silver beam:
And saw the bright boy-knight, and bound it on
　　him,
Saying, 'My knight, my love, my knight of Heaven,
O thou, my love, whose love is one with mine,
I, maiden, round thee, maiden, bind my belt.
Go forth, for thou shalt see what I have seen.
And break thro' all, till one will crown thee king
Far in the spiritual city:' and as she spake
She sent the deathless passion in her eyes
Thro' him, and made him hers, and laid her mind
On him, and he believed in her belief.

"Then came a year of miracle: O brother,
In our great hall there stood a vacant chair,
Fashion'd by Merlin ere he past away,
And carven with strange figures, and in and out
(The figures, like a serpent,)ran a scroll
Of letters in a tongue no man could read.
And Merlin call'd it 'The Siege perilous.'
Perilous for good and ill; 'for there,' he said,
'No man could sit but he should lose himself:'
And once by misadvertence Merlin sat
In his own chair, and so was lost; but he,
Galahad, when he heard of Merlin's doom,
Cried, 'If I lose myself I save myself!'

"Then on a summer night it came to pass,
While the great banquet lay along the hall,
That Galahad would sit down in Merlin's chair.

"And all at once, as there we sat, we heard
A cracking and a riving of the roofs,
And rending, and a blast, and overhead
Thunder, and in the thunder was a cry.
And in the blast there smote along the hall
A beam of light seven times more clear than day:
And down the long beam stole the Holy Grail
All over cover'd with a luminous cloud,
And none might see who bare it, and it past.
But every knight beheld his fellow's face
As in a glory, and all the knights arose,
And staring each at other like dumb men
Stood, till I found a voice and sware a vow.

"I sware a vow before them all, that I,
Because I had not seen the Grail, would ride
A twelvemonth and a day in quest of it,
Until I found and saw it, as the nun
My sister saw it; and Galahad sware the vow,
And good Sir Bors, our Lancelot's cousin, sware,
And Lancelot sware, and many among the knights,
And Gawain sware, and louder than the rest."

Then spake the monk Ambrosius, asking him,
"What said the King? Did Arthur take the vow?"

"Nay, for my lord," said Percivale, "the King,
Was not in hall: for early that same day,
Scaped thro' a cavern from a bandit hold,
An outraged maiden sprang into the hall
Crying on help: for all her shining hair
Was smear'd with earth, and either milky arm
Red-rent with hooks of bramble, and all she wore
Torn as a sail that leaves the rope is torn

In tempest: so the King arose and went
To smoke the scandalous hive of those wild bees
That made such honey in his realm. Howbeit
Some little of this marvel he too saw,
Returning o'er the plain that then began
To darken under Camelot: whence the King
Look'd up, calling aloud, 'Lo, there! the roofs
Of our great hall are roll'd in thunder-smoke!
Pray Heaven, they be not smitten by the bolt.'
For dear to Arthur was that hall of ours,
As having there so oft with all his knights
Feasted, and as the stateliest under heaven.

"O brother, had you known our mighty hall,
Which Merlin built for Arthur long ago!
For all the sacred mount of Camelot,
And all the dim rich city, roof by roof,
Tower after tower, spire beyond spire,
By grove, and garden-lawn, and rushing brook,
Climbs to the mighty hall that Merlin built.
And four great zones of sculpture, set betwixt
With many a mystic symbol, gird the hall:
And in the lowest beasts are slaying men,
And in the second men are slaying beasts,
And on the third are warriors, perfect men,
And on the fourth are men with growing wings,
And over all one statue in the mould
Of Arthur, made by Merlin, with a crown,
And peak'd wings pointed to the Northern Star.
And eastward fronts the statue, and the crown
And both the wings are made of gold, and flame
At sunrise till the people in far fields,
Wasted so often by the heathen hordes,
Behold it, crying, 'We have still a King.'

"And, brother, had you known our hall within,
Broader and higher than any in all the lands!
Where twelve great windows blazon Arthur's wars,
And all the light that falls upon the board
Streams thro' the twelve great battles of our King.
Nay, one there is, and at the eastern end,
Wealthy with wandering lines of mount and mere,
Where Arthur finds the brand Excalibur.
And also one to the west, and counter to it,
And blank: and who shall blazon it? when and
　　how?—
Oh, there, perchance, when all our wars are done,
The brand Excalibur will be cast away.

"So to this hall full quickly rode the King,
In horror lest the work by Merlin wrought,
Dreamlike, should on the sudden vanish, wrapt
In unremorseful folds of rolling fire.
And in he rode, and up I glanced, and saw
The golden dragon sparkling over all:
And many of those who burnt the hold, their arms
Hack'd, and their foreheads grimed with smoke, and
　　sear'd,
Follow'd, and in among bright faces, ours,
Full of the vision, prest: and then the King
Spake to me, being nearest, 'Percivale'
(Because the hall was all in tumult—some
Vowing, and some protesting), 'what is this?'

"O brother, when I told him what had chanced,
My sister's vision, and the rest, his face
Darken'd, as I have seen it more than once,
When some brave deed seem'd to be done in vain,
Darken; and 'Woe is me, my knights,' he cried,
'Had I been here, ye had not sworn the vow.'
Bold was mine answer, 'Had thyself been here,
My King, thou wouldst have sworn.' 'Yea, yea,'
　　said he,
'Art thou so bold and hast not seen the Grail?'

"'Nay, lord, I heard the sound, I saw the light,
But since I did not see the Holy Thing,
I sware a vow to follow it till I saw.'

"Then when he ask'd us, knight by knight, if any
Had seen it, all their answers were as one:
'Nay, lord, and therefore have we sworn our vows.'

"'Lo, now,' said Arthur, 'have you seen a cloud?
What go ye into the wilderness to see?'

"Then Galahad on the sudden, and in a voice
Shrilling along the hall to Arthur, call'd,
'But I, Sir Arthur, saw the Holy Grail,
I saw the Holy Grail and heard a cry—
"O Galahad, and O Galahad, follow me."'

"'Ah, Galahad, Galahad,' said the King, 'for such
As thou art is the vision, not for these.
Thy holy nun and thou have seen a sign—
Holier is none, my Percivale, than she—
A sign to maim this Order which I made.
But ye, that follow but the leader's bell'
(Brother, the King was hard upon his knights)
'Taliessin is our fullest throat of song,
And one hath sung and all the dumb will sing.
Lancelot is Lancelot, and hath overborne
Five knights at once, and every younger knight,
Unproven, holds himself as Lancelot,
Till overborne by one, he learns—and ye,
What are ye? Galahads?—no, nor Percivales'
(For thus it pleased the King to range me close
After Sir Galahad); 'nay,' said he, 'but men
With strength and will to right the wrong'd, of power
To lay the sudden heads of violence flat,
Knights that in twelve great battles splash'd and
    dyed
The strong White Horse in his own heathen blood—
But one hath seen, and all the blind will see.
Go, since your vows are sacred, being made:
Yet—for ye know the cries of all my realm
Pass thro' this hall—how often, O my knights,
Your places being vacant at my side,
This chance of noble deeds will come and go
Unchallenged, while ye follow wandering fires
Lost in the quagmire! Many of you, yea most,
Return no more: ye think I show myself
Too dark a prophet: come now, let us meet
The morrow morn once more in one full field
Of gracious pastime, that once more the King,
Before ye leave him for this Quest, may count
The yet unbroken strength of all his knights,
Rejoicing in that Order which he made.'

"So when the sun broke next from under ground,
All the great table of our Arthur closed
And clash'd in such a tourney and so full,
So many lances broken—never yet
Had Camelot seen the like, since Arthur came;
And I myself and Galahad, for a strength
Was in us from the vision, overthrew
So many knights that the people cried,
And almost burst the barriers in their heat,
Shouting, 'Sir Galahad and Sir Percivale!'

"But when the next day brake from under ground—
O brother, had you known our Camelot,
Built by old kings, age after age, so old
The King himself had fears that it would fall,
So strange, and rich, and dim; for where the roofs
Totter'd toward each other in the sky,
Met foreheads all along the street of those
Who watch'd us pass; and lower, and where the long
Rich galleries, lady-laden, weigh'd the necks
Of dragons clinging to the crazy walls,
Thicker than drops from thunder, showers of flowers
Fell as we past; and men and boys astride
On wyvern, lion, dragon, griffin, swan,
At all the corners, named us each by name,
Calling 'God speed!' but in the ways below
The knights and ladies wept, and rich and poor
Wept, and the King himself could hardly speak

For grief, and all in middle street the Queen,
Who rode by Lancelot, wail'd and shriek'd aloud,
'This madness has come on us for our sins.'
So to the Gate of the three Queens we came,
Where Arthur's wars are render'd mystically,
And thence departed every one his way.

"And I was lifted up in heart, and thought
Of all my late-shown prowess in the lists,
How my strong lance had beaten down the knights,
So many and famous names; and never yet
Had heaven appear'd so blue, nor earth so green,
For all my blood danced in me, and I knew
That I should light upon the Holy Grail.

"Thereafter the dark warning of our King,
That most of us would follow wandering fires,
Came like a driving gloom across my mind.
Then every evil word I had spoken once,
And every evil thought I had thought of old,
And every evil deed I ever did,
Awoke and cried, 'This Quest is not for thee.'
And lifting up mine eyes, I found myself
Alone, and in a land of sand and thorns,
And I was thirsty even unto death;
And I, too, cried, 'This Quest is not for thee.'

"And on I rode, and when I thought my thirst
Would slay me, saw deep lawns, and then a brook,
With one sharp rapid, where the crisping white
Play'd ever back upon the sloping wave,
And took both ear and eye; and o'er the brook
Were apple-trees, and apples by the brook
Fallen, and on the lawns. 'I will rest here,'
I said, 'I am not worthy of the Quest;'
But even while I drank the brook, and ate
The goodly apples, all these things at once
Fell into dust, and I was left alone,
And thirsting, in a land of sand and thorns.

"And then behold a woman at a door
Spinning; and fair the house whereby she sat,
And kind the woman's eyes and innocent,
And all her bearing gracious; and she rose
Opening her arms to meet me, as who should say,
'Rest here;' but when I touch'd her, lo! she, too,
Fell into dust and nothing, and the house
Became no better than a broken shed,
And in it a dead babe; and also this
Fell into dust, and I was left alone.

"And on I rode, and greater was my thirst.
Then flash'd a yellow gleam across the world,
And where it smote the ploughshare in the field,
The ploughman left his ploughing, and fell down
Before it; where it glitter'd on her pail,
The milkmaid left her milking, and fell down
Before it, and I knew not why, but thought
'The sun is rising,' tho' the sun had risen.
Then was I ware of one that on me moved
In golden armor with a crown of gold
About a casque all jewels; and his horse
In golden armor jewell'd everywhere:
And on the splendor came, flashing me blind;
And seem'd to me the Lord of all the world,
Being so huge. But when I thought he meant
To crush me, moving on me, lo! he, too,
Open'd his arms to embrace me as he came,
And up I went and touch'd him, and he, too,
Fell into dust, and I was left alone
And wearying in a land of sand and thorns.

"And I rode on and found a mighty hill,
And on the top, a city wall'd: the spires
Prick'd with incredible pinnacles into heaven.
And by the gateway stirr'd a crowd; and these
Cried to me climbing, 'Welcome, Percivale!
Thou mightiest and thou purest among men!'

And glad was I and clomb, but found at top
No man, nor any voice. And thence I past
Far thro' a ruinous city, and I saw
That man had once dwelt there; but there I found
Only one man of an exceeding age.
'Where is that goodly company,' said I,
'That so cried out upon me?' and he had
Scarce any voice to answer, and yet gasp'd,
'Whence and what art thou?' and even as he spoke
Fell into dust, and disappear'd, and I
Was left alone once more, and cried in grief,
'Lo, if I find the Holy Grail itself
And touch it, it will crumble into dust.'

"And thence I dropt into a lowly vale,
Low as the hill was high, and where the vale
Was lowest, found a chapel, and thereby
A holy hermit in a hermitage,
To whom I told my phantoms, and he said:

"'O son, thou hast not true humility,
The highest virtue, mother of them all;
For when the Lord of all things made himself
Naked of glory for His mortal change,
"Take thou my robe," she said, "for all is thine,"
And all her form shone forth with sudden light
So that the angels were amazed, and she
Follow'd him down, and like a flying star
Led on the gray-hair'd wisdom of the East;
But her thou hast not known: for what is this
Thou thoughtest of thy prowess and thy sins?
Thou hast not lost thyself to save thyself
As Galahad.' When the hermit made an end,
In silver armor suddenly Galahad shone
Before us, and against the chapel door
Laid lance, and enter'd, and we knelt in prayer.
And there the hermit slaked my burning thirst,
And at the sacring of the mass I saw
The holy elements alone; but he,
'Saw ye no more? I, Galahad, saw the Grail,
The Holy Grail, descend upon the shrine:
I saw the fiery face as of a child
That smote itself into the bread and went;
And hither am I come; and never yet
Hath what thy sister taught me first to see,
This Holy Thing, fail'd from my side, nor come
Cover'd, but moving with me night and day,
Fainter by day, but always in the night
Blood-red, and sliding down the blacken'd marsh
Blood-red, and on the naked mountain top
Blood-red, and in the sleeping mere below
Blood-red. And in the strength of this I rode,
Shattering all evil customs everywhere,
And past thro' Pagan realms, and made them mine,
And clash'd with Pagan hordes, and bore them down,
And broke thro' all, and in the strength of this
Come victor. But my time is hard at hand,
And hence I go; and one will crown me king
Far in the spiritual city; and come thou, too,
For thou shalt see the vision when I go.'

"While thus he spake, his eye, dwelling on mine,
Drew me, with power upon me, till I grew
One with him, to believe as he believed.
Then, when the day began to wane, we went.

"There rose a hill that none but man could climb,
Scarr'd with a hundred wintry watercourses—
Storm at the top, and when we gain'd it, storm
Round us and death; for every moment glanced
His silver arms and gloom'd: so quick and thick
The lightnings here and there to left and right
Struck, till the dry old trunks about us, dead,
Yea, rotten with a hundred years of death,
Sprang into fire: and at the base we found
On either hand, as far as eye could see,
A great black swamp and of an evil smell,
Part black, part whiten'd with the bones of men,

Not to be crost, save that some ancient king
Had built a way, where, link'd with many a bridge,
A thousand piers ran into the great Sea.
And Galahad fled along them bridge by bridge,
And every bridge as quickly as he crost
Sprang into fire and vanish'd, tho' I yearn'd
To follow; and thrice above him all the heavens
Open'd and blazed with thunder such as seem'd
Shoutings of all the sons of God: and first
At once I saw him far on the great Sea,
In silver-shining armor starry-clear;
And o'er his head the holy vessel hung
Clothed in white samite or a luminous cloud.
And with exceeding swiftness ran the boat,
If boat it were—I saw not whence it came.
And when the heavens open'd and blazed again
Roaring, I saw him like a silver star—
And had he set the sail, or had the boat
Become a living creature clad with wings?
And o'er his head the Holy Vessel hung
Redder than any rose, a joy to me,
For now I knew the veil had been withdrawn.
Then in a moment when they blazed again
Opening, I saw the least of little stars
Down on the waste, and straight beyond the star
I saw the spiritual city and all her spires
And gateways in a glory like one pearl—
No larger, tho' the goal of all the saints—
Strike from the sea; and from the star there shot
A rose-red sparkle to the city, and there
Dwelt, and I knew it was the Holy Grail,
Which never eyes on earth again shall see.
Then fell the floods of heaven drowning the deep.
And how my feet recrost the deathful ridge
No memory in me lives; but that I touch'd
The chapel-doors at dawn I know; and thence
Taking my war-horse from the holy man,
Glad that no phantom vext me more, return'd
To whence I came, the gate of Arthur's wars."

"O brother," ask'd Ambrosius—"for in sooth
These ancient books (and they would win thee)
    teem,
Only I find not there this Holy Grail,
With miracles and marvels like to these,
Not all unlike; which oftentime I read,
Who read but on my breviary with ease,
Till my head swims; and then go forth and pass
Down to the little thorpe that lies so close,
And almost plaster'd like a martin's nest
To these old walls, and mingle with our folk;
And knowing every honest face of theirs
As well as ever shepherd knew his sheep,
And every homely secret in their hearts,
Delight myself with gossip and old wives,
And ills and aches, and teethings, lyings-in,
And mirthful sayings, children of the place,
That have no meaning half a league away:
Or lulling random squabbles when they rise,
Chafferings and chatterings at the market-cross,
Rejoice, small man, in this small world of mine,
Yea, even in their hens and in their eggs—
O brother, saving this Sir Galahad,
Came ye on none but phantoms in your quest,
No man, no woman?"

                Then Sir Percivale:
"All men, to one so bound by such a vow,
And women were as phantoms. O my brother,
Why wilt thou shame me to confess to thee
How far I falter'd from my quest and vow?
For after I had lain so many nights,
A bedmate of the snail and eft and snake,
In grass and burdock, I was changed to wan
And meagre, and the vision had not come;
And then I chanced upon a goodly town
With one great dwelling in the middle of it:
Thither I made, and there was I disarm'd

By maidens each as fair as any flower:
But when they led me into hall, behold,
The Princess of that castle was the one,
Brother, and that one only, who had ever
Made my heart leap; for when I moved of old
A slender page about her father's hall,
And she a slender maiden, all my heart
Went after her with longing: yet we twain
Had never kiss'd a kiss, or vow'd a vow.
And now I came upon her once again,
And one had wedded her, and he was dead,
And all his land and wealth and state were hers.
And while I tarried, every day she set
A banquet richer than the day before
By me; for all her longing and her will
Was toward me as of old; till one fair morn,
I walking to and fro beside a stream
That flash'd across her orchard underneath
Her castle-walls, she stole upon my walk,
And calling me the greatest of all knights,
Embraced me, and so kiss'd me the first time,
And gave herself and all her wealth to me.
Then I remember'd Arthur's warning word,
That most of us would follow wandering fires,
And the Quest faded in my heart. Anon,
The heads of all her people drew to me,
With supplication both of knees and tongue:
'We have heard of thee: thou art our greatest knight,
Our Lady says it, and we well believe:
Wed thou our Lady, and rule over us,
And thou shalt be as Arthur in our land.'
O me, my brother! but one night my vow
Burnt me within, so that I rose and fled,
But wail'd and wept, and hated mine own self,
And ev'n the Holy Quest, and all but her;
Then after I was join'd with Galahad
Cared not for her, nor anything upon earth."

Then said the monk, "Poor men, when yule is cold,
Must be content to sit by little fires.
And this am I, so that ye care for me
Ever so little; yea, and blest be Heaven
That brought thee here to this poor house of ours,
Where all the brethren are so hard, to warm
My cold heart with a friend: but oh, the pity
To find thine own first love once more—to hold,
Hold her a wealthy bride within thine arms,
Or all but hold, and then—cast her aside,
Foregoing all her sweetness, like a weed.
For we that want the warmth of double life,
We that are plagued with dreams of something sweet
Beyond all sweetness in a life so rich,—
Ah, blessed Lord, I spake too earthlywise,
Seeing I never stray'd beyond the cell,
But live like an old badger in his earth,
With earth about him everywhere, despite
All fast and penance. Saw ye none beside?
None of your knights?"

                "Yea so," said Percivale:
"One night my pathway swerving east, I saw
The pelican on the casque of our Sir Bors
All in the middle of the rising moon:
And toward him spurr'd, and hail'd him, and he me,
And each made joy of either; then he ask'd,
'Where is he? hast thou seen him—Lancelot?—Once,'
Said good Sir Bors, 'he dash'd across me—mad,
And maddening what he rode: and when I cried,
"Ridest thou then so hotly on a quest
So holy," Lancelot shouted, "Stay me not!
I have been the sluggard, and I ride apace,
For now there is a lion in the way."
So vanish'd.'

        "Then Sir Bors had ridden on
Softly, and sorrowing for our Lancelot,
Because his former madness, once the talk
And scandal of our table, had return'd;

For Lancelot's kith and kin so worship him
That ill to him is ill to them; to Bors
Beyond the rest: he well had been content
Not to have seen, so Lancelot might have seen
The Holy Cup of healing; and, indeed,
Being so clouded with his grief and love,
Small heart was his after the Holy Quest:
If God would send the vision, well: if not,
The Quest and he were in the hands of Heaven.

"And then, with small adventure met, Sir Bors
Rode to the lonest tract of all the realm,
And found a people there among their crags,
Our race and blood, a remnant that were left
Paynim amid their circles, and the stones
They pitch up straight to heaven: and their wise men
Were strong in that old magic which can trace
The wandering of the stars, and scoff'd at him
And this high Quest as at a simple thing:
Told him he follow'd—almost Arthur's words—
A mocking fire: 'what other fire than he,
Whereby the blood beats, and the blossom blows,
And the sea rolls, and all the world is warm'd?'
And when his answer chafed them, the rough crowd,
Hearing he had a difference with their priests,
Seized him, and bound and plunged him into a cell
Of great piled stones; and lying bounden there
In darkness thro' innumerable hours
He heard the hollow-ringing heavens sweep
Over him, till by miracle—what else?—
Heavy as it was, a great stone slipt and fell,
Such as no wind could move: and thro' the gap
Glimmer'd the streaming scud: then came a night
Still as the day was loud; and thro' the gap
The seven clear stars of Arthur's Table Round—
For, brother, so one night, because they roll
Thro' such a round in heaven, we named the stars
Rejoicing in ourselves and in our King—
And these, like bright eyes of familiar friends,
In on him shone: 'And then to me, to me,'
Said good Sir Bors, 'beyond all hopes of mine,
Who scarce had pray'd or ask'd it for myself—
Across the seven clear stars—oh, grace to me—
In color like the fingers of a hand
Before a burning taper, the sweet Grail
Glided and past, and close upon it peal'd
A sharp quick thunder.' Afterwards, a maid,
Who kept our holy faith among her kin
In secret, entering, loosed and let him go."

To whom the monk: "And I remember now
That pelican on the casque: Sir Bors it was
Who spake so low and sadly at our board;
And mighty reverent at our grace was he:
A square-set man and honest; and his eyes,
An outdoor sign of all the warmth within,
Smiled with his lips—a smile beneath a cloud,
But Heaven had meant it for a sunny one:
Ay, ay, Sir Bors, who else? But when ye reach'd
The city, found ye all your knights return'd,
Or was there sooth in Arthur's prophecy,
Tell me, and what said each, and what the King?"

Then answer'd Percivale: "And that can I,
Brother, and truly; since the living words
Of so great men as Lancelot and our King
Pass not from door to door and out again,
But sit within the house. Oh, when we reach'd
The city, our horses stumbling as they trod
On heaps of ruin, hornless unicorns,
Crack'd basilisks and splinter'd cockatrices,
And shatter'd talbots, which had left the stones
Raw, that they fell from, brought us to the hall.

"And there sat Arthur on the dais-throne,
And those that had gone out upon the Quest,
Wasted and worn, and but a tithe of them,
And those that had not, stood before the King,

Who, when he saw me, rose, and bade me hail,
Saying, 'A welfare in thine eye reproves
Our fear of some disastrous chance for thee
On hill, or plain, at sea, or flooding ford.
So fierce a gale made havoc here of late
Among the strange devices of our kings;
Yea, shook this newer, stronger hall of ours,
And from the statue Merlin moulded for us
Half-wrench'd a golden wing; but now—the Quest,
This vision—hast thou seen the Holy Cup,
That Joseph brought of old to Glastonbury?'

"So when I told him all thyself hast heard,
Ambrosius, and my fresh but fixt resolve
To pass away into the quiet life,
He answer'd not, but, sharply turning, ask'd
Of Gawain, 'Gawain, was this Quest for thee?'

"'Nay, lord,' said Gawain, 'not for such as I.
Therefore I communed with a saintly man,
Who made me sure the Quest was not for me;
For I was much awearied of the Quest:
But found a silk pavilion in a field,
And merry maidens in it; and then this gale
Tore my pavilion from the tenting-pin,
And blew my merry maidens all about
With all discomfort; yea, and but for this,
My twelvemonth and a day were pleasant to me.'

"He ceased; and Arthur turn'd to whom at first
He saw not, for Sir Bors, on entering, push'd
Athwart the throng to Lancelot, caught his hand,
Held it, and there, half-hidden by him, stood,
Until the King espied him, saying to him,
'Hail, Bors! if ever loyal man and true
Could see it, thou hast seen the Grail;' and Bors,
'Ask me not, for I may not speak of it,
I saw it:' and the tears were in his eyes.

"Then there remain'd but Lancelot, for the rest
Spake but of sundry perils in the storm;
Perhaps, like him of Cana in Holy Writ,
Our Arthur kept his best until the last;
'Thou too, my Lancelot,' ask'd the King, 'my friend,
Our mightiest, hath this Quest avail'd for thee?'

"'Our mightiest!' answer'd Lancelot, with a groan;
'O King!'—and when he paused, methought I spied
A dying fire of madness in his eyes—
'O King, my friend, if friend of thine I be,
Happier are those that welter in their sin,
Swine in the mud, that cannot see for slime,
Slime of the ditch: but in me lived a sin
So strange, of such a kind, that all of pure,
Noble, and knightly in me twined and clung
Round that one sin, until the wholesome flower
And poisonous grew together, each as each,
Not to be pluck'd asunder; and when thy knights
Sware, I sware with them only in the hope
That could I touch or see the Holy Grail
They might be pluck'd asunder. Then I spake
To one most holy saint, who wept and said,
That save they could be pluck'd asunder, all
My Quest were but in vain; to whom I vow'd
That I would work according as he will'd.
And forth I went, and while I yearn'd and strove
To tear the twain asunder in my heart,
My madness came upon me as of old,
And whipt me into waste fields far away.
There was I beaten down by little men,
Mean knights, to whom the moving of my sword
And shadow of my spear had been enow
To scare them from me once; and then I came
All in my folly to the naked shore,
Wide flats, where nothing but coarse grasses grew,
But such a blast, my King, began to blow,
So loud a blast along the shore and sea,
Ye could not hear the waters for the blast,

Tho' heapt in mounds and ridges all the sea
Drove like a cataract, and all the sand
Swept like a river, and the clouded heavens
Were shaken with the motion and the sound.
And blackening in the sea-foam sway'd a boat,
Half-swallow'd in it, anchor'd with a chain;
And in my madness to myself I said,
"I will embark and I will lose myself,
And in the great sea wash away my sin."
I burst the chain, I sprang into the boat.
Seven days I drove along the dreary deep,
And with me drove the moon and all the stars;
And the wind fell, and on the seventh night
I heard the shingle grinding in the surge,
And felt the boat shock earth, and looking up,
Behold, the enchanted towers of Carbonek,
A castle like a rock upon a rock,
With chasm-like portals open to the sea,
And steps that met the breaker! there was none
Stood near it but a lion on each side
That kept the entry, and the moon was full.
Then from the boat I leapt, and up the stairs.
There drew my sword. With sudden-flaring manes
Those two great beasts rose upright like a man,
Each gript a shoulder, and I stood between;
And, when I would have smitten them, heard a voice,
"Doubt not, go forward; if thou doubt, the beasts
Will tear thee piecemeal." Then with violence
The sword was dash'd from out my hand, and fell.
And up into the sounding hall I past;
But nothing in the sounding hall I saw,
No bench nor table, painting on the wall,
Or shield of knight; only the rounded moon
Thro' the tall oriel on the rolling sea.
But always in the quiet house I heard,
Clear as a lark, high o'er me as a lark,
A sweet voice singing in the topmost tower
To the eastward: up I climb'd a thousand steps
With pain: as in a dream I seem'd to climb
For ever: at the last I reach'd a door,
A light was in the crannies, and I heard,
"Glory and joy and honor to our Lord
And to the Holy Vessel of the Grail."
Then in my madness I essay'd the door:
It gave; and thro' a stormy glare, a heat
As from a seventimes-heated furnace, I,
Blasted and burnt, and blinded as I was,
With such a fierceness that I swoon'd away—
Oh, yet methought I saw the Holy Grail,
All pall'd in crimson, samite, and around
Great angels, awful shapes, and wings and eyes.
And but for all my madness and my sin,
And then my swooning, I had sworn I saw
That which I saw; but what I saw was veil'd
And cover'd; and this Quest was not for me.'

"So speaking, and here ceasing, Lancelot left
The hall long silent, till Sir Gawain—nay,
Brother, I need not tell thee foolish words—
A reckless and irreverent knight was he,
Now bolden'd by the silence of his King—
Well, I will tell thee: 'O King, my liege,' he said,
'Hath Gawain fail'd in any quest of thine?
When have I stinted stroke in 'foughten field?
But as for thine, my good friend Percivale,
Thy holy nun and thou have driven men mad,
Yea, made our mightiest madder than our least.
But by mine eyes and by mine ears I swear,
I will be deafer than the blue-eyed cat,
And thrice as blind as any noonday owl,
To holy virgins in their ecstasies,
Henceforward.'

"'Deafer,' said the blameless King,
'Gawain, and blinder unto holy things
Hope not to make thyself by idle vows,
Being too blind to have desire to see.
But if indeed there came a sign from Heaven,

Blessed are Bors, Lancelot, and Percivale,
For these have seen according to their sight.
For every fiery prophet in old times,
And all the sacred madness of the bard,
When God made music thro' them, could but speak
His music by the framework and the chord;
And as ye saw it ye have spoken truth.

"'Nay—but thou errest, Lancelot: never yet
Could all of true and noble in knight and man
Twine round one sin, whatever it might be,
With such a closeness, but apart there grew,
Save that he were the swine thou spakest of,
Some root of knighthood and pure nobleness;
Whereto see thou, that it may bear its flower.

"'And spake I not too truly, O my knights?
Was I too dark a prophet when I said
To those who went upon the Holy Quest,
That most of them would follow wandering fires,
Lost in the quagmire?—lost to me and gone,
And left me gazing at a barren board,
And a lean Order—scarce return'd a tithe—
And out of those to whom the vision came
My greatest hardly will believe he saw;
Another hath beheld it afar off,
And leaving human wrongs to right themselves,
Cares but to pass into the silent life.
And one hath had the vision face to face,
And now his chair desires him here in vain,
However they may crown him otherwhere.

"'And some among you held, that if the King
Had seen the sight he would have sworn the vow:
Not easily, seeing that the King must guard
That which he rules, and is as but the hind
To whom a space of land is given to plough,
Who may not wander from the allotted field
Before his work be done; but, being done,
Let visions of the night or of the day
Come, as they will; and many a time they come,
Until this earth he walks on seems not earth,
This light that strikes his eyeball is not light,
This air that smites his forehead is not air
But vision—yea, his very hand and foot—
In moments when he feels he cannot die,
And knows himself no vision to himself,
Nor the high God a vision, nor that One
Who rose again: ye have seen what ye have seen.'

"So spake the King: I knew not all he meant."

PELLEAS AND ETTARRE.

KING ARTHUR made new knights to fill the gap
Left by the Holy Quest; and as he sat
In hall at old Caerleon, the high doors
Were softly sunder'd, and thro' these a youth,
Pelleas, and the sweet smell of the fields
Past, and the sunshine came along with him.

"Make me thy knight, because I know, Sir King,
All that belongs to knighthood, and I love."
Such was his cry; for having heard the King
Had let proclaim a tournament—the prize
A golden circlet and a knightly sword,
Full fain had Pelleas for his lady won
The golden circlet, for himself the sword:
And there were those who knew him near the King,
And promised for him: and Arthur made him knight.

And this new knight, Sir Pelleas of the isles—
But lately come to his inheritance,

And lord of many a barren isle was he—
Riding at noon, a day or twain before,
Across the forest call'd of Dean, to find
Caerleon and the King, had felt the sun
Beat like a strong knight on his helm, and reel'd
Almost to falling from his horse; but saw
Near him a mound of even-sloping side,
Whereon a hundred stately beeches grew,
And here and there great hollies under them,
But for a mile all round was open space,
And fern and heath: and slowly Pelleas drew
To that dim day, then binding his good horse
To a tree, cast himself down; and as he lay
At random looking over the brown earth
Thro' that green-glooming twilight of the grove,
It seem'd to Pelleas that the fern without
Burnt as a living fire of emeralds,
So that his eyes were dazzled looking at it.
Then o'er it crost the dimness of a cloud
Floating, and once the shadow of a bird
Flying, and then a fawn; and his eyes closed.
And since he loved all maidens, but no maid
In special, half-awake he whisper'd, "Where?
Oh, where? I love thee, tho' I know thee not.
For fair thou art and pure as Guinevere,
And I will make thee with my spear and sword
As famous—O my Queen, my Guinevere,
For I will be thine Arthur when we meet."

Suddenly waken'd with a sound of talk
And laughter at the limit of the wood,
And glancing thro' the hoary boles, he saw,
Strange as to some old prophet might have seem'd
A vision hovering on a sea of fire,
Damsels in divers colors like the cloud
Of sunset and sunrise, and all of them
On horses, and the horses richly trapt
Breast-high in that bright line of bracken stood:
And all the damsels talk'd confusedly,
And one was pointing this way, and one that,
Because the way was lost.

                              And Pelleas rose,
And loosed his horse, and led him to the light.
There she that seem'd the chief among them said,
"In happy time behold our pilot-star!
Youth, we are damsels-errant, and we ride,
Arm'd as ye see, to tilt against the knights
There at Caerleon, but have lost our way:
To right? to left? straight forward? back again?
Which? tell us quickly."

                         And Pelleas gazing thought,
"Is Guinevere herself so beautiful?"
For large her violet eyes look'd, and her bloom
A rosy dawn kindled in stainless heavens,
And round her limbs, mature in womanhood;
And slender was her hand and small her shape;
And but for those large eyes, the haunts of scorn,
She might have seem'd a toy to trifle with,
And pass and care no more. But while he gazed
The beauty of her flesh abash'd the boy,
As tho' it were the beauty of her soul:
For as the base man, judging of the good,
Puts his own baseness in him by default
Of will and nature, so did Pelleas lend
All the young beauty of his own soul to hers,
Believing her; and when she spake to him,
Stammer'd, and could not make her a reply.
For out of the waste islands had he come,
Where saving his own sisters he had known
Scarce any but the women of his isles,
Rough wives, that laugh'd and scream'd against the gulls,
Makers of nets, and living from the sea.

Then with a slow smile turn'd the lady round
And look'd upon her people; and as when

A stone is flung into some sleeping tarn,
The circle widens till it lip the marge,
Spread the slow smile thro' all her company.
Three knights were thereamong; and they too
    smiled,
Scorning him; for the lady was Ettarre,
And she was a great lady in her land.

Again she said, "O wild and of the woods,
Knowest thou not the fashion of our speech?
Or have the heavens but given thee a fair face,
Lacking a tongue?"

            "O damsel," answer'd he,
"I woke from dreams; and coming out of gloom
Was dazzled by the sudden light. and crave
Pardon: but will ye to Caerleon? I
Go likewise: shall I lead you to the King?"

"Lead then," she said; and thro' the woods they
    went.
And while they rode, the meaning in his eyes,
His tenderness of manner, and chaste awe,
His broken utterances and bashfulness,
Were all a burthen to her, and in her heart
She mutter'd, "I have lighted on a fool,
Raw, yet so stale!" But since her mind was bent
On hearing, after trumpet blown, her name
And title, "Queen of Beauty," in the lists
Cried—and beholding him so strong, she thought
That peradventure he will fight for me,
And win the circlet: therefore flatter'd him,
Being so gracious, that he wellnigh deem'd
His wish by hers was echo'd; and her knights
And all her damsels too were gracious to him,
For she was a great lady.

                And when they reach'd
Caerleon, ere they past to lodging, she,
Taking his hand, "O the strong hand," she said,
"See! look at mine! but wilt thou fight for me,
And win me this fine circlet, Pelleas,
That I may love thee?"

            Then his helpless heart
Leapt, and he cried, "Ay! wilt thou if I win?"
"Ay, that will I," she answer'd. and she laugh'd,
And straitly nipt the hand, and flung it from her;
Then glanced askew at those three knights of hers,
Till all her ladies laugh'd along with her.

"O happy world," thought Pelleas, "all, meseems,
Are happy; I the happiest of them all."
Nor slept that night for pleasure in his blood,
And green wood-ways, and eyes among the leaves;
Then being on the morrow knighted, sware
To love one only. And as he came away,
The men who met him rounded on their heels
And wonder'd after him, because his face
Shone like the countenance of a priest of old
Against the flame about a sacrifice
Kindled by fire from heaven: so glad was he.

Then Arthur made vast banquets, and strange
    knights
From the four winds came in: and each one sat,
Tho' served with choice from air, land, stream, and
    sea,
Oft in mid-banquet measuring with his eyes
His neighbor's make and might: and Pelleas look'd
Noble among the noble, for he dream'd
His lady loved him, and he knew himself
Loved of the King· and him his new-made knight
Worshipt, whose lightest whisper moved him more
Than all the ranged reasons of the world.

Then blush'd and brake the morning of the jousts,
And this was call'd "The Tournament of Youth;"

For Arthur, loving his young knight, withheld
His older and his mightier from the lists,
That Pelleas might obtain his lady's love,
According to her promise, and remain
Lord of the tourney. And Arthur had the jousts
Down in the flat field by the shore of Usk
Holden: the gilded parapets were crown'd
With faces, and the great tower fill'd with eyes
Up to the summit, and the trumpets blew.
There all day long Sir Pelleas kept the field
With honor: so by that strong hand of his
The sword and golden circlet were achieved.

Then rang the shout his lady loved: the heat
Of pride and glory fired her face; her eye
Sparkled; she caught the circlet from his lance,
And there before the people crown'd herself:
So for the last time she was gracious to him.

Then at Caerleon for a space—her look
Bright for all others, cloudier on her knight—
Linger'd Ettarre: and seeing Pelleas droop,
Said Guinevere. "We marvel at thee much,
O damsel, wearing this unsunny face
To him who won thee glory?" And she said,
"Had ye not held your Lancelot in your bower,
My Queen, he had not won." Whereat the Queen,
As one whose foot is bitten by an ant,
Glanced down upon her, turn'd and went her way.

But after, when her damsels and herself,
And those three knights all set their faces home,
Sir Pelleas follow'd. She that saw him cried,
"Damsels—and yet I should be shamed to say it—
I cannot bide Sir Baby. Keep him back
Among yourselves. Would rather that we had
Some rough old knight who knew the worldly way,
Albeit grizzlier than a bear, to ride
And jest with: take him to you, keep him off,
And pamper him with papmeat, if ye will,
Old milky fables of the wolf and sheep,
Such as the wholesome mothers tell their boys.
Nay, should ye try him with a merry one
To find his mettle, good: and if he fly us,
Small matter! let him." This her damsels heard,
And mindful of her small and cruel hand,
They, closing round him thro' the journey home,
Acted her hest, and always from her side
Restrain'd him with all manner of device,
So that he could not come to speak with her.
And when she gain'd her castle, upsprang the bridge,
Down rang the grate of iron thro' the groove,
And he was left alone in open field.

"These be the ways of ladies," Pelleas thought,
"To those who love them, trials of our faith.
Yea, let her prove me to the uttermost,
For loyal to the uttermost am I."
So made his moan: and, darkness falling, sought
A priory not far off, there lodged, but rose
With morning every day, and, moist or dry,
Full-arm'd upon his charger all day long
Sat by the walls, and no one open'd to him.

And this persistence turn'd her scorn to wrath.
Then calling her three knights, she charged them,
        "Out!
And drive him from the walls." And out they came,
But Pelleas overthrew them as they dash'd
Against him one by one; and these return'd,
But still he kept his watch beneath the wall.

Thereon her wrath became a hate: and once,
A week beyond, while walking on the walls
With her three knights, she pointed downward,
        "Look,
He haunts me—I cannot breathe—besieges me;
Down! strike him! put my hate into your strokes,

And drive him from my walls." And down they went,
And Pelleas overthrew them one by one;
And from the tower above him cried Ettarre,
"Bind him, and bring him in."

                    He heard her voice;
Then let the strong hand, which had overthrown
Her minion-knights, by those he overthrew
Be bounden straight, and so they brought him in.

Then when he came before Ettarre, the sight
Of her rich beauty made him at one glance
More bondsman in his heart than in his bonds.
Yet with good cheer he spake, "Behold me, Lady,
A prisoner, and the vassal of thy will;
And if thou keep me in thy donjon here,
Content am I so that I see thy face
But once a day: for I have sworn my vows,
And thou hast given thy promise, and I know
That all these pains are trials of my faith,
And that thyself when thou hast seen me strain'd
And sifted to the utmost, wilt at length
Yield me thy love and know me for thy knight."

Then she began to rail so bitterly,
With all her damsels, he was stricken mute:
But when she mock'd his vows and the great King,
Lighted on words: "For pity of thine own self,
Peace, Lady, peace: is he not thine and mine?"

"Thou fool," she said, "I never heard his voice
But long'd to break away. Unbind him now,
And thrust him out of doors: for save he be
Fool to the midmost marrow of his bones,
He will return no more." And those, her three,
Laugh'd, and unbound, and thrust him from the
          gate.

And after this, a week beyond, again
She call'd them, saying, "There he watches yet,
There like a dog before his master's door!
Kick'd, he returns: do ye not hate him, ye?
Ye know yourselves: how can ye bide at peace,
Affronted with his fulsome innocence?
Are ye but creatures of the board and bed,
No men to strike? Fall on him all at once,
And if ye slay him I reck not: if ye fail,
Give ye the slave mine order to be bound,
Bind him as heretofore, and bring him in:
It may be ye shall slay him in his bonds."

          She spake; and at her will they couch'd their
          spears,
Three against one: and Gawain passing by,
Bound upon solitary adventure, saw
Low down beneath the shadow of those towers
A villainy, three to one: and thro' his heart
The fire of honor and all noble deeds
Flash'd, and he call'd, "I strike upon thy side—
The caitiffs!" "Nay," said Pelleas, "but forbear;
He needs no aid who doth his lady's will."

So Gawain, looking at the villainy done,
Forbore, but in his heat and eagerness
Trembled and quiver'd, as the dog, withheld
A moment from the vermin that he sees
Before him, shivers, ere he springs and kills.

And Pelleas overthrew them, one to three;
And they rose up, and bound, and brought him in.
Then first her anger, leaving Pelleas, burn'd
Full on her knights in many an evil name
Of craven, weakling, and thrice-beaten hound:
"Yet, take him, ye that scarce are fit to touch,
Far less to bind, your victor, and thrust him out,
And let who will release him from his bonds,
And if he comes again—" There she brake short;
And Pelleas answer'd, "Lady, for indeed

I loved you and I deem'd you beautiful,
I cannot brook to see your beauty marr'd
Thro' evil spite: and if ye love me not,
I cannot bear to dream you so forsworn:
I had liefer ye were worthy of my love,
Than to be loved again of you—farewell;
And tho' ye kill my hope, not yet my love,
Vex not yourself: ye will not see me more."

While thus he spake, she gazed upon the man
Of princely bearing, tho' in bonds, and thought,
"Why have I push'd him from me? this man loves,
If love there be: yet him I loved not. Why?
I deem'd him fool? yea, so? or that in him
A something—was it nobler than myself?—
Seem'd my reproach? He is not of my kind.
He could not love me, did he know me well.
Nay, let him go—and quickly." And her knights
Laugh'd not, but thrust him bounden out of door.

Forth sprang Gawain, and loosed him from his
          bonds
And flung them o'er the walls; and afterward,
Shaking his hands, as from a lazar's rag,
"Faith of my body," he said, "and art thou not—
Yea, thou art he, whom late our Arthur made
Knight of his Table: yea and he that won
The circlet? wherefore hast thou so defamed
Thy brotherhood in me and all the rest,
As let these caitiffs on thee work their will?"

And Pelleas answer'd, "Oh, their wills are hers
For whom I won the circlet; and mine, hers,
Thus to be bounden, so to see her face,
Marr'd tho' it be with spite and mockery now,
Other than when I found her in the woods;
And tho' she hath me bounden but in spite,
And all to flout me, when they bring me in,
Let me be bounden, I shall see her face;
Else must I die thro' mine unhappiness."

And Gawain answer'd kindly tho' in scorn,
"Why, let my lady bind me if she will,
And let my lady beat me if she will:
But an she send her delegate to thrall
These fighting hands of mine—Christ kill me then
But I will slice him handless by the wrist,
And let my lady sear the stump for him,
Howl as he may. But hold me for your friend:
Come, ye know nothing: here I pledge my troth,
Yea, by the honor of the Table Round,
I will be leal to thee and work thy work,
And tame thy jailing princess to thine hand.
Lend me thine horse and arms, and I will say
That I have slain thee. She will let me in
To hear the manner of thy fight and fall;
Then, when I come within her counsels, then
From prime to vespers will I chant thy praise
As prowest knight and truest lover, more
Than any have sung thee living, till she long
To have thee back in lusty life again,
Not to be bound, save by white bonds and warm,
Dearer than freedom. Wherefore now thy horse
And armor: let me go: be comforted:
Give me three days to melt her fancy, and hope
The third night hence will bring thee news of gold."

Then Pelleas lent his horse and all his arms,
Saving the goodly sword, his prize, and took
Gawain's, and said, "Betray me not, but help—
Art thou not he whom men call light-of-love?"

"Ay," said Gawain, "for women be so light."
Then bounded forward to the castle walls,
And raised a bugle hanging from his neck,
And winded it, and that so musically
That all the old echoes hidden in the wall
Rang out like hollow woods at huntingtide.

Up ran a score of damsels to the tower;
"Avaunt," they cried, "our lady loves thee not."
But Gawain lifting up his vizor said,
"Gawain am I, Gawain of Arthur's court,
And I have slain this Pelleas whom ye hate:
Behold his horse and armor. Open gates,
And I will make you merry."

                    And down they ran,
Her damsels, crying to their lady, "Lo!
Pelleas is dead—he told us—he that hath
His horse and armor: will ye let him in?
He slew him! Gawain, Gawain of the court,
Sir Gawain—there he waits below the wall,
Blowing his bugle as who should say him nay."

And so, leave given, straight on thro' open door
Rode Gawain, whom she greeted courteously.
"Dead, is it so?" she ask'd. "Ay, ay," said he,
"And oft in dying cried upon your name."
"Pity on him," she answer'd, "a good knight,
But never let me bide one hour at peace."
"Ay," thought Gawain, "and you be fair enow:
But I to your dead man have given my troth,
That whom ye loathe, him will I make you love."

So those three days, aimless about the land,
Lost in a doubt, Pelleas wandering
Waited, until the third night brought a moon
With promise of large light on woods and ways.

Hot was the night and silent; but a sound
Of Gawain ever coming, and this lay—
Which Pelleas had heard sung before the Queen,
And seen her sadden listening—vext his heart,
And marr'd his rest—"A worm within the rose."

"A rose, but one, none other rose had I,
A rose, one rose, and this was wondrous fair,
One rose, a rose that gladden'd earth and sky,
One rose, my rose, that sweeten'd all mine air—
I cared not for the thorns; the thorns were there.

"One rose, a rose to gather by and by,
One rose, one rose, to gather and to wear,
No rose but one—what other rose had I?
One rose, my rose; a rose that will not die—
He dies who loves it—if the worm be there."

This tender rhyme, and evermore the doubt,
"Why lingers Gawain with his golden news?"
So shook him that he could not rest, but rode
Ere midnight to her walls, and bound his horse
Hard by the gates. Wide open were the gates,
And no watch kept; and in thro' these he past,
And heard but his own steps, and his own heart
Beating, for nothing moved but his own self,
And his own shadow. Then he crost the court,
And spied not any light in hall or bower,
But saw the postern portal also wide
Yawning; and up a slope of garden, all
Of roses white and red, and brambles mixt
And overgrowing them, went on, and found,
Here too, all hush'd below the mellow moon,
Save that one rivulet from a tiny cave
Came lightening downward, and so spilt itself
Among the roses, and was lost again.

Then was he ware of three pavilions rear'd
Above the bushes, gilden-peakt: in one,
Red after revel, droned her hurdane knights
Slumbering, and their three squires across their feet:
In one, their malice on the placid lip
Froz'n by sweet sleep, four of her damsels lay:
And in the third, the circlet of the jousts
Bound on her brow, were Gawain and Ettarre.

Back, as a hand that pushes thro' the leaf

To find a nest and feels a snake, he drew:
Back, as a coward slinks from what he fears
To cope with, or a traitor proven, or hound
Beaten, did Pelleas in an utter shame
Creep with his shadow thro' the court again,
Fingering at his sword-handle until he stood
There on the castle-bridge once more, and thought,
"I will go back, and slay them where they lie."

And so went back, and seeing them yet in sleep
Said, "Ye, that so dishallow the holy sleep,
Your sleep is death," and drew the sword, and
        thought,
"What! slay a sleeping knight? the King hath
        bound
And sworn me to this brotherhood;" again,
"Alas that ever a knight should be so false!"
Then turn'd, and so return'd, and groaning laid
The naked sword athwart their naked throats,
There left it, and them sleeping; and she lay,
The circlet of the tourney round her brows,
And the sword of the tourney across her throat.

And forth he past, and mounting on his horse
Stared at her towers that, larger than themselves
In their own darkness, throng'd into the moon.
Then crush'd the saddle with his thighs, and clench'd
His hands, and madden'd with himself and moan'd:

"Would they have risen against me in their blood
At the last day? I might have answer'd them
Even before high God. O towers so strong,
Huge, solid, would that even while I gaze
The crack of earthquake shivering to your base
Split you, and Hell burst up your harlot roofs
Bellowing, and charr'd you thro' and thro' within,
Black as the harlot's heart—hollow as a skull!
Let the fierce east scream thro' your eyelet-holes,
And whirl the dust of harlots round and round
In dung and nettles! hiss, snake—I saw him there—
Let the fox bark, let the wolf yell. Who yells
Here in the still sweet summer night, but I—
I, the poor Pelleas whom she call'd her fool?
Fool, beast—he, she, or I? myself most fool;
Beast too, as lacking human wit—disgraced,
Dishonor'd all for trial of true love—
Love?—we be all alike: only the King
Hath made us fools and liars. O noble vows!
O great and sane and simple race of brutes
That own no lust because they have no law!
For why should I have loved her to my shame?
I loathe her, as I loved her to my shame.
I never loved her, I but lusted for her—
Away—"

                He dash'd the rowel into his horse,
And bounded forth and vanish'd thro' the night.

Then she, that felt the cold touch on her throat,
Awaking knew the sword, and turn'd herself
To Gawain: "Liar, for thou hast not slain
This Pelleas! here he stood, and might have slain
Me and thyself." And he that tells the tale
Says that her ever-veering fancy turn'd
To Pelleas, as the one true knight on earth,
And only lover; and thro' her love her life
Wasted and pined, desiring him in vain.

But he by wild and way, for half the night,
And over hard and soft, striking the sod
From out the soft, the spark from off the hard,
Rode till the star above the wakening sun,
Beside that tower where Percivale was cowl'd,
Glanced from the rosy forehead of the dawn.
For so the words were flash'd into his heart
He knew not whence or wherefore: "O sweet star,
Pure on the virgin forehead of the dawn!"
And there he would have wept, but felt his eyes

Harder and drier than a fountain bed
In summer: thither came the village girls
And linger'd talking, and they come no more
Till the sweet heavens have fill'd it from the heights
Again with living waters in the change
Of seasons: hard his eyes; but so weary were his limbs, that he,
Seem'd; but so weary were his limbs, that he,
Gasping, "Of Arthur's hall am I, but here,
Here let me rest and die," cast himself down,
And gulf'd his griefs in inmost sleep; so lay,
Till shaken by a dream, that Gawain fired
The hall of Merlin, and the morning star   .
Reel'd in the smoke, brake into flame, and fell.

He woke, and being ware of some one nigh,
Sent hands upon him, as to tear him, crying,
"False! I held thee as pure as Guinevere."

But Percivale stood near him and replied,
"Am I but false as Guinevere is pure?
Or art thou mazed with dreams? or being one
Of our free-spoken Table hast not heard
That Lancelot"—there he check'd himself and paused.

Then fared it with Sir Pelleas as with one
Who gets a wound in battle, and the sword
That made it plunges thro' the wound again,
And pricks it deeper; and he shrank and wail'd,
"Is the Queen false?" and Percivale was mute.
"Have any of our Round Table held their vows?"
And Percivale made answer not a word.
"Is the King true?" "The King!" said Percivale.
"Why then let men couple at once with wolves.
What! art thou mad?"

                        But Pelleas, leaping up,
Ran thro' the doors and vaulted on his horse
And fled: small pity upon his horse had he,
Or on himself, or any, and when he met
A cripple, one that held a hand for alms—
Hunch'd as he was, and like an old dwarf-elm
That turns its back on the salt blast, the boy
Paused not, but overrode him, shouting, "False,
And false with Gawain!" and so left him bruised
And batter'd, and fled on, and hill and wood
Went ever streaming by him till the gloom,
That follows on the turning of the world,
Darken'd the common path: he twitch'd the reins,
And made his beast, that better knew it, swerve
Now off it and now on; but when he saw
High up in heaven the hall that Merlin built,
Blackening against the dead-green stripes of even,
"Black nest of rats," he groan'd, "ye build too high."

Not long thereafter from the city gates
Issued Sir Lancelot riding airily,
Warm with a gracious parting from the Queen,
Peace at his heart, and gazing at a star
And marvelling what it was: on whom the boy,
Across the silent seeded meadow-grass
Borne, clash'd: and Lancelot, saying, "What name
         hast thou
That ridest here so blindly and so hard?"
"I have no name," he shouted, "a scourge am I,
To lash the treasons of the Table Round."
"Yea, but thy name?" "I have many names," he
         cried:
"I am wrath and shame and hate and evil fame,
And like a poisonous wind I pass to blast
And blaze the crime of Lancelot and the Queen."
"First over me," said Lancelot, "shalt thou pass."
"Fight therefore," yell'd the other, and either knight
Drew back a space, and when they closed, at once
The weary steed of Pelleas floundering flung
His rider, who call'd out from the dark field,
"Thou art false as Hell: slay me: I have no sword."
Then Lancelot, "Yea, between thy lips—and sharp;
But here will I disedge it by thy death."

"Slay then," he shriek'd, "my will is to be slain."
And Lancelot, with his heel upon the fall'n,
Rolling his eyes, a moment stood, then spake:
"Rise, weakling; I am Lancelot; say thy say."

And Lancelot slowly rode his warhorse back
To Camelot, and Sir Pelleas in brief while
Caught his unbroken limbs from the dark field,
And follow'd to the city. It chanced that both
Brake into hall together, worn and pale.
There with her knights and dames was Guinevere.
Full wonderingly she gazed on Lancelot
So soon return'd, and then on Pelleas, him
Who had not greeted her, but cast himself
Down on a bench, hard - breathing. "Have ye
         fought?"
She ask'd of Lancelot. "Ay, my Queen," he said.
"And thou hast overthrown him?" "Ay, my Queen."
Then she, turning to Pelleas, "O young knight,
Hath the great heart of knighthood in thee fail'd
So far thou canst not bide, unfrowardly,
A fall from him?" Then, for he answer'd not,
"Or hast thou other griefs? If I, the Queen,
May help them, loose thy tongue, and let me know."
But Pelleas lifted up an eye so fierce
She quail'd; and he, hissing, "I have no sword,"
Sprang from the door into the dark. The Queen
Look'd hard upon her lover, he on her;
And each foresaw the dolorous day to be:
And all talk died, as in a grove all song
Beneath the shadow of some bird of prey;
Then a long silence came upon the hall,
And Modred thought, "The time is hard at hand."

<hr>

THE LAST TOURNAMENT.

" Danced like a wither'd leaf before the hall."

DAGONET, the fool, whom Gawain in his mood
Had made mock-knight of Arthur's Table Round,
At Camelot, high above the yellowing woods,
Danced like a wither'd leaf before the hall.
And toward him from the hall, with harp in hand,
And from the crown thereof a carcanet
Of ruby swaying to and fro, the prize

Of Tristram in the jousts of yesterday,
Came Tristram, saying, "Why skip ye so, Sir Fool?"

For Arthur and Sir Lancelot riding once
Far down beneath a winding wall of rock
Heard a child wail. A stump of oak half-dead,
From roots like some black coil of carven snakes,
Clutch'd at the crag, and started thro' mid-air
Bearing an eagle's nest: and thro' the tree
Rush'd ever a rainy wind, and thro' the wind
Pierced ever a child's cry: and crag and tree
Scaling, Sir Lancelot from the perilous nest,
This ruby necklace thrice around her neck,
And all unscarr'd from beak or talon, brought
A maiden babe; which Arthur pitying took,
Then gave it to his Queen to rear: the Queen
But coldly acquiescing, in her white arms
Received, and after loved it tenderly,
And named it Nestling; so forgot herself
A moment, and her cares; till that young life
Being smitten in mid-heaven with mortal cold
Past from her; and in time the carcanet
Vext her with plaintive memories of the child:
So she, delivering it to Arthur, said,
"Take thou the jewels of this dead innocence,
And make them, an thou wilt, a tourney-prize."

To whom the King, "Peace to thine eagle-borne
Dead nestling, and this honor after death,
Following thy will! but, O my Queen, I muse
Why ye not wear on arm, or neck, or zone
Those diamonds that I rescued from the tarn,
And Lancelot won, methought, for thee to wear."

"Would rather you had let them fall," she cried,
"Plunge and be lost—ill-fated as they were,
A bitterness to me!—ye look amazed,
Not knowing they were lost as soon as given—
Slid from my hands, when I was leaning out
Above the river—that unhappy child
Past in her barge: but rosier luck will go
With these rich jewels, seeing that they came
Not from the skeleton of a brother-slayer,
But the sweet body of a maiden babe.
Perchance—who knows?—the purest of thy knights
May win them for the purest of my maids."

She ended, and the cry of a great joust
With trumpet-blowings ran on all the ways
From Camelot in among the faded fields
To furthest towers; and everywhere the knights
Arm'd for a day of glory before the King.

But on the hither side of that loud morn
Into the hall stagger'd, his visage ribb'd
From ear to ear with dogwhip-weals, his nose
Bridge-broken, one eye out, and one hand off,
And one with shatter'd fingers dangling lame,
A churl, to whom indignantly the King,

"My churl, for whom Christ died, what evil beast
Hath drawn his claws athwart thy face? or fiend?
Man was it who marr'd heaven's image in thee thus?"

Then, sputtering thro' the hedge of splinter'd teeth,
Yet strangers to the tongue, and with blunt stump
Pitch-blacken'd sawing the air, said the maim'd churl,

"He took them and he drave them to his tower—
Some hold he was a table-knight of thine—
A hundred goodly ones—the Red Knight, he—
Lord, I was tending swine, and the Red Knight
Brake in upon me and drave them to his tower;
And when I call'd upon thy name as one
That doest right by gentle and by churl,
Maim'd me and maul'd, and would outright have slain,
Save that he sware me to a message, saying,

'Tell thou the King and all his liars, that I
Have founded my Round Table in the North,
And whatsoever his own knights have sworn
My knights have sworn the counter to it—and say
My tower is full of harlots, like his court,
But mine are worthier, seeing they profess
To be none other than themselves—and say
My knights are all adulterers like his own,
But mine are truer, seeing they profess
To be none other; and say his hour is come,
The heathen are upon him, his long lance
Broken, and his Excalibur a straw.'"

Then Arthur turn'd to Kay, the seneschal,
"Take thou my churl, and tend him curiously
Like a king's heir, till all his hurts be whole.
The heathen—but that ever-climbing wave,
Hurl'd back again so often in empty foam,
Hath lain for years at rest—and renegades,
Thieves, bandits, leavings of confusion, whom
The wholesome realm is purged of otherwhere,
Friends, thro' your manhood and your fealty—now
Make their last head like Satan in the North.
My younger knights, new-made, in whom your flower
Waits to be solid fruit of golden deeds,
Move with me toward their quelling, which achieved,
The loneliest ways are safe from shore to shore.
But thou, Sir Lancelot, sitting in my place
Enchair'd to-morrow, arbitrate the field;
For wherefore shouldst thou care to mingle with it,
Only to yield my Queen her own again?
Speak, Lancelot, thou art silent: is it well?"

Thereto Sir Lancelot answer'd, "It is well:
Yet better if the King abide, and leave
The leading of his younger knights to me.
Else, for the King has will'd it, it is well.'

Then Arthur rose and Lancelot follow'd him,
And while they stood without the doors, the King
Turn'd to him saying, "Is it then so well?
Or mine the blame that oft I seem as he
Of whom was written, 'A sound is in his ears?'
The foot that loiters, bidden go—the glance
That only seems half-loyal to command—
A manner somewhat fall'n from reverence—
Or have I dream'd the bearing of our knights
Tells of a manhood ever less and lower?
Or whence the fear lest this my realm, uprear'd,
By noble deeds at one with noble vows,
From flat confusion and brute violences,
Reel back into the beast, and be no more?"

He spoke, and taking all his younger knights,
Down the slope city rode, and sharply turn'd
North by the gate. In her high bower the Queen,
Working a tapestry, lifted up her head,
Watch'd her lord pass, and knew not that she sigh'd.
Then ran across her memory the strange rhyme
Of bygone Merlin, "Where is he who knows?
From the great deep to the great deep he goes."

But when the morning of a tournament,
By these in earnest those in mockery call'd
The Tournament of the Dead Innocence,
Brake with a wet wind blowing, Lancelot,
Round whose sick head all night, like birds of prey,
The words of Arthur flying shriek'd, arose,
And down a streetway hung with folds of pure
White samite, and by fountains running wine,
Where children sat in white with cups of gold,
Moved to the lists, and there, with slow sad steps
Ascending, fill'd his double-dragon'd chair.

He glanced and saw the stately galleries,
Dame, damsel, each thro' worship of their Queen
White-robed in honor of the stainless child,
And some with scatter'd jewels, like a bank

Of maiden snow mingled with sparks of fire.
He look'd but once, and veil'd his eyes again.

The sudden trumpet sounded as in a dream
To ears but half-awaked, then one low roll
Of Autumn thunder, and the jousts began:
And ever the wind blew, and yellowing leaf
And gloom and gleam, and shower and shorn plume,
Went down it. Sighing wearicdly, as one
Who sits and gazes on a faded fire,
When all the goodlier guests are past away,
Sat their great umpire, looking o'er the lists.
He saw the laws that ruled the tournament
Broken, but spake not; once, a knight cast down
Before his throne of arbitration cursed
The dead babe and the follies of the King;
And once the laces of a helmet crack'd,
And show'd him, like a vermin in its hole,
Modred, a narrow face: anon he heard
The voice that billow'd round the barriers roar
An ocean-sounding welcome to one knight,
But newly enter'd, taller than the rest,
And armor'd all in forest green, whereon
There tript a hundred tiny silver deer,
And wearing but a holly spray for crest,
With ever-scattering berries, and on shield
A spear, a harp, a bugle—Tristram—late
From overseas in Brittany return'd,
And marriage with a princess of that realm,
Isolt the White—Sir Tristram of the Woods—
Whom Lancelot knew, had held sometime with pain
His own against him, and now yearn'd to shake
The burthen off his heart in one full shock
With Tristram ev'n to death: his strong hands gript
And dinted the gilt dragons right and left,
Until he groan'd for wrath—so many of those,
That wore their ladies' colors on the casque,
Drew from before Sir Tristram to the bounds,
And there with gibes and flickering mockeries
Stood, while he mutter'd, "Craven crests! O shame!
What faith have these in whom they sware to love?
The glory of our Round Table is no more."

So Tristram won, and Lancelot gave, the gems,
Not speaking other word than "Hast thou won?
Art thou the purest, brother? See, the hand
Wherewith thou takest this, is red!" to whom
Tristram, half plagued by Lancelot's langnorous
          mood,
Made answer, "Ay, but wherefore toss me this
Like a dry bone cast to some hungry hound?
Let be thy fair Queen's fantasy. Strength of heart
And might of limb, but mainly use and skill,
Are winners in this pastime of our King.
My hand—belike the lance hath dript upon it—
No blood of mine, I trow; but, O chief knight,
Right arm of Arthur in the battlefield,
Great brother, thou nor I have made the world;
Be happy in thy fair Queen as I in mine."

And Tristram round the gallery made his horse
Caracole; then bow'd his homage, bluntly saying,
"Fair damsels, each to him who worships each
Sole Queen of Beauty and of love, behold
This day my Queen of Beauty is not here."
And most of these were mute, some anger'd, one
Murmuring, "All courtesy is dead," and one,
"The glory of our Round Table is no more."

Then fell thick rain, plume droopt and mantle
          clung,
And pettish cries awoke, and the wan day
Went glooming down in wet and weariness:
But under her black brows a swarthy one
Laugh'd shrilly, crying, "Praise the patient saints,
Onr one white day of Innocence hath past,
Tho' somewhat draggled at the skirt. So be it.
The snowdrop only, flowering thro' the year,

Would make the world as blank as Winter-tide.
Come—let us gladden their sad eyes, our Queen's
And Lancelot's, at this night's solemnity
With all the kindlier colors of the field."

So dame and damsel glitter'd at the feast
Variously gay: for he that tells the tale
Liken'd them, saying, as when an honr of cold
Falls on the mountain in midsummer snows,
And all the purple slopes of mountain flowers
Pass under white, till the warm honr returns
With veer of wind, and all are flowers again;
So dame and damsel cast the simple white,
And glowing in all colors, the live grass,
Rose-campion, blue-bell, kingcup, poppy, glanced
About the revels, and with mirth so loud
Beyond all use, that, half-amazed, the Queen,
And wroth at Tristram and the lawless jousts,
Brake up their sports, then slowly to her bower
Parted, and in her bosom pain was lord.

And little Dagonet on the morrow morn,
High over all the yellowing Autumn-tide,
Danced like a wither'd leaf before the hall.
Then Tristram saying, "Why skip ye so, Sir Fool?"
Wheel'd round on either heel, Dagonet replied,
"Belike for lack of wiser company:
Or being fool, and seeing too much wit
Makes the world rotten, why, belike I skip
To know myself the wisest knight of all."
"Ay, fool," said Tristram, "but 'tis eating dry
To dance without a catch, a roundelay
To dance to." Then he twangled on his harp,
And while he twangled little Dagonet stood,
Quiet as any water-sodden log
Stay'd in the wandering warble of a brook;
But when the twangling ended, skipt again;
And being ask'd, "Why skipt ye not, Sir Fool?"
Made answer, "I had liefer twenty years
Skip to the broken mnsic of my brains
Than any broken music thou canst make."
Then Tristram, waiting for the qnip to come,
"Good now, what music have I broken, fool?"
And little Dagonet, skipping, "Arthnr, the King's;
For when thou playest that air with Queen Isolt,
Thon makest broken music with thy bride,
Her daintier namesake down in Brittany—
And so thou breakest Arthur's music too."
"Save for that broken music in thy brains,
Sir Fool," said Tristram, "I would break thy head.
Fool, I came late, the heathen wars were o'er,
The life had flown, we sware but by the shell—
I am but a fool to reason with a fool—
Come, thou art crabb'd and sour; but lean me down,
Sir Dagonet, one of thy long asses' ears,
And hearken if my music be not true.

"'Free love—free field—we love but while we may:
The woods are hush'd, their music is no more:
The leaf is dead, the yearning past away:
New leaf, new life—the days of frost are o'er:
New life, new love, to suit the newer day:
New loves are sweet as those that went before:
Free love—free field—we love but while we may.'

"Ye might have moved slow-measure to my tune,
Not stood stockstill. I made it in the woods,
And heard it ring as true as tested gold."

But Dagonet, with one foot poised in his hand,
"Friend, did ye mark that fountain yesterday
Made to run wine?—but this had run itself
All out like a long life to a sour end—
And them that round it sat with golden cups
To hand the wine to whosoever came—
The twelve small damosels white as Innocence,
In honor of poor Innocence the babe,
Who left the gems which Innocence the Queen

" But Dagonet, with one foot poised in his hand."

Lent to the King, and Innocence the King
Gave for a prize—and one of those white slips
Handed her cup and piped, the pretty one,
'Drink, drink, Sir Fool,' and thereupon I drank,
Spat—pish—the cup was gold, the draught was mud."

And Tristram, "Was it muddier than thy gibes?
Is all the laughter gone dead out of thee?—
Not marking how the knighthood mock thee, fool—
'Fear God: honor the King—his one true knight—
Sole follower of the vows'—for here be they
Who knew thee swine enow before I came,
Smuttier than blasted grain: but when the King
Had made thee fool, thy vanity so shot up
It frighted all free fool from out thy heart:
Which left thee less than fool, and less than swine,
A naked nught—yet swine I hold thee still,
For I have flung thee pearls and find thee swine."

And little Dagonet mincing with his feet,
"Knight, an ye fling those rubies round my neck
In lieu of hers, I'll hold thou hast some touch
Of music, since I care not for thy pearls.
Swine? I have wallow'd, I have wash'd—the world
Is flesh and shadow—I have had my day.
The dirty nurse, Experience, in her kind
Hath fool'd me—an I wallow'd, then I wash'd—
I have had my day and my philosophies—
And thank the Lord I am King Arthur's fool.
Swine, say ye? swine, goats, asses, rams, and geese
Troop'd round a Paynim harper once, who thrumm'd
On such a wire as musically as thou
Some such fine song—but never a king's fool."

And Tristram, "Then were swine, goats, asses, geese,
The wiser fools, seeing thy Paynim bard
Had such a mastery of his mystery
That he could harp his wife up out of hell."

Then Dagonet, turning on the ball of his foot,

"And whither harp'st thou thine? down! and thy-
self
Down! and two more: a helpful harper thou,
That harpest downward! Dost thou know the star
We call the harp of Arthur up in heaven?"

And Tristram, "Ay, Sir Fool, for when our King
Was victor wellnigh day by day, the knights,
Glorying in each new glory, set his name
High on all hills, and in the signs of heaven."

And Dagonet answer'd, "Ay, and when the land
Was freed, and the Queen false, ye set yourself
To babble about him, all to show your wit—
And whether he were King by courtesy,
Or King by right—and so went harping down
The black king's highway, got so far, and grew
So witty that ye play'd at ducks and drakes
With Arthur's vows on the great lake of fire.
Tuwhoo! do you see it? do you see the star?"

"Nay, fool," said Tristram, "not in open day."
And Dagonet, "Nay, nor will: I see it and hear.
It makes a silent music up in heaven,
And I, and Arthur and the angels hear,
And then we skip." "Lo, fool," he said, "ye talk
Fool's treason: is the King thy brother fool?"
Then little Dagonet clapt his hands and shrill'd,
"Ay, ay, my brother fool, the king of fools!
Conceits himself as God that he can make
Figs out of thistles, silk from bristles, milk
From burning spurge, honey from hornet-combs,
And men from beasts—Long live the king of fools!"

And down the city Dagonet danced away;
But thro' the slowly-mellowing avenues
And solitary passes of the wood
Rode Tristram toward Lyonnesse and the west.
Before him fled the face of Queen Isolt
With ruby-circled neck, but evermore
Past, as a rustle or twitter in the wood

Made dull his inner, keen his outer eye
For all that walk'd, or crept, or perch'd, or flew.
Anon the face, as, when a gust hath blown,
Unruffling waters re-collect the shape
Of one that in them sees himself, return'd;
But at the slot or fewmets of a deer,
Or ev'n a fall'n feather, vanish'd again.

So on for all that day from lawn to lawn
Thro' many a league-long bower he rode.   At length
A lodge of intertwisted beechen-boughs
Furze-cramm'd, and bracken-rooft, the which himself
Built for a summer day with Queen Isolt
Against a shower, dark in the golden grove
Appearing, sent his fancy back to where
She lived a moon in that low lodge with him:
Till Mark her lord had past, the Cornish king,
With six or seven, when Tristram was away,
And snatch'd her thence; yet dreading worse than
      shame
Her warrior Tristram, spake not any word,
But bode his hour, devising wretchedness.

And now that desert lodge to Tristram lookt
So sweet, that halting, in he past, and sank
Down on a drift of foliage random-blown;
But could not rest for musing how to smoothe
And sleek his marriage over to the Queen.
Perchance in lone Tintagil far from all
The tonguesters of the court she had not heard.
But then what folly had sent him overseas
After she left him lonely here? a name?
Was it the name of one in Brittany,
Isolt, the daughter of the King?   "Isolt
Of the white hands" they call'd her: the sweet name
Allured him first, and then the maid herself,
Who served him well with those white hands of hers,
And loved him well, until himself had thought
He loved her also, wedded easily,
But left her all as easily, and return'd.
The black-blue Irish hair and Irish eyes
Had drawn him home—what marvel? then he laid
His brows upon the drifted leaf and dream'd.

He seem'd to pace the strand of Brittany
Between Isolt of Britain and his bride,
And show'd them both the ruby chain, and both
Began to struggle for it, till his Queen
Graspt it so hard, that all her hand was red.
Then cried the Breton, "Look, her hand is red!
These be no rubies, this is frozen blood,
And melts within her hand—her hand is hot
With ill desires, but this I gave thee, look,
Is all as cool and white as any flower."
Follow'd a rush of eagle's wings, and then
A whimpering of the spirit of the child,
Because the twain had spoilt her carcanet.

He dream'd; but Arthur with a hundred spears
Rode far, till o'er the illimitable reed,
And many a glancing plash and sallowy isle,
The wide-wing'd sunset of the misty marsh
Glared on a huge machicolated tower
That stood with open doors, whereout was roll'd
A roar of riot, as from men secure
Amid their marshes, ruffians at their ease
Among their harlot-brides, an evil song.
"Lo there," said one of Arthur's youth, for there,
High on a grim dead tree before the tower,
A goodly brother of the Table Round
Swung by the neck; and on the boughs a shield
Showing a shower of blood in a field noir,
And therebeside a horn, inflamed the knights
At that dishonor done the gilded spur,
Till each would clash the shield, and blow the horn.
But Arthur waved them back. Alone he rode,
Then at the dry harsh roar of the great horn,
That sent the face of all the marsh aloft

An ever upward-rushing storm and cloud
Of shriek and plume, the Red Knight heard, and all,
Even to tipmost lance and topmost helm,
In blood-red armor sallying, howl'd to the King,

  "The teeth of hell flay bare and gnash thee flat!—
Lo! art thou not that eunuch-hearted King
Who fain had clipt free manhood from the world—
The woman-worshiper? Yea, God's curse, and I!
Slain was the brother of my paramour
By a knight of thine, and I that heard her whine
And snivel, being eunuch-hearted too,
Sware by the scorpion-worm that twists in hell,
And stings itself to everlasting death,
To hang whatever knight of thine I fought
And tumbled. Art thou King?—Look to thy life!"

He ended: Arthur knew the voice; the face
Welluigh was helmet-hidden, and the name
Went wandering somewhere darkling in his mind,
And Arthur deign'd not use of word or sword,
But let the drunkard, as he stretch'd from horse
To strike him, overbalancing his bulk,
Down from the causeway heavily to the swamp
Fall, as the crest of some slow-arching wave,
Heard in dead night along that table-shore,
Drops flat, and after the great waters break
Whitening for half a league, and thin themselves,
Far over sands marbled with moon and cloud,
From less and less to nothing; thus he fell
Head-heavy; then the knights, who watch'd him,
      roar'd
And shouted and leapt down upon the fall'n;
There trampled out his face from being known,
And sank his head in mire, and slimed themselves:
Nor heard the King for their own cries, but sprang
Thro' open doors, and swording right and left
Men, women, on their sodden faces, hurl'd
The tables over and the wines, and slew
Till all the rafters rang with woman-yells,
And all the pavement stream'd with massacre:
Then, yell with yell echoing, they fired the tower,
Which half that autumn night, like the live North,
Red-pulsing up thro' Alioth and Alcor,
Made all above it, and a hundred meres
About it, as the water Moab saw
Come round by the East, and out beyond them
      flush'd
The long low dune, and lazy-plunging sea.

So all the ways were safe from shore to shore,
But in the heart of Arthur pain was lord.

Then, out of Tristram waking, the red dream
Fled with a shout, and that low lodge return'd,
Mid-forest, and the wind among the boughs.
He whistled his good warhorse left to graze
Among the forest greens, vaulted upon him,
And rode beneath an ever-showering leaf,
Till one lone woman, weeping near a cross,
Stay'd him. "Why weep ye?" "Lord," she said,
      "my man
Hath left me or is dead;" whereon he thought—
"What, if she hate me now? I would not this.
What, if she love me still? I would not that.
I know not what I would"—but said to her,
"Yet weep not thou, lest, if thy mate return,
He find thy favor changed and love thee not"—
Then pressing day by day thro' Lyonnesse
Last in a rocky hollow, belling, heard
The hounds of Mark, and felt the goodly hounds
Yelp at his heart, but turning, past and gain'd
Tintagil, half in sea, and high on land,
A crown of towers.

                          Down in a casement sat,
A low sea-sunset glorying round her hair
And glossy-throated grace, Isolt the Queen.

And when she heard the feet of Tristram grind
The spiring stone that scaled about her tower,
Flush'd, started, met him at the doors, and there
Belted his body with her white embrace,
Crying aloud. "Not Mark—not Mark, my soul!
The footstep flutter'd me at first: not he:
Catlike thro' his own castle steals my Mark,
But warrior-wise thou stridest thro' his halls
Who hates thee, as I him—ev'n to the death.
My soul, I felt my hatred for my Mark
Quicken within me, and knew that thou wert nigh."
To whom Sir Tristram smiling, "I am here.
Let be thy Mark, seeing he is not thine."

And drawing somewhat backward, she replied,
"Can he be wrong'd who is not ev'n his own,
But save for dread of thee had beaten me,
Scratch'd, bitten, blinded, marr'd me somehow—
        Mark?
What rights are his that dare not strike for them?
Not lift a hand—not, tho' he found me thus!
But hearken! have ye met him? hence he went
To-day for three days' hunting—as he said—
And so returns belike within an hour.
Mark's way, my soul!—but eat not thou with Mark,
Because he hates thee even more than fears;
Nor drink: and when thou passest any wood
Close vizor, lest an arrow from the bush
Should leave me all alone with Mark and hell.
My God, the measure of my hate for Mark
Is as the measure of my love for thee."

So, pluck'd one way by hate and one by love,
Drain'd of her force, again she sat, and spake
To Tristram, as he knelt before her, saying,
"O hunter, and O blower of the horn,
Harper, and thou hast been a rover too,
For, ere I mated with my shambling king,
Ye twain had fallen out about the bride
Of one—his name is out of me—the prize,
If prize she were—(what marvel—she could see)—
Thine, friend; and ever since my craven seeks
To wreck thee villainously: but, O Sir Knight,
What dame or damsel have ye kneel'd to last?"

And Tristram, "Last to my Queen Paramount,
Here now to my Queen Paramount of love
And loveliness—ay, lovelier than when first
Her light feet fell on our rough Lyonnesse,
Sailing from Ireland."

                Softly laugh'd Isolt;
"Flatter me not, for hath not our great Queen
My dole of beauty trebled?" and he said,
"Her beauty is her beauty, and thine thine,
And thine is more to me—soft, gracious, kind—
Save when thy Mark is kindled on thy lips
Most gracious; but she, haughty, ev'n to him,
Lancelot; for I have seen him wan enow
To make one doubt if ever the great Queen
Have yielded him her love."

                To whom Isolt,
"Ah, then, false hunter and false harper, thou
Who breakest thro' the scruple of my bond,
Calling me thy white hind, and saying to me
That Guinevere had sinn'd against the highest,
And I—misyoked with such a want of man—
That I could hardly sin against the lowest."

He answer'd, "O my soul, be comforted!
If this be sweet, to sin in leading-strings,
If here be comfort, and if ours be sin,
Crown'd warrant had we for the crowning sin
That made us happy: but how ye greet me—fear
And fault and doubt—no word of that fond tale—
Thy deep heart-yearnings, thy sweet memories
Of Tristram in that year he was away."

        14

And, saddening on the sudden, spake Isolt,
"I had forgotten all in my strong joy
To see thee—yearnings?—ay! for, hour by hour,
Here in the never-ended afternoon,
O sweeter than all memories of thee,
Deeper than any yearnings after thee
Seem'd those far-rolling, westward-smiling seas,
Watch'd from this tower. Isolt of Britain dash'd
Before Isolt of Brittany on the strand,
Would that have chill'd her bride-kiss? Wedded
        her?
Fought in her father's battles? wounded there?
The King was all fulfill'd with gratefulness,
And she, my namesake of the hands, that heal'd
Thy hurt and heart with unguent and caress—
Well—can I wish her any huger wrong
Than having known thee? Her too hast thou left
To pine and waste in those sweet memories.
Oh, were I not my Mark's, by whom all men
Are noble, I should hate thee more than love."

And Tristram, fondling her light hands, replied,
"Grace, Queen, for being loved: she loved me well.
Did I love her? the name at least I loved.
Isolt?—I fought his battles for Isolt!
The night was dark; the true star set. Isolt!
The name was ruler of the dark— Isolt?
Care not for her! patient, and prayerful, meek,
Pale-blooded, she will yield herself to God."

And Isolt answer'd, "Yea, and why not I?
Mine is the larger need, who am not meek,
Pale-blooded, prayerful. Let me tell thee now.
Here one black, mute midsummer night I sat,
Lonely, but musing on thee, wondering where,
Murmuring a light song I had heard thee sing,
And once or twice I spake thy name aloud.
Then flash'd a levin-brand; and near me stood,
In fuming sulphur blue and green, a fiend—
Mark's way to steal behind one in the dark—
For there was Mark: 'He has wedded her,' he said,
Not said, but hiss'd it: then this crown of towers
So shook to such a roar of all the sky,
That here in utter dark I swoon'd away,
And woke again in utter dark, and cried,
'I will flee hence and give myself to God'—
And thou wert lying in thy new leman's arms."

Then Tristram, ever dallying with her hand,
"May God be with thee, sweet, when old and gray,
And past desire!" a saying that anger'd her.
"'May God be with thee, sweet, when thou art old,
And sweet no more to me!' I need Him now.
For when had Lancelot utter'd aught so gross
Ev'n to the swineherd's malkin in the mast?
The greater man, the greater courtesy.
Far other was the Tristram, Arthur's knight!
But then, thro' ever harping thy wild beasts—
Save that to touch a harp, tilt with a lance
Becomes thee well—art grown wild beast thyself.
How darest thou, if lover, push me even
In fancy from thy side, and set me far
In the gray distance, half a life away,
Her to be loved no more? Unsay it, unswear—
Flatter me rather, seeing me so weak,
Broken with Mark and hate and solitude,
Thy marriage and mine own, that I should suck
Lies like sweet wines: lie to me: I believe.
Will ye not lie? not swear, as there ye kneel,
And solemnly as when ye sware to him,
The man of men, our King—My God, the power
Was once in vows when men believed the King!
They lied not then, who sware, and thro' their vows
The King prevailing made his realm:—I say,
Swear to me thou wilt love me ev'n when old,
Gray-hair'd, and past desire, and in despair."

Then Tristram, pacing moodily up and down,

"Ay, ay, oh ay!"

"Vows! did you keep the vow you made to Mark
More than I mine? Lied, say ye? Nay, but learnt,'
The vow that binds too strictly snaps itself—
My knighthood taught me this—ay, being snapt—
We run more counter to the soul thereof
Than had we never sworn. I swear no more.
I swore to the great King, and am forsworn.
For once—ev'n to the height—I honor'd him.
'Man, is he man at all?' methought, when first
I rode from our rough Lyonnesse, and beheld
That victor of the Pagan throned in hall—
His hair, a sun that ray'd from off a brow
Like hillsnow high in heaven, the steel-blue eyes,
The golden beard that clothed his lips with light—
Moreover, that weird legend of his birth,
With Merlin's mystic babble about his end
Amazed me; then, his foot was on a stool

Shaped as a dragon; he seem'd to me no man,
But Michaël trampling Satan; so I sware,
Being amazed: but this went by—The vows!
Oh ay—the wholesome madness of an hour—
They served their use, their time: for every knight
Believed himself a greater than himself,
And every follower eyed him as a God;
Till he, being lifted up beyond himself,
Did mightier deeds than elsewise he had done,
And so the realm was made: but then their vows—
First mainly thro' that sullying of our Queen—
Began to gall the knighthood, asking whence
Had Arthur right to bind them to himself?
Dropt down from heaven? wash'd up from out the
    deep?
They fail'd to trace him thro' the flesh and blood
Of our old kings: whence then? a doubtful lord

To bind them by inviolable vows,
Which flesh and blood perforce would violate:
For feel this arm of mine—the tide within
Red with free chase and heather-scented air,
Pulsing full man ; can Arthur make me pure
As any maiden child ? lock up my tongue
From uttering freely what I freely hear?
Bind me to one ? The wide world laughs at it.
And worldling of the world am I, and know
The ptarmigan that whitens ere his hour
Wooes his own end ; we are not angels here
Nor shall be: vows—I am woodman of the woods,
And hear the garnet-headed yaffingale
Mock them : my soul, we love but while we may ;
And therefore is my love so large for thee,
Seeing it is not bounded save by love."

Here ending, he moved toward her, and she said,
"Good : an I turn'd away my love for thee
To some one thrice as courteous as thyself—
For courtesy wins woman all as well
As valor may, but he that closes both
Is perfect, he is Lancelot—taller indeed,
Rosier and comelier, thou—but say I loved
This knightliest of all knights, and cast thee back
Thine own small saw, 'We love but while we may,'
Well then, what answer ?"

        He that while she spake,
Mindful of what he brought to adorn her with,
The jewels, had let one finger lightly touch
The warm white apple of her throat, replied,
"Press this a little closer, sweet, until—
Come, I am hunger'd and half-anger'd—meat,
Wine, wine—and I will love thee to the death,
And out beyond into the dream to come."

So then, when both were brought to full accord,
She rose, and set before him all he will'd ;
And after these had comforted the blood
With meats and wines, and satiated their hearts—
Now talking of their woodland paradise,
The deer, the dews, the fern, the founts, the lawns ;
Now mocking at the much ungainliness,
And craven shifts, and long crane legs of Mark—
Then Tristram laughing caught the harp, and sang :

"Ay, ay, oh ay—the winds that bend the brier !
A star in heaven, a star within the mere !
Ay, ay, oh ay—a star was my desire,
And one was far apart, and one was near :
Ay, ay, oh ay—the winds that bow the grass !
And one was water and one star was fire,
And one will ever shine and one will pass.
Ay, ay, oh ay—the winds that move the mere."

Then in the light's last glimmer Tristram show'd
And swung the ruby carcanet. She cried,
"The collar of some Order, which our King
Hath newly founded, all for thee, my soul,
For thee, to yield thee grace beyond thy peers."

"Not so, my Queen," he said, "but the red fruit
Grown on a magic oak-tree in mid-heaven,
And won by Tristram as a tourney-prize,
And hither brought by Tristram for his last
Love-offering and peace-offering unto thee."

He rose, he turn'd, then, flinging round her neck,
Claspt it, and cried, "Thine Order, O my Queen !"
But, while he bow'd to kiss the jewell'd throat,
Out of the dark, just as the lips had touch'd,
Behind him rose a shadow and a shriek—
"Mark's way," said Mark, and clove him thro' the
    brain.

    That night came Arthur home, and while he
    climb'd,

"I am thy fool,
And I shall never make thee smile again."

All in a death-dumb, autumn-dripping gloom,
The stairway to the hall, and look'd and saw
The great Queen's bower was dark—about his feet
A voice clung sobbing till he question'd it,
"What art thou ?" and the voice about his feet
Sent up an answer, sobbing, "I am thy fool,
And I shall never make thee smile again."

            —⊲⊳—

GUINEVERE.

Queen Guinevere had fled the court, and sat
There in the holy house at Almesbury
Weeping, none with her save a little maid,
A novice: one low light betwixt them burn'd
Blurr'd by the creeping mist, for all abroad,
Beneath a moon unseen albeit at full,
The white mist, like a face-cloth to the face,
Clung to the dead earth, and the land was still.

For hither had she fled, her cause of flight
Sir Modred ; he that like a subtle beast
Lay couchant with his eyes upon the throne,
Ready to spring, waiting a chance : for this
He chill'd the popular praises of the King
With silent smiles of slow disparagement ;
And tamper'd with the Lords of the White Horse,
Heathen, the brood by Hengist left ; and sought
To make disruption in the Table Round
Of Arthur, and to splinter it into feuds
Serving his traitorous end ; and all his aims
Were sharpen'd by strong hate for Lancelot.

For thus it chanced one morn when all the court,
Green-suited, but with plumes that mock'd the may,
Had been, their wont, a-maying and return'd,
That Modred still in green, all ear and eye,
Climb'd to the high top of the garden-wall
To spy some secret scandal if he might,

And saw the Queen who sat betwixt her best
Enid, and lissome Vivien, of her court
The wiliest and the worst; and more than this
He saw not, for Sir Lancelot passing by
Spied where he couch'd, and as the gardener's hand
Picks from the colewort a green caterpillar,
So from the high wall and the flowering grove
Of grasses Lancelot pluck'd him by the heel,
And cast him as a worm upon the way;
But when he knew the Prince tho' marr'd with dust,
He, reverencing king's blood in a bad man,
Made such excuses as he might, and these
Full knightly without scorn; for in those days
No knight of Arthur's noblest dealt in scorn;
But, if a man were halt or hunch'd, in him
By those whom God had made full-limb'd and tall,
Scorn was allow'd as part of his defect,
And he was answer'd softly by the King
And all his Table. So Sir Lancelot holp
To raise the Prince. who rising twice or thrice
Full sharply smote his knees, and smiled, and went:
But, ever after, the small violence done
Rankled in him and ruffled all his heart,
As the sharp wind that ruffles all day long
A little bitter pool about a stone
On the bare coast.

          But when Sir Lancelot told
This matter to the Queen, at first she laugh'd
Lightly, to think of Modred's dusty fall,
Then shudder'd, as the village wife who cries
"I shudder, some one steps across my grave;"
Then laugh'd again, but faintlier, for indeed
She half-foresaw that he, the subtle beast,
Would track her guilt until he found, and hers
Would be for evermore a name of scorn.
Henceforward rarely could she front in hall,
Or elsewhere, Modred's narrow foxy face,
Heart-hiding smile. and gray persistent eye:
Henceforward too, the Powers that tend the soul,
To help it from the death that cannot die,
And save it even in extremes, began
To vex and plague her. Many a time for hours,
Beside the placid breathings of the King,
In the dead night, grim faces came and went
Before her, or a vague spiritual fear—
Like to some doubtful noise of creaking doors,
Heard by the watcher in a haunted house,
That keeps the rust of murder on the walls—
Held her awake: or if she slept, she dream'd
An awful dream; for then she seem'd to stand
On some vast plain before a setting sun,
And from the sun there swiftly made at her
A ghastly something, and its shadow flew
Before it, till it touch'd her, and she turn'd—
When lo! her own, that broadening from her feet,
And blackening, swallow'd all the land, and in it
Far cities burnt, and with a cry she woke.
And all this trouble did not pass but grew;
Till ev'n the clear face of the guileless King,
And trustful courtesies of household life,
Became her bane; and at the last she said,
"O Lancelot, get thee hence to thine own land,
For if thou tarry we shall meet again,
And if we meet again, some evil chance
Will make the smouldering scandal break and blaze
Before the people, and our lord the King."
And Lancelot ever promised, but remain'd,
And still they met and met. Again she said,
"O Lancelot, if thou love me get thee hence."
And then they were agreed upon a night
(When the good King should not be there) to meet
And part for ever. Passion-pale they met
And greeted: hands in hands, and eye to eye,
Low on the border of her couch they sat
Stammering and staring: it was their last hour,
A madness of farewells. And Modred brought
His creatures to the basement of the tower

For testimony; and crying with full voice
"Traitor, come out. ye are trapt at last," aroused
Lancelot, who rushing outward lionlike
Leapt on him, and hurl'd him headlong, and he fell
Stunn'd, and his creatures took and bare him off,
And all was still: then she, "The end is come,
And I am shamed for ever;" and he said,
"Mine be the shame; mine was the sin: but rise,
And fly to my strong castle overseas:
There will I hide thee, till my life shall end,
There hold thee with my life against the world."
She answer'd "Lancelot, wilt thou hold me so?
Nay, friend, for we have taken our farewells.
Would God that thou couldst hide me from myself!
Mine is the shame, for I was wife, and thou
Unwedded: yet rise now, and let us fly,
For I will draw me into sanctuary,
And bide my doom." So Lancelot got her horse,
Set her thereon, and mounted on his own,
And then they rode to the divided way,
There kiss'd, and parted weeping: for he past,
Love-loyal to the least wish of the Queen,
Back to his land; but she to Almesbury
Fled all night long by glimmering waste and weald,
And heard the Spirits of the waste and weald
Moan as she fled, or thought she heard them moan:
And in herself she moan'd "Too late, too late!"
Till in the cold wind that foreruns the morn,
A blot in heaven, the Raven, flying high,
Croak'd, and she thought, "He spies a field of
     death;
For now the Heathen of the Northern Sea,
Lured by the crimes and frailties of the court,
Begin to slay the folk, and spoil the land."

   And when she came to Almesbury she spake
There to the nuns, and said, "Mine enemies
Pursue me, but, O peaceful Sisterhood,
Receive, and yield me sanctuary, nor ask
Her name to whom ye yield it, till her time
To tell you:" and her beauty, grace, and power,
Wrought as a charm upon them, and they spared
To ask it.

        So the stately Queen abode
For many a week, unknown, among the nuns;
Nor with them mix'd, nor told her name, nor sought,
Wrapt in her grief, for housel or for shrift,
But communed only with the little maid,
Who pleased her with a babbling heedlessness
Which often lured her from herself; but now,
This night, a rumor wildly blown about
Came, that Sir Modred had usurp'd the realm,
And leagued him with the heathen, while the King
Was waging war on Lancelot: then she thought,
"With what a hate the people and the King
Must hate me," and bow'd down upon her hands
Silent, until the little maid, who brook'd
No silence, brake it, uttering, "Late! so late!
What hour, I wonder, now?" and when she drew
Nor answer, by and by began to hum
An air the nuns had taught her: "Late, so late!"
Which when she heard, the Queen look'd up, and said,
"O maiden, if indeed ye list to sing,
Sing, and unbind my heart that I may weep."
Whereat full willingly sang the little maid.

   "Late, late, so late! and dark the night and chill
Late, late, so late! but we can enter still.
Too late, too late! ye cannot enter now.

   "No light had we: for that we do repent;
And learning this, the bridegroom will relent.
Too late, too late! ye cannot enter now.

   "No light: so late! and dark and chill the night!
Oh, let us in, that we may find the light!
Too late, too late! ye cannot enter now.

"Have we not heard the bridegroom is so sweet?
Oh, let us in, tho' late, to kiss his feet!
No, no, too late! ye cannot enter now."

So sang the novice, while full passionately,
Her head upon her hands, remembering
Her thought when first she came, wept the sad Queen.
Then said the little novice, prattling to her,

"Oh, pray you, noble lady, weep no more:
But let my words, the words of one so small,
Who knowing nothing knows but to obey,
And if I do not there is penance given—
Comfort your sorrows; for they do not flow
From evil done; right sure am I of that,
Who see your tender grace and stateliness.
But weigh your sorrows with our lord the King's,
And weighing find them less; for gone is he
To wage grim war against Sir Lancelot there,
Round that strong castle where he holds the Queen;
And Modred whom he left in charge of all,
The traitor—Ah! sweet lady, the King's grief
For his own self, and his own Queen, and realm,
Must needs be thrice as great as any of ours.
For me, I thank the saints, I am not great.
For if there ever come a grief to me
I cry my cry in silence, and have done:
None knows it, and my tears have brought me good:
But even were the griefs of little ones
As great as those of great ones, yet this grief
Is added to the griefs the great must bear,
That howsoever much they may desire
Silence, they cannot weep behind a cloud:
As even here they talk at Almesbury
About the good King and his wicked Queen,
And were I such a King with such a Queen,
Well might I wish to veil her wickedness;
But were I such a King, it could not be."

Then to her own sad heart mutter'd the Queen,
"Will the child kill me with her innocent talk?"
But openly she answer'd, "Must not I,
If this false traitor have displaced his lord,
Grieve with the common grief of all the realm?"

"Yea," said the maid, "this is all woman's grief,
That she is woman, whose disloyal life
Hath wrought confusion in the Table Round
Which good King Arthur founded, years ago,
With signs and miracles and wonders, there
At Camelot, ere the coming of the Queen."

Then thought the Queen within herself again,
"Will the child kill me with her foolish prate?"
But openly she spake and said to her,
"O little maid, shut in by nunnery walls,
What canst thou know of Kings and Tables Round,
Or what of signs and wonders, but the signs
And simple miracles of thy nunnery?"

To whom the little novice garrulously,
"Yea, but I know: the land was full of signs
And wonders ere the coming of the Queen.
So said my father, and himself was knight
Of the great Table—at the founding of it;
And rode thereto from Lyonnesse, and he said
That as he rode, an hour or maybe twain
After the sunset, down the coast, he heard
Strange music, and he paused, and turning—there,
All down the lonely coast of Lyonnesse,
Each with a beacon-star upon his head,
And with a wild sea-light about his feet,
He saw them—headland after headland flame
Far on into the rich heart of the west:
And in the light the white mermaiden swam,
And strong man-breasted things stood from the sea,
And sent a deep sea-voice thro' all the land,
To which the little elves of chasm and cleft

Made answer, sounding like a distant horn.
So said my father—yea, and furthermore,
Next morning, while he past the dim-lit woods,
Himself beheld three spirits mad with joy
Come dashing down on a tall wayside flower,
That shook beneath them, as the thistle shakes
When three gray linnets wrangle for the seed:
And still at evenings on before his horse
The flickering fairy-circle wheel'd and broke
Flying, and link'd again, and wheel'd and broke
Flying, for all the land was full of life.
And when at last he came to Camelot,
A wreath of airy dancers hand-in-hand
Swung round the lighted lantern of the hall;
And in the hall itself was such a feast
As never man had dream'd; for every knight
Had whatsoever meat he long'd for served
By hands unseen; and even as he said
Down in the cellars merry bloated things
Shoulder'd the spigot, straddling on the butts
While the wine ran: so glad were spirits and men
Before the coming of the sinful Queen."

Then spake the Queen and somewhat bitterly,
"Were they so glad? ill prophets were they all,
Spirits and men: could none of them foresee,
Not even thy wise father with his signs
And wonders, what has fall'n upon the realm?"

To whom the novice garrulously again,
"Yea, one, a bard; of whom my father said,
Full many a noble war-song had he sung,
Ev'n in the presence of an enemy's fleet,
Between the steep cliff and the coming wave;
And many a mystic lay of life and death
Had chanted on the smoky mountain-tops,
When round him bent the spirits of the hills
With all their dewy hair blown back like flame:
So said my father—and that night the bard
Sang Arthur's glorious wars, and sang the King
As wellnigh more than man, and rail'd at those
Who call'd him the false son of Gorloïs:
For there was no man knew from whence he came.
But after tempest, when the long wave broke
All down the thundering shores of Bude and Bos,
There came a day as still as heaven, and then
They found a naked child upon the sands
Of dark Tintagil by the Cornish sea:
And that was Arthur; and they foster'd him
Till he by miracle was approven King:
And that his grave should be a mystery
From all men, like his birth; and could he find
A woman in her womanhood as great
As he was in his manhood, then, he sang,
The twain together well might change the world.
But even in the middle of his song
He falter'd, and his hand fell from the harp,
And pale he turn'd, and reel'd, and would have
                                                    fall'n,
But that they stay'd him up; nor would he tell
His vision; but what doubt that he foresaw
This evil work of Lancelot and the Queen?"

Then thought the Queen, "Lo! they have set her
                                                    on,
Our simple-seeming Abbess and her nuns,
To play upon me," and bowed her head nor spake.
Whereat the novice crying, with clasp'd hands,
Shame on her own garrulity garrulously,
Said the good nuns would check her gadding tongue
Full often, "and, sweet lady, if I seem
To vex an ear too sad to listen to me,
Unmannerly, with prattling and the tales
Which my good father told me, check me too:
Nor let me shame my father's memory, one
Of noblest manners, tho' himself would say
Sir Lancelot had the noblest; and he died,
Kill'd in a tilt, come next, five summers back,

And left me; but of others who remain,
And of the two first-famed for courtesy—
And pray you check me if I ask amiss—
But pray you, which had noblest, while you moved
Among them, Lancelot, or our lord the King?"

  Then the pale Queen look'd up and answer'd her,
"Sir Lancelot, as became a noble knight,

Then Lancelot's needs must be a thousand-fold
Less noble, being, as all rumor runs,
The most disloyal friend in all the world."

  To which a mournful answer made the Queen:
"Oh, closed about by narrowing nunnery-walls,
What knowest thou of the world, and all its light
And shadows, all the wealth and all the woe?

"While he past the dim-lit woods,
Himself beheld three spirits mad with joy
Come dashing down on a tall wayside flower."

Was gracious to all ladies, and the same
In open battle or the tilting-field
Forbore his own advantage, and the King
In open battle or the tilting-field
Forbore his own advantage, and these two
Were the most nobly-manner'd men of all;
For manners are not idle, but the fruit
Of loyal nature, and of noble mind."

  "Yea." said the maid. "be manners such fair fruit?

If ever Lancelot, that most noble knight,
Were for one hour less noble than himself,
Pray for him that he 'scape the doom of fire,
And weep for her who drew him to his doom."

  "Yea," said the little novice, "I pray for both;
But I should all as soon believe that his,
Sir Lancelot's, were as noble as the King's,
As I could think, sweet lady, yours would be
Such as they are, were you the sinful Queen."

So she, like many another babbler, hurt
Whom she would soothe, and harm'd where she
    would heal;
For here a sudden flush of wrathful heat
Fired all the pale face of the Queen, who cried,
"Such as thou art be never maiden more
For ever! thou their tool, set on to plague
And play upon, and harry me, petty spy
And traitress." When that storm of anger brake
From Guinevere, aghast the maiden rose,
White as her veil, and stood before the Queen
As tremulously as foam upon the beach
Stands in a wind, ready to break and fly,
And when the Queen had added "Get thee hence,"
Fled frighted. Then that other left alone
Sigh'd, and began to gather heart again,
Saying in herself, "The simple, fearful child
Meant nothing, but my own too-fearful guilt,
Simpler than any child, betrays itself.
But help me, heaven, for surely I repent.
For what is true repentance but in thought—
Not ev'n in inmost thought to think again
The sins that made the past so pleasant to us:
And I have sworn never to see him more,
To see him more."

    And ev'n in saying this,
Her memory from old habit of the mind
Went slipping back upon the golden days
In which she saw him first, when Lancelot came,
Reputed the best knight and goodliest man,
Ambassador, to lead her to his lord
Arthur, and led her forth, and far ahead
Of his and her retinue moving, they,
Rapt in sweet talk or lively, all on love
And sport and tilts and pleasure (for the time
Was Maytime, and as yet no sin was dream'd),
Rode under groves that look'd a paradise
Of blossom, over sheets of hyacinth
That seem'd the heavens upbreaking thro' the earth,
And on from hill to hill, and every day
Beheld at noon in some delicious dale
The silk pavilions of King Arthur raised
For brief repast or afternoon repose
By couriers gone before; and on again,
Till yet once more ere set of sun they saw
The Dragon of the great Pendragonship,
That crown'd the state pavilion of the King,
Blaze by the rushing brook or silent well.

But when the Queen immersed in such a trance,
And moving thro' the past unconsciously,
Came to that point where first she saw the King
Ride toward her from the city, sigh'd to find
Her journey, done, glanced at him, thought him cold,
High, self-contain'd, and passionless, not like him,
"Not like my Lancelot"—while she brooded thus
And grew half-guilty in her thoughts again,
There rode an armed warrior to the doors.
A murmuring whisper thro' the nunnery ran,
Then on a sudden a cry, "The King." She sat
Stiff-stricken, listening; but when armed feet
Thro' the long gallery from the outer doors
Rang coming, prone from off her seat she fell,
And grovell'd with her face against the floor:
There with her milkwhite arms and shadowy hair
She made her face a darkness from the King:
And in the darkness heard his armed feet
Pause by her; then came silence, then a voice,
Monotonous and hollow like a ghost's
Denouncing judgment, but tho' changed, the King's:

"Liest thou here so low, the child of one
I honor'd, happy, dead before thy shame?
Well is it that no child is born of thee.
The children born of thee are sword and fire,
Red ruin, and the breaking-up of laws,
The craft of kindred and the godless hosts

Of heathen swarming o'er the Northern Sea;
Whom I, while yet Sir Lancelot, my right arm,
The mightiest of my knights, abode with me,
Have everywhere about this land of Christ
In twelve great battles ruining overthrown.
And knowest thou now from whence I come—from
    him,
From waging bitter war with him: and he,
That did not shun to smite me in worse way,
Had yet that grace of courtesy in him left,
He spared to lift his hand against the King
Who made him knight: but many a knight was
    slain;
And many more, and all his kith and kin
Clave to him, and abode in his own land.
And many more when Modred raised revolt,
Forgetful of their troth and fealty, clave
To Modred, and a remnant stays with me.
And of this remnant will I leave a part,
True men who love me still, for whom I live,
To guard thee in the wild hour coming on,
Lest but a hair of this low head be harm'd.
Fear not: thou shalt be guarded till my death.
Howbeit I know, if ancient prophecies
Have err'd not, that I march to meet my doom.
Thou hast not made my life so sweet to me,
That I the King should greatly care to live;
For thou hast spoilt the purpose of my life.
Bear with me for the last time while I show,
Ev'n for thy sake, the sin which thou hast sinn'd.
For when the Roman left us, and their law
Relax'd its hold upon us, and the ways
Were fill'd with rapine, here and there a deed
Of prowess done redress'd a random wrong.
But I was first of all the kings who drew
The knighthood-errant of this realm and all
The realms together under me, their Head,
In that fair Order of my Table Round,
A glorious company, the flower of men,
To serve as model for the mighty world,
And be the fair beginning of a time.
I made them lay their hands in mine and swear
To reverence the King, as if he were
Their conscience, and their conscience as their King,
To break the heathen and uphold the Christ,
To ride abroad redressing human wrongs,
To speak no slander, no, nor listen to it,
To honor his own word as if his God's,
To lead sweet lives in purest chastity,
To love one maiden only, cleave to her,
And worship her by years of noble deeds,
Until they won her; for indeed I knew
Of no more subtle master under heaven
Than is the maiden passion for a maid,
Not only to keep down the base in man,
But teach high thought, and amiable words
And courtliness, and the desire of fame,
And love of truth, and all that makes a man.
And all this throve before I wedded thee,
Believing, 'lo mine helpmate, one to feel
My purpose and rejoicing in my joy.'
Then came thy shameful sin with Lancelot;
Then came the sin of Tristram and Isolt;
Then others, following these my mightiest knights,
And drawing foul ensample from fair names,
Sinn'd also, till the loathsome opposite
Of all my heart had destined did obtain,
And all thro' thee! so that this life of mine
I guard as God's high gift from scathe and wrong,
Not greatly care to lose; but rather think
How sad it were for Arthur, should he live,
To sit once more within his lonely hall,
And miss the wonted number of my knights,
And miss to hear high talk of noble deeds
As in the golden days before thy sin.
For which of us, who might be left, could speak
Of the pure heart, nor seem to glance at thee?
And in thy bowers of Camelot or of Usk

Thy shadow still would glide from room to room,
And I should evermore be vext with thee
Oɪ hanging robe or vacant ornament,
Oɪ ghostly footfall echoing on the stair.
For think not, tho' thou wouldst not love thy lord,
Thy lord has wholly lost his love for thee.
I am not made of so slight elements.
Yet must I leave thee, woman, to thy shame.
I hold that man the worst of public foes
Who either for his own or children's sake,
To save his blood from scandal, lets the wife
Whom he knows false, abide and rule the house:
For being thro' his cowardice allow'd
Her station, taken everywhere for pure,
She like a new disease, unknown to men,
Creeps, no precaution used, among the crowd,
Makes wicked lightnings of her eyes, and saps
The fealty of our friends, and stirs the pulse
With devil's leaps, and poisons half the young.
Worst of the worst were that man he that reigns!
Better the King's waste hearth and aching heart
Than thou resented in thy place of light,
The mockery of my people, and their bane."

He paused, and in the pause she crept an inch
Nearer, and laid her hands about his feet.
Far off a solitary trumpet blew.
Then waiting by the doors the warhorse neigh'd
As at a friend's voice, and he spake again:

"Yet think not that I come to urge thy crimes,
I did not come to curse thee, Guinevere,
I, whose vast pity almost makes me die
To see thee, laying there thy golden head,
My pride in happier summers, at my feet.
The wrath which forced my thoughts on that fierce law,
The doom of treason and the flaming death
(When first I learnt thee hidden here), is past.
The pang—which while I weigh'd thy heart with one
Too wholly true to dream untruth in thee,
Made my tears burn—is also past, in part.
And all is past, the sin is sinn'd, and I,
Lo! I forgive thee, as Eternal God
Forgives: do thou for thine own soul the rest.
But how to take last leave of all I loved?
O golden hair, with which I used to play
Not knowing! O imperial-moulded form,
And beauty such as woman never wore,
Until it came a kingdom's curse with thee—
I cannot touch thy lips, they are not mine,
But Lancelot's: nay, they never were the King's.
I cannot take thy hand; that too is flesh,
And in the flesh thou hast sinn'd; and mine own flesh,
Here looking down on thine polluted, cries,
'I loathe thee:' yet not less, O Guinevere,
For I was ever virgin save for thee,
My love thro' flesh hath wrought into my life
So far, that my doom is, I love thee still.
Let no man dream but that I love thee still,
Perchance, and so thou purify thy soul,
And so thou lean on our fair father Christ,
Hereafter in that world where all are pure
We two may meet before high God, and thou
Wilt spring to me, and claim me thine, and know
I am thine husband—not a smaller soul,
Nor Lancelot, nor another. Leave me that,
I charge thee, my last hope. Now must I hence.
Thro' the thick night I hear the trumpet blow:
They summon me their King to lead mine hosts
Far down to that great battle in the west,
Where I must strike against the man they call
My sister's son—no kin of mine, who leagues
With Lords of the White Horse, heathen, and knights,
Traitors—and strike him dead, and meet myself
Death, or I know not what mysterious doom.
And thou remaining here wilt learn the event;

But hither shall I never come again,
Never lie by thy side; see thee no more—
Farewell!"

And while she grovell'd at his feet,
She felt the King's breath wander o'er her neck,
And in the darkness o'er her fallen head,
Perceived the waving of his hands that blest.

Then, listening till those armed steps were gone,
Rose the pale Queen, and in her anguish found
The casement: "peradventure," so she thought,
"If I might see his face, and not be seen."
And lo, he sat on horseback at the door!
And near him the sad nuns with each a light
Stood, and he gave them charge about the Queen,
To guard and foster her for evermore.
And while he spake to these his helm was lower'd,
To which for crest the golden dragon clung
Of Britain; so she did not see the face
Which then was as an angel's, but she saw,
Wet with the mists and smitten by the lights,
The Dragon of the great Pendragonship
Blaze, making all the night a steam of fire:
And even then he turn'd; and more and more
The moony vapor rolling round the King,
Who seem'd the phantom of a Giant in it,
Enwound him fold by fold, and made him gray
And grayer, till himself became as mist
Before her, moving ghostlike to his doom.

Then she stretch'd out her arms and cried aloud
"O Arthur!" there her voice brake suddenly,
Then—as a stream that spouting from a cliff
Fails in mid-air, but gathering at the base
Re-makes itself, and flashes down the vale—
Went on in passionate utterance:

"Gone—my lord!
Gone thro' my sin to slay and to be slain!
And he forgave me, and I could not speak.
Farewell? I should have answer'd his farewell.
His mercy choked me. Gone, my lord the King,
My own true lord! how dare I call him mine?
The shadow of another cleaves to me,
And makes me one pollution: he, the King,
Call'd me polluted: shall I kill myself?
What help in that? I cannot kill my sin,
If soul be soul; nor can I kill my shame;
No, nor by living can I live it down.
The days will grow to weeks, the weeks to months,
The months will add themselves and make the years,
The years will roll into the centuries,
And mine will ever be a name of scorn.
I must not dwell on that defeat of fame.
Let the world be; that is but of the world.
What else? what hope? I think there was a hope,
Except he mock'd me when he spake of hope;
His hope he call'd it; but he never mocks,
For mockery is the fume of little hearts.
And blessed be the King, who hath forgiven
My wickedness to him, and let me hope
That in mine own heart I can live down sin
And be his mate hereafter in the heavens
Before high God. Ah, great and gentle lord,
Who wast, as is the conscience of a saint
Among his warring senses, to thy knights—
To whom my false voluptuous pride, that took
Full easily all impressions from below,
Would not look up, or half-despised the height
To which I would not or I could not climb—
I thought I could not breathe in that fine air
That pure severity of perfect light—
I wanted warmth and color which I found
In Lancelot—now I see thee what thou art,
Thou art the highest and most human too,
Not Lancelot, nor another. Is there none
Will tell the King I love him tho' so late?

Now—ere he goes to the great Battle? none:
Myself must tell him in that purer life,
But now it were too daring. Ah my God,
What might I not have made of thy fair world,
Had I but loved thy highest creature here?
It was my duty to have loved the highest:
It surely was my profit had I known:
It would have been my pleasure had I seen.
We needs must love the highest when we see it,
Not Lancelot, nor another."

    Here her hand
Grasp'd, made her veil her eyes: she look'd and saw
The novice, weeping, suppliant, and said to her,
"Yea, little maid, for am I not forgiven?"
Then glancing up beheld the holy nuns
All round her, weeping; and her heart was loosed
Within her, and she wept with these and said,

"Ye know me then, that wicked one, who broke
The vast design and purpose of the King.
Oh, shut me round with narrowing nunnery-walls,
Meek maidens, from the voices crying 'shame.'
I must not scorn myself: he loves me still.
Let no one dream but that he loves me still.
So let me, if you do not shudder at me
Nor shun to call me sister, dwell with you;
Wear black and white, and be a nun like you,
Fast with your fasts, not feasting with your feasts;
Grieve with your griefs, not grieving at your joys,
But not rejoicing; mingle with your rites:
Pray and be pray'd for; lie before your shrines;
Do each low office of your holy house;
Walk your dim cloister, and distribute dole
To poor sick people, richer in His eyes
Who ransom'd us, and haler too than I;
And treat their loathsome hurts and heal mine own,
And so wear out in almsdeed and in prayer
The sombre close of that voluptuous day,
Which wrought the ruin of my lord the King."

She said: they took her to themselves; and she,
Still hoping, fearing, "is it yet too late?"
Dwelt with them, till in time their Abbess died,
Then she, for her good deeds and her pure life,
And for the power of ministration in her,
And likewise for the high rank she had borne,
Was chosen Abbess; there, an Abbess, lived
For three brief years; and there, an Abbess, past
To where beyond these voices there is peace.

---◇◇◇---

THE PASSING OF ARTHUR.

THAT story which the bold Sir Bedivere,
First made and latest left of all the knights,
Told, when the man was no more than a voice
In the white winter of his age, to those
With whom he dwelt, new faces, other minds.

For on their march to westward Bedivere,
Who slowly paced among the slumbering host,
Heard in his tent the moanings of the King:

"I found Him in the shining of the stars,
I mark'd Him in the flowering of His fields,
But in His ways with men I find Him not.
I waged His wars, and now I pass and die.
O me! for why is all around us here
As if some lesser god had made the world,
But had not force to shape it as he would,
Till the High God behold it from beyond,
And enter it, and make it beautiful?
Or else as if the world were wholly fair,
But that these eyes of men are dense and dim,
And have not power to see it as it is

Perchance, because we see not to the close:
For I, being simple, thought to work His will,
And have but stricken with the sword in vain;
And all whereon I lean'd in wife and friend
Is traitor to my peace, and all my realm
Reels back into the beast, and is no more.
My God, thou hast forgotten me in my death:
Nay—God my Christ—I pass, but shall not die."

Then, ere that last weird battle in the west,
There came on Arthur sleeping, Gawain kill'd
In Lancelot's war, the ghost of Gawain blown
Along a wandering wind, and past his ear
Went shrilling, "Hollow, hollow all delight!
Hail, King! to-morrow thou shalt pass away.
Farewell! there is an isle of rest for thee.
And I am blown along a wandering wind,
And hollow, hollow, hollow all delight."
And fainter onward, like wild birds that change
Their season in the night and wail their way
From cloud to cloud, down the long wind the dream
Shrill'd: but in going mingled with dim cries
Far in the moonlit haze among the hills,
As of some lonely city sack'd by night,
When all is lost, and wife and child with wail
Pass to new lords; and Arthur woke and call'd,
"Who spake? A dream. Oh, light upon the wind,
Thine, Gawain, was the voice—are these dim cries
Thine? or doth all that haunts the waste and wild
Mourn, knowing it will go along with me?"

This heard the bold Sir Bedivere and spake:
"O me, my King, let pass whatever will,
Elves, and the harmless glamour of the field;
But in their stead thy name and glory cling
To all high places like a golden cloud
For ever: but as yet thou shalt not pass.
Light was Gawain in life, and light in death
Is Gawain, for the ghost is as the man;
And care not thou for dreams from him, but rise—
I hear the steps of Modred in the west,
And with him many of thy people, and knights
Once thine, whom thou hast loved, but grosser grown
Than heathen, spitting at their vows and thee.
Right well in heart they know thee for the King.
Arise, go forth and conquer as of old."

Then spake King Arthur to Sir Bedivere:
"Far other is this battle in the west
Whereto we move, than when we strove in youth,
And brake the petty kings, and fought with Rome,
Or thrust the heathen from the Roman wall,
And shook him thro' the north. Ill doom is mine
To war against my people and my knights.
The king who fights his people fights himself.
And they my knights, who loved me once, the stroke
That strikes them dead is as my death to me.
Yet let us hence, and find or feel a way
Thro' this blind haze, which ever since I saw
One lying in the dust at Almesbury,
Hath folded in the passes of the world."

Then rose the King and moved his host by night,
And ever push'd Sir Modred, league by league,
Back to the sunset bound of Lyonnesse—
A land of old upheaven from the abyss
By fire, to sink into the abyss again;
Where fragments of forgotten peoples dwelt,
And the long mountains ended in a coast
Of ever-shifting sand, and far away
The phantom circle of a moaning sea.
There the pursuer could pursue no more,
And he that fled no further fly the King;
And there, that day when the great light of heaven
Burn'd at his lowest in the rolling year,
On the waste sand by the waste sea they closed.
Nor ever yet had Arthur fought a fight
Like this last, dim, weird battle of the west.

A deathwhite mist slept over sand and sea:
Whereof the chill, to him who breathed it, drew
Down with his blood, till all his heart was cold
With formless fear; and ev'n on Arthur fell
Confusion, since he saw not whom he fought,
For friend and foe were shadows in the mist,
And friend slew friend not knowing whom he slew;
And some had visions out of golden youth,
And some beheld the faces of old ghosts
Look in upon the battle; and in the mist
Was many a noble deed, many a base,
And chance and craft and strength in single fights,
And ever and anon with host to host
Shocks, and the splintering spear, the hard mail
    hewn,
Shield-breakings, and the clash of brands, the crash
Of battleaxes on shatter'd helms, and shrieks
After the Christ, of those who falling down
Look'd up for heaven, and only saw the mist;
And shouts of heathen and the traitor knights,
Oaths, insult, filth, and monstrous blasphemies,
Sweat, writhings, anguish, laboring of the lungs,
In that close mist, and cryings for the light,
Moans of the dying, and voices of the dead.

Last, as by some one deathbed after wail
Of suffering, silence follows, or thro' death
Or deathlike swoon, thus over all that shore,
Save for some whisper of the seething seas,
A dead hush fell; but when the dolorous day
Grew drearier toward twilight falling, came
A bitter wind, clear from the north, and blew
The mist aside, and with that wind the tide
Rose, and the pale King glanced across the field
Of battle: but no man was moving there;
Nor any cry of Christian heard thereon,
Nor yet of heathen; only the wan wave
Brake in among dead faces, to and fro
Swaying the helpless hands, and up and down
Tumbling the hollow helmets of the fallen,
And shiver'd brands that once had fought with Rome,
And rolling far along the gloomy shores
The voice of days of old and days to be.

Then spake King Arthur to Sir Bedivere,
And whiter than the mist that all day long
Had held the field of battle was the King:

"Hearest thou this great voice that shakes the
    world,
And wastes the narrow realm whereon we move,
And beats upon the faces of the dead,
My dead, as tho' they had not died for me?—
O Bedivere, for on my heart hath fall'n
Confusion, till I know not what I am,
Nor whence I am, nor whether I be King,
Behold, I seem but King among the dead."

Then spake the bold Sir Bedivere: "My King,
King everywhere! and so the dead have kings,
There also will I worship thee as King.
Yet still thy life is whole, and still I live
Who love thee; but who hates thee, he that brought
The heathen back among us, yonder stands,
Modred, unharm'd, the traitor of thine house."

Then spake the King: "My house hath been my
    doom.
But call not thou this traitor of my house
Who hath but dwelt beneath one roof with me.
My house are rather they who sware my vows,
Yea, even while they brake them, own'd me King.
And well for thee, saying in my dark hour,
When all the purport of my throne hath fail'd,
That quick or dead thou holdest me for King.
King am I, whatsoever be their cry;
And one last act of kinghood shalt thou see
Yet, ere I pass." And uttering this the King

Made at the man: then Modred smote his liege
Hard on that helm which many a heathen sword
Had beaten thin; while Arthur at one blow,
Striking the last stroke with Excalibur,
Slew him, and all but slain himself, he fell.

So all day long the noise of battle roll'd
Among the mountains by the winter sea;
Until King Arthur's Table, man by man,
Had fall'n in Lyonnesse about their lord,
King Arthur. Then, because his wound was deep,
The bold Sir Bedivere uplifted him,
And bore him to a chapel nigh the field,
A broken chancel with a broken cross,
That stood on a dark strait of barren land:
On one side lay the Ocean, and on one
Lay a great water, and the moon was full.

Then spake King Arthur to Sir Bedivere:
"The sequel of to-day unsolders all
The goodliest fellowship of famous knights
Whereof this world holds record. Such a sleep
They sleep—the men I loved. I think that we
Shall never more, at any future time,
Delight our souls with talk of knightly deeds,
Walking about the gardens and the halls
Of Camelot, as in the days that were.
I perish by this people which I made—
Tho' Merlin sware that I should come again
To rule once more: but, let what will be, be,
I am so deeply smitten thro' the helm
That without help I cannot last till morn.
Thou therefore take my brand Excalibur,
Which was my pride: for thou rememberest how
In those old days, one summer noon, an arm
Rose up from out the bosom of the lake,
Clothed in white samite, mystic, wonderful,
Holding the sword—and how I row'd across
And took it, and have worn it, like a king;
And, wheresoever I am sung or told
In aftertime, this also shall be known:
But now delay not: take Excalibur,
And fling him far into the middle mere:
Watch what thou seëst, and lightly bring me word."

To him replied the bold Sir Bedivere:
"It is not meet, Sir King, to leave thee thus,
Aidless, alone, and smitten thro' the helm—
A little thing may harm a wounded man;
Yet I thy hest will all perform at full,
Watch what I see, and lightly bring thee word."

So saying, from the ruin'd shrine he stept,
And in the moon athwart the place of tombs,
Where lay the mighty bones of ancient men,
Old knights, and over them the sea-wind sang
Shrill, chill, with flakes of foam. He, stepping down
By zigzag paths, and juts of pointed rock,
Came on the shining levels of the lake.

There drew he forth the brand Excalibur,
And o'er him, drawing it, the winter moon,
Brightening the skirts of a long cloud, ran forth
And sparkled keen with frost against the hilt:
For all the haft twinkled with diamond sparks,
Myriads of topaz-lights, and jacinth-work
Of subtlest jewelry. He gazed so long
That both his eyes were dazzled as he stood,
This way and that dividing the swift mind,
In act to throw: but at the last it seem'd
Better to leave Excalibur conceal'd
There in the many-knotted waterflags,
That whistled stiff and dry about the marge.
So strode he back slow to the wounded King.

Then spake King Arthur to Sir Bedivere:
"Hast thou perform'd my mission which I gave?
What is it thou hast seen? or what hast heard?"

And answer made the bold Sir Bedivere:
"I heard the ripple washing in the reeds,
And the wild water lapping on the crag."

To whom replied King Arthur, faint and pale:
"Thou hast betray'd thy nature and thy name,
Not rendering true answer, as beseem'd
Thy fealty, nor like a noble knight:
For surer sign had follow'd, either hand,
Or voice, or else a motion of the mere.
This is a shameful thing for men to lie.
Yet now, I charge thee, quickly go again,
As thou art lief and dear, and do the thing
I bade thee, watch, and lightly bring me word."

Then went Sir Bedivere the second time
Across the ridge, and paced beside the mere,
Counting the dewy pebbles, fix'd in thought;
But when he saw the wonder of the hilt,
How curiously and strangely chased, he smote
His palms together, and he cried aloud:

"And if indeed I cast the brand away,
Surely a precious thing, one worthy note,
Should thus be lost for ever from the earth,
Which might have pleased the eyes of many men.
What good should follow this, if this were done?
What harm, undone? Deep harm to disobey,
Seeing obedience is the bond of rule.
Were it well to obey then, if a king demand
An act unprofitable, against himself?
The King is sick, and knows not what he does.
What record, or what relic of my lord
Should be to aftertime, but empty breath
And rumors of a doubt? But were this kept,
Stored in some treasure-house of mighty kings,
Some one might show it at a joust of arms,
Saying, 'King Arthur's sword, Excalibur,
Wrought by the lonely maiden of the Lake.
Nine years she wrought it, sitting in the deeps
Upon the hidden bases of the hills.'
So might some old man speak in the aftertime
To all the people, winning reverence.
But now much honor and much fame were lost."

So spake he, clouded with his own conceit,
And hid Excalibur the second time,
And so strode back slow to the wounded King.

Then spoke King Arthur, breathing heavily:
"What is it thou hast seen? or what hast heard?"

And answer made the bold Sir Bedivere:
"I heard the water lapping on the crag,
And the long ripple washing in the reeds."

To whom replied King Arthur, much in wrath:
"Ah, miserable and unkind, untrue,
Unknightly, traitor-hearted! Woe is me!
Authority forgets a dying king,
Laid widow'd of the power in his eye
That bow'd the will. I see thee what thou art,
For thou, the latest-left of all my knights,
In whom should meet the offices of all,
Thou wouldst betray me for the precious hilt;
Either from lust of gold, or like a girl
Valuing the giddy pleasure of the eyes.
Yet, for a man may fail in duty twice,
And the third time may prosper, get thee hence:
But, if thou spare to fling Excalibur,
I will arise and slay thee with my hands."

Then quickly rose Sir Bedivere, and ran,
And, leaping down the ridges lightly, plunged
Among the bulrush beds, and clutch'd the sword,
And strongly wheel'd, and threw it. The great brand
Made lightnings in the splendor of the moon,
And flashing round and round, and whirl'd in an arch,

Shot like a streamer of the northern morn,
Seen where the moving isles of winter shock
By night, with noises of the Northern Sea.
So flash'd and fell the brand Excalibur:
But ere he dipt the surface, rose an arm
Clothed in white samite, mystic, wonderful,
And caught him by the hilt, and brandish'd him
Three times, and drew him under in the mere.
And lightly went the other to the King.

Then spoke King Arthur, drawing thicker breath:
"Now see I by thine eyes that this is done.
Speak out: what is it thou hast heard, or seen?"

And answer made the bold Sir Bedivere:
"Sir King, I closed mine eyelids, lest the gems
Should blind my purpose, for I never saw,
Nor shall see, here or elsewhere, till I die,
Not tho' I live three lives of mortal men,
So great a miracle as yonder hilt.
Then with both hands I flung him, wheeling him;
But when I look'd again, behold an arm,
Clothed in white samite, mystic, wonderful,
That caught him by the hilt and brandish'd him
Three times, and drew him under in the mere."

And answer made King Arthur, breathing hard:
"My end draws nigh; 'tis time that I were gone.
Make broad thy shoulders to receive my weight,
And bear me to the margin; yet I fear
My wound hath taken cold, and I shall die."

So saying, from the pavement he half rose,
Slowly, with pain, reclining on his arm,
And looking wistfully with wide blue eyes
As in a picture. Him Sir Bedivere
Remorsefully regarded thro' his tears,
And would have spoken, but he found not words;
Then took with care, and kneeling on one knee,
O'er both his shoulders drew the languid hands,
And rising bore him thro' the place of tombs.

But, as he walk'd, King Arthur panted hard,
Like one that feels a nightmare on his bed
When all the house is mute. So sigh'd the King,
Muttering and murmuring at his ear, "Quick, quick!
I fear it is too late, and I shall die."
But the other swiftly strode from ridge to ridge,
Clothed with his breath, and looking, as he walk'd,
Larger than human on the frozen hills.
He heard the deep behind him, and a cry
Before. His own thought drove him like a goad.
Dry clash'd his harness in the icy caves
And barren chasms, and all to left and right
The bare black cliff clang'd round him, as he based
His feet on juts of slippery crag that rang
Sharp-smitten with the dint of armed heels—
And on a sudden, lo! the level lake,
And the long glories of the winter moon.

Then saw they how there hove a dusky barge,
Dark as a funeral scarf from stem to stern,
Beneath them; and descending they were ware
That all the decks were dense with stately forms,
Black-stoled, black-hooded, like a dream—by these
Three queens with crowns of gold: and from them
rose
A cry that shiver'd to the tingling stars,
And, as it were one voice, an agony
Of lamentation, like a wind that shrills
All night in a waste land, where no one comes,
Or hath come, since the making of the world.

Then murmur'd Arthur, "Place me in the barge."
So to the barge they came. There those three queens
Put forth their hands, and took the King, and wept.
But she, that rose the tallest of them all
And fairest, laid his head upon her lap,

And loosed the shatter'd casque, and chafed his hands,
And call'd him by his name, complaining loud,
And dropping bitter tears against a brow
Striped with dark blood: for all his face was white
And colorless, and like the wither'd moon
Smote by the fresh beam of the springing east:
And all his greaves and cuisses dash'd with drops
Of onset; and the light and lustrous curls—
That made his forehead like a rising sun
High from the daïs-throne—were parch'd with dust;
Or, clotted into points and hanging loose,
Mix'd with the knightly growth that fringed his lips.
So like a shatter'd column lay the King;
Not like that Arthur who, with lance in rest,
From spur to plume a star of tournament,
Shot thro' the lists at Camelot, and charged
Before the eyes of ladies and of kings.

Then loudly cried the bold Sir Bedivere:
"Ah! my Lord Arthur, whither shall I go?
Where shall I hide my forehead and my eyes?
For now I see the true old times are dead,
When every morning brought a noble chance,
And every chance brought out a noble knight.
Such times have been not since the light that led
The holy Elders with the gift of myrrh.
But now the whole Round Table is dissolved,
Which was an image of the mighty world,
And I, the last, go forth companionless,
And the days darken round me, and the years,
Among new men, strange faces, other minds."

And slowly answer'd Arthur from the barge:
"The old order changeth, yielding place to new,
And God fulfils himself in many ways,
Lest one good custom should corrupt the world.
Comfort thyself: what comfort is in me?
I have lived my life, and that which I have done
May He within himself make pure! but thou,
If thou shouldst never see my face again,
Pray for my soul. More things are wrought by prayer
Than this world dreams of. Wherefore, let thy voice
Rise like a fountain for me night and day.
For what are men better than sheep or goats
That nourish a blind life within the brain,
If, knowing God, they lift not hands of prayer
Both for themselves and those who call them friend?
For so the whole round earth is every way
Bound by gold chains about the feet of God.
But now farewell. I am going a long way

With these thou seëst—if indeed I go
(For all my mind is clouded with a doubt)—
To the island-valley of Avilion;
Where falls not hail, or rain, or any snow,
Nor ever wind blows loudly; but it lies
Deep-meadow'd, happy, fair with orchard lawns
And bowery hollows crown'd with summer sea,
Where I will heal me of my grievous wound."

So said he, and the barge with oar and sail
Moved from the brink, like some full-breasted swan
That, fluting a wild carol ere her death,
Ruffles her pure cold plume, and takes the flood
With swarthy webs. Long stood Sir Bedivere
Revolving many memories, till the hull
Look'd one black dot against the verge of dawn,
And on the mere the wailing died away.

But when that moan had past for evermore,
The stillness of the dead world's winter dawn
Amazed him, and he groan'd, "The King is gone."
And therewithal came on him the weird rhyme,
"From the great deep to the great deep he goes."

Whereat he slowly turn'd and slowly clomb
The last hard footstep of that iron crag;
Thence mark'd the black hull moving yet, and cried,
"He passes to be King among the dead,
And after healing of his grievous wound
He comes again; but—if he come no more—
O me, be yon dark queens in yon black boat,
Who shriek'd and wail'd, the three whereat we gazed
On that high day, when, clothed with living light,
They stood before his throne in silence, friends
Of Arthur, who should help him at his need?"

Then from the dawn it seem'd there came, but faint
As from beyond the limit of the world,
Like the last echo born of a great cry,
Sounds, as if some fair city were one voice
Around a king returning from his wars.

Thereat once more he moved about, and clomb
Ev'n to the highest he could climb, and saw,
Straining his eyes beneath an arch of hand,
Or thought he saw, the speck that bare the King,
Down that long water opening on the deep
Somewhere far off, pass on and on, and go
From less to less and vanish into light.
And the new sun rose bringing the new year.

TO THE QUEEN.

O LOYAL to the royal in thyself,
And loyal to thy land, as this to thee—
Bear witness, that remembrable day,
When, pale as yet, and fever-worn, the Prince
Who scarce had pluck'd his flickering life again
From halfway down the shadow of the grave,
Past with thee thro' thy people and their love,
And London roll'd one tide of joy thro' all
Her trebled millions, and loud leagues of man
And welcome! witness, too, the silent cry,
The prayer of many a race and creed and clime—
Thunderless lightnings striking under sea
From sunset and sunrise of all thy realm,
And that true North, whereof we lately heard
A strain to shame us "keep you to yourselves;
So loyal is too costly! friends—your love
Is but a burthen: loose the bond, and go."
Is this the tone of empire? here the faith
That made us rulers? this, indeed, her voice
And meaning, whom the roar of Hougoumont

Left mightiest of all peoples under heaven?
What shock has fool'd her since, that she should speak
So feebly? wealthier—wealthier—hour by hour!
The voice of Britain, or a sinking land,
Some third-rate isle half-lost among her seas?
There rang her voice, when the full city peal'd
Thee and thy Prince! The loyal to their crown
Are loyal to their own far sons, who love
Our ocean-empire with her boundless homes
For ever-broadening England, and her throne
In our vast Orient, and one isle, one isle,
That knows not her own greatness: if she knows
And dreads it we are fall'n.—But thou, my Queen,
Not for itself, but thro' thy living love
For one to whom I made it o'er his grave
Sacred, accept this old imperfect tale,
New-old, and shadowing Sense at war with Soul
Rather than that gray king, whose name, a ghost,
Streams like a cloud, man-shaped, from mountain
        peak,

And cleaves to cairn and cromlech still; or him
Of Geoffrey's book, or him of Malleor's, one
Touch'd by the adulterous finger of a time
That hover'd between war and wantonness,
And crownings and dethronements: take withal
Thy poet's blessing, and his trust that Heaven
Will blow the tempest in the distance back
From thine and ours: for some are scared, who mark,
Or wisely or unwisely, signs of storm,
Waverings of every vane with every wind,
And wordy trucklings to the transient hour,
And fierce or careless looseners of the faith,
And Softness breeding scorn of simple life,

Or Cowardice, the child of lust for gold,
Or Labor, with a groan and not a voice,
Or Art with poisonous honey stol'n from France,
And that which knows, but careful for itself,
And that which knows not, ruling that which knows
To its own harm: the goal of this great world
Lies beyond sight: yet—if our slowly-grown
And crown'd Republic's crowning common-sense,
That saved her many times, not fail—their fears
Are morning shadows huger than the shapes
That cast them, not those gloomier which forego
The darkness of that battle in the West,
Where all of high and holy dies away.

ELAINE.

And the dead
Steer'd by the dumb went upward with the flood—
In her right hand the lily, in her left
The letter.

[See page 190.

ENOCH ARDEN.

Long lines of cliff breaking have left a chasm;
And in the chasm are foam and yellow sands;
Beyond, red roofs about a narrow wharf
In cluster; then a moulder'd church; and higher
A long street climbs to one tall-tower'd mill;
And high in heaven behind it a gray down
With Danish barrows; and a hazel-wood,
By autumn nutters haunted, flourishes
Green in a cuplike hollow of the down.

Here on this beach a hundred years ago,
Three children of three houses, Annie Lee,
The prettiest little damsel in the port,
And Philip Ray, the miller's only son,
And Enoch Arden, a rough sailor's lad
Made orphan by a winter shipwreck, play'd
Among the waste and lumber of the shore,
Hard coils of cordage, swarthy fishing-nets,
Anchors of rusty fluke, and boats up-drawn;
And built their castles of dissolving sand
To watch them overflow'd, or following up
And flying the white breaker, daily left
The little footprint daily wash'd away.

A narrow cave ran in beneath the cliff:
In this the children play'd at keeping house.
Enoch was host one day, Philip the next,
While Annie still was mistress; but at times
Enoch would hold possession for a week:
"This is my house and this my little wife."
"Mine too," said Philip, "turn and turn about:"
When, if they quarrell'd, Enoch stronger-made
Was master: then would Philip, his blue eyes
All flooded with the helpless wrath of tears,
Shriek out, "I hate you, Enoch," and at this
The little wife would weep for company,
And pray them not to quarrel for her sake,
And say she would be little wife to both.

But when the dawn of rosy childhood past,
And the new warmth of life's ascending sun
Was felt by either, either fixt his heart
On that one girl; and Enoch spoke his love,
But Philip loved in silence; and the girl
Seem'd kinder unto Philip than to him;
But she loved Enoch; tho' she knew it not,
And would if ask'd deny it. Enoch set
A purpose evermore before his eyes,
To hoard all savings to the uttermost,
To purchase his own boat, and make a home
For Annie: and so prosper'd that at last
A luckier or a bolder fisherman,
A carefuller in peril, did not breathe
For leagues along that breaker-beaten coast
Than Enoch. Likewise had he served a year
On board a merchantman, and made himself
Full sailor; and he thrice had pluck'd a life
From the dread sweep of the down-streaming seas:
And all men look'd upon him favorably:
And ere he touch'd his one-and-twentieth May,
He purchased his own boat, and made a home
For Annie, neat and nestlike, half-way up
The narrow street that clamber'd toward the mill.

Then on a golden autumn eventide,
The younger people making holiday,
With bag and sack and basket, great and small,
Went nutting to the hazels. Philip stay'd

(His father lying sick and needing him)
An hour behind; but as he climbed the hill,
Just where the prone edge of the wood began
To feather toward the hollow, saw the pair,
Enoch and Annie, sitting hand-in-hand,
His large gray eyes and weather-beaten face
All-kindled by a still and sacred fire,
That burned as on an altar. Philip look'd,
And in their eyes and faces read his doom;
Then, as their faces grew together, groan'd
And slipt aside, and like a wounded life
Crept down into the hollows of the wood;
There, while the rest were loud with merry-making,
Had his dark hour unseen, and rose and past
Bearing a lifelong burden in his heart.

So these were wed, and merrily rang the bells,
And merrily ran the years, seven happy years,
Seven happy years of health and competence,
And mutual love and honorable toil;
With children; first a daughter. In him woke,
With his first babe's first cry, the noble wish
To save all earnings to the uttermost,
And give his child a better bringing-up
Than his had been, or hers; a wish renew'd,
When two years after came a boy to be
The rosy idol of her solitudes,
While Enoch was abroad on wrathful seas,
Or often journeying landward; for in truth
Enoch's white horse, and Enoch's ocean-spoil
In ocean-smelling osier. and his face,
Rough-redden'd with a thousand winter-gales,
Not only to the market-cross were known,
But in the leafy lanes behind the down,
Far as the portal-warding lion-whelp,
And peacock-yewtree of the lonely Hall,
Whose Friday fare was Enoch's ministering.

Then came a change, as all things human change.
Ten miles to northward of the narrow port
Open'd a larger haven: thither used
Enoch at times to go by land or sea;
And once when there, and clambering on a mast
In harbor, by mischance he slipt and fell:
A limb was broken when they lifted him:
And while he lay recovering there, his wife
Bore him another son, a sickly one:
Another hand crept too across his trade
Taking her bread and theirs: and on him fell,
Altho' a grave and staid God-fearing man,
Yet lying thus inactive, doubt and gloom.
He seem'd, as in a nightmare of the night,
To see his children leading evermore
Low miserable lives of hand-to-mouth,
And her, he loved, a beggar: then he pray'd
"Save them from this, whatever comes to me."
And while he pray'd, the master of that ship
Enoch had served in, hearing his mischance,
Came, for he knew the man and valued him,
Reporting of his vessel China-bound.
And wanting yet a boatswain. Would he go?
There yet were many weeks before she sail'd,
Sail'd from this port. Would Enoch have the place?
And Enoch all at once assented to it,
Rejoicing at that answer to his prayer.

So now that shadow of mischance appear'd
No graver than as when some little cloud

Cuts off the fiery highway of the sun,
And isles a light in the offing: yet the wife —
When he was gone — the children — what to do?
Then Enoch lay long-pondering on his plans;
To sell the boat — and yet he loved her well —
How many a rough sea had he weather'd in her!
He knew her, as a horseman knows his horse —
And yet to sell her — then with what she brought
Buy goods and stores — set Annie forth in trade
With all that seamen needed or their wives —
So might she keep the house while he was gone.
Should he not trade himself out yonder? go
This voyage more than once? yea twice or thrice —
As oft as needed — last, returning rich,
Become the master of a larger craft,
With fuller profits lead an easier life,
Have all his pretty young ones educated.
And pass his days in peace among his own.

Thus Enoch in his heart determined all:
Then moving homeward came on Annie pale,
Nursing the sickly babe, her latest-born.
Forward she started with a happy cry,
And laid the feeble infant in his arms:
Whom Enoch took, and handled all his limbs,
Appraised his weight, and fondled fatherlike,
But had no heart to break his purposes
To Annie, till the morrow, when he spoke.

Then first since Enoch's golden ring had girt
Her finger, Annie fought against his will:
Yet not with brawling opposition she,
But manifold entreaties, many a tear,
Many a sad kiss by day by night renew'd
(Sure that all evil would come out of it)
Besought him, supplicating, if he cared
For her or his dear children, not to go.
He not for his own self caring but for her,
Her and her children, let her plead in vain;
So grieving held his will, and bore it thro'.

For Enoch parted with his old sea-friend,
Bought Annie goods and stores, and set his hand
To fit their little streetward sitting-room
With shelf and corner for the goods and stores.
So all day long till Enoch's last at home,
Shaking their pretty cabin, hammer and axe,
Auger and saw, while Annie seem'd to hear
Her own death-scaffold rising, shrill'd and rang,
Till this was ended, and his careful hand,—
The space was narrow,— having order'd all
Almost as neat and close as Nature packs
Her blossom or her seedling, paused; and he,
Who needs would work for Annie to the last,
Ascending tired, heavily slept till morn.

And Enoch faced this morning of farewell
Brightly and boldly. All his Annie's fears,
Save as his Annie's, were a laughter to him.
Yet Enoch as a brave God-fearing man
Bow'd himself down, and in that mystery
Where God-in-man is one with man-in-God,
Pray'd for a blessing on his wife and babes
Whatever came to him: and then he said,
"Annie, this voyage by the grace of God
Will bring fair weather yet to all of us.
Keep a clean hearth and a clear fire for me.
For I'll be back, my girl, before you know it."
Then lightly rocking baby's cradle. "and he,
This pretty, puny, weakly little one,—
Nay — for I love him all the better for it—
God bless him, he shall sit upon my knees,
And I will tell him tales of foreign parts,
And make him merry when I come home again.
Come Annie, come, cheer up before I go."

Him running on thus hopefully she heard,
And almost hoped herself; but when he turn'd

The current of his talk to graver things
In sailor fashion roughly sermonizing
On providence and trust in Heaven, she heard,
Heard and not heard him . as the village girl,
Who sets her pitcher underneath the spring,
Musing on him that used to fill it for her,
Hears and not hears, and lets it overflow.

At length she spoke, "O Enoch, you are wise;
And yet for all your wisdom well know I
That I shall look upon your face no more."

"Well then," said Enoch, "I shall look on yours.
Annie, the ship I sail in passes here
(He named the day): get you a seaman's glass,
Spy out my face, and laugh at all your fears."

But when the last of those last moments came,
"Annie, my girl, cheer up, be comforted,
Look to the babes, and till I come again,
Keep everything shipshape, for I must go.
And fear no more for me; or if you fear
Cast all your cares on God; that anchor holds.
Is He not yonder in those uttermost
Parts of the morning? if I flee to these
Can I go from Him? and the sea is His,
The sea is His: He made it."

                              Enoch rose,
Cast his strong arms about his drooping wife,
And kiss'd his wonder-stricken little ones;
But for the third, the sickly one, who slept
After a night of feverous wakefulness,
When Annie would have raised him Enoch said.
"Wake him not; let him sleep; how should the
    child
Remember this?" and kiss'd him in his cot,
But Annie from her baby's forehead clipt
A tiny curl, and gave it: this he kept
Thro' all his future; but now hastily caught
His bundle, waved his hand, and went his way.

She, when the day that Enoch mention'd came,
Borrow'd a glass, but all in vain: perhaps
She could not fix the glass to suit her eye;
Perhaps her eye was dim, hand tremulous:
She saw him not: and while he stood on deck
Waving, the moment and the vessel past.

Ev'n to the last dip of the vanishing sail
She watch'd it, and departed weening for him;
Then, tho' she mourn'd his absence as his grave,
Set her sad will no less to chime with his,
But throve not in her trade, not being bred
To barter, nor compensating the want
By shrewdness, neither capable of lies,
Nor asking overmuch and taking less,
And still foreboding "What would Enoch say?"
For more than once, in days of difficulty
And pressure, had she sold her wares for less
Than what she gave in buying what she sold:
She fail'd and sadden'd knowing it; and thus,
Expectant of that news which never came,
Gain'd for her own a scanty sustenance,
And lived a life of silent melancholy.

Now the third child was sickly born and grew
Yet sicklier, tho' the mother cared for it
With all a mother's care: nevertheless,
Whether her business often call'd her from it,
Or thro' the want of what it needed most,
Or means to pay the voice who best could tell
What most it needed—howsoe'er it was,
After a lingering,—ere she was aware,—
Like the caged bird escaping suddenly,
The little innocent soul flitted away.

In that same week when Annie buried it,

Philip's true heart. which hunger'd for her peace
(Since Enoch left he had not look'd upon her),
Smote him, as having kept aloof so long.
"Surely," said Philip, "I may see her now,
May be some little comfort;" therefore went,
Past thro' the solitary room in front,
Paused for a moment at an inner door,
Then struck it thrice. and, no one opening,
Enter'd; but Annie, seated with her grief,
Fresh from the burial of her little one,
Cared not to look on any human face,
But turn'd her own toward the wall and wept.
Then Philip standing up said falteringly,
"Annie, I came to ask a favor of you."

He spoke; the passion in her moan'd reply,
"Favor from one so sad and so forlorn
As I am!" half abash'd him, yet unask'd,
His bashfulness and tenderness at war,
He set himself beside her, saying to her:

"I came to speak to you of what he wish'd,
Enoch, your husband: I have ever said
You chose the best among us—a strong man·
For where he fixt his heart he set his hand
To do the thing he will'd, and bore it thro'.
And wherefore did he go this weary way,
And leave you lonely? not to see the world—
For pleasure?—nay, but for the wherewithal
To give his babes a better oringing-up
Than his had been, or yours· that was his wish.
And if he come again, vext will he be
To find the precious morning hours were lost.
And it would vex him even in his grave,
If he could know his babes were running wild
Like colts about the waste. So, Annie, now—
Have we not known each other all our lives?
I do beseech you by the love you bear
Him and his children not to say me nay—
For, if you will, when Enoch comes again
Why then he shall repay me—if you will,
Annie—for I am rich and well-to-do.
Now let me put the boy and girl to school·
This is the favor that I came to ask."

Then Annie with her brows against the wall
Answer'd, "I cannot look you in the face;
I seem so foolish and so broken down.
When you came in my sorrow broke me down;
And now I think your kindness breaks me down;
But Enoch lives; that is borne in on me:
He will repay you: money can be repaid;
Not kindness such as yours."

                                And Philip ask'd
"Then you will let me, Annie?"

                                There she turn'd,
She rose, and fixt her swimming eyes upon him,
And dwelt a moment on his kindly face,
Then calling down a blessing on his head
Caught at his hand and wrung it passionately,
And past into the little garth beyond.
So lifted up in spirit he moved away.

Then Philip put the boy and girl to school,
And bought them needful books, and every way,
Like one who does his duty by his own,
Made himself theirs; and tho' for Annie's sake,
Fearing the lazy gossip of the port,
He oft denied his heart his dearest wish,
And seldom crost her threshold, yet he sent
Gifts by the children, garden-herbs and fruit,
The late and early roses from his wall,
Or conies from the down, and now and then,
With some pretext of fineness in the meal
To save the offence of charitable, flour
From his tall mill that whistled on the waste.

But Philip did not fathom Annie's mind:
Scarce could the woman when he came upon her,
Out of full heart and boundless gratitude
Light on a broken word to thank him with.
But Philip was her children's all-in-all;
From distant corners of the street they ran
To greet his hearty welcome heartily;
Lords of his house and of his mill were they;
Worried his passive ear with petty wrongs
Or pleasures, hung upon him, play'd with him
And call'd him Father Philip. Philip gain'd
As Enoch lost; for Enoch seem'd to them
Uncertain as a vision or a dream,
Faint as a figure seen in early dawn
Down at the far end of an avenue,
Going we know not where; and so ten years,
Since Enoch left his hearth and native land,
Fled forward, and no news of Enoch came.

It chanced one evening Annie's children long'd
To go with others, nutting to the wood,
And Annie would go with them; then they begg'd
For Father Philip (as they him call'd) too:
Him, like the working-bee in blossom-dust,
Blanch'd with his mill, they found; and saying to
        him,
"Come with us, Father Philip," he denied;
But when the children pluck'd at him to go,
He laugh'd, and yielded readily to their wish,
For was not Annie with them? and they went.

But after scaling half the weary down,
Just where the prone edge of the wood began
To feather toward the hollow, all her force
Fail'd her, and sighing "Let me rest" she said·
So Philip rested with her well-content;
While all the younger ones with jubilant cries
Broke from their elders. and tumultuously
Down thro' the whitening hazels made a plunge
To the bottom, and dispersed, and bent or broke
The lithe reluctant boughs to tear away
Their tawny clusters, crying to each other
And calling, here and there, about the wood.

But Philip sitting at her side forgot
Her presence, and remember'd one dark hour
Here in this wood, when like a wounded life
He crept into the shadow: at last he said,
Lifting his honest forehead, "Listen, Annie,
How merry they are down yonder in the wood."
"Tired, Annie?" for she did not speak a word.
"Tired?" but her face had fall'n upon her hands;
At which, as with a kind of anger in him,
"The ship was lost," he said, "the ship was lost!
No more of that! why should you kill yourself
And make them orphans quite?" And Annie said,
"I thought not of it: but—I know not why—
Their voices make me feel so solitary."

Then Philip coming somewhat closer spoke.
"Annie, there is a thing upon my mind,
And it has been upon my mind so long,
That tho' I know not when it first came there,
I know that it will out at last. O Annie,
It is beyond all hope, against all chance,
That he who left you ten long years ago
Should still be living; well then—let me speak:
I grieve to see you poor and wanting help:
I cannot help you as I wish to do
Unless—they say that women are so quick—
Perhaps you know what I would have you know·
I wish you for my wife. I fain would prove
A father to your children: I do think
They love me as a father: I am sure
That I love them as if they were mine own:
And I believe, if you were fast my wife,
That after all these sad uncertain years,
We might be still as happy as God grants

To any of His creatures. Think upon it:
For I am well-to-do—no kin, no care,
No burthen, save my care for you and yours;
And we have known each other all our lives,
And I have loved you longer than you know."

Then answer'd Annie; tenderly she spoke:
"You have been as God's good angel in our house.
God bless you for it, God reward you for it,
Philip, with something happier than myself.
Can one love twice? can you be ever loved
As Enoch was? what is it that you ask?"
"I am content," he answer'd, "to be loved
A little after Enoch." "O," she cried,
Scared as it were, "dear Philip, wait a while:
If Enoch comes—but Enoch will not come—
Yet wait a year, a year is not so long:
Surely I shall be wiser in a year:
O wait a little!" Philip sadly said,
"Annie, as I have waited all my life
I well may wait a little." "Nay," she cried,
"I am bound: you have my promise—in a year:
Will you not bide your year as I bide mine?"
And Philip answered, "I will bide my year."

Here both were mute, till Philip glancing up
Beheld the dead flame of the fallen day
Pass from the Danish barrow overhead;
Then fearing night and chill for Annie rose,
And sent his voice beneath him thro' the wood.
Up came the children laden with their spoil;
Then all descended to the port, and there
At Annie's door he paused and gave his hand,
Saying gently, "Annie, when I spoke to you,
That was your hour of weakness. I was wrong.
I am always bound to you, but you are free."
Then Annie weeping answer'd, "I am bound."

She spoke; and in one moment as it were,
While yet she went about her household ways,
Ev'n as she dwelt upon his latest words,
That he had loved her longer than she knew,
That autumn into autumn flash'd again,
And there he stood once more before her face,
Claiming her promise. "Is it a year?" she ask'd.
"Yes, if the nuts," he said, "be ripe again:
Come out and see." But she—she put him off—
So much to look to—such a change—a month—
Give her a month—she knew that she was bound—
A month—no more. Then Philip with his eyes
Full of that lifelong hunger, and his voice
Shaking a little like a drunkard's hand,
"Take your own time, Annie, take your own time."
And Annie could have wept for pity of him;
And yet she held him on delayingly
With many a scarce-believable excuse,
Trying his truth and his long-sufferance,
Till half-another year had slipt away.

By this the lazy gossips of the port,
Abhorrent of a calculation crost,
Began to chafe as at a personal wrong.
Some thought that Philip did but trifle with her;
Some that she but held off to draw him on;
And others laugh'd at her and Philip too,
As simple folk that knew not their own minds;
And one, in whom all evil fancies clung
Like serpent eggs together, laughingly
Would hint at worse in either. Her own son
Was silent, tho' he often look'd his wish;
But evermore the daughter prest upon her
To wed the man so dear to all of them
And lift the household out of poverty;
And Philip's rosy face contracting grew
Careworn and wan; and all these things fell on her
Sharp as reproach.
　　　　　　At last one night it chanced
That Annie could not sleep, but earnestly
Pray'd for a sign, "my Enoch, is he gone?"

15

Then compass'd round by the blind wall of night
Brook'd not the expectant terror of her heart,
Started from bed, and struck herself a light,
Then desperately seized the holy Book,
Suddenly set it wide to find a sign,
Suddenly put her finger on the text,
"Under a palmtree." That was nothing to her:
No meaning there: she closed the book and slept:
When lo! her Enoch sitting on a height,
Under a palmtree, over him the Sun:
"He is gone," she thought, "he is happy, he is sing
　　　　ing
Hosanna in the highest: yonder shines
The Sun of Righteousness, and these be palms
Whereof the happy people strowing cried
'Hosanna in the highest!'" Here she woke,
Resolved, sent for him and said wildly to him,
"There is no reason why we should not wed."
"Then for God's sake," he answer'd, "both our
　　　　sakes,
So you will wed me, let it be at once."

So these were wed and merrily rang the bells,
Merrily rang the bells and they were wed.
But never merrily beat Annie's heart.
A footstep seem'd to fall beside her path,
She knew not whence; a whisper on her ear,
She knew not what; nor loved she to be left
Alone at home, nor ventured out alone.
What ail'd her then, that ere she enter'd, often
Her hand dwelt lingeringly on the latch,
Fearing to enter: Philip thought he knew:
Such doubts and fears were common to her state,
Being with child: but when her child was born,
Then her new child was as herself renew'd,
Then the new mother came about her heart,
Then her good Philip was her all-in-all,
And that mysterious instinct wholly died.

And where was Enoch? Prosperously sail'd
The ship "Good Fortune," tho' at setting forth
The Biscay, roughly ridging eastward, shook
And almost overwhelm'd her, yet unvext
She slipt across the summer of the world,
Then after a long tumble about the Cape
And frequent interchange of foul and fair,
She passing thro' the summer world again,
The breath of Heaven came continually
And sent her sweetly by the golden isles,
Till silent in her oriental haven.

There Enoch traded for himself, and bought
Quaint monsters for the market of those times,
A gilded dragon, also, for the babes.

Less lucky her home-voyage: at first indeed
Thro' many a fair sea-circle, day by day,
Scarce-rocking, her full-busted figure-head
Stared o'er the ripple feathering from her bows:
Then follow'd calms, and then winds variable,
Then baffling, a long course of them: and last
Storm, such as drove her under moonless heavens
Till hard upon the cry of "breakers" came
The crash of ruin, and the loss of all
But Enoch and two others. Half the night,
Buoy'd upon floating tackle and broken spars,
These drifted, stranding on an isle at morn
Rich, but the loneliest in a lonely sea.

No want was there of human sustenance,
Soft fruitage, mighty nuts and nourishing roots;
Nor save for pity was it hard to take
The helpless life so wild that it was tame
There in a seaward-gazing mountain-gorge
They built, and thatch'd with leaves of palm, a hut,
Half hut, half native cavern. So the three,
Set in this Eden of all plenteousness,
Dwelt with eternal summer, ill-content-

For one, the youngest, hardly more than boy,
Hurt in that night of sudden ruin and wreck,
Lay lingering out a three-years' death-in-life.
They could not leave him. After he was gone,
The two remaining found a fallen stem ;
And Enoch's comrade, careless of himself,
Fire-hollowing this in Indian fashion, fell
Sun-stricken, and that other lived alone.
In those two deaths he read God's warning "wait."

The mountain wooded to the peak, the lawns
And winding glades high up like ways to Heaven,
The slender coco's drooping crown of plumes,
The lightning flash of insect and of bird,
The lustre of the long convolvuluses
That coil'd around the stately stems, and ran
Ev'n to the limit of the land, the glows
And glories of the broad belt of the world,
All these he saw ; but what he fain had seen
He could not see, the kindly human face,
Nor ever hear a kindly voice, but heard
The myriad shriek of wheeling ocean-fowl,
The league-long roller thundering on the reef.
The moving whisper of huge trees that branch'd
And blossom'd in the zenith, or the sweep
Of some precipitous rivulet to the wave,
As down the shore he ranged, or all day long
Sat often in the seaward-gazing gorge,
A shipwreck'd sailor, waiting for a sail :
No sail from day to day, but every day
The sunrise broken into scarlet shafts
Among the palms and ferns and precipices ;
The blaze upon the waters to the east ;
The blaze upon his island overhead ;
The blaze upon the waters to the west ;
Then the great stars that globed themselves in
  Heaven,
The hollower-bellowing ocean, and again
The scarlet shafts of sunrise—but no sail.

There, often as he watch'd or seem'd to watch,
So still, the golden lizard on him paused,
A phantom made of many phantoms moved
Before him haunting him, or he himself
Moved haunting people, things and places, known
Far in a darker isle beyond the line ;
The babes, their babble, Annie, the small house,
The climbing street, the mill, the leafy lanes,
The peacock-yewtree and the lonely Hall,
The horse he drove, the boat he sold, the chill
November dawns and dewy-glooming downs,
The gentle shower, the smell of dying leaves,
And the low moan of leaden-colour'd seas.

Once likewise, in the ringing of his ears,
Tho' faintly, merrily—far and far away—
He heard the pealing of his parish bells :
Then, tho' he knew not wherefore, started up
Shuddering, and when the beauteous hateful isle
Return'd upon him, had not his poor heart
Spoken with That, which being everywhere
Lets none, who speaks with Him, seem all alone,
Surely the man had died of solitude.

Thus over Enoch's early-silvering head
The sunny and rainy seasons came and went
Year after year. His hopes to see his own,
And pace the sacred old familiar fields,
Not yet had perish'd, when his lonely doom
Came suddenly to an end. Another ship
(She wanted water) blown by baffling winds
Like the Good Fortune, from her destined course,
Stay'd by this isle, not knowing where she lay ;
For since the mate had seen at early dawn
Across a break on the mist-wreathen isle
The silent water slipping from the hills,
They sent a crew that landing burst away
In search of stream or fount, and fill'd the shores

With clamor. Downward from his mountain gorge
Stept the long-haired long-bearded solitary,
Brown, looking hardly human, strangely clad,
Muttering and mumbling, idiotlike it seem'd,
With inarticulate rage, and making signs
They knew not what : and yet he led the way
To where the rivulets of sweet water ran ;
And ever as he mingled with the crew,
And heard them talking, his long-bounden tongue
Was loosen'd, till he made them understand ;
Whom, when their casks were fill'd they took aboard,
And there the tale he utter'd brokenly,
Scarce credited at first but more and more,
Amazed and melted all who listen'd to it :
And clothes they gave him and free passage home
But oft he work'd among the rest and shook
His isolation from him. None of these
Came from his county, or could answer him,
If question'd, aught of what he cared to know.
And dull the voyage was with long delays,
The vessel scarce sea-worthy ; but evermore
His fancy fled before the lazy wind
Returning, till beneath a clouded moon
He like a lover down thro' all his blood
Drew in the dewy meadowy morning-breath
Of England, blown across her ghostly wall :
And that same morning officers and men
Levied a kindly tax upon themselves,
Pitying the lonely man, and gave him it :
Then moving up the coast they landed him,
Ev'n in that harbor whence he sail'd before.

There Enoch spoke no word to any one,
But homeward,—home,—what home ? had he a home ?
His home he walk'd. Bright was that afternoon,
Sunny but chill ; till drawn thro' either chasm,
Where either haven open'd on the deeps,
Roll'd a sea-haze and whelm'd the world in gray ·
Cut off the length of highway on before,
And left but narrow breadth to left and right
Of wither'd holt or tilth or pasturage.
On the nigh-naked tree the Robin piped
Disconsolate, and thro' the dripping haze
The dead weight of the dead leaf bore it down
Thicker the drizzle grew, deeper the gloom ;
Last, as it seem'd, a great mist-blotted light
Flared on him, and he came upon the place.

Then down the long street having slowly stolen,
His heart foreshadowing all calamity,
His eyes upon the stones, he reach'd the home
Where Annie lived and loved him, and his babes
In those far-off seven happy years were born ;
But finding neither light nor murmur there
(A bill of sale gleam'd thro' the drizzle) crept
Still downward thinking "dead or dead to me !"

Down to the pool and narrow wharf he went,
Seeking a tavern which of old he knew,
A front of timber-crost antiquity,
So propt, worm-eaten, ruinously old.
He thought it must have gone ; but he was gone
Who kept it : and his widow, Miriam Lane,
With daily-dwindling profits held the house ;
A haunt of brawling seamen once, but now
Stiller, with yet a bed for wandering men.
There Enoch rested silent many days.

But Miriam Lane was good and garrulous,
Nor let him be, but often breaking in,
Told him, with other annals of the port,
Not knowing—Enoch was so brown, so bow'd,
So broken—all the story of his house.
His baby's death, her growing poverty,
How Philip put her little ones to school,
And kept them in it, his long wooing her,
Her slow consent, and marriage, and the birth
Of Philip's child : and o'er his countenance

No shadow past, nor motion; any one,
Regarding, well had deem'd he felt the tale
Less than the teller: only when she closed,
"Enoch, poor man, was cast away and lost,"
He, shaking his gray head pathetically,
Repeated muttering "Cast away and lost;"
Again in deeper inward whispers "Lost!"

But Enoch yearn'd to see her face again;
"If I might look on her sweet face again
And know that she is happy." So the thought
Haunted and harass'd him, and drove him forth
At evening when the dull November day
Was growing duller twilight, to the hill.
There he sat down gazing on all below:
There did a thousand memories roll upon him,
Unspeakable for sadness. By and by
The ruddy square of comfortable light,
Far-blazing from the rear of Philip's house,
Allured him, as the beacon-blaze allures
The bird of passage, till he madly strikes
Against it, and beats out his weary life.

For Philip's dwelling fronted on the street,
The latest house to landward; but behind,
With one small gate that open'd on the waste,
Flourish'd a little garden square and wall'd:
And in it throve an ancient evergreen,
A yewtree, and all round it ran a walk
Of shingle, and a walk divided it:
But Enoch shunn'd the middle walk and stole
Up by the wall, behind the yew; and thence
That which he better might have shunn'd, if griefs
Like his have worse or better, Enoch saw.

For cups and silver on the burnish'd board
Sparkled and shone; so genial was the hearth;
And on the right hand of the hearth he saw
Philip, the slighted suitor of old times,
Stout, rosy, with his babe across his knees;
And o'er her second father stoopt a girl,
A later but a loftier Annie Lee,
Fair-hair'd and tall, and from her lifted hand
Dangled a length of ribbon and a ring
To tempt the babe, who rear'd his creasy arms,
Caught at and ever miss'd it, and they laugh'd:
And on the left hand of the hearth he saw
The mother glancing often toward her babe,
But turning now and then to speak with him,
Her son, who stood beside her tall and strong,
And saying that which pleased him, for he smiled.

Now when the dead man come to life beheld
His wife his wife no more, and saw the babe
Hers, yet not his, upon the father's knee,
And all the warmth, the peace, the happiness,
And his own children tall and beautiful,
And him, that other, reigning in his place,
Lord of his rights and of his children's love,—
Then he, tho' Miriam Lane had told him all,
Because things seen are mightier than things heard,
Stagger'd and shook, holding the branch, and fear'd
To send abroad a shrill and terrible cry,
Which in one moment, like the blast of doom,
Would shatter all the happiness of the hearth.

He therefore turning softly like a thief,
Lest the harsh shingle should grate underfoot,
And feeling all along the garden-wall,
Lest he should swoon and tumble and be found,
Crept to the gate, and open'd it, and closed,
As lightly as a sick man's chamber-door,
Behind him, and came out upon the waste.

And there he would have knelt, but that his
        knees
Were feeble, so that falling prone he dug
His fingers into the wet earth, and pray'd.

"Too hard to bear! why did they take me thence?
O God Almighty, blessed Saviour, Thou
That didst uphold me on my lonely isle,
Uphold me, Father, in my loneliness
A little longer! aid me, give me strength
Not to tell her, never to let her know.
Help me not to break in upon her peace.
My children too! must I not speak to these?
They know me not. I should betray myself.
Never: no father's kiss for me,—the girl
So like her mother, and the boy, my son."

There speech and thought and nature fail'd a little.
And he lay tranced; but when he rose and paced
Back toward his solitary home again,
All down the long and narrow street he went
Beating it in upon his weary brain,
As tho' it were the burthen of a song,
"Not to tell her, never to let her know."

He was not all unhappy. His resolve
Upbore him, and firm faith, and evermore
Prayer from a living source within the will,
And beating up thro' all the bitter world,
Like fountains of sweet water in the sea,
Kept him a living soul. "This miller's wife,"
He said to Miriam, "that you told me of,
Has she no fear that her first husband lives?"
"Ay, ay, poor soul," said Miriam, "fear enow!
If you could tell her you had seen him dead,
Why, that would be her comfort:" and he thought
"After the Lord has call'd me she shall know,
I wait His time," and Enoch set himself,
Scorning an alms, to work whereby to live.
Almost to all things could he turn his hand.
Cooper he was and carpenter, and wrought
To make the boatmen fishing-nets, or help'd
At lading and unlading the tall barks,
That brought the stinted commerce of those days
Thus earn'd a scanty living for himself:
Yet since he did but labor for himself,
Work without hope, there was not life in it
Whereby the man could live; and as the year
Roll'd itself round again to meet the day
When Enoch had return'd, a languor came
Upon him, gentle sickness, gradually
Weakening the man, till he could do no more,
But kept the house, his chair, and last his bed
And Enoch bore his weakness cheerfully.
For sure no gladlier does the stranded wreck
See thro' the gray skirts of a lifting squall
The boat that bears the hope of life approach
To save the life despair'd of, than he saw
Death dawning on him, and the close of all.

For thro' that dawning gleam'd a kindlier hope
On Enoch thinking, "After I am gone,
Then may she learn I loved her to the last."
He call'd aloud for Miriam Lane and said,
"Woman, I have a secret—only swear,
Before I tell you—swear upon the book
Not to reveal it, till you see me dead."
"Dead," clamor'd the good woman, "hear him talk
I warrant, man, that we shall bring you round."
"Swear," added Enoch sternly, "on the book."
And on the book, half-frighted, Miriam swore.
Then Enoch rolling his gray eyes upon her,
"Did you know Enoch Arden of this town?"
"Know him?" she said, "I knew him far away.
Ay, ay, I mind him coming down the street:
Held his head high, and cared for no man, he."
Slowly and sadly Enoch answer'd her;
"His head is low, and no man cares for him.
I think I have not three days more to live;
I am the man." At which the woman gave
A half incredulous, half-hysterical cry.
"You Arden, you! nay,—sure he was a foot
Higher than you be." Enoch said again,

"My God has bow'd me down to what I am;
My grief and solitude have broken me;
Nevertheless, know you that I am he
Who married — but that name has twice been
          changed—
I married her who married Philip Ray.
Sit. listen." Then he told her of his voyage,
His wreck, his lonely life, his coming back,
His gazing in on Annie, his resolve,
And how he kept it. As the woman heard,
Fast flow'd the current of her easy tears,
While in her heart she yearn'd incessantly
To rush abroad all round the little haven,
Proclaiming Enoch Arden and his woes;
But awed and promise-bounden she forbore,
Saying only, "See your bairns before you go!
Eh, let me fetch 'em, Arden." and arose
Eager to bring them down, for Enoch hung
A moment on her words, but then replied:

"Woman, disturb me not now at the last,
But let me hold my purpose till I die.
Sit down again; mark me and understand,
While I have power to speak. I charge you now,
When you shall see her, tell her that I died
Blessing her, praying for her, loving her;
Save for the bar between us, loving her
As when she laid her head beside my own.
And tell my daughter Annie, whom I saw
So like her mother, that my latest breath
Was spent in blessing her and praying for her.
And tell my son that I died blessing him.
And say to Philip that I blest him too;

He never meant us anything but good.
But if my children care to see me dead,
Who hardly knew me living, let them come,
I am their father; but she must not come,
For my dead face would vex her after-life.
And now there is but one of all my blood,
Who will embrace me in the world-to-be:
This hair is his: she cut it off and gave it,
And I have borne it with me all these years,
And thought to bear it with me to my grave:
But now my mind is changed, for I shall see him,
My babe in bliss: wherefore when I am gone,
Take, give her this, for it may comfort her;
It will moreover be a token to her
That I am he."

          He ceased; and Miriam Lane
Made such a voluble answer promising all,
That once again he roll'd his eyes upon her
Repeating all he wish'd, and once again
She promised.

          Then the third night after this,
While Enoch slumber'd motionless and pale,
And Miriam watch'd and dozed at intervals,
There came so loud a calling of the sea,
That all the houses in the haven rang.
He woke, he rose, he spread his arms abroad
Crying with a loud voice "A sail! a sail!
I am saved;" and so fell back and spoke no more

So past the strong heroic soul away.
And when they buried him the little port
Had seldom seen a costlier funeral.

ADDITIONAL POEMS.

AYLMER'S FIELD.

1793.

Dust are our frames; and, gilded dust, our pride
Looks only for a moment whole and sound;
Like that long-buried body of the king,
Found lying with his urns and ornaments,
Which at a touch of light, an air of heaven,
Slipt into ashes and was found no more.

Here is a story which in rougher shape
Came from a grizzled cripple, whom I saw
Sunning himself in a waste field alone—
Old, and a mine of memories—who had served,
Long since, a bygone Rector of the place,
And been himself a part of what he told.

Sir Aylmer Aylmer, that almighty man,
The county God—in whose capacious hall,
Hung with a hundred shields, the family tree
Sprang from the midriff of a prostrate king—
Whose blazing wyvern weathercock'd the spire,
Stood from his walls and wing'd his entry-gates
And swang besides on many a windy sign—
Whose eyes from under a pyramidal head
Saw from his windows nothing save his own—
What lovelier of his own had he than her,
His only child, his Edith, whom he loved
As heiress and not heir regretfully?
But "he that marries her marries her name"
This fiat somewhat soothed himself and wife,
His wife a faded beauty of the Baths,
Insipid as the queen upon a card;
Her all of thought and bearing hardly more
Than his own shadow in a sickly sun.

A land of hops and poppy-mingled corn,
Little about it stirring save a brook!
A sleepy land where under the same wheel
The same old rut would deepen year by year;
Where almost all the village had one name;
Where Aylmer follow'd Aylmer at the Hall
And Averill Averill at the Rectory
Thrice over: so that Rectory and Hall,
Bound in an immemorial intimacy,
Were open to each other: tho' to dream
That Love could bind them closer well had made
The hoar hair of the Baronet bristle up
With horror, worse than had he heard his priest
Preach an inverted scripture, sons of men
Daughters of God; so sleepy was the land.

And might not Averill, had he will'd it so,
Somewhere beneath his own low range of roofs,
Have also set his many-shielded tree?
There was an Aylmer-Averill marriage once,
When the red rose was redder than itself,
And York's white rose as red as Lancaster's,
With wounded peace which each had prick'd to
    death.
"Not proven," Averill said, or laughingly,
"Some other race of Averills"—prov'n or no,
What cared he? what, if other or the same?
He lean'd not on his fathers but himself.
But Leolin, his brother, living oft

With Averill, and a year or two before
Call'd to the bar, but ever call'd away
By one low voice to one dear neighborhood,
Would often, in his walks with Edith, claim
A distant kinship to the gracious blood
That shook the heart of Edith hearing him.

Sanguine he was: a but less vivid hue
Than of that islet in the chestnut-bloom
Flamed in his cheek; and eager eyes, that still
Took joyful note of all things joyful, beam'd
Beneath a manlike mass of rolling gold,
Their best and brightest, when they dwelt on hers
Edith, whose pensive beauty, perfect else,
But subject to the season or the mood,
Shone like a mystic star between the less
And greater glory varying to and fro,
We know not wherefore; bounteously made,
And yet so finely, that a troublous touch
Thinn'd, or would seem to thin her in a day,
A joyous to dilate, as toward the light.
And these had been together from the first.
Leolin's first nurse was, five years after, hers;
So much the boy foreran; but when his date
Doubled her own, for want of playmates, he
(Since Averill was a decade and a half
His elder, and their parents underground)
Had tost his ball and flown his kite, and roll'd
His hoop to pleasure Edith, with her dipt
Against the rush of the air in the prone swing,
Made blossom-ball or daisy-chain, arranged
Her garden, sow'd her name and kept it green
In living letters, told her fairy-tales,
Show'd her the fairy footings on the grass,
The little dells of cowslip, fairy palms,
The petty marestail forest, fairy pines,
Or from the tiny pitted target blew
What look'd a flight of fairy arrows aim'd
All at one mark, all hitting: make-believes
For Edith and himself: or else he forged,
But that was later, boyish histories
Of battle, bold adventure, dungeon, wreck,
Flights, terrors, sudden rescues, and true love
Crown'd after trial; sketches rude and faint,
But where a passion yet unborn perhaps
Lay hidden as the music of the moon
Sleeps in the plain eggs of the nightingale.
And thus together, save for college-times
Or Temple-eaten terms, a couple, fair
As ever painter painted, poet sang,
Or Heav'n in lavish bounty moulded, grew.
And more and more, the maiden woman-grown,
He wasted hours with Averill; there, when first
The tented winter-field was broken up
Into that phalanx of the summer spears
That soon should wear the garland; there again
When burr and bine were gather'd; lastly there
At Christmas; ever welcome at the Hall,
On whose dull sameness his full tide of youth
Broke with a phosphorescence cheering even
My lady; and the Baronet yet had laid
No bar between them: dull and self-involved,
Tall and erect, but bending from his height
With half-allowing smiles for all the world,
And mighty courteous in the main—his pride

Lay deeper than to wear it as his ring—
He, like an Aylmer in his Aylmerism,
Would care no more for Leolin's walking with her
Than for his old Newfoundland's, when they ran
To loose him at the stables; for he rose
Twofooted at the limit of his chain,
Roaring to make a third: and how should Love,
Whom the cross-lightnings of four chance-met eyes
Flash into fiery life from nothing, follow
Such dear familiarities of dawn?
Seldom, but when he does, Master of all.

So these young hearts not knowing that they loved,
Not she at least, nor conscious of a bar
Between them, nor by plight or broken ring
Bound, but an immemorial intimacy,
Wander'd at will, but oft accompanied
By Averill: his, a brother's love, that hung
With wings of brooding shelter o'er her peace,
Might have been other, save for Leolin's—
Who knows? but so they wander'd, hour by hour
Gather'd the blossom that rebloom'd, and drank
The magic cup that fill'd itself anew.

A whisper half reveal'd her to herself.
For out beyond her lodges, where the brook
Vocal, with here and there a silence, ran
By sallowy rims, arose the laborers' homes,
A frequent haunt of Edith, on low knolls
That dimpling died into each other, huts
At random scatter'd, each a nest in bloom.
Her art, her hand, her counsel all had wrought
About them: here was one that, summer-blanch'd,
Was parcel-bearded with the traveller's-joy
In Autumn, parcel ivy-clad; and here
The warm-blue breathings of a hidden hearth
Broke from a bower of vine and honeysuckle:
One look'd all rosetree, and another wore
A close-set robe of jasmine sown with stars:
This had a rosy sea of gillyflowers
About it; this a milky-way on earth,
Like visions in the Northern dreamer's heavens,
A lily-avenue climbing to the doors;
One, almost to the martin-haunted eaves
A summer burial deep in hollyhocks;
Each, its own charm: and Edith's everywhere;
And Edith ever visitant with him,
He but less loved than Edith, of her poor:
For she—so lowly-lovely and so loving,
Queenly responsive when the loyal hand
Rose from the clay it work'd in as she past,
Not sowing hedgerow texts and passing by,
Nor dealing goodly counsel from a height
That makes the lowest hate it, but a voice
Of comfort and an open hand of help,
A splendid presence flattering the poor roofs
Revered as theirs, but kindlier than themselves
To ailing wife or wailing infancy
Or old bedridden palsy,—was adored:
He, loved for her and for himself. A grasp
Having the warmth and muscle of the heart,
A childly way with children, and a laugh
Ringing like proven golden coinage true,
Were no false passport to that easy realm,
Where once with Leolin at her side the girl,
Nursing a child, and turning to the warmth
The tender pink five-headed baby-soles,
Heard the good mother softly whisper "Bless,
God bless 'em; marriages are made in Heaven."

A flash of semi-jealousy clear'd it to her.
My Lady's Indian kinsman unannounced
With half a score of swarthy faces came.
His own, tho' keen and bold and soldierly,
Scar'd by the close ecliptic, was not fair;
Fairer his talk, a tongue that ruled the hour,
Tho' seeming boastful: so when first he dash'd
Into the chronicle of a deedful day,

Sir Aylmer half forgot his lazy smile
Of patron "Good! my lady's kinsman! good!"
My lady with her fingers interlock'd,
And rotatory thumbs on silken knees,
Call'd all her vital spirits into each ear
To listen: unawares they flitted off,
Busying themselves about the flowerage
That stood from out a stiff brocade in which,
The meteor of a splendid season, she,
Once with this kinsman, ah so long ago,
Stept thro' the stately minuet of those days:
But Edith's eager fancy hurried with him
Snatch'd thro' the perilous passes of his life:
Till Leolin ever watchful of her eye
Hated him with a momentary hate.
Wife-hunting, as the rumor ran, was he:
I know not, for he spoke not, only shower'd
His oriental gifts on every one
And most on Edith: like a storm he came,
And shook the house, and like a storm he went.

Among the gifts he left her (possibly
He flow'd and ebb'd uncertain, to return
When others had been tested) there was one,
A dagger, in rich sheath with jewels on it
Sprinkled about in gold that branch'd itself
Fine as ice-ferns on January panes
Made by a breath. I know not whence at first,
Nor of what race, the work; but as he told
The story, storming a hill-fort of thieves
He got it; for their captain after fight,
His comrades having fought their last below,
Was climbing up the valley; at whom he shot:
Down from the beetling crag to which he clung
Tumbled the tawny rascal at his feet,
This dagger with him, which when now admired
By Edith whom his pleasure was to please,
At once the costly Sahib yielded to her.

And Leolin, coming after he was gone,
Tost over all her presents petulantly:
And when she show'd the wealthy scabbard, saying
"Look what a lovely piece of workmanship!"
Slight was his answer "Well—I care not for it:"
Then playing with the blade he prick'd his hand.
"A gracious gift to give a lady, this!"
"But would it be more gracious," ask'd the girl,
"Were I to give this gift of his to one
That is no lady?" "Gracious? No," said he.
"Me?—but I cared not for it. O pardon me,
I seem to be ungraciousness itself."
"Take it," she added sweetly, "tho' his gift;
For I am more ungracious ev'n than you,
I care not for it either;" and he said
"Why then I love it;" but Sir Aylmer past,
And neither loved nor liked the thing he heard.

The next day came a neighbor. Blues and reds
They talk'd of: blues were sure of it, he thought:
Then of the latest fox—where started—kill'd
In such a bottom: "Peter had the brush,
My Peter, first;" and did Sir Aylmer know
That great pock-pitten fellow had been caught?
Then made his pleasure echo, hand to hand,
And rolling as it were the substance of it
Between his palms a moment up and down—
"The birds were warm, the birds were warm upon
him;
We have him now;" and had Sir Aylmer heard—
Nay, but he must—the land was ringing of it—
This blacksmith-border marriage—one they knew—
Raw from the nursery—who could trust a child?
That cursed France with her egalities!
And did Sir Aylmer (deferentially
With nearing chair and lower'd accent) think—
For people talk'd—that it was wholly wise
To let that handsome fellow Averill walk
So freely with his daughter? people talk'd—

The boy might get a notion into him ;
The girl might be entangled ere she knew.
Sir Aylmer slowly stiffening spoke :
"The girl and boy, Sir, know their differences !"
"Good," said his friend, "but watch !" and he
   "enough,
More than enough, Sir ! I can guard my own."
They parted, and Sir Aylmer Aylmer watch'd.

Pale, for on her the thunders of the house
Had fallen first, was Edith that same night :
Pale as the Jephtha's daughter, a rough piece
Of early rigid color, under which
Withdrawing by the counter door to that
Which Leolin open'd, she cast back upon him
A piteous glance, and vanish'd. He, as one
Caught in a burst of unexpected storm,
And pelted with outrageous epithets,
Turning beheld the Powers of the House
On either side the hearth, indignant ; her,
Cooling her false cheek with a feather-fan,
Him glaring, by his own stale devil spurr'd,
And, like a beast hard-ridden, breathing hard.
"Ungenerous, dishonorable, base,
Presumptuous ! trusted as he was with her,
The sole succeeder to their wealth, their lands,
The last remaining pillar of their house,
The one transmitter of their ancient name,
Their child." "Our child !" "Our heiress !" "Ours !"
   for still,
Like echoes from beyond a hollow, came
Her sicklier iteration. Last he said
"Boy, mark me ! for your fortunes are to make.
I swear you shall not make them out of mine.
Now inasmuch as you have practised on her,
Perplext her, made her half forget herself,
Swerve from her duty to herself and us—
Things in an Aylmer deem'd impossible,
Far as we track ourselves—I say that this,—
Else I withdraw favor and countenance
From you and yours forever—shall you do.
Sir, when you see her—but you shall not see her—
No, you shall write, and not to her, but me :
And you shall say that having spoken with me,
And after look'd into yourself, you find
That you meant nothing—as indeed you know
That you meant nothing. Such a match as this !
Impossible, prodigious !" These were words,
As meted by his measure of himself,
Arguing boundless forbearance : after which,
And Leolin's horror-stricken answer, "I
So foul a traitor to myself and her,
Never, O never," for about as long
As the wind-hover hangs in balance, paused
Sir Aylmer reddening from the storm within,
Then broke all bonds of courtesy, and crying
"Boy, should I find you by my doors again
My men shall lash you from them like a dog ;
Hence !" with a sudden execration drove
The footstool from before him, and arose ;
So, stammering "scoundrel" out of teeth that ground
As in a dreadful dream, while Leolin still
Retreated half-aghast, the fierce old man
Follow'd, and under his own lintel stood
Storming with lifted hands, a hoary face
Meet for the reverence of the hearth, but now,
Beneath a pale and unimpassion'd moon,
Vext with unworthy madness, and deform'd.

Slowly and conscious of the rageful eye
That watch'd him, till he heard the ponderous door
Close, crashing with long echoes thro' the land,
Went Leolin ; then, his passions all in flood
And masters of his motion, furiously
Down thro' the bright lawns to his brother's ran,
And foam'd away his heart at Averill's ear :
Whom Averill solaced as he might, amazed :
The man was his, had been his father's friend ·

He must have seen, himself had seen it long ;
He must have known, himself had known : besides,
He never yet had set his daughter forth
Here in the woman-markets of the west,
Where our Caucasians let themselves be sold.
Some one, he thought, had slander'd Leolin to him.
"Brother, for I have loved you more as son
Than brother, let me tell you : I myself—
What is their pretty saying ? jilted, is it ?
Jilted I was : I say it for your peace.
Pain'd, and, as bearing in myself the shame
The woman should have borne, humiliated,
I lived for years a stunted sunless life ;
Till after our good parents past away
Watching your growth, I seem'd again to grow.
Leolin, I almost sin in envying you :
The very whitest lamb in all my fold
Loves you : I know her : the worst thought she has
Is whiter even than her pretty hand :
She must prove true : for, brother, where two fight
The strongest wins, and truth and love are strength,
And you are happy : let her parents be."

But Leolin cried out the more upon them—
Insolent, brainless, heartless ! heiress, wealth,
Their wealth, their heiress ! wealth enough was theirs
For twenty matches. Were he lord of this,   •
Why twenty boys and girls should marry on it,
And forty blest ones bless him, and himself
Be wealthy still, ay wealthier. He believed
This filthy marriage-hindering Mammon made
The harlot of the cities ; nature crost
Was mother of the foul adulteries
That saturate soul with body. Name, too ! name,
Their ancient name ! they might be proud ; its worth
Was being Edith's. Ah how pale she had look'd
Darling, to-night ! they must have rated her
Beyond all tolerance. These old pheasant-lords,
These partridge-breeders of a thousand years,
Who had mildew'd in their thousands, doing nothing
Since Egbert—why, the greater their disgrace !
Fall back upon a name ! rest, rot in that !
Not keep it noble, make it nobler ? fools,
With such a vantage-ground for nobleness.
He had known a man, a quintessence of man,
The life of all—who madly loved—and he.
Thwarted by one of those old father-fools,
Had rioted his life out, and made an end.
He would not do it ! her sweet race and faith
Held him from that : but he had powers, he knew it
Back would he to his studies, make a name,
Name, fortune too : the world should ring of him
To shame these mouldy Aylmers in their graves ·
Chancellor, or what is greatest would he be—
"O brother, I am grieved to learn your grief—
Give me my fling, and let me say my say."

At which, like one that sees his own excess,
And easily forgives it as his own,
He laugh'd ; and then was mute : but presently
Wept like a storm : and honest Averill seeing
How low his brother's mood had fallen, fetch'd
His richest beeswing from a bin reserved
For banquets, praised the waning red, and told
The vintage—when this Aylmer came of age—
Then drank and past it : till at length the two,
Tho' Leolin flamed and fell again, agreed
That much allowance must be made for men
After an angry dream this kindlier glow
Faded with morning, but his purpose held.

Yet once by night again the lovers met,
A perilous meeting under the tall pines
That darken'd all the northward of her Hall.
Him, to her meek and modest bosom prest
In agony, she promised that no force,
Persuasion, no, nor death could alter her :
He, passionately hopefuller, would go,

Labor for his own Edith, and return
In such a sunlight of prosperity
He should not be rejected. "Write to me!
They loved me, and because I love their child
They hate me: there is war between us, dear,
Which breaks all bonds but ours; we must remain
Sacred to one another." So they talk'd,
Poor children, for their comfort: the wind blew;
The rain of heaven, and their own bitter tears,
Tears, and the careless rain of heaven, mixt
Upon their faces, as they kiss'd each other
In darkness, and above them roar'd the pine.

So Leolin went; and as we task ourselves
To learn a language known but smatteringly
In phrases here and there at random, toil'd
Mastering the lawless science of our law,
That codeless myriad of precedent,
That wilderness of single instances,
Thro' which a few, by wit or fortune led,
May beat a pathway out to wealth and fame.
The jests, that flash'd about the pleader's room,
Lightning of the hour, the pun, the scurrilous tale,—
Old scandals buried now seven decades deep
In other scandals that have lived and died,
And left the living scandal that shall die—
Were dead to him already; bent as he was
To make disproof of scorn, and strong in hopes,
And prodigal of all brain-labor he,
Charier of sleep, and wine and exercise,
Except when for a breathing-while at eve
Some niggard fraction of an hour he ran
Beside the river-bank: and then indeed
Harder the times were, and the hands of power
Were bloodier, and the according hearts of men
Seem'd harder too; but the soft river-breeze,
Which fann'd the gardens of that rival rose
Yet fragrant in a heart remembering
His former talks with Edith, on him breathed
Far purelier in his rushings to and fro,
After his books, to flush his blood with air,
Then to his books again. My lady's cousin,
Half-sickening of his pensioned afternoon,
Drove in upon the student once or twice,
Ran a Malayan muck against the times,
Had golden hopes for France and all mankind,
Answer'd all queries touching those at home
With a heaved shoulder and a saucy smile,
And fain had haled him out into the world,
And air'd him there: his nearer friend would say,
"Screw not the cord too sharply lest it snap."
Then left alone he pluck'd her dagger forth
From where his worldless heart had kept it warm,
Kissing his vows upon it like a knight.
And wrinkled benchers often talk'd of him
Approvingly, and prophesied his rise:
For heart, I think, help'd head: her letters too,
Tho' far between, and coming fitfully
Like broken music, written as she found
Or made occasion, being strictly watch'd,
Charm'd him thro' every labyrinth till he saw
An end, a hope, a light breaking upon him.

But they that cast her spirit into flesh,
Her worldly-wise begetters, plagued themselves
To sell her, those good parents, for her good.
Whatever eldest-born of rank or wealth
Might lie within their compass, him they lured
Into their net made pleasant by the baits
Of gold and beauty, wooing him to woo.
So month by month the noise about their doors,
And distant blaze of those dull banquets, made
The nightly wirer of their innocent hare
Falter before he took it. All in vain.
Sullen, defiant, pitying, wroth, return'd
Leolin's rejected rivals from their suit
So often, that the folly taking wings
Slipt o'er those lazy limits down the wind

With rumor, and became in other fields
A mockery to the yeomen over ale,
And laughter to their lords: but those at home,
As hunters round a hunted creature draw
The cordon close and closer toward the death,
Narrow'd her goings out and comings in;
Forbade her first the house of Averill,
Then closed her access to the wealthier farms,
Last from her own home-circle of the poor
They barr'd her: yet she bore it: yet her cheek
Kept color: wondrous! but, O mystery!
What amulet drew her down to that old oak,
So old, that twenty years before, a part
Falling had let appear the brand of John—
Once grovelike, each huge arm a tree, but now
The broken base of a black tower, a cave
Of touchwood, with a single flourishing spray.
There the manorial lord too curiously
Raking in that millennial touchwood-dust
Found for himself a bitter treasure-trove:
Burst his own wyvern on the seal, and read
Writhing a letter from his child, for which
Came at the moment Leolin's emissary,
A crippled lad, and coming turn'd to fly,
But scared with threats of jail and halter gave
To him that fluster'd his poor parish wits
The letter which he brought, and swore besides
To play their go-between as heretofore
Nor let them know themselves betray'd, and then,
Soul-stricken at their kindness to him, went
Hating his own lean heart and miserable.

Thenceforward oft from out a despot dream
Panting he woke, and oft as early as dawn
Aroused the black republic on his elms,
Sweeping the frothfly from the fescue, brush'd
Thro' the dim meadow toward his treasure-trove,
Seized it, took home, and to my lady, who made
A downward crescent of her minion mouth,
Listless in all despondence, read; and tore,
As if the living passion symbol'd there
Were living nerves to feel the rent; and burnt,
Now chafing at his own great self defied,
Now striking on huge stumbling-blocks of scorn
In babyisms, and dear diminutives
Scatter'd all over the vocabulary
Of such a love as like a chidden babe,
After much wailing, hush'd itself at last
Hopeless of answer: then tho' Averill wrote
And bade him with good heart sustain himself—
All would be well—the lover heeded not,
But passionately restless came and went,
And rustling once at night about the place,
There by a keeper shot at, slightly hurt,
Raging return'd: nor was it well for her
Kept to the garden now, and grove of pines,
Watch'd even there: and one was set to watch
The watcher, and Sir Aylmer watch'd them all,
Yet bitterer from his readings: once indeed,
Warm'd with his wines, or taking pride in her,
She look'd so sweet, he kiss'd her tenderly,
Not knowing what possess'd him: that one kiss
Was Leolin's one strong rival upon earth;
Seconded, for my lady follow'd suit,
Seem'd hope's returning rose: and then ensued
A Martin's summer of his faded love,
Or ordeal by kindness; after this
He seldom crost his child without a sneer;
The mother flow'd in shallower acrimonies:
Never one kindly smile, one kindly word:
So that the gentle creature shut from all
Her charitable use, and face to face
With twenty months of silence, slowly lost
Nor greatly cared to lose, her hold on life.
Last, some low fever ranging round to spy
The weakness of a people or a house,
Like flies that haunt a wound, or deer, or men,
Or almost all that is, hurting the hurt—

Save Christ as we believe him—found the girl
And flung her down upon a couch of fire,
Where careless of the household faces near,
And crying upon the name of Leolin,
She, and with her the race of Aylmer, past.

Star to star vibrates light: may soul to soul
Strike thro' a finer element of her own?
So,—from afar,—touch as at once? or why
That night, that moment, when she named his name,
Did the keen shriek, " Yes love, yes Edith, yes,"
Shrill, till the comrade of his chambers woke,
And came upon him half-arisen from sleep,
With a weird bright eye, sweating and trembling,
His hair as it were crackling into flames,
His body half flung forward in pursuit,
And his long arms stretch'd as to grasp a flyer:
Nor knew he wherefore he had made the cry:
And being much befool'd and idioted
By the rough amity of the other, sank
As into sleep again. The second day,
My lady's Indian kinsman rushing in,
A breaker of the bitter news from home,
Found a dead man, a letter edged with death
Beside him, and the dagger which himself
Gave Edith, redden'd with no bandit's blood
"From Edith" was engraven on the blade.

Then Averill went and gazed upon his death.
And when he came again, his flock believed—
Beholding how the years which are not Time's
Had blasted him—that many thousand days
Were clipt by horror from his term of life.
Yet the sad mother, for the second death
Scarce touch'd her thro' that nearness of the first,
And being used to find her pastor texts,
Sent to the harrow'd brother, praying him
To speak before the people of her child,
And fixt the Sabbath. Darkly that day rose:
Autumn's mock sunshine of the faded woods
Was all the life of it; for hard on these,
A breathless burthen of low-folded heavens
Stifled and chill'd at once: but every roof
Sent out a listener: many too had known
Edith among the hamlets round, and since
The parents' harshness and the hapless loves
And double death were widely murmur'd, left
Their own gray tower, or plain-faced tabernacle,
To hear him; all in mourning these, and those
With blots of it about them, ribbon, glove
Or kerchief; while the church,—one night, except
For greenish glimmerings thro' the lancets,—made
Still paler the pale head of him, who tower'd
Above them, with his hopes in either grave.

Long o'er his bent brows linger'd Averill,
His face magnetic to the hand from which
Livid he pluck'd it forth, and labor'd thro'
His brief prayer-prelude, gave the verse "Behold,
Your house is left unto you desolate!"
But lapsed into so long a pause again
As half amazed, half frighted all his flock:
Then from his height and loneliness of grief
Bore down in flood, and dash'd his angry heart
Against the desolations of the world.

Never since our bad earth became one sea,
Which rolling o'er the palaces of the proud,
And all but those who knew the living God—
Eight that were left to make a purer world—
When since had flood, fire, earthquake, thunder, wrought
Such waste and havoc as the idolatries,
Which from the low light of mortality
Shot up their shadows to the Heaven of Heavens.
And worshipt their own darkness as the Highest?
"Gash thyself, priest, and honor thy brute Baäl,

And to thy worst self sacrifice thyself,
For with thy worst self hast thou clothed thy God."
Then came a Lord in no wise like to Baäl.
The babe shall lead the lion. Surely now
The wilderness shall blossom as the rose.
Crown thyself, worm, and worship thine own lusts!—
No coarse and blockish God of acreage
Stands at thy gate for thee to grovel to—
Thy God is far diffused in noble groves
And princely halls, and farms, and flowing lawns,
And heaps of living gold that daily grow,
And title-scrolls and gorgeous heraldries.
In such a shape dost thou behold thy God.
Thou wilt not gash thy flesh for him; for thine
Fares richly, in fine linen, not a hair
Ruffled upon the scarfskin, even while
The deathless ruler of thy dying house
Is wounded to the death that cannot die;
And tho' thou numberest with the followers
Of One who cried "Leave all and follow me,"
Thee therefore with His light about thy feet,
Thee with His message ringing in thine ears,
Thee shall thy brother man, the Lord from Heaven,
Born of a village girl, carpenter's son,
Wonderful, Prince of peace, the Mighty God,
Count the more base idolater of the two;
Crueller: as not passing thro' the fire
Bodies, but souls—thy children's—thro' the smoke,
The blight of low desires—darkening thine own
To thine own likeness; or if one of these,
Thy better born unhappily from thee,
Should, as by miracle, grow straight and fair—
Friends, I was bid to speak of such a one
By those who most have cause to sorrow for her—
Fairer than Rachel by the palmy well,
Fairer than Ruth among the fields of corn,
Fair as the Angel that said "hail" she seem'd,
Who entering fill'd the house with sudden light.
For so mine own was brighten'd: where indeed
The roof so lowly but that beam of Heaven
Dawn'd sometimes thro' the doorway? whose the babe
Too ragged to be fondled on her lap,
Warm'd at her bosom? The poor child of shame,
The common care whom no one cared for, leapt
To greet her, wasting his forgotten heart,
As with the mother he had never known,
In gambols; for her fresh and innocent eyes
Had such a star of morning in their blue,
That all neglected places of the field
Broke into nature's music when they saw her.
Low was her voice, but won mysterious way
Thro' the seal'd ear, to which a louder one
Was all but silence—free of alms her hand—
The hand that robed your cottage-walls with flowers
Has often toil'd to clothe your little ones;
How often placed upon the sick man's brow
Cool'd it, or laid his feverous pillow smooth!
Had you one sorrow and she shared it not?
One burthen and she would not lighten it?
One spiritual doubt she did not soothe?
Or when some heat of difference sparkled out,
How sweetly would she glide between your wraths,
And steal you from each other! for she walk'd
Wearing the light yoke of that Lord of love,
Who still'd the rolling wave of Galilee!
And one—of him I was not bid to speak—
Was always with her, whom you also knew.
Him too you loved, for he was worthy love.
And these had been together from the first;
They might have been together till the last.
Friends, this frail bark of ours, when sorely tried,
May wreck itself without the pilot's guilt,
Without the captain's knowledge: hope with me.
Whose shame is that, if he went hence with shame?
Nor mine the fault, if losing both of these
I cry to vacant chairs and widow'd walls,
"My house is left unto me desolate."

While thus he spoke, his hearers wept; But some,
Sons of the glebe, with other frowns than those
That knit themselves for summer shadow, scowl'd
At their great lord. He, when it seem'd he saw
No pale sheet-lightnings from afar, but fork'd
Of the near storm, and aiming at his head,
Sat anger-charm'd from sorrow, soldier-like,
Erect: but when the preacher's cadence flow'd
Softening thro' all the gentle attributes
Of his lost child, the wife, who watch'd his face,
Paled at a sudden twitch of his iron mouth;
And, "O pray God that he hold up," she thought,
"Or surely I shall shame myself and him."

"Nor yours the blame—for who beside your hearths
Can take her place—if echoing me you cry
'Our house is left unto us desolate?'
But thou, O thou that killest, hadst thou known,
O thou that stonest, hadst thou understood
The things belonging to thy peace and ours!
Is there no prophet but the voice that calls
Doom upon kings, or in the waste 'Repent?'
Is not our own child on the narrow way,
Who down to those that saunter in the broad
Cries 'Come up hither,' as a prophet to us?
Is there no stoning save with flint and rock?
Yes, as the dead we weep for testify—
No desolation but by sword and fire?
Yes, as your moanings witness, and myself
Am lonelier, darker, earthlier for my loss.
Give me your prayers, for he is past your prayers,
Not past the living fount of pity in Heaven.
But I that thought myself long-suffering, meek,
Exceeding 'poor in spirit'—how the words
Have twisted back upon themselves and mean
Vileness, we are grown so proud—I wish'd my voice
A rushing tempest of the wrath of God
To blow these sacrifices thro' the world—
Sent like the twelve-divided concubine
To inflame the tribes; but there—out yonder—earth
Lightens from her own central Hell—O there
The red fruit of an old idolatry—
The heads of chiefs and princes fall so fast,
They cling together in the ghastly sack—
The land all shambles—naked marriages
Flash from the bridge, and ever-murder'd France,
By shores that darken with the gathering wolf,
Runs in a river of blood to the sick sea.
Is this a time to madden madness then?
Was this a time for these to flaunt their pride?
May Pharaoh's darkness, folds as dense as those
Which hid the Holiest from the people's eyes
Ere the great death, shroud this great sin from all:
Doubtless our narrow world must canvass it;
O rather pray for those and pity them
Who thro' their own desire accomplish'd bring
Their own gray hairs with sorrow to the grave—
Who broke the bond which they desired to break—
Which else had link'd their race with times to
  come—
Who wove coarse webs to snare her purity,
Grossly contriving their dear daughter's good—
Poor souls, and knew not what they did, but sat
Ignorant, devising their own daughter's death
May not that earthly chastisement suffice?
Have not our love and reverence left them bare?
Will not another take their heritage?
Will there be children's laughter in their hall
Forever and forever, or one stone
Left on another, or is it a light thing
That I their guest, their host, their ancient friend,
I made by these the last of all my race
Must cry to these the last of theirs, as cried
Christ ere His agony to those that swore
Not by the temple but the gold, and made
Their own traditions God, and slew the Lord,
And left their memories a world's curse—'Behold,
Your house is left unto you desolate?'"

Ended he had not, but she brook'd no more:
Long since her heart had beat remorselessly,
Her crampt-up sorrow pain'd her, and a sense
Of meanness in her unresisting life.
Then their eyes vext her; for on entering
He had cast the curtains of their seat aside—
Black velvet of the costliest—she herself
Had sewn to that: fain had she closed them now,
Yet dared not stir to do it, only near'd
Her husband inch by inch, but when she laid,
Wifelike, her hand in one of his, he veil'd
His face with the other, and at once, as falls
A creeper when the prop is broken, fell
The woman shrieking at his feet, and swoon'd.
Then her own people bore along the nave
Her pendent hands, and narrow meagre face
Seam'd with the shallow cares of fifty years;
And her the Lord of all the landscape round
Ev'n to its last horizon, and of all
Who peer'd at him so keenly, follow'd out
Tall and erect, but in the middle aisle
Reel'd, as a footsore ox in crowded ways
Stumbling across the market to his death,
Unpitied; for he groped as blind, and seem'd
Always about to fall, grasping the pews
And oaken finials till he touch'd the door;
Yet to the lychgate, where his chariot stood,
Strode from the porch, tall and erect again.

But nevermore did either pass the gate
Save under pall with bearers. In one month,
Thro' weary and yet ever wearier hours,
The childless mother went to seek her child;
And when he felt the silence of his house
About him, and the change and not the change,
And those fixt eyes of painted ancestors
Staring forever from their gilded walls
On him their last descendant, his own head
Began to droop, to fall; the man became
Imbecile; his one word was "desolate;"
Dead for two years before his death was he;
But when the second Christmas came, escaped
His keepers, and the silence which he felt,
To find a deeper in the narrow gloom
By wife and child; nor wanted at his end
The dark retinue reverencing death
At golden thresholds; nor from tender hearts,
And those who sorrow'd o'er a vanish'd race,
Pity, the violet on the tyrant's grave.
Then the great Hall was wholly broken down,
And the broad woodland parcell'd into farms;
And where the two contrived their daughter's good,
Lies the hawk's cast, the mole has made his run,
The hedgehog underneath the plantain bores,
The rabbit fondles his own harmless face,
The slow-worm creeps, and the thin weasel there
Follows the mouse, and all is open field.

SEA DREAMS.

A city clerk, but gently born and bred;
His wife, an unknown artist's orphan child—
One babe was theirs, a Margaret, three years old:
They, thinking that her clear germander eye
Droopt in the giant-factoried city-gloom,
Came, with a month's leave given them, to the sea:
For which his gains were dock'd, however small:
Small were his gains, and hard his work; besides,
Their slender household fortunes (for the man
Had risk'd his little) like the little thrift,
Trembled in perilous places o'er a deep;
And oft, when sitting all alone, his face
Would darken, as he cursed his credulousness,
And that one unctuous mouth which lured him, rogue,
To buy strange shares in some Peruvian mine.
Now seaward-bound for health they gain'd a coast,

All sand and cliff and deep-inrunning cave,
At close of day: slept, woke, and went the next,
The Sabbath, pious varlets from the church,
To chapel; where a heated pulpiteer,
Not preaching simple Christ to simple men,
Announced the coming doom, and fulminated
Against the scarlet woman and her creed:
For sideways up he swung his arms, and shriek'd,
"Thus, thus with violence," ev'n as if he held
The Apocalyptic millstone, and himself
Were that great Angel; "thus with violence
Shall Babylon be cast into the sea;
Then comes the close." The gentle-hearted wife
Sat shuddering at the ruin of a world;
He at his own: but when the wordy storm
Had ended, forth they came and paced the shore,
Ran in and out the long sea-framing caves,
Drank the large air, and saw, but scarce believed
(The sootflake of so many a summer still
Clung to their fancies) that they saw, the sea.
So now on sand they walk'd, and now on cliff,
Lingering about the thymy promontories,
Till all the sails were darken'd in the west,
And rosed in the east: then homeward and to bed:
Where she, who kept a tender Christian hope
Haunting a holy text, and still to that
Returning, as the bird returns, at night,
"Let not the sun go down upon your wrath,"
Said, "Love, forgive him:" but he did not speak;
And silenced by that silence lay the wife,
Remembering her dear Lord who died for all,
And musing on the little lives of men,
And how they mar this little by their feuds.

But while the two were sleeping, a full tide
Rose with ground-swell, which, on the foremost rocks
Touching, uplifted in spirts of wild sea-smoke,
And scaled in sheets of wasteful foam, and fell
In vast sea-cataracts—ever and anon
Dead claps of thunder from within the cliffs
Heard thro' the living roar. At this the babe,
Their Margaret cradled near them, wail'd and woke
The mother, and the father suddenly cried,
"A wreck, a wreck!" then turn'd, and groaning said

"Forgive! How many will say 'forgive,' and find
A sort of absolution in the sound
To hate a little longer! No; the sin
That neither God nor man can well forgive,
Hypocrisy, I saw it in him at once.
Is it so true that second thoughts are best?
Not first, and third, which are a riper first?
Too ripe, too late! they come too late for use.
Ah love, there surely lives in man and beast
Something divine to warn them of their foes:
And such a sense, when first I fronted him,
Said, 'Trust him not:' but after, when I came
To know him more, I lost it, knew him less:
Fought with what seem'd my own uncharity;
Sat at his table: drank his costly wines;
Made more and more allowance for his talk:
Went further, fool! and trusted him with all,
All my poor scrapings from a dozen years
Of dust and deskwork; there is no such mine,
None; but a gulf of ruin, swallowing gold,
Not making. Ruin'd! ruin'd! the sea roars
Ruin: a fearful night!"

"Not fearful; fair,"
Said the good wife, "if every star in heaven
Can make it fair: you do but hear the tide.
Had you ill dreams?"

"O yes," he said. "I dream'd
Of such a tide swelling toward the land,
And I from out the boundless outer deep
Swept with it to the shore, and enter'd one
Of those dark caves that run beneath the cliffs.

I thought the motion of the boundless deep
Bore through the cave, and I was heaved upon it
In darkness: then I saw one lovely star
Larger and larger. 'What a world,' I thought,
'To live in!' but in moving on I found
Only the landward exit of the cave,
Bright with the sun upon the stream beyond:
And near the light a giant woman sat.
All over earthy, like a piece of earth,
A pickaxe in her hand: then out I slipt
Into a land all sun and blossom, trees
As high as heaven, and every bird that sings:
And here the night-light flickering in my eyes
Awoke me."

"That was then your dream," she said,
"Not sad, but sweet."

"So sweet, I lay," said he,
"And mused upon it, drifting up the stream
In fancy, till I slept again, and pieced
The broken vision; for I dream'd that still
The motion of the great deep bore me on,
And that the woman walk'd upon the brink:
I wonder'd at her strength, and ask'd her of it:
'It came,' she said, 'by working in the mines:'
O then to ask her of my shares, I thought:
And ask'd; but not a word; she shook her head.
And then the motion of the current ceased,
And there was rolling thunder; and we reach'd
A mountain, like a wall of burrs and thorns:
But she with her strong feet up the steep hill
Trod out a path: I follow'd; and at top
She pointed seaward: there a fleet of glass,
That seem'd a fleet of jewels under me,
Sailing along before a gloomy cloud
That not one moment ceased to thunder, past
In sunshine; right across its track there lay,
Down in the water, a long reef of gold,
Or what seem'd gold: and I was glad at first
To think that in our often-ransacked world
Still so much gold was left; and then I fear'd
Lest the gray navy there should splinter on it,
And fearing waved my arm to warn them off;
An idle signal, for the brittle fleet
(I thought I could have died to save it) near'd,
Touch'd, clink'd, and clash'd, and vanish'd, and I
woke,
I heard the clash so clearly. Now I see
My dream was Life; the woman honest Work;
And my poor venture but a fleet of glass,
Wreck'd on a reef of visionary gold."

"Nay," said the kindly wife to comfort him,
"You raised your arm, you tumbled down and broke
The glass with little Margaret's medicine in it;
And, breaking that, you made and broke your
dream:
A trifle makes a dream, a trifle breaks."

"No trifle," groan'd the husband; "yesterday
I met him suddenly in the street, and ask'd
That which I ask'd the woman in my dream.
Like her, he shook his head. 'Show me the books!'
He dodged me with a long and loose account.
'The books, the books!' but he, he could not wait,
Bound on a matter he of life and death:
When the great Books (see Daniel seven and ten)
Were open'd, I should find he meant me well:
And then began to bloat himself, and ooze
All over with the fat affectionate smile
That makes the widow lean. 'My dearest friend,
Have faith, have faith! We live by faith,' said he;
'And all things work together for the good
Of those'—it makes me sick to quote him—last
Gript my hand hard, and with God-bless-you went
I stood like one that had received a blow:
I found a hard friend in his loose accounts,

A loose one in the hard grip of his hand,
A curse in his God-bless-you: then my eyes
Pursued him down the street, and far away,
Among the honest shoulders of the crowd,
Read rascal in the motions of his back,
And scoundrel in the supple-sliding knee."

"Was he so bound, poor soul?" said the good
     wife;
"So are we all: but do not call him, love,
Before you prove him, rogue, and proved, forgive.
His gain is loss; for he that wrongs his friend
Wrongs himself more, and ever bears about
A silent court of justice in his breast,
Himself the judge and jury, and himself
The prisoner at the bar, ever condemn'd:
And that drags down his life: then comes what
     comes
Hereafter: and he meant, he said he meant,
Perhaps he meant, or partly meant, you well."

"'With all his conscience and one eye askew'—
Love, let me quote these lines, that you may learn
A man is likewise counsel for himself,
Too often in that silent court of yours—
'With all his conscience and one eye askew,
So false, he partly took himself for true:
Whose pious talk, when most his heart was dry,
Made wet the crafty crowsfoot round his eye;
Who, never naming God except for gain,
So never took that useful name in vain;
Made Him his catspaw and the Cross his tool,
And Christ the bait to trap his dupe and fool;
Nor deeds of gift, but gifts of grace he forged,
And snakelike slimed his victim ere he gorged;
And oft at Bible meetings, o'er the rest
Arising, did his holy oily best,
Dropping the too rough H in Hell and Heaven,
To spread the Word by which himself had thriven.'
How like you this old satire?"

                        "Nay," she said,
"I loathe it: he had never kindly heart,
Nor ever cared to better his own kind,
Who first wrote satire with no pity in it.
But will you hear my dream, for I had one
That altogether went to music? Still
It awed me."

                Then she told it, having dream'd
Of that same coast.

            —"But round the North, a light,
A belt, it seem'd, of luminous vapor, lay,
And ever in it a low musical note
Swell'd up and died; and, as it swell'd, a ridge
Of breaker issued from the belt, and still
Grew with the growing note, and when the note
Had reach'd a thunderous fullness on those cliffs
Broke, mixt with awful light (the same as that
Living within the belt) whereby she saw
That all those lines of cliffs were cliffs no more,
But huge cathedral fronts of every age,
Grave, florid, stern, as far as eye could see,
One after one: and then the great ridge drew,
Lessening to the lessening music, back,
And past into the belt and swell'd again
Slowly to music: ever when it broke
The statues, king or saint, or founder, fell;
Then from the gaps and chasms of ruin left
Came men and women in dark clusters round,
Some crying 'Set them up! they shall not fall!'
And others, 'Let them lie, for they have fall'n.'
And still they strove and wrangled: and she grieved
In her strange dream, she knew not why, to find
Their wildest wailings never out of tune
With that sweet note; and ever as their shrieks
Ran highest up the gamut, that great wave

Returning, while none mark'd it, on the crowd
Broke, mixt with awful light, and show'd their eyes
Glaring, and passionate looks, and swept away
The men of flesh and blood, and men of stone,
To the waste deeps together.

                        "Then I fixt
My wistful eyes on two fair images,
Both crown'd with stars and high among the stars,—
The Virgin Mother standing with her child
High up on one of those dark minster-fronts—
Till she began to totter, and the child
Clung to the mother, and sent out a cry
Which mixt with little Margaret's, and I woke,
And my dream awed me:—well—but what are
     dreams?
Yours came but from the breaking of a glass,
And mine but from the crying of a child."

"Child? No!" said he, "but this tide's roar, and
     his,
Our Boanerges, with his threats of doom,
And loud-lung'd Antibabylonianisms
(Altho' I grant but little music there)
Went both to make your dream: but if there were
A music harmonizing our wild cries,
Sphere-music such as that you dream'd about,
Why, that would make our passions far too like
The discords dear to the musician. No—
One shriek of hate would jar all the hymns of
     heaven:
True Devils with no ear, they howl in tune
With nothing but the Devil!"

                        "'True' indeed!
One of our town, but later by an hour
Here than ourselves, spoke with me on the shore;
While you were running down the sands, and made
The dimpled flounce of the sea-furbelow flap,
Good man, to please the child. She brought strange
     news.
Why were you silent when I spoke to-night?
I had set my heart on your forgiving him
Before you knew. We must forgive the dead."

"Dead! who is dead?"

                        "The man your eye pursued.
A little after you had parted with him,
He suddenly dropt dead of heart-disease."

"Dead? he? of heart-disease? what heart had he
To die of? dead!"

                        "Ah, dearest, if there be
A devil in man, there is an angel too,
And if he did that wrong you charge him with,
His angel broke his heart. But your rough voice
(You spoke so loud) has roused the child again.
Sleep, little birdie, sleep! will she not sleep
Without her 'little birdie?' well then, sleep,
And I will sing you 'birdie.'"

                        Saying this,
The woman half turn'd round from him she loved,
Left him one hand, and reaching thro' the night
Her other, found (for it was close beside)
And half embraced the basket cradle-head
With one soft arm, which, like the pliant bough
That moving moves the nest and nestling, sway'd
The cradle, while she sang this baby song.

            What does little birdie say
            In her nest at peep of day?
            Let me fly, says little birdie,
            Mother, let me fly away.
            Birdie, rest a little longer,
            Till the little wings are stronger.

So she rests a little longer,
Then she flies away.

What does little baby say,
In her bed at peep of day?
Baby says, like little birdie,
Let me rise and fly away.
Baby, sleep a little longer,
Till the little limbs are stronger.
If she sleeps a little longer,
Baby too shall fly away.

"She sleeps: let us too, let all evil, sleep.
He also sleeps—another sleep than ours.
He can do no more wrong: forgive him, dear,
And I shall sleep the sounder!"

　　　　　　　　　Then the man,
"His deeds yet live, the worst is yet to come.
Yet let your sleep for this one night be sound:
I do forgive him!"

　　　　　　　　"Thanks, my love," she said,
"Your own will be the sweeter," and they slept.

———◇◇———

THE GRANDMOTHER.

I.

And Willy, my eldest-born, is gone, you say, little Anne?
Ruddy and white, and strong on his legs, he looks like a man.
And Willy's wife has written: she never was over-wise,
Never the wife for Willy: he would n't take my advice.

II.

For, Annie, you see, her father was not the man to save,
Had n't a head to manage, and drank himself into his grave.
Pretty enough, very pretty! but I was against it for one.
Eh!—but he would n't hear me—and Willy, you say, is gone.

III.

Willy, my beauty, my eldest-born, the flower of the flock;
Never a man could fling him: for Willy stood like a rock.
"Here's a leg for a baby of a week!" says doctor: and he would be bound,
There was not his like that year in twenty parishes round.

IV.

Strong of his hands, and strong on his legs, but still of his tongue!
I ought to have gone before him: I wonder he went so young.
I cannot cry for him, Annie: I have not long to stay;
Perhaps I shall see him the sooner, for he lived far away.

V.

Why do you look at me, Annie? you think I am hard and cold;
But all my children have gone before me, I am so old:
I cannot weep for Willy, nor can I weep for the rest;
Only at your age, Annie, I could have wept with the best.

VI.

For I remember a quarrel I had with your father, my dear,
All for a slanderous story, that cost me many a tear.
I mean your grandfather, Annie: it cost me a world of woe,
Seventy years ago, my darling, seventy years ago.

VII.

For Jenny, my cousin, had come to the place, and I knew right well
That Jenny had tript in her time: I knew, but I would not tell.
And she to be coming and slandering me, the base little liar!
But the tongue is a fire, as you know, my dear, the tongue is a fire.

VIII.

And the parson made it his text that week, and he said likewise,
That a lie which is half a truth is ever the blackest of lies,
That a lie which is all a lie may be met and fought with outright,
But a lie which is part a truth is a harder matter to fight.

IX.

And Willy had not been down to the farm for a week and a day;
And all things look'd half-dead, tho' it was the middle of May.
Jenny, to slander me, who knew what Jenny had been!
But soiling another, Annie, will never make one's self clean.

X.

And I cried myself wellnigh blind, and all of an evening late
I climb'd to the top of the garth, and stood by the road at the gate.
The moon like a rick on fire was rising over the dale,
And whit, whit, whit, in the bush beside me chirrupt the nightingale.

XI.

All of a sudden he stopt: there past by the gate of the farm,
Willy,—he did n't see me,—and Jenny hung on his arm.
Out into the road I started, and spoke I scarce knew how;
Ah, there's no fool like the old one—it makes me angry now.

XII.

Willy stood up like a man, and look'd the thing that he meant;
Jenny, the viper, made me a mocking courtesy and went.
And I said, "Let us part: in a hundred years it 'll all be the same,
You cannot love me at all, if you love not my good name."

XIII.

And he turn'd, and I saw his eyes all wet, in the sweet moonshine:
"Sweetheart, I love you so well that your good name is mine.
And what do I care for Jane, let her speak of you well or ill;
But marry me out of hand: we too shall be happy still."

XIV.

'Marry you, Willy!" said I, "but I needs must speak my mind,
And I fear you'll listen to tales, be jealous and hard and unkind."
But he turn'd and claspt me in his arms, and answer'd, "No, love, no;"
Seventy years ago, my darling, seventy years ago.

XV.

So Willy and I were wedded: I wore a lilac gown;
And the ringers rang with a will, and he gave the ringers a crown.
But the first that ever I bare was dead before he was born,
Shadow and shine is life, little Annie, flower and thorn.

XVI.

That was the first time, too, that ever I thought of death.
There lay the sweet little body that never had drawn a breath.
I had not wept, little Annie, not since I had been a wife;
but I wept like a child that day, for the babe had fought for his life.

XVII.

His dear little face was troubled, as if with anger or pain:
I look'd at the still little body—his trouble had all been in vain.
For Willy I cannot weep, I shall see him another morn:
But I wept like a child for the child that was dead before he was born.

XVIII.

But he cheer'd me, my good man, for he seldom said me nay:
Kind, like a man, was he; like a man, too, would have his way:
Never jealous—not he: we had many a happy year;
And he died, and I could not weep—my own time seem'd so near.

XIX.

But I wish'd it had been God's will that I, too, then could have died:
I began to be tired a little, and fain had slept at his side.
And that was ten years back, or more, if I don't forget:
But as to the children, Annie, they 're all about me yet.

XX.

Pattering over the boards, my Annie who left me at two,
Patter she goes, my own little Annie, an Annie like you:
Pattering over the boards, she comes and goes at her will,
While Harry is in the five-acre and Charlie ploughing the hill.

XXI.

And Harry and Charlie, I hear them too—they sing to their team:
Often they come to the door in a pleasant kind of a dream.
They come and sit by my chair, they hover about my bed—
I am not always certain if they be alive or dead.

XXII.

And yet I know for a truth, there 's none of them left alive;
For Harry went at sixty, your father at sixty-five:
And Willy, my eldest-born, at nigh threescore and ten;
I knew them all as babies, and now they 're elderly men.

XXIII.

For mine is a time of peace, it is not often I grieve;
I am oftener sitting at home in my father's farm at eve:
And the neighbors come and laugh and gossip, and so do I;
I find myself often laughing at things that have long gone by.

XXIV.

To be sure the preacher says, our sins should make us sad :
But mine is a time of peace, and there is Grace to be had :
And God, not man, is the Judge of us all when life shall cease ;
And in this Book, little Annie, the message is one of Peace.

XXV.

And age is a time of peace, so it be free from pain,
And happy has been my life ; but I would not live it again.
I seem to be tired a little, that 's all, and long for rest :
Only at your age, Annie, I could have wept with the best.

XXVI.

So Willy has gone, my beauty, my eldest-born, my flower ;
But how can I weep for Willy, he has but gone for an hour,—
Gone for a minute, my son, from this room into the next ;
I, too, shall go in a minute. What time have I to be vext ?

XXVII.

And Willy's wife has written, she never was over-wise.
Get me my glasses, Annie : thank God that I keep my eyes.
There is but a trifle left you, when I shall have past away.
But stay with the old woman now : you cannot have long to stay.

NORTHERN FARMER.

OLD STYLE.

I.

Wheer 'asta beän saw long and meä liggin' 'ere aloän ?
Noorse ? thoort nowt o' a noorse : whoy, doctor 's abeän an' agoän :
Says that I moänt 'a naw moor yaäle : but I beänt a fool :
Git ma my yaäle, for I beänt a-gooin' to break my rule.

II.

Doctors, they knaws nowt, for a says what 's nawways true :
Naw soort o' koind o' use to saäy the things that a do.
I 've 'ed my point o' yaäl ivry noight sin' I beän 'ere,
An' I 've 'ed my quart ivry market-noight for foorty year.

III.

Parson 's a beän loikewoise, an' a sittin 'ere o' my bed.
"The amoighty 's a taäkin o' you to 'issen, my friend," a said,
An' a towd ma my sins, an 's toithe were due, an' I gied it in hond ;
I done my duty by un, as I 'a done by the lond.

IV.

Larn'd a ma' beä. I reckons I 'annot sa mooch to larn.
But a cost oop, thot a did, 'boot Bessy Marris's barn.
Thof a knaws I hallus voäted wi' Squoire an' choorch an staäte,
An' i' the woost o' toimes I wur niver agin the raäte.

V.

An' I hallus comed to 's choorch afoor my Sally wur deäd,
An' 'eerd un a bummin' awaäy loike a buzzard-clock* ower my yeäd,
An' I niver knaw'd whot a meän'd but I thowt a 'ad summut to saäy,
An' I thowt a said whot a owt to 'a said an' I comed awaäy.

VI.

Bessy Marris's barn ! tha knaws she laäid it to meä.
Mowt 'a beän, mayhap, for she wur a bad un, sheä.
'Siver, I kep un, I kep un, my lass, tha mun understond ;
I done my duty by un as I 'a done by the lond.

VII.

But Parson a comes an' a goos, an' a says it easy an' freeä
"The amoighty 's a taäkin o' you to 'issen, my friend," says 'eä.
I weänt saäy men be loiars, thof summun said it in 'aäste :
But a reäds wonn sarmin a weeäk, an' I 'a stubb'd Thornaby waäste.

VIII.

D' ya moind the waäste, my lass ? naw, naw, tha was not born then :
Theer wur a boggle in it, I often 'eerd un mysen ;
Moä∗t loike a butter-bump,† for I 'eerd un aboot an aboot,
But I stubb'd un oop wi' the lot, and raäved an' rembled un oot.

---

* Cockchafer.   † Bittern.

IX.

Keäper's it wur; fo' they fun un theer a laäid on 'is faäce
Doon i' the woild 'enemies* afoor I comed to the plaäce.
Noäks or Thimbleby—toner 'ed shot an as deäd as a naäil.
Noäks wur 'ang'd for it oop at 'soize—but git ma my yaäle.

X.

Dubbut looäk at the waäste: theer war n't not feäd for a cow;
Nowt at all but bracken an' fuzz, an' looäk at it now—
War n't worth nowt a haäcre, an' now theer's lots o' feäd,
Fourscore yows upon it an' some on it doon in seäd.

XI.

Nobbut a bit on it 's left, an' I mean'd to 'a stubb'd it at fall,
Done it ta-year I meän'd, an' runn'd plow thruff it an' all,
If godamoighty an' parson 'ud nobbut let ma aloän,
Meä, wi' haäte oonderd haäcre o' Squoire's an' loäd o' my oän.

XII.

Do godamoighty knaw what a 's doing a-taäkin' o' meä?
I beänt wonn as saws 'ere a beän an' yonder a peä;
An' Squoire 'ull be sa mad an' all—a' dear a' dear!
And I 'a mounaged for Squoire come Michaelmas thirty year.

XIII.

A mowt 'a taäken Joänes, as 'ant a 'aäpoth o' sense,
Or a mowt 'a taäken Robins—a niver mended a fence:
But godamoighty a moost taäke meä an' taäke ma now
Wi' auf the cows to cauve an' Thornaby holms to plow!

XIV.

Looäk 'ow quoloty smoiles when they sees ma a passin' by,
Says to thessen naw doot "what a mon a be eewer-ly!"
For they knaws what I beän to Squoire sin fust a comed to the 'All;
I done my duty by Squoire an' I done my duty by all.

XV.

Squoire 's in Lunnon, an' summun I reckons 'ull 'a to wroite,
For who 's to howd the lond ater meä thot muddles ma quoit;
Sartin-sewer I beä, thot a weänt niver give it to Joänes,
Noither a moänt to Robins—a niver rembles the stoäns.

XVI.

But summun 'ull come ater meä mayhap wi' 'is kittle o' steäm
Huzzin' an' maäzin' the blessed feälds wi' the Divil's oän teäm.
Gin I mun doy I mun doy, an' loife they says is sweet,
But gin I mun doy I mun doy, for I couldn abear to see it.

XVII.

What atta stannin' theer for, an' doesn bring ma the yaäle?
Doctor 's a 'tottler, lass, and a 's hallus i' the owd taäle;
I weänt breäk rules for Doctor, a knaws naw moor nor a floy:
Git ma my yaäle I tell tha, an' gin I mun doy I mun doy.

TITHONUS.

The woods decay, the woods decay and fall,
The vapors weep their burthen to the ground,
Man comes and tills the field and lies beneath,
And after many a summer dies the swan.
Me only cruel immortality
Consumes: I wither slowly in thine arms,
Here at the quiet limit of the world.
A white-hair'd shadow roaming like a dream
The ever silent spaces of the East,
Far-folded mists, and gleaming halls of morn.
  Alas! for this gray shadow, once a man—
So glorious in his beauty and thy choice,
Who madest him thy chosen, that he seem'd
To his great heart none other than a God!
I ask'd thee "Give me immortality."
Then did'st thou grant mine asking with a smile,
Like wealthy men who care not how they give.

But thy strong Hours indignant work'd their wills,
And beat me down and marred and wasted me.
And tho' they could not end me, left me maim'd
To dwell in presence of immortal youth,
Immortal age beside immortal youth,
And all I was, in ashes. Can thy love,
Thy beauty, make amends, tho' even now,
Close over us, the silver star, thy guide,
Shines in those tremulous eyes that fill with tears
To hear me? Let me go: take back thy gift:
Why should a man desire in any way
To vary from the kindly race of men,
Or pass beyond the goal of ordinance
Where all should pause, as is most meet for all?

  A soft air fans the cloud apart: there comes
A glimpse of that dark world where I was born.
Once more the old mysterious glimmer steals
From thy pure brows, and from thy shoulders pure.

* Anemones.

And bosom beating with a heart renew'd.
Thy cheek begins to redden thro' the gloom,
Thy sweet eyes brighten slowly close to mine,
Ere yet they blind the stars, and the wild team
Which love thee, yearning for thy yoke, arise,
And shake the darkness from their loosen'd manes,
And beat the twilight into flakes of fire.

Lo! ever thus thou growest beautiful
In silence, then before thine answer given
Departest, and thy tears are on my cheek.

Why wilt thou ever scare me with thy tears,
And make me tremble lest a saying learnt
In days far-off, on that dark earth, be true?
"The Gods themselves cannot recall their gifts."

Ay me! ay me! with what another heart
In days far-off, and with what other eyes
I used to watch—if I be he that watch'd—
The lucid outline forming round thee; saw
The dim curls kindle into sunny rings;
Changed with thy mystic change, and felt my blood
Glow with the glow that slowly crimson'd all
Thy presence and thy portals, while I lay,
Mouth, forehead, eyelids, growing dewy-warm
With kisses balmier than half-opening buds
Of April, and could hear the lips that kiss'd
Whispering I knew not what of wild and sweet,
Like that strange song I heard Apollo sing,
While Ilion like a mist rose into towers.

Yet hold me not forever in thine East:
How can my nature longer mix with thine?
Coldly thy rosy shadows bathe me, cold
Are all thy lights, and cold my wrinkled feet
Upon thy glimmering thresholds, when the steam
Floats up from those dim fields about the homes
Of happy men that have the power to die,
And grassy barrows of the happier dead.
Release me, and restore me to the ground:
Thou seest all things, thou wilt see my grave:
Thou wilt renew thy beauty morn by morn;
I earth in earth forget these empty courts,
And thee returning on thy silver wheels.

———◇———

THE VOYAGE.

I.

We left behind the painted buoy
  That tosses at the harbor-mouth:
And madly danced our hearts with joy,
  As fast we fleeted to the South:
How fresh was every sight and sound
  On open main or winding shore!
We knew the merry world was round,
  And we might sail forevermore.

II.

Warm broke the breeze against the brow,
  Dry sang the tackle, sang the sail:
The Lady's-head upon the prow
  Caught the shrill salt, and sheer'd the gale.
The broad seas swell'd to meet the keel,
  And swept behind: so quick the run,
We felt the good ship shake and reel,
  We seem'd to sail into the Sun!

III.

How oft we saw the Sun retire,
  And burn the threshold of the night,
Fall from his Ocean-lane of fire,
  And sleep beneath his pillar'd light!
How oft the purple-skirted robe
  Of twilight slowly downward drawn,
As thro' the slumber of the globe
  Again we dash'd into the dawn!

16

IV.

New stars all night above the brim
  Of waters lighten'd into view;
They climb'd as quickly, for the rim
  Changed every moment as we flew.
Far ran the naked moon across
  The houseless ocean's heaving field,
Or flying shone, the silver boss
  Of her own halo's dusky shield;

V.

The peaky islet shifted shapes,
  High towns on hills were dimly seen,
We past long lines of Northern capes
  And dewy Northern meadows green.
We came to warmer waters, and deep
  Across the boundless east we drove,
Where those long swells of breaker sweep
  The nutmeg rocks and isles of clove.

VI.

By peaks that flamed, or, all in shade,
  Gloom'd the low coast and quivering brine
With ashy rains, that spreading made
  Fantastic plume or sable pine:
By sands and steaming flats, and floods
  Of mighty mouth, we scudded fast,
And hills and scarlet-mingled woods
  Glow'd for a moment as we past.

VII.

O hundred shores of happy climes,
  How swiftly stream'd ye by the bark!
At times the whole sea burn'd, at times
  With wakes of fire we tore the dark;
At times a carven craft would shoot
  From havens hid in fairy bowers,
With naked limbs and flowers and fruit,
  But we nor paused for fruits nor flowers.

VIII.

For one fair Vision ever fled
  Down the waste waters day and night,
And still we follow'd where she led,
  In hope to gain upon her flight.
Her face was evermore unseen,
  And fixt upon the far sea-line;
But each man murmur'd, "O my Queen,
  I follow till I make thee mine."

IX.

And now we lost her, now she gleam'd
  Like Fancy made of golden air,
Now nearer to the prow she seem'd
  Like Virtue firm, like Knowledge fair,
Now high on waves that idly burst
  Like Heavenly Hope she crown'd the sea,
And now, the bloodless point reversed,
  She bore the blade of Liberty.

X.

And only one among us—him
  We pleased not—he was seldom pleased:
He saw not far: his eyes were dim:
  But ours he swore were all diseased.
"A ship of fools," he shriek'd in spite,
  "A ship of fools," he sneer'd and wept.
And overboard one stormy night
  He cast his body, and on we swept.

XI.

And never sail of ours was furl'd,
  Nor anchor dropt at eve or morn;
We loved the glories of the world,
  But laws of nature were our scorn;
For blasts would rise and rave and cease,
  But whence were those that drove the sail
Across the whirlwind's heart of peace,
  And to and thro' the counter-gale?

XII.

Again to colder climes we came,
 For still we follow'd where she led:
Now mate is blind and captain lame,
 And half the crew are sick or dead.
But blind or lame or sick or sound,
 We follow that which flies before:
We know the merry world is round,
 And we may sail forevermore.

IN THE VALLEY OF CAUTERETZ.

ALL along the valley, stream that flashest white,
Deepening thy voice with the deepening of the night,
All along the valley, where thy waters flow,
I walk'd with one I loved two and thirty years ago.
All along the valley, while I walk'd to-day,
The two and thirty years were a mist that rolls away;
For all along the valley, down thy rocky bed,
Thy living voice to me was as the voice of the dead,
And all along the valley, by rock and cave and tree,
The voice of the dead was a living voice to me.

THE FLOWER.

ONCE in a golden hour
 I cast to earth a seed.
Up there came a flower,
 The people said, a weed.

To and fro they went
 Thro' my garden-bower,
And muttering discontent
 Cursed me and my flower.

Then it grew so tall
 It wore a crown of light,
But thieves from o'er the wall
 Stole the seed by night.

Sow'd it far and wide
 By every town and tower,
Till all the people cried,
 "Splendid is the flower."

Read my little fable:
 He that runs may read.
Most can raise the flowers now,
 For all have got the seed.

And some are pretty enough,
 And some are poor indeed;
And now again the people
 Call it but a weed.

THE ISLET.

"WHITHER, O whither, love, shall we go,
For a score of sweet little summers or so?"
The sweet little wife of the singer said
On the day that follow'd the day she was wed:
'Whither, O whither, love, shall we go?'
And the singer shaking his curly head
Turn'd as he sat, and struck the keys
There at his right with a sudden crash,
Singing, "And shall it be over the seas
With a crew that is neither rude nor rash,
But a bevy of Eroses apple-cheek'd,
In a shallop of crystal ivory-beak'd,
With a satin sail of a ruby glow,
To a sweet little Eden on earth that I know,
A mountain islet pointed and peak'd;
Waves on a diamond shingle dash,

Cataract brooks to the ocean run,
Fairily-delicate palaces shine
Mixt with myrtle and clad with vine,
And overstream'd and silvery-streak'd
With many a rivulet high against the Sun
The facets of the glorious mountain flash
Above the valleys of palm and pine."

"Thither, O thither, love, let us go."

"No, no, no!
For in all that exquisite isle, my dear,
There is but one bird with a musical throat,
And his compass is but of a single note,
That it makes one weary to hear."
"Mock me not! mock me not! love, let us go."

"No, love. no.
For the bud ever breaks into bloom on the tree,
And a storm never wakes on the lonely sea,
And a worm is there in the lonely wood,
That pierces the liver and blackens the blood,
And makes it a sorrow to be."

REQUIESCAT.

FAIR is her cottage in its place,
 Where yon broad water sweetly slowly glides.
It sees itself from thatch to base
 Dream in the sliding tides.

And fairer she, but ah, how soon to die!
 Her quiet dream of life this hour may cease.
Her peaceful being slowly passes by
 To some more perfect peace.

THE SAILOR-BOY.

HE rose at dawn and, fired with hope,
 Shot o'er the seething harbor-bar,
And reach'd the ship and caught the rope,
 And whistled to the morning star.

And while he whistled long and loud
 He heard a fierce mermaiden cry,
"O Boy, tho' thou art young and proud,
 I see the place where thou wilt lie.

"The sands and yensty surges mix
 In caves about the dreary bay,
And on thy ribs the limpet sticks,
 And in thy heart the scrawl shall play."

"Fool," he answer'd, "death is sure
 To those that stay and those that roam,
But I will nevermore endure
 To sit with empty hands at home.

"My mother clings about my neck,
 My sisters crying, 'Stay, for shame;'
My father raves of death and wreck,
 They are all to blame, they are all to blame.

"God help me! save I take my part
 Of danger on the roaring sea,
A devil rises in my heart,
 Far worse than any death to me."

THE RINGLET.

"YOUR ringlets, your ringlets,
 That look so golden-gay,
If you will give me one, but one
 To kiss it night and day,

Then never chilling touch of Time
  Will turn it silver-gray,
And then shall I know it is all true gold
To flame and sparkle and stream as of old,
Till all the comets in heaven are cold,
  And all her stars decay."
" Then take it, love, and put it by;
This cannot change, nor yet can I."

2.

"My ringlet, my ringlet,
  That art so golden-gay,
Now never chilling touch of Time
  Can turn thee silver-gray;
And a lad may wink, and a girl may hint,
  And a fool may say his say;
For my doubts and fears were all amiss,
And I swear henceforth by this and this,
That a doubt will only come for a kiss,
  And a fear to be kiss'd away."
"Then kiss it, love, and put it by:
If this can change, why so can I."

II.

O Ringlet, O Ringlet,
  I kiss'd you night and day,
And Ringlet, O Ringlet,
  You still are golden-gay,
But Ringlet, O Ringlet,
  You should be silver-gray:
For what is this which now I'm told,
I that took you for true gold,
She that gave you 's bought and sold,
      Sold, sold.

2.

O Ringlet, O Ringlet,
  She blush'd a rosy red,
When Ringlet, O Ringlet,
  She clipt you from her head,
And Ringlet, O Ringlet,
  She gave you me, and said,
" Come, kiss it, love, and put it by :
If this can change, why so can I."
O fie, you golden nothing, fie
      Yon golden lie.

3.

O Ringlet, O Ringlet,
  I count you much to blame,
For Ringlet, O Ringlet,
  You put me much to shame,
So Ringlet, O Ringlet,
  I doom you to the flame.
For what is this which now I learn,
Has given all my faith a turn?
Burn, you glossy heretic, burn,
      Burn, burn.

———∞———

A WELCOME TO ALEXANDRA.

MARCH 7, 1863.

SEA-KINGS' daughter from over the sea,
                      Alexandra!
Saxon and Norman and Dane are we,
But all of us Danes in our welcome of thee,
                      Alexandra!
Welcome her, thunders of fort and of fleet!
Welcome her, thundering cheer of the street!
Welcome her, all things youthful and sweet,
Scatter the blossom under her feet!
Break, happy land, into earlier flowers!
Make music, O bird, in the new-budded bowers!
Blazon your mottoes of blessing and prayer!
Welcome her, welcome her, all that is ours!

Warble, O bugle, and trumpet, blare!
Flags, flutter out upon turrets and towers!
Flames, on the windy headland flare!
Utter your jubilee, steeple and spire!
Clash, ye bells, in the merry March air!
Flash, ye cities, in rivers of fire!
Rush to the roof, sudden rocket, and higher
Melt into the stars for the land's desire!
Roll and rejoice, jubilant voice,
Roll as a ground-swell dash'd on the strand,
Roar as the sea when he welcomes the land,
And welcome her, welcome the land's desire,
The sea-kings' daughter as happy as fair,
Blissful bride of a blissful heir,
Bride of the heir of the kings of the sea—
O joy to the people, and joy to the throne,
Come to us, love us, and make us your own.
For Saxon or Dane or Norman we,
Teuton or Celt, or whatever we be,
We are each all Dane in our welcome of thee,
                      Alexandra!

———∞———

ODE SUNG AT THE OPENING OF THE INTERNATIONAL EXHIBITION.

UPLIFT a thousand voices full and sweet,
  In this wide hall with earth's invention stored,
  And praise th' invisible universal Lord,
Who lets once more in peace the nations meet,
  Where Science, Art, and Labor have outpour'd
  Their myriad horns of plenty at our feet.

O silent father of our Kings to be
Mourn'd in this golden hour of jubilee,
For this, for all, we weep our thanks to thee!

        The world-compelling plan was thine,
        And lo! the long laborious miles,
        Of Palace: lo! the giant aisles,
        Rich in model and design;
        Harvest-tool and husbandry,
        Loom and wheel and engin'ry,
        Secrets of the sullen mine,
        Steel and gold, and corn and wine,
        Fabric rough, or Fairy fine,
        Sunny tokens of the Line,
        Polar marvels, and a feast
        Of wonder out of West and East,
        And shapes and hues of Art divine!
        All of beauty, all of use,
        That one fair planet can produce,
          Brought from under every star,
          Blown from over every main,
          And mixt, as life is mixt with pain,
          The works of peace with works of war.

O ye, the wise who think, the wise who reign,
From growing commerce loose her latest chain,
And let the fair white-winged peacemaker fly
To happy havens under all the sky,
And mix the seasons and the golden hours,
Till each man finds his own in all men's good,
And all men work in noble brotherhood,
Breaking their mailed fleets and armed towers,
And ruling by obeying Nature's powers,
And gathering all the fruits of peace and crown'd
  with all her flowers.

———∞———

A DEDICATION.

DEAR, near and true—no truer Time himself
Can prove you, tho' he make you evermore
Dearer and nearer, as the rapid life
Shoots to the fall—take this, and pray that he,

Who wrote it, honoring your sweet faith in him,
May trust himself: and spite of praise and scorn,
As one who feels the immeasurable world,
Attain the wise indifference of the wise;
And after Autumn past—if left to pass
His autumn into seeming-leafless days—
Draw toward the long frost and longest night,
Wearing his wisdom lightly, like the fruit
Which in our winter woodland looks a flower.*

THE CAPTAIN.

A LEGEND OF THE NAVY.

He that only rules by terror
　Doeth grievous wrong.
Deep as Hell I count his error,
　Let him hear my song.
Brave the Captain was: the seaman
　Made a gallant crew,
Gallant sons of English freemen,
　Sailors bold and true.
But they hated his oppression,
　Stern he was and rash;
So for every light transgression
　Doom'd them to the lash.
Day by day more harsh and cruel
　Seem'd the Captain's mood.
Secret wrath like smother'd fuel
　Burnt in each man's blood.
Yet he hoped to purchase glory,
　Hoped to make the name
Of his vessel great in story,
　Wheresoe'er he came.
So they past by capes and islands,
　Many a harbor-mouth,
Sailing under palmy highlands
　Far within the South.
On a day when they were going
　O'er the lone expanse,
In the North, her canvas flowing,
　Rose a ship of France.
Then the Captain's color heighten'd
　Joyful came his speech:
But a cloudy gladness lighten'd
　In the eyes of each.
"Chase," he said: the ship flew forward,
　And the wind did blow:
Stately, lightly, went she Norward,
　Till she near'd the foe.
Then they look'd at him they hated,
　Had what they desired:
Mute with folded arms they waited—
　Not a gun was fired.
But they heard the foeman's thunder
　Roaring out their doom;
All the air was torn in sunder,
　Crashing went the boom.
Spars were splinter'd, decks were shatter'd,
　Bullets felt like rain;
Over mast and deck were scatter'd
　Blood and brains of men.
Spars were splinter'd: decks were broken:
　Every mother's son—
Down they dropt—no word was spoken—
　Each beside his gun.
On the decks as they were lying,
　Were their faces grim.
In their blood, as they lay dying,
　Did they smile on him.
Those, in whom he had reliance
　For his noble name,
With one smile of still defiance
　Sold him unto shame.
Shame and wrath his heart confounded,
　Pale he turn'd and red,

* The fruit of the Spindle-tree (*Euonymus Europæus*).

Till himself was deadly wounded
　Falling on the dead.
Dismal error! fearful slaughter!
　Years have wander'd by,
Side by side beneath the water
　Crew and Captain lie;
There the sunlit ocean tosses
　O'er them mouldering,
And the lonely seabird crosses
　With one waft of the wing.

THREE SONNETS TO A COQUETTE.

Caress'd or chidden by the dainty hand,
　And singing airy trifles this or that,
Light Hope at Beauty's call would perch and stand,
　And run thro' every change of sharp and flat:
And Fancy came and at her pillow sat,
　When Sleep had bound her in his rosy band,
And chased away the still-recurring gnat,
　And woke her with a lay from fairy land.
But now they live with Beauty less and less,
　For Hope is other Hope and wanders far,
　Nor cares to lisp in love's delicious creeds:
And Fancy watches in the wilderness,
　Poor Fancy sadder than a single star,
　That sets at twilight in a land of reeds.

2.

The form, the form alone is eloquent!
　A nobler yearning never broke her rest
　Than but to dance and sing, be gayly drest,
And win all eyes with all accomplishment:
Yet in the waltzing-circle as we went,
　My fancy made me for a moment blest
　To find my heart so near the beauteous breast
That once had power to rob it of content.
A moment came the tenderness of tears,
　The phantom of a wish that once could move,
　A ghost of passion that no smiles restore—
For ah! the slight coquette, she cannot love,
And if you kiss'd her feet a thousand years,
　She still would take the praise, and care no
　　more.

3.

Wan Sculptor, weepest thou to take the cast
　Of those dead lineaments that near thee lie?
O sorrowest thou, pale Painter, for the past,
　In painting some dead friend from memory?
Weep on: beyond his object Love can last:
　His object lives: more cause to weep have I:
My tears, no tears of love, are flowing fast,
　No tears of love, but tears that Love can die.
I pledge her not in any cheerful cup,
　Nor care to sit beside her where she sits—
　Ah pity—hint it not in human tones,
But breathe it into earth and close it up
　With secret death forever, in the pits
　Which some green Christmas crams with weary
　　bones.

ON A MOURNER.

Nature, so far as in her lies,
　Imitates God, and turns her face
To every land beneath the skies,
　Counts nothing that she meets with base,
　But lives and loves in every place;

2.

Fills out the homely quick-set screens,
　And makes the purple lilac ripe,
Steps from her airy hill, and greens
　The swamp, where hums the dropping snipe,
　With moss and braided marish-pipe;

3.

And on thy heart a finger lays,
　Saying, "Beat quicker, for the time
Is pleasant, and the woods and ways
　Are pleasant, and the beech and lime
　Put forth and feel a gladder clime."

4.

And murmurs of a deeper voice,
　Going before to some far shrine,
Teach that sick heart the stronger choice,
　Till all thy life one way incline
　With one wide will that closes thine.

5.

And when the zoning eve has died
　Where yon dark valleys wind forlorn,
Come Hope and Memory, spouse and bride,
　From out the borders of the morn,
　With that fair child betwixt them born.

6.

And when no mortal motion jars
　The blackness round the tombing sod,
Thro' silence and the trembling stars
　Comes Faith from tracts no feet have trod,
　And Virtue, like a household god,

7.

Promising empire; such as those
　That once at dead of night did greet
Troy's wandering prince, so that he rose
　With sacrifice, while all the fleet
　Had rest by stony hills of Crete.

SONG.

Lady, let the rolling drums
Beat to battle where thy warrior stands:
　Now thy face across his fancy comes,
And gives the battle to his hands.

Lady, let the trumpets blow,
Clasp thy little babes about thy knee:
　Now their warrior father meets the foe,
And strikes him dead for thine and thee.

SONG.

Home they brought him slain with spears.
　They brought him home at even-fall:
All alone she sits and hears
　Echoes in his empty hall,
　　Sounding on the morrow.

The Sun peep'd in from open field,
　The boy began to leap and prance,
Rode upon his father's lance,
Beat upon his father's shield—
　"O hush, my joy, my sorrow."

EXPERIMENTS.

BOÄDICÉA.

While about the shore of Mona those Neronian legionaries
Burnt and broke the grove and altar of the Druid and Druidess,
Far in the east Boädicéa, standing loftily charioted,
Mad and maddening all that heard her in her fierce volubility,
Girt by half the tribes of Britain, near the colony Cámulodúne.
Yell'd and shriek'd between her daughters o'er a wild confederacy.

　　"They that scorn the tribes and call us Britain's barbarous populaces,
Did they hear me, would they listen, did they pity me supplicating?
Shall I heed them in their anguish? shall I brook to be supplicated?
Hear Icenian, Catieuchlanian, hear Coritanian, Trinobant!
Must their ever-ravening eagle's beak and talon annihilate us?
Tear the noble heart of Britain, leave it gorily quivering?
Bark an answer, Britain's raven! bark and blacken innumerable,
Blacken round the Roman carrion, make the carcass a skeleton,
Kite and kestrel, wolf and wolfkin, from the wilderness, wallow in it,
Till the face of Bel be brighten'd, Taranis be propitiated.
Lo their colony half-defended! lo their colony, Cámulodúne!
There the horde of Roman robbers mock at a barbarous adversary.
There the hive of Roman liars worship a gluttonous emperor-idiot.
Such is Rome, and this her deity: hear it, Spirit of Cássivélaún!

　　"Hear it, Gods! the Gods have heard it, O Icenian, O Coritanian!
Doubt not ye the Gods have answer'd, Catieuchlanian, Trinobant.
These have told us all their anger in miraculous utterances,
Thunder, a flying fire in heaven, a murmur heard aërially,
Phantom sound of blows descending, moan of an enemy massacred,
Phantom wail of women and children, multitudinous agonies.
Bloodily flow'd the Tamesa rolling phantom bodies of horses and men;
Then a phantom colony smoulder'd on the refluent estuary;
Lastly yonder yester-even, suddenly giddily tottering—
There was one who watch'd and told me—down their statue of Victory fell.
Lo their precious Roman bantling, lo the colony Cámulodúne,
Shall we teach it a Roman lesson? shall we care to be pitiful?
Shall we deal with it as an infant? shall we dandle it amorously?

　　"Hear Icenian, Catieuchlanian, hear Coritanian, Trinobant!
While I roved about the forest, long and bitterly meditating,

There I heard them in the darkness, at the mystical ceremony,
Loosely robed in flying raiment, sang the terrible prophetesses.
'Fear not, isle of blowing woodland, isle of silvery parapets!
Tho' the Roman eagle shadow thee, tho' the gathering enemy narrow thee,
Thou shalt wax and he shall dwindle, thou shalt be the mighty one yet!
Thine the liberty, thine the glory, thine the deeds to be celebrated.
Thine the myriad-rolling ocean, light and shadow illimitable,
Thine the lands of lasting summer, many-blossoming Paradises,
Thine the North and thine the South and thine the battle-thunder of God.'
So they chanted: how shall Britain light upon auguries happier?
So they chanted in the darkness, and there cometh a victory now.

"Hear Icenian, Catieuchlanian, hear Coritanian, Trinobant!
Me the wife of rich Prasutagus, me the lover of liberty,
Me they seized and me they tortured, me they lash'd and humiliated,
Me the sport of ribald Veterans, mine of ruffian violators!
See they sit, they hide their faces, miserable in ignominy!
Wherefore in me burns an anger, not by blood to be satiated.
Lo the palaces and the temple, lo the colony Cámulodúne!
There they ruled, and thence they wasted all the flourishing territory,
Thither at their will they haled the yellow-ringleted Britoness—
Bloodily, bloodily fall the battle-axe, unexhausted, inexorable.
Shout Icenian, Catieuchlanian, shout Coritanian, Trinobant,
Till the victim hear within and yearn to hurry precipitously
Like the leaf in a roaring whirlwind, like the smoke in a hurricane whirl'd.
Lo the colony, there they rioted in the city of Cúnobeline?
There they drank in cups of emerald, there at tables of ebony lay,
Rolling on their purple couches in their tender effeminacy.
There they dwelt and there they rioted; there—there—they dwell no more.
Burst the gates, and burn the palaces, break the works of the statuary,
Take the hoary Roman head and shatter it, hold it abominable,
Cut the Roman boy to pieces in his lust and voluptuousness,
Lash the maiden into swooning, me they lash'd and humiliated,
Chop the breasts from off the mother, dash the brains of the little one out,
Up my Britons, on my chariot, on my chargers, trample them under us."

So the Queen Boädícéa, standing loftily charioted,
Brandishing in her hand a dart and rolling glances lioness-like,
Yell'd and shrieked between her daughters in her fierce volubility,
Till her people all around the royal chariot agitated,
Madly dash'd the darts together, writhing barbarous lineäments.
Made the noise of frosty woodlands, when they shiver in January.
Roar'd as when the rolling breakers boom and blanch on the precipices,
Yell'd as when the winds of winter tear an oak on a promontory.
So the silent colony hearing her tumultuous adversaries
Clash the darts and on the buckler beat with rapid unanimous hand,
Thought on all her evil tyrannies, all her pitiless avarice,
Till she felt the heart within her fall and flutter tremulously,
Then her pulses at the clamoring of her enemy fainted away.
Out of evil evil flourishes, out of tyranny tyranny buds.
Ran the land with Roman slaughter, multitudinous agonies.
Perish'd many a maid and matron, many a valorous legionary.
Fell the colony, city and citadel, London, Vernlam, Cámulodúne.

———◦✕◦———

IN QUANTITY.

MILTON.

Alcaics.

O mighty-mouth'd inventor of harmonies,
O skill'd to sing of Time or Eternity,
   God-gifted organ-voice of England,
      Milton, a name to resound for ages,
Whose Titan angels, Gabriel, Abdiel,
Starr'd from Jehovah's gorgeous armories,
   Tower, as the deep-domed empyrean
      Rings to the roar of an angel onset—
Me rather all that bowery loneliness,
The brooks of Eden mazily murmuring,
   And bloom profuse and cedar arches
      Charm, as a wanderer out in ocean,
Where some refulgent sunset of India
Streams o'er a rich ambrosial ocean isle,
   And crimson-hued the stately palmwoods
      Whisper in odorous heights of even.

Hendecasyllabics.

O you chorus of indolent reviewers,
Irresponsible, indolent reviewers,
Look, I come to the test, a tiny poem
All composed in a metre of Catullus,
All in quantity, careful of my motion,
Like the skater on ice that hardly bears him,
Lest I fall unawares before the people,
Waking laughter in indolent reviewers.
Should I flounder awhile without a tumble
Thro' this metrification of Catullus,
They should speak to me not without a welcome,
All that chorus of indolent reviewers.
Hard, hard, hard is it, only not to tumble,
So fantastical is the dainty metre.
Wherefore slight me not wholly, nor believe me
Too presumptuous, indolent reviewers.
O blatant Magazines, regard me rather—
Since I blush to belaud myself a moment—
As some rare little rose, a piece of inmost
Horticultural art, or half coquette-like
Maiden, not to be greeted unbenignly.

SPECIMEN OF A TRANSLATION OF THE ILIAD IN BLANK VERSE.

So Hector said, and sea-like roar'd his host;
Then loosed their sweating horses from the yoke
And each beside his chariot bound his own;
And oxen from the city, and goodly sheep
In haste they drove, and honey-hearted wine
And bread from out the houses brought, and heap'd
Their firewood, and the winds from off the plain
Roll'd the rich vapor far into the heaven.
And these all night upon the *bridge of war
Sat glorying; many a fire before them blazed;
As when in heaven the stars about the moon

> * Or, ridge.

Look beautiful, when all the winds are laid,
And every height comes out, and jutting peak
And valley, and the immeasurable heavens
Break open to their highest, and all the stars
Shine, and the Shepherd gladdens in his heart:
So many a fire between the ships and stream
Of Xanthus blazed before the towers of Troy,
A thousand on the plain; and close by each
Sat fifty in the blaze of burning fire;
And champing golden grain, the horses stood
Hard by their chariots, waiting for the dawn.[2]

Iliad, viii. 542–565.

> * Or more literally,—
>
> And eating hoary grain and pulse, the steeds
> Stood by their cars, waiting the throned morn.

ON TRANSLATIONS OF HOMER.

Hexameters and Pentameters.

THESE lame hexameters the strong-wing'd music of Homer:
No—but a most burlesque barbarous experiment.
When was a harsher sound ever heard, ye Muses, in England?
When did a frog coarser croak upon our Helicon?
Hexameters no worse than daring Germany gave us,
Barbarous experiment, barbarous hexameters.

MISCELLANEOUS.

THE NORTHERN FARMER.

NEW STYLE.

I.

Doesn't thou 'ear my 'erse's legs, as they canters awaäy?
Proputty, proputty, proputty—that 's what I 'ears 'em saäy.
Proputty, proputty, proputty—Sam, thou 's an ass for thy paaïns.
Theer 's moor sense i' one o' 'is legs nor in all thy braäïns.

II.

Woä—theer 's a craw to pluck wi' tha, Sam: yon 's parson's 'ouse—
Dosn't thou knaw that a man muu be eäither a man or a mouse?
Time to think on it then; for thou 'll be twenty to weeak.*
Proputty, proputty—woä then woä—let ma 'ear mysén speäk.

III.

Me an' thy muther, Sammy, 'as beän a-talkin' o' thee;
Thou 's been taäkin' to muther, an' she beän a tellin' it me.
Thou 'll not marry for munny—thou 's sweet upo' parson's lass—
Noä—thou 'll marry for luvv—an' we boäth on us thinks tha an ass.

IV.

Seeä'd her todaäy goä by—Saäïnt's-daäy—thay was ringing the bells.
She 's a beauty thou thinks—an' soä is scoors o' galls.
Them as 'as munny an' all—wot 's a beauty?—the flower as blaws.
But proputty, proputty sticks, an' proputty, proputty graws.

V.

Do'ant be stunt;† taäke time: I knaws what maäkes tha sa mad.
Warn't I craäzed fur the lasses mysén when I wur a lad?
But I knaw'd a Quaäker feller as often 'as towd ma this:
"Doänt thou marry for munny, but goä wheer munny is!"

VI.

An' I went wheer munny war: an' thy mother coom to 'and,
Wi' lots o' munny laäïd by, an' a nicetish bit o' land.
Maäybe she warn't a beauty:—I niver giv it a thowt—
But warn't she as good to cuddle an' kiss as a lass as 'ant nowt?

VII.

Parson's lass 'ant nowt, an' she weänt 'a nowt when 'e 's deäd,
Mun be a gavness, lad, or summut, and addle‡ her bread:
Why? fur 'e 's nobbut a curate, an' weänt nivir git naw 'igher;
An' 'e maäde the bed as 'e ligs on afoor 'e coom'd to the shire.

VIII.

And thin 'e coom'd to the parish wi' lots o' 'Varsity debt,
Stook to his taäïl they did, an' 'e 'ant got shut on 'em yet.
An' 'e ligs on 'is back i' the grip, wi' noän to lend 'im a shove,
Woorse nor a far-welter'd§ yowe: fur, Sammy, 'e married fur luvv.

IX.

Luvv? what 's luvv? thou can luvv thy lass an' 'er munny too,
Maäkin' 'em goä togither as they 've good right to do.
Could'n I luvv thy muther by cause o' 'er munny laäïd by?
Naäy—fur I luvv'd 'er a vast sight moor fur it: reäson why.

---

* This week.   † Obstinate.   ‡ Earn.   § Or fow weltered—said of a sheep lying on its back in the furrow.

X.

Ay, an' thy muther says thou wants to marry the lass,
Cooms of a gentleman burn : an' we boäth on us thinks tha an ass.
Woä then, proputty, wiltha?—an ass as near as mays nowt—*
Woä then, wiltha? dangtha!—the bees is as fell as owt.†

XI.

Breäk me a bit o' the esh for his 'eäd, lad, out o' the fence!
Gentleman burn! what 's gentleman burn? is it shillins an' pence?
Proputty, proputty 's ivrything 'ere, an', Sammy, I 'm blest
If it is n't the saäme oop yonder, fur them as 'as it 's the best.

XII.

Tis'n them as 'as munny as breäks into 'ouses an' steäls,
Them as 'as coäts to their backs an' taäkes their regular meäls.
Noä, but it 's them as niver knaws wheer a meäl 's to be 'ad.
Taäke my word for it, Sammy, the poor in a loomp is bad.

XIII.

Them or thir feythers, tha sees, mun 'a beän a lazzy lot,
Fur work mun 'a gone to the gittin' whiniver munny was got.
Feyther 'ad ammost nowt ; leästwaays 'is munny was 'id.
But 'e tued an' moil'd 'issén dead, an' 'e died a good un, 'e did.

XIV.

Look thou theer wheer Wrigglesby beck comes out by the 'ill!
Feyther run up to the farm, an' I runs up to the mill;
An' I 'll run up to the brig, an' that thou 'll live to see ;
And if thou marries a good un, I 'll leäve the land to thee.

XV.

Thim 's my noätions, Sammy, wheerby I means to stick ;
But if thou marries a bad un, I 'll leäve the land to Dick.—
Coom oop, proputty, proputty—that 's what I 'ears 'im saäy—
Proputty, proputty, proputty—canter an' canter awaäy.

THE VICTIM.

1.

A PLAGUE upon the people fell,
    A famine after laid them low,
Then thorpe and byre arose in fire,
    For on them brake the sudden foe ;
So thick they died the people cried
    "The Gods are moved against the land."
The Priest in horror about his altar
    To Thor and Odin lifted a hand :
        "Help us from famine
        And plague and strife!
        What would you have of us?
        Human life?
        Were it our nearest,
        Were it our dearest,
        (Answer, O answer)
        We give you his life."

2.

But still the foeman spoil'd and burn'd,
    And cattle died, and deer in wood,
And bird in air, and fishes turn'd
    And whiten'd all the rolling flood ;
And dead men lay all over the way,
    Or down in a furrow scathed with flame :
And ever and aye the Priesthood moan'd
    Till at last it seem'd that an answer came :
        "The King is happy
        In child and wife ;
        Take you his dearest,
        Give us a life."

3.

The Priest went out by heath and hill;
    The King was hunting in the wild ;
They found the mother sitting still ;
    She cast her arms about the child.
The child was only eight summers old,
    His beauty still with his years increased,
His face was ruddy, his hair was gold,
    He seem'd a victim due to the priest.
        The priest beheld him,
        And cried with joy,
        "The Gods have answer'd :
        We give them the boy."

4.

The King return'd from out the wild,
    He bore but little game in hand ;
The mother said : "They have taken the child
    To spill his blood and heal the land :
The land is sick, the people diseased,
    And blight and famine on all the len :
The holy Gods, they must be appeased,
    So I pray you tell the truth to me.
        They have taken our son,
        They will have his life.
        Is he your dearest?
        Or I, the wife?"

5.

The King bent low, with hand on brow,
    He stay'd his arms upon his knee :
"O wife, what use to answer now?
    For now the Priest has judged for me."

The King was shaken with holy fear;
"The Gods," he said, "would have chosen well;
Yet both are near, and both are dear,
And which the dearest I cannot tell!"
   But the Priest was happy,
     His victim won:
  "We have his dearest,
    His only son!"

6.

The rites prepared, the victim bared,
  The knife uprising toward the blow,
To the altar-stone she sprang alone,
  "Me, not my darling, no!"
He caught her away with a sudden cry;
  Suddenly from him brake his wife,
And shrieking "*I* am his dearest, I—
  I am his dearest!" rush'd on the knife.
   And the Priest was happy,
    "O, Father Odin,
    We give you a life.
   Which was his nearest?
   Who was his dearest?
   The Gods have answer'd;
   We give them the wife!"

WAGES.

Glory of warrior, glory of orator, glory of song,
Paid with a voice flying by to be lost on an end-
   less sea—
Glory of Virtue, to fight, to struggle, to right the
   wrong—
  Nay, but she aim'd not at glory, no lover of glory
   she:
Give her the glory of going on, and still to be.

The wages of sin is death: if the wages of Virtue
   be dust,
  Would she have heart to endure for the life of the
   worm and the fly?
She desires no isles of the blest, no quiet seats of
   the just,
  To rest in a golden grove, or to bask in a summer sky:
Give her the wages of going on, and not to die.

THE HIGHER PANTHEISM.

The sun, the moon, the stars, the seas, the hills and
   the plains—
Are not these, O Soul, the Vision of Him who reigns?

Is not the Vision He? tho' He be not that which He
   seems?
Dreams are true while they last, and do we not live
   in dreams?

Earth, these solid stars, this weight of body and
   limb,
Are they not sign and symbol of thy division from
   Him?

Dark is the world to thee: thyself art the reason
   why;
For is He not all but thou, that hast power to feel
   "I am I?"

Glory about thee, without thee: and thou fulfillest
   thy doom,
Making Him broken gleams, and a stifled splendor
   and gloom.

Speak to Him thou for He hears, and Spirit with
   Spirit can meet—
Closer is He than breathing, and nearer than hands
   and feet.

God is law, say the wise, O Soul, and let us rejoice.
For if He thunder by law the thunder is yet His
   voice.

Law is God, say some: no God at all, says the fool;
For all we have power to see is a straight staff bent
   in a pool;

And the ear of man cannot hear, and the eye of man
   cannot see;
But if we could see and hear, this Vision—were it
   not He?

Flower in the crannied wall,
I pluck you out of the crannies,—
Hold you here, root and all, in my hand,
Little flower—but if I could understand
What you are, root and all, and all in all,
I should know what God and man is.

LUCRETIUS.

Lucilia, wedded to Lucretius, found
Her master cold; for when the morning flush
Of passion and the first embrace had died
Between them, tho' he loved her none the less,
Yet often when the woman heard his foot
Return from pacings in the field, and ran
To greet him with a kiss, the master took
Small notice, or austerely, for—his mind
Half buried in some weightier argument,
Or fancy-borne perhaps upon the rise
And long roll of the Hexameter—he past
To turn and ponder those three hundred scrolls
Left by the Teacher whom he held divine.
She brook'd it not; but wrathful, petulant,
Dreaming some rival, sought and found a witch
Who brew'd the philter which had power, they said
To lead an errant passion home again.
And this, at times, she mingled with his drink,
And this destroy'd him; for the wicked broth
Confused the chemic labor of the blood,
And tickling the brute brain within the man's,
Made havoc among those tender cells, and check'd
His power to shape: he loath'd himself, and once
After a tempest woke upon a morn
That mock'd him with returning calm, and cried.'

"Storm in the night! for thrice I heard the rain
Rushing; and once the flash of a thunderbolt—
Methought I never saw so fierce a fork—
Struck out the streaming mountain-side, and show'd
A riotous confluence of watercourses
Blanching and billowing in a hollow of it,
Where all but yester-eve was dusty-dry.

"Storm, and what dreams, ye holy Gods, what
   dreams!
For thrice I waken'd after dreams. Perchance
We do but recollect the dreams that come
Just ere the waking: terrible! for it seem'd
A void was made in Nature; all her bonds
Crack'd; and I saw the flaring atom-streams
And torrents of her myriad universe,
Raining along the illimitable inane,
Fly on to clash together again, and make
Another and another frame of things

Forever: that was mine, my dream, I knew it
Of and belonging to me, as the dog
With inward yelp and restless forefoot plies
His function of the woodland: but the next!
I thought that all the blood by Sylla shed
Came driving rainlike down again on earth,
And where it dashed the reddening meadow, sprang
No dragon warriors from Cadmean teeth,
For these I thought my dream would show to me,
But girls, Hetairai, curious in their art,
Hired animalisms, vile as those that made
The mulberry-faced Dictator's orgies worse
Than aught they fable of the quiet Gods.
And hands they mixt, and yell'd and round me drove
In narrowing circles till I yell'd again
Half suffocated, and sprang up, and saw—
Was it the first beam of my latest day?

"Then, then, from utter gloom stood out the
        breasts,
The breasts of Helen, and hoveringly a sword
Now over and now under, now direct,
Pointed itself to pierce, but sank down shamed
At all that beauty; and as I stared, a fire,
The fire that left a roofless Ilion,
Shot out of them, and scorch'd me that I woke.

"Is this thy vengeance, holy Venus, thine,
Because I would not one of thine own doves,
Not ev'n a rose, were offer'd to thee? thine,
Forgetful how my rich procemion makes
Thy glory fly along the Italian field,
In lays that will outlast thy Deity?

"Deity? nay, thy worshippers. My tongue
Trips, or I speak profanely. Which of these
Angers thee most, or angers thee at all?
Not if thou be'st of those who far aloof
From envy, hate and pity, and spite and scorn,
Live the great life which all our greatest fain
Would follow, centred in eternal calm.

"Nay, if thou canst, O Goddess, like ourselves
Touch, and be touched, then would I cry to thee
To kiss thy Mavors, roll thy tender arms
Round him, and keep him from the lust of blood
That makes a steaming slaughter-house of Rome.

"Ay, but I meant not thee; I meant not her,
Whom all the pines of Ida shook to see
Slide from that quiet heaven of hers, and tempt
The Trojan, while his neat-herds were abroad;
Nor her that o'er her wounded hunter wept
Her Deity false in human-amorous tears;
Nor whom her beardless apple-arbiter
Decided fairest. Rather, O ye Gods,
Poet-like, as the great Sicilian called
Calliope to grace his golden verse—
Ay, and this Kypris also—did I take
That popular name of thine to shadow forth
The all-generating powers and genial heat
Of Nature, when she strikes through the thick blood
Of cattle, and light is large and lambs are glad
Nosing the mother's udder, and the bird
Makes his heart voice amid the blaze of flowers
Which things appear the work of mighty Gods.

"The Gods! and if I go my work is left
Unfinish'd—if I go. The Gods, who haunt
The lucid interspace of world and world,
Where never creeps a cloud, or moves a wind,
Nor ever falls the least white star of snow,
Nor ever lowest roll of thunder moans,
Nor sound of human sorrow mounts to mar
Their sacred everlasting calm! and such,
Not all so fine, nor so divine a calm,
Not such, nor all unlike it, man may gain
Letting his own life go. The Gods, the Gods!

If all be atoms, how then should the Gods
Being atomic not be dissoluble,
Not follow the great law? My master held
That Gods there are, for all men so believe.
I press'd my footsteps into his, and meant
Surely to lead my Memmius in a train
Of flowery clauses onward to the proof
That Gods there are, and deathless. Meant? I
        meant?
I have forgotten what I meant: my mind
Stumbles, and all my faculties are lamed.

"Look where another of our Gods, the Sun,
Apollo, Delius, or of older use
All-seeing Hyperion—what you will—
Has mounted yonder; since he never sware,
Except his wrath were wreak'd on wretched man,
That he would only shine among the dead
Hereafter; tales! for never yet on earth
Could dead flesh creep, or bits of roasting ox
Moan round the spit—nor knows he what he sees;
King of the East altho' he seem, and girt
With song and flame and fragrance, slowly lifts
His golden feet on those empurpled stairs
That climb into the windy halls of heaven,
And here he glances on an eye new-born,
And gets for greeting but a wail of pain;
And here he stays upon a freezing orb
That fain would gaze upon him to the last;
And here upon a yellow eyelid fall'n
And closed by those who mourn a friend in vain,
Not thankful that his troubles are no more.
And me, altho' his fire is on my face
Blinding, he sees not, nor at all can tell
Whether I mean this day to end myself,
Or lend an ear to Plato where he says,
That men like soldiers may not quit the post
Allotted by the Gods: but he that holds
The Gods are careless, wherefore need he care
Greatly for them, nor rather plunge at once,
Being troubled, wholly out of sight, and sink
Past earthquake—ay, and gout and stone, that break
Body toward death, and palsy, death-in-life,
And wretched age—and worst disease of all,
Those prodigies of myriad nakednesses,
And twisted shapes of lust, unspeakable,
Abominable, strangers at my hearth
Not welcome, harpies miring every dish,
The phantom husks of something foully done,
And fleeting through the boundless universe,
And blasting the long quiet of my breast
With animal heat and dire insanity.

"How should the mind, except it loved them, clasp
These idols to herself? or do they fly
Now thinner, and now thicker, like the flakes
In a fall of snow, and so press in, perforce
Of multitude, as crowds that in an hour
Of civic tumult jam the doors, and bear
The keepers down, and throng, their rags and they,
The basest, far into that council-hall
Where sit the best and stateliest of the land?

"Can I not fling this horror off me again,
Seeing with how great ease Nature can smile,
Balmier and nobler from her bath of storm,
At random ravage? and how easily
The mountain there has cast his cloudy slough,
Now towering o'er him in serenest air,
A mountain o'er a mountain, ay, and within
All hollow as the hopes and fears of men.

"But who was he, that in the garden snared
Pieus and Faunus, rustic Gods? a tale
To laugh at—more to laugh at in myself—
For look! what is it? there? yon arbutus
Totters: a noiseless riot underneath
Strikes through the wood, sets all the tops quiver
        ing—

The mountain quickens into Nymph and Faun;
And here an Oread — how the sun delights
To glance and shift about her slippery sides,
And rosy knees and supple roundedness,
And budded bosom-peaks — who this way runs
Before the rest — A satyr, a satyr, see —
Follows; but him I proved impossible;
Twy-natured is no nature; yet he draws
Nearer and nearer, and I scan him now
Beastlier than any phantom of his kind
That ever butted his rough brother-brute
For lust or lusty blood or provender:
I hate, abhor, spit, sicken at him; and she
Loathes him as well; such a precipitate heel,
Fledged as it were with Mercury's ankle-wing,
Whirls her to me: but will she fling herself,
Shameless upon me? Catch her, goatfoot: nay,
Hide, hide them, mill'on-myrtled wilderness,
And cavern-shadowing laurels, hide! do I wish —
What? — that the bush were leafless? or to whelm
All of them in one massacre? O ye Gods,
I know you careless, yet, behold, to you
From childly wont and ancient use I call —
I thought I lived securely as yourselves —
No lewdness, narrowing envy, monkey-spite,
No madness of ambition, avarice, none:
No larger feast that under plane or pine
With neighbors laid along the grass, to take
Only such cups as left us friendly warm,
Affirming each his own philosophy —
Nothing to mar the sober majesties
Of settled, sweet, Epicurean life.
But now it seems some unseen monster lays
His vast and filthy hands upon my will,
Wrenching it backward into his; and spoils
My bliss in being; and it was not great;
For save when shutting reasons up in rhythm,
Or Heliconian honey in living words,
To make a truth less harsh, I often grew
Tired of so much within our little life,
Or of so little in our little life —
Poor little life that toddles half an hour
Crown'd with a flower or two, and there an end —
And since the nobler pleasure seems to fade,
Why should I, beastlike as I find myself,
Not manlike end myself? — our privilege —
What beast has heart to do it? And what man,
What Roman would be dragged in triumph thus?
Not I; not he, who bears one name with her,
Whose death-blow struck the dateless doom of kings,
When brooking not the Tarquin in her veins,
She made her blood in sight of Collatine
And all his peers, flushing the guiltless air,
Spout from the maiden fountain in her heart.
And from it sprang the Commonwealth, which breaks
As I am breaking now!

"And therefore now
Let her, that is the womb and tomb of all,
Great Nature, take, and forcing far apart
Those blind beginnings that have made me man,
Dash them anew together at her will
Through all her cycles — into man once more
Or beast or bird or fish, or opulent flower —
But till this cosmic order everywhere
Shatter'd into one earthquake in one day
Cracks all to pieces, — and that hour perhaps
Is not so far when momentary man
Shall seem no more a something to himself,
But he, his hopes and hates, his homes and fanes,
And even his bones long laid within the grave,
The very sides of the grave itself shall pass,
Vanishing, atom and void, atom and void,
Into the unseen forever, — till that hour,
My golden work in which I told a truth
That stays the rolling Ixionian wheel.
And numbs the Fury's ringlet-snake, and plucks
The mortal soul from out immortal hell,

Shall stand: ay, surely: then it falls at last,
And perishes as I must; for O Thou,
Passionless bride, divine Tranquillity,
Yearned after by the wisest of the wise,
Who fail to find thee, being as thou art
Without one pleasure and without one pain,
Howbeit I know thou surely must be mine
Or soon or late, yet out of season, thus
I woo thee roughly, for thou carest not
How roughly men may woo thee so they win —
Thus — thus: the soul flies out and dies in the air.

With that he drove the knife into his side:
She heard him raging, heard him fall: ran in,
Beat breast, tore hair, cried out upon herself
As having failed in duty to him, shriek'd
That she but meant to win him back, fell on him,
Clasp'd, kiss'd him, wail'd: he answer'd, "Care not thou
What matters? All is over: Fare thee well!"

THE VOICE AND THE PEAK.

The voice and the Peak
  Far over summit and lawn,
The lone glow and long roar
  Green-rushing from the rosy thrones of dawn!

All night have I heard the voice
  Rave over the rocky bar,
But thou wert silent in heaven,
  Above thee glided the star.

Hast thou no voice, O Peak,
  That standest high above all?
"I am the voice of the Peak,
  I roar and rave for I fall.

"A thousand voices go
  To North, South, East, and West;
They leave the heights and are troubled,
  And moan and sink to their rest.

"The fields are fair beside them,
  The chestnut towers in his bloom;
But they — they feel the desire of the deep —
  Fall, and follow their doom.

"The deep has power on the height,
  And the height has power on the deep;
They are raised for ever and ever,
  And sink again into sleep."

Not raised for ever and ever,
  But when their cycle is o'er,
The valley, the voice, the peak, the star
  Pass and are found no more.

The Peak is high and flush'd
  At his highest with sunrise fire;
The peak is high, and the stars are high,
  And the thought of a man is higher.

A voice below the voice,
  And a height beyond the height!
Our hearing is not hearing,
  And our seeing is not sight.

The voice and the Peak
  Far into heaven withdrawn,
The lone glow and long roar
  Green-rushing from the rosy thrones of dawn!

THE DUKE AND DUCHESS OF EDINBURGH.

I.

THE Son of him with whom we strove for power—
 Whose will is lord thro' all his world-domain—
 Who made the serf a man, and burst his chain—
Has given our Prince his own Imperial Flower,
                                         Alexandrovna.
And welcome, Russian flower, a people's pride,
 To Britain, when her flowers begin to blow!
 From love to love, from home to home you go,
From mother unto mother, stately bride,
                                 Marie-Alexandrovna.

II.

The golden news along the steppes is blown,
 And at thy name the Tartar tents are stirred;
 Elburz and all the Caucasus have heard;
And all the sultry palms of India known,
                                        Alexandrovna.
The voices of our universal sea,
 On capes of Afric as on cliffs of Kent,
 The Maoris and that Isle of Continent,
And loyal pines of Canada murmur thee,
                                 Marie-Alexandrovna!

III.

Fair empires branching, both, in lusty life!—
 Yet Harold's England fell to Norman swords;
 Yet thine own land has bow'd to Tartar hordes
Since English Harold gave its throne a wife,
                                        Alexandrovna!
For thrones and peoples are as waifs that swing,
 And float or fall, in endless ebb and flow;
 But who love best have best the grace to know
That Love by right divine is deathless king,
                                 Marie-Alexandrovna!

IV.

And love has led thee to the stranger land,
 Where men are bold and strongly say their say;—
 See empire upon empire smiles to-day,
As thou with thy young lover hand in hand,
                                        Alexandrovna!
So now thy fuller life is in the West,
 Whose hand at home was gracious to thy poor:
 Thy name was blest within the narrow door;
Here, also, Marie, shall thy name be blest,
                                 Marie-Alexandrovna!

V.

Shall fears and jealous hatreds flame again?
 Or at thy coming, Princess, everywhere,
 The blue heaven break, and some diviner air
Breathe thro' the world and change the hearts of
      men,
                                        Alexandrovna?
But hearts that change not, love that cannot cease,
 And peace be yours, the peace of soul in soul!
 And howsoever this wild world may roll,
Between your peoples truth and manful peace,
                                 Alfred—Alexandrovna!

IN THE GARDEN AT SWAINSTON.

NIGHTINGALES warbled without—
 Within was weeping for thee;
Shadows of three dead men
 Walked in the walks with me;
Shadows of three dead men,
 And thou wast one of the three.

Nightingales sang in the woods—
 The master was far away;
Nightingales warbled and sang
 Of a passion that lasts but a day;
Still in the house in his coffin
 The prince of courtesy lay.

Two dead men have I known
 In courtesy like to thee;
Two dead men have I loved
 With a love that ever will be;
Three dead men have I loved,
 And thou art last of the three.

————

CHILD-SONGS.

THE CITY CHILD.

DAINTY little maiden, whither would you wander?
 Whither from this pretty home, the home where
  mother dwells?
"Far and far away," said the dainty little maiden,
"All among the gardens, auriculas, anemones,
 Roses and lilies and Canterbury-bells."

Dainty little maiden, whither would you wander?
 Whither from this pretty house, this city-house of
  ours?
"Far and far away," said the dainty little maiden,
"All among the meadows, the clover and the clematis,
 Daisies and kingcups and honeysuckle-flowers."

MINNIE AND WINNIE.

MINNIE and Winnie
 Slept in a shell.
Sleep, little ladies!
 And they slept well.

Pink was the shell within,
 Silver without;
Sounds of the great sea
 Wander'd about.

Sleep, little ladies!
 Wake not soon!
Echo on echo
 Dies to the moon.

Two bright stars
 Peep'd into the shell.
"What are they dreaming of?
 Who can tell?"

Started a green linnet
 Out of the croft;
Wake, little ladies,
 The sun is aloft!

THE WINDOW;

OR,

THE SONGS OF THE WRENS.

Four years ago Mr. Sullivan requested me to write a little song-cycle, German fashion, for him to exercise his art upon. He had been very successful in setting such old songs as "Orpheus with his lute," and I drest up for him, partly in the old style, a puppet whose almost only merit is, perhaps, that it can dance to Mr. Sullivan's instrument. I am sorry that my four-year-old puppet should have to dance at all in the dark shadow of these days; but the music is now completed, and I am bound by my promise.   A. Tennyson.

December, 1870.

ON THE HILL.

The lights and shadows fly!
Yonder it brightens and darkens down on the plain.
A jewel, a jewel dear to a lover's eye!
O is it the brook, or a pool, or her window-pane,
    When the winds are up in the morning?

Clouds that are racing above,
And winds and lights and shadows that cannot be
    still.
All running on one way to the home of my love,
You are all running on, and I stand on the slope of
    the hill,
    And the winds are up in the morning!

Follow, follow the chase!
And my thoughts are as quick and as quick, ever on,
    on, on.
O lights, are you flying over her sweet little face?
And my heart is there before you are come and gone,
    When the winds are up in the morning!

Follow them down the slope!
And I follow them down to the window-pane of my
    dear,
And it brightens and darkens and brightens like
    my hope,
And it darkens and brightens and darkens like my
    fear,
    And the winds are up in the morning.

AT THE WINDOW.

Vine, vine and eglantine,
Clasp her window, trail and twine!
Rose, rose and clematis,
Trail and twine and clasp and kiss,
Kiss, kiss; and make her a bower
All of flowers, and drop me a flower,
    Drop me a flower.

Vine, vine and eglantine,
Cannot a flower, a flower, be mine?
Rose, rose and clematis,
Drop me a flower, a flower, to kiss,
Kiss, kiss—And out of her bower
All of flowers, a flower, a flower,
    Dropt, a flower.

GONE!

Gone!
Gone till the end of the year,
Gone, and the light gone with her and left me in
    shadow here!

Gone—flitted away,
Taken the stars from the night and the sun from
    the day!
Gone, and a cloud in my heart, and a storm in the
    air!
Flown to the east or the west, flitted I know not
    where!
Down in the south is a flash and a groan: she is
    there! she is there!

WINTER.

The frost is here,
And fuel is dear,
And woods are sear,
And fires burn clear,
And frost is here
And has bitten the heel of the going year.

Bite, frost, bite!
You roll up away from the light
The blue woodlouse, and the plump dormouse,
And the bees are still'd, and the flies are kill'd,
And you bite far into the heart of the house,
But not into mine.

Bite, frost, bite!
The woods are all the searer,
The fuel is all the dearer,
The fires are all the clearer,
My spring is all the nearer,
You have bitten into the heart of the earth,
But not into mine.

SPRING.

Birds' love and birds' song
    Flying here and there,
Birds' song and birds' love,
    And you with gold for hair!
Birds' song and birds' love,
    Passing with the weather,
Men's song and men's love,
    To love once and for ever.

Men's love and birds' love,
    And women's love and men's:
And you my wren with a crown of gold,
    You my Queen of the wrens!
You the Queen of the wrens—
    We'll be birds of a feather,
I'll be King of the Queen of the wrens,
    And all in a nest together.

THE LETTER.

WHERE is another sweet as my sweet,
   Fine of the fine, and shy of the shy?
Fine little hands, fine little feet—
   Dewy blue eye.
Shall I write to her? shall I go?
   Ask her to marry me by and by?
Somebody said that she'd say no:
   Somebody knows that she'll say ay!

Ay or no, if ask'd to her face?
   Ay or no, from shy of the shy?
Go, little letter, apace, apace,
   Fly!
Fly to the light in the valley below—
   Tell my wish to her dewy blue eye:
Somebody said that she'd say no:
   Somebody knows that she'll say ay!

—◇◇—

NO ANSWER.

THE mist and the rain, the mist and the rain!
Is it ay or no? is it ay or no?
And never a glimpse of her window-pane!
   And I may die but the grass will grow,
And the grass will grow when I am gone,
And the wet west wind and the world will go on.

Ay is the song of the wedded spheres,
   No is trouble and cloud and storm,
Ay is life for a hundred years,
   No will push me down to the worm,
And when I am there and dead and gone,
The wet west wind and the world will go on.

The wind and the wet, the wind and the wet!
   Wet west wind, how you blow, you blow!
And never a line from my lady yet!
   Is it ay or no? is it ay or no?
Blow then, blow, and when I am gone,
The wet west wind and the world may go on.

—◇◇—

NO ANSWER.

WINDS are loud and you are dumb:
   Take my love, for love will come,
   Love will come but once a life.
Winds are loud and winds will pass!
Spring is here with leaf and grass:
   Take my love and be my wife.
After-loves of maids and men
Are but dainties drest again:
Love me now, you'll love me then:
   Love can love but once a life.

—◇◇—

THE ANSWER.

Two little hands that meet,
Claspt on her seal, my sweet!
Must I take you and break you,
Two little hands that meet?
I must take you, and break you,
And loving hands must part—
Take, take—break, break—
Break—you may break my heart.
   Faint heart never won—
   Break, break, and all's done.

AY!

BE merry, all birds, to-day,
   Be merry on earth as you never were merry before
Be merry in heaven, O larks, and far away,
   And merry for ever and ever, and one day more.
      Why?
      For it's easy to find a rhyme.

Look, look, how he flits,
   The fire-crown'd king of the wrens, from out of
      the pine!
Look how they tumble the blossom, the mad little tits!
   "Cuck-oo! Cuck-oo!" was ever a May so fine?
      Why?
      For it's easy to find a rhyme.

O merry the linnet and dove,
   And swallow and sparrow and throstle, and have
      your desire!
O merry my heart, you have gotten the wings of love,
   And flit like the king of the wrens with a crown
      of fire.
            Why?
      For it's ay ay ay, ay ay.

—◇◇—

WHEN?

SUN comes, moon comes,
   Time slips away.
Sun sets, moon sets,
   Love, fix a day.

"A year hence, a year hence."
   "We shall both be gray."
"A month hence, a month hence."
   "Far, far away."

"A week hence, a week hence."
   "Ah, the long delay."
"Wait a little, wait a little,
   You shall fix a day."   ·

"To-morrow, love, to-morrow,
   And that's an age away."
Blaze upon her window, sun,
   And honour all the day.

—◇◇—

MARRIAGE MORNING.

LIGHT, so low upon earth,
   You send a flash to the sun.
Here is the golden close of love,
   All my wooing is done.
O the woods and the meadows,
   Woods where we hid from the wet,
Stiles where we stay'd to be kind,
   Meadows in which we met!
Light, so low in the vale,
   You flash and lighten afar:
For this is the golden morning of love,
   And you are his morning star.
Flash, I am coming, I come,
   By meadow and stile and wood:
O lighten into my eyes and my heart,
   Into my heart and my blood!
Heart, are you great enough
   For a love that never tires?
O heart, are you great enough for love?
   I have heard of thorns and briers.
Over the thorns and briers,
   Over the meadows and stiles,
Over the world to the end of it
   Flash for a million miles.

DISCARDED POEMS.

[This division includes early and occasional poems, omitted by Mr. Tennyson from his collected works. A few have been replaced by him in his later editions. With these exceptions, these poems are printed exclusively in this edition.]

TIMBUCTOO.*

"Deep in that lion-haunted inland lies
A mystic city, goal of high emprise."— CHAPMAN.

I STOOD upon the Mountain which o'erlooks
The narrow seas, whose rapid interval
Parts Afric from green Europe, when the Sun
Had fall'n below th' Atlantic, and above
The silent heavens were blench'd with faery light,
Uncertain whether faery light or cloud,
Flowing Southward, and the chasms of deep, deep blue
Slumber'd unfathomable, and the stars
Were flooded over with clear glory and pale.
I gazed upon the sheeny coast beyond,
There where the Giant of old Time infix'd
The limits of his prowess, pillars high
Long time erased from earth: even as the Sea
When weary of wild inroad buildeth up
Huge mounds whereby to stay his yeasty waves.
And much I mused on legends quaint and old
Which whilome won the hearts of all on earth
Toward their brightness, ev'n as flame draws air,
But had their being in the heart of men
As air is th' life of flame: and thou wert than
A center'd glory-circled memory,
Divinest Atalantis, whom the waves
Have buried deep, and thou of later name,
Imperial Eldorado, roof'd with gold:
Shadows to which, despite all shocks of change,
All on-set of capricious accident,
Men clung with yearning hope which would not die.
As when in some great city where the walls
Shake, and the streets with ghastly faces thronged,
Do utter forth a subterranean voice,
/mong the inner columns far retired
At midnight, in the lone Acropolis,
Before the awful genius of the place
Kneels the pale Priestess in deep faith, the while
Above her head the weak lamp dips and winks
Unto the fearful summoning without:
Nathless she ever clasps the holy knees,
Bathes the cold hand with tears, and gazeth on
Those eyes which wear no light but that wherewith
Her phantasy informs them.

Where are ye,
Thrones of the Western wave, fair Islands green?
Where are your moonlight halls, your cedarn glooms,
The blossoming abysses of your hills?
Your flowering capes, and your gold-sanded bays
Blown round with happy airs of odorous winds?
Where are the infinite ways, which, seraph-trod,
Wound through your great Elysian solitudes,
Whose lowest deeps were, as with visible love,
Filled with Divine effulgence, circumfused,
Flowing between the clear and polished stems,
And ever circling round their emerald cones
In coronals and glories, such as gird
The unfading foreheads of the Saints in Heaven?
For nothing visible, they say, had birth
In that blest ground, but it was played about
With its peculiar glory. Then I raised
My voice and cried, "Wide Afric, doth thy Sun
Lighten, thy hills enfold a city as fair

* A Poem which obtained the Chancellor's Medal at the Cambridge Commencement, MDCCCXXIX. By A. TENNYSON, of Trinity College.

As those which starred the night o' the elder world?
Or is the rumor of thy Timbuctoo
A dream as frail as those of ancient time?"
A curve of whitening, flashing, ebbing light!
A rustling of white wings! the bright descent
Of a young Seraph! and he stood beside me
There on the ridge, and looked into my face
With his unutterable, shining orbs,
So that with hasty motion I did veil
My vision with both hands, and saw before me
Such colored spots as dance athwart the eyes
Of those that gaze upon the noonday Sun.
Girt with a zone of flashing gold beneath
His breast, and compassed round about his brow
With triple arch of everchanging bows,
And circled with the glory of living light
And alternation of all hues, he stood.
"O child of man, why muse you here alone
Upon the Mountain, on the dreams of old
Which filled the earth with passing loveliness,
Which flung strange music on the howling winds,
And odors rapt from remote Paradise?
Thy sense is clogged with dull mortality:
Open thine eyes and see."

I looked, but not
Upon his face, for it was wonderful
With its exceeding brightness, and the light
Of the great Angel Mind which looked from out
The starry glowing of his restless eyes.
I felt my soul grow mighty, and my spirit
With supernatural excitation bound
Within me, and my mental eye grew large
With such a vast circumference of thought,
That in my vanity I seemed to stand
Upon the outward verge and bound alone
Of full beatitude. Each failing sense,
As with a momentary flash of light,
Grew thrillingly distinct and keen. I saw
The smallest grain that dappled the dark earth,
The indistinctest atom in deep air,
The Moon's white cities, and the opal width
Of her small glowing lakes, her silver heights
Unvisited with dew of vagrant cloud,
And the unsounded, undescended depth
Of her black hollows. The clear galaxy
Shorn of its hoary lustre, wonderful,
Distinct and vivid with sharp points of light,
Blaze within blaze, an unimagined depth
And harmony of planet-girded suns
And moon-encircled planets, wheel in wheel,
Arched the wan sapphire. Nay—the hum of men
Or other things talking in unknown tongues,
And notes of busy life in distant worlds
Beat like a far wave on my anxious ear.
A maze of piercing, trackless, thrilling thoughts,
Involving and embracing each with each,
Rapid as fire, inextricably linked,
Expanding momently with every sight
And sound which struck the palpitating sense,
The issue of strong impulse, hurried through
The riven rapt brain; as when in some large lake
From pressure of descendant crags, which lapse
Disjointed, crumbling from their parent slope
At slender interval, the level calm
Is ridged with restless and increasing spheres
Which break upon each other, each th' effect
Of separate impulse, but more fleet and strong

Than its precursor, till the eye in vain
Amid the wild unrest of swimming shade
Dappled with hollow and alternate rise
Of interpenetrated arc, would scan
Definite round.

      I know not if I shape
These things with accurate similitude
From visible objects, for but dimly now,
Less vivid than a half-forgotten dream,
The memory of that mental excellence
Comes o'er me, and it may be I entwine
The indecision of my present mind
With its past clearness, yet it seems to me
As even then the torrent of quick thought
Absorbed me from the nature of itself
With its own fleetness. Where is he, that borne
Adown the sloping of an arrowy stream,
Could link his shalop to the fleeting edge,
And muse midway with philosophic calm
Upon the wondrous laws which regulate
The fierceness of the bounding element?

My thoughts which long had grovelled in the slime
Of this dull world, like dusky worms which house
Beneath unshaken waters, but at once
Upon some earth-awakening day of Spring
Do pass from gloom to glory, and aloft
Winnow the purple, bearing on both sides
Double display of star-lit wings, which burn
Fan-like and fibred with intensest bloom;
Even so my thoughts erewhile so low, now felt
Unutterable buoyancy and strength
To bear them upward through the trackless fields
Of undefined existence far and free.

Then first within the South methought I saw
A wilderness of spires, and crystal pile
Of rampart upon rampart, dome on dome,
Illimitable range of battlement
On battlement, and the Imperial height
Of canopy o'ercanopied.

      Behind
In diamond light up spring the dazzling peaks
Of Pyramids, as far surpassing earth's
As heaven than earth is fairer. Each aloft
Upon his narrowed eminence bore globes
Of wheeling suns, or stars, or semblances
Of either, showering circular abyss
Of radiance. But the glory of the place
Stood out a pillared front of burnished gold,
Interminably high, if gold it were
Or metal more ethereal, and beneath
Two doors of blinding brilliance, where no gaze
Might rest, stood open, and the eye could scan,
Through length of porch and valve and boundless
    hall,
Part of a throne of fiery flame, wherefrom
The snowy skirting of a garment hung,
And glimpse of multitude of multitudes
That ministered around it—if I saw
These things distinctly, for my human brain
Staggered beneath the vision, and thick night
Came down upon my eyelids, and I fell.

With ministering hand he raised me up:
Then with a mournful and ineffable smile,
Which but to look on for a moment filled

17

My eyes with irresistible sweet tears,
In accents of majestic melody,
Like a swoln river's gushings in still night
Mingled with floating music, thus he spake:
  "There is no mightier Spirit than I to sway
The heart of man; and teach him to attain
By shadowing forth the Unattainable;
And step by step to scale that mighty stair
Whose landing-place is wrapt about with clouds
Of glory of heaven.* With earliest light of Spring
And in the glow of sallow Summertide,
And in red Autumn when the winds are wild
With gambols, and when full-voiced Winter roofs
The headland with inviolate white snow,
I play about his heart a thousand ways,
Visit his eyes with visions, and his ears
With harmonies of wind and wave and wood,
—Of winds which tell of waters, and of waters
Betraying the close kisses of the wind—
And win him unto me: and few there be
So gross of heart who have not felt and known
A higher than they see: they with dim eyes
Behold me darkling. Lo! I have given thee
To understand my presence, and to feel
My fullness: I have filled thy lips with power.
I have raised thee nigher to the spheres of heaven.
Man's first, last home: and thou with ravished sense
Listenest the lordly music flowing from
The illimitable years. I am the Spirit,
The permeating life which courseth through
All th' intricate and labyrinthine veins
Of the great vine of Fable, which, outspread
With growth of shadowing leaf and clusters rare,
Reacheth to every corner under heaven,
Deep-rooted in the living soil of truth:
So that men's hopes and fears take refuge in
The fragrance of its complicated glooms,
And cool impleached twilights. Child of man,
Seest thou yon river, whose translucent wave,
Forth issuing from the darkness, windeth through
The argent streets o' the city, imaging
The soft inversion of her tremulous domes,
Her gardens frequent with the stately palm,
Her pagods hung with music of sweet bells,
Her obelisks of rangèd chrysolite,
Minarets and towers? Lo! how he passeth by,
And gulphs himself in sands, as not enduring
To carry through the world those waves, which bore
The reflex of my city in their depths.
Oh city! oh latest throne! where I was raised
To be a mystery of loveliness
Unto all eyes, the time is well-nigh come
When I must render up this glorious home
To keen Discovery: soon yon brilliant towers
Shall darken with the waving of her wand;
Darken and shrink and shiver into huts,
Black specks amid a waste of dreary sand,
Low-built, mud-walled, barbarian settlements.
How changed from this fair city!"

           Thus far the Spirit.
Then parted heaven-ward on the wing: and I
Was left alone on Calpe, and the moon
Had fallen from the night, and all was dark!

* "Be ye perfect, even as your father in heaven is perfect."

POEMS PUBLISHED IN THE EDITION OF 1830, AND OMITTED IN LATER EDITIONS.

ELEGIACS.

LOWFLOWING breezes are roaming the broad valley
  dimmed in the gloming:
Thro' the blackstemmed pines only the far river
  shines.
Creeping through blossomy rushes and bowers of
  roseblowing bushes,
Down by the poplar tall rivulets babble and fall.
Barketh the shepherd-dog cheerly; the grasshopper
  carolleth clearly;
Deeply the turtle coos; shrilly the owlet halloos;
Winds creep: dews fall chilly: in her first sleep
  earth breathes stilly:
Over the pools in the burn waterguats murmur and
  mourn.
Sadly the far kine loweth: 'the glimmering water
  outfloweth:
Twin peaks shadowed with pine slope to the dark
  hyaline.
Lowthroned Hesper is stayed between the two
  peaks; but the Naiad
Throbbing in wild unrest holds him beneath in her
  breast.
The ancient poetess singeth that Hesperus all things
  bringeth,
Smoothing the wearied mind: bring me my love,
  Rosalind.
Thou comest morning and even; she cometh not
  morning or even.
False-eyed Hesper, unkind, where is my sweet Ro-
  salind?

THE "HOW" AND THE "WHY."

?

I AM any man's suitor,
  If any will be my tutor:
Some say this life is pleasant,
  Some think it speedeth fast,
In time there is no present,
  In eternity no future,
    In eternity no past.
We laugh, we cry, we are born, we die,
Who will riddle me the *how* and the *why?*

The bulrush nods unto its brother.
The wheatears whisper to each other:
What is it they say? what do they there?
Why two and two make four? why round is not
  square?
Why the rock stands still, and the light clouds fly?
Why the heavy oak groans, and the white willows
  sigh?
Why deep is not high, and high is not deep?
Whether we wake, or whether we sleep?
Whether we sleep, or whether we die?
How you are you? why I am I?
Who will riddle me the *how* and the *why?*

The world is somewhat; it goes on somehow:
But what is the meaning of *then* and *now?*
  I feel there is something; but how and what?
I know there is somewhat: but what and why?
I cannot tell if that somewhat be I.

The little bird pipeth—"why? why?"
In the summer woods when the sun falls low,
And the great bird sits on the opposite bough,
And stares in his face, and shouts "how? how?"
And the black owl scuds down the mellow twilight,
And chants "how? how?" the whole of the night,

Why the life goes when the blood is spilt?
  What the life is? where the soul may lie?
Why a church is with a steeple built;
  And a house with a chimney-pot?
Who will riddle me the how and the what?
Who will riddle me the what and the why?

SUPPOSED CONFESSIONS

OF A SECOND-RATE SENSITIVE MIND NOT IN
UNITY WITH ITSELF.

OH GOD! my God! have mercy now.
I faint, I fall. Men say that thou
Didst die for me, for such as me,
Patient of ill, and death, and scorn,
And that my sin was as a thorn
Among the thorns that girt thy brow,
Wounding thy soul.—That even now,
In this extremest misery
Of ignorance, I should require
A sign! and if a bolt of fire
Would rive the slumbrous summer noon
While I do pray to thee alone,
Think my belief would stronger grow!
Is not my human pride brought low?
The boastings of my spirit still?
The joy I had in my free will
All cold, and dead, and corpse-like grown?
And what is left to me, but thou,
And faith in thee? Men pass me by:
Christians with happy countenances—
And children all seem full of thee!
And women smile with saintlike glances
Like thine own mother's when she bowed
Above thee, on that happy morn,
When angels spake to men aloud,
And thou and peace to earth were born.
Goodwill to me as well as all—
—I one of them: my brothers they:
Brothers in Christ—a world of peace
  And confidence, day after day;
And trust and hope till things should cease,
  And then one Heaven receive us all.

How sweet to have a common faith!
To hold a common scorn of death!
And at a burial to hear
  The creaking cords which wound and eat
Into my human heart, whene'er
Earth goes to earth, with grief, not fear,
  With hopeful grief, were passing sweet!
A grief not uninformed, and dull,
Hearted with hope, of hope as full
As is the blood with life, or night
And a dark cloud with rich moonlight.
To stand beside a grave, and see
The red small atoms wherewith we

Are built, and smile in calm, and say—
"These little motes and grains shall be
Clothed on with immortality
More glorious than the noon of day.
　All that is pass'd into the flowers,
And into beasts and other men,
And all the Norland whirlwind showers
From open vaults, and all the sea
O'erwashes with sharp salts, again
Shall fleet together all, and be
Indued with immortality."

Thrice happy state again to be
The trustful infant on the knee!
Who lets his waxen fingers play
About his mother's neck, and knows
Nothing beyond his mother's eyes.
They comfort him by night and day,
They light his little life alway;
He hath no thought of coming woes;
He hath no care of life or death,
Scarce outward signs of joy arise,
Because the Spirit of happiness
And perfect rest so inward is;
And loveth so his innocent heart,
Her temple and her place of birth,
Where she would ever wish to dwell,
Life of the fountain there, beneath
Its salient springs, and far apart,
Hating to wander out on earth,
Or breathe into the hollow air,
Whose chillness would make visible
Her subtil, warm, and golden breath,
Which mixing with the infant's blood,
Fulfills him with beatitude.
Oh! sure it is a special care
Of God, to fortify from doubt,
To arm in proof, and guard about
With triple mailéd trust, and clear
Delight, the infant's dawning year.
Would that my gloomed fancy were
As thine, my mother, when with brows
Propped on thy knees, my hands upheld
In thine, I listened to thy vows,
For me outpoured in holiest prayer—
For me unworthy!—and beheld
Thy mild deep eyes upraised, that knew
The beauty and repose of faith,
And the clear spirit shining through.
Oh! wherefore do we grow awry
From roots which strike so deep? why dare
Paths in the desert? Could not I
Bow myself down, where thou hast knelt,
To th' earth—until the ice would melt
Here, and I feel as thou hast felt?
What Devil had the heart to scathe
Flowers thou hadst reared—to brush the dew
From thine own lily, when thy grave
Was deep, my mother, in the clay?
Myself? Is it thus? Myself? Had I
So little love for thee? But why
Prevailed not thy pure prayers? Why pray
To one who heeds not, who can save
But will not? Great in faith, and strong
Against the grief of circumstance
Wert thou, and yet unheard? What if
Thou pleadest still, and seest me drive
Through utter dark a full-sailed skiff,
Unpiloted i' the echoing dance
Of reboant whirlwinds, stooping low
Unto the death, not sunk! I know
At matins and at evensong,
That thou, if thou wert yet alive,
In deep and daily prayers would'st strive
To reconcile me with thy God,
Albeit, my hope is gray, and cold
At heart, thou wouldest murmur still—
"Bring this lamb back into thy fold.

My Lord, if so it be thy will."
Would'st tell me I must brook the rod,
And chastisement of human pride;
That pride, the sin of devils, stood
Betwixt me and the light of God!
That hitherto I had defied,
And had rejected God—that Grace
Would drop from his o'erbrimming love,
As manna on my wilderness,
If I would pray—that God would move
And strike the hard, hard rock, and thence,
Sweet in their utmost bitterness,
Would issue tears of penitence
Which would keep green hope's life. Alas:
I think that pride hath now no place
Or sojourn in me. I am void,
Dark, formless, utterly destroyed.

Why not believe then? Why not yet
Anchor thy frailty there, where man
Hath moored and rested? Ask the sea
At midnight, when the crisp slope waves
After a tempest, rib and fret
The broadimbaséd beach, why he
Slumbers not like a mountain torn?
Wherefore his ridges are not curls
And ripples of an inland meer?
Wherefore he moaneth thus, nor can
Draw down into his vexéd pools
All that blue heaven which hues and paves
The other? I am too forlorn,
Too shaken: my own weakness fools
My judgment, and my spirit whirls,
Moved from beneath with doubt and fear.

"Yet," said I, in my morn of youth,
The unsunned freshness of my strength,
When I went forth in quest of truth,
"It is man's privilege to doubt,
If so be that from doubt at length,
Truth may stand forth unmoved of change,
An image with profulgent brows,
And perfect limbs, as from the storm
Of running fires and fluid range
Of lawless airs at last stood out
This excellence and solid form
Of constant beauty. For the Ox
Feeds in the herb, and sleeps, or fills
The hornéd valleys all about,
And hollows of the fringed hills
In summerheats, with placid lows
Unfearing, till his own blood flows
About his hoof. And in the flocks
The lamb rejoiceth in the year,
And raceth freely with his fere,
And answers to his mother's calls
From the flowered furrow. In a time,
Of which he wots not, run short pains
Through his warm heart: and then, from whence
He knows not, on his light there falls
A shadow; and his native slope,·
Where he was wont to leap and climb,
Floats from his sick and filmed eyes,
And something in the darkness draws
His forehead earthward, and he dies.
Shall men live thus, in joy and hope
As a young lamb, who cannot dream,
Living, but that he shall live on?
Shall we not look into the laws
Of life and death, and things that seem,
And things that be, and analyze
Our double nature, and compare
All creeds till we have found the one,
If one there be?" Ay me! I fear
All may not find, but every where
Some must clasp Idols. Yet, my God,
Whom call I Idol? Let thy dove
Shadow me over, and my sins

Be unremembered, and thy love
Enlighten me. Oh teach me yet
Somewhat before the heavy clod
Weighs on me, and the busy fret
Of that sharp-headed worm begins
In the gross blackness underneath.

Oh weary life! oh weary death!
Oh spirit and heart made desolate!
Oh damnèd vacillating state!

———

THE BURIAL OF LOVE.

His eyes in eclipse,
Palecold his lips,
The light of his hopes unfed,
Mute his tongue,
His bow unstrung
With the tears he hath shed,
Backward drooping his graceful head,
    Love is dead:
His last arrow is sped;
He hath not another dart;
Go—carry him to his dark deathbed;
Bury him in the cold, cold heart—
    Love is dead.

Oh, truest love! art thou forlorn,
And unrevenged? thy pleasant wiles
Forgotten, and thine innocent joy?
Shall hollowhearted apathy,
The cruellest form of perfect scorn,
With languor of most hateful smiles,
    For ever write,
    In the withered light
Of the tearless eye,
An epitaph that all may spy?
No! sooner she herself shall die.

For her the showers shall not fall,
Nor the round sun shine that shineth to all;
Her light shall into darkness change;
For her the green grass shall not spring,
Nor the rivers flow, nor the sweet birds sing,
Till Love have his full revenge.

———

TO ———.

Sainted Juliet! dearest name!
If to love be life alone,
    Divinest Juliet,
I love thee, and live; and yet
Love unreturned is like the fragrant flame
Folding the slaughter of the sacrifice
Offered to gods upon an altar-throne;
My heart is lighted at thine eyes,
Changed into fire, and blown about with sighs.

———

SONG.

I.

I' the glooming light
Of middle night
    So cold and white,
Worn Sorrow sits by the moaning wave,
    Beside her are laid
    Her mattock and spade,
For she hath half delved her own deep grave.
    Alone she is there:
The white clouds drizzle: her hair falls loose.
    Her shoulders are bare:
Her tears are mixed with the beaded dews.

II.

Death standeth by;
She will not die;
    With glazèd eye
She looks at her grave: she cannot sleep;
    Ever alone
    She maketh her moan:
She cannot speak: she can only weep,
    For she will not hope.
The thick snow falls on her flake by flake,
    The dull wave mourns down the slope,
The world will not change, and her heart will not
    break.

———

SONG.

I.

The lintwhite and the throstlecock
Have voices sweet and clear;
    All in the bloomèd May.
They from the blosmy brere
Call to the fleeting year,
    If that he would them hear
        And stay.
Alas! that one so beautiful
Should have so dull an ear.

II.

Fair year, fair year, thy children call.
But thou art deaf as death;
    All in the bloomèd May.
When thy light perisheth
That from thee issueth,
    Our life evanisheth:
        Oh! stay.
Alas! that lips so cruel-dumb
Should have so sweet a breath?

III.

Fair year, with brows of royal love
Thou comest, as a king,
    All in the bloomèd May.
Thy golden largess fling,
And longer hear us sing;
    Though thou art fleet of wing,
        Yet stay.
Alas! that eyes so full of light
Should be so wandering!

IV.

Thy locks are all of sunny sheen
In rings of gold yronne,*
    All in the bloomèd May.
We pri'thee pass not on;
If thou dost leave the sun,
    Delight is with thee gone.
        Oh! stay.
Thou art the fairest of thy feres.
We pri'thee pass not on.

———

SONG.

I.

Every day hath its night:
Every night its morn:
Thorough dark and bright
Wingèd hours are borne:
    Ah! welaway!
Seasons flower and fade;
Golden calm and storm
    Mingle day by day.
There is no bright form
Doth not cast a shade—
    Ah! welaway!

* "His crispe hair in ringis was yronne."—Chaucer, *Knight's Tale.*

II.

When we laugh, and our mirth
Apes the happy vein,
We're so kin to earth,
Pleasaunce fathers pain —
Ah! welaway!
Madness laugheth loud:
Laughter bringeth tears:
Eyes are worn away
Till the end of fears
Cometh in the shroud,
Ah! welaway!

III.

All is change, woe or weal;
Joy is Sorrow's brother;
Grief and gladness steal
Symbols of each other;
Ah! welaway!
Larks in heaven's cope
Sing: the culvers mourn
All the livelong day.
Be not all forlorn:
Let us weep in hope —
Ah! welaway!

NOTHING WILL DIE.

When will the stream be aweary of flowing
Under my eye?
When will the wind be aweary of blowing
Over the sky?
When will the clouds be aweary of fleeting?
When will the heart be aweary of beating?
And nature die?
Never, oh! never, nothing will die;
The stream flows,
The wind blows,
The cloud fleets,
The heart beats,
Nothing will die.

Nothing will die;
All things will change
Through eternity.
'Tis the world's winter;
Autumn and summer
Are gone long ago.
Earth is dry to the centre,
But spring a new comer—
A spring rich and strange,
Shall make the winds blow
Round and round,
Through and through,
Here and there,
Till the air
And the ground
Shall be filled with life anew.
The world was never made;
It will change, but it will not fade.
So let the wind range;
For even and morn
Ever will be
Through eternity.
Nothing was born;
Nothing will die;
All things will change.

ALL THINGS WILL DIE.

Clearly the blue river chimes in its flowing
Under my eye;
Warmly and broadly the south winds are blowing
Over the sky.
One after another the white clouds are fleeting;
Every heart this Maymorning in joyance is beating
Full merrily;

Yet all things must die.
The stream will cease to flow;
The wind will cease to blow;
The clouds will cease to fleet;
The heart will cease to beat;
For all things must die.

All things must die.
Spring will come never more.
Oh! vanity!
Death waits at the door.
See! our friends are all forsaking
The wine and merrymaking.
We are called — we must go.
Laid low, very low,
In the dark we must lie.
The merry glees are still;
The voice of the bird
Shall no more be heard,
Nor the wind on the hill.
Oh! misery!
Hark! death is calling
While I speak to ye,
The jaw is falling,
The red cheek paling,
The strong limbs failing;
Ice with the warm blood mixing;
The eyeballs fixing.
Nine times goes the passing bell:
Ye merry souls, farewell.

The old earth
Had a birth,
As all men know
Long ago.
And the old earth must die.
So let the warm winds range,
And the blue wave beat the shore;
For even and morn
Ye will never see
Through eternity.
All things were born.
Ye will come never more,
For all things must die.

HERO TO LEANDER.

Oh go not yet, my love,
The night is dark and vast;
The white moon is hid in her heaven above,
And the waves climb high and fast.
Oh! kiss me, kiss me, once again,
Lest thy kiss should be the last.
Oh kiss me ere we part;
Grow closer to my heart.
My heart is warmer surely than the bosom of the
main.
O joy! O bliss of blisses!
My heart of hearts art thou.
Come bathe me with thy kisses,
My eyelids and my brow.
Hark how the wild rain hisses,
And the loud sea roars below.

Thy heart beats through thy rosy limbs,
So gladly doth it stir;
Thine eye in drops of gladness swims.
I have bathed thee with the pleasant myrrh,
Thy locks are dripping balm;
Thou shalt not wander hence to-night,
I'll stay thee with my kisses.
To-night the roaring brine
Will rend thy golden tresses;
The ocean with the morrow light
Will be both blue and calm;
And the billow will embrace thee with a kiss as soft
as mine.

No Western odours wander
  On the black and moaning sea,
And when thou art dead, Leander,
  My soul must follow thee !
Oh go not yet, my love,
  Thy voice is sweet and low;
The deep salt wave breaks in above
  Those marble steps below.
The turretstairs are wet
  That lead into the sea.
Leander! go net yet.
The pleasant stars have set:
Oh! go not, go not yet,
  Or I will follow thee.

———∞———

THE MYSTIC.

Angels have talked with him, and showed him
    thrones:
Ye knew him not; he was not one of ye,
Ye scorned him with an undiscerning scorn:
Ye could not read the marvel in his eye,
The still serene abstraction: he hath felt
The vanities of after and before;
Albeit, his spirit and his secret heart
The stern experiences of converse lives,
The linkèd woes of many a fiery change
Had purified, and chastened, and made free.
Always there stood before him, night and day,
Of wayward varycolored circumstance
The imperishable presences serene,
Colossal, without form, or sense, or sound,
Dim shadows but unwaning presences
Fourfacèd to four corners of the sky:
And yet again, three shadows, fronting one,
One forward, one respectant, three but one;
And yet again, again and evermore,
For the two first were not, but only seemed,
One shadow in the midst of a great light,
One reflex from eternity on time,
One mighty countenance of perfect calm,
Awful with most invariable eyes.
For him the silent congregated hours,
Daughters of time, divinely tall, beneath
Severe and youthful brows, with shining eyes
Smiling a godlike smile (the innocent light
Of earliest youth pierced through and through with
    all
Keen knowledges of low-embowèd eld)
Upheld, and ever hold aloft the cloud
Which droops lowhung on either gate of life,
Both birth and death: he in the centre fixt,
Saw far on each side through the grated gates
Most pale and clear and lovely distances.
He often lying broad awake, and yet
Remaining from the body, and apart
In intellect and power and will, hath heard
Time flowing in the middle of the night,
And all things creeping to a day of doom.
How could ye know him? Ye were yet within
The narrower circle; he had wellnigh reached
The last, which with a region of white flame,
Pure without heat, into a larger air
Upburning, and an ether of black blue,
Investeth and ingirds all other lives.

———∞———

THE GRASSHOPPER.

I.

Voice of the summerwind,
Joy of the summerplain,
Life of the summerhours,
Carol clearly, bound along.
No Tithon thou as poets feign
(Shame fall 'em they are deaf and blind),

But an insect lithe and strong,
Bowing the seeded summer flowers.
Prove their falsehood and thy quarrel,
Vaulting on thine airy feet.
Clap thy shielded sides and carol,
  Carol clearly, chirrup sweet.
Thou art a mailèd warrior in youth and strength
    complete;
      Armed cap-a-pie
      Full fair to see;
      Unknowing fear,
      Undreading loss,
    A gallant cavalier,
    Sans peur et sans reproche,
    In sunlight and in shadow,
    The Bayard of the meadow.

II.

I would dwell with thee,
  Merry grasshopper,
Thou art so glad and free,
  And as light as air;
Thou hast no sorrow or tears,
Thou hast no compt of years,
No withered immortality,
But a short youth sunny and free.
Carol clearly, bound along,
  Soon thy joy is over,
A summer of loud song,
  And slumbers in the clover.
What hast thou to do with evil
In thine hour of love and revel,
  In thy heat of summer pride,
Pushing the thick roots aside
Of the singing flowered grasses,
That brush thee with their silken tresses?
What hast thou to do with evil,
Shooting, singing, ever springing
  In and out the emerald glooms,
  Ever leaping, ever singing,
  Lighting on the golden blooms?

———∞———

LOVE, PRIDE, AND FORGETFULNESS

Ere yet my heart was sweet Love's tomb,
  Love laboured honey busily.
I was the hive, and Love the bee,
  My heart the honeycomb.
One very dark and chilly night
  Pride came beneath and held a light.

The cruel vapours went through all,
  Sweet Love was withered in his cell;
Pride took Love's sweets, and by a spell
  Did change them into gall;
And Memory, though fed by Pride,
  Did wax so thin on gall,
Awhile she scarcely lived at all.
  What marvel that she died?

———∞———

CHORUS

IN AN UNPUBLISHED DRAMA, WRITTEN VERY EARLY.

The varied earth, the moving heaven,
  The rapid waste of roving sea,
The fountainpregnant mountains riven
  To shapes of wildest anarchy.
By secret fire and midnight storms
  That wander round their windy cones,
The subtle life, the countless forms
  Of living things, the wondrous tones
    Of man and beast are full of strange
    Astonishment and boundless change.

The day, the diamonded night,
  The echo, feeble child of sound,
The heavy thunder's griding might,
  The herald lightning's starry bound,
The vocal spring of bursting bloom,
  The naked summer's glowing birth,
The troublous autumn's sallow gloom,
  The hoarhead winter paving earth
    With sheeny white, are full of strange
    Astonishment and boundless change.

Each sun which from the centre flings
  Grand music and redundant fire,
The burning belts, the mighty rings,
  The murm'rous planets' rolling choir,
The globefilled arch that, cleaving air,
  Lost in its own effulgence sleeps,
The lawless comets as they glare,
  And thunder through the sapphire deeps
    In wayward strength, are full of strange
    Astonishment and boundless change.

LOST HOPE.

You cast to ground the hope which once was mine:
  But did the while your harsh decree deplore,
Embalming with sweet tears the vacant shrine,
  My heart, where Hope had been and was no more.

So on an oaken sprout
  A goodly acorn grew:
But winds from heaven shook the acorn out,
  And filled the cup with dew.

THE TEARS OF HEAVEN.

Heaven weeps above the earth all night till morn,
  In darkness weeps as all ashamed to weep,
Because the earth hath made her state forlorn
  With self-wrought evil of unnumbered years,
And doth the fruit of her dishonor reap.
And all the day heaven gathers back her tears
  Into her own blue eyes so clear and deep,
And showering down the glory of lightsome day,
Smiles on the earth's worn brow to win her if she
  may.

LOVE AND SORROW.

O maiden, fresher than the first green leaf
With which the fearful springtide flecks the lea,
Weep not, Almeida, that I said to thee
That thou hast half my heart, for bitter grief
Doth hold the other half in sovranty.
Thou art my heart's sun in love's crystalline:
Yet on both sides at once thou canst not shine:
Thine is the bright side of my heart, and thine
My heart's day, but the shadow of my heart,
Issue of its own substance, my heart's night
Thou canst not lighten even with *thy* light,
Allpowerful in beauty as thou art.
Almeida, if my heart were substanceless,
Then might thy rays pass through to the other side,
So swiftly, that they nowhere would abide,
But lose themselves in utter emptiness.
Half-light, half-shadow, let my spirit sleep:
They never learned to love who never knew to weep.

TO A LADY SLEEPING.

O thou whose fringèd lids I gaze upon,
  Through whose dim brain the wingèd dreams are
    borne,

Unroof the shrines of clearest vision,
In honor of the silver-flecked morn;
Long hath the white wave of the virgin light
Driven back the billow of the dreamful dark.
Thou all unwittingly prolongest night,
Though long ago listening the poisèd lark,
With eyes dropt downward through the blue serene,
Over heaven's parapet the angels lean.

SONNET.

Could I outwear my present state of woe
With one brief winter, and induc i' the spring
Hues of fresh youth, and mightily outgrow
The wan dark coil of faded suffering—
Forth in the pride of beauty issuing
A sheeny snake. the light of vernal bowers,
Moving his crest to all sweet plots of flowers
And watered valleys where the young birds sing:
Could I thus hope my lost delight's renewing,
I straightly would command the tears to creep
From my charged lids; but inwardly I weep;
Some vital heat as yet my heart is wooing:
That to itself hath drawn the frozen rain
From my cold eyes, and melted it again.

SONNET.

Though Night hath climbed her peak of highest
  noon,
And bitter blasts the screaming autumn whirl,
All night through archways of the bridged pearl,
And portals of pure silver, walks the moon.
Walk on, my soul, nor crouch to agony.
Turn cloud to light, and bitterness to joy,
And dross to gold with glorious alchemy,
Basing thy throne above the world's annoy.
Reign thou above the storms of sorrow and ruth
That roar beneath; unshaken peace hath won thee;
So shalt thou pierce the woven glooms of truth;
So shall the blessing of the meek be on thee;
So in thine hour of dawn, the body's youth,
An honourable eld shall come upon thee.

SONNET.

Shall the hag Evil die with child of Good,
Or propagate again her loathèd kind,
Thronging the cells of the diseasèd mind,
Hateful with hanging cheeks, a withered brood,
Though hourly pastured on the salient blood?
Oh! that the wind which bloweth cold or heat
Would shatter and o'erbear the brazen beat
Of their broad vans, and in the solitude
Of middle space confound them, and blow back
Their wild cries down their cavern throats, and slake
With points of blastborne hail their heated eyne!
So their wan limbs no more might come between
The moon and the moon's reflex in the night,
Nor blot with floating shades the solar light.

SONNET.

The pallid thunderstricken sigh for gain,
Down an ideal stream they ever float,
And sailing on Pactolus in a boat,
Drown soul and sense, while wistfully they strain
Weak eyes upon the glistening sands that robe
The understream. The wise, could he behold
Cathedralled caverns of thickribbèd gold
And branching silvers of the central globe,
Would marvel from so beautiful a sight

How scorn and ruin, pain and hate could flow.
But Hatred in a gold cave sits below:
Pleached with her hair, in mail of argent light
Shot into gold, a snake her forehead clips,
And skins the colour from her trembling lips.

LOVE.

I.

Thou, from the first, unborn, undying love,
Albeit we gaze not on thy glories near,
Before the face of God didst breathe and move,
Though night and pain and ruin and death reign
        here.
Thou foldest, like a golden atmosphere,
The very throne of the eternal God:
Passing through thee the edicts of his fear
Are mellowed into music, borne abroad
By the loud winds, though they uprend the sea,
Even from its central deeps: thine empery
Is over all; thou wilt not brook eclipse;
Thou goest and returnest to His lips
Like lightning: thou dost ever brood above
The silence of all hearts, unutterable Love.

II.

To know thee is all wisdom, and old age
Is but to know thee: dimly we behold thee
Athwart the veils of evils which infold thee.
We beat upon our aching hearts in rage;
We cry for thee; we deem the world thy tomb.
As dwellers in lone planets look upon
The mighty disk of their majestic sun,
Hollowed in awful chasme of wheeling gloom,
Making their day dim, so we gaze on thee.
Come, thou of many crowns, whiterobed love.
Oh! rend the veil in twain: all men adore thee;
Heaven crieth after thee; earth waiteth for thee;
Breathe on thy wingèd throne, and it shall move
In music and in light o'er land and sea.

III.

And now — methinks I gaze upon thee now,
As on a serpent in his agonies
Awestricken Indians; what time laid low
And crushing the thick fragrant reeds he lies,
When the new year warmbreathèd on the Earth,
Waiting to light him with her purple skies,
Calls to him by the fountain to uprise.
Already with the pangs of a new birth
Strain the hot spheres of his convulsèd eyes,
And in his writhings awful hues begin
To wander down his sable-sheeny sides.
Like light on troubled waters: from within
Anon he rusheth forth with merry din,
And in him light and joy and strength abides;
And from his brows a crown of living light
Looks through the thickstemmed woods by day and
        night.

THE KRAKEN.

Below the thunders of the upper deep;
Far, far beneath in the abysmal sea,
His ancient, dreamless, uninvaded sleep,
The Kraken sleepeth: faintest sunlights flee
About his shadowy sides: above him swell
Huge sponges of millennial growth and height;
And far away into the sickly light,
From many a wondrous grot and secret cell
Unnumbered and enormous polypi
Winnow with giant fins the slumbering green.
There hath he lain for ages and will lie
Battening upon huge seaworms in his sleep,
Until the latter fire shall heat the deep;
Then once by man and angels to be seen,
In roaring he shall rise and on the surface die.

ENGLISH WAR-SONG.

Who fears to die? Who fears to die?
    Is there any here who fears to die?
He shall find what he fears; and none shall grieve
    For the man who fears to die:
But the withering scorn of the many shall cleave
    To the man who fears to die.
        Chorus. — Shout for England!
            Ho! for England!
            George for England!
            Merry England!
            England for aye!

The hollow at heart shall crouch forlorn,
    He shall eat the bread of common scorn;
It shall be steeped in the salt, salt tear,
    Shall be steeped in his own salt tear:
Far better, far better he never were born
    Than to shame merry England here.
        Chorus. — Shout for England! etc.

There standeth our ancient enemy;
    Hark! he shouteth — the ancient enemy!
On the ridge of the hill his banners rise;
    They stream like fire in the skies;
Hold up the Lion of England on high
    Till it dazzle and blind his eyes.
        Chorus. — Shout for England! etc.

Come along! we alone of the earth are free;
    The child in our cradles is bolder than he:
For where is the heart and strength of slaves?
    Oh! where is the strength of slaves?
He is weak! we are strong: he a slave, we are free
    Come along! we will dig their graves.
        Chorus. — Shout for England! etc.

There standeth our ancient enemy,
    Will he dare to battle with the free?
Spur along! spur amain! charge to the fight
    Charge! charge to the fight!
Hold up the Lion of England on high!
    Shout for God and our right!
        Chorus. — Shout for England! etc.

NATIONAL SONG.

There is no land like England
    Where'er the light of day be;
There are no hearts like English hearts,
    Such hearts of oak as they be.
There is no land like England
    Where'er the light of day be;
There are no men like Englishmen,
    So tall and bold as they be.
Chorus. — For the French the Pope may shrive 'em
        For the devil a whit we heed 'em:
    As for the French, God speed 'em
        Unto their heart's desire,
    And the merry devil drive 'em
        Through the water and the fire.
Full Chor. — Our glory is our freedom,
        We lord it o'er the sea;
    We are the sons of freedom,
        We are free.

There is no land like England,
    Where'er the light of day be;
There are no wives like English wives,
    So fair and chaste as they be.
There is no land like England,
    Where'er the light of day be;
There are no maids like English maids,
    So beautiful as they be.
Chorus. — For the French, etc.

DUALISMS.

Two bees within a crystal flowerbell rock'd,
    Hum a lovelay to the westwind at noontide.
Both alike, they buzz together,
Both alike, they hum together,
Through and through the flowered heather.
Where in a creeping cove the wave unshock'd
    Lays itself calm and wide.
Over a stream two birds of glancing feather
Do woo each other, carolling together.
Both alike, they glide together,
            Side by side;
Both alike, they sing together,
Arching blue-gloss'd necks beneath the purple
    weather.

Two children lovelier than Love adown the lea are
    singing,
As they gambol, lilygarlands ever stringing:
    Both in blossnwhite silk are frock'd:
Like, unlike, they roam together
Under a summervault of golden weather;
Like, unlike, they sing together
            Side by side,
        MidMay's darling golden lock'd,
        Summer's tanling diamond eyed.

———

WE ARE FREE.

The winds, as at their hour of birth,
    Leaning upon the winged sea,

Breathed low around the rolling earth
    With mellow preludes, "We are free."
The streams through many a lilied row
    Down-carolling to the crisped sea,
Low-tinkled with a bell-like flow
    Atween the blossoms, "We are free."

———

Οἱ ῥέοντες.

I.

All thoughts, all creeds, all dreams are true,
    All visions wild and strange;
Man is the measure of all truth
    Unto himself. All truth is change.
All men do walk in sleep, and all
    Have faith in that they dream:
For all things are as they seem to all,
    And all things flow like a stream.

II.

There is no rest, no calm, no pause,
    Nor good nor ill, nor light nor shade,
Nor essence nor eternal laws:
    For nothing is, but all is made.
But if I dream that all these are,
    They are to me for that I dream;
For all things are as they seem to all,
    And all things flow like a stream.

Argal—this very opinion is only true relatively to
the flowing philosophers.

———

POEMS PUBLISHED IN THE EDITION OF 1833,
AND OMITTED IN LATER EDITIONS.

SONNET.

Mine be the strength of spirit fierce and free,
Like some broad river rushing down alone,
With the selfsame impulse wherewith he was thrown
From his loud fount upon the echoing lea:—
Which with increasing might doth forward flee
By town, and tower, and hill, and cape, and isle,
And in the middle of the green salt sea
Keeps his blue waters fresh for many a mile.
Mine be the Power which ever to its sway
Will win the wise at once, and by degrees
May into uncongenial spirits flow:
Even as the great gulfstream of Florida
Floats far away into the Northern seas
The lavish growths of southern Mexico.

TO ———.

I.

All good things have not kept aloof,
    Nor wandered into other ways;
I have not lacked thy mild reproof,
    Nor golden largess of thy praise,
But life is full of weary days.

II.

Shake hands, my friend, across the brink
    Of that deep grave to which I go.
Shake hands once more: I cannot sink
    So far—far down, but I shall know
    Thy voice, and answer from below.

III.

When, in the darkness over me,
    The four-handed mole shall scrape,
Plant thou no dusky cypress tree,
    Nor wreathe thy cap with doleful crape,
    But pledge me in the flowing grape.

IV.

And when the sappy field and wood
    Grow green beneath the showery gray,
And rugged barks begin to bud,
    And through damp holts, newflushed with May,
    Ring sudden laughters of the Jay;

V.

Then let wise Nature work her will,
    And on my clay the darnels grow.
Come only when the days are still,
    And at my headstone whisper low,
    And tell me if the woodbines blow,

VI.

If thou art blest, my mother's smile
    Undimmed, if bees are on the wing:
Then cease, my friend, a little while,
    That I may hear the throstle sing
    His bridal song, the boast of spring.

VII.

Sweet as the noise in parched plains
    Of bubbling wells that fret the stones
(If any sense in me remains).
    Thy words will be; thy cheerful tones
    As welcome to my crumbling bones.

BUONAPARTE.

He thought to quell the stubborn hearts of oak,
Madman!—to chain with chains, and bind with bands
That island queen that sways the floods and lands
From Ind to Ind, but in fair daylight woke,
When from her wooden walls, lit by sure hands,
With thunders, and with lightnings, and with smoke,
Peal after peal, the British battle broke,
Lulling the brine against the Coptic sands.
We taught him lowlier moods, when Elsinore
Heard the war moan along the distant sea,
Rocking with shattered spars, with sudden fires
Flamed over: at Trafalgar yet once more
We taught him: late he learned humility   [ers.
Perforce, like those whom Gideon schooled with bri-

SONNETS.

I.

O beauty, passing beauty! sweetest Sweet!
How canst thou let me waste my youth in sighs?
I only ask to sit beside thy feet.
Thou knowest I dare not look into thine eyes.
Might I but kiss thy hand! I dare not fold
My arms about thee — scarcely dare to speak.
And nothing seems to me so wild and bold,
As with one kiss to touch thy blessèd cheek.
Methinks if I should kiss thee, no control
Within the thrilling brain could keep afloat
The subtle spirit. Even while I spoke,
The bare word Kiss hath made my inner soul
To tremble like a lutestring, ere the note
Hath melted in the silence that it broke.

II.

But were I loved, as I desire to be,
What is there in the great sphere of the earth,
And range of evil between death and birth,
That I should fear,—if I were loved by thee?
All the inner, all the outer world of pain
Clear Love would pierce and cleave, if thou wert mine,
As I have heard that, somewhere in the main,
Fresh-water springs come up through bitter brine.
'Twere joy, not fear, clasped hand-in-hand with thee,
To wait for death—mute—careless of all ills,
Apart upon a mountain, though the surge
Of some new deluge from a thousand hills
Flung leagues of roaring foam into the gorge
Below us, as far on as eye could see.

THE HESPERIDES.

Hesperus and his daughters three,
That sing about the golden tree.—COMUS.

The Northwind fall'n, in the newstarred night
Zidonian Hanno, voyaging beyond
The hoary promontory of Soloë
Past Thymiaterion, in calmèd bays,
Between the southern and the western Horn.
Heard neither warbling of the nightingale,
Nor melody of the Libyan lotus flute
Blown seaward from the shore; but from a slope
That ran bloombright into the Atlantic blue,
Beneath a highland leaning down a weight
Of cliffs, and zoned below with cedar shade,
Came voices, like the voices in a dream,
Continuous, till he reached the outer sea.

SONG.

1.

The golden apple, the golden apple, the hallowed
Guard it well, guard it warily,   [fruit,
Singing airily,
Standing about the charmèd root.
Round about all is mute,
As the snowfield on the mountain-peaks,
As the sandfield at the mountain-foot.
Crocodiles in briny creeks
Sleep and stir not: all is mute.
If ye sing not, if ye make false measure,
We shall lose eternal pleasure,
Worth eternal want of rest.
Laugh not loudly: watch the treasure
Of the wisdom of the West.
In a corner wisdom whispers. Five and three
(Let it not be preached abroad) make an awful mys-
tery.
For the blossom unto threefold music bloweth;
Evermore it is born anew;
And the sap to threefold music floweth,
From the root
Drawn in the dark,
Up to the fruit,
Creeping under the fragrant bark,
Liquid gold, honeysweet, thro' and thro'.
Keen-eyed Sisters, singing airily,
Looking warily
Every way,
Guard the apple night and day,
Lest one from the East come and take it away.

II.

Father Hesper, Father Hesper, watch, watch, ever and aye,
Looking under silver hair with a silver eye.
Father, twinkle not thy steadfast sight;
Kingdoms lapse, and climates change, and races die;
Honour comes with mystery;
Hoarded wisdom brings delight.
Number, tell them over and number
How many the mystic fruit tree holds
Lest the redcombed dragon slumber
Rolled together in purple folds.
Look to him, father, lest he wink, and the golden apple be stol'n away,
For his ancient heart is drunk with overwatchings night and day,
Round about the hallowed fruit tree curled—
Sing away, sing aloud evermore in the wind, without stop,
Lest his scalèd eyelid drop,
For he is older than the world.
If he waken, we waken,
Rapidly levelling eager eyes.
If he sleep, we sleep,
Dropping the eyelid over the eyes.
If the golden apple be taken,
The world will be overwise.
Five links, a golden chain, are we,
Hesper, the dragon, and sisters three,
Bound about the golden tree.

III.

Father Hesper, Father Hesper, watch, watch, night and day,
Lest the old wound of the world be healed,
The glory unsealed,
The golden apple stolen away.
And the ancient secret revealed.
Look from west to east along:
Father, old Himala weakens, Caucasus is bold and strong.
Wandering waters unto wandering waters call·
Let them clash together, foam and fall.
Out of watchings, out of wiles,
Comes the bliss of secret smiles.
All things are not told to all.
Half-round the mantling night is drawn,
Purple fringèd with even and dawn.
Hesper hateth Phosphor, evening hateth morn.

IV.

Every flower and every fruit the redolent breath
Of this warm sea wind ripeneth,
Arching the billow in his sleep;
But the land wind wandereth,
Broken by the highland-steep,
Two streams upon the violet deep;
For the western sun and the western star,
And the low west wind, breathing afar,
The end of day and beginning of night
Make the apple holy and bright;
Holy and bright, round and full, bright and blest,
Mellowed in a land of rest;
Watch it warily day and night;
All good things are in the west.
Till mid noon the cool east light
Is shut out by the tall hillbrow;
But when the fulfaced sunset yellowly
Stays on the flowering arch of the bough,
The luscious fruitage clustereth mellowly,
Goldenkernelled, goldencored,
Sunset-ripened above on the tree.
The world is wasted with fire and sword,
But the apple of gold hangs over the sea.
Five links, a golden chain are we,
Hesper, the dragon, and sisters three,
Daughters three,
Bound about
The gnarlèd bole of the charmèd tree.
The golden apple, the golden apple, the hallowed
    fruit,
Guard it well, guard it warily,
Watch it warily,
Singing airily,
Standing about the charmèd root.

ROSALIND.

I.

My Rosalind, my Rosalind,
My frolic falcon, with bright eyes,
Whose free delight, from any height of rapid flight,
Stoops at all game that wing the skies,
My Rosalind, my Rosalind,
My bright-eyed, wild-eyed falcon, whither,
Careless both of wind and weather,
Whither fly ye, what game spy ye,
Up or down the streaming wind?

II.

The quick lark's closest-carolled strains,
The shadow rushing up the sea,
The lighting flash atween the rains,
The sunlight driving down the lea,
The leaping stream, the very wind,
That will not stay, upon his way,
To stoop the cowslip to the plains,
Is not so clear and bold and free
As you, my falcon Rosalind.
You care not for another's pains,
Because you are the soul of joy,
Bright metal all without alloy.
Life shoots and glances thro' your veins,
And flashes off a thousand ways,
Through lips and eyes in subtle rays.
Your hawkeyes are keen and bright,
Keen with triumph, watching still
To pierce me through with pointed light:
But oftentimes they flash and glitter
Like sunshine on a dancing rill,
And your words are seeming-bitter,
Sharp and few, but seeming-bitter
From excess of swift delight.

III.

Come down, come home, my Rosalind,
My gay young hawk, my Rosalind:

Too long you keep the upper skies;
Too long you roam and wheel at will;
But we must hood your random eyes,
That care not whom they kill,
And your cheek, whose brilliant hue
Is so sparkling-fresh to view,
Some red heath flower in the dew,
Touched with sun rise. We must bind
And keep you fast, my Rosalind,
Fast, fast, my wild-eyed Rosalind,
And clip your wings, and make you love:
When we have lured you from above,
And that delight of frolic flight, by day or night,
From north to south;
Will bind you fast in silken cords,
And kiss away the bitter words
From off your rosy mouth.

NOTE TO ROSALIND.

Perhaps the following lines may be allowed to stand as a separate poem; originally they made part of the text, where they were manifestly improper.

My Rosalind, my Rosalind,
Bold, subtle, careless Rosalind,
Is one of those who know no strife
Of inward woe or outward fear;
To whom the slope and stream of Life,
The life before, the life behind,
In the ear, from far and near,
Chimeth musically clear.
My falconhearted Rosalind,
Fullsailed before a vigorous wind,
Is one of those who cannot weep
For others' woes, but overleap
All the petty shocks and fears
That trouble life in early years,
With a flash of frolic scorn
And keen delight, that never falls
Away from freshness, selfupborne
With such gladness as, whenever
The freshflushing springtime calls
To the flooding waters cool,
Young fishes, on an April morn,
Up and down a rapid river,
Leap the little waterfalls
That sing into the pebbled pool.
My happy falcon, Rosalind,
Hath daring fancies of her own,
Fresh as the dawn before the day,
Fresh as the early seasmell blown
Through vineyards from an inland bay.
My Rosalind, my Rosalind,
Because no shadow on you falls,
Think you hearts are tennisballs,
To play with, wanton Rosalind?

SONG.

Who can say
Why Today
Tomorrow will be yesterday?
Who can tell
Why to smell
The violet, recalls the dewy prime
Of youth and buried time?
The cause is nowhere found in rhyme.

KATE.

I KNOW her by her angry air,
Her bright black eyes, her bright black hair,
Her rapid laughters wild and shrill,
As laughters of the woodpecker

From the bosom of a hill.
'Tis Kate—she sayeth what she will:
For Kate hath an unbridled tongue,
Clear as the twanging of a harp.
Her heart is like a throbbing star.
Kate hath a spirit ever strung
Like a new bow, and bright and sharp
As edges of the scymetar.
Whence shall she take a fitting mate?
For Kate no common love will feel;
My woman-soldier, gallant Kate,
As pure and true as blades of steel.

Kate saith "the world is void of might."
Kate saith "the men are gilded flies."
Kate snaps her fingers at my vows;
Kate will not hear of lovers' sighs.
I would I were an armèd knight,
Far famed for wellwon enterprise,
And wearing on my swarthy brows
The garland of new-wreathed emprise;
For in a moment I would pierce
The blackest files of clanging fight,
And strongly strike to left and right,
In dreaming of my lady's eyes.
Oh! Kate loves well the bold and fierce:
But none are bold enough for Kate,
She cannot find a fitting mate.

———◇◇◇———

SONNET

WRITTEN ON HEARING OF THE OUTBREAK OF THE
POLISH INSURRECTION.

BLOW ye the trumpet, gather from afar
The hosts to battle: be not bought and sold.
Arise, brave Poles, the boldest of the bold;
Break through your iron shackles—fling them far.
O for those days of Piast, ere the Czar
Grew to his strength among his deserts cold;
When even to Moscow's cupolas were rolled
The growing murmurs of the Polish war!
Now must your noble anger blaze out more
Than when from Sobieski, clan by clan,
The Moslem myriads fell, and fled before—
Than when Zamoysky smote the Tatar Khan;
Than earlier, when on the Baltic shore
Boleslas drove the Pomeranian.

———◇◇◇———

SONNET

ON THE RESULT OF THE LATE RUSSIAN INVASION
OF POLAND.

HOW long, O God, shall men be ridden down,
And trampl'd under by the last and least
Of men? The heart of Poland hath not ceased
To quiver, though her sacred blood doth drown
The fields; and out of every mouldering town
Cries to Thee, lest brute Power be increased,
Till that o'ergrown Barbarian in the East
Transgress his ample bound to some new crown:—
Cries to Thee, "Lord, how long shall these things be?
How long shall the icy-hearted Muscovite
Oppress the region?" Us, O Just and Good,
Forgive, who smiled when she was torn in three;
Us, who stand now, when we should aid the right—
A matter to be wept with tears of blood!

———◇◇◇———

SONNET.

AS when with downcast eyes we muse and brood,
And ebb into a former life, or seem
To lapse far back in a confusèd dream
To states of mystical similitude;

If one but speaks or hems or stirs his chair,
Ever the wonder waxeth more and more,
So that we say, "All this hath been before,
All this hath been, I know not when or where."
So, friend, when first I looked upon your face,
Our thought gave answer, each to each, so true,
Opposed mirrors each reflecting each—
Altho' I knew not in what time or place,
Methought that I had often met with you,
And each had lived in the other's mind and speech.

———◇◇◇———

ENGLAND AND AMERICA IN 1782.

O THOU, that sendest out the man
To rule by land and sea,
Strong mother of a Lion-line,
Be proud of those strong sons of thine
Who wrench'd their rights from thee!

What wonder, if in noble heat
Those men thine arms withstood,
Retaught the lesson thou hadst taught,
And in thy spirit with thee fought—
Who sprang from English blood!

But Thou rejoice with liberal joy,
Lift up thy rocky face,
And shatter, when the storms are black,
In many a streaming torrent back,
The seas that shock thy base!

Whatever harmonies of law
The growing world assume,
Thy work is thine—The single note
From that deep chord which Hampden smote
Will vibrate to the doom.

———◇◇◇———

O DARLING ROOM.

I.

O DARLING room, my heart's delight
Dear room, the apple of my sight,
With thy two couches soft and white,
There is no room so exquisite,
No little room so warm and bright,
Wherein to read, wherein to write.

II.

For I the Nonnenwerth have seen,
And Oberwinter's vineyards green,
Musical Lurlei: and between
The hills to Bingen have I been,
Bingen in Darmstadt, where the Rhene
Curves toward Mentz, a woody scene.

III.

Yet never did there meet my sight,
In any town to left or right,
A little room so exquisite,
With two such couches, soft and white;
Not any room so warm and bright,
Wherein to read, wherein to write.

———◇◇◇———

TO CHRISTOPHER NORTH.

YOU did late review my lays,
Crusty Christopher;
You did mingle blame and praise,
Rusty Christopher.
When I learnt from whom it came,
I forgave you all the blame,
Musty Christopher;
I could not forgive the praise,
Fusty Christopher.

OCCASIONAL POEMS.

NO MORE.*

Oh sad *No More!* Oh sweet *No More!*
  Oh strange *No More!*
By a mossed brookbank on a stone
I smelt a wildweed flower alone;
There was a ringing in my ears,
  And both my eyes gushed out with tears.
Surely all pleasant things had gone before,
Lowburied fathom deep beneath with thee, No More!

---- ----

ANACREONTICS.

With roses muskybreathed,
And drooping daffodilly,
And silverleaved lily,
And ivy darkly-wreathed.
I wove a crown before her,
For her I love so dearly,
A garland for Lenora.
With a silken cord I bound it.
Lenora, laughing clearly
A light and thrilling laughter,
About her forehead wound it,
And loved me ever after.

---- ----

A FRAGMENT.

Where is the Giant of the Sun, which stood
In the midnoon the glory of old Rhodes,
A perfect Idol with profulgent brows
Farsheening down the purple seas to those
Who sailed from Mizraim underneath the star
Named of the Dragon—and between whose limbs
Of brassy vastness broadblown Argosies
Drave into haven? Yet endure unscathed
Of changeful cycles the great Pyramids
Broadbased amid the fleeting sands, and sloped
Into the slumbrous summer noon; but where,
Mysterious Egypt, are thine obelisks
Graven with gorgeous emblems undiscerned?
Thy placid Sphinxes brooding o'er the Nile?
Thy shadowing Idols in the solitudes.
Awful Memnonian countenances calm
Looking athwart the burning flats, far off
Seen by the highnecked camel on the verge
Journeying southward? Where are thy monuments
Piled by the strong and sunborn Anakim
Over their crowned brethren On and Oph?
Thy Memnon when his peaceful lips are kist
With earliest rays, that from his mother's eyes
Flow over the Arabian bay, no more
Breathes low into the charmed ears of morn
Clear melody flattering the crisped Nile   [down;
By columned Thebes. Old Memphis hath gone
The Pharoahs are no more: somewhere in death
They sleep with staring eyes and gilded lips,
Wrapped round with spiced cerements in old grots
Rockhewn and sealed for ever.

*This and the two following poems are from the *Gem,* a literary
annual for 1831.

SONNET.*

Me my own fate to lasting sorrow doometh:
  Thy woes are birds of passage, transitory:
  Thy spirit, circled with a living glory,
In summer still a summer joy resumeth.
Alone my hopeless melancholy gloometh,
  Like a lone cypress, through the twilight hoary,
From an old garden where no flower bloometh,
  One cypress on an island promontory.
But yet my lonely spirit follows thine,
  As round the rolling earth night follows day:
But yet thy lights on my horizon shine
  Into my night, when thou art far away
I am so dark, alas! and thou so bright,
When we two meet there's never perfect light.

---- ----

SONNET.*

Check every outflash, every ruder sally
  Of thought and speech; speak low and give up
    wholly
Thy spirit to mild-minded melancholy;
This is the place. Through yonder poplar valley
  Below the blue-green river windeth slowly;
But in the middle of the sombre valley
The crispèd waters whisper musically,
  And all the haunted place is dark and holy.
The nightingale, with long and low preamble,
  Warbled from yonder knoll of solemn larches,
  And in and out the woodbine's flowery arches
The summer midges wove their wanton gambol
  And all the white-stemmed pinewood slept above—
When in this valley first I told my love.

---- ----

THE SKIPPING-ROPE.†

Sure never yet was Antelope
  Could skip so lightly by.
Stand off, or else my skipping-rope
  Will hit you in the eye.
How lightly whirls the skipping-rope!
  How fairy-like you fly!
Go, get you gone, you muse and mope—
  I hate that silly sigh.
Nay, dearest, teach me how to hope,
  Or tell me how to die.
There, take it, take my skipping-rope,
  And hang yourself thereby.

---- ----

THE NEW TIMON AND THE POETS.‡

We know him, out of Shakspeare's art,
  And those fine curses which he spoke;
The old Timon, with his noble heart,
  That, strongly loathing, greatly broke.

* Friendship's Offering, 1833.
† Omitted from the edition of 1842.
‡ Published in Punch, Feb. 1846, signed "Alcibiades."

So died the Old: here comes the New.
    Regard him: a familiar face:
I thought we knew him: What, it's you,
    The padded man—that wears the stays—

Who killed the girls and thrilled the boys
    With dandy pathos when you wrote!
A Lion, you, that made a noise,
    And shook a mane en papillotes.

And once you tried the Muses too:
    You failed, Sir: therefore now you turn,
To fall on those who are to you
    As Captain is to Subaltern.

But men of long-enduring hopes,
    And careless what this hour may bring,
Can pardon little would-be Popes
    And Brummels, when they try to sting.

An Artist, Sir, should rest in Art,
    And wave a little of his claim;
To have the deep Poetic heart
    Is more than all poetic fame.

But you, Sir, you are hard to please;
    You never look but half content:
Nor like a gentleman at ease,
    With moral breadth of temperament.

And what with spites and what with fears,
    You can not let a body be:
It's always ringing in your ears,
    "They call this man as good as me."

What profits now to understand
    The merits of a spotless shirt—
A dapper boot—a little hand—
    If half the little soul is dirt?

You talk of tinsel! why, we see
    The old mark of rouge upon your cheeks.
You prate of Nature! you are he
    That spilt his life about the cliques.

A Timon you! Nay, nay, for shame:
    It looks too arrogant a jest—
The fierce old man—to take his name,
    You bandbox. Off, and let him rest.

————◇————

LITERARY SQUABBLES.*

Ah, God! the petty fools of rhyme,
    That shriek and sweat in pigmy wars
Before the stony face of Time,
    And look'd at by the silent stars;—

That hate each other for a song,
    And do their little best to bite,
That pinch their brothers in the throng,
    And scratch the very dead for spite;—

And strive to make an inch of room
    For their sweet selves, and can not hear
The sullen Lethe rolling down
    On them and theirs, and all things here;—

When one small touch of Charity
    Could lift them nearer Godlike State,
Than if the crowded Orb should cry
    Like those that cried Diana great.

And I too talk, and lose the touch
    I talk of. Surely, after all,
The noblest answer unto such
    Is kindly silence when they bawl.

* Punch, March 7, 1846, signed "Alcibiades."

STANZAS.*

What time I wasted youthful hours,
One of the shining winged powers,
Show'd me vast cliffs with crown of towers

As towards the gracious light I bow'd,
They seem'd high palaces and proud,
Hid now and then with sliding cloud.

He said, "The labor is not small;
Yet winds the pathway free to all:—
Take care thou dost not fear to fall!"

————◇————

SONNET

TO WILLIAM CHARLES MACREADY.†

Farewell, Macready, since to-night we part.
    Full-handed thunders often have confest
    Thy power, well-used to move the public breast.
We thank thee with one voice, and from the heart
Farewell, Macready: since this night we part.
    Go, take thine honors home: rank with the best,
    Garrick, and stateller Kemble, and the rest
Who made a nation purer thro' their art.
Thine is it, that our Drama did not die,
    Nor flicker down to brainless pantomime,
    And those gilt gauds men-children swarm to see.
Farewell, Macready; moral, grave, sublime.
Our Shakspeare's bland and universal eye   [thee.
    Dwells pleased, thro' twice a hundred years, on

————◇————

BRITONS, GUARD YOUR OWN.‡

Rise, Britons, rise, if manhood be not dead,
The world's last tempest darkens overhead,
        The Pope has bless'd him;
        The Church caress'd him:
He triumphs; may be we shall stand alone.
        Britons, guard your own.

His ruthless host is bought with plunder'd gold,
By lying priests the peasants' votes controll'd.
        All freedom vanish'd,
        The true men banish'd,
He triumphs: may be we shall stand alone.
        Britons, guard your own.

Peace-lovers we—sweet Peace we all desire—
Peace-lovers we—but who can trust a liar?—
        Peace-lovers, haters
        Of shameless traitors,
We hate not France, but this man's heart of stone
        Britons, guard your own.

We hate not France, but France has lost her voice.
This man is France, the man they call her choice.
        By tricks and spying,
        By craft and lying,
And murder was her freedom overthrown.
        Britons, guard your own.

"Vive l'Empereur" may follow bye and bye;
"God save the Queen" is here a truer cry.
        God save the Nation,
        The toleration,
And the free speech that makes a Briton known.
        Britons, guard your own.

Rome's dearest daughter now is captive France,
The Jesuit laughs, and reckoning on his chance,

* The Keepsake, 1851.
† Read by Mr. John Forster at a dinner given to Mr. Macready
March 1, 1851, on his retirement from the stage.
‡ The Examiner, 1852.

Would unrelenting,
Kill all dissenting,
Till we were left to fight for truth alone.
Britons, guard your own.

Call home your ships across Biscayan tides,
To blow the battle from their oaken sides.
Why waste they yonder
Their idle thunder?
Why stay they there to guard a foreign throne?
Seamen, guard your own.

We were the best of marksmen long ago,
We won old battles with our strength, the bow.
Now practice, yeomen,
Like those bowmen,
Till your balls fly as their shafts have flown.
Yeomen, guard your own.

His soldier-ridden Highness might incline
To take Sardinia, Belgium, or the Rhine:
Shall we stand idle,
Nor seek to bridle
His rude aggressions, till we stand alone?
Make their cause your own.

Should he land here, and for one hour prevail,
There must no man go back to bear the tale:
No man to bear it—
Swear it! we swear it!
Although we fight the banded world alone,
We swear to guard our own.

———◁○▷———

THE THIRD OF FEBRUARY, 1852.*

My lords, we heard you speak; you told us all
That England's honest censure went too far;
That our free press should cease to brawl,
Not sting the fiery Frenchman into war.
It was an ancient privilege, my lords,
To fling whate'er we felt, not fearing, into words.

We love not this French God, this child of Hell,
Wild War, who breaks the converse of the wise;
But though we love kind Peace so well,
We dare not, e'en by silence, sanction lies.
It might safe be our censures to withdraw;
And yet, my lords, not well; there is a higher law.

As long as we remain, we must speak free,
Though all the storm of Europe on us break:
No little German state are we,
But the one voice in Europe: we must speak;
That if to-night our greatness were struck dead,
There might remain some record of the things we
    said.

If you be fearful, then must we be bold.
Our Britain can not salve a tyrant o'er.
Better the waste Atlantic roil'd
On her and us and ours forevermore.
What! have we fought for freedom from our prime,
At last to dodge and palter with a public crime?

Shall we fear him? our own we never feared.
From our first Charles by force we wrung our
    claims,
Prick'd by the Papal spur, we rear'd,
And flung the burthen of the second James.
I say we never fear'd! and as for these,   [seas.
We broke them on the land, we drove them on the

And you, my lords, you make the people muse,
In doubt if you be of our Barons' breed—

* The Examiner, 1852, and signed " Merlin."

Were those your sires who fought at Lewes?
Is this the manly strain of Runnymede?
O fall'n nobility, that, overawed,
Would lisp in honey'd whispers of this monstrous
    fraud.

We feel, at least, that silence here were sin.
Not ours the fault if we have feeble hosts—
If easy patrons of their kin
Have left the last free race with naked coasts!
They knew the precious things they had to guard:
For us, we will not spare the tyrant one hard word.

Though niggard throats of Manchester may bawl,
What England was, shall her true sons forget?
We are not cotton-spinners all,
But some love England, and her honor yet.
And these in our Thermopylæ shall stand,
And hold against the world the honor of the land.

———◁○▷———

HANDS ALL ROUND.

First drink a health, this solemn night,
    A health to England, every guest;
That man's the best cosmopolite
    Who loves his native country best.
May Freedom's oak for ever live
    With stronger life from day to day;
That man's the best Conservative
    Who lops the mouldered branch away.
            Hands all round!
God the tyrant's hope confound!
To this great cause of Freedom drink, my friends,
    And the great name of England, round and round.

A health to Europe's honest men!
    Heaven guard them from her tyrants' jails!
From wronged Poerio's noisome den,
    From ironed limbs and tortured nails!
We curse the crimes of southern kings,
    The Russian whips and Austrian rods—
We likewise have our evil things;
    Too much we make our Ledgers, Gods.
            Yet hands all round!
God the tyrant's cause confound!
To Europe's better health we drink, my friends,
    And the great name of England, round and round!

What health to France, if France be she,
    Whom martial progress only charms?
Yet tell her—better to be free
    Than vanquish all the world in arms.
Her frantic city's flashing heats
    But fire, to blast, the hopes of men.
Why change the titles of your streets?
    You fools, you'll want them all again.
            Hands all round!
God the tyrant's cause confound!
To France, the wiser France, we drink, my friends,
    And the great name of England, round and round

Gigantic daughter of the West,
    We drink to thee across the flood,
We know thee and we love thee best,
    For art thou not of British blood?
Should war's mad blast again be blown,
    Permit not thou the tyrant powers
To fight thy mother here alone.
    But let thy broadsides roar with ours.
            Hands all round!
God the tyrant's cause confound!
To our dear kinsmen of the West, my friends,
    And the great name of England, round and round

O rise, our strong Atlantic sons,
    When war against our freedom springs!

O speak to Europe through your guns!
  They *can* be understood by kings.
You must not mix our Queen with those
  That wish to keep their people fools;
Our freedom's foemen are her foes,
  She comprehends the race she rules.
      Hands all round!
God the tyrant's cause confound!
To our dear kinsman in the West, my friends,
  And the great name of England, round and round.

───⟫⟨───

THE WAR.

There is a sound of thunder afar,
  Storm in the South that darkens the day,
Storm of battle and thunder of war,
  Well, if it do not roll our way.
    Form! form! Riflemen, form!
    Ready, be ready to meet the storm!
    Riflemen, riflemen, riflemen, form!

Be not deaf to the sound that warns!
  Be not gull'd by a despot's plea!
Are figs of thistles, or grapes of thorns?
  How should a despot set men free?
    Form! form! Riflemen, form!
    Ready, be ready to meet the storm!
    Riflemen, riflemen, riflemen, form!

Let your Reforms for a moment go,
  Look to your butts and take good aims.
Better a rotten borough or so,
  Than a rotten fleet or a city in flames!
    Form! form! Riflemen, form!
    Ready, be ready to meet the storm!
    Riflemen, riflemen, riflemen, form!

Form, be ready to do or die!
  Form in Freedom's name and the Queen's!
True, that we have a faithful ally,
  But only the Devil knows what he means.
    Form! form! Riflemen, form!
    Ready, be ready to meet the storm!
    Riflemen, riflemen, riflemen, form!

───⟫⟨───

1865–1866.

I stood on a tower in the wet.
And New Year and Old Year met,
And winds were roaring and blowing;
And I said, "O years that meet in tears,
Have ye aught that is worth the knowing?
Science enough and exploring,
Wanderers coming and going,
Matter enough for deploring,
But aught that is worth the knowing?"
Seas at my feet were flowing,
Waves on the shingle pouring,
Old Year roaring and blowing,
And New Year blowing and roaring.

───⟫⟨───

ON A SPITEFUL LETTER.

Here, it is here—the close of the year,
  And with it a spiteful letter.
My fame in song has done him much wrong,
  For himself has done much better.

O foolish bard, is your lot so hard,
  If men neglect your pages?
I think not much of yours or of mine:
  I hear the roll of the ages.

This fall'n leaf, isn't fame as brief?
  My rhymes may have been the stronger.
Yet hate me not, but abide your lot;
  I last but a moment longer.

O faded leaf, isn't fame as brief?
  What room is here for a hater?
Yet the yellow leaf hates the greener leaf,
  For it hangs one moment later.

Greater than I—isn't that your cry?
  And I shall live to see it.
Well, if it be so, so it is, you know;
  And if it be so—so be it!

O summer leaf, isn't Life as brief?
  But this is the time of hollies.
And my heart, my heart is an evergreen:
  I hate the spites and the follies.

───⟫⟨───

ALEXANDER.

Warrior of God, whose strong right arm debased
The throne of Persia, when her Satrap bled
At Issus by the Syrian gates, or fled
Beyond the Memnian naphtha-pits, disgraced
For ever—thee (thy pathway sand-erased)
Gliding with equal crowns two serpents led
Joyful to that palm-planted fountain-fed
Ammonian Oasis in the waste.
There in a silent shade of laurel brown
Apart the Chamian Oracle divine
Shelter'd his unapproached mysteries:
High things were spoken there, unhanded down;
Only they saw thee from the secret shrine
Returning with hot cheek and kindled eyes.

───⟫⟨───

THE BRIDESMAID.

O bridesmaid, ere the happy knot was tied,
Thine eyes so wept that they could hardly see;
Thy sister smiled and said, "No tears for me!
A happy bridesmaid makes a happy bride."
And then, the couple standing side by side,
Love lighted down between them full of glee,
And over his left shoulder laugh'd at thee,
"O happy bridesmaid, make a happy bride."
And all at once a pleasant truth I learn'd,
For while the tender service made thee weep,
I loved thee for the tear thou couldst not hide,
And prest thy hand, and knew the press return'd,
And thought, "My life is sick of single sleep:
O happy bridesmaid, make a happy bride!"

───⟫⟨───

═══════════════

I.

My life is full of weary days,
  But good things have not kept aloof,
  Nor wander'd into other ways:
I have not lack'd thy mild reproof,
Nor golden largess of thy praise.

And now shake hands across the brink,
  Of that deep grave to which I go:
Shake hands once more: I cannot sink
  So far—far down, but I shall know
Thy voice, and answer from below.

II.

When in the darkness over me
  The four-handed mole shall scrape,
Plant thou no dusky cypress-tree,
  Nor wreathe thy cap with doleful crape,
  But pledge me in the flowing grape.

And when the sappy field and wood
  Grow green beneath the showery gray,
And rugged barks begin to bud,
  And thro' damp holts new-flush'd with may,
  Ring sudden scritches of the jay,

Then let wise Nature work her will,
  And on my clay her darnel grow;
Come only, when the days are still,
  And at my headstone whisper low,
  And tell me if the woodbines blow.

—⊰⊱—

SONNET.*

There are three things which fill my heart with sighs,
And steep my soul in laughter (when I view
Fair maiden-forms moving like melodies)—
Dimples, roselips, and eyes of any hue.
There are three things beneath the blessed skies
For which I live—black eyes and brown and blue:
I hold them all most dear; but oh! black eyes,
I live and die, and only die in you.
Of late such eyes looked at me—while I mused,
At sunset, underneath a shadowy plane.
In old Bayona nigh the southern sea—
From an half-open lattice looked at *me*.
I saw no more—only those eyes—confused
And dazzled to the heart with glorious pain.

ADDITIONAL VERSES

To "God Save the Queen!" written for the marriage of the Princess
Royal of England with the Crown Prince of Prussia, Jan. 25, 1858.

God bless our Prince and Bride!
God keep their lands allied,
  God save the Queen!
Clothe them with righteousness,
Crown them with happiness,
Them with all blessings bless,
  God save the Queen!

Fair fall this hallow'd hour,
Farewell, our England's flower,
  God save the Queen!
Farewell, first rose of May!
Let both the peoples say,
God bless thy marriage-day,
  God bless the Queen!

—⊰⊱—

SONNET ON CAMBRIDGE UNIVERSITY.

Therefore your Halls, your ancient Colleges,
Your portals statued with old kings and queens,
Your gardens, myriad-volumed libraries,
Wax-lighted chapels, and rich carven screens,
Your doctors, and your proctors, and your deans
Shall not avail you, when the Day-beam sports
New-risen o'er awaken'd Albion—No!
Nor yet your solemn organ-pipes that blow
Melodious thunders thro' your vacant courts
At morn and eve--because your manner sorts
Not with this age wherefrom ye stand apart—
Because the lips of little children preach
Against you, you that do profess to teach
And teach us nothing, feeding not the heart.

—⊰⊱—

LINES.†

Here often, when a child, I lay reclined,
  I took delight in this locality.
Here stood the infant Ilion of the mind,
  And here the Grecian ships did seem to be.
And here again I come, and only find
  The drain-cut levels of the marshy lea,—
Gray sandbanks, and pale sunsets,—dreary wind,
  Dim shores, dense rains, and heavy-clouded sea!

---

* Yorkshire Literary Annual, 1832.   † Manchester Athenæum Album, 1850.

18

DRAMATIS PERSONÆ.

—◇✕◇—

QUEEN MARY.

PHILIP (King of Naples and Sicily, afterward King of Spain).

THE PRINCESS ELIZABETH.

REGINALD POLE (Cardinal and Papal Legate).

SIMON RENARD (Spanish Ambassador).

LE SIEUR DE NOAILLES (French Ambassador).

THOMAS CRANMER (Archbishop of Canterbury).

SIR NICHOLAS HEATH (Archbishop of York; Lord Chancellor after Gardiner).

EDWARD COURTENAY (Earl of Devon).

LORD WILLIAM HOWARD (afterward Lord Howard and Lord High Admiral).

LORD WILLIAMS OF THAME.

LORD PAGET.

LORD PETRE.

STEPHEN GARDINER (Bishop of Winchester and Lord Chancellor).

EDMUND BONNER (Bishop of London).

THOMAS THIRLBY (Bishop of Ely).

SIR THOMAS WYATT }
SIR THOMAS STAFFORD } (Insurrectionary Leaders).

SIR RALPH BAGENHALL.

SIR ROBERT SOUTHWELL.

SIR HENRY BEDINGFIELD.

SIR WILLIAM CECIL.

SIR THOMAS WHITE (Lord Mayor of London).

THE DUKE OF ALVA }
THE COUNT DE FERIA } (attending on Philip).

PETER MARTYR.

FATHER COLE.

FATHER BOURNE.

VILLA GARCIA.

SOTO.

CAPTAIN BRETT }
ANTONY KNYVETT } (Adherents of Wyatt).

PETERS (Gentleman of Lord Howard).

ROGER (Servant to Noailles).

WILLIAM (Servant to Wyatt).

STEWARD OF HOUSEHOLD to the Princess Elizabeth.

OLD NOKES and NOKES.

MARCHIONESS OF EXETER (Mother of Courtenay).

LADY CLARENCE }
LADY MAGDALEN DACRES } (Ladies in waiting to the Queen).
ALICE }

MAID OF HONOR to the Princess Elizabeth.

JOAN }
TIB } (Two Country Wives).

Lords and other Attendants, Members of the Privy Council, Members of Parliament, two Gentlemen, Aldermen, Citizens, Peasants, Ushers, Messengers, Guards, Pages, etc.

QUEEN MARY.

ACT I.

SCENE I.—ALDGATE RICHLY DECORATED.

CROWD. MARSHALMEN.

Marshalman. Stand back, keep a clear lane. When will her Majesty pass, sayst thou? why, now, even now; wherefore draw back your heads and your horns before I break them, and make what noise you will with your tongues, so it be not treason. Long live Queen Mary, the lawful and legitimate daughter of Harry the Eighth! Shout, knaves!

Citizens. Long live Queen Mary!

First Citizen. That's a hard word, legitimate; what does it mean?

Second Citizen. It means a bastard.

Third Citizen. Nay, it means true-born.

First Citizen. Why, didn't the Parliament make her a bastard?

Second Citizen. No; it was the Lady Elizabeth.

Third Citizen. That was after, man; that was after.

First Citizen. Then which is the bastard?

Second Citizen. Troth, they be both bastards by Act of Parliament and Council.

Third Citizen. Ay, the Parliament can make every true-born man of us a bastard. Old Nokes, can't it make thee a bastard? thou shouldst know, for thou art as white as three Christmasses.

Old Nokes (dreamily). Who's a-passing? King Edward or King Richard?

Third Citizen. No, old Nokes.

Old Nokes. It's Harry!

Third Citizen. It's Queen Mary.

Old Nokes. The blessed Mary's a-passing!

[*Falls on his knees.*

Nokes. Let father alone, my masters! he's past your questioning.

Third Citizen. Answer thou for him, then! thou art 'no such cockerel thyself, for thou was born i' the tail end of old Harry the Seventh.

Nokes. Eh! that was afore bastard-making began. I was born true man at five in the forenoon i' the tail of old Harry, and so they can't make me a bastard.

Third Citizen. But if Parliament can make the Queen a bastard, why, it follows all the more that they can make thee one, who art fray'd i' the knees, and out at elbow, and bald o' the back, and bursten at the toes, and down at heels.

Nokes. I was born of a true man and a ring'd wife, and I can't argue upon it; but I and my old woman 'ud burn upon it, that would we.

Marshalman. What are you cackling of bastardy under the Queen's own nose? I'll have you flogg'd and burnt too, by the Rood I will!

First Citizen. He swears by the Rood. Whew!

Second Citizen. Hark! the trumpets.

[*The Procession passes, MARY and ELIZABETH riding side by side, and disappears under the gate.*

Citizens. Long live Queen Mary! Down with all traitors! God save her Grace; and death to Northumberland! [*Exeunt.*

Manent TWO GENTLEMEN.

First Gentleman. By God's light, a noble creature, right royal.

Second Gentleman. She looks comelier than ordinary to-day; but to my mind the Lady Elizabeth is the more noble and royal.

First Gentleman. I mean the Lady Elizabeth. Did you hear (I have a daughter in her service who reported it) that she met the Queen at Wanstead with five hundred horse, and the Queen (tho' some say they be much divided) took her hand, called her sweet sister, and kiss'd not her alone, but all the ladies of her following.

Second Gentleman. Ay, that was in her hour of joy, there will be plenty to sunder and unsister them again; this Gardiner for one, who is to be made Lord Chancellor, and will pounce like a wild beast out of his cage to worry Cranmer.

First Gentleman. And furthermore, my daughter said that when there rose a talk of the late rebellion, she spoke even of Northumberland pitifully, and of the good Lady Jane as a poor innocent child who had but obeyed her father; and furthermore, she said that no one in her time should be burnt for heresy.

Second Gentleman. Well, sir, I look for happy times.

First Gentleman. There is but one thing against them. I know not if you know.

Second Gentleman. I suppose you touch upon the rumor that Charles, the master of the world, has offer'd her his son Philip, the Pope, and the Devil. I trust it is but a rumor.

First Gentleman. She is going now to the Tower to loose the prisoners there, and among them Courtenay, to be made Earl of Devon, of royal blood, of splendid feature, whom the council and all her people wish her to marry. May it be so, for we are many of us Catholics, but few Papists, and the Hot Gospellers will go mad upon it.

Second Gentleman. Was she not betroth'd in her babyhood to the Great Emperor himself?

First Gentleman. Ay, but he's too old.

Second Gentleman. And again to her cousin Reginald Pole, now Cardinal, but I hear that he too is full of aches and broken before his day.

First Gentleman. O, the Pope could dispense with his Cardinalate, and his achage, and his breakage, if that were all: but will you not follow the procession?

Second Gentleman. No, I have seen enough for this day.

First Gentleman. Well, I shall follow: if I can get near enough I shall judge with my own eyes whether her Grace incline to this splendid scion of Plantagenet. [*Exeunt.*

SCENE II.—A ROOM IN LAMBETH PALACE.

CRANMER.

Cranmer. To Strasburg, Antwerp, Frankfort, Zurich, Worms,
Geneva, Basle—our bishops from their sees
Or fled, they say, or flying—Poinet, Barlow,
Bale, Scory, Coverdale; besides the Deans
Of Christchurch, Durham, Exeter, and Wells—
Ailmer and Bullingham, and hundreds more;
So they report: I shall be left alone.
No: Hooper, Ridley, Latimer will not fly.

Enter Peter Martyr.

Peter Martyr. Fly, Cranmer! were there nothing
else, your name
Stands first of those who sign'd the Letters Patent
That gave her royal crown to Lady Jane.
Cranmer. Stand first it may, but it was written
last:
Those that are now her Privy Council, sign'd
Before me: nay, the judges had pronounced
That our young Edward might bequeath the crown
Of England, putting by his father's will.
Yet I stood out, till Edward sent for me.
The wan boy-king, with his fast-fading eyes
Fixt hard on mine, his frail transparent hand,
Damp with the sweat of death, and griping mine,
Whisper'd me, if I loved him, not to yield
His Church of England to the Papal wolf
And Mary; then I could no more—I sign'd.
Nay, for bare shame of inconsistency,
She cannot pass her traitor council by,
To make me headless.
Peter Martyr. That might be forgiven.
I tell you, fly, my Lord. You do not own
The bodily presence in the Eucharist,
Their wafer and perpetual sacrifice:
Your creed will be your death.
Cranmer. Step after step,
Thro' many voices crying right and left,
Have I climb'd back into the primal church,
And stand within the porch, and Christ with me:
My flight were such a scandal to the faith,
The downfall of so many simple souls,
I dare not leave my post.
Peter Martyr. But you divorced
Queen Catharine and her father; hence, her hate
Will burn till you are burn'd.
Cranmer. I can not help it.
The Canonists and Schoolmen were with me.
"Thou shalt not wed thy brother's wife."—'Tis writ-
ten,
"They shall be childless." True, Mary was born,
But France would not accept her for a bride
As being born from incest; and this wrought
Upon the King; and child by child, you know,
Were momentary sparkles out as quick
Almost as kindled; and he brought his doubts
And fears to me. Peter, I'll swear for him
He *did* believe the bond incestuous.
But wherefore am I trenching on the time
That should already have seen your steps a mile
From me and Lambeth? God be with you! Go.
Peter Martyr. Ah, but how fierce a letter you wrote
against
Their superstition when they slander'd you
For setting up a mass at Canterbury
To please the Queen.
Cranmer. It was a wheedling monk
Set up the mass.
Peter Martyr. I know it, my good Lord.
But you so bubbled over with hot terms
Of Satan, liars, blasphemy, Antichrist,
She never will forgive you. Fly, my Lord, fly!
Cranmer. I wrote it, and God grant me power to
burn!
Peter Martyr. They have given me a safe conduct:
for all that
I dare not stay. I fear, I fear, I see you,
Dear friend, for the last time; farewell, and fly.
Cranmer. Fly and farewell, and let me die the
death [*Exit* Peter Martyr.

Enter Old Servant.

O, kind and gentle master, the Queen's Officers
Are here in force to take you to the Tower.
Cranmer. Ay, gentle friend, admit them. I will
go.
I thank my God it is too late to fly. [*Exeunt.*

SCENE III.—ST. PAUL'S CROSS.

Father Bourne *in the pulpit. A crowd.* Marchioness of Exeter, Courtenay. *The* Sieur de Noailles *and his man* Roger *in front of the stage.*
Hubbub.

Noailles. Hast thou let fall those papers in the palace?
Roger. Ay, sir.
Noailles. "There will be no peace for Mary till Eliz-
abeth lose her head."
Roger. Ay, sir.
Noailles. And the other. "Long live Elizabeth the
Queen!"
Roger. Ay, sir; she needs must tread upon them.
Noailles. Well.
These beastly swine make such a grunting here,
I cannot catch what Father Bourne is saying.
Roger. Quiet a moment, my masters; hear what the
shaveling has to say for himself.
Crowd. Hush—hear.
Bourne. —and so this unhappy land, long divided in
itself, and sever'd from the faith, will return into the
one true fold, seeing that our gracious Virgin Queen
hath—
Crowd. No pope! no pope!
Roger (to those about him, mimicking Bourne).
—hath sent for the holy legate of the holy father the
Pope, Cardinal Pole, to give us all that holy absolu-
tion which—
First Citizen. Old Bourne to the life!
Second Citizen. Holy Absolution! holy Inquisition!
Third Citizen. Down with the Papist! [*Hubbub.*
Bourne. —and now that your good bishop, Bonner,
who hath lain so long under bonds for the faith—
[*Hubbub.*
Noailles. Friend Roger, steal thou in among the
crowd,
And get the swine to shout Elizabeth.
You gray old Gospeller, sour as midwinter,
Begin with him.
Roger (goes). By the mass, old friend, we'll have no
pope here while the Lady Elizabeth lives.
Gospeller. Art thou of the true faith, fellow, that
swearest by the mass?
Roger. Ay, that am I, new converted, but the old
leaven sticks to my tongue yet.
First Citizen. He says right; by the mass, we'll have
no mass here.
Voices of the Crowd. Peace! hear him; let his own
words damn the Papist. From thine own mouth I
judge thee—tear him down.
Bourne. —and since our Gracious Queen, let me call
her our second Virgin Mary, hath begun to re-edify
the true temple—
First Citizen. Virgin Mary! we'll have no virgins
here—we'll have the Lady Elizabeth!
[*Swords are drawn, a knife is hurled, and sticks in
the pulpit. The mob throng to the pulpit stairs.*
Marchioness of Exeter. Son Courtenay, wilt thou see
the holy father
Murder'd before thy face? Up, son, and save him!
They love thee, and thou canst not come to harm.
Courtenay (in the pulpit). Shame, shame, my mas-
ters! are you English-born,
And set yourselves by hundreds against one?
Crowd. A Courtenay! a Courtenay!
[*A train of Spanish servants crosses at the back
of the stage.*
Noailles. These birds of passage come before their
time:
Stave off the crowd upon the Spaniard there.
Roger. My masters, yonder's fatter game for you
Than this old gaping gurgoyle: look you there—
The Prince of Spain coming to wed our Queen!
After him, boys! and pelt him from the city.
[*They seize stones and follow the Spaniards. Exe-
unt on the other side* Marchioness of Exeter *and
Attendants.*

Noailles (to Roger). Stand from me. If Elizabeth lose
her head—
That makes for France.
And if her people, anger'd thereupon,
Arise against her and dethrone the Queen—
That makes for France.
And if I breed confusion anyway—
That makes for France.
    Good-day, my Lord of Devon;
A bold heart yours to beard that raging mob!
Courtenay. My mother said, Go up: and up I went.
I knew they would not do me any wrong,
For I am mighty popular with them, Noailles.
Noailles. You look'd a king.
Courtenay.   Why not? I am king's blood.
Noailles. And in the whirl of change may come to be
one.
Courtenay. Ah!
Noailles. But does your gracious Queen entreat you
king-like?
Courtenay. 'Fore God, I think she entreats me like
a child.
Noailles. You've but a dull life in this Maiden court,
I fear, my Lord.
Courtenay.   A life of nods and yawns.
Noailles. So you would honor my poor house to-
night,
We might enliven you. Divers honest fellows,
The Duke of Suffolk lately freed from prison,
Sir Peter Carew and Sir Thomas Wyatt,
Sir Thomas Stafford, and some more—we play.
Courtenay. At what?
Noailles.   The game of chess.
Courtenay.   The game of chess!
I can play well, and I shall beat you there.
Noailles. Ay, but we play with Henry, King of France,
And certain of his Court.
His Highness makes his moves across the channel,
We answer him with ours, and there are messengers
That go between us.
Courtenay. Why, such a game, sir, were whole years
a playing.
Noailles. Nay; not so long I trust. That all depends
Upon the skill and swiftness of the players.
Courtenay. The King is skilful at it?
Noailles.   Very, my Lord.
Courtenay. And the stakes high?
Noailles.   But not beyond your means.
Courtenay. Well, I'm the first of players. I shall
win.
Noailles. With our advice and in our company,
And so you well attend to the King's moves,
I think you may.
Courtenay.   When do you meet?
Noailles.   To-night.
Courtenay (aside). I will be there; the fellow's at
his tricks—
Deep—I shall fathom him. *(Aloud.)* Good-morning,
Noailles.   [*Exit* COURTENAY.
Noailles. Good-day, my Lord. Strange game of
chess! a King
That with her own pawns plays against a Queen,
Whose play is all to find herself a King.
Ay; but this fine blue-blooded Courtenay seems
Too princely for a pawn. Call him a Knight,
That, with an ass's, not an horse's head,
Skips every way, from levity or from fear.
Well, we shall use him somehow, so that Gardiner
And Simon Renard spy not out our game
Too early. Roger, thinkest thou that any one
Suspected thee to be my man?
Roger.   Not one, sir.
Noailles. No! the disguise was perfect. Let's away!
    [*Exeunt.*

SCENE IV.—LONDON. A ROOM IN THE
PALACE.

ELIZABETH. *Enter* COURTENAY.

Courtenay. So yet am I,
Unless my friends and mirrors lie to me,
A goodlier-looking fellow than this Philip.
Pah!
The Queen is ill advised: shall I turn traitor?
They've almost talk'd me into it: yet the word
Affrights me somewhat: to be such a one
As Harry Bolingbroke hath a lure in it.
Good now, my Lady Queen, tho' by your age,
And by your looks, you are not worth the having,
Yet by your crown you are. [*Seeing* ELIZABETH.
    The Princess there?
If I tried her and la—she's amorous.
Have we not heard of her in Edward's time,
Her freaks and frolics with the late Lord Admiral?
I do believe she'd yield. I should be still
A party in the state; and then, who knows—
Elizabeth. What are you musing on, my Lord of
Devon?
Courtenay. Has not the Queen—
Elizabeth.   Done what, sir?
Courtenay.   —Made you follow
The Lady Suffolk and the Lady Lennox;
You,
The heir presumptive?
Elizabeth.   Why do you ask? you know it.
Courtenay. You needs must bear it hardly.
Elizabeth.   No, indeed!
I am utterly submissive to the Queen.
Courtenay. Well, I was musing upon that; the Queen
Is both my foe and yours: we should be friends.
Elizabeth. My Lord, the hatred of another to us
Is no true bond of friendship.
Courtenay.   Might it not
Be the rough preface of some closer bond?
Elizabeth. My Lord, you late were loosed from out
the Tower,
Where, like a butterfly in a chrysalis,
You spent your life: that broken, out you flutter
Thro' the new world, go zigzag, now would settle
Upon this flower, now that; but all things here
At Court are known: you have solicited
The Queen, and been rejected.
Courtenay.   Flower, she!
Half faded! but you, cousin, are fresh and sweet
As the first flower no bee has ever tried.
Elizabeth. Are you the bee to try me? why, but now
I called you butterfly.
Courtenay.   You did me wrong,
I love not to be called a butterfly:
Why do you call me butterfly?
Elizabeth.   Why do you go so gay then?
Courtenay. Velvet and gold.
This dress was made me as the Earl of Devon
To take my seat in; looks it not right royal?
Elizabeth. So royal that the Queen forbade you
wearing it.
Courtenay. I wear it then to spite her.
Elizabeth. My Lord, my Lord:
I see you in the Tower again. Her Majesty
Hears you affect the Prince—prelates kneel to you.—
Courtenay. I am the noblest blood in Europe, Mad-
am,
A Courtenay of Devon, and her cousin.
Elizabeth. She hears you make your boast that after
all
She means to wed you. Folly, my good Lord.
Courtenay. How folly? a great party in the state
Wills me to wed her.
Elizabeth.   Failing her, my Lord,
Doth not as great a party in the state
Will you to wed me?
Courtenay.   Even so, fair lady.

Elizabeth. You know to flatter ladies.

Courtenay.   Nay, I meant
True matters of the heart.

Elizabeth.   My heart, my Lord,
Is no great party in the state as yet.

Courtenay. Great, said you? nay, you shall be great.
  I love you,
Lay my life in your hands. Can you be close?

Elizabeth. Can you, my Lord?

Courtenay.   Close as a miser's casket.
Listen:
The King of France, Noailles the ambassador,
The Duke of Suffolk and Sir Peter Carew,
Sir Thomas Wyatt, I myself, some others,
Have sworn this Spanish marriage shall not be.
If Mary will not hear us—well—conjecture—
Were I in Devon with my wedded bride,
The people there so worship me—Your ear;
You shall be Queen.

Elizabeth.   You speak too low, my Lord;
I cannot hear you.

Courtenay.   I'll repeat it.

Elizabeth.   No!
Stand further off, or you may lose your head.

Courtenay. I have a head to lose for your sweet
  sake.

Elizabeth. Have you, my Lord? Best keep it for
  your own.
Nay, pout not, cousin.
Not many friends are mine, except indeed
Among the many. I believe you mine;
And so you may continue mine, farewell,
And that at once.

Enter MARY, *behind.*

Mary.   Whispering—leagued together
To bar me from my Philip.

Courtenay.   Pray—consider—

Elizabeth (seeing the Queen). Well, that's a noble
  horse of yours, my Lord.
I trust that he will carry you well to-day,
And heal your headache.

Courtenay.   You are wild; what headache?
Heartache, perchance; not headache.

Elizabeth (aside to Courtenay).   Are you blind?
[*Courtenay sees the* QUEEN *and exit. Exit* MARY.

Enter LORD WILLIAM HOWARD.

Howard. Was that my Lord of Devon? Do not you
Be seen in corners with my Lord of Devon.
He hath fallen out of favor with the Queen.
She fears the Lords may side with you and him
Against her marriage; therefore is he dangerous.
And if this Prince of fluff and feather come
To woo you, niece, he is dangerous every way.

Elizabeth. Not very dangerous that way, my good
  uncle.

Howard. But your own state is full of danger here.
The disaffected, heretics, reformers,
Look to you as the one to crown their ends.
Mix not yourself with any plot, I pray you:
Nay, if by chance you hear of any such,
Speak not thereof—no, not to your best friend,
Lest you should be confounded with it. Still—
Perinde ac cadaver—as the priest says,
You know your Latin—quiet as a dead body.
What was my Lord of Devon telling you?

Elizabeth. Whether he told me any thing or not,
I follow your good counsel, gracious uncle.
Quiet as a dead body.

Howard.   You do right well.
I do not care to know; but this I charge you,
Tell Courtenay nothing. The Lord Chancellor
(I count it as a kind of virtue in him,
He hath not many), as a mastiff dog
May love a puppy cur for no more reason
Than that the twain have been tied up together,

Thus Gardiner—for the two were fellow-prisoners
So many years in yon accursed Tower—
Hath taken to this Courtenay. Look to it, niece,
He hath no fence when Gardiner questions him;
All oozes out; yet him—because they know him
The last White Rose, the last Plantagenet
(Nay, there is Cardinal Pole, too), the people
Claim as their natural leader—ay, some say
That you shall marry him, make him King belike.

Elizabeth. Do they say so, good uncle?

Howard.   Ay, good niece!
You should be plain and open with me, niece.
You should not play upon me.

Elizabeth.   No, good uncle.

Enter GARDINER.

Gardiner. The Queen would see your Grace upon
  the moment.

Elizabeth. Why, my Lord Bishop?

Gardiner. I think she means to counsel your withdrawing
To Ashridge, or some other country house.

Elizabeth. Why, my Lord Bishop?

Gardiner. I do but bring the message, know no
  more.
Your Grace will hear her reasons from herself.

Elizabeth. 'Tis mine own wish fulfill'd before the
  word
Was spoken, for in truth I had meant to crave
Permission of her Highness to retire
To Ashridge, and pursue my studies there.

Gardiner. Madam, to have the wish before the
  word
Is man's good Fairy—and the Queen is yours.
I left her with rich jewels in her hand,
Whereof 'tis like enough she means to make
A farewell present to your Grace.

Elizabeth.   My Lord,
I have the jewel of a loyal heart.

Gardiner. I doubt it not, Madam, most loyal.
            [*Bows low and exit.*

Howard.   See,
This comes of parleying with my Lord of Devon.
Well, well, you must obey; and I myself
Believe it will be better for your welfare.
Your time will come.

Elizabeth.   I think my time will come.
Uncle,
I am of sovereign nature, that I know,
Not to be quell'd; and I have felt within me
Stirrings of some great doom when God's just hour
Peals—but this fierce old Gardiner—his big bald-
  ness,
That irritable forelock which he rubs,
His buzzard beak and deep-lucavern'd eyes
Half fright me.

Howard.   You've a bold heart; keep it so.
He cannot touch you save that you turn traitor;
And so take heed I pray you—you are one
Who love that men should smile upon you, niece.
They'd smile you into treason—some of them.

Elizabeth. I spy the rock beneath the smiling
  sea.
But if this Philip, the proud Catholic prince,
And this bald priest, and she that hates me, seek,
In that lone house, to practise on my life,
By poison, fire, shot, stab—

Howard.   They will not, niece.
Mine is the fleet and all the power at sea—
Or will be in a moment. If they dared
To harm you, I would blow this Philip and all
Your trouble to the dogstar and the devil.

Elizabeth. To the Pleiads, uncle; they have lost a
  sister.

Howard. But why say that? what have you done to
  lose her?
Come, come, I will go with you to the Queen.
            [*Exeunt.*

SCENE V.—A ROOM IN THE PALACE.

MARY, *with* PHILIP's *miniature,* ALICE.

Mary (kissing the miniature). Most goodly, king-
like, and an emperor's son,—
A king to be,—is he not noble, girl ?
    Alice. Goodly enough, your Grace, and yet, me-
thinks,
I have seen goodlier.
    Mary. Ay ; some waxen doll
Thy baby eyes have rested on, belike ;
All red and white, the fashion of our land,
But my good mother came (God rest her soul)
Of Spain, and I am Spanish in myself,
And in my likings.
    Alice.   By your Grace's leave
Your royal mother came of Spain, but took
To the English red and white. Your royal father
(For so they say) was all pure lily and rose
In his youth, and like a lady.
    Mary.   O just God !
Sweet mother, you had time and cause enough
To sicken of his lilies and his roses.
Cast off, betray'd, defamed, divorced, forlorn !
And then the King—that traitor past forgiveness,
The false archbishop fawning on him, married
The mother of Elizabeth—a heretic
Ev'n as *she* is ; but God hath sent me here
To take such order with all heretics
That it shall be, before I die, as tho'
My father and my brother had not lived.
What wast thou saying of this Lady Jane,
Now in the Tower ?
    Alice.   Why, Madam, she was passing
Some chapel down in Essex, and with her
Lady Anne Wharton, and the Lady Anne
Bow'd to the Pyx ; but Lady Jane stood up
Stiff as the very backbone of heresy.
And wherefore bow ye not, says Lady Anne,
To him within there who made heaven and earth ?
I cannot, and I dare not, tell your Grace
What Lady Jane replied.
    Mary.   But I will have it.
    Alice. She said—pray pardon me, and pity her—
She hath hearken'd evil counsel—ah ! she said,
The baker made him.
    Mary.   Monstrous ! blasphemous !
She ought to burn. Hence, thou (*Exit* ALICE). No—
        being traitor
Her head will fall : shall it ? she is but a child.
We do not kill the child for doing that
His father whipt him into doing—a head
So full of grace and beauty ! would that mine
Were half as gracious ! O, my lord to be,
My love, for thy sake only.
I am eleven years older than he is.
But will he care for that ?
No, by the Holy Virgin, being noble,
But love me only : then the bastard sprout,
My sister, is far fairer than myself.
Will he be drawn to her ?
No, being of the true faith with myself.
Paget is for him—for to wed with Spain
Would treble England—Gardiner is against him ;
The Council, people, Parliament against him ;
But I will have him ! My hard father hated me ;
My brother rather hated me than loved ;
My sister cowers and hates me. Holy Virgin,
Plead with thy blessed Son ; grant me my prayer ;
Give me my Philip ; and we two will lead
The living waters of the Faith again
Back thro' their widow'd channel here, and watch
The parch'd banks rolling incense, as of old,
To heaven, and kindled with the palms of Christ !

        Enter USHER.

Who waits, sir ?

Usher. Madam, the Lord Chancellor.
    Mary. Bid him come in. (*Enter* GARDINER.) Good-
morning, my good Lord.   [*Exit* USHER.
    Gardiner. That every morning of your Majesty
May be most good, is every morning's prayer
Of your most loyal subject, Stephen Gardiner.
    Mary. Come you to tell me this, my Lord ?
    Gardiner.   And more.
Your people have begun to learn your worth.
Your pious wish to pay King Edward's debts,
Your lavish household curb'd, and the remission
Of half that subsidy levied on the people,
Make all tongues praise and all hearts beat for you.
I'd have you yet more loved : the realm is poor,
The exchequer at neap-ebb : we might withdraw
Part of our garrison at Calais.
    Mary.   Calais !
Our one point on the main, the gate of France !
I am Queen of England : take mine eyes, mine heart,
But do not lose me Calais.
    Gardiner.   Do not fear it.
Of that hereafter. I say your Grace is loved.
That I may keep you thus, who am your friend
And ever faithful counsellor, might I speak ?
    Mary. I can forespeak your speaking. Would I
    marry
Prince Philip, if all England hate him ? That is
Your question, and I front it with another :
Is it England, or a party ? Now, your answer.
    Gardiner. My answer is, I wear beneath my dress
A shirt of mail : my house hath been assaulted,
And when I walk abroad, the populace,
With fingers pointed like so many daggers,
Stab me in fancy, hissing Spain and Philip ;
And when I sleep, a hundred men-at-arms
Guard my poor dreams for England. Men would
        murder me,
Because they think me favorer of this marriage.
    Mary. And that were hard upon you, my Lord
        Chancellor.
    Gardiner. But our young Earl of Devon—
    Mary.   Earl of Devon ?
I freed him from the Tower, placed him at Court ;
I made him Earl of Devon, and—the fool—
He wrecks his health and wealth on courtesans,
And rolls himself in carrion like a dog.
    Gardiner. More like a school-boy that hath broken
        bounds,
Sickening himself with sweets.
    Mary.   I will not hear of him.
Good, then, they will revolt : but I am Tudor,
And shall control them.
    Gardiner.   I will help you, Madam,
Even to the utmost. All the church is grateful.
You have ousted the mock priest, reinstated
The shepherd of St. Peter, raised the Rood again,
And brought us back the mass. I am all thanks
To God and to your Grace : yet I know well,
Your people, and I go with them so far,
Will brook nor Pope nor Spaniard here to play
The tyrant, or in commonwealth or church.
    Mary (showing the picture). Is this the face of one
        who plays the tyrant ?
Peruse it ; is it not goodly, ay, and gentle ?
    Gardiner. Madam, methinks a cold face and a
        haughty.
And when your Highness talks of Courtenay—
Ay, true—a goodly one. I would his life
Were half as goodly (*aside*).
    Mary.   What is that you mutter ?
    Gardiner. Oh, Madam, take it bluntly : marry Phil-
        ip,
And be stepmother of a score of sons !
The prince is known in Spain, in Flanders, ha !
For Philip—
    Mary.   You offend us ; you may leave us.
You see thro' warping glasses.
    Gardiner.   If your Majesty—

Mary. I have sworn upon the body and blood of
Christ
I'll none but Philip.
Gardiner.   Hath your Grace so sworn?
Mary. Ay, Simon Renard knows it.
Gardiner.   News to me!
It then remains for your poor Gardiner,
So you still care to trust him somewhat less
Than Simon Renard, to compose the event
In some such form as least may harm your Grace.
Mary. I'll have the scandal sounded to the mud.
I know it a scandal.
Gardiner.   All my hope is now
It may be found a scandal.
Mary.   You offend us.
Gardiner (*aside*). These princes are like children,
must be physick'd,
The bitter in the sweet. I have lost mine office,
It may be, thro' mine honesty, like a fool.   [*Exit.*

Enter USHER.

Mary. Who waits?
Usher. The ambassador from France, your Grace.
Mary. Bid him come in. Good-morning, Sir de
Noailles.   [*Exit* USHER.
Noailles (*entering*). A happy morning to your Ma\
esty.
Mary. And I should some time have a happy morn-
ing;
I have had none yet. What says the King, your mas-
ter?
Noailles. Madam, my master hears with much alarm
That you may marry Philip, Prince of Spain—
Foreseeing, with whate'er unwillingness,
That if this Philip be the titular king
Of England, and at war with him, your Grace
And kingdom will be suck'd into the war,
Ay, tho' you long for peace: wherefore, my master,
If but to prove your Majesty's good-will,
Would fain have some fresh treaty drawn between
you.
Mary. Why some fresh treaty? wherefore should I
do it?
Sir, if we marry, we shall still maintain
All former treaties with his Majesty.
Our royal word for that! and your good master,
Pray God he do not be the first to break them,
Must be content with that; and so, farewell.
Noailles (*going, returns*). I would your answer had
been other, Madam,
For I foresee dark days.
Mary.   And so do I, sir;
Your master works against me in the dark.
I do believe he help Northumberland
Against me.
Noailles.   Nay, pure phantasy, your Grace.
Why should he move against you?
Mary.   Will you hear why?
Mary of Scotland,—for I have not own'd
My sister, and I will not,—after me
Is heir of England; and my royal father,
To make the crown of Scotland one with ours,
Had mark'd her for my brother Edward's bride
Ay, but your King stole her a babe from Scotland
In order to betroth her to your Dauphin.
See then:
Mary of Scotland, married to your Dauphin,
Would make our England, France;
Mary of England, joining hands with Spain,
Would be too strong for France.
Yea, were there issue born to her, Spain and we,
One crown, might rule the world. There lies your fear.
That is your drift. You play at hide and seek.
Show me your faces!
Noailles.   Madam, I am amazed:
French, I must needs wish all good things for France.
That must be pardon'd me; but I protest
Your Grace's policy hath a farther flight

Than mine into the future. We but seek
Some settled ground for peace to stand upon.
Mary. Well, we will leave all this, sir, to our Council.
Have you seen Philip ever?
Noailles.   Only once.
Mary. Is this like Philip?
Noailles.   Ay, but nobler-looking.
Mary. Hath he the large ability of the Emperor?
Noailles. No, surely.
Mary.   I can make allowance for thee,
Thou speakest of the enemy of thy King.
Noailles. Make no allowance for the naked truth.
He is every way a lesser man than Charles;
Stone-hard, ice-cold — no dash of daring in him.
Mary. If cold, his life is pure.
Noailles.   Why (*smiling*), no, indeed.
Mary. Sayst thou?
Noailles.   A very wanton life indeed (*smiling*).
Mary. Your audience is concluded, sir.
                              [*Exit* NOAILLES.
                              You cannot
Learn a man's nature from his natural foe.

Enter USHER.

Who waits?
Usher.   The ambassador of Spain, your Grace.
                                            [*Exit.*

Enter SIMON RENARD.

Mary. Thou art ever welcome, Simon Renard. Hast
thou
Brought me the letter which thine Emperor promised
Long since, a formal offer of the hand
Of Philip?
Renard. Nay, your Grace, it hath not reach'd me.
I know not wherefore—some mischance of flood,
And broken bridge, or spavin'd horse, or wave
And wind at their old battle; he must have written.
Mary. But Philip never writes me one poor word,
Which in his absence had been all my wealth.
Strange in a wooer!
Renard.   Yet I know the Prince,
So your king-parliament suffer him to land,
Yearns to set foot upon your island shore.
Mary. God change the pebble which his kingly foot
First presses into some more costly stone
Than ever blinded eye. I'll have one mark it
And bring it me. I'll have it burnish'd firelike;
I'll set it round with gold, with pearl, with diamond.
Let the great angel of the church come with him;
Stand on the deck and spread his wings for sail!
God lay the waves and strew the storms at sea,
And here at land among the people. O Renard,
I am much beset, I am almost in despair.
Paget is ours. Gardiner perchance is ours;
But for our heretic Parliament—
Renard.   O Madam,
You fly your thoughts like kites. My master, Charles
Bade you go softly with your heretics here,
Until your throne had ceased to tremble. Then
Spit them like larks, for aught I care. Besides,
When Henry broke the carcass of your church
To pieces, there were many wolves among you
Who dragg'd the scatter'd limbs into their den.
The Pope would have you make them render these;
So would your cousin, Cardinal Pole; ill counsel!
These let them keep at present; stir not yet
This matter of the church lands. At his coming
Your star will rise.
Mary.   My star! a baleful one.
I see but the black night, and hear the wolf.
What star?
Renard.   Your star will be your princely son,
Heir of this England and the Netherlands!
And if your wolf the while should howl for more
We'll dust him from a bag of Spanish gold.
I do believe, I have dusted some already,
That, soon or late, your Parliament is ours

Mary. Why do they talk so foully of your Prince,
Renard?
Renard. The lot of princes. To sit high
Is to be lied about.
Mary. They call him cold,
Haughty, ay, worse.
Renard. Why, doubtless, Philip shows
Some of the bearing of your blue blood—still
All within measure—nay, it well becomes him.
Mary. Hath he the large ability of his father?
Renard. Nay, some believe that he will go beyond him.
Mary. Is this like him?
Renard. Ay, somewhat; but your Philip
Is the most princelike Prince beneath the sun.
This is a daub to Philip.
Mary. Of a pure life?
Renard. As an angel among angels. Yea, by Heaven,
The text—Your Highness knows it, "Whosoever
Looketh after a woman," would not graze
The Prince of Spain. You are happy in him there,
Chaste as your Grace!
Mary. I am happy in him there.
Renard. And would be altogether happy, Madam,
So that your sister were but look'd to closer.
You have sent her from the Court, but then she goes,
I warrant, not to hear the nightingales,
But hatch you some new treason in the woods.
Mary. We have our spies abroad to catch her trip-
ping,
And then if caught, to the Tower.
Renard. The Tower! the block.
The word has turn'd your Highness pale; the thing
Was no such scarecrow in your father's time.
I have heard, the tongue yet quiver'd with the jest
When the head leapt—so common! I do think
To save your crown that it must come to this.
Mary. I love her not, but all the people love her,
And would not have her even to the Tower.
Renard. Not yet; but your old traitors of the Tower,
Why, when you put Northumberland to death,
The sentence having past upon them all,
Spared you the Duke of Suffolk, Guildford Dudley.
Ev'n that young girl who dared to wear your crown?
Mary. Dared, no, not that; the child obey'd her fa-
ther.
Spite of her tears her father forced it on her.
Renard. Good Madam, when the Roman wish'd to
reign,
He slew not him alone who wore the purple,
But his assessor in the throne, perchance
A child more innocent than Lady Jane.
Mary. I am English Queen, not Roman Emperor.
Renard. Yet too much mercy is a want of mercy,
And wastes more life. Stamp out the fire, or this
Will smoulder and re-flame, and burn the throne
Where you should sit with Philip: he will not come
Till she be gone.
Mary. Indeed, if that were true—
But I must say farewell. I am somewhat faint
With our long talk. Tho' Queen, I am not Queen
Of mine own heart, which every now and then
Beats me half dead: yet stay, this golden chain—
My father on a birthday gave it me.
And I have broken with my father—take
And wear it as memorial of a morning
Which found me full of foolish doubts, and leaves me
As hopeful.
Renard (aside). Whew—the folly of all follies
Is to be love-sick for a shadow. (*Aloud.*) Madam,
This chains me to your service, not with gold,
But dearest links of love. Farewell, and trust me,
Philip is yours. [*Exit.*
Mary. Mine—but not yet all mine.

Enter USHER.

Usher. Your Council is in session, please your Majesty.

Mary. Sir, let them sit. I must have time to breathe.
No, say I come. (*Exit* USHER.) I won by boldness once.
The Emperor counsell'd me to fly to Flanders.
I would not; but a hundred miles I rode,
Sent out my letters, call'd my friends together,
Struck home, and won.
And when the Council would not crown me—thought
To bind me first by oaths I could not keep,
And keep with Christ and conscience—was it bold-
ness
Or weakness that won there? when I, their Queen,
Cast myself down upon my knees before them,
And those hard men brake into woman tears,
Ev'n Gardiner, all amazed, and in that passion
Gave me my crown.

Enter ALICE.

Girl, hast thou ever heard
Slanders against Prince Philip in our Court?
Alice. What slanders? I, your Grace; no, never.
Mary. Nothing?
Alice. Never, your Grace.
Mary. See that you neither hear them nor repeat!
Alice (aside). Good Lord! but I have heard a thou-
sand such.
Ay, and repeated them as often—mum!
Why comes that old fox-Fleming back again?

Enter RENARD.

Renard. Madam, I scarce had left your Grace's pres-
ence
Before I chanced upon the messenger
Who brings that letter which we waited for—
The formal offer of Prince Philip's hand.
It craves an instant answer, Ay or No?
Mary. An instant, Ay or No! the Council sits.
Give it me quick.
Alice (stopping before her). Your Highness is all
trembling.
Mary. Make way. [*Exit into the Council Chamber.*
Alice. O Master Renard, Master Renard,
If you have falsely painted your fine Prince;
Praised, where you should have blamed him, I pray
God
No woman ever love you, Master Renard.
It breaks my heart to hear her moan at night
As tho' the nightmare never left her bed.
Renard. My pretty maiden, tell me, did you ever
Sigh for a beard?
Alice. That's not a pretty question.
Renard. Not prettily put? I mean, my pretty maid-
en,
A pretty man for such a pretty maiden.
Alice. My Lord of Devon is a pretty man.
I hate him. Well, but if I have, what then?
Renard. Then, pretty maiden, you should know that
whether
A wind be warm or cold, it serves to fan
A kindled fire.
Alice. According to the song.

"His friends would praise him, I believed 'em,
His foes would blame him, and I scorned 'em;
His friends—as angels I received 'em,
His foes—the Devil had suborn'd 'em."

Renard. Peace, pretty maiden.
I hear them stirring in the Council Chamber.
Lord Paget's "Ay" is sure—who else? and yet,
They are all too much at odds to close at once
In one full-throated No! Her Highness comes.

Enter Mary

Alice. How deathly pale!—a chair, your Highness.
[*Bringing one to the* QUEEN.
Renard. Madam,
The Council?
Mary. Ay! My Philip is all mine.
[*Sinks into chair, half fainting.*

ACT II.

SCENE I.—ALLINGTON CASTLE.

Sir Thomas Wyatt.

Wyatt. I do not hear from Carew or the Duke
Of Suffolk, and till then I should not move.
The Duke hath gone to Leicester: Carew stirs
In Devon: that fine porcelain Courtenay,
Save that he fears he might be crack'd in using,
(I have known a semi-madman in my time
So fancy-ridd'n) should be in Devon too.

Enter William.

News abroad, William?
   William. None so new, Sir Thomas, and none so old,
Sir Thomas. No new news that Philip comes to wed
Mary; no old news that all men hate it. Old Sir Thom-
as would have hated it. The bells are ringing at Maid-
stone. Doesn't your worship hear?
   Wyatt. Ay, for the saints are come to reign again.
Most like it is a saint's-day. There's no call
As yet for me; so in this pause, before
The mine be fired, it were a pious work
To string my father's sonnets, left about
Like loosely-scatter'd jewels, in fair order,
And bead them with a lamer rhyme of mine,
To grace his memory.
   William. Ay, why not, Sir Thomas? He was a fine
courtier, he; Queen Anne loved him. All the women
loved him. I loved him, I was in Spain with him. I
couldn't eat in Spain, I couldn't sleep in Spain. I hate
Spain, Sir Thomas.
   Wyatt. But thou could'st drink in Spain if I remem-
ber.
   William. Sir Thomas, we may grant the wine. Old
Sir Thomas always granted the wine.
   Wyatt. Hand me the casket with my father's son-
nets.
   William. Ay—sonnets—a fine courtier of the old
Court, old Sir Thomas.   [*Exit.*
   Wyatt. Courtier of many courts, he loved the more
His own gray towers, plain life and letter'd peace,
To read and rhyme in solitary fields,
The lark above, the nightingale below,
And answer them in song. The sire begets
Not half his likeness in the son. I fail
Where he was fullest: yet—to write it down.
                                             [*He writes.*

Re-enter William.

   William. There *is* news, there *is* news, and no call
for sonnet-sorting now, nor for sonnet-making either,
but ten thousand men on Penenden Heath all calling
after your worship, and your worship's name heard
into Maidstone market, and your worship the first
man in Kent and Christendom, for the world's up, and
your worship a-top of it.
   Wyatt. Inverted Æsop—mountain out of mouse.
Say for ten thousand ten—and pothouse knaves,
Brain-dizzied with a draught of morning-ale.

Enter Antony Knyvett.

   William. Here's Antony Knyvett.
   Knyvett.   Look you, Master Wyatt,
Tear up that woman's work there.
   Wyatt.   No; not these,
Dumb children of my father, that will speak
When I and thou and all rebellions lie
Dead bodies without voice. Song flies, you know,
For ages

   Knyvett. Tut, your sonnet's a flying ant,
Wing'd for a moment.
   Wyatt.   Well, for mine own work,
                                      [*tearing the paper.*
It lies there in six pieces at your feet;
For all that I can carry it in my head.
   Knyvett. If you can carry your head upon your shoul-
ders.
   Wyatt. I fear you come to carry it off my shoulders,
And sonnet-making's safer.
   Knyvett.   Why, good Lord,
Write you as many sonnets as you will.
Ay, but not now; what, have you eyes, ears, brains?
This Philip and the black-faced swarms of Spain,
The hardest, cruellest people in the world,
Come locusting upon us, eat us up,
Confiscate lands, goods, money—Wyatt, Wyatt,
Wake, or the stout old island will become
A rotten limb of Spain. They roar for you
On Penenden Heath, a thousand of them—more—
All arm'd, waiting a leader; there's no glory
Like his who saves his country: and you sit
Sing-songing here; but, if I'm any judge,
By God, you are as poor a poet, Wyatt,
As a good soldier.
   Wyatt.   You as poor a critic
As an honest friend: you stroke me on one cheek,
Buffet the other. Come, you bluster, Antony!
You know I know all this. I must not move
Until I hear from Carew and the Duke.
I fear the mine is fired before the time.
   Knyvett (*showing a paper*). But here's some He-
    · brew. Faith, I half forgot it.
Look; can you make it English? A strange youth
Suddenly thrust it on me, whisper'd, "Wyatt,"
And, whisking round a corner, show'd his back
Before I read his face.
   Wyatt.   Ha! Courtenay's cipher. [*Reads.*
"Sir Peter Carew fled to France: it is thought the Duke will be
taken. I am with you still, but, for appearance' sake stay with the
Queen. Gardiner knows, but the Council are all at odds, and the
Queen hath no force for resistance. Move, if you move, at once."

Is Peter Carew fled? Is the Duke taken?
Down scabbard, and out sword! and let Rebellion
Roar till throne rock, and crown fall. No; not that;
But we will teach Queen Mary how to reign.
Who are those that shout below there?
   Knyvett.   Why, some fifty
That follow'd me from Penenden Heath in hope
To hear you speak.
   Wyatt.   Open the window, Knyvett;
The mine is fired. and I will speak to them.
Men of Kent—England of England—you that have
kept your old customs upright, while all the rest of
England bow'd theirs to the Norman,—The cause that
hath brought us together is not the cause of a county
or a shire, but of this England, in whose crown our
Kent is the fairest jewel. Philip shall not wed Mary:
and ye have called me to be your leader. I know Spain.
I have been there with my father; I have seen them
in their own land: have marked the haughtiness of
their nobles; the cruelty of their priests. If this man
marry our Queen, however the Council and the Commons may fence round his power with restriction, he
will be King, King of England, my masters; and the
Queen, and the laws, and the people, his slaves. What?
shall we have Spain on the throne and in the Parliament; Spain in the pulpit and on the law-bench;

Spain in all the great offices of state; Spain in our
ships, in our forts, in our houses, in our beds?

Crowd. No! no! no Spain.

William. No Spain in our beds—that were worse
than all. I have been there with old Sir Thomas, and
the beds I know. I hate Spain.

A Peasant. But, Sir Thomas, must we levy war
against the Queen's Grace?

Wyatt. No, my friend; war *for* the Queen's Grace
—to save her from herself and Philip—war against
Spain. And think not we shall be alone—thousands
will flock to us. The Council, the Court itself, is on
our side. The Lord Chancellor himself is on our side.
The King of France is with us; the King of Denmark
is with us; the world is with us—war against Spain!
And if we move not now, yet it will be known that
we have moved; and if Philip come to be King, O
my God! the rope, the rack, the thumb-screw, the
stake, the fire. If we move not now, Spain moves,
bribes our nobles with her gold, and creeps, creeps
snake-like about our legs till we cannot move at all;
and ye know, my masters, that wherever Spain hath
ruled she hath wither'd all beneath her. Look at the
New World—a paradise made hell; the red man, that
good helpless creature, starved, maim'd, flogg'd,
flay'd, burn'd, boil'd, buried alive, worried by dogs;
and here, nearer home, the Netherlands, Sicily, Naples,
Lombardy. I say no more—only this, their lot is
yours. Forward to London with me! forward to London! If ye love your liberties or your skins, forward
to London!

Crowd. Forward to London! A Wyatt! a Wyatt!

Wyatt. But first to Rochester, to take the guns
From out the vessels lying in the river.
Then on.

A Peasant. Ay, but I fear we be too few, Sir Thomas.

Wyatt. Not many yet. The world as yet, my friend,
Is not half-waked; but every parish tower
Shall clang and clash alarum as we pass,
And pour along the land, and swoll'n and fed
With indraughts and side-currents, in full force
Roll upon London.

Crowd. A Wyatt! a Wyatt! Forward!

Knyvett. Wyatt, shall we proclaim Elizabeth?

Wyatt. I'll think upon it, Knyvett.

Knyvett. Or Lady Jane?

Wyatt. No, poor soul; no.
Ah, gray old castle of Allington, green field
Beside the brimming Medway, it may chance
That I shall never look upon you more.

Knyvett. Come, now, you're sonnetting again.

Wyatt. Not I.
I'll have my head set higher in the state;
Or—if the Lord God will it—on the stake. [*Exeunt.*

SCENE II.—GUILDHALL.

Sir Thomas White (the Lord Mayor), Lord William
Howard, Sir Ralph Bagenhall, Aldermen and
Citizens.

White. I trust the Queen comes hither with her
Guards.

Howard. Ay, all in arms.
[*Several of the Citizens move hastily out of the hall.*
Why do they hurry out there?

White. My Lord, cut out the rotten from your apple,
Your apple eats the better. Let them go.
They go like those old Pharisees in John
Convicted by their conscience, arrant cowards,
Or tamperers with that treason out of Kent.
When will her Grace be here?

Howard. In some few minutes.
She will address your guilds and companies.
I have striven in vain to raise a man for her.
But help her in this exigency, make

Your city loyal, and be the mightiest man
This day in England.

White. I am Thomas White.
Few things have fail'd to which I set my will.
I do my most and best.

Howard. You know that after
The Captain Brett, who went with your train bands
To fight with Wyatt, had gone over to him
With all his men, the Queen in that distress
Sent Cornwallis and Hastings to the traitor,
Feigning to treat with him about her marriage—
Know too what Wyatt said.

White. He'd sooner be,
While this same marriage question was being argued,
Trusted than trust—the scoundrel—and demanded
Possession of her person and the Tower.

Howard. And four of her poor Council too, my Lord
As hostages.

White. I know it. What do and say
Your Council at this hour?

Howard. I will trust you.
We fling ourselves on you, my Lord. The Council,
The Parliament as well, are troubled waters:
And yet like waters of the fen they know not
Which way to flow. All hangs on her address.
And upon you, Lord Mayor.

White. How look'd the city
When now you past it? Quiet?

Howard. Like our Council,
Your city is divided. As we past,
Some hail'd, some hiss'd us. There were citizens
Stood each before his shut-up booth, and look'd
As grim and grave as from a funeral.
And here a knot of ruffians all in rags,
With execrating execrable eyes,
Glared at the citizen. Here was a young mother,
Her face on flame, her red hair all blown back,
She shrilling "Wyatt," while the boy she held
Mimick'd and piped her "Wyatt," as red as she
In hair and cheek; and almost elbowing her,
So close they stood, another, mute as death,
And white as her own milk; her babe in arms
Had felt the faltering of his mother's heart,
And look'd as bloodless. Here a pious Catholic,
Mumbling and mixing up in his scared prayers
Heaven and earth's Maries; over his bow'd shoulder
Scowl'd that world-hated and world-hating beast,
A haggard Anabaptist. Many such groups.
The names of Wyatt, Elizabeth, Courtenay,
Nay the Queen's right to reign—'fore God, the
rogues—
Were freely buzz'd among them. So I say
Your city is divided, and I fear
One scruple, this or that way, of success
Would turn it thither. Wherefore now the Queen,
In this low pulse and palsy of the state,
Bade me to tell you that she counts on you
And on myself as her two hands; on you,
In your own city, as her right, my Lord,
For you are loyal.

White. Am I Thomas White?
One word before she comes. Elizabeth—
Her name is much abused among these traitors.
Where is she? She is loved by all of us.
I scarce have heart to mingle in this matter.
If she should be mishandled?

Howard. No; she shall not.
The Queen had written her word to come to court.
Methought I smelt out Renard in the letter,
And, fearing for her, sent a secret missive,
Which told her to be sick. Happily or not,
It found her sick indeed.

White. God send her well;
Here comes her Royal Grace.

Enter Guards, Mary, *and* Gardiner. Sir Thomas
White *leads her to a raised seat on the dais.*

White. I, the Lord Mayor, and these our companies

And guilds of London, gathered here, beseech
Your Highness to accept our lowliest thanks
For your most princely presence ; and we pray
That we, your true and loyal citizens,
From your own royal lips, at once may know
The wherefore of this coming, and so learn
Your Royal will, and do it.—I, Lord Mayor
Of London, and our guilds and companies.

Mary. In mine own person am I come to you,
To tell you what indeed ye see and know,
How traitorously these rebels out of Kent
Have made strong head against ourselves and you.
They would not have me wed the Prince of Spain ;
That was their pretext—so they spake at first—
But we sent divers of our Council to them,
And by their answers to the question ask'd,
It doth appear this marriage is the least
Of all their quarrel.
They have betray'd the treason of their hearts:
Seek to possess our person, hold our Tower,
Place and displace our councillors, and use
Both us and them according as they will.
Now what am I ye know right well—your Queen ;
To whom, when I was wedded to the realm
And the realm's laws (the spousal ring whereof,
Not ever to be laid aside, I wear
Upon this finger), ye did promise full
Allegiance and obedience to the death.
Ye know my father was the rightful heir
Of England, and his right came down to me,
Corroborate by your acts of Parliament :
And as ye were most loving unto him,
So doubtless will ye show yourselves to me.
Wherefore, ye will not brook that anyone
Should seize our person, occupy our state,
More specially a traitor so presumptuous
As this same Wyatt, who hath tamper'd with
A public ignorance, and, under color
Of such a cause as hath no color, seeks
To bend the laws to his own will, and yield
Full scope to persons rascal and forlorn,
To make free spoil and havoc of your goods.
Now as your Prince, I say,
I, that was never mother, cannot tell
How mothers love their children : yet, methinks,
A prince as naturally may love his people
As these their children : and be sure your Queen
So loves you, and so loving, needs must deem
This love by you return'd as heartily ;
And thro' this common knot and bond of love,
Doubt not they will be speedily overthrown.
As to this marriage, ye shall understand
We made thereto no treaty of ourselves,
And set no foot theretoward unadvised
Of all our Privy Council ; furthermore,
This marriage had the assent of those to whom
The King, my father, did commit his trust ;
Who not alone esteem'd it honorable,
But for the wealth and glory of our realm,
And all our loving subjects, most expedient.
As to myself,
I am not so set on wedlock as to choose
But where I list, nor yet so amorous
That I must needs be husbanded ; I thank God,
I have lived a virgin, and I noway doubt
But that, with God's grace, I can live so still.
Yet if it might please God that I should leave
Some fruit of mine own body after me,
To be your king, ye would rejoice thereat,
And it would be your comfort, as I trust ;
And truly, if I either thought or knew
This marriage should bring loss or danger to you,
My subjects, or impair in any way
This royal state of England, I would never
Consent thereto, nor marry while I live ;
Moreover, if this marriage should not seem,
Before our own High Court of Parliament,
To be of rich advantage to our realm,

We will refrain, and not alone from this,
Likewise from any other, out of which
Looms the least chance of peril to our realm.
Wherefore be bold, and with your lawful Prince
Stand fast against our enemies and yours,
And fear them not. I fear them not. My Lord,
I leave Lord William Howard in your city,
To guard and keep you whole and safe from all
The spoil and sackage aim'd at by these rebels,
Who mouth and foam against the Prince of Spain.

Voices. Long live Queen Mary !
                                      Down with Wyatt !
                                                  The Queen !

White. Three voices from our guilds and companies !
You are shy and proud like Englishmen, my masters,
And will not trust your voices. Understand :
Your lawful Prince hath come to cast herself
On loyal hearts and bosoms, hoped to fall
Into the wide-spread arms of fealty,
And finds you statues. Speak at once—and all !
For whom ?
Our sovereign Lady by King Harry's will ;
The Queen of England—or the Kentish Squire ?
I know you loyal. Speak ! in the name of God !
The Queen of England or the rabble of Kent ?
The reeking dungfork master of the mace !
Your havings wasted by the scythe and spade—
Your rights and charters hobnail'd into slush—
Your houses fired—your gutters bubbling blood—
    Acclamation. No ! No ! The Queen ! the Queen !
White.   Your Highness hears
This burst and bass of loyal harmony,
And how we each and all of us abhor
The venomous, bestial, devilish revolt
Of Thomas Wyatt. Hear us now make oath
To raise your Highness thirty thousand men,
And arm and strike as with one hand, and brush
This Wyatt from our shoulders, like a flea
That might have leapt upon us unawares.
Swear with me, noble fellow-citizens, all,
With all your trades, and guilds, and companies.

    Citizens. We swear !

Mary. We thank your Lordship and your loyal city.
                              [*Exit* MARY, *attended.*

White. I trust this day, thro' God, I have saved the
    crown.

First Alderman. Ay, so my Lord of Pembroke in
    command
Of all her force be safe ; but there are doubts.

Second Alderman. I hear that Gardiner, coming
    with the Queen,
And meeting Pembroke, bent to his saddle-bow,
As if to win the man by flattering him.
Is he so safe to fight upon her side ?

First Alderman. If not, there's no man safe.
White.   Yes, Thomas White.
I am safe enough ; no man need flatter me.

Second Alderman. Nay, no man need ; but did you
    mark our Queen ?
The color freely play'd into her face,
And the half sight which makes her look so stern,
Seem'd, thro' that dim dilated world of hers,
To read our faces ; I have never seen her
So queenly or so goodly.

White.   Courage, sir,
That makes or man or woman look their goodliest.
Die like the torn fox, dumb, but never whine
Like that poor heart, Northumberland, at the block.

Bagenhall. The man had children, and he whined
    for those.
Methinks most men are but poor-hearted, else
Should we so doat on courage, were it commoner ?
The Queen stands up, and speaks for her own self ;
And all men cry, she is queenly, she is goodly.
Yet she's no goodlier : tho' my Lord Mayor here,
By his own rule, he hath been so bold to-day,
Should look more goodly than the rest of us.

White. Goodly ? I feel most goodly heart and hand,

And strong to throw ten Wyatts and all Kent.
Ha! ha! sir; but you jest; I love it: a jest
In time of danger shows the pulses even,
Be merry! yet, Sir Ralph, you look but sad.
I dare avouch you'd stand up for yourself,
Tho' all the world should bay like winter wolves.

Bagenhall. Who knows? the man is proven by the
hour.

White. The man should make the hour, not this the
man;
And Thomas White will prove this Thomas Wyatt,
And he will prove an Iden to this Cade,
And he will play the Walworth to this Wat;
Come, sirs, we prate; hence all—gather your men—
Myself must bustle. Wyatt comes to Southwark;
I'll have the drawbridge hewn into the Thames,
And see the citizen arm'd. Good day; good day.
[*Exit* WHITE.

Bagenhall. One of much outdoor bluster.

Howard. For all that,
Most honest, brave, and skilful; and his wealth
A fountain of perennial alms—his fault
So thoroughly to believe in his own self.

Bagenhall. Yet thoroughly to believe in one's own
self,
So one's own self be thorough, were to do
Great things, my Lord.

Howard. It may be.

Bagenhall. I have heard
One of your Council fleer and jeer at him.

Howard. The nursery-cocker'd child will jeer at
aught
That may seem strange beyond his nursery.
The statesman that shall jeer and fleer at men,
Makes enemies for himself and for his king;
And if he jeer not seeing the true man
Behind his folly, he is thrice the fool;
And if he see the man and still will jeer,
He is child and fool, and traitor to the state.
Who is he? let me shun him.

Bagenhall. Nay, my Lord,
He is damn'd enough already.

Howard. I must set
The guard at Ludgate. Fare you well, Sir Ralph.

Bagenhall. "Who knows?" I am for England. But
who knows,
That knows the Queen, the Spaniard, and the Pope,
Whether I be for Wyatt, or the Queen? [*Exeunt.*

SCENE III.—LONDON BRIDGE.

Enter SIR THOMAS WYATT *and* BRETT.

Wyatt. Brett, when the Duke of Norfolk moved
against us
Thou cried'st "a Wyatt," and, flying to our side,
Left his all bare, for which I love thee, Brett.
Have for thine asking aught that I can give,
For thro' thine help we are come to London Bridge;
But how to cross it balks me. I fear we cannot.

Brett. Nay, hardly, save by boat, swimming, or
wings.

Wyatt. Last night I climb'd into the gate-house,
Brett,
And scared the gray old porter and his wife.
And then I crept along the gloom and saw
They had hewn the drawbridge down into the river.
It roll'd as black as death; and that same tide
Which, coming with our coming, seem'd to smile
And sparkle like our fortune as thou saidest,
Ran sunless down, and moan'd against the piers.
But o'er the chasm I saw Lord William Howard
By torchlight, and his guard; four guns gaped at me,
Black, silent mouths: had Howard spied me there
And made them speak, as well he might have done,
Their voice had left me none to tell you this.
What shall we do?

Brett. On somehow. To go back
Were to lose all.

Wyatt. On over London Bridge
We cannot: stay we cannot; there is ordnance
On the White Tower and on the Devil's Tower,
And pointed full at Southwark: we must round
By Kingston Bridge.

Brett. Ten miles about.

Wyatt. Ev'n so.
But I have notice from our partisans
Within the city that they will stand by us
If Ludgate can be reach'd by dawn to-morrow.

Enter one of WYATT's *men.*

Man. Sir Thomas, I've found this paper, pray your
worship read it; I know not my letters; the old priests
taught me nothing.

Wyatt (reads). "Whosoever will apprehend the traitor Thomas Wyatt shall have a hundred pounds for
reward."

Man. Is that it? That's a big lot of money.

Wyatt. Ay, ay, my friend; not read it? 'tis not writ-
ten
Half plain enough. Give me a piece of paper!
[*Writes* "THOMAS WYATT" *large.*
There, any man can read that. [*Sticks it in his cap.*

Brett. But that's foolhardy.

Wyatt. No! boldness, which will give my followers
boldness.

Enter MAN *with a prisoner.*

Man. We found him, your worship, a-plundering o'
Bishop Winchester's house; he says he's a poor gentleman.

Wyatt. Gentleman, a thief! Go hang him. Shall
we make
Those that we come to serve our sharpest foes.

Brett. Sir Thomas—

Wyatt. Hang him, I say.

Brett. Wyatt, but now you promised me a boon.

Wyatt. Ay, and I warrant this fine fellow's life.

Brett. Ev'n so; he was my neighbor once in Kent.
He's poor enough, has drunk and gambled out
All that he had, and gentleman he was.
We have been glad together: let him live.

Wyatt. He has gambled for his life, and lost, he hangs.
No, no, my word's my word. Take thy poor gentleman!
Gamble thyself at once out of my sight,
Or I will dig thee with my dagger. Away!
Women and children!

Enter a Crowd of Women *and* Children.

First Woman. O Sir Thomas, Sir Thomas! pray you
go away, Sir Thomas, or you'll make the White Tower
a black 'un for us this blessed day. He'll be the death
on us: and you'll set the Divil's Tower a-spitting, and
he'll smash all our bits o' things worse than Philip o'
Spain.

Second Woman. Don't ye now go to think that we
be for Philip o' Spain.

Third Woman. No, we know that ye be come to kill
the Queen, and we'll pray for you all on our bended
knees. But o' God's mercy don't ye kill the Queen
here, Sir Thomas: look ye, here's little Dickon, and
little Robin, and little Jenny—though she's but a side-
cousin—and all on our knees, we pray you to kill the
Queen further off, Sir Thomas.

Wyatt. My friends. I have not come to kill the Queen
Or here or there: I come to save you all.
And I'll go further off.

Crowd. Thanks, Sir Thomas, we be beholden to you,
and we'll pray for you on our bended knees till our
lives' end.

Wyatt. Be happy, I am your friend.
To Kingston, forward!
[*Exeunt.*

SCENE IV.—ROOM IN THE GATEHOUSE OF WESTMINSTER PALACE.

MARY, ALICE, GARDINER, RENARD, LADIES.

Alice. O madam, if Lord Pembroke should be false?
Mary. No, girl; most brave and loyal, brave and loyal.
His breaking with Northumberland broke Northumberland.
At the park gate he hovers with our guards.
These Kentish ploughmen cannot break the guards.

Enter MESSENGER.

Messenger. Wyatt, your Grace, hath broken thro' the guards
And gone to Ludgate.
Gardiner. Madam, I much fear
That all is lost; but we can save your Grace.
The river still is free. I do beseech you,
There yet is time, take boat and pass to Windsor.
Mary. I pass to Windsor and I lose my crown.
Gardiner. Pass, then, I pray your Highness, to the Tower.
Mary. I shall but be their prisoner in the Tower.
[*Cries without.*
The traitor! treason! Pembroke!
Ladies. Treason! treason!
Mary. Peace.
False to Northumberland, is he false to me?
Bear witness, Renard, that I live and die
The true and faithful bride of Philip—A sound
Of feet and voices thickening hither—blows—
Hark, there is battle at the palace gates,
And I will out upon the gallery.
Ladies. No, no, your Grace; see there the arrows flying.
Mary. I am Harry's daughter, Tudor, and not fear.
[*Goes out on the Gallery.*
The guards are all driven in, skulk into corners
Like rabbits to their holes. A gracious guard
Truly; shame on them! they have shut the gates!

Enter SIR ROBERT SOUTHWELL.

Southwell. The porter, please your Grace, hath shut the gates
On friend and foe. Your gentlemen-at-arms,
If this be not your Grace's order, cry
To have the gates set wide again, and they
With their good battleaxes will do you right
Against all traitors.
Mary. They are the flower of England; set the gates wide.
[*Exit* SOUTHWELL.

Enter COURTENAY.

Courtenay. All lost, all lost, all yielded; a barge, a barge,
The Queen must to the Tower.
Mary. Whence come you, sir?
Courtenay. From Charing Cross; the rebels broke us there,

And sped hither with what haste I might
To save my royal cousin.
Mary. Where is Pembroke?
Courtenay. I left him somewhere in the thick of it.
Mary. Left him and fled; and thou that would'st be King,
And hast nor heart nor honor. I myself
Will down into the battle, and there bide
The upshot of my quarrel, or die with those
That are no cowards and no Courtenays.
Courtenay. I do not love your Grace should call me coward.

Enter another MESSENGER.

Messenger. Over, your Grace, all crush'd; the brave Lord William
Thrust him from Ludgate, and the traitor flying
To Temple Bar, there by Sir Maurice Berkeley
Was taken prisoner.
Mary. To the Tower with him!
Messenger. 'Tis said he told Sir Maurice there was one
Cognisant of this, and party thereunto,
My Lord of Devon.
Mary. To the Tower with him!
Courtenay. O la, the Tower, the Tower, always the Tower,
I shall grow into it—I shall be the Tower.
Mary. Your Lordship may not have so long to wait.
Remove him!
Courtenay. La, to whistle out my life,
And carve my coat upon the walls again!
[*Exit* COURTENAY *guarded.*
Messenger. Also this Wyatt did confess the Princess
Cognisant thereof, and party thereunto.
Mary. What? whom—whom did you say?
Messenger. Elizabeth,
Your Royal sister.
Mary. To the Tower with her!
My foes are at my feet and I am Queen.
[GARDINER *and her* LADIES *kneel to her.*
Gardiner (*rising*). There let them lie, your footstool! (*Aside.*) Can I strike
Elizabeth?—not now and save the life
Of Devon: if I save him, he and his
Are bound to me—may strike hereafter. (*Aloud.*)
Madam,
What Wyatt said, or what they said he said,
Cries of the moment and the street—
Mary. He said it.
Gardiner. Your courts of justice will determine that.
Renard (*advancing*). I trust by this your Highness will allow
Some spice of wisdom in my telling you,
When last we talk'd, that Philip would not come
Till Guildford Dudley and the Duke of Suffolk,
And Lady Jane had left us.
Mary. They shall die.
Renard. And your so loving sister?
Mary. She shall die.
My foes are at my feet, and Philip King. [*Exeunt.*

ACT III.

SCENE I. — THE CONDUIT IN GRACE-CHURCH,

Painted with the Nine Worthies, among them King Henry VIII. holding a book, on it inscribed "Verbum Dei."

Enter SIR RALPH BAGENHALL *and* SIR THOMAS STAFFORD.

Bagenhall. A hundred here and hundreds hang'd in Kent.
The tigress had unsheath'd her nails at last,
And Renard and the Chancellor sharpen'd them.
In every London street a gibbet stood.
They are down to-day. Here by this house was one;
The traitor husband dangled at the door,
And when the traitor wife came out for bread
To still the petty treason therewithin,
Her cap would brush his heels.
   Stafford.   It is Sir Ralph,
And muttering to himself as heretofore.
Sir, see you aught up yonder?
   Bagenhall.   I miss something.
The tree that only bears dead fruit is gone.
   Stafford. What tree, sir?
   Bagenhall.   Well, the tree in Virgil, sir,
That bears not its own apples.
   Stafford.   What! the gallows?
   Bagenhall. Sir, this dead fruit was ripening overmuch,
And had to be removed lest living Spain
Should sicken at dead England.
   Stafford.   Not so dead,
But that a shock may rouse her.
   Bagenhall.   I believe
Sir Thomas Stafford?
   Stafford. I am ill disguised.
   Bagenhall. Well, are you not in peril here?
   Stafford.   I think so.
I came to feel the pulse of England, whether
It beats hard at this marriage. Did you see it?
   Bagenhall. Stafford, I am a sad man and a serious.
Far liefer had I in my country hall
Been reading some old book, with mine old hound
Couch'd at my hearth, and mine old flask of wine
Beside me, than have seen it, yet I saw it.
   Stafford. Good; was it splendid?
   Bagenhall.   Ay, if dukes, and earls,
And counts, and sixty Spanish cavaliers,
Some six or seven bishops, diamonds, pearls,
That royal commonplace too, cloth of gold,
Could make it so.
   Stafford.   And what was Mary's dress?
   Bagenhall. Good faith, I was too sorry for the woman
To mark the dress. She wore red shoes!
   Stafford.   Red shoes!
   Bagenhall. Scarlet, as if her feet were wash'd in blood,
As if she had waded in it.
   Stafford.   Were your eyes
So bashful that you look'd no higher?
   Bagenhall.   A diamond,
And Philip's gift, as proof of Philip's love,
Who hath not any for any,—tho' a true one,
Blazed false upon her heart.
   Stafford.   But this proud Prince—

   Bagenhall. Nay, he is King, you know, the King of Naples.
The father ceded Naples, that the son,
Being a King, might wed a Queen. O, he
Flamed in brocade; white satin his trunk-hose,
Inwrought with silver; on his neck a collar,
Gold, thick with diamonds; hanging down from this
The Golden Fleece; and round his knee, misplaced,
Our English Garter, studded with great emeralds,
Rubies, I know not what. Have you had enough
Of all this gear?
   Stafford. Ay, since you hate the telling it.
How look'd the Queen?
   Bagenhall.   No fairer for her jewels.
And I could see that as the new-made couple
Came from the minister, moving side by side
Beneath one canopy, ever and anon
She cast on him a vassal smile of love,
Which Philip with a glance of some distaste,
Or so methought, return'd. I may be wrong, sir.
This marriage will not hold.
   Stafford.   I think with you.
The King of France will help to break it.
   Bagenhall.   France!
We once had half of France, and hurl'd our battles
Into the heart of Spain; but England now
Is but a ball chuck'd between France and Spain,
His in whose hand she drops: Harry of Bolingbroke
Had holpen Richard's tottering throne to stand,
Could Harry have foreseen that all our nobles
Would perish on the civil slaughter-field,
And leave the people naked to the crown,
And the crown naked to the people; the crown
Female, too! Sir, no woman's regimen
Can save us. We are fallen, and, as I think,
Never to rise again.
   Stafford. You are too black-blooded.
I'd make a move myself to hinder that:
I know some lusty fellows there in France.
   Bagenhall. You would but make us weaker, Thomas Stafford.
Wyatt was a good soldier, yet he fail'd,
And strengthen'd Philip.
   Stafford.   Did not his last breath
Clear Courtenay and the Princess from the charge
Of being his co-rebels?
   Bagenhall.   Ay, but then
What such a one as Wyatt says is nothing:
We have no men among us. The new Lords
Are quieted with their sop of Abbeylands,
And ev'n before the Queen's face Gardiner buys them
With Philip's gold. All greed, no faith, no courage!
Why, ev'n the haughty Prince, Northumberland,
The leader of our Reformation, knelt
And blubber'd like a lad, and on the scaffold
Recanted, and resold himself to Rome.
   Stafford. I swear you do your country wrong, Sir Ralph.
I know a set of exiles over there,
Dare-devils, that would eat fire and spit it out
At Philip's beard: they pillage Spain already.
The French King winks at it. An hour will come
When they will sweep her from the seas. No men?
Did not Lord Suffolk die like a true man?
Is not Lord William Howard a true man?
Yea, yon yourself, altho' you are black-blooded:-
And I, by God, believe myself a man.

Ay, even in the church there is a man—
Cranmer.
Fly, would he not, when all men bade him fly.
And what a letter he wrote against the Pope!
There's a brave man, if any.
   Bagenhall.   Ay; if it hold.
   Crowd (coming on). God save their Graces!
   Stafford.   Bagenhall, I see
The Tudor green and white. (*Trumpets.*) They are
   coming now.
And here's a crowd as thick as herring-shoals.
   Bagenhall. Be limpets to this pillar, or we are torn
Down the strong wave of brawlers.
   Crowd.   God save their Graces!
   [*Procession of Trumpeters, Javelin-men, etc.; then
     Spanish and Flemish Nobles intermingled.*
   Stafford. Worth seeing, Bagenhall! These black
     dog-Dons
Garb themselves bravely. Who's the long-face there,
Looks very Spain of very Spain?
   Bagenhall.   The Duke
Of Alva, an iron soldier.
   Stafford.   And the Dutchman,
Now laughing at some jest?
   Bagenhall.   William of Orange,
William the Silent.
   Stafford.   Why do they call him so?
   Bagenhall. He keeps, they say, some secret that may
   cost
Philip his life.
   Stafford.   But then he looks so merry.
   Bagenhall. I cannot tell you why they call him so.
   [*The* KING *and* QUEEN *pass, attended by Peers of
    the Realm, Officers of State, etc. Cannon shot off.*
   Crowd. Philip and Mary! Philip and Mary!
Long live the King and Queen, Philip and Mary!
   Stafford. They smile as if content with one another.
   Bagenhall. A smile abroad is oft a scowl at home.
        [KING *and* QUEEN *pass on. Procession.*
   First Citizen. I thought this Philip had been one
of those black devils of Spain, but he hath a yellow
beard.
   Second Citizen. Not red like Iscariot's.
   First Citizen. Like a carrot's, as thou say'st, and
English carrot's better than Spanish licorice; but I
thought he was a beast.
   Third Citizen. Certain I had heard that every Spaniard carries a tail like a devil under his trunk-hose.
   Tailor. Ay, but see what trunk-hoses! Lord! they
be fine: I never stitch'd none such. They make
amends for the tails.
   Fourth Citizen. Tut! every Spanish priest will tell
you that all English heretics have tails.
   Fifth Citizen. Death and the Devil—if he find I
have one—
   Fourth Citizen. Lo! thou hast call'd them up! here
they come—a pale horse for Death, and Gardiner for
the Devil.

   Enter GARDINER (*turning back from the procession*).

   Gardiner. Knave, wilt thou wear thy cap before the
Queen?
   Man. My Lord, I stand so squeezed among the
   crowd
I cannot lift my hands unto my head.
   Gardiner. Knock off his cap there, some of you about
   him!
See there be others that can use their hands.
Thou art one of Wyatt's men?
   Man.   No, my Lord, no.
   Gardiner. Thy name, thou knave?
   Man.   I am nobody, my Lord.
   Gardiner (*shouting*). God's passion! knave, thy
name?
   Man. I have ears to hear.
   Gardiner. Ay, rascal, if I leave thee ears to hear.
Find out his name and bring it me (*to Attendant*).
   Attendant.   Ay, my Lord.

   Gardiner. Knave, thou shalt lose thine ears and find
   thy tongue,
And shalt be thankful if I leave thee that.
          [*Coming before the Conduit.*
The conduit painted—the nine worthies—ay!
But then what's here? King Harry with a scroll.
Ha—Verbum Dei—verbum—word of God!
God's passion! do you know the knave that painted it?
   Attendant. I do, my Lord.
   Gardiner.   Tell him to paint it out,
And put some fresh device in lieu of it—
A pair of gloves, a pair of gloves, sir; ha?
There is no heresy there.
   Attendant.   I will, my Lord,
The man shall paint a pair of gloves. I am sure
(Knowing the man) he wrought it ignorantly,
And not from any malice.
   Gardiner.   Word of God
In English! over this the brainless loons,
That cannot spell Esaias from St. Paul,
Make themselves drunk and mad, fly out and flare
Into rebellions. I'll have their Bibles burnt.
The Bible is the priest's! Ay! fellow, what!
Stand staring at me! shout, you gaping rogue.
   Man. I have, my Lord, shouted till I am hoarse.
   Gardiner. What hast thou shouted, knave?
   Man.   Long live Queen Mary!
   Gardiner. Knave, there be two. There be both
   King and Queen,
Philip and Mary. Shout.
   Man.   Nay, but, my Lord,
The Queen comes first, Mary and Philip.
   Gardiner.   Shout, then,
Mary and Philip.
   Man.   Mary and Philip!
   Gardiner.   Now,
Thou hast shouted for thy pleasure, shout for mine:
Philip and Mary!
   Man.   Must it be so, my Lord?
   Gardiner. Ay, knave.
   Man.   Philip and Mary.
   Gardiner.   I distrust thee.
Thine is a half voice and a lean assent.
What is thy name?
   Man.   Sanders.
   Gardiner.   What else?
   Man.   Zeruhbabel.
   Gardiner. Where dost thou live?
   Man.   In Cornhill.
   Gardiner.   Where, knave, where?
   Man. Sign of the Talbot.
   Gardiner.   Come to me to-morrow.—
Rascal!—this land is like a hill of fire,
One crater opens when another shuts.
But so I get the laws against the heretic,
Spite of Lord Paget and Lord William Howard,
And others of our Parliament, revived,
I will show fire on my side—stake and fire—
Sharp work and short. The knaves are easily cow'd.
Follow their Majesties. [*Exit. The crowd following.*
   Bagenhall.   As proud as Becket.
   Stafford. You would not have him murder'd as
   Becket was?
   Bagenhall. No—murder fathers murder: but I say
There is no man—there was one woman with us—
It was a sin to love her married, dead
I cannot choose but love her.
   Stafford.   Lady Jane?
   Crowd (going off). God save their Graces!
   Stafford.   Did you see her die?
   Bagenhall. No, no: her innocent blood had blind-
   ed me.
You call me too black-blooded—true enough,
Her dark dead blood is in my heart with mine.
If ever I cry out against the Pope,
Her dark dead blood that ever moves with mine
Will stir the living tongue and make the cry.
   Stafford. Yet doubtless you can tell me how she died?

Bagenhall. Seventeen—and knew eight languages—
in music
Peerless—her needle perfect, and her learning
Beyond the churchmen ; yet so meek, so modest,
So wife-like humble to the trivial boy
Mismatch'd with her for policy ! I have heard
She would not take a last farewell of him,
She fear'd it might unman him for his end.
She could not be unmann'd—no, nor outwoman'd—
Seventeen—a rose of grace !
Girl never breathed to rival such a rose ;
Rose never blew that equall'd such a bud.
  Stafford. Pray you go on.
  Bagenhall.   She came upon the scaffold,
And said she was condemn'd to die for treason ;
She had but follow'd the device of those
Her nearest kin : she thought they knew the laws.
But for herself, she knew but little law,
And nothing of the titles to the crown ;
She had no desire for that, and wrung her hands,
And trusted God would save her thro' the blood
Of Jesus Christ alone.
  Stafford.   Pray you go on.
  Bagenhall. Then knelt and said the Miserere Mei—
But all in English, mark you ; rose again,
And, when the headsman pray'd to be forgiven,
Said, "You will give me my true crown at last,
But do it quickly ;" then all wept but she,
Who changed not color when she saw the block
But ask'd him, childlike : "Will you take it off
Before I lay me down ?" "No, madam," he said,
Gasping ; and when her innocent eyes were bound,
She, with her poor blind hands feeling—"Where is it ?
Where is it ?"—You must fancy that which follow'd,
If you have heart to do it !
  Crowd (in the distance). God save their Graces !
  Stafford. Their Graces, our disgraces ! God con-
        found them !
Why, she's grown bloodier ! When I last was here,
This was against her conscience—would be murder !
  Bagenhall. The "Thou shalt do no murder," which
        God's hand
Wrote on her conscience, Mary rubbed out pale—
She could not make it white—and over that,
Traced in the blackest text of Hell—"Thou shalt !"
And sign'd it—Mary!
  Stafford.   Philip and the Pope
Must have sign'd too. I hear this Legate's coming
To bring us absolution from the Pope.
The Lords and Commons will bow down before him—
You are of the house ? what will you do, Sir Ralph ?
  Bagenhall. And why should I be bolder than the rest,
Or honester than all ?
  Stafford.   But, sir, if I—
And oversea they say this state of yours
Hath no more mortice than a tower of cards ;
And that a puff would do it—then if I
And others made that move I touch'd upon,
Back'd by the power of France, and landing here,
Came with a sudden splendor, shout, and show,
And dazzled men and deafen'd by some bright
Loud venture, and the people so unquiet—
And I the race of murder'd Buckingham—
Not for myself, but for the kingdom—sir,
I trust that you would fight along with us.
  Bagenhall. No ; you would fling your lives into the
        gulf.
  Stafford. But if this Philip, as he's like to do,
Left Mary a wife-widow here alone,
Set up a viceroy, sent his myriads hither
To seize upon the forts and fleet, and make us
A Spanish province ; would you not fight then ?
  Bagenhall. I think I should fight then.
  Stafford.   I am sure of it.
Hist ! there's the face coming on here of one
Who knows me. I must leave you. Fare you well,
You'll hear of me again.
  Bagenhall. Upon the scaffold.   [*Exeunt.*
                        19

SCENE II.—ROOM IN WHITEHALL PALACE.

MARY. *Enter* PHILIP *and* CARDINAL POLE.

  Pole. Ave Maria, gratia plena, Benedicta tu in mu-
        lieribus.
  Mary. Loyal and royal cousin, humblest thanks.
Had you a pleasant voyage up the river ?
  Pole. We had your royal barge, and that same chair,
Or rather throne of purple, on the deck.
Our silver cross sparkled before the prow,
The ripples twinkled at their diamond-dance,
The boats that follow'd were as glowing-gay
As regal gardens ; and your flocks of swans,
As fair and white as angels ; and your shores
Wore in mine eyes the green of Paradise.
My foreign friends, who dream'd us blanketed
In ever-closing fog, were much amazed
To find as fair a sun as might have flash'd
Upon their lake of Garda, fire the Thames ;
Our voyage by sea was all but miracle ;
And here the river flowing from the sea,
Not toward it (for they thought not of our tides),
Seem'd as a happy miracle to make glide—
In quiet—home your banish'd countryman.
  Mary. We heard that you were sick in Flanders,
        cousin.
  Pole. A dizziness.
  Mary.   And how came you round again ?
  Pole. The scarlet thread of Rahab saved her life ;
And mine, a little letting of the blood.
  Mary. Well ? now ?
  Pole.   Ay, cousin, as the heathen giant
Had but to touch the ground, his force return'd—
Thus, after twenty years of banishment,
Feeling my native land beneath my foot
I said thereto : "Ah, native land of mine,
Thou art much beholden to this foot of mine,
That hastes with full commission from the Pope
To absolve thee from thy guilt of heresy.
Thou hast disgraced me and attainted me,
And mark'd me ev'n as Cain, and I return
As Peter, but to bless thee : make me well."
Methinks the good land heard me, for to-day
My heart beats twenty, when I see you, cousin.
Ah, gentle cousin, since your Herod's death,
How oft hath Peter knock'd at Mary's gate !
And Mary would have risen and let him in,
But, Mary, there were those within the house
Who would not have it.
  Mary.   True, good cousin Pole ;
And there were also those without the house
Who would not have it.
  Pole.   I believe so, cousin.
State-policy and church-policy are conjoint,
But Janus-faces looking diverse ways.
I fear the Emperor much misvalued me.
But all is well : 'twas ev'n the will of God,
Who, waiting till the time had ripen'd, now,
Makes me his mouth of holy greeting. "Hail,
Daughter of God, and saver of the faith.
Sit benedictus fructus ventris tui !"
  Mary. Ah, heaven !
  Pole.   Unwell, your Grace ?
  Mary.   No, cousin, happy—
Happy to see you ; never yet so happy
Since I was crown'd.
  Pole.   Sweet cousin, you forget
That long low minster where you gave your hand
To this great Catholic King.
  Philip.   Well said, Lord Legate.
  Mary. Nay, not well said ; I thought of you, my
        liege,
Ev'n as I spoke.
  Philip.   Ay, Madam ; my Lord Paget
Waits to present our Council to the Legate.
Sit down here, all ; Madam, between us you.

Pole. Lo, now you are enclosed with boards of cedar,
Our little sister of the Song of Songs!
You are doubly fenced and shielded sitting here
Between the two most high-set thrones on earth,
The Emperor's highness happily symboll'd by
The King your husband, the Pope's Holiness
By mine own self.

Mary.   True, cousin, I am happy.
When will you that we summon both our houses
To take this absolution from your lips,
And be regather'd to the Papal fold?

Pole. In Britain's calendar the brightest day
Beheld our rough forefathers break their gods,
And clasp the faith in Christ; but after that
Might not St. Andrew's be her happiest day?

Mary. Then these shall meet upon St. Andrew's day.

Enter PAGET, *who presents the Council.   Dumb show.*

Pole. I am an old man wearied with my journey,
Ev'n with my joy.   Permit me to withdraw.
To Lambeth?

Philip.   Ay, Lambeth has ousted Cranmer.
It was not meet the heretic swine should live
In Lambeth.

Mary.   There or anywhere, or at all.

Philip. We have had it swept and garnish'd after him.

Pole. Not for the seven devils to enter in?

Philip. No, for we trust they parted in the swine.

Pole. True, and I am the Angel of the Pope.
Farewell, your Graces.

Philip.   Nay, not here—to me;
I will go with you to the waterside.

Pole. Not be my Charon to the counter side?

Philip. No, my Lord Legate, the Lord Chancellor goes.

Pole. And unto no dead world; but Lambeth palace,
Henceforth a centre of the living faith.
                          [*Exeunt* PHILIP, POLE, PAGET, *etc.*

Mary. He hath awaked! he hath awaked!
He stirs within the darkness!
Oh, Philip, husband! now thy love to mine
Will cling more close, and those bleak manners thaw,
That make me shamed and tongue-tied in my love.
The second Prince of Peace—
The great unborn defender of the Faith,
Who will avenge me of mine enemies—
He comes, and my star rises.
The stormy Wyatts and Northumberlands,
The proud ambitions of Elizabeth,
And all her fieriest partisans—are pale
Before my star!
The light of this new learning wanes and dies:
The ghosts of Luther and Zuinglius fade
Into the deathless hell which is their doom
Before my star!
His sceptre shall go forth from Ind to Ind!
His sword shall hew the heretic peoples down;
His faith shall clothe the world that will be his,
Like universal air and sunshine! Open,
Ye everlasting gates! The King is here!—
My star, my son!

Enter PHILIP, DUKE OF ALVA, *etc.*

                          Oh, Philip, come with me;
Good news have I to tell you, news to make
Both of us happy—ay, the kingdom too.
Nay come with me—one moment!

Philip (to Alva).   More than that:
There was one here of late—William the Silent
They call him—he is free enough in talk,
But tells me nothing.   You will be, we trust,
Sometime the viceroy of those provinces—
He must deserve his surname better.

Alva.   Ay, sir,
Inherit the Great Silence.

Philip.   True; the provinces
Are hard to rule and must be hardly ruled;
Most fruitful, yet, indeed, an empty rind,
All hollow'd out with stinging heresies;
And for their heresies, Alva, they will fight:
You must break them or they break you.

Alva (proudly).   The first.

Philip. Good!
Well, Madam, this new happiness of mine.   [*Exeunt.*

Enter THREE PAGES.

First Page. News, mates! a miracle, a miracle! news!
The bells must ring; Te Deums must be sung;
The Queen hath felt the motion of her babe!

Second Page. Ay; but see here!

First Page.   See what?

Second Page.   This paper, Dickon.
I found it fluttering at the palace gates:--
"The Queen of England is delivered of a dead dog!"

Third Page. These are the things that madden her.
Fie upon it.

First Page. Ay; but I hear she hath a dropsy, lad,
Or a high-dropsy, as the doctors call it.

Third Page. Fie on her dropsy, so she have a drop-sy!
I know that she was ever sweet to me.

First Page. For thou and thine are Roman to the core.

Third Page. So thou and thine must be.   Take heed!

First Page.   Not I,
And whether this flash of news be false or true,
So the wine run, and there be revelry,
Content am I.   Let all the steeples clash,
Till the sun dance, as upon Easter day.   [*Exeunt.*

SCENE III. — GREAT HALL IN WHITE-HALL.

[*At the far end a daïs.   On this three chairs, two under one canopy for* MARY *and* PHILIP, *another on the right of these for* POLE.   *Under the daïs on* POLE'S *side, ranged along the wall, sit all the Spiritual Peers, and along the wall opposite, all the Temporal.   The Commons on cross benches in front, a line of approach to the daïs between them.   In the foreground* SIR RALPH BAGENHALL *and other* MEMBERS *of the* COMMONS.]

First Member. St. Andrew's day; sit close, sit close,
we are friends.
Is reconciled the word? the Pope again?
It must be thus; and yet, cocksbody! how strange
That Gardiner, once so one with all of us
Against this foreign marriage, should have yielded
So utterly!—strange! but stranger still that he,
So fierce against the headship of the Pope,
Should play the second actor in this pageant
That brings him in; such a cameleon he!

Second Member. This Gardiner turn'd his coat in Henry's time:
The serpent that hath slough'd will slough again.

Third Member. Tut, then we all are serpents.

Second Member.   Speak for yourself.

Third Member. Ay, and for Gardiner! being English citizen,
How should he bear a bridegroom out of Spain?
The Queen would have him! being English churchman
How should he bear the headship of the Pope?
The Queen would have it! Statesmen that are wise
Shape a necessity, as the sculptor clay,
To their own model.

Second Member.   Statesmen that are wise
Take truth herself for model, what say you?
                          [*To* SIR RALPH BAGENHALL.

Bagenhall. We talk and talk.
First Member.　　　Ay, and what use to talk?
Philip's no sudden alien—the Queen's husband,
He's here, and King, or will be—yet, cockshody!
So hated here! I watch'c a hive of late;
My seven-years' friend was with me, my young boy;
Out crept a wasp, with half the swarm behind.
"Philip," says he. I had to cuff the rogue
For infant treason.
Third Member.　　But they say that bees,
If any creeping life invade their hive
Too gross to be thrust out, will build him round,
And bind him in from harming of their combs.
And Philip by these articles is bound
From stirring hand or foot to wrong the realm.
　　Second Member. By bonds of beeswax, like your
　　　　creeping thing;
But your wise bees had stung him first to death.
　　Third Member. Hush, hush!
You wrong the Chancellor: the clauses added
To that same treaty which the Emperor sent us
Were mainly Gardiner's: that no foreigner
Hold office in the household, fleet, forts, army;
That if the Queen should die without a child,
The bond between the kingdoms be dissolved;
That Philip should not mix us any way
With his French wars—
　　Second Member.　　　Ay, ay, but what security,
Good sir, for this, if Philip—
　　Third Member.　　　Peace—the Queen,
Philip, and Pole.　　　[*All rise, and stand.*

　　　　Enter MARY, PHILIP, *and* POLE.

　　[GARDINER *conducts them to the three chairs of
　　state.* PHILIP *sits on the* QUEEN's *left,* POLE *on
　　her right.*
　　Gardiner. Our short-lived sun, before his winter
　　　plunge,
Laughs at the last red leaf, and Andrew's day.
　　Mary. Should not this day be held in after-years
More solemn than of old?
　　Philip.　　　Madam, my wish
Echoes your Majesty's.
　　Pole.　　　It shall be so.
　　Gardiner. Mine echoes both your Graces'; *(aside)*
　　　but the Pope—
Can we not have the Catholic church as well
Without as with the Italian? if we cannot,
Why then the Pope.

　　　　　　My Lords of the upper house,
And ye, my masters, of the lower house,
Do ye stand fast by that which ye resolved?
　　Voices. We do.
　　Gardiner. And be you all one mind to supplicate
The Legate here for pardon, and acknowledge
The primacy of the Pope?
　　Voices.　　　We are all one mind.
　　Gardiner. Then must I play the vassal to this Pole.
　　　　　　　　　　　　　　[*Aside.*
　　[He *draws a paper from under his robes and pre-
　　sents it to the* KING *and* QUEEN, *who took through
　　it and return it to him; then ascends a tribune,
　　and reads.*
We, the Lords Spiritual and Temporal,
And Commons here in Parliament assembled,
Presenting the whole body of this realm
Of England, and dominions of the same,
Do make most humble suit unto your Majesties,
In our own name and that of all the state,
That by your gracious means and intercession
Our supplication be exhibited
To the Lord Cardinal Pole, sent here as Legate
From our Most Holy Father, Julius, Pope,
And from the apostolic see of Rome;
And do declare our penitence and grief
For our long schism and disobedience,
Either in making laws and ordinances

Against the Holy Father's primacy,
Or else by doing or by speaking aught
Which might impugn or prejudice the same;
By this our supplication promising,
As well for our own selves as all the realm,
That now we be and ever shall be quick,
Under and with your Majesties' authorities,
To do to the utmost all that in us lies
Towards the abrogation and repeal
Of all such laws and ordinances made;
Whereon we humbly pray your Majesties,
As persons undefiled with our offence,
So to set forth this humble suit of ours
That we the rather by your intercession
May from the apostolic see obtain,
Thro' this most reverend Father, absolution,
And full release from danger of all censures
Of Holy Church that we be fall'n into,
So that we may, as children penitent,
Be once again received into the bosom
And unity of Universal Church;
And that this noble realm thro' after-years
May in this unity and obedience
Unto the holy see and reigning Pope
Serve God and both your Majesties.
　　Voices.　　　Amen.　[*All so.*
　　[He *again presents the petition to the* KING *and
　　*QUEEN, *who hand it reverentialy to* POLE.
　　Pole (sitting). This is the loveliest day that ever
　　　smiled
On England. All her breath should, incenselike,
Rise to the heavens in grateful praise of Him
Who now recalls her to his ancient fold.
Lo! once again God to this realm hath given
A token of His more especial Grace:
For as this people were the first of all
The islands call'd into the dawning church
Out of the dead, deep night of heathendom,
So now are these the first whom God hath given
Grace to repent and sorrow for their schism;
And if your penitence be not mockery,
Oh how the blessed angels who rejoice
Over one saved do triumph at this hour
In the reborn salvation of a land
So noble!　　　　　[*A pause.*
　　　　　　For ourselves we do protest
That our commission is to heal, not harm;
We come not to condemn, but reconcile;
We come not to compel, but call again;
We come not to destroy, but edify;
Nor yet to question things already done;
These are forgiven—matters of the past—
And range with jetsam and with offal thrown
Into the blind sea of forgetfulness.　　　[*A pause.*
Ye have reversed the attainder laid on us
By him who sack'd the house of God; and we,
Amplier than any field on our poor earth
Can render thanks in fruit for being sown,
Do here and now repay you sixty-fold,
A hundred, yea, a thousand thousand-fold,
With heaven for earth.
　　[*Rising and stretching forth his hands. All kneel
　　but* SIR RALPH BAGENHALL, *who rises and re-
　　mains standing.*
　　　　　　The Lord who hath redeem'd us
With His own blood, and wash'd us from our sins,
To purchase for Himself a stainless bride;
He, whom the Father hath appointed Head
Of all his church, He by His mercy absolve you!
　　　　　　　　　　　　　[*A pause.*
And we by that authority apostolic
Given unto us, his Legate, by the Pope,
Our Lord and Holy Father, Julius,
God's Vicar and Vicegerent upon earth,
Do here absolve you and deliver you
And every one of you, and all the realm
And its dominions from all heresy,
All schism, and from all and every censure,

Judgment, and pain accruing thereupon;
And also we restore you to the bosom
And unity of Universal Church.
　　　　　　　　　　[*Turning to* GARDINER.
Our letters of commission will declare this plainlier.
　　　[QUEEN *heard sobbing.　　Cries of* Amen! Amen!
　　　Some of the members embrace one another.　All
　　　but SIR RALPH BAGENHALL *pass out into the*
　　　neighboring chapel, whence is heard the Te Deum.
　Bagenhall. We strove against the papacy from the
　　　first,
In William's time, in our first Edward's time,
And in my master Henry's time; but now,
The unity of Universal Church,
Mary would have it; and this Gardiner follows;
The unity of Universal Hell.
Philip would have it; and this Gardiner follows!
A Parliament of imitative apes!
Sheep at the gap which Gardiner takes, who not
Believes the Pope, nor any of them believe—
These spaniel-Spaniard English of the time,
Who rub their fawning noses in the dust,
For that is Philip's gold-dust, and adore
This Vicar of their Vicar.　Would I had been
Born Spaniard!　I had held my head up then.
I am ashamed that I am Bagenhall,
English.

　　　　　　　Enter OFFICER.

　Officer. Sir Ralph Bagenhall.
　Bagenhall.　　　　　　　　What of that?
　Officer. You were the one sole man in either house
Who stood upright when both the houses fell.
　Bagenhall. The houses fell!
　Officer.　　　　　　I mean the houses knelt
Before the Legate.
　Bagenhall.　　　　Do not scrimp your phrase,
But stretch it wider; say when England fell.
　Officer. I say you were the one sole man who stood.
　Bagenhall. I am the one sole man in either house,
Perchance in England, loves her like a son.
　Officer. Well, you one man, because you stood up-
　　　right,
Her Grace the Queen commands you to the Tower.
　Bagenhall. As traitor, or as heretic, or for what?
　Officer. If any man in any way would be
The one man, he shall be so to his cost.
　Bagenhall. What! will she have my head?
　Officer.　　　　　　A round fine likelier.
Your pardon.　　　　　[*Calling to attendant.*
　　　By the river to the Tower.
　　　　　　　　　　　　[*Exeunt.*

　　　　────

SCENE IV.—WHITEHALL.　A ROOM IN
　　　　THE PALACE.

　MARY, GARDINER, POLE, PAGET, BONNER, *etc.*

　Mary. The King and I, my Lords, now that all trai-
　　　tors
Against our royal state have lost the heads
Wherewith they plotted in their treasonous malice,
Have talk'd together, and are well agreed
That those old statutes touching Lollardism
To bring the heretic to the stake, should be
No longer a dead letter, but requicken'd.
　One of the Council. Why, what hath fluster'd Gar-
　　　diner?　How he rubs
His forelock!
　Paget.　　　I have changed a word with him
In coming, and may change a word again.
　Gardiner. Madam, your Highness is our sun, the
　　　King
And you together our two suns in one;
And so the beams of both may shine upon us,
The faith that seem'd to droop will feel your light,
Lift head, and flourish; yet not light alone.
There must be heat—there must be heat enough
To scorch and wither heresy to the root.

For what saith Christ?　"Compel them to come in."
And what saith Paul?　"I would they were cut off
That trouble you."　Let the dead letter live!
Trace it in fire, that all the louts to whom
Their A B C is darkness, clowns and grooms
May read it! so you quash rebellion too,
For heretic and traitor are all one:
Two vipers of one breed—an amphisbœna.
Each end a sting.　Let the dead letter burn!
　Paget. Yet there be some disloyal Catholics,
And many heretics loyal; heretic throats
Cried no God-bless-her to the Lady Jane,
But shouted in Queen Mary.　So there be
Some traitor-heretic, there is axe and cord.
To take the lives of others that are loyal,
And by the churchman's pitiless doom of fire,
Were but a thankless policy in the crown,
Ay, and against itself; for there are many.
　Mary. If we could burn out heresy, my Lord Paget,
We reck not tho' we lost this crown of England—
Ay! tho' it were ten Englands!
　Gardiner.　　　　　　　　Right, your Grace.
Paget, you are all for this poor life of ours,
And care but little for the life to be.
　Paget. I have some time, for curiousness, my Lord,
Watch'd children playing at *their* life to be,
And cruel at it, killing helpless flies;
Such is our time—all times for aught I know.
　Gardiner. We kill the heretics that sting the soul—
They, with right reason, flies that prick the flesh.
　Paget. They had not reach'd right reason; little
　　　children!
They kill'd but for their pleasure and the power
They felt in killing.
　Gardiner.　　　　A spice of Satan, ha!
Why, good! what then? granted!—we are fallen creat-
　　　ures;
Look to your Bible, Paget! we are fallen.
　Paget. I am but of the laity, my Lord Bishop,
And may not read your Bible, yet I found
One day, a wholesome scripture, "Little children,
Love one another."
　Gardiner.　　　　Did you find a scripture,
"I come not to bring peace, but a sword?"　The sword
Is in her Grace's hand to smite with.　Paget,
You stand up here to fight for heresy,
You are more than guess'd at as a heretic,
And on the steep-up track of the true faith
Your lapses are far seen.
　Paget.　　　　　　The faultless Gardiner!
　Mary. You brawl beyond the question; speak, Lord
　　　Legate.
　Pole. Indeed, I can not follow with your Grace,
Rather would say—the shepherd doth not kill
The sheep that wander from his flock, but sends
His careful dog to bring them to the fold.
Look to the Netherlands, wherein have been
Such holocausts of heresy! to what end?
For yet the faith is not establish'd there.
　Gardiner. The end's not come.
　Pole.　　　　　　No—nor this way will come,
Seeing there lie two ways to every end,
A better and a worse—the worse is here
To persecute, because to persecute
Makes a faith hated, and is furthermore
No perfect witness of a perfect faith
In him who persecutes: when men are tost
On tides of strange opinion, and not sure
Of their own selves, they are wroth with their own
　　　selves,
And thence with others; then, who lights the fag-
　　　got?
Not the full faith, no, but the lurking doubt.
Old Rome, that first made martyrs in the Church,
Trembled for her own gods, for these were trembling—
But when did our Rome tremble?
　Paget.　　　　　　　Did she not
In Henry's time and Edward's?

Pole.   What, my Lord!
The Church on Peter's rock? never! I have seen
A pine in Italy that cast its shadow
Athwart a cataract; firm stood the pine—
The cataract shook the shadow. To my mind,
The cataract typed the headlong plunge and full
Of heresy to the pit: the pine was Rome.
You see, my Lords,
It was the shadow of the Church that trembled;
Your church was but a shadow of a church,
Wanting the triple mitre.
    Gardiner (muttering).   Here be tropes.
    Pole. And tropes are good to clothe a naked truth,
And make it look more seemly.
    Gardiner.   Tropes again!
    Pole. You are hard to please. Then without tropes,
        my Lord,
An overmuch severeness, I repeat,
When faith is wavering makes the waverer pass
Into more settled hatred of the doctrines
Of those who rule, which hatred by-and-by
Involves the ruler (thus there springs to light
That Centaur of a monstrous Commonweal,
The traitor-heretic); then, tho' some may quail,
Yet others are that dare the stake and fire,
And their strong torment bravely borne, begets
An admiration and an indignation,
And hot desire to imitate; so the plague
Of schism spreads; were there but three or four
Of these misleaders, yet I would not say
Burn! and we cannot burn whole towns; they are
        many,
As my Lord Paget says.
    Gardiner.   Yet, my Lord Cardinal—
    Pole. I am your Legate; please you let me finish.
Methinks that under our Queen's regimen
We might go softlier than with crimson rowel
And streaming lash. When Herod-Henry first
Began to batter at your English Church,
This was the cause, and hence the judgment on her.
She seethed with such adulteries, and the lives
Of many among your churchmen were so foul
That heaven wept and earth blush'd. I would advise
That we should thoroughly cleanse the Church within
Before these bitter statutes be requicken'd.
So after that when she once more is seen
White as the light, the spotless bride of Christ,
Like Christ Himself on Tabor, possibly
The Lutheran may be won to her again;
Till when, my Lords, I counsel tolerance.
    Gardiner. What, if a mad dog bit your hand, my
        Lord,
Would you not chop the bitten finger off,
Lest your whole body should madden with the poison?
I would not, were I Queen, tolerate the heretic,
No, not an hour. The ruler of a land
Is bounden by his power and place to see
His people be not poison'd. Tolerate them!
Why? do they tolerate you? Nay, many of them
Would burn—have burnt each other; call they not
The one true faith a loathsome idol-worship?
Beware, Lord Legate, of a heavier crime
Than heresy is itself; beware, I say,
Lest men accuse you of indifference
To all faiths, all religion; for you know
Right well that you yourself have been supposed
Tainted with Lutheranism in Italy.
    Pole (angered). But you, my Lord, beyond all sup-
        position,
In clear and open day are congruent
With that vile Cranmer in the accursed lie
Of good Queen Catherine's divorce—the spring
Of all those evils that have flow'd upon us;
For you yourself have truckled to the tyrant,
And done your best to bastardize our Queen,
For which God's righteous judgment fell upon you
In your five years of imprisonment, my Lord,
Under young Edward. Who so bolster'd up

The gross King's headship of the Church, or more
Denied the Holy Father?
    Gardiner.   Ha! what I eh?
But you, my Lord, a polish'd gentleman,
A bookman, flying from the heat and tussle,
You lived among your vines and oranges,
In your soft Italy yonder! You were sent for,
You were appeal'd to, but you still preferr'd
Your learned leisure. As for what I did,
I suffer'd and repented. You, Lord Legate
And Cardinal-Deacon, have not now to learn
That ev'n St. Peter in his time of fear
Denied his master, ay, and thrice, my Lord.
    Pole. But not for five-and-twenty years, my Lord.
    Gardiner. Ha! good! it seems then I was sum-
        mon'd hither
But to be mock'd and baited. Speak, friend Bonner,
And tell this learned Legate he lacks zeal.
The Church's evil is not as the King's,
Cannot be heal'd by stroking. The mad bite
Must have the cautery—tell him—and at once.
What would'st thou do had'st thou his power, thou
That layest so long in heretic bonds with me.
Would'st thou not burn and blast them root and
        branch?
    Bonner. Ay, after you, my Lord.
    Gardiner. Nay, God's passion, before me! speak.
    Bonner. I am on fire until I see them flame.
    Gardiner. Ay, the psalm-singing weavers, cobblers,
        scum—
But this most noble prince Plantagenet,
Our good Queen's cousin—dallying over seas
Even when his brother's, nay, his noble mother's,
Head fell—
    Pole.   Peace, madman!
Thou stirrest up a grief thou canst not fathom.
Thou Christian Bishop, thou Lord Chancellor
Of England! no more rein upon thine anger
Than any child! Thou mak'st me much ashamed
That I was for a moment wroth at thee.
    Mary. I come for counsel, and ye give me feuds,
Like dogs that, set to watch their master's gate,
Fall, when the thief is ev'n within the walls,
To worrying one another. My Lord Chancellor,
You have an old trick of offending us;
And but that you are art and part with us
In purging heresy, well we might, for this
Your violence and much roughness to the Legate,
Have shut you from our counsels. Cousin Pole,
You are fresh from brighter lands. Retire with me.
His Highness and myself (so you allow us)
Will let you learn in peace and privacy
What power this cooler sun of England hath
In breeding godless vermin. And pray Heaven
That you may see according to our sight.
Come, cousin.   [*Exeunt* QUEEN *and* POLE, *etc.*
    Gardiner. Pole has the Plantagenet face,
But not the force made them our mightiest kings.
Fine eyes—but melancholy, irresolute—
A fine beard, Bonner, a very full fine beard.
But a weak mouth, an indeterminate—ha?
    Bonner. Well, a weak mouth, perchance.
    Gardiner.   And not like thine,
To gorge a heretic whole, roasted or raw.
    Bonner. I'd do my best, my Lord; but yet the
        Legate
Is here as Pope and Master of the Church,
And if he go not with you—
    Gardiner.   Tut, Master Bishop,
Our bashful Legate, saw'st not how he flush'd?
Touch him upon his old heretical talk,
He'll burn a diocese to prove his orthodoxy.
And let him call me truckler. In those times,
Thou knowest we had to dodge, or duck, or die;
I kept my head for use of Holy Church;
And see you, we shall have to dodge again,
And let the Pope trample our rights, and plunge
His foreign fist into our island Church

To plump the leaner pouch of Italy.
For a time, for a time.
Why? that these statutes may be put in force,
And that his fan may thoroughly purge his floor.
  Bonner. So then you hold the Pope—
  Gardiner.   I hold the Pope!
What do I hold him? what do I hold the Pope?
Come, come, the morsel stuck—this Cardinal's fault—
I have gulpt it down. I am wholly for the Pope,
Utterly and altogether for the Pope,
The Eternal Peter of the changeless chair,
Crown'd slave of slaves, and mitred King of kings,
God upon earth! What more? what would you have?
Hence, let's be gone.

              Enter Usher.

  Usher.   Well that you be not gone,
My Lord. The Queen, most wroth at first with you,
Is now content to grant you full forgiveness,
So that you crave full pardon of the Legate.
I am sent to fetch you.
  Gardiner.   Doth Pole yield, sir, ha!
Did you hear 'em? were you by?
  Usher.   I cannot tell you,
His bearing is so courtly-delicate;
And yet methinks he falters: their two Graces
Do so dear-cousin and royal-cousin him,
So press on him the duty which as Legate
He owes himself, and with such royal smiles—
  Gardiner. Smiles that burn men. Bonner, it will be
carried.
He falters, ha? 'fore God we change and change;
Men now are bow'd and old, the doctors tell you,
At three-score years; then, if we change at all,
We needs must do it quickly; it is an age
Of brief life, and brief purpose, and brief patience,
As I have shown to-day. I am sorry for it
If Pole be like to turn. Our old friend Cranmer,
Your more especial love, hath turn'd so often,
He knows not where he stands, which, if this pass,
We two shall have to teach him; let 'em look to it,
Cranmer and Hooper, Ridley and Latimer,
Rogers and Ferrar, for their time is come,
Their hour is hard at hand, their "dies iræ,"
Their "dies illa," which will test their sect.
I feel it but a duty—you will find in it
Pleasure as well as duty, worthy Bonner—
To test their sect. Sir, I attend the Queen
To crave most humble pardon—of her most
Royal, Infallible, Papal Legate-cousin.   [*Exeunt.*

SCENE V.—WOODSTOCK.

Elizabeth, Lady in Waiting.

  Lady. The colors of our Queen are green and white,
These fields are only green, they make me gape.
  Elizabeth. There's whitethorn, girl.
  Lady.   Ay, for an hour in May.
But court is always May, buds out in masques,
Breaks into feather'd merriments, and flowers
In silken pageants. Why do they keep us here?
Why still suspect your Grace?
  Elizabeth.   Hard upon both.
  [*Writes on the window with a diamond:*

    Much suspected, of me
    Nothing proven can be,
        Quoth Elizabeth, prisoner.

  Lady. What hath your Highness written?
  Elizabeth.   A true rhyme.
  Lady. Cut with a diamond; so to last like truth.
  Elizabeth. Ay, if truth last.
  Lady.   But truth, they say, will out,
So it must last. It is not like a word,
That comes and goes in uttering.
  Elizabeth.   Truth, a word!
The very Truth and very Word are one.

But truth of story, which I glanced at, girl,
Is like a word that comes from olden days,
And passes thro' the peoples: every tongue
Alters it passing, till it spells and speaks
Quite other than at first.
  Lady.   I do not follow.
  Elizabeth. How many names in the long sweep of
     time
That so foreshortens greatness, may but hang
On the chance mention of some fool that once
Brake bread with us, perhaps; and my poor chronicle
Is but of glass. Sir Henry Bedingfield
May split it for a spite.
  Lady.   God grant it last,
And witness to your Grace's innocence,
Till doom's-day melt it.
  Elizabeth.   Or a second fire,
Like that which lately crackled underfoot
And in this very chamber, fuse the glass,
And char us back again into the dust
We grew from. Never peacock against rain
Scream'd as you did for water.
  Lady.   And I got it.
I woke Sir Henry—and he's true to you—
I read his honest horror in his eyes.
  Elizabeth. Or true to you?
  Lady.   Sir Henry Bedingfield!
I will have no man true to me, your Grace,
But one that pares his nails; to me? the clown!
For, like his cloak, his manners want the nap
And gloss of court; but of this fire he says—
Nay, swears—it was no wicked willfulness,
Only a natural chance.
  Elizabeth.   A chance—perchance
One of those wicked willfuls that men make,
Nor shame to call it nature. Nay, I know
They hunt my blood. Save for my daily range
Among the pleasant fields of Holy Writ,
I might despair. But there hath some one come;
The house is all in movement. Hence, and see.
                     [*Exit* Lady.

  Milkmaid (singing without).

    Shame upon you, Robin,
      Shame upon you now!
    Kiss me would you? with my hands
      Milking the cow!
      Daisies grow again,
      Kingcups blow again,
    And you came and kiss'd me milking the cow

    Robin came behind me,
      Kiss'd me well, I vow;
    Caff him could I? with my hands
      Milking the cow?
      Swallows fly again,
      Cuckoos cry again,
    And you came and kiss'd me milking the cow.

    Come, Robin, Robin,
      Come and kiss me now;
    Help it can I? with my hands
      Milking the cow!
      Ringdoves coo again,
      All things woo again,
    Come behind and kiss me milking the cow!

  Elizabeth. Right honest and red-cheek'd; Robin
     was violent,
And she was crafty—a sweet violence,
And a sweet craft. I would I were a milkmaid,
To sing, love, marry, churn, brew, bake, and die,
Then have my simple headstone by the church,
And all things lived and ended honestly.
I could not if I would. I am Harry's daughter:
Gardiner would have my head. They are not sweet,
The violence and the craft that do divide
The world of nature; what is weak must lie;
The lion needs but roar to guard his young;
The lapwing lies, says "here" when they are there.
Threaten the child, "I'll scourge you if you did it."
What weapon hath the child, save his soft tongue,
To say "I did not?" and my rod's the block.

I never lay my head upon the pillow
But that I think, "Wilt thou lie there to-morrow?"
How oft the falling axe, that never fell,
Hath shock'd me back into the daylight truth
That it may fall to-day! Those damp, black, dead
Nights in the Tower; dead—with the fear of death.
Too dead ev'n for a death-watch! Toll of a bell,
Stroke of a clock, the scurrying of a rat
Affrighted me, and then delighted me,
For there was life—and there was life in death—
The little murder'd princes, in a pale light,
Rose hand in hand, and whisper'd, "Come away;
The civil wars are gone for evermore:
Thou last of all the Tudors, come away,
With us is peace!" The last? It was a dream;
I must not dream, nor wink, but watch. She has
gone,
Maid Marian to her Robin—by-and-by
Both happy! A fox may filch a hen by night,
And make a morning outcry in the yard;
But there's no Renard here to "catch her tripping."
Catch me who can; yet, sometime I have wish'd
That I were caught, and kill'd away at once
Out of the flutter. The gray rogue, Gardiner,
Went on his knees, and pray'd me to confess
In Wyatt's business, and to cast myself
Upon the good Queen's mercy; ay, when, my Lord?
God save the Queen. My jailor—

Enter Sir Henry Bedingfield.

Bedingfield.   One, whose bolts,
That jail you from free life, bar you from death.
There haunt some Papist ruffians hereabout
Would murder you.
Elizabeth.   I thank you heartily, sir;
But I am royal, tho' your prisoner,
And God hath blest or cursed me with a nose—
Your boots are from the horses.
Bedingfield.   Ay, my Lady.
When next there comes a missive from the Queen
It shall be all my study for one hour
To rose and lavender my horsiness,
Before I dare to glance upon your Grace.
Elizabeth. A missive from the Queen: last time she
wrote,
I had like to have lost my life: it takes my breath:
O God, sir, do you look upon your boots,
Are you so small a man? Help me: what think you,
Is it life or death?
Bedingfield.   I thought not on my boots;
The devil take all boots were ever made
Since man went barefoot. See, I lay it here,
For I will come no nearer to your Grace;
                              [*Laying down the letter.*
And, whether it bring you bitter news or sweet,
And God have given your Grace a nose, or not,
I'll help you, if I may.
Elizabeth.   Your pardon, then:
It is the heat and narrowness of the cage
That make the captive testy; with free wing
The world were all one Araby. Leave me now,
Will you, companion to myself, sir?
Bedingfield.   Will I?
With most exceeding willingness, I will;
You know I never come till I be call'd.   [*Exit.*
Elizabeth. It lies there folded: is there venom in it?
A snake—and if I touch it, it may sting.
Come, come, the worst!
Best wisdom is to know the worst at once. [*Reads:*

"It is the King's wish that you should wed Prince Philibert of
Savoy. You are to come to Court on the instant; and think of this
in your coming.   MARY THE QUEEN."

Think! I have many thoughts;
I think there may be birdlime here for me;
I think they fain would have me from the realm;
I think the Queen may never bear a child;
I think that I may be some time the Queen,

Then, Queen indeed: no foreign prince or priest
Should fill my throne, myself upon the steps.
I think I will not marry anyone,
Specially not this landless Philibert
Of Savoy; but, if Philip menace me,
I think that I will play with Philibert—
As once the Holy Father did with mine,
Before my father married my good mother—
For fear of Spain.

Enter LADY.

Lady.   O Lord! your Grace, your Grace,
I feel so happy: it seems that we shall fly
These bald, blank fields, and dance into the sun
That shines on princes.
Elizabeth.   Yet, a moment since,
I wish'd myself the milkmaid singing here,
To kiss and cuff among the birds and flowers—
A right rough life and healthful.
Lady.   But the wench
Hath her own troubles; she is weeping now;
For the wrong Robin took her at her word.
Then the cow kick'd, and all her milk was spilt.
Your Highness such a milkmaid?
Elizabeth.   I had kept
My Robins and my cows in sweeter order
Had I been such.
Lady (slyly).   And had your Grace a Robin.
Elizabeth. Come, come, you are chill here: you
want the sun
That shines at Court; make ready for the journey.
Pray God, we 'scape the sunstroke. Ready at once.
                                          [*Exeunt.*

SCENE VI.—LONDON. A ROOM IN THE PALACE.

LORD PETRE *and* LORD WILLIAM HOWARD.

Petre. You cannot see the Queen. Renard denied
her,
Ev'n now to me.
Howard.   Their Flemish go-between
And all-in-all. I came to thank her Majesty
For freeing my friend Bagenhall from the Tower;
A grace to me! Mercy, that herb-of-grace,
Flowers now but seldom.
Petre.   Only now, perhaps,
Because the Queen hath been three days in tears
For Philip's going—like the wild hedge-rose
Of a soft winter, possible, not probable,
However, you have prov'n it.
Howard.   I must see her.

Enter RENARD.

Renard. My Lords, you cannot see her Majesty.
Howard. Why then the King! for I would have him
bring it
Home to the leisure wisdom of his Queen,
Before he go, that since these statutes past,
Gardiner out-Gardiners Gardiner in his heat,
Bonner cannot out-Bonner his own self—
Beast!—but they play with fire as children do,
And burn the house. I know that these are breeding
A fierce resolve and fixt heart-hate in men
Against the King, the Queen, the Holy Father,
The faith itself. Can I not see him?
Renard.   Not now.
And in all this, my Lord, her Majesty
Is flint of flint, you may strike fire from her,
Not hope to melt her. I will give your message.
                              [*Exeunt* PETRE *and* HOWARD.

Enter PHILIP (*musing*).

Philip. She will not have Prince Philibert of Savoy;
I talk'd with her in vain—says she will live

And die true maid—a goodly creature too.
Would *she* had been the Queen! yet she must have
  him;
She troubles England: that she breathes in England
Is life and lungs to every rebel birth
That passes out of embryo.

              Simon Renard!—
This Howard, whom they fear, what was he saying?
  Renard. What your imperial father said, my liege,
To deal with heresy gentlier. Gardiner burns,
And Bonner burns; and it would seem this people
Care more for our brief life in their wet land,
Than yours in happier Spain. I told my Lord
He should not vex her Highness: she would say
These are the means God works with, that His church
May flourish.
  Philip.   Ay, sir, but in statesmanship
To strike too soon is oft to miss the blow.
Thou knowest I bade my chaplain, Castro, preach
Against these burnings.
  Renard.   And the Emperor
Approved you, and, when last he wrote, declared
His comfort in your Grace that you were bland
And affable to men of all estates,
In hope to charm them from their hate of Spain.
  Philip. In hope to crush all heresy under Spain.
But, Renard, I am sicker staying here
Than any sea could make me passing hence,
Tho' I be ever deadly sick at sea.
So sick am I with biding for this child.
Is it the fashion in this clime for women
To go twelve months in bearing of a child?
The nurses yawn'd, the cradle gaped, they led
Processions, chanted litanies, clash'd their bells,
Shot off their lying cannon, and her priests
Have preach'd, the fools, of this fair prince to come,
Till, by St. James! I find myself the fool.
Why do you lift your eyebrow at me thus?
  Renard. I never saw your Highness moved till now.
  Philip. So, weary am I of this wet land of theirs,
And every soul of man that breathes therein.
  Renard. My liege, we must not drop the mask before
The masquerade is over—
  Philip.   —Have I dropt it?
I have but shown a loathing face to you,
Who knew it from the first.

           Enter MARY.

  Mary (aside).   With Renard. Still
Parleying with Renard, all the day with Renard,
And scarce a greeting all the day for me—
And goes to-morrow.   [*Exit* MARY.
  Philip (to RENARD, *who advances to him).* Well, sir,
  is there more?
  Renard (who has perceived the QUEEN*).* May Simon
    Renard speak a single word?
  Philip. Ay.
  Renard. And be forgiven for it?
  Philip.   Simon Renard
Knows me too well to speak a single word
That could not be forgiven.
  Renard.   Well, my liege,
Your Grace hath a most chaste and loving wife.
  Philip. Why not? The Queen of Philip should be
  chaste.
  Renard. Ay, but, my Lord, you know what Virgil
  sings,
Woman is various and most mutable.
  Philip. She play the harlot! never.
  Renard.   No, sire, no.
Not dream'd of by the rabidest Gospeller.
There was a paper thrown into the palace,
"The King hath wearied of his barren bride."
She came upon it, read it, and then rent it,
With all the rage of one who hates a truth
He cannot but allow. Sire, I would have you—
What should I say, I cannot pick my words—
Be somewhat less—majestic to your Queen.

  Philip. Am I to change my manners, Simon Renard,
Because these islanders are brutal beasts?
Or would you have me turn a sonneteer,
And warble those brief-sighted eyes of hers?
  Renard. Brief-sighted tho' they be, I have seen them,
  sire,
When you perchance were trifling royally
With some fair dame of Court, suddenly fill
With such fierce fire—had it been fire indeed
It would have burnt both speakers.
  Philip.   Ay, and then?
  Renard. Sire, might it not be policy in some matter
Of small importance now and then to cede
A point to her demand?
  Philip.   Well, I am going.
  Renard. For should her love, when you are gone, my
  liege,
Witness these papers, there will not be wanting
Those that will urge her injury. Should her love—
And I have known such women more than one—
Veer to the counterpoint (and jealousy
Hath in it an alchemic force to fuse
Almost into one metal love and hate),
And she impress her wrongs upon her Council,
And these again upon her Parliament—
We are not loved here, and would be then perhaps
Not so well holpen in our wars with France,   ,
As else we might be. Here she comes.

           Enter MARY.

  Mary.   O Philip!
Nay, must you go indeed?
  Philip.   Madam, I must.
  Mary. The parting of a husband and a wife
Is like the cleaving of a heart; one half
Will flutter here, one there.
  Philip.   You say true, Madam.
  Mary. The Holy Virgin will not have me yet
Lose the sweet hope that I may bear a prince.
If such a prince were born and you not here!
  Philip. I should be here if such a prince were
  born.
  Mary. But must you go?
  Philip.   Madam, you know my father,
Retiring into cloistral solitude
To yield the remnant of his years to heaven,
Will shift the yoke and weight of all the world
From off his neck to mine. We meet at Brussels.
But since mine absence will not be for long,
Your Majesty shall go to Dover with me,
And wait my coming back.
  Mary.   To Dover? no,
I am too feeble. I will go to Greenwich,
So you will have me with you; and there watch
All that is gracious in the breath of heaven
Draw with your sails from our poor land, and pass
And leave me, Philip, with my prayers for you.
  Philip. And doubtless I shall profit by your prayers.
  Mary. Methinks that would you tarry one day more
(The news was sudden) I could mould myself
To bear your going better; will you do it?
  Philip. Madam, a day may sink or save a realm.
  Mary. A day may save a heart from breaking too.
  Philip. Well, Simon Renard, shall we stop a day?
  Renard. Your Grace's business will not suffer, sire,
For one day more, so far as I can tell.
  Philip. Then one day more to please her Majesty.
  Mary. The sunshine sweeps across my life again.
Oh if I knew you felt this parting, Philip,
As I do!
  Philip. By St. James! I do protest,
Upon the faith and honor of a Spaniard,
I am vastly grieved to leave your Majesty.
Simon, is supper ready?
  Renard.   Ay, my liege,
I saw the covers laying.
  Philip.   Let us have it.
                  [*Exeunt.*

ACT IV.

SCENE I.—A ROOM IN THE PALACE.

MARY, CARDINAL POLE.

Mary. What have you there?
Pole.   So please your Majesty,
A long petition from the foreign exiles
To spare the life of Cranmer. Bishop Thirlby,
And my Lord Paget and Lord William Howard,
Crave, in the same cause, hearing of your Grace.
Hath he not written himself—infatuated—
To sue you for his life?
Mary.   His life? Oh, no;
Not sued for that—he knows it were in vain.
But so much of the anti-papal leaven
Works in him yet, he hath pray'd me not to sully
Mine own prerogative, and degrade the realm
By seeking justice at a stranger's hand
Against my natural subject. King and Queen,
To whom he owes his loyalty after God,
Shall these accuse him to a foreign prince?
Death would not grieve him more. I cannot be
True to this realm of England and the Pope
Together, says the heretic.
Pole.   And there errs:
As he hath ever err'd thro' vanity.
A secular kingdom is but as the body
Lacking a soul; and in itself a beast.
The Holy Father in a secular kingdom
Is as the soul descending out of heaven
Into a body generate.
Mary.   Write to him, then.
Pole. I will.
Mary.   And sharply, Pole.
Pole.   Here come the Cranmerites!

Enter THIRLBY, LORD PAGET, LORD WILLIAM HOWARD.

Howard. Health to your Grace! Good morrow, my
     Lord Cardinal;
We make our humble prayer unto your Grace
That Cranmer may withdraw to foreign parts,
Or into private life within the realm.
In several bills and declarations, Madam,
He hath recanted all his heresies.
Paget. Ay, ay; if Bonner have not forged the bills.
                                              [*Aside.*
Mary. Did not More die, and Fisher? he must burn.
Howard. He hath recanted, Madam.
Mary.   The better for him.
He burns in purgatory, not in hell.
Howard. Ay, ay, your Grace; but it was never seen
That any one recanting thus at full,
As Cranmer hath, came to the fire on earth.
Mary. It will be seen now, then.
Thirlby.   O Madam, Madam!
I thus implore you, low upon my knees,
To reach the hand of mercy to my friend.
I have err'd with him; with him I have recanted.
What human reason is there why my friend
Should meet with lesser mercy than myself?
Mary. My Lord of Ely, this: After a riot
We hang the leaders, let their following go.
Cranmer is head and fount of these heresies,
New learning, as they call it; yea, may God
Forget me at most need when I forget
Her foul divorce—my sainted mother—No!—
Howard. Ay, ay, but mighty doctors doubted there.
The Pope himself waver'd; and more than one
Row'd in that galley—Gardiner, to wit,

Whom truly I deny not to have been
Your faithful friend and trusty councillor.
Hath not your Highness ever read his book,
His tractate upon True Obedience,
Writ by himself and Bonner?
Mary.   I will take
Such order with all bad, heretical books
That none shall hold them in his house and live,
Henceforward. No, my Lord.
Howard.   Then never read it.
The truth is here. Your father was a man
Of such colossal kinghood, yet so courteous,
Except when wroth, you scarce could meet his eye
And hold your own; and were he wroth indeed,
You held it less, or not at all. I say,
Your father had a will that beat men down;
Your father had a brain that beat men down—
Pole. Not me, my Lord.
Howard.   No, for you were not here;
You sit upon this fallen Cranmer's throne;
And it would more become you, my Lord Legate,
To join a voice, so potent with her Highness,
To ours in plea for Cranmer than to stand
On naked self-assertion.
Mary.   All your voices
Are waves on flint. The heretic must burn.
Howard. Yet once he saved your Majesty's own life;
Stood out against the King in your behalf,
At his own peril.
Mary.   I know not if he did;
And if he did I care not, my Lord Howard.
My life is not so happy, no such boon,
That I should spare to take a heretic priest's
Who saved it or not saved. Why do you vex me?
Paget. Yet to save Cranmer were to serve the
     Church,
Your Majesty's, I mean; he is effaced,
Self-blotted out; so wounded in his honor,
He can but creep down into some dark hole
Like a hurt beast, and hide himself and die;
But if you burn him,—well, your Highness knows
The saying, "Martyr's blood—seed of the Church."
Mary. Of the true Church; but his is none, nor
     will be.
You are too politic for me, my Lord Paget.
And if he have to live so loath'd a life,
It were more merciful to burn him now.
Thirlby. O yet relent. O Madam, if you knew him
As I do, ever gentle, and so gracious,
With all his learning—
Mary.   Yet a heretic still.
His learning makes his burning the more just.
Thirlby. So worship of all those that came across
     him;
The stranger at his hearth, and all his house—
Mary. His children and his concubine, belike.
Thirlby. To do him any wrong was to beget
A kindness from him, for his heart was rich,
Of such fine mould that if you sow'd therein
The seed of Hate, it blossom'd Charity.
Pole. "After his kind it costs him nothing," there's
An old-world English adage to the point.
These are but natural graces, my good Bishop,
Which in the Catholic garden are as flowers,
But on the heretic dunghill only weeds.
Howard. Such weeds make dunghills gracious.
Mary.   Enough, my Lords.
It is God's will, the Holy Father's will,

And Philip's will, and mine, that he should burn.
He is pronounced anathema.
Howard.   Farewell, Madam.
God grant you ampler mercy at your call
Than you have shown to Cranmer.   [*Exeunt* LORDS.
Pole.   After this,
Your Grace will hardly care to overlook
This same petition of the foreign exiles
For Cranmer's life.
    Mary.   Make out the writ to-night.
                                        [*Exeunt.*

SCENE II.—OXFORD. CRANMER IN PRISON.

Cranmer. Last night, I dream'd the faggots were
      alight,
And that myself was fasten'd to the stake,
And found it all a visionary flame,
Cool as the light in old decaying wood;
And then King Harry look'd from out a cloud,
And bade me have good courage; and I heard
An angel cry, "There is more joy in heaven,"—
And after that, the trumpet of the dead.
                        [*Trumpets without.*
Why, there are trumpets blowing now: what is it?

Enter FATHER COLE.

Cole. Cranmer, I come to question you again:
Have you remain'd in the true Catholic faith
I left you in?
    Cranmer.   In the true Catholic faith,
By Heaven's grace, I am more and more confirm'd.
Why are the trumpets blowing, Father Cole?
    Cole. Cranmer, it is decided by the Council
That you to-day should read your recantation
Before the people in Saint Mary's Church.
And there be many heretics in the town,
Who loathe you for your late return to Rome,
And might assail you passing through the street,
And tear you piecemeal: so you have a guard.
    Cranmer. Or seek to rescue me. I thank the Council.
    Cole. Do you lack any money?
    Cranmer.   Nay, why should I?
The prison fare is good enough for me.
    Cole. Ay, but to give the poor.
    Cranmer.   Hand it me, then!
I thank you.
    Cole.   For a little space, farewell;
Until I see you in St. Mary's Church.   [*Exit* COLE.
    Cranmer. It is against all precedent to burn
One who recants; they mean to pardon me.
To give the poor—they give the poor who die.
Well, burn me or not burn me, I am fixt;
It is but a communion, not a mass:
A holy supper, not a sacrifice;
No man can make his maker—Villa Garcia.

Enter VILLA GARCIA.

Villa Garcia. Pray you write out this paper for me,
      Cranmer.
    Cranmer. Have I not writ enough to satisfy you?
    Villa Garcia. It is the last.
    Cranmer.   Give it me, then.
                                        [*He writes.*
    Villa Garcia.   Now sign.
    Cranmer. I have sign'd enough, and I will sign no
      more.
    Villa Garcia. It is no more than what you have
      sign'd already,
The public form thereof.
    Cranmer.   It may be so;
I sign it with my presence, if I read it.
    Villa Garcia. But this is idle of you. Well, sir, well,
You are to beg the people to pray for you;
Exhort them to a pure and virtuous life;
Declare the Queen's right to the throne; confess

Your faith before all hearers; and retract
That eucharistic doctrine in your book.
Will you not sign it now?
    Cranmer.   No, Villa Garcia,
I sign no more. Will they have mercy on me?
    Villa Garcia. Have you good hopes of mercy ! So,
      farewell.   [*Exit.*
    Cranmer. Good hopes, not theirs, have I that I am
      fixt,
Fixt beyond fall; however, in strange hours,
After the long brain-dazing colloquies,
And thousand-times-recurring argument
Of those two friars ever in my prison,
When left alone in my despondency,
Without a friend, a book, my faith would seem
Dead or half-drown'd, or else swam heavily
Against the huge corruptions of the Church,
Monsters of mis-tradition, old enough
To scare me into dreaming, "What am I,
Cranmer, against whole ages?" was it so,
Or am I slandering my most inward friend,
To veil the fault of my most outward foe—
The soft and tremulous coward in the flesh?
O higher, holier, earlier, purer church,
I have found thee, and not leave thee any more.
It is but a communion, not a mass—
No sacrifice, but a life-giving feast !
(*Writes*). So, so; this will I say—thus will I pray.
                        [*Puts up the paper.*

Enter BONNER.

Bonner. Good day, old friend. What ! you look
      somewhat worn:
And yet it is a day to test your health
Ev'n at the best. I scarce have spoken with you
Since when?—your degradation. At your trial
Never stood up a bolder man than you;
You would not cap the Pope's commissioner—
Your learning, and your stoutness, and your heresy,
Dumbfounded half of us. So, after that,
We had to dis-archbishop and unlord,
And make you simple Cranmer once again.
The common barber clipt your hair, and I
Scraped from your finger-points the holy oil;
And, worse than all, you had to kneel to *me:*
Which was not pleasant for you, Master Cranmer.
Now you, that would not recognize the Pope,
And you, that would not own the Real Presence,
Have found a real presence in the stake,
Which frights you back into the ancient faith ;
And so you have recanted to the Pope.
How are the mighty fallen, Master Cranmer !
    Cranmer. You have been more fierce against the
      Pope than I ;
But why fling back the stone he strikes me with?
                                        [*Aside.*
O Bonner, if I ever did you kindness—
Power hath been given you to try faith by fire—
Pray you, remembering how yourself have changed,
Be somewhat pitiful, after I have gone,
To the poor flock—to women and to children—
That when I was archbishop held with me.
    Bonner. Ay—gentle as they call you—live or die !
Pitiful to this pitiful heresy?
I must obey the Queen and Council, and
Win thro' this day with honor to yourself,
And I'll say something for you ; so, good-bye. [*Exit.*
    Cranmer. This hard coarse man of old hath crouch'd
      to me
Till I myself was half ashamed for him.

Enter THIRLBY.

Weep not, good Thirlby.
    Thirlby.   Oh, my Lord, my Lord !
My heart is no such block as Bonner's is:
Who would not weep?
    Cranmer.   Why do you so my-lord me,
Who am disgraced?

Thirlby.   On earth; but saved in heaven
By your recanting.
    Cranmer.   Will they burn me, Thirlby?
    Thirlby. Alas, they will! These burnings will not
    help
The purpose of the faith; but my poor voice
Against them is a whisper to the roar
Of a spring-tide.
    Cranmer.   And they will surely burn me?
    Thirlby. Ay; and, besides, will have you in the
    church
Repeat your recantation in the ears
Of all men, to the saving of their souls,
Before your execution. May God help you
Thro' that hard hour.
    Cranmer.   And may God bless you, Thirlby.
Well, they shall hear my recantation there.
                       [*Exit* THIRLBY.
Disgraced, dishonor'd!—not by them, indeed,
By mine own self—by mine own hand!
O thin-skinn'd hand and jutting veins, 'twas you
That sign'd the burning of poor Joan of Kent!
But then she was a witch. You have written much,
But you were never raised to plead for Frith,
Whose dogmas I have reach'd: he was deliver'd,
To the secular arm to burn; and there was Lambert;
Who can foresee himself? Truly these burnings,
As Thirlby says, are profitless to the burners,
And help the other side. You shall burn too,
Burn first when I am burnt.
Fire—inch by inch to die in agony! Latimer
Had a brief end—not Ridley. Hooper burn'd
Three-quarters of an hour. Will my faggots
Be wet as his were? It is a day of rain.
I will not muse upon it.
My fancy takes the burner's part, and makes
The fire seem even crueller than it is.
No, I not doubt that God will give me strength,
Albeit I have denied him.

       Enter SOTO *and* VILLA GARCIA.

    Villa Garcia.   We are ready
To take you to St. Mary's, Master Cranmer.
    Cranmer. And I: lead on; ye loose me from my
    bonds.   [*Exeunt.*

SCENE III.—ST. MARY'S CHURCH.

COLE *in the Pulpit,* LORD WILLIAMS *of* THAME *presiding.* LORD WILLIAM HOWARD, LORD PAGET, *and others.* CRANMER *enters between* SOTO *and* VILLA GARCIA, *and the whole Choir strike up* "Nunc Dimittis." CRANMER *is set upon a Scaffold before the people.*

    Cole. Behold him—
           [*A pause; people in the foreground.*
    People. Oh, unhappy sight!
    First Protestant. See how the tears run down his
fatherly face.
    Second Protestant. James, didst thou ever see a car-
    rion crow
Stand watching a sick beast before he dies?
    First Protestant. Him perch'd up there? I wish
some thunderbolt
Would make this Cole a cinder, pulpit and all.
    Cole. Behold him, brethren: he hath cause to
weep!—
So have we all: weep with him if ye will,
Yet—
It is expedient for one man to die,
Yea, for the people, lest the people die.
Yet wherefore should he die that hath return'd
To the one Catholic Universal Church,
Repentant of his errors?
    Protestant murmurs. Ay, tell us that.
    Cole. Those of the wrong side will despise the man,
Deeming him one that thro' the fear of death

Gave up his cause, except he seal his faith
In sight of all with flaming martyrdom.
    Cranmer.   Ay.
    Cole. Ye hear him, and albeit there may seem
According to the canons pardon due
To him that so repents, yet are there causes
Wherefore our Queen and Council at this time
Adjudge him to the death. He hath been a traitor,
A shaker and confounder of the realm;
And when the King's divorce was sued at Rome,
He here, this heretic metropolitan,
As if he had been the Holy Father, sat
And judged it. Did I call him heretic?
A huge heresiarch! Never was it known
That any man so writing, preaching so,
So poisoning the Church, so long continuing,
Hath found his pardon: therefore he must die,
For warning and example.
                   Other reasons
There be for this man's ending, which our Queen
And Council at this present deem it not
Expedient to be known.
    Protestant murmurs. I warrant you.
    Cole. Take therefore, all, example by this man;
For if our holy Queen not pardon him,
Much less shall others in like cause escape,
That all of you, the highest as the lowest,
May learn there is no power against the Lord.
There stands a man, once of so high degree,
Chief prelate of our Church, archbishop, first
In Council, second person in the realm,
Friend for so long time of a mighty King;
And now ye see downfallen and debased
From councillor to caitiff—fallen so low,
The leprous flutterings of the byway. scum
And offal of the city, would not change
Estates with him: in brief, so miserable,
There is no hope of better left for him,
No place for worse.
             Yet, Cranmer, be thou glad.
This is the work of God. He is glorified
In thy conversion: lo! thou art reclaim'd;
He brings thee home: nor fear but that to-day
Thou shalt receive the penitent thief's award,
And be with Christ the Lord in Paradise.
Remember how God made the fierce fire seem
To those three children like a pleasant dew.
Remember, too,
The triumph of St. Andrew on his cross,
The patience of St. Lawrence in the fire.
Thus, if thou call on God and all the saints,
God will beat down the fury of the flame,
Or give thee saintly strength to undergo.
And for thy soul shall masses here be sung
By every priest in Oxford. Pray for him.
    Cranmer. Ay, one and all, dear brothers, pray for
me;
Pray with one breath, one heart, one soul for me.
    Cole. And now, lest anyone among yon doubt
The man's conversion and remorse of heart,
Yourselves shall hear him speak. Speak, Master Cran-
    mer,
Fulfil your promise made me, and proclaim
Your true undoubted faith, that all may hear.
    Cranmer. And that I will. O God, Father of heav-
en!
O Son of God, Redeemer of the world!
O Holy Ghost! proceeding from them both,
Three persons and one God, have mercy on me,
Most miserable sinner, wretched man.
I have offended against heaven and earth
More grievously than any tongue can tell.
Then whither should I flee for any help?
I am ashamed to lift my eyes to heaven,
And I can find no refuge upon earth.
Shall I despair then? God forbid! O God,
For thou art merciful, refusing none
That come to Thee for succor, unto Thee,

Therefore, I come: humble myself to Thee;
Saying, O Lord God, although my sins be great,
For thy great mercy have mercy! O God the Son,
Not for slight faults alone, when thou becamest
Man in the Flesh, was the great mystery wrought;
O God the Father, not for little sins
Didst thou yield up thy Son to human death;
But for the greatest sin that can be sinn'd,
Yea, even such as mine, incalculable,
Unpardonable,—sin against the light,
The truth of God, which I had proven and known.
Thy mercy must be greater than all sin.
Forgive me, Father, for no merit of mine,
But that Thy name by man be glorified,
And Thy most blessed Son's, who died for man.
Good people, every man at time of death
Would fain set forth some saying that may live
After his death and better humankind;
For death gives life's last word a power to live,
And, like the stone-cut epitaph, remain
After the vanish'd voice, and speak to men.
God grant me grace to glorify my God!
And first I say it is a grievous case,
Many so dote upon this bubble world,
Whose colors in a moment break and fly,
They care for nothing else. What saith St. John?—
"Love of this world is hatred against God."
Again, I pray you all that, next to God,
You do unmurmuringly and willingly
Obey your King and Queen, and not for dread
Of these alone, but from the fear of Him
Whose ministers they be to govern you.
Thirdly, I pray you all to love together
Like brethren; yet what hatred Christian men
Bear to each other, seeming not as brethren,
But mortal foes! But do you good to all
As much as in you lieth. Hurt no man more
Than you would harm your loving natural brother
Of the same roof, same breast. If any do,
Albeit he think himself at home with God,
Of this be sure, he is whole worlds away.
    Protestant murmurs. What sort of brothers then be
        those that lust
To burn each other?
    Williams.   Peace among you, there.
    Cranmer. Fourthly, to those that own exceeding
        wealth,
Remember that sore saying spoken once
By Him that was the truth, "How hard it is
For the rich man to enter into heaven!"
Let all rich men remember that hard word.
I have not time for more: if ever, now
Let them flow forth in charity, seeing now
The poor so many, and all food so dear.
Long have I lain in prison, yet have heard
Of all their wretchedness. Give to the poor,
Ye give to God. He is with us in the poor.
And now, and forasmuch as I have come
To the last end of life, and thereupon
Hangs all my past, and all my life to be,
Either to live with Christ in heaven with joy,
Or to be still in pain with devils in hell;
And, seeing in a moment I shall find
                        [*Pointing upwards.*
Heaven or else hell ready to swallow me,
                        [*Pointing downwards.*
I shall declare to you my very faith
Without all color.
    Cole.   Hear him, my good brethren.
    Cranmer. I do believe in God, Father of all:
In every article of the Catholic faith,
And every syllable taught us by our Lord,
His prophets, and apostles, in the Testaments,
Both Old and New.
    Cole.   Be plainer, Master Cranmer.
    Cranmer. And now I come to the great cause that
        weighs
Upon my conscience more than anything

Or said or done in all my life by me;
For there be writings I have set abroad
Against the truth I knew within my heart,
Written for fear of death, to save my life,
If that might be: the papers by my hand
Sign'd since my degradation—by this hand
                        [*Holding out his right hand.*
Written and sign'd—I here renounce them all;
And, since my hand offended, having written
Against my heart, my hand shall first be burnt,
So I may come to the fire.
                        [*Protestant murmurs.*
    First Protestant. I knew it would be so.
    Second Protestant.   Our prayers are heard!
    Third Protestant. God bless him!
    Catholic murmurs. Out upon him! out upon him!
Liar! dissembler! traitor! to the fire!
    Williams (raising his voice). You know that you re-
        canted all you said
Touching the sacrament in that same book
You wrote against my Lord of Winchester.
Dissemble not; play the plain Christian man.
    Cranmer. Alas! my Lord,
I have been a man loved plainness all my life;
I *did* dissemble, but the hour has come
For utter truth and plainness: wherefore, I say,
I hold by all I wrote within that book,
Moreover,
As for the Pope I count him Antichrist,
With all his devil's doctrines; and refuse,
Reject him, and abhor him. I have said.
    [*Cries on all sides,* "Pull him down! Away with
        him!"
    Cole. Aye, stop the heretic's mouth. Hale him away.
    Williams. Harm him not, harm him not, have him
        to the fire.
    [*Cranmer goes out between two Friars, smiling;
    hands are reached to him from the crowd.* Lord
    William Howard *and* Lord Paget *are left alone
    in the church.*
    Paget. The nave and aisles all empty as a fool's jest!
No, here's Lord William Howard. What, my Lord!
You have not gone to see the burning?
    Howard.   Fie!
To stand at ease, and stare as at a show,
And watch a good man burn. Never again.
I saw the deaths of Latimer and Ridley.
Moreover, tho' a Catholic, I would not,
For the pure honor of our common nature,
Hear what I might—another recantation
Of Cranmer at the stake.
    Paget.   You'd not hear that.
He pass'd out smiling, and he walk'd upright;
His eye was like a soldier's, whom the general
He looks to and he leans on as his God,
Hath rated for some backwardness and bidd'n him
Charge one against a thousand, and the man
Hurls his soil'd life against the pikes and dies.
    Howard. Yet that he might not, after all those papers
Of recantation, yield again, who knows?
    Paget. Papers of recantation! Think you then
That Cranmer read all papers that he sign'd?
Or sign'd all those they tell us that he sign'd?
Nay, I trow not; and you shall see, my Lord,
That howsoever hero-like the man
Dies in the fire, this Bonner or another
Will in some lying fashion misreport
His ending to the glory of their church.
And you saw Latimer and Ridley die?
Latimer was eighty, was he not? His best
Of life was over then.
    Howard.   His eighty years
Look'd somewhat crooked on him in his frieze;
But after they had stript him to his shroud,
He stood upright, a lad of twenty-one,
And gather'd with his hands the starting flame,
And wash'd his hands and all his face therein,
Until the powder suddenly blew him dead.

Ridley was longer burning, but he died
As manfully and boldly: and, 'fore God,
I know them heretics, but right English ones.
If ever, as Heaven grant, we clash with Spain,
Our Ridley-soldiers and our Latimer-sailors
Will teach her something.

Paget.   Your mild Legate Pole
Will tell you that the devil helpt them thro' it.

[*A murmur of the crowd in the distance.*
Hark, how those Roman wolfdogs howl and bay him.

Howard. Might it not be the other side rejoicing
In his brave end?

Paget.   They are too crush'd, too broken,
They can but weep in silence.

Howard.   Ay, ay, Paget,
They have brought it in large measure on them-
selves.
Have I not heard them mock the blessed Host
In songs so lewd, the beast might roar his claim
To being in God's image more than they?
Have I not seen the gamekeeper, the groom,
Gardener, and huntsman, in the parson's place,
The parson from his own spire swung out dead,
And Ignorance crying in the streets, and all men
Regarding her? I say they have drawn the fire
On their own heads: yet, Paget, I do hold
The Catholic, if he have the greater right,
Hath been the crueller.

Paget.   Action and reaction,
The miserable see-saw of our child-world,
Make us despise it at odd hours, my Lord.
Heaven help that this reaction not react,
Yet fiercelier under Queen Elizabeth,
So that she come to rule us.

Howard.   The world's mad.

Paget. My Lord, the world is like a drunken man,
Who cannot move straight to his end—but reels
Now to the right, then as far to the left,
Push'd by the crowd beside—and underfoot
An earthquake; for since Henry for a doubt—
Which a young lust had clapt upon the back,
Crying, "Forward"—set our old church rocking, men
Have hardly known what to believe, or whether
They should believe in anything: the currents
So shift and change, they see not how they are borne,
Nor whither. I conclude the King a beast:
Verily a lion, if you will—the world
A most obedient beast and fool—myself
Half beast and fool as appertaining to it;
Altho' your Lordship hath as little of each
Cleaving to your original Adam-clay
As may be consonant with mortality.

Howard. We talk, and Cranmer suffers.
The kindliest man I ever knew: see, see,
I speak of him in the past. Unhappy land!
Hard-natured Queen, half Spanish in herself,
And grafted on the hard-grain'd stock of Spain—
Her life, since Philip left her, and she lost
Her fierce desire of bearing him a child,
Hath, like a brief and bitter winter's day,
Gone narrowing down and darkening to a close.
There will be more conspiracies, I fear.

Paget. Ay, ay, beware of France.

Howard.   O Paget, Paget!
I have seen heretics of the poorer sort,
Expectant of the rack from day to day,
To whom the fire were welcome, lying chain'd
In breathless dungeons over steaming sewers,
Fed with rank bread that crawl'd upon the tongue,
And putrid water, every drop a worm,
Until they died of rotten limbs; and then
Cast on the dunghill naked, and become
Hideously alive again from head to heel,
Made even the carrion-nosing mongrel vomit
With hate and horror.

Paget.   Nay, you sicken *me*
To hear you.

Howard.   Fancy-sick; these things are done,

Done right against the promise of this Queen
Twice given.

Paget. No faith with heretics, my Lord!
Hist! there be two old gossips—Gospellers,
I take it; stand behind the pillar here:
I warrant you they talk about the burning.

Enter TWO OLD WOMEN. JOAN, *and after her* TIB.

Joan. Why, it be Tib.

Tib. I cum behind tha, gall, and couldn't make tha
hear. Eh, the wind and the wet! What a day, what
a day! nigh upo' judgment-daay loike. Pwoaps be
pretty things, Joan, but they wunt set i' the Lord's
cheer o' that day.

Joan. I must set down myself, Tib: it be a var waay
vor my owld legs up vro' Islip. Eh, my rheumatizy be
that bad howiver be I to win 'the burnin'.

Tib. I should saay 'twur ower by now. I'd ha' been
here avore, but Dumble wur blow'd wi' the wind, and
Dumble's the best milcher in Islip.

Joan. Our Daisy's as good 'z her.

Tib. Noa, Joan.

Joan. Our Daisy's butter's as good 'z hern.

Tib. Noa, Joan.

Joan. Our Daisy's cheeses be better.

Tib. Noa, Joan.

Joan. Eh, then ha' thy way wi' me, Tib; ez thou
hast wi' thy owld man.

Tib. Ay, Joan, and my owld man wur up and awaay
betimes wi' dree hard eggs for a good pleace at the
burnin'; and barrin' the wet, Hodge 'nd ha' been a-har-
rowin' o' white pea-zen i' the ontfield—and barrin' the
wind, Dumble wur blow'd wi' the wind, so 'z we was
forced to stick her, but we fetched her round at last.
Thank the Lord, therevore. Dumble's the best milcher
in Islip.

Joan. Thou's thy way wi' man and beast, Tib. I
wonder at tha', it beats me! Eh, but I do know ez
Pwoaps and vires be bad things; tell 'ee now, I heerd
summat as summun towld summun o' owld Bishop
Gardiner's eud; there wur an owld lord a-cum to dine
wi' un, and a wur so owld a couldn't bide vor his dinner, but a had to bide howsomiver, vor "I wunt dine,"
says my Lord Bishop, says he, "not till I hears ez Latimer and Ridley be a-vire;" and so they bided on and
on till vour o' the clock, till his man cum in post vro'
here, and tells un ez the vire has tuk holt, "Now,"
says the bishop, says he, "we'll gwo to dinner;" and
the owld lord fell to 's meat wi' a will. God bless un:
but Gardiner wur strnck down llke by the haud o' God
avore a could taste a mossel, and a set him all a-vire,
so 'z the tongue on un cum a-lolluping out o' 'is mouth
as black as a rat. Thank the Lord, therevore.

Paget. The fools!

Tib. Ay, Joan; and Queen Mary gwoes on a-burnin' and a-burniu', to git her banby born; but all her
burnin's 'ill never burn out the hypocrisy that makes
the water in her. There's nought but the vire of God's
hell ez can burn out that.

Joan. Thank the Lord, therevore.

Paget. The fools!

Tib. A-burnin', and a-burnin', and a-makin' o' volk
madder and madder; but tek thou my word vor't,
Joan—and I bean't wrong not twice i' ten year—the
burnin' o' the owld archbishop 'ill burn the Pwoap
out o' this 'ere land vor iver and iver.

Howard. Out of the church, you brace of cursed
crones,
Or I will have you duck'd. (*Women hurry out.*) Said
I not right?
For how should reverend prelate or throned prince
Brook for an hour such brute malignity?
Ah, what an acrid wine has Luther brew'd!

Paget. Pooh, pooh, my Lord! poor garrulous coun-
try wives.
Buy you their cheeses, and they'll side with you;
You cannot judge the liquor from the lees.

Howard. I think that in some sort we may. But see,

Enter PETERS.

Peters, my gentleman, an honest Catholic,
Who follow'd with the crowd to Cranmer's fire.
One that would neither misreport nor lie,
Not to gain paradise: no, nor if the Pope
Charged him to do it—he is white as death.
Peters, how pale you look! you bring the smoke
Of Cranmer's burning with you.
   Peters.   Twice or thrice
The smoke of Cranmer's burning wrapt me round.
   Howard. Peters, you know me Catholic, but English.
Did he die bravely? Tell me that, or leave
All else untold.
   Peters.   My Lord, he died most bravely.
   Howard. Then tell me all.
   Paget.   Ay, Master Peters, tell us.
   Peters. You saw him how he past among the crowd;
And ever as he walk'd the Spanish friars
Still plied him with entreaty and reproach:
But Cranmer, as the helmsman at the helm
Steers, ever looking to the happy haven
Where he shall rest at night, moved to his death;
And I could see that many silent hands
Came from the crowd and met his own; and thus,
When we had come where Ridley burnt with Latimer,
He, with a cheerful smile, as one whose mind
Is all made up, in haste put off the rags
They had mock'd his misery with, and all in white,

His long white beard, which he had never shaven
Since Henry's death, down-sweeping to the chain
Wherewith they bound him to the stake, he stood,
More like an ancient father of the Church
Than heretic of these times; and still the friars
Plied him, but Cranmer only shook his head,
Or answer'd them in smiling negatives;
Whereat Lord Williams gave a sudden cry:—
"Make short! make short!" and so they lit the wood.
Then Cranmer lifted his left hand to heaven,
And thrust his right into the bitter flame;
And crying, in his deep voice, more than once,
"This hath offended—this unworthy hand!"
So held it till it all was burn'd, before
The flame had reach'd his body. I stood near—
Mark'd him—he never uttered moan of pain;
He never stirr'd or writhed, but, like a statue,
Unmoving in the greatness of the flame,
Gave up the ghost; and so past martyr-like—
Martyr I may not call him—past—but whither?
   Paget. To purgatory, man, to purgatory.
   Peters. Nay, but, my Lord, he denied purgatory.
   Paget. Why, then to heaven, and God ha' mercy on
     him.
   Howard. Paget, despite his fearful heresies,
I loved the man, and needs must moan for him;
O Cranmer!
   Paget.   But your moan is useless now:
Come out, my Lord, it is a world of fools. [*Exeunt.*

ACT V.

SCENE I.—LONDON. HALL IN THE PALACE.

QUEEN, SIR NICHOLAS HEATH.

Heath. Madam,
I do assure you that it must be look'd to:
Calais is but ill-garrison'd, in Guisnes
Are scarce two hundred men, and the French fleet
Rule in the narrow seas, and wherefore could you not
If war should fall between yourself and France;
Or you will lose your Calais.
   Mary.   It shall be look'd to;
I wish you a good-morning, good Sir Nicholas:
Here is the King.   [*Exit* HEATH.

Enter PHILIP.

Ph'ip.   Sir Nicholas tells you true,
And you must look to Calais when I go.
   Mary. Go! must you go, indeed—again—so soon?
Why, nature's licensed vagabond, the swallow,
That might live always in the sun's warm heart,
Stays longer here in our poor north than you—
Knows where he nested—ever comes again.
   Philip. And, Madam, so shall I.
   Mary.   Oh, will you? will you?
I am faint with fear that you will come no more.
   Philip. Ay, ay; but many voices call me hence.
   Mary. Voices—I hear unhappy rumors—nay,
I say not, I believe. What voices call you
Dearer than mine that should be dearest to you?
Alas, my Lord! what voices, and how many?
   Philip. The voices of Castile and Aragon,
Granada, Naples, Sicily, and Milan—
The voices of Franche-Comté and the Netherlands,
The voices of Peru and Mexico,
Tunis, and Oran, and the Philippines,
And all the fair spice-islands of the East.
   Mary (*admiringly*). You are the mightiest monarch
    upon earth,

I but a little Queen; and so, indeed,
Need you the more; and wherefore could you not
Helm the huge vessel of your state, my liege,
Here, by the side of her who loves you most?
   Philip. No, Madam, no! a candle in the sun
Is all but smoke—a star beside the moon
Is all but lost; your people will not crown me—
Your people are as cheerless as your clime;
Hate me and mine: witness the brawls, the gibbets,
Here swings a Spaniard—there an Englishman;
The peoples are unlike as their complexion;
Yet will I be your swallow and return—
But now I cannot bide.
   Mary.   Not to help me?
They hate me also for my love to you,
My Philip; and these judgments on the land—
Harvestless autumns, horrible agues, plague—
   Philip. The blood and sweat of heretics at the stake
Is God's best dew upon the barren field.
Burn more!
   Mary.   I will, I will; and you will stay.
   Philip. Have I not said? Madam, I came to sue
Your Council and yourself to declare war.
   Mary. Sir, there are many English in your ranks
To help your battle.
   Philip.   So far, good. I say
I came to sue your Council and yourself
To declare war against the King of France.
   Mary. Not to see me?
   Philip.   Ay, Madam, to see you.
Unalterably and pesteringly fond!   [*Aside.*
But, soon or late you must have war with France;
King Henry warms your traitors at his hearth.
Carew is there, and Thomas Stafford there.
Courtenay, belike—
   Mary.   A fool and featherhead!
   Philip. Ay, but they use his name. In brief, this
    Henry
Stirs up your land against you to the intent
That you may lose your English heritage.

And then, your Scottish namesake marrying
The Dauphin, he would weld France, England, Scot-
     land,
Into one sword to hack at Spain and me.
   Mary. And yet the Pope is now colleagued with
France;
You make your wars upon him down in Italy:—
Philip, can that be well?
   Philip.   Content you, Madam:
You must abide my judgment, and my father's,
Who deems it a most just and holy war.
The Pope would cast the Spaniard out of Naples:
He calls us worse than Jews, Moors, Saracens.
The Pope has push'd his horns beyond his mitre—
Beyond his province. Now,
Duke Alva will but touch him on the horns,
And he withdraws; and of his holy head—
For Alva is true son of the true church—
No hair is harm'd. Will you not help me here?
   Mary. Alas! the Council will not hear of war.
They say your wars are not the wars of England.
They will not lay more taxes on a land
So hunger-nipt and wretched; and you know
The crown is poor. We have given the church-lands
     back:
The nobles would not; nay, they clapt their hands
Upon their swords when ask'd; and therefore God
Is hard upon the people. What's to be done?
Sir, I will move them in your cause again,
And we will raise us loans and subsidies
Among the merchants; and Sir Thomas Gresham
Will aid us. There is Antwerp and the Jews.
   Philip. Madam, my thanks.
   Mary.   And you will stay your going?
   Philip. And further to discourage and lay lame
The plots of France, altho' you love her not,
You must proclaim Elizabeth your heir.
She stands between you and the Queen of Scots.
   Mary. The Queen of Scots at least is Catholic.
   Philip. Ay, Madam, Catholic; but I will not have
The King of France the King of England too.
   Mary. But she's a heretic, and, when I am gone,
Brings the new learning back.
   Philip.   It must be done.
You must proclaim Elizabeth your heir.
   Mary. Then it is done; but you will stay your going
Somewhat beyond your settled purpose?
   Philip.   No!
   Mary. What, not one day?
   Philip.   You beat upon the rock.
   Mary. And I am broken there.
   Philip.   Is this a place
To wail in, Madam? what! a public hall!
Go in, I pray you.
   Mary.   Do not seem so changed.
Say go; but only say it lovingly.
   Philip. You do mistake. I am not one to change.
I never loved you more.
   Mary.   Sire, I obey you.
Come quickly.
   Philip. Ay.   [*Exit* MARY.

           Enter COUNT DE FERIA.

   Feria (*aside*).   The Queen in tears.
   Philip.   Feria!
Hast thou not mark'd—come closer to mine ear—
How doubly aged this Queen of ours hath grown
Since she lost hope of bearing us a child?
   Feria. Sire, if your Grace hath mark'd it, so have I.
   Philip. Hast thou not likewise mark'd Elizabeth,
How fair and royal—like a Queen, indeed?
   Feria. Allow me the same answer as before—
That if your Grace hath mark'd her, so have I.
   Philip. Good, now; methinks my Queen is like
     enough
To leave me by-and-by.
   Feria.   To leave you, sire?
   Philip. I mean not like to live. Elizabeth—

To Philibert of Savoy, as you know,
We meant to wed her; but I am not sure
She will not serve me better—so my Queen
Would leave me—as—my wife.
   Feria.   Sire, even so.
   Philip. She will not have Prince Philibert of Savoy.
   Feria. No, sire.
   Philip. I have to pray you, some odd time,
To sound the Princess carelessly on this;
Not as from me, but as your phantasy;
And tell me how she takes it.
   Feria.   Sire, I will.
   Philip. I am not certain but that Philibert
Shall be the man; and I shall urge his suit
Upon the Queen, because I am not certain:
You understand, Feria?
   Feria.   Sire, I do.
   Philip. And if you be not secret in this matter.
You understand me there, too?
   Feria.   Sire, I do.
   Philip. You must be sweet and supple, like a French-
     man.
She is none of those who loathe the honeycomb.
                                        [*Exit* FERIA.

              Enter RENARD.

   Renard. My liege, I bring you goodly tidings.
   Philip.   Well.
   Renard. There *will* be war with France, at last, my
     liege;
Sir Thomas Stafford, a bull-headed ass,
Sailing from France, with thirty Englishmen,
Hath taken Scarboro' Castle, north of York;
Proclaims himself protector, and affirms
The Queen has forfeited her right to reign
By marriage with an alien—other things
As idle; a weak Wyatt! Little doubt
This buzz will soon be silenced! but the Council
(I have talk'd with some already) are for war.
This is the fifth conspiracy hatch'd in France;
They show their teeth upon it; and your Grace,
So you will take advice of mine, should stay
Yet for awhile, to shape and guide the event.
   Philip. Good! Renard, I will stay then.
   Renard.   Also, sire,
Might I not say—to please your wife, the Queen?
   Philip. Ay, Renard, if you care to put it so.
                                        [*Exeunt.*

                    ———

SCENE II.—A ROOM IN THE PALACE.

           MARY *and* CARDINAL POLE.

   LADY CLARENCE *and* ALICE *in the background.*

   Mary. Reginald Pole, what news hath plagued thy
     heart?
What makes thy favor like the bloodless head
Fall'n on the block, and held up by the hair?
Philip?—
   Pole. No, Philip is as warm in life
As ever.
   Mary. Ay, and then as cold as ever.
Is Calais taken?
   Pole.   Cousin, there hath chanced
A sharper harm to England and to Rome,
Than Calais taken. Julius the Third
Was ever just and mild, and fatherlike;
But this new Pope Caraffa, Paul the Fourth,
Not only reft me of that legate-ship
Which Julius gave me, and the legate-ship
Annex'd to Canterbury—nay, but worse—
And yet I must obey the Holy Father,
And so must you, good cousin;—worse than all,
A passing bell toll'd in a dying ear—
He hath cited me to Rome, for heresy,
Before his Inquisition.

Mary.   I knew it, cousin,
But held from you all papers sent by Rome,
That you might rest among us, till the Pope,
To compass which I wrote myself to Rome,
Reversed his doom, and that you might not seem
To disobey his Holiness.

Pole.   He hates Philip;
He is all Italian, and he hates the Spaniard;
He cannot dream that *I* advised the war;
He strikes thro' me at Philip and yourself.
Nay, but I know it of old, he hates me too;
So brands me in the stare of Christendom
A heretic!
Now, even now, when bow'd before my time,
The house half-ruin'd ere the lease be out;
When I should guide the Church in peace at home,
After my twenty years of banishment,
And all my lifelong labor to uphold
The primacy—a heretic. Long ago,
When I was ruler in the patrimony,
I was too lenient to the Lutheran,
And I and learned friends among ourselves
Would freely canvass certain Lutheranisms.
What then! he knew I was no Lutheran.
A heretic!
He drew this shaft against me to the head,
When it was thought I might be chosen Pope,
But then withdrew it. In full con-istory,
When I was made archbishop, he approved me.
And how should he have sent me Legate hither,
Deeming me heretic? and what heresy since?
But he was evermore mine enemy,
And hates the Spaniard—fiery-choleric,
A drinker of black, strong, volcanic wines,
That ever make him fierier. I, a heretic!
Your Highness knows that in pursuing heresy
I have gone beyond your late Lord Chancellor,—
He cried "Enough! enough!" before his death,—
Gone beyond him and mine own natural man
(It was God's cause); so far they call me now
The scourge and butcher of their English church.

Mary. Have courage, your reward is heaven itself.

Pole. They groan amen; they swarm into the fire
Like flies—for what? No dogma. They know nothing;
They burn for nothing.

Mary.   You have done your best.

Pole. Have done my best, and as a faithful son,
That all day long hath wrought his father's work,
When back he comes at evening, hath the door
Shut on him by the father whom he loved,
His early follies cast into his teeth,
And the poor son turn'd out into the street
To sleep, to die—I shall die of it, cousin.

Mary. I pray you be not so disconsolate;
I still will do mine utmost with the Pope.
Poor cousin!
Have I not been the fast friend of your life
Since mine began? and it was thought we two
Might make one flesh, and cleave unto each other
As man and wife.

Pole.   Ah, cousin, I remember
How I would dandle you upon my knee
At lisping-age. I watch'd you dancing once
With your huge father; he look'd the Great Harry,
You but his cockboat: prettily you did it,
And innocently. No—we were not made
One flesh in happiness: no happiness here;
But now we are made one flesh in misery;
Our bridemaids are not lovely—Disappointment,
Ingratitude, Injustice, Evil-tongue,
Labor-in-vain.

Mary.   Surely, not all in vain.
Peace, cousin, peace! I am sad at heart myself.

Pole. Our altar is a mound of dead men's clay,
Dug from the grave that yawns for us beyond;
And there is one Death stands behind the Groom,
And there is one Death stands behind the Bride—

Mary. Have you been looking at the "Dance of
Death?"

Pole. No; but these libellous papers which I found
Strewn in your palace. Look you here—the Pope
Pointing at me with "Pole, the heretic,
Thou hast burnt others, do thou burn thyself,
Or I will burn thee;" and this other; see!—
"We pray continually for the death
Of our accursed Queen and Cardinal Pole."
This last—I dare not read it her.   [*Aside.*

Mary.   Away!
Why do you bring me these?
I thought you knew me better. I never read,
I tear them; they come back upon my dreams.
The hands that write them should be burnt clean
off
As Cranmer's, and the fiends that utter them
Tongue-torn with pincers, lash'd to death, or lie
Famishing in black cells, while famish'd rats
Eat them alive. Why do they bring me these?
Do you mean to drive me mad?

Pole.   I had forgotten
How these poor libels trouble you. Your pardon,
Sweet cousin, and farewell, "O bubble world,
Whose colors in a moment break and fly!"
Why, who said that? I know not—true enough!
[*Puts up the papers, all but the last, which falls.
Exit* POLE.

Alice. If Cranmer's spirit were a mocking one,
And heard these two, there might be sport for him.
.   [*Aside.*

Mary. Clarence, they hate me; even while I speak
There lurks a silent dagger, listening
In some dark closet, some long gallery, drawn,
And panting for my blood as I go by.

Lady Clarence. Nay, Madam, there be loyal papers
too,
And I have often found them.

Mary.   Find me one!

Lady Clarence. Ay, Madam; but Sir Nicholas Heath,
the Chancellor,
Would see your Highness.

Mary.   Wherefore should I see him?

Lady Clarence. Well, Madam, he may bring you
news from Philip.

Mary. So, Clarence.

Lady Clarence.   Let me first put up your hair;
It tumbles all abroad.

Mary.   And the gray dawn
Of an old age that never will be mine
Is all the clearer seen. No, no; what matters?
Forlorn I am, and let me look forlorn.

Enter SIR NICHOLAS HEATH.

Heath. I bring your Majesty such grievous news
I grieve to bring it. Madam, Calais is taken.

Mary. What traitor spoke? Here, let my Cousin
Pole
Seize him and burn him for a Lutheran.

Heath. Her Highness is unwell. I will retire.

Lady Clarence. Madam, your Chancellor, Sir Nicholas Heath.

Mary. Sir Nicholas? I am stunn'd—Nicholas Heath?
Methought some traitor smote me on the head.
What said you, my good Lord, that our brave English
Had sallied out from Calais and driven back
The Frenchmen from their trenches?

Heath.   Alas! no
That gateway to the mainland over which
Our flag hath floated for two hundred years
Is France again.

Mary.   So: but it is not lost—
Not yet. Send out: let England, as of old,
Rise lionlike, strike hard and deep into
The prey they are rending from her—ay, and rend
The renders too. Send out! send out! and make
Musters in all the counties; gather all

From sixteen years to sixty; collect the fleet;
Let every craft that carries sail and gun
Steer toward Calais. Guisnes is not taken yet?
  Heath. Guisnes is not taken yet.
  Mary.   There yet is hope.
  Heath. Ah, Madam, but your people are so cold;
I do much fear that England will not care.
Methinks there is no manhood left among us.
  Mary. Send out: I am too weak to stir abroad:
Tell my mind to the Council—to the Parliament:
Proclaim it to the winds. Thou art cold thyself
To babble of their coldness. Oh, would I were
My father for an hour! Away now—quick!
                                [*Exit* HEATH.
I hoped I had served God with all my might!
It seems I have not. Ah! much heresy
Shelter'd in Calais. Saints, I have rebuilt
Your shrines, set up your broken images;
Be comfortable to me. Suffer not
That my brief reign in England be defamed
Thro' all her angry chronicles hereafter
By loss of Calais. Grant me Calais. Philip,
We have made war upon the Holy Father
All for your sake: what good could come of that?
  Lady Clarence. No, Madam, not against the Holy
          Father;
You did but help King Philip's war with France.
Your troops were never down in Italy.
  Mary. I am a byword. Heretic and rebel
Point at me and make merry. Philip gone!
And Calais gone! Time that I were gone too!
  Lady Clarence. Nay, if the fœtid gutter had a voice
And cried I was not clean, what should I care?
Or you, for heretic cries? And I believe,
Spite of your melancholy Sir Nicholas,
Your England is as loyal as myself.
  Mary (seeing the paper dropt by POLE). There, there!
          another paper! Said you not
Many of these were loyal? Shall I try
If this be one of such?
  Lady Clarence.   Let it be, let it be.
God pardon me! I have never yet found one. [*Aside.*
  Mary (reads). "Your people hate you as your hus-
          band hates you."
Clarence, Clarence, what have I done? what sin
Beyond all grace, all pardon? Mother of God,
Thou knowest never woman meant so well
And fared so ill in this disastrous world.
My people hate me and desire my death.
  Lady Clarence. No, Madam, no.
  Mary. My husband hates me and desires my death.
  Lady Clarence. No, Madam; these are libels.
  Mary. I hate myself, and I desire my death.
  Lady Clarence. Long live your Majesty! Shall Alice
          sing you
One of her pleasant songs? Alice, my child,
Bring us your lute (ALICE *goes*). They say the gloom
      of Saul
Was lighten'd by young David's harp.
  Mary.   Too young!
And never knew a Philip (*re-enter* ALICE). Give me
      the lute.
He hates me!

                (*She sings.*)

Hapless doom of woman happy in betrothing!
Beauty passes like a breath, and love is lost in loathing:
Low, my lute; speak low, my lute, but say the world is nothing—
          Low, lute, low!
Love will hover round the flowers when they first awaken;
Love will fly the fallen leaf, and not be overtaken;
Low, my lute! oh low, my lute! we fade, and are forsaken—
          Low, dear lute, low!

Take it away! not low enough for me!
  Alice. Your Grace hath a low voice.
  Mary. How dare you say it?
Even for that he hates me. A low voice
Lost in a wilderness where none can hear!
A voice of shipwreck on a shoreless sea!

A low voice from the dust and from the grave (*sitting
      on the ground*).
There, am I low enough now?
  Alice. Good Lord! how grim and ghastly looks her
          Grace,
With both her knees drawn upward to her chin.
There was an old-world tomb beside my father's,
And this was open'd, and the dead were found
Sitting, and in this fashion; she looks a corpse.

          Enter LADY MAGDALEN DACRES.

  Lady Magdalen. Madam, the Count de Feria waits
      without,
In hopes to see your Highness.
  Lady Clarence (pointing to MARY). Wait he must—
Her trance again. She neither sees nor hears,
And may not speak for hours.
  Lady Magdalen.   Unhappiest
Of queens and wives and women.
  Alice (in the foreground with LADY MAGDALEN). And
      all along
Of Philip.
  Lady Magdalen. Not so loud! Our Clarence there
Sees ever such an aureole round the Queen.
It gilds the greatest wronger of her peace,
Who stands the nearest to her.
  Alice.   Ay, this Philip:
I used to love the Queen with all my heart—
God help me, but methinks I love her less
For such a dotage upon such a man.
I would I were as tall and strong as you.
  Lady Magdalen. I seem half-shamed at times to be
      so tall.
  Alice. You are the stateliest deer in all the herd—
Beyond his aim; but I am small and scandalous,
And love to hear bad tales of Philip.
  Lady Magdalen.   Why?
I never heard him utter worse of you
Than that you were low-statured.
  Alice.   Does he think
Low stature is low nature, or all women's
Low as his own?
  Lady Magdalen. There you strike in the nail.
This coarseness is a want of phantasy.
It is the low man thinks the woman low;
Sin is too dull to see beyond himself.
  Alice. Ah, Magdalen, sin is bold as well as dull.
How dared he?
  Lady Magdalen. Stupid soldiers oft are bold.
Poor lads, they see not what the general sees,
A risk of utter ruin. I am *not*
Beyond his aim, or was not.
  Alice.   Who? Not you?
Tell, tell me: save my credit with myself.
  Lady Magdalen. I never breathed it to a bird in the
      eaves,
Would not for all the stars and maiden moon
Our drooping Queen should know! In Hampton Court
My window look'd upon the corridor;
And I was robing;—this poor throat of mine,
Barer than I should wish a man to see it—
When he we speak of drove the window back,
And, like a thief, push'd in his royal hand;
But by God's providence a good stout staff
Lay near me; and you know me strong of arm;
I do believe I lamed his Majesty's
For a day or two, tho', give the Devil his due,
I never found he bore me any spite.
  Alice. I would she could have wedded that poor youth,
My Lord of Devon—light enough, God knows,
And mixt with Wyatt's rising, and the boy
Not out of him; but neither cold, coarse, cruel,
And, more than all, no Spaniard.
  Lady Clarence.   Not so loud.
Lord Devon, girls! what are you whispering here?
  Alice. Probing an old state-secret—how it chanced
That this young Earl was sent on foreign travel,
Not lost his head.

Lady Clarence. There was no proof against him.

Alice. Nay, Madam, did not Gardiner intercept
A letter which the Count de Noailles wrote
To that dead traitor, Wyatt, with full proof
Of Courtenay's treason? What became of that?

Lady Clarence. Some say that Gardiner, out of love
for him,
Burnt it, and some relate that it was lost
When Wyatt sack'd the Chancellor's house in South-
wark.
Let dead things rest.

Alice. Ay, and with him who died
Alone in Italy.

Lady Clarence. Much changed, I hear,
Had put off levity and put graveness on.
The foreign courts report him in his manner
Noble as his young person and old shield.
It might be so—but all is over now;
He caught a chill in the lagoons of Venice,
And died in Padua.

Mary (looking up suddenly). Died in the true faith?

Lady Clarence. Ay, Madam, happily.

Mary. Happier he than I.

Lady Magdalen. It seems her Highness hath awak-
en'd. Think you
That I might dare to tell her that the Count—

Mary. I will see no man hence for evermore,
Saving my confessor and my cousin Pole.

Lady Magdalen. It is the Count de Feria, my dear
lady.

Mary. What Count?

Lady Magdalen. The Count de Feria, from his Majesty,
King Philip.

Mary. Philip! quick! loop up my hair!
Throw cushions on that seat, and make it throne-
like.
Arrange my dress—the gorgeous Indian shawl
That Philip brought me in our happy days!—
That covers all. So—am I somewhat queenlike,
Bride of the mightiest sovereign upon earth?

Lady Clarence. Ay, so your Grace would bide a
moment yet.

Mary. No, no, he brings a letter. I may die
Before I read it. Let me see him at once.

Enter COUNT DE FERIA *(kneels).*

Feria. I trust your Grace is well. *(Aside.)* How her
hand burns!

Mary. I am not well, but it will better me,
Sir Count, to read the letter which you bring.

Feria. Madam, I bring no letter.

Mary. How! no letter?

Feria. His Highness is so vex'd with strange affairs—

Mary. That his own wife is no affair of his.

Feria. Nay, Madam, nay! he sends his veriest love,
And says he will come quickly.

Mary. Doth he, indeed?
You, sir, do *you* remember what *you* said
When last you came to England?

Feria. Madam, I brought
My King's congratulations; it was hoped
Your Highness was once more in happy state
To give him an heir male.

Mary. Sir, you said more:
You said he would come quickly. I had horses
On all the road from Dover, day and night;
On all the road from Harwich, night and day;
But the child came not, and the husband came not;
And yet he will come quickly. Thou hast learnt
Thy lesson, and I mine. There is no need
For Philip so to shame himself again.
Return,
And tell him that I know he comes no more.
Tell him at last I know his love is dead,
And that I am in state to bring forth dead—
Thou art commission'd to Elizabeth,
And not to me!

Feria. Mere compliments and wishes.
But shall I take some message from your Grace?

Mary. Tell her to come and close my dying eyes,
And wear my crown, and dance upon my grave.

Feria. Then I may say your Grace will see your sis-
ter?
Your Grace is too low-spirited. Air and sunshine.
I would we had you, Madam, in our warm Spain.
You droop in your dim London.

Mary. Have him away;
I sicken of his readiness.

Lady Clarence. My Lord Count,
Her Highness is too ill for colloquy.

Feria (kneels and kisses her hand). I wish her Highness better. *(Aside.)* How her hand burns!
[*Exeunt.*

SCENE III.—A HOUSE NEAR LONDON.

ELIZABETH, STEWARD OF THE HOUSEHOLD, ATTEND-
ANTS.

Elizabeth. There's half an angel wrong'd in your
account:
Methinks I am all angel, that I bear it
Without more ruffling. Cast it o'er again.

Steward. I were whole devil if I wrong'd you, Madam.
[*Exit* STEWARD.

Attendant. The Count de Feria, from the King of
Spain.

Elizabeth. Ah!—let him enter. Nay, you need not
go: [*To her* LADIES.
Remain within the chamber, but apart.
We'll have no private conference. Welcome to England!

Enter FERIA.

Feria. Fair island star.

Elizabeth. I shine! What else, Sir Count?

Feria. As far as France, and into Philip's heart.
My King would know if you be fairly served,
And lodged, and treated.

Elizabeth. You see the lodging, sir,
I am well-served, and am in everything
Most loyal and most grateful to the Queen.

Feria. You should be grateful to my master, too;
He spoke of this; and unto him you owe
That Mary hath acknowledged you her heir.

Elizabeth. No, not to her, nor him; but to the peo-
ple,
Who know my right, and love me, as I love
The people! whom God aid!

Feria. You will be Queen,
And, were I Philip—

Elizabeth. Wherefore pause you—what?

Feria. Nay, but I speak from mine own self, not
him:
Your royal sister cannot last; your hand
Will be much coveted! What a delicate one!
Our Spanish ladies have none such—and there,
Were you in Spain, this fine fair gossamer gold—
Like sun-gilt breathings on a frosty dawn—
That hovers round your shoulder—

Elizabeth. Is it so fine?
Truth, some have said so.

Feria. —would be deemed a miracle.

Elizabeth. Your Philip hath gold hair and golden
beard;
There must be ladies many with hair like mine.

Feria. Some few of Gothic blood have golden hair,
But none like yours.

Elizabeth. I am happy you approve it.

Feria. But as to Philip and your Grace, consider,
If such a one as you should match with Spain,
What hinders but that Spain and England join'd
Should make the mightiest empire earth has known.
Spain would be England on her seas, and England
Mistress of the Indies.

Elizabeth.   It may chance that England
Will be the Mistress of the Indies yet,
Without the help of Spain.
    Feria.   Impossible;
Except you put Spain down.
Wide of the mark ev'n for a madman's dream.
    Elizabeth. Perhaps; but we have seamen. Count
de Feria.
I take it that the King hath spoken to you;
But is Don Carlos such a goodly match?
    Feria. Don Carlos, Madam, is but twelve years old.
    Elizabeth. Ay, tell the King that I will muse upon it;
He is my good friend, and I would keep him so;
But—he would have me Catholic of Rome,
And that I scarce can be; and, sir, till now
My sister's marriage, and my father's marriages,
Make me full fain to live and die a maid.
But I am much beholden to your King.
Have you aught else to tell me?
    Feria.   Nothing, Madam,
Save that methought I gather'd from the Queen
That she would see your Grace before she—died.
    Elizabeth. God's death! and wherefore spake you
not before?
We dally with our lazy moments here,
And hers are number'd. Horses there, without!
I am much beholden to the King, your master.
Why did you keep me prating? Horses, there!
                  [*Exit* Elizabeth, *etc.*
    Feria. So from a clear sky falls the thunderbolt!
Don Carlos? Madam, if you marry Philip,
Then I and he will snaffle your "God's death,"
And break your paces in, and make you tame;
God's death, forsooth—you do not know King Philip.
                          [*Exit.*

SCENE IV. — LONDON. BEFORE THE PALACE.

A light burning within. Voices *of the night passing.*

    First. Is not yon light in the Queen's chamber?
    Second.   Ay,
They say she's dying.
    First.   So is Cardinal Pole.
May the great angels join their wings, and make
Down for their heads to heaven!
    Second.   Amen. Come on.
                          [*Exeunt.*

Two Others.

    First. There's the Queen's light. I hear she cannot
live.
    Second. God curse her and her Legate! Gardiner
burns
Already; but to pay them full in kind,
The hottest hold in all the devil's den
Were but a sort of winter; sir, in Guernsey,
I watch'd a woman burn; and in her agony
The mother came upon her—a child was born—
And, sir, they hurl'd it back into the fire,
That, being but baptized in fire, the babe
Might be in fire forever. Ah, good neighbor,
There should be something fierier than fire
To yield them their deserts.
    First.   Amen to all
You wish, and further.
    A Third Voice. Deserts! Amen to what? Whose
deserts? Yours? You have a gold ring on your fin-
ger, and soft raiment about your body; and is not the
woman up yonder sleeping, after all she has done, in
peace and quietness, on a soft bed, in a closed room,
with light, fire, physic, tendance; and I have seen the
true men of Christ lying famine-dead by scores, and
under no ceiling but the cloud that wept on them, not
for them.
    First. Friend, tho' so late, it is not safe to preach.
You had best go home. What are you?

    Third. What am I? One who cries continually with
sweat and tears to the Lord God that it would please
Him out of His infinite love to break down all kingship and queenship, all priesthood and prelacy; to
cancel and abolish all bonds of human allegiance, all
the magistracy, all the nobles, and all the wealthy;
and to send us again, according to his promise, the
one King, the Christ, and all things in common, as in
the day of the first church, when Christ Jesus was
King.
    First. If ever I heard a madman—let's away!
Why, you long-winded —— sir, you go beyond me.
I pride myself on being moderate.
Good-night! Go home. Besides, you curse so loud,
The watch will hear you. Get you home at once.
                          [*Exeunt.*

SCENE V.—LONDON. A ROOM IN THE PALACE.

*A gallery on one side. The moonlight streaming
through a range of windows on the wall opposite.*
Mary, Lady Clarence, Lady Magdalen Dacres,
Alice. Queen *pacing the gallery. A writing-ta-
ble in front.* Queen *comes to the table and writes,
and goes again, pacing the gallery.*

    Lady Clarence. Mine eyes are dim: what hath she
written? Read.
    Alice. "I am dying, Philip; come to me."
    Lady Magdalen. There—up and down. poor lady, up
and down.
    Alice. And how her shadow crosses one by one
The moonlight casements pattern'd on the wall,
Following her like her sorrow. She turns again.
            [Queen *sits and writes, and goes again.*
    Lady Clarence. What hath she written now?
    Alice. Nothing; but "come, come, come," and all
awry,
And blotted by her tears. This cannot last.
                        [Queen *returns.*
    Mary. I whistle to the bird has broken cage,
And all in vain.   [*Sitting down.*
Calais gone—Guisnes gone, too—and Philip gone.
    Lady Clarence. Dear Madam, Philip is but at the
wars;
I cannot doubt but that he comes again;
And he is with you in a measure still.
I never look'd upon so fair a likeness
As your great King in armor there, his hand
Upon his helmet.
      [*Pointing to the portrait of* Philip *on the wall.*
    Mary.   Doth he not look noble?
I had heard of him in battle over seas,
And I would have my warrior all in arms.
He said it was not courtly to stand helmeted
Before the Queen. He had his gracious moment,
Altho' you'll not believe me. How he smiles,
As if he loved me yet!
    Lady Clarence.   And so he does.
    Mary. He never loved me—nay, he could not love
me.
It was his father's policy against France.
I am eleven years older than he,
Poor boy.   [*Weeps.*
    Alice. That was a lusty boy of twenty-seven; [*Aside*
Poor enough in God's grace!
    Mary.   —And all in vain!
The Queen of Scots is married to the Dauphin,
And Charles, the lord of this low world, is gone;
And all his wars and wisdoms past away;
And in a moment I shall follow him.
    Lady Clarence. Nay, dearest Lady, see your good
physician.
    Mary. Drugs—but he knows they cannot help me—
says
That rest is all—tells me I must not think—

That I must rest—I shall rest by-and-by.
Catch the wild cat, cage him, and when he springs
And maims himself against the bars, say "Rest:"
Why, you must kill him if you would have him rest—
Dead or alive, you cannot make him happy.
        Lady Clarence. Your Majesty has lived so pure a
                life,
And done such mighty things by Holy Church,
I trust that God will make you happy yet.
        Mary. What is the strange thing happiness?   Sit
                down here;
Tell me thine happiest hour.
        Lady Clarence.   I will, if that
May make your Grace forget yourself a little.
There runs a shallow brook across our field
For twenty miles, where the black crow flies five,
And doth so bound and babble all the way
As if itself were happy. It was May-time,
And I was walking with the man I loved.
I loved him, but I thought I was not loved.
And both were silent, letting the wild brook
Speak for us—till he stoop'd and gather'd one
From out a bed of thick forget-me-nots,
Look'd hard and sweet at me, and gave it me.
I took it, tho' I did not know I took it,
And put it in my bosom, and all at once
I felt his arms about me, and his lips—
        Mary. O God! I have been too slack, too slack;
There are Hot Gospellers even among our guards—
Nobles we dared not touch. We have but burnt
The heretic priest, workmen, and women and chil-
        dren.
Wet, famine, ague, fever, storm, wreck, wrath—
We have so play'd the coward; but, by God's grace,
We'll follow Philip's leading, and set up
The Holy Office here—garner the wheat,
And burn the tares with unquenchable fire!
Burn!—
Fie, what a savor! Tell the cooks to close
The doors of all the offices below.
Latimer!
Sir, we are private with our women here—
Ever a rough, blunt, and uncourtly fellow—
Thou light a torch that never will go out!
'Tis out—mine flames. Women, the Holy Father
Has ta'en the legateship from our cousin Pole—
Was that well done? and poor Pole pines of it,
As I do, to the death. I am but a woman,
I have no power. Ah, weak and meek old man,
Seven-fold dishonor'd even in the sight
Of thine own sectaries—No, no. No pardon!—
Why, that was false: there is the right hand still
Beckons me hence.
Sir, you were burnt for heresy, not for treason,
Remember that! 'Twas I and Bonner did it,
And Pole; we are three to one. Have you found
        mercy there,
Grant it me here; and see he smiles and goes,
Gentle as in life.
        Alice.   Madam, who goes? King Philip?
        Mary. No, Philip comes and goes, but never goes.
Women, when I am dead,
Open my heart, and there you will find written
Two names, Philip and Calais; open his—
So that he have one—
You will find Philip only. policy, policy—
Ay, worse than that—not one hour true to me!
Foul maggots crawling in a fester'd vice!
Adulterous to the very heart of hell.
Hast thou a knife?
        Alice. Ay, Madam, but o' God's mercy—
        Mary. Fool, think'st thou I would peril mine own
                soul
By slaughter of the body? I could not, girl,
Not this way—callous with a constant stripe,
Unwoundable. Thy knife!
        Alice.   Take heed, take heed!
The blade is keen as death.

        Mary.   This Philip shall not
Stare in upon me in my haggardness;
Old, miserable, diseased,
Incapable of children. Come thou down.
        [*Cuts out the picture and throws it down,*
Lie there. (*Wails.*) O God, I have kill'd my Philip.
        Alice.   No,
Madam, you have but cut the canvas out;
We can replace it.
        Mary.   All is well then; rest—
I will to rest; he said I must have rest.
        [*Cries of "* ELIZABETH *" in the street.*
A cry! What's that? Elizabeth? revolt?
A new Northumberland, another Wyatt?
I'll fight it on the threshold of the grave.
        Lady Clarence. Madam, your royal sister comes to
                see you.
        Mary. I will not see her.
Who knows if Boleyn's daughter be my sister?
I will see none except the priest. Your arm.
        [*To* LADY CLARENCE.
O Saint of Aragon, with that sweet worn smile
Among thy patient wrinkles, help me hence.
        [*Exeunt.*

The PRIEST *passes.*   *Enter* ELIZABETH *and* SIR WIL-
        LIAM CECIL.

        Elizabeth. Good counsel yours—
                No one in waiting? Still,
As if the chamberlain were Death himself!
The room she sleeps in—is not this the way?
No, that way there are voices. Am I too late?
Cecil....God guide me lest I lose the way.
        [*Exit* ELIZABETH.
        Cecil. Many points weather'd, many perilous ones,
At last a harbor opens; but therein
Sunk rocks—they need fine steering—much it is
To be nor mad, nor bigot—have a mind—
Not let priests' talk, or dream of worlds to be,
Miscolor things about her—sudden touches
For him, or him—sunk rocks; no passionate faith—
But—if let be—balance and compromise;
Brave, wary, sane to the heart of her—a Tudor
School'd by the shadow of death—a Boleyn, too,
Glancing across the Tudor—not so well.

        Enter ALICE.

How is the good Queen now?
        Alice.   Away from Philip.
Back in her childhood—prattling to her mother
Of her betrothal to the Emperor Charles,
And childlike-jealous of him again—and once
She thank'd her father sweetly for his book
Against that godless German. Ah, those days
Were happy. It was never merry world
In England, since the Bible came among us.
        Cecil. And who says that?
        Alice. It is a saying among the Catholics.
        Cecil. It never will be merry world in England,
Till all men have their Bible, rich and poor.
        Alice. The Queen is dying, or you dare not say it.

        Enter ELIZABETH.

        Elizabeth. The Queen is dead.
        Cecil.   Then here she stands! My homage.
        Elizabeth. She knew me, and acknowledged me her
                heir,
Pray'd me to pay her debts, and keep the Faith;
Then clasp't the cross, and pass'd away in peace.
I left her lying still and beautiful,
More beautiful than in life. Why would you vex your-
        self,
Poor sister? Sir, I swear I have no heart
To be your Queen. To reign is restless fence,
Tierce, quart, and trickery. Peace is with the
        dead.
Her life was winter, for her spring was nipt:
And she loved much: pray God she be forgiven.

Cecil. Peace with the dead, who never were at
   peace !
Yet she loved one so much—I needs must say—
That never English monarch dying left
England so little.
   Elizabeth.   But with Cecil's aid
And others, if our person be secured
From traitor stabs, we will make England great.

Enter PAGET, *and other* LORDS OF THE COUNCIL, SIR
       RALPH BAGENHALL, *etc.*

Lords. God save Elizabeth, the Queen of England !
Bagenhall. God save the Crown : the Papacy is no
   more.
Paget (aside). Are we so sure of that ?
Acclamation.   God save the Queen !

TO HIS EXCELLENCY

THE RIGHT HON. LORD LYTTON,

VICEROY AND GOVERNOR-GENERAL OF INDIA.

—◇◇—

My dear Lord Lytton,—After old-world records—such as the Bayeux tapestry and the Roman de Rou—Edward Freeman's History of the Norman Conquest, and your father's Historical Romance treating of the same times, have been mainly helpful to me in writing this Drama. Your father dedicated his "Harold" to my father's brother; allow me to dedicate my "Harold" to yourself.

A. TENNYSON.

SHOW-DAY AT BATTLE ABBEY, 1876.

A GARDEN here—May breath and bloom of spring—
The cuckoo yonder from an English elm
Crying "with my false egg I overwhelm
The native nest:" and fancy hears the ring
Of harness, and that deathful arrow sing,
And Saxon battle-axe clang on Norman helm.
Here rose the dragon-banner of our realm:

Here fought, here fell, our Norman-slander'd king.
O Garden blossoming out of English blood!
O strange hate-healer Time! We stroll and stare
Where might made right eight hundred years ago;
Might, right? ay good, so all things make for good—
But he and he, if soul be soul, are where
Each stands full face with all he did below.

DRAMATIS PERSONÆ.

KING EDWARD THE CONFESSOR.
STIGAND (created Archbishop of Canterbury by the Antipope Benedict).
ALDRED (Archbishop of York).
THE NORMAN BISHOP OF LONDON.
HAROLD, Earl of Wessex, afterwards King of England,⎫
TOSTIG, Earl of Northumbria,⎪
GURTH, Earl of East Anglia,⎬ Sons of Godwin.
LEOFWIN, Earl of Kent and Essex,⎪
WULFNOTH,⎭
COUNT WILLIAM OF NORMANDY.
WILLIAM RUFUS.
WILLIAM MALET (a Norman Noble).*
EDWIN, Earl of Mercia,⎫ Sons of Alfgar of Mercia.
MORCAR, Earl of Northumbria after Tostig,⎭
GAMEL (a Northumbrian Thane).
GUY (Count of Ponthieu).
ROLF (a Ponthieu Fisherman).
HUGH MARGOT (a Norman Monk).
OSGOD and ATHELRIC (Canons from Waltham).
THE QUEEN (Edward the Confessor's Wife, Daughter of Godwin).
ALDWYTH (Daughter of Alfgar and Widow of Griffyth, King of Wales).
EDITH (Ward of King Edward).

Courtiers, Earls and Thanes, Men-at-Arms, Canons of Waltham, Fishermen, etc.

* ....quidam partim Normannus et Anglus
Compater Heraldi. (*Guy of Amiens*, 557.)

HAROLD.

ACT I.

SCENE I.—LONDON. THE KING'S PALACE.

(*A comet seen through the open window.*)

ALDWYTH, GAMEL, COURTIERS *talking together.*

First Courtier. Lo! there once more—this is the seventh night!
You grimly-glaring, treble-brandish'd scourge
Of England!
Second Courtier. Horrible!
First Courtier. Look you, there's a star
That dances in it as mad with agony!
Third Courtier. Ay, like a spirit in hell who skips and flies ·
To right and left, and cannot scape the flame.
Second Courtier. Steam'd upward from the undescendable
Abysm.
First Courtier. Or floated downward from the throne
Of God Almighty.
Aldwyth. Gamel, son of Orm,
What thinkest thou this means?
Gamel. War, my dear lady!
Aldwyth. Doth this affright thee?
Gamel. Mightily, my dear lady!
Aldwyth. Stand by me then, and look upon my face,
Not on the comet.

Enter MORCAR.

Brother, why so pale?
Morcar. It glares in heaven, it flares upon the Thames,
The people are as thick as bees below,
They hum like bees,—they cannot speak—for awe;
Look to the skies, then to the river, strike
Their hearts, and hold their babies up to it.
I think that they would Molochize them too,
To have the heavens clear.
Aldwyth. They fright not me.

(*Enter* LEOFWIN, *after him* GURTH.)

Ask thou Lord Leofwin what he thinks of this!
Morcar. Lord Leofwin, dost thou believe that these
Three rods of blood-red fire up yonder mean
The doom of England and the wrath of Heaven?
Bishop of London (passing). Did ye not cast with bestial violence
Our holy Norman bishops down from all
Their thrones in England? I alone remain.
Why should not Heaven be wroth?
Leofwin. With us, or thee?
Bishop of London. Did ye not outlaw your archbishop Robert,
Robert of Jumiéges—well-nigh murder him too?
Is there no reason for the wrath of Heaven?
Leofwin. Why then the wrath of Heaven hath three tails,
The devil only one. [*Exit* BISHOP OF LONDON.

(*Enter* ARCHBISHOP STIGAND.)

Ask *our* Archbishop.
Stigand should know the purposes of Heaven.
Stigand. Not I. I cannot read the face of heaven,
Perhaps our vines will grow the better for it.
Leofwin (laughing). He can but read the King's face on his coins.
Stigand. Ay, ay, young lord, *there* the King's face is power.
Gurth. O father, mock not at a public fear,
But tell us, is this pendent hell in heaven
A harm to England?
Stigand. Ask it of King Edward!
And he may tell thee, *I* am a harm to England.
Old uncanonical Stigand—ask of *me*
Who had my pallium from an Antipope!
Not he the man—for in our windy world
What's up is faith, what's down is heresy.
Our friends, the Normans, help to shake his chair.
I have a Norman fever on me, son,
And cannot answer sanely....What it means?
Ask our broad Earl. [*Pointing to* HAROLD, *who enters.*
Harold (seeing Gamel). Hail, Gamel, son of Orm!
Albeit no rolling stone, my good friend Gamel,
Thou hast rounded since we met. Thy life at home
Is easier than mine here. Look! am I not
Work-wan, flesh-fallen?
Gamel. Art thou sick, good Earl?
Harold. Sick as an autumn swallow for a voyage,
Sick for an idle week of hawk and hound
Beyond the seas—a change! When camest thou hither?
Gamel. To-day, good Earl.
Harold. Is the North quiet, Gamel?
Gamel. Nay, there be murmurs, for thy brother breaks us
With over-taxing—quiet, ay, as yet—
Nothing as yet.
Harold. Stand by him, mine old friend,
Thou art a great voice in Northumberland!
Advise him: speak him sweetly, he will hear thee.
He is passionate, but honest. Stand thou by him!
More talk of this to-morrow, if you weird sign
Not blast us in our dreams.—Well, father Stigand—
[*To* STIGAND, *who advances to him.*
Stigand (pointing to the comet). War there, my son?
Is that the doom of England?
Harold. Why not the doom of all the world as well?
For all the world sees it as well as England.
These meteors came and went before our day,
Not harming any: it threatens us no more
Than French or Norman. War? the worst that follows
Things that seem jerk'd out of the common rut
Of Nature is the hot religious fool,
Who, seeing war in heaven, for heaven's credit
Makes it on earth: but look, where Edward draws
A faint foot hither, leaning upon Tostig.
He hath learnt to love our Tostig much of late.
Leofwin. And *he* hath learnt, despite the tiger in him,
To sleek and supple himself to the King's hand.
Gurth. I trust the kingly touch that cures the evil
May serve to charm the tiger out of him.
Leofwin. He hath as much of cat as tiger in him.
Our Tostig loves the hand, and not the man.
Harold. Nay! Better die than lie!

Enter KING, QUEEN *and* TOSTIG.

Edward.   In heaven signs!
Signs upon earth! signs everywhere! your Priests
Gross, worldly, simoniacal, unlearn'd!
They scarce can read their Psalter: and your churches
Uncouth, unhandsome, while in Normanland
God speaks thro' abler voices, as He dwells
In statelier shrines. I say not this as being
Half Norman-blooded, nor, as some have held,
Because I love the Norman better—no,
But dreading God's revenge upon this realm
For narrowness and coldness; and I say it
For the last time perchance, before I go
To find the sweet refreshment of the Saints.
I have lived a life of utter purity:
I have builded the great church of Holy Peter:
I have wrought miracles—to God the glory—
And miracles will in my name be wrought
Hereafter.—I have fought the fight and go—
I see the flashing of the gates of pearl—
And it is well with me, tho' some of you
Have scorn'd me—ay—but after I am gone
Woe, woe to England! I have had a vision;
The seven sleepers in the cave at Ephesus
Have turn'd from right to left.
Harold.   My most dear Mas'er,
What matters? Let them turn from left to right
And sleep again.
Tostig.   Too hardy with thy King!
A life of prayer and fasting well may see
Deeper into the mysteries of heaven
Than thou, good brother.
Aldwyth (*aside*).   Sees he into thine,
That thou wouldst have his promise for the crown?
Edward. Tostig says true: my son, thou art too
hard,
Not stagger'd by this ominous earth and heaven:
But heaven and earth are threads of the same loom,
Play into one another, and weave the web
That may confound thee yet.
Harold.   Nay, I trust not,
For I have served thee long and honestly.
Edward. I know it, son ; i am not thankless: thou
Hast broken all my foes, lighten'd for me
The weight of this poor crown, and left me time
And peace for prayer to gain a better one.
Twelve years of service! England loves thee for it.
Thou art the man to rule her!
Aldwyth (*aside*).   So, not Tostig!
Harold. And after those twelve years a boon, my
King,
Respite, a holiday: thyself wast wont
To love the chase: thy leave to set my feet
On board, and hunt and hawk beyond the seas!
Edward. What, with this flaming horror overhead?
Harold. Well, when it passes then.
Edward.   Ay, if it pass.
Go not to Normandy—go not to Normandy.
Harold. And wherefore not, my King, to Norman-
dy?
Is not my brother Wulfnoth hostage there
For my dead father's loyalty to thee?
I pray thee, let me hence and bring him home.
Edward. Not thee, my son; some other messen-
ger.
Harold. And why not me, my lord, to Normandy?
Is not the Norman Count thy friend and mine?
Edward. I pray thee, do not go to Normandy.
Harold. Because my father drove the Normans out
Of England?—That was many a summer gone—
Forgotten and forgiven by them and thee.
Edward. Harold, I will not yield thee leave to go.
Harold. Why then to Flanders. I will hawk and
hunt
In Flanders.
Edward.   Be there not fair woods and fields
In England? Wilful, wilful. Go—the Saints

Pilot and prosper all thy wandering out
And homeward. Tostig, I am faint again.
Son Harold, I will in and pray for thee.
    [*Exit, leaning on* TOSTIG, *and followed by*
        STIGAND, MORCAR, *and* Courtiers.
Harold. What lies upon the mind of our good
King,
That he should harp this way on Normandy?
Queen. Brother, the King is wiser than he seems;
And Tostig knows it; Tostig loves the King.
Harold. And love should know; and, be the King
so wise,
Then Tostig too were wiser than he seems.
I love the man, but not his phantasies.

                    (*Re-enter* TOSTIG.)

Well, brother,
When didst thou hear from thy Northumbria?
Tostig. When did I hear aught but this "*When*"
from thee?
Leave me alone, brother, with my Northumbria:
She is *my* mistress, let *me* look to her!
The King hath made me Earl; make me not fool!
Nor make the King a fool, who made me Earl!
Harold. No, Tostig—lest I make myself a fool
Who made the King who made thee, make thee
Earl.
Tostig. Why chafe me then? Thou knowest I soon
go wild.
Gurth. Come, come! as yet thou art not gone so
wild
But thou canst hear the best and wisest of us.
Harold. So says old Gurth, not I: yet hear! thine
earldom,
Tostig, hath been a kingdom. Their old crown
Is yet a force among them, a sun set
But leaving light enough for Alfgar's house
To strike thee down by—nay, this ghastly glare
May heat their fancies.
Tostig.   My most worthy brother,
That art the quietest man in all the world—
Ay, ay, and wise in peace and great in war—
Pray God the people choose thee for their king!
But all the powers of the house of Godwin
Are not entranced in thee.
Harold.   Thank the Saints, no!
But thou hast drain'd them shallow by thy tolls,
And thou art ever here about the King:
Thine absence well may seem a want of care.
Cling to their love ; for, now the sons of Godwin
Sit topmost in the field of England, envy,
Like the rough bear beneath the tree, good brother,
Waits till the man let go.
Tostig.   Good counsel truly!
I heard from my Northumbria yesterday.
Harold. How goes it then with thy Northumbria?
Well?
Tostig. And wouldst thou that it went aught else
than well?
Harold. I would it went as well as with mine
earldom,
Leofwin's and Gurth's.
Tostig.   Ye govern milder men.
Gurth. We have made them milder by just govern-
ment.
Tostig. Ay, ever give yourselves your own good
word.
Leofwin. An honest gift, by all the Saints, if given
And taken be but honest! but they bribe
Each other, and so often, an honest world
Will not believe them.
Harold.   I may tell thee, Tostig,
I heard from thy Northumberland to-day.
Tostig. From spies of thine to spy my nakedness
In my poor North!
Harold.   There is a movement there,
A blind one—nothing yet.
Tostig.   Crush it at once

With all the power I have!—I must—I will!—
Crush it half-born! Fool still? or wisdom there,
My wise head-shaking Harold?

Harold. Make not thou
The nothing something. Wisdom, when in power
And wisest, should not frown as Power, but smile
As kindness, watching all, till the true *must*
Shall make her strike as Power: but when to
 strike—
O Tostig, O dear brother—if they prance,
Rein in, not lash them, lest they rear and run
And break both neck and axle.

Tostig. Good again!
Good counsel, tho' scarce needed. Pour not water
In the full vessel running out at top
To swamp the house.

Leofwin. Nor thou be a wild thing
Out of the waste, to turn and bite the hand
Would help thee from the trap.

Tostig. Thou playest in tune.
Leofwin. To the deaf adder thee, that wilt not
 dance,
However wisely charm'd.

Tostig. No more, no more!
Gurth. I likewise cry "no more." Unwholesome
 talk
For Godwin's house! Leofwin, thou hast a tongue!
Tostig, thou lookst as thou wouldst spring upon him.
Saint Olaf, not while I am by! Come, come,
Join hands, let brethren dwell in unity;
Let kith and kin stand close as our shield-wall,
Who breaks us then? I say thou hast a tongue,
And Tostig is not stout enough to bear it.
Vex him not, Leofwin.

Tostig. No, I am not vext,—
Altho' ye seek to vex me, one and all.
I have to make report of my good earldom
To the good King who gave it—not to you—
Not any of you.—I am not vext at all.

Harold. The King? the King is ever at his pray-
 ers;
In all that handles matter of the State
I am the King.

Tostig. That shalt thou never be
If I can thwart thee.

Harold. Brother, brother!
Tostig. Away! [*Exit* Tostig.
Queen. Spite of this grisly star ye three must gall
Poor Tostig.

Leofwin. Tostig, sister, galls himself.
He cannot smell a rose but pricks his nose
Against the thorn, and rails against the rose.

Queen. I am the only rose of all the stock
That never thorn'd him; Edward loves him, so
Ye hate him. Harold always hated him.
Why—how they fought when boys—and, Holy Mary!
How Harold used to beat him!

Harold. Why, boys will fight.
Leofwin would often fight me, and I beat him.
Even old Gurth would fight. I had much ado
To hold mine own against old Gurth. Old Gurth,
We fought like great states for grave cause; but
 Tostig—
On a sudden—at a something—for a nothing—
The boy would fist me hard, and when we fought
I conquer'd, and he loved me none the less,
Till thou wouldst get him all apart, and tell him
That where he was but worsted, he was wrong'd.
Ah! thou hast taught the King to spoil him too;
Now the spoilt child sways both. Take heed, take
 heed;
Thou art the Queen; ye are boy and girl no more:
Side not with Tostig in any violence,
Lest thou be sideways guilty of the violence.

Queen. Come, fall not foul on me. I leave thee,
 brother.

Harold. Nay, my good sister—
 [*Exeunt* Queen, Harold, Gurth, *and* Leofwin.

Aldwyth. Gamel, son of Orm,
What thinkest thou this means?
 [*Pointing to the comet.*
Gamel. War, my dear lady,
War, waste, plague, famine, all malignities.

Aldwyth. It means the fall of Tostig from his earl-
 dom.
Gamel. That were too small a matter for a comet!
Aldwyth. It means the lifting of the house of Alf-
 gar.
Gamel. Too small! a comet would not show for
 that!
Aldwyth. Not small for thee, if thou canst com-
 pass it.
Gamel. Thy love?
Aldwyth. As much as I can give thee, man;
This Tostig is, or like to be, a tyrant;
Stir up thy people: oust him!
Gamel. And thy love?
Aldwyth. As much as thou canst bear.
Gamel. I can bear all,
And not be giddy.
Aldwyth. No more now: to-morrow.

SCENE II.—IN THE GARDEN. THE KING'S HOUSE NEAR LONDON. SUN-SET.

Edith.

Edith. Mad for thy mate, passionate nightin-
 gale....
I love thee for it—ay, but stay a moment;
He can but stay a moment: he is going.
I fain would hear him coming!.... near me ....
 near,
Somewhere—to draw him nearer with a charm
Like thine to thine.

(*Singing.*)

Love is come with a song and a smile,
 Welcome Love with a smile and a song:
Love can stay but a little while.
 Why cannot he stay? They call him away:
Ye do him wrong, ye do him wrong;
 Love will stay for a whole life-long.

Enter Harold.

Harold. The nightingales at Havering-in-the-bower
Sang out their loves so loud, that Edward's prayers
Were deafen'd, and he pray'd them dumb, and thus
I dumb thee too, my wingless nightingale!
 [*Kissing her.*
Edith. Thou art my music! Would their wings
 were mine
To follow thee to Flanders! Must thou go?
Harold. Not must, but will. It is but for one
 moon.

Edith. Leaving so many foes in Edward's hall
To league against thy weal. The Lady Aldwyth
Was here to-day, and when she touch'd on thee,
She stammer'd in her hate; I am sure she hates
 thee,
Pants for thy blood.

Harold. Well, I have given her cause—
I fear no woman.

Edith. Hate not one who felt
Some pity for thy hater! I am sure
Her morning wanted sunlight, she so praised
The convent and lone life—within the pale—
Beyond the passion. Nay—she held with Edward,
At least methought she held with holy Edward,
That marriage was half sin.

Harold. A lesson worth
Finger and thumb—thus (*snaps his fingers*). And
 my answer to it—
See here—an interwoven H and E!
Take thou this ring; I will demand his ward

From Edward when I come again. Ay, would she?
She to shut up my blossom in the dark!
Thou art *my* nun, thy cloister in mine arms.
  Edith (taking the ring). Yea, but Earl Tostig—
  Harold.   That's a truer fear!
For if the North take fire, I should be back;
I shall be, soon enough.
  Edith.   Ay, but last night
An evil dream that ever came and went—
  Harold. A gnat that vext thy pillow! Had I
    been by
I would have spoil'd his horn. My girl, what was
    it?
  Edith. Oh that thou wert not going!
For so methought it was our marriage-morn,
And while we stood together, a dead man
Rose from behind the altar, tore away
My marriage-ring, and rent my bridal veil;
And then I turn'd, and saw the church all fill'd
With dead men upright from their graves, and all
The dead men made at thee to murder thee,
But thou didst back thyself against a pillar,
And strike among them with thy battle-axe—
There, what a dream!
  Harold.   Well, well—a dream—no more!
  Edith. Did not Heaven speak to men in dreams
    of old?
  Harold. Ay—well—of old. I tell thee what, my
    child;
Thou hast misread this merry dream of thine,
Taken the rifted pillars of the wood
For smooth stone columns of the sanctuary,
The shadows of a hundred fat dead deer
For dead men's ghosts. True, that the battle-axe
Was out of place; it should have been the bow.—
Come, thou shalt dream no more such dreams; I
    swear it,
By mine own eyes—and these two sapphires—these
Twin rubies, that are amulets against all
The kisses of all kind of womankind
In Flanders, till the sea shall roll me back
To tumble at thy feet.
  Edith.   That would but shame me,
Rather than make me vain. The sea may roll
Sand, shingle, shore-weed, not the living rock
Which guards the land.
  Harold.   Except it be a soft one,
And undereaten to the fall. Mine amulet....
This last....upon thine eyelids, to shut in
A happier dream. Sleep, sleep, and thou shalt see
My greyhounds fleeting like a beam of light,
And hear my peregrine and her bells in heaven;
And other bells on earth, which yet are heaven's;
Guess what they be.
  Edith.   He cannot guess who knows.
Farewell, my king.
  Harold.   Not yet, but then—my queen. [*Exeunt.*

    Enter ALDWYTH *from the thicket.*

  Aldwyth. The kiss that charms thine eyelids into
    sleep
Will hold mine waking. Hate him? I could love
    him
More, tenfold, than this fearful child can do;
Griffyth I hated: why not hate the foe
Of England? Griffyth, when I saw him flee,
Chased deer-like up his mountains, all the blood
That should have only pulsed for Griffyth, beat
For his pursuer. I love him or think I love him.

If he were king of England, I his queen,
I might be sure of it. Nay, I do love him—
She must be cloister'd somehow, lest the King
Should yield his ward to Harold's will. What
    harm?
She hath but blood enough to live, not love.—
When Harold goes and Tostig, shall I play
The craftier Tostig with him? fawn upon him?
Chime in with all? "O thou more saint than king!"
And that were true enough. "O blessed relics!"
"O Holy Peter!" If he found me thus,
Harold might hate me; he is broad and honest,
Breathing an easy gladness....not like Aldwyth....
For which I strangely love him. Should not En-
    gland
Love Aldwyth, if she stay the feuds that part
The sons of Godwin from the sons of Alfgar
By such a marrying? Courage, noble Aldwyth!
Let all thy people bless thee!
            Our wild Tostig,
Edward hath made him Earl: he would be king:—
The dog that snapt the shadow, dropt the bone.—
I trust he may do well, this Gamel, whom
I play upon, that he may play the note
Whereat the dog shall howl and run, and Harold
Hear the king's music, all alone with him,
Pronounced his heir of England.
I see the goal and half the way to it.—
Peace-lover is our Harold for the sake
Of England's wholeness—so—to shake the North
With earthquake and disruption—some divi-ion—
Then fling mine own fair person in the gap
A sacrifice to Harold, a peace-offering,
A scape-goat marriage—all the sins of both
The houses on mine head—then a fair life
And bless the Queen of England.
  Morcar (coming from the thicket). Art thou assured
By this, that Harold loves but Edith?
  Aldwyth.   Morcar!
Why creepst thou like a timorous beast of prey
Out of the bush by night?
  Morcar.   I follow'd thee.
  Aldwyth. Follow my lead, and I will make thee Earl.
  Morcar. What lead then?
  Aldwyth.   Thou shalt flash it secretly
Among the good Northumbrian folk, that I—
That Harold loves me—yea, and presently
That I and Harold are betroth'd—and last—
Perchance that Harold wrongs me; tho' I would not
That it should come to that.
  Morcar.   I will both flash
And thunder for thee.
  Aldwyth.   I said "secretly;"
It is the flash that murders, the poor thunder
Never harm'd head.
  Morcar.   But thunder may bring down
That which the flash hath stricken.
  Aldwyth.   Down with Tostig!
That first of all.—And when doth Harold go?
  Morcar. To-morrow—first to Bosham, then to Flan-
    ders.
  Aldwyth. Not to come back till Tostig shall have
    shown
And redden'd with his people's blood the teeth
That shall be broken by us—yea, and thou
Chair'd in his place. Good-night, and dream thyself
Their chosen Earl. [*Exit* ALDWYTH.
  Morcar.   Earl first, and after that
Who knows I may not dream myself their king!

ACT II.

SCENE I. — SEASHORE. PONTHIEU. NIGHT.

HAROLD and his Men wrecked.

Harold. Friends, in that last inhospitable plunge
Our boat hath burst her ribs; but ours are whole;
I have but bark'd my hands.
Attendant. I dug mine into
My old fast friend the shore, and clinging thus
Felt the remorseless outdraught of the deep
Haul like a great strong fellow at my legs,
And then I rose and ran. The blast that came
So suddenly hath fallen as suddenly—
Put thou the comet and this blast together—
Harold. Put thou thyself and mother-wit together.
Be not a fool!

(Enter Fishermen *with torches,* HAROLD *going up to one of them,* ROLF.)

Wicked sea-will-o'-the-wisp!
Wolf of the shore! dog, with thy lying lights
Thou hast betray'd us on these rocks of thine!
Rolf. Ay, but thou liest as loud as the black her-
ring-pond behind thee. We be fishermen; I came to
see after my nets.
Harold. To drag us into them. Fishermen? devils!
Who, while ye fish for men with your false fires,
Let the great Devil fish for your own souls.
Rolf. Nay then, we be liker the blessed Apostles;
they were fishers of men, Father Jean says.
Harold. I had liefer that the fish had swallowed me,
Like Jonah, than have known there were such devils.
What's to be done?
[*To his* Men—*goes apart with them.*
Fisherman. Rolf, what fish did swallow Jonah?
Rolf. A whale!
Fisherman. Then a whale to a whelk we have
swallowed the King of England. I saw him over
there. Look thee, Rolf, when I was down in the fever, *she* was down with the hunger, and thou didst
stand by her and give her thy crabs, and set her up
again, till now, by the patient Saints, she's as crabb'd
as ever.
Rolf. And I'll give her my crabs again, when thou
art down again.
Fisherman. I thank thee, Rolf. Run thou to Count
Guy; he is hard at hand. Tell him what hath crept
into our creel, and he will fee thee as freely as he will
wrench this outlander's ransom out of him—and why
not? for what right had he to get himself wrecked
on another man's land?
Rolf. Thou art the human-heartedest, Christian-
charitiest of all crab-catchers! Share and share
alike! [*Exit.*
Harold (to Fisherman). Fellow, dost thou catch
crabs?
Fisherman. As few as I may in a wind, and less
than I would in a calm. Ay!
Harold. I have a mind that thou shalt catch no
more.
Fisherman. How?
Harold. I have a mind to brain thee with mine axe.
Fisherman. Ay, do, do, and our great Count-crab
will make his nippers meet in thine heart; he'll
sweat it out of thee, he'll sweat it out of thee. Look,
he's here! He'll speak for himself! Hold thine
own, if thou canst!

Enter GUY, COUNT OF PONTHIEU.

Harold. Guy, Count of Ponthieu!
Guy. Harold, Earl of Wessex!
Harold. Thy villains with their lying lights have
wreck'd us!
Guy. Art thou not Earl of Wessex?
Harold. In mine earldom
A man may hang gold bracelets on a bush,
And leave them for a year, and coming back
Find them again.
Guy. Thou art a mighty man
In thine own earldom!
Harold. Were such murderous liars
In Wessex—if I caught them, they should hang
Cliff-gibbeted for sea-marks; our sea-mew
Winging their only wail!
Guy. Ay, but my men
Hold that the shipwreckt are accursed of God;—
What hinders me to hold with mine own men?
Harold. The Christian manhood of the man who
reigns!
Guy. Ay, rave thy worst, but in our oubliettes
Thou shalt or rot or ransom. Hale him hence!
[*To one of his* Attendants.
Fly thou to William: tell him we have Harold.

SCENE II.—BAYEUX. PALACE.

COUNT WILLIAM *and* WILLIAM MALET.

William. We hold our Saxon woodcock in the
springe,
But he begins to flutter. As I think,
He was thine host in England when I went
To visit Edward.
Malet. Yea, and there, my lord,
To make allowance for their rougher fashions,
I found him all a noble host should be.
William. Thou art his friend: thou know'st my
claim on England
Thro' Edward's promise: we have him in the toils.
And it were well if thou shouldst let him feel
How dense a fold of danger nets him round,
So that he bristle himself against my will.
Malet. What would I do, my lord, if I were you?
William. What wouldst thou do?
Malet. My lord, he is thy guest.
William. Nay, by the splendor of God, no guest
of mine.
He came not to see me, had past me by
To hunt and hawk elsewhere, save for the fate
Which hunted *him* when that un-Saxon blast,
And bolts of thunder moulded in high heaven
To serve the Norman purpose, drave and crack'd
His boat on Ponthieu beach; where our friend Guy
Had wrung his ransom from him by the rack,
But that I stept between and purchased him,
Translating his captivity from Guy
To mine own hearth at Bayeux, where he sits
My ransom'd prisoner.
Malet. Well, if not with gold,
With golden deeds and iron strokes that brought
Thy war with Brittany to a goodlier close
Than else had been, he paid his ransom back.
William. So that henceforth they are not like to
league
With Harold against *me.*

Malet.   A marvel, how
He from the liquid sands of Coesnon
Haled thy shore-swallow'd, armor'd Normans up
To fight for thee again!
William.   Perchance against
Their saver, save thou save him from himself.
Malet. But I should let him home again, my lord.
William. Simple! let fly the bird within the hand,
To catch the bird again within the bush!
No.
Smooth thou my way, before he clash with me;
I want his voice in England for the crown.
I want thy voice with him to bring him round;
And being brave he must be subtly cow'd,
And being truthful wrought upon to swear
Vows that he dare not break. England our own
Thro' Harold's help, he shall be my dear friend
As well as thine, and thou thyself shalt have
Large lordship there of lands and territory.
Malet. I knew thy purpose; he and Wulfnoth never
Have met, except in public; shall they meet
In private? I have often talk'd with Wulfnoth,
And stuffed the boy with fears that these may act
On Harold when they meet.
William.   Then let them meet!
Malet. I can but love this noble, honest Harold.
William. Love him! why not? thine is a loving
office.
I have commission'd thee to save the man:
Help the good ship, showing the sunken rock,
Or he is wreckt for ever.

Enter WILLIAM RUFUS.

William Rufus.   Father.
William.   Well, boy.
William Rufus. They have taken away the toy thou
gavest me,
The Norman knight.
William.   Why, boy?
William Rufus.   Because I broke
The horse's leg—it was mine own to break;
I like to have my toys, and break them too.
William. Well, thou shalt have another Norman
knight!
William Rufus. And may I break his legs?
William.   Yea,—get thee gone!
William Rufus. I'll tell them I have had my way
with thee.   [*Exit.*
Malet. I never knew thee check thy will for aught
Save for the prattling of thy little ones.
William. Who shall be kings of England. I am heir
Of England by the promise of her King.
Malet. But there the great Assembly choose their
King,
The choice of England is the voice of England.
William. I will be King of England by the laws,
The choice, and voice of England.
Malet.   Can that be?
William. The voice of any people is the sword
That guards them, or the sword that beats them
down.
Here comes the would-be what I will be .... king-
like....
Tho' scarce at ease; for, save our meshes break,
More king-like he than like to prove a king.

(*Enter HAROLD, musing, with his eyes on the ground.*)

He sees me not—not dreams of me.
Earl, wilt thou fly my falcons this fair day?
They are of the best, strong-wing'd against the wind.
*Harold (looking up suddenly, having caught but the
last word). Which* way does it blow?
William.   Blowing for England, ha?
Not yet. Thou hast not learnt thy quarters here.
The winds so cross and jostle among these towers.
Harold. Conut of the Normans, thou hast ransom'd
us,
Maintain'd, and entertain'd us royally!

William. And thou for us hast fought as loyally,
Which binds us friendship-fast for ever!
Harold.   Good!
But lest we turn the scale of courtesy
By too much pressure on it, I would fain,
Since thou hast promised Wulfnoth home with us,
Be home again with Wulfnoth.
William.   Stay—as yet
Thou hast but seen how Norman hands can strike,
But walk'd our Norman field, scarce touch'd of
tasted
The splendors of our Court.
Harold.   I am in no mood:
I should be as the shadow of a cloud
Crossing your light.
William.   Nay, rest a week or two,
And we will fill thee full of Norman sun,
And send thee back among thine island mists
With laughter.
Harold.   Conut, I thank thee, but had rather
Breathe the free wind from off our Saxon downs,
Tho' charged with all the wet of all the west.
William. Why, if thou wilt, so let it be—thou shalt.
That were a graceless hospitality
To chain the free guest to the banquet-board;
To-morrow we will ride with thee to Harfleur,
And see thee shipt, and pray in thy behalf
For happier homeward winds than that which
crack'd
Thy bark at Ponthieu,—yet to us, in faith.
A happy one,—whereby we came to know
Thy valor and thy value, noble earl.
Ay, and perchance a happy one for thee,
Provided—I will go with thee to-morrow—
Nay—but there be conditions, easy ones,
So thou, fair friend, will take them easily.

Enter PAGE.

Page. My lord, there is a post from over the seas
With news for thee.   [*Exit Page.*
William.   Come, Malet, let us hear!
                    [*Exeunt COUNT WILLIAM and MALET.*
Harold. Conditions? What conditions? pay him
back
His ransom? "easy"—that were easy—nay—
No money-lover he! What said the King?
"I pray you do not go to Normandy."
And fate hath blown me hither, bound me too
With bitter obligation to the Count—
Have I not fought it out? What did he mean?
There lodged a gleaming grimness in his eyes,
Gave his shorn smile the lie. The walls oppress me,
And you huge keep that hinders half the heaven.
Free air! free field!
            [*Moves to go out. A Man-at-arms follows him.*
Harold (to the Man-at-arms). I need thee not. Why
dost thou follow me?
Man-at-arms. I have the Count's commands to fol-
low thee.
Harold. What then? Am I in danger in this court?
Man-at-arms. I cannot tell. I have the Count's
commands.
Harold. Stand out of earshot then, and keep me
still
In eyeshot.
Man-at-arms. Yea, lord Harold.   [*Withdraws.*
Harold.   And arm'd men
Ever keep watch beside my chamber door,
And if I walk within the lonely wood,
There is an arm'd man ever glides behind!

(*Enter MALET.*)

Why am I follow'd, haunted, harass'd, watch'd?
See yonder!   [*Pointing to the Man-at-arms.*
Malet.   'Tis the good Count's care for thee!
The Normans love thee not, nor thou the Normans,
Or—so they deem.
Harold.   But wherefore is the wind,

Which way soever the vane-arrow swing, ·
Not ever fair for England? Why but now
He said (thou heardst him) that I must not hence
Save on conditions.
   Malet.   So in truth he said.
   Harold. Malet, thy mother was an Englishwoman:
There somewhere beats an English pulse in thee!
   Malet. Well—for my mother's sake I love your Eu-
     gland,
But for my father I love Normandy.
   Harold. Speak for thy mother's sake, and tell me
     true.
   Malet. Then for my mother's sake, and England's
     sake
That suffers in the daily want of thee,
Obey the Count's conditions, my good friend.
   Harold. How, Malet, if they be not honorable!
   Malet. Seem to obey them.
   Harold.   Better die than lie!
   Malet. Choose therefore whether thou wilt have
     thy conscience
White as a maiden's hand, or whether England
Be shatter'd into fragments.
   Harold.   News from England?
   Malet. Morcar and Edwin have stirr'd up the Thanes
Against thy brother Tostig's governance;
And all the North of Humber is one storm.
   Harold. I should be there, Malet, I should be there!
   Malet. And Tostig in his own hall on suspicion
Hath massacred the Thane that was his guest,
Gamel, the son of Orm: and there be more
As villainously slain.
   Harold.   The wolf! the beast!
Ill news for guests, ha, Malet! More? What more?
What do they say? did Edward know of this?
   Malet. They say, his wife was knowing and abetting.
   Harold. They say, his wife!—To marry and have
     no husband
Makes the wife fool. My God, I should be there.
I'll hack my way to the sea.
   Malet.   Thou canst not, Harold;
Our Duke is all between thee and the sea,
Our Duke is all about thee like a God;
All passes block'd. Obey him, speak him fair,
For he is only debonair to those
That follow where he leads, but stark as death
To those that cross him.—Look thou, here is Wulf-
     noth!
I leave thee to thy talk with him alone;
How wan, poor lad! how sick and sad for home!
                    [*Exit* MALET.
   Harold (*muttering*). Go not to Normandy—go not
     to Normandy!

          (*Enter* WULFNOTH.)

Poor brother! still a hostage!
   Wulfnoth.   Yea, and I
Shall see the dewy kiss of dawn no more
Make blush the maiden-white of our tall cliffs,
Nor mark the sea-bird rouse himself and hover
Above the windy ripple, and fill the sky
With free sea-laughter—never—save indeed
Thou canst make yield this iron-mooded Duke
To let me go.
   Harold. Why, brother, so he will;
But on conditions. Canst thou guess at them?
   Wulfnoth. Draw nearer,—I was in the corridor;
I saw him coming with his brother Odo
The Bayeux bishop, and I hid myself.
   Harold. They did thee wrong who made thee host-
     age; thou
Wast ever fearful.
   Wulfnoth.   And he spoke—I heard him—
"This Harold is not of the royal blood,
Can have no right to the crown," and Odo said,
"Thine is the right, for thine the might; he is here,
And yonder is thy keep."
   Harold.   No, Wulfnoth, no.

   Wulfnoth. And William laugh'd and swore that
     might was right,
Far as he knew in this poor world of ours—
" Marry, the Saints must go along with us,
And, brother, we will find a way," said he—
Yea, yea, he would be King of England.
   Harold.   Never!
   Wulfnoth. Yea, but thou must not this way an-
     swer *him.*
   Harold. Is it not better still to speak the truth?
   Wulfnoth. Not here, or thou wilt never hence nor I;
For in the racing towards this golden goal
He turns not right or left, but tramples flat
Whatever thwarts him; hast thou never heard
His savagery at Alençon,—the town
Hung out raw hides along their walls, and cried
"Work for the tanner."
   Harold.   That had anger'd me
Had I been William.
   Wulfnoth.   Nay, but he had prisoners,
He tore their eyes out, sliced their hands away,
And flung them streaming o'er the battlements
Upon the heads of those who walk'd within—
Oh, speak him fair, Harold, for thine own sake.
   Harold. Your Welshman says, "The Truth against
     the World,"
Much more the truth against myself.
   Wulfnoth.   Thyself?
But for my sake, O brother! oh! for my sake!
   Harold. Poor Wulfnoth! do they not entreat thee
     well?
   Wulfnoth. I see the blackness of my dungeon loom
Across their lamps of revel, and beyond
The merriest murmurs of their banquet clank
The shackles that will bind me to the wall.
   Harold. Too fearful still!
   Wulfnoth.   Oh no, no—speak him fair!
Call it to temporize, and not to lie;
Harold, I do not counsel thee to lie.
The man that hath to foil a murderous aim
May, surely, play with words.
   Harold.   Words are the man.
Not ev'n for thy sake, brother, would I lie.
   Wulfnoth. Then for thine Edith?
   Harold.   There thou prick'st me deep.
   Wulfnoth. And for our Mother England?
   Harold.   Deeper still.
   Wulfnoth. And deeper still the deep-down oubliette,
Down thirty feet below the smiling day—
In blackness—dogs' food thrown upon thy head.
And over thee the suns arise and set,
And the lark sings, the sweet stars come and go,
And men are at their markets, in their fields,
And woo their loves and have forgotten thee;
And thou art upright in thy living grave,
Where there is barely room to shift thy side,
And all thine England hath forgotten thee;
And he our lazy-pious Norman King,
With all his Normans round him once again,
Counts his old beads, and hath forgotten thee.
   Harold. Thou art of my blood, and so methinks,
     my boy,
Thy fears infect me beyond reason. Peace!
   Wulfnoth. And then our fiery Tostig, while thy
     hands
Are palsied here, if his Northumbrians rise
And hurl him from them—I have heard the Normans
Count upon this confusion—may he not make
A league with William, so to bring him back?
   Harold. That lies within the shadow of the chance.
   Wulfnoth. And like a river in flood thro' a burst
     dam
Descends the ruthless Norman—our good King
Kneels mumbling some old bone—our helpless folk
Are wash'd away, wailing, in their own blood—
   Harold. Wailing! not warring? Boy, thou hast
     forgotten
That thou art English.

Wulfnoth.   Then our modest women—
I know the Norman license—thine own Edith—
Harold. No more! I will not hear thee—William
comes.
Wulfnoth. I dare not well be seen in talk with
thee.
Make thou not mention that I spake with thee.
          [*Moves away to the back of the stage.*

          Enter WILLIAM, MALET, *and* Officer.

Officer. We have the man that rail'd against thy
birth.
William. Tear out his tongue.
Officer.   He shall not rail again.
He said that he should see confusion fall
On thee and on thine house.
William.   Tear out his eyes,
And plunge him into prison.
Officer.   It shall be done.
                    [*Exit* Officer.
William. Look not amazed, fair earl! Better leave
undone
Than do by halves—tongueless and eyeless, prison'd—
Harold. Better methinks have slain the man at
once!
William. We have respect for man's immortal soul,
We seldom take man's life, except in war;
It frights the traitor more to maim and blind.
Harold. In mine own land I should have scorn'd
the man,
Or lash'd his rascal back, and let him go.
William. And let him go? To slander thee again!
Yet in thine own land in thy father's day
They blinded my young kinsman, Alfred—ay,
Some said it was thy father's deed.
Harold.   They lied.
William. But thou and he—whom at thy word, for
thou
Art known a speaker of the truth, I free
From this foul charge—
Harold.   Nay, nay, he freed himself
By oath and compurgation from the charge.
The King, the lords, the people clear'd him of it.
William. But thou and he drove our good Nor-
mans out
From England, and this rankles in us yet.
Archbishop Robert hardly scaped with life.
Harold. Archbishop Robert! Robert the Arch-
bishop!
Robert of Jumiéges, he that—
Malet.   Quiet! quiet!
Harold. Count! if there sat within thy Norman
chair
A ruler all for England—one who fill'd
All offices, all bishopricks with English—
We could not move from Dover to the Humber
Saving thro' Norman bishopricks—I say
Ye would applaud that Norman who should drive
The stranger to the fiends!
William.   Why, that is reason!
Warrior thou art, and mighty wise withal!
Ay, ay, but many among our Norman lords
Hate thee for this, and press upon me—saying
God and the sea have given thee to our hands—
To plunge thee into life-long prison here:—
Yet I hold out against them, as I may,
Yea—would hold out, yea, tho' they should revolt—
For thou hast done the battle in my cause;
I am thy fastest friend in Normandy.
Harold. I am doubly bound to thee....if this be so.
William. And I would bind thee more, and would
myself
Be bounden to thee more.
Harold.   Then let me hence
With Wulfnoth to King Edward.
William.   So we will.
We hear he hath not long to live.
Harold.   It may be.

William. Why, then, the heir of England, who is
he?
Harold. The Atheling is nearest to the throne.
William. But sickly, slight, half-witted and a child,
Will England have him King?
Harold.   It may be, no.
William. And hath King Edward not pronoun
his heir?
Harold. Not that I know.
William.   When he was here in Normandy,
He loved us and we him, because we found him
A Norman of the Normans.
Harold.   So did we.
William. A gentle, gracious, pure and saintly man!
And grateful to the hand that shielded him,
He promised that if ever he were King
In England, he would give his kingly voice
To me as his successor. Knowest thou this?
Harold. I learn it now.
William.   Thou knowest I am his cousin,
And that my wife descends from Alfred?
Harold.   Ay.
William. Who hath a better claim then to the
crown
So that ye will not crown the Atheling?
Harold. None that I know....if that but hung upon
King Edward's will.
William.   Wilt *thou* uphold my claim?
Malet (aside to Harold). Be careful of thine an-
swer, my good friend.
Wulfnoth (aside to Harold). Oh, Harold! for my
sake and for thine own!
Harold. Ay....if the King have not revoked his
promise.
William. But hath he done it then?
Harold.   Not that I know.
William. Good, good, and thou wilt help me to the
crown.
Harold. Ay....if the Witan will consent to this.
William. Thou art the mightiest voice in England,
man,
Thy voice will lead the Witan—shall I have it?
Wulfnoth (aside to Harold). Oh, Harold! if thou
love thine Edith, ay.
Harold. Ay, if—
Malet (aside to Harold). Thine "ifs" will scar
thine eyes out—ay.
William. I ask thee, wilt thou help me to the
crown?
And I will make thee my great Earl of Earls,
Foremost in England and in Normandy:
Thou shalt be verily King—all but the name—
For I shall most sojourn in Normandy;
And thou be my vice-king in England. Speak.
Wulfnoth (aside to Harold). Ay, brother — for the
sake of England—ay.
Harold. My lord—
Malet (aside to Harold). Take heed now.
Harold.   Ay.
William.   I am content,
For thou art truthful, and thy word thy bond.
To-morrow will we ride with thee to Harflenr.
                    [*Exit* WILLIAM.
Malet. Harold, I am thy friend, one life with thee,
And even as I should bless thee saving mine,
I thank thee now for having saved thyself.
                    [*Exit* MALET.
Harold. For having lost myself to save myself,
Said "ay" when I meant "no," lied like a lad
That dreads the pendent scourge, said "ay" for
"no!"
Ay! no!—he hath not bound me by an oath —
Is "ay" an oath? is "ay" strong as an oath?
Or is it the same sin to break my word
As break mine oath? He call'd my word my bond!
He is a liar who knows I am a liar,
And makes believe that he believes my word—
The crime be on his head—not bounden—no.

[Suddenly doors are flung open, discovering in an inner hall COUNT WILLIAM *in his state robes, seat'd upon his throne, between two Bishops,* ODO OF BAYEUX *being one; in the centre of the hall an ark covered with cloth of gold; and on either side of it the Norman barons.*

Enter a Jailor before WILLIAM'S *throne.*

William (to Jailor). Knave, hast thou let thy prisoner scape?

Jailor.   Sir Count,
He had but one foot, he must have hopt away,
Yea, some familiar spirit must have help'd him.

William. Woe, knave, to thy familiar and to thee!
Give me thy keys.   *[They fall clashing.*
Nay, let them lie. Stand there and wait my will.
                            [The Jailor stands aside.

William (to Harold). Hast thou such trustless jailors
in thy North?

Harold. We have few prisoners in mine earldom
there,
So less chance for false keepers.

William.   We have heard
Of thy just, mild, and equal governance;
Honor to thee! thou art perfect in all honor!
Thy naked word thy bond! confirm it now
Before our gather'd Norman baronage,
For they will not believe thee—as I believe.
            [Descends from his throne and stands by the ark.
Let all men here bear witness of our bond!
        [Beckons to HAROLD, *who advances. Enter*
                            MALET *behind him.*
Lay thou thy hand upon this golden pall!
Behold the jewel of Saint Pancratius
Woven into the gold. Swear thou on this!

Harold. What should I swear? Why should I
swear on this?

William (savagely). Swear thou to help me to the
crown of England.

Malet (whispering Harold). My friend, thou hast
gone too far to palter now.

Wulfnoth (whispering Harold). Swear thou to-day;
to-morrow is thine own.

Harold. I swear to help thee to the crown of England....
According as King Edward promises.

William. Thou must swear absolutely, noble Earl.

Malet (whispering). Delay is death to thee, ruin to
England.

Wulfnoth (whispering). Swear, dearest brother, I
beseech thee, swear!

Harold (putting his hand on the jewel). I swear to
help thee to the crown of England.

William. Thanks, truthful Earl; I did not doubt
thy word,
But that my barons might believe thy word,
And that the Holy Saints of Normandy,
When thou art home in England with thine own,
Might strengthen thee in keeping of thy word,
I made thee swear.—Show him by whom he hath
sworn.

[The two Bishops *advance, and raise the cloth of gold. The bodies and bones of Saints are seen lying in the ark.*
The holy bones of all the Canonized
From all the holiest shrines in Normandy!

Harold. Horrible!   *[They let the cloth fall again*

William. Ay, for thou hast sworn an oath
Which, if not kept, would make the hard earth rive
To the very Devil's horns, the bright sky cleave
To the very feet of God, and send her hosts
Of injured Saints to scatter sparks of plague
Thro' all your cities, blast your infants, dash
The torch of war among your standing corn,
Dabble your hearths with your own blood.—Enough!
Thou wilt not break it! I, the Count—the King—
Thy friend—am grateful for thine honest oath,
Not coming fiercely like a conqueror, now,
But softly as a bridegroom to his own.
For I shall rule according to your laws,
And make your ever-jarring Earldoms move
To music and in order—Angle, Jute,
Dane, Saxon, Norman, help to build a throne
Out-towering hers of France....The wind is fair
For England now....To-night we will be merry.
To-morrow will I ride with thee to Harfleur.
        [Exeunt WILLIAM *and all the Norman barons, etc.*

Harold. To-night we will be merry—and to-morrow—
Juggler and bastard—bastard—he hates that most—
William the tanner's bastard! Would he heard me!
O God, that I were in some wide, waste field
With nothing but my battle-axe and him
To spatter his brains! Why let earth rive, gulf in
These cursed Normans—yea, and mine own self.
Cleave heaven, and send thy saints that I may say
Ev'n to their faces, "If ye side with William,
Ye are not noble." How their pointed fingers
Glared at me! Am I Harold, Harold son
Of our great Godwin? Lo! I touch mine arms,
My limbs—they are not mine—they are a liar's—
I mean to be a liar—I am not bound—
Stigand shall give me absolution for it—
Did the chest move? did it move? I am utter craven!
O Wulfnoth, Wulfnoth, brother, thou hast betray'd
me!

Wulfnoth. Forgive me, brother, I will live here and
die.

Enter Page.

Page. My lord! the Duke awaits thee at the banquet.

Harold. Where they eat dead men's flesh, and
drink their blood.

Page. My lord—

Harold. I know your Norman cookery is so spiced,
It masks all this.

Page.   My lord! thou art white as death.

Harold. With looking on the dead. Am I so
white?
Thy Duke will seem the darker. Hence, I follow.
                            [Exeunt.

ACT III.

SCENE I.—THE KING'S PALACE.
LONDON.

KING EDWARD *dying on a couch, and by him standing the* QUEEN, HAROLD, ARCHBISHOP STIGAND, GURTH, LEOFWIN, ARCHBISHOP ALDRED, ALDWYTH, *and* EDITH.

Stigand. Sleeping or dying there? If this be death,
Then our great Council wait to crown thee King—
Come hither, I have a power; [*To* HAROLD.
They call me near, for I am close to thee
And England—I, old shrivell'd Stigand, I,
Dry as an old wood-fungus on a dead tree,
I have a power!
See here this little key about my neck!
There lies a treasure buried down in Ely:
If e'er the Norman grow too hard for thee,
Ask me for this at thy most need, son Harold,
At thy most need—not sooner.
Harold.   So I will.
Stigand. Red gold—a hundred purses—yea, and more!
If thou canst make a wholesome use of these
To chink against the Norman, I do believe
My old crook'd spine would bud out two young wings
To fly to heaven straight with.
Harold.   Thank thee, father!
Thou art English; Edward too is English now,
He hath clean repented of his Normanism.
Stigand. Ay, as the libertine repents who cannot
Make done undone, when thro' his dying sense
Shrills "lost thro' thee." They have built their castles here;
Our priories are Norman; the Norman adder
Hath bitten us; we are poison'd: our dear England
Is demi-Norman. He!—
                [*Pointing to* KING EDWARD, *sleeping.*
Harold.   I would I were
As holy and as passionless as he!
That I might rest as calmly! Look at him—
The rosy face, and long down-silvering beard,
The brows unwrinkled as a summer mere.—
Stigand. A summer mere with sudden wreckful gusts
From a side-gorge. Passionless? How he flamed
When Tostig's anger'd earldom flung him! Nay,
He fain had calcined all Northumbria
To one black ash, but that thy patriot passion,
Siding with our great Council against Tostig,
Out-passion'd his! Holy? ay, ay, forsooth,
A conscience for his own soul, not his realm;
A twilight conscience lighted thro' a chink;
Thine by the sun; nay, by some sun to be.
When all the world hath learnt to speak the truth,
And lying were self-murder by that state
Which was the exception.
Harold.   That sun may God speed!
Stigand. Come, Harold, shake the cloud off!
Harold.   Can I, father?
Our Tostig parted cursing me and England;
Our sister hates us for his banishment:
He hath gone to kindle Norway against England,
And Wulfnoth is alone in Normandy.
For when I rode with William down to Harfleur,
"Wulfnoth is sick," he said; "he cannot follow;"
Then with that friendly-fiendly smile of his,

"We have learnt to love him, let him a little longer
Remain a hostage for the loyalty
Of Godwin's house." As far as touches Wulfnoth,
I that so prized plain word and naked truth
Have sinn'd against it—all in vain.
Leofwin.   Good brother,
By all the truths that ever priest hath preach'd,
Of all the lies that ever men have lied,
Thine is the pardonablest.
Harold.   May be so!
I think it so, I think I am a fool
To think it can be otherwise than so.
Stigand. Tut, tut, I have absolved thee; dost thou scorn me,
Because I had my Canterbury pallium
From one whom they disposed?
Harold.   No, Stigand, no!
Stigand. Is naked truth actable in true life?
I have heard a saying of thy father Godwin,
That, were a man of state nakedly true,
Men would but take him for the craftier liar.
Leofwin. Be men less delicate than the Devil himself?
I thought that naked Truth would shame the Devil,
The Devil is so modest.
Gurth.   He never said it!
Leofwin. Be thou not stupid-honest, brother Gurth!
Harold. Better to be a liar's dog, and hold
My master honest, than believe that lying
And ruling men are fatal twins that cannot
Move one without the other. Edward wakes!—
Dazed—he hath seen a vision.
Edward.   The green tree!
Then a great Angel past along the highest,
Crying "the doom of England," and at once
He stood beside me, in his grasp a sword
Of lightnings, wherewithal he cleft the tree
From off the bearing trunk, and hurl'd it from him
Three fields away, and then he dash'd and drench'd,
He dyed, he soak'd the trunk with human blood,
And brought the sunder'd tree again, and set it
Straight on the trunk, that thus baptized in blood
Grew ever high and higher, beyond my seeing,
And shot out sidelong boughs across the deep
That dropt themselves, and rooted in far isles
Beyond my seeing: and the great Angel rose
And past again along the highest, crying
"The doom of England!"—Tostig, raise my head!
                [*Falls back senseless.*
Harold (*raising him*). Let Harold serve for Tostig!
Queen.   Harold served
Tostig so ill, he cannot serve for Tostig! .
Ay, raise his head, for thou hast laid it low!
The sickness of our saintly King, for whom
My prayers go up as fast as my tears fall,
I well believe, hath mainly drawn itself
From lack of Tostig—thou hast banish'd him.
Harold. Nay—but the Council, and the King himself!
Queen. Thou hatest him, hatest him.
Harold (*coldly*).   Ay—Stigand, unriddle
This vision, canst thou?
Stigand.   Dotage!
Edward (*starting up*).   It is finish'd.
I have built the Lord a house—the Lord hath dwelt
In darkness. I have built the Lord a house—
Palms, flowers, pomegranates, golden cherubim
With twenty-cubit wings from wall to wall—
I have built the Lord a house—sing, Asaph! clash

The cymbal, Heman! blow the trumpet, priest!
Fall, cloud, and fill the house—lo! my two pillars,
Jachin and Boaz!— [*Seeing* HAROLD *and* GURTH.
Harold, Gurth—where am I?
Where is the charter of our Westminster?
Stigand. It lies beside thee, King, upon thy bed.
Edward. Sign, sign at once—take, sign it, Stigand,
Aldred!
Sign it, my good son Harold, Gurth, and Leofwin!
Sign it, my Queen!
All. We have sign'd it.
Edward. It is finish'd!
The kingliest Abbey in all Christian lands,
The lordliest, loftiest minster ever built
To Holy Peter in our English isle!
Let me be buried there, and all our kings,
And all our just and wise and holy men
That shall be born hereafter. It is finish'd!
Hast thou had absolution for thine oath?
[*To* HAROLD.
Harold. Stigand hath given me absolution for it.
Edward. Stigand is not canonical enough
To save thee from the wrath of Norman Saints.
Stigand. Norman enough! Be there no Saints of
England
To help us from their brethren yonder?
Edward. Prelate,
The Saints are one, but those of Normanland
Are mightier than our own. Ask it of Aldred.
[*To* HAROLD.
Aldred. It shall be granted him, my King; for he
Who vows a vow to strangle his own mother
Is guiltier keeping this, than breaking it.
Edward. O friends, I shall not overlive the day.
Stigand. Why then the throne is empty. Who in-
herits?
For tho' we be not bound by the King's voice
In making of a king, yet the King's voice
Is much toward his making. Who inherits?
Edgar the Atheling?
Edward. No, no, but Harold.
I love him: he hath served me: none but he
Can rule all England. Yet the curse is on him
For swearing falsely by those blessed bones:
He did not mean to keep his vow.
Harold. Not mean
To make our England Norman.
Edward. There spake Godwin,
Who hated all the Normans; but their Saints
Have heard thee, Harold.
Edith. Oh! my lord, my King!
He knew not whom he sware by.
Edward. Yea, I know
He knew not; but those heavenly ears have heard,
Their curse is on him; wilt thou bring another,
Edith, upon his head?
Edith. No, no, not I.
Edward. Why then, thou must not wed him.
Harold. Wherefore, wherefore?
Edward. O son, when thou didst tell me of thine
oath,
I sorrow'd for my random promise given
To you fox-lion. I did not dream then
I should be king.—My son, the Saints are virgins;
They love the white rose of virginity,
The cold white lily blowing in her cell:
I have been myself a virgin; and I sware
To consecrate my virgin here to Heaven—
The silent, cloister'd, solitary life,
A life of life-long prayer against the curse
That lies on thee and England.
Harold. No, no, no.
Edward. Treble denial of the tongue of flesh,
Like Peter's when he fell, and thou wilt have
To wail for it like Peter. O my son!
Are all oaths to be broken then, all promises
Made in our agony for help from Heaven?
Son, there is one who loves thee: and a wife,

21

What matters who, so she be serviceable
In all obedience, as mine own hath been:
God bless thee, wedded daughter.
[*Laying his hand on the* QUEEN's *head.*
Queen. Bless thou too
That brother whom I love beyond the rest,
My banish'd Tostig.
Edward. All the sweet Saints bless him!
Spare and forbear him, Harold, if he comes!
And let him pass unscathed: he loves me, Harold! .
Be kindly to the Normans left among us,
Who follow'd me for love! and, dear son, swear
When thou art King to see my solemn vow
Accomplish'd!
Harold. Nay, dear lord, for I have sworn
Not to swear falsely twice.
Edward. Thou wilt not swear?
Harold. I cannot.
Edward. Then on thee remains the curse,
Harold, if thou embrace her: and on thee,
Edith, if thou abide it,—
[*The* KING *swoons;* EDITH *falls and kneels by the*
couch.
Stigand. He hath swoon'd!
Death?....no, as yet a breath.
Harold. Look up! look up!
Edith!
Aldred. Confuse her not; she hath begun
Her life-long prayer for thee.
Aldwyth. O noble Harold,
I would thou couldst have sworn.
Harold. For thine own pleasure?
Aldwyth. No, but to please our dying King, and
those
Who make thy good their own—all England, Earl.
Aldred. I would thou couldst have sworn. Our
holy King
Hath given his virgin lamb to Holy Church
To save thee from the curse.
Harold. Alas! poor man,
His promise brought it on me.
Aldred. O good son!
That knowledge made him all the carefuller
To find a means whereby the curse might glance
From thee and England.
Harold. Father, we so loved—
Aldred. The more the love, the mightier is the
prayer;
The more the love, the more acceptable
The sacrifice of both your loves to Heaven.
No sacrifice to Heaven, no help from Heaven;
That runs thro' all the faiths of all the world.
And sacrifice there must be, for the King
Is holy, and hath talk'd with God, and seen
A shadowing horror; there are signs in heaven—
Harold. Your comet came and went.
Aldred. And signs on earth!
Knowest thou Senlac hill?
Harold. I know all Sussex;
A good entrenchment for a perilous hour!
Aldred. Pray God that come not suddenly! There
is one
Who passing by that hill three nights ago—
He shook so that he scarce could out with it—
Heard, heard—
Harold. The wind in his hair?
Aldred. A ghostly horn
Blowing continually, and faint battle-hymns,
And cries, and clashes, and the groans of men;
And dreadful shadows strove upon the hill,
And dreadful lights crept up from out the marsh—
Corpse-candles gliding over nameless graves—
Harold. At Senlac?
Aldred. Senlac.
Edward (waking). Senlac! Sanguelac,
The Lake of Blood!
Stigand. This lightning before death
Plays on the word,—and Normanizes too!

Harold. Hush, father, hush!

Edward.   Thou uncanonical fool,
Wilt *thou* play with the thunder? North and South
Thunder together, showers of blood are blown
Before a never-ending blast, and hiss
Against the blaze they cannot quench—a lake,
A sea of blood—we are drown'd in blood—for God
Has fill'd the quiver, and Death has drawn the bow—
Sanguelac! Sanguelac! the arrow! the arrow!
                                        [*Dies.*

Stigand. It is the arrow of death in his own heart—
And our great Council wait to crown thee King.

SCENE II.—IN THE GARDEN. THE KING'S HOUSE NEAR LONDON.

EDITH.

Edith. Crown'd, crown'd and lost, crown'd King—
and lost to me!

(*Singing.*)

Two young lovers in winter weather,
    None to guide them,
Walk'd at night on the misty heather;
Night, as black as a raven's feather;
Both were lost and found together,
    None beside them.

That is the burthen of it—lost and found
Together in the cruel river Swale
A hundred years ago; and there's another,

    Lost, lost, the light of day,

To which the lover answers lovingly,

    "I am beside thee."
    Lost, lost, we have lost the way.
    "Love, I will guide thee."

Whither, O whither? into the river,
Where we two may be lost together,
And lost for ever? "Oh! never, oh! never,
Tho' we be lost and be found together."

Some think they loved within the pale forbidden
By Holy Church: but who shall say? the truth
Was lost in that fierce North, where *they* were lost,
Where all good things are lost, where Tostig lost
The good hearts of his people. It is Harold!

(*Enter* HAROLD.)

Harold the King!
    Harold.   Call me not King, but Harold.
    Edith. Nay, thou art King!
    Harold.   Thine, thine, or King or churl!
My girl, thou hast been weeping: turn not thou
Thy face away, but rather let me be
King of the moment to thee, and command
That kiss my one own subject, which will make
My kingship kinglier to me than to reign
King of the world without it.
    Edith.   Ask me not,
Lest I should yield it, and the second curse
Descend upon thine head, and thou be only
King of the moment over England.
    Harold.   Edith,
Tho' somewhat less a king to my true self
Than ere they crown'd me one, for I have lost
Somewhat of upright stature thro' mine oath,
Yet thee I would not lose, and sell not thou
Our living passion for a dead man's dream;
Stigand believed he knew not what he spake.
O God! I cannot help it, but at times
They seem to me too narrow, all the faiths
Of this grown world of ours, whose baby eye
Saw them sufficient. Fool and wise, I fear

This curse, and scorn it. But a little light!—
And on it falls the shadow of the priest;
Heaven yield us more! for better, Woden, all
Our cancell'd warrior-gods, our grim Walhalla,
Eternal war, than that the Saints at peace
The Holiest of our Holiest one should be
This William's fellow-tricksters;—better die
Than credit this, for death is death, or else
Lifts us beyond the lie. Kiss me—thou art not
A holy sister yet, my girl, to fear
There might be more than brother in my kiss,
And more than sister in thine own.
    Edith.   I dare not.
    Harold. Scared by the church—"Love for a whole
        life long"
When was that sung?
    Edith.   Here to the nightingales.
    Harold. Their anthems of no church. how sweet
        they are!
Nor kingly priest, nor priestly king to cross
Their billings ere they nest.
    Edith.   They are but of spring,
They fly the winter change—not so with us—
No wings to come and go.
    Harold.   But wing'd souls flying
Beyond all change and in the eternal distance
To settle on the Truth.
    Edith.   They are not so true,
They change their mates.
    Harold.   Do they? I did not know it.
    Edith. They say thou art to wed the Lady Ald-
        wyth.
    Harold. They say, they say.
    Edith.   If this be politic,
And well for thee and England—and for her—
Care not for me who love thee.
    Gurth (*calling*).   Harold, Harold!
    Harold. The voice of Gurth! (*Enter* GURTH.) Good
        even, my good brother!
    Gurth. Good even, gentle Edith.
    Edith.   Good even, Gurth.
    Gurth. Ill news hath come! Our hapless brother,
        Tostig—
He, and the giant King of Norway, Harold
Hardrada—Scotland, Ireland, Iceland, Orkney,
Are landed North of Humber, and in a field
So packt with carnage that the dikes and brooks
Were bridged and damm'd with dead, have over-
        thrown
Morcar and Edwin.
    Harold.   Well then, we must fight.
How blows the wind?
    Gurth.   Against St. Valery
And William.
    Harold.   Well, then, we will to the North.
    Gurth. Ay, but worse news: this William sent to
        Rome,
Swearing thou swarest falsely by his Saints:
The Pope and that Archdeacon Hildebrand
His master, heard him, and have sent him back
A holy gonfanon, and a blessed hair
Of Peter; and all France, all Burgundy,
Poitou, all Christendom is raised against thee;
He hath cursed thee, and all those who fight for
        thee,
And given thy realm of England to the bastard.
    Harold. Ha! ha!
    Edith. Oh! laugh not!....Strange and ghastly in
        the gloom
And shadowing of this double thunder-cloud
That lours on England—laughter!
    Harold.   No, not strange!
This was old human laughter in old Rome
Before a pope was born, when that which reign'd
Call'd itself God.—A kindly rendering
Of "Render unto Cæsar."....The Good Shepherd!
Take this, and render that.
    Gurth.   They have taken York.

Harold. The Lord was God and came as man—the
    Pope
Is man and comes as God.—York taken?
Garth.   Yea,
Tostig hath taken York!
Harold.   To York then.   Edith,
Hadst thou been braver, I had better braved
All—but I love thee, and thou me—and that
Remains beyond all chances and all churches,
And that thou knowest.
Edith.   Ay, but take back thy ring.

It burns my hand—a curse to thee and me.
I dare not wear it.
                    [*Proffers* HAROLD *the ring, which he takes.*
Harold.   But I dare.   God with thee!
                              [*Exeunt* HAROLD *and* GARTH.
Edith. The King hath cursed him, if he marry me·
The Pope hath cursed him, marry me or no!
God help me!   I know nothing—can but pray
For Harold—pray, pray, pray—no help but prayer,
A breath that fleets beyond this iron world,
And touches Him that made it.

ACT IV.

SCENE I.—IN NORTHUMBRIA.

ARCHBISHOP ALDRED, MORCAR, EDWIN, *and* Forces.
Enter HAROLD. *The standard of the Golden Dragon
of Wessex preceding him.*

Harold. What! are thy people sullen from defeat?
Our Wessex dragon flies beyond the Humber,
No voice to greet it.
Edwin.   Let not our great King
Believe us sullen—only shamed to the quick
Before the King—as having been so bruised
By Harold, King of Norway; but our help
Is Harold, King of England.   Pardon us, thou!
Our silence is our reverence for the King!
Harold. Earl of the Mercians! if the truth be gall,
Cram me not thou with honey, when our good hive
Needs every sting to save it.
Voices.   Aldwyth! Aldwyth!
Harold. Why cry thy people on thy sister's name?
Morcar. She hath won upon our people thro' her
    beauty,
And pleasantness among them.
Voices.   Aldwyth, Aldwyth!
Harold. They shout as they would have her for a
    queen.
Morcar. She hath followed with our host, and suf-
    fer'd all.
Harold. What would ye, men?
Voice.   Our old Northumbrian crown,
And kings of our own choosing.
Harold.   Your old crown
Were little help without our Saxon carles
Against Hardrada.
Voice.   Little! we are Danes,·
Who conquer'd what we walk on, our own field.
Harold. They have been plotting here!   [*Aside.*
Voice.   He calls us little!
Harold. the kingdoms of this world began with
    little,
A hill, a fort, a city—that reach'd a hand
Down to the field beneath it, "Be thou mine;"
Then to the next, "Thou also—" if the field
Cried out "I am mine own;" another hill,
Or fort, or city, took it, and the first
Fell, and the next became an Empire.
Voice.   Yet
Thou art but a West Saxon: we are Danes!
Harold. My mother is a Dane, and I am English;
There is a pleasant fable in old books,
Ye take a stick, and break it; bind a score
All in one faggot, snap it over knee
Ye cannot.
Voice.   Hear King Harold! he says true!
Harold. Would ye be Norsemen?
Voices.   No!
Harold.   Or Norman?
Voices.   No!

Harold. Snap not the faggot-band then.
Voice.   That is true!
Voice. Ay, but thou art not kingly, only grandson
To Wulfnoth, a poor cow-herd.
Harold.   This old Wulfnoth
Would take me on his knees and tell me tales
Of Alfred and of Athelstan the Great
Who drove you Danes; and yet he held that Dane,
Jute, Angle, Saxon, were or should be all
One England, for this cow-herd, like my father,
Who shook the Norman scoundrels off the throne,
Had in him kingly thoughts—a king of men,
Not made, but born, like the great King of all,
A light among the oxen.
Voice.   That is true!
Voice. Ay, and I love him now, for mine own father
Was great, and cobbled.
Voice.   Thou art Tostig's brother,
Who wastes the land.
Harold.   This brother comes to save
Your land from waste; I saved it once before,
For when your people banish'd Tostig hence,
And Edward would have sent a host against you,
Then I, who loved my brother, bade the King,
Who doted on him, sanction your decree
Of Tostig's banishment, and choice of Morcar,
To help the realm from scattering.
Voice.   King! thy brother,
If one may dare to speak the truth. was wrong'd
Wild was he, born so: but the plots against him
Had madden'd tamer men.
Morcar.   Thou art one of those
Who brake into Lord Tostig's treasure-house
And slew two hundred of his following,
And now, when Tostig hath come back with power,
Are frighted back to Tostig.
Old Thane.   Ugh! Plots and feuds!
This is my ninetieth birthday.   Can ye not
Be brethren?   Godwin still at feud with Alfgar,
And Alfgar hates King Harold.   Plots and feuds!
This is my ninetieth birthday!
Harold.   Old man, Harold
Hates nothing; not *his* fault, if our two houses
Be less than brothers.
Voices.   Aldwyth, Harold, Aldwyth!
Harold. Again! Morcar! Edwin!   What do they
    mean?
Edwin. So the good King would deign to lend an
    ear
Not overscornful, we might chance—perchance—
To guess their meaning.
Morcar.   Thine own meaning, Harold,
To make all England one, to close all feuds,
Mixing our bloods, that thence a king may rise
Half Godwin and half Alfgar, one to rule
All England beyond question, beyond quarrel.
Harold. Who sow'd this fancy here among the
    people?

Morcar. Who knows what sows itself among the people?
A goodly flower at times.
Harold.   The Queen of Wales?
Why, Morcar, it is all but duty in her
To hate me; I have heard she hates me.
Morcar.   No!
For I can swear to that, but cannot swear
That these will follow thee against the Norsemen,
If thou deny them this.
Harold.   Morcar and Edwin,
When will ye cease to plot against my house?
Edwin. The King can scarcely dream that we, who know
His prowess in the mountains of the West,
Should care to plot against him in the North.
Morcar. Who dares arraign us, King, of such a plot?
Harold. Ye-heard one witness even now.
Morcar.   The craven!
There is a faction risen again for Tostig,
Since Tostig came with Norway—fright not love.
Harold. Morcar and Edwin, will ye, if I yield,
Follow against the Norseman?
Morcar.   Surely, surely!
Harold. Morcar and Edwin, will ye, upon oath,
Help us against the Norman?
Morcar.   With good will;
Yea, take the Sacrament upon it, King.
Harold. Where is thy sister?
Morcar.   Somewhere hard at hand;
Call and she comes.
                    [*One goes out, then enter* ALDWYTH.
Harold.   I doubt not but thou knowest
Why thou art summon'd.
Aldwyth.   Why?—I stay with these,
Lest thy fierce Tostig spy me out alone,
And flay me all alive.
Harold.   Canst thou love one
Who did discrown thine husband, unqueen thee?
Didst thou not love thine husband?
Aldwyth.   Oh! my lord,
The nimble, wild, red, wiry, savage King—
That was, my lord, a match of policy.
Harold.   Was it?
I knew him brave: he loved his land: he fain
Had made her great: his finger on her harp
(I heard him more than once) had in it Wales,
Her floods, her woods, her hills: had I been his,
I had been all Welsh.
Aldwyth.   Oh, ay—all Welsh—and yet
I saw thee drive him up his hills—and women
Cling to the conquer'd, if they love, the more;
If not, they cannot hate the conqueror.
We never—oh! good Morcar, speak for us,
His conqueror conquer'd Aldwyth.
Harold.   Goodly news!
Morcar. Doubt it not thou! Since Griffyth's head
was sent
To Edward, she hath said it.
Harold.   I had rather
She would have loved her husband. Aldwyth, Aldwyth,
Canst thou love me, thou knowing where I love?
Aldwyth. I can, my lord, for mine own sake, for thine,
For England, for thy poor white dove, who flutters
Between thee and the porch, but then would find
Her nest within the cloister, and be still.
Harold. Canst thou love one who cannot love again?
Aldwyth. Full hope have I that love will answer love.
Harold. Then, in the name of the great God, so be it!
Come, Aldred, join our hands before the hosts,
That all may see.
          [ALDRED *joins the hands of* HAROLD *and*
              ALDWYTH *and blesses them.*

Voices.   Harold, Harold and Aldwyth!
Harold. Set forth our Golden Dragon, let him flap
The wings that beat down Wales!
Advance our Standard of the Warrior,
Dark among gems and gold; and thou, brave banner,
Blaze like a night of fatal stars on those
Who read their doom and die.
Where lie the Norsemen? on the Derwent? ay,
At Stamford-bridge.
Morcar. collect thy men; Edwin, my friend—
Thou lingerest.—Garth,—
Last night King Edward came to me in dreams—
The rosy face and long down-silvering beard—
He told me I should conquer:—
I am no woman to put faith in dreams.
(*To his Army.*) Last night King Edward came to me
          in dreams,
And told me we should conquer.
Voices.   Forward! Forward!
Harold and Holy Cross!
Aldwyth.   The day is won!

SCENE II.—A PLAIN. BEFORE THE
BATTLE OF STAMFORD-BRIDGE.

HAROLD *and his* Guard.

Harold. Who is it comes this way? Tostig?

          (*Enter* TOSTIG *with a small force.*)
                              O brother,
What art thou doing here?
Tostig.   I am foraging
For Norway's army.
Harold.   I could take and slay thee.
Thou art in arms against us.
Tostig.   Take and slay me,
For Edward loved me.
Harold.   Edward bade me spare thee.
Tostig. I hate King Edward, for he join'd with thee
To drive me outlaw'd. Take and slay me, I say,
Or I shall count thee fool.
Harold.   Take thee, or free thee,
Free thee or slay thee, Norway will have war;
No man would strike with Tostig, save for Norway.
Thou art nothing in thine England, save for Norway,
Who loves not thee, but war. What dost thou here,
Trampling thy mother's bosom into blood?
Tostig. She hath wean'd me from it with such bitterness.
I come for mine own Earldom, my Northumbria;
Thou hast given it to the enemy of our house.
Harold. Northumbria threw thee off, she will not have thee:
Thou hast misused her: and. O crowning crime!
Hast murder'd thine own guest, the son of Orm,
Gamel, at thine own hearth.
Tostig.   The slow, fat fool!
He drawl'd and prated so. I smote him suddenly,
I knew not what I did.
Harold.   Come back to us,
Know what thou dost, and we may find for thee,
So thou be chasten'd by thy banishment,
Some easier Earldom.
Tostig.   What for Norway then?
He looks for land among you, he and his.
Harold. Seven feet of English land, or something more,
Seeing he is a giant.
Tostig.   O brother, brother,
O Harold—
Harold. Nay then come thou back to us!
Tostig. Never shall any man say that I, that Tostig
Conjured the mightier Harold from his North

To do the battle for me here in England,
Then left him for the meaner! thee!—
Thou hast no passion for the House of Godwin—
Thou hast but cared to make thyself a King—
Thou hast sold me for a cry—
Thou gavest thy voice against me in the Council—
I hate thee, and despise thee, and defy thee.
Farewell for ever!   [*Exit.*
    Harold.   On to Stamford-bridge!

SCENE III. — AFTER THE BATTLE OF STAMFORD-BRIDGE. BANQUET.

HAROLD *and* ALDWYTH. GURTH, LEOFWIN, MORCAR, EDWIN, *and other Earls and Thanes.*

Voices. Hail, Harold! Aldwyth! hail, bridegroom
    and bride!
Aldwyth (talking with Harold). Answer them thou!
Is this our marriage-banquet? Would the wines
Of wedding had been dash'd into the cups
Of victory, and our marriage and thy glory
Been drunk together! these poor hands but sew,
Spin, broider—would that they were man's to have
    held
The battle-axe by thee!
    Harold.   There *was* a moment
When being forced aloof from all my guard,
And striking at Hardrada and his madmen
I had wish'd for any weapon.
    Aldwyth.   Why art thou sad?
Harold. I have lost the boy who play'd at ball
    with me,
With whom I fought another fight than this
Of Stamford-bridge.
    Aldwyth.   Ay! ay! thy victories
Over our own poor Wales, when at thy side
He conquer'd with thee.
    Harold.   No—the childish fist
That cannot strike again.
    Aldwyth.   Thou art too kindly.
Why didst thou let so many Norsemen hence?
Thy fierce forekings had clench'd their pirate hides
To the bleak church doors, like kites upon a barn.
    Harold. Is there so great a need to tell thee why?
    Aldwyth. Yea, am I not thy wife?
    Voices.   Hail, Harold, Aldwyth!
Bridegroom and bride!
    Aldwyth (to Harold). Answer them!
    Harold (to all).   Earls and Thanes!
Full thanks for your fair greeting of my bride!
Earls, Thanes, and all our countrymen! the day,
Our day beside the Derwent will not shine
Less than a star among the goldenest hours
Of Alfred, or of Edward his great son,
Or Athelstan, or English Ironside
Who fought with Knut, or Knut who, coming Dane,
Died English. Every man about his King
Fought like a king; the King like his own man,
No better: one for all, and all for one,
One soul! and therefore have we shatter'd back
The hugest wave from Norseland ever yet
Surged on us, and our battle-axes broken
The Raven's wing, and dumb'd his carrion croak
From the gray sea for ever. Many are gone—
Drink to the dead who died for us, the living
Who fought and would have died, but happier lived,
If happier be to live: they both have life
In the large mouth of England, till *her* voice
Die with the world. Hail—hail!
    Morcar. May all invaders perish like Hardrada!
All traitors fail like Tostig! [*All drink but* HAROLD.
    Aldwyth.   Thy cup's full!
    Harold. I saw the hand of Tostig cover it.
Our dear, dead, traitor-brother, Tostig, him
Reverently we buried. Friends, had I been here,

Without too large self-lauding I must hold
The sequel had been other than his league
With Norway, and this battle. Peace be with him!
He was not of the worst. If there be those
At banquet in this hall, and hearing me—
For there be those I fear who prick'd the lion
To make him spring, that sight of Danish blood
Might serve an end not English—peace with them
Likewise, if *they* can be at peace with what
God gave us to divide us from the wolf!
    Aldwyth (aside to Harold). Make not our Morcar
    sullen: it is not wise.
    Harold. Hail to the living who fought, the dead
    who fell!
    Voices. Hail, hail!
    First Thane. How ran that answer which King
    Harold gave
To his dead namesake, when he ask'd for England?
    Leofwin. "Seven feet of English earth, or some-
        thing more,
Seeing he is a giant!"
    First Thane.   Then for the bastard
Six feet and nothing more!
    Leofwin.   Ay, but belike
Thou hast not learnt his measure.
    First Thane.   By St. Edmund,
I over-measure him. Sound sleep to the man
Here by dead Norway without dream or dawn!
    Second Thane. What, is he bragging still that he
    will come
To thrust our Harold's throne from under him?
My nurse would tell me of a molehill crying
To a mountain "Stand aside and room for me.
    First Thane. Let him come! let him come. Here's
    to him, sink or swim!   [*Drinks.*
    Second Thane. God sink him!
    First Thane. Cannot hands which had the strength
To shove that stranded iceberg off our shores,
And send the shatter'd North again to sea,
Scuttle his cockle-shell? What's Brunanburg
To Stamford-bridge? a war-crash, and so hard,
So loud, that, by St. Dunstan, old St. Thor—
By God, we thought him dead—but our old Thor
Heard his own thunder again, and woke and came
Among us again, and mark'd the sons of those
Who made this Britain England break the North:

        Mark'd how the war-axe swang,
        Heard how the war-horn sang,
        Mark'd how the spear-head sprang,
        Heard how the shield-wall rang,
        Iron on iron clang,
        Anvil on hammer bang—

    Second Thane. Hammer on anvil, hammer on an-
    vil. Old dog!
Thou art drunk, old dog!
    First Thane.   Too drunk to fight with thee!
    Second Thane. Fight thou with thine own double,
    not with me:
Keep that for Norman William!
    First Thane.   Down with William!
    Third Thane. The washerwoman's brat!
    Fourth Thane.   The tanner's bastard!
    Fifth Thane. The Falaise byblow!
        [*Enter a Thane, from Pevensey, spattered
            with mud.*
    Harold.   Ay, but what late guest,
As haggard as a fast of forty days,
And caked and plaster'd with a hundred mires,
Hath stumbled on our cups?
    Thane from Pevensey.   My lord the King!
William the Norman, for the wind had changed—
    Harold. I felt it in the middle of that fierce fight
At Stamford-bridge. William hath landed, ha?
    Thane from Pevensey. Landed at Pevensey—I am
    from Pevensey—
Hath wasted all the land at Pevensey—
Hath harried mine own cattle—God confound him!

I have ridden night and day from Pevensey—
A thousand ships, a hundred thousand men—
Thousands of horses, like as many lions
Neighing and roaring as they leapt to land—
  Harold. How oft in coming hast thou broken
    bread?
  Thane from Pevensey. Some thrice, or so.
  Harold.   Bring not thy hollowness
On our full feast. Famine is fear, were it but
Of being starved. Sit down, sit down, and eat,
And, when again red-blooded, speak again :
(*Aside.*) The men that guarded England to the South
Were scatter'd to the harvest.....No power mine
To hold their force together.....Many are fallen

At Stamford-bridge....the people, stupid-sure,
Sleep like their swine....in South and North at once
I could not be.
  (*Aloud.*)   Gurth, Leofwin, Morcar, Edwin !
(*Pointing to the revellers.*) The curse of England ! these
  are drown'd in wassail,
And cannot see the world but thro' their wines !
I leave them ! and thee too, Aldwyth, must I leave—
Harsh is the news ! hard is our honeymoon !
Thy pardon. (*Turing round to his attendants.*) Break
    the banquet up....Ye four !
And thou, my carrier-pigeon of black news,
Cram thy crop full, but come when thou art call'd.
                [*Exit* HAROLD.

ACT V.

SCENE I.—A TENT ON A MOUND, FROM WHICH CAN BE SEEN THE FIELD OF SENLAC.

HAROLD, *sitting; by him standing* HUGH MARGOT *the Monk,* GURTH, LEOFWIN.

  Harold. Refer my cause, my crown to Rome !....
    The wolf
Mudded the brook, and predetermined all.
  Monk,
Thou hast said thy say, and had my constant "No"
For all but instant battle. I hear no more.
  Margot. Hear me again—for the last time. Arise,
Scatter thy people home, descend the hill,
Lay hands of full allegiance in thy Lord's
And crave his mercy, for the Holy Father
Hath given this realm of England to the Norman.
  Harold. Then for the last time, monk. I ask again
When had the Lateran and the Holy Father
To do with England's choice of her own king?
  Margot. Earl, the first Christian Cæsar drew to the
    East
To leave the Pope dominion in the West.
He gave him all the kingdoms of the West.
  Harold. So !—did he ?—Earl—I have a mind to play
The William with thine eyesight and thy tongue.
Earl—ay—thou art but a messenger of William.
I am weary—go : make me not wroth with thee !
  Margot. Mock-king, I am the messenger of God,
His Norman Daniel ! Mene, Mene, Tekel !
Is thy wrath hell, that I should spare to cry,
You heaven is wroth with *thee ?* Hear me again !
Our Saints have moved the Church that moves the
    world,
And all the heavens and very God : they heard—
They know King Edward's promise and thine—thine.
  Harold. Should they not know free England crowns
    herself?
Not know that he nor I had power to promise ?
Not know that Edward cancell'd his own promise?
And for *my* part therein—Back to that juggler,
                (*Rising*)
Tell him the Saints are nobler than he dreams,
Tell him that God is nobler than the Saints,
And tell him we stand arm'd on Senlac Hill,
And bide the doom of God.
  Margot.   Hear it thro' me.
The realm for which thou art forsworn is cursed,
The babe enwomb'd and at the breast is cursed,
The corpse thou whelmest with thine earth is cursed,
The soul who fighteth on thy side is cursed,
The seed thou sowest in thy field is cursed,
The steer wherewith thou plowest thy field is cursed,

The fowl that fleeth o'er thy field is cursed,
And thou, usurper, liar—
  Harold.   Out, beast monk !
    [*Lifting his hand to strike him.* GURTH
             stops the blow.
I ever hated monks.
  Margot.   I am but a voice
Among you : murder, martyr me if ye will—
  Harold. Thanks, Gurth ! The simple, silent, self-
    less man
Is worth a world of tonguesters. (*To Margot.*) Get
    thee gone !
He means the thing he says. See him out safe !
  Leofwin. He hath blown himself as red as fire with
    curses.
An honest fool ! Follow me, honest fool,
But if thou blurt thy curse among our folk,
I know not—I may give that egg-bald head
The tap that silences.
  Harold.   See him out safe.
    [*Exeunt* LEOFWIN *and* MARGOT.
  Gurth. Thou hast lost thine even temper, brother
    Harold !
  Harold. Gurth, when I past by Waltham, my foun-
    dation
For men who serve the neighbor, not themselves,
I cast me down prone, praying ; and, when I rose,
They told me that the Holy Rood had lean'd
And bow'd above me ; whether that which held it
Had weaken'd, and the Rood itself were bound
To that necessity which binds us down ;
Whether it bow'd at all but in their fancy ;
Or if it bow'd, whether it symbol'd ruin
Or glory, who shall tell ? but they were sad,
And somewhat sadden'd me.
  Gurth.   Yet if a fear,
Or shadow of a fear, lest the strange Saints
By whom thou swarest should have power to balk
Thy puissance in this fight with him who made
And heard thee swear—brother—*I* have not sworn—
If the King fall, may not the kingdom fall ?
But if I fall, I fall, and thou art King ;
And if I win, I win, and thou art King ;
Draw thou to London, there make strength to breast
Whatever chance, but leave this day to me.
  Leofwin (*entering*). And waste the land about thee
    as thou goest,
And be thy hand as winter on the field,
To leave the foe no forage.
  Harold.   Noble Gurth !
Best son of Godwin ! If I fall, I fall—
The doom of God ! How should the people fight
When the King flies ? And, Leofwin, art thou mad !
How should the King of England waste the fields

Of England, his own people?—No glance yet
Of the Northumbrian helmet on the heath?
   Leofwin. No, but a shoal of wives upon the heath,
And someone saw thy willy-nilly nun
Vying a tress against our golden fern.
   Harold. Vying a tear with our cold dews, a sigh
With these low-mourning heavens. Let her be
fetch'd.
We have parted from our wife without reproach,
Tho' we have dived thro' all her practices;
And that is well.
   Leofwin. I saw her even now:
She hath not left us.
   Harold. Nought of Morcar then?
   Gurth. Nor seen, nor heard; thine, William's, or
his own
As wind blows, or tide flows: belike he watches,
If this war-storm in one of its rough rolls
Wash up that old crown of Northumberland.
   Harold. I married her for Morcar—a sin against
The truth of love. Evil for good, it seems,
Is oft as childless of the good as evil
For evil.
   Leofwin. Good for good hath borne at times
A bastard false as William.
   Harold. Ay, if Wisdom
Pair'd not with Good. But I am somewhat worn,
A snatch of sleep were like the peace of God.
Gurth, Leofwin, go once more about the hill—
What did the dead man call it—Sanguelac,
The Lake of Blood?
   Leofwin. A lake that dips in William
As well as Harold.
   Harold. Like enough. I have seen
The trenches dug, the palisades uprear'd
And wattled thick with ash and willow wands;
Yea, wrought at them myself. Go round once more;
See all be sound and whole. No Norman horse
Can shatter England, standing shield by shield;
Tell that again to all.
   Gurth. I will, good brother.
   Harold. Our guardsman hath but toil'd his hand
and foot,
I hand, foot, heart and head. Some wine! (*One
pours wine into a goblet, which he hands to
Harold.*) Too much!
What? we must use our battle-axe to-day.
Our guardsmen have slept well, since we came in?
   Leofwin. Ay, slept and snored. Your second-sight-
ed man
That scared the dying conscience of the King,
Misheard their snores for groans. They are up again
And chanting that old song of Brunanburg
Where England conquer'd.
   Harold. That is well. The Norman,
What is he doing?
   Leofwin. Praying for Normandy.
Our scouts have heard the tinkle of their bells.
   Harold. And our old songs are prayers for England
too!
But by all Saints—
   Leofwin. Barring the Norman!
   Harold. Nay,
Were the great trumpet blowing doomsday dawn,
I needs must rest. Call when the Norman moves—
             [*Exeunt all but* HAROLD.
No horse—thousands of horses—our shield wall—
Wall—break it not—break not—break—   [*Sleeps.*
   Vision of Edward. Son Harold, I thy King, who
came before
To tell thee thou shouldst win at Stamford-bridge
Come yet once more, from where I am at peace,
Because I loved thee in my mortal day,
To tell thee thou shalt die on Senlac hill—
Sanguelac!
   Vision of Wulfnoth. O brother, from my ghastly
oubliette
I send my voice across the narrow seas—

No more, no more, dear brother, nevermore—
Sanguelac!
   Vision of Tostig. O brother, most unbrotherlike to
me,
Thou gavest thy voice against me in my life,
I give my voice against thee from the grave—
Sanguelac!
   Vision of Norman Saints. O hapless Harold! King
but for an hour!
Thou swarest falsely by our blessed bones.
We give our voice against thee out of heaven!
Sanguelac! Sanguelac! The arrow! the arrow!
   Harold (*starting up, battle-axe in hand*). Away!
My battle-axe against your voices. Peace!
The King's last word—"the arrow!" I shall die—
I die for England then, who lived for England—
What nobler? men must die.
I cannot fall into a falser world—
I have done no man wrong. Tostig, poor brother,
Art thou so anger'd?
Fain had I kept thine earldom in thy hands
Save for thy wild and violent will that wrench'd
All hearts of freemen from thee. I could do
No other than this way advise the King
Against the race of Godwin. Is it possible
That mortal men should bear their earthly heats
Into yon bloodless world, and threaten us thence
Unschool'd of Death? Thus then thou art re-
venged—
I left our England naked to the South
To meet thee in the North. The Norseman's raid
Hath helpt the Norman, and the race of Godwin
Hath ruin'd Godwin. No—our waking thoughts
Suffer a stormless shipwreck in the pools
Of sullen slumber, and arise again
Disjointed: only dreams—where mine own self
Takes part against myself! Why? for a spark
Of self-disdain born in me when I sware
Falsely to him, the falser Norman, over
His gilded ark of mummy-saints, by whom
I knew not that I sware,—not for myself—
For England—yet not wholly—

          (*Enter* EDITH.)

                  Edith, Edith,
Get thou into thy cloister as the King
Will'd it: be safe: the perjury-mongering Count
Hath made too good an use of Holy Church
To break her close! There the great God of truth
Fill all thine hours with peace!—A lying devil
Hath haunted me—mine oath—my wife—I fain
Had made my marriage not a lie; I could not:
Thou art my bride! and thou in after-years
Praying perchance for this poor soul of mine
In cold, white cells beneath an icy moon—
This memory to thee!—and this to England,
My legacy of war against the Pope
From child to child, from Pope to Pope, from age
to age,
Till the sea wash her level with her shores,
Or till the Pope be Christ's.

          Enter ALDWYTH.

   Aldwyth (*to Edith*). Away from him!
   Edith. I will....I have not spoken to the King
One word; and one I must. Farewell!   [*Going.*
   Harold. Not yet.
Stay.
   Edith. To what use?
   Harold. The King commands thee, woman!
(*To Aldwyth*). Have thy two brethren sent their forces
in?
   Aldwyth. Nay, I fear not.
   Harold. Then there's no force in thee!
Thou didst possess thyself of Edward's ear
To part me from the woman that I loved!
Thou didst arouse the fierce Northumbrians!
Thou hast been false to England and to me!—

As....in some sort....I have been false to thee.
Leave me. No more—pardon on both sides. Go!
Aldwyth. Alas, my lord, I love thee.
Harold (*bitterly*).   With a love
Passing thy love for Griffyth! wherefore now
Obey my first and last commandment. Go!
Aldwyth. O Harold! husband!   Shall we meet
    again?
Harold. After the battle—after the battle. Go.
Aldwyth. I go. (*Aside*). That I could stab her
    standing there!   [*Exit* ALDWYTH.
Edith. Alas, my lord, she loved thee.
Harold.   Never! never!
Edith. I saw it in her eyes!
Harold.   I see it in thine.
And not on thee—nor England—fall God's doom!
Edith. On *thee?* on me. And thou art England!
    Alfred
Was England. Ethelred was nothing. England
Is but her King, and thou art Harold!
Harold.   Edith,
The sign in heaven—the sudden blast at sen—
My fatal oath—the dead Saints—the dark dreams—
The Pope's Anathema—the Holy Rood
That bow'd to me at Waltham—Edith, if
I, the last English King of England—
Edith.   No,
First of a line that coming from the people,
And chosen by the people—
Harold.   And fighting for
And dying for the people—
Edith.   Living! living!
Harold. Yea so, good cheer! thou art Harold, I am
    Edith!
Look not thus wan!
Edith.   What matters how I look?
Have we not broken Wales and Norseland? slain,
Whose life was all one battle, incarnate war,
Their giant-king, a mightier man-in-arms
Than William.
Harold.   Ay, my girl, no tricks in him—
No bastard he! when all was lost, he yell'd,
And bit his shield, and dash'd it on the ground,
And swaying his two-handed sword about him,
Two deaths at every swing, ran in upon us
And died so. and I loved him as I hate
This liar who made me liar. If Hate can kill,
And Loathing wield a Saxon battle-axe—
Edith. Waste not thy might before the battle!
Harold.   No,
And thou must hence. Stigand will see thee safe,
And so—farewell.   [*He is going, but turns back.*
                    The ring thou darest not wear,
I have had it fashion'd, see. to meet my hand.
    [HAROLD *shows the ring which is on his*
        finger.
Farewell!   [*He is going, but turns back again.*
I am dead as Death this day to aught of earth's
Save William's death or mine.
Edith.   Thy death!—to-day!
Is it not thy birthday?
Harold.   Ay, that happy day!
A birthday welcome! happy days and many!
One—this!   [*They embrace.*
Look, I will bear thy blessing into the battle
And front the doom of God.
    Norman cries (*heard in the distance*). Ha Rou! Ha
    Rou!

            Enter GURTH.

Gurth. The Norman moves!
Harold.   Harold and Holy Cross!
                    [*Exeunt* HAROLD *and* GURTH.

            Enter STIGAND.

Stigand. Our Church in arms—the lamb the lion—
    not
Swear into pruning-hook—the counter way—
Cowl, helm; and crozier, battle-axe. Abbot Alfwig,

Leofric, and all the monks of Peterboro'
Strike for the King; but I, old wretch, old Stigand,
With hands too limp to brandish iron—and yet
I have a power—would Harold ask me for it—
I have a power.
Edith.   What power, holy father?
Stigand. Power now from Harold to command thee
    hence
And see thee safe from Senlac.
Edith.   I remain!
Stigand. Yea, so will I, daughter, until I find
Which way the battle balance. I can see it
From where we stand: and, live or die, I would
I were among them!

    CANONS *from Waltham* (*singing without*).
            Salva patriam
            Sancte Pater,
            Salva Fili,
            Salva Spiritus,
            Salva patriam,
            Sancta Mater.*

Edith. Are those the blessed angels quiring, fa-
    ther?
Stigand. No, daughter, but the canons out of Walt-
    ham,
The King's foundation, that have follow'd him.
Edith. O God of battles, make their wall of shields
Firm as thy cliffs, strengthen their palisades!
What is that whirring sound?
Stigand.   The Norman arrow!
Edith. Look out upon the battle—is he safe?
Stigand. The King of England stands between his
    banners.
He glitters on the crowning of the hill.
God save King Harold!
Edith.   —Chosen by his people
And fighting for his people!
Stigand.   There is one
Come as Goliath came of yore—he flings
His brand in air and catches it again:
He is chanting some old war-song.
Edith.   And no David
To meet him?
Stigand. Ay, there springs a Saxon on him,
Falls—and another falls.
Edith.   Have mercy on us!
Stigand. Lo! our good Gurth hath smitten him to
    the death.
Edith. So perish all the enemies of Harold!

            CANONS (*singing*).
            Hostis in Angliam
            Ruit prædator,
            Illorum, Domine,
            Scutum scindatur!
            Hostis per Angliæ
            Plagas bacchatur;
            Casa crematur,
            Pastor fugatur
            Grex trucidatur—

Stigand. Illos trucida, Domine.
Edith.   Ay, good father.

            CANONS (*singing*).
            Illorum scelera
            Pœna sequatur!

English Cries. Harold and Holy Cross! Out! out!
Stigand.   Our javelins
Answer their arrows. All the Norman foot
Are storming up the hill. The range of knights
Sit, each a statue on his horse, and wait.

―――――――――

* The *a* throughout these hymns should be sounded broad, as in
" father."

English Cries. Harold and God Almighty!
Norman Cries. Ha Rou! Ha Rou!

CANONS (*singing*).

Eques cum pedite
Præpediatur!
Illorum in lacrymas
Cruor fundatur!
Pereant, pereant,
Anglia precatur.

Stigand. Look, daughter, look.
Edith. Nay, father, look for *me!*
Stigand. Our axes lighten with a single flash
About the summit of the hill, and heads
And arms are sliver'd off and splinter'd by
Their lightning—and they fly—the Norman flies.
Edith. Stigand, O father, have we won the day?
Stigand. No, daughter, no—they fall behind the
horse—
Their horse are thronging to the barricades;
I see the gonfanon of Holy Peter
Floating above their helmets—ha! he is down!
Edith. He down! Who down?
Stigand. The Norman Count is down.
Edith. So perish all the enemies of England!
Stigand. No, no, he hath ri-en again—he bares his
face—
Shouts something—he points onward—all their horse
Swallow the hill locust-like, swarming up.
Edith. O God of battles, make his battle-axe keen
As thine own sharp-dividing justice, heavy
As thine own bolts that fall on crimeful heads
Charged with the weight of heaven wherefrom they
fall!

CANONS (*singing*).

Jacta tonitrua
Dens bellator!
Surgas e tenebris,
Sis vindicator!
Fulmina, fulmina
Deus vastator!

Edith. O God of battles, they are three to one,
Make thou one man as three to roll them down!

CANONS (*singing*).

Equus cum equite
Dejiciatur!
Acies, Acies
Prona sternatur!
Illorum lanceas
Frange Creator!

Stigand. Yea, yea, for how their lances snap and
shiver
Against the shifting blaze of Harold's axe!
War-woodman of old Woden, how he fells
The mortal copse of faces! There! And there
The horse and horseman cannot meet the shield.
The blow that brains the horseman cleaves the
horse;
The horse and horseman roll along the hill:
They fly once more, they fly, the Norman flies!

Equus cum equite
Præcipitatur.

Edith. O God, the God of truth hath heard my
cry.
Follow them, follow them, drive them to the sea!

Illorum scelera
Pœna sequatur!

Stigand. Truth! no; a lie; a trick, a Norman
trick!
They turn on the pursuer, horse against foot,
They murder all that follow.
Edith. Have mercy on us!

Stigand. Hot-headed fools—to burst the wall of
shields!
They have broken the commandment of the King!
Edith. His oath was broken—O holy Norman
Saints,
Ye that are now of heaven, and see beyond
Your Norman shrines, pardon it, pardon it,
That he forsware himself for all he loved,
Me, me and all! Look out upon the battle!
Stigand. They thunder again upon the barricades.
My sight is eagle, but the strife so thick—
This is the hottest of it: hold, ash! hold, willow!
English Cries. Out, out!
Norman Cries. Ha Rou!
Stigand. Ha! Gurth hath leapt upon him
And slain him: he hath fallen.
Edith. And I am heard.
Glory to God in the Highest! fallen, fallen!
Stigand. No, no, his horse—he mounts another—
wields
His war-club, dashes it on Gurth, and Gurth,
Our noble Gurth, is down!
Edith. Have mercy on us!
Stigand. And Leofwin is down!
Edith. Have mercy on us!
O Thou that knowest, let not my strong prayer
Be weaken'd in thy sight, because I love
The husband of another!
Norman Cries. Ha Rou! Ha Rou!
Edith. I do not hear our English war-cry.
Stigand. No.
Edith. Look out upon the battle—is he safe?
Stigand. He stands between the banners, with the
dead
So piled about him he can hardly move.
Edith (*takes up the war-cry*). Out! out!
Norman Cries. Ha Rou!
Edith (*cries out*). Harold and Holy Cross!
Norman Cries. Ha Rou! Ha Rou!
Edith. What is that whirring sound?
Stigand. The Norman sends his arrows up to heav-
en,
They fall on those within the palisade!
Edith. Look out upon the hill—is Harold there?
Stigand. Sanguelac—Sanguelac—the arrow—the ar-
row!—away!

SCENE II. — FIELD OF THE DEAD. NIGHT.

ALDWYTH *and* EDITH.

Aldwyth. O Edith, art thou here? O Harold, Har-
old—
Our Harold—we shall never see him more.
Edith. For there was more than sister in my kiss,
And so the saints were wroth. I cannot love them,
For they are Norman saints—and yet I should—
They are so much holier than their harlot's son
With whom they play'd their game against the King!
Aldwyth. The King is slain, the kingdom over-
thrown!
Edith. No matter!
Aldwyth. How no matter, Harold slain?—
I cannot find his body. Oh, help me thou!
O Edith, if I ever wrought against thee,
Forgive me thou, and help me here!
Edith. No matter!
Aldwyth. Not help me, nor forgive me?
Edith. So thou saidest.
Aldwyth. I say it now, forgive me!
Edith. Cross me not!
I am seeking one who wedded me in secret.
Whisper! God's angels only know it. Ha!
What art *thou* doing here among the dead?
They are stripping the dead bodies naked yonder,
And thou art come to rob them of their rings!

Aldwyth. O Edith, Edith, I have lost both crown
And husband.

Edith.   So have I.

Aldwyth.   I tell thee, girl,
I am seeking my dead Harold.

Edith.   And I mine!
The Holy Father strangled him with a hair
Of Peter, and his brother Tostig helpt;
The wicked sister clapt her hands and laugh'd;
Then all the dead fell on him.

Aldwyth.   Edith, Edith—

Edith. What was he like, this husband? like to
    thee?
Call not for help from me. I knew him not.
He lies not here: not close beside the standard.
Here fell the truest, manliest hearts of England.
Go further hence and find him.

Aldwyth.   She is crazed!

Edith. That doth not matter either. Lower the
    light.
He must be here.

*Enter two Canons, Osgod and Athelric, with torches.
  They turn over the dead bodies and examine them as
  they pass.*

Osgod.   I think that this is Thurkill.

Athelric. More likely Godric.

Osgod.   I am sure this body
Is Alfwig, the King's uncle.

Athelric.   So it is!
No, no—brave Gurth, one gash from brow to knee!

Osgod. And here is Leofwin.

Edith.   And here is *He!*

Aldwyth. Harold? Oh no—nay, if it were—my
    God,
They have so maim'd and murder'd all his face
There is no man can swear to him.

Edith.   But one woman!
Look you, we never mean to part again.
I have found him, I am happy.
Was there not someone ask'd me for forgiveness?
I yield it freely, being the true wife
Of this dead King, who never bore revenge.

Enter Count William *and* William Malet.

William. Who be these women? And what body
    is this?

Edith. Harold, thy better!

William.   Ay, and what art thou?

Edith. His wife!

Malet.   Not true, my girl, here is the Queen!
                    [*Pointing out* Aldwyth.

William (*to Aldwyth*). Wast thou his Queen?

Aldwyth.   I was the Queen of Wales.

William. Why then of England. Madam, fear us
    not.
(*To Malet*). Knowest thou this other?

Malet.   When I visited England,
Some held she was his wife in secret—some—
Well—some believed she was his paramour.

Edith. Norman, thou liest! liars all of you,
Your Saints and all! *I* am his wife! and she—
For look, our marriage-ring!
                [*She draws it off the finger of* Harold.
                        I lost it somehow—

I lost it, playing with it when I was wild.
That bred the doubt! but I am wiser now....
I am too wise....Will none among you all
Bear me true witness—only for this once—
That I have found it here again? [*She puts it on.*
                        And thou,
Thy wife am I for ever and evermore.
                [*Falls on the body and dies.*

William. Death!—and enough of death for this
    one day,
The day of Saint Calixtus, and the day,
My day, when I was born.

Malet.   And this dead King's,
Who, King or not, hath kinglike fought and fallen,
His birthday, too. It seems but yester-even
I held it with him in his English halls,
His day, with all his rooftree ringing "Harold,"
Before he fell into the snare of Guy;
When all men counted Harold would be king,
And Harold was most happy.

William.   Thou art half English.
Take them away!
Malet, I vow to build a church to God
Here on this hill of battle: let our high altar
Stand where their standard fell....where these two
    lie.
Take them away, I do not love to see them.
Pluck the dead woman off the dead man, Malet!

Malet. Faster than ivy. Must I hack her arms
    off?
How shall I part them?

William.   Leave them. Let them be!
Bury him and his paramour together.
He that was false in oath to me, it seems
Was false to his own wife. We will not give him
A Christian burial: yet he was a warrior,
And wise, yea truthful, till that blighted vow
Which God avenged to-day.
Wrap them together in a purple cloak
And lay them both upon the waste sea-shore
At Hastings, there to guard the land for which
He did forswear himself—a warrior—ay,
And but that Holy Peter fought for us,
And that the false Northumbrian held aloof,
And save for that chance arrow which the Saints
Sharpen'd and sent against him—who can tell?—
Three horses had I slain beneath me: twice
I thought that all was lost. Since I knew battle,
And that was from my boyhood, never yet—
No, by the splendor of God—have I fought men
Like Harold and his brethren, and his guard
Of English. Every man about his King
Fell where he stood. They loved him: and, pray God
My Normans may but move as true with me
To the door of death. Of one self-stock at first,
Make them again one people—Norman, English;
And English, Norman;—we should have a hand
To grasp the world with, and a foot to stamp it
Flat. Praise the Saints. It is over. No more
    blood!
I am King of England, so they thwart me not,
And I will rule according to their laws.
(*To Aldwyth*). Madam, we will entreat thee with all
    honor.

Aldwyth. My punishment is more than I can bear.

POEMS,

BY TWO BROTHERS.*

[ALFRED AND CHARLES TENNYSON.]

" Hæc nos novimus esse nihil."—MARTIAL.

ADVERTISEMENT.

THE following Poems were written from the ages of fifteen to eighteen, not conjointly, but individually; which may account for their difference of style and matter. To light upon any novel combination of images, or to open any vein of sparkling thought untouched before, were no easy task ; indeed, the remark itself is as old as the truth is clear ; and, no doubt, if submitted to the microscopic eye of periodical criticism, a long list of inaccuracies and imitations would result from the investigation. But so it is : we have passed the Rubicon, and we leave the rest to fate ; though its edict may create a fruitless regret that we ever emerged from "the shade," and courted notoriety.

March, 1827.

'Tis sweet to lead from stage to stage,
Like infancy to a maturer age,
The fleeting thoughts that crowd quick Fancy's
    view,
And the coy image into form to woo:
Till all its charms to life and shape awake,
Wrought to the finest polish they can take:
Now out of sight the crafty Proteus steals,
The mind's quick emissaries at his heels,
Its nature now a partial light reveals.
Each moment's labor, easier than before,
Embodies the illusive image more:
Brings it more closely underneath the eye,
And lends it form and palpability.
What late in shadowy vision fleeted by,
Receives at each essay a deepening dye ;
Till diction gives us, modell'd into song,
The fairy phantoms of the motley throng;
Detaining and elucidating well
Her airy embryos with binding spell;
For when the mind reflects its image true—
Sees its own aim—expression must ensue ;
If all but language is supplied before,
She quickly follows, and the task is o'er.
Thus when the hand of pyrotechnic skill
Has stored the spokes of the fantastic wheel,
Apply the flame—it spreads as is design'd,
And glides and lightens o'er the track defined ;
Unerring on its faithful pathway burns,
Searches each nook, and tracks its thousand
    turns;

The well-fill'd tubes in flexile flame arrays,
And fires each winding of the pregnant maze;
Feeding on prompt materials, spurns delay,
Till o'er the whole the lambent glories play.
I know no joy so well deserves the name,
None that more justly may that title claim,
Than that of which the poet is possess'd
When warm imagination fires his breast,
And countless images like claimants throng,
Prompting the ardent ecstasy of song.
He walks his study in a dreaming mood,
Like Pythia's priestess panting with the god ;
His varying brow, betraying what he feels,
The labor of his plastic mind reveals:
Now roughly furrow'd into anxious storms,
If with much toil his lab'ring lines he forms;
Now brightening into triumph as, the skein
Unravelling, he cons them o'er again,
As each correction of his favorite piece
Confers more smoothness, elegance, or ease.

Such are the sweets of song—and in this age,
Perchance too many in its lists engage:
And they who now would fain awake the lyre,
May swell this supernumerary choir:
But ye, who deign to read, forget t' apply
The searching microscope of scrutiny:
Few from too near inspection fail to lose,
Distance on all a mellowing haze bestows ;
And who is not indebted to that aid
Which throws his failures into welcome shade?

* London : Printed for W. Simpkin, and R. Marshall, Stationers-hall Court : and J. and J. Jackson, Louth. MDCCCXXVII.

POEMS.

STANZAS.

Yon star of eve, so soft and clear,
Beams mildly from the realms of rest;
And, sure, some deathless angel there
Lives in its light supremely blest:
Yet if it be a spirit's shrine,
I think, my love, it must be thine.

Oh! if in happier worlds than this
The just rejoice—to thee is giv'n
To taste the calm, undying bliss
Eternally in that blue heav'n,
Whither thine earnest soul would flow,
While yet it linger'd here below.

If Beauty, Wit, and Virtue find
In heav'n a more exalted throne,
To thee such glory is assign'd,
And thou art matchless and alone:
Who lived on earth so pure—may grace
In heav'n the brightest seraph's place.

For tho' on earth thy beauty's bloom
Blush'd in its spring, and faded then,
And, mourning o'er thine early tomb,
I weep thee still, but weep in vain;
Bright was the transitory gleam
That cheer'd thy life's short wav'ring dream.

Each youthful rival may confess
Thy look, thy smile, beyond compare,
Nor ask the palm of loveliness,
When thou wert more than doubly fair:
Yet ev'n the magic of that form
Drew from thy mind its loveliest charm.

Be thou as the immortal are,
Who dwell beneath their God's own wing;
A spirit of light, a living star,
A holy and a searchless thing:
But oh! forget not those who mourn,
Because thou canst no more return.

"IN EARLY YOUTH I LOST MY SIRE."

"Hinc mild prima mali labes."—VIRGIL.

In early youth I lost my sire,
That fost'ring guide, which all require,
But chief in youth, when passion glows,
And, if uncheck'd, to frenzy grows,
The fountain of a thousand woes.
To flowers it is an hurtful thing
To lose the sunshine in the spring;
Without the sun they cannot bloom,
And seldom to perfection come,
E'en so my soul, that might have borne
The fruits of virtue, left forlorn,
By every blast of vice was torn.
Why lowers my brow, dost thou enquire?
Why burns mine eye with feverish fire?
With hatred now, and now with ire?
In early youth I lost my sire.

From this I date whatever vice
Has numb'd my feelings into ice;
From this—the frown upon my brow;
From this—the pangs that rack me now.
My wealth, I can with safety say,
Ne'er bought me one unruffled day,
But only wore my life away.
The pruning-knife ne'er lopp'd a bough;
My passions spread, and strengthen'd too.
The chief of these was vast ambition,
That long'd with eagle-wing to soar;
Nor ever soften'd in contrition,
Tho' that wild wing were drench'd in gore.
And other passions play'd their part
On stage most fit—a youthful heart;
Till far beyond all hope I fell,
A play-thing for the fiends of hell—
A vessel, tost upon a deep
Whose stormy waves would never sleep.
Alas! when virtue once has flown,
We need not ask why peace is gone:
If she at times a moment play'd
With bright beam on my mind's dark shade,
I knew the rainbow soon would fade!
Why thus it is, dost thou enquire?
Why bleeds my breast with tortures dire?
Loathes the rank earth, yet soars not higher?
In early youth I lost my sire.

MEMORY.

"The memory is perpetually looking back when we have nothing present to entertain us: it is like those repositories in animals that are filled with stores of food on which they may ruminate when their present pasture fails."—ADDISON.

Memory! dear enchanter!
Why bring back to view
Dreams of youth, which banter
All that e'er was true?

Why present before me
Thoughts of years gone by,
Which, like shadows o'er me,
Dim in distance fly?

Days of youth, now shaded
By twilight of long years,
Flowers of youth, now faded,
Though bathed in sorrow's tears:

Thoughts of youth, which waken
Mournful feelings now,
Fruits which time hath shaken
From off their parent bough:

Memory! why, oh why,
This fond heart consuming,
Show me years gone by,
When those hopes were blooming?

Hopes which now are parted,
Hopes which then I prized,
Which this world, cold-hearted,
Ne'er has realized?

I knew not then its strife,
I knew not then its rancor;
In every rose of life,
. Alas! there lurks a canker.

Round every palm-tree, springing
With bright fruit in the waste,
A mournful asp is clinging,
Which sours it to our taste.

O'er every fountain, pouring
Its waters thro' the wild,
Which man imbibes, adoring,
And deems it undefiled,

The poison-shrubs are dropping
Their dark dews day by day;
And Care is hourly lopping
Our greenest boughs away!

Ah! these are thoughts that grieve me
Then, when others rest.
Memory! why deceive me
By thy visions blest?

Why lift the veil, dividing
The brilliant courts of spring—
Where gilded shapes are gliding
In fairy coloring—

From age's frosty mansion,
So cheerless and so chill?
Why bid the bleak expansion
Of past life meet us still?

Where's now that peace of mind
O'er youth's pure bosom stealing,
So sweet and so refined,
So exquisite a feeling?

Where's now the heart exulting
In pleasure's buoyant sense,
And gaiety, resulting
From conscious innocence?

All, all have past and fled,
And left me lorn and lonely;
All those dear hopes are dead,
Remembrance wakes them only!

I stand like some lone tower
Of former days remaining,
Within whose place of power
The midnight owl is plaining;—

Like oak-tree old and gray,
Whose trunk with age is failing,
Thro' whose dark boughs for aye
The winter winds are wailing.

Thus, Memory, thus thy light
O'er this worn soul is gleaming,
Like some far fire at night
Along the dun deep streaming.

———◇◇◇———

"YES—THERE BE SOME GAY SOULS WHO NEVER WEEP."

"O Lachrymarum fons, tenero sacros
Ducentium ortus ex animo."
GRAY'S *Poemata.*

YES—there be some gay souls who never weep,
And some who, weeping, hate the tear they shed;
But sure in them the heart's fine feelings sleep,
And all its loveliest attributes are dead.

For oh! to feel it swelling to the eye,
When melancholy thoughts have sent it there,
Is something so akin to ecstasy,
So true a balm to misery and care,

That those are cold, I ween, who cannot feel
The soft, the sweet, the exquisite control,
Which tears, as down the moisten'd cheek they steal,
Hold o'er the yielding empire of the soul.

They soothe, they ease, and they refine the breast,
And blunt the agonizing stings of grief,
And lend the tortured mind a healing rest,
A welcome opiate, and a kind relief.

Then, if the pow'r of woe thou wouldst disarm,
The tear thy burning wounds will gently close;
The rage of grief will sink into a calm,
And her wild frenzy find the wish'd repose.

———◇◇◇———

"HAVE YE NOT SEEN THE BUOYANT ORB?"

"A bubble........
That in the act of seizing shrinks to naught."
CLARE

HAVE ye not seen the buoyant orb, which oft
The tube and childhood's playful breath produce?
Fair, but impalpable—it mounts aloft,
While o'er its surface rove the restless hues;
And sun-born tints their gliding bloom diffuse:
But 'twill not brook the touch—the vision bright,
Dissolved with instantaneous burst, we lose;
Breaks the thin globe with its array of light
And shrinks at once to naught, at contact e'er so slight.

So the gay hopes we chase with ardent zeal—
Which view'd at distance to our gaze appear
Sweetly embodied, tangible, and real—
Elude our grasp, and melt away to air:
The test of touch too delicate to bear,
In unsubstantial loveliness thy glow
Before our wistful eyes, too passing fair
For earth to realize or man to know,
Whose life is but a scene of fallacy and woe.

———◇◇◇———

THE EXILE'S HARP.

I WILL hang thee, my harp, by the side of the fountain,
On the whispering branch of the lone-waving willow:
Above thee shall rush the hoarse gale of the mountain,
Below thee shall tumble the dark breaking billow.
The winds shall blow by thee, abandon'd, forsaken,
The wild gales alone shall arouse thy sad strain;
For where is the heart or the hand to awaken
The sounds of thy soul-soothing sweetness again?
Oh! harp of my fathers!
Thy chords shall decay,
One by one with the strings
Shall thy notes fade away;
Till the fiercest of tempests
Around thee may yell,
And not waken one sound
Of thy desolate shell!

Yet, oh! yet, ere I go, will I fling a wreath round thee,
With the richest of flowers in the green valley springing;

Those that see shall remember the hand that hath
   crown'd thee,
When, wither'd and dead, to thee still they are
   clinging.
There! now I have wreathed thee—the roses are
   twining
Thy chords with their bright blossoms glowing
   and red:
Though the lapse of one day see their freshness
   declining,
Yet bloom for one day when thy minstrel has
   fled!
     Oh! harp of my fathers!
      No more in the hall,
     The souls of the chieftains
      Thy strains shall enthral:
     One sweep will I give thee,
      And wake thy bold swell;
     Then, thou friend of my bosom,
      Forever farewell!

—⋄—

"WHY SHOULD WE WEEP FOR THOSE WHO DIE?"

" Quamobrem, si dolorum finem mors affert, si securioris et me-
lioris initium vitæ : si futura mala avertit—cur eam tantopere ac-
cusare, ex qua potius consolationem et lætitiam haurire fas esset ?"
                       CICERO.

WHY should we weep for those who die?
  They fall—their dust returns to dust;
Their souls shall live eternally
  Within the mansions of the just.

They die to live—they sink to rise,
  They leave this wretched mortal shore;
But brighter suns and bluer skies
  Shall smile on them forevermore.

Why should we sorrow for the dead?
  Our life on earth is but a span;
They tread the path that all must tread,
  They die the common death of man.

The noblest songster of the gale
  Must cease, when Winter's frowns appear;
The reddest rose is wan and pale,
  When Autumn tints the changing year.

The fairest flower on earth must fade,
  The brightest hopes on earth must die:
Why should we mourn that man was made
  To droop on earth, but dwell on high?

The soul, th' eternal soul, must reign
  In worlds devoid of pain and strife:
Then why should mortal man complain
  Of death, which leads to happier life?

—⋄—

"RELIGION! THO' WE SEEM TO SPURN."

" Sublatam ex oculis quærimus."—HORACE.

RELIGION! tho' we seem to spurn
Thy hallow'd joys, their loss we mourn,
  With many a secret tear;
Tho' we have long dissolved the tie,
The hour we broke it claims a sigh,
  And Virtue still is dear.

Our hearts forget not she was fair,
And her pure feelings, ling'ring there,
  Half win us back from ill;

And—tho' so long to Vice resign'd
'Twould seem we've left her far behind—
  Pursue and haunt us still.

Thus light's all-penetrating glow
Attends us to the deeps below,
  With wav'ring, rosy gleam:
To the bold inmates of the bell
Faint rays of distant sunlight* steal,
  And thro' the waters beam.

By the rude blasts of passion tost,
We sigh for bliss we ne'er had lost,
  Had Conscience been our guide:
She burns a lamp we need not trim,
Whose steady flame is never dim,
  But throws its lustre wide.

—⋄—

REMORSE.

" ….Sudant tacita præcordia culpa."—JUVENAL.

OH! 'tis a fearful thing to glance
  Back on the gloom of misspent years:
What shadowy forms of guilt advance,
  And fill me with a thousand fears!
The vices of my life arise,
  Portray'd in shapes, alas! too true;
And not one beam of hope breaks through,
To cheer my old and aching eyes,
T' illume my night of wretchedness
My age of anguish and distress.
If I am damn'd, why find I not
Some comfort in this earthly spot?
But no! this world and that to come
Are both to me one scene of gloom!
Lest ought of solace I should see,
  Or lose the thoughts of what I do,
Remorse, with soul-felt agony,
  Holds up the mirror to my view.
And I was cursèd from my birth,
A reptile made to creep on earth,
An hopeless outcast, born to die
A living death eternally!
With too much conscience to have rest,
Too little to be ever blest,
To you vast world of endless woe,
  Unlighted by the cheerful day,
My soul shall wing her weary way;
  To those dread depths where aye the same
Throughout the waste of darkness, glow
  The glimmerings of the boundless flame.
And yet I cannot here below
Take my full cup of guilt, as some,
And laugh away my doom to come.
I would I'd been all-heartless! then
I might have sinn'd like other men;
But all this side the grave is fear,
A wilderness so dank and drear,
That never wholesome plant would spring;
  And all behind—I dare not think!
I would not risk th' imagining—
  From the full view my spirits shrink;
And starting backwards, yet I cling
To life, whose every hour to me
Hath been increase of misery.
But yet I cling to it, for well
  I know the pangs that rack me now
Are trifles, to the endless hell
  That waits me, when my burning brow
And my wrung eyes shall hope in vain
For one small drop to cool the pain,
The fury of that madd'ning flame
That then shall scorch my writhing frame!

* A vermeil color plays on the hands and faces of those who
descend in this machine.

Fiends! who have goaded me to ill!
Distracting fiends, who goad me still!
If e'er I work'd a sinful deed,
  Ye know how bitter was the draught;
Ye know my inmost soul would bleed,
  And ye have look'd at me and laugh'd
Triumphing that I could not free
My spirit from your slavery!
Yet is there that in me which says,
  Should these old feet their course retread
From out the portal of my days,
  That I should lead the life I've led:
My agony, my torturing shame,
My guilt, my errors all the same!
O God! that thou wouldst grant that ne'er
  My soul its clay-cold bed forsake,
That I might sleep, and never wake
Unto the thrill of conscious fear;
For when the trumpet's piercing cry
Shall burst upon my slumb'ring ear,
  And countless seraphs throng the sky,
How shall I cast my shroud away,
And come into the blaze of day?
How shall I brook to hear each crime,
Here veil'd by secrecy and time,
Read out from thine eternal book?
  How shall I stand before thy throne,
    While earth shall like a furnace burn?
How shall I bear the with'ring look
    Of men and angels, who will turn
Their dreadful gaze on me alone?

⸎

'ON GOLDEN EVENINGS, WHEN THE SUN."

"The bliss to meet,
And the pain to part!"—MOORE.

On golden evenings, when the sun
  In splendor sinks to rest,
How we regret, when they are gone,
  Those glories of the west,
That o'er the crimson-mantled sky
Threw their broad flush of deepest dye!

But when the wheeling orb again
  Breaks gorgeous on the view,
And tints the earth and fires the main
  With rich and ruddy hue,
We soon forget the eve of sorrow,
For joy at that more brilliant morrow.

E'en so when much-loved friends depart,
  Their farewell rends the swelling heart;
But when those friends again we see,
  We glow with soul-felt ecstasy,
That far exceeds the tearful feeling
That o'er our bosoms then was stealing.
The rapture of that joyous day
Bids former sorrows fade away;
And Memory dwells no more on sadness
When breaks that sudden morn of gladness!

⸎

THE DELL OF E——.

"Tantum ævi longinqua valet mutare vetustas!"
                                    VIRGIL.

There was a long, low, rushy dell, emboss'd
  With knolls of grass and clumps of copsewood
    green;
Midway a wandering burn the valley cross'd,
  And streak'd with silvery line the woodland scene;

High hills on either side to heaven upsprung,
  Y-clad with groves of undulating pine,
Upon whose heads the hoary vapors hung,
  And far—far off the heights were seen to shine
In clear relief against the sapphire sky,
  And many a blue stream wander'd thro' the shade
Of those dark groves that clomb the mountains high,
  And glistening 'neath each lone entangled glade,
At length with brawling accent loudly fell
Within the limpid brook that wound along the dell.
How pleasant was the ever-varying light
Beneath that emerald coverture of boughs!
How often, at th' approach of dewy night,
Have those tall pine-trees heard the lover's vows!
How many a name was carved upon the trunk
Of each old hollow willow-tree, that stoop'd
To lave its branches in the brook, and drank
Its freshening dew! How many a cypress droop'd
From those fair banks, where bloom'd the earliest
    flowers,
Which the young year from her abounding horn
Scatters profuse within her secret bowers!
What rapturous gales from that wild dell were
    borne!
And, floating on the rich spring breezes, flung
Their incense o'er that wave on whose bright banks
    they sprung!

Long years had past, and there again I came,
  But man's rude hand had sorely scathed the dell;
And though the cloud-capt mountains, still the same,
  Uprear'd each heaven-invading pinnacle:
Yet were the charms of that lone valley gone,
  And the gray winding of the stream was gone;
The brook once murmuring o'er its pebbly bed,
  Now deeply—straightly—noiselessly went on.
Slow turn'd the sluggish wheel beneath its force,
  Where clattering mills disturb'd the solitude:
Where was the prattling of its former course?
  Its shelving, sedgy sides y-crown'd with wood?
The willow trunks were fell'd, the names erased
From one broad shatter'd pine which still its sta-
    tion graced.

Remnant of all its brethren, there it stood,
  Braving the storms that swept the cliffs above,
Where once, throughout th' impenetrable wood,
  Were heard the plainings of the pensive dove.
But man had bid th' eternal forests bow
That bloom'd upon the earth-imbedded base
Of the strong mountain, and perchance they now
  Upon the billows were the dwelling-place
Of their destroyers, and bore terror round
  The trembling earth:—ah! lovelier had they still
Whisper'd unto the breezes with low sound,
  And greenly flourish'd on their native hill,
And flinging their proud arms in state on high,
Spread out beneath the sun their glorious canopy!

⸎

MY BROTHER.

"Meorum prime sodalium."—HORACE.

With falt'ring step I came to see,
In Death's unheeding apathy,
That friend so dear in life to me.
                          My brother!

'Mid flowers of loveliest scent and hue
That strew'd thy form, 'twas sad to view
Thy lifeless face peep wanly through,
                          My brother!

Why did they (there they did not feel!)
With studious care all else conceal,
But thy cold face alone reveal,
                          My brother!

They might have known, what used to glow
With smiles, and oft dispell'd my woe,
Would chill me most, when faded so,
    My brother!

The tolling of thy funeral bell,
The nine low notes that spoke thy knell,
I know not how I bore so well,
    My brother!

But oh! the chill, dank mould that slid,
Dull-sounding, on thy coffin-lid,
That drew more tears than all beside,
    My brother!

And then I hurried fast away;
How could I e'er have borne to stay
Where careless hand inhumed thy clay,
    My brother!

ANTONY TO CLEOPATRA.

O Cleopatra! fare thee well,
 We two can meet no more;
This breaking heart alone can tell
 The love to thee I bore.
But wear not thou the conqueror's chain
 Upon thy race and thee;
And though we ne'er can meet again,
 Yet still be true to me:
For I for thee have lost a throne,
To wear the crown of love alone.

Fair daughter of a regal line!
 To thraldom bow not tame;
My every wish on earth was thine,
 My every hope the same.
And I have moved within thy sphere,
 And lived within thy light;
And oh! thou wert to me so dear,
 I breathed but in thy sight!
A subject world I lost for thee,
For thou wert all my world to me!

Then when the shriekings of the dying
 Were heard along the wave,
Soul of my soul! I saw thee flying;
 I follow'd thee, to save.
The thunder of the brazen prows
 O'er Actium's ocean rung;
Fame's garland faded from my brows,
 Her wreath away I flung.
I sought, I saw, I heard but thee:
For what to love was victory?

Thine on the earth, and on the throne,
 And in the grave, am I;
And, dying, still I am thine own,
 Thy bleeding Antony.
How shall my spirit joy to hear
 That thou art ever true!
Nay—weep not—dry that burning tear,
 That bathes thine eyes' dark hue.
Shades of my fathers! lo! I come;
I hear your voices from the tomb!

"I WANDER IN DARKNESS AND SORROW."

I wander in darkness and sorrow,
 Unfriended, and cold, and alone,
As dismally gurgles beside me
 The bleak river's desolate moan.

The rise of the volleying thunder
 The mountain's lone echoes repeat:
The roar of the wind is around me,
 The leaves of the year at my feet.

I wander in darkness and sorrow,
 Uncheer'd by the moon's placid ray;
Not a friend that I lov'd but is dead,
 Not a hope but has faded away!
Oh! when shall I rest in the tomb,
 Wrapt about with the chill winding-sheet?
For the roar of the wind is around me,
 The leaves of the year at my feet.

I heed not the blasts that sweep o'er me,
 I blame not the tempests of night;
They are not the foes who have banish'd
 The visions of youthful delight:
I hail the wild sound of their raving,
 Their merciless presence I greet;
Though the roar of the wind be around me,
 The leaves of the year at my feet.

In this waste of existence, for solace,
 On whom shall my lone spirit call?
Shall I fly to the friends of my bosom?
 My God! I have buried them all!
They are dead, they are gone, they are cold,
 My embraces no longer they meet;
Let the roar of the wind be around me,
 The leaves of the year at my feet.

Those eyes that glanced love unto mine,
 With motionless slumbers are prest;
Those hearts which once throbb'd but for me,
 Are chill as the earth where they rest.
Then around on my wan wither'd form
 Let the pitiless hurricanes beat;
Let the roar of the wind be around me,
 The leaves of the year at my feet!

Like the voice of the owl in the hall,
 Where the song and the banquet have ceased,
Where the green weeds have mantled the hearth
 Whence arose the proud flame of the feast;
So I cry to the storm, whose dark wing
 Scatters on me the wild-driving sleet—
"Let the roar of the wind be around me,
 The fall of the leaves at my feet!"

"TO ONE WHOSE HOPE REPOSED ON THEE."

"She's gone . . . .
 She's sunk, with her my joys entombing!"
      Byron.

To one whose hope reposed on thee,
 Whose very life was in thine own,
How deep a wound thy death must be,
 And the wild thought that thou art gone!

Oh! must the earth-born reptiles prey
 Upon that cheek of late so blooming?
Alas! this heart must wear away
 Long ere that cheek they've done consuming!

For hire the sexton toll'd thy bell—
 But why should he receive a meed
Who work'd at least no mortal's weal,
 And made one lonely bosom bleed?

For hire with ready mould he stood—
 But why should gain his care repay
Who told, as harshly as he could,
 That all I loved was past away?

For, sure, it was too rude a blow
  For Misery's ever-wakeful ear,
To cast the earth with sudden throw
  Upon the grave of one so dear:

For aye these bitter tears must swell,
  Tho' the sad scene is past and gone;
And still I hear the tolling bell,
  For Memory makes each sense her own.

But stay, my soul! thy plaint forbear,
  And be thy murm'ring song forgiven!
Tread but the path of Virtue here,
  And thou shalt meet with her in heaven!

—⊸◦⊶—

THE OLD SWORD.

Old Sword! tho' dim and rusted
  Be now thy sheeny blade,
Thy glitt'ring edge encrusted
  With cankers Time hath made:
    Yet once around thee swell'd the cry
    Of triumph's fierce delight,
    The shoutings of the victory,
    The thunders of the fight!

Tho' age hath past upon thee
  With still corroding breath,
Yet once stream'd redly on thee
  The purpling tide of death:
    What time amid the war of foes
    The dastard's cheek grew pale,
    As through the feudal field arose
    The ringing of the mail.

Old Sword! what arm hath wielded
  Thy richly gleaming brand,
'Mid lordly forms who shielded
  The maidens of their land?
    And who hath clov'n his foes in wrath
    With thy puissant fire,
    And scatter'd in his perilous path
    The victims of his ire?

Old Sword! whose fingers clasp'd thee
  Around thy carvèd hilt?
And with that hand which grasp'd thee
  What heroes' blood was spilt:
    When fearlessly, with open hearts,
    And lance to lance opposed,
    Beneath the shade of barbed darts
    The dark-eyed warriors closed?

Old Sword! I would not burnish
  Thy venerable rust,
Nor sweep away the tarnish
  Of darkness and of dust!
    Lie there, in slow and still decay,
    Unfamed in olden rhyme,
    The relic of a former day,
    A wreck of ancient time!

—⊸◦⊶—

THE GONDOLA.

        " 'Tis sweet to hear
At midnight, o'er the blue and moonlit deep,
The song and oar of Adria's gondolier."
              Don Juan.

O'er ocean's curling surges borne along,
  Arion sung—the dolphin caught the strain,
As soft the mellow'd accents of his tongue
  Stole o'er the surface of the watery plain.
    22

And do those silver sounds, so deep, so clear,
  Possess less magic than Arion's lay?
Swell they less boldly on the ravish'd ear,
  Or with less cadence do they die away?

Yon gondola, that skims the moonlight sea,
  Yields me those notes more wild than Houri's lyre,
That, as they rise, exalt to ecstasy,
  And draw the tear as, length'ning, they expire.

An arch of purest azure beams above,
  A sea, as blue, as beauteous, spreads below;
In this voluptuous clime of song and love
  What room for sorrow? who shall cherish woe?

False thought! tho' pleasure wing the careless hours,
  Their stores tho' Cyprus and Arabia send,
Tho' for the ear their fascinating power
  Divine Timotheus and Cecilia blend;—

All without Virtue's relish fail to please,
  Venetian charms the cares of Vice alloy,
Joy's swiftest, brightest current they can freeze,
  And all the genuine sweets of life destroy!

—⊸◦⊶—

"WE MEET NO MORE."

We meet no more—the die is cast,
  The chain is broke that tied us,
Our every hope on earth is past,
  And there's no helm to guide us:
We meet no more—the roaring blast
  And angry seas divide us!

And I stand on a distant shore,
  The breakers round me swelling;
And lonely thoughts of days gone o'er
  Have made this breast their dwelling:
We meet no more—We meet no more:
  Farewell forever, Ellen!

—⊸◦⊶—

WRITTEN

BY AN EXILE OF BASSORAH,

WHILE SAILING DOWN THE EUPHRATES.

Thou land of the lily! thy gay flowers are blooming
  In joy on thine hills, but they bloom not for me;
For a dark gulf of woe, all my fond hopes entombing,
  Has roll'd its black waves 'twixt this lone heart and thee.

The far-distant hills, and the groves of my childhood,
  Now stream in the light of the sun's setting ray;
And the tall-waving palms of my own native wildwood
  In the blue haze of distance are melting away.

I see thee, Bassorah! in splendor retiring,
  Where thy waves and thy walls in their majesty meet;
I see the bright glory thy pinnacles firing,
  And the broad vassal river that rolls at thy feet.

I see thee but faintly—thy tall towers are beaming
  On the dusky horizon so far and so blue;

And minaret and mosque in the distance are gleaming,
  While the coast of the stranger expands on my
    view.

I see thee no more: for the deep waves have parted
  The land of my birth from her desolate son;
And I am gone from thee, though half broken-
   hearted.
  To wander thro' climes where thy name is un-
    known.

Farewell to my harp, which I hung in my anguish
  On the lonely palmetto that nods to the gale;
For its sweet-breathing tones in forgetfulness lan-
   guish,
  And around it the ivy shall weave a green veil.

Farewell to the days which so smoothly have glided
  With the maiden whose look was like Cama's
   young glance.
And the sheen of whose eyes was the load-star
   which guided
  My course on this earth thro' the storms of mis-
    chance!

—◇—

MARIA TO HER LUTE,

THE GIFT OF HER DYING LOVER.

"O laborum
Dulce lenimen!"—HORACE.

I love thee, Lute! my soul is link'd to thee
  As by some tie—'tis not a groundless love;
I cannot rouse thy plaintive melody,
  And fail its magic influence to prove.

I think I found thee more than ever dear
  (If thought can work within this fever'd brain)
Since Edward's lifeless form was buried here,
  And I deplored his hapless fate in vain.

'Twas then to thee my strange affection grew,
  For thou wert his—I've heard him wake thy
   strain:
Oh! if in heaven each other we shall view,
  I'll bid him sweep thy mournful chords again.

I would not change thee for the noblest lyre
  That ever lent its music to the breeze:
How could Maria taste its note of fire?
  How wake a harmony that could not please?

Then, till mine eye shall glaze, and cheek shall fade,
  I'll keep thee, prize thee as my dearest friend;
And oft I'll hasten to the green-wood shade,
  My hours in sweet, tho' fruitless grief to spend.

For in the tear there is a nameless joy;
  The full warm gush relieves the aching soul:
So still, to ease my hopeless agony,
  My lute shall warble and my tears shall roll.

—◇—

THE VALE OF BONES.

"Albis informem—ossibus agrum '—HORACE.

Along yon vapor-mantled sky
The dark-red moon is riding high;
At times her beams in beauty break
Upon the broad and silv'ry lake;
At times more bright they clearly fall
On some white castle's ruin'd wall;
At times her partial splendor shines
Upon the grove of deep-black pines,

Through which the dreary night-breeze moans,
Above this Vale of scatter'd bones.

The low, dull gale can scarcely stir
The branches of that black'ning fir,
Which betwixt me and heav'n flings wide
Its shadowy boughs on either side,
And o'er yon granite rock uprears
Its giant form of many years.
And the shrill owlet's desolate wail
Comes to mine ear along the gale,
As, list'ning to its lengthen'd tones,
I dimly pace the Vale of Bones.

Dark Valley! still the same art thou,
Unchanged thy mountain's cloudy brow:
Still from yon cliffs, that part asunder,
Falls down the torrent's echoing thunder;
Still from this mound of reeds and rushes
With bubbling sound the fountain gushes:
Thence, winding thro' the whisp'ring ranks
Of sedges on the willowy banks,
Still brawling, chafes the rugged stones
That strew this dismal Vale of Bones.

Unchanged art thou! no storm hath rent
Thy rude and rocky battlement;
Thy rioting mountains sternly piled,
The screen of nature, wide and wild:
But who were they whose bones bestrew
The heather, cold with midnight dew,
Upon whose slowly-rotting clay
The raven long hath censed to prey,
But, mould'ring in the moonlight air,
Their wan, white sculls show bleak and bare?
And, aye, the dreary night-breeze moans
Above them in this Vale of Bones!

I knew them all—a gallant band,
The glory of their native land,
And on each lordly brow elate
Sat valor and contempt of fate,
Fierceness of youth, and scorn of foe,
And pride to render blow for blow.
In the strong war's tumultuous crash
How darkly did their keen eyes flash!
How fearlessly each arm was raised!
How dazzlingly each broad-sword blazed!
Though now the dreary night-breeze moans
Above them in this Vale of Bones.

What lapse of time shall sweep away
The memory of that gallant day,
When on to battle proudly going,
Your plumage to the wild winds blowing,
Your tartans far behind ye flowing,
Your pennons raised, your clarions sounding,
Fiercely your steeds beneath ye bounding,
Ye mix'd the strife of warring foes
In fiery shock and deadly close?
What stampings in the madd'ning strife,
What thrusts, what stabs, with brand and knife,
What desp'rate strokes for death or life,
Were there! What cries, what thrilling groans,
Re-echoed thro' the Vale of Bones!

Thou peaceful Vale, whose mountains lonely
Sound to the torrent's chiding only,
Or wild goat's cry from rocky ledge,
Or bull-frog from the rustling sedge,
Or eagle from her airy cairn,
Or screaming of the startled hern—
How did thy million echoes waken
Amid thy caverns deeply shaken!
How with the red dew o'er thee rain'd
Thine emerald turf was darkly stain'd!
How did each innocent flower, that sprung
Thy greenly-tangled glades among,

Blush with the big and purple drops
That dribbled from the leafy copse!
I paced the valley, when the yell
Of triumph's voice had ceased to swell;
When battle's brazen throat no more
Raised its annihilating roar.
There lay ye on each other piled,
Your brows with noble dust defiled;[*]
There, by the loudly-gushing water,
Lay man and horse in mingled slaughter.
Then wept I not, thrice gallant band;
For though no more each dauntless hand
The thunder of the combat hurl'd.
Yet still with pride your lips were curl'd;
And e'en in death's o'erwhelming shade
Your fingers linger'd round the blade!
I deem'd, when gazing proudly there
Upon the fix'd and haughty air
That mark'd each warrior's bloodless face,
Ye would not change the narrow space
Which each cold form of breathless clay
Then cover'd, as on earth ye lay,
For realms, for sceptres, or for thrones—
I dream'd not on this Vale of Bones!

But years have thrown their veil between,
And alter'd is that lonely scene;
And dreadful emblems of thy might,
Stern Dissolution! meet my sight;
The eyeless socket, dark and dull,
The hideous grinning of the skull,
Are sights which Memory disowns,
Thou melancholy Vale of Bones!

TO FANCY.

Bright angel of heavenliest birth!
Who dwellest among us unseen,
O'er the gloomiest spot on the earth
There's a charm where thy footsteps have been.
We feel thy soft sunshine in youth,
While our joys like young blossoms are new;
For oh! thou art sweeter than Truth,
And fairer and lovelier too!

The exile, who mourneth alone.
Is glad in the glow of thy smile,
Tho' far from the land of his own,
In the ocean's most desolate isle:
And the captive, who pines in his chain,
Sees the banners of glory unroll'd,
As he dreams of his own native plain,
And the forms of the heroes of old.

In the earliest ray of the morn,
In the last rosy splendor of even,
We view thee—thy spirit is borne
On the murmuring zephyrs of heaven:
Thou art in the sunbeam of noon,
Thou art in the azure of air,
If I pore on the sheen of the moon,
If I search the bright stars, thou art there!

Thou art in the rapturous eye
Of the bard, when his visions rush o'er him;
And like the fresh iris on high
Are the wonders that sparkle before him.
Thou stirrest the thunders of song,
Those transports that brook not control;
Thy voice is the charm of his tongue,
Thy magic the light of his soul!

Like the day-star that heralds the sun,
Thou seem'st, when our young hopes are dawning;

But ah! when the day is begun,
Thou art gone like the star of the morning!
Like a beam in the winter of years,
When the joys of existence are cold,
Thine image can dry up our tears,
And brighten the eyes of the old!

Tho' dreary and dark be the night
Of affliction that gathers around,
There is something of heaven in thy light,
Glad spirit! where'er thou art found:
As calmly the sea-maid may lie
In her pearly pavilion at rest,
The heart-broken and friendless may fly
To the shade of thy bower, and be blest!

BOYHOOD.

"Ah, happy years! once more who would not be a boy?"
Childe Harold.

Boyhood's blest hours! when yet unfledged and callow,
We prove those joys we never can retain,
In riper years with fond regret we hallow,
Like some sweet scene we never see again.

For youth—whate'er may be its petty woes,
Its trivial sorrows—disappointments—fears,
As on in haste life's wintry current flows—
Still claims, and still receives, its debt of tears.

Yes! when, in grim alliance, grief and time
Silver our heads and rob our hearts of ease,
We gaze along the deeps of care and crime
To the far, fading shore of youth and peace;

Each object that we meet the more endears
That rosy morn before a troubled day;
That blooming dawn—that sunrise of our years—
That sweet voluptuous vision past away!

For by the welcome, tho' embittering power
Of wakeful memory, we too well behold
That lightsome—careless—unreturning hour,
Beyond the reach of wishes or of gold.

And ye, whom blighted hopes or passion's heat
Have taught the pangs that care-worn hearts endure,
Ye will not deem the vernal rose so sweet!
Ye will not call the driven snow so pure!

"DID NOT THY ROSEATE LIPS OUTVIE."

"Ulla si juris tibi pejerati
Pœna, Barine, nocuisset unquàm;
Denti si nigro fieres, vel uno
Turpior ungui
Crederem."—HORACE.

Did not thy roseate lips outvie
The gay anann's spicy bloom;[*]
Had not thy breath its luxury,
The richness of its deep perfume—

Were not the pearls it fans more clear
Than those which grace the valvèd shell;
Thy foot more airy than the deer,
When startled from his lonely dell—

*"Non indecoro pulvere sordidos.'—HORACE.

* Ulloa says that the blossom of the West-Indian anana is of
so elegant a crimson as even to dazzle the eye, and that the fragrancy of the fruit discovers the plant, though concealed from
sight.—See ULLOA'S Voyages, vol. i., p. 72.

Were not thy bosom's stainless whiteness,
　Where angel loves their vigils keep.
More heavenly than the dazzling brightness
　Of the cold crescent on the deep—

Were not thine eye a star might grace
　Yon sapphire concave beaming clear,
Or fill the vanish'd Pleiad's place,
　And shine for aye as brightly there—

Had not thy locks the golden glow
　That robes the gay and early east,
Thus falling in luxuriant flow
　Around thy fair but faithless breast:

I might have deem'd that thou wert she
　Of the Cumæan cave, who wrote
Each fate-involving mystery
　Upon the feathery leaves that float,

Borne thro' the boundless waste of air,
　Wherever chance might drive along.
But she was wrinkled—thou art fair:
　And she was old—but thou art young.

Her years were as the sands that strew
　The fretted ocean-beach; but thou—
Triumphant in that eye of blue,
　Beneath thy smoothly-marble brow;

Exulting in thy form thus moulded,
　By nature's tenderest touch design'd;
Proud of the fetters thou hast folded
　Around this fond deluded mind—

Deceivest still with practised look,
　With fickle vow, and well-feign'd sigh.
I tell thee, that I will not brook
　Reiterated perjury!

Alas! I feel thy deep control,
　E'en now when I would break thy chain:
But while I seek to gain thy soul,
　Ah! say—hast thou a soul to gain?

———◇◇———

HUNTSMAN'S SONG.

"Who the melodies of morn can tell?"—BEATTIE.

Oh! what is so sweet as a morning in spring,
When the gale is all freshness, and larks, on the
　　wing,
In clear liquid carols their gratitude sing?

I rove o'er the hill as it sparkles with dew,
And the red flush of Phœbus with ecstasy view,
As he breaks thro' the east o'er thy crags, Benvenue!

And boldly I bound o'er the mountainous scene,
Like the roe which I hunt thro' the woodlands so
　　green,
Or the torrent which leaps from the height to the
　　plain.

The life of the hunter is chainless and gay,
As the wing of the falcon that wins him his prey;
No song is so glad as his blithe roundelay.

His eyes in soft arbors the Moslem may close,
And Fayoum's rich odors may breathe from the
　　rose,
To scent his bright harem and lull his repose:

Th' Italian may vaunt of his sweet harmony,
And mingle soft sounds of voluptuous glee;
But the lark's airy music is sweeter to me.

Then happy the man who upsprings with the morn,
But not from a couch of effeminate lawn,
And slings o'er his shoulder his loud bugle-horn!

———◇◇———

PERSIA.

"The flower and choice
Of many provinces from bound to bound."
MILTON.

Land of bright eye and lofty brow!
　Whose every gale is balmy breath
　Of incense from some sunny flower,
Which on tall hill or valley low,
　In clustering maze or circling wreath,
　Sheds perfume; or in blooming bower
Of Schiraz or of Ispahan,
In bower untrod by foot of man,
Clasps round the green and fragrant stem
　Of lotos, fair and fresh and blue,
And crowns it with a diadem
　Of blossoms, ever young and new;
Oh! lives there yet within thy soul
　Aught of the fire of him who led
Thy troops, and bade thy thunder roll
　O'er lone Assyria's crownless head?
I tell thee, had that conqueror red
　From Thymbria's plain beheld thy fall,
When stormy Macedonia swept
　Thine honors from thee one and all,
He would have wail'd, he would have wept,
That thy proud spirit should have bow'd
To Alexander, doubly proud.
Oh, Iran! Iran! had he known
The downfall of his mighty throne,
Or had he seen that fatal night,
　When the young king of Macedon
　In madness led his veterans on,
And Thais held the funeral light,
Around that noble pile which rose
Irradiant with the pomp of gold,
　In high Persepolis of old,
Encompass'd with its frenzied foes;
He would have groan'd, he would have spread
The dust upon his laurell'd head,
To view the setting of that star,
Which beam'd so gorgeously and far
O'er Anatolia and the fane
Of Belus, and Caïster's plain,
　And Sardis, and the glittering sands
　Of bright Pactolus, and the lands
Where Crœsus held his rich domain:
On fair Diarbeck's land of spice,*
Adiabene's plains of rice,
Where down th' Euphrates, swift and strong,
The shield-like kuphars bound along;†
And sad Cunaxa's field, where, mixing
　With host to adverse host opposed,
'Mid clashing shield and spear transfixing,
　The rival brothers sternly closed.
And further east, where, broadly roll'd,
Old Indus pours his stream of gold;
And there where, tumbling deep and hoarse,
Blue Ganga leaves her vaccine source;‡
Loveliest of all the lovely streams
That meet immortal Titan's beams,
And smile upon their fruitful way
Beneath his golden Orient ray:
And southward to Cilicia's shore,
Where Cydnus meets the billows' roar,

---

* Xenophon says that every shrub in these wilds had an aromatic odor.
† Rennel on Herodotus.
‡ The cavern in the ridge of Himmalah, whence the Ganges seems to derive its original springs, has been moulded, by the mind of Hindoo superstition, into the head of a cow.

And where the Syrian gates divide
The meeting realms on either side;*
E'en to the land of Nile, whose crops
  Bloom rich beneath his bounteous swell,
  To hot Syene's wondrous well,
Nigh to the long-lived Æthiops.
And northward far to Trebizonde,
  Renown'd for kings of chivalry,
Near where old Ilyssus, rolling from the strand,
  Disgorges in the Euxine Sea—
The Euxine, falsely named, which whelms
  The mariner in the heaving tide,
To high Sinope's distant realms,
  Whence cynics rail'd at human pride.

—————◇—————

EGYPT.

"Egypt's palmy groves,
Her grots, and sepulchres of kings."
         MOORE's *Lalla Rookh*.

THE sombre pencil of the dim-gray dawn
  Draws a faint sketch of Egypt to mine eye,
As yet uncolor'd by the brilliant morn,
  And her gay orb careering up the sky.

And see! at last he comes in radiant pride,
  Life in his eye, and glory in his ray;
No veiling mists his growing splendor hide,
  And hang their gloom around his golden way.

The flowery region brightens in his smile,
  Her lap of blossoms freights the passing gale,
That robs the odors of each balmy i-le,
  Each fragrant field and aromatic vale.

But the first glitter of his rising beam
  Falls on the broad-based pyramids sublime,
As proud to show us with his earliest gleam
  Those vast and hoary enemies of Time.

E'en History's self, whose certain scrutiny
  Few eras in the list of Time beguile,
Pauses, and scans them with astonish'd eye,
  As unfamiliar with their aged pile.

Awful, august, magnificent, they tower
  Amid the waste of shifting sands around;
The lapse of year and month and day and hour,
  Alike unfelt, perform th' unwearied round.

How often hath yon day-god's burning light,
  From the clear sapphire of his stainless heaven,
Bathed their high peaks in noontide brilliance
    bright,
  Gilded at morn, and purpled them at even!†

—————◇—————

THE DRUID'S PROPHECIES.‡

MONA! with flame thine oaks are streaming,
  Those sacred oaks we rear'd on high:
Lo! Mona, lo! the swords are gleaming
  Adown thine hills confusedly.

Hark! Mona, hark! the chargers' neighing!
  The clang of arms and helmets bright!
The crash of steel, the dreadful braying
  Of trumpets thro' the madd'ning fight!

---

* See Xenophon's "Expeditio Cyri."
† See Savary's letters.
‡ "Stabat pro littore diversa acies, densa armis virisque, inter-cursantibus feminis in modum Furiarum, quæ veste ferali, crinibus dejectis, faces præferebant. Druidæque circum, preces diras, sublatis ad cœlum manibus, fundentes," etc.—TACIT., *Annal.*, xiv., c. 30.

Exalt your torches, raise your voices;
  Your thread is spun—your day is brief;
Yea! howl for sorrow! Rome rejoices,
  But Mona—Mona bends in grief!

But woe to Rome, though now she raises
  You eagles of her haughty power;
Though now her sun of conquest blazes,
  Yet soon shall come her darkening hour!

Woe, woe to him who sits in glory,
  Enthroned on thine hills of pride!
Can he not see the poignard gory
  With his best heart's-blood deeply dyed?

Ah! what avails his gilded palace,
  Whose wings the seven-hill'd town enfold?*
The costly bath, the crystal chalice?
  The pomp of gems, the glare of gold?

See where, by heartless anguish driven,
  Crownless he creeps 'mid circling thorns;†
Around him flash the bolts of heaven,
  And angry earth before him yawns.‡

Then, from his pinnacle of splendor,
  The feeble king,§ with locks of gray,
Shall fall, and sovereign Rome shall render
  Her sceptre to the usurper's‖ sway.

Who comes with sounds of mirth and gladness,
  Triumphing o'er the prostrate dead?¶
Ay, me! thy mirth shall change to sadness,
  When Vengeance strikes thy guilty head.

Above thy noonday feast suspended,
  High hangs in air a naked sword:
Thy days are gone, thy joys are ended,
  The cup, the song, the festal board.

Then shall the eagle's shadowy pinion
  Be spread beneath the eastern skies;**
And dazzling far with wide dominion,
  Five brilliant stars shall brightly rise.††

Then, coward king!‡‡ the helpless agèd
  Shall bow beneath thy dastard blow;
But reckless hands and hearts, enragèd,
  By double fate shall lay thee low.§§

And two,‖‖ with death-wounds deeply mangled,
  Low on their parent earth shall lie:
Fond wretches! ah! too soon entangled
  Within the snares of royalty.

Then comes that mighty one victorious
  In triumph o'er this earthly ball,¶¶

---

* Pliny says that the golden palace of Nero extended all round the city.
† "Ut ad diverticulum ventum est, dimissis equis inter fruticeta ac vepres, per arundineti semitam ægre, nec nisi strata sub pedibus veste, ad adversum villæ parietem evasit."—SUETON., *Vit. Cæsar.*
‡ Statimque tremore terræ, et fulgure adverso pavefactus, audiit ex proximis castris clamorem," etc.—*Ibid.*
§ Galba.   ‖ Otho.
¶ "Utque campos, in quibus pugnatum est, adiit [*i. e.*, Vitellius] plurimum meri propalam hausit," etc.—SUETON.
** At the siege of Jerusalem.
†† The five good emperors: Nerva, Trajan, Adrian, Antoninus Pius, and Marcus Aurelius, or Antoninus the Philosopher. Perhaps the best commentary on the life and virtues of the last is his own volume of "Meditations."
‡‡ "Debiles pedibus, et eos qui ambulare non possent, in gigantum modum, ita ut a genibus de pannis et linteis quasi dracones dige-rerentur; eosdemque sagittis confecit."—ÆL. LAMPRID. *in Vita Commod.* Such were the laudable amusements of Commodus!
§§ He was first poisoned; but the operation not fully answering the wishes of his beloved, he was afterward strangled by a robust wrestler.
‖‖ Pertinax and Didius Julian.
¶¶ Severus, who was equally victorious in the Eastern and West-

Exulting in his conquests glorious—
Ah! glorious to his country's fall!

But thou shalt see the Romans flying,
O Albyn! with yon dauntless ranks :*
And thou shalt view the Romans dying,
Blue Carun! on thy mossy banks.

But lo! what dreadful visions o'er me
Are bursting on this aged eye!
What length of bloody train before me
In slow succession passes by!†

Thy hapless monarchs fall together,
Like leaves in winter's stormy ire;
Some by the sword, and some shall wither
By lightning's flame and fever's fire.‡

They come! they leave their frozen regions,
Where Scandinavia's wilds extend;
And Rome, though girt with dazzling legions,
Beneath their blasting power shall bend.

Woe, woe to Rome! though tall and ample
She rears her domes of high renown;
Yet fiery Goths shall fiercely trample
The grandeur of her temples down!

She sinks to dust; and who shall pity
Her dark despair and hopeless groans?
There is a wailing in her city—
Her babes are dash'd against the stones!

Then, Mona! then, though wan and blighted
Thy hopes be now by Sorrow's dearth,
Then all thy wrongs shall be requited—
The Queen of Nations bows to earth!

———◇———

LINES.§

The eye must catch the point that shows
The pensile dew-drop's twinkling gleam,
Where on the trembling blade it glows,
Or hueless hangs the liquid gem.

Thus do some minds unmark'd appear
By aught that's generous or divine,
Unless we view them in the sphere
Where with their fullest light they shine.

Occasion—circumstance—give birth
To charms that else unheeded lie,
And call the latent virtues forth
To break upon the wond'ring eye.

E'en he your censure has enroll'd
So rashly with the cold and dull,
Waits but occasion to unfold
An ardor and a force of soul.

Go then, impetuous youth, deny
The presence of the orb of day,
Because November's cloudy sky
Transmits not his resplendent ray.

Time, and the passing throng of things,
Full well the mould of minds betray,
And each a clearer prospect brings:—
Suspend thy judgment for a day.

———◇———

SWISS SONG.

I love St. Gothard's head of snows,
That shoots into the sky,
Where, yet unform'd, in grim repose
Ten thousand avalanches lie.

I love Lucerne's transparent lake,
And Jura's hills of pride,
Whence infant rivers, gushing, break
With small and scanty tide.

And thou, Mont Blanc! thou mighty pile
Of crags and ice and snow;
The Gallic toes in wonder smile
That we should love thee so!

But we were nurst within thy breast,
And taught to brave thy storms:
Thy tutorage was well confest
Against the Frank in arms—

The Frank who basely, proudly came
To rend us from our home,
With flashing steel and wasting flame.—
How could he, dare he come?

———◇———

THE EXPEDITION OF NADIR SHAH INTO HINDOSTAN.

"Quoi! vous allez combattre un roi, dont la puissance
Semble forcer le ciel de prendre sa défense,
Sous qui toute l'Asie a vu tomber ses rois
Et qui tient la fortune attachée a ses lois!"
                              RACINE's *Alexandre*.

"Squallent populatibus agri."
                              CLAUDIAN.

As the host of the locusts in numbers, in might
As the flames of the forest that redden the night,
They approach: but the eye may not dwell on the glare
Of standard and sabre that sparkle in air.

Like the fiends of destruction they rush on their way,
The vulture behind them is wild for his prey;
And the spirits of death, and the demons of wrath,
Wave the gloom of their wings o'er their desolate path.

Earth trembles beneath them, the dauntless, the bold;
Oh! weep for thy children, thou region of gold;*
For thy thousands are bow'd to the dust of the plain,
And all Delhi runs red with the blood of her slain.

For thy glory is past, and thy splendor is dim,
And the cup of thy sorrow is full to the brim;
And where is the chief in thy realms to abide,
The "Monarch of Nations,"† the strength of his pride?

---

cra World : but those conquests, however glorious, were conducive to
the ruin of the Roman Empire —See GIBBON, vol. vi, chap. v., p. 203.
   * In allusion to the real or feigned victory obtained by Fingal over
Caracul, or Caracalla.—See OSSIAN.
   † Very few of the emperors after Severus escaped assassination.
   ‡ Macrinus, Heliogabalus, Alexander, Maximin Papienus, Balbi-
nus, Gordian, Philip, etc., were assassinated ; Claudius died of a
pestilential fever ; and Carus was struck dead by lightning in his
tent.
   § To one who entertained a light opinion of an eminent character,
because too impatient to wait for its gradual development.

   * This invader required as a ransom for Mohammed Shah no less
than thirty millions, and amassed in the rich city of Delhi the enormous sum of two hundred and thirty-one millions sterling. Others,
however, differ considerably in their account of this treasure.
   † Such pompous epithets the Oriental writers are accustomed to
bestow on their monarchs ; of which sufficient specimens may be
seen in Sir William Jones's translation of the "History of Nadir
Shah." We can scarcely read one page of this work without meeting with such sentences as these : "Le roi des rois ;" "Les (tendards

Like a thousand dark streams from the mountain
  they throng,
With the fife and the horn and the war-beating
  gong:
The land like an Eden before them is fair.
But behind them a wilderness dreary and bare.*

The shrieks of the orphan, the lone widow's wail,
The groans of the childless, are loud on the gale;
For the star of thy glory is blasted and wan,
And wither'd the flower of thy fame, Hindostan!

———⟨⟩———

GREECE.

"Exoritur clamorque virum, clangorque tubarum."
VIRGIL.

WHAT wakes the brave of yon isle-throng'd wave?
  And why does the trumpet bray?
And the tyrant groan on his gory throne,
  In fear and wild dismay?

Why, he sees the hosts around his coasts
  Of those who will be f.ee;
And he views the bands of trampled lands
  In a dreadful league agree.

"Revenge!" they call, "for one, for all—
  In the page of song and story
Be their name erased, and ours replaced
  In all its pristine glory!

"Too long in pain has Slavery's chain
  Our listless limbs encumber'd;
Too long beneath her freezing breath
  Our torpid souls have slumber'd.

"But now we rise—the great, the wise
  Of ages past inspire us!
Oh! what could inflame our love of fame,
  If that should fail to fire us?

"Let Cecrops' town of old renown
  Her bands and chieftains muster;
With joy unsheathe the blade of death,
  And crush the foes who crush'd her!

"We come, we come, with trump and drum,
  To smite the hand that smote us,
And spread the blaze of freedom's rays
  From Athens to Eurotas!"

———⟨⟩———

THE MAID OF SAVOY.

DOWN Savoy's hills of stainless white
  A thousand currents run,
And sparkle bright in the early light
  Of the slowly-rising sun:
    But brighter far,
    Like the glance of a star
    From regions above,
    Is the look of love
    In the eye of the Maid of Savoy!

Down Savoy's hills of lucid snow
  A thousand roebucks leap,

And headlong they go when the bugles blow,
  And sound from steep to steep:
    But lighter far,
    Like the motion of air
    On the smooth river's bed,
    Is the noiseless tread
    Of the foot of the Maid of Savoy!

In Savoy's vales, with green array'd,
  A thousand blossoms flower,
'Neath the odorous shade by the larches made,
  In their own ambrosial bower:
    But sweeter still,
    Like the cedars which rise
    On Lebanon's hill
    To the pure blue skies,
    Is the breath of the Maid of Savoy!

In Savoy's groves full merrily sing
  A thousand songsters gay,
When the breath of spring calls them forth on the
    wing,
  To sport in the sun's mild ray:
    But softer far,
    Like the holy song
    Of angels in air,
    When they sweep along,
    Is the voice of the Maid of Savoy!

———⟨⟩———

IGNORANCE OF MODERN EGYPT.

DAY's genial beams expand the flowers
That bloom in Damietta's bowers;
Beneath the night's descending dew
They close those leaves of finest hue:
So Science droops in Egypt's land,
Beneath the Turkish despot's hand;
The damps of Ignorance and Pride
Close up its leaves, its beauties hide:
The morrow's rays her flowers may woo—
Is there no ray for Science too?

———⟨⟩———

MIDNIGHT.

'Tis midnight o'er the dim mere's lonely bosom,
  Dark, dusky, windy midnight: swift are driven
The swelling vapors onward: every blossom
  Bathes its bright petals in the tears of heaven.
Imperfect, half-seen objects meet the sight,
  The other half our fancy must portray;
A wan, dull, lengthen'd sheet of swimming light
  Lies the broad lake: the moon conceals her ray,
Sketch'd faintly by a pale and lurid gleam
  Shot thro' the glimmering clouds: the lovely
    planet
Is shrouded in obscurity; the scream
  Of owl is silenced; and the rocks of granite
Rise tall and drearily, while damp and dank
Hang the thick willows on the reedy bank.
Beneath, the gurgling eddies slowly creep,
  Blacken'd by foliage; and the glutting wave,
That saps eternally the cold gray steep,
  Sounds heavily within the hollow cave.
All earth is restless—from his glossy wing*
  The heath-fowl lifts his head at intervals;
Wet, driving, rainy, come the bursting squalls;
All nature wears her dun dead covering.
Tempest is gather'd, and the brooding storm
Spreads its black mantle o'er the mountain's form;

qui subjuguent le monde ;" "L'âme rayonnante de sa majesté ;"
"Le rayonnant monarque du monde ;" "Sa majesté conquérante
du monde ;" etc.
* "The land is as the Garden of Eden before them, and behind
them a desolate wilderness."—Joel.

* The succeeding lines are a paraphrase of Ossian.

And, mingled with the rising roar, is swelling,
From the far hunter's booth, the blood-hound's yell-
  ing,
The water-falls in various cadence chiming,
  Or in one loud unbroken sheet descending,
  Salute each other thro' the night's dark womb;
The moaning pine-trees to the wild blast bend-
  ing,
  Are pictured faintly thro' the chequer'd gloom:
The forests, half-way up the mountain climbing,
Resound with crash of falling branches; quiver
  Their aged mossy trunks: the startled doe
Leaps from her leafy lair: the swelling river
  Winds his broad stream majestic, deep, and slow.

———⟨∘⟩———

"IN SUMMER, WHEN ALL NATURE GLOWS."

"Nature in every form inspires delight." —COWPER.

In summer, when all nature glows,
  And lends its fragrance to the rose,
And tints the sky with deeper blue,
  And copious sheds the fruitful dew;
When odors come with every gale,
  And nature holds her carnival;
When all is bright and pure and calm,
The smallest herb or leaf can charm
The man whom nature's beauties warm.

The glitt'ring tribes of insects gay,
  Disporting in their parent-ray,
Each full of life and careless joy,
  He views with philosophic eye:
For well he knows the glorious Hand,
That bade th' eternal mountains stand,
And spread the vast and heaving main,
And studded heaven's resplendent plain,
Gave life to nature's humbler train.

Nor less admires his mighty pow'r
  In the fine organs of a flow'r,
Than when he bids the thunder roll,
  Rebellowing o'er the stormy pole;
Or launches forth his bolts of fire
On the lost objects of his ire;
Or with the yawning earthquake shocks
The reeling hills and shatter'd rocks,
And every mortal project mocks.

No skeptic he—who bold essays
  T' unravel all the mystic maze
Of the Creator's mighty plan—
  A task beyond the pow'rs of man;
Who, when his reason fails to soar
High as his will, believes no more—
No!—calmly thro' the world he steals,
Nor seeks to trace what God conceals,
Content with what that God reveals.

———⟨∘⟩———

SCOTCH SONG.

There are tears o' pity, an' tears o' wae,
An' tears for excess o' joy will fa',
Yet the tears o' luve are sweeter than a'!

There are sighs o' pity, an' sighs o' wae,
An' sighs o' regret frae the saul will gae;
Yet the sighs o' luve are sweeter than a'!

There's the look o' pity, the look o' wae,
The look o' frien,' an' the look o' fae;
Yet the look o' luve is sweeter than a'!

There's the smile o' friends when they come frae far,
There's the smile o' joy in the festive ha';
Yet the smile o' luve is sweeter than a'!

———⟨∘⟩———

"BORNE ON LIGHT WINGS OF BUOY-
ANT DOWN."

"Nunc mihi, nunc alii benigna."
            HORACE.

Borne on light wings of buoyant down,
  Mounts the hoar thistle-beard aloft;
An air scarce felt can bear it on,
  A touch propel, tho' e'er so soft:
Dislodged from yonder thistle's head,
Upon the passing gale it fled.

See! to each object on its way
  A faithless moment it adheres;
But if one breeze upon it play,
  Breaks its slight bonds and disappears:
Its silken sail each zephyr catches,
A breath its airy hold detaches.

The man who wins thy love awhile,
  Should never dream it will remain;
For one fond word, one courteous smile,
  Will set thy heart afloat again.
But he whose eye the light can chase,
That sports above the trembling vase,

Attend its roving sheen, pursue
  Its rapid movements here and there,
And with a firm unwavering view
  Arrest the fleeting phantom fair,
May fix inconstancy—ensure
Thy love, thy fickle faith secure!

How many have—for many ask—
  The kiss I fondly deem'd my own!
And hundreds in succession bask
  In eye-beams due to me alone:
Tho' all, like me, in turn must prove
The wandering nature of thy love.

Thou saw'st the glow-worm on our way,
  Last eve, with mellow lustre shine—
Clad in pellucid flame she lay,
  And glimmer'd in her amber shrine—
Would that those eyes of heavenly blue
Were half as faithful and as true!

And lo! the blush, quick mantling, breaks
  In rich suffusion o'er thy cheek;
In sudden vermeil Conscience speaks,
  No further, fuller proof I seek:
The rosy herald there was sent,
To bid thee own it and repent.

———⟨∘⟩———

SONG.

It is the solemn even-time,
  And the holy organ's pealing:
And the vesper chime, oh! the vesper chime!
  O'er the clear blue wave is stealing.

It is the solemn mingled swell
  Of the monks in chorus singing:
And the vesper bell, oh! the vesper bell!
  To the gale is its soft note flinging.

'Tis the sound of the voices sweeping along,
  Like the wind thro' a grove of larches:
And the vesper song, oh! the vesper song!
  Echoes sad thro' the cloister'd arches.

"THE STARS OF YON BLUE PLACID SKY."

"....supereminet omnes."—VIRGIL.

THE stars of yon blue placid sky
In vivid thousands burn,
And beaming from their orbs on high,
On radiant axes turn:
The eye with wonder gazes there,
And could but gaze on sight so fair.

But should a comet, brighter still,
His blazing train unfold
Among the many lights that fill
The sapphirine with gold;
More wonder then would one bestow
Than millions of a meaner glow.

E'en so, sweet maid! thy beauties shine
With light so peerless and divine,
That others, who have charm'd before,
When match'd with thee, attract no more.

FRIENDSHIP.

" Neque ego nunc de vulgari aut de mediocri, quæ tamen ipsa et delectat et prodest, sed de vera et perfecta loquor [amicitia] qualis eorum, qui pauci nominantur, fuit."—CICERO.

O THOU most holy Friendship! whereso'er
Thy dwelling be—for in the courts of man
But seldom thine all-heavenly voice we hear,
Sweet'ning the moments of our narrow span;
And seldom thy bright footsteps do we scan
Along the weary waste of life unblest,
For faithless is its frail and wayward plan,
And perfidy is man's eternal guest,
With dark suspicion link'd and shameless interest!

'Tis thine, when life has reach'd its final goal,
Ere the last sigh that frees the mind be giv'n,
To speak sweet solace to the parting soul,
And pave the bitter path that leads to heav'n:
'Tis thine, whene'er the heart is rack'd and riv'n
By the hot shafts of baleful calumny,
When the dark spirit to despair is driv'n,
To teach its lonely grief to lean on thee,
And pour within thine ear the tale of misery.

But where art thou, thou comet of an age,
Thou phœnix of a century? Perchance
Thou art but of those fables which engage
And hold the minds of men in giddy trance.
Yet, be it so, and be it all romance,
The thought of thine existence is so bright
With beautiful imaginings—the glance
Upon thy fancied being such delight,
That I will deem thee Truth, so lovely is thy might!

ON THE DEATH OF MY GRAND-MOTHER.

" Cui pudor et justitiæ soror
Incorrupta fides nudaque veritas,
Quando ullum invenient parem?"
HORACE.

THREE on her bier she sleeps!
E'en yet her face its native sweetness keeps.
Ye need not mourn above that faded form,
Her soul defies the ravage of the worm;
Her better half has sought its heavenly rest,
Unstain'd, unharm'd, unfetter'd, unopprest;
And far above all worldly pain and woe,
She sees that God she almost saw below.
She trod the path of virtue from her birth,
And finds in Heaven what she sought on earth;
She wins the smile of her eternal King,
And sings his praise where kindred angels sing.
Her holy patience, her unshaken faith,
How well they smooth'd the rugged path of Death!
She met his dread approach without alarm,
For Heaven in prospect makes the spirit calm.
In steadfast trust and Christian virtue strong,
Hope on her brow, and Jesus on her tongue;
Her faith, like Stephen's, soften'd her distress—
Scarce less her anguish, scarce her patience less!

"AND ASK YE WHY THESE SAD TEARS STREAM?"

"Te somnia nostra reducunt."—OVID.

AND ask ye why these sad tears stream?
Why these wan eyes are dim with weeping?
I had a dream—a lovely dream,
Of her that in the grave is sleeping.

I saw her as 'twas yesterday,
The bloom upon her cheek still glowing;
And round her play'd a golden ray,
And on her brows were gay flowers blowing.

With angel-hand she swept a lyre,
A garland red with roses bound it;
Its strings were wreath'd with lambent fire,
And amaranth was woven round it.

I saw her mid the realms of light,
In everlasting radiance gleaming;
Co-equal with the seraphs bright,
Mid thousand thousand angels beaming.

I strove to reach her, when, behold,
Those fairy forms of bliss Elysian,
And all that rich scene wrapt in gold
Faded in air—a lovely vision!

And I awoke, but oh! to me
That waking hour was doubly weary;
And yet I could not envy thee,
Although so blest, and I so dreary.

ON SUBLIMITY.

"The sublime always dwells on great objects and terrible."
BURKE.

O TELL me not of vales in tenderest green,
The poplar's shade, the plantain's graceful tree;
Give me the wild cascade, the rugged scene,
The loud surge bursting o'er the purple sea:
On such sad views my soul delights to pore.
By Teneriffe's peak, or Kilda's giant height,
Or dark Loffoden's melancholy shore,
What time gray eve is fading into night;
When by that twilight beam I scarce descry
The mingled shades of earth and sea and sky.

Give me to wander at midnight alone,
Through some august cathedral, where, from high,
The cold, clear moon on the mosaic stone
Comes glancing in gay colors gloriously,
Through windows rich with gorgeous blazonry,
Gilding the niches dim, where, side by side,
Stand antique mitred prelates, whose bones lie
Beneath the pavement, where their deeds of pride

Were graven, but long since are worn away
By constant feet of ages day by day.

Then, as Imagination aids, I hear
　Wild heavenly voices sounding from the choir,
And more than mortal music meets mine ear,
　Whose long, long notes among the tombs expire,
With solemn rustling of cherubic wings,
　Round those vast columns which the roof upbear;
While sad and undistinguishable things
　Do flit athwart the moonlit windows there;
And my blood curdles at the chilling sound
Of lone, unearthly steps, that pace the hallow'd
　　ground!

I love the starry spangled heav'n, resembling
　A canopy with fiery gems o'erspread,
When the wide loch with silvery sheen is trembling,
　Far stretch'd beneath the mountain's hoary head.
But most I love that sky, when, dark with storms,
　It frowns terrific o'er this wilder'd earth,
While the black clouds, in strange and uncouth forms,
　Come hurrying onward in their ruinous wrath;
And shrouding in their deep and gloomy robe
The burning eyes of heav'n and Dian's lucid globe!

I love your voice, ye echoing winds, that sweep
　Thro' the wide womb of midnight, when the veil
Of darkness rests upon the mighty deep,
　The laboring vessel, and the shatter'd sail—
Save when the forked bolts of lightning leap
　On flashing pinions, and the mariner pale
Raises his eyes to heav'n. Oh! who would sleep
　What time the rushing of the angry gale
Is loud upon the waters?—Hail, all hail!
Tempest and clouds and night and thunder's rend-
　ing peal!

All hail, Sublimity! thou lofty one,
　For thou dost walk upon the blast, and gird
Thy majesty with terrors, and thy throne
　Is on the whirlwind, and thy voice is heard
In thunders and in shakings: thy delight
　Is in the secret wood, the blasted heath,
The ruin'd fortress, and the dizzy height,
　The grave, the ghastly charnel-house of death.
In vaults, in cloisters, and in gloomy piles,
Long corridors and towers and solitary aisles!

Thy joy is in obscurity, and plain
　Is naught with thee; and on thy steps attend
Shadows but half distinguish'd: the thin train
　Of hovering spirits round thy pathway bend,
With their low tremulous voice and airy tread,*
　What time the tomb above them yawns and gapes:
For thou dost hold communion with the dead
　Phantoms and phantasies and grisly shapes;
And shades and headless spectres of St. Mark,†
Seen by a lurid light, formless and still and dark!

What joy to view the varied rainbow smile
　On Niagara's flood of matchless might,
Where all around the melancholy isle‡
　The billows sparkle with their hues of light!
While, as the restless surges roar and rave,
　The arrowy stream descends with awful sound,
Wheeling and whirling with each breathless wave,§
　Immense, sublime, magnificent, profound!

---

* According to Burke, a low, tremulous, intermitted sound is conducive to the sublime.
† It is a received opinion, that on St. Mark's Eve all the persons
who are to die in the following year make their appearances without their heads in the churches of their respective parishes. See Dr.
Langhorne's Notes to Collins.
‡ This Island, on both sides of which the waters rush with aston-
ishing swiftness, is 900 or 900 feet long, and its lower edge is just at
the perpendicular edge of the fall.
§ "Undis Phlegethon perlustrat anhelis."—CLAUDIAN.

If thou hast seen all this, and could'st not feel,
Then know, thine heart is framed of marble or of
　steel.

The hurricane fair earth to darkness changing,
　Kentucky's chambers of eternal gloom.*
The swift-paced columns of the desert ranging
　Th' uneven waste, the violent Simoom,
Thy snow-clad peaks, stupendous Gungotree!
　Whence springs the hallow'd Jumna's echoing tide,
Hoar Cotopaxi's cloud-capt majesty,
　Enormous Chimborazo's naked pride,
The dizzy cape of winds that cleaves the sky,†
　Whence we look down into eternity,

The pillar'd cave of Morven's giant king,‡
　The Yanar,§ and the Geyser's boiling fountain,
The deep volcano's inward murmuring,
　The shadowy Colossus of the mountain;‖
Antiparos, where sunbeams never enter;
　Loud Stromboli, amid the quaking isles;
The terrible Maelstroom, around his centre
　Wheeling his circuit of unnumber'd miles:
These, these are sights and sounds that freeze the
　blood,
Yet charm the awe-struck soul which doats on
　solitude.

Blest be the bard, whose willing feet rejoice
　To tread the emerald green of Fancy's vales,
Who hears the music of her heavenly voice,
　And breathes the rapture of her nectar'd gales!
Blest be the bard, whom golden Fancy loves,
　He strays forever thro' her blooming bowers,
Amid the rich profusion of her groves,
　And wreathes his forehead with her spicy flowers
Of sunny radiance; but how blest is he
Who feels the genuine force of high Sublimity!

———◆———

THE DEITY.

"Immutable—immortal—infinite!"—MILTON.

WHERE is the wonderful abode,
　The holy, secret, searchless shrine,
Where dwells the immaterial God,
　The all-pervading and benign?

Oh that he were reveal'd to me,
　Fully and palpably display'd
In all the awful majesty
　Of Heaven's consummate pomp array'd—

How would the overwhelming light
　Of his tremendous presence beam!
And how insufferably bright
　Would the broad glow of glory stream!

What tho' this flesh would fade like grass,
　Before th' intensity of day?
One glance at Him who always was,
　The fiercest pangs would well repay.

---

* See Dr. Nahum Ward's account of the great Kentucky cavern,
in the *Monthly Magazine*, October, 1816.
† In the Ukraine.
‡ Fingal's Cave in the Island of Staffa. If the Colossus of Rhodes
bestrid a harbor, Fingal's powers were certainly far from despica-
ble:

A chos air Cromleach druim-ard
Chos eile air Crommeal dubh
Thoga Fion le lamh mhoir
An d'uisge o Lubhair na fruth.

With one foot on Cromleach his brow,
The other on Crommeal the dark,
Fion took up with his large hand
The water from Lubhair of streams.

See the Dissertations prefixed to Ossian's Poems.
§ Or perpetual fire.　　‖ Alias, the Spectre of the Broken.

When Moses on the mountain's brow
 Had met th' Eternal face to face,
While anxious Israel stood below,
 Wond'ring and trembling at its base;

His visage, as he downward trod,
 Shone starlike on the shrinking crowd,
With lustre borrow'd from his God:
 They could not brook it, and they bow'd.

The mere reflection of the blaze
 That lighten'd round creation's Lord,
Was too puissant for their gaze;
 And he that caught it was adored.

Then how ineffably august,
 How passing wond'rous must He be,
Whose presence lent to earthly dust
 Such permanence of brilliancy!

Throned in sequester'd sanctity,
 And with transcendent glories crown'd;
With all His works beneath His eye,
 And suns and systems burning round,—

How shall I hymn Him? How aspire
 His holy Name with song to blend,
And bid my rash and feeble lyre
 To such an awless flight ascend?

—⁂—

THE REIGN OF LOVE.

"In freta dum fluvii current," etc.—VIRGIL.

WHILE roses boast a purple dye,
 While seas obey the blast,
Or glowing rainbows span the sky—
 The reign of love shall last.

While man exults o'er present joy,
 Or mourns o'er joy that's past,
Feels virtue soothe, or vice alloy—
 The reign of love shall last.

While female charms attract the mind,
 In moulds of beauty cast;
While man is warm, or woman kind—
 The reign of love shall last.

—⁂—

"'TIS THE VOICE OF THE DEAD."

"Non omnis moriar."—HORACE.

'Tis the voice of the dead
 From the depth of their glooms:
Hark! they call me away
 To the world of the tombs!
I come, lo! I come
 To your lonely abodes,
For my dust is the earth's
 But this soul is my God's!

Thine is not the triumph,
 O invincible Death!
Thou hast not prevail'd,
 Tho' I yield thee my breath:
Thy sceptre shall wave
 O'er a fragment of clay,
But my spirit, thou tyrant,
 Is bounding away!

I fear not, I feel not
 The pang that destroys,

In the bliss of that thought—
 That the blest shall rejoice:
For why should I shrink?
 One moment shall sever
My soul from its chain,
 Then it liveth forever!

Then weep not for me,
 Tho' I sink, I shall rise;
I shall live, tho' I sleep—
 'Tis the guilty who dies.
E'en now in mine ear
 'Tis a seraph who sings:
Farewell!—for I go
 On the speed of his wings!

—⁂—

TIME: AN ODE.

I SEE the chariot, where,
Throughout the purple air,
 The forelock'd monarch rides:
Arm'd like some antique vehicle for war,
Time, hoary Time! I see thy scythèd car,
 In voiceless majesty,
Cleaving the clouds of ages that float by,
 And change their many-color'd sides,
  Now dark, now dun, now richly bright,
  In an ever-varying light.
The great, the lowly, and the brave
  Bow down before the rushing force
  Of thine unconquerable course;
Thy wheels are noiseless as the grave,
Yet fleet as Heaven's red bolt they hurry on,
They pass above us, and are gone!

Clear is the track which thou hast past;
 Strew'd with the wrecks of frail renown,
 Robe, sceptre, banner, wreath, and crown,
 The pathway that before thee lies,
An undistinguishable waste,
 Invisible to human eyes,
 Which fain would scan the various shapes which
  glide
  In dusky cavalcade,
Imperfectly descried,
  Through that intense, impenetrable shade.

Four gray steeds thy chariot draw;
In th' obdurate, tameless jaw
 Their rusted iron bits they sternly champ;
 Ye may not hear the echoing tramp
  Of their light-bounding, windy feet,
  Upon that cloudy pavement beat.
Four wings have each, which, far outspread,
 Receive the many blasts of heav'n,
As with unwearied speed,
 Throughout the long extent of ether driv'n,
Onward they rush forever and for aye:
 Thy voice, thou mighty Charioteer!
 Always sounding in their ear,
Throughout the gloom of night and heat of day.

Fast behind thee follows Death,
 Thro' the ranks of wan and weeping,
That yield their miserable breath,
 On with his pallid courser proudly sweeping.
Arm'd is he in full mail,[*]
 Bright breastplate and high crest,
 Nor is the trenchant falchion wanting:
So fiercely does he ride the gale,
 On Time's dark car, before him, rest
 The dew-drops of his charger's panting,

* I am indebted for the idea of Death's armor to that famous chorus in "Caractacus" beginning with—

  "Hark! heard ye not that footstep dread?"

On, on they go along the boundless skies,
    All human grandeur fades away
Before their flashing, fiery, hollow eyes;
        Beneath the terrible control
        Of those vast arméd orbs, which roll
Oblivion on the creatures of a day.
Those splendid monuments alone he spares
    Which, to her deathless votaries,
Bright Fame, with glowing hand, uprears
Amid the waste of countless years.

"Live ye!" to these he crieth; "live!
To ye eternity I give—
Ye, upon whose blessed birth
    The noblest star of heaven hath shone;
Live, when the ponderous pyramids of earth
    Are crumbling in oblivion!
Live, when, wrapt in sullen shade,
The golden hosts of heaven shall fade;
Live, when yon gorgeous sun on high
Shall veil the sparkling of his eye!
Live, when imperial Time and Death himself shall
    die!"

———

GOD'S DENUNCIATIONS AGAINST PHA-RAOH-HOPHRA, OR APRIES.

Thou beast of the flood, who hast said in thy soul,
"I have made me a stream that forever shall roll!"[*]
Thy strength is the flower that shall last but a day,
And thy might is the snow in the sun's burning ray.

Arm, arm from the east, Babylonia's son!
Arm, arm for the battle—the Lord leads thee on!
With the shield of thy fame, and the power of thy
    pride,
Arm, arm in thy glory—the Lord is thy guide.

Thou shalt come like a storm when the moonlight
    is dim,
And the lake's gloomy bosom is full to the brim;
Thou shalt come like the flash in the darkness of
    night,
When the wolves of the forest shall howl for af-
    fright.

Woe, woe to thee, Tanis![†] thy babes shall be thrown
By the barbarous hands on the cold marble-stone;
Woe, woe to thee, Nile! for thy stream shall be red
With the blood that shall gush o'er thy billowy bed!

Woe, woe to thee, Memphis![†] the war-cry is near,
And the child shall be toss'd on the murderer's
    spear;
For fiercely he comes in the day of his ire,
With wheels like a whirlwind, and chariots of fire!

———

"ALL JOYOUS IN THE REALMS OF DAY."

"Hominum divomque pater."—VIRGIL.

ALL joyous in the realms of day,
    The radiant angels sing,
In incorruptible array,
    Before the Eternal King:

---

[*] "Pliny's reproach to the Egyptians, for their vain and foolish pride with regard to the inundations of the Nile, points out one of their most distinguishing characteristics, and recalls to my mind a fine passage of Ezekiel, where God thus speaks to Pharaoh, one of their kings: Behold, I am against thee, Pharaoh king of Egypt, the great dragon that lieth in the midst of his rivers, that hath said, My river is mine own, and I have made it for myself."—ROLLIN, vol. i., p. 216.

[†] The Scriptural appellations are "Zoan" and "Noph."

Who, hymn'd by archangelic tongues,
    In majesty and might,
The subject of ten thousand songs,
    Sits veil'd in circling light.

Benignly great, serenely dread,
    Amid th' immortal choir,
How glory plays around his head
    In rays of heavenly fire!

Before the blaze of Deity
    The deathless legions bend,
And to the grand co-equal Three
    Their choral homage lend.

They land that God, who has no peers,
    High—holy—searchless—pure;
Who has endured for countless years,
    And ever will endure:

Who spoke, and fish, fowl, beast, in pairs,
    Or swam, or flew, or trod;
Space glitter'd with unnumber'd stars,
    And heaving oceans flow'd.

Then let us join our feeble praise
    To that which angels give;
And hymns to that great Parent raise,
    In whom we breathe and live!

———

THE BATTLE-FIELD.

"When all is o'er, it is humbling to tread
O'er the weltering field of the tombless dead!"
                    BYRON.

THE heat and the chaos of contest are o'er,
To mingle no longer—to madden no more:
And the cold forms of heroes are stretch'd on the
    plain;
Those lips cannot breathe thro' the trumpet again!

For the globes of destruction have shatter'd their
    might,
The swift and the burning—and wrapt them in night;
Like lightning, electric and sudden they came;
They took but their life, and they left them their
    fame!

I heard, oh! I heard, when, with barbarous bray,
They leapt from the mouth of the cannon away;
And the loud-rushing sound of their passage in air
Seem'd to speak in a terrible language—"Beware!"

Farewell to ye, chieftains; to one and to all,
Who this day have perish'd by sabre or ball;
Ye cannot awake from your desolate sleep—
Unbroken and silent and dreamless and deep!

———

THE THUNDER-STORM.

"Non imitabile fulmen "—VIRGIL.

THE storm is brooding!—I would see it pass,
Observe its tenor, and its progress trace.
How dark and dun the gathering clouds appear,
Their rolling thunders seem to rend the ear!
But faint at first, they slowly, sternly rise,
From mutt'rings low to peals which rock the skies.
As if at first their fury they forbore,
And nursed their terrors for a closing roar.
And hark! they rise into a loftier sound,
Creation's trembling objects quake around;
In silent awe the subject-nations hear
Th' appalling crash of elemental war:

The lightning too each eye in dimness shrouds,
The fiery progeny of clashing clouds,
That carries death upon its blazing wing,
And the keen tortures of th' electric sting:
Not like the harmless flash on summer's eve
(When no rude blasts their silent slumbers leave),
Which, like a radiant vision to the eye,
Expands serenely in the placid sky:
It rushes fleeter than the swiftest wind,
And bids attendant thunders wait behind:
Quick—forked—livid, thro' the air it flies,
A moment blazes—dazzles—bursts—and dies:
Another, and another yet, and still
To each replies its own allotted peal.
But see, at last, its force and fury spent,
The tempest slackens, and the clouds are rent:
How sweetly opens on th' enchanted view
The deep-blue sky, more fresh and bright in hue!
A finer fragrance breathes in every vale,
A fuller luxury in every gale;
My ravish'd senses catch the rich perfume,
And Nature smiles in renovated bloom!

—◇○◇—

THE GRAVE OF A SUICIDE.

Hark! how the gale, in mournful notes and stern,
Sighs thro' yon grove of aged oaks, that wave
(While down these solitary walks I turn)
    Their mingled branches o'er yon lonely grave!

Poor soul! the dawning of thy life was dim;
Frown'd the dark clouds upon thy natal day;
Soon rose thy cup of sorrow to the brim,
    And hope itself but shed a doubtful ray.

That hope had fled, and all within was gloom;
That hope had fled—thy woe to frenzy grew;
For thou, wed to misery from the womb—
    Scarce one bright scene thy night of darkness
        knew!

Oft when the moonbeam on the cold bank sleeps,
Where 'neath the dewy turf thy form is laid,
In silent woe thy wretched mother weeps,
    By this lone tomb, and by this oak-tree's shade.

"Oh! softly tread: in death he slumbers here;
'Tis here," she cries, "within his narrow cell!"—
The bitter sob, the wildly-starting tear,
    The quivering lip, proclaim the rest too well!

—◇○◇—

ON THE DEATH OF LORD BYRON.

"Unus tanta dedit?—dedit et majora daturus
Ni celeri letho corriperetur, erat."
Don Manuel de Souza Coutino's *Epitaph on Camoens.*

The hero and the bard is gone!
His bright career on earth is done,
Where with a comet's blaze he shone.

He died—where vengeance arms the brave,
Where buried freedom quits her grave,
In regions of the eastern wave.

Yet not before his ardent lay
Had bid them chase all fear away,
And taught their trumps a bolder bray.

Thro' him their ancient valor glows,
And, stung by thraldom's scathing woes,
They rise again, as once they rose.*

* A little exaggeration may be pardoned on a subject so inspir-
ing.

As once in conscious glory bold,
To war their sounding cars they roll'd,
Uncrush'd, untrampled, uncontroll'd!

Each drop that gushes from their side,
Will serve to swell the crimson tide,
That soon shall whelm the Moslem's pride!

At last upon their lords they turn,
At last the shame of bondage learn,
At last they feel their fetters burn!*

Oh! how the heart expands to see
An injured people all agree
To burst those fetters and be free!

Each far-famed mount that cleaves the skies,
Each plain where buried glory lies,
All, all exclaim—"Awake! arise!"

Who would not feel their wrongs? and who
Departed freedom would not rue,
With all her trophies in his view?

To see imperial Athens reign,
And, towering o'er the vassal main,
Rise in embattled strength again—

To see rough Sparta train once more
Her infants' ears for battle's roar,
Stern, dreadful, chainless, as before—

Was Byron's hope—was Byron's aim:
With ready heart and hand he came;
But perish'd in that path of fame!

—◇○◇—

THE WALK AT MIDNIGHT.

"Tremulo sub lumine."—Virgil.

Soft, shadowy moonbeam! by thy light
    Sleeps the wide meer serenely pale:
How various are the sounds of night,
    Borne on the scarcely-rising gale!

The swell of distant brook is heard,
    Whose far-off waters faintly roll;
And piping of the shrill small bird,
    Arrested by the wand'ring owl.

Come hither! let us thread with care
    The maze of this green path, which binds
The beauties of the broad parterre,
    And thro' yon fragrant alley winds.

Or on this old bench will we sit,
    Round which the clust'ring woodbine wreathes:
While birds of night around us flit;
    And thro' each lavish wood-walk breathes,

Unto my ravish'd senses, brought
    From yon thick-woven odorous bowers,
The still rich breeze, with incense fraught
    Of glowing fruits and spangled flowers.

The whispering leaves, the gushing stream,
    Where trembles the uncertain moon,
Suit more the poet's pensive dream,
    Than all the jarring notes of noon.

Then, to the thickly-crowded mart
    The eager sons of interest press:
Then, shine the tinsel works of art—
    Now, all is Nature's loneliness!

* The enthusiasm the noble poet excited reminds us of Tyrtæus.

Then, wealth aloft in state displays
  The glittering of her gilded cars;
Now, dimly stream the mingled rays
  Of yon far-twinkling, silver stars.

Yon church, whose cold gray spire appears
  In the black outline of the trees,
Conceals the object of my tears,
  Whose form in dreams my spirit sees.

There in the chilling bed of earth
  The chancel's letter'd stone above—
There sleepeth she who gave me birth,
  Who taught my lips the hymn of love!

Yon mossy stems of ancient oak,
  So widely crown'd with sombre shade,
Those ne'er have heard the woodman's stroke
  Their solemn, secret depths invade.

How oft the grassy way I've trod
  That winds their knotty boles between,
And gather'd from the blooming sod
  The flowers that flourish'd there unseen!

Rise! let us trace that path once more,
  While o'er our track the cold beams shine;
Down this low shingly vale, and o'er
  Yon rude, rough bridge of prostrate pine.

MITHRIDATES PRESENTING BERE-NICE WITH THE CUP OF POISON.

Oh! Berenice, lorn and lost,
  This wretched soul with shame is bleeding:
Oh! Berenice, I am tost
  By griefs, like wave to wave succeeding.

Fall'n Pontus! all her fame is gone,
  And dim the splendor of her glory;
Low in the west her evening sun,
  And dark the lustre of her story.

Dead is the wreath that round her brow
  The glowing hands of Honor braided:
What change of fate can wait her now,
  Her sceptre spoil'd, her throne degraded?

And wilt thou, wilt thou basely go,
  My love, thy life, thy country shaming,
In all the agonies of woe,
  'Mid madd'ning shouts, and standards flaming?

And wilt thou, wilt thou basely go,
  Proud Rome's triumphal car adorning?
Hark! hark! I hear thee answer "No!"
  The proffer'd life of thraldom scorning.

Lone, crownless, destitute, and poor,
  My heart with bitter pain is burning;
So thick a cloud of night hangs o'er,
  My daylight into darkness turning.

Yet though my spirit, bow'd with ill,
  Small hope from future fortune borrows;
One glorious thought shall cheer me still,
  That thou art free from abject sorrows—

Art free forever from the strife
  Of slavery's pangs and tearful anguish;
For life is death, and death is life,
  To those whose limbs in fetters languish.

Fill high the bowl! the draught is thine!
  The Romans!—now thou need'st not heed them!

'Tis nobler than the noblest wine—
  It gives thee back to fame and freedom!

The scalding tears my cheek bedew;
  My life, my love, my all—we sever!
One last embrace, one long adieu,
  And then farewell—farewell forever!

In reality Mithridates had no personal interview with Monima and Berenice before the deaths of those princesses, but only sent his eunuch Bacchides to signify his intention that they should die. I have chosen Berenice as the more general name, though Monima was his peculiar favorite.

THE BARD'S FAREWELL.

"The king, sensible that nothing kept alive the ideas of military valor and of ancient glory so much as the traditional poetry of the people—which, assisted by the power of music and the jollity of festivals, made deep impression on the minds of the youth—gathered together all the Welsh bards, and, from a barbarous though not absurd policy, ordered them to be put to death."—HUME.

SNOWDON! thy cliffs shall hear no more
  This deep-toned harp again;
But banner-cry and battle-roar
  Shall form a fiercer strain!

O'er thy sweet chords, my magic lyre!
  What future hand shall stray?
What brain shall feel thy master's fire,
  Or frame his matchless lay?

Well might the crafty Edward fear:
  Should I but touch thy chord,
Its slightest sound would couch the spear,
  And bare the indignant sword!

Full well he knew the wizard-spell
  That dwelt upon thy string;
And trembled, when he heard thy swell
  Thro' Snowdon's caverns ring!

These eyes shall sleep in death's dull night,
  This hand all nerveless lie,
Ere once again yon orb of light
  Break o'er the clear blue sky!

And then, by Hell's own furies nurst,
  Unfurl thy banner's pride!
But know that, living, thee I cursed;
  And, cursing thee, I died!

EPIGRAM.

MEDEA's herbs her magic gave—
  They taught her how to kill or save:
No foreign aid couldst thou devise,
  For in thyself thy magic lies.

ON BEING ASKED FOR A SIMILE,

TO ILLUSTRATE THE ADVANTAGE OF KEEPING THE PAS-SIONS SUBSERVIENT TO REASON.

As the sharp, pungent taste is the glory of mustard,
  But, if heighten'd, would trouble your touchy papillæ;
As a few laurel-leaves add a relish to custard,
  But, if many, would fight with your stomach and kill ye:—

So the passions, if freed from the precincts of reason,
  Have noxious effects—but if duly confined, sir,
Are useful, no doubt—this each writer agrees on:
  So I've dish'd up a simile just to your mind, sir.

EPIGRAM ON A MUSICIAN,

WHOSE HARP-STRINGS WERE CRACKED FROM WANT
OF USING.

"Why dost thou not *string thine old harp?*" says a
friend:
"Thy complaints," replied Dolce, "I think never
end;
I've reason enough to remember the thing,
For you always are *harping upon the old string.*"

THE OLD CHIEFTAIN.

"And said I, that my limbs were old!"—SCOTT.

Raise, raise the song of the hundred shells!
    Though my hair is gray and my limbs are cold;
Yet in my bosom proudly dwells
    The memory of the days of old;

When my voice was high, and my arm was strong,
    And the foeman before my stroke would bow,
And I could have raised the sounding song
    As loudly as I hear ye now.

For when I have chanted the bold song of death,
    Not a page would have stay'd in the hall,
Not a lance in the rest, not a sword in the sheath,
    Not a shield on the dim gray wall.

And who might resist the united powers
    Of battle and music that day,
When, all martiall'd in arms on the heaven-kissing
        towers,
    Stood the chieftains in peerless array?

When our enemies sunk from our eyes as the snow
    Which falls down the stream in the dell,
When each word that I spake was the death of a
        foe,
    And each note of my harp was his knell?

So raise ye the song of the hundred shells;
    Though my hair is gray and my limbs are cold,
Yet in my bosom proudly dwells
    The memory of the days of old!

APOLLONIUS RHODIUS'S COMPLAINT.*

With cutting taunt they bade me lay
    My high-strung harp aside,
As if I dare not soar away
    On Fancy's plume of pride!

Oh! while there's image in my brain
    And vigor in my hand,
The first shall frame the soul-fraught strain,
    The last these chords command!

'Tis true, I own, the starting tear
    Has swell'd into mine eye,
When she, whose hand the plant should rear,
    Could bid it fade and die:

But, deaf to cavil, spite, and scorn,
    I still must wake the lyre;
And still, on Fancy's pinions borne,
    To Helicon aspire.

* This eminent poet, resenting the unworthy treatment of the
Alexandrians, quitted their city, where he had been for some time
librarian, and retired to Rhodes.

And all the ardent lays I pour,
    Another realm shall claim;
My name shall live—a foreign shore
    Shall consecrate my name.

My country's* scorn I will not brook,
    But she shall rue it long;
And Rhodes shall bless the hour she took
    The exiled child of song.

THE FALL OF JERUSALEM.

Jerusalem! Jerusalem!
    Thou art low! thou mighty one,
How is the brilliance of thy diadem,
    How is the lustre of thy throne
Rent from thee, and thy sun of fame
    Darken'd by the shadowy pinion
        Of the Roman bird, whose sway
        All the tribes of earth obey,
    Crouching 'neath his dread dominion,
And the terrors of his name!

How is thy royal seat—whereon
    Sat in days of yore
Lowly Jesse's godlike son,
    And the strength of Solomon,
        In those rich and happy times
        When the ships from Tarshish bore
        Incense, and from Ophir's land,
        With silken sail and cedar oar,
        Wafting to Judea's strand
All the wealth of foreign climes—
    How is thy royal seat o'erthrown!
    Gone is all thy majesty:
        Salem! Salem! city of kings,
    Thou sittest desolate and lone,
        Where once the glory of the Most High
        Dwelt visibly enshrined between the wings
    Of Cherubims, within whose bright embrace
        The golden mercy-seat remain'd:
    Land of Jehovah! view that sacred place
        Abandon'd and profaned!

Wail! fallen Salem! Wail:
    Mohammed's votaries pollute thy fane;
    The dark division of thine holy veil
        Is rent in twain!
Thrice hath Sion's crowned rock
    Seen thy temple's marble state,
    Awfully, serenely great,
        Towering on his sainted brow,
        Rear its pinnacles of snow:
    Thrice, with desolating shock,
        Down to earth hath seen it driv'n
        From his heights, which reach to heav'n!

Wail, fallen Salem! Wail:
    Though not one stone above another
There was left to tell the tale
        Of the greatness of thy story,
    Yet the long lapse of ages cannot smother
        The blaze of thine abounding glory;
Which thro' the mist of rolling years,
O'er history's darken'd page appears,
Like the morning star, whose gleam
    Gazeth thro' the waste of night,
What time old Ocean's purple stream
    In his cold surge hath deeply laved
    Its ardent front of dewy light.
        Oh! who shall e'er forget thy bands, which
            braved

* Alexandria, however, was not his native city: he was born at
Naucratis.

The terrors of the desert's barren reign,
And that strong arm which broke the chain
  Wherein ye foully lay enslaved,
  Or that sublime Theocracy which paved
Your way thro' ocean's vast domain,
And on, far on to Canaan's emerald plain
  Led the Israelitish crowd
  With a pillar and a cloud?

  Signs on earth and signs on high
  Prophesied thy destiny;
    A trumpet's voice above thee rung,
    A starry sabre o'er thee hung:
Visions of fiery armies, redly flashing
  In the many-color'd glare
  Of the setting orb of day;
And flaming chariots, fiercely dashing,
  Swept along the peopled air,
  In magnificent array:
The temple doors, on brazen hinges crashing,
  Burst open with appalling sound,
  A wondrous radiance streaming round!

  "Our blood be on our heads!" ye said:
    Such your awless imprecation:
Full bitterly at length 'twas paid
    Upon your captive nation!
  Arms of adverse legions bound thee,
  Plague and pestilence stood round thee;
  Seven weary suns had brighten'd Syria's sky,
  Yet still was heard th' unceasing cry—
  "From south, north, east, and west, a voice,
  Woe unto thy sons and daughters!
    Woe to Salem! thou art lost!"
A sound divine
Came from the sainted, secret, inmost shrine:
" Let us go hence!"—and then a noise—
  The thunders of the parting Deity,
    Like the rush of countless waters,
    Like the murmur of a host!

  Though now each glorious hope be blighted,
Yet an hour shall come, when ye,
Though scatter'd like the chaff, shall be
  Beneath one standard once again united:
  When your wandering race shall own,
  Prostrate at the dazzling throne
  Of your high Almighty Lord,
  The wonders of His searchless word,
  Th' unfading splendors of His Son!

LAMENTATION OF THE PERUVIANS.

The foes of the East have come down on our shore,
And the state and the strength of Peru are no more:
Oh! cursed, doubly cursed, was that desolate hour,
When they spread o'er our land in the pride of their
  power!
Lament for the Inca, the son of the Sun;
Atahlba's fallen—Peru is undone!

Pizarro! Pizarro! though conquest may wing
  Her course round thy banners that wanton in air;
Yet remorse to thy grief-stricken conscience shall
  cling,
  And shriek o'er thy banquets in sounds of despair.
It shall tell thee, that he who beholds from his throne
  The blood thou hast spilt and the deeds thou hast
  done,
Shall mock at thy fear, and rejoice at thy groan,
  And arise in his wrath for the death of his son!
Why blew ye, ye gales, when the murderer came?
Why fann'd ye the fire, and why fed ye the flame?
Why sped ye his sails o'er the ocean so blue?
Are ye also combined for the fall of Peru?

And thou, whom no prayers, no entreaties can bend,
Thy crimes and thy murders to heav'n shall ascend:
For vengeance the ghosts of our forefathers call;
At thy threshold, Pizarro, in death shalt thou fall!
Ay, there—even there, in the halls of thy pride,
With the blood of thine heart shall thy portals be
  dyed!

Lo! dark as the tempests that frown from the
  North,
From the cloud of past time Manco Capac looks
  forth—
Great Inca! to whom the gay day-star gave birth,
Whose throne is the heav'n, and whose foot-stool
  the earth—
His visage is sad as the vapors that rise
From the desolate mountain of fire to the skies;
But his eye flashes flame as the lightnings that
  streak
Those volumes that shroud the volcano's high peak.
Hark! he speaks—bids us fly to our mountains, and
  cherish
Bold freedom's last spark ere forever it perish;
Bids us leave these wild condors to prey on each
  other,
Each to bathe his fierce beak in the gore of his
  brother!
This symbol we take of our godhead the Sun,
And curse thee and thine for the deeds thou hast
  done.
May the curses pursue thee of those thou hast slain,
Of those that have fallen in war on the plain,
When we went forth to greet ye—but foully ye
  threw
Your dark shots of death on the sons of Peru.
May the curse of the widow—the curse of the brave—
The curse of the fatherless, cleave to thy grave!
And the words which they spake with their last
  dying breath
Embitter the pangs and the tortures of death!

May he that assists be childless and poor,
With famine behind him, and death at his door:
May his nights be all sleepless, his days spent alone,
And ne'er may he list to a voice but his own!
Or, if he shall sleep, in his dreams may he view
The ghost of our Inca, the fiends of Peru:
May the flames of destruction that here he was
  spread
Be tenfold return'd on his murderous head!

SHORT EULOGIUM ON HOMER.

Immortal bard! thy warlike lay
Demands the greenest, brightest bay,
  That ever wreathed the brow
Of minstrel bending o'er his lyre,
With ardent hand and soul of fire,
  Or then, or since, or now!

"A SISTER, SWEET ENDEARING
NAME!"

"Why should we mourn for the blest?"—BYRON.

A sister, sweet endearing name!
  Beneath this tombstone sleeps;
A brother (who such tears could blame?)
  In pensive anguish weeps.

I saw her when in health she wore
  A soft and matchless grace,
And sportive pleasures wanton'd o'er
  The dimples of her face.

I saw her when the icy wind
  Of sickness froze her bloom;
I saw her (bitterest stroke!) consign'd
  To that cold cell—the tomb!

Oh! when I heard the crumbling mould
  Upon her coffin fall,
And thought within she lay so cold,
  And knew that worms would crawl

O'er her sweet cheek's once lovely dye,
  I shudder'd as I turn'd
From the sad spot, and in mine eye
  The full warm tear-drop burn'd.

Again I come—again I feel
  Reflection's poignant sting,
As I retrace my sister's form,
  And back her image bring.

Herself I cannot—from the sod
  She will not rise again;
But this sweet thought, "She rests with God,"
  Relieves a brother's pain.

———&——

"THE SUN GOES DOWN IN THE DARK BLUE MAIN."

"Irreparabile tempus."—VIRGIL.

THE sun goes down in the dark blue main,
  To rise the brighter to-morrow;
But oh! what charm can restore again
  Those days now consign'd to sorrow?

The moon goes down on the calm still night,
  To rise sweeter than when she parted;
But oh! what charm can restore the light
  Of joy to the broken-hearted?

The blossoms depart in the wintry hour,
  To rise in vernal glory;
But oh! what charm can restore the flower
  Of youth to the old and hoary?

———&——

"STILL, MUTE, AND MOTIONLESS SHE LIES."

"Belle en sa fleur d'adolescence."—BERQUIN.
"Lovely in death the beauteous ruin lay"—YOUNG.

STILL, mute, and motionless she lies,
The mist of death has veil'd her eyes,
And is that bright-red lip so pale,
Whose hue was freshen'd by a gale
More sweet than summer e'er could bring
To fan her flowers with balmy wing!
Thy breath, the summer gale, is fled,
And leaves thy lip, the flower, decay'd.
When I was young, with fost'ring care
I rear'd a tulip bright and fair,
And saw its lovely leaves expand,
The labor of my infant hand.
But winter came—its varied dye
Each morn grew fainter to mine eye;
Till, with'ring, it was bright no more,
Nor bloom'd as it was wont before:
And gazing there in boyish grief,
Upon the dull and alter'd leaf,
"Alas! sweet flower," I cried in vain,
"Would I could bid thee blush again!"
So now, "Return, thou crimson dye.
To Celia's lip!" I wildly cry:

23

And steal upon my hopeless view,
  And flush it with reviving hue,
  Soft as the early vermeil given
  To the dim paleness of the heaven
  When slowly gaining on the sight.
  It breaks upon the cheerless white.
It is an idle wish—a dream—
I may not see the glazed eye beam;
I may not warm the damps of death,
  Or link again the scatter'd wreath;
Array in leaves the wintry scene,
  Or make parch'd Afric's deserts green;
Replace the rose-bud on the tree,
  Or breathe the breath of life in thee.

———&——

"OH! NEVER MAY FROWNS AND DISSENSION MOLEST."

"Ipse meique
Ante Larem proprium."—HORACE.

OH! never may frowns and dissension molest
  The pleasure I find at the social hearth;
A pleasure the dearest—the purest—the best
  Of all that are found or enjoy'd on the earth!

For who could e'er traverse this valley of tears,
  Without the dear comforts of friendship and home;
And bear all the dark disappointments and fears,
  Which chill most of our joys and annihilate some?

Vain, bootless pursuers of honor and fame!
  'Tis idle to tell ye, what soon ye must prove—
That honor's a bauble, and glory a name,
  When put in the balance with friendship and love.

For when by fruition their pleasure is gone,
  We think of them no more—they but charm for a
    while;
When the objects of love and affection are flown,
  With pleasure we cling to their memories still!

———&——

ON A DEAD ENEMY.

"Non odi mortuum."—CICERO.

I CAME in haste with cursing breath,
  And heart of hardest steel;
But when I saw thee cold in death,
  I felt as man should feel.

For when I look upon that face,
  That cold, unheeding, frigid brow,
Where neither rage nor fear has place,
  By Heaven! I cannot hate thee now!

———&——

LINES.*

"Cur pendet tacita fistula cum lyra?"—HORACE.

WHEREON is it, friend, that thine enchanting lyre
  Of wizard charm, should thus in silence lie?
Ah! why not boldly sweep its chords of fire,
  And rouse to life its latent harmony?

Thy fancy, fresh, exuberant, boundless, wild,
  Like the rich herbage of thy Plata's shore,
By Song's resistless witchery beguiled
  Would then transport us, since it charm'd before!

* Occasioned by hearing an ardent and beautiful description of the scenery of Southern America given by a gentleman whom the author persuaded to put his ideas into the language of poetry.

For if thy vivid thoughts possess'd a spell,
Which chain'd our ears, and fix'd attention's gaze,
As at the social board we heard thee tell
Of Chili's woods and Orellana's maze—

How will they, deck'd in Song's enlivening grace,
Demand our praise, with added beauties told;
How in thy potent language shall we trace
Those thoughts more vigorous and those words
more bold!

———

THE DUKE OF ALVA'S OBSERVATION ON KINGS.*

Kings, when to private audience they descend,
And make the baffled courtier their prey,
Do use an orange, as they treat a friend—
Extract the juice, and cast the rind away.

When thou art favor'd by thy sovereign's eye,
Let not his glance thine inmost thoughts discover;
Or he will scan thee through, and lay thee by,
Like some old book which he has read all over.

———

"AH! YES, THE LIP MAY FAINTLY SMILE."

Ah! yes, the lip may faintly smile,
The eye may sparkle for a while;
But never from that wither'd heart
The consciousness of ill shall part!

That glance, that smile of passing light,
Are as the rainbow of the night;
But seldom seen, it dares to bloom
Upon the bosom of the gloom.

Its tints are sad and coldly pale,
Dim-glimmering thro' their misty veil;
Unlike the ardent hues which play
Along the flowery bow of day.

The moonbeams sink in dark-robed shades,
Too soon the airy vision fades;
And double night returns, to shroud
The volumes of the showery cloud.

———

"THOU CAMEST TO THY BOWER, MY LOVE."

"Virgo egregia forma."- TERENCE.

Thou camest to thy bower, my love, across the
musky grove,
To fan thy blooming charms within the coolness of
the shade;
Thy locks were like a midnight cloud with silver
moonbeams wove,†
And o'er thy face the varying tints of youthful passion play'd.

Thy breath was like the sandal-wood that casts a
rich perfume,
Thy blue eyes mock'd the lotos in the noonday of
his bloom;

---

* See D'Israeli's "Curiosities of Literature."
† A simile elicited from the songs of Jayadeva, the Horace of
India.

Thy cheeks were like the beamy flush that gilds
the breaking day,
And in th' ambrosia of thy smiles the god of
rapture lay.*

Fair as the cairba-stone art thou, that stone of daz-
zling white,†
Ere yet unholy fingers changed its milk-white hue
to-night;
And lovelier than the loveliest glance from Even's
placid star,
And brighter than the sea of gold,‡ the gorgeous
Himsagar.

In high Mohammed's boundless heaven Al Caw-
thor's stream may play,
The fount of youth may sparkling gush beneath
the western ray;§
And Tasnim's wave in crystal cups may glow with
musk and wine,
But oh! their lustre could not match one beauteous
tear of thine!

———

TO ——.

And shall we say the rose is sweet,
Nor grant that claim to thee,
In whom the loveliest virtues meet
In social harmony?

And shall we call the lily pure,
Nor grant that claim to thee,
Whose taintless, spotless soul is, sure,
The shrine of purity?

And shall we say the sun is bright,
Nor grant that claim to thee,
Whose form and mind with equal light
Both beam so radiantly?

———

THE PASSIONS.

"You have passions in your heart—scorpions; they sleep now—
beware how you awaken them! they will sting you even to death!"
—Mysteries of Udolpho, vol. iii.

Beware, beware, ere thou takest
The draught of misery!
Beware, beware ere thou wakest
The scorpions that sleep in thee!

The woes which thou canst not number,
As yet are wrapt in sleep;
Yet oh! yet they slumber,
But their slumbers are not deep.

Yet oh! yet while the rancor
Of hate has no place in thee,
While thy buoyant soul has an anchor
In youth's bright tranquil sea:

Yet oh! yet while the blossom
Of hope is blooming fair,
While the beam of bliss lights thy bosom—
Oh! rouse not the serpent there!

For bitter thy tears will trickle
'Neath misery's heavy load,
When the world has put in its sickle
To the crop which fancy sow'd.

---

* Vide Horace's ode, " Pulchris EXCUBAT in genis."
† Vide Sale's "Koran."
‡ See Sir William Jones on Eastern plants.
§ The fabled fountain of youth in the Bahamas, in search of which
Juan Ponce de Leon discovered Florida.

When the world has rent the cable
  That bound thee to the shore,
And launch'd thee weak and unable
  To bear the billow's roar;

Then the slightest touch will waken
  Those pangs that will always grieve thee,
And thy soul will be fiercely shaken
  With storms that will never leave thee!

So beware, beware, ere thou takest
  The draught of misery!
Beware, beware, ere thou wakest
  The scorpions that sleep in thee!

THE HIGH-PRIEST TO ALEXANDER.

"Derrame en todo el orbe de la tierra
Las armas, el furor, y nueva guerra."
La Araucana, Canto xvi.

Go forth, thou man of force!
  The world is all thine own;
Before thy dreadful course
  Shall totter every throne.
Let India's jewels glow
  Upon thy diadem:
Go, forth to conquest go,
  But spare Jerusalem.
    For the God of gods, which liveth
      Through all eternity.
    'Tis He alone which giveth
      And taketh victory:
    'Tis He the bow that blasteth,
      And breaketh the proud one's quiver;
    And the Lord of armies resteth
      In His Holy of Holies forever!

For God is Salem's spear,
  And God is Salem's sword:
What mortal man shall dare
  To combat with the Lord?
Every knee shall bow
  Before His awful sight;
Every thought sink low
  Before the Lord of might.
    For the God of gods, which liveth
      Through all eternity.
    'Tis He alone which giveth
      And taketh victory:
    'Tis He the bow that blasteth,
      And breaketh the proud one's quiver;
    And the Lord of armies resteth
      In His Holy of Holies forever!

"THE DEW, WITH WHICH THE EARLY MEAD IS DREST."

"Spes nunquam implenda."—LUCRETIUS.

The dew, with which the early mead is drest,
  Which fell by night inaudible and soft,
Mocks the foil'd eye that would its hues arrest,
  That glance and change so quickly and so oft.

So in this fruitless sublunary waste,
  This trance of life, this unsubstantial show,
Each hope we grasp at flies, to be replaced
  By one as fair and as fallacious too.

His limbs encased in aromatic wax,
  The joenud bee hies home his hoard to fill:
On human joys there lies the heavy tax
  Of hope unrealized, and beck'ning still.

But why with earth's vile fuel should we feed
  Those hopes which Heaven, and Heaven alone,
    should claim?
Why should we lean upon a broken reed,
  Or chase a meteor's evanescent flame?

O man! relinquish Passion's baleful joys,
  And bend at Virtue's bright unsullied shrine;
Oh! learn her chaste and hallow'd glow to prize,
  Pure—unalloy'd—ineffable—divine!

ON THE MOONLIGHT SHINING UPON A FRIEND'S GRAVE.

Show not, O moon! with pure and liquid beam,
  That mournful spot, where Memory fears to tread;
Glance on the grove, or quiver in the stream,
  Or tip the hills—but shine not on the dead:
It wounds the lonely hearts that still survive,
  And after buried friends are doom'd to live.

A CONTRAST.

Dost ask why Laura's soul is riv'n
  By pangs her prudence can't command?
To one who heeds not she has giv'n
  Her *heart*, alas! *without her hand.*

But Chloe claims our sympathy,
  To wealth a martyr and a slave;
For when the knot she dared to tie,
  Her hand without her heart she gave.

EPIGRAM.

A SAINT by soldiers fetter'd lay;
An angel took his bonds away.
An angel put the chains on me;
And 'tis a soldier sets me free.*

THE DYING CHRISTIAN.

"It cannot die, it cannot stay,
But leaves its darken'd dust behind."—BYRON.

I DIE—my limbs with icy feeling
  Bespeak that Death is near;
His frozen hand each pulse is stealing;
  Yet still I do not fear!

There is a hope—not frail as that
  Which rests on human things—
The hope of an immortal state,
  And with the King of kings!

And ye may gaze upon my brow,
  Which is not sad, tho' pale;
These hope-illumined features show
  But little to bewail.

Death should not chase the wonted bloom
  From off the Christian's face;
Ill prelude of the bliss to come,
  Prepared by heavenly grace.

* The reader must suppose a young man deeply in love, but persuaded by a friend in the army to lead a military life, and forgot the charms of the siren who cramped the vigor of his soul.

Lament no more—no longer weep
That I depart from men;
Brief is the intermediate sleep,
And bliss awaits me then!

"THOSE WORLDLY GOODS THAT, DISTANT, SEEM."

Those worldly goods that, distant, seem
With every joy and bliss to teem,
Are spurn'd as trivial when possess'd,
And, when acquired, delight us least:
As torrent-rainbows,* which appear
Still dwindling as we still draw near;
And yet contracting on the eye,
Till the bright circling colors die.

"HOW GAYLY SINKS THE GORGEOUS SUN WITHIN HIS GOLDEN BED."

" Tu fais naître la lumière
Du sein de l'obscurité."—ROUSSEAU.

How gayly sinks the gorgeous sun within his golden
bed,
As heaven's immortal azure glows and deepens into
red!
How gayly shines the burnish'd main beneath that
living light,
And trembles with his million waves magnificently
bright!
But ah! how soon that orb of day must close his
burning eye,
And night, in sable pall array'd, involve yon lovely
sky!
E'en thus in life our fairest scenes are preludes to
our woe;
For fleeting as that glorious beam is happiness
below.
But what? though evil fates may frown upon our
mortal birth,
Yet Hope shall be the star that lights our night of
grief on earth:
And she shall point to sweeter morns, when brighter
suns shall rise,
And spread the radiance of their rays o'er earth, and
sea, and skies!

"OH! YE WILD WINDS, THAT ROAR AND RAVE."

" It is the great army of the dead returning on the northern blast."
Song of the Five Bards in Ossian.

Oh! ye wild winds, that roar and rave
Around the headland's stormy brow,
That toss and heave the Baltic wave,
And bid the sounding forest bow,

---

* The term "rainbows" is not exactly applicable here, as I mean
the bow after it has assumed the circular figure. " The sun shining
full upon it (viz., the Fall of Staubbach) formed toward the bottom
of the fall a miniature rainbow extremely bright; while I stood at
some distance, the rainbow assumed a semicircular figure; as I ap-
proached, the extreme points gradually coincided, and formed a
complete circle of the most lively and brilliant colors. In order to
have a still fairer view, I ventured nearer and nearer, the circle at
the same time lessening smaller and smaller; and as I stood quite
under the fall, it suddenly disappeared."—COXE's Switzerland.

Whence is your course? and do ye bear
The sigh of other worlds along,
When through the dark immense of air
Ye rush in tempests loud and strong?

Methinks, upon your moaning course
I hear the army of the dead;
Each on his own invisible horse,
Triumphing in his trackless tread.

For when the moon conceals her ray,
And midnight spreads her darkest veil,
Borne on the air, and far away,
Upon the eddying blasts they sail.

Then, then their thin and feeble bands
Along the echoing winds are roll'd;
The bodiless tribes of other lands!
The formless, misty sons of old!

And then at times their wailings rise,
The shrilly wailings of the grave!
And mingle with the madden'd skies,
The rush of wind, and roar of wave.

Heard you that sound? It was the hum
Of the innumerable host,
As down the northern sky they come,
Lamenting o'er their glories lost.   .

Now for a space each shadowy king,
Who sway'd of old some mighty realm,
Mounts on the tempest's squally wing,
And grimly frowns thro' barred helm.

Now each dim ghost, with awful yells,
Uprears on high his cloudy form;
And with his feeble accent swells
The hundred voices of the storm.

Why leave ye thus the narrow cell,
Ye lords of night and anarchy!
Your robes the vapors of the dell,
Your swords the meteors of the sky?

Your bones are whitening on the heath;
Your fame is in the minds of men:
And would ye break the sleep of death,
That ye might live to war again?

SWITZERLAND.

"Tous les objets de mon amour,
Nos clairs ruisseaux,
Nos hameaux,
Nos coteaux,
Nos montagnes?"
Ranz des Vaches.

With Memory's eye,
Thou land of joy!
I view thy cliffs once more;
And tho' thy plains
Red slaughter stains,
'Tis Freedom's blessed gore.

Thy woody dells,
And shadowy fells,
Exceed a monarch's halls;
Thy pine-clad hills,
And gushing rills,
And foaming water-falls.

The Gallic foe
Has work'd thee woe,

But trumpet never scared thee;
How could he think
That thou wouldst shrink,
With all thy rocks to guard thee?

E'en now the Gaul,
That wrought thy fall,
At his own triumph wonders;
So long the strife
For death and life,
So lond our rival thunders!

Oh! when shall Time
Avenge the crime,
And to our rights restore us?
And bid the Seine
Be choked with slain,
And Paris quake before us?

———⁂———

A GLANCE.

Lady! you threw a glance at me,
I knew its meaning well;
He who has loved, and only he,
Its mysteries can tell:
That hieroglyphic of the brain,
Which none but Cupid's priests explain.[*]

———⁂———

BABYLON.

"Come down, and sit in the dust, O virgin daughter of Babylon, sit on the ground : there is no throne."—*Isaiah* xlvii.. 1.

Bow, daughter of Babylon, bow thee to dust!
Thine heart shall be quell'd, and thy pride shall be crush'd;
Weep, Babylon, weep! for thy splendor is past;
And they come like the storm in the day of the blast.

Howl, desolate Babylon, lost one and lone!
And bind thee in sackcloth—for where is thy throne?
Like a wine-press in wrath will I trample thee down,
And rend from thy temples the pride of thy crown.

Though thy streets be a hundred, thy gates be all brass,
Yet thy proud ones of war shall be wither'd like grass;
Thy gates shall be broken, thy strength be laid low,
And thy streets shall resound to the shouts of the foe!

Though thy chariots of power on thy battlements bound,
And the grandeur of waters encompass thee round;
Yet thy walls shall be shaken, thy waters shall fail,
Thy matrons shall shriek, and thy king shall be pale.

The terrible day of thy fall is at hand,
When my rage shall descend on the face of thy land;
The lances are pointed, the keen sword is bared,
The shields are anointed,[†] the helmets prepared.

I call upon Cyrus! He comes from afar,
And the armies of nations are gather'd to war:
With the blood of thy children his path shall be red,
And the bright sun of conquest shall blaze o'er his head!

Thou glory of kingdoms! thy princes are drunk,[*]
But their loins shall be loosed, and their hearts shall be sunk;
They shall crouch to the dust, and be counted as slaves,
At the roll of his wheels, like the rushing of waves!

For I am the Lord, who have mightily spann'd
The breadth of the heavens, and the sea and the land;
And the mountains shall flow at my presence,[†] and earth
Shall reel to and fro in the glance of my wrath!

Your proud domes of cedar on earth shall be thrown,
And the rank grass shall wave o'er the lonely hearth-stone;
And your sons and your sires and your daughters shall bleed
By the barbarous hands of the murdering Mede!

I will sweep ye away in destruction and death,
As the whirlwind that scatters the chaff with its breath;
And the fanes of your gods shall be sprinkled with gore,
And the course of your stream shall be heard of no more![‡]

There the wandering Arab shall ne'er pitch his tent,
But the beasts of the desert shall wail and lament;
In their desolate houses the dragons shall lie,
And the satyrs shall dance, and the bittern shall cry![§]

———⁂———

"OH! WERE THIS HEART OF HARD-EST STEEL."

"Vultus nimium lubricus aspici."—HORACE.

Oh! were this heart of hardest steel,
That steel should yield to thee;
And tho' naught else could make it feel,
'Twould melt thy form to see:
That eye, that cheek, that lip, possess
Such fascinating loveliness!

The first may claim whatever praise
By amorous bard is paid;
In the dark lightning of its rays
I view thy soul portray'd:
And in that soul what light must be,
When it imparts so bounteously!

Thy cheek, e'en in its humblest bloom,
Like rich carnation glows;
But when the mantling blushes come,
How fades the brightest rose!
Dead the fine hues, the beauty dead,
And coarse the velvet of its head.

Th' anemone's deep crimson dye
Beams on thy lip's red charm;
Thy voice is more than harmony,
Thy breath as sweet as balm:
But still more balmy would it be,
Would it but waft one sigh for me.

[*] None but the priests could interpret the Egyptian hieroglyphics.
[†] " Arise, ye princes, and anoint the shield."—*Isaiah* xxi., 5.

[*] "I will make drunk her princes."—*Jeremiah* li., 57.
[†] " The mountains melted from before the Lord."—*Judges* v., 5. "Oh that the mountains might flow down at thy presence !"—*Isaiah* lxiv., 1 ; and again, ver. 3, " The mountains flowed down at thy presence."
[‡] "A drought is upon her waters."—*Jeremiah* l., 38.
[§] *Vide* Isaiah xiii., 20.

To gaze on thee is ecstasy,
  Is ecstasy—but pain:
Such is thy lip, thy cheek, thine eye,
  I gaze, and gaze again:
Oh! might those three bright features bear
For me a kiss—a blush—a tear!

―――◇―――

THE SLIGHTED LOVER.

"Spes animi credula mutui."—HORACE.

I LOVED a woman, and too fondly thought
  The vows she made were constant and sincere;
But now, alas! in agony am taught,
  That she is faithless—I no longer dear!

Why was I frenzied when her bright black eye,
  With ray pernicious, flash'd upon my gaze?
Why did I burn with feverish ecstasy,
  Stung with her scorn, and ravish'd with her praise?

Would that her loveliness of form and mind
  Had only kindled friendship's calmer glow!
Then had I been more tranquil and resign'd,
  And her neglect had never touch'd me so.

But with such peerless charms before his sight,
  Who would not own resistless Love's control?
Feel the deep thrilling of intense delight,
  And lose at once the balance of his soul?

Such was my fate—one sole enchanting hope,
  One darling object from all else I chose:
That hope is gone—its blighted blossoms droop;
  And where shall hopeless passion find repose?

―――◇―――

"CEASE, RAILER, CEASE! UNTHINK-ING MAN."

"Cur in amicorum vitiis tam cernis acutum,
Quam aut aquila, aut serpens Epidaurius?"
HORACE.

CEASE, railer, cease! unthinking man,
  Is every virtue found in thee?
How plain another's faults we scan,
  Our own how faintly do we see!

So one who roves o'er marshy ground
  When evening fogs the scene obscure,
Sees vapor hung on all things round,
  And falsely deems his station pure!

―――◇―――

ANACREONTIC.

"Insanire juvat."—HORACE.

LET others of wealth and emolument dream,
  At profits exult, and at losses repine:
Far different my object, far different my theme—
  Warm love and frank friendship, and roses and wine!

Let other dull clods, without fancy or fire,
  Give my dear friend of Teos a mere poet's due;
Discarding his morals, his fancy admire,
  I deem him a bard, and a moralist too.

Ye sober, ye specious, ye sage, ye discreet!
  Your joys in perspective I never could brook;
With rapture I seize on whatever is sweet,
  Real, positive, present—no further I look.

I will not be fetter'd by maxims or duties:
  The cold charms of ethics I wholly despise:
My hours glide along amid bottles and beauties—
  There's nothing to match with old crust and bright eyes!

I vary my cups as his fashions the dandy,
  And one day the creatures of gin haunt my brain;
And the next I depute the same office to brandy;
  And so on, and so on, and the same round again!

I'm a flighty young spark—but I deem myself blest,
  And as happy a soul as my clerical brother;
Tho' the wish of a moment's first half's dispossest
  Of its sway o'er my mind, by the wish of the other.

And thou who this wild mode of living despisest,
  Sententious and grave, of thy apophthegms boast,
Cry shame of my nostrums; but I know who's wisest,
  Makes the best use of life, and enjoys it the most.

―――◇―――

"IN WINTER'S DULL AND CHEER-LESS REIGN."

"Deme supercilio nubem."—HORACE.

IN winter's dull and cheerless reign,
  What flower could ever glow?
Beneath the ice of thy disdain,
  What song could ever flow?

Restore thy smile!—beneath its ray
  The flower of verse shall rise:
And all the ice that froze my lay
  Be melted by thine eyes!

―――◇―――

SUNDAY MOBS.

Tho' we at times amid the mob may find
A beauteous face, with many a charm combined;
Yet still it wants the signature of mind.
On such a face no fine expression dwells,
That eye no inborn dignity reveals;
Tho' bright its jetty orb, as all may see,
The glance is vacant—has no charms for me.
When Sunday's sun is sinking in the west,
Our streets all swarm with numbers gayly drest;
Prank'd out in ribbons, and in silks array'd,
To catch the eyes of passing sons of trade.
Then giggling milliners swim pertly by,
Obliquely glancing with a roguish eye;
With short and airy gait they trip along,
And vulgar volubility of tongue:
Their minds well pictured in their every tread,
And that slight backward tossing of the head:
But no idea, 'faith, that harbors there,
Is independent of a stomacher.
Their metaphors from gowns and caps are sought,
And stays incorporate with every thought;
And if in passing them I can but spare
A moment's glance—far better thrown elsewhere—
They deem my admiration caught, nor wist
They turn it on an ancient fabulist,
Who aptly pictured, in the jackdaw's theft,
These pert aspirers of their wits bereft.
To these, as well as any under heaven,
A well-form'd set of features may be given:
But where's the halo? where's the spell divine?
And the sweet, modest, captivating mien?
"Those tenderer tints that shun the careless eye,"
Where are they?—far from these low groups they fly:

Yes, far indeed!—for here you cannot trace
The flash of intellect along the face;
No vermeil blush e'er spreads its lovely dye,
Herald of genuine sensibility.
These extras, e'en in beauty's absence, a charm;
But when combined with beauty, how they warm!
These are the charms that will not be withstood,
Sure signs of generous birth and gentle blood.
There is a something I cannot describe,
Beyond th' all-gaining influence of a bribe,
Which stamps the lady in the meanest rout,
And by its sure criterion marks her out;
Pervades each feature, thro' each action flows,
And lends a charm to every thing she does;
Which not the weeds of Irus could disguise,
And soon detected wheresoe'er it lies.

———————

PHRENOLOGY.

"Quorsum hæc tam putida tendunt?"—Horace.

A curious sect's in vogue, who deem the soul
Of man is legible upon his poll:
Give them a squint at yonder doctor's pate,
And they'll soon tell you why he dines on plate:
Ask why yon bustling statesman, who for years
Has pour'd his speeches in the senate's ears,
Tho' always in a politician's sweat,
Has hardly grasp'd the seals of office yet?
The problem gravels me—the man's possest
Of talents—this his many schemes attest.
The drawback, what?—they tell me, looking big,
"His skull was never moulded for intrigue."
Whence'er a culprit has consign'd his breath,
And proved the Scripture adage—death for death,
With peering eyes the zealous throng appear,
To see if murder juts behind his ear.
So far 'tis barely plausible:—but stay!
I ne'er can muster brass enough to say
That a rude lump, or bunch too prominent,
Is a bad symbol of a vicious bent.
But when the sages strike another key,
Consorting things that never will agree,
And my consistency of conduct rate
By inequalities upon my pate,[*]
And make an inharmonious bump the test
Of my delight in concord†—'tis at best
An awkward system, and not overwise,
And badly built on incoherences.
Another lustrum will behold our youth,
With eager souls all panting after truth,
Shrewd Spurzheim's visionary pages turn,
And, with Napoleon's bust before them, learn
Without the agency of what small bone
Quicklime had ne'er upon a host been thrown:
In what rough rise a trivial sink had saved
The towns he burnt, the nations he enslaved.‡
E'en now, when Harold's minstrel left the scene,
Where such a brilliant meteor he had been.
Thus with the same officiousness of pains,
Gazettes announced the volume of his brains.
Rise, sons of Science and Invention, rise!
Make some new inroad on the starry skies;
Draw from the main some truths unknown before,
Rummage the strata, every nook explore,
To lead mankind from this fantastic lore:
Solve the long-doubted problems pending still,
And these few blanks in nature's annals fill:
Tell us why Saturn rolls begirt with flame?
Whence the red depth of Mars's aspect came?
Are the dark tracts the silver moon displays
Dusk with the gloom of caverns or of seas?

* The bump of firmness. † The bump of tune.
‡ The Corsican's organ of destructiveness must have been very prominent.

Think ye, with Olbers, that her glow intense,
Erst deem'd volcanic, is reflected hence?
Are the black spots, which in yon sun appear
Long vistas thro' his flaming atmosphere,
Rents in his fiery robe, thro' which the eye
Gains access to his secret sanctuary?
Or may we that hypothesis explode,
Led by your science nearer to our God?
Shall we, with Glasgow's learned Watt, maintain
That yon bright bow is not produced by rain?
Or deem the theory but ill surmised,
And call it light (as Brewster) polarized?
Tell when the clouds their fleecy load resign,
How the frail nitre-moulded points combine;
What secret cause, when heaven and ocean greet,
Commands their close, or dictates their retreat.*
On you we rest, to check th' encroaching sway
This outré science gains from day to day;
Investigation's blood-hound scent employ
On themes more worthy of our scrutiny:
Rob this attractive magnet of its force,
And check this torrent's inundating course.

———————

LOVE.

I.

Almighty Love! whose nameless pow'r
  This glowing heart defines too well,
Whose presence cheers each fleeting hour,
  Whose silken bonds our souls compel,
  Diffusing such a sainted spell,

As gilds our being with the light
  Of transport and of rapturous bliss,
And almost seeming to unite
  The joys of other worlds to this,
  The heavenly smile, the rosy kiss;—

Before whose blaze my spirits shrink,
  My senses all are wrapt in thee,
Thy force I own too much, to think
  (So full, so great thine ecstasy)
  That thou art less than deity!

Thy golden chains embrace the land,
  The starry sky, the dark blue main;
And at the voice of thy command
  (So vast, so boundless is thy reign)
  All nature springs to life again!

II.

The glittering fly, the wondrous things
  That microscopic art descries;
The lion of the waste, which springs,
  Bounding upon his enemies;
The mighty sea-snake of the storm,
The vorticella's viewless form,†

The vast leviathan, which takes
  His pastime in the sounding floods;
The crafty elephant, which makes
  His haunts in Ceylon's spicy woods—
Alike confess thy magic sway,
Thy soul-enchanting voice obey!

Oh! whether thou, as bards have said,
  Of bliss or pain the partial giver,
Wingest thy shaft of pleasing dread
  From out thy well-stored golden quiver,
O'er earth thy cherub wings extending,
Thy sea-born mother's side attending;—

* The waterspout.
† See Baker on animalculæ.

Or else, as Indian fables say,
  Upon thine emerald lory riding,
Through gardens, 'mid the restless play
  Of fountains, in the moonbeam gliding,
'Mid sylph-like shapes of maidens dancing,
Thy scarlet standard high advancing;—

Thy fragrant bow of cane thou bendest,*
  Twanging the string of honey'd bees,
And thence the flower-tipp'd arrow sendest,
  Which gives or robs the heart of ease;
Camdeo, or Cupid, oh be near
To listen, and to grant my prayer!

———

TO ———.

The dew that sits upon the rose
The brilliant hue beneath it shows;
Nor can it hide the velvet dye
O'er which it glitters tremblingly.
The fine-wove veil thrown o'er thy face,
Betrays its bloom—thro' it we trace
A loveliness, tho' veil'd, reveal'd,
Too bright to be by ought conceal'd.

———

SONG.

To sit beside a crystal spring,
Cool'd by the passing zephyr's wing,
And bend my every thought to thee,
Is life, is bliss, is ecstasy!

And as within that spring I trace
Each line, each feature of my face;
The faithful mirror tells me true—
It tells me that I think of *you!*

———

IMAGINATION.

Perennial source of rapturous pleasure, hail!
Whose inexhaustive stores can never fail;
Thou ardent inmate of the poet's brain,
Bright as the sun and restless as the main,
From all material Nature's stores at will
Creating, blending, and arranging still;
Things in themselves both beautiful and grand,
Receive fresh lustre from thy kindling hand;
And even those whose abstract charms are few,
Thy spell-like touch arrays in colors bright and
  new.
Oh! thou art Poetry's informing soul,
Detach'd from thee she stagnates and is dull:
She has no sweets without thee, and from thee
Derives her magic and her majesty;
Thou art th' essential adjunct of her charms,
'Tis by thy aid that she transports and warms:
Nor will I e'er with that weak sect concur,
Who on obscurity alone confer
Thy misapplied and prostituted name—
A false and spurious and ungrounded claim!—
Construct a mass of thoughts uncouth and wild,
Their words involved, and meaning quite exiled;
A mazy labyrinth without a clue,
Wherein they lose themselves and readers too;
The crude abortions of a heated brain,
Where sense and symmetry are sought in vain!

  * See Sir William Jones's works, vol. vi., p. 318.

  "He bends the luscious cane, and twists the string;
  With bees how sweet, but ah! how keen the sting!
  He with five flowrets tips thy ruthless darts,
  Which tho' five senses pierce enraptured hearts."

But images both bright and sorted well,
And perspicuity, that crowning spell,
Fervor chastised by judgment and by taste,
And language vivid, elegant, and chaste—
These form the poet; in such garb array'd,
Then, Fancy, all thy beauties are display'd;
We feel thy loveliness and own thy sway.
Confess thy magic pow'r, and praise the glowing lay!

———

THE OAK OF THE NORTH.

  " Quæ quantum vertice ad auras
  Æthereas, tantum radice in Tartara tendit,
  Ergo non hyemes illam, non flabra, neque imbres
  Convellunt; immota manet, multosque nepotes
  Multa virum volvens durando sæcula vincit."
                                          VIRGIL.

Thou forest lord! whose deathless arms
    Full many an age of rolling time
Have mock'd the madness of the storms,
    Unfaded in thy shadowy prime
Thou livest still—and still shalt stay,
Tho' the destroying tyrant bow
The temple, and the tower, and lay
    The pomp and pride of empires low.
And it thy stately form be riven
And blasted by the fiery levin,
Still dost thou give that giant front,
Undaunted, to the pitiless brunt
    Of angry winds, that vainly rave;
And, like the scars by battle graven
Upon the bosoms of the brave,
The tokens of resistless heaven
Deep in thy rugged breast are seen.
The marks of frays that once have been;
The lightning's stroke, the whirlwind's force,
Have marr'd thee in their furious course,
But they have left thee unsubdued;
And if they bend thy crest awhile,
Thou dost arise in might renew'd,
    Tameless in undiminish'd toil,
Singly against an hostile host
    Contending, like th' immortal king,
Who quell'd the Titans' impious boast
    With thunder, tho' he stood alone
Defender of his starry throne,
    Dashing th' aspiring mountains down,
Dark Ossa, like a powerless thing,
And Pelion with his nodding pines;
    Then bound with adamantine chains,
Where the glad sunlight never shines,
    The earth-born in eternal pains.
Of many who were born with thee,
    Scarce now a thought survives to tell;
War hath ta'en some—their memory
    But faintly lives of those who fell:
Even the conqueror's glorious name,
    That boasts a life beyond the tomb,
Borne on the wings of rushing fame,
    May bow before the common doom,
Before the measure of its praise
Hath fill'd thy multitude of days.

And ere the poet's hallow'd star,
    Refulgent o'er his voiceless urn,
Glance thro' the gloom of years so far,
    Its living fires may cease to burn.
Thy mere existence shall be more
    Than others' immortality;
The spirits of the great, who bore
    A sway on earth, and still would be
Remember'd when they are not seen,
    Shall die like echoes on the wind,
Nor leave of all that they have been
    In living hearts one thrill behind;

Their very names shall be forgot,
  Ancient of days! ere thou art not.

The druid's mystic harp, that hung
  So long upon thy stormy boughs,
Mute as its master's magic tongue,
  Who slumbereth in that deep repose,
No earthly sound shall wake again,
  Nor glare of sacrificial fire,
Nor howl of victims in their pain,
  Or the weird priestess in her ire,
Hath mingled with th' oblivious dust
  Of him who called its spirit forth.
In those prophetic tones which hush'd
  The enraptured children of the north,
Binding them with a holy fear.
And smiting each enchanted ear
  With such a sound as seem'd to raise
The hidden forms of future days:
Sleep on!—no Roman foe alarms
  Your rest: and over ye shall wave
A guardian God's protecting arms,
  And flowers shall deck your grassy grave!

And he who gazeth on thee now,
  Ere long shall lie as low as they:
The daring heart, the intrepid brow,
  Not long can feel youth's joyous glow,
The strength of life must soon decay.
A few short years fleet swiftly by,
And rayless is the sparkling eye,
Mute the stern voice of high command,
And still oppression's iron hand:
The lords of earth shall waste away
Beneath the worm, and many a day
Of wintry frost and summer sun,
Ere yet thy number'd hours be done;
For thou art green and flourishing,
The mountain-forest's stately king,
Unshaken as the granite stone
That stands thine everlasting throne.

There was a tower, whose haughty head
  Erewhile rose darkly by thy side,
But they are number'd with the dead,
  Who ruled within its place of pride;
For time and overwhelming war
  Have crumbled it, and overthrown
Bulwark, and battlement, and bar,
  Column, and arch, and sculptured stone;
Around thy base are rudely strewn
  The tokens of departed power,
The wrecks of unrecorded fame
  Lie mouldering in the frequent shower:
But thou art there, the very same
As when those hearts, which now are cold,
First beat in triumph to behold
The shadow of its form, which fell
At distance o'er the darken'd dell.
No more the battle's black array
Shall sternly meet the rising day;
No beacon-fire's disastrous light
Flame fiercely in the perilous night.
Forgotten is that fortress now,
  Deserted is the feudal hall,
But here and there the red flowers blow
  Upon its bare and broken wall.
And ye may hear the night-wind moan
Thro' shatter'd hearths with moss o'ergrown,
  Wild grasses wave above the gate;
And where the trumpets sung at morn,
The tuneless night-bird dwells forlorn,
  And the unanswer'd ravens prate,
Till silence is more desolate.
For thou hast heard the clarion's breath
Pour from thy heights its blast of death,
While gathering multitudes replied
  Defiance with a shout that hurl'd

Back on their foes the curse of pride,
  And bended bows, and flags unfurl'd;
And swiftly from the hollow vale
Their arrowy vengeance glanced, like hail,
What time some fearless son of war,
  Emerging to the upper air,
Gain'd the arm'd steep's embattled brows,
  Thro' angry swords around him waving,
'Mid the leagued thousands of his foes,
  Their fury like a lion braving:
And faster than the summer rain
Stream'd forth the life-blood of the slain,
  Whom civil hate and feudal power
Mingled in that tempestuous hour,
Steeping thy sinewy roots, that drew
Fresh vigor from that deadly dew,
And still shall live—tho' monarchs fail;
  And those who waged the battle then
Are made the marvel of a tale,
  To warm the hearts of future men.
On such a sight did Cambria gaze,
  When Freedom on that dismal day
Saw Edward's haughty banners blaze
  Triumphant, and the dread array
In the deep vales beneath her gleam,
  Then started from her ancient throne,
That mighty song could not redeem
  From ruthless hands and hearts of stone.
While ages yield their fleeting breath,
  Art thou the only living thing
On earth, which all-consuming death
  Blasts not with his destroying wing?
No! thou shalt die!—tho' gloriously
  Those proud arms beat the azure air,
Some hour in Time's dark womb shall see
  The strength they boast no longer there.
Tho' to thy life, as to thy God's,
  Unnumber'd years are as a day,
When He, who is eternal, nods,
  Thy mortal strength must pass away.
Unconquer'd Fate, with viewless hand,
  Hath mark'd the moment of thy doom,
For He, who could create, hath spann'd
  Thy being, and its hour shall come:
Some thunderbolt more dread than all
  That ever scathed thee with their fire,
Arm'd with the force of heaven, shall fall
  Upon thee, and thou shalt expire!
Or age, that curbs a giant's might,
  Shall bow thee down and fade thy bloom,
The last of all, the bitterest blight
  That chills our hearts, except the tomb.
And then thou canst but faintly strive
  Against the foes thou has defied,
Returning spring shall not revive
  The beauty of thy summer pride:
And the green earth no more shall sleep
  Beneath thy dark and stilly shade,
Where silvery dews were wont to weep,
  And the red day-beam never stray'd,
But flow'rets of the tenderest hue,
  That live not in the garish noon,
Pale violets of a heavenly blue,
  Unfaded by the sultry sun,
Unwearied by the blasts that shook
  Thy lofty head, securely throve,
Nor heeded in that grassy nook
  The ceaseless wars that raged above.
The revelling elves at noon of night
  Shall throng no more beneath thy boughs,
When moonbeams shed a solemn light,
  And every star intensely glows;
No verdant canopy shall screen
  From view the orgies of their race,
But the blue heaven's unclouded sheen
  Shall pierce their secret dwelling-place.
Tho' now the lavrock pours at morn,
  Shrined in thy leaves, his rapturous lay,

Then shall the meanest songster scorn
   To hail thee, as he wings his way,
The troubled eagle, when he flies
   Before the lightnings, and the wrath
Of gathering winds and stormy skies,
   That darken o'er his cloudy path,
With ruffled breast and angry eye
   Shall pass thee, and descend in haste
Amid the sheltering bowers that lie
   Far down beneath the rolling blast.
Thine awful voice, that swells on high
   Above the rushing of the north,
Above the thunders of the sky,
   When midnight hurricanes come forth,
Like some fall'n conqueror's, who bewails
   His laurels torn, his humbled fame,
Shall murmur to the passing gales
   At once thy glory and thy shame!

———◇———

EXHORTATION TO THE GREEKS.

"En illa, illa quam sæpe optastis, libertas!"—SALLUST.

Arouse thee, O Greece! and remember the day,
When the millions of Xerxes were quell'd on their
   way!
Arouse thee, O Greece! let the pride of thy name
Awake in thy bosom the light of thy fame!
Why hast thou shone in the temple of glory?
   Why hast thou blazed in those annals of fame?
For know that the former bright page of thy story
Proclaims but thy bondage and tells but thy
   shame:
Proclaims from how high thou art fallen!—how low
Thou art plunged in the dark gulf of thraldom and
   woe!
Arouse thee, O Greece! from the weight of thy
   slumbers!
The chains are upon thee!—arise from thy sleep!
Remember the time, when nor nations nor numbers
   Could break thy thick phalanx embodied and
   deep.
Old Athens and Sparta remember the morning,
   When the swords of the Grecians were red to the
   hilt:
And, the bright gem of conquest her chaplet adorn-
   ing,
   Platæa rejoiced at the blood that ye spilt!
Remember the night, when, in shrieks of affright,
   The fleets of the East in your ocean were sunk!
Remember each day, when, in battle array,
   From the fountain of glory how largely ye drunk!
For there is not ought that a freeman can fear,
   As the fetters of insult, the name of a slave;
And there is not a voice to a nation so dear,
   As the war-song of freedom that calls on the brave.

———◇———

.

KING CHARLES'S VISION.

A vision somewhat resembling the following, and prophetic of the
Northern Alexander, is said to have been witnessed by Charles XI.
of Sweden, the antagonist of Sigismund. The reader will exclaim,
" Credat Judæus Apella !"

KING CHARLES was sitting all alone,
   In his lonely palace-tower,
When there came on his ears a heavy groan
   At the silent midnight hour.

He turn'd him round where he heard the sound,
   But nothing might he see;
And he only heard the nightly bird
   That shriek'd right fearfully.

He turn'd him round where he heard the sound,
   To his casement's arched frame;
"And he was aware of a light that was there,"*
   But he wist not whence it came.

He looked forth into the night,
   'Twas calm as night might be;
But broad and bright the flashing light
   Stream'd red and radiantly.

From ivory sheath his trusty brand
   Of stalwart steel he drew;
And he raised the lamp in his better hand,
   But its flame was dim and blue.

And he open'd the door of that palace-tower,
   But harsh turn'd the jarring key:
"By the Virgin's might," cried the king that night,
   "All is not as it should be!"

Slow turn'd the door of the crazy tower,
   And slowly again did it close;
And within and without, and all about,
   A sound of voices rose.

The king he stood in dreamy mood,
   For the voices his name did call;
Then on he past, till he came at last
   To the pillar'd audience-hall.

Eight-and-forty columns wide,
   Many and carved and tall
(Four-and-twenty on each side),
   Stand in that lordly hall.

The king had been pight† in the mortal fight,
   And struck the deadly blow;
The king he had strode in the red red blood,
   Often, afore, and now:

Yet his heart had ne'er been so harrow'd with fear
   As it was this fearful hour;
For his eyes were not dry, and his hair stood on
   high,
   And his soul had lost its power.

For a blue livid flame, round the hall where he
   came,
   In fiery circles ran;
And sounds of death, and chattering teeth,
   And gibbering tongues began.

He saw four-and-twenty statesmen old
   Round a lofty table sit;
And each in his hand did a volume hold,
   Wherein mighty things were writ.

In burning steel were their limbs all cased;
   On their cheeks was the flush of ire:
Their armor was braced, and their helmets were
   laced,
   And their hollow eyes darted fire.

With sceptre of might, and with gold crown bright,
   And locks like the raven's wing,
And in regal state at that board there sat
   The likeness of a king.

With crimson tinged, and with ermine fringed,
   And with jewels spangled o'er,

———

* " And he was aware of a Gray-friar."
                            The Gray Brother.
   " And he was aware of a knight that was there."
                        The Baron of Smalhome.

†   " A hideous rock is *pight*
   Of mighty magnes-stone."—SPENSER.
   " You vile abominable tents,
   Thus proudly *pight* upon our Phrygian plains!"
                           SHAKSPEARE.

And rich as the beam of the sun on the stream,
A sparkling robe he wore.*

Yet though fair shone the gem on his proud dia-
  dem,
  Though his robe was jewell'd o'er,
Though brilliant the vest on his mailed breast,
  Yet they all were stain'd with gore!

And his eye darted ire, and his glance shot fire,
  And his look was high command;
And each, when he spoke, struck his mighty book,
  And raised his shadowy hand.

And a headman stood by, with his axe on high,
  And quick was his ceaseless stroke;
And loud was the shock on the echoing block,
  As the steel shook the solid oak.

While short and thick came the mingled shriek
  Of the wretches who died by his blow;
And fast fell each head on the pavement red,
  And warm did the life-blood flow.

Said the earthly king to the ghostly king,
  "What fearful sights are those?"
Said the ghostly king to the earthly king,
  "They are signs of future woes!"

---

* This is, perhaps, an unpardonable falsehood, since it is well
known that Charles was so great an enemy to finery as even to object to the appearance of the Duke of Marlborough on that account.
Let those readers, therefore, whose critical nicety this passage offends substitute the following stanza, which is "the whole truth, and
nothing but the truth :"

  With buttons of brass that glitter'd like glass,
    And brows that were crown'd with bays,
  With large blue coat, and with black jack-boot,
    The theme of his constant praise.

Nothing indeed could exceed Charles's affection for his boots: he
eat, drank, and slept in them; nay, he never went on a bootless er-
rand. When the dethroned monarch Augustus waited upon him with
proposals of peace, Charles entertained him with a long dissertation
on his unparalleled aforesaid jack-boots: he even went so far as to
threaten (according to Voltaire), in an authoritative epistle to the
Senate at Stockholm, that unless they proved less refractory, he
would send them one of his boots as regent ! Now this, we must
allow, was a step beyond Caligula's consul.

Said the earthly king to the ghostly king,
  "By St. Peter, who art thou ?"
Said the ghostly king to the earthly king,
  "I shall be, but I am not now."

Said the earthly king to the ghostly king,
  "But when will thy time draw nigh ?"
"Oh! the sixth after thee will a warrior be,
  And that warrior am I.

"And the lords of the earth shall be pale at my birth,
  And conquest shall hover o'er me;
And the kingdoms shall shake, and the nations shall
    quake,
  And the thrones fall down before me.

"And Cracow shall bend to my majesty,
  And the haughty Dane shall bow;
And the Pole shall fly from my piercing eye,
  And the scowl of my clouded brow.

"And around my way shall the hot balls play,
  And the red-tongued flames arise;
And my pathway shall be on the midnight sea,
  'Neath the frown of the wintry skies.

"Thro' narrow pass, over dark morass,
  And the waste of the weary plain,
Over ice and snow, where the dark streams flow,
  Thro' the woods of the wild Ukraine.

"And though sad be the close of my life and my
    woes,
  And the hand that shall slay me unshown;
Yet in every clime, thro' the lapse of all time,
  Shall my glorious conquests be known.

"And blood shall be shed, and the earth shall be red
  With the gore of misery;
And swift as this flame shall the light of my fame
  O'er the world as brightly fly."

As the monarch spoke, crew the morning cock,
  When all that pageant bright,
And the glitter of gold, and the statesmen old,
  Fled into the gloom of night !

THE LOVER'S TALE.

THE original Preface to "The Lover's Tale" states that it was composed in my nineteenth year. Two only of the three parts then written were printed, when, feeling the imperfection of the poem, I withdrew it from the press. One of my friends, however, who, boy-like, admired the boy's work, distributed among our common associates of that hour some copies of these two parts, without my knowledge, without the omissions and amendments which I had in contemplation, and marred by the many misprints of the compositor. Seeing that these two parts have of late been mercilessly pirated, and that what I had deemed scarce worthy to live is not allowed to die, may I not be pardoned if I suffer the whole poem at last to come into the light, accompanied with a reprint of the sequel—a work of my mature life—"The Golden Supper?"

May, 1879.

ARGUMENT.

JULIAN, whose cousin and foster-sister, Camilla, has been wedded to his friend and rival, Lionel, endeavors to narrate the story of his own love for her, and the strange sequel. He speaks (in Parts II. and III.) of having been haunted by visions and the sound of bells, tolling for a funeral, and at last ringing for a marriage; but he breaks away, overcome, as he approaches the Event, and a witness to it completes the tale.

I.

HEAR far away, seen from the topmost cliff,
Filling with purple gloom the vacancies
Between the tufted hills, the sloping seas
Hung in mid-heaven, and half-way down rare sails,
White as white clouds, floated from sky to sky.
Oh! pleasant breast of waters, quiet bay,
Like to a quiet mind in the loud world,
Where the chafed breakers of the outer sea
Sank powerless, as anger falls aside
And withers on the breast of peaceful love;
Thou didst receive the growth of pines that fledged
The hills that watched thee, as Love watcheth Love,
In thine own essence, and delight thyself
To make it wholly thine on sunny days.
Keep thou thy name of "Lover's Bay." See, sirs,
Even now the Goddess of the Past, that takes
The heart, and sometimes touches but one string
That quivers, and is silent, and sometimes
Sweeps suddenly all its half-moulder'd chords
To some old melody, begins to play
That air which pleased her first. I feel thy breath;
I come, great Mistress of the ear and eye:
Thy breath is of the pinewood; and tho' years
Have hollow'd out a deep and stormy strait
Betwixt the native land of Love and me,
Breathe but a little on me, and the sail
Will draw me to the rising of the sun,
The lucid chambers of the morning star,
And East of Life.

            Permit me, friend, I prithee,
To pass my hand across my brows, and muse
On those dear hills, that never more will meet
The sight that throbs and aches beneath my touch,
As tho' there beat a heart in either eye;
For when the outer lights are darken'd thus,
The memory's vision hath a keener edge.
It grows upon me now—the semicircle
Of dark blue waters and the narrow fringe
Of curving beach—its wreaths of dripping green—
Its pale pink shells—the summer-house aloft
That open'd on the pines with doors of glass,
A mountain nest—the pleasure-boat that rock'd,
Light green with its own shadow, keel to keel,
Upon the dappled dimplings of the wave,
That blanch'd upon its side.

                O Love, O Hope!
They come, they crowd upon me all at once—
Moved from the cloud of unforgotten things,
That sometimes on the horizon of the mind
Lies folded, often sweeps athwart in storm—
Flash upon flash they lighten thro' me—days
Of dewy dawning and the amber eves
When thou and I, Camilla, thou and I
Were borne about the bay or safely moor'd
Beneath a low-brow'd cavern, where the tide
Plash'd, sapping its worn ribs; and all without
The slowly ridging rollers on the cliffs
Clash'd, calling to each other, and thro' the arch
Down those loud waters, like a setting star,
Mixt with the gorgeous west the light-house shone,
And silver-smiling Venus ere she fell
Would often loiter in her balmy blue,
To crown it with herself.

                Here, too, my love
Waver'd at anchor with me, when day hung
From his mid-dome in Heaven's airy halls;
Gleams of the water-circles as they broke,
Flicker'd like doubtful smiles about her lips,
Quiver'd a flying glory on her hair,
Leapt like a passing thought across her eyes;
And mine with one that will not pass, till earth
And heaven pass too, dwelt on my heaven, a face
Most starry-fair, but kindled from within
As 'twere with dawn. She was dark-haired, dark-eyed.
Oh, such dark eyes! a single glance of them
Will govern a whole life from birth to death,
Careless of all things else, led on with light
In trances and in visions: look at them,
You lose yourself in utter ignorance;
You can not find their depth; for they go back,
And farther back, and still withdraw themselves
Quite into the deep soul, that evermore
Fresh springing from her fountains in the brain,
Still pouring thro' floods with redundant life
Her narrow portals.

                Trust me, long ago
I should have died, if it were possible
To die in gazing on that perfectness
Which I do bear within me: I had died,
But from my farthest lapse, my latest ebb,
Thine image, like a charm of light and strength
Upon the waters, push'd me back again
On these deserted sands of barren life.
Tho' from the deep vault where the heart of Hope
Fell into dust, and crumbled in the dark—
Forgetting how to render beautiful
Her countenance with quick and healthful blood—
Thou didst not sway me upward; could I perish
While thou, a meteor of the sepulchre,

Didst swathe thyself all round Hope's quiet urn
Forever? He, that saith it, hath o'erslept
The slippery footing of his narrow wit,
And fall'n away from judgment. Thou art light,
To which my spirit leaneth all her flowers,
And length of days, and immortality
Of thought, and freshness ever self-renew'd.
For Time and Grief abode too long with Life,
And, like all other friends i' the world, at last
They grew aweary of her fellowship:
So Time and Grief did beckon unto Death,
And Death drew nigh and beat the doors of Life;
But thou didst sit alone in the inner house,
A wakeful portress, and didst parle with Death,—
" This is a charmèd dwelling which I hold;"
So Death gave back, and would no farther come.
Yet is my life nor in the present time,
Nor in the present place. To me alone,
Push'd from his chair of regal heritage,
The Present is the vassal of the Past:
So that, in that I *have* lived, do I live,
And can not die, and am, in having been—
A portion of the pleasant yesterday,
Thrust forward on to-day and out of place;
A body journeying onward, sick with toil,
The weight as if of age upon my limbs,
The grasp of hopeless grief about my heart,
And all the senses weaken'd, save in that,
Which long ago they had glean'd and garner'd up
Into the granaries of memory—
The clear brow, bulwark of the precious brain,
Chink'd as you see, and seam'd—and all the while
The light soul twines and mingles with the growths
Of vigorous early days, attracted, won,
Married, made one with, molten into all
The beautiful in Past of act or place,
And like the all-enduring camel, driven
Far from the diamond fountain by the palms,
Who toils across the middle moon lit nights,
Or when the white heats of the blinding noons
Beat from the concave sand; yet in him keeps
A draught of that sweet fountain that he loves,
To stay his feet from falling, and his spirit
From bitterness of death.

Ye ask me, friends,
When I began to love. How should I tell you?
Or from the after-fullness of my heart,
Flow back again unto my slender spring
And first of love, tho' every turn and depth
Between is clearer in my life than all
Its present flow. Ye know not what ye ask.
How should the broad and open flower tell
What sort of bud it was, when, prest together
In its green sheath, close-lapt in silken folds,
It seem'd to keep its sweetness to itself,
Yet was not the less sweet for that it seem'd?
For young Life knows not when young Life was born,
But takes it all for granted: neither Love,
Warm in the heart, his cradle, can remember
Love in the womb, but resteth satisfied,
Looking on her that brought him to the light:
Or as men know not when they fall asleep
Into delicious dreams, our other life,
So know I not when I began to love.
This is my sum of knowledge—that my love
Grew with myself—say rather, was my growth,
My inward sap, the hold I have on earth,
My outward circling air wherewith I breathe,
Which yet upholds my life, and evermore
Is to me daily life and daily death:
For how should I have lived and not have loved?
Can ye take off the sweetness from the flower,
The color and the sweetness from the rose,
And place them by themselves; or set apart
Their motions and their brightness from the stars,
And then point out the flower or the star?
Or build a wall betwixt my life and love,

And tell me where I am? 'Tis even thus:
In that I live I love; because I love
I live: whate'er is fountain to the one
Is fountain to the other; and whene'er
Our God unknits the riddle of the one,
There is no shade or fold of mystery
Swathing the other.

Many, many years
(For they seem many and my most of life,
And well I could have linger'd in that porch,
So unproportion'd to the dwelling-place),
In the May dews of childhood, opposite
The flush and dawn of youth, we lived together,
Apart, alone together on those hills.

Before he saw my day my father died,
And he was happy that he saw it not;
But I and the first daisy on his grave
From the same clay came into light at once.
As Love and I do number equal years,
So she, my love, is of an age with me.
How like each other was the birth of each!
On the same morning, almost the same hour,
Under the selfsame aspect of the stars
(Oh falsehood of all starcraft!), we were born.
How like each other was the birth of each!
The sister of my mother—she that bore
Camilla close beneath her beating heart,
Which to the imprison'd spirit of the child,
With its true-touch'd pulses in the flow
And hourly visitation of the blood,
Sent notes of preparation manifold,
And mellow'd echoes of the outer world—
My mother's sister, mother of my love,
Who had a twofold claim upon my heart,
One twofold mightier than the other was,
In giving so much beauty to the world,
And so much wealth as God had charged her with—
Loathing to put it from herself forever,
Left her own life with it; and dying thus,
Crown'd with her highest act the placid face
And breathless body of her good deeds past.

So were we born, so orphan'd. She was motherless
And I without a father. So from each
Of those two pillars which from earth uphold
Our childhood, one had fallen away, and all
The careful burden of our tender years
Trembled upon the other. He that gave
Her life, to me delightedly fulfill'd
All loving-kindnesses, all offices
Of watchful care and trembling tenderness.
He waked for both: he pray'd for both: he slept
Dreaming of both: nor was his love the less
Because it was divided, and shot forth
Boughs on each side, laden with wholesome shade,
Wherein we nested sleeping or awake,
And sang aloud the matin-song of life.

She was my foster-sister: on one arm
The flaxen ringlets of our infancies
Wander'd, the while we rested: one soft lap
Pillow'd us both: a common light of eyes
Was on us as we lay: our baby lips,
Kissing one bosom, ever drew from thence
The stream of life, one stream, one life, one blood,
One sustenance, which, still as thought grew large,
Still larger moulding all the house of thought,
Made all our tastes and fancies like, perhaps—
All—all but one; and strange to me, and sweet,
Sweet thro' strange years to know that whatsoe'er
Our general mother meant for me alone,
Our mutual mother dealt to both of us:
So what was earliest mine in earliest life,
I shared with her in whom myself remains.
As was our childhood, so our infancy,
They tell me, was a very miracle

Of fellow-feeling and communion.
They tell me that we would not be alone,—
We cried when we were parted; when I wept,
Her smile lit up the rainbow on my tears,
Staid on the cloud of sorrow; that we loved
The sound of one another's voices more
Than the gray cuckoo loves his name, and learnt
To lisp in tune together; that we slept
In the same cradle always, face to face,
Heart beating time to heart, lip pressing lip,
Folding each other, breathing on each other,
Dreaming together (dreaming of each other
They should have added), till the morning light
Sloped thro' the pines, upon the dewy pane
Falling, unseal'd our eyelids, and we woke
To gaze upon each other. If this be true,
At thought of which my whole soul languishes
And faints, and hath no pulse, no breath—as tho'
A man in some still garden should infuse
Rich atar in the bosom of the rose,
Till, drunk with its own wine, and overfull
Of sweetness, and in smelling of itself,
It fall on its own thorns—if this be true—
And that way my wish leads me evermore
Still to believe it—'tis so sweet a thought,
Why in the utter stillness of the soul
Doth question'd memory answer not, nor tell
Of this our earliest, our closest-drawn,
Most loveliest, earthly-heavenliest harmony?

O blossom'd portal of the lonely house,
Green prelude, April promise, glad new-year
Of Being, which with earliest violets
And lavish carol of clear-throated larks
Fill'd all the March of life!—I will not speak of thee;
These have not seen thee, these can never know thee,
They can not understand me. Pass we then
A term of eighteen years. Ye would but laugh,
If I should tell you how I hoard in thought
The faded rhymes and scraps of ancient crones.
Gray relics of the nurseries of the world,
Which are as gems set in my memory,
Because she learnt them with me; or what use
To know her father left us just before
The daffodil was blown? or how we found
The dead man cast upon the shore? All this
Seems to the quiet daylight of your minds
But cloud and smoke, and in the dark of mine
Is traced with flame. Move with me to the event.

There came a glorious morning, such a one
As dawns but once a season. Mercury
On such a morning would have flung himself
From cloud to cloud, and swum with balanced wings
To some tall mountain: when I said to her,
"A day for Gods to stoop," she answered, "Ay,
And men to soar;" for as that other gazed,
Shading his eyes till all the fiery cloud,
The prophet and the chariot and the steeds,
Suck'd into oneness like a little star
Were drunk into the inmost blue, we stood,
When first we came from out the pines at noon,
With hands for eaves, uplooking and almost
Waiting to see some blessed shape in heaven,
So bathed we were in brilliance. Never yet
Before or after have I known the spring
Pour with such sudden deluges of light
Into the middle summer; for that day
Love, rising, shook his wings, and charged the winds
With spiced May-sweets from bound to bound, and
    blew
Fresh fire into the sun, and from within
Burst thro' the heated buds, and sent his soul
Into the songs of birds, and touch'd far off
His mountain-altars, his high hills, with flame
Milder and purer.

            Thro' the rocks we wound:
The great pine shook with lonely sounds of joy
That came on the sea-wind. As mountain streams
Our bloods ran free: the sunshine seem'd to brood
More warmly on the heart than on the brow.
We often paused, and, looking back, we saw
The clefts and openings in the mountains fill'd
With the blue valley and the glistening brooks,
And all the low dark groves, a land of love!
A land of promise, a land of memory,
A land of promise flowing with the milk
And honey of delicious memories!
And down to sea, and far as eye could ken,
Each way from verge to verge a Holy Land,
Still growing holier as you near'd the bay,
For there the Temple stood.

            When we had reach'd
The grassy platform on some hill, I stoop'd,
I gather'd the wild herbs, and for her brows
And mine made garlands of the selfsame flower,
Which she took smiling, and with my work thus
Crown'd her clear forehead. Once or twice she told me
(For I remember all things) to let grow
The flowers that ran poison in their veins.
She said, "The evil flourish in the world."
Then playfully she gave herself the lie—
"Nothing in nature is unbeautiful,
So, brother, pluck, and spare not." So I wove
Ev'n the dull-blooded poppy-stem, "whose flower,
Hued with the scarlet of a fierce sunrise,
Like to the wild youth of an evil prince,
Is without sweetness, but who crowns himself
Above the secret poisons of his heart
In his old age." A graceful thought of hers
Grav'n on my fancy! And oh, how like a nymph,
A stately mountain nymph she look'd! how native
Unto the hills she trod on! While I gazed,
My coronal slowly disentwined itself
And fell between us both; tho' while I gazed
My spirit leapt as with those thrills of bliss
That strike across the soul in prayer, and show us
That we are surely heard. Methought a light
Burst from the garland I had wov'n, and stood
A solid glory on her bright black hair;
A light methought broke from her dark, dark eyes,
And shot itself into the singing winds;
A mystic light flash'd ev'n from her white robe
As from a glass in the sun, and fell about
My footsteps on the mountains.

            Last we came
To what our people call "The Hill of Woe."
A bridge is there, that, look'd at from beneath,
Seems but a cobweb filament to link
The yawning of an earthquake-cloven chasm.
And thence one night, when all the winds were loud,
A woful man (for so the story went)
Had thrust his wife and child and dash'd himself
Into the dizzy depth below. Below,
Fierce in the strength of far descent, a stream
Flies with a shatter'd foam along the chasm.
The path was perilous, loosely strewn with crags:
We mounted slowly: yet to both there came
The joy of life in steepness overcome,
And victories of ascent, and looking down
On all that had look'd down on us; and joy
In breathing nearer heaven; and joy to me,
High over all the azure-circled earth,
To breathe with her as if in heaven itself;
And more than joy that I to her became
Her guardian and her angel, raising her
Still higher, past all peril, until she saw
Beneath her feet the region far away,
Beyond the nearest mountain's bosky brows,
Burst into open prospect—heath and hill,
And hollow lined and wooded to the lips,
And steep-down walls of battlemented rock
Gilded with broom, or shatter'd into spires,
And glory of broad waters interfused,

Whence rose as it were breath and steam of gold,
And over all the great wood rioting
And climbing, streak'd or starr'd at intervals
With falling brook or blossom'd bush—and last,
Framing the mighty landscape to the west,
A purple range of mountain-cones, between
Whose interspaces gush'd in blinding bursts
The incorporate blaze of sun and sea.

           At length
Descending from the point and standing both,
There on the tremulous bridge, that from beneath
Had seem'd a gossamer filament up in air,
We paused amid the splendor. All the west
And ev'n unto the middle south was ribb'd
And barr'd with bloom on bloom. The sun below,
Held for a space 'twixt cloud and wave, shower'd down
Rays of a mighty circle, weaving over
That various wilderness a tissue of light
Unparallel'd. On the other side, the moon,
Half melted into thin blue air, stood still,
And pale and fibrous as a wither'd leaf,
Nor yet endured in presence of His eyes
To indue his lustre; most unlover-like,
Since in his absence full of light and joy,
And giving light to others. But this most,
Next to her presence whom I loved so well,
Spoke loudly even unto my inmost heart
As to my outward hearing: the loud stream,
Forth issuing from his portals in the crag
(A visible link unto the home of my heart),
Ran amber toward the west, and nigh the sea
Parting my own loved mountains was received,
Shorn of its strength, into the sympathy
Of that small bay, which out to open main
Glow'd intermingling close beneath the sun.
Spirit of Love! that little hour was bound
Shut in from Time, and dedicate to thee.
Thy fires from heaven had touch'd it, and the earth
They fell on became hallow'd evermore.

  We turn'd: our eyes met: hers were bright, and mine
Were dim with floating tears, that shot the sunset
In lightnings round me, and my name was borne
Upon her breath. Henceforth my name has been
A hallow'd memory like the names of old,
A centred, glory-circled memory,
And a peculiar treasure, brooking not
Exchange or currency; and in that hour
A hope flow'd round me, like a golden mist
Charm'd amid eddies of melodious airs,
A moment, ere the onward whirlwind shatter it,
Waver'd and floated—which was less than Hope,
Because it lack'd the power of perfect Hope;
But which was more and higher than all Hope,
Because all other Hope had lower aim;
Even that this name to which her gracious lips
Did lend such gentle utterance, this one name,
In some obscure hereafter, might inwreathe
(How lovelier, nobler then!) her life, her love,
With my life, love, soul, spirit, and heart and strength.
  "Brother," she said, "let this be call'd henceforth
The Hill of Hope;" and I replied, "O sister,
My will is one with thine, the Hill of Hope."
Nevertheless, we did not change the name.
  I did not speak: I could not speak my love.
Love lieth deep: Love dwells not in lip-depths.
Love wraps his wings on either side the heart,
Constraining it with kisses close and warm,
Absorbing all the incense of sweet thoughts
So that they pass not to the shrine of sound.
Else had the life of that delighted hour
Drunk in the largeness of the utterance
Of Love; but how should Earthly measure mete
The Heavenly-unmeasured or unlimited Love,
Who scarce can tune his high majestic sense
Unto the thunder-song that wheels the spheres,
Scarce living in the Æolian harmony,   .

And flowing odor of the spacious air,
Scarce housed within the circle of this Earth,
Be cabin'd up in words and syllables,
Which pass with that which breathes them? Sooner
    Earth
Might go round Heaven, and the strait girth of Time
Inswathe the fullness of Eternity,
Than language grasp the infinite of Love.

  O day which did enwomb that happy hour,
Thou art blessed in the years, divinest day!
O Genius of that hour which dost uphold
Thy coronal of glory like a God,
Amid thy melancholy mates far-seen,
Who walk before thee, ever turning round
To gaze upon thee till their eyes are dim
With dwelling on the light and depth of thine,
Thy name is ever worshipp'd among hours!
Had I died then, I had not seem'd to die,
For bliss stood round me like the light of Heaven—
Had I died then, I had not known the death;
Yea had the Power from whose right hand the light
Of Life issueth, and from whose left hand floweth
The Shadow of Death, perennial effluences,
Whereof to all that draw the wholesome air,
Somewhile the one must overflow the other;
Then had he stemm'd my day with night, and driven
My current to the fountain whence it sprang,—
Even his own abiding excellence—
On me, methinks, that shock of gloom had full'n
Unfelt, and in this glory I had merged
The other, like the sun I gazed upon,
Which seeming for the moment due to death,
And dipping his head low beneath the verge,
Yet bearing round about him his own day,
In confidence of unabated strength,
Steppeth from Heaven to Heaven, from light to light,
And holdeth his undimmed forehead far
Into a clearer zenith, pure of cloud.

  We trod the shadow of the downward hill;
We past from light to dark. On the other side
Is scoop'd a cavern and a mountain hall,
Which none have fathom'd. If you go far in
(The country people rumor) yon may hear
The moaning of the woman and the child,
Shut in the secret chambers of the rock.
I too have heard a sound—perchance of streams
Running far on within its inmost halls,
The home of darkness; but the cavern-mouth,
Half overtrailed with a wanton weed,
Gives birth to a brawling brook, that passing lightly
Adown a natural stair of tangled roots,
Is presently received in a sweet grave
Of eglantines, a place of burial
Far lovelier than its cradle; for unseen,
But taken with the sweetness of the place,
It makes a constant bubbling melody
That drowns the nearer echoes. Lower down
Spreads out a little lake, that, flooding, leaves
Low banks of yellow sand; and from the woods
That belt it rise three dark, tall cypresses,—
Three cypresses, symbols of mortal woe,
That men plant over graves.

              .   Hither we came,
And sitting down upon the golden moss,
Held converse sweet and low—low converse sweet,
In which our voices bore least part. The wind
Told a love tale beside us, how he woo'd
The waters, and the waters answering lisp'd
To kisses of the wind, that, sick with love,
Fainted at intervals, and grew again
To utterance of passion. Ye can not shape
Fancy so fair as is this memory.
Methought all excellence that ever was
Had drawn herself from many thousand years,
And all the separate Edens of this earth,

To centre in this place and time. I listen'd,
And her words stole with most prevailing sweetness
Into my heart, as thronging fancies come
To boys and girls when summer days are new,
And soul and heart and body are all at ease:
What marvel my Camilla told me all?
It was so happy an hour, so sweet a place,
And I was the brother of her blood,
And by that name I moved upon her breath;
Dear name, which had too much of nearness in it
And heralded the distance of this time!
At first her voice was very sweet and low,
As if she were afraid of utterance;
But in the onward current of her speech
(As echoes of the hollow-banked brooks
Are fashion'd by the channel which they keep),
Her words did of their meaning borrow sound,
Her cheek did catch the color of her words.
I heard and trembled, yet I could but hear:
My heart paused—my raised eyelids would not fall,
But still I kept my eyes upon the sky.
I seem'd the only part of Time stood still.
And saw the motion of all other things;
While her words, syllable by syllable,
Like water, drop by drop, upon my ear
Fell; and I wish'd, yet wish'd her not to speak;
But she spake on, for I did name no wish.
What marvel my Camilla told me all
Her maiden dignities of Hope and Love—
"Perchance," she said, "return'd." Even then the stars
Did tremble in their stations as I gazed;
But she spake on, for I did name no wish,
No wish—no hope. Hope was not wholly dead.
But breathing hard at the approach of Death,—
Camilla, my Camilla, who was mine
No longer in the dearest sense of mine—
For all the secret of her inmost heart,
And all the maiden empire of her mind,
Lay like a map before me, and I saw
There, where I hoped myself to reign as king,
There, where that day I crown'd myself as king,
There in my realm and even on my throne,
Another! then it seem'd as tho' a link
Of some tight chain within my inmost frame
Was riven in twain: that life I heeded not
Flow'd from me, and the darkness of the grave,
The darkness of the grave and utter night,
Did swallow up my vision; at her feet,
Even the feet of her I loved, I fell,
Smit with exceeding sorrow unto Death.

Then had the earth beneath me yawning cloven
With such a sound as when an iceberg splits
From cope to base—had Heaven from all her doors,
With all her golden thresholds clashing, roll'd
Her heaviest thunder—I had lain as dead,
Mute, blind, and motionless as then I lay;
Dead, for henceforth there was no life for me!
Mute, for henceforth what use were words to me!
Blind, for the day was as the night to me!
The night to me was kinder than the day:
The night in pity took away my day,
Because my grief as yet was newly born
Of eyes too weak to look upon the light;
And thro' the hasty notice of the ear
Frail Life was startled from the tender love
Of him she brooded over. Would I had lain
Until the plaited ivy-tress had wound
Round my worn limbs, and the wild brier had driven
Its knotted thorns thro' my unpaining brows,
Leaning its roses on my faded eyes.
The wind had blown above me, and the rain
Had fall'n upon me, and the gilded snake
Had nestled in this bosom-throne of Love,
But I had been at rest for evermore.

Long time entrancement held me. All too soon

Life (like a wanton too-officious friend,
Who will not hear denial, vain and rude
With proffer of unwished-for services)
Entering all the avenues of sense
Past thro' into his citadel, the brain,
With hated warmth of apprehensiveness.
And first the chillness of the sprinkled brook
Smote on my brows, and then I seem'd to hear
Its murmur, as the drowning seaman hears,
Who with his head below the surface dropt
Listens the muffled booming indistinct
Of the confused floods, and dimly knows
His head shall rise no more: and then came in
The white light of the weary moon above.
Diffused and molten into flaky cloud.
Was my sight drunk that it did shape to me
Him who should own that name? Were it not well
If so be that the echo of that name
Ringing within the fancy had updrawn
A fashion and a phantasm of the form
It should attach to? Phantom!—had the ghastliest
That ever lasted for a body, sucking
The foul steam of the grave to thicken by it,
There in the shuddering moonlight brought its face
And what it has for eyes as close to mine
As he did—better that than his, than he
The friend, the neighbor, Lionel, the beloved,
The loved, the lover, the happy Lionel,
The low-voiced, tender-spirited Lionel,
All joy, to whom my agony was a joy.
O how her choice did leap forth from his eyes!
O how her love did clothe itself in smiles
About his lips! and—not one moment's grace—
Then when the effect weigh'd seas upon my head
To come my way! to twit me with the cause!

Was not the land as free thro' all her ways
To him as me? Was not his wont to walk
Between the going light and growing night?
Had I not learnt my loss before he came?
Could that be more because he came my way?
Why should he not come my way if he would?
And yet to-night, to-night—when all my wealth
Flash'd from me in a moment and I fell
Beggar'd forever—why should he come my way
Robed in those robes of light I must not wear,
With that great crown of beams about his brows—
Come like an angel to a damned soul,
To tell him of the bliss he had with God—
Come like a careless and a greedy heir
That scarce can wait the reading of the will
Before he takes possession? Was mine a mood
To be invaded rudely, and not rather
A sacred, secret, unapproached woe,
Unspeakable? I was shut up with Grief;
She took the body of my past delight,
Narded and swathed and balm'd it for herself,
And laid it in a sepulchre of rock
Never to rise again. I was led mute
Into her temple like a sacrifice;
I was the High Priest in her holiest place,
Not to be loudly broken in upon.

Oh friend, thoughts deep and heavy as these well nigh
O'erbore the limits of my brain: but he
Bent o'er me, and my neck his arm upstay'd.
I thought it was an adder's fold, and once
I strove to disengage myself, but fail'd,
Being so feeble: she bent above me, too;
Wan was her cheek; for whatsoe'er of blight
Lives in the dewy touch of pity had made
The red rose there a pale one—and her eyes—
I saw the moonlight glitter on their tears—
And some few drops of that distressful rain
Fell on my face, and her long ringlets moved,
Drooping and beaten by the breeze, and brush'd
My fallen forehead in their to and fro,

For in the sudden anguish of her heart
Loosed from their simple thrall they had flow'd abroad,
And floated on and parted round her neck,
Mantling her form half way. She, when I woke,
Something she ask'd, I know not what, and ask'd,
Unanswer'd, since I spake not; for the sound
Of that dear voice so musically low,
And now first heard with any sense of pain,
As it had taken life away before,
Choked all the syllables, that strove to rise
From my full heart.

   The blissful lover, too,
From his great hoard of happiness distill'd
Some drops of solace; like a vain rich man,
That, having always prosper'd in the world,
Folding his hands, deals comfortable words
To hearts wounded forever; yet, in truth,
Fair speech was his and delicate of phrase,
Falling in whispers on the sense, address'd
More to the inward than the outward ear,
As rain of the midsummer midnight soft,
Scarce heard, recalling fragrance of the green
Of the dead spring: but mine was wholly dead,
No bud, no leaf, no flower, no fruit for me.
Yet who had done, or who had suffer'd wrong?
And why was I to darken their pure love,
If, as I found, they two did love each other,
Because my own was darken'd? Why was I
To cross between their happy star and them?
To stand a shadow by their shining doors,
And vex them with my darkness? Did I love her?
Ye know that I did love her; to this present
My full-orb'd love has waned not. Did I love her,
And could I look upon her tearful eyes?
What had she done to weep? Why should she weep?
O innocent of spirit—let my heart
Break rather—whom the gentlest airs of Heaven
Should kiss with an unwonted gentleness.
Her love did murder mine? What then? She deem'd
I wore a brother's mind: she call'd me brother:
She told me all her love, she shall not weep.

  The brightness of a burning thought, awhile
In battle with the glooms of my dark will,
Moon-like emerged, and to itself lit up
There on the depth of an unfathom'd woe
Reflex of action. Starting up at once,
As from a dismal dream of my own death,
I, for I loved her, lost my love in Love;
I, for I loved her, graspt the hand she lov'd,
And laid it in her own, and sent my cry
Thro' the blank night to Him who loving made
The happy and the unhappy love, that He
Would hold the hand of blessing over them,
Lionel, the happy, and her, and her, his bride!
Let them so love that men and boys may say,
"Lo! how they love each other!" till their love
Shall ripen to a proverb, unto all
Known, when their faces are forgot in the land—
One golden dream of love, from which may death
Awake them with heaven's music in a life
More living to some happier happiness,
Swallowing its precedent in victory.
And as for me, Camilla, as for me,—
The dew of tears is an unwholesome dew,
They will but sicken the sick plant the more.
Deem that I love thee but as brothers do,
So shalt thou love me still as sisters do;
Or if thou dream aught farther, dream but how
I could have loved thee, had there been none else
To love as lovers, loved again by thee.

  Or this, or somewhat like to this, I spake,
When I beheld her weep so ruefully;
For sure my love should ne'er indue the front
And mask of Hate, who lives on others' moans.
Shall Love pledge Hatred in her bitter draughts,

And batten on her poisons? Love forbid!
Love passeth not the threshold of cold Hate,
And Hate is strange beneath the roof of Love.
O Love, if thou be'st Love, dry up these tears
Shed for the love of Love; for tho' mine image,
The subject of thy power, be cold in her,
Yet, like cold snow, it melteth in the source
Of these sad tears, and feeds their downward flow.
So Love, arraign'd to judgment and to death,
Received unto himself a part of blame,
Being guiltless, as an innocent prisoner,
Who, when the woful sentence hath been past,
And all the clearness of his fame hath gone
Beneath the shadow of the curse of man,
First falls asleep in swoon, wherefrom awaked,
And looking round upon his tearful friends,
Forthwith and in his agony conceives
A shameful sense as of a cleaving crime—
For whence without some guilt should such grief be?

  So died that hour, and fell into the abysm
Of forms outworn, but not to me outworn,
Who never hail'd another—was there one?
There might be one—one other, worth the life
That made it sensible. So that hour died
Like odor rapt into the winged wind
Borne into alien lands and far away.

  There be some hearts so airily built, that they,
They—when their love is wreck'd—if Love can wreck—
On that sharp ridge of utmost doom ride highly
Above the perilous seas of Change and Chance;
Nay, more, hold out the lights of cheerfulness;
As the tall ship, that many a dreary year
Knit to some dismal sand-bank far at sea,
All thro' the livelong hours of utter dark,
Showers slanting light upon the dolorous wave.
For me—what light, what gleam on those black ways
Where Love could walk with banish'd Hope no more?

  It was ill done to part you, Sisters fair;
Love's arms were wreath'd about the neck of Hope,
And Hope kiss'd Love, and Love drew in her breath
In that close kiss, and drank her whisper'd tales.
They said that Love would die when Hope was gone,
And Love mourn'd long, and sorrow'd after Hope;
At last she sought out Memory, and they trod
The same old paths where Love had walk'd with Hope,
And Memory fed the soul of Love with tears.

II.

From that time forth I would not see her more;
But many weary moons I lived alone—
Alone, and in the heart of the great forest.
Sometimes upon the hills beside the sea
All day I watch'd the floating isles of shade,
And sometimes on the shore, upon the sands
Insensibly I drew her name, until
The meaning of the letters shot into
My brain; anon the wanton billow wash'd
Them over, till they faded like my love.
The hollow caverns heard me—the black brooks
Of the mid-forest heard me—the soft winds,
Laden with thistle-down and seeds of flowers,
Paused in their course to hear me, for my voice
Was all of thee: the merry linnet knew me,
The squirrel knew me, and the dragon-fly
Shot by me like a flash of purple fire.
The rough brier tore my bleeding palms; the hemlock
Brow-high, did strike my forehead as I past;
Yet trod I not the wildflower in my path.
Nor bruised the wildbird's egg.

      Was this the end?
Why grew we then together in one plot?
Why fed we from one fountain? drew one sun?
Why were our mothers' branches of one stem?

Why were we one in all things, save in that
Where to have been one had been the cope and
    crown
Of all I hoped and fear'd ?—If that same nearness
Were father to this distance, and that *one*
Vauntcourier to this *double?* if Affection
Living slew Love, and Sympathy hew'd out
The bosom-sepulchre of Sympathy ?

   Chiefly I sought the cavern and the hill
Where last we roam'd together, for the sound
Of the loud stream was pleasant, and the wind
Came woolngly with woodbine smells. Sometimes
All day I sat within the cavern-mouth,
Fixing my eyes on those three cypress-cones
That spired above the wood ; and with mad hand
Tearing the bright leaves of the ivy-screen,
I cast them in the noisy brook beneath,
And watch'd them till they vanish'd from my sight
Beneath the bower of wreathed eglantines :
And all the fragments of the living rock
(Huge blocks, which some old trembling of the world
Had loosen'd from the mountain, till they fell
Half digging their own graves), these in my agony
Did I make bare of all the golden moss,
Wherewith the dashing runnel in the spring
Had liveried them all over. In my brain
The spirit seem'd to flag from thought to thought,
As moonlight wandering thro' a mist. my blood
Crept like marsh drains thro' all my languid limbs ;
The motions of my heart seem'd far within me,
Unfrequent, low, as tho' it told its pulses ;
And yet it shook me, that my frame would shudder,
As if 'twere drawn asunder by the rack.
But over the deep graves of Hope and Fear,
And all the broken palaces of the Past,
Brooded one master-passion evermore,
Like to a low-hung and a fiery sky
Above some fair metropolis, earth-shock'd,—
Hung round with ragged rims and burning folds,—
Embathing all with wild and woful hues,
Great hills of ruins, and collapsed masses
Of thunder-shaken columns indistinct,
And fused together in the tyrannous light—
Ruins, the ruin of all my life and me!

   Sometimes I thought Camilla was no more,
Some one had told she was dead, and ask'd me
If I would see her burial : then I seem'd
To rise, and through the forest-shadow borne
With more than mortal swiftness, I ran down
The steepy sea-bank, till I came upon
The rear of a procession, curving round
The silver-sheeted bay : in front of which
Six stately virgins, all in white, upbare
A broad earth-sweeping pall of whitest lawn,
Wreathed round the bier with garlands in the dis-
    tance,
From out the yellow woods upon the hill
Look'd forth the summit and the pinnacles
Of a gray steeple—thence at intervals
A low bell tolling. All the pageantry,
Save those six virgins which upheld the bier,
Were stoled from head to foot in flowing black ;
One walk'd abreast with me, and veil'd his brow,
And he was loud in weeping and in praise
Of her we follow'd ; a strong sympathy
Shook all my soul : I flung myself upon him
In tears and cries : I told him all my love,
How I had loved her from the first ; whereat
He shrank and howl'd, and from his brow drew back
His hand to push me from him ; and the face,
The very face and form of Lionel
Flash'd thro' my eyes into my innermost brain,
And at his feet I seem'd to faint and fall,
To fall and die away. I could not rise
Albeit I strove to follow. They past on,
The lordly Phantasms! in their floating folds

They past and were no more : but I had fallen
Prone by the dashing runnel on the grass.

   Alway the inaudible invisible thought,
Artificer and subject, lord and slave,
Shaped by the audible and visible,
Moulded the audible and visible ;
All crisped sounds of wave and leaf and wind
Flatter'd the fancy of my fading brain,
The cloud-pavilion'd element, the wood,
The mountain, the three cypresses, the cave,
Storm, sunset, glows and glories of the moon
Below black firs, when silent-creeping winds
Laid the long night in silver streaks and bars,
Were wrought into the tissue of my dream :
The moanings in the forest, the loud brook,
Cries of the partridge like a rusty key
Turn'd in a lock, owl-whoop and dorhawk-whir,
Awoke me not, but were a part of sleep,
And voices in the distance calling to me
And in my vision bidding me dream on,
Like sounds without the twilight realm of dreams,
Which wander round the bases of the hills,
And murmur at the low-dropt eaves of sleep,
Half-entering the portals. Oftentimes
The vision had fair prelude, in the end
Opening on darkness, stately vestibules
To caves and shows of Death : whether the mind,
With some revenge—even to itself unknown,—
Made strange division of its suffering
With her, whom to have suffering view'd had been
Extremest pain ; or that the clear-eyed Spirit,
Being blunted in the Present, grew at length
Prophetical and prescient of whate'er
The Future had in store : or that which most
Enchains belief, the sorrow of my spirit
Was of so wide a compass it took in
All I had loved, and my dull agony,
Ideally to her transferr'd, became
Anguish intolerable.

          The day waned ;
Alone I sat with her : about my brow
Her warm breath floated in the utterance
Of silver-chorded tones, her lips were sunder'd
With smiles of tranquil bliss, which broke in light
Like morning from her eyes—her eloquent eyes
(As I have seen them many a hundred times),
Filled all with pure clear fire, thro' mine down rain'd
Their spirit-searching splendors. As a vision
Unto a haggard prisoner, iron-stay'd
In damp and dismal dungeons under-ground,
Confined on points of faith, when strength is shock'd
With torment, and expectancy of worse
Upon the morrow, thro' the ragged walls,
All unawares before his half-shut eyes,
Comes in upon him in the dead of night,
And with the excess of sweetness and of awe,
Makes the heart tremble, and the sight run over
Upon his steely gyves ; so those fair eyes
Shone on my darkness, forms which ever stood
Within the magic cirque of memory,
Invisible but deathless, waiting still
The edict of the will to re-assume
The semblance of those rare realities
Of which they were the mirrors. Now the light
Which was their life bursts through the cloud of
    thought
Keen, irrepressible.

          It was a room
Within the summer-house of which I spake,
Hung round with paintings of the sea, and one
A vessel in mid-ocean, her heaved prow
Clambering, the mast bent and the ravin wind
In her sail roaring. From the outer day,
Betwixt the close-set ivies came a broad
And solid beam of isolated light,

Crowded with driving atomies, and fell
Slanting upon that picture, from prime youth
Well known, well loved. She drew it long ago
Forth-gazing on the waste and open sea,
One morning when the upblown billow ran
Shoreward beneath red clouds, and I had pour'd
Into the shadowing pencil's naked forms
Color and life: it was a bond and seal
Of friendship, spoken of with tearful smiles;
A monument of childhood and of love;
The poesy of childhood; my lost love
Symbol'd in storm. We gazed on it together
In mute and glad remembrance, and each heart
Grew closer to the other, and the eye
Was riveted and charm-bound, gazing like
The Indian on a still-eyed snake, low-couch'd—
A beauty which is death; when all at once
That painted vessel, as with inner life,
Began to heave upon that painted sea;
An earthquake, my loud heart-beats, made the ground
Reel under us, and all at once, soul, life
And breath and motion, past and flow'd away
To those unreal billows: round and round
A whirlwind caught and bore us; mighty gyres
Rapid and vast, of hissing spray wind-driven
Far thro' the dizzy dark. Aloud she shriek'd;
My heart was cloven with pain; I wound my arms
About her: we whirl'd giddily; the wind
Sung: but I claspt her without fear: her weight
Shrank in my grasp, and over my dim eyes,
And parted lips which drank her breath, down hung
The jaws of Death: I, groaning, from me flung
Her empty phantom: all the sway and whirl
Of the storm dropt to windless calm, and I
Down welter'd thro' the dark ever and ever.

III.

I CAME one day and sat among the stones
Strewn in the entry of the moaning cave;
A morning air, sweet after rain, ran over
The rippling levels of the lake, and blew
Coolness and moisture and all smells of bud
And foliage from the dark and dripping woods
Upon my fever'd brows that shook and throbb'd
From temple unto temple. To what height
The day had grown I know not. Then came on me
The hollow tolling of the bell, and all
The vision of the bier. As heretofore,
I walk'd behind with one who vell'd his brow.
Methought by slow degrees the sullen bell
Toll'd quicker, and the breakers on the shore
Sloped into louder surf: those that went with me,
And those that held the bier before my face,
Moved with one spirit round about the bay,
Trod swifter steps; and while I walk'd with these
In marvel at that gradual change, I thought
Four bells instead of one began to ring,
Four merry bells, four merry marriage bells,
In clanging cadence jangling peal on peal—
A long loud clash of rapid marriage bells.
Then those who led the van, and those in rear,
Rush'd into dance, and like wild Bacchanals
Fled onward to the steeple in the woods:
I, too, was borne along, and felt the blast
Beat on my heated eyelids: all at once
The front rank made a sudden halt; the bells
Lapsed into frightful stillness; the surge fell
From thunder into whispers; those six maids
With shrieks and ringing laughter on the sand
Threw down the bier; the woods upon the hill
Waved with a sudden gust that sweeping down
Took the edges of the pall, and blew it far
Until it hung, a little silver cloud,
Over the sounding seas: I turn'd: my heart
Shrank in me, like a snow-flake in the hand,
Waiting to see the settled countenance
Of her I loved, adorn'd with fading flowers.

But she from out her death-like chrysalis,
She from her bier, as into fresher life,
My sister, and my cousin, and my love,
Leapt lightly, clad in bridal white—her hair
Studded with one rich Provence rose—a light
Of smiling welcome round her lips—her eyes
And cheeks as bright as when she climb'd the hill.
One hand she reach'd to those that came behind,
And while I mused nor yet endured to take
So rich a prize, the man who stood with me
Stept gayly forward, throwing down his robes,
And claspt her hand in his: again the bells
Jangled and clang'd: again the stormy surf
Crash'd in the shingle: and the whirling rout
Led by those two rush'd into dance, and fled
Wind-footed to the steeple in the woods,
Till they were swallow'd in the leafy bowers,
And I stood sole beside the vacant bier.

There, there, my latest vision—then the event!

IV.

THE GOLDEN SUPPER.

(Another speaks.)

HE flies the event: he leaves the event to me:
Poor Julian—how he rush'd away; the bells,
Those marriage bells, echoing in ear and heart—
But cast a parting glance at me, you saw,
As who should say "Continue." Well, he had
One golden hour—of triumph shall I say?
Solace at least—before he left his home.

Would you had seen him in that hour of his!
He moved thro' all of it majestically—
Restrain'd himself quite to the close—but now—

Whether they *were* his lady's marriage bells,
Or prophets of them in his fantasy,
I never asked: but Lionel and the girl
Were wedded, and our Julian came again
Back to his mother's house among the pines.
But these, their gloom, the mountains and the Bay,
The whole land, weigh'd him down as Ætna does
The Giant of Mythology: he would go,
Would leave the land forever, and had gone
Surely, but for a whisper, "Go not yet,"
Some warning—sent divinely—as it seem'd
By that which follow'd—but of this I deem
As of the visions that he told—the event
Glanced back upon them in his after-life,
And partly made them—tho' he knew it not.

And thus he staid and would not look at her—
No not for months, but, when the eleventh moon
After their marriage lit the lover's Bay,
Heard yet once more the tolling bell, and said,
Would you could tell me out of life, but found—
All softly as his mother broke it to him—
A crueller reason than a crazy ear,
For that low knell tolling his lady dead—
Dead—and had lain three days without a pulse:
All that look'd on her had pronounced her dead.
And so they bore her (for in Julian's land
They never nail a dumb head up in elm),
Bore her free-faced to the free airs of heaven,
And laid her in the vault of her own kin.

What did he then? not die: he is here and hale—
Not plunge head-foremost from the mountain there,
And leave the name of Lover's Leap: not he:
He knew the meaning of the whisper now.
Thought that he knew it. "This, I staid for this;
O love, I have not seen you for so long.
Now, now, will I go down into the grave,
I will be all alone with all I love,

And kiss her on the lips. She is his no more:
The dead returns to me, and I go down
To kiss the dead."

      The fancy stirr'd him so
He rose and went, and entering the dim vault,
And, making there a sudden light, beheld
All round about him that which all will be.
The light was but a flash, and went again.
Then at the far end of the vault he saw
His lady with the moonlight on her face;
Her breast as in a shadow-prison, bars
Of black and bands of silver, which the moon
Struck from an open grating overhead
High in the wall, and all the rest of her
Drown'd in the gloom and horror of the vault.

"It was my wish," he said, "to pass, to sleep,
To rest, to be with her—till the great day
Peal'd on us with that music which rights all,
And raised us hand in hand." And kneeling there
Down in the dreadful dust that once was man,
Dust, as he said, that once was loving hearts,
Hearts that had beat with such a love as mine—
Not such as mine, no, nor for such as her—
He softly put his arm about her neck
And kissed her more than once, till helpless death
And silence made him bold—nay, but I wrong him,
He reverenced his dear lady even in death;
But, placing his true hand upon her heart,
"O, you warm heart," he moaned, "not even death
Can chill you all at once:" then starting, thought
His dreams had come again. "Do I wake or sleep?
Or am I made immortal, or my love
Mortal once more?" It beat—the heart—it beat:
Faint—but it beat: at which his own began
To pulse with such a vehemence that it drowned
The feebler motion underneath his hand.
But when at last his doubts were satisfied,
He raised her softly from the sepulchre,
And wrapping her all over with the cloak
He came in, and now striding fast, and now
Sitting awhile to rest, but evermore
Holding his golden burden in his arms,
So bore her thro' the solitary land
Back to the mother's house where she was born.

There the good mother's kindly ministering,
With half a night's appliances, recall'd
Her fluttering life: she raised an eye that ask'd
"Where?" till the things familiar to her youth
Had made a silent answer: then she spoke
"Here! and how came I here?" and learning it
(They told her somewhat rashly as I think),
At once began to wander and to wail,
"Ay, but you know that you must give me back:
Send! bid him come;" but Lionel was away—
Stung by his loss had vanished, none knew where.
"He casts me out," she wept, "and goes"—a wail
That seeming something, yet was nothing, born
Not from believing mind, but shatter'd nerve,
Yet haunting Julian, as her own reproof
At some precipitance in her burial.
Then, when her own true spirit had return'd,
"O yes, and you," she said, "and none but you,
For you have given me life and love again,
And none but you yourself shall tell him of it,
And you shall give me back when he returns."
"Stay then a little," answered Julian, "here,
And keep yourself, none knowing, to yourself;
And I will do your will. I may not stay,
No, not an hour; but send me notice of him
When he returns, and then will I return,
And I will make a solemn offering of you
To him you love." And faintly she replied,
"And I will do *your* will, and none shall know."

Not know? with such a secret to be known.

But all their house was old and loved them both,
And all the house had known the loves of both;
Had died almost to serve them any way,
And all the land was waste and solitary:
And then he rode away; but after this,
An hour or two, Camilla's travail came
Upon her, and that day a boy was born,
Heir of his face and land, to Lionel.

And thus our lonely lover rode away,
And pausing at a hostel in a marsh,
There fever seized upon him: myself was then
Travelling that land, and meant to rest an hour;
And sitting down to such a base repast,
It makes me angry yet to speak of it—
I heard a groaning overhead, and climb'd
The moulder'd stairs (for every thing was vile),
And in a loft, with none to wait on him,
Found, as it seem'd, a skeleton alone,
Raving of dead men's dust and beating hearts.

A dismal hostel in a dismal land,
A flat malarian world of reed and rush!
But there from fever and my care of him
Sprang up a friendship that may help us yet.
For while we roam'd along the dreary coast,
And waited for her message, piece by piece
I learnt the drearier story of his life;
And tho' he loved and honor'd Lionel,
Found that the sudden wail his lady made
Dwelt in his fancy: did he know her worth,
Her beauty even? should he not be taught,
Ev'n by the price that others set upon it,
The value of that jewel he had to guard?

Suddenly came her notice, and we past,
I with our lover to his native Bay.

This love is of the brain, the mind, the soul:
That makes the sequel pure; tho' some of us
Beginning at the sequel know no more.
Not such am I: and yet I say, the bird
That will not hear my call, however sweet,
But if my neighbor whistle answers him—
What matter? there are others in the wood.
Yet when I saw her (and I thought him crazed,
Tho' not with such a craziness as needs
A cell and keeper), those dark eyes of hers—
Oh! such dark eyes! and not her eyes alone,
But all from these to where she touch'd on earth,
For such a craziness as Julian's look'd
No less than one divine apology.

So sweetly and so modestly she came
To greet us, her young hero in her arms!
"Kiss him," she said. "You gave me life again.
He, but for you, had never seen it once.
His other father you! Kiss him, and then
Forgive him, if his name be Julian too."

Talk of lost hopes and broken heart! his own
Sent such a flame into his face, I knew
Some sudden vivid pleasure hit him there.

But he was all the more resolved to go,
And sent at once to Lionel, praying him
By that great love they both had borne the dead,
To come and revel for one hour with him
Before he left the land for evermore;
And then to friends—they were not many—who lived
Scatteringly about that lonely land of his,
And bade them to a banquet of farewells.

And Julian made a solemn feast: I never
Sat at a costlier: for all round his hall
From column on to column, as in a wood,
Not such as here—an equatorial one—
Great garlands swung and blossom'd; and beneath,

Heirlooms, and ancient miracles of Art,
Chalice and salver, wines that, Heaven knows when,
Had suck'd the fire of some forgotten sun,
And kept it thro' a hundred years of gloom,
Yet glowing in a heart of ruby—cups
Where nymph and god ran ever round in gold—
Others of glass as costly—some with gems
Movable and resettable at will,
And trebling all the rest in value—Ah heavens!
Why need I tell you all?—suffice to say
That whatsoever such a house as his,
And his was old, has in it rare or fair
Was brought before the guest: and they, the guests,
Wonder'd at some strange light in Julian's eyes
(I told you that he had his golden hour),
And such a feast, ill suited as it seem'd
To such a time, to Lionel's loss and his,
And that resolved self-exile from a land
He never would revisit, such a feast
So rich, so strange, and stranger ev'n than rich,
But rich as for the nuptials of a king.

And stranger yet, at one end of the hall
Two great funereal curtains, looping down,
Parted a little ere they met the floor,
About a picture of his lady, taken
Some years before, and falling hid the frame.
And just above the parting was a lamp:
So the sweet figure folded round with night
Seem'd stepping out of darkness with a smile.

Well, then—our solemn feast—we ate and drank,
And might—the wines being of such nobleness—
Have jested also, but for Julian's eyes,
And something weird and wild about it all:
What was it? for our lover seldom spoke,
Scarce touch'd the meats; but ever and anon
A priceless goblet with a priceless wine
Arising, show'd he drank beyond his use;
And when the feast was near an end, he said:

"There is a custom in the Orient, friends—
I read of it in Persia—when a man
Will honor those who feast with him, he brings
And shows them whatsoever he accounts
Of all his treasures the most beautiful,
Gold, jewels, arms, whatever it may be.
This custom—"

Pausing here a moment, all
The guests broke in upon him with meeting hands
And cries about the banquet—"Beautiful!
Who could desire more beauty at a feast?"

The lover answer'd, "There is more than one
Here sitting who desires it. Laud me not
Before my time, but hear me to the close.
This custom steps yet further when the guest
Is loved and honor'd to the uttermost.
For after he hath shown him gems or gold,
He brings and sets before him in rich guise
That which is thrice as beautiful as these,
The beauty that is dearest to his heart—
'O my heart's lord, would I could show you,' he
says,
'Ev'n my heart too.' And I propose to-night
To show you what is dearest to my heart,
And my heart too.

"But solve me first a doubt.
I knew a man, nor many years ago;
He had a faithful servant, one who loved
His master more than all on earth beside.
He falling sick, and seeming close on death,
His master would not wait until he died,
But bade his menials bear him from the door,
And leave him in the public way to die.
I knew another, not so long ago,
Who found the dying servant, took him home,

And fed, and cherish'd him, and saved his life.
I ask you now, should this first master claim
His service, whom does it belong to? him
Who thrust him out, or him who saved his life?"

This question, so flung down before the guests,
And balanced either way by each, at length,
When some were doubtful how the law would hold,
Was handed over by consent of all
To one who had not spoken, Lionel.

Fair speech was his, and delicate of phrase.
And he, beginning languidly—his loss
Weigh'd on him yet—but warming as he went,
Glanced at the point of law, to pass it by,
Affirming that as long as either lived,
By all the laws of love and gratefulness,
The service of the one so saved was due
All to the saver—adding, with a smile,
The first for many weeks—a semi-smile
As at a strong conclusion—"body and soul
And life and limbs, all his to work his will."

Then Julian made a secret sign to me
To bring Camilla down before them all.
And crossing her own picture as she came,
And looking as much lovelier as herself
Is lovelier than all others—on her head
A diamond circlet, and from under this
A veil, that seemed no more than gilded air,
Flying by each fine ear, an Eastern gauze
With seeds of gold—so, with that grace of hers,
Slow-moving as a wave against the wind,
That flings a mist behind it in the sun—
And bearing high in arms the mighty babe,
The younger Julian, who himself was crown'd
With roses, none so rosy as himself—
And over all her babe and her the jewels
Of many generations of his house
Sparkled and flash'd, for he had deck'd them out
As for a solemn sacrifice of love—
So she came in:—I am long in telling it,
I never yet beheld a thing so strange,
Sad, sweet, and strange together—floated in—
While all the guests in mute amazement rose—
And slowly pacing to the middle hall,
Before the board, there paused and stood, her breast
Hard-heaving, and her eyes upon her feet,
Not daring yet to glance at Lionel.
But him she carried, him nor lights nor feast
Dazed or amazed, nor eyes of men; who cared
Only to use his own, and staring wide
And hungering for the gilt and jewell'd world
About him, look'd, as he is like to prove,
When Julian goes, the lord of all he saw.

"My guests," said Julian: "you are honor'd now
Ev'n to the uttermost: in her behold
Of all my treasures the most beautiful,
Of all things upon earth the dearest to me."
Then waving us a sign to seat ourselves,
Led his dear lady to a chair of state.
And I, by Lionel sitting, saw his face
Fire, and dead ashes and all fire again
Thrice in a second, felt him tremble too,
And heard him muttering, "So like, so like;
She never had a sister. I knew none.
Some cousin of his and hers—O God, so like!"
And then he suddenly ask'd her if she were.
She shook, and cast her eyes down, and was dumb
And then some other question'd if she came
From foreign lands, and still she did not speak.
Another, if the boy were hers: but she
To all their queries answer'd not a word,
Which made the amazement more, till one of them
Said, shuddering, "Her spectre!" But his friend
Replied, in half a whisper, "Not at least
The spectre that will speak if spoken to.

Terrible pity, if one so beautiful
Prove, as I almost dread to find her, dumb!"

But Julian, sitting by her, answer'd all:
"She is but dumb because in her you see
That faithful servant whom we spoke about,
Obedient to her second master now;
Which will not last. I have here to-night a guest
So bound to me by common love and loss—
What! shall I bind him more? In his behalf,
Shall I exceed the Persian, giving him
That which of all things is the dearest to me,
Not only showing? and he himself pronounced
That my rich gift is wholly mine to give.

"Now all be dumb, and promise all of you
Not to break in on what I say by word
Or whisper, while I show you all my heart."
And then began the story of his love
As here to-day, but not so wordily—
The passionate moment would not suffer that—
Past thro' his visions to the burial; thence
Down to this last strange hour in his own hall;
And then rose up, and with him all his guests
Once more as by enchantment; all but he,
Lionel, who fain had risen, but fell again,
And sat as if in chains—to whom he said:

"Take my free gift, my cousin, for your wife:
And were it only for the giver's sake,
And tho' she seem so like the one you lost,
Yet cast her not away so suddenly,
Lest there be none left here to bring her back:
I leave this land forever." Here he ceased.

Then taking his dear lady by one hand,
And bearing on one arm the noble babe,
He slowly brought them both to Lionel.
And there the widower husband and dead wife
Rush'd each at each with a cry, that rather seem'd
For some new death than for a life renew'd;
Whereat the very babe began to wail;
At once they turn'd, and caught and brought him in
To their charm'd circle, and, half killing him
With kisses, round him closed and claspt again.
But Lionel, when at last he freed himself
From wife and child, and lifted up a face
All over glowing with the sun of life,
And love, and boundless thanks—the sight of this
So frighted our good friend, that, turning to me
And saying, "It is over: let us go"—
There were our horses ready at the doors—
We bade them no farewell, but mounting these
He past forever from his native land:
And I with him, my Julian, back to mine.

BALLADS AND OTHER POEMS.

TO

ALFRED TENNYSON

MY GRANDSON.

GOLDEN-HAIR'D Ally whose name is one with mine,
Crazy with laughter and babble and earth's new wine,
Now that the flower of a year and a half is thine,
O little blossom, O mine, and mine of mine,
Glorious poet who never hast written a line,
Laugh, for the name at the head of my verse is thine.
May'st thou never be wrong'd by the name that is mine!

THE CHARGE OF THE HEAVY BRIGADE AT BALACLAVA.*

OCTOBER 25, 1854.

I.

THE charge of the gallant three hundred, the Heavy
Brigade!—
Down the hill, down the hill, thousands of Russians,
Thousands of horsemen, drew to the valley—and
stay'd;
For Scarlett and Scarlett's three hundred were rid-
ing by
When the points of the Russian lances broke in on
the sky;
And he call'd "Left wheel into line!" and they
wheel'd and obey'd.
Then he look'd at the host that had halted he knew
not why,
And he turn'd half round, and he bade his trumpeter
sound
To the charge, and he rode on ahead, as he waved
his blade
To the gallant three hundred whose glory will never
die—
"Follow," and up the hill, up the hill, up the hill,
Follow'd the Heavy Brigade.

II.

The trumpet, the gallop, the charge, and the might
of the fight!—
Down the hill, slowly, thousands of Russians
Drew to the valley, and halted at last on the height,
With a wing push'd out to the left, and a wing to
the right—
But Scarlett was far on ahead, and he dash'd up
alone
Thro' the great gray slope of men,
And he wheel'd his sabre, he held his own
Like an Englishman there and then;
And the three that were nearest him follow'd with
force,
Wedged themselves in between horse and horse,

* The "three hundred" of the "Heavy Brigade" who made this
famous charge were the Scots Greys and the second squadron of Inniskillens; the remainder of the "Heavy Brigade" subsequently dashing
up to their support.
The "three" were Elliot, Scarlett's aide-de-camp, who had been
riding by his side, and the trumpeter, and Shegog the orderly, who had
been close behind him.

Fought for their lives in the narrow gap they had
made,
Four amid thousands; and up the hill, up the hill
Gallopt the gallant three hundred, the Heavy Brigade.

III.

Fell like a cannon-shot,
Burst like a thunder-bolt,
Crash'd like a hurricane,
Broke thro' the mass from below,
Drove thro' the midst of the foe,
Plunged up and down, to and fro,
Rode flashing blow upon blow,
Brave Inniskillens and Greys
Whirling their sabres in circles of light!
And some of us, all in amaze,
Who were held for a while from the fight,
And were only standing at gaze,
When the dark-muffled Russian crowd
Folded its wings from the left and the right,
And roll'd them around like a cloud—
O mad for the charge and the battle were we,
When our own good redcoats sank from sight,
Like drops of blood in a dark-gray sea,
And we turn'd to each other, muttering, all dis-
may'd,
Lost are the gallant three hundred, the Heavy Bri-
gade!

IV.

But they rode like Victors and Lords
Thro' the forest of lances and swords
In the heart of the Russian hordes;
They rode, or they stood at bay—
Struck with the sword-hand and slew,
Down with the bridle-hand drew
The foe from the saddle and threw
Underfoot there in the fray—
Ranged like a storm or stood like a rock
In the wave of a stormy day;
Till suddenly shock upon shock
Stagger'd the mass from without,
For our men gallopt up with a cheer and a shout,
And the Russian surged, and waver'd, and reel'd
Up the hill, up the hill, up the hill, out of the field,
Over the brow and away.

V.

Glory to each and to all, and the charge that they
made!
Glory to all the three hundred, the Heavy Brigade!

"THE REVENGE."

A BALLAD OF THE FLEET.

I.

At Flores in the Azores Sir Richard Grenville lay,
And a pinnace, like a flutter'd bird, came flying from
far away:
"Spanish ships of war at sea! we have sighted fifty-
three!"
Then sware Lord Thomas Howard: "'Fore God I am
no coward;
But I can not meet them here, for my ships are out
of gear,
And the half my men are sick. I must fly, but follow
quick.
We are six ships of the line; can we fight with fifty-
three?"

II.

Then spake Sir Richard Grenville: "I know you are
no coward;
You fly them for a moment to fight with them again.
But I've ninety men and more that are lying sick
ashore.
I should count myself the coward if I left them, my
Lord Howard,
To these Inquisition dogs and the devildoms of
Spain."

III.

So Lord Howard past away with five ships of war
that day,
Till he melted like a cloud in the silent summer
heaven:
But Sir Richard bore in hand all his sick men from
the land
Very carefully and slow,
Men of Bideford in Devon,
And we laid them on the ballast down below;
For we brought them all aboard,
And they blest him in their pain, that they were not
left to Spain,
To the thumbscrew and the stake, for the glory of
the Lord.

IV.

He had only a hundred seamen to work the ship and
to fight,
And he sail'd away from Flores till the Spaniard
came in sight,
With his huge sea-castles heaving upon the weather
bow.
"Shall we fight or shall we fly?
Good Sir Richard, let us know,
For to fight is but to die!
There'll be little of us left by the time this sun be
set."
And Sir Richard said again: "We be all good English
men.
Let us bang these dogs of Seville, the children of the
devil,
For I never turn'd my back upon Don or devil yet."

V.

Sir Richard spoke and he laugh'd, and we roar'd a
hurrah, and so
The little *Revenge* ran on sheer into the heart of the
foe,
With her hundred fighters on deck, and her ninety
sick below:
For half of their fleet to the right and half to the
left were seen,
And the little *Revenge* ran on thro' the long sea-lane
between.

VI.

Thousands of their soldiers look'd down from their
decks and laugh'd,
Thousands of their seamen made mock at the mad
little craft
Running on and on, till delay'd
By their mountain-like *San Philip* that, of fifteen
hundred tons,
And up-shadowing high above us with her yawning
tiers of guns,
Took the breath from our sails, and we stay'd.

VII.

And while now the great *San Philip* hung above us
like a cloud
Whence the thunder-bolt will fall
Long and loud,
Four galleons drew away
From the Spanish fleet that day,
And two upon the larboard and two upon the star-
board lay,
And the battle-thunder broke from them all.

VIII.

But anon the great *San Philip*, she bethought herself
and went,
Having that within her womb that had left her ill
content;
And the rest they came aboard us, and they fought
us hand to hand,
For a dozen times they came with their pikes and
musqueteers,
And a dozen times we shook 'em off as a dog that
shakes his ears
When he leaps from the water to the land.

IX.

And the sun went down, and the stars came out far
over the summer sea,
But never a moment ceased the fight of the one and
the fifty-three.
Ship after ship, the whole night long, their high-built
galleons came,
Ship after ship, the whole night long, with her battle-
thunder and flame;
Ship after ship, the whole night long, drew back with
her dead and her shame.
For some were sunk and many were shatter'd, and
so could fight us no more—
God of battles, was ever a battle like this in the world
before?

X.

For he said, "Fight on! fight on!"
Tho' his vessel was all but a wreck;
And it chanced that, when half of the summer night
was gone,
With a grisly wound to be drest he had left the deck,
But a bullet struck him that was dressing it suddenly
dead,
And himself he was wounded again in the side and
the head,
And he said, "Fight on! fight on!"

XI.

And the night went down, and the sun smiled out
far over the summer sea,
And the Spanish fleet with broken sides lay round
us all in a ring;
But they dared not touch us again, for they fear'd
that we still could sting,
So they watch'd what the end would be.
And we had not fought them in vain,

But in perilous plight were we,
Seeing forty of our poor hundred were slain,
And half of the rest of us maim'd for life
In the crash of the cannonades and the desperate
strife;
And the sick men down in the hold were most of
them stark and cold,
And the pikes were all broken or bent, and the pow-
der was all of it spent;
And the masts and the rigging were lying over the
side:
But Sir Richard cried, in his English pride,
"We have fought such a fight for a day and a night
As may never be fought again!
We have won great glory, my men!
And a day less or more,
At sea or ashore,
We die—does it matter when?
Sink me the ship, Master Gunner—sink her, split her
in twain!
Fall into the hands of God, not into the hands of
Spain!"

XII.

And the gunner said, "Ay, ay," but the seamen made
reply:
"We have children, we have wives,
And the Lord hath spared our lives.
We will make the Spaniard promise, if we yield, to
let us go;
We shall live to fight again and to strike another
blow."
And the lion there lay dying, and they yielded to the
foe.

XIII.

And the stately Spanish men to their flag-ship bore
him then,
Where they laid him by the mast, old Sir Richard
caught at last,
And they praised him to his face with their courtly
foreign grace;
But he rose upon their decks, and he cried:
"I have fought for Queen and Faith like a valiant
man and true;
I have only done my duty as a man is bound to do:
With a joyful spirit I, Sir Richard Grenville, die!"
And he fell upon their decks, and he died.

XIV.

And they stared at the dead that had been so valiant
and true,
And had holden the power and glory of Spain so cheap
That he dared her with one little ship and his Eng-
lish few;
Was he devil or man? He was devil for aught they
knew,
But they sank his body with honor down into the
deep,
And they mann'd the *Revenge* with a swarthier alien
crew,
And away she sail'd with her loss and long'd for her
own;
When a wind from the lands they had ruin'd awoke
from sleep,
And the water began to heave and the weather to
moan,
And or ever that evening ended a great gale blew,
And a wave like the wave that is raised by an earth-
quake grew,
Till it smote on their hulls and their sails and their
masts and their flags,
And the whole sea plunged and fell on the shot-
shatter'd navy of Spain,
And the little *Revenge* herself went down by the isl-
and crags
To be lost evermore in the main.

THE DEFENCE OF LUCKNOW.

DEDICATORY POEM TO THE PRINCESS ALICE.

DEAD PRINCESS, living Power, if that, which lived
True life, live on—and if the fatal kiss,
Born ot true life and love, divorce thee not
From earthly love and life—if what we call
The spirit flash not all at once from out
This shadow into Substance—then perhaps
The mellow'd murmur of the people's praise
From thine own State, and all our breadth of realm,
Where Love and Longing dress thy deeds in light,
Ascends to thee; and this March morn that sees
Thy Soldier-brother's bridal orange-bloom
Break thro' the yews and cypress of thy grave,
And thine Imperial mother smile again,
May send one ray to thee! and who can tell—
Thou—England's England-loving daughter—thou
Dying so English thou wouldst have her flag
Borne on thy coffin—where is he can swear
But that some broken gleam from our poor earth
May touch thee, while remembering thee, I lay
At thy pale feet this ballad of the deeds
Of England, and her banner in the East?

THE DEFENCE OF LUCKNOW.

I.

BANNER of England, not for a season, O banner of
Britain, hast thou
Floated in conquering battle or flapt to the battle-cry!
Never with mightier glory than when we had rear'd
thee on high,
Flying at top of the roofs in the ghastly siege of
Lucknow—
Shot thro' the staff or the halyard, but ever we raised
thee anew,
And ever upon the topmost roof our banner of Eng-
land blew.

II.

Frail were the works that defended the hold that we
held with our lives—
Women and children among us, God help them, our
children and wives!
Hold it we might—and for fifteen days or for twenty at most.
"Never surrender, I charge you, but every man die
at his post!"
Voice of the dead whom we loved, our Lawrence the
best of the brave:
Cold were his brows when we kiss'd him—we laid
him that night in his grave.
"Every man die at his post!" and there hail'd on our
houses and halls
Death from their rifle-bullets, and death from their
cannon-balls,
Death in our innermost chamber, and death at our
slight barricade,
Death while we stood with the musket, and death
while we stoopt to the spade,
Death to the dying, and wounds to the wounded, for
often there fell,
Striking the hospital wall, crashing thro' it, their shot
and their shell;
Death—for their spies were among us, their marksmen were told of our best,
So that the brute bullet broke thro' the brain that
could think for the rest;
Bullets would sing by our foreheads, and bullets
would rain at our feet—
Fire from ten thousand at once of the rebels that
girdled us round—
Death at the glimpse of a finger from over the
breadth of a street,

Death from the heights of the mosque' and the palace, and death in the ground!

Mine? yes, a mine! Countermine! down, down! and creep thro' the hole!

Keep the revolver in hand! You can hear him—the murderous mole.

Quiet, ah! quiet—wait till the point of the pickaxe be thro'!

Click with the pick, coming nearer and nearer again than before—

Now let it speak, and you fire, and the dark pioneer is no more;

And ever upon the topmost roof our banner of England blew.

III.

Ay, but the foe sprung his mine many times, and it chanced on a day

Soon as the blast of that under-ground thunder-clap echo'd away,

Dark thro' the smoke and the sulphur, like so many fiends in their hell—

Cannon-shot, musket-shot, volley on volley, and yell upon yell—

Fiercely on all the defences our myriad enemy fell.

What have they done? where is it? Out yonder. Guard the Redan!

Storm at the Water-gate! storm at the Bailey-gate! storm; and it ran

Surging and swaying all round us, as ocean on every side

Plunges and heaves at a bank that is daily drown'd by the tide—

So many thousands that, if they be bold enough, who shall escape?

Kill or be kill'd, live or die, they shall know we are soldiers and men!

Ready! take aim at their leaders—their masses are gapp'd with our grape—

Backward they reel like the wave, like the wave flinging forward again.

Flying and foil'd at the last by the handful they could not subdue;

And ever upon the topmost roof our banner of England blew.

IV.

Handful of men as we were, we were English in heart and in limb;

Strong with the strength of the race to command, to obey, to endure,

Each of us fought as if hope for the garrison hung but on him;

Still—could we watch at all points? we were every day fewer and fewer.

There was a whisper among us, but only a whisper that past:

" Children and wives—if the tigers leap into the fold unawares—

Every man die at his post—and the foe may outlive us at last—

Better to fall by the hands that they love, than to fall into theirs!"

Roar upon roar in a moment two mines by the enemy sprung

Clove into perilous chasms our walls and our poor palisades.

Rifleman, true is your heart, but be sure that your hand be as true!

Sharp is the fire of assault, better aim'd are your flank fusillades—

Twice do we hurl them to earth from the ladders to which they had clung,

Twice from the ditch where they shelter we drive them with hand-grenades;

And ever upon the topmost roof our banner of England blew.

V.

Then on another wild morning another wild earthquake out-tore

Clean from our lines of defence ten or twelve good paces or more.

Rifleman, high on the roof, hidden there from the light of the sun—

One has leapt up on the breach, crying out, " Follow me, follow me!"

Mark him—he falls! then another, and *him* too, and down goes he.

Had they been bold enough then, who can tell but the traitors had won?

Boardings and rafters and doors—an embrasure! make way for the gun!

Now double-charge it with grape! It is charged and we fire, and they run!

Praise to our Indian brothers, and let the dark face have his due:

Thanks to the kindly dark faces who fought with us, faithful and few,

Fought with the bravest among us, and drove them, and smote them, and slew,

That ever upon the topmost roof our banner in India blew.

VI.

Men will forget what we suffer and not what we do. We can fight!

But to be soldier all day and be sentinel all thro' the night—

Ever the mine and assault, our sallies, their lying alarms,

Bugles and drums in the darkness, and shoutings and soundings to arms,

Ever the labor of fifty that had to be done by five,

Ever the marvel among us that one should be left alive,

Ever the day with its traitorous death from the loopholes around,

Ever the night with its coffinless corpse to be laid in the ground,

Heat like the month of a hell, or a deluge of cataract skies,

Stench of old offal decaying, and infinite torment of flies,

Thoughts of the breezes of May blowing over an English field,

Cholera, scurvy, and fever, the wound that *would* not be heal'd,

Lopping away of the limb by the pitiful-pitiless knife—

Torture and trouble in vain—for it never could save us a life,

Valor of delicate women who tended the hospital bed,

Horror of women in travail among the dying and dead,

Grief for our perishing children, and never a moment for grief,

Toil and ineffable weariness, faltering hopes of relief,

Havelock baffled, or beaten, or butcher'd for all that we knew—

Then day and night, day and night, coming down on the still-shatter'd walls

Millions of musket-bullets, and thousands of cannonballs—

But ever upon the topmost roof our banner of England blew.

VII.

Hark cannonade, fusillade! is it true what was told by the scout?

Outram and Havelock breaking their way thro' the fell mutineers!

Surely the pibroch of Europe is ringing again in our ears!

All on a sudden the garrison utter a jubilant shout,

Havelock's glorious Highlanders answer with conquering cheers,
Forth from their holes and their hidings our women
and children come out,
Blessing the wholesome white faces of Havelock's
good fusileers,
Kissing the war-harden'd hand of the Highlander wet
with their tears!
Dance to the pibroch!—saved! we are saved!—is it
you? is it you?
Saved by the valor of Havelock, saved by the blessing of Heaven!
"Hold it for fifteen days!" we have held it for
eighty-seven!
And ever aloft on the palace roof the old banner
of England blew.

———∞———

DE PROFUNDIS.

TWO GREETINGS.

I.

Out of the deep, my child, out of the deep,
Where all that was to be in all that was
Whirl'd for a million æons thro' the vast
Waste dawn of multitudinous-eddying light—
Out of the deep, my child, out of the deep,
Thro' all this changing world of changeless law,
And every phase of ever-heightening life,
And nine long months of antenatal gloom,
With this last moon, this crescent—her dark orb
Touch'd with earth's light—thou comest, darling boy;
Our own; a babe in lineament and limb
Perfect, and prophet of the perfect man;
Whose face and form are hers and mine in one,
Indissolubly married like our love;
Live and be happy in thyself, and serve
This mortal race thy kin so well that men
May bless thee as we bless thee, O young life
Breaking with laughter from the dark, and may
The fated channel where thy motion lives
Be prosperously shaped, and sway thy course
Along the years of haste and random youth
Unshatter'd, then full-current thro' full man,
And last in kindly curves, with gentlest fall,
By quiet fields, a slowly-dying power,
To that last deep where we and thou are still

II.

1.

Out of the deep, my child, out of the deep,
From that great deep before our world begins
Whereon the Spirit of God moves as he will—
Out of the deep, my child, out of the deep,
From that true world within the world we see,
Whereof our world is but the bounding shore—
Out of the deep, Spirit, out of the deep,
With this ninth moon which sends the hidden sun
Down yon dark sea, thou comest, darling boy.

2.

For in the world, which is not ours, They said
"Let us make man" and that which should be man,
From that one light no man can look upon,
Drew to this shore lit by the suns and moons
And all the shadows. O dear Spirit half-lost
In thine own shadow and this fleshly sign
That thou art thou—who wailest being born
And banish'd into mystery, and the pain
Of this divisible-indivisible world
Among the innumerable-innumerable
Sun, sun, and sun, thro' finite-infinite space
In finite-infinite time—our mortal veil
And shatter'd phantom of that infinite One,
Who made thee unconceivably thy-self
Out of His whole World-self and all in all—
Live thou, and of the grain and husk, the grape

And ivy-berry, choose; and still depart
From death to death thro' life and life, and find
Nearer and ever nearer Him who wrought
Not Matter, nor the finite-infinite,
But this main miracle, that thou art thou,
With power on thine own act and on the world.

THE HUMAN CRY.

I.

Hallowèd be thy Name—Halleluiah!—
Infinite Ideality!
Immeasurable Reality!
Infinite Personality!
Hallowèd be Thy name—Halleluiah!

II.

We feel we are nothing—for all is Thou and in Thee;
We feel we are something—*that* also has come from
Thee:
We are nothing, O Thou—but Thou wilt help us to be.
Hallowèd be Thy name—Halleluiah!

———∞———

THE FIRST QUARREL.

(IN THE ISLE OF WIGHT.)

I.

"Wait a little," you say, "you are sure it 'll all
come right,"
But the boy was born i' trouble, an' looks so wan
an' so white:
Wait! an' once I ha' waited—I hadn't to wait for long.
Now I wait, wait, wait for Harry.—No, no, you are
doing me wrong!
Harry and I were married: the boy can hold up
his head,
The boy was born in wedlock, but after my man
was dead;
I ha' work'd for him fifteen years, an' I work an' I
wait to the end.
I am all alone in the world, an' you are my only
friend.

II.

Doctor, if *you* can wait, I'll tell you the tale o' my life.
When Harry an' I were children, he call'd me his
own little wife;
I was happy when I was with him, an' sorry when
he was away,
An' when we play'd together, I loved him better
than play;
He workt me the daisy chain—he made me the
cowslip ball,
He fought the boys that were rude, an' I loved him
better than all.
Passionate girl tho' I was, an' often at home in
disgrace,
I never could quarrel with Harry—I had but to look
in his face.

III.

There was a farmer in Dorset of Harry's kin, that
had need
Of a good stout lad at his farm; he sent, an' the
father agreed;
So Harry was bound to the Dorsetshire farm for
years an' for years;
I walked with him down to the quay, poor lad, an'
we parted in tears.
The boat was beginning to move, we heard them
a-ringing the bell,
"I'll never love any but you, God bless you, my
own little Nell."

IV.

I was a child, an' he was a child, an' he came to
    harm;
There was a girl, a hussy, that workt with him up
    at the farm,
One had deceived her an' left her alone with her
    sin an' her shame,
And so she was wicked with Harry; the girl was
    the most to blame.

V.

And years went over till I that was little had grown
    so tall,
The men would say of the maids "Our Nelly's the
    flower of 'em all."
I didn't take heed o' *them*, but I taught myself all
    I could
To make a good wife for Harry, when Harry came
    home for good.

VI.

Often I seem'd unhappy, and often as happy too,
For I heard it abroad in the fields "I'll never love
    any but you;"
"I'll never love any but you" the morning song of
    the lark,
"I'll never love any but you" the nightingale's hymn
    in the dark.

VII.

And Harry came home at last, but he look'd at me
    sidelong and shy,
Vext me a bit, till he told me that so many years
    had gone by,
I had grown so handsome and tall—that I might ha'
    forgot him somehow—
For he thought—there were other lads—he was
    fear'd to look at me now.

VIII.

Hard was the frost in the field, we were married o'
    Christmas-day,
Married among the red berries, an' all as merry as
    May—
Those were the pleasant times, my house an' my
    man were my pride,
We seem'd like ships i' the Channel a-sailing with
    wind an' tide.

IX.

But work was scant in the Isle, tho' he tried the
    villages round,
So Harry went over the Solent to see if work could
    be found;
An' he wrote "I ha' six weeks' work, little wife, so
    far as I know;
I'll come for an hour to-morrow, an' kiss you before
    I go."

X.

So I set to righting the house, for wasn't he coming
    that day?
An' I hit on an old deal-box that was push'd in a
    corner away,
It was full of old odds an' ends, an' a letter along
    wi' the rest,
I had better ha' put my naked hand in a hornets'
    nest.

XI.

"Sweetheart"—this was the letter—this was the let-
    ter I read—
"You promised to find me work near you, an' I wish
    I was dead—
Didn't you kiss me an' promise? you haven't done
    it, my lad,
An' I almost died o' your going away, an' I wish
    that I had."

XII.

I too wish that I had—in the pleasant times that
    had past,
Before I quarrell'd with Harry—*my* quarrel—the first
    an' the last.

XIII.

For Harry came in, an' I flung him the letter that
    drove me wild,
An' he told it me all at once, as simple as any
    child,
"What can it matter, my lass, what I did wi' my
    single life?
I ha' been as true to you as ever a man to his wife;
An' *she* wasn't one o' the worst." "Then," I said,
    "I'm none o' the best."
An' he smiled at me, "Ain't you, my love? Come,
    come, little wife, let it rest!
The man isn't like the woman, no need to make such
    a stir."
But he anger'd me all the more, an' I said "You
    were keeping with her,
When I was a-loving you all along an' the same as
    before."
An' he didn't speak for a while, an' he anger'd me
    more and more.
Then he patted my hand in his gentle way, "Let by-
    gones be!"
"Bygones! you kept yours hushed," I said, "when
    you married me!
By-gones ma' be come-agains; an' *she*—in her
    shame an' her sin—
You'll have her to nurse my child, if I die o' my
    lying in!
You'll make her its second mother! I hate her—
    an' I hate you!"
Ah, Harry, my man, you had better ha' beaten me
    black and blue
Than ha' spoken as kind as you did, when I were
    so crazy wi' spite,
"Wait a little, my lass, I am sure it 'ill all come
    right."

XIV.

An' he took three turns in the rain, an' I watch'd
    him, an' when he came in
I felt that my heart was hard, he was all wet thro'
    to the skin,
An' I never said "off wi' the wet," I never said "on
    wi' the dry,"
So I knew my heart was hard, when he came to bid
    me good-bye.
"You said that you hated me, Ellen, but that isn't
    true, you know;
I am going to leave you a bit—you'll kiss me before
    I go?"

XV.

"Going! you're going to her—kiss her—if you will,"
    I said,—
I was near my time wi' the boy, I must ha' been
    light i' my head—
"I had sooner be cursed than kiss'd!"—I didn't
    know well what I meant,
But I turn'd my face from *him*, an' he turn'd *his*
    face an' he went.

XVI.

And then he sent me a letter, "I've gotten my work
    to do;
You wouldn't kiss me, my lass, an' I never loved
    any but you;
I am sorry for all the quarrel an' sorry for what she
    wrote,
I ha' six weeks' work in Jersey an' go to-night by
    the boat."

XVII.

An' the wind began to rise, an' I thought of him out
    at sea,
An' I felt I had been to blame; he was always kind
    to me.
"Wait a little, my lass, I am sure it 'ill all come
    right "—
An' the boat went down that night—the boat went
    down that night.

RIZPAH.

17—.

I.

WAILING, wailing, wailing, the wind over land and
sea—
And Willy's voice in the wind, "O mother, come ont
to me."
Why should he call me to-night, when he knows
that I cannot go?
For the downs are as bright as day, and the full
moon stares at the snow.

II.

We should be seen, my dear; they would spy us ont
of the town.
The loud black nights for us, and the storm rushing over the down,
When I cannot see my own hand, but am led by the
creak of the chain,
And grovel and grope for my son till I find myself
drenched with the rain.

III.

Anything fallen again? nay—what was there left to
fall?
I have taken them home, I have number'd the bones,
I have hidden them all.
What am I saying? and what are *you?* do you come
as a spy?
Falls? what falls? who knows? As the tree falls so
must it lie.

IV.

Who let her in? how long has she been? you—what
have you heard?
Why did you sit so quiet? you never have spoken a
word.
O—to pray with me—yes—a lady—none of their
spies—
But the night has crept into my heart, and begun
to darken my eyes.

V.

Ah—you, that have lived so soft, what should *you*
know of the night,
The blast and the burning shame and the bitter
frost and the fright?
I have done it, while you were asleep—you were
only made for the day.
I have gather'd my baby together—and now you may
go your way.

VI.

Nay—for it's kind of you, Madam, to sit by an old
dying wife.
But say nothing hard of my boy, I have only an
hour of life.
I kiss'd my boy in the prison, before he went out to
die.
"They dared me to do it," he said, and he never has
told me a lie.
I whipt him for robbing an orchard once when he
was but a child—
"The farmer dared me to do it," he said; he was
always so wild—
And idle—and couldn't be idle—my Willy—he never
could rest.
The King should have made him a soldier, he would
have been one of his best.

VII.

But he lived with a lot of wild mates, and they
never would let him be good;
They swore that he dare not rob the mail, and he
swore that he would;
And he took no life, but he took one purse, and
when all was done
He flung it among his fellows—I'll none of it, said
my son.

VIII.

I came into court to the Judge and the lawyers. I
told them my tale,
God's own truth—but they kill'd him, they kill'd him
for robbing the mail.
They hang'd him in chains for a show—we had always borne a good name—
To be hang'd for a thief—and then put away—isn't
that enough shame?
Dust to dust—low down—let us hide! but they set
him so high
That all the ships of the world could stare at him,
passing by.
God 'ill pardon the hell-black raven and horrible
fowls of the air,
But not the black heart of the lawyer who kill'd
him and hang'd him there.

IX.

And the jailer forced me away. I had bid him my
last goodbye;
They had fasten'd the door of his cell. "O mother!"
I heard him cry.
I couldn't get back tho' I tried, he had something
further to say,
And now I never shall know it. The jailer forced
me away.

X.

Then since I couldn't but hear that cry of my boy
that was dead,
They seized me and shut me up: they fasten'd me
down on my bed.
"Mother, O mother!"—he call'd in the dark to me
year after year—
They beat me for that, they beat me—you know
that I couldn't but hear;
And then at the last they found I had grown so
stupid and still
They let me abroad again—but the creatures had
worked their will.

XI.

Flesh of my flesh was gone, but bone of my bone
was left—
I stole them all from the lawyers—and you, will
you call it a theft?—
My baby, the bones that had suck'd me, the bones
that had laughed and had cried—
Theirs? O no! they are mine—not theirs—they had
moved in my side.

XII.

Do you think I was scared by the bones? I kiss'd
'em, I buried 'em all—
I can't dig deep, I am old—in the night by the
churchyard wall.
My Willy 'ill rise up whole when the trumpet of
judgment 'ill sound,
But I charge you never to say that I laid him in
holy ground.

XIII.

They would scratch him up—they would hang him
again on the cursed tree.
Sin? O yes—we are sinners, I know—let all that be,
And read me a Bible verse of the Lord's good will
toward men—
"Full of compassion and mercy, the Lord"—let me
hear it again:
"Full of compassion and mercy—long-suffering."
Yes, O yes!
For the lawyer is born but to murder—the Saviour
lives but to bless.
He'll never put on the black cap except for the
worst of the worst,
And the first may be last—I have heard it in church
—and the last may be first.

Suffering—O long-suffering—yes, as the Lord must know,
Year after year in the mist and the wind and the shower and the snow.

XIV.

Heard, have you? what? they have told you he never repented his sin.
How do they know it? are *they* his mother? are *you* of his kin?
Heard! have you ever heard, when the storm on the downs began,
The wind that 'ill wail like a child and the sea that 'ill moan like a man?

XV.

Election, Election and Reprobation—it's all very well,
But I go to-night to my boy, and I shall not find him in Hell.
For I cared so much for my boy that the Lord has look'd into my care,
And He means me, I'm sure, to be happy with Willy, I know not where.

XVI.

And if *he* be lost—but to save *my* soul, that is all your desire:
Do you think that I care for *my* soul if my boy be gone to the fire?
I have been with God in the dark—go, go, you may leave me alone—
You never have borne a child—you are just as hard as a stone.

XVII.

Madam, I beg your pardon! I think that you mean to be kind,
But I cannot hear what you say for my Willy's voice in the wind—
The snow and the sky so bright—he used but to call in the dark,
And he calls to me now from the church and not from the gibbet—for hark!
Nay—you can hear it yourself—it is coming—shaking the walls—
Willy—the moon's in a cloud——Good-night. I am going. He calls.

THE NORTHERN COBBLER.

I.

Waait till our Sally cooms in, fur thou mun a' sights* to tell.
Eh, but I be maäin glad to seeä tha sa 'arty an' well.
"Cast awaäy on a disolnt laäd wi' a vartical soont!"
Strange fur to goä fur to think what saäilors a' seeän an' a' doon:
"Summat to drink—sa' 'ot?" I 'a nowt but Adam's wine:
What's the 'eät o' this little 'ill-side to the 'eät o' the line?

II.

"What's i' tha bottle a-stanning theer?" I'll tell tha. Gin.
But if thou wants thy grog, tha mun goä fur it down to the inn.

---

* The vowels *aï*, pronounced separately though in the closest con-junction, best render the sound of the long *i* and *y* in this dialect. But since such words as *craïn', daïïn', whaï, aï* (I), etc., look awkward except in a page of express phonetics, I have thought it better to leave the simple *i* and *y*, and to trust that my readers will give them the broader pronunciation.
† The *oo* short, as in "wood."

Naay—fur I be maäin-glad, but thaw tha was iver sa dry,
Thou gits naw gin fro' the bottle theer, an' I'll tell tha why.

III.

Meä an' thy sister was married, when wur it? back-end o' Juue,
Ten year sin', and wa 'greed as well as a fiddle i' tune:
I could fettle and clump owd booöts and shoes wi' the best on 'em all,
As fer as fro' Thursby thurn hup to Harmsby and Hutterby Hall.
We was busy as beeäs i' the bloom an' as 'appy as 'art could think,
An' then the babby wur burn, and then I taäkes to the drink.

IV.

An' weänt gaäinsaäy it, my lad, thaw I be hafe shaämed on it now,
We could sing a good song at the Plow, we could sing a good song at the Plow;
Thaw once of a frosty night I slither'd an' hurted my huck,*
An' I coom'd neck-an-crop soomtimes slaäpe down i' the squad an' the muck:
An' once I fowt wi' the Taäilor—not hafe ov a man, my lad—
Fur he scrawm'd an' scratted my faäce like a cat, an' it maäde 'er sa mad
That Sally she turn'd a tongue-banger,† an' raäted ma, "Sottin' thy braäins
Guzzlin' an' soäkin' an' smoäkin' an' hawmin'‡ about i' the laanes,
Soä sow-droonk that tha doesn not touch thy 'at to the Squire;"
An' I looök'd cock-eyed at my noäse an' I seeäd 'im a-gittin' o' fire:
But sin' I wur hallus i' liquor an' hallus as droonk as a king,
Foälks' coostom flitted awaäy like a kite wi' a brok-ken string.

V.

An' Sally she wesh'd foälks' cloäths to keep the wolf fro' the door,
Eh but the moor she riled me, she druv me to drink the moor,
Fur I fun', when 'er back wur turn'd, wheer Sally's owd stockin' wur 'id,
An' I grabb'd the munny she maäde, and I weär'd it o' liquor, I did.

VI.

An' one night I cooms 'oäm like a bull gotten loose at a faäir,
An' she wur a-waäitin' fo'mma, au' cryin' and teär-in' 'er 'aäir,
An' I tummled athurt the craädle an' sweär'd as I'd breäk ivry stick
O' furnitur 'ere i' the 'ouse, an' I gied our Sally a kick,
An' I mash'd the taäbles an' chairs, an' she an' the babby beäl'd,§
Fur I knaw'd naw moor what I did nor a mortal beäst o' the feäld.

VII.

An' when I waäked i' the murnin' I seeäd that our Sally went laämed
Cos' o' the kick as I gied 'er, an' I wur dreädful ashaämed;
An' Sally wur sloomy‖ an' draggle-taäil'd in an owd turn gown,
An' the babby's faäce wurn't wesh'd, an' the 'ole 'ouse hupside down.

---

* Hip.   † Scold.   ‡ Lounging.
§ Bellowed, cried out.   ‖ Sluggish, out of spirits.

VIII.

An' then I minded our Sally sa pratty an' neät an'
sweeat,
Straït as a pole an' cleän as a flower fro' 'eäd to
feeät:
An' then I minded the fust kiss I gied 'er by Thurs-
by thurn;
Theer wur a lark a-singin' 'is best of a Sunday at
murn,
Couldn't see 'im, we 'eärd im a-mountin' oop 'igher
an' 'igher,
An' then 'e turn'd to the sun, an' 'e shined like a
sparkle o' fire,
"Doesn't tha see 'im," she axes, "fur I can see
'im ?" an I
Seeäd nobbut the smile o' the sun as danced in 'er
pratty blue eye ;
An' I says "I mun gie tha a kiss," an' Sally says
"Noä, thou moänt,"
But I gied 'er a kiss, an' then anoother, an' Sally
says "Doänt !"

IX.

An' when we coom'd into Meeätin', at fust she wur
all in a tew,
But, arter, we sing'd the 'ymn togither like birds on
a beugh ;
An' Muggins 'e preäch'd o' Hell-fire an' the loov o'
God fur men,
An' then upo' coomin' awaäy Sally gied me a kiss
ov 'ersen.

X.

Heer wur a fall fro' a kiss to a kick like Saätan as
fell
Down out o' heaven i' Hell-fire—thaw theer's naw
drinkin' i' Hell ;
Meä fur to kick our Sally as kep the wolf fro' the
door,
All along o' the drink, fur I loov'd 'er as well as
afoor.

XI.

Sa like a graät num-cumpus I blubber'd awaäy o'
the bed—
"Weänt niver do it naw moor;" an' Sally looökt up
an' she said.
"I'll upowd it* tha weänt ; thou'rt laïke the rest o'
the men,
Thou'll goä sniffin' about the tap till tha does it
ageän.
Theer's thy hennemy, man, an' I knaws, as knaws
tha sa well,
That, if tha seeäs 'im an' smells 'im tha'll foller 'im
slick into Hell."

XII.

"Naäy," says I, "fur I weänt goä sniffin' about the
tap."
"Weänt tha ?" she says, an' mysen I thowt i' mysen
"mayhap."
"Noä;" an' I started awaäy like a shot, an' down
to the Hinn,
An' I browt what tha seeäs stannin' theer, yon big
black bottle o' gin.

XIII.

"That caps owt,"† says Sally, an' saw she begins to
cry,
But I puts it inter 'er 'ands an' I says to 'er, "Sally," says I,
"Stan' 'im theer i' the naäme o' the Lord an' the
power ov 'is Graäce,
Stan' 'im theer, fur I'll looök my hennemy straït i'
the faäce,
Stan' 'im theer i' the winder, an' let ma looök at 'im
then,
E' seeäms naw moor nor watter, an' 'e's the Divil's
oän sen."

XIV.

Au' I wur down i' tha mouth, couldn't do naw work
an' all,
Nasty an' snaggy an' shaäky, an' poonch'd my 'and
wi' the bawl,
But she wur a power o' coomfut, an' settled 'ersen
o' my knee,
An' coäxd an' coodled me oop till ageän I feel'd
mysen free.

XV.

An' Sally she tell'd it about, an' foälk stood a-gawm-
in'* in,
As thaw it wur summat bewitch'd istead of a quart
o' gin ;
Au' some on 'em said it wur watter—an' I wur
chousin' the wife,
Fur I couldn't 'owd 'ands off gin, wur it nobbut to
saave my life ;
An' blacksmith 'e strips me the thick ov 'is airm,
an' 'e shaws it to me,
"Feeäl thou this ! thou can't graw this upo' watter !"
says he.
An' Doctor 'e calls o' Sunday an' just as candles was
lit,
"Thou moänt do it," he says, "tha mun breäk 'im
off bit by bit."
"Thou'rt but a Methody-man," says Parson, and
laäys down 'is 'at,
An' 'e points to the bottle o' gin, "but I respecks
tha fur that :"
An' Squire, his oän very sen, walks down fro' the
'All to see,
An' 'e spanks 'is 'and into mine, "fur I respecks
tha," says 'e ;
Au' coostom ageän draw'd in like a wind fro' far 'an
wide,
And browt me the booöts to be cobbled fro' hafe the
coontryside.

XVI.

An' theer 'e stans an' theer 'e shall stan to my dying daäy;
I 'a gotten to loov 'im ageän in anoother kind of a
waäy.
Proud on 'im, like, my lad, an' I keeäps 'im cleän
an' bright,
Loovs 'im, an' roobs 'im, an' doosts 'im, and puts 'im
back i' the light.

XVII.

Wouldn't a pint a' sarved as well as a quart? Naw
doubt ;
But I liked a bigger feller to fight wi' an' fowt it
out.
Fine an' meller 'e mun be by this, if I cared to
taäste,
But I moänt, my lad, and I weänt, fur I'd feäl mysen cleän disgraäced.

XVIII.

An' once I said to the Missis, "My lass, when I
cooms to die,
Smash the bottle to smithers, the Divil's in 'im,"
said I.
But arter I chaänged my mind, an' if Sally be left
aloän,
I'll hev 'em a-buried wi'mma an' taäke 'im afoor the
Throän.

XIX.

Coom thou 'eer—yon laädy a-steppin' along the
streeät,
Doesn't tha knaw 'er—sa pratty, an' feät, an' neät,
an' sweeät ?
Look at the cloäths on 'er back, thebbe ammost
spick-span-new,
An' Tommy's faäce is as fresh as a codlin 'at's
wesh'd i' the dew.

---

* I'll uphold it.   † That's beyond everything.   * Staring vacantly.

XX.

'Ere's our Sally an' Tommy, an' we be a-goin' to
    dine,
Bāācon an' taātes, an' a beslings-puddin'* an' Adam's
    wine;
But if tha wants ony grog tha mun goā fur it down
    to the Hinn,
Fur I weänt shed a drop on 'is blood, noa, not fur
    Sally's oān kin.

THE SISTERS.

They have left the door ajar; and by their clash,
And prelude on the keys, I know the song,
Their favorite—which I call "The Tables Turned."
Evelyn begins it "O diviner Air."

EVELYN.

'O diviner Air,
    Thro' the heat, the drouth, the dust, the glare,
    Far from out the west in shadowing showers,
    Over all the meadow baked and bare,
    Making fresh and fair
    All the bowers and the flowers,
    Fainting flowers, faded bowers,
    Over all this weary world of ours,
    Breathe, diviner Air!
                            ,

A sweet voice that—you scarce could better that.
Now follows Edith echoing Evelyn.

EDITH.

O diviner light,
    Thro' the cloud that roofs our noon with night,
    Thro' the blotting mist, the blinding showers,
    Far from out a sky forever bright,
    Over all the woodland's flooded bowers,
    Over all the meadow's drowning flowers,
    Over all this ruin'd world of ours,
    Break, diviner light!

Marvellously like, their voices—and themselves!
Tho' one is somewhat deeper than the other,
As one is somewhat graver than the other—
Edith than Evelyn. Your good Uncle, whom
You count the father of your fortune, longs
For this alliance: let me ask you then,
Which voice most takes you? for I do not doubt,
Being a watchful parent, you are taken
With one or other: tho' sometimes I fear
You may be flickering, fluttering in a doubt
Between the two—which must not be—which might
Be death to one: they both are beautiful:
Evelyn is gayer, wittier, prettier, says
The common voice, if one may trust it: she?
No! but the paler and the graver, Edith.
Woo her and gain her then: no wavering, boy!
The graver is perhaps the one for you
Who jest and laugh so easily and so well.
For love will go by contrast, as by likes.

No sisters ever prized each other more.
Not so: their mother and her sister loved
More passionately still.
                        But that my best
And oldest friend, your Uncle, wishes it,
And that I know you worthy everyway
To be my son, I might, perchance, be loath
To part them, or part from them: and yet one
Should marry, or all the broad lands in your view
From this bay window—which our house has held
Three hundred years—will pass collaterally.

* A pudding made with the first milk of the cow after calving.

My father with a child on either knee,
A hand upon the head of either child,
Smoothing their locks, as golden as his own
Were silver, "get them wedded" would he say.
And once my prattling Edith ask'd him "why?"
Ay, why? said he, "for why should I go lame?"
Then told them of his wars, and of his wound.
For see—this wine—the grape from whence it flow'd
Was blackening on the slopes of Portugal,
When that brave soldier, down the terrible ridge
Plunged in the last fierce charge at Waterloo,
And caught the laming bullet. He left me this,
Which yet retains a memory of its youth,
As I of mine, and my first passion. Come!
Here's to your happy union with my child!

Yet must you change your name: no fault of mine!
You say that you can do it as willingly
As birds make ready for their bridal-time
By change of feather: for all that, my boy,
Some birds are sick and sullen when they moult.
An old and worthy name! but mine that stirr'd
Among our civil wars and earlier too
Among the Roses, the more venerable.
I care not for a name—no fault of mine.
Once more—a happier marriage than my own!

You see yon Lombard poplar on the plain.
The highway running by it leaves a breadth
Of sward to left and right, where, long ago,
One bright May morning in a world of song,
I lay at leisure, watching overhead
The aërial poplar wave, an amber spire.

I dozed; I woke. An open landaulet
Whirl'd by, which, after it had past me, show'd
Turning my way, the loveliest face on earth.
The face of one there sitting opposite,
On whom I brought a strange unhappiness,
That time I did not see.
                        Love at first sight
May seem—with goodly rhyme and reason for it—
Possible—at first glimpse, and for a face
Gone in a moment—strange. Yet once, when first
I came on lake Llanberris in the dark,
A moonless night with storm—one lightning-fork
Flash'd out the lake; and tho' I loiter'd there
The full day after, yet in retrospect
That less than momentary thunder-sketch
Of lake and mountain conquers all the day.

The Sun himself has limn'd the face for me.
Not quite so quickly, no, nor half as well.
For look you here—the shadows are too deep,
And like the critic's blurring comment make
The veriest beauties of the work appear
The darkest faults: the sweet eyes frown: the lips
Seem but a gash. My sole memorial ,
Of Edith—no the other,—both indeed.

So that bright face was flash'd thro' sense and soul
And by the poplar vanish'd—to be found
Long after, as it seem'd, beneath the tall
Tree-bowers, and those long-sweeping beechen
    boughs
Of our New Forest. I was there alone:
The phantom of the whirling landaulet
For ever past me by: when one quick peal
Of laughter drew me thro' the glimmering glades
Down to the snowlike sparkle of a cloth
On fern and foxglove. Lo, the face again,
My Rosalind in this Arden—Edith—all
One bloom of youth, health, beauty, happiness,
And moved to merriment at a passing jest.

There one of those about her knowing me
Call'd me to join them; so with these I spent
What seem'd my crowning hour, my day of days.

I woo'd her then, nor unsuccessfully,
The worse for her, for me! was I content?
Ay—no, not quite; for now and then I thought
Laziness, vague love-longings, the bright May,
Had made a heated haze to magnify
The charm of Edith—that a man's ideal
Is high in Heaven, and lodged with Plato's God,
Not findable here—content, and not content,
In some such fashion as a man may be
That having had the portrait of his friend
Drawn by an artist, looks at it, and says,
"Good! very like! not altogether he."

As yet I had not bound myself by words,
Only, believing I loved Edith, made
Edith love *me*. Then came the day when I,
Flattering myself that all my doubts were fools
Born of the fool this Age that doubts of all—
Not I that day of Edith's love or mine—
Had braced my purpose to declare myself:
I stood upon the stairs of Paradise.
The golden gates would open at a word.
I spoke it—told her of my passion, seen
And lost and found again, had got so far,
Had caught her hand, her eyelids fell—I heard
Wheels, and a noise of welcome at the doors—
On a sudden, after two Italian years
Had set the blossom of her health again,
The younger sister, Evelyn, enter'd—there,
There was the face, and altogether she.
The mother fell about the daughter's neck,
The sisters closed in one another's arms,
Their people throng'd about them from the hall,
And in the thick of question and reply
I fled the house, driven by one angel face,
And all the Furies.
                        I was bound to her;
I could not free myself in honor—bound
Not by the sounded letter of the word,
But counterpressures of the yielded hand
That timorously and faintly echoed mine,
Quick blushes, the sweet dwelling of her eyes
Upon me when she thought I did not see—
Were these not bonds? nay, nay, but could I wed
her
Loving the other? do her that great wrong?
Had I not dream'd I loved her yestermorn?
Had I not known where Love, at first a fear,
Grew after marriage to full height and form?
Yet after marriage, that mock-sister there—
Brother-in-law—the fiery nearness of it—
Unlawful and disloyal brotherhood—
What end but darkness could ensue from this
For all the three? So Love and Honor jarr'd,
Tho' Love and Honor join'd to raise the full
High-tide of doubt that sway'd me up and down
Advancing nor retreating.
                           Edith wrote:
"My mother bids me ask" (I did not tell you—
A widow with less guile than many a child.
God help the wrinkled children that are Christ's
As well as the plump cheek—she wrought us harm,
Poor soul, not knowing) "are you ill?" (so ran
The letter) "you have not been here of late.
You will not find me here. At last I go
On that long-promised visit to the North.
I told your wayside story to my mother
And Evelyn. She remembers you. Farewell.
Pray come and see my mother. Almost blind
With ever-growing cataract, yet she thinks
She sees you when she hears. Again farewell."

Cold words from one I had hoped to warm so far
That I could stamp my image on her heart!
"Pray come and see my mother, and farewell."
Cold, but as welcome as free airs of heaven
After a dungeon's closeness. Selfish, strange!
What dwarfs are men! my strangled vanity
25

Utter'd a stifled cry—to have vext myself
And all in vain for her—cold heart or none—
No bride for me. Yet so my path was clear
To win the sister.
                   Whom I woo'd and won.
For Evelyn knew not of my former suit,
Because the simple mother work'd upon
By Edith pray'd me not to whisper of it.
And Edith would be brides-maid on the day.
But on that day, not being all at ease,
I from the altar glancing back upon her,
Before the first "I will" was utter'd, saw
The brides-maid pale, statuelike, passionless—
"No harm, no harm," I turn'd again, and placed
My ring upon the finger of my bride.

So, when we parted, Edith spoke no word,
She wept no tear, but round my Evelyn clung
In utter silence for so long, I thought
"What will she never set her sister free?"

We left her, happy each in each, and then,
As tho' the happiness of each in each
Were not enough, must fain have torrents, lakes,
Hills, the great things of Nature and the fair,
To lift us as it were from commonplace,
And help us to our joy. Better have sent
Our Edith thro' the glories of the earth,
To change with her horizon, if true Love
Were not his own imperial all-in-all.
Far off we went. My God, I would not live
Save that I think this gross hard-seeming world
Is our misshaping vision of the Powers
Behind the world, that make our griefs our gains.

For on the dark night of our marriage-day
The great Tragedian, that had quench'd herself
In that assumption of the brides-maid—she
That loved me—our true Edith—her brain broke
With over-acting, till she rose and fled
Beneath a pitiless rush of Autumn rain
To the deaf church—to be let in—to pray
Before *that* altar—so I think: and there
They found her beating the hard Protestant doors.
She died and she was buried ere we knew.

I learnt it first. I had to speak. At once
The bright quick smile of Evelyn, that had sunn'd
The morning of our marriage, past away:
And on our home-return the daily want
Of Edith in the house, the garden, still
Haunted us like her ghost; and by-and-by,
Either from that necessity for talk
Which lives with blindness, or plain innocence
Of nature, or desire that her lost child
Should earn from both the praise of heroism,
The mother broke her promise to the dead,
And told the living daughter with what love
Edith had welcomed my brief wooing of her,
And all her sweet self-sacrifice and death.

Henceforth that mystic bond betwixt the twins—
Did I not tell you they were twins?—prevail'd
So far that no caress could win my wife
Back to that passionate answer of full heart
I had from her at first. Not that her love,
Tho' scarce as great as Edith's power of love,
Had lessen'd, but the mother's garrulous wail
For ever woke the unhappy Past again,
Till that dead brides-maid, meant to be my bride,
Put forth cold hands between us, and I fear'd
The very fountains of her life were chill'd;
So took her thence, and brought her here, and here
She bore a child, whom reverently we call'd
Edith; and in the second year was born
A second—this I named from her own self,
Evelyn; then two weeks—no more—she joined,
In and beyond the grave, that one she loved.

Now in this quiet of declining life,
Thro' dreams by night and trances of the day,
The sisters glide about me hand in hand,
Both beautiful alike, nor can I tell
One from the other, no, nor care to tell
One from the other, only know they come,
They smile upon me, till, remembering all
The love they both have borne me, and the love
I bore them both—divided as I am
From either by the stillness of the grave—
I know not which of these I love the best.

But *you* love Edith; and her own true eyes
Are traitors to her; our quick Evelyn—
The merrier, prettier, wittier, as they talk,
And not without good reason, my good son—
Is yet untouch'd: and I that hold them both
Dearest of all things—well, I am not sure—
But if there lie a preference eitherway,
And in the rich vocabulary of Love
"Most dearest" be a true superlative—
I think *I* likewise love your Edith most.

THE VILLAGE WIFE; OR, THE ENTAIL.*

I.

'OUSE-KEEPER sent tha, my lass, fur New Squire coom'd last night.
Butter an' heggs—yis—yis. I'll goä wi' tha back: all right;
Butter I warrants be prime, an' I warrants the heggs be as well,
Hafe a pint o' milk runs out when ya breäks the shell.

II.

Sit thysen down fur a bit: hev a glass o' cowslip wine!
I liked the owd Squire an' 'is gells as thaw they was gells o' mine,
Fur then we was all es one, the Squire an' 'is darters an' me,
Hall but Miss Annie, the heldest, I nivir not took to she:
But Nelly, the last o' the cletch,† I liked 'er the fust on 'em all,
Fur hoffens we talkt o' my darter es died o' the fever at fall:
An' I thowt 'twur the will o' the Lord, but Miss Annie she said it wur draäins,
Fur she hedn't naw coomfut in 'er, an' arn'd naw thanks fur 'er paäins.
Eh! thebbe all wi' the Lord my childer, I han't gotten none!
Sa new Squire's coom'd wi' 'is taäil in 'is 'and, an' owd Squire's gone.

III.

Fur 'staäte be i' taäil, my lass: tha dosn' knaw what that be?
But I knaws the law, I does, for the lawyer ha towd it me.
"When theer's naw 'eäd to a 'Ouse by the fault o' that ere maäle—
The gells they counts fur nowt, and the next un he taäkes the taäil."

IV.

What be the next un like? can tha tell ony harm on 'im, lass?—
Nany sit down—naw 'urry—sa cowd!—hev another glass!

Straänge an' cowd fur the time! we may happen a fall o' snaw—
Not es I cares fur to hear ony harm, but I likes to knaw.
An' I 'oäps es 'e beänt boooklarn'd: but 'e dosn not coom fro' the shere;
We'd anew o' that wi' the Squire, an' we haätes boooklarnin' ere.

V.

Fur Squire wur a Varsity scholard, an' niver lookt arter the land—
Whoäts or turmuts or taätes—'e 'ed hallus a boook i' 'is 'and,
Hallus aloän wi' 'is boooks, thaw nigh upo' seventy year.
An' boooks, what's boooks? thou knaws thebbe neyther 'ere nor theer.

VI.

An' the gells, they hedn't naw taäils, an' the lawyer he towd it me
That 'is taäil were soä tied up es he couldn't cut down a tree!
"Drat the trees," says I, to be sewer I haätes 'em, my lass,
Fur we puts the muck o' the land, an' they sucks the muck fro' the grass.

VII.

An' Squire wur hallus a-smilin', an' gied to the tramps goin' by—
An' all o' the wust i' the parish—wi' hoffens a drop in 'is eye.
An' ivry durter o' Squire's hed her awn ridin-erse to 'er-en,
An' they rampaged about wi' their grooms, an' was 'untin' arter the men,
An' hallus a-dallackt* an' dizen'd out, an' a-buyin' new cloäthes,
While 'e sit like a graät glimmer-gowk† wi' 'is glasses athurt 'is noäse,
An' 'is noä-e sa grufted wi' snuff es it couldn't be scroob'd awaäy,
Fur atween 'is reädin' an' writin' 'e snift up a box in a daäy,
An' 'e niver runn'd arter the fox, nor arter the birds wi' 'is gun,
An' 'e niver not shot one 'are, but 'e leäved it to Charlie 'is son,
An' 'e niver not fish'd 'is awn ponds, but Charlie 'e cotch'd the pike,
Fur 'e warn't not burn to the land, an' 'e didn't take kind to it like;
But I cärs es 'e'd gie fur a howry‡ owd book thutty pound an' moor,
An' 'e'd wrote an owd book, his awn sen, sa I knaw'd es 'e'd coom to be poor;
An' 'e gied—I be fear'd fur to tell tha 'ow much—fur an owd scratted stoän,
An' 'e digg'd up a loomp i' the land an' 'e got a brown pot an' a boän,
An' 'e bowt owd money, es wouldn't goä, wi' good gowd o' the Queen,
An' 'e bowt little statutes all-naäkt an' which was a shaäme to be seen;
But 'e niver looökt ower a bill, nor 'e niver not seed to owt,
An' 'e niver knawd nowt but boooks, an' boooks, as thou knaws, beänt nowt.

VIII.

But owd Squire's laädy es long es she lived she kep 'em all cleär,
Thaw es long es she lived I niver had none of 'er darters 'ere;

---

* See note to "Northern Cobbler." † A brood of chickens.

* Overdrest in gay colors. † Owl. ‡ Filthy.

But arter she died we was all es one, the childer an'
me,
Au' survints runn'd in an' out, an' offens we hed 'em
to tea.
Lawk! 'ow I laugh'd when the lasses 'ud talk o'
their Missis's waäys,
An' the Missis's talk'd o' the lasses.—I'll tell tha
some o' these daäys.
Hoänly Miss Annie were saw stuck oop, like 'er
mother afoor—
'Er an' 'er blessed darter—they niver derken'd my
door.

IX.

An' Squire 'e smiled an' 'e smiled till 'e 'd gotten a
fright at last,
An' e' calls fur 'is son, fur the 'turney's letters they
foller'd sa fast;
But Squire war afear'd o' 'is son, an' 'e says to 'im,
meek as a mouse,
"Lad, thou mun cut off thy taäil, or the gells 'ull
goä to the 'Ouse,
Fur I finds es I be that i' debt, es I 'oäps es thou'll
'elp me a bit,
An' if thou'll 'gree to cut off thy taäil I may saäve
mysen yit."

X.

But Charlie 'e sets back 'is ears, an' 'e sweärs, an'
'e says to 'im "Noä.
I've gotten the 'staäte by the taäil an' be dang'd
if I iver let goä!
Coom! coom! feyther," 'e says, "why shouldn't thy
booöks be sowd?
I hears es soom o' thy booöks mebbe worth their
weight i' gowd."

XI.

Heäps an' heäps o' booöks, I ha' see'd 'em, belong'd
to the Squire,
But the lasses 'ed teäred out leaves i' the middle to
kindle the fire;
Sa moäst on 'is owd big booöks fetch'd nigh to
nowt at the saäle,
Aud Squire were at Charlie ageän to git 'im to cut
off 'is taäil.

XII.

Ya wouldn't find Charlie's likes—'e were that out-
dacious at 'oäm,
Not thaw ya went fur to raäke out Hell wi' a small-
tooth coämb—
Droonk wi' the Quoloty's wine, an' droonk wi' the
farmer's aäle,
Mad wi' the lasses an' all—an' 'e wouldn't cut off
the taäil.

XIII.

Thou's coom'd oop by the beck; and a thuru be
a-grawin' theer,
I niver ha seed it sa white wi' the Maäy es I see'd
it to-year—
Theerabouts Charlie joompt—and it gied me a scare
tother night.
Fur I thowt it war Charlie's ghoäst i' the derk, fur
it loöökt sa white.
"Billy," says 'e, "hev a joomp!"—thaw the banks
o' the beck be sa high,
Fur he ca'd 'is 'erse Billy-rough-un, thaw niver a
hair war awry;
But Billy fell bakkuds o' Charlie, an' Charlie 'e brok
'is neck.
So theer war a hend o' the taäil, fur 'e lost 'is taäil
i' the beck.

XIV.

Sa 'is taäil wur lost an' 'is booöks wur gone an' 'is
boy war deäd,
An' Squire 'e smiled an' 'e smiled, but 'e niver not
lift oop 'is eäd:
Hallus a soft un Squire! an' 'e smiled, fur 'e hedn't
naw friend,
Sa feyther an' son was buried togither, an' this wur
the hend.

XV.

An' Parson as hesn't the call, nor the mooney, but
hes the pride,
'E reäds of a sewer an' sartan 'oäp o' the tother
side;
But I beänt that sewer es the Lord, howsiver they
praäy'd an' praäy'd,
Lets them inter 'eaven eäsy es leäves their debts to
be paäid.
Siver the mou'ds rattled down upo' poor owd Squire
i' the wood,
An' I cried along wi' the gells, fur they weänt niver coom to naw good.

XVI.

Fur Molly the youngest she walkt awaäy wi' a
hofficer lad,
An' nawbody 'eärd ou 'er sin, sa o' coorse she be
gone to the bad!
An' Lucy war laäme o' one leg, sweet-'arts she niv-
er 'ed none—
Straänge an' unheppen* Miss Lucy! we naämed her
"Dot an' gaw one!"
An' Hetty wur weak i' the hattics, wi'out ony harm
i' the legs,
An' the fever 'ed baäked Jinny's 'eäd as bald as one
o' them beggs,
An' Nelly wur up fro' the craädle as big i' the
mouth as a cow,
An' saw she mun hammergrate,† lass, or she weänt
git a maäte onyhow!
An' es fur Miss Annie es call'd me afoor my awn
foälks to my faäce
"A hignorant village wife as 'ud hev to be laru'd
her awn plaäce,"
Hes fur Miss Hnunie the heldest hes now be a-graw-
in' sa howd.
I knaws that mooch o' sheä, es it beänt not fit to
be towd!

XVII.

Sa I didn't not taäke it kindly ov owd Miss Annie
to saäy
Es I should be talkin' ageän 'em, es soon es they
went awaäy,
Fur, lawks! 'ow I cried when they went, an' our
Nelly she gied me 'er 'aud,
Fur I'd ha done owt fur the Squire an' 'is gells es
belong'd to the land;
Booöks, es I said afoor, thebbe neyther 'ere nor
theer!
But I sarved 'em wi' butter an' heggs fur huppuds
o' twenty year.

XVIII.

An' they hallus paäid what I hax'd, sa I hallus
deal'd wi' the Hall,
An' they knaw'd what butter wur, an' they knaw'd
what a hegg wur an' all;
Hugger-mugger they lived, but they wasn't that eäsy
to pleäse,
Till I gied 'em Hinjian curn, an' they laäid big
heggs es tha seeas;
An' I niver puts saämet i' my butter, they does it
at Willis's farm,
Taäste another drop o' the wine—tweänt do tha
naw harm.

XIX.

Sa new Squire's coom'd wi' 'is taäil in 'is 'and, an'
owd Squire's gone ;
I heard 'im a roomlin' by, but arter my nightcap
wur on ;
Sa I han't clapt eyes on 'im yit, fur he coom'd last
night sa laäte—
Plaksh! ! !§ the hens i' the peäs! why didn't tha
hesp tha gaäte?

---

* Ungainly, awkward.   † Emigrate.   ‡ Lard.
§ A cry accompanied by a clapping of hands to scare trespassing
fowl.

TO THE REV. W. H. BROOKFIELD.

BROOKS, for they call'd you so that knew you best,
Old Brooks, who loved so well to mouth my rhymes,
How oft we two have heard St. Mary's chimes!
How oft the Cantab supper, host and guest,
Would echo helpless laughter to your jest!
How oft with him we paced that walk of limes,
Him, the lost light of those dawn-golden times,
Who loved you well! Now both are gone to rest.
You man of humorous melancholy mark,
Dead of some inward agony—is it so?
Our kindlier, trustier Jaques, past away!
I cannot land this life, it looks so dark:
Σκιᾶς ὄναρ—dream of a shadow, go—
God bless you. I shall join you in a day.

IN THE CHILDREN'S HOSPITAL.

EMMIE.

I.

OUR doctor had call'd in another, I never had seen
   him before,
But he sent a chill to my heart when I saw him
   come in at the door,
Fresh from the surgery-schools of France and of
   other lands—
Harsh red hair, big voice, big chest, big merciless
   hands!
Wonderful cures he had done, O yes, but they said
   too of him
He was happier using the knife than in trying to
   save the limb,
And that I can well believe, for he look'd so coarse
   and so red,
I could think he was one of those who would break
   their jests on the dead,
And mangle the living dog that had loved him and
   fawn'd at his knee—
Drench'd with the hellish oorali—that ever such
   things should be!

II.

Here was a boy—I am sure that some of our chil-
   dren would die
But for the voice of Love, and the smile, and the
   comforting eye—
Here was a boy in the ward, every bone seem'd out
   of its place—
Caught in a mill and crush'd—it was all but a hope-
   less case:
And he handled him gently enough; but his voice
   and his face were not kind,
And it was but a hopeless case, he had seen it and
   made up his mind,
And he said to me roughly "The lad will need little
   more of your care."
"All the more need," I told him, "to seek the Lord
   Jesus in prayer:
They are all his children here, and I pray for them
   all as my own:"
But he turned to me, "Ay, good woman, can prayer
   set a broken bone?"
Then he mutter'd half to himself, but I know that I
   heard him say
"All very well—but the good Lord Jesus has had
   his day."

III.

Had? has it come? It has only dawn'd. It will
   come by-and-by.
O how could I serve in the wards if the hope of the
   world were a lie?
How could I bear with the sights and the loathsome
   smells of disease,
But that He said "Ye do it to me, when ye do it to
   these?"

IV.

So he went. And we past to this ward where the
   younger children are laid:
Here is the cot of our orphan, our darling, our meek
   little maid;
Empty you see just now! We have lost her who
   loved her so much—
Patient of pain tho' as quick as a sensitive plant to
   the touch;
Hers was the prettiest prattle, it often moved me to
   tears,
Hers was the gratefullest heart I have found in a
   child of her years—
Nay you remember our Emmie; you used to send
   her the flowers;
How she would smile at 'em, play with 'em, talk to
   'em hours after hours!
They that can wander at will where the works of
   the Lord are reveal'd
Little guess what joy can be got from a cowslip out
   of the field;
Flowers to these "spirits in prison" are all they
   can know of the spring,
They freshen and sweeten the wards like the waft
   of an Angel's wing;
And she lay with a flower in one hand and her thin
   hands crost on her breast—
Wan, but as pretty as heart can desire, and we
   thought her at rest,
Quietly sleeping—so quiet, our doctor said, "Poor
   little dear,
Nurse, I must do it to-morrow; she'll never live
   thro' it, I fear."

V.

I walk'd with our kindly old Doctor as far as the
   head of the stair,
Then I return'd to the ward; the child didn't see I
   was there.

VI.

Never since I was nurse, had I been so grieved and
   so vext!
Emmie had heard him. Softly she call'd from her
   cot to the next,
"He says I shall never live thro' it, O Annie, what
   shall I do?"
Annie consider'd. "If I," said the wise little Annie,
   "was you,
I should cry to the dear Lord Jesus to help me, for,
   Emmie, you see,
It's all in the picture there: "Little children should
   come to me.'"
(Meaning the print that you gave us, I find that it
   always can please
Our children, the dear Lord Jesus with children
   about his knees.)
"Yes, and I will," said Emmie, "but then if I call
   to the Lord,
How should he know that it's me? such a lot of
   beds in the ward!"
That was a puzzle for Annie. Again she consider'd
   and said:
"Emmie, you put out your arms, and you leave 'em
   outside on the bed—
The Lord has so much to see to! but, Emmie, you
   tell it him plain,
It's the little girl with her arms lying out on the
   counterpane."

VII.

I had sat three nights by the child—I could not
   watch her for four—
My brain had begun to reel—I felt I could do it no
   more.
That was my sleeping-night, but I thought that it
   never would pass.
There was a thunderclap once, and the clatter of
   hail on the glass,

And there was a phantom cry that I heard as I tost
about,
The motherless bleat of a lamb in the storm and the
darkness without;
My sleep was broken besides with dreams of the
dreadful knife
And fears for our delicate Emmie who scarce would
escape with her life;
Then in the gray of the morning it seem'd she stood
by me and smiled,
And the doctor came at his hour, and we went to
see the child.

VIII.

He had brought his ghastly tools: we believed her
asleep again—
Her dear, long, lean, little arms lying out on the
counterpane;
Say that His day is done! Ah, why should we care
what they say?
The Lord of the children had heard her, and Emmie
had past away.

—————

SIR JOHN OLDCASTLE, LORD COBHAM.

(IN WALES.)

My friend should meet me somewhere hereabout
To take me to that hiding in the hills.

I have broke their cage, no gilded one, I trow—
I read no more the prisoner's mate wail
Scribbled or carved upon the pitiless stone:
I find hard rocks, hard life, hard cheer, or none,
For I am emptier than a friar's brains;
But God is with me in this wilderness,
These wet black passes and foam-churning chasms,—
And God's free air, and hope of better things.

I would I knew their speech; not now to glean,
Not now—I hope to do it—some scatter'd ears,
Some ears for Christ in this wild field of Wales—
But, bread, merely for bread. This tongue that
wagg'd
They said with such heretical arrogance
Against the proud archbishop Arundel—
So much God's cause was fluent in it—is here
But as a Latin Bible to the crowd:
"Bara!"—what use? The Shepherd, when I speak,
Vailing a sullen eyelid with his hard
"Dim Saesneg" passes, wroth at things of old—
No fault of mine. Had he God's word in Welsh
He might be kindlier: happily come the day!

Not least art thou, thou little Bethlehem
In Judah, for in thee the Lord was born;
Nor thou in Britain, little Lutterworth,
Least, for in thee the word was born again.

Heaven-sweet Evangel, ever-living word,
Who whilome spakest to the South in Greek
About the soft Mediterranean shores,
And then in Latin to the Latin need,
As good need was—thou hast come to talk our isle.
Hereafter thou, fulfilling Pentecost,
Must learn to use the tongues of all the world,
Yet art thou thine own witness that thou bringest
Not peace, a sword, a fire.
                    What did he say,
My frighted Wiclif-preacher whom I crost
In flying hither? that one night a crowd
Throng'd the waste field about the city gates:
The king was on them suddenly with a host.
Why there? they came to hear their preacher. Then
Some cried on Cobham, on the good Lord Cobham;
Ay, for they love me! but the king—nor voice
Nor finger raised against him—took and hang'd,
Took, hang'd and burnt—how many—thirty-nine—

Call'd it rebellion—hang'd, poor friends, as rebels
And burn'd alive as heretics! for your Priest
Labels—to take the king along with him—
All heresy, treason: but to call men traitors
May make men traitors.
                    Rose of Lancaster,
Red in thy birth, redder with household war,
Now reddest with the blood of holy men,
Redder to be, red rose of Lancaster—
If somewhere in the North, as Rumor sang,
Fluttering the hawks of this crown-lusting line—
By firth and loch thy silver sister grow,*
That were my rose, there my allegiance due.
Self-starved, they say—nay, murder'd, doubtless dead.
So to this king I cleaved; my friend was he.
Once my fast friend; I would have given my life
To help his own from scathe, a thousand lives
To save his soul. He might have come to learn
Our Wiclif's learning: but the worldly Priests,
Who fear the king's hard common-sense should
find
What rotten piles uphold their masonwork,
Urge him to foreign war. O had he will'd
I might have stricken a lusty stroke for him,
But he would not; far liever led my friend
Back to the pure and universal church,
But he would not: whether that heirless flaw
In his throne's title make him feel so frail,
He leans on Antichrist; or that his mind,
So quick, so capable in soldiership,
In matters of the faith, alas the while!
More worth than all the kingdoms of this world,
Runs in the rut, a coward to the Priest.

Burnt—good Sir Roger Acton, my dear friend!
Burnt too, my faithful preacher, Beverley!
Lord, give thou power to thy two witnesses!
Lest the false faith make merry over them!
Two—nay, but thirty-nine have risen and stand,
Dark with the smoke of human sacrifice,
Before thy light, and cry continually—
Cry—against whom?
                Him, who should bear the sword
Of Justice—what! the kingly, kindly boy;
Who took the world so easily heretofore,
My boon companion, tavern-fellow—him
Who gibed and japed—in many a merry tale
That shook our sides—at Pardoners, Summoners,
Friars, absolution-sellers, monkeries
And nunneries, when the wild hour and the wine
Had set the wits aflame.
                    Harry of Monmouth,
Or Amurath of the East?
                    Better to sink
Thy fleurs-de-lys in slime again, and fling
Thy royalty back into the riotous fits
Of wine and harlotry—thy shame, and mine,
Thy comrade—than to persecute the Lord,
And play the Saul that never will be Paul.

Burnt, burnt! and while this mitred Arundel
Dooms our unlicensed preacher to the flame,
The mitre-sanction'd harlot draws his clerks
Into the suburb—their hard celibacy,
Sworn to be veriest ice of pureness, molten
Into adulterous living, or such crimes
As holy Paul—a shame to speak of them—
Among the heathen—
                    Sanctuary granted
To bandit, thief, assassin—yea to him
Who hacks his mother's throat—denied to him,
Who finds the Saviour in his mother tongue.
The Gospel, the Priest's pearl, flung down to swine—
The swine, lay-men, lay-women, who will come,
God willing, to onlearn the filthy friar.
Ah rather, Lord, than that thy Gospel, meant

_____

* Richard II.

To course and range thro' all the world, should be
Tether'd to these dead pillars of the Church—
Rather than so, if thou wilt have it so,
Burst vein, snap sinew, and crack heart, and life
Pass in the fire of Babylon! but how long,
O Lord, how long!
         My friend should meet me here.
Here is the copse, the fountain and—a Cross!
To thee, dead wood, I bow, not bend nor knees.
Rather to thee, green boscage, work of God,
Black holly, and white-flower'd wayfaring-tree!
Rather to thee, thou living water, drawn
By this good Wiclif mountain down from heaven,
And speaking clearly in thy native tongue—
No Latin—He that thirsteth, come and drink!

Eh! how I anger'd Arundel asking me
To worship Holy Cross! I spread mine arms.
God's work, I said, a cross of flesh and blood,
And holier. That was heresy. (My good friend
By this time should be with me.) "Images?"
"Bury them as God's truer images
Are daily buried." "Heresy.—Penance?" "Fast,
Hairshirt and scourge—nay, let a man repent,
Do penance in his heart, God hears him." "Her-
     esy—
Not shriven, not saved?" "What profits an ill
     Priest
Between me and my God? I would not spurn
Good counsel of good friends, but shrive myself
No, not to an Apostle." "Heresy."
(My friend is long in coming.) "Pilgrimages?"
"Drink, bagpipes, revelling, devil's-dances, vice,
The poor man's money gone to fat the friar.
Who reads of begging saints in Scripture?"—"Her-
     esy"—
(Hath he been here—not found me—gone again?
Have I mislearnt our place of meeting?) "Bread—
Bread left after the blessing?" how they stared,
That was their main test-question—glared at me!
"He veil'd Himself in flesh, and now He veils
His flesh in bread, body and bread together."
Then rose the howl of all the cassock'd wolves,
"No bread, no bread. God's body!" Archbishop,
     Bishop,
Priors, Canons, Friars, bellringers, Parish-clerks—
"No bread, no bread!"—"Authority of the Church,
Power of the keys!"—Then I, God help me, I
So mock'd, so spurn'd, so baited two whole days—
I lost myself and fell from evenness,
And rail'd at all the Popes, that ever since
Sylvester shed the venom of world-wealth
Into the church, had only prov'n themselves
Poisoners, murderers. Well—God pardon all—
Me, them, and all the world—yea, that proud Priest,
That mock-meek month of utter Antichrist,
That traitor to King Richard and the truth,
Who rose and doom'd me to the fire.
                 Amen!
Nay, I can burn, so that the Lord of life
Be by me in my death.
            Those three! the fourth
Was like the son of God. Not burnt were they.
On *them* the smell of burning had not past.
That was a miracle to convert the king.
These Pharisees, this Caiaphas-Arundel
What miracle could turn? *He* here again,
He thwarting their traditions of Himself,
He would be found a heretic to Himself,
And doom'd to burn alive.
            So, caught, I burn.
Burn? heathen men have borne as much as this,
For freedom, or the sake of those they loved,
Or some less cause, some cause far less than mine;
For every other cause is less than mine.
The moth will singe her wings, and singed return,
Her love of light quenching her fear of pain—
How now, my soul, we do not heed the fire?

Faint-hearted? tut!—faint-stomach'd! faint as I am,
God willing, I will burn for Him.
                 Who comes?
A thousand marks are set upon my head,
Friend?—foe perhaps—a tussle for it then!
Nay, but my friend. Thou art so well disguised,
I knew thee not. Hast thou brought bread with
     thee?
I have not broken bread for fifty hours.
None? I am damn'd already by the Priest
For holding there was bread where bread was
     none—
No bread. My friends await me yonder? Yes.
Lead on then. *Up* the mountain? Is it far?
Not far. Climb first and reach me down thy hand.
I am not like to die for lack of bread,
For I must live to testify by fire.*

※

COLUMBUS.

CHAINS, my good lord: in your raised brows I read
Some wonder at our chamber ornaments.
We brought this iron from our isles of gold.

Does the king know you deign to visit him
Whom once he rose from off his throne to greet
Before his people, like his brother king?
I saw your face that morning in the crowd.

At Barcelona—tho' you were not then
So bearded. Yes. The city deck'd herself
To meet me, roar'd my name; the king, the queen
Bad me be seated, speak, and tell them all
The story of my voyage, and while I spoke
The crowd's roar fell as at the "Peace, be still!"
And when I ceased to speak, the king, the queen,
Sank from their thrones, and melted into tears,
And knelt, and lifted hand and heart and voice
In praise to God who led me thro' the waste.
And then the great "Laudamus" rose to heaven.

Chains for the Admiral of the Ocean! chains
For him who gave a new heaven, a new earth,
As holy John had prophesied of me,
Gave glory and more empire to the kings
Of Spain than all their battles! chains for him
Who push'd his prows into the setting sun,
And made West East, and sail'd the Dragon's mouth,
And came upon the Mountain of the World,
And saw the rivers roll from Paradise!

Chains! we are Admirals of the Ocean, we,
We and our sons forever. Ferdinand
Hath sign'd it and our Holy Catholic queen—
Of the Ocean—of the Indies—Admirals we—
Our title, which we never mean to yield,
Our guerdon not alone for what we did, ·
But our amends for all we might have done—
The vast occasion of our stronger life—
Eighteen long years of waste, seven in your Spain,
Lost, showing courts and kings a truth the babe
Will suck in with his milk hereafter—earth
A sphere.
         Were *you* at Salamanca? No.
We fronted there the learning of all Spain,
All their cosmogonies, their astronomies:
Guess-work *they* guess'd it, but the golden guess
Is morning-star to the full round of truth.
No guess-work! I was certain of my goal;
Some thought it heresy, but that would not hold,
King David call'd the heavens a hide, a tent
Spread over earth, and so this earth was flat;
Some cited old Lactantius: could it be
That trees grew downward, rain fell upward, men

---

       * He was burnt on Christmas-day, 1417.

Walk'd like the fly on ceilings? and besides,
The great Augustine wrote that none could breathe
Within the zone of heat; so might there be
Two Adams, two mankinds, and that was clean
Against God's word: thus was I beaten back,
And chiefly to my sorrow by the Church,
And thought to turn my face from Spain, appeal
Once more to France or England; but our Queen
Recall'd me, for at last their Highnesses
Were half-assured this earth might be a sphere.

All glory to the all-blessed Trinity,
All glory to the mother of our Lord,
And Holy Church, from whom I never swerved
Not even by one hair's-breadth of heresy,
I have accomplish'd what I came to do.

Not yet—not all—last night a dream—I sail'd
On my first voyage, harass'd by the frights
Of my first crew, their curses and their groans.
The great flame-banner borne by Teneriffe,
The compass, like an old friend false at last
In our most need, appall'd them, and the wind
Still westward, and the weedy seas—at length
The landbird, and the branch with berries on it,
The carven staff—and last the light, the light
On Guanahani! but I changed the name;
San Salvador I call'd it; and the light
Grew as I gazed, and brought out a broad sky
Of dawning over—not those alien palms,
The marvel of that fair new nature—not
That Indian isle, but our most ancient East,
Moriah with Jerusalem; and I saw
The glory of the Lord flash up, and beat
Thro' all the homely town from jasper, sapphire,
Chalcedony, emerald, sardonyx, sardius,
Chrysolite, beryl, topaz, chrysoprase,
Jacynth, and amethyst—and those twelve gates,
Pearl—and I woke, and thought—death—I shall die—
I am written in the Lamb's own Book of Life
To walk within the glory of the Lord
Sunless and moonless, utter light—but no!
The Lord had sent this bright, strange dream to me
To mind me of the secret vow I made
When Spain was waging war against the Moor—
I strove myself with Spain against the Moor.
There came two voices from the Sepulchre,
Two friars crying that if Spain should oust
The Moslem from her limit, he, the fierce
Soldan of Egypt, would break down and raze
The blessed tomb of Christ; whereon I vow'd
That, if our Princes harken'd to my prayer,
Whatever wealth I brought from that new world
Should, in this old, be consecrate to lead
A new crusade against the Saracen,
And free the Holy Sepulchre from thrall.

Gold? I had brought your Princes gold enough
If left alone! Being but a Genovese,
I am handled worse than had I been a Moor,
And breach'd the belting wall of Cambalu,
And given the Great Khan's palaces to the Moor,
Or clutch'd the sacred crown of Prester John,
And cast it to the Moor: but had I brought
From Solomon's now-recover'd Ophir all
The gold that Solomon's navies carried home,
Would that have gilded me? Blue blood of Spain,
Tho' quartering your own royal arms of Spain,
I have not: blue blood and black blood of Spain,
The noble and the convict of Castile,
Howl'd me from Hispaniola; for you know
The flies at home, that ever swarm about
And cloud the highest heads, and murmur down
Truth in the distance—these outbuzz'd me so
That even our prudent king, our righteous queen—
I pray'd them being so calumniated,
They would commission one of weight and worth
To judge between my slander'd self and me—

Fonseca my main enemy at their court,
They send me out his tool, Bovadilla, one
As ignorant and impolitic as a beast—
Blockish irreverence, brainless greed—who sack'd
My dwelling, seized upon my papers, loosed
My captives, feed the rebels of the crown,
Sold the crown-farms for all but nothing, gave
All but free leave for all to work the mines,
Drove me and my good brothers home in chains,
And gathering ruthless gold—a single piece
Weigh'd nigh four thousand Castillanos—so
They tell me—weigh'd him down into the abysm—
The hurricane of the latitude on him fell,
The seas of our discovering over-roll
Him and his gold; the frailer caravel,
With what was mine, came happily to the shore.
There was a glimmering of God's hand.
                            And God
Hath more than glimmer'd on me. O my lord,
I swear to you I heard his voice between
The thunders in the black Veragua nights,
"O soul of little faith, slow to believe!
Have I not been about thee from thy birth?
Given thee the keys of the great Ocean-sea?
Set thee in light till time shall be no more?
Is it I who have deceived thee or the world?
Endure! thou hast done so well for men, that men
Cry out against thee: was it otherwise
With mine own Son?"
                            And more than once in days
Of doubt and cloud and storm, when drowning hope
Sank all but out of sight, I heard his voice,
"Be not cast down. I lead thee by the hand,
Fear not." And I shall hear his voice again—
I know that he has led me all my life,
I am not yet too old to work his will—
His voice again.
                            Still for all that, my lord,
I lying here bedridden and alone,
Cast off, put by, scouted by court and king—
The first discoverer starves—his followers, all
Flower into fortune—our world's way—and I,
Without a roof that I can call mine own,
With scarce a coin to buy a meal withal,
And seeing what a door for scoundrel scum
I open'd to the West, thro' which the lust,
Villany, violence, avarice, of your Spain
Pour'd in on all those happy naked isles—
Their kindly native princes slain or slaved,
Their wives and children Spanish concubines,
Their innocent hospitalities quench'd in blood,
Some dead of hunger, some beneath the scourge,
Some over-labor'd, some by their own hands,—
Yea, the dear mothers, crazing Nature, kill
Their babies at the breast for hate of Spain—
Ah God, the harmless people whom we found
In Hispaniola's island-Paradise!
Who took us for the very Gods from Heaven,
And we have sent them very fiends from Hell;
And I myself, myself not blameless, I
Could sometimes wish I had never led the way.

Only the ghost of our great Catholic Queen
Smiles on me, saying, "Be thou comforted!
This creedless people will be brought to Christ
And own the holy governance of Rome."

But who could dream that we, who bore the Cross
Thither, were excommunicated there,
For curbing crimes that scandalized the Cross,
By him, the Catalonian Minorite,
Rome's Vicar in our Indies? who believe
These hard memorials of our truth to Spain
Clung closer to us for a longer term
Than any friend of ours at Court? and yet
Pardon—too harsh, unjust. I am rack'd with pains.

You see that I have hung them by my bed,
And I will have them buried in my grave.

Sir, in that flight of ages which are God's
Own voice to justify the dead—perchance
Spain once the most chivalric race on earth,
Spain then the mightiest, wealthiest realm on earth,
So made by me, may seek to unbury me,
To lay me in some shrine of this old Spain,
Or in that vaster Spain I leave to Spain.
Then some one standing by my grave will say,
"Behold the bones of Christopher Colòn"—
"Ay, but the chains, what do *they* mean—the
  chains?"
I sorrow for that kindly child of Spain
Who then will have to answer, "These same chains
Bound these same bones back thro' the Atlantic
  sea,
Which he unchain'd for all the world to come."

O Queen of Heaven who seest the souls in Hell
And purgatory, I suffer all as much
As they do—for the moment. Stay, my son
Is here anon : my son will speak for me
Ablier than I can in these spasms that grind
Bone against bone. You will not. One last word.

You move about the Court, I pray you tell
King Ferdinand who plays with me, that one,
Whose life has been no play with him and his
Hidalgos—shipwrecks, famines, fevers, fights,
Mutinies, treacheries—wink'd at, and condoned—
That I am loyal to him till the death,
And ready—tho' our Holy Catholic Queen,
Who fain had pledged her jewels on my first voy-
  age,
Whose hope was mine to spread the Catholic faith,
Who wept with me when I return'd in chains,
Who sits beside the blessed Virgin now,
To whom I send my prayer by night and day—
She is gone—but you will tell the King, that I,
Rack'd as I am with gout, and wrench'd with pains
Gain'd in the service of His Highness, yet
Am ready to sail forth on one last voyage,
And readier, if the King would hear, to lead
One last crusade against the Saracen,
And save the Holy Sepulchre from thrall.

Going? I am old and slighted : you have dared
Somewhat perhaps in coming? my poor thanks !
I am but an alien and a Genovese.

———

THE VOYAGE OF MAELDUNE.

(FOUNDED ON AN IRISH LEGEND. A.D. 700.)

I.

I was the chief of the race—he had stricken my fa-
  ther dead—
But I gather'd my fellows together, I swore I would
  strike off his head.
Each of them look'd like a king, and was noble in
  birth as in worth,
And each of them boasted he sprang from the oldest
  race upon earth.
Each was as brave in the fight as the bravest hero
  of song,
And each of them liefer had died than have done
  one another a wrong.
He lived on an isle in the ocean—we sail'd on a
  Friday morn—
He that had slain my father the day before I was
  born.

II.

And we came to the isle in the ocean, and there on
  the shore was he.
But a sudden blast blew us out and away thro' a
  boundless sea.

III.

And we came to the Silent Isle that we never had
  touch'd at before,
Where a silent ocean always broke on a silent shore,
And the brooks glitter'd on in the light without
  sound, and the long waterfalls
Pour'd in a thunderless plunge to the base of the
  mountain walls,
And the poplar and cypress unshaken by storm
  flourish'd up beyond sight,
And the pine shot aloft from the crag to an unbe-
  lievable height,
And high in the heaven above it there flicker'd a
  songless lark,
And the cock couldn't crow, and the bull couldn't
  low, and the dog couldn't bark,
And round it we went, and thro' it, but never a
  murmur, a breath—
It was all of it fair as life, it was all of it quiet as death,
And we hated the beautiful Isle, for whenever we
  strove to speak
Our voices were thinner and fainter than any flitter-
  mouse-shriek ;
And the men that were mighty of tongue and could
  raise such a battle-cry
That a hundred who heard it would rush on a
  thousand lances and die—
O they to be dumb'd by the charm !—so fluster'd
  with anger were they
They almost fell on each other ; but after we sail'd
  away.

IV.

And we came to the Isle of Shouting, we landed, a
  score of wild birds
Cried from the topmost summit with human voices
  and words ;
Once in an hour they cried, and whenever their
  voices peal'd
The steer fell down at the plow and the harvest
  died from the field,
And the men dropt dead in the valleys and half of
  the cattle went lame,
And the roof sank in on the hearth, and the dwelling broke into flame ;
And the shouting of these wild birds ran into the
  hearts of my crew,
Till they shouted along with the shouting and seized
  one another and slew ;
But I drew them the one from the other ; I saw that
  we could not stay,
And we left the dead to the birds and we sail'd with
  our wounded away.

V.

And we came to the Isle of Flowers : their breath
  met us out on the seas,
For the Spring and the middle Summer sat each on
  the lap of the breeze ;
And the red passion-flower to the cliffs, and the dark
  blue clematis, clung,
And starr'd with a myriad blossom the long con-
  volvulus hung ;
And the topmost spire of the mountain was lilies in
  in lieu of snow,
And the lilies like glaciers winded down, running
  out below
Thro' the fire of the tulip and poppy, the blaze of
  gorse, and the blush
Of millions of roses that sprang without leaf or a
  thorn from the bush ;
And the whole isle-side flashing down from the peak
  without ever a tree
Swept like a torrent of gems from the sky to the
  blue of the sea ;
And we roll'd upon capes of crocus and vaunted our
  kith and our kin,
And we wallow'd in beds of lilies, and chanted the
  triumph of Finn,

Till each like a golden image was pollen'd from head
to feet,
And each was as dry as a cricket, with thirst in the
middle-day heat.
Blossom and blossom, and promise of blossom, but
never a fruit!
And we hated the Flowering Isle, as we hated the
isle that was mute,
And we tore up the flowers by the million and flung
them in bight and bay,
And we left but a naked rock, and in anger we sail'd
away.

VI.

And we came to the Isle of Fruits: all round from
the cliffs and the capes,
Purple or amber, dangled a hundred fathom of
grapes,
And the warm melon lay like a little sun on the
tawny sand,
And the fig ran up from the beach and rioted over
the land,
And the mountain arose like a jewell'd throne thro'
the fragrant air,
Glowing with all-color'd plums and with golden
masses of pear,
And the crimson and scarlet of berries that flamed
upon hine and vine,
But in every berry and fruit was the poisonous
pleasure of wine:
And the peak of the mountain was apples, the hugest
that ever were seen,
And they prest, as they grew, on each other, with
hardly a leaflet between,
And all of them redder than rosiest health or than
utterest shame.
And setting, when Even descended, the very sunset
aflame;
And we stay'd three days, and we gorged and we
madden'd, till every one drew
His sword on his fellow to slay him, and ever they
struck and they slew;
And myself, I had eaten but sparely, and fought till
I sunder'd the fray,
Then I had them remember my father's death, and
we sail'd away.

VII.

And we came to the Isle of Fire: we were lured by
the light from afar,
For the peak sent up one league of fire to the North-
ern Star;
Lured by the glare and the blare, but scarcely could
stand upright,
For the whole isle shudder'd and shook like a man
in a mortal affright;
We were giddy besides with the fruits we had
gorged, and so crazed that at last
There were some leap'd into the fire; and away we
sail'd, and we past
Over that undersea isle, where the water is clearer
than air;
Down we look'd: what a garden! O bliss, what a
Paradise there!
Towers of a happier time, low down in a rainbow
deep
Silent palaces, quiet fields of eternal sleep!
And three of the gentlest and best of my people,
whate'er I could say,
Plunged head down in the sea, and the Paradise
trembled away.

VIII.

And we came to the Bounteous Isle, where the
heavens lean low on the land,
And ever at dawn from the cloud glitter'd o'er us a
sunbright hand,
Then it open'd and dropt at the side of each man,
as he rose from his rest,
Bread enough for his need till the laborless day
dipt under the West;

And we wander'd about it and thro' it. O never
was time so good!
And we sang of the triumphs of Finn, and the boast
of our ancient blood,
And we gazed at the wandering wave as we sat by
the gurgle of springs,
And we chanted the songs of the Bards and the
glories of fairy kings;
But at length we began to be weary, to sigh, and to
stretch and yawn,
Till we hated the Bounteous Isle and the sunbright
hand of the dawn,
For there was not an enemy near, but the whole
green isle was our own,
And we took to playing at ball, and we took to
throwing the stone,
And we took to playing at battle, but that was a
perilous play,
For the passion of battle was in us, we slew and
we sail'd away.

IX.

And we came to the Isle of Witches and heard their
musical cry—
"Come to us, O come, come" in the stormy red of
a sky
Dashing the fires and the shadows of dawn on the
beautiful shapes,
For a wild witch naked as heaven stood on each
of the loftiest capes,
And a hundred ranged on the rock like white sea-
birds in a row,
And a hundred gamboll'd and pranced on the
wrecks in the sand below,
And a hundred splash'd from the ledges, and bosom'd
the burst of the spray,
But I knew we should fall on each other, and hastily sail'd away.

X.

And we came in an evil time to the Isle of the
Double Towers:
One was of smooth-cut stone, one carved all over
with flowers;
But an earthquake always moved in the hollows
under the dells,
And they shock'd on each other and butted each
other with clashing of bells,
And the daws flew out of the Towers and jangled
and wrangled in vain,
And the clash and boom of the bells rang into the
heart and the brain,
Till the passion of battle was on us, and all took
sides with the Towers,
There were some for the clean-cut stone, there were
more for the carven flowers,
And the wrathful thunder of God peal'd over us all
the day,
For the one half slew the other, and after we sail'd
away.

XI.

And we came to the Isle of a Saint who had sail'd
with St. Brendan of yore,
He had lived ever since on the Isle, and his winters
were fifteen score,
And his voice was low as from other worlds, and
his eyes were sweet,
And his white hair sank to his heels and his white
beard fell to his feet,
And he spake to me, "O Maeldune, let be this pur-
pose of thine!
Remember the words of the Lord when he told us
'Vengeance is mine!'
His fathers have slain thy fathers in war or in sin-
gle strife,
Thy fathers have slain his fathers, each taken a life
for a life,

Thy father had slain his father, how long shall the
    murder last?
Go back to the Isle of Finn and suffer the Past to
    be Past."
And we kiss'd the fringe of his beard, and we pray'd
    as we heard him pray,
And the Holy man he assoil'd us, and sadly we
    sail'd away.

XII.

And we came to the Isle we were blown from, and
    there on the shore was he,
The man that had slain my father. I saw him and
    let him be.
O weary was I of the travel, the trouble, the strife
    and the sin,
When I landed again, with a tithe of my men, on
    the Isle of Finn.

TO VIRGIL.

WRITTEN AT THE REQUEST OF THE MANTUANS FOR
THE NINETEENTH CENTENARY OF VIRGIL'S DEATH.

I.

ROMAN VIRGIL, thou that singest
    Ilion's lofty temples robed in fire,
Ilion falling, Rome arising,
        wars, and filial faith, and Dido's pyre;

II.

Landscape-lover, lord of language
        more than he that sang the Works and Days,
All the chosen coin of fancy
        flashing out from many a golden phrase;

III.

Thou that singest wheat and woodland,
        tilth and vineyard, hive and horse and herd;
All the charm of all the Muses
        often flowering in a lonely word;

IV.

Poet of the happy Tityrus
        piping underneath his beechen bowers;
Poet of the poet-satyr   [flowers;
        whom the laughing shepherd bound with

V.

Chanter of the Pollio, glorying
        in the blissful years again to be,
Summers of the snakeless meadow,
        unlaborious earth and oarless sea;

VI.

Thou that seëst Universal
        Nature moved by Universal Mind;
Thou majestic in thy sadness
        at the doubtful doom of human kind;

VII.

Light among the vanish'd ages;
        star that gildest yet this phantom shore;
Golden branch amid the shadows,
        kings and realms that pass to rise no more;

VIII.

Now thy Forum roars no longer,
        fallen every purple Cæsar's dome—
Tho' thine ocean-roll of rhythm
        sound for ever of Imperial Rome—

IX.

Now the Rome of slaves hath perish'd,
        and the Rome of freemen holds her place,
I, from out the Northern Island
        sunder'd once from all the human race,

X.

I salute thee, Mantovano,
        I that loved thee since my day began,
Wielder of the stateliest measure
        ever moulded by the lips of man.

TRANSLATIONS, ETC.

BATTLE OF BRUNANBURH.

Constantinus, King of the Scots, after having sworn allegiance to
Athelstan, allied himself with the Danes of Ireland under Anlaf, and
invading England, was defeated by Athelstan and his brother Edmund with great slaughter at Brunanburh in the year 937.

I.

*ATHELSTAN King,
    Lord among Earls,
    Bracelet-bestower, and
    Baron of Barons,
    He with his brother,
    Edmund Atheling,
    Gaining a lifelong
    Glory in battle,
    Slew with the sword-edge
    There by Brunanburh,
    Brake the shield-wall,
    Hew'd the lindenwood,†
    Hack'd the battleshield,
Sons of Edward with hammer'd brands.

II.

    Theirs was a greatness
    Got from their Grandsires—
    Theirs that so often in
    Strife with their enemies
Struck for their hoards and their hearths and their
    homes.

III.

    Bow'd the spoiler,
    Bent the Scotsman,
    Fell the shipcrews
    Doom'd to the Death.
    All the field with blood of the fighters
    Flow'd, from when first the great
    Sun-star of morningtide,
    Lamp of the Lord God
    Lord everlasting,
Glode over earth till the glorious creature
    Sunk to his setting.

IV.

    There lay many a man
    Marr'd by the javelin,
    Men of the Northland
    Shot over shield.
    There was the Scotsman
    Weary of war.

V.

    We the West-Saxons,
    Long as the daylight
    Lasted, in companies
Troubled the track of the host that we hated,
Grimly with swords that were sharp from the grind-
    stone,
Fiercely we hack'd at the flyers before us.

* I have more or less availed myself of my son's prose translation
of this poem in the *Contemporary Review* (November, 1876).
† Shields of lindenwood.

vi.

Mighty the Mercian,
Hard was his hand play,
Sparing not any of
Those that with Anlaf,
Warriors over the
Weltering waters
Borne in the bark's-bosom,
Drew to this island,
Doom'd to the death.

vii.

Five young kings put asleep by the sword-stroke,
Seven strong Earls of the army of Anlaf
Fell on the war-field, numberless numbers,
Shipmen and Scot-men.

viii.

Then the Norse leader,
Dire was his need of it,
Few were his following,
Fled to his warship:
Fleeted his vessel to sea with the king in it,
Saving his life on the fallow flood.

ix.

Also the crafty one,
Constantinus,
Crept to his North again,
Hoar-headed hero!

x.

Slender reason had
He to be proud of
The welcome of war-knives—
He that was reft of his
Folk and his friends that had
Fallen in conflict,
Leaving his son too
Lost in the carnage,
Mangled to morsels,
A youngster in war!

xi.

Slender reason had
He to be glad of
The clash of the war-glaive—
Traitor and trickster
And spurner of treaties—
He nor had Anlaf
With armies so broken
A reason for bragging
That they had the better
In perils of battle
On places of slaughter—
The struggle of standards,
The rush of the javelins,
The crash of the charges,*
The wielding of weapons—
The play that they play'd with
The children of Edward.

xii.

Then with their nail'd prows
Parted the Norsemen, a
Blood-redden'd relic of
Javelins over
The jarring breaker, the deepsea billow,
Shaping their way toward Dyflen† again,
Shamed in their souls.

* Lit. " the gathering of men."
† Dublin.

xiii.

Also the brethren,
King and Atheling,
Each in his glory,
Went to his own in his own West-Saxonland,
Glad of the war.

xiv.

Many a carcase they left to be carrion,
Many a livid one, many a sallow-skin—
Left for the white-tail'd eagle to tear it, and
Left for the horny-nibb'd raven to rend it, and
Gave to the garbaging war-hawk to gorge it, and
That gray beast, the wolf of the weald.

xv.

Never had huger
Slaughter of heroes
Slain by the sword-edge—
Such as old writers
Have writ of in histories—
Hapt in this isle, since
Up from the East hither
Saxon and Angle from
Over the broad billow
Broke into Britain with
Haughty war-workers who
Harried the Welshman, when
Earls that were lured by the
Hunger of glory gat
Hold of the land.

TO THE PRINCESS FREDERICA ON HER MARRIAGE.

O You that were eyes and light to the king till he
    past away
    From the darkness of life—
He saw not his daughter—he blest her: the blind
    King sees you to-day,
    He blesses the wife.

SIR JOHN FRANKLIN.

ON THE CENOTAPH IN WESTMINSTER ABBEY.

Not here! the white North has thy bones; and thou,
    Heroic sailor-soul,
Art passing on thine happier voyage now
    Toward no earthly pole.

TO DANTE.

WRITTEN AT REQUEST OF THE FLORENTINES.

King, that hast reign'd six hundred years, and
    grown
In power, and ever growest, since thine own
Fair Florence honoring thy nativity,
Thy Florence now the crown of Italy,
Hath sought the tribute of a verse from me,
I, wearing but the garland of a day,
Cast at thy feet one flower that fades away.

ACHILLES OVER THE TRENCH.

ILIAD, xviii., 202.

So saying, light-foot Iris pass'd away.
Then rose Achilles dear to Zeus; and round
The warrior's puissant shoulders Pallas flung
Her fringèd ægis, and around his head
The glorious goddess wreathed a golden cloud,
And from it lighted an all-shining flame.
As when a smoke from a city goes to heaven
Far off from out an island girt by foes,
All day the men contend in grievous war
From their own city, and with set of sun
Their fires flame thickly, and aloft the glare
Flies streaming, if perchance the neighbors round
May see, and sail to help them in the war:
So from his head the splendor went to heaven.
From wall to dyke he stept, he stood, nor join'd
The Achæans—honoring his wise mother's word—
There standing, shouted; Pallas far away
Call'd; and a boundless panic shook the foe.
For like the clear voice when a trumpet shrills,
Blown by the fierce beleaguerers of a town,
So rang the clear voice of Æakidês:
And when the brazen cry of Æakidês
Was heard among the Trojans, all their hearts
Were troubled, and the full-maned horses whirl'd
The chariots backward, knowing griefs at hand;
And sheer-astounded were the charioteers
To see the dread, unweariable fire
That always o'er the great Peleion's head
Burnt, for the bright-eyed goddess made it burn.
Thrice from the dyke he sent his mighty shout,
Thrice backward reel'd the Trojans and allies:
And there and then twelve of their noblest died
Among their spears and chariots.

PREFATORY SONNET TO THE "NINE-TEENTH CENTURY."

THOSE that of late had fleeted far and fast
To touch all shores, now leaving to the skill
Of others their old craft seaworthy still,
Have charter'd this; where, mindful of the past,
Our true co-mates regather round the mast,
Of diverse tongue, but with a common will
Here, in this roaring moon of daffodil
And crocus, to put forth and brave the blast;
For some, descending from the sacred peak
Of hoar high-templed Faith, have leagued again
Their lot with ours to rove the world about;
And some are wilder comrades, sworn to seek
If any golden harbor be for men
In seas of Death and sunless gulfs of Doubt.

MONTENEGRO.

THEY rose to where their sovran eagle sails,
They kept their faith, their freedom, on the height,
Chaste, frugal, savage, arm'd by day and night
Against the Turk; whose inroad nowhere scales
Their headlong passes, but his footstep fails,
And red with blood the Crescent reels from fight
Before their dauntless hundreds, in prone flight
By thousands down the crags and thro' the vales.
O smallest among peoples! rough rock-throne
Of Freedom! warriors beating back the swarm
Of Turkish Islam for five hundred years,
Great Tsernagora! never since thine own
Black ridges drew the cloud and brake the storm
Has breathed a race of mightier mountaineers.

TO VICTOR HUGO.

VICTOR in Drama! Victor in Romance!
Cloud weaver of phantasmal hopes and fears!
French of the French and lord of human tears!
Child lover, bard, whose fame-lit laurels glance,
Darkening the wreaths of all that would advance
Beyond our strait their claim to be thy peers!
Weird Titan, by thy wintry weight of years
As yet unbroken! Stormy voice of France,
Who dost not love our England, so they say;
I know not! England, France, all men to be
Will make one people ere man's race be run;
And I, desiring that diviner day,
Yield thee full thanks for thy full courtesy
To younger England in the boy, my son.

THE CUP:

A TRAGEDY.

DRAMATIS PERSONÆ.

Galatians.

SYNORIX, an ex-Tetrarch.
SINNATUS, a Tetrarch.
PHŒBE.
CAMMA, wife of Sinnatus, afterwards Priest-
ess in the Temple of Artemis.
Attendant. Boy. Maid.

Romans.

ANTONIUS, a Roman General.
PUBLIUS.
Nobleman.
Messenger.

ACT I.

SCENE I.—DISTANT VIEW OF A CITY OF GALATIA.—AFTERNOON.

As the curtain rises, Priestesses are heard singing in the Temple. Boy discovered on a pathway among rocks, picking grapes. A party of Roman Soldiers, guarding a prisoner in chains, come down the pathway and exeunt.

Enter SYNORIX (*looking round*). *Singing ceases.*

Synorix. Pine, beech, and plane, oak, walnut, apri-
cot,
Vine, cypress, poplar, myrtle, bowering-in
The city where she dwells. She past me here
Three years ago when I was flying from
My tetrarchy to Rome. I almost touch'd her—
A maiden slowly moving on to music
Among her maidens to this Temple—O Gods!
She is my fate—else wherefore has my fate
Brought me again to her own city?—married
Since—married Sinnatus, the Tetrarch here—
But if he be conspirator, Rome will chain,
Or slay him. I may trust to gain her then
When I shall have my tetrarchy restored
By Rome, our mistress, grateful that I show'd her
The weakness and the dissonance of our clans,
And how to crush them easily. Wretched race!
And once I wish'd to scourge them to the bones.
But in this narrow breathing-time of life
Is vengeance for its own sake worth the while,
If once our ends are gain'd? and now this cup—
I never felt such passion for a woman.

[*Brings out a cup and scroll from under his cloak.*
What have I written to her?

[*Reading the scroll.*

" To the admired Camma, wife of Sinnatus, the Tetrarch, one who
years ago, himself an adorer of our great goddess, Artemis, beheld you
afar off worshipping in her Temple, and loved you for it, sends you
this cup, rescued from the burning of one of her shrines in a city thro'
which he past with the Roman army . it is the cup we use in our marriages. Receive it from one who cannot at present write himself other
than

" A GALATIAN SERVING BY FORCE IN THE ROMAN LEGION."

[*Turns and looks up to Boy.*
Boy, dost thou know the house of Sinnatus?
Boy. These grapes are for the house of Sinnatus—
Close to the Temple.
Synorix. Yonder?
Boy. Yes.
Synorix (*aside*). That I

With all my range of women should yet shun
To meet her face to face at once! My boy,

[*Boy comes down rocks to him.*
Take thou this letter and this cup to Camma,
The wife of Sinnatus.
Boy. Going or gone to-day
To hunt with Sinnatus.
Synorix. That matters not.
Take thou this cup and leave it at her doors.

[*Gives the cup and scroll to the Boy.*
Boy. I will, my lord.

[*Takes his basket of grapes, and exit.*

Enter ANTONIUS.

Antonius (*meeting the Boy as he goes out*). Why,
whither runs the boy?
Is that the cup you rescued from the fire?
Synorix. I send it to the wife of Sinnatus,
One half besotted in religious rites.
You come here with your soldiers to enforce
The long-withholden tribute: you suspect
This Sinnatus of playing patriotism,
Which in your sense is treason. You have yet
No proof against him: now this pious cup
Is passport to their house, and open arms
To him who gave it; and once there I warrant
I worm thro' all their windings.
Antonius. If you prosper,
Our Senate, wearied of their tetrarchies,
Their quarrels with themselves, their spites at Rome,
Is like enough to cancel them, and throne
One king above them all, who shall be true
To the Roman: and from what I heard in Rome,
This tributary crown may fall to you.
Synorix. The king, the crown! their talk in Rome?
is it so?

[ANTONIUS *nods.*
Well—I shall serve Galatia taking it,
And save her from herself, and be to Rome
More faithful than a Roman.

[*Turns and sees* CAMMA *coming.*
Stand aside.
Stand aside: here she comes!

[*Watching* CAMMA *as she enters with her Maid.*
Camma (*to Maid*). Where is he, girl?
Maid. You know the waterfall
That in the summer keeps the mountain side,
But after rain o'erleaps a jutting rock
And shoots three hundred feet.
Camma. The stag is there?

Maid. Seen in the thicket at the bottom there
But yester-even.
 Camma.   Good then, we will climb
The mountain opposite and watch the chase.
     [*They descend the rocks, and exeunt.*
 Synorix (watching her). (*Aside.*) The bust of Juno
  and the brows and eyes
Of Venus; face and form unmatchable!
 Antonius. Why do you look at her so lingeringly?
 Synorix. To see if years have changed her.
 Antonius (sarcastically). Love her, do you?
 Synorix. I envied Sinnatus when he married her.
 Antonius. She knows it? Ha!
 Synorix.   She—no, nor ev'n my face.
 Antonius. Nor Sinnatus either?
 Synorix.   No, nor Sinnatus.
 Antonius. Hot-blooded! I have heard them say in
  Rome,
That your own people cast you from their bounds,
For some unprincely violence to a woman,
As Rome did Tarquin.
 Synorix.   Well, if this were so,
I here return like Tarquin—for a crown.
 Antonius. And may be foil'd like Tarquin, if you
  follow
Not the dry light of Rome's straight-going policy,
But the fool-fire of love or lust, which well
May make you lose yourself, may even drown you
In the good regard of Rome.
 Synorix.   Tut—fear me not;
I ever had my victories among women.
I am most true to Rome.
 Antonius (aside). I hate the man!
What filthy tools our Senate works with! Still
I must obey them. (*Aloud.*) Fare you well. [*Going.*
 Synorix.   Farewell!
 Antonius (stopping). A moment! If you track this
  Sinnatus
In any treason, I give you here an order
     [*Produces a paper.*
To seize upon him. Let me sign it. (*Signs it.*) There
"Antonius leader of the Roman Legion."
   [*Hands the paper to* SYNORIX. *Goes up*
    pathway, and exit.
 Synorix. Woman again!—but I am wiser now.
No rushing on the game—the net,—the net.
  [*Shouts of* "Sinnatus! Sinnatus!" *Then horn.*
(*Looking off stage.*) He comes, a rough, bluff, simple-
  looking fellow.
If we may judge the kernel by the husk,
Not one to keep a woman's fealty when
Assailed by Craft and Love. I'll join with him:
I may reap something from him—come upon *her*
Again, perhaps, to-day—*her*. Who are with him?
I see no face that knows me. Shall I risk it?
I am a Roman now, they dare not touch me.
I will.

   Enter SINNATUS, HUNTSMEN, *and hounds.*

   Fair Sir, a happy day to you!
You reck but little of the Roman here,
While you can take your pastime in the woods.
 Sinnatus. Ay, ay, why not? What would you with
  me, man?
 Synorix. I am a life-long lover of the chase,
And tho' a stranger fain would be allow'd
To join the hunt.
 Sinnatus. Your name?
 Synorix.   Strato, my name.
 Sinnatus. No Roman name?
 Synorix.   A Greek, my lord; you know
That we Galatians are both Greek and Gaul.
   [*Shouts and horns in the distance.*
 Sinnatus. Hillo, the stag! (*To* SYNORIX.) What,
  you are all unfurnish'd?
Give him a bow and arrows—follow—follow.
     [*Exit, followed by Huntsmen.*
 Synorix. Slowly but surely—till I see my way.

It is the one step in the dark beyond
Our expectation, that amazes us.
     [*Distant shouts and horns.*
 Hillo! Hillo! [*Exit* SYNORIX. *Shouts and horns.*

SCENE II.—A ROOM IN THE TE-
TRARCH'S HOUSE.—EVENING.

*Frescoed figures on the walls. Moonlight outside. A
couch with cushions on it. A small table with flag-
on of wine, cups, plate of grapes, etc., also the cup
of Scene I. A chair with drapery on it.*

 CAMMA *enters, and opens curtains of window.*
 Camma. No Sinnatus yet—and there the rising
  moon.
   [*Takes up a cithern and sits on couch. Plays
    and sings.*

  "Moon on the field and the foam,
   Moon on the waste and the wold,
  Moon bring him home, bring him home
   Safe from the dark and the cold,
  Home, sweet moon, bring him home,
   Home with the flock to the fold—
  Safe from the wolf"—

(*Listening.*) Is he coming? I thought I heard
A footstep. No not yet. They say that Rome
Sprang from a wolf. I fear my dear lord mixt
With some conspiracy against the wolf.
This mountain shepherd never dream'd of Rome.
 (*Sings.*) "Safe from the wolf to the fold"—
And that great break of precipice that runs
Thro' all the wood, where twenty years ago
Huntsman, and hound, and deer were all neck-broken!
Nay, here he comes.

   Enter SINNATUS, *followed by* SYNORIX.

 Sinnatus (angrily). I tell thee, my good fellow,
My arrow struck the stag.
 Synorix. But was it so?
Nay, you were further off: besides the wind
Went with *my* arrow.
 Sinnatus. I am sure *I* struck him.
 Synorix. And I am just as sure, my lord, *I* struck
  him.
(*Aside.*) And I may strike your game when you are
  gone.
 Camma. Come, come, we will not quarrel about the
  stag.
I have had a weary day in watching you.
Yours must have been a wearier. Sit and eat,
And take a hunter's vengeance on the meats.
 Sinnatus. No, no—we have eaten—we are heated.
Wine!
 Camma. Who is our guest?
 Sinnatus. Strato he calls himself.
  [CAMMA *offers wine to* SYNORIX, *while* SINNATUS
   helps himself.
 Sinnatus. I pledge you, Strato. [*Drinks.*
 Synorix. And I you, my lord. [*Drinks.*
 Sinnatus (seeing the cup sent to CAMMA). What's
  here?
 Camma. A strange gift sent to me to-day.
A sacred cup saved from a blazing shrine
Of our great Goddess, in some city where
Antonius past. I had believed that Rome
Made war upon the peoples not the Gods.
 Synorix. Most like the city rose against Antonius,
Whereon he fired it, and the sacred shrine
By chance was burnt along with it.
 Sinnatus. Had you then
No message with the cup?
 Camma. Why, yes, see here. [*Gives him the scroll.*
 Sinnatus (reads).
"To the admired Camma,—behold you afar off—loved you—sends
you this cup—the cup we use in our marriages—cannot at present
write himself other than

"A GALATIAN SERVING BY FORCE IN THE ROMAN LEGION,"

Serving by force! Were there no boughs to hang on.

Rivers to drown in? Serve by force? No force
Could make me serve by force.
    Synorix.   How then, my lord?
The Roman is encampt without your city—
The force of Rome a thousand-fold our own.
Must all Galatia hang or drown herself?
And you a Prince and Tetrarch in this province—
    Sinnatus. Province!
    Synorix.   Well, well, they call it so in Rome.
    Sinnatus (angrily).   Province!
    Synorix. A noble anger! but Antonius
To-morrow will demand your tribute—you,
Can you make war? Have you alliances?
Bithynia, Pontus, Paphlagonia?
We have had our leagues of old with Eastern kings.
There is my hand—if such a league there be.
What will you do?
    Sinnatus.   Not set myself abroach
And run my mind out to a random guest
Who join'd me in the hunt. You saw my hounds
True to the scent; and we have two-legg'd dogs
Among us who can smell a true occasion,
And when to bark and how.
    Synorix.   My good Lord Sinnatus,
I once was at the hunting of a lion.
Roused by the clamor of the chase he woke,
Came to the front of the wood—his monarch mane
Bristled about his quick ears—he stood there
Staring upon the hunter. A score of dogs
Gnaw'd at his ankles: at the last he felt
The trouble of his feet, put forth one paw,
Slew four, and knew it not, and so remain'd
Staring upon the hunter: and this Rome
Will crush you if you wrestle with her; then
Save for some slight report in her own Senate
Scarce know what she has done.
        (Aside.) Would I could move him,
Provoke him any way! *(Aloud.)* The Lady Camma,
Wise I am sure as she is beautiful,
Will close with me that you submit at once
Is better than a wholly-hopeless war,
Our gallant citizens murder'd all in vain,
Son, husband, brother gash'd to death in vain,
And the small state more cruelly trampled on
Than had she never moved.
    Camma.   Sir, I had once
A boy who died a babe; but were he living
And grown to man and Sinnatus will'd it, I
Would set him in the front rank of the fight
With scarce a pang. *(Rises.)* Sir, if a state submit
At once, she may be blotted out at once
And swallow'd in the conqueror's chronicle.
Whereas in wars of freedom and defence
The glory and grief of battle won or lost
Solders a race together—yea—tho' they fail,
The names of those who fought and fell are like
A bank'd-up fire that flashes out again
From century to century, and at last
May lead them on to victory—I hope so—
Like phantoms of the Gods.
    Sinnatus.   Well spoken, wife.
    Synorix (bowing). Madam, so well I yield.
    Sinnatus   I should not wonder
If Synorix, who has dwelt three years in Rome
And wrought his worst against his native land,
Returns with this Antonius.
    Synorix.   What is Synorix?
    Sinnatus. Galatian, and not know? This Synorix
Was Tetrarch here, and tyrant also—did
Dishonour to our wives.
    Synorix.   Perhaps you judge him
With feeble charity: being as you tell me
Tetrarch, there might be willing wives enough
To feel dishonor, honor.
    Camma.   Do not say so.
I know of no such wives in all Galatia.
There may be courtesans for aught I know
Whose life is one dishonor.

                Enter ATTENDANT.
    Attendant (aside).   My lord, the men!
    Sinnatus (aside). Our anti-Roman faction?
    Attendant (aside).   Ay, my lord.
    Synorix (overhearing). (Aside.) I have enough—
    their anti-Roman faction.
    Sinnatus (aloud). Some friends of mine would speak
    with me without.
You, Strato, make good cheer till I return.   *[Exit.*
    Synorix. I have much to say, no time to say it in.
First, lady, know myself am that Galatian
Who sent the cup.
    Camma.   I thank you from my heart.
    Synorix. Then that I serve with Rome to serve
    Galatia.
That is my secret: keep it, or you sell me
To torment and to death.   *[Coming closer.*
        `For your ear only—
I love you—for your love to the great Goddess.
The Romans sent me here a spy upon you,
To draw you and your husband to your doom.
I'd sooner die than do it.
        [Takes out paper given him by Antonius.
              This paper sign'd
Antonius—will you take it, read it? there!
    Camma (Reads).

     " You are to seize on Sinnatus,—if—"

    Synorix (snatches paper).   No more.
What follows is for no wife's eyes. O Camma,
Rome has a glimpse of this conspiracy;
Rome never yet hath spar'd conspirator.
Horrible! flaying, scourging, crucifying—
    Camma. I am tender enough. Why do you practise
    on me?
    Synorix. Why should I practise on you? How you
    wrong me!
I am sure of being every way malign'd.
And if you should betray me to your husband—
    Camma. Will *you* betray him by this order?
    Synorix.   See,
I tear it all to pieces, never dream'd
Of acting on it.   *[Tears the paper.*
    Camma.   I owe you thanks for ever.
    Synorix. Hath Sinnatus never told you of this plot?
    Camma. What plot?
    Synorix.   A child's sand-castle on the beach
For the next wave—all seen,—all calculated,
All known by Rome. No chance for Sinnatus.
    Camma. Why said you not as much to my brave
    Sinnatus?
    Synorix. Brave—ay—too brave, too over-confident,
Too like to ruin himself, and you, and me!
Who else, with this black thunderbolt of Rome
Above him, would have chased the stag to-day
In the full face of all the Roman camp?
A miracle that they let him home again,
Not caught, maim'd, blinded him.   *[*CAMMA *shudders.*
            (Aside.) I have made her tremble.
(Aloud.) I know they mean to torture him to death.
I dare not tell him how I came to know it;
I durst not trust him with—my serving Rome
To serve Galatia; you heard him on the letter.
Not say as much? I all but said as much.
I am sure I told him that his plot was folly.
I say it to you—you are wiser—Rome knows all,
But you know not the savagery of Rome.
    Camma. O—have you power with Rome? use it for
    him!
    Synorix. Alas! I have no such power with Rome.
    All that
Lies with Antonius.
    [As if struck by a sudden thought. Comes over to her
               He will pass to-morrow
In the gray dawn before the Temple doors.
You have beauty,—O great beauty,—and Antonius,
So gracious toward women, never yet

Flung back a woman's prayer. Plend to him,
I am sure you will prevail
      Camma.   Still—I should tell
My husband.
      Synorix.   Will he let you plead for him
To a Roman?
      Camma.   I fear not.
      Synorix.   Then do not tell him.
Or tell him, if you will, when you return,
When you have charm'd our general into mercy,
And all is safe again. O dearest lady,
      [*Murmurs of* "Synorix! Synorix!" *heard outside.*
Think,—torture,—death,—and come.
      Camma.   I will, I will.
And I will not betray you.
      Synorix (aside). (*As* Sinnatus *enters.*) Stand apart.

                  Enter Sinnatus *and* Attendant.

      Sinnatus. Thou art that Synorix! One whom thou
            hast wrong'd
Without there, knew thee with Antonius.
They howl for thee, to rend thee head from limb.
      Synorix. I am much malign'd. I thought to serve
            Galatia.
      Sinnatus. Serve thyself first, villain! They shall
            not harm
My guest within my house. There! (*points to door*)
      there! this door
Opens upon the forest! Out, begone!
Henceforth I am thy mortal enemy.
      Synorix. However I thank thee (*draws his sword*);
            thou hast saved my life.   [*Exit.*
      Sinnatus (to Attendant). Return and tell them Sy-
            norix is not here.   [*Exit Attendant.*
What did that villain Synorix say to you?
      Camma. Is he—that—Synorix?
      Sinnatus.   Wherefore should you doubt it?
One of the men there knew him.
      Camma.   Only one,
And he perhaps mistaken in the face.
      Sinnatus. Come, come, could he deny it? What
            did he say?
      Camma. What *should* he say?
      Sinnatus.   What *should* he say, my wife!
He should say this, that being Tetrarch once
His own true people cast him from their doors
Like a base coin.
      Camma.   Not kindly to them?
      Sinnatus.   Kindly?
O the most kindly Prince in all the world!
Would clap his honest citizens on the back,
Bandy their own rude jests with them, be curious
About the welfare of their babes, their wives,
O ay—their wives—their wives. What should he say?
He should say nothing to my wife if I
Were by to throttle him! He steep'd himself
In all the lust of Rome. How should *you* guess
What manner of beast it is?
      Camma.   Yet he seem'd kindly,
And said he loathed the cruelties that Rome
Wrought on her vassals.
      Sinnatus.   Did he, *honest* man?
      Camma. And you, that seldom brook the stranger
            here,
Have let him hunt the stag with you to-day.
      Sinnatus. I warrant you now, he said *he* struck the
            stag.
      Camma. Why no, he never touch'd upon the stag.
      Sinnatus. Why so I said, *my* arrow. Well, to sleep.
            [*Goes to close door.*
      Camma. Nay, close not yet the door upon a night
That looks half day.
      Sinnatus. True; and my friends may spy him
And slay him as he runs.
      Camma.   He is gone already,
Oh look,—yon grove upon the mountain,—white
In the sweet moon as with a lovelier snow!
But what a blotch of blackness underneath!

Sinnatus, you remember—yea, you must,
That there three years ago—the vast vine-bowers
Ran to the summit of the trees, and dropt
Their streamers earthward, which a breeze of May
Took ever and anon, and open'd out
The purple zone of hill and heaven; there
You told your love; and like the swaying vines—
Yea,—with our eyes,—our hearts, our prophet hopes
Let in the happy distance, and that all
But cloudless heaven which we have found together
In our three married years! You kiss'd me there
For the first time. Sinnatus, kiss me now.
      Sinnatus. First kiss. (*Kisses her.*) There then.
            You talk almost as if it
Might be the last.
      Camma.   Will you not eat a little?
      Sinnatus. No, no, we found a goat-herd's hut and
            shared
His fruits and milk. Liar! You will believe
Now that he never struck the stag—a brave one
Which you shall see to-morrow.
      Camma.   I rise to-morrow
In the gray dawn, and take this holy cup
To lodge it in the shrine of Artemis.
      Sinnatus. Good!
      Camma.   If I be not back in half an hour,
Come after me.
      Sinnatus. What! is there danger?
      Camma.   Nay,
None that I know: 'tis but a step from here
To the Temple.
      Sinnatus. All my brain is full of sleep.
Wake me before you go, I'll after you—
After *me* now!   [*Closes door and exit.*
      Camma (drawing curtains). Your shadow. Synorix—
His face was not malignant, and he said
That men malign'd him. Shall I go? Shall I go?
Death, torture—
"He never yet flung back a woman's prayer"—
I go, but I will have my dagger with me.   [*Exit.*

———

            SCENE III.—SAME AS SCENE I.
                  Dawn.

            Music and Singing in the Temple.

Enter Synorix *watchfully, after him* Publius *and*
                  Soldiers
      Synorix. Publius!
      Publius.   Here!
      Synorix.   Do you remember what
I told you?
      Publius. When you cry "Rome, Rome," to seize
On whomsoever may be talking with you,
Or man, or woman, as traitors unto Rome.
      Synorix. Right. Back again. How many of you
are there?
      Publius. Some half a score.
            [*Exeunt Soldiers and* Publius.
      Synorix.   I have my guard about me.
I need not fear the crowd that hunted me
Across the woods, last night. I hardly gain'd
The camp at midnight. Will she come to me
Now that she knows me Synorix? Not if Sinnatus
Has told her all the truth about me. Well,
I cannot help the mould that I was cast in.
I fling all that upon my fate. my star.
I know that I am genial, I would be
Happy, and make all others happy so
They did not thwart me. Nay, she will not come,
Yet if she be a true and loving wife
She may, perchance, to save this husband. Ay!
See, see, my white bird stepping toward the snare.
Why now I count it all but miracle,
That this brave heart of mine should shake me so,
As helplessly as some unbearded boy's
When first he meets his maiden in a bower.

Enter CAMMA (*with cup*).

Synorix. The lark first takes the sunlight on his
wing,
But you, twin sister of the morning star,
Forelead the sun.
Camma.   Where is Antonius?
Synorix. Not here as yet. You are too early for
him.   [*She crosses towards Temple.*
Synorix. Nay, whither go you now?
Camma.   To lodge this cup
Within the holy shrine of Artemis,
And so return.
Synorix.   To find Antonius here.
[*She goes into the Temple, he looks after her.*
The loveliest life that ever drew the light
From heaven to brood upon her, and enrich
Earth with her shadow! I trust she *will* return.
These Romans dare not violate the Temple.
No, I must lure my game into the camp.
A woman I could live and die for. What!
Die for a woman, what new faith is this?
I am not mad, not sick, not old enough
To dote on one alone. Yes, mad for her,
Camma the stately, Camma the great-hearted,
So mad, I fear some strange and evil chance
Coming upon me, for by the Gods I seem
Strange to myself.

Re-enter CAMMA.

Camma.   Where is Antonius?
Synorix. Where? As I said before, you are still too
early.
Camma. Too early to be here alone with thee;
For whether men malign thy name, or no,
It bears an evil savor among women.
Where is Antonius? (*Loud.*)
Synorix.   Madam, as you know
The camp is half a league without the city;
If you will walk with me we needs must meet
Antonius coming, or at least shall find him
There in the camp.
Camma.   No, not one step with thee.
Where is Antonius? (*Louder.*)
Synorix (*advancing towards her*). Then for your own
sake,
Lady, I say it with all gentleness,
And for the sake of Sinnatus your husband,
I must compel you.
Camma (*drawing her dagger*). Stay! - too near is
death.
Synorix (*disarming her*). Is it not easy to disarm a
woman?

Enter SINNATUS (*seizes him from behind by the
throat*).

Synorix (*throttled and scarce audible*). Rome! Rome!
Sinnatus. Adulterous dog!

Synorix (*stabbing him with* CAMMA'S *dagger*). What!
will you have it?
[CAMMA *utters a cry and runs to* SINNATUS.
Sinnatus (*falls backward*). I have it in my heart—
to the Temple—fly—
For *my* sake—or they seize on thee. Remember!
Away—farewell!   [*Dies.*
Camma (*runs up the steps into the Temple, looking
back*). Farewell!
Synorix (*seeing her escape*). The women of the Tem-
ple drag her in.
Publius! Publius! No,
Antonius would not suffer me to break
Into the sanctuary. She hath escaped.
[*Looking down at* SINNATUS.
"Adulterous dog!" that red-faced rage at me!
Then with one quick short stab—eternal peace.
So end all passions. Then what use in passions?
To warm the cold bounds of our dying life
And, lest we freeze in mortal apathy,
Employ us, heat us, quicken us, help us, keep us
From seeing all too near that urn, those ashes
Which all must be. Well used, they serve us well.
I heard a saying in Egypt, that ambition
Is like the sea wave, which the more you drink,
The more you thirst—yea—drink too much, as men
Have done on rafts of wreck—it drives you mad.
I will be no such wreck, am no such gamester
As, having won the stake, would dare the chance
Of double, or losing all. The Roman Senate,
For I have always play'd into their hands,
Means me the crown. And Camma for my bride—
The people love her—if I win her love,
They too will cleave to me, as one with her.
There then I rest, Rome's tributary king.
[*Looking down on* SINNATUS.
Why did I strike him?—having proof enough
Against the man, I surely should have left
That stroke to Rome. He saved my life too. Did he?
It seem'd so. I have play'd the sudden fool.
And that sets her against me—for the moment.
Camma—well, well, I never found the woman
I could not force or wheedle to my will.
She will be glad at last to wear my crown.
And I will make Galatia prosperous too,
And we will chirp among our vines, and smile
At bygone things till that (*pointing to* SINNATUS) eter-
nal peace.
Rome! Rome!

Enter PUBLIUS *and Soldiers.*

Twice I cried Rome. Why came ye not before?
Publius. Why come we now? Whom shall we seize
upon?
Synorix (*pointing to the body of* SINNATUS). The body
of that dead traitor Sinnatus.
Bear him away.
            Music and Singing in Temple.

ACT II.

SCENE.—INTERIOR OF THE TEMPLE
OF ARTEMIS.

*Small gold gates on platform in front of the veil before
the colossal statue of the Goddess, and in the centre
of the Temple a tripod altar, on which is a lighted
lamp. Lamps (lighted) suspended between each pillar. Tripods, vases, garlands of flowers, etc., about
stage. Altar at back close to Goddess, with two cups.
Solemn music. Priestesses decorating the Temple.*

Enter a PRIESTESS.

Priestess. Phœbe, that man from Synorix, who has
been

So oft to see the Priestess waits once more
Before the Temple.
Phœbe. We will let her know.
[*Signs to one of the Priestesses, who goes out.*
Since Camma fled from Synorix to our Temple,
And for her beauty, stateliness, and power,
Was chosen Priestess here, have you not mark'd
Her eyes were ever on the marble floor?
To-day they are fixt and bright—they look straight
out.
Hath she made up her mind to marry him?
Priestess. To marry him who stabb'd her Sinnatus.
You will not easily make me credit that.
Phœbe. Ask her.

26

Enter CAMMA *as Priestess (in front of the curtains).*

Priestess.   You will not marry Synorix?
Camma. My girl, I am the bride of Death, and only
Marry the dead.
Priestess.   Not Synorix then?
Camma.   My girl,
At times this oracle of great Artemis
Has no more power than other oracles
To speak directly.
Phœbe.   Will you speak to him,
The messenger from Synorix who waits
Before the Temple?
Camma. Why not? Let him enter.
            [*Comes forward on to step by tripod.*

Enter a MESSENGER.

Messenger (*kneels*). Greeting and health from Syno-
  rix! More than once
You have refused his hand. When last I saw you,
You all but yielded. He entreats you now
For your last answer. When he struck at Sinnatus—
As I have many a time declared to you—
He knew not at the moment who had fasten'd
About his throat—he begs you to forget it
As scarce his act:—a random stroke: all else
Was love for you: he prays you to believe him.
Camma. I pray him to believe—that I believe him.
Messenger. Why that is well. You mean to marry
  him?
Camma. I mean to marry him—if that be well.
Messenger. This very day the Romans crown him
  king
For all his faithful services to Rome.
He wills you then this day to marry him,
And so be throned together in the sight
Of all the people, that the world may know
You twain are reconciled, and no more feuds
Disturb our peaceful vassalage to Rome.
Camma. To-day? Too sudden. I will brood upon it.
When do they crown him?
Messenger.   Even now.
Camma.   And where?
Messenger. Here by your Temple.
Camma.   Come once more to me
Before the crowning,—I will answer you.
                [*Exit Messenger.*
Phœbe. Great Artemis! O Camma, can it be well,
Or good, or wise, that you should clasp a hand
Red with the sacred blood of Sinnatus?
Camma. Good! mine own dagger driven by Synorix
  found
All good in the true heart of Sinnatus,
And quench'd it there for ever. Wise!
Life yields to death and wisdom bows to Fate,
Is wisest, doing so. Did not this man
Speak well? We cannot fight imperial Rome,
But he and I are both Galatian-born,
And, tributary sovereigns, he and I
Might teach this Rome—from knowledge of our peo-
  ple—
Where to lay on her tribute—heavily here
And lightly there. Might I not live for that,
And drown all poor self-passion in the sense
Of public good?
Phœbe.   I am sure you will not marry him.
Camma. Are you so sure? I pray you wait and see.
    [*Shouts (from the distance),* "Synorix! Synorix!"
Camma. Synorix, Synorix! So they cried Sinnatus
Not so long since—they sicken me. The One
Who shifts his policy suffers something, must
Accuse himself, excuse himself; the Many
Will feel no shame to give themselves the lie.
Phœbe. Most like it was the Roman soldier shouted.
Camma. Their shield-borne patriot of the morning
  star
Hang'd at mid-day, their traitor of the dawn
The clamor'd darling of their afternoon!

And that same head they would have play'd at ball
  with,
And kick'd it featureless—they now would crown.
                [*Flourish of trumpets.*

Enter a Galatian NOBLEMAN *with crown on a cushion.*

Nobleman (*kneels*). Greeting and health from Synorix.
    He sends you
This diadem of the first Galatian Queen,
That you may feed your fancy on the glory of it,
And join your life this day with his, and wear it
Beside him on his throne. He waits your answer.
Camma. Tell him there is one shadow among the
  shadows,
One ghost of all the ghosts—as yet so new,
So strange among them—such an alien there,
So much of husband in it still—that if
The shout of Synorix and Camma sitting
Upon one throne, should reach it, *it* would rise
He!... He, with that red star between the ribs,
And my knife there—and blast the king and me,
And blanch the crowd with horror. I dare not, sir!
Throne him—and then the marriage—ay and tell
  him
That I accept the diadem of Galatia—
                [*All are amazed.*
Yea, that ye saw me crown myself withal.
                [*Puts on the crown.*
I wait him his crown'd queen.
Nobleman.   So will I tell him.
                        [*Exit.*
[*Music. Two Priestesses go up the steps before the
  shrine, draw the curtains on either side (discovering the Goddess), then open the gates and remain
  on steps, one on either side, and kneel. A Priestess goes off and returns with a veil of marriage,
  then assists* PHŒBE *to veil* CAMMA. *At the same
  time Priestesses enter and stand on either side of
  the Temple.* CAMMA *and all the Priestesses kneel,
  raise their hands to the Goddess, and bow down.*
        [*Shouts,* "Synorix! Synorix!" *All rise.*
Camma. Fling wide the doors, and let the new-
  made children
Of our imperial mother see the show.
            [*Sunlight pours through the doors.*
I have no heart to do it. (*To* PHŒBE.) Look for
  me!   [*Crouches.* PHŒBE *looks out.*
            [*Shouts,* "Synorix! Synorix!"
Phœbe. He climbs the throne. Hot blood, ambi-
  tion, pride
So bloat and redden his face—O would it were
His third last apoplexy! O bestial!
O how unlike our goodly Sinnatus.
Camma (*on the ground*). You wrong him surely; far
  as the face goes
A goodlier-looking man than Sinnatus.
Phœbe (*aside*). How dare she say it? I could hate
  her for it
But that she is distracted.   [*A flourish of trumpets.*
Camma.   Is he crown'd?
Phœbe. Ay, there they crown him.
        [*Crowd without shout,* "Synorix! Synorix!"
Camma (*rises*). Rouse the dead altar-flame, fling in
  the spices.
    [*A Priestess brings a box of spices to* CAMMA, *who
      throws them on the altar-flame.*
Nard, cinnamon, amomum, benzoin.
Let all the air reel into a mist of odor,
As in the midmost heart of Paradise.
Lay down the Lydian carpets for the king.
The king should pace on purple to his bride,
And music there to greet my lord the king.   [*Music.*
(*To* PHŒBE.) Dost thou remember when I wedded
  Sinnatus?
Ay, thou wast there—whether from maiden fears
Or reverential love for him I loved,
Or some strange second-sight, the marriage-cup
Wherefrom we make libation to the Goddess

So shook within my hand, that the red wine
Ran down the marble and lookt like blood, like blood.
 Phœbe. I do remember your first-marriage fears.
 Camma. I have no fears at this my second marriage.
See here—I stretch my hand out—hold it there.
How steady it is!
 Phœbe.   Steady enough to stab him!
 Camma. O hush! O peace! This violence ill be-
comes
The silence of our Temple. Gentleness,
Low words best chime with this solemnity.
  [*Enter a procession of Priestesses and Children
  bearing garlands and golden goblets, and strewing
  flowers.*

Enter Synorix (*as King, with gold laurel-wreath crown
 and purple robes*), *followed by* Antonius, Publius,
 Noblemen, Guards, and the Populace.

 Camma. Hail, King!
 Synorix.   Hail, Queen!
The wheel of Fate has roll'd me to the top.
I would that happiness were gold, that I
Might cast my largess of it to the crowd!
I would that every man made feast to-day
Beneath the shadow of our pines and planes!
For all my truer life begins to-day.
The past is like a travell'd land now sunk
Below the horizon—like a barren shore
That grew salt weeds, but now all drown'd in love
And glittering at full tide—the bounteous bays
And havens filling with a blissful sea.
Nor speak I now too mightily, being King
And happy! happiest, Lady, in my power
To make you happy.
 Camma.   Yes, sir.
 Synorix.   Our Antonius,
Our faithful friend of Rome, tho' Rome may set
A free foot where she will, yet of his courtesy
Entreats he may be present at our marriage.
 Camma. Let him come—a legion with him, if he will.
(*To* Antonius.) Welcome, my lord Antonius, to our
 Temple.
(*To* Synorix.) You on this side the altar. (*To* An-
 tonius.) You on that.
Call first upon the Goddess, Synorix.
  [*All face the Goddess. Priestesses, Children, Popu-
  lace, and Guards kneel—the others remain stand-
  ing.*
 Synorix. O Thou, that dost inspire the germ with life,
The child, a thread within the house of birth,
And give him limbs, then air, and send him forth
The glory of his father—Thou whose breath
Is balmy wind to robe our hills with grass,
And kindle all our vales with myrtle-blossom,
And roll the golden oceans of our grain,
And sway the long grape-bunches of our vines,
And fill all hearts with fatness and the lust
Of plenty—make me happy in my marriage!
 Chorus (*chanting*). Artemis, Artemis, hear him,
  Ionian Artemis!
 Camma. O Thou that slayest the babe within the
  womb
Or in the being born, or after slayest him
As boy or man, great Goddess, whose storm-voice
Unsockets the strong oak, and rears his root
Beyond his head, and strows our fruits, and lays
Our golden grain, and runs to sea and makes it
Foam over all the fleeted wealth of kings
And peoples, hear.
Whose arrow is the plague—whose quick flash splits
The mid-sea mast, and rifts the tower to the rock,
And hurls the victor's column down with him
That crowns it, hear.
Who causest the safe earth to shudder and gape,
And gulf and flatten in her closing chasm
Domed cities, hear.
Whose lava-torrents blast and blacken a province
To a cinder, hear.

Whose winter-cataracts find a realm and leave it
A waste of rock and ruin, hear. I call thee
To make my marriage prosper to my wish!
 Chorus. Artemis, Artemis, hear her, Ephesian Ar-
  temis!
 Camma. Artemis, Artemis, hear me, Galatian Arte-
  mis!
I call on our own Goddess in our own Temple.
 Chorus. Artemis, Artemis, hear her, Galatian Arte-
  mis!   [*Thunder. All rise.*
 Synorix (*aside*). Thunder! Ay, ay, the storm was
  drawing hither
Across the hills when I was being crown'd.
I wonder if I look as pale as she?
 Camma. Art thou—still bent—on marrying?
 Synorix.   Surely—yet
These are strange words to speak to Artemis.
 Camma. Words are not always what they seem, my
  King.
I will be faithful to thee till thou die.
 Synorix. I thank thee, Camma,—I thank thee.
 Camma (*turning to* Antonius). Antonius,
Much graced are we that our Queen Rome in yon
Deigns to look in upon our barbarisms.
  [*Turns, goes up steps to altar before the Goddess.
  Takes a cup from off the altar. Holds it towards
  Antonius. Antonius goes up to the foot of the
  steps, opposite to* Synorix.
You see this cup, my lord.   [*Gives it to him.*
 Antonius.   Most curious!
The many-breasted mother Artemis
Emboss'd upon it.
 Camma.   It is old, I know not
How many hundred years. Give it me again.
It is the cup belonging our own Temple.
  [*Puts it back on altar, and takes up the cup of Act I.
  Showing it to* Antonius.
Here is another cup belonging our own Temple.
The gift of Synorix; and the Goddess, being
For this most grateful, wills, thro' me her Priestess,
In honour of his gift and of our marriage,
That Synorix should drink from his own cup.
 Synorix. I thank thee, Camma,—I thank thee.
 Camma.   For—my lord—
It is our ancient custom in Galatia
That ere two souls be knit for life and death,
They two should drink together from one cup,
In symbol of their married unity,
Making libation to the Goddess. Bring me
The costly wines we use in marriages.
  [*They bring in a large jar of wine.* Camma *pours
  wine into cup.*
(*To* Synorix.) See here, I fill it. (*To* Antonius.) Will
 you drink, my lord?
 Antonius. I? Why should I? I am not to be married.
 Camma. But that might bring a Roman blessing on
  us.
 Antonius. (*refusing cup*). Thy pardon, Priestess!
 Camma.   Thou art in the right.
This blessing is for Synorix and for me.
See first I make libation to the Goddess,
     [*Makes libation.*
And now I drink. [*Drinks and fills the cup again.*
    Thy turn, Galatian King.
Drink and drink deep—our marriage will be fruitful.
Drink and drink deep, and thou wilt make me happy.
  [Synorix *goes up to her. She hands him the cup.
  He drinks.*
 Synorix. There, Camma! I have almost drain'd the
  cup—
A few drops left.
 Camma.   Libation to the Goddess.
  [*He throws the remaining drops on the altar and
  gives* Camma *the cup.*
 Camma (*placing the cup on the altar*). Why then
  the Goddess hears.
  [*Comes down and forward to tripod.* Antonius
  follows.

Antonius,
Where wast thou on that morning when I came
To plead to thee for Sinnatus's life,
Beside this temple half a year ago?
  Antonius. I never heard of this request of thine.
  Synorix (coming forward hastily to foot of tripod steps). I sought him and I could not find him.
Pray you,
Go on with the marriage rites.
  Camma.   *Antonius—*
"Camma!" who spake?
  Antonius.   Not I.
  Phœbe.   Nor any here.
  Camma. I am all but sure that some one spake.
      Antonius,
If you had found him plotting against Rome,
Would you have tortured Sinnatus to death?
  Antonius. No thought was mine of torture or of death,
But had I found him plotting, I had counsell'd him
To rest from vain resistance. Rome is fated
To rule the world. Then, if he had not listen'd,
I might have sent him prisoner to Rome.
  Synorix. Why do you palter with the ceremony?
Go on with the marriage rites.
  Camma.   They are fiuish'd.
  Synorix.   How!
  Camma. Thou hast drunk deep enough to make me happy.
Dost thou not feel the love I bear to thee
Glow thro' thy veins?
  Synorix.   The love I bear to thee
Glows thro' my veins since first I look'd on thee.
But wherefore slur the perfect ceremony?
The sovereign of Galatia weds his Queen.
Let all be done to the fullest in the sight
Of all the Gods. *(Starts.)* This pain—what is it?—again?
I had a touch of this last year—in—Rome.
Yes, yes. *(To* ANTONIUS.*)* Your arm—a moment—It will pass.
I reel beneath the weight of utter joy—
This all too happy day, crown—queen at once.
                     [Staggers.
O all ye Gods—Jupiter!—Jupiter!   *[Falls backward.*
  Camma. Dost thou cry out upon the Gods of Rome.
Thou art Galatian-born? Our Artemis
Has vanquish'd their Diana.
  Synorix (on the ground).   I am poison'd.
She—close the Temple doors. Let her not fly.
  Camma (leaning on tripod). Have I not drunk of the same cup with thee?
  Synorix. Ay, by the Gods of Rome and all the world.

She too—she too—the bride! the Queen! and I—
Monstrous! I that loved her.
  Camma.   I loved *him.*
  Synorix. O murderous mad-woman! I pray you lift me
And make me walk awhile. I have heard these poisons
May be walk'd down.
        *[*ANTONIUS *and* PUBLIUS *raise him up.*
         My feet are tons of lead,
They will break in the earth—I am sinking—hold me—
Let me alone.
      [They leave him; he sinks down on ground.
       Too late—thought myself wise—
A woman's dupe. Antonius, tell the Senate
I have been most true to Rome—would have been true
To *her*—if—if—   *[Falls as if dead.*
  Camma (coming and leaning over him). So falls the throne of an hour.
  Synorix (half rising). Throne? is it thou? the Fates are throned, not we—
Not guilty of ourselves—thy doom and mine—
Thou—coming my way too—Camma—good-night.
                     [Dies.
  Camma (upheld by weeping Priestesses). Thy way? poor worm, crawl down thine own black hole
To the lowest Hell. Antonius, is *he* there?
I meant thee to have follow'd—better thus.
Nay, if my people must be thralls of Rome,
He is gentle, tho' a Roman.
      [Sinks back into the arms of the Priestesses
  Antonius.   Thou art one
With thine own people, and tho' a Roman I
Forgive thee, Camma.
  Camma (raising herself). "CAMMA!"—why there again
I am most sure that some one call'd. O women,
Ye will have Roman masters. I am glad
I shall not see it. Did not some old Greek
Say death was the chief good? He had my fate for it,
Poison'd. *(Sinks back again.)* Have I the crown on?
       I will go
To meet him, crown'd! crown'd victor of my will—
On my last voyage—but the wind has fail'd—
Growing dark too—but light enough to row.
Row to the blessed Isles! the blessed Isles!—
Sinnatus!
Why comes he not to meet me? It is the crown
Offends him—and my hands are too sleepy
To lift it off.   *[*PHŒBE *takes the crown off.*
    Who touch'd me then? I thank you.
              [Rises, with outspread arms.
There—league on league of ever-shining shore
Beneath an ever-rising sun—I see him—
" Camma, Camma!" Sinnatus, Sinnatus!   *[Dies.*

THE FALCON.

DRAMATIS PERSONÆ.

THE COUNT FEDERIGO DEGLI ALBERIGHI.
FILIPPO, the Count's foster-brother.

THE LADY GIOVANNA.
ELISABETTA, the Count's nurse.

SCENE.—AN ITALIAN COTTAGE. CAS-
TLE AND MOUNTAINS SEEN
THROUGH WINDOW.

ELISABETTA *discovered seated on stool in window, darning. The* COUNT, *with Falcon on his hand, comes
down through the door at back. A withered wreath
on the wall.*

Elisabetta. So, my lord, the Lady Giovanna, who
hath been away so long, came back last night with
her son to the castle.
 Count. Hear that, my bird! Art thou not jealous
of her?
My princess of the cloud, my plumed purveyor,
My far-eyed queen of the winds — thou that canst
 soar
Beyond the morning lark, and howsoe'er
Thy quarry wind and wheel, swoop down upon him
Eagle-like, lightning-like—strike, make his feathers
Glance in mid heaven. [*Crosses to chair.*
 I would thou hadst a mate!
Thy breed will die with thee, and mine with me:
I am as lone and loveless as thyself. [*Sits in chair.*
Giovanna here! Ay, ruffle thyself—be jealous!
Thou should'st be jealous of her. Tho' I bred thee
The full-train'd marvel of all falconry,
And love thee and thou me, yet if Giovanna
Be here again—No, no! Buss me, my bird!
The stately widow has no heart for me.
Thou art the last friend left me upon earth—
No, no again to that. [*Rises and turns.*
 My good old nurse,
I had forgotten thou wast sitting there.
 Elisabetta. Ay, and forgotten thy foster-brother too.
 Count. Bird-babble for my falcon! Let it pass.
What art thou doing there?
 Elisabetta. Darning, your lordship.
We cannot flaunt it in new feathers now:
Nay, if we *will* buy diamond necklaces
To please our lady, we must darn, my lord.
This old thing here (*points to necklace round her neck*),
 they are but blue beads—my Piero,
God rest his honest soul, he bought 'em for me,
Ay, but he knew I meant to marry him.
How couldst thou do it, my son? How couldst thou
 do it?
 Count. She saw it at a dance, upon a neck
Less lovely than her own, and long'd for it.
 Elisabetta. She told thee as much?
 Count. No, no—a friend of hers.
 Elisabetta. Shame on her that she took it at thy
 hands,
She rich enough to have bought it for herself!
 Count. She would have robb'd me then of a great
 pleasure.

Elisabetta. But hath she yet return'd thy love?
 Count. Not yet!
 Elisabetta. She should return thy necklace then.
 Count. Ay, if
She knew the giver; but I bound the seller
To silence, and I left it privily
At Florence, in her palace.
 Elisabetta. And sold thine own
To buy it for her. She not know? She knows
There's none such other——
 Count. Madman anywhere.
Speak freely, tho' to call a madman mad
Will hardly help to make him sane again.

Enter FILIPPO.

Filippo. Ah, the women, the women! Ah, Monna
Giovanna, you here again! you that have the face of
an angel and the heart of a—that's too positive! You
that have a score of lovers and have not a heart for
any of them—that's positive-negative: you that have
not the head of a toad, and *not* a heart like the jewel
in it—that's too negative: you that have a cheek like
a peach and a heart like the stone in it—that's positive
again—that's better!
 Elisabetta. Sh—sh—Filippo!
 Filippo (*turns half round*). Here has our master
been a-glorifying and a-velveting and a-silking himself, and a-peacocking and a-spreading to catch her
eye for a dozen year, till he hasn't an eye left in his
own tail to flourish among the peahens, and all along
o' you, Monna Giovanna, all along o' you!
 Elisabetta. Sh—sh—Filippo! Can't you hear that
you are saying behind his back what you see you are
saying afore his face?
 Count. Let him—he never spares me to my face!
 Filippo. No, my lord, I never spare your lordship
to your lordship's face, nor behind your lordship's
back, nor to right, nor to left, nor to round about and
back to your lordship's face again, for I'm honest, your
lordship.
 Count. Come, come, Filippo, what is there in the
larder?
 [ELISABETTA *crosses to fireplace and puts on wood.*
 Filippo. Shelves and hooks, shelves and hooks, and
when I see the shelves I am like to hang myself on
the hooks.
 Count. No bread?
 Filippo. Half a breakfast for a rat!
 Count. Milk?
 Filippo. Three laps for a cat!
 Count. Cheese?
 Filippo. A supper for twelve mites.
 Count. Eggs?
 Filippo. One, but addled.
 Count. No bird?
 Filippo. Half a tit and a hern's bill.

Count. Let be thy jokes and thy jerks, man! Any-thing or nothing?

Filippo. Well, my lord, if all-but-nothing be any-thing, and one plate of dried prunes be all-but-nothing, then there is anything in your lordship's larder at your lordship's service, if your lordship care to call for it.

Count. Good mother, happy was the prodigal son, For he return'd to the rich father; I But add my poverty to thine. And all Thro' following of my fancy. Pray thee make Thy slender meal out of those scraps and shreds Filippo spoke of. As for him and me, There sprouts a salad in the garden still. (*To the Falcon.*) Why didst thou miss thy quarry yes-ter-even? To-day, my beauty, thou must dash us down Our dinner from the skies. Away, Filippo!

[*Exit, followed by* FILIPPO.

Elisabetta. I knew it would come to this. She has beggar'd him. I always knew it would come to this! (*Goes up to table as if to resume darning, and looks out of window.*) Why, as I live, there is Monna Giovanna coming down the hill from the castle. Stops and stares at our cottage. Ay, ay! stare at it: it's all you have left us. Shame upon you! *She* beautiful! sleek as a miller's mouse! Meal enough, meat enough, well fed; but beautiful—bah! Nay, see, why she turns down the path through our little vineyard, and I sneezed three times this morning. Coming to visit my lord, for the first time in her life too! Why, bless the saints! I'll be bound to confess her love to him at last. I forgive her, I forgive her! I knew it would come to this—I always knew it must come to this! (*Going up to door during latter part of speech and opens it.*) Come in, Madonna, come in. (*Retires to front of table and curtseys as the* LADY GIOVANNA *enters, then moves chair towards the hearth.*) Nay, let me place this chair for your ladyship.

[LADY GIOVANNA *moves slowly down stage, then crosses to chair, looking about her, bows as she sees the Madonna over fireplace, then sits in chair.*

Lady Giovanna. Can I speak with the Count?

Elisabetta. Ay, my lady, but won't you speak with the old woman first, and tell her all about it and make her happy? for I've been on my knees every day for these half-dozen years in hope that the saints would send us this blessed morning: and he always took you so kindly, he always took the world so kindly. When he was a little one, and I put the bitters on my breast to wean him, he made a wry mouth at it, but he took it so kindly, and your ladyship has given him bitters enough in this world, and he never made a wry mouth at you, he always took you so kindly—which is more than I did, my lady, more than I did—and he so handsome—and bless your sweet face, you look as beautiful this morning as the very Madonna her own self—and better late than never—but come when they will—then or now—it's all for the best, come when they will—they are made by the blessed saints—these marriages. [*Raises her hands.*

Lady Giovanna. Marriages? I shall never marry again!

Elisabetta (*rises and turns*). Shame on her then!

Lady Giovanna. Where is the Count?

Elisabetta. Just gone To fly his falcon.

Lady Giovanna. Call him back and say I come to breakfast with him.

Elisabetta. Holy mother! To breakfast! Oh sweet saints! one plate of prunes! Well, Madam, I will give your message to him. [*Exit.*

Lady Giovanna. His falcon, and I come to ask for his falcon, The pleasure of his eyes—boast of his hand— Pride of his heart—the solace of his hours— His one companion here—nay, I have heard That, thro' his late magnificence of living And this last costly gift to mine own self,

[*Shows diamond necklace.*

He hath become so beggar'd, that his falcon Ev'n wins his dinner for him in the field. That must be talk, not truth, but truth or talk, How can I ask for his falcon?

[*Rises and moves as she speaks.*

O my sick boy! My daily fading Florio, it is thou Hath set me this hard task, for when I say What can I do—what can I get for thee? He answers, " Get the Count to give me his falcon, And that will make me well." Yet if I ask, He loves me, and he knows I know he loves me! Will he not pray me to return his love— To marry him?—(*pause*)—I can never marry him. His grandsire struck my grandsire in a brawl At Florence, and my grandsire stabb'd him there. The feud between our houses is the bar I cannot cross; I dare not brave my brother, Break with my kin. My brother hates him, scorns The noblest-natured man alive, and I— Who have that reverence for him that I scarce Dare beg him to receive his diamonds back— How can I, dare I, ask him for his falcon?

[*Puts diamonds in her casket.*

Re-enter COUNT *and* FILIPPO. COUNT *turns to* FILIPPO.

Count. Do what I said; I cannot do it myself.

Filippo. Why then, my lord, we are pauper'd out and out.

Count. Do what I said! [*Advances and bows low.* Welcome to this poor cottage, my dear lady.

Lady Giovanna. And welcome turns a cottage to a palace.

Count. 'Tis long since we have met!

Lady Giovanna. To make amends I come this day to break my fast with you.

Count. I am much honour'd—yes—

[*Turns to* FILIPPO.

Do what I told thee. Must I do it myself?

Filippo. I will, I will. (*Sighs.*) Poor fellow! [*Exit.*

Count. Lady, you bring your light into my cottage Who never deign'd to shine into my palace. My palace wanting you was but a cottage; My cottage, while you grace it, is a palace.

Lady Giovanna. In cottage or in palace, being still Beyond your fortunes, you are still the king Of courtesy and liberality.

Count. I trust I still maintain my courtesy; My liberality perforce is dead Thro' lack of means of giving.

Lady Giovanna. Yet I come To ask a gift. [*Moves towards him a little.*

Count. It will be hard, I fear, To find one shock upon the field when all The harvest has been carried.

Lady Giovanna. But my boy—

(*Aside.*) No, no! not yet—I cannot!

Count. Ay, how is he, That bright inheritor of your eyes—your boy?

Lady Giovanna. Alas, my Lord Federigo, he hath fallen Into a sickness, and it troubles me.

Count. Sick! is it so? why, when he came last year To see me hawking, he was well enough: And then I taught him all our hawking-phrases.

Lady Giovanna. Oh yes, and once you let him fly your falcon.

Count. How charm'd he was! what wonder?—A gallant boy, A noble bird, each perfect of the breed.

Lady Giovanna (*sinks in chair*). What do you rate her at?

Count. My bird? a hundred Gold pieces once were offer'd by the Duke. I had no heart to part with her for money.

Lady Giovanna. No, not for money.

[Count *turns away and sighs.*
Wherefore do you sigh?

Count. I have lost a friend of late.

Lady Giovanna. I could sigh with you
For fear of losing more than friend, a son;
And if he leave me—all the rest of life—
That wither'd wreath were of more worth to me.

[*Looking at wreath on wall.*

Count. That wither'd wreath is of more worth to me
Than all the blossom, all the leaf of this
New-wakening year. [*Goes and takes down wreath.*

Lady Giovanna. And yet I never saw
The land so rich in blossom as this year.

Count (holding wreath towards her). Was not the
year when this was gather'd richer?

Lady Giovanna. How long ago was that?

Count. Alas, ten summers!
A lady that was beautiful as day
Sat by me at a rustic festival
With other beauties on a mountain meadow,
And she was the most beautiful of all;
Then but fifteen, and still as beautiful.
The mountain flowers grew thickly round about.
I made a wreath with some of these; I ask'd
A ribbon from her hair to bind it with;
I whisper'd, Let me crown you Queen of Beauty,
And softly placed the chaplet on her head.
A color, which has color'd all my life,
Flush'd in her face; then I was call'd away;
And presently all rose, and so departed.
Ah! she had thrown my chaplet on the grass,
And there I found it.

[*Lets his hands fall, holding wreath despondingly.*

Lady Giovanna (after pause). How long since do you
say?

Count. That was the very year before you married.

Lady Giovanna. When I was married you were at
the wars.

Count. Had she not thrown my chaplet on the grass,
It may be I had never seen the wars.

[*Replaces wreath whence he had taken it.*

Lady Giovanna. Ah, but, my lord, there ran a ru-
mor then
That you were kill'd in battle. I can tell you
True tears that year were shed for you in Florence.

Count. It might have been as well for me. Un-
happily
I was but wounded by the enemy there
And then imprison'd.

Lady Giovanna. Happily, however,
I see you quite recover'd of your wound.

Count. No, no, not quite, Madonna, not yet, not yet.

Re-enter FILIPPO.

Filippo. My lord, a word with you.

Count. Pray, pardon me!

[*LADY GIOVANNA crosses, and passes behind chair
and takes down wreath; then goes to chair by
table.*

Count (to Filippo). What is it, Filippo?

Filippo. Spoons, your lordship.

Count. Spoons!

Filippo. Yes, my lord, for wasn't my lady born with
a golden spoon in her ladyship's mouth, and we
haven't never so much as a silver one for the golden
lips of her ladyship.

Count. Have we not half a score of silver spoons?

Filippo. Half o' one, my lord!

Count. How half of one?

Filippo. I trod upon him even now, my lord, in my
hurry, and broke him.

Count. And the other nine?

Filippo. Sold! but shall I not mount with your
lordship's leave to her ladyship's castle, in your lordship's and her ladyship's name, and confer with her
ladyship's seneschal, and so descend again with some
of her ladyship's own appurtenances?

Count. Why—no, man. Only see your cloth be
clean. [*Exit* FILIPPO.

Lady Giovanna. Ay, ay, this faded ribbon was the
mode
In Florence ten years back. What's here? a scroll
Pinn'd to the wreath.

My lord, you have said so much
Of this poor wreath that I was bold enough
To take it down, if but to guess what flowers
Had made it; and I find a written scroll
That seems to run in rhymings. Might I read?

Count. Ay, if you will.

Lady Giovanna. It should be if you can.

(Reads.) "Dead mountain." Nay, for who could
trace a hand
So wild and staggering?

Count. This was penn'd, Madonna,
Close to the grating on a winter morn
In the perpetual twilight of a prison,
When he that made it, having his right hand
Lamed in the battle, wrote it with his left.

Lady Giovanna. Oh heavens! the very letters seem
to shake
With cold, with pain perhaps, poor prisoner! Well,
Tell me the words—or better—for I see
There goes a musical score along with them,
Repeat them to their music.

Count. You can touch
No chord in me that would not answer you
In music.

Lady Giovanna. That is musically said.

[*Count takes guitar. LADY GIOVANNA sits listening with wreath in her hand, and quietly removes
scroll and places it on table at the end of the song.*

Count (sings, playing guitar).

"Dead mountain flowers, dead mountain-meadow flowers,
   Dearer than when you made your mountain gay,
   Sweeter than any violet of to-day,
   Richer than all the wide world-wealth of May,
To me, tho' all your bloom has died away,
You bloom again, dead mountain-meadow flowers."

Enter ELISABETTA, *with cloth.*

Elisabetta. A word with you, my lord!

Count (singing). "O mountain flowers!"

Elisabetta. A word, my lord! *(Louder.)*

Count (sings). "Dead flowers!"

Elisabetta. A word, my lord! *(Louder.)*

Count. I pray you pardon me again!

[*LADY GIOVANNA, looking at wreath.*

Count (to Elisabetta.) What is it?

Elisabetta. My lord, we have but one piece of earth-
enware to serve the salad in to my lady, and that
cracked!

Count. Why then, that flower'd bowl my ancestor
Fetch'd from the farthest east—we never use it
For fear of breakage—but this day has brought
A great occasion. You can take it, nurse!

Elisabetta. I did take it, my lord, but what with my
lady's coming that had so flurried me, and what with
the fear of breaking it, I did break it, my lord: it is
broken!

Count. My one thing left of value in the world!
No matter! see your cloth be white as snow!

Elisabetta (pointing thro' window) White? I warrant thee, my son, as the snow yonder on the very tip-
top o' the mountain.

Count. And yet to speak white truth, my good old
mother,
I have seen it like the snow on the morning.

Elisabetta. How can your lordship say so? There,
my lord! [*Lays cloth.*
O my dear son, be not unkind to me.
And one word more. [*Going—returns.*

Count (touching guitar). Good! let it be but one.

Elisabetta. Hath she return'd thy love?

Count. Not yet!

Elisabetta. And will she?

Count (looking at Lady Giovanna). I scarce believe
  it!

. *Elisabetta.*   Shame upon her then ! [*Exit.*

Count (sings). " Dead mountain flowers "—

Ah well, my nurse has broken
The thread of my dead flowers, as she has broken
My china bowl. My memory is as dead.

                           [*Goes and replaces guitar*
Strange that the words at home with me so long
Should fly like bosom friends when needed most.
So by your leave if you would hear the rest,
The writing.

Lady Giovanna (holding wreath towards him). There !
  my lord, you are a poet,
And can you not imagine that the wreath,
Set, as you say, so lightly on her head,
Fell with her motion as she rose, and she,
A girl, a child, then but fifteen, however
Flutter'd or flatter'd by your notice of her,
Was yet too bashful to return for it ?

Count. Was it so indeed ? was it so ? was it so ?
  [*Leans forward to take wreath, and touches* LADY
  GIOVANNA's *hand, which she withdraws hastily ;
  he places wreath on corner of chair.*

Lady Giovanna (with dignity). I did not say, my
  lord, that it was so ;
I said you might imagine it was so.

Enter FILIPPO *with bowl of salad, which he places
  on table.*

Filippo. Here's a fine salad for my lady, for tho' we
have been a soldier, and ridden by his lordship's side,
and seen the red of the battle-field, yet are we now
drill-sergeant to his lordship's lettuces, and profess to
be great in green things and in garden-stuff.

Lady Giovanna. I thank you, good Filippo.

                                       [*Exit* FILIPPO.

Enter ELISABETTA *with bird on a dish which she places
  on table.*

Elisabetta (close to table). Here's a fine fowl for my
lady : I had scant time to do him in. I hope he be
not underdone, for we be undone in the doing of him.

Lady Giovanna. I thank you, my good nurse.

Filippo (re-entering with plate of prunes). And here
are fine fruits for my lady—prunes, my lady, from the
tree that my lord himself planted here in the blossom
of his boyhood—and so I, Filippo, being, with your
ladyship's pardon, and as your ladyship knows, his
lordship's own foster-brother, would commend them
to your ladyship's most peculiar appreciation.

                                   [*Puts plate on table.*

Elisabetta. Filippo !

Lady Giovanna (Count leads her to table). Will you
  not eat with me, my lord ?

Count.   I cannot,
Not a morsel, not one morsel. I have broken
My fast already. I will pledge you. Wine !

Filippo, wine !
  [*Sits near table ; Filippo brings flask, fills the
  Count's goblet, then Lady Giovanna's ; Elisabetta
  stands at the back of Lady Giovanna's chair.*

Count.   It is but thin and cold,
Not like the vintage blowing round your castle.
We lie too deep down in the shadow here.
Your ladyship lives higher in the sun.

                    [*They pledge each other and drink.*

Lady Giovanna. If I might send you down a flask or
  two
Of that same vintage ? There is iron in it.
It has been much commended as a medicine.
I give it my sick son, and if you be
Not quite recover'd of your wound, the wine
Might help you. None has ever told me yet
The story of your battle and your wound.

Filippo (coming forward). I can tell you, my lady,
I can tell you.

Elisabetta. Filippo ! will you take the word out of
your master's own mouth ?

Filippo. Was it there to take ? Put it there, my
lord.

Count. Giovanna, my dear lady, in this same battle
We had been beaten—they were ten to one.
The trumpets of the fight had echo'd down,
I and Filippo here had done our best,
And, having passed unwounded from the field,
Were seated sadly at a fountain side,
Our horses grazing by us, when a troop,
Laden with booty and with a flag of ours
Ta'en in the fight—

Filippo.   Ay, but we fought for it back,
And kill'd—

Elisabetta. Filippo !

Count.   A troop of horse—

Filippo.   Five hundred !

Count. Say fifty !

Filippo.   And we kill'd 'em by the score !

Elisabetta. Filippo !

Filippo. Well, well, well ! I bite my tongue.

Count. We may have left their fifty less by five.
However, staying not to count how many,
But anger'd at their flaunting of our flag,
We mounted, and we dashed into the heart of 'em.
I wore the lady's chaplet round my neck ;
It served me for a blessed rosary.
I am sure that more than one brave fellow owed
His death to the charm in it.

Elisabetta.   Hear that, my lady !

Count. I cannot tell how long we strove before
Our horses fell beneath us : down we went
Crush'd, hack'd at, trampled underfoot. The night,
As some cold-manner'd friend may strangely do us
The truest service, had a touch of frost
That help'd to check the flowing of the blood.
My last sight ere I swoon'd was one sweet face
Crown'd with the wreath. *That* seem'd to come and
  go.
They left us there for dead !

Elisabetta.   Hear that, my lady !

Filippo. Ay, and I left two fingers there for dead.
See, my lady ! (*Showing his hand.*)

Lady Giovanna. I see, Filippo !

Filippo. And I have small hope of the gentleman
gout in my great toe.

Lady Giovanna. And why, Filippo ?

                                       [*Smiling absently.*

Filippo. I left him there for dead too !

Elisabetta. She smiles at him—how hard the woman
  is !
My lady, if your ladyship were not
Too proud to look upon the garland, you
Would find it stain'd—

Count (rising).   Silence, Elisabetta !

Elisabetta. Stain'd with the blood of the best heart
  that ever
Beat for one woman. [*Points to wreath on chair.*

Lady Giovanna (rising slowly). I can eat no more !

Count. You have but trifled with our homely salad,
But dallied with a single lettuce-leaf ;
Not eaten anything.

Lady Giovanna.   Nay, nay, I cannot.
You know, my lord, I told you I was troubled.
My one child Florio lying still so sick,
I bound myself, and by a solemn vow,
That I would touch no flesh till he were well
Here, or else well in Heaven, where all is well.

  [*Elisabetta clears table of bird and salad : Filippo
  snatches up the plate of prunes and holds them to
  Lady Giovanna.*

Filippo. But the prunes, my lady, from the tree that
his lordship—

Lady Giovanna. Not now, Filippo. My lord Federigo,
Can I not speak with you once more alone ?

Count. You hear, Filippo ? My good fellow, go !

Filippo. But the prunes that your lordship—

Elisabetta. Filippo!

Count. Ay, prune our company of thine own and go!

Elisabetta. Filippo!

Filippo (turning). Well, well! the women! [*Exit.*

Count. And thou too leave us, my dear nurse, alone.

Elisabetta (folding up cloth and going). And me too? Ay, the dear nurse will leave you alone; but, for all that, she that has eaten the yolk is scarce like to swallow the shell.

[*Turns and curtseys stiffly to* Lady Giovanna, *then exit.* Lady Giovanna *takes out diamond necklace from casket.*

Lady Giovanna. I have anger'd your good nurse: these old-world servants
Are all but flesh and blood with those they serve.
My lord, I have a present to return you,
And afterwards a boon to crave of you.

Count. No, my most honor'd and long-worshipt lady,
Poor Federigo degli Alberighi
Takes nothing in return from you except
Return of his affection—can deny
Nothing to you that you require of him.

Lady Giovanna. Then I require you to take back your diamonds— [*Offering necklace.*
I doubt not they are yours. No other heart
Of such magnificence in courtesy
Beats—out of heaven. They seem'd too rich a prize
To trust with any messenger. I came
In person to return them. [*Count draws back.*
If the phrase
" Return " displease you, we will say—exchange them
For your—for your—

Count (takes a step towards her and then back). For mine—and what of mine?

Lady Giovanna. Well, shall we say this wreath and your sweet rhymes?

Count. But have you ever worn my diamonds?

Lady Giovanna. No!
For that would seem accepting of your love.
I cannot brave my brother—but be sure
That I shall never marry again, my lord!

Count. Sure?

Lady Giovanna. Yes!

Count. Is this your brother's order?

Lady Giovanna. No!
For he would marry me to the richest man
In Florence; but I think you know the saying—
" Better a man without riches, than riches without a man."

Count. A noble saying—and acted on would yield
A nobler breed of men and women. Lady,
I find you a shrewd bargainer. The wreath
That once you wore outvalues twentyfold
The diamonds that you never deign'd to wear.
But lay them there for a moment!

[*Points to table.* Lady Giovanna *places necklace on table.*

And be you
Gracious enough to let me know the boon
By granting which, if aught be mine to grant,
I should be made more happy than I hoped
Ever to be again.

Lady Giovanna. Then keep your wreath,
But you will find me a shrewd bargainer still.
I cannot keep your diamonds, for the gift
I ask for, to *my* mind and at this present
Outvalues all the jewels upon earth.

Count. It should be love that thus outvalues all.
You speak like love, and yet you love me not.
I have nothing in this world but love for you.

Lady Giovanna. Love? it *is* love, love for my dying boy,
Moves me to ask it of you.

Count. What? my time?
Is it my time? Well, I can give my time

To him that is a part of you, your son,
Shall I return to the castle with you? Shall I
Sit by him, read to him, tell him my tales,
Sing him my songs? You know that I can touch
The ghittern to some purpose.

Lady Giovanna. No, not that!
I thank you heartily for that—and you,
I doubt not from your nobleness of nature,
Will pardon me for asking what I ask.

Count. Giovanna, dear Giovanna, I that once
The wildest of the random youth of Florence
Before I saw you—all my nobleness
Of nature, as you deign to call it, draws
From you, and from my constancy to you.
No more, but speak.

Lady Giovanna. I will. You know sick people,
More specially sick children, have strange fancies,
Strange longings; and to thwart them in their mood
May work them grievous harm at times, may even
Hasten their end. I would you had a son!
It might be easier then for you to make
Allowance for a mother—her—who comes
To rob you of your one delight on earth.
How often has my sick boy yearn'd for this!
I have put him off as often; but to-day
I dared not—so much weaker, so much worse
For last day's journey. I was weeping for him:
He gave me his hand: "I should be well again
If the good Count would give me—"

Count. Give me.

Lady Giovanna. His falcon.

Count (starts back). My falcon!

Lady Giovanna. Yes, your falcon, Federigo!

Count. Alas, I cannot!

Lady Giovanna. Cannot? Even so!
I fear'd as much. O this unhappy world!
How shall I break it to him? how shall I tell him?
The boy may die: more blessed were the rags
Of some pale beggar-woman seeking alms
For her sick son, if he were like to live,
Than all my childless wealth, if mine must die.
I was to blame—the love you said you bore me—
My lord, we thank you for your entertainment,
[*With a stately curtsey.*
And so return—Heaven help him!—to our son.
[*Turns.*

Count (rushes forward). Stay, stay, I am most unlucky, most unhappy.
You never had look'd in on me before,
And when you came and dipt your sovereign head
Thro' these low doors, you ask'd to eat with me.
I had but emptiness to set before you,
No not a draught of milk, no not an egg,
Nothing but my brave bird, my noble falcon,
My comrade of the house, and of the field.
She had to die for it—she died for you.
Perhaps I thought with those of old, the nobler
The victim was, the more acceptable
Might be the sacrifice. I fear you scarce
Will thank me for your entertainment now.

Lady Giovanna (returning). I bear with him no longer.

Count. No, Madonna!
And he will have to bear with it as he may!

Lady Giovanna. I break with him for ever!

Count. Yes, Giovanna,
But he will keep his love to you for ever!

Lady Giovanna. You? you? not you! My brother! my hard brother!
O Federigo, Federigo, I love you!
Spite of ten thousand brothers, Federigo
[*Falls at his feet.*

Count (impetuously). Why then the dying of my noble bird
Hath served me better than her living—then
[*Takes diamonds from table.*
These diamonds are both yours and mine—have won
Their value again—beyond all markets—there

I lay them for the first time round your neck.

[Lays necklace round her neck.

And then this chaplet—No more feuds, but peace,
Peace and conciliation!   I will make
Your brother love me.   See, I tear away
The leaves were darken'd by the battle—

[Pulls leaves off and throws them down.

—crown you
Again with the same crown my Queen of Beauty.

[Places wreath on her head.

Rise—I could almost think that the dead garland
Will break once more into the living blossom.
Nay, nay, I pray you rise.

[Raises her with both hands.

We two together
Will help to heal your son—your son and mine—
We shall do it—we shall do it.   *[Embraces her.*
The purpose of my being is accomplish'd,
And I am happy !

Lady Giovanna.   And I too, Federigo.

LATEST POEMS.

DESPAIR: A DRAMATIC MONOLOGUE.*

[A man and his wife having lost faith in a God, and hope of a life to come, and being utterly miserable in this, resolve to end themselves by drowning. The woman is drowned, but the man is rescued by a minister of the sect he had abandoned.]

Is it you, that preach'd in the chapel there looking over the sand?
Follow'd us too that night, and dogg'd us, and drew me to land?

What did I feel that night? You are curious. How should I tell?
Does it matter so much what I felt? You rescued me—yet—was it well
That you came unwish'd for, uncall'd, between me and the deep and my doom
Three days since, three more dark days of the Godless gloom
Of a life without sun, without health, without hope, without any delight
In anything here upon earth? but ah God, that night, that night
When the rolling eyes of the light-house there on the fatal neck
Of land running out into rock—they had saved many hundreds from wreck—
Glared on our way toward death, I remember I thought as we past
Does it matter how many they saved? we are all of us wreck'd at last—
"Do you fear," and there came thro' the roar of the breaker a whisper, a breath
"Fear? am I not with you? I am frighted at life not death."

And the suns of the limitless Universe sparkled and shone in the sky,
Flashing with fires as of God, but we knew that their light was a lie—
Bright as with deathless hope—but, however they sparkled and shone,
The dark little worlds running round them were worlds of woe like our own—
No soul in the heaven above, no soul on the earth below,
A fiery scroll written over with lamentation and woe.

See, we were nursed in the dark night-fold of your fatalist creed,
And we turn'd to the growing dawn, we had hoped for a dawn indeed,
When the light of a Sun that was coming would scatter the ghosts of the Past,
And the cramping creeds that had madden'd the peoples would vanish at last,
And we broke away from the Christ, our human brother and friend,
For He spoke, or it seem'd that He spoke, of a Hell without help, without end.

Hoped for a dawn and it came, but the promise had faded away;
We had past from a cheerless night to the glare of a drearier day;
He is only a cloud and a smoke who was once a pillar of fire,
The guess of a worm in the dust and the shadow of its desire—
Of a worm as it writhes in a world of the weak trodden down by the strong,
Of a dying worm in a world, all massacre, murder, and wrong.

O we poor orphans of nothing—alone on that lonely shore—
Born of the brainless Nature who knew not that which she bore!
Trusting no longer that earthly flower would be heavenly fruit—
Come from the brute, poor souls—no souls—and to die with the brute—

Nay, but I am not claiming your pity: I know you of old—
Small pity for those that have ranged from the narrow warmth of your fold,
Where you bawl'd the dark side of your faith and a God of eternal rage,
Till you flung us back on ourselves, and the human heart, and the Age.

But pity—the Pagan held it a vice—was in her and in me.
Helpless, taking the place of the pitying God that should be!
Pity for all that aches in the grasp of an idiot power,
And pity for our own selves on an earth that bore not a flower;
Pity for all that suffers on land or in air or the deep,
And pity for our own selves till we long'd for eternal sleep

"Lightly step over the sands! the waters—you hear them call!
Life with its anguish, and horrors, and errors—away with it all!"
And she laid her hand in my own—she was always loyal and sweet—
Till the points of the foam in the dusk came playing about our feet.
There was a strong sea-current would sweep us out to the main.
"Ah God" tho' I felt as I spoke I was taking the name in vain—

* Nineteenth Century, November, 1881.

"Ah God" and we turn'd to each other, we kiss'd, we embraced, she and I,
Knowing the Love we were used to believe everlasting would die:
We had read their know-nothing books and we lean'd to the darker side—
Ah God, should we find Him, perhaps, perhaps, if we died, if we died?
We never had found Him on earth—this earth is a fatherless Hell—
"Dear Love, for ever and ever, for ever and ever farewell!"
Never a cry so desolate, not since the world began;
Never a kiss so sad, no, not since the coming of man.

But the blind wave cast me ashore, and you saved me, a valueless life.
Not a grain of gratitude mine! You have parted the man from the wife.
I am left alone on the land, she is all alone in the sea,
If a curse meant ought, I would curse you for not having let me be.

Visions of youth—for my brain was drunk with the water, it seems;
I had past into perfect quiet at length out of pleasant dreams,
And the transient trouble of drowning—what was it when match'd with the pains
Of the hellish heat of a wretched life rushing back thro' the veins?

Why should I live? one son had forged on his father and fled,
And if I believed in a God, I would thank him, the other is dead,
And there was a baby-girl, that had never look'd on the light:
Happiest she of us all, for she past from the night to the night.

But the crime, if a crime, of her eldest-born, her glory, her boast,
Struck hard at the tender heart of the mother, and broke it almost;
Tho', name and fame dying out for ever in endless time,
Does it matter so much whether crown'd for a virtue, or hang'd for a crime?

And ruin'd by *him*, by *him*, I stood there, naked, amazed
In a world of arrogant opulence, fear'd myself turning crazed,
And I would not be mock'd in a madhouse! and she, the delicate wife,
With a grief that could only be cured, if cured, by the surgeon's knife,—

Why should we bear with an hour of torture, a moment of pain,
If every man die for ever, if all his griefs are in vain,
And the homeless planet at length will be wheel'd thro' the silence of space,
Motherless evermore of an ever-vanishing race,
When the worm shall have writhed its last, and its last brother-worm will have fled
From the dead fossil skull that is left in the rocks of an earth that is dead?

Have I crazed myself over their horrible infidel writings? O yes,
For these are the new dark ages, you see, of the popular press,
When the bat comes out of his cave, and the owls are whooping at noon,
And Doubt is the lord of this dunghill and crows to the sun and the moon,
Till the Sun and the Moon of our science are both of them turn'd into blood,
And Hope will have broken her heart, running after a shadow of good:
For their knowing and know-nothing books are scatter'd from hand to hand—
We have knelt in your know-all chapel too looking over the sand.

What! I should call on that Infinite Love that has served us so well?
Infinite wickedness rather that made everlasting Hell,
Made us, foreknew us, foredoom'd us, and does what he will with his own;
Better our dead brute mother who never has heard us groan!

Hell? if the souls of men were immortal, as men have been told,
The lecher would cleave to his lusts, and the miser would yearn for his gold,
And so there were Hell for ever! but were there a God as you say,
His Love would have power over Hell till it utterly vanish'd away.

Ah yet—I have had some glimmer, at times, in my gloomiest woe,
Of a God behind all—after all—the great God for aught that I know;
But the God of Love and of Hell together—they cannot be thought;
If there be such a God, may the Great God curse him and bring him to nought!

Blasphemy! whose is the fault? is it mine? for why would you save
A madman to vex you with wretched words, who is best in his grave?
Blasphemy! ay, why not, being damn'd beyond hope of grace?
O would I were yonder with her, and away from your faith and your face!
Blasphemy! true! I have scared you pale with my scandalous talk,
But the blasphemy to *my* mind lies all in the way that you walk.

Hence! she is gone! can I stay? can I breathe divorced from the Past?
You needs must have good lynx-eyes if I do not escape you at last.
Our orthodox coroner doubtless will find it a felo-de-se,
And the stake and the cross-road, fool, if you will, does it matter to me?

MIDNIGHT, JUNE 30, 1879.*

I.

MIDNIGHT—in no midsummer tune
The breakers lash the shores:
The cuckoo of a joyless June
Is calling out-of-doors:

And thou hast vanish'd from thine own
To that which looks like rest,
True brother, only to be known
By those who love thee best.

II.

Midnight—and joyless June gone by,
And from the deluged park
The cuckoo of a worse July
Is calling thro' the dark:

But thou art silent under-ground,
And o'er thee streams the rain,
True poet, surely to be found
When Truth is found again.

III.

And, now to these unsummer'd skies
The summer bird is still,
Far off a phantom cuckoo cries
From out a phantom hill;

And thro' this midnight breaks the sun
Of sixty years away,
The light of days when life begun,
The days that seem to-day,

When all my griefs were shared with thee,
And all my hopes were thine—
As all thou wert was one with me,
May all thou art be mine!

EARLY SPRING.†

Once more the Heavenly Power
Makes all things new,
And domes the red-plough'd hills
With loving blue;
The blackbirds have their wills,
The throstles too.

Opens a door in Heaven;
From skies of glass
A Jacob's-ladder falls
On greening grass,
And o'er the mountain-walls
Young angels pass.

Before them fleets the shower,
And burst the buds,
And shine the level lands,
And flash the floods;
The stars are from their hands
Flung thro' the woods;

The woods by living airs
How freshly fann'd,
Light airs from where the deep,
All down the sand,
Is breathing in his sleep,
Heard by the land!

O follow, leaping blood,
The season's lure!
O heart, look down and up,
Serene, secure,
Warm as the crocus-cup,
Like snowdrops, pure!

Past, future, glimpse and fade
Thro' some slight spell,
Some gleam from yonder vale,
Some far blue fell,
And sympathies, how frail,
In sound and smell.

Till, at thy chuckled note,
Thou twinkling bird,
The fairy fancies range,
And, lightly stirr'd,
Ring little bells of change
From word to word.

For now the Heavenly Power
Makes all things new,
And thaws the cold, and fills
The flower with dew;
The blackbirds have their wills,
The poets too.

"FRATER AVE ATQUE VALE."‡

Row us out from Desenzano, to your Sirmione row!
So they row'd, and there we landed—"O venusta Sirmio!"
There to me thro' all the groves of olive in the summer glow,
There beneath the Roman ruin where the purple flowers grow,
Came that "Ave atque Vale" of the Poet's hopeless woe,
Tenderest of Roman poets nineteen-hundred years ago,
"Frater Ave atque Vale"—as we wander'd to and fro
Gazing at the Lydian laughter of the Garda-lake below
Sweet Catullus's all-but-island, olive-silvery Sirmio!

Prefixed to Sonnets by Charles Tennyson Turner.   † Youth's Companion, Dec., 1883.   ‡ Nineteenth Century, March, 1882.